THE GROLIER ATLAS OF NORTH AMERICA AND THE WORLD

GROLIER INC.

Edited by
Bill Willett, Cartographic Editor,
David Gaylard, Assistant Cartographic Editor,
and Geoffrey Atkinson, Lilla Prince-Smith, Raymond Smith
and Joan Williamson

Maps prepared under the direction of Alan Poynter,
Director of Cartography

The maps of the United States are based on material appearing in
the National Atlas of the United States. The material was supplied
by the National Cartographic Information Center, U.S. Geological
Survey, Reston, Va.

Printed in Hong Kong

First printing for Grolier Inc., 1984

ISBN 0-7172-8519-7

PREFACE

This atlas is purposefully entitled an atlas of North America and the World for nearly half of the pages are devoted to maps covering the United States, Canada and Central America and the other half to the rest of the World. The dimensions of the atlas make it easily handleable; it is not too large to be cumbersome or too small for the maps to have no value as a reference atlas. Within the page size the scale of 1:2.5 million (40 miles to the inch) has been used as far as possible for the State maps; the more densely populated and really smaller states in the east are shown at twice this basic scale, namely 1:1.25 million (20 miles to the inch) and the geographically larger Alaska, Montana and Texas are shown at smaller scales. Each state is shown on a separate page and is arranged in the atlas alphabetically except where the shape of two or more states taken together fit more comfortably on to the page, Vermont and New Hampshire being examples. In these cases one or two states are out of alphabetical sequence and these exceptions are clearly indicated.

Each of the State maps shows the boundaries of the State, naturally, and also the county boundaries together with the county seat. Recreation areas and reservations, roads, rails and airports are shown. The land surface is depicted with contours and hill shading. The symbols and type for the cities and towns are graded according to their population at the 1980 Census.

An atlas, a collection of maps, contains a lot of information and to answer a specific query the reader can find the particular map that he requires in two ways; via the contents list and the index. In the contents lists which follow this preface there are lists of states and map titles and also outline maps of the United States and the Continents showing the extent of individual map pages. The index gives the page number of the map which holds the place name required. The reader is then directed to a point on that page by way of the geographical co-ordinates.

The forms of place names on the map and in the index are those that are used locally in the country concerned. The normally-used name form in English, if it differs from the local form, often appears on the map in brackets and in the index it is cross-referenced to the locally spelled form (Vienna = Wien, for example). In countries that do not use a Roman script the place names have been transcribed using a system which is accepted by the U.S. and British authorities on geographic names. In China the Pinyin system is used. This is the system which the Chinese themselves prefer and which is being increasingly used outside China.

The reader is reminded that a map is a scaled down representation of the Earth. The General Reference at the beginning of the map section shows the symbols that are used on the maps and the introduction to the index explains how to use it in conjunction with the maps.

B. M. WILLETT

CONTENTS I

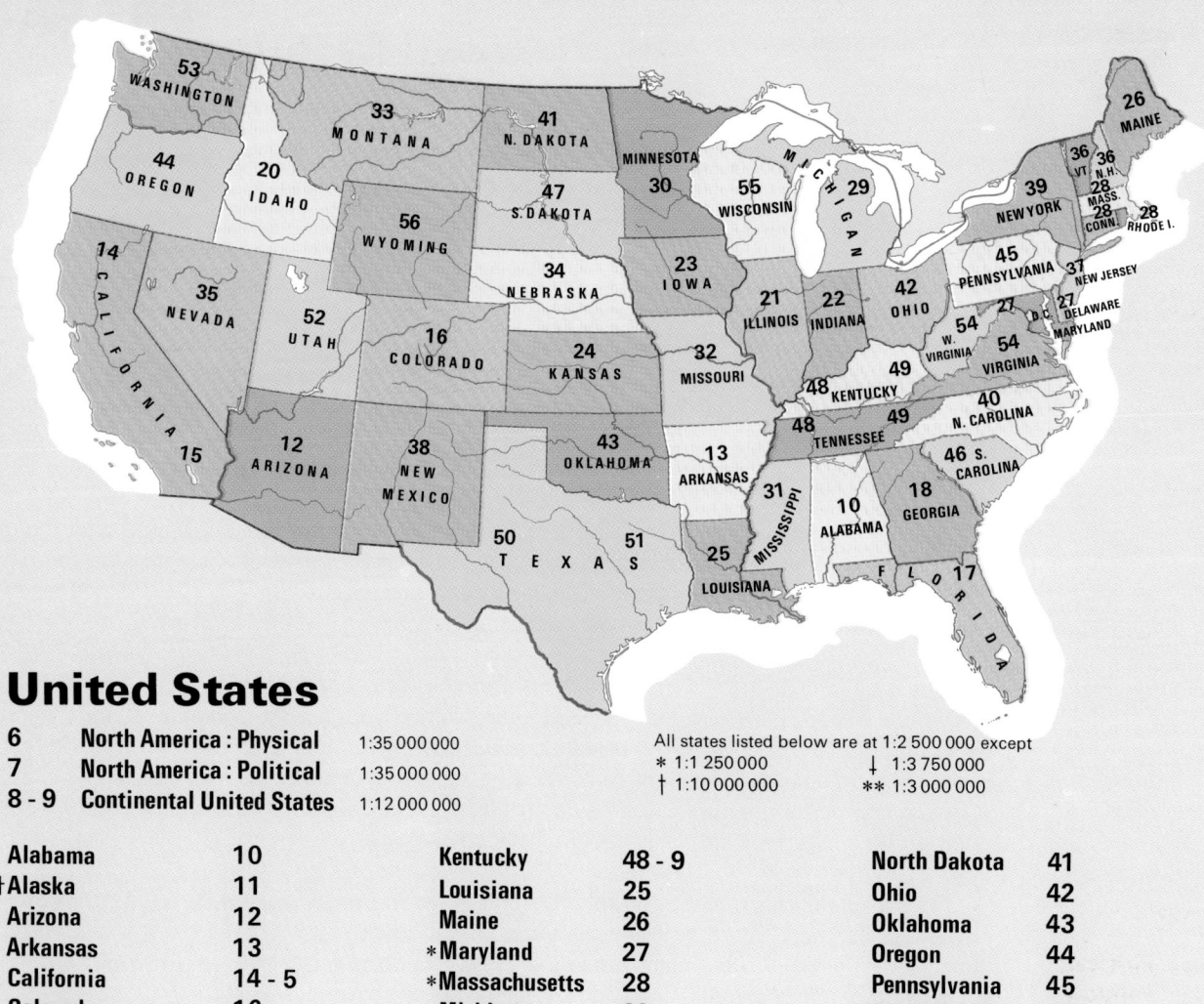

United States

CONTENTS II

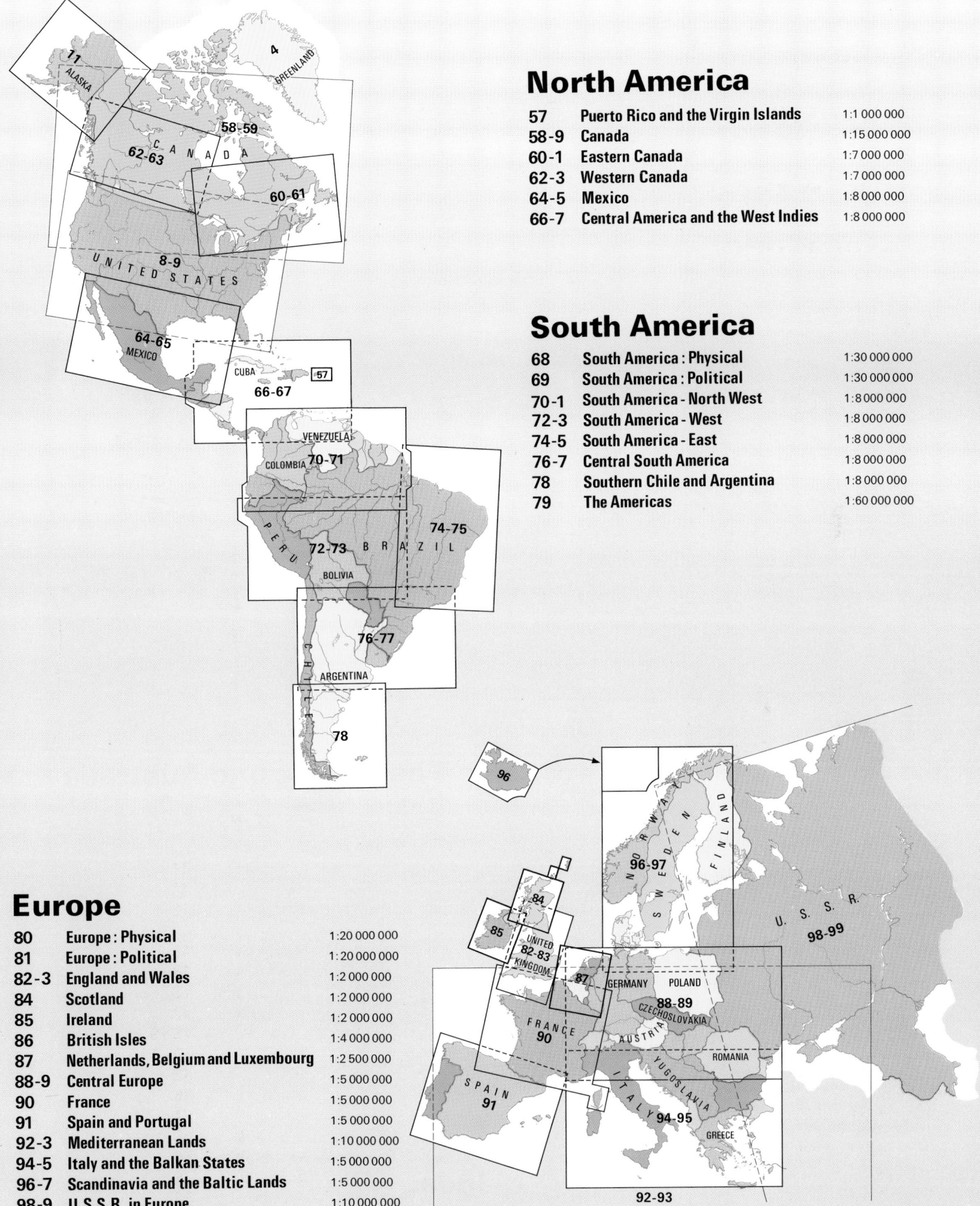

North America

South America

Europe

CONTENTS III

Asia

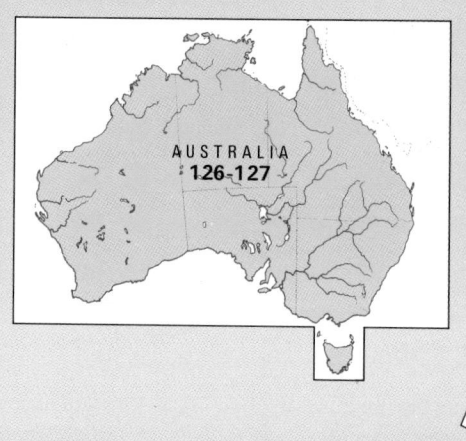

Africa

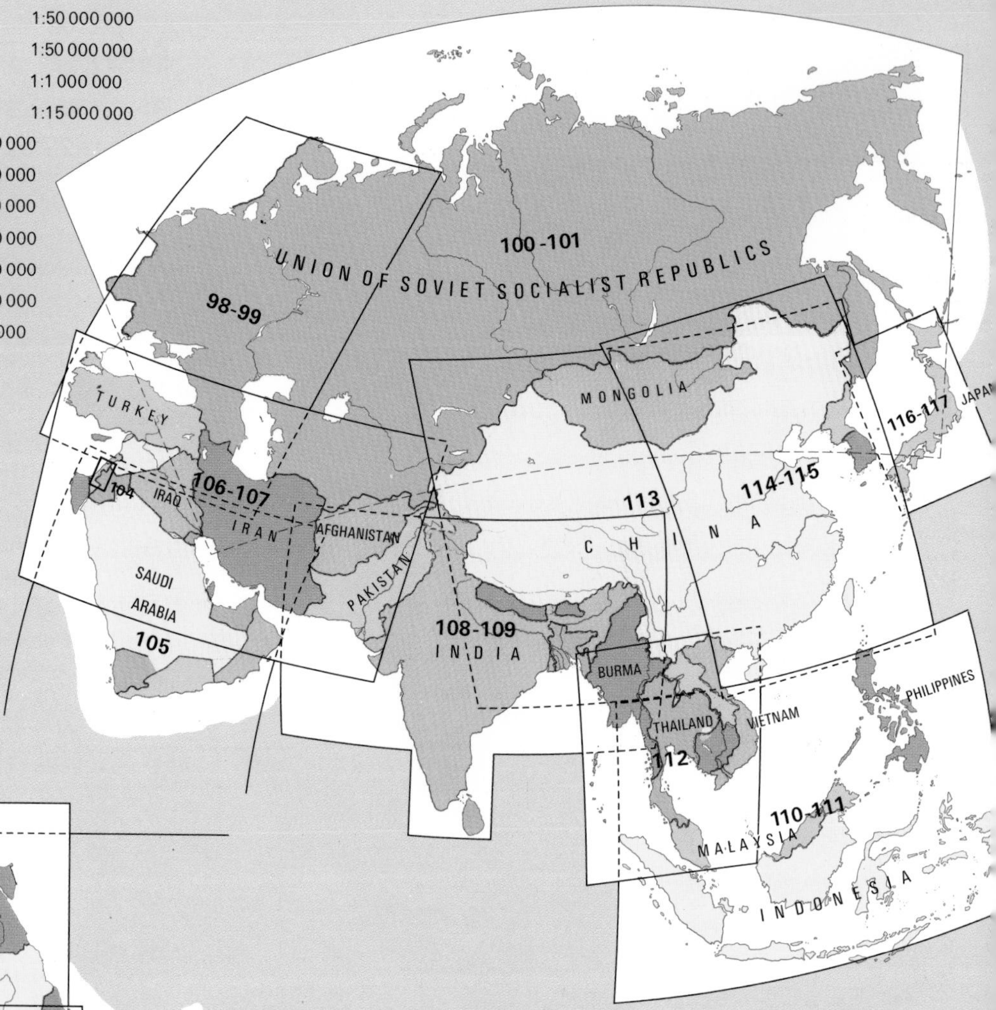

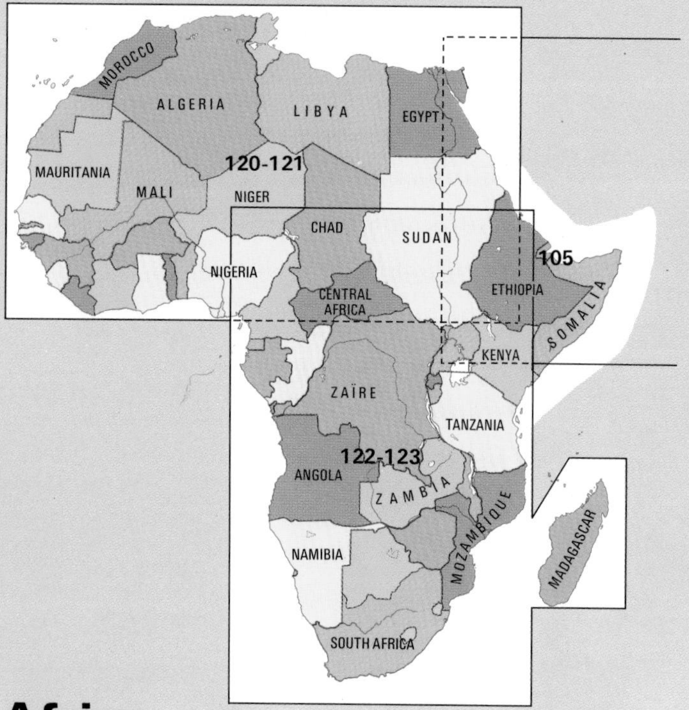

The Pacific and Australia

Index

PRINCIPAL COUNTRIES OF THE WORLD

Country	Area in thousands of square km.	Population in thousands	Density of population per sq. km.	Capital Population in thousands
Afghanistan	647	17 222	27	Kabul (1 036)
Albania	29	2 841	98	Tiranë (202)
Algeria	2 382	20 500	9	Algiers (1 740)
Angola	1 247	8 339	7	Luanda (700)
Argentina	2 767	29 627	11	Buenos Aires (9 927)
Australia	7 687	15 369	2	Canberra (251)
Austria	84	7 549	90	Vienna (1 516)
Bangladesh	144	94 651	657	Dhaka (3 459)
Belgium	31	9 856	318	Brussels (989)
Belize	23	156	5	Belmopan (3)
Benin	113	3 720	33	Porto-Novo (132)
Bhutan	47	1 360	29	Thimphu (60)
Bolivia	1 099	6 082	5	Sucre (63) La Paz (881)
Botswana	600	1 007	2	Gaborone (60)
Brazil	8 512	129 662	15	Brasilia (1 306)
Brunei	6	209	35	Bandar Seri Begawan (58)
Bulgaria	111	8 946	81	Sofia (1 064)
Burkina Faso	274	6 607	24	Ouagadougou (286)
Burma	677	36 750	54	Rangoon (2 276)
Burundi	28	4 540	162	Bujumbura (157)
Cambodia (Kampuchea)	181	6 981	39	Phnom Penh (400)
Cameroon	475	9 165	19	Yaoundé (485)
Canada	9 976	24 907	2	Ottawa (738)
Central African Rep.	623	2 450	4	Bangui (302)
Chad	1 284	4 789	4	Ndjamena (303)
Chile	757	11 682	15	Santiago (4 132)
China	9 597	1 039 677	108	Peking (9 231)
Colombia	1 139	27 190	24	Bogota (4 056)
Congo	342	1 651	5	Brazzaville (422)
Costa Rica	51	2 379	47	San José (272)
Cuba	115	9 884	86	Havana (1 951)
Cyprus	9	655	73	Nicosia (161)
Czechoslovakia	128	15 415	120	Prague (1 186)
Denmark	43	5 118	119	Copenhagen (1 382)
Djibouti	22	332	15	Djibouti (150)
Dominican Republic	49	5 962	121	Santo Domingo (1 313)
Ecuador	284	9 251	32	Quito (881)
Egypt	1 001	45 915	46	Cairo (5 074)
El Salvador	21	5 232	249	San Salvador (429)
Equatorial Guinea	28	381	14	Rey Malabo (37)
Ethiopia	1 222	33680	28	Addis Abeba (1 478)
Fiji	18	670	37	Suva (68)
Finland	337	4 863	14	Helsinki (922)
France	547	54 652	99	Paris (8 510)
French Guiana	91	78	1	Cayenne (39)
Gabon	268	1 127	4	Libréville (252)
Gambia	11	696	63	Banjul (109)
Germany, East	108	16 864	156	East Berlin (1 173)
Germany, West	249	61 638	248	Bonn (294)
Ghana	239	12 700	53	Accra (738)
Greece	132	9 848	75	Athens (3 027)
Greenland	2 176	52	0.02	Godthåb (10)
Guatemala	109	7 699	71	Guatemala (793)
Guinea	246	5 704	23	Conakry (763)
Guinea-Bissau	36	836	23	Bissau (109)
Guyana	215	922	4	Georgetown (188)
Haiti	28	5 201	186	Port-au-Prince (888)
Honduras	112	4 092	37	Tegucigalpa (485)
Hong Kong	1	5 313	5 313	Hong Kong (1 184)
Hungary	93	10 702	115	Budapest (2 067)
Iceland	103	236	2	Reykjavik (84)
India	3 288	732 256	223	Delhi (5 729)
Indonesia	2 027	156 442	77	Jakarta (6 503)
Iran	1 648	42 070	26	Tehran (4 496)
Iraq	435	14 654	34	Baghdad (2 969)
Irish Republic	70	3 508	50	Dublin (525)
Israel	21	4 097	195	Jerusalem (424)
Italy	301	56 836	189	Rome (2 831)
Ivory Coast	322	9 300	29	Abidjan (850)
Jamaica	11	2 260	205	Kingston (671)
Japan	372	119 259	320	Tokyo (8 139)
Jordan	98	3 489	36	Ammān (681)
Kenya	583	18 784	32	Nairobi (1 048)
Korea, North	121	19 185	158	Pyŏngyang (1 500)
Korea, South	98	39 951	408	Seoul (8 367)
Kuwait	18	1 672	93	Kuwait (775)
Laos	237	4 209	18	Vientiane (90)
Lebanon	10	2 739	274	Beirut (702)
Lesotho	30	1 444	48	Maseru (45)
Liberia	111	2 113	19	Monrovia (306)
Libya	1 760	3 356	2	Tripoli (980)
Luxembourg	3	365	121	Luxembourg (79)
Madagascar	587	9 400	16	Antananarivo (400)
Malawi	118	6 429	54	Lilongwe (103)
Malaysia	330	14 860	45	Kuala Lumpur (938)
Mali	1 240	7 528	6	Bamako (419)
Malta	0.3	377	1 256	Valletta (14)
Mauritania	1 031	1 779	2	Nouakchott (135)
Mauritius	2	993	496	Port Louis (149)
Mexico	1 973	75 103	38	Mexico (14 750)
Mongolia	1 565	1 803	1	Ulan Bator (419)
Morocco	447	22 110	49	Rabat (842)
Mozambique	783	13 311	17	Maputo (384)
Namibia	824	1 040	1	Windhoek (61)
Nepal	141	15 738	112	Katmandu (210)
Netherlands	41	14 362	350	Amsterdam (936)
New Zealand	269	3 203	12	Wellington (343)
Nicaragua	130	3 058	23	Managua (820)
Niger	1 267	6 040	5	Niamey (225)
Nigeria	924	89 022	96	Lagos (1 477)
Norway	324	4 129	13	Oslo (624)
Oman	212	1 131	5	Muscat (25)
Pakistan	804	89 729	112	Islamabad (201)
Panama	76	2 089	27	Panama (655)
Papua New Guinea	462	3 190	7	Port Moresby (123)
Paraguay	407	3 472	8	Asunción (602)
Peru	1 285	18 790	15	Lima (4 601)
Philippines	300	52 055	173	Manila (1 630)
Poland	313	36 571	117	Warsaw (1 641)
Portugal	92	10 056	109	Lisbon (818)
Puerto Rico	9	3 350	372	San Juan (1 086)
Romania	238	22 638	95	Bucharest (1 979)
Rwanda	26	5 700	219	Kigali (116)
Saudi Arabia	2 150	10 421	5	Riyadh (667)
Senegal	196	6 316	32	Dakar (799)
Sierra Leone	72	3 672	51	Freetown (214)
Singapore	0.6	2 502	4 170	Singapore (2 517)
Somali Republic	638	5 269	8	Mogadishu (400)
South Africa	1 221	31 008	25	Pretoria (739) Cape Town (2 517)
Spain	505	38 228	76	Madrid (3 159)
Sri Lanka	66	15 416	234	Colombo (1 412)
Sudan	2 506	20 362	8	Khartoum (561)
Surinam	163	407	2	Paramaribo (151)
Swaziland	17	605	36	Mbabane (23)
Sweden	450	8 331	19	Stockholm (1 409)
Switzerland	41	6 482	158	Bern (289)
Syria	185	9 660	52	Damascus (1 251)
Taiwan	36	18 700	519	Taipei (2 271)
Tanzania	945	20 378	22	Dar-es-Salaam (757)
Thailand	514	49 459	96	Bangkok (5 468)
Togo	56	2 756	49	Lomé (247)
Trinidad and Tobago	5	1 202	240	Port of Spain (66)
Tunisia	164	6 886	42	Tunis (597)
Turkey	781	47 279	61	Ankara (2 239)
Uganda	236	14 625	62	Kampala (332)
United Arab Emirates	84	1 206	14	Abu Dhabi (449)
U.S.S.R.	22 402	272 500	12	Moscow (8 396)
United Kingdom	245	56 377	230	London (6 755)
United States	9 363	234 496	25	Washington (3 061)
Uruguay	178	2 968	17	Montevideo (1 173)
Venezuela	912	16 394	18	Caracas (2 944)
Vietnam	330	57 181	173	Hanoi (2 571)
Western Samoa	3	159	53	Apia (36)
Yemen, North	195	6 232	32	Sana' (448)
Yemen, South	288	2 158	7	Aden (285)
Yugoslavia	256	22 800	89	Belgrade (1 407)
Zaïre	2 345	31 151	13	Kinshasa (2 242)
Zambia	753	6 242	8	Lusaka (641)
Zimbabwe	391	7 740	20	Harare (656)

PRINCIPAL CITIES OF THE WORLD

The population figures used are from censuses or more recent estimates and are given in thousands for towns and cities over 500,000 (over 750,000 in China, India, the U.S.S.R. and the U.S.A.) Where possible the population of the metropolitan area is given e.g. Greater London, Greater New York, etc.

AFRICA

ALGERIA (1977)
Alger 1 740
Oran 543

ANGOLA (1982)
Luanda 700

CAMEROON (1983)
Douala 708

EGYPT (1976)
El Qâhira 5 074
El Iskandarîya 2 318
El Giza 1 230

ETHIOPIA (1983)
Addis Abeba 1 478

GHANA (1970)
Accra 738

GUINEA (1980)
Conakry 763

IVORY COAST (1976)
Abidjan 850

KENYA (1983)
Nairobi 1 048

MOROCCO (1981)
Casablanca 2 409
Rabat-Salé 842
Fès 562
Marrakech 549

NIGERIA (1975)
Lagos 1 477
Ibadan 847

SENEGAL (1976)
Dakar 779

SOUTH AFRICA (1980)
Johannesburg ... 1 726
Cape Town 1 491
Durban 961
Pretoria 739
Port Elizabeth 585

SUDAN (1980)
El Khartûm, ... 561

TANZANIA (1978)
Dar-es-Salaam 757

TUNISIA (1984)
Tunis 597

ZAIRE (1975)
Kinshasa 2 242

ZAMBIA (1980)
Lusaka 641

ZIMBABWE (1983)
Harare 681

ASIA

AFGHANISTAN (1979)
Kābul 1 036

BANGLADESH (1982)
Dhaka 3 459
Chittagong 1 388
Khulna 623

BURMA (1977)
Rangoon 2 276

CHINA (1970)
Shanghai 11 860
Beijing 9 231
Tianjin 7 764
Shenyang 2 800
Wuhan 2 560
Guangzhou 2 500
Chongqing 2 400
Nanjing 1 750
Harbin 1 670
Dalian 1 650
Xi'an 1 600
Lanzhou 1 450
Taiyuan 1 350
Qingdao 1 300
Chengdu 1 250

Changchun 1 200
Kunming 1 100
Jinan 1 100
Fushun 1 080
Anshan 1 050
Zhengzhou 1 050
Hangzhou 960
Tangshan 950
Baotou 920
Zibo 850
Changsha 825
Shijiazhuang 800
Qiqihar 760

HONG KONG (1981)
Kowloon 2 450
Hong Kong 1 184
Tsuen Wan 599

INDIA (1981)
Calcutta 9 194
Bombay 8 243
Delhi 5 729
Madras 4 289
Bangalore 2 922
Ahmedabad 2 548
Hyderabad 2 546
Pune 1 686
Kanpur 1 639
Nagpur 1 302
Jaipur 1 015
Lucknow 1 008
Coimbatore 920
Patna 919
Surat 914
Madurai 908
Indore 829
Varanasi 797
Jabalpur 757

INDONESIA (1980)
Jakarta 6 503
Surabaya 2 028
Bandung 1 462
Medan 1 379
Semarang 1 026
Palembang 787
Ujung Pandang ... 709
Malang 512

IRAN (1976)
Tehrān 4 496
Esfahān 672
Mashhad 670
Tabrīz 599

IRAQ (1970)
Baghdād 2 969

JAPAN (1982)
Tōkyō 11 676
Yokohama 2 848
Ōsaka 2 623
Nagoya 2 093
Kyōto 1 480
Sapporo 1 465
Kobe 1 383
Fukuoka 1 121
Kitakyūshū 1 065
Kawasaki 1 055
Hiroshima 898
Sakai 809
Chiba 756
Sendai 662
Okayama 551
Kumamoto 522
Kagoshima 514
Amagasaki 510
Higashiōsaka ... 501

JORDAN (1981)
'Ammān 681

KOREA, NORTH (1972)
Pyŏngyang 1 500

KOREA, SOUTH (1980)
Sŏul 8 367
Pusan 3 160
Taegu 1 607

Inchŏn 1 085
Kwangju 728
Taejon 652

KUWAIT (1975)
Al-Kuwayt 775

LEBANON (1980)
Bayrūt 702

MALAYSIA (1980)
Kuala Lumpur 938

PAKISTAN (1981)
Karachi 5 103
Lahore 2 922
Faisalabad 1 092
Rawalpindi 806
Hyderabad 795
Multan 730
Gujranwala 597
Peshawar 555

PHILIPPINES (1981)
Manila 1 630
Quezon City 1 166
Davao 610

SAUDI ARABIA (1974)
Ar Riyād 667
Jiddah 561

SINGAPORE (1983)
Singapore 2 517

SRI LANKA (1981)
Colombo 1 412

SYRIA (1982)
Dimashq 1 112
Halab 985

TAIWAN (1981)
Taipei 2 271
Kaohsiung 1 227
Taichung 607
Tainan 595

THAILAND (1982)
Bangkok 5 468

TURKEY (1982)
İstanbul 2 949
Ankara 2 276
İzmir 1 083
Adana 864
Konya 691
Bursa 658
Gaziantep 526

VIETNAM (1973-79)
Phanh Bho Ho Chi
Minh 3 420
Hanoi 2 571
Haiphong 1 279

AUSTRALIA AND NEW ZEALAND

AUSTRALIA (1982)
Sydney 3 310
Melbourne 2 837
Brisbane 1 124
Adelaide 960
Perth 948

NEW ZEALAND (1982)
Auckland 839

EUROPE

AUSTRIA (1981)
Wien 1 516

BELGIUM (1983)
Brussel 989

BULGARIA (1982)
Sofiya 1 064

CZECHOSLOVAKIA (1983)
Praha 1 186

DENMARK (1981)
København 1 382

FINLAND (1982)
Helsinki 922

FRANCE (1982)
Paris 8 510
Lyon 1 170
Marseille 1 080
Lille 935
Bordeaux 628
Toulouse 523

GERMANY, EAST (1982)
East Berlin 1 173
Leipzig 557
Dresden 521

GERMANY, WEST (1980)
West Berlin 1 896
Hamburg 1 645
München 1 299
Köln 977
Essen 648
Frankfurt am Main 629
Dortmund 608
Düsseldorf 590
Stuttgart 581
Duisburg 558
Bremen 555
Hannover 535

GREECE (1981)
Athínai 3 027
Thessaloníki 706

HUNGARY (1983)
Budapest 2 067

IRISH REPUBLIC (1981)
Dublin 525

ITALY (1981)
Roma 2 831
Milano 1 635
Napoli 1 211
Torino 1 104
Genova 760
Palermo 700

NETHERLANDS (1983)
Rotterdam 1 025
Amsterdam 936
's-Gravenhage ... 674

NORWAY (1980)
Oslo 624

POLAND (1983)
Warszawa 1 641
Łodz 848
Kraków 735
Wrocław 631
Poznań 571

PORTUGAL (1981)
Lisboa 818

ROMANIA (1982)
Bucureşti 1 979

SPAIN (1981)
Madrid 3 159
Barcelona 1 753
Valencia 745
Sevilla 646
Zaragoza 572
Málaga 502

SWEDEN (1983)
Stockholm 1 409

SWITZERLAND (1982)
Zürich 705

U.S.S.R. (1983)
Moskva 8 396
Leningrad 4 779
Kiyev 2 355
Tashkent 1 944
Baku 1 638
Kharkov 1 519
Minsk 1 405
Gorkiy 1 382
Novosibirsk 1 370
Sverdlovsk 1 269
Kuybyshev 1 242
Dnepropetrovsk .. 1 128
Tbilisi 1 125

Odessa 1 097
Yerevan 1 095
Omsk 1 080
Chelyabinsk 1 077
Donetsk 1 055
Perm 1 037
Ufa 1 034
Kazan 1 031
Alma-Ata 1 023
Rostov 977
Volgograd 962
Saratov 887
Riga 867
Krasnoyarsk 845
Zaporozhye 835
Voronezh 831

UNITED KINGDOM (1983)
London 6 754
Birmingham 1 013
Glasgow 751
Leeds 714
Sheffield 543
Liverpool 502

YUGOSLAVIA (1981)
Beograd 1 407
Zagreb 1 175
Skopje 507

SOUTH AMERICA

ARGENTINA (1980)
Buenos Aires 9 927
Córdoba 982
Rosario 955
Mendoza 597
La Plata 560

BOLIVIA (1982)
La Paz 881

BRAZIL (1980)
São Paulo 8 732
Rio de Janeiro .. 5 539
Belo Horizonte .. 1 937
Salvador 1 502
Recife 1 433
Fortaleza 1 307
Brasilia 1 306
Pôrto Alegre ... 1 221
Nova Iguaçu ... 1 184
Curitiba 943
Belém 934
Goiánia 680
Duque de Caxias . 666
São Gonçalo ... 660
Santo André ... 634
Campinas 587

CHILE (1983)
Santiago 4 132

COLOMBIA (1978)
Bogotá 4 056
Medellin 1 507
Cali 1 316
Barranquilla 855

ECUADOR (1982)
Guayaquil 1 279
Quito 881

PARAGUAY (1978)
Asunción 602

PERU (1981)
Lima 4 601

URUGUAY (1981)
Montevideo 1 173

VENEZUELA (1980)
Caracas 2 944
Maracaibo 901
Valencia 506

NORTH AMERICA

CANADA (1983)
Toronto 3 067
Montréal 2 862

Vancouver 1 311
Ottawa 738
Edmonton 699
Calgary 634
Winnipeg 601
Québec 580
Hamilton 548

CUBA (1981)
La Habana 1 925

DOMINICAN REP. (1981)
Santo Domingo ... 1 313

GUATEMALA (1979)
Guatemala 793

HAITI (1982)
Port-au-Prince 888

JAMAICA (1980)
Kingston 671

MEXICO (1979)
Mexico 14 750
Guadalajara 2 468
Netzahualcóyotl . 2 331
Monterrey 2 019
Puebla de Zaragoza 711
Ciudad Juárez .. 625
León de los
  Aldamas 625
Tijuana 566

NICARAGUA (1981)
Managua 820

PANAMA (1981)
Panama 655

PUERTO RICO (1980)
San Juan 1 086

UNITED STATES (1980)
New York 16 121
Los Angeles ... 11 498
Chicago 7 870
Philadelphia ... 5 548
San Francisco .. 5 180
Detroit 4 618
Boston 3 448
Houston 3 101
Washington ... 3 061
Dallas 2 975
Cleveland 2 834
Miami 2 644
St. Louis 2 356
Pittsburgh 2 264
Baltimore 2 174
Minneapolis-St.
  Paul 2 114
Seattle 2 093
Atlanta 2 030
San Diego 1 817
Cincinnati 1 660
Denver 1 621
Milwaukee 1 570
Tampa 1 569
Phoenix 1 509
Kansas City ... 1 327
Indianapolis ... 1 306
Portland 1 243
Buffalo 1 243
New Orleans ... 1 187
Providence 1 096
Columbus 1 093
San Antonio ... 1 072
Sacramento ... 1 014
Dayton 1 014
Rochester 971
Salt Lake City .. 936
Memphis 913
Louisville 906
Nashville 851
Birmingham ... 847
Oklahoma 834
Greensboro 827
Norfolk 807
Albany 795
Toledo 792
Honolulu 763

Chart of the Stars

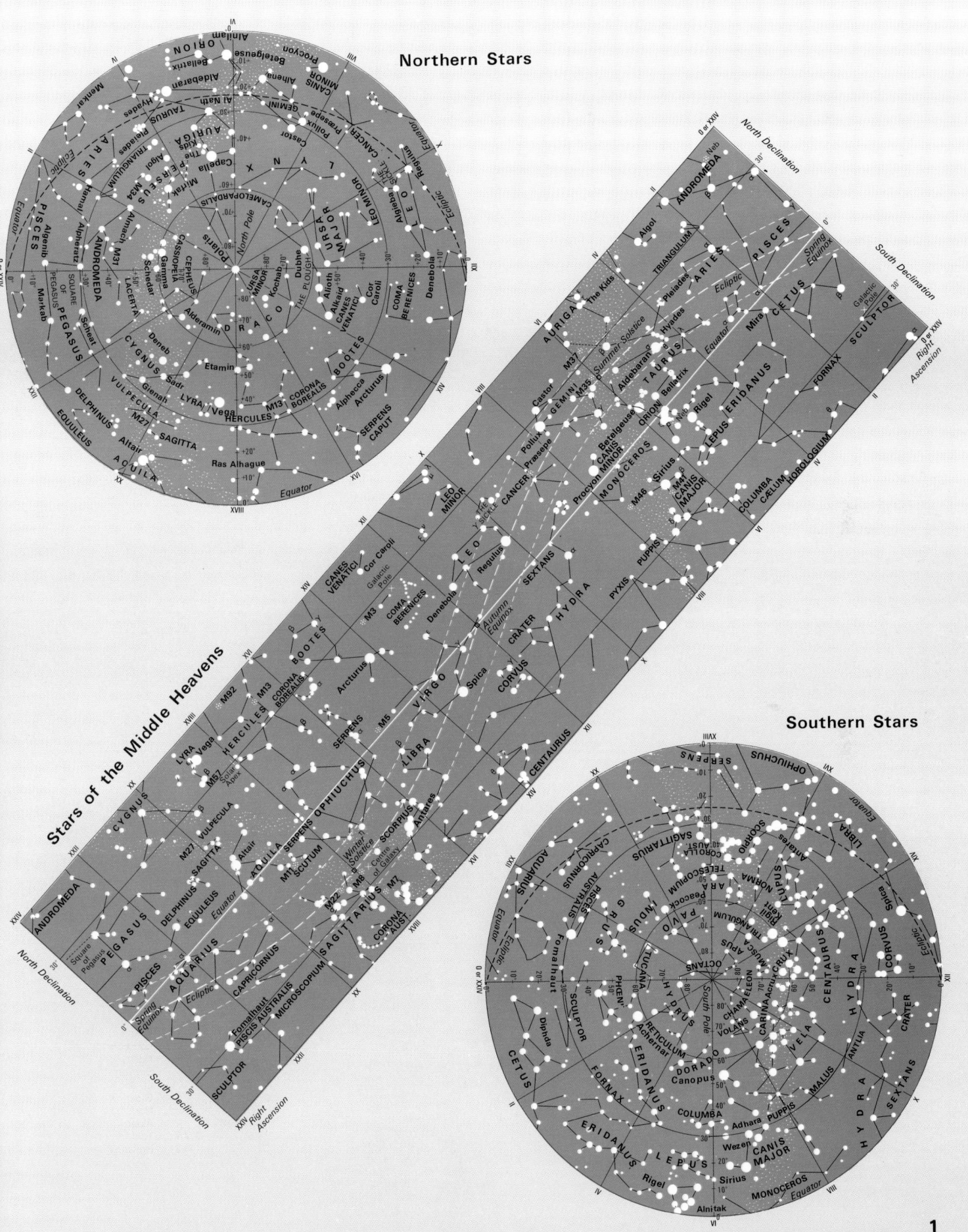

Northern Stars

Stars of the Middle Heavens

Southern Stars

1

Continents of the World

3

Oceans of the World

5

Facts and Comparisons

Earth's Dimensions

	Distance in miles	*Distance in kilometers*
Equatorial circumference	24,902	40,076
Polar circumference	24,860	40,008
Equatorial diameter	7,927	12,757
Polar diameter	7,900	12,714
Equatorial radius	3,963	6,378
Polar radius	3,950	6,357

Surface Area	197,000,000 mi^2
Land surface	57,000,000 mi^2
Land surface as % of total area	29.2%
Water surface	139,000,000 mi^2
Volume of the Earth	672,686 x 10^6 mi^3
Mass of the Earth	5.9 x 10^{21} tonnes

Continental Comparisons

Continent	*Area in Square Miles (Square Kilometers)*	*Population Estimated June 1980*	*Highest Elevation*	*Lowest Elevation*	*Hottest Recorded Temperature*	*Coldest Recorded Temperature*
Africa	11,685,000 (30,264,150)	476,053,000	Mt. Kilimanjaro, Tanzania 19,340 ft. 5,895 m.	Lac Assal, Djibouti 509 ft. below sea level	Al'Aziziyah, Libya 136°F Sept. 13, 1922	Ifrane, Morocco –11°F Feb. 11, 1935
Antarctica	5,100,000 (13,209,000)	Uninhabited	Vinson Massif 16,864 ft. 5,140 m.	Unknown	Esperanza 58°F Oct. 20, 1956	Vostok –127°F Aug. 24, 1960
Asia	17,085,000 (44,250,150)	2,636,525,000	Mt. Everest, China-Nepal 29,028 ft. 8,848 m.	Dead Sea, Israel-Jordan 1,299 ft. below sea level	Tirat Tsvi, Israel 129°F June 21, 1942	Oymyakon, Soviet Union –90°F Feb. 6, 1933
Australia	2,967,909 (7,686,884)	14,726,000	Mt. Kosciusko 7,314 ft. 2,230 m.	Lake Eyre 52 ft. below sea level	Cloncurry 128°F Jan. 16, 1889	Charlotte Pass –8°F July 22, 1947
Europe	3,825,000 (9,906,750)	680,375,000	Mt. Elbrus, Soviet Union 18,481 ft. 5,633 m.	Caspian Sea, Soviet Union-Iran 92 ft. below sea level	Seville, Spain 122°F Aug. 4, 1881	Ust-Shchugor, Soviet Union –67°F date unknown
North America	9,420,000 (24,397,800)	367,515,000	Mt. McKinley, United States 20,320 ft. 6,194 m.	Death Valley, United States 282 ft. below sea level	Death Valley, United States 134°F July 10, 1913	Snag, Canada –81°F Feb. 3, 1947
South America	6,870,000 (17,793,300)	239,207,000	Mt. Aconcagua, Argentina 22,831 ft. 6,959 m.	Salinas Chicas, Argentina 138 ft. below sea level	Rivadavia, Argentina 120°F Dec. 11, 1905	Sarmiento, Argentina –27°F June 1, 1907
Oceania (including Australia)	3,295,000 (8,534,050)	24,800,000	Mt. Wilhelm, Papua New Guinea 15,400 ft. 4,694 m.	Lake Eyre, Australia 52 ft. below sea level	Cloncurry, Australia 128°F Jan. 16, 1889	Charlotte Pass, Australia –8°F July 22, 1947

Mt. Everest

Dead Sea

Oceans and Seas

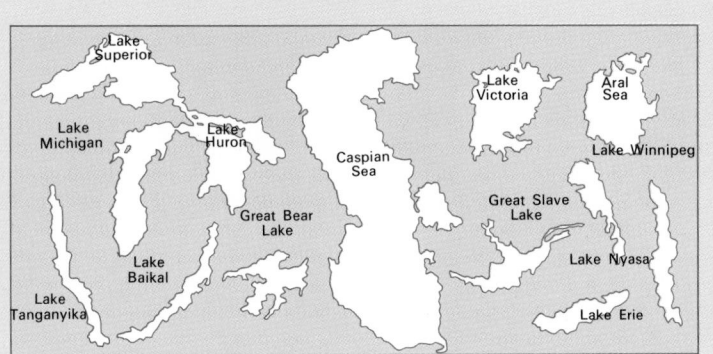

	Area in Square Miles	Area in Square Kilometers
Pacific Ocean	64,186,300	166,242,527
Atlantic Ocean	33,420,000	86,557,800
Indian Ocean	28,350,500	73,427,795
Arctic Ocean	5,105,700	13,223,763
Caribbean Sea	971,400	2,515,926
Mediterranean Sea	969,100	2,509,969
Bering Sea	873,000	2,261,070
Gulf of Mexico	582,100	1,507,639
Sea of Okhotsk	537,500	1,392,125
Sea of Japan	391,100	1,012,949
Hudson Bay	281,900	730,121
East China Sea	256,600	664,594
Black Sea	196,100	507,899
Red Sea	174,900	452,991
North Sea	164,900	427,091
Baltic Sea	147,500	382,025
Persian Gulf	88,800	229,992
Gulf of California	59,100	153,069

Lakes and Inland Seas

	Continent	Area in Square Miles	Area in Square Kilometers
Caspian Sea	Asia-Europe	143,550	371,795
Lake Superior	North America	31,700	82,103
Lake Victoria	Africa	26,828	69,485
Aral Sea	Asia	25,300	65,527
Lake Huron	North America	23,100	59,829
Lake Michigan	North America	22,300	57,757
Lake Tanganyika	Africa	12,700	32,893
Great Bear Lake	North America	12,096	31,329
Lake Baikal	Asia	11,780	30,510
Lake Nyasa	Africa	11,430	29,604
Great Slave Lake	North America	11,031	28,570
Lake Erie	North America	9,910	25,667
Lake Winnipeg	North America	9,417	24,390

Longest Rivers in the World

	Continent	Length in Miles	Length in Kilometers
Nile	Africa	4,145	6,670
Amazon	South America	4,000	6,437
Mississippi-Missouri	North America	3,710	5,971
Ob-Irtysh	Asia	3,460	5,568
Yangtze	Asia	3,434	5,526
Hwang	Asia	2,903	4,672
Amur	Asia	2,744	4,416
Lena	Asia	2,734	4,400
Zaire (Congo)	Africa	2,718	4,374
Mackenzie	North America	2,635	4,241
Mekong	Asia	2,600	4,184
Niger	Africa	2,600	4,184
Yenisey	Asia	2,566	4,130

Flags of the World

Canada

United States

Iceland

Norway

Finland

Sweden

Denmark

United Kingdom

German Dem. Rep.

Poland

Netherlands

Ireland

Fed. Rep. of Germany

Czechoslovakia

Belgium

Luxembourg

Hungary

France

Switzerland

Austria

Yugoslavia

Portugal

Spain

Italy

Albania

Antigua & Barbuda

Bahamas

St. Kitts & Nevis

Mexico

Cuba

Haiti

Belize

Guatemala

Jamaica

Dominica

Dominican Republic

Barbados

Cape Verde Is.

Morocco

Algeria

Tunisia

El Salvador

Honduras

Grenada

Trinidad & Tobago

St. Lucia

Mauritania

Mali

Libya

Costa Rica

Nicaragua

Venezuela

St. Vincent

Senegal

Burkina Faso

Niger

Panama

Colombia

Guyana

Gambia

Guinea

Ghana

Nigeria

Ecuador

Surinam

Guinea-Bissau

Ivory Coast

Benin

Central African F

Sierra Leone

Togo

Cameroon

Equatorial Guinea

Liberia

Brazil

São Tomé

Gabon

Peru

Angola

Bolivia

Z

Paraguay

Botsw

Chile

Argentina

Le

Uruguay

South Africa

8

United Nations

Vatican City

U.S.S.R.

Mongolia

Japan

North Korea

China

South Korea

Turkey

Syria

Iraq

Afghanistan

Lebanon

Iran

Kuwait

Bhutan

Taiwan
Republic of China

Pakistan

Nepal

Jordan

Qatar

Bahrain

Bangladesh

Hong Kong

Israel

United Arab Emirates

India

Burma

Saudi Arabia

Laos

Ethiopia

Oman

Philippines

Yemen,

South Yemen

Thailand

Djibouti

Vietnam

Uganda

Sri Lanka

Kampuchea

Kiribati

Somalia

Malaysia

Brunei

Rwanda

Maldive Islands

Nauru

Burundi

Kenya

Singapore

Solomon Is.

Tuvalu

Seychelles

Indonesia

Tanzania

Western Samoa

Comoros

Papua New Guinea

Malawi

Mauritius

Vanuatu

Fiji

Zimbabwe

Mozambique

Madagascar

Australia

Tonga

Swaziland

New Zealand

Landsat Images — Introduction

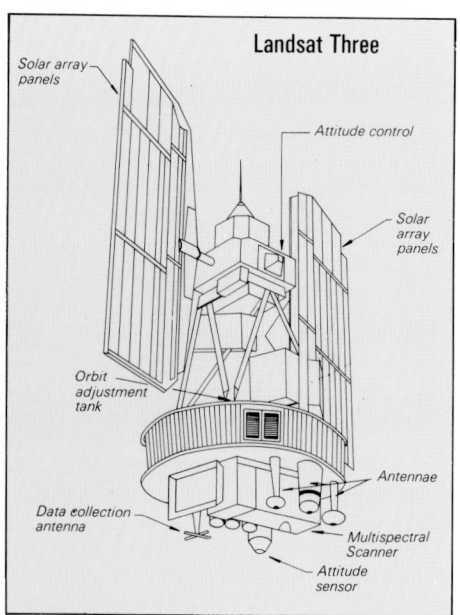

Landsat Three

Solar array panels

Attitude control

Solar array panels

Orbit adjustment tank

Antennae

Data collection antenna

Multispectral Scanner

Attitude sensor

The National Aeronautics and Space Administration (NASA) of the United States established its Earth Resources Survey Programme in 1965. It has developed the space programmes of Gemini, Apollo, Skylab and Landsat. The first Landsat was launched in 1972 and the fourth in 1982. The satellite is put into orbit and gathers its information by "remote sensing", that is viewing the Earth from a great height and signalling what it sees back to Earth.

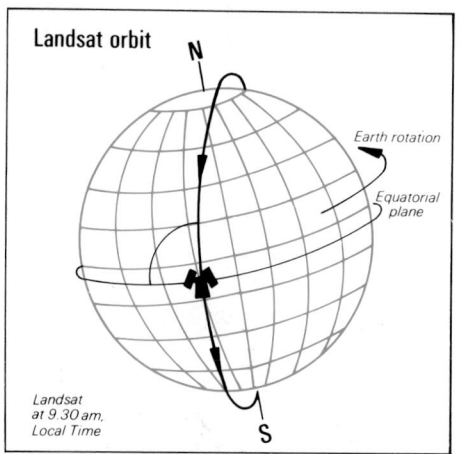

Landsat orbit

N

Earth rotation

Equatorial plane

Landsat at 9.30 am, Local Time

S

The Landsat spacecraft circles the Earth at a height of 919km and nearly crosses the Poles, cutting the Equator at 9° from a rightangle. It weighs 959kg. It takes 103 minutes to complete a revolution of the Earth and crosses the Equator at the same local time, about 9.30 in the morning, always therefore on the sunlit side of the Earth. It circles the Earth fourteen times a day and on the fifteenth orbit is overhead, 159km west of its original point. It returns to the original point eighteen days later. When Landsat 2 and 3 were working together this "same image" period was reduced to nine days. The instruments on board record a view of the Earth along its path to a width of 185km and an area of approximately 35,000km² per scene. The fourth Landsat was launched in 1982, flies at an altitude of 705km and has a sixteen day cycle.

Landsat carries a number of instruments and the one responsible for the images on the following pages is the Multi Spectral Scanner (MSS). The word "image" is used rather than photograph because they are not produced by a camera or are they true in colour. On board the spacecraft a

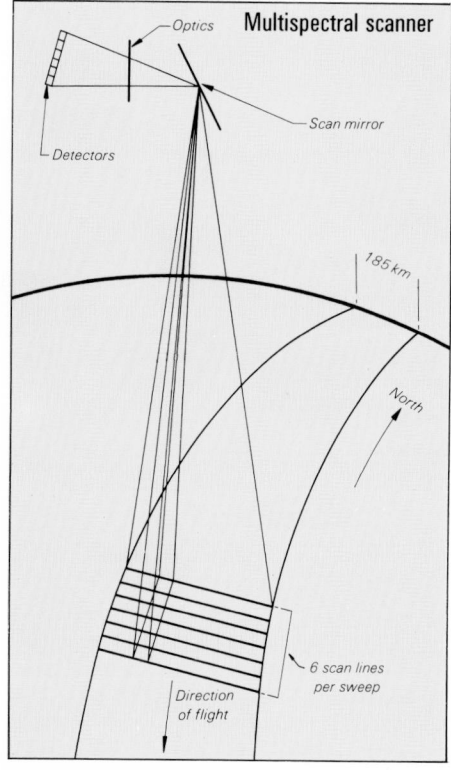

Multispectral scanner

Optics

Scan mirror

Detectors

185 km

North

Direction of flight

6 scan lines per sweep

mirror oscillates slightly, scanning a swathe of the Earth at rightangles to the orbit path. The light from the ground is broken down through filters into four selected parts of the spectrum, two of visible light and two in the infra-red. The intensity in each of these bands for a small area of the Earth is measured and converted into a signal which is sent to the Earth receiving station. If the satellite is out of sight the material is recorded and transmitted when it is in contact with a ground station.

Four black and white images are made for each of the spectral bands by reproducing the intensity for the given area on a grey scale. To produce the false colour images in the following pages, the black and white images of the two visible bands and the longer infra-red are passed through colour filters.

In such a false colour image, growing vegetation being highly reflective in the near infra-red appears in shades of red. Water areas appear as black if clear and deep, but if it has sediment in it, it will be blue. This can be seen at the mouths of rivers and along coastal bays. Soils and rocks appear bluish but can range through yellow and browns; where there is a high water content, as in peats, they will be black. Cities and principal roads which can be detected on the image will be white to blue-grey. These are only indications of the colour for their actual hue can be affected by the angle of illumination of the sun on the original scene, the atmospheric conditions, the season in the vegetational growth cycle and minor variations in the image processing and printing.

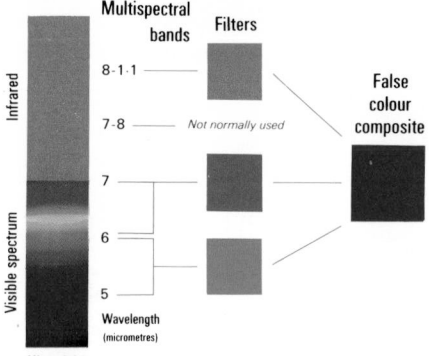

Landsat false colour

Infrared

Visible spectrum

Ultraviolet

Multispectral bands

Filters

8-1-1

7-8   Not normally used

7

6

5

Wavelength (micrometres)

False colour composite

On each of the following pages are presented a false colour image of part of the Earth at a scale of 1:1 000 000 (1cm = 10km), a map of the same area and a brief description. The map is normally at a scale of 1:2 500 000 (1cm = 25km) but if it is at a smaller scale the image area is shown on the map by a red square.

Some applications of Landsat

Geology	recognition of rock types, landforms and specific minerals
Water resources	area of surface water, water availability; extent of snow cover or ice, glaciers, floods and irrigation; sediment and mapping of shallow waters; shoreline changes
Environment	effects of natural disasters; air pollution; mapping of remote areas
Agriculture	crop, timber, vegetation—surveys and health; soil conditions; crop areas and yield; land-use surveys

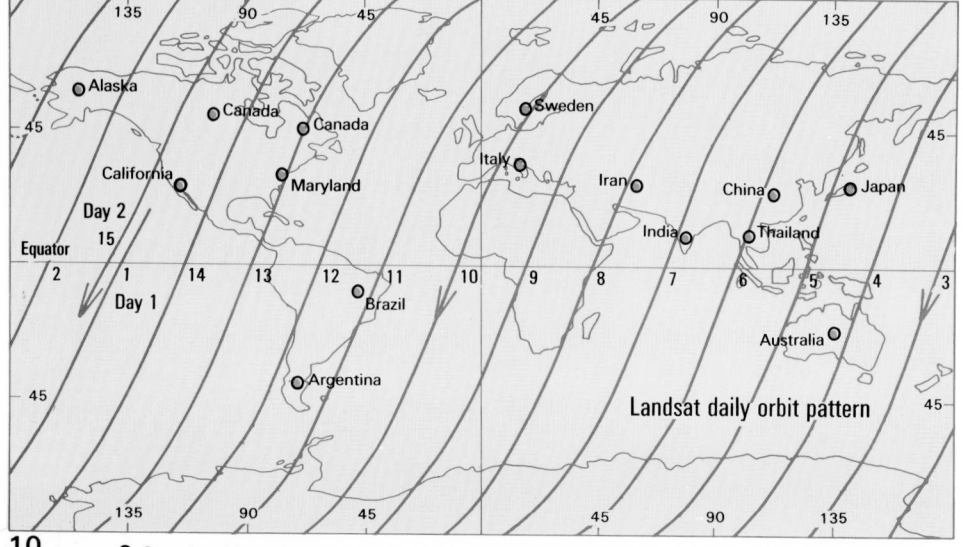

Landsat daily orbit pattern

Alaska

Canada

Canada

Sweden

Italy

Iran

China

Japan

California

Maryland

India

Thailand

Day 2

15

Equator

2   1   14   13   12   11   10   9   8   7   6   5   4   3

Day 1

Brazil

Australia

Argentina

Ground receiving station

A quarter of a million years ago, a huge ice-cap covered much of North America. When it melted, water collected in huge depressions, becoming what we know as the Great Lakes. The pattern of rivers is now much changed since before the glaciation: the Niagara, between Lakes Erie and Ontario, makes a spectacular waterfall as it flows over the edge of a great limestone escarpment, the product of erosion by an ancient drainage system. Another legacy of the Ice Age has been a coating of fertile clays and sands spread over this region. In consequence, Canada's "Golden Horseshoe", bordering Lake Ontario from Toronto to the U.S. frontier, is rich crop and fruit-growing country, lately experiencing industrial and urban growth. *(Image taken in September)*

Cape Cod

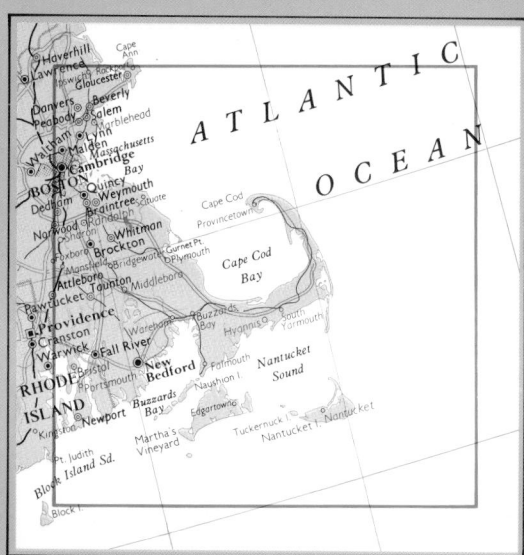

The remarkable outline of Cape Cod, poking out to sea like a scorpion's tail, is the work of two of nature's most potent agents: ice and sea. Ice-transported debris, or *moraine*, piled up where the Ice Age glaciers reached their southernmost extent, were left above the rising sea level as the islands and peninsulas around Nantucket Sound. By steadily removing sand alongshore, ocean waves have subsequently produced bars and spits, Cape Cod being the most spectacular of a number of examples shown in this image. The landscape provides for the nearby East Coast cities in several ways – holiday resorts, fishing harbours, and fertile land for garden produce. *(Image taken in July)*

The Tennessee Valley

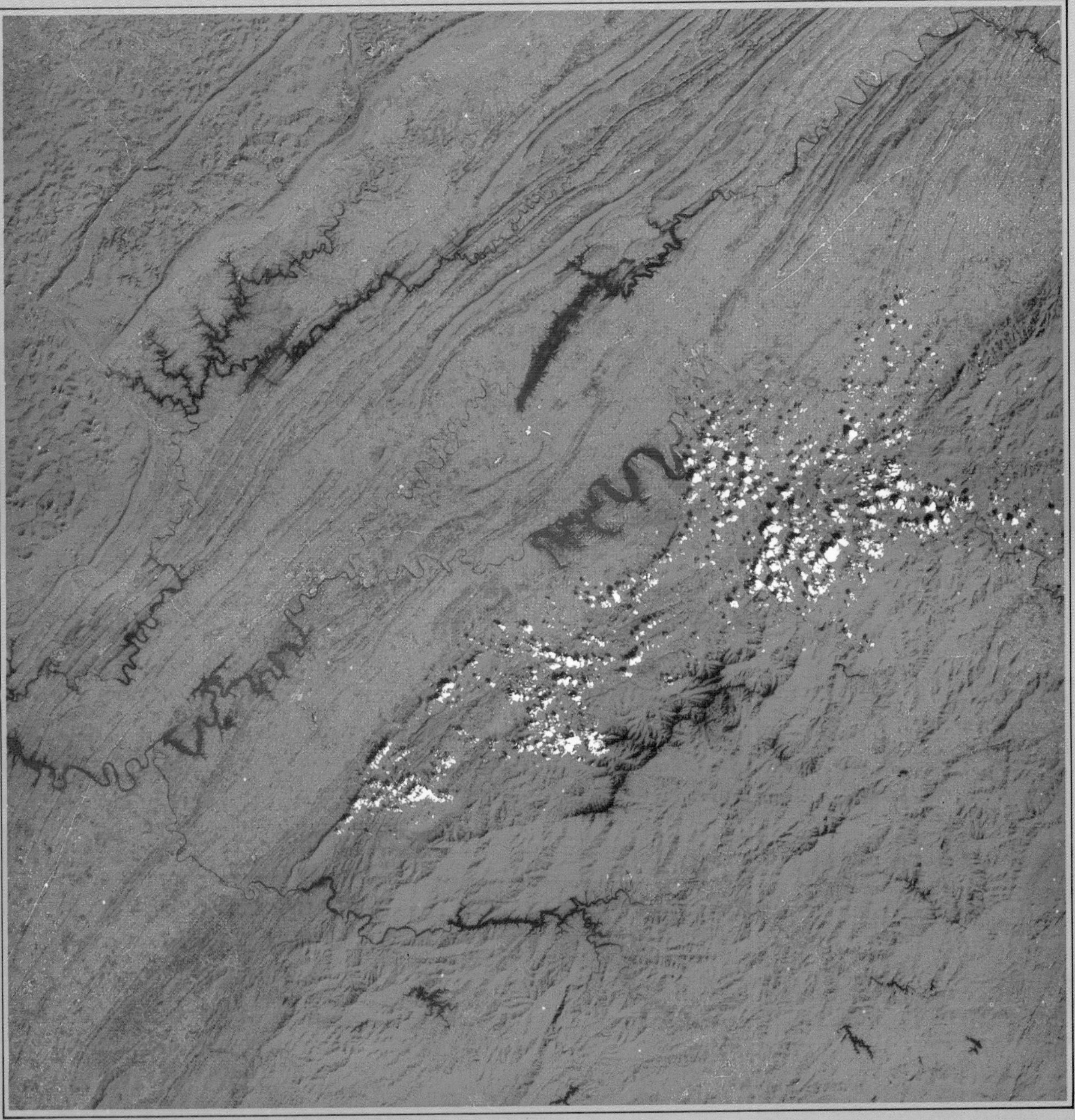

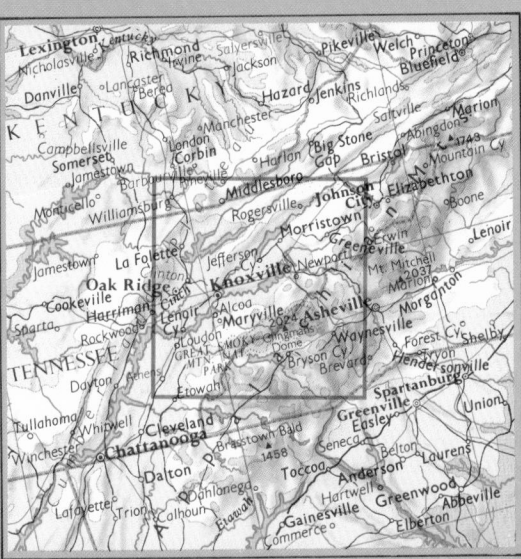

Three regions can be identified running northeast-southwest across this view of the Appalachian Mountains in Tennessee. The heavily-forested Great Smoky Mountains are the highest in Eastern United States, with Clingman's Dome rising above 2000m. Several rivers, many dammed to provide hydroelectric power, meander across the Appalachian Valley, a fertile agricultural corridor characterized by a succession of parallel limestone ridges cloaked in woodland. Separated from the valley by a faulted edge is the isolated Cumberland Plateau, a region of forested upland and limestone gorges, inhabited by poor mining communities. *(Image taken in October)*

Washington — Baltimore

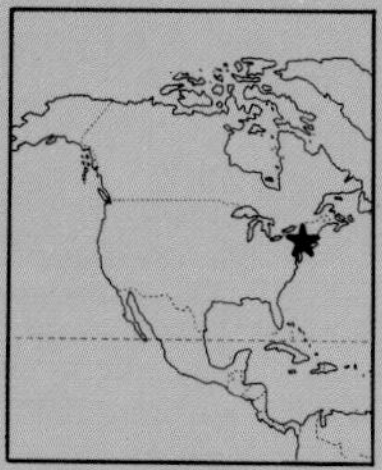

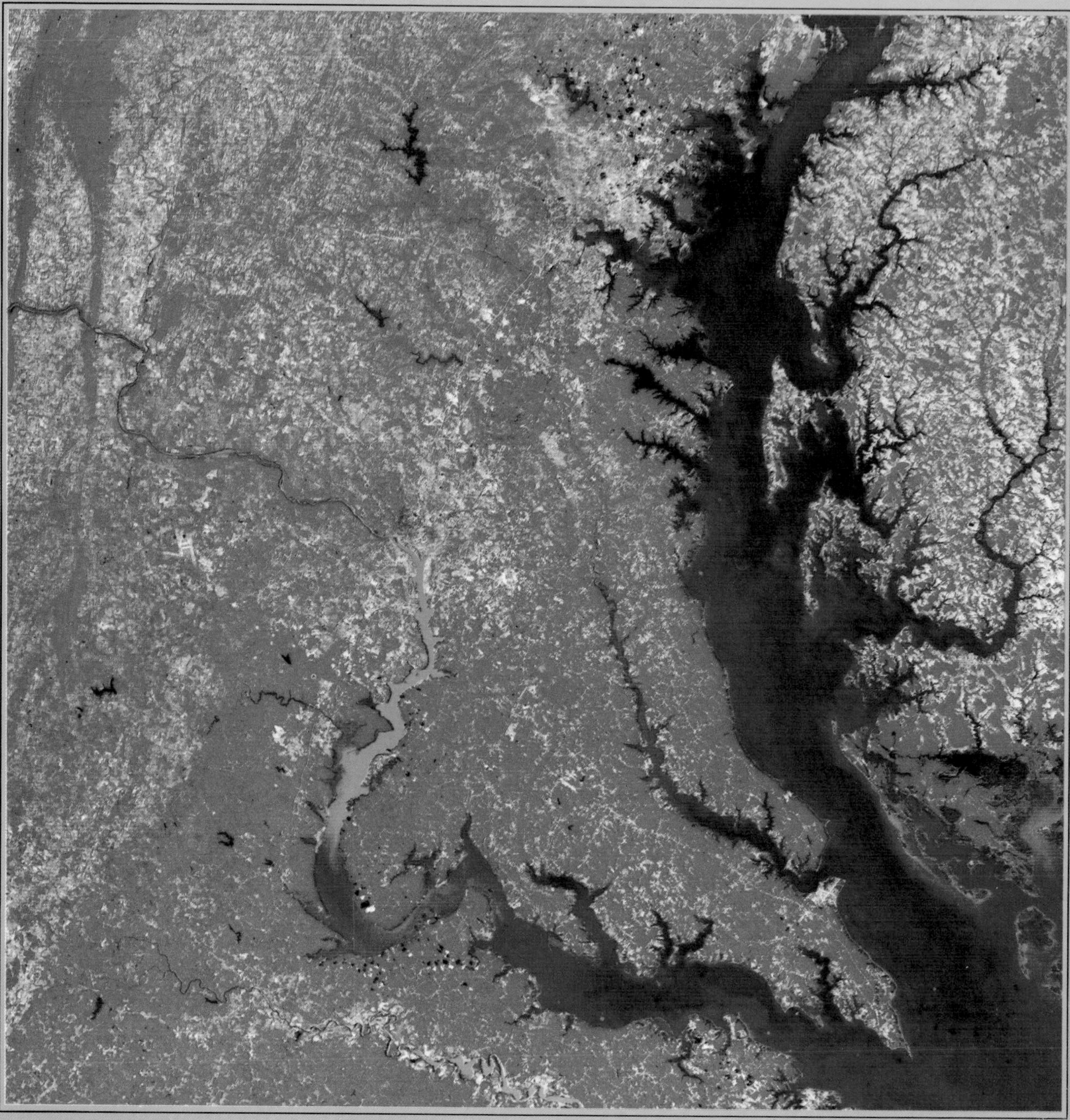

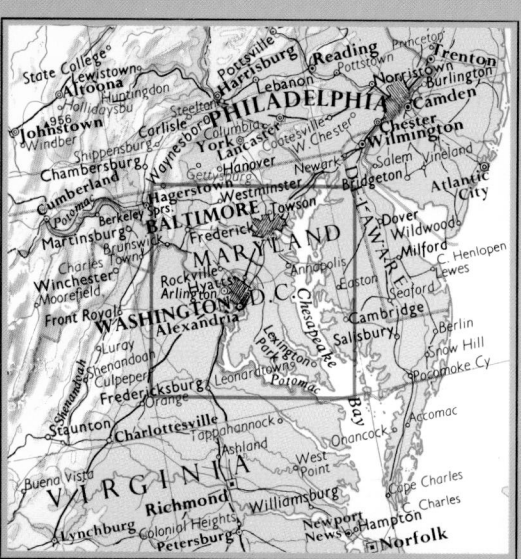

The cities of Washington and Baltimore may be thought of as forming the southern end of a virtually continuous urban agglomeration or *megalopolis* extending as far as Boston in the north. The use of intermediate land not yet swallowed up for urban use is typified here: orchards, vegetable gardens and dairying for city markets lie among stands of dense woodland. Washington's transitional position between the industrial North and agricultural South was considered an important factor when it was chosen as capital of the United States. Some of the city's landmarks are visible here: the Capitol and White House grounds, and the Mall which runs between them. *(Image taken in October)*

St. Louis, Missouri

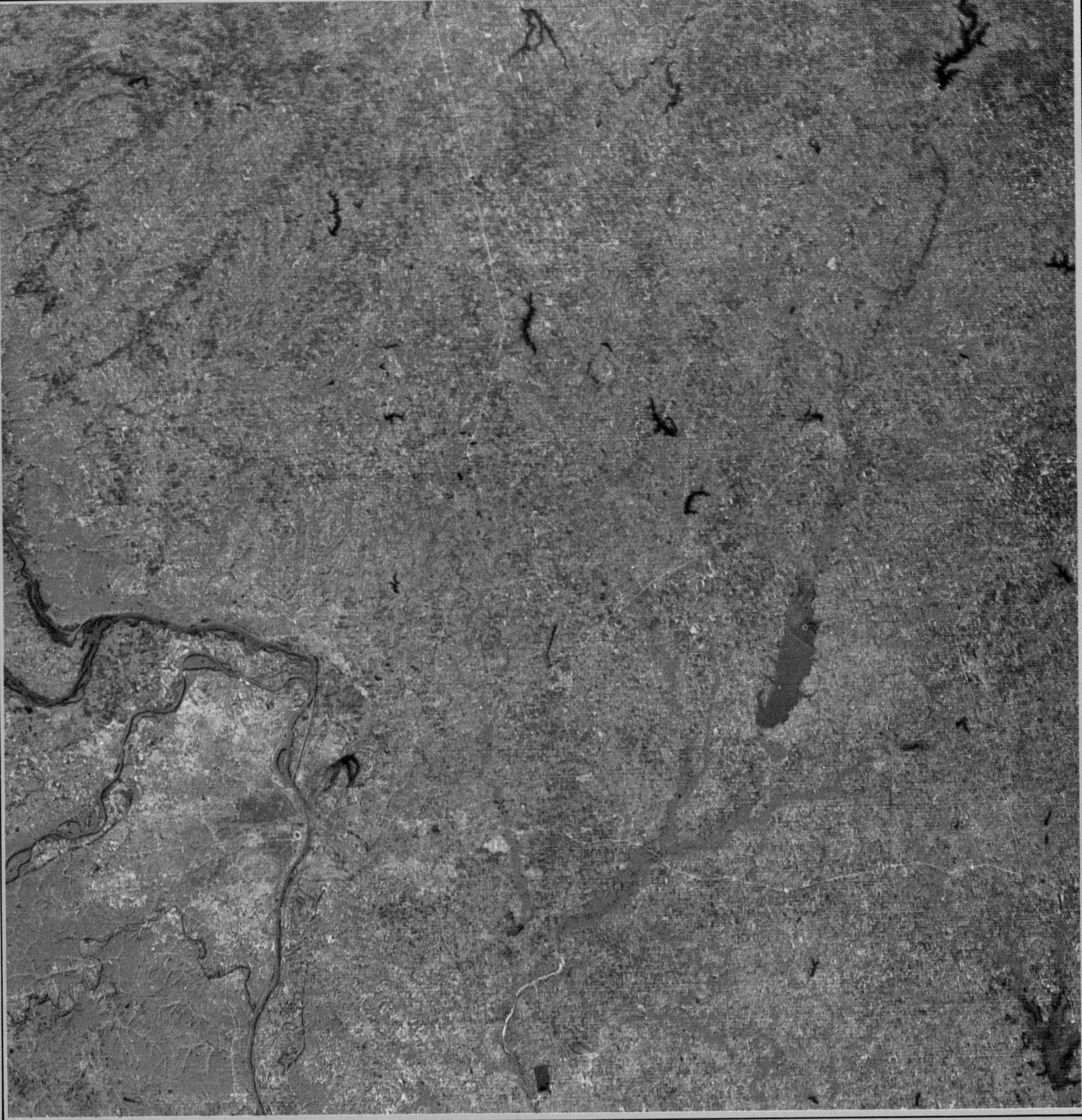

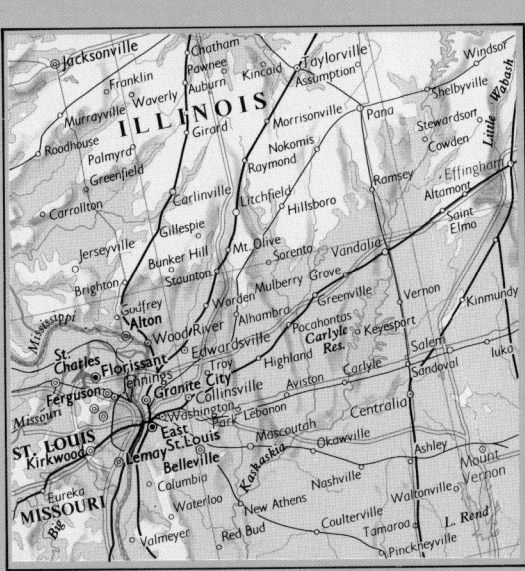

St. Louis, standing at the meeting-place of major rivers and highways, could also be said to lie at the geographical crossroads of the United States. The Mississippi river is generally regarded as the border between the industrialized East and the open country of the West. Below St. Louis, the Mississippi valley opens out into the Gulf Plains of the Deep South. Most of the scene belongs, however, to the continent's agricultural heartland, the lowland prairies that stretch away to the north, beyond the Great Lakes into Canada. Here in Illinois, the corn, wheat and soyabean fields – now harvested – are laced with the deeper red of woods and meadows that follow the river courses and so display their intricate patterns on the landscape.
(Image taken in October)

The Mississippi River

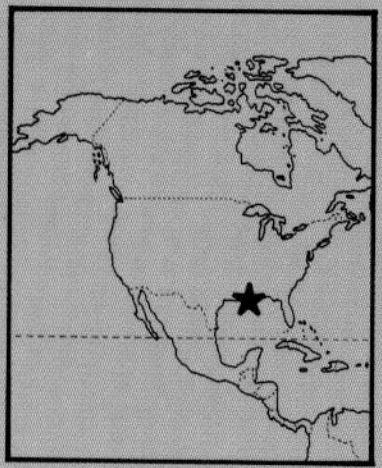

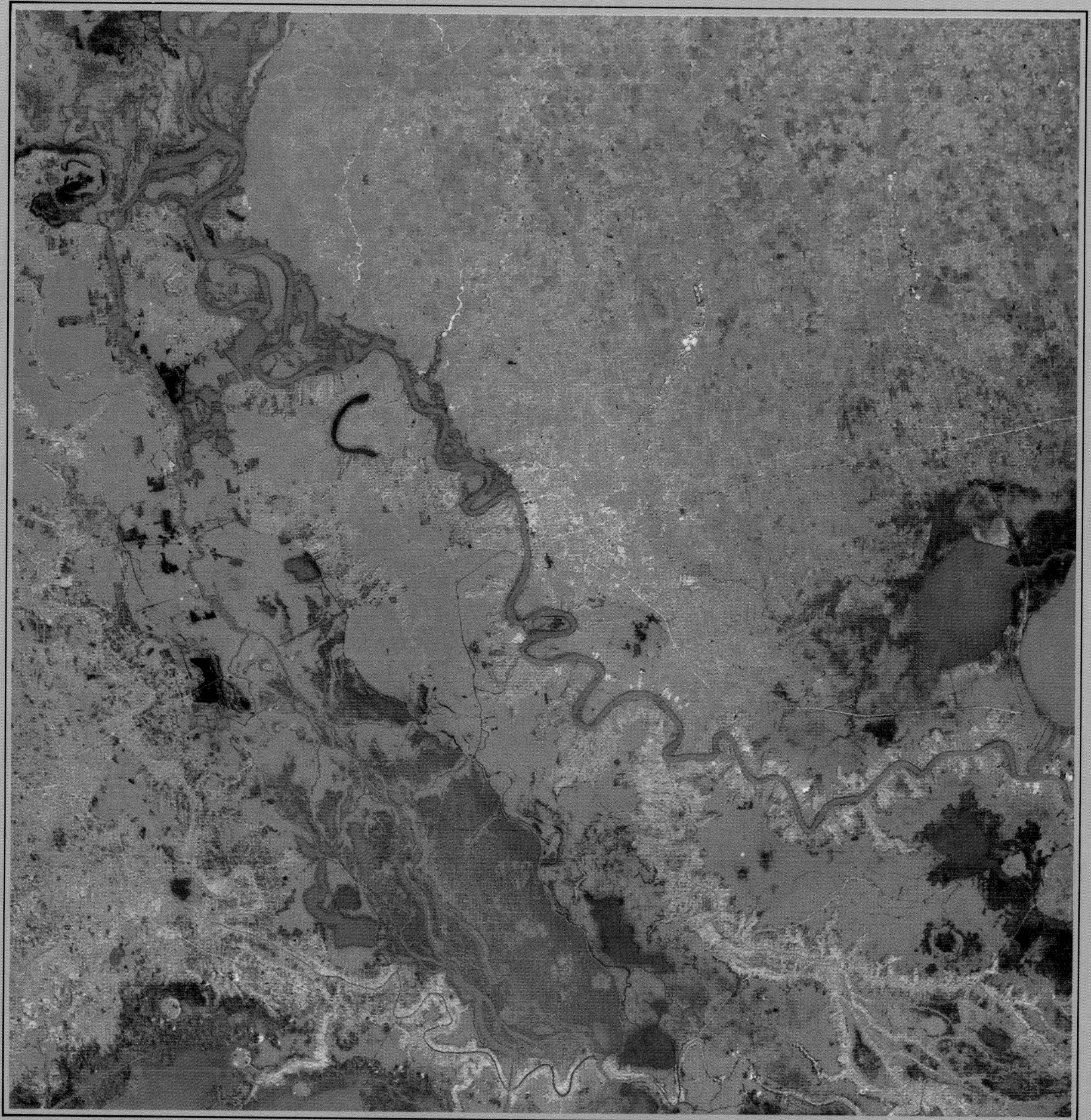

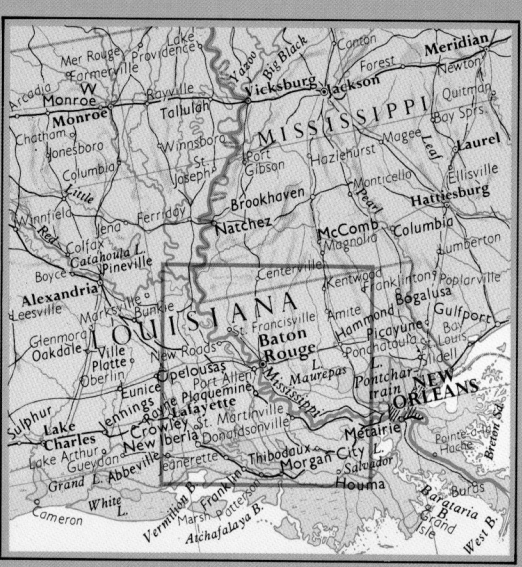

Meandering across the flat plains of Louisiana, the Mississippi is nearing the end of its journey to the Gulf of Mexico. Seen at high water during a spring flood, it is pale blue on the image with the great volume of sediment carried at that time. Especially to the west of the river, there is dense, swampy forest amid a jumble of smaller streams and lakes that represent older courses taken by the Mississippi to the sea. The farmland occupies the areas of higher land that envelop the river course in the southern part of the image. The distinctive field pattern, long strips of land perpendicular to the river-bank, was inherited from early French settlers. *(Image taken in May)*

Southern Florida

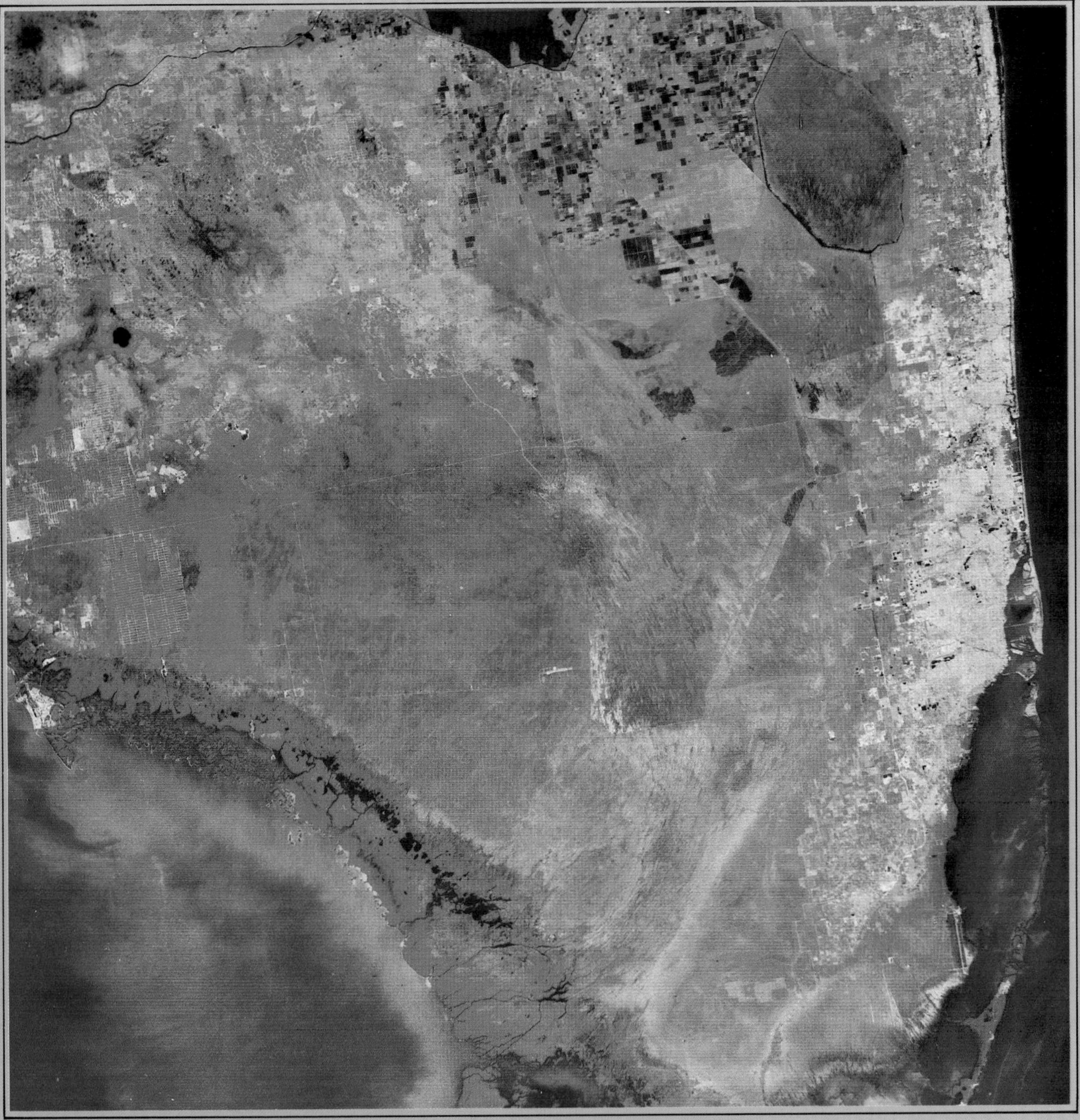

Southern Florida is a unique region of the United States. Almost entirely flat lowland, enjoying a tropical climate and covered by swamp and sand, it is also both a tourist boom area and rich farming country. Trapped behind the sand bars thrown up by Atlantic waves, the vast Everglades tall saw-grass swamp dominates this image – a grey mass, flecked with red marking the "tree-islands" of slightly higher rises. Man's shaping of the land-scape is betrayed by straight lines and rectangular patterns: the streets and blocks of the Eastern Gold Coast cities from Palm Beach to Miami, the orchards, gardens and sugar-cane fields around the southern shores of Lake Okeechobee. *(Image taken in March)*

The Canadian Rockies

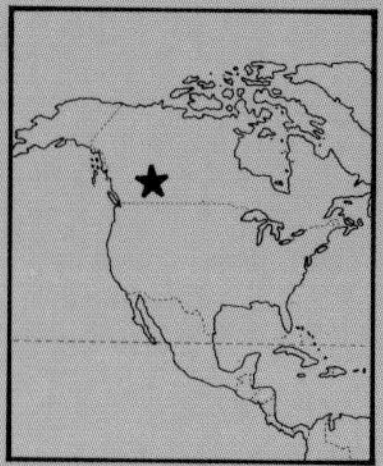

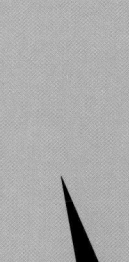

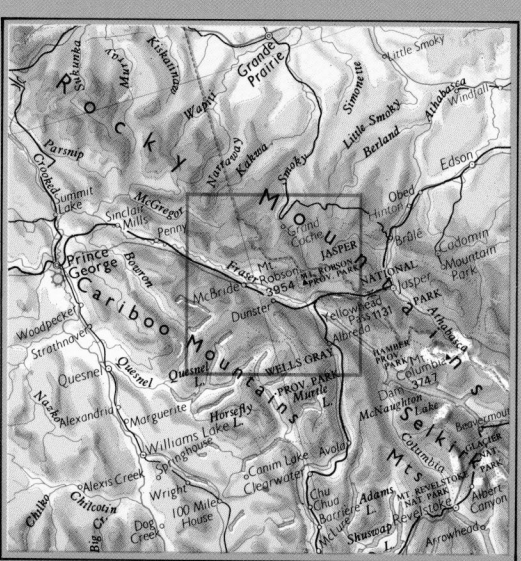

The Rocky Mountain Trench cuts across the Canadian Cordilleras pictured in this image – and for hundreds of miles northwest to the Yukon and southeast to Montana in the United States. This remarkably straight depression, occupied here by the Fraser river sharply divides the Rocky mountains from the Cariboo and Selkirk ranges, though, as the image illustrates, the landscape to either side is one of snow-capped summits and deep valleys with evidence of faulting and glacial erosion. From its linearity and geology, the Trench itself is obviously the product of faulting, but its exact origin is less clear. Could it have been carved by ice along a line of weakness, or was it simply dropped between long parallel cracks in the Earth's surface? *(Image taken in September)*

Lethbridge, Alberta

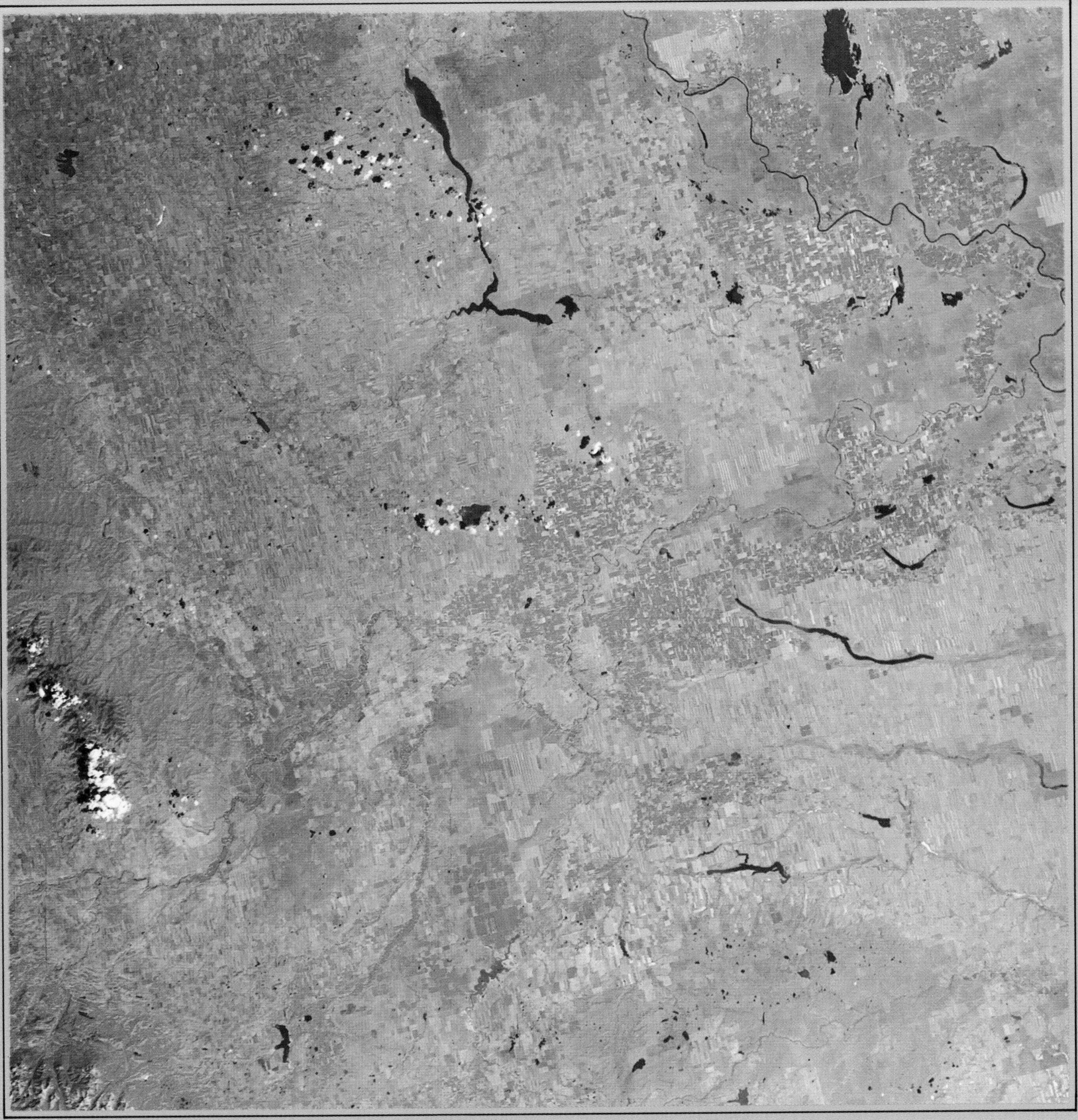

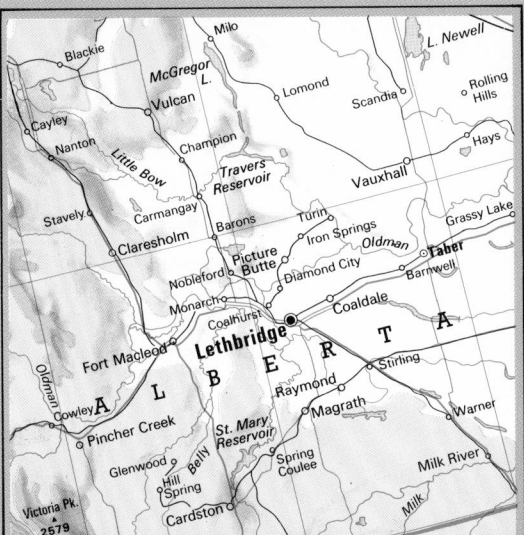

Nearly all this image of the Prairies just east of the Rockies in Southern Alberta is agricultural land of one type or another, although this even-surfaced countryside is of varying fertility and can suffer excessive temperature ranges and near-aridity. Different crops have found their best cultivation sites according to local conditions. Narrow wheat fields occupy the driest areas east of Lethbridge, while to the northeast lies expansive pasture land or, showing as bright red patches, irrigated fields of corn, sugar beet and potatoes. The fine mosaic of the remaining land identifies the many small farms that both raise cattle and grow fodder crops on the wetter black soils east of the foothills. (*Image taken in August*)

The Canyon Lands of Utah

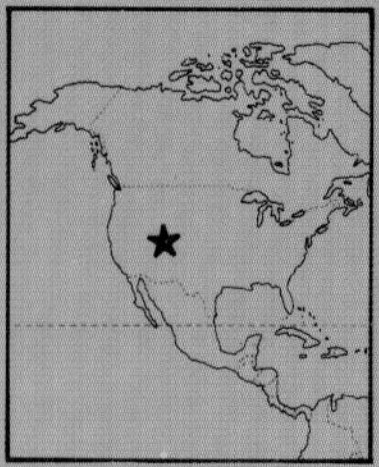

By the same process which created the Grand Canyon further downstream, the upper Colorado and its tributaries have found renewed energy from the uplifting of the Colorado Plateau to carve deep, if less impressive canyons for themselves. The region's climate is not too harsh – there is enough rainfall to support grasslands and dense pine forest on higher ground, masked by snow in this winter scene. It is the ruggedness and inaccessibility that has made farming and settlement difficult. Instead, other potential qualities have been exploited: plentiful supplies of fresh water are dammed in reservoirs, and the natural beauty of the canyonlands draws tourists to the area every year. *(Image taken in February)*

San Francisco

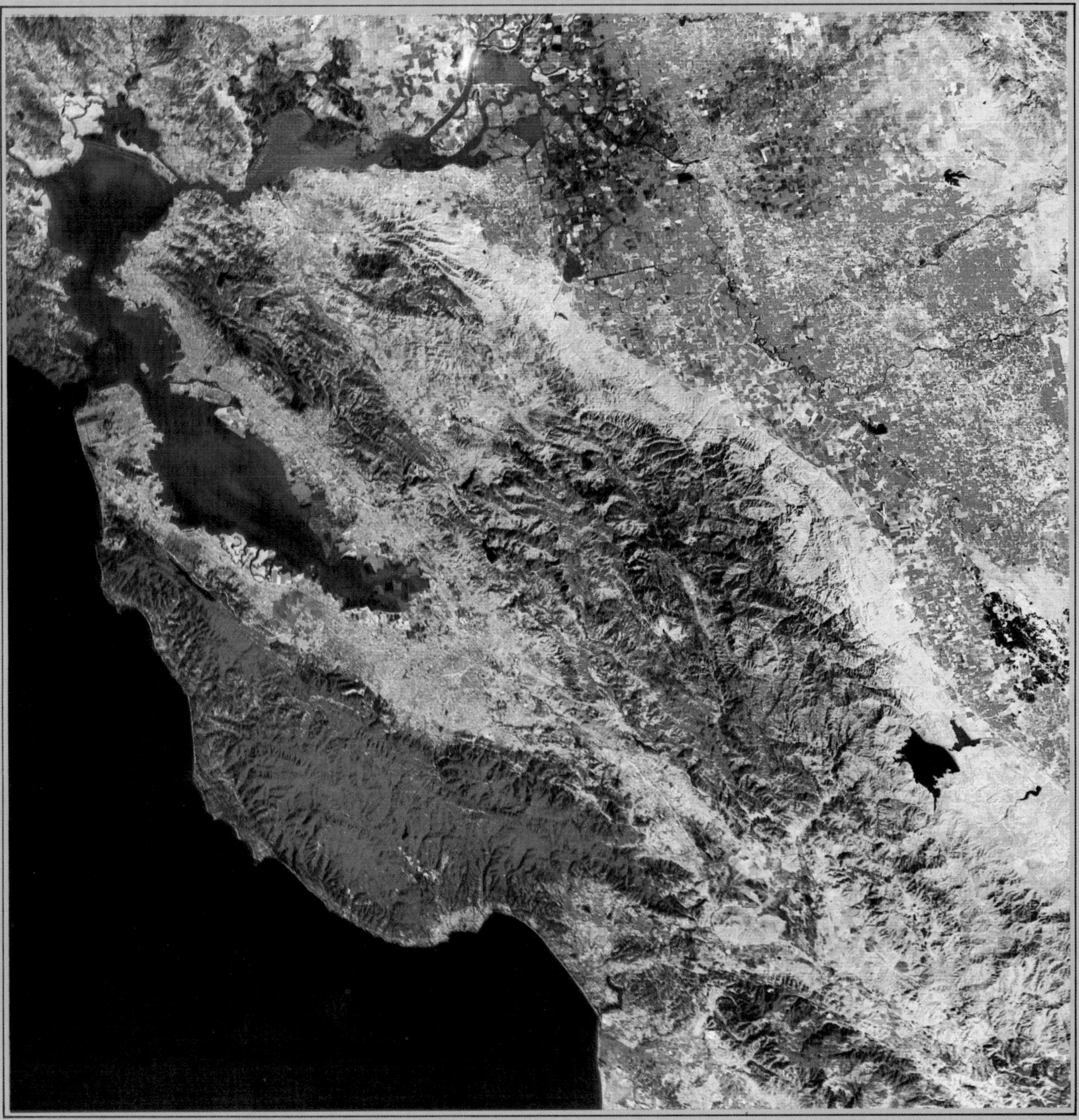

Faults, great fissures in the Earth's crust, run the length of America's west coast. Troughs, like San Francisco Bay and San Joaquin Valley, have been created where land has slumped between them. The former was drowned when the sea breached the Golden Gate, creating a magnificent deepwater harbour, around which San Francisco and the Bay Area cities grew up. The San Joaquin Valley, with its fertile soils and perfect Mediterranean climate, produces fruit, vegetables, wine, cotton and rice for sale in the rest of the world. Marking the edge of the redwood-forested Santa Cruz Mountains is the notorious San Andreas fault, responsible for earthquakes which destroyed San Francisco in 1906 and always threaten to do so again. *(Image taken in October)*

The Grand Canyon

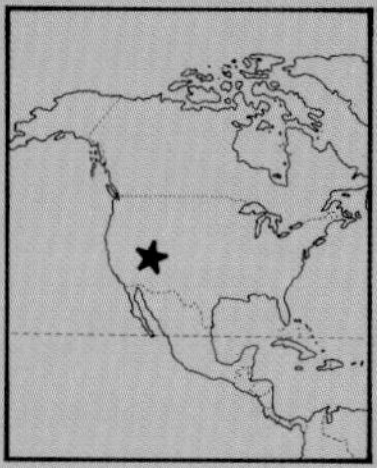

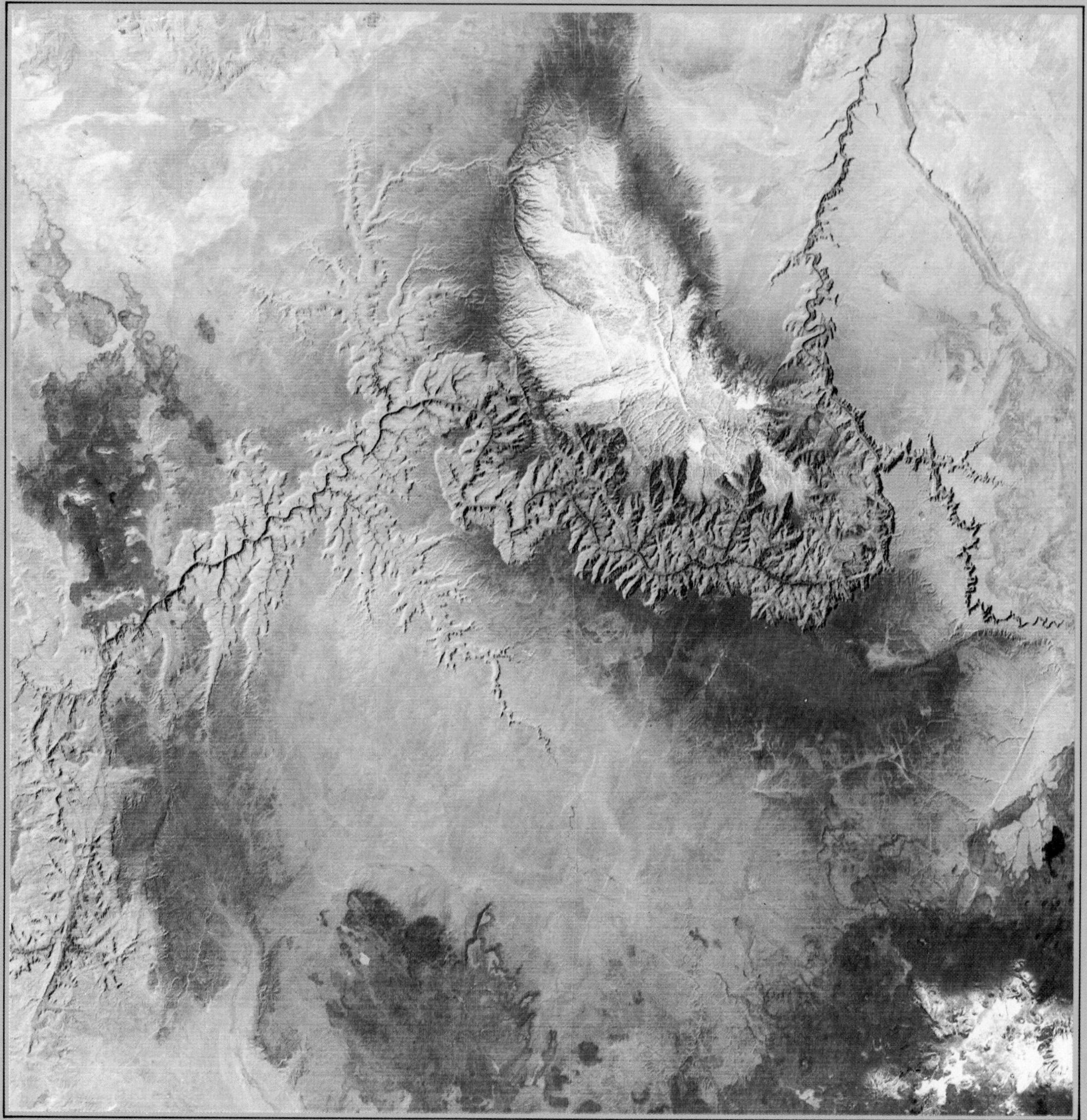

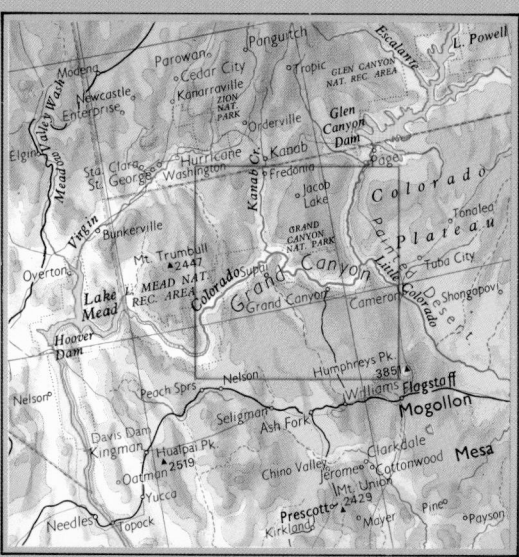

The Colorado River, maintaining its course by cutting deeply into the plateau that has been uplifted in geologically recent times, has sculpted one of the world's most spectacular natural features. 20 km by 1.6 km at its widest and deepest, the Grand Canyon has been hewn from rocks laid down successively in more or less horizontal, undisturbed layers. The resulting profile, weathered back through time, offers both an unparallelled insight into geological history – and breathtaking scenery that draws thousands of tourists every year to this largely semi-desert region. *(Image taken in May)*

Salton Sea, California

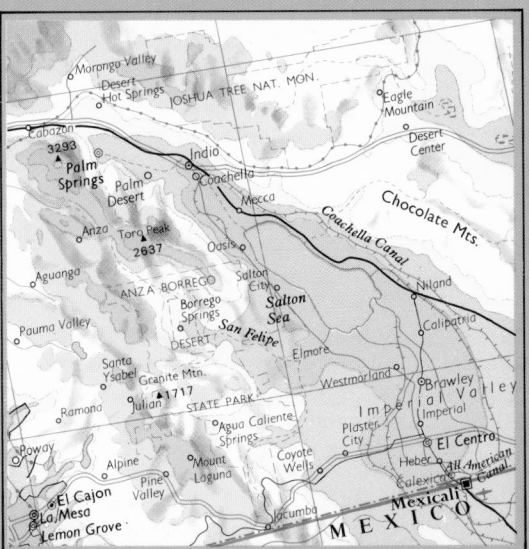

The Colorado River flows well to the East of this image, but its waters are responsible for bringing life to this eternally dry, sun-baked region. A trough between the arid Chocolate Mountains and the scrub-vegetated ranges to the west, its lowest depths reach 80m below sea-level. Here, water was channelled from the Colorado in the early 20th century and collected to form the Salton Sea. A modern irrigation system built from the All-American and Coachella canals that draw water from the Imperial Reservoir, sustains the level of the Sea, and the rich variety of fruit and grain crops filling the Imperial Valley to the south in a bright mosaic. Note how the character of land-use changes across the border at Mexicali. *(Image taken in July)*

Mexico City

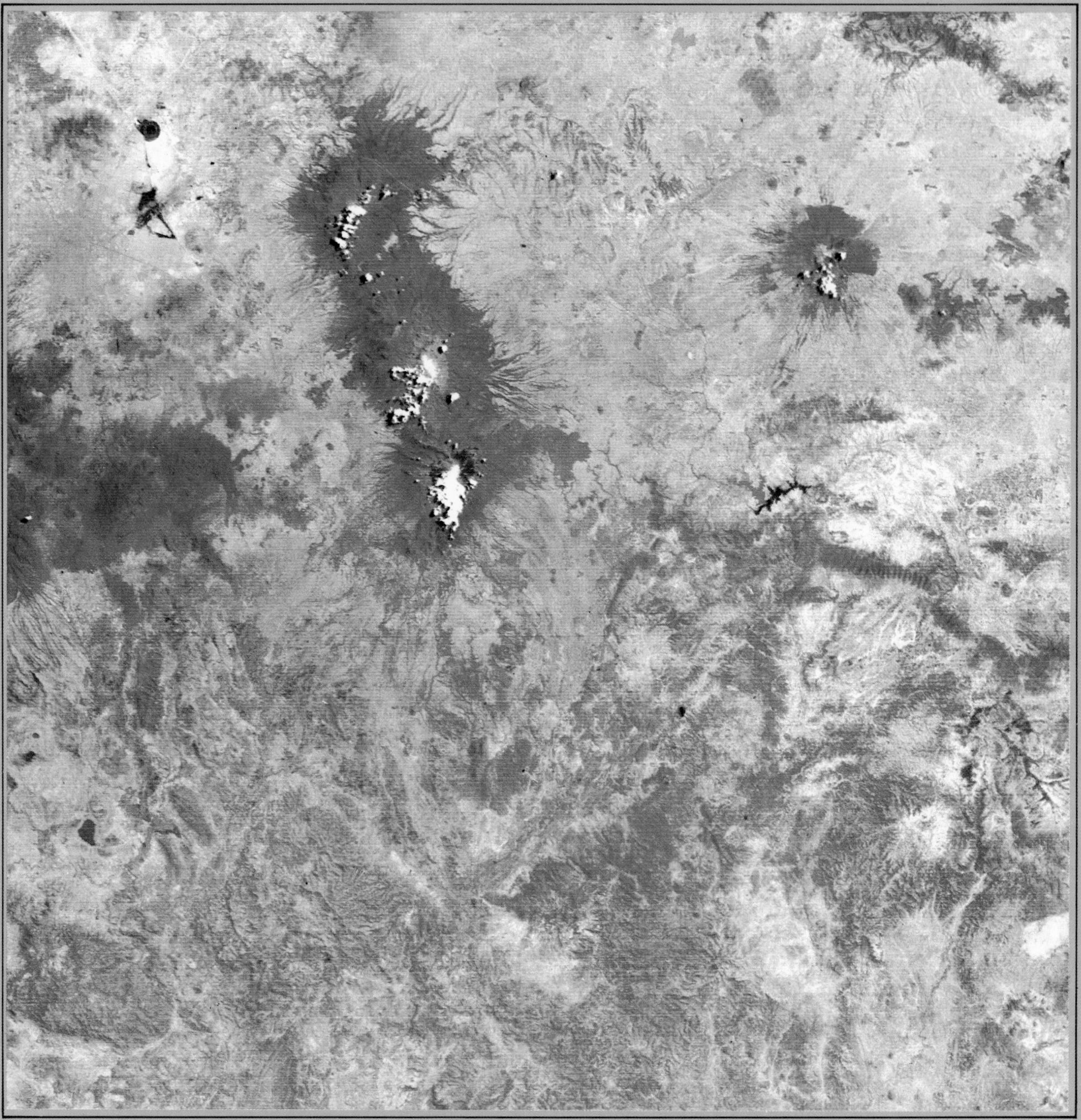

High above the Mesa Central soar the grand volcanoes, Popocatepetl, Iztacihuatl and La Malinche, snow-clad summits atop thickly-forested slopes. To this land of temperate climate and fertile volcanic soils, came the Indians, who farmed the land and founded cities where they settled. The great Aztec civilization originated at Tenochtitlán, by the shores of Lake Texcoco in the Valley of Mexico. Today, as in ancient times, maize and beans are the main crops of the plateau, and the old Aztec city, now called Mexico City, is one of the largest urban areas in the world, with a population of over 10 millions. *(Image taken in May)*

U.S.A.

SETTLEMENTS

Settlement symbols in order of size

BALTIMORE ■**NEWARK** ■ **Allentown** ● **Trenton** ◉**Norristown** ◎ Bridgeton ○ Quakertown ○ Parkesburg ○ Avondale

ADMINISTRATION

County seat towns have red infill   **RICHMOND** State Capital   **WASHINGTON** National Capital

—— County Boundary
(census area in Alaska)

OHIO / INDIANA State Boundary

ADDISON Counties

National Parks, Recreation Areas, Monuments, Seashores, Lakeshores

Indian Reservations   MARK TWAIN NATIONAL FOREST National Forests

COMMUNICATIONS

Interstates and Major Turnpikes

Other Highways

—— Railroads

→- - ← Railroad Tunnels

≍ Passes

Transportation Canals

Other Canals

✈ Major Airfields

+ Other Airfields

PHYSICAL FEATURES

Perennial Streams

Intermittent Streams

Waterfalls

Perennial Lakes

Swamps, Marshes

Intermittent Lakes

Dry Lakes

Glaciers, Icefields

Dams with Reservoirs

▲ 733 Elevation in meters

▼ 329 Sea Depth in meters

174 Height of Lake Surface Above Sea Level in meters

WORLD

SETTLEMENTS

Settlement symbols in order of size

LONDON ■ **Stuttgart** ● **Sevilla** ◎ **Bergen** ◎ Bath ○ Biarritz ○ Srikolayatji

Settlement symbols and type styles vary according to the scale of each map and indicate the importance of towns on map rather than specific population figures

ADMINISTRATION

—— International Boundaries

- - - International Boundaries
(Undemarcated or undefined)

······· Internal Boundaries

National and Provincial Parks

International boundaries show the **de facto** situation where there are rival claims to territory

COMMUNICATIONS

—— Principal Roads

Other Roads

≍ Passes

Principal Railroads

Other Railroads

Railroads (under construction)

········ Principal Canals

Principal Oil Pipelines

3386 Principal Shipping Routes

Trails and Seasonal Roads

✧ Airfields

PHYSICAL FEATURES

Perennial Streams

Intermittent Streams

Perennial Lakes

Swamps, Marshes

Intermittent Lakes

Permanent Ice

Wells in Desert

▲▼ 8848 Elevation, Sea Depth in meters

1134 Height of Lake Surface Above Sea Level in meters

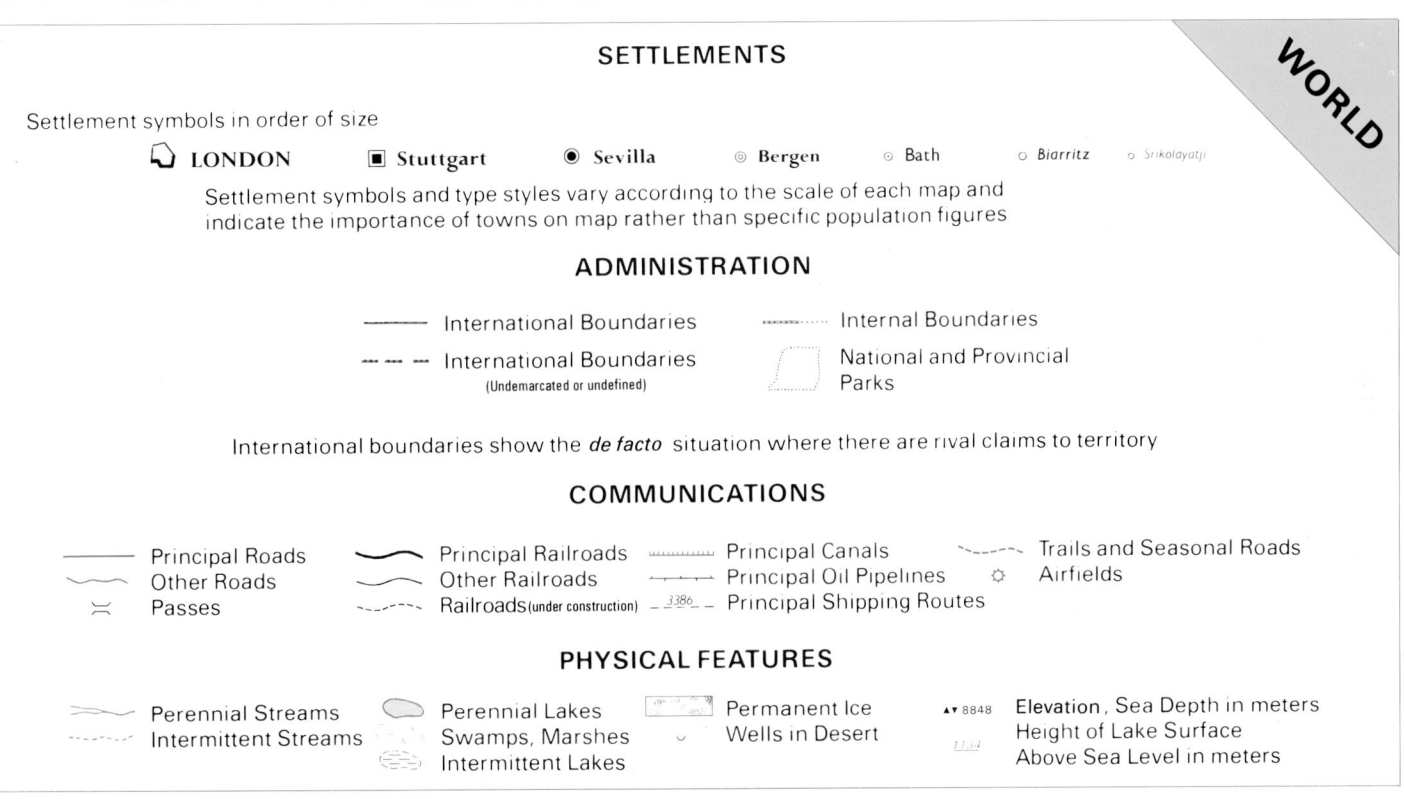

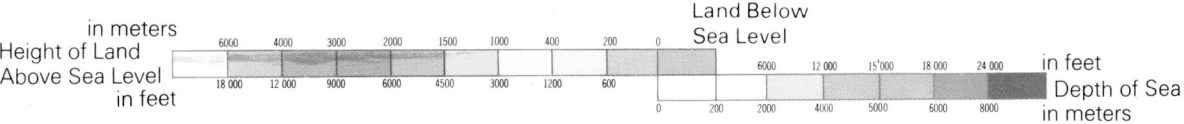

in meters
Height of Land Above Sea Level in feet

Land Below Sea Level

in feet
Depth of Sea in meters

6060 4000 3000 2000 1500 1000 400 200   6000 12 000 15'000 18 000 24 000

18 000 12 000 9000 6000 4500 3000 1200 600   0 200 2000 4000 5000 6000 8000

Some of the maps have different contours to highlight and clarify the principal relief features

Abbreviations of measures used   mm Millimeters   m. Meters   km. Kilometers

Beaufort
Sea

Queen Elizabeth Is.
Ellesmere I.
GREENLAND
(Den.)

Pt Barrow
Banks I.
Parry Is.
N. Magnetic
Pole 1980
Devon I.
Baffin
Bay
Thule

Wrangel I.
Dezhnev Str.
Victoria I.
Baffin I.
Davis
Strait
Godthåb
Denmark Str.
ICELAND
Reykjavik
Faroe Is.
(Den.)

Bering Str.
St. Lawrence I.
Yukon
Fairbanks
Bear L.
Gt. Coppermine
Yellowknife
Gt. Slave L.
Hudson
Bay
Churchill
C. Chidley

ALASKA
(U.S.)
Anchorage
Dawson
Mackenzie
Scheffervile
UNITED
KINGDOM
Glasg

Kodiak
Is.
Prince Rupert
Juneau
Edmonton
C A N A D A
Nelson
Newfoundland
St. John's
C. Race
Dubli
IRELAND

Gulf of
Alaska
Queen
Charlotte Is.
Calgary
Winnipeg
L. Superior
Montréal
Québec
Halifax
Sable I.

Aleutian Islands
(U.S.)
Vancouver
Vancouver I.
Minneapolis-
St. Paul
Michigan
L. Huron
Ottawa
Toronto
Buffalo
Boston
C. Cod
C. Finisterre

Seattle
Portland
Missouri
Milwaukee
Chicago
Detroit
Cleveland
Pittsburgh
New York
Philadelphia

Salt Lake
City
Denver
Omaha
Indianapolis
St. Louis
Cincinnati
Ohio
Baltimore
Washington
PORTUGAL
Lisboa

San Francisco
Sacramento
Kansas City
UNITED STATES
Norfolk
Azores
(Port.)

Los Angeles
San Diego
Phoenix
Oklahoma
Colorado
Mississippi
Memphis
Atlanta
Bermuda
(Br.)
Gibralta
Tanger
Rabat
MOR

El Paso
Dallas
Birmingham
Madeira Casablanca
(Port.)
Marrakech

Ciudad Juárez
Houston
Rio Grande
San
Antonio
New
Orleans
Jacksonville
Canary Is.
(Span.)
WESTERN
SAHARA

Tropic of Cancer
Monterrey
Gulf of
Mexico
Miami
BAHAMAS
ATLANTIC
MAURITANIA
Nouakchott
Ton

C. San Lucas
La Habana
CUBA
West
Hispaniola
HAITI
DOM. REP
San Juan
Leeward
CAPE VERDE
IS.
C. Verde
SENEGAL
Dakar

Guadalajara
México
Puebla
BELIZE
GUATEMALA
HONDURAS
Indies
Port-au-Prince
JAMAICA
Kingston
Santo
Domingo
DOMINICA
ANTIGUA & BARBUDA
ST. CHRISTOPHER-NEVIS
GAMBIA
GUINEA-BISSAU
GUINEA

Revilla
Gigedo Is.
(Mexico)
Guatemala
San Salvador
EL SALVADOR
Tegucigalpa
NICARAGUA
Caribbean
Sea
Windward
Is.
ST. LUCIA
BARBADOS
ST. VINCENT
Conakry
Freetown
SIERRA LEONE
LIBERIA
IVO
COA

Managua
San José
Barranquilla
GRENADA
TRINIDAD &
TOBAGO
Monrovia
Abid

Clipperton I.
(Fr.)
COSTA RICA
Panamá
PANAMA
Maracaibo
Caracas
VENEZUELA
Orinoco
Georgetown
GUYANA
Paramaribo
SURINAM
Cayenne
FR. GUIANA

Medellín
Bogotá
St. Paul
(Brazil)
G

Cali
COLOMBIA
Quito
Negro
Belém
Fortaleza
Fernando de Noronha
(Brazil)

ECUADOR
Galapagos Is.
(Ecuador)
Guayaquil
Iquitos
Japurá
Manaus
Amazon
B R A Z I L
C. de São Roque
Natal

Equator
Marañón
Ucayali
Madeira
Tapajós
Xingu
Tocantins
São Francisco
Recife
Ascension
(Br.)

P A C I F I C
PERÚ
Callao
Lima
Salvador

Palmyra I.
(U.S.)
Kiritimati
Brasília
St. Helena
(Br.)

Baker Is.
(U.S.)
Jarvis I.
(U.S.)
Malden I.
Starbuck I.
L. Titicaca
La Paz
Belo Horizonte

Abariringa
Phoenix Is.
Penrhyn I.
BOLIVIA
Arequipa
Paraná

Tokelau Is.
Manihiki I.
Flint I.
Marquesas Is.
(Fr.)
O C E A N
São Paulo
Rio de Janeiro

W. SAMOA
Samoan Is.
Tutuila
(U.S.)
Cook Is.
Society Is.
(Fr.)
Tahiti
Tuamotu
Archipelago
(Fr.)
PARAGUAY
Asunción
Santos
Curitiba

TONGA
(Friendly Is.)
Niue
(N.Z.)
Tongatapu Rarotonga
Tubuai Is.
(Fr.)
Tropic of Capricorn
Antofagasta
Tucumán
Paraguay
Paraná
Pôrto Alegre
Rio Grande do Sul

S. Ambrosio
(Chile)
ARGENTINA
Córdoba
Paraná
Uruguay
URUGUAY

Ducie I.
(Br.)
Pitcairn I.
(Br.)
Easter I.
(Chile)
Sala-y-Gómez
(Chile)
Valparaíso
Rosario
Montevideo
Tristan da
(Br.)

Rapa
(Fr.)
Arch. de Juan Fernández
(Chile)
Santiago
Buenos Aires
Goug
(Br.)

Kermadec Is.
(N.Z.)
Chatham Is.
(N.Z.)
Talcahuano
Bahia Blanca

International Date Line
CHILE
Chiloé
Falkland Is.
(Br.)
S. Georgia

Punta Arenas
Tierra del Fuego
C. Horn
Scotia Sea
S. Sandwich Is.

FALKLAND IS. DEPENDENCIES

Drake Passage
South Orkney Is.

ROSS
DEPENDENCY
Antarctic Circle
S. Shetland Is.
Antarctic
Peninsula
Graham Ld.
Weddell
Sea

Amundsen Sea
Bellingshausen Sea
Alexander
Palmer Ld.

Byrd Land
Ellsworth Land
BRITISH ANTARCTIC
TERRITORY
West from Gree

Projection: Hammer Equal Area

ARCTIC OCEAN
Zemlya Frantsa Iosifa
Novaya Zemlya
Laptev Sea   New Siberian Is.
East Siberian Sea
Severnaya Zemlya
Nord Kapp   Barents Sea   Kara Sea   Tiksi   Verkhoyansk   Nizhne-Kolymsk   Arctic Circle   Anadyr
Narvik   Murmansk   Ust Port   Yenisey   Lena   Vilyuysk   Yakutsk
FINLAND   Arkhangelsk   Salekhard   Ob   SOCIALIST   Vilyuysk   REPUBLICS   Bering Sea
SWEDEN   Helsinki   UNION OF SOVIET   RUSSIAN   FEDERATIVE   YAKUTSK   Okhotsk   Kamchatka   Petropavlovsk-
Stockholm   Leningrad   Perm   Sverdlovsk   SOCIALIST   SOCIALIST   REPUBLIC   Sea of   Kamchatskiy
EST.   LATVIA   Yaroslavl   Kazan   Tomsk   Krasnoyarsk   Okhotsk   C. Lopatka
POLAND   Moskva   Kuybyshev   Ufa   Novosibirsk   Omsk   Komsomolsk
WHITE   Minsk   Voronezh   Orenburg   Chelyabinsk   Novokuznetsk   Sakhalin   Kuril Is.
Warszawa   RUSSIA   Kiyev   Saratov   Volga   Irtysh   Barnaul   Irkutsk   Ulan   Khabarovsk   Sapporo
Praha   CZECH   UKRAINE   Rostov   Volgograd   KAZAKHSTAN   L. Baykal   Ude   Amur   Hakodate
Wien   HUNG   Odessa   Astrakhan   Karaganda   Ulaanbaatar   Vladivostok
Budapest   ROMANIA   Groznyy   Caspian   L. Balkhash   MONGOLIA   Harbin   N. KOREA
Beograd   Bucuresti   Black   Tbilisi   Aral   Alma Ata   Changchun   Pyŏngyang   Sea of   Sapporo
YUGOSLAVIA   BULGARIA   Sea   Yerevan   Sea   KIRGIZIA   Shenyang   KOREA   Japan
Sofiya   Istanbul   Ankara   Baku   UZBEK ISTAN   Tashkent   Beijing   Dalian   Sŏul   Kyoto   JAPAN
Athinai   Izmir   TURKEY   TURKMENISTAN   Samarkand   Tianjin   Taiyuan   Jinan   Qingdao   Pusan   Kōbe   Yokohama
GREECE   Halab   SYRIA   Tabriz   Ashkhabad   Dushanbe   Lanzhou   Xi'an   Huang   Nanjing   Kitakyūshū   Nagoya
Crete   Bayrūt   Dimashq   Tehrān   AFGHANISTAN   Srinagar   CHINA   Chengdu   Wuhan   Shanghai   Ōsaka
Mediterranean Sea   Tel Aviv-Yafo   Baghdād   IRAN   Kabul   Lahore   XIZANG   Lhasa   Chongqing   Changsha   East China   Ryukyu Is.
Iskandariya   ISR.   Ammān   IRAQ   (PERSIA)   Rawalpindi   (TIBET)   Chang Jiang   Sea
El Qâhira   Jerusalem   JORDAN   Ābādān   Shiraz   Delhi   NEPAL   Katmandu   Kunming   Fuzhou   Taibei
LIBYA   EGYPT   KUWAIT   Agra   Lucknow   BANGLA-   Taibei   (FORMOSA)   PACIFIC
BAHRAIN   QATAR   Karachi   Kanpur   DESH   Dhaka   Guangzhou   Hong Kong   (Br.)   Tropic of Cancer
Aswân   Ar Riyāḍ   U.A.E.   INDIA   Calcutta   BURMA   Hainan   South   Northern   Wake I.
SAUDI   OMAN   Ahmadābād   Nagpur   Mandalay   VIET.   China   Marianas   (U.S.)
Red   Makkah   ARABIA.   Arabian   Bombay   Pune   Bay of   Rangoon   Hanoi   Sea   (U.S.)
CHAD   SUDAN   El Khartum   Sea   SOUTH   Bengal   THAILAND   NAM
NIGER   Omdurmân   YEMEN   Hyderabad   Bangkok   Manila   OCEAN
L. Chad   Asmera   Aden   Bangalore   Madras   CAMBODIA   Guam   PHILIPPINES
NIGERIA   Ndjamena   DJIBOUTI   Gulf of Aden   Andaman Is.   Phnom   (U.S.)
CAMEROON   Addis Abeba   Socotra   Lakshadweep Is.   (India)   Penh   Phanh Bho   Cebu   Yap   TRUST TERRITORY OF   Marshall Is.
Douala   SOMALI REP.   Nicobar Is.   Ho Chi Minh   Belau
CENTRAL   ETHIOPIA   SRI LANKA   (India)   MALAYSIA   Caroline Is.   Ponape   THE PACIFIC ISLANDS (U.S.)
AFRICAN   Colombo   (CEYLON)   BRUNEI   SABAH
EQU. GUINEA   REPUBLIC   Bangui   MALDIVES   Dondra Hd.   Kuala Lumpur   KIRIBATI
Yaoundé   Zaire   L. Turkana   PEN. MALAYSIA   Kuching   NAURU
GABON   ZAÏRE   Kisangani   UGANDA   KENYA   Equator   SINGAPORE   Borneo
(Congo)   Kampala   Medan   Banjarmasin   Sulawesi   Irian   PAPUA   New Ireland
Brazzaville   (CONGO)   Victoria   Nairobi   Sumatera   INDONESIA   Jaya   Rabaul
CABINDA   Kinshasa   BUR.   INDIAN   Palembang   Ujung Pandang   New   New Britain   SOLOMON   TUVALU
Kasai   L.   SEYCHELLES   Chagos Arch.   GUINEA   Is.
Luanda   Kananga   Tanganyika   Mombasa   (Br.)   Jakarta   Surabaya   Port   Louisiade   Santa Cruz Is.
ANGOLA   Lubumbashi   TANZANIA   Dar es Salaam   Diego Garcia   OCEAN   Bandung   Jawa   Timor   Arafura Sea   Moresby   Arch.
Benguela   Zanzibar   Amirante   (Br.)   Timor Sea   C. York   VANUATU
ZAMBIA   Aldabra   Cocos   Darwin   Vanua Levu
Lusaka   COMORO   (Keeling Is.)   NORTHERN   Cairns   FIJI   Viti Levu
NAMIBIA   Zomba   MADAGASCAR   (Australia)   Christmas I.   TERRITORY   Townsville   Suva
Harare   Antananarivo   (Australia)   New
ZIMBABWE   Bulawayo   Réunion   MAURITIUS   Rodriguez   North West C.   WESTERN   QUEENSLAND   Caledonia
BOTSWANA   (Fr.)   Rodriguez   Tropic of Capricorn   Alice Springs   Rockhampton
Windhoek   Gaborone   Pretoria   AUSTRALIA   Norfolk I.
SOUTH   Johannesburg   SWAZ.   Maputo   Amsterdam   AUSTRÁLIA   SOUTH   Brisbane   (Australia)
WEST   LES.   (Fr.)   Perth   Kalgoorlie-   AUSTRALIA   Lord Howe
AFRICA   SOUTH   Durban   St. Paul   Fremantle   Boulder   NEW SOUTH   I. (Australia)
Cape Town   AFRICA   (Fr.)   C. Leeuwin   Darling   WALES   Newcastle
C. of Good Hope   Port Elizabeth   McDonald I.   Heard I.   Great   Adelaide   Sydney
Pr. Edward Is.   Crozet Is.   (Australia)   (Australia)   Australian   VICTORIA   Canberra   Auckland
(South Africa)   (Fr.)   Bight   Tasman   North I.
Kerguelen   Melbourne   Sea   NEW
(Fr.)   TASMANIA   ZEALAND
SOUTHERN   OCEAN   Hobart   C. Farewell   Wellington
Antarctic Circle   Christchurch
Enderby   Wilkes Land   S. Magnetic Pole   Balleny Is.   South I.
Land   1980   Stewart I.   Dunedin
AUSTRALIAN DEPENDENCY   TERRE ADÉLIE   Ross Sea   Antipodes Is.   (N.Z.)
from Greenwich   McDonald I.   Macquarie I.   Campbell I.   Auckland Is.
(Australia)   (N.Z.)   (N.Z.)

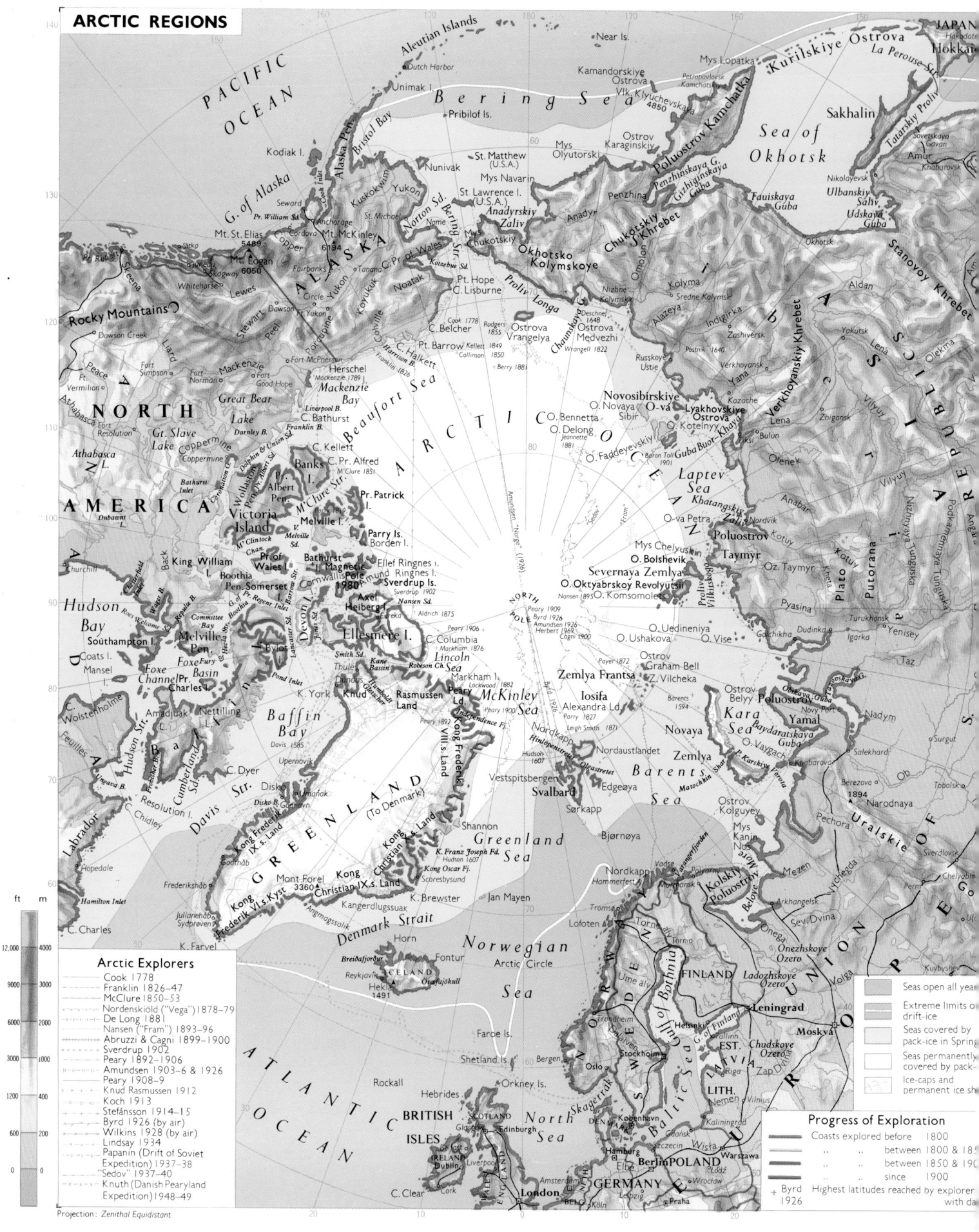

ARCTIC REGIONS

Arctic Explorers
Cook 1778
Franklin 1826–47
McClure 1850–53
Nordenskiöld ("Vega") 1878–79
De Long 1881
Nansen ("Fram") 1893–96
Abruzzi & Cagni 1899–1900
Sverdrup 1902
Peary 1892–1906
Amundsen 1903–6 & 1926
Peary 1908–9
Knud Rasmussen 1912
Koch 1913
Stefánsson 1914–15
Byrd 1926 (by air)
Wilkins 1928 (by air)
Lindsay 1934
Papanin (Drift of Soviet Expedition) 1937–38
"Sedov" 1937–40
Knuth (Danish Pearyland Expedition) 1948–49

Projection: Zenithal Equidistant

Seas open all year
Extreme limits of drift-ice
Seas covered by pack-ice in Spring
Seas permanently covered by pack-ice
Ice-caps and permanent ice shelf

Progress of Exploration
Coasts explored before 1800
"   "   "   between 1800 & 1850
"   "   "   between 1850 & 1900
"   "   "   since 1900
+ Byrd 1926   Highest latitudes reached by explorer with date

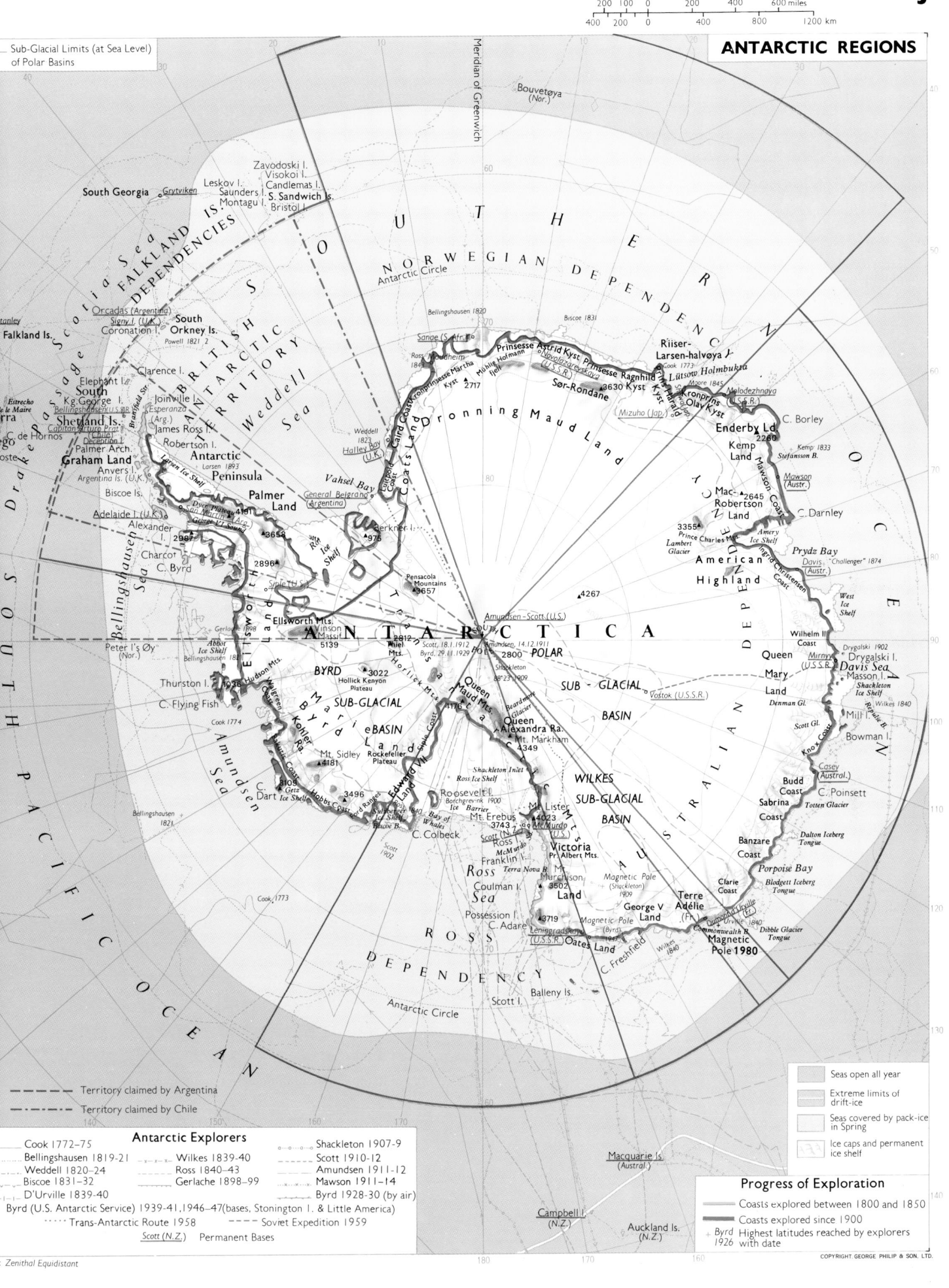

1:35 000 000

200   0   200   400   600   800 miles
400   0   400   800   1200 km

Asia

ARCTIC OCEAN

Greenland

Iceland

Bering Strait
Bering Sea

Beaufort Sea

Brooks Range

Axel Heiberg
Sverdrup Land
Ellesmere I.
Kane Basin
Thule

Queen Elizabeth Islands

Parry Is.
Melville I.
Magnetic
Banks I.
M'Clure Strait
Victoria I.
Devon I.
Lancaster Sound
Baffin Bay

Prince of Wales
Gulf of Boothia
Boothia Pen.
Melville Pen.
Foxe Basin
Baffin Island

Cumberland Sound

Arctic Circle

Great Bear L.
Great Slave L.

Mackenzie Mts.

Alaska Range
Mt. McKinley 6194

Alaska Pen.
Kodiak I.
Gulf of Alaska
Mt. St. Elias 5489
Mt. Logan 6050

Alexander Archipelago

Queen Charlotte Islands
Queen Charlotte Sound

Vancouver I.
Juan de Fuca Strait
C. Flattery

ROCKY MOUNTAINS

Mt. Robson 3954
Yellowhead Pass
Kicking Horse Pass
Crowsnest Pass

Athabasca L.
Reindeer L.
Churchill

Nelson
Lake Winnipeg

Hudson Bay
James Bay

Southampton I.
Chesterfield Inlet
Foxe Channel
Hudson Strait
Resolution
Frobisher Bay

Ungava Peninsula
Labrador

Newfoundland
Gulf of St. Lawrence
Nova Scotia
Anticosti
C. Breton
C. Race

Laurentian Plateau

Québec
Montreal
Ottawa
Toronto
Lake Ontario
Niagara Falls
New York
Philadelphia
Washington
Chesapeake Bay

APPALACHIAN Mts.
Alleghany Mts.
Blue Ridge

Mt. Washington 1917

L. Superior
L. Huron
L. Michigan
Detroit
Chicago
Minneapolis

Edmonton
Calgary
Regina
Winnipeg

Seattle
Portland
Columbia
Snake
Mt. Rainier 4392
Mt. Shasta 4317

Coast Range
Sierra Nevada
Mt. Whitney 4418

San Francisco
Los Angeles

Great Basin
Great Salt Lake
Wasatch Mountains
Mt. Elbert 4399
Denver

Colorado
Grand Canyon
Colorado Plateau

C. Mendocino
C. Blanco

Mendocino Seascarp
Murray Seascarp
Clarion Fracture Zone

PACIFIC OCEAN

Tropic of Cancer

Lower California
Gulf of California
C. San Lucas
Revilla Gigedo Is.

Western Sierra Madre
Eastern Sierra Madre
Mexican Plateau

Guadalajara
C. Corrientes
Santiago
Mexico
Puebla
Popocatepetl 5452
Orizaba 5700

Isthmus of Tehuantepec
G. of Tehuantepec
Guatemala
Guatemala Trench 6662

Great Plains

Kansas City
St. Louis
Memphis
Dallas
Houston
New Orleans
Mississippi Delta
Atlanta

Ozark Plateau
Cumberland Plateau

Red
Arkansas
Missouri
Mississippi

ATLANTIC OCEAN
Bermuda
C. Hatteras

Gulf of Mexico

Rio Grande
Monterrey
Gulf of Campeche
Yucatán Peninsula
Yucatán Basin
C. Catoche
Yucatán Strait
Gulf of Honduras

Florida
Bahama Islands
C. Sable
Florida Strait
Havana
Cuba
Greater Antilles
Jamaica
Hispaniola
Puerto Rico
Milwaukee Deep 9200
Coyman Trough 7680

Caribbean Sea
Colombian Basin
Gracias á Dios
Nicaragua
L. Nicaragua
Panama Canal
G. of Darien
G. of Panama

Andes
Sa. Nevada de Sta. Marta 5800
Maracaibo
Venezuela
Magdalena
Sierra de Merida

Projection: Bonne   West from Greenwich   COPYRIGHT. GEORGE PHILIP & SON. LTD.

1:35 000 000

200   0   200   400   600   800 miles
400   0   400   800   1200 km

ARCTIC OCEAN

U.S.S.R.

Bering Strait

Bering Sea

GREENLAND (Denmark)

Denmark Strait

Reykjavik ICELAND

Beaufort Sea

Queen Elizabeth Is.

Ellesmere I.

Baffin Bay

Davis Strait

C. Farvel

Godhåb

ALASKA

Yukon

Arctic Circle

Fairbanks

Anchorage

Gulf of Alaska

Juneau

Porcupine

INUVIK

YUKON TERRITORY

KITIKMEOT

Victoria I.

NORTHWEST TERRITORIES

KEEWATIN

BAFFIN

Baffin I.

Hudson Strait

NEWFOUNDLAND

BRITISH COLUMBIA

FORT SMITH

Great Bear L.

Mackenzie

Great Slave L.

Back

Dubawnt

C A N A D A

Hudson Bay

Labrador

Liard

ALBERTA

Finlay

Peace

L. Athabasca

Edmonton

N. Saskatchewan

Athabasca

SASKATCHEWAN

Churchill

Nelson

MANITOBA

Eastmain

QUÉBEC

St. John's

SPM

Sheena

Fraser

Calgary

S. Saskatchewan

Regina

L. Winnipeg

Winnipeg

ONTARIO

St. Lawrence

Québec

PR. EDWARD I.

Charlottetown

NEW BRUNS. WICK

NOVA SCOTIA

Halifax

Fredericton

Victoria

Vancouver

WASHINGTON

Seattle

Olympia

Columbia

Portland

Salem

OREGON

IDAHO

Boise

Snake

MONTANA

Helena

Missouri

NORTH DAKOTA

Bismarck

MINNESOTA

St. Paul

Minneapolis

SOUTH DAKOTA

Pierre

WISCONSIN

Madison

L. Superior

L. Michigan

L. Huron

MICHIGAN

Lansing

Toronto

L. Ontario

VT.

MAINE

N.H.

Concord

Montpelier

Augusta

Boston

MASS.

Providence R.I.

Hartford

Albany

NEW YORK

Buffalo

Montréal

Ottawa

WYOMING

Milwaukee

Detroit

Cleveland

PENNSYLVANIA

Pittsburgh

Harrisburg

Trenton N.J.

Philadelphia

NEW YORK

Sacramento

Carson City

San Francisco

San Jose

NEVADA

Salt Lake City

UTAH

Cheyenne

N. Platte

NEBRASKA

Lincoln

Des Moines

IOWA

Chicago

ILLINOIS

Springfield

INDIANA

Indianapolis

Columbus

OHIO

Cincinnati

Frankfort

WEST VIRGINIA

Charleston

Richmond

VIRGINIA

Baltimore

Annapolis M.D.

D.C.

Dover DEL.

Washington

CALIFORNIA

Denver

COLORADO

Arkansas

KANSAS

Topeka

Kansas City

St. Louis

MISSOURI

Jefferson City

KENTUCKY

Nashville

TENNESSEE

Tennessee

NORTH CAROLINA

Raleigh

Columbia

SOUTH CAROLINA

Bermuda

Las Vegas

Colorado

LOS ANGELES

San Diego

ARIZONA

Phoenix

Tucson

Gila

Santa Fe

NEW MEXICO

Albuquerque

OKLAHOMA

Oklahoma City

ARKANSAS

Little Rock

Memphis

Mississippi

Birmingham

MISSISSIPPI

ALABAMA

Alabama

Jackson

Atlanta

GEORGIA

Montgomery

Jacksonville

U N I T E D   S T A T E S

El Paso

Red River

T E X A S

Dallas

Fort Worth

Austin

LOUISIANA

Baton Rouge

New Orleans

FLORIDA

Tallahassee

Tampa

Miami

C. Sable

Str. of Florida

Houston

Rio Grande

Monterrey

PACIFIC OCEAN

Tropic of Cancer

Golfo de California

M E X I C O

Revillagigedo Is.

Guadalajara

MEXICO

ATLANTIC OCEAN

BAHAMAS

Nassau

Havana

C U B A

Gulf of Mexico

DOMINICAN REP.

HAITI

Port-au-Prince

Santo Domingo

San Juan

PUERTO RICO

JAMAICA

Kingston

Caribbean Sea

Belmopan

BELIZE

GUATEMALA

Guatemala

San Salvador

EL SALVADOR

HONDURAS

Tegucigalpa

NICARAGUA

Managua

L. de Nicaragua

COSTA RICA

San José

P A N A M Á

Panamá

Maracaibo

Barranquilla

VENEZUELA

Medellín

COLOMBIA

Bogotá

SOUTH AMERICA

Montgomery : State capital ⊙

C.	CONNECTICUT	N.H.	NEW HAMPSHIRE
D.	DELAWARE	N.J.	NEW JERSEY
D.C.	DISTRICT OF COLUMBIA	R.I.	RHODE ISLAND
M.	MARYLAND	VER.	VERMONT
MASS.	MASSACHUSETTS	SPM	ST. PIERRE ET MIQUELON

Projection: Bonne

West from Greenwich

COPYRIGHT GEORGE PHILIP & SON. LTD.

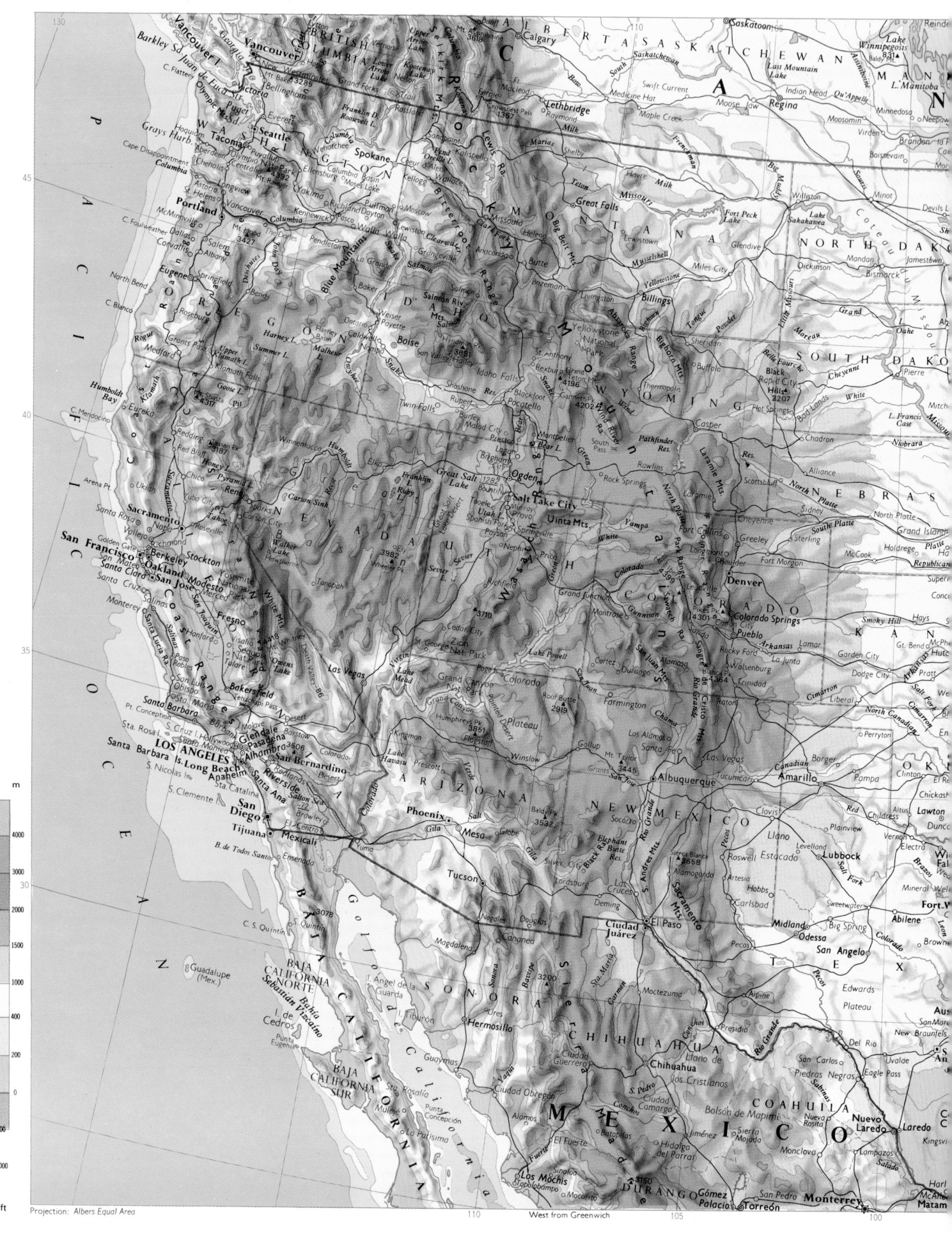

1:12 000 000

50   100   150   200   250   300 miles
50   0   50   100   150   200 250 300 350 400 450 km

CANADA

Winnipeg
Lake of the Woods

MINNESOTA   Lake Superior   Sault Ste. Marie   MAINE

MONTRÉAL   Québec   NEW BRUNSWICK

Ottawa   Hull   VERMONT   N.H.   MASS.   Boston

Minneapolis   St. Paul   WISCONSIN   Lake Michigan   Lake Huron   TORONTO   Lake Ontario   Rochester   Buffalo   NEW YORK   Albany   Hartford   Providence

Madison   Milwaukee   Grand Rapids   Lansing   Detroit   Lake Erie   Cleveland   PENNSYLVANIA   Scranton   NEW YORK   New Haven

Des Moines   CHICAGO   Toledo   Akron   Youngstown   Pittsburgh   Allentown   Newark   NEW YORK   Jersey City   PHILADELPHIA

IOWA   Peoria   OHIO   Columbus   Wheeling   Harrisburg   Baltimore   Atlantic City

Kansas City   ILLINOIS   INDIANA   Indianapolis   Dayton   Cincinnati   WEST VIRGINIA   Washington D.C.   Delaware Bay

St. Louis   MISSOURI   Louisville   Lexington   Charleston   VIRGINIA   Richmond   Newport News   Norfolk

Springfield   KENTUCKY   Huntington   Roanoke   Virginia Beach   Cape Hatteras

TENNESSEE   Nashville   Knoxville   NORTH CAROLINA   Winston   Greensboro   Durham   Raleigh   Pamlico Sd.

Memphis   Chattanooga   Asheville   Charlotte   Greenville   Columbia   SOUTH CAROLINA   Long Bay

ARKANSAS   Little Rock   Birmingham   Atlanta   GEORGIA   Augusta   Charleston   Savannah

MISSISSIPPI   ALABAMA   Columbus   Macon

Shreveport   Jackson   Montgomery   Albany   Brunswick

LOUISIANA   Baton Rouge   Mobile   Pensacola   Tallahassee   Jacksonville   St. Augustine   Daytona Beach

Houston   New Orleans   FLORIDA   Orlando   Ft. Pierce   West Palm Beach   BAHAMAS

Galveston   Delta of the Mississippi   Tampa   St. Petersburg   Sarasota   Ft. Myers   Ft. Lauderdale   Miami

GULF OF MEXICO   Everglades   Key West   Florida Bay   ATLANTIC OCEAN

COPYRIGHT. GEORGE PHILIP & SON. LTD.

1:2 500 000

10 0 10 20 30 40 50 miles
10 0 20 40 60 80 km

TENNESSEE
MISSISSIPPI ALABAMA
GEORGIA
FLORIDA

GULF OF MEXICO

Chattanooga
Huntsville
Decatur
Florence Sheffield
Muscle Shoals
Tuscumbia
Gadsden
Rome
ATLANTA
Tupelo
Columbus
BIRMINGHAM
Bessemer
Fairfield
Homewood
Mountain Brook
Talladega
Anniston
Tuscaloosa
Northport
Meridian
Selma
Montgomery
Auburn
Opelika
Phenix City
Columbus
Albany
Laurel
Monroeville
Andalusia
Enterprise
Dothan
Mobile
Prichard
Chickasaw
Gulfport
Biloxi
Pascagoula
Moss Point
Pensacola
W. Pensacola
Fort Walton Beach
Panama City
Tallahassee
Apalachicola

Mississippi Sound
Mobile Bay
Pensacola Bay
Chandeleur Sound
CHANDELEUR ISLANDS
DAUPHIN ISLAND
Perdido Bay
Choctawhatchee Bay
GULF ISLANDS NAT. SEASHORE

W. B. BANKHEAD NATIONAL FOREST
TALLADEGA NATIONAL FOREST
TOMBIGBEE NAT. FOREST
DE SOTO NATIONAL FOREST
CONECUH NATIONAL FOREST
APALACHICOLA NATIONAL FOREST
HOLLY RINGS NATIONAL FOREST

Cumberland Plateau
Lookout Mt.
Pine Mt.

Pickwick Lake
Wilson Lake
Wheeler Lake
Guntersville Lake
Lewis Smith Lake
Weiss Lake
Logan Martin Res.
Mitchell Lake
Martin Lake
Lake Harding
Walter F. George Res.
Lake Eufaula
Lake Seminole
William 'Bill' Dannelly Res.

Cheaha Mt. 734
Woodall Mt. 246

Projection: Albers Equal Area
West from Greenwich
COPYRIGHT GEORGE PHILIP & SON. LTD

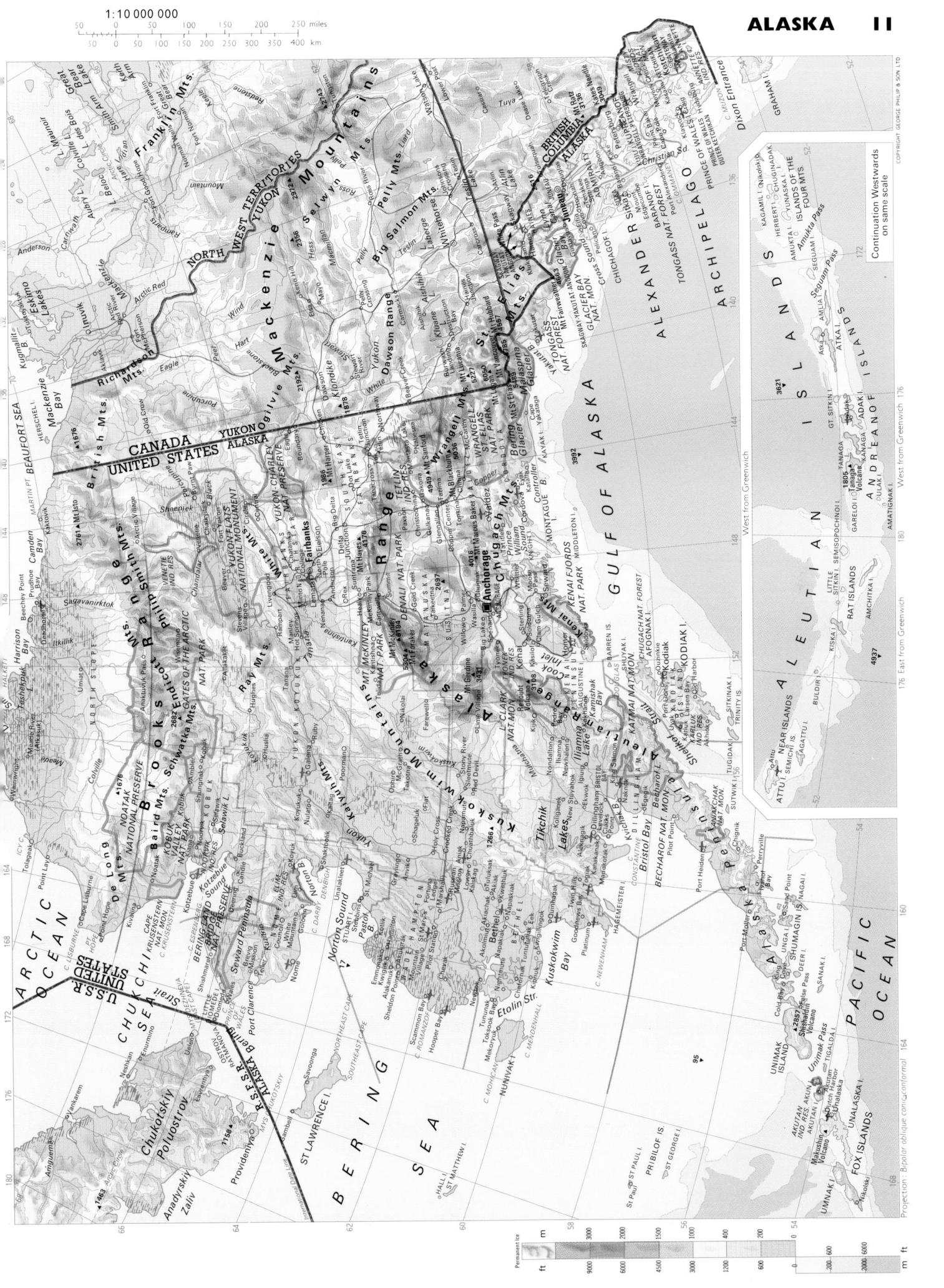

ALASKA 11

1:2 500 000

Projection: Albers Equal Area

West from Greenwich

COPYRIGHT. GEORGE PHILIP & SON. LTD.

1:2 500 000

Projection: Albers Equal Area

West from Greenwich

COPYRIGHT GEORGE PHILIP & SON. LTD.

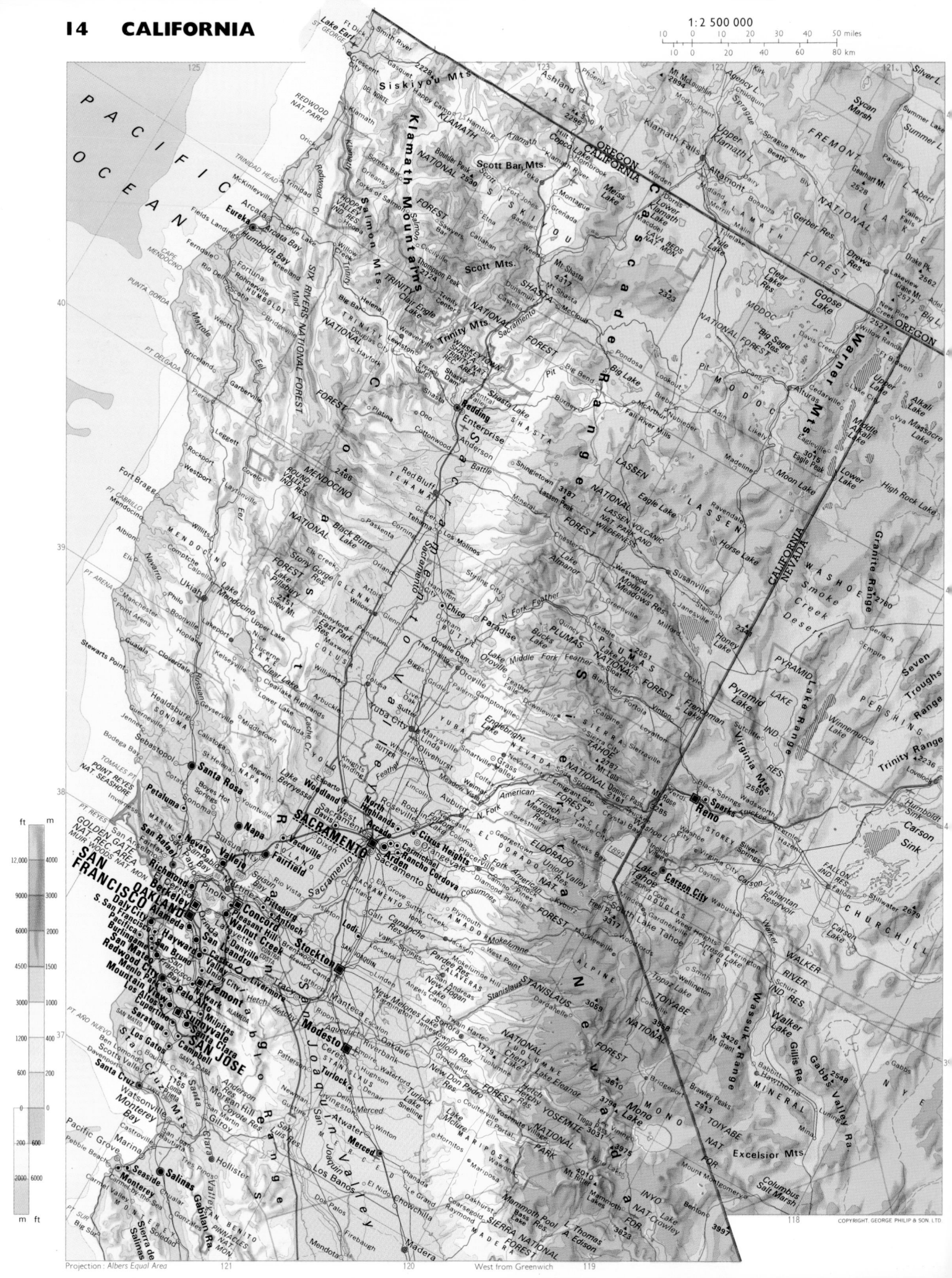

1:2 500 000

Projection: Albers Equal Area

West from Greenwich

PACIFIC

OCEAN

CHANNEL ISLANDS

Gulf of Santa Catalina

LOS ANGELES

LONG BEACH

SAN DIEGO

TIJUANA

MEXICALI

Fresno

Bakersfield

Hillcrest Center

Visalia

San Luis Obispo

Santa Maria

Lompoc

Santa Barbara

Ventura

Oxnard

SEQUOIA NATIONAL PARK

KINGS CANYON NATIONAL PARK

Death Valley

Mojave Desert

San Bernardino

Riverside

Salton Sea

Imperial Valley

UNITED STATES
MEXICO

CALIF.
BAJA CALIFORNIA

1 : 2 500 000

10   0   10   20   30   40   50 miles
10   0   20   40   60   80 km

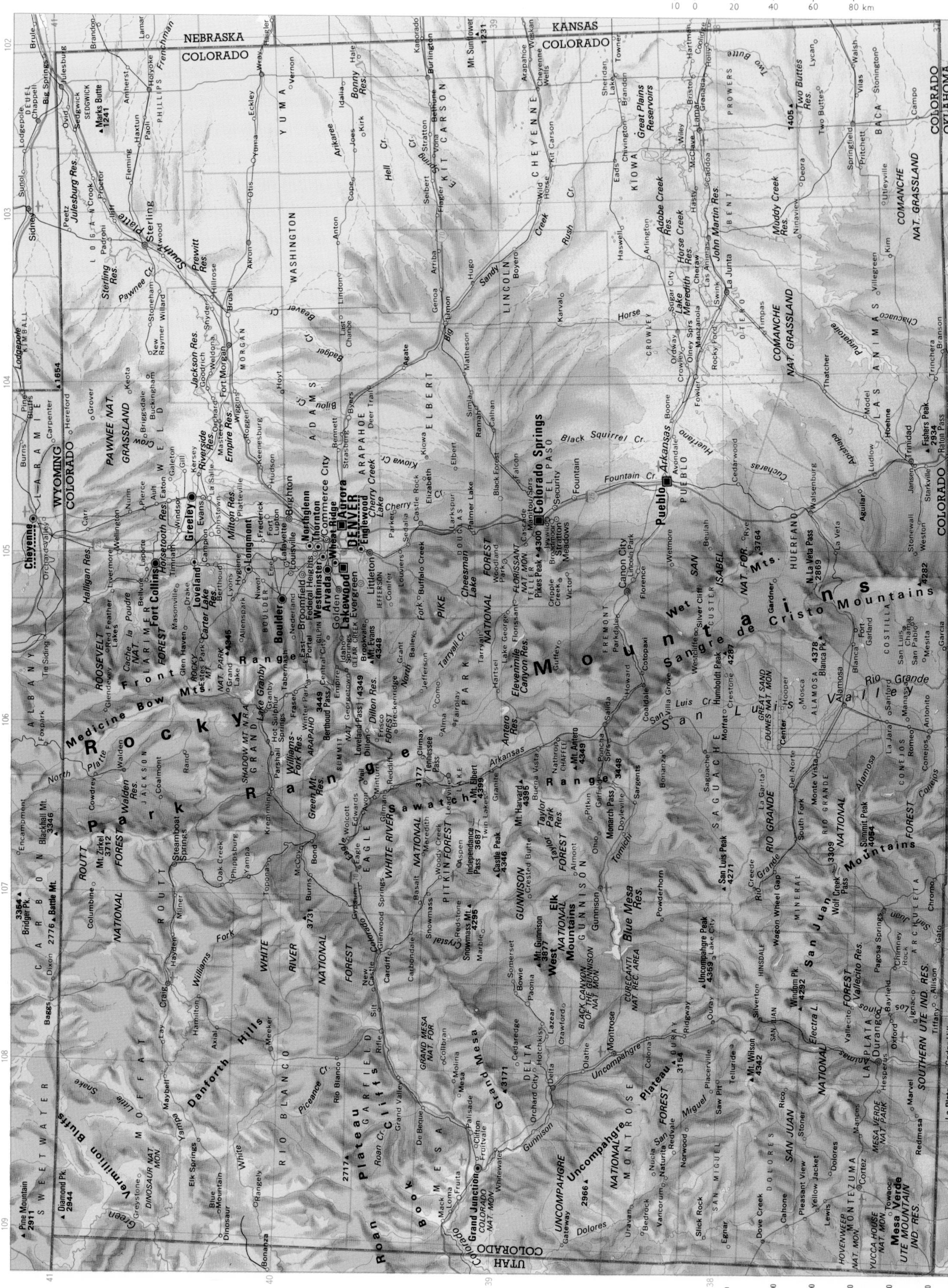

NEBRASKA
COLORADO
KANSAS
COLORADO
WYOMING
COLORADO
COLORADO
OKLAHOMA
COLORADO
NEW MEXICO
COLORADO
UTAH
COLORADO

DENVER
Colorado Springs
Pueblo
Aurora
Boulder
Fort Collins
Greeley
Longmont
Lakewood
Grand Junction
Cheyenne

Rocky Mountains
Front Range
Park Range
Sawatch Range
Sangre de Cristo Mountains
San Juan Mountains
San Luis Valley

m 4000 3000 2000 1500 1000
ft 12000 9000 6000 4500 3000

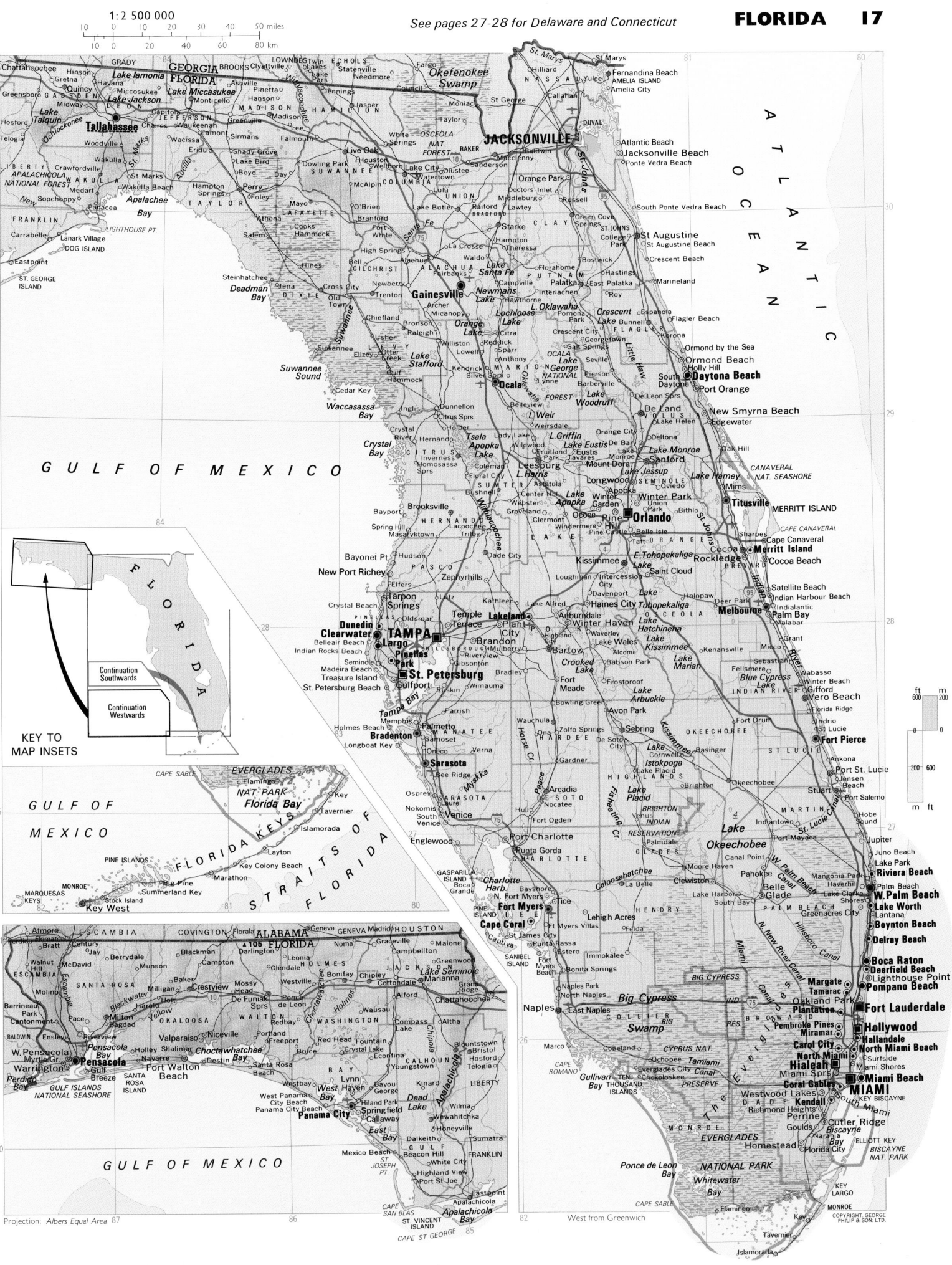

1 : 2 500 000

10 0 10 20 30 40 50 miles
10 0 20 40 60 80 km

GEORGIA
FLORIDA

Okefenokee
Swamp

Tallahassee

ATLANTIC OCEAN

JACKSONVILLE

Atlantic Beach
Jacksonville Beach
Ponte Vedra Beach

Fernandina Beach
AMELIA ISLAND
Amelia City

South Ponte Vedra Beach

St Augustine
St Augustine Beach
Crescent Beach

Marineland

APALACHICOLA
NATIONAL FOREST

Apalachee
Bay

LIGHTHOUSE PT.

Deadman
Bay

Gainesville

Ormond by the Sea
Ormond Beach
Holly Hill
Daytona Beach
South
Daytona
Port Orange

New Smyrna Beach
Edgewater

GULF OF MEXICO

Ocala

Crystal
Bay

Waccasassa
Bay

Suwannee
Sound

OCALA
NATIONAL
FOREST

CANAVERAL
NAT. SEASHORE

Leesburg

Mount Dora
Sanford

Titusville
MERRITT ISLAND

Winter Park

Orlando
Cocoa
Cape Canaveral
Merritt Island
Cocoa Beach
Rockledge

Satellite Beach
Indian Harbour Beach

Melbourne
Palm Bay

Vero Beach

Fort Pierce

Port St. Lucie

TAMPA
Clearwater
Largo
Pinellas
Park
St. Petersburg

Lakeland
Plant
City

Sarasota

Bradenton

Haines City

Lake
Okeechobee

Riviera Beach
Palm Beach
W. Palm Beach
Lake Worth

Boynton Beach

Delray Beach

Boca Raton
Deerfield Beach
Lighthouse Point
Pompano Beach
Margate
Tamarac
Oakland Park
Plantation
Fort Lauderdale

Naples

Big Cypress
Swamp

Fort Myers
Cape Coral

Hollywood
Hallandale
Carol City
North Miami Beach
North Miami
Hialeah
Miami Sprs
Coral Gables
Miami
Miami Beach
KEY BISCAYNE

Kendall

Homestead
Florida City

ft   m
600 200

0

200 600
m   ft

FLORIDA
Continuation
Southwards
Continuation
Westwards

KEY TO
MAP INSETS

EVERGLADES
NAT. PARK
Florida Bay

GULF OF
MEXICO

STRAITS OF FLORIDA

FLORIDA KEYS

Key West

ALABAMA
FLORIDA

Pensacola

GULF ISLANDS
NATIONAL SEASHORE

Panama City

GULF OF MEXICO

Projection: Albers Equal Area

West from Greenwich

COPYRIGHT GEORGE
PHILIP & SON: LTD.

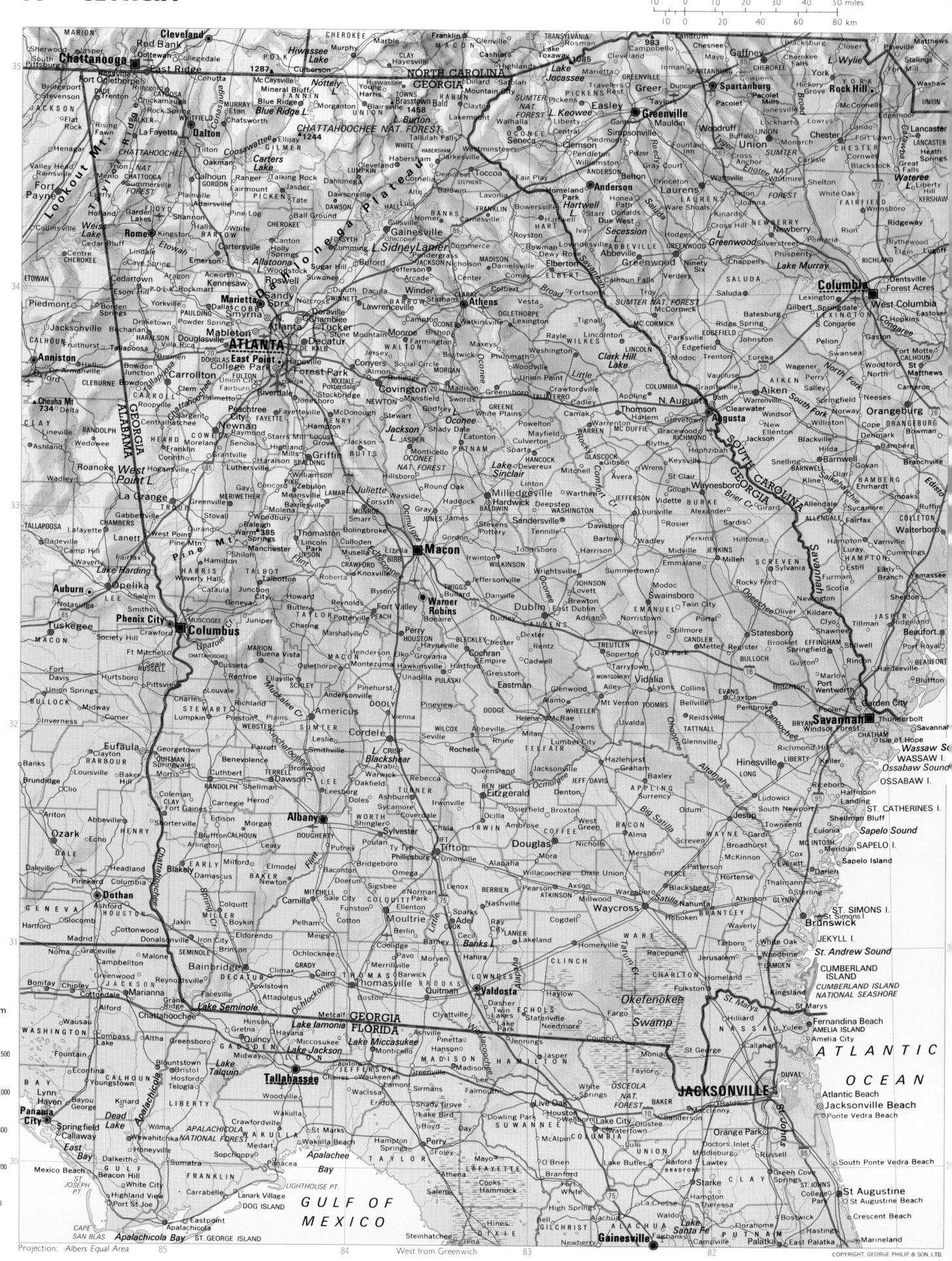

1:2 500 000

1:2 500 000
10 0 10 20 30 40 50 miles
10 0 20 40 60 80 km

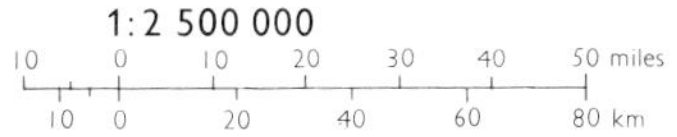

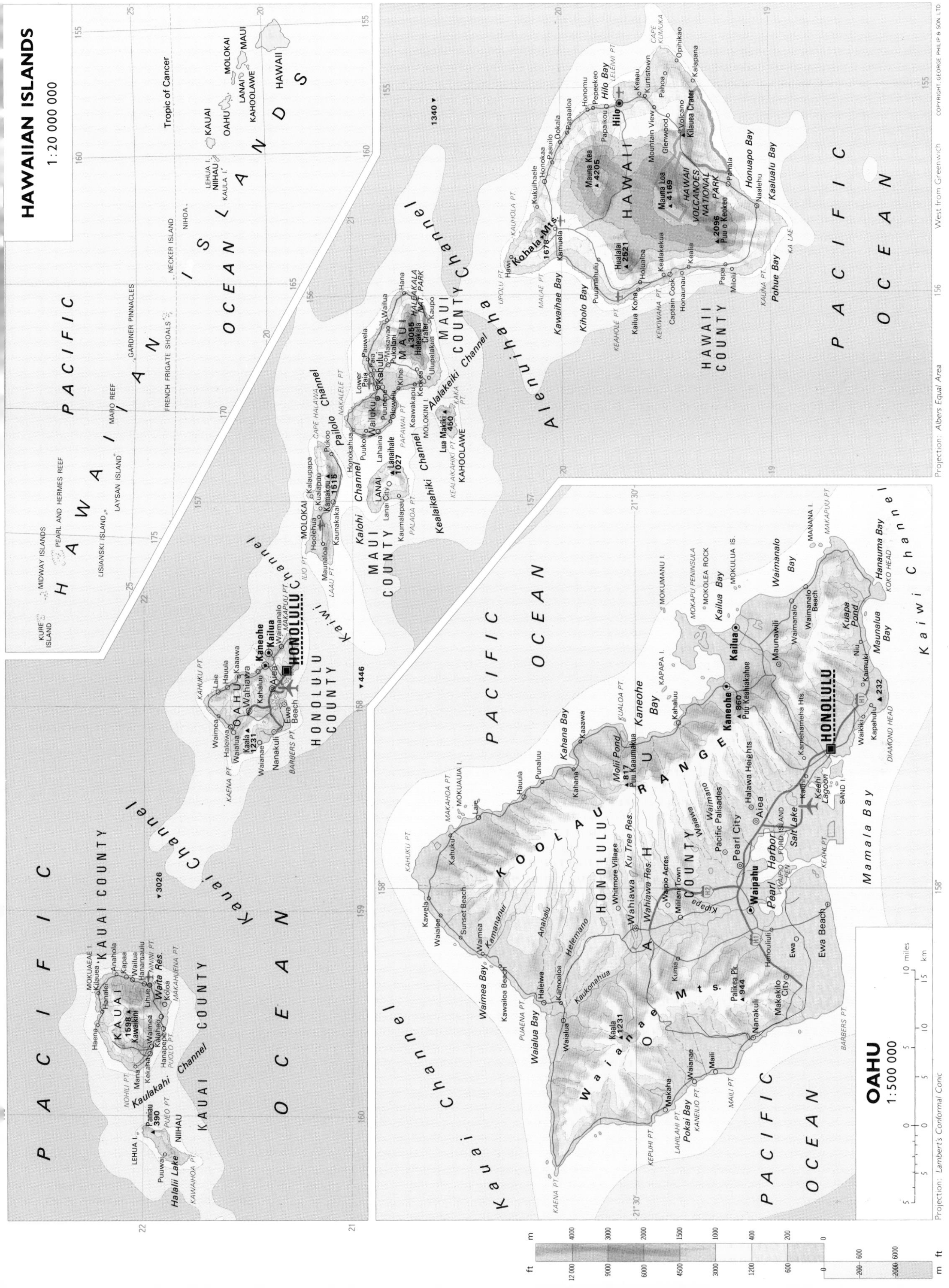

HAWAIIAN ISLANDS
1:20 000 000
P A C I F I C
H A W A I I A N   I S L A N D S
O C E A N
Tropic of Cancer
KURE ISLAND
MIDWAY ISLANDS
PEARL AND HERMES REEF
LISIANSKI ISLAND
LAYSAN ISLAND
MARO REEF
GARDNER PINNACLES
FRENCH FRIGATE SHOALS
NECKER ISLAND
NIHOA
LEHUA I.
NIIHAU
KAULA I.
KAUAI
OAHU
MOLOKAI
LANAI
MAUI
KAHOOLAWE
HAWAII
P A C I F I C   O C E A N
KAUAI COUNTY
HONOLULU COUNTY
MAUI COUNTY
HAWAII COUNTY
Kauai Channel
Kaiwi Channel
Kalohi Channel
Pailolo Channel
Kealaikahiki Channel
Alalakeiki Channel
Alenuihaha Channel
Kaulakahi Channel
HONOLULU
Kaneohe
Kailua
Hilo
Mauna Kea 4205
Mauna Loa 4169
Kilauea Crater
Hualalai 2521
Kohala Mts. 1678
Haleakala 3055
HAWAII VOLCANOES NATIONAL PARK
HALEAKALA NAT. PARK
Kawaikini 1598
Waialeale
Puu o Keokeo 2096
Lanaihale 1027
Kamakou 1515
Kaala 1231
Lua Makiki 450
Paniau 390
Projection: Albers Equal Area
West from Greenwich
COPYRIGHT GEORGE PHILIP & SON, LTD
OAHU
1:500 000
0 5 10 miles
0 5 10 15 km
K O O L A U   R A N G E
W a i a n a e   M t s.
HONOLULU COUNTY
P A C I F I C   O C E A N
Kauai Channel
Kaiwi Channel
Mamala Bay
Pearl Harbor
Kaneohe Bay
Kailua Bay
Waimanalo Bay
Hanauma Bay
Maunalua Bay
Kahana Bay
Waimea Bay
Waialua Bay
Pokai Bay
Waipahu
Pearl City
Aiea
Wahiawa
Ewa Beach
Kaneohe
Kailua
DIAMOND HEAD
KAENA PT
KAHUKU PT
MAKAPUU PT
BARBERS PT
Kaala 1231
Puu Kaaumakua 817
Puu Keahiakahoe 860
Palikea Pk. 944
Projection: Lambert's Conformal Conic
m ft
4000 12 000
3000 9000
2000 6000
1500 4500
1000 3000
400 1200
200 600
0 0
200 600
2000 6000

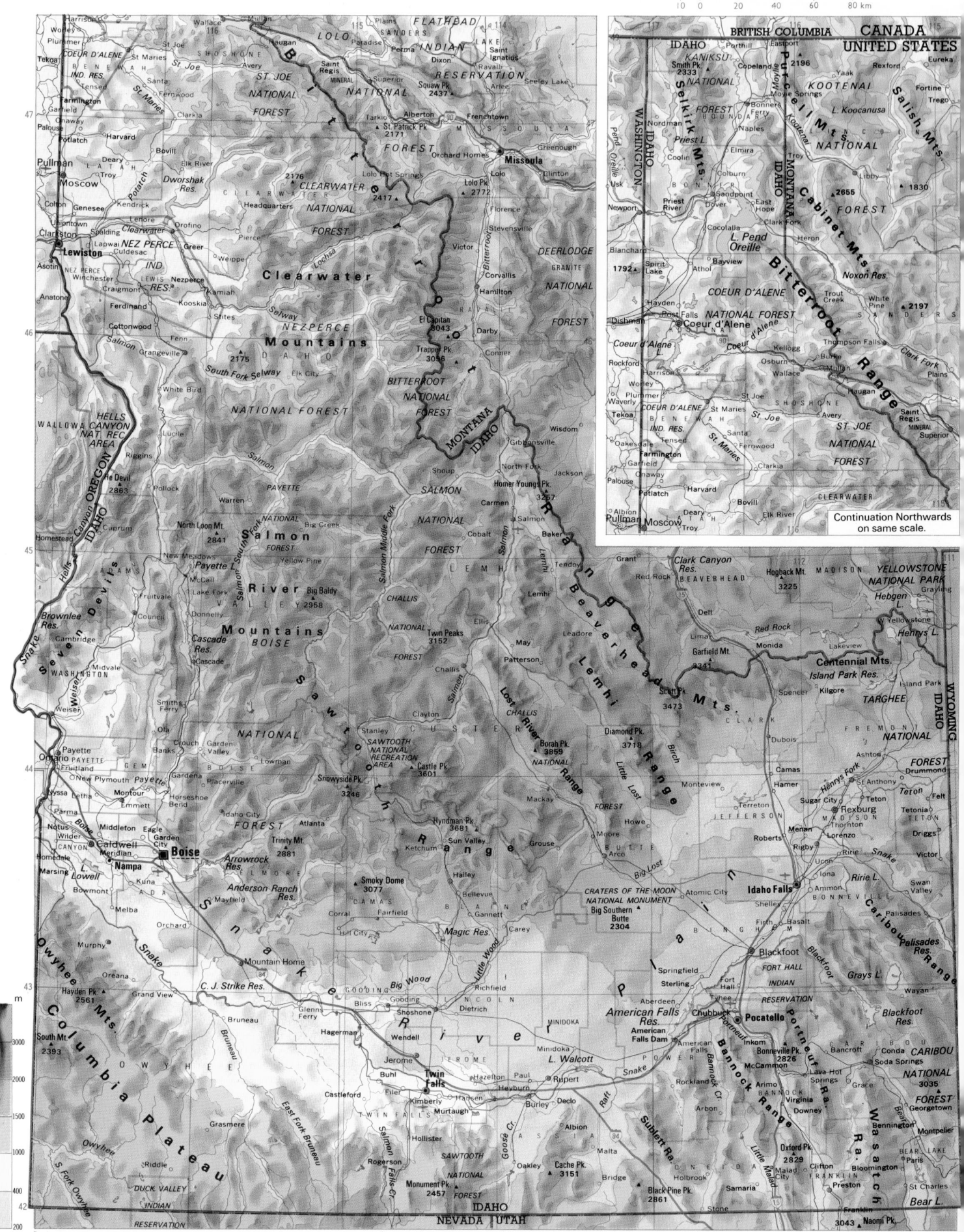

1 : 2 500 000

10   0   10   20   30   40   50 miles
10   0   20   40   60   80 km

BRITISH COLUMBIA   CANADA
UNITED STATES

Continuation Northwards
on same scale.

ft   m

9000 3000
6000 2000
4500 1500
1200 400
600   200

Projection: Albers Equal Area

West from Greenwich

COPYRIGHT: GEORGE PHILIP & SON, LTD.

1 : 2 500 000

WISCONSIN
ILLINOIS

LAKE MICHIGAN

CHICAGO

Rockford

Cedar Rapids

Iowa City

Davenport Rock Island Moline E. Moline

Peoria East Peoria

Bloomington Normal

Decatur

Springfield

Champaign Urbana

Quincy

Galesburg

SAINT LOUIS E. St. Louis

Terre Haute

Evansville

Owensboro

South Bend Gary

INDIANA

MISSOURI

KENTUCKY

IOWA

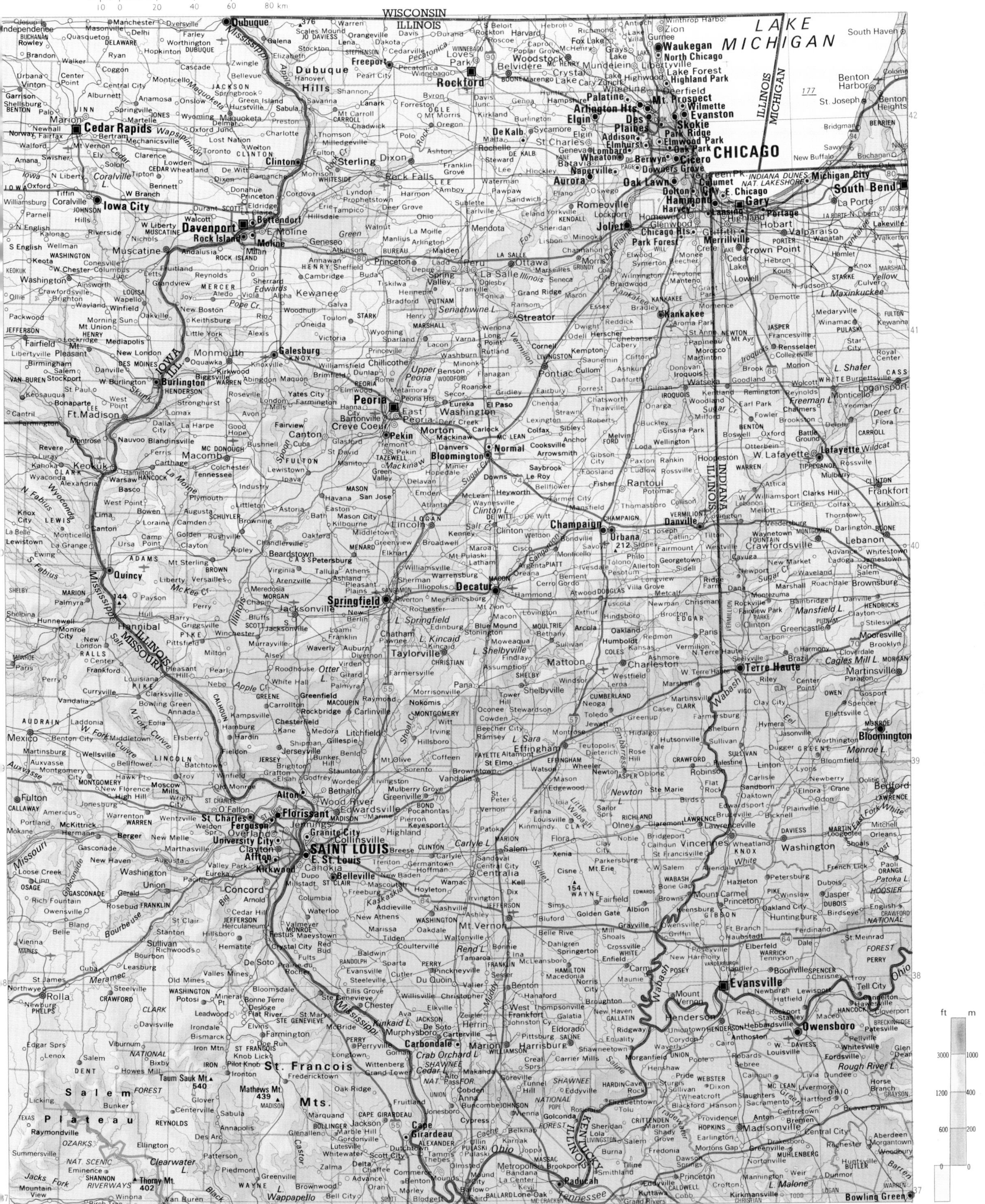

Projection: Albers Equal Area

West from Greenwich

COPYRIGHT GEORGE PHILIP & SON LTD

1:2 500 000

WISCONSIN

LAKE MICHIGAN

CHICAGO

MICHIGAN

INDIANA

OHIO

TOLEDO

ILLINOIS

Ft. Wayne

Lima

Rockford

South Bend

Elkhart

INDIANAPOLIS

Terre Haute

Bloomington

CINCINNATI

Evansville

Owensboro

LOUISVILLE

Frankfort

Lexington

KENTUCKY

Dayton

Springfield

Muncie

Anderson

Kokomo

Lafayette

Champaign

Decatur

Normal

Bloomington

Kankakee

Joliet

Gary

Hammond

Kalamazoo

Battle Creek

Jackson

Ann Arbor

Bowling Green

Findlay

Van Wert

Marion

Hamilton

Middletown

Kettering

Projection: Albers Equal Area

West from Greenwich

COPYRIGHT. GEORGE PHILIP & SON, LTD.

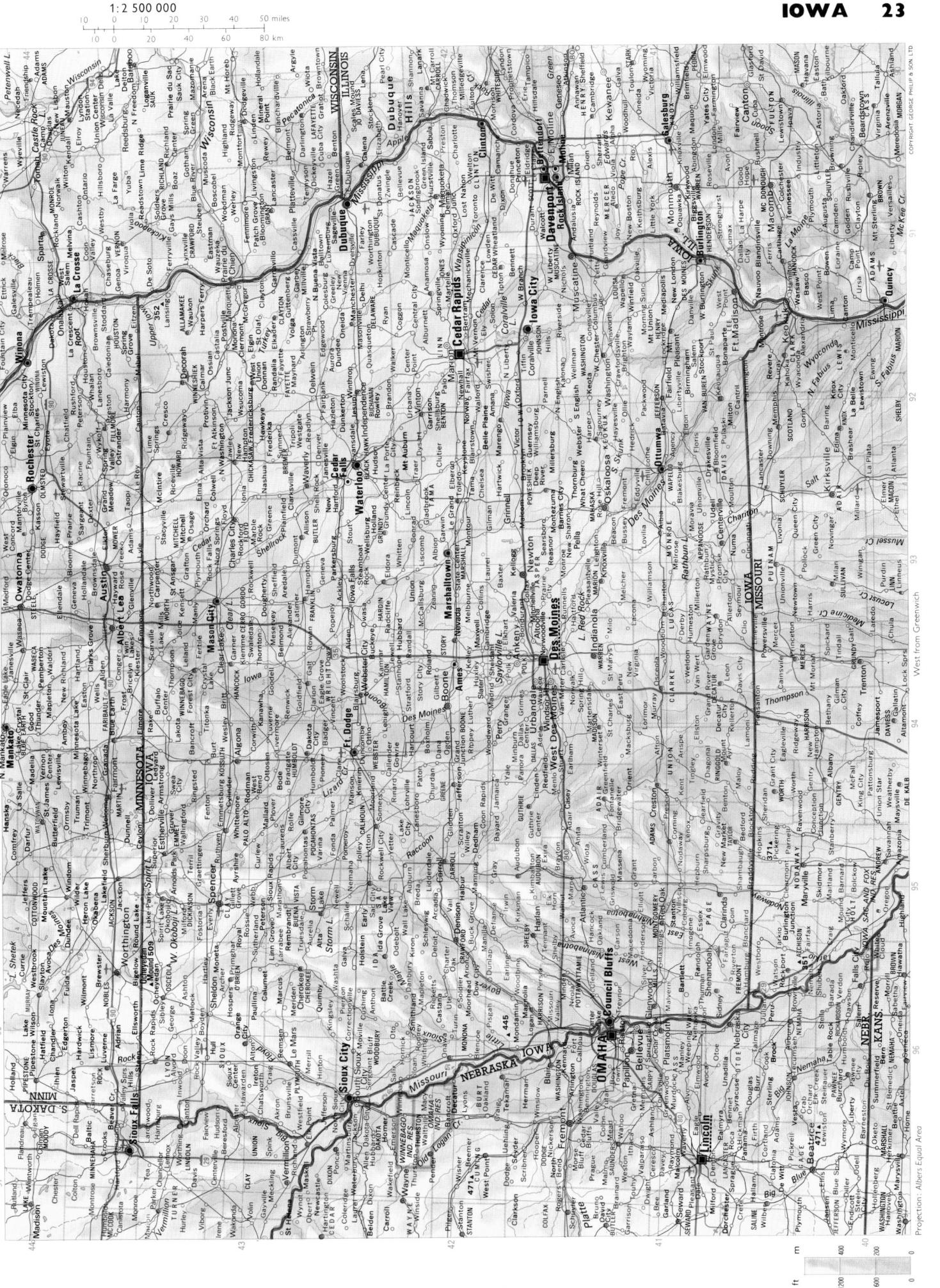

1 : 2 500 000

Projection: Albers Equal Area

West from Greenwich

1:2 500 000

10　　0　　10　　20　　30　　40　　50 miles
10　　0　　20　　40　　60　　80 km

1:2 500 000

10 0 10 20 30 40 50 miles
10 0 20 40 60 80 km

COPYRIGHT GEORGE PHILIP & SON, LTD.

West from Greenwich

Projection: Albers Equal Area

GULF OF MEXICO

NEW ORLEANS

Baton Rouge

Mobile

Jackson

MISSISSIPPI

ALABAMA

LOUISIANA

ARKANSAS

TEXAS

Shreveport

Bossier City

Monroe

Alexandria

Lafayette

Lake Charles

Beaumont

Port Arthur

Houma

El Dorado

Meridian

Hattiesburg

Biloxi

Gulfport

Pascagoula

Vicksburg

Natchez

CHANDELEUR ISLANDS

Chandeleur Sound

Breton Sound

Mississippi River Delta

Atchafalaya Bay

Lake Pontchartrain

Lake Borgne

Mississippi Sound

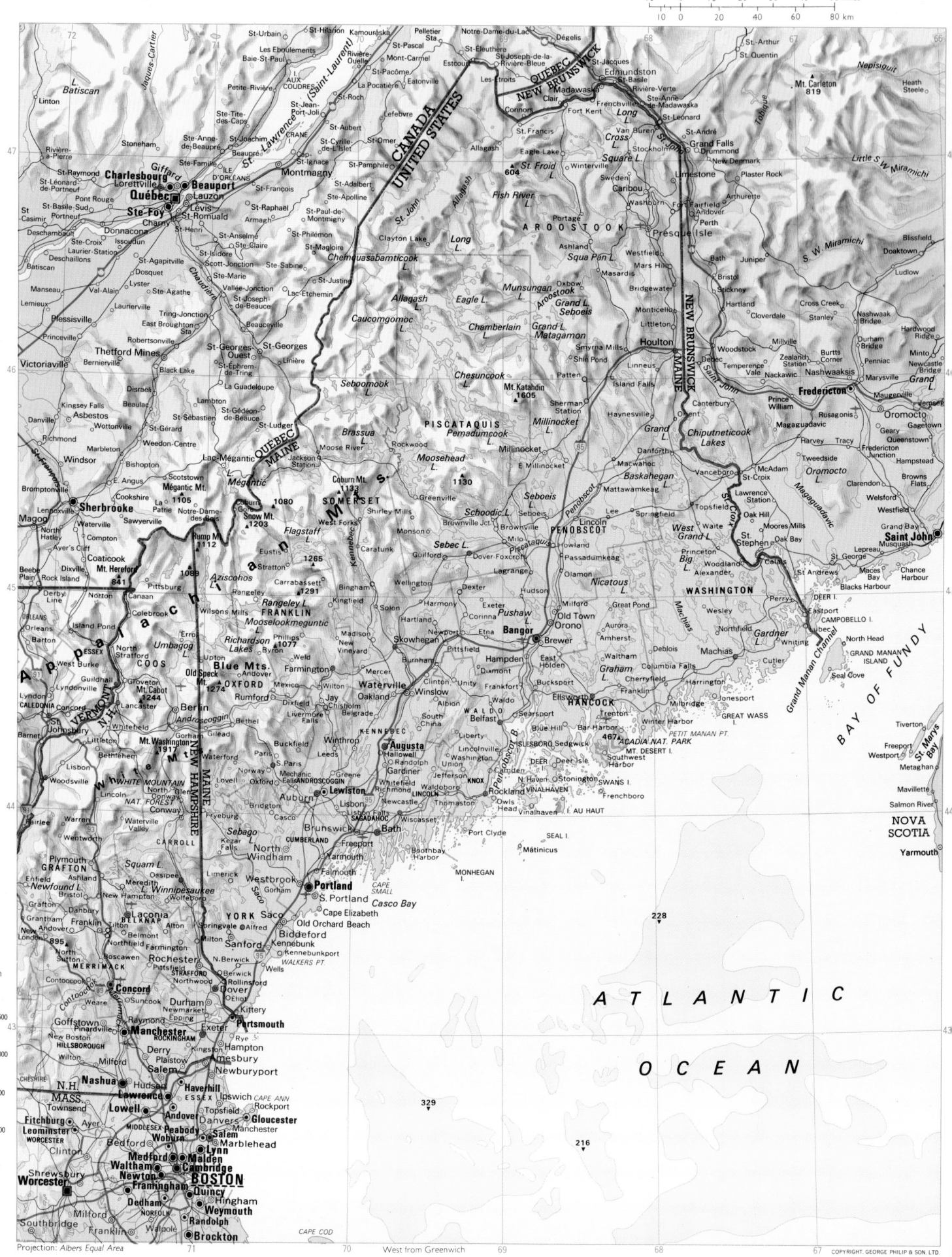

1:2 500 000

Projection: Albers Equal Area

West from Greenwich

COPYRIGHT. GEORGE PHILIP & SON. LTD.

1:1 250 000

10   10   20 miles
10   0   10   20   30 km

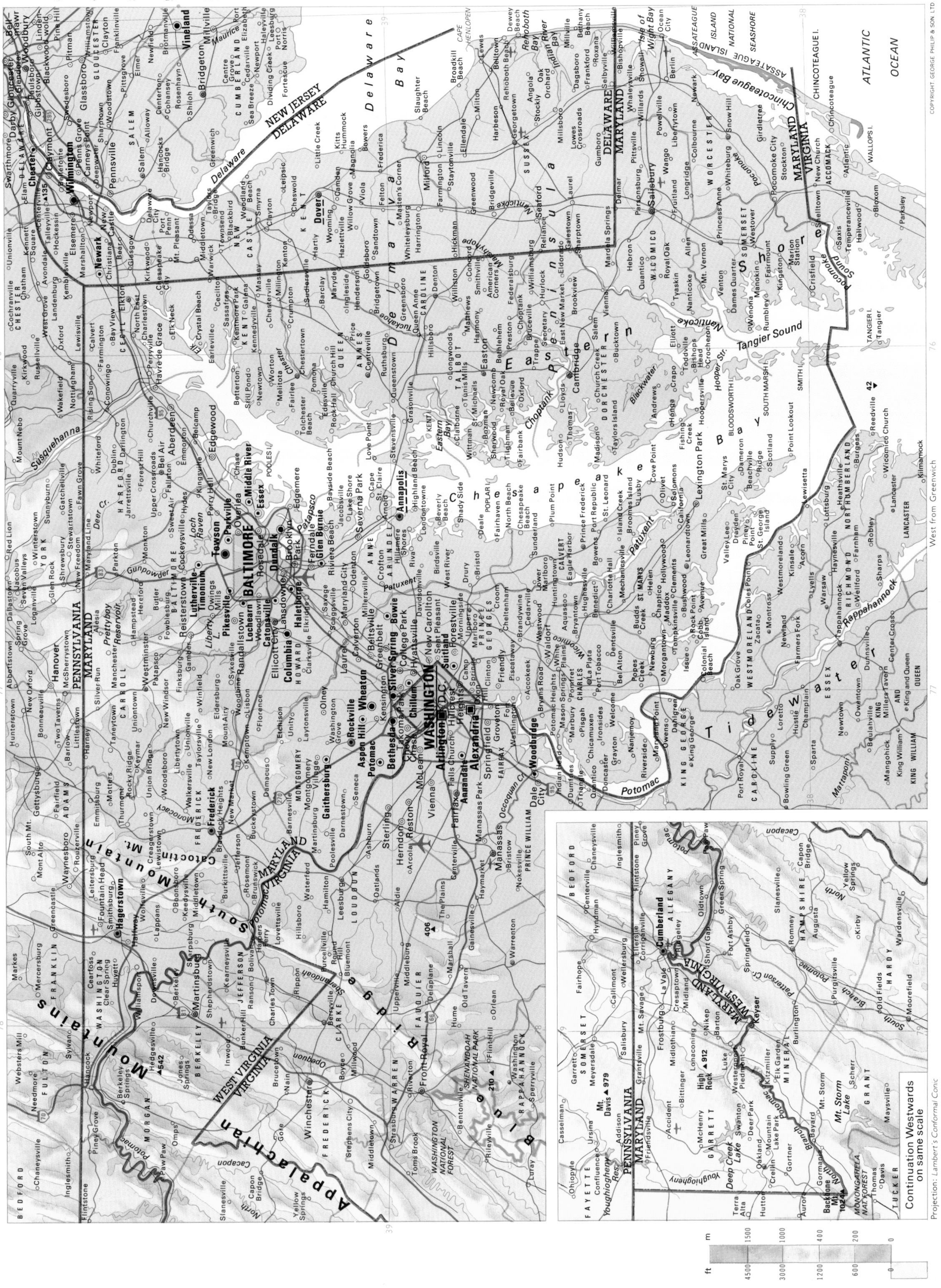

PENNSYLVANIA

NEW JERSEY

DELAWARE

Delaware Bay

MARYLAND

VIRGINIA

WEST VIRGINIA

WASHINGTON D.C.

BALTIMORE

Chesapeake Bay

ATLANTIC OCEAN

Delmarva Peninsula

Eastern Shore

Tidewater

Blue Ridge

Appalachian Mountains

South Mountain

Catoctin Mt.

Tangier Sound

Pocomoke Sound

ASSATEAGUE ISLAND NATIONAL SEASHORE

Chincoteague Bay

West from Greenwich

COPYRIGHT GEORGE PHILIP & SON LTD

Projection: Lambert's Conformal Conic

Continuation Westwards on same scale

Mt. Davis ▲979   High Rock ▲912

ALLEGANY   GARRETT

Cumberland   Keyser

WEST VIRGINIA

Deep Creek Lake

m   1500   1000   400   200   0
ft   4500   3000   1200   600   0

1:1 250 000

10   0   10   20 miles
10   0   10   20   30 km

ATLANTIC   OCEAN

Massachusetts

Bay

CAPE COD

CAPE COD NATIONAL SEASHORE

Cape Cod

Bay

Nantucket Sound

NANTUCKET ISLAND

MARTHA'S VINEYARD

NOMANS LAND

ATLANTIC   OCEAN

NEW HAMPSHIRE

Manchester
Nashua
Lowell
Lawrence
Haverhill
Gloucester
Salem
Beverly
Peabody
Lynn
Cambridge
BOSTON
Somerville
Medford
Newton
Quincy
Weymouth
Braintree
Brockton
Taunton
New Bedford
Fall River

Worcester
Leominster
Fitchburg

VERMONT

Keene

MASSACHUSETTS

Greenfield
Northampton
Holyoke
Chicopee
Springfield
West Springfield
Westfield

Pittsfield

NEW YORK

BERKSHIRE HILLS

Hoosac Range

GREEN MOUNTAIN NAT. FOR.

CONNECTICUT

Hartford
East Hartford
West Hartford
New Britain
Meriden
Waterbury
Bristol
New Haven
West Haven
East Haven
Hamden
Milford
Stratford
Bridgeport
Fairfield
Norwalk
Westport
Stamford
Greenwich
Danbury
Torrington

New London
Norwich
Groton

RHODE ISLAND

Providence
Pawtucket
Cranston
Warwick
West Warwick
East Providence
North Providence
Central Falls
Woonsocket
Newport
Middletown

Narragansett Bay

Rhode Island Sound

BLOCK I. (R.I.)

Block Island Sound

LONG ISLAND

Long Island Sound

MONTAUK POINT

MASS.
R.I.
CONN.

Projection: Lambert's Conformal Conic
West from Greenwich

1 : 2 500 000

10 0 10 20 30 40 50 miles
10 0 10 20 30 40 60 80 km

LAKE SUPERIOR

Extension Northwards on same scale

CANADA
UNITED STATES
ISLE ROYALE NAT. PARK
ISLE ROYALE
GRAND PORTAGE IND. RES.
Grand Portage
Hovland
CUMBERLAND PT.
KEWEENAW
Jarvis River
PIE I.
BLAKE PT.

Extension Westwards on same scale

APOSTLE ISLANDS
OUTER I.
APOSTLE ISLANDS NAT. LAKESHORE
STOCKTON I.
MICHIGAN I.
ASHLAND
FOURTEEN MILE PT.
Silver City
Ontonagon
564 Government Pk.
597
Porcupine Mts.
Greenland
Rockland
White Pine
MICHIGAN
WISCONSIN
Ironwood Bessemer Wakefield Ramsay
Hurley Iron Belt
GOGEBIC
OTTAWA NATIONAL FOREST
Bond Falls Flowage
Watersmeet
Lac Vieux Desert
Manitowish Waters
Phelps
VILAS

Keweenaw Peninsula
Copper Harbor
MANITOU I.
KEWEENAW PT.
PT. ISABELLE
331
Mohawk Calumet Laurium
Hancock Houghton
Lake Linden Hubbell
Painesdale
TRAVERSE PT.
PT. ABBAYE
Keweenaw Bay
L'ANSE INDIAN RES.
Baraga L'Anse
604 Mt. Curwood
Prickett
Huron Mts. Big Bay
BARAGA
Michigamme
Sidnaw
Amasa
Michigamme Res.
Champion Ishpeming Negaunee
Republic
MARQUETTE
Princeton
GRANITE PT.
LAUGHING FISH PT.
AU SABLE PT.
PICTURED ROCKS NAT. LAKESHORE
GRAND
Marquette
Munising Chatham
ALGER
Shingleton

PT. PATTERSON
Grand Marais
Paradise
WHITEFISH BAY
Whitefish Point
ÎLE PARISIENNE
Whitefish Bay
Sault Ste. Marie
Sault Ste. Marie
Echo Bay
BAY MILLS IND. RES.
Brimley
Batchawana Bay
CRISP PT.

LAKE MICHIGAN

HIAWATHA
NATIONAL
FOREST
Indian L.
Manistique L.
SCHOOLCRAFT
Blaney Park
Gould City
Naubinway
MACKINAC
Brevort
Moran
St. Ignace
Mackinac Island
Mackinaw City
Str. of Mackinac
BOIS BLANC

NORTH CHANNEL
CANADA
UNITED STATES
MANITOULIN ISLAND
WESTERN DUCK
GREAT DUCK
Meldrum Bay
Silver Water
BARRIE
COCKBURN

LAKE HURON

ONTARIO
MICHIGAN

Escanaba
Gladstone
Rapid River
Nahma
Garden
Manistique
SEUL CHOIX PT.
PT. AUX BARQUES
BEAVER I.
CHARLEVOIX
Charlevoix
HOG I.
GARDEN I.
HIGH I.
St. James
WAUGOSHANCE
Cross Village
Levering
Cheboygan
Mullett Lake
Mullett L.
Burt L.
Indian River
Onaway
Millersburg
Rogers City
PRESQUE ISLE
Presque Isle
Posen
Long L.
Alpena
THUNDER B.
NORTH PT.

Petoskey
Walloon L.
Boyne City
Boyne Falls
East Jordan
Ellsworth
Central Lake
Bellaire
Mancelona
Gaylord
OTSEGO
Vanderbilt
Wolverine
Hillman
MONTMORENCY
Atlanta
Lewiston
Fletcher Pond
Hubbard L.
Ossineke

Grand Traverse Bay
Traverse City
Elk Rapids
Kalkaska
Grayling
Frederic
CRAWFORD
OSCODA
Mio
Au Sable
ALCONA
Lincoln
Harrisville
HURON NATIONAL FOREST
Oscoda
AU SABLE PT.
East Tawas
Tawas City

SLEEPING BEAR DUNES NAT. LAKESHORE
Empire
Glen L.
Leland
Leelanau
N. MANITOU I.
S. MANITOU I.

Frankfort Elberta
Beulah Benzie
Honor
Crystal L.
Arcadia
Copemish
Bear Lake
Onekama
Kaleva
Manistee
East Lake
Thompsonville
Buckley
Mesick
WEXFORD
Cadillac
Manton
MISSAUKEE
Lake City
Falmouth
McBain
Houghton Lake
ROSCOMMON
Roscommon
Higgins L.
Houghton L.
Prudenville
Rose City
West Branch
OGEMAW
Whittemore
Prescott
RIFLE
ARENAC
Omer
Standish
Sterling
Gladwin
GLADWIN
Beaverton
Au Gres
PT. AU GRES
PT. LOOKOUT
CHARITY I.
SAGINAW BAY
Pigeon
Caseville
Kinde
Port Austin
Port Hope
Harbor Beach
Bad Axe
HURON
Ubly
Minden City
Deckerville

MANISTEE
NATIONAL
FOREST
BIG SABLE PT.
Ludington
MASON
Scottville
Hamlin L.
LITTLE SABLE PT.
Pentwater
Hart
OCEANA
Shelby
Hesperia
New Era
Montague
Whitehall
N Muskegon
Muskegon
Muskegon Hts.
Norton Shores
Ferrysburg
Grand Haven
Spring Lake

Freesoil
Fountain
Luther
Le Roy
LAKE
Baldwin
Reed City
OSCEOLA
Evart
Hersey
Farwell
Clare
CLARE
Coleman
BAY
MIDLAND
Midland
Auburn
Bay City
Carrollton
Saginaw
SAGINAW
Bridgeport
Frankenmuth
Vassar
Caro
TUSCOLA
Reese
Kingston
Marlette
Sandusky
SANILAC
Snover
Applegate
Croswell
Port Sanilac
Lexington

Big Rapids
MECOSTA
Mecosta
ISABELLA
Mt. Pleasant
Shepherd
St. Louis
Alma
Ithaca
GRATIOT
Chesaning
Montrose
St. Charles
Birch Run
Clio
Flushing
Otisville
Columbiaville
Mill
Yale
Brown City
Capac
Imlay City
LAPEER
Lapeer
Almont
Memphis
Marine City
ST. CLAIR
St. Clair
Marysville
Port Huron

Newaygo
White Cloud
Morley
Lakeview
Edmore
Merrill
Breckenridge
NEWAYGO
Hardy Dam Pond
Fremont
Grant
Howard City
McBrides
Stanton
MONTCALM
Carson City
Elsie
Ovid
Owosso
SHIAWASSEE
Corunna
Durand
Byron
Linden
Fenton
Holly
Lake Orion
Oxford
Romeo
New Haven
Rochester
Mt. Clemens
New Baltimore
MACOMB
Algonac

Sand Lake
Cedar Sprs.
Rockford
Greenville
Belding
Maple Rapids
Muir
Maple
St. Johns
CLINTON
Fowler
Westphalia
Laingsburg
Perry
LIVINGSTON
Howell
Brighton
Milford
Wixom
OAKLAND
Pontiac
Waterford
Drayton Plains
Clarkston
Sterling Hts.
Troy
Warren
Roseville
St. Clair Shores

Grand Rapids
Walker
Kentwood
Wyoming
Jenison
OTTAWA
Hudsonville
Zeeland
Holland
Saugatuck
ALLEGAN
Allegan
Fennville
Glenn
S. Haven
Bangor

Coopersville
Comstock Pk.
Ionia
IONIA
Saranac
Portland
Clarksville
Lake Odessa
Freeport
Hastings
BARRY
Middleville
Wayland
Caledonia
Cutlerville
Dorr
Hopkins
Martin
Plainwell
Otsego
Gobles
Paw Paw Lake
Coloma
Lawrence
Paw Paw
VAN BUREN
Hartford
Lawton
Decatur
Gobles
Richland
KALAMAZOO
Kalamazoo
Portage
Parchment
Climax
Vicksburg
Schoolcraft
Marcellus
Mendon
CASS
Cassopolis
Dowagiac
Three Rivers
Constantine
White Pigeon
Sturgis
Edwardsburg
Niles
Buchanan
New Buffalo
Bridgman
Sawyer
Stevensville
St. Joseph
Benton Harbor
Benton Heights
St. Joseph
Fair Plain
Eau Claire
Berrien Sprs.
BERRIEN
Three Oaks

East Lansing
Lansing
Okemos
Holt
Mason
INGHAM
Williamston
Dansville
Stockbridge
Fowlerville
Webberville
Looking Glass
DeWitt
Grand Ledge
Charlotte
EATON
Eaton Rapids
Springport
Olivet
Bellevue
CALHOUN
Battle Creek
Marshall
Albion
Homer
Tekonsha
Union City
Athens
Colon
Burr Oak
Bronson
Coldwater
BRANCH
Quincy
Reading
HILLSDALE
Hillsdale
Osseo
Jonesville
Litchfield
Jackson
JACKSON
Michigan Center
Grass Lake
Concord
Hanover
Brooklyn
Manchester
Clinton
WASHTENAW
Chelsea
Dexter
Ann Arbor
Ypsilanti
Saline
Milan
Dundee
LENAWEE
Adrian
Tecumseh
Blissfield
Petersburg
Hudson
Morenci
Waldron

Detroit
Windsor
Dearborn
Livonia
Westland
Taylor
Wayne
Southfield
Royal Oak
Oak Park
Ferndale
Lincoln Park
Wyandotte
Trenton
Grosse Pointe
MONROE
Monroe
Flat Rock
Rockwood
Carleton
Stony Point
LAKE ERIE

South Lyon
Northville
Plymouth
Garden City
Inkster
Romulus
Belleville
Flint
Burton
Grand Blanc
Swartz Creek
GENESEE
Fenton
Davison
Metamora
Imlay City

WISCONSIN
MICHIGAN

Green Bay
De Pere
Allouez
Kaukauna
Appleton
Menasha
Neenah
Oshkosh
Lake Winnebago
Fond du Lac
Sheboygan
Sheboygan Falls
Plymouth
West Bend
Menomonee Falls
Brookfield
Wauwatosa
MILWAUKEE
West Allis
Waukesha
New Berlin
Cudahy
S. Milwaukee
Oak Creek
Racine
Sturtevant
Kenosha
Waukegan
North Chicago
Zion
Winthrop Harbor
Gurnee
Mundelein
Libertyville
Lake Forest
Highland Park
Deerfield
Wheeling
Arlington Hts.
Mt. Prospect
Des Plaines
Palatine
Elgin
Wilmette
Evanston
CHICAGO

Oconto
Oconto Falls
Shawano
Pulaski
Seymour
OUTAGAMIE
Hortonville
Greenville
Brillion
Chilton
Kiel
New Holstein
Plymouth
Random Lake
Cedar Grove
Oostburg
Port Washington
Grafton
Mequon
Thiensville
Brown Deer
Shorewood
Whitefish Bay
Hartland
Sussex
Delafield
Dousman
Pewaukee
Mukwonago
East Troy
Elkhorn
WALWORTH
Lake Geneva
Genoa City
Antioch
Fox Lake
McHenry
Crystal Lake
Woodstock
MCHENRY

Marinette
Menominee
Peshtigo
Coleman
Pound
Crivitz
Suring
Gillett
MENOMINEE IND. RES.
Keshena
Wausaukee
Amberg
Stephenson
Powers
Hermansville
Vulcan
Norway
Iron Mountain
Kingsford
Niagara
Pembine
Goodman
Laona
Wabeno
Crystal Falls
IRON
Alpha
Caspian
Florence
FLORENCE
DICKINSON
Felch
Channing
Sagola
MENOMINEE
Carney
Cedar
Daggett
Nadeau
Wallace

Two Rivers
Manitowoc
MANITOWOC
Whitelaw
Valders
Reedsville
Brillion
Denmark
Casco
Luxemburg
Algoma
Kewaunee
KEWAUNEE
Forestville
Sturgeon Bay
DOOR
Baileys Harbor
Sister Bay
Ellison Bay
Egg Harbor
CHAMBERS I.
Washington I.
WASHINGTON
WISCONSIN ISLANDS WILDERNESS
N. MANITOU I.
Northport
Leland
CAT HEAD PT.
LEELANAU
Suttons Bay
PT. DETOUR
SUMMER I.
ST. MARTIN I.
Big Bay de Noc

Projection: Albers Equal Area

West from Greenwich

MICHIGAN
OHIO
COPYRIGHT. GEORGE PHILIP & SON. LTD.

ft m
1200 400
600 200
0 0
200 600

m ft

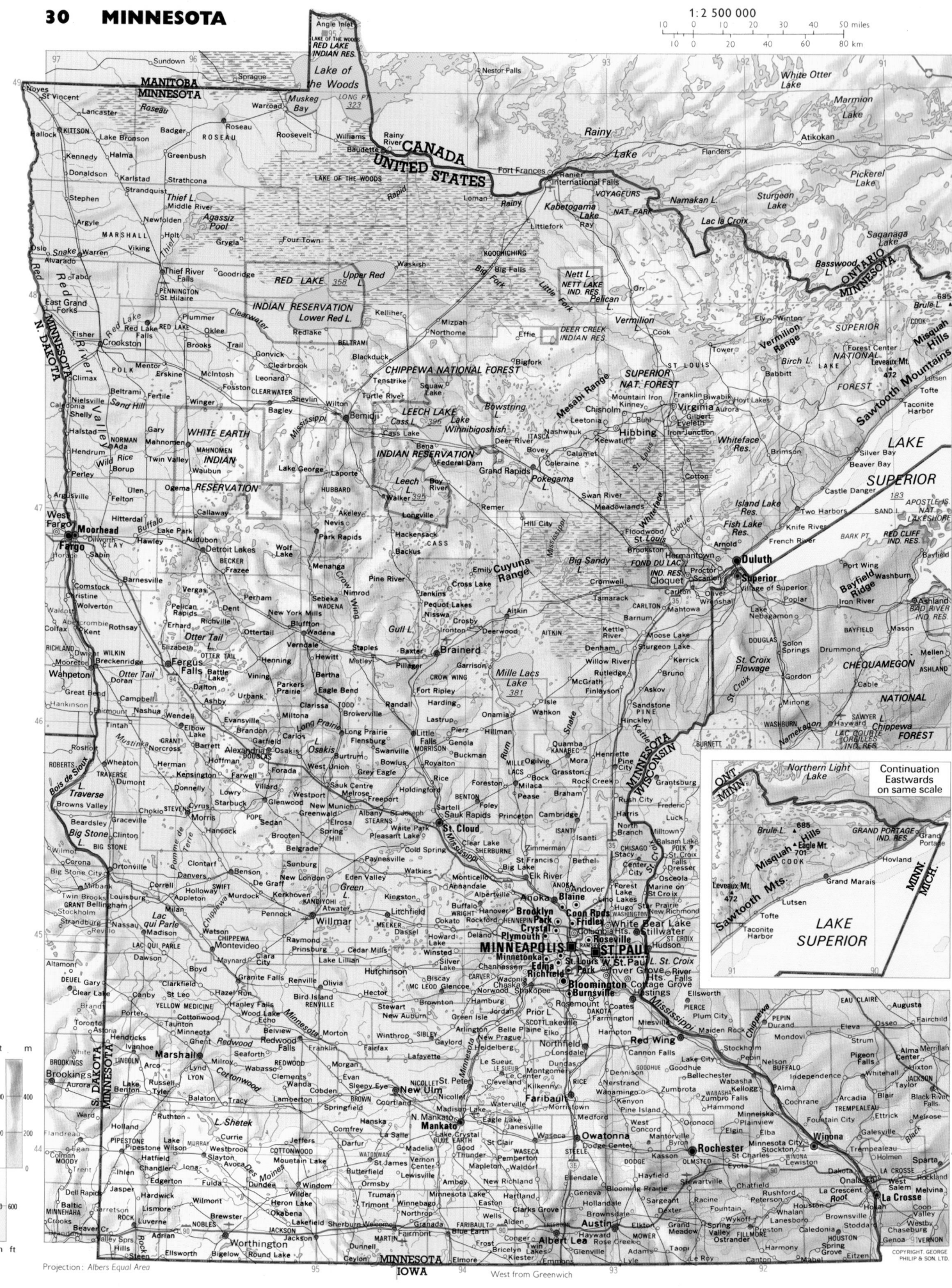

1:2 500 000

Projection: Albers Equal Area

West from Greenwich

1:2 500 000

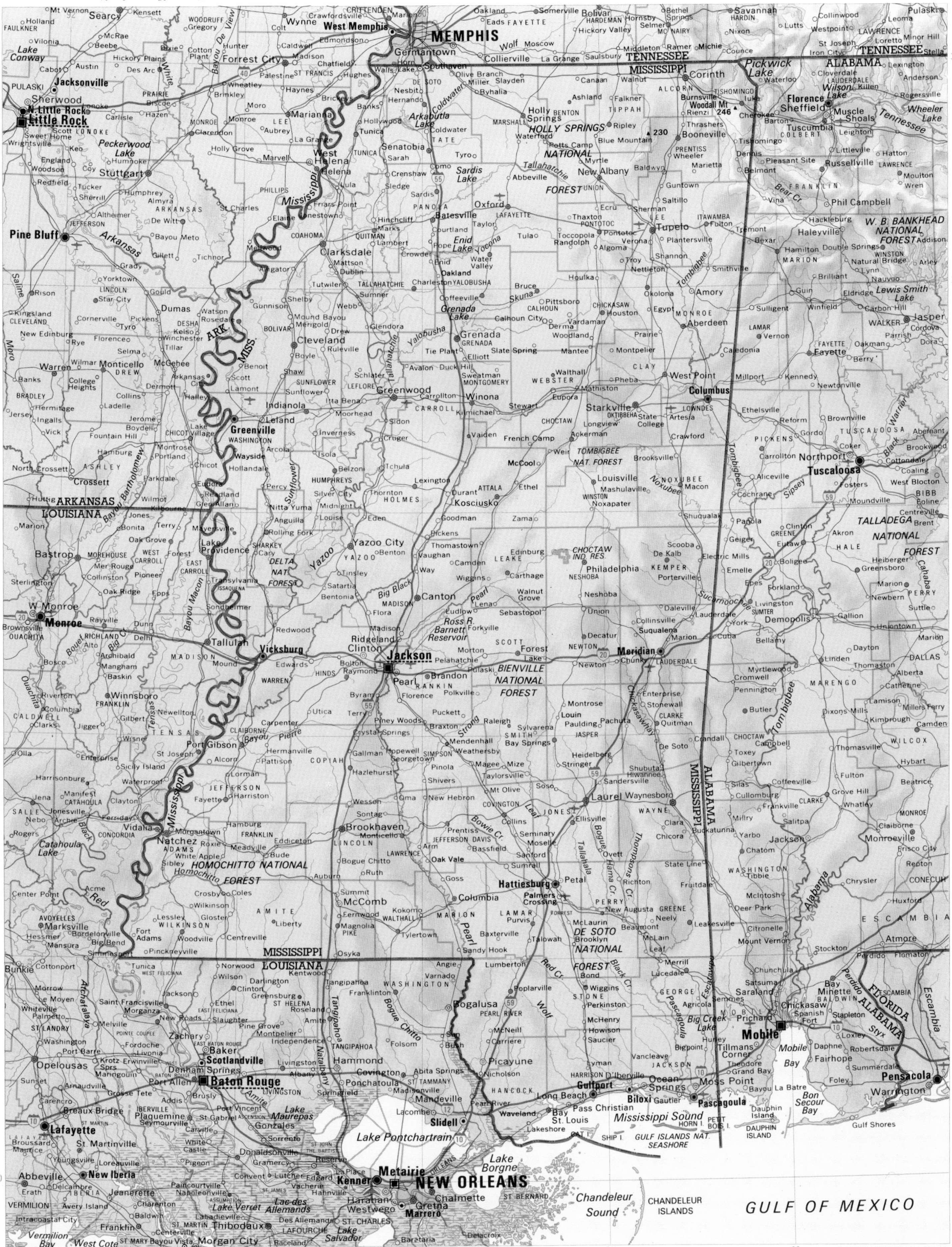

Projection: Albers Equal Area

West from Greenwich

COPYRIGHT GEORGE PHILIP & SON LTD.

MEMPHIS

MISSISSIPPI

TENNESSEE

ALABAMA

ARKANSAS

LOUISIANA

NEW ORLEANS

Jackson

GULF OF MEXICO

Little Rock
N. Little Rock
Pine Bluff
Forrest City
West Helena
Helena
Clarksdale
Greenville
Greenwood
Grenada
Oxford
Tupelo
Columbus
Starkville
West Point
Aberdeen
Tuscaloosa
Northport
Vicksburg
Clinton
Ridgeland
Brandon
Pearl
Meridian
Monroe
W Monroe
Tallulah
Natchez
Brookhaven
McComb
Hattiesburg
Laurel
Columbia
Baton Rouge
Scotlandville
Baker
Lafayette
New Iberia
Slidell
Metairie
Kenner
Gretna
Marrero
Biloxi
Gulfport
Pascagoula
Moss Point
Mobile
Pensacola
Warrington

Mississippi Sound

Chandeleur Sound
CHANDELEUR ISLANDS

Lake Pontchartrain
Lake Borgne

HOLLY SPRINGS NATIONAL FOREST
DELTA NAT. FOREST
BIENVILLE NATIONAL FOREST
HOMOCHITTO NATIONAL FOREST
TOMBIGBEE NAT. FOREST
DE SOTO NATIONAL FOREST
W. B. BANKHEAD NATIONAL FOREST
TALLADEGA NATIONAL FOREST
CHOCTAW IND. RES.
GULF ISLANDS NAT. SEASHORE

Pickwick Lake
Sardis Lake
Enid Lake
Grenada Lake
Ross R. Barnett Reservoir

FLORIDA

1:2 500 000

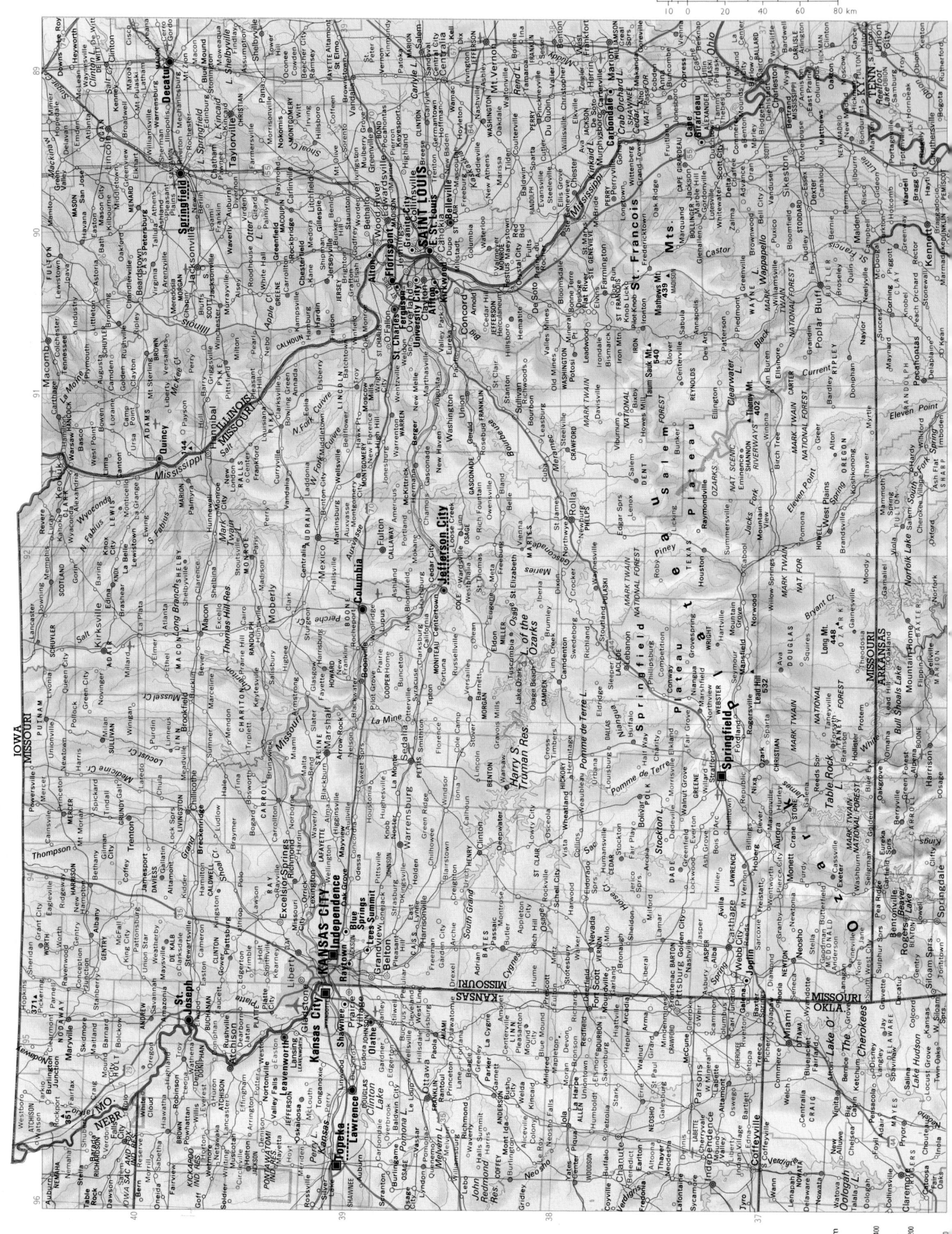

1:3 750 000

20 0 20 40 60 80 100 miles
20 0 20 40 60 80 100 120 140 160 km

NORTH DAKOTA
MONTANA
S.D.
MONT.

SASKATCHEWAN
MONTANA

CANADA
UNITED STATES

ALBERTA
MONTANA

B.C.
MONTANA

IDAHO
MONTANA

MONTANA
WYOMING

Williston Basin

FORT PECK INDIAN RESERVATION
ROOSEVELT

Big Sheep Mountain 1105

CROW INDIAN RESERVATION

Big Horn Mts.

Little Rocky Mts.

Bearpaw Mts.

Little Belt Mts.

Big Snowy Mts.

Crazy Mts.

Beartooth Ra.

YELLOWSTONE NATIONAL PARK

R O C K Y   M O U N T A I N S

Bitterroot Range

Clearwater Mountains

Salmon River Mountains

Sawtooth Range

Lemhi Range

Beaverhead Range

Billings

Great Falls

Helena

Butte

Missoula

Medicine Hat

Lethbridge

Cypress Hills

Projection: Albers' Equal Area

COPYRIGHT GEORGE PHILIP & SON LTD.

110° West from Greenwich

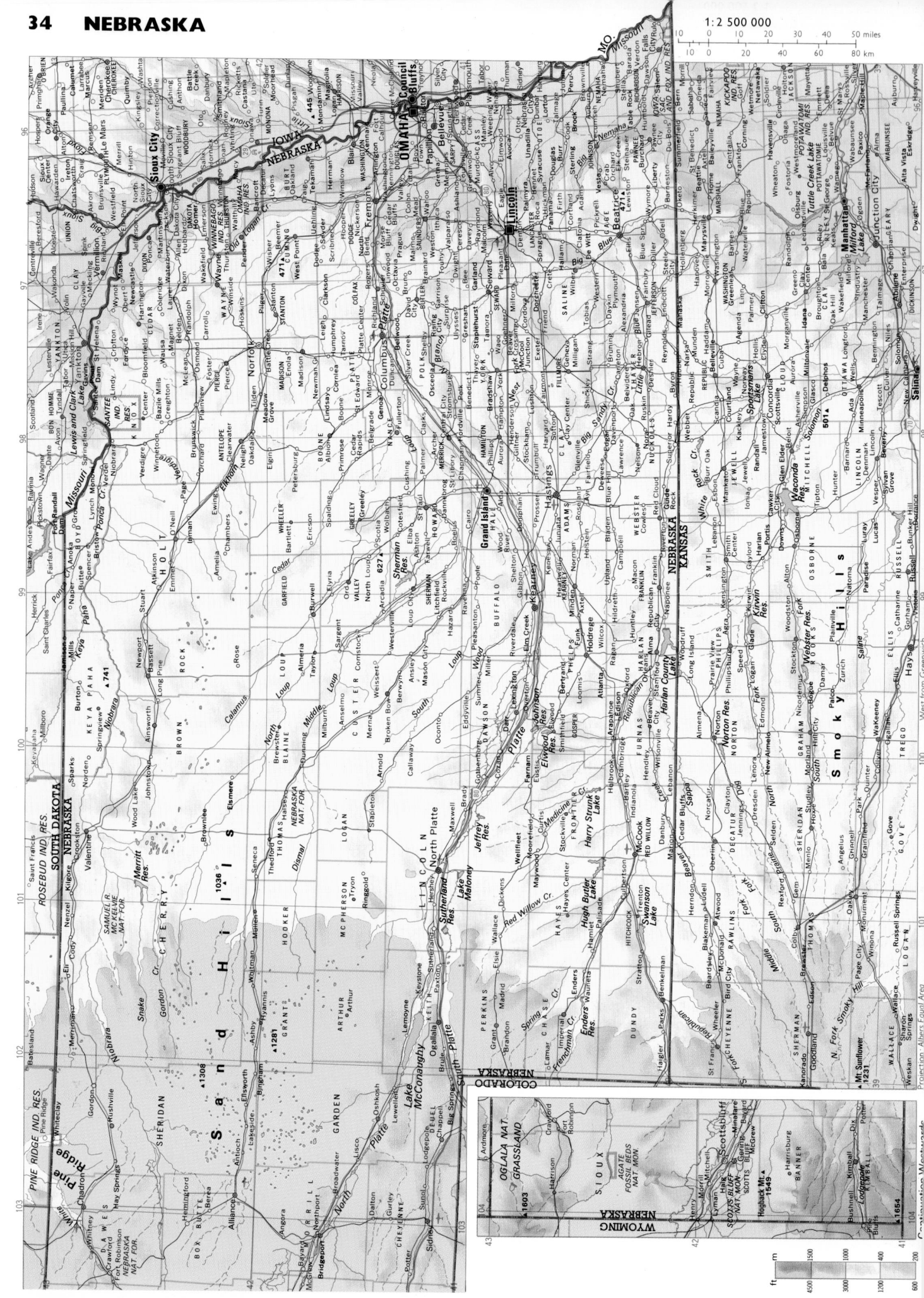

1 : 2 500 000

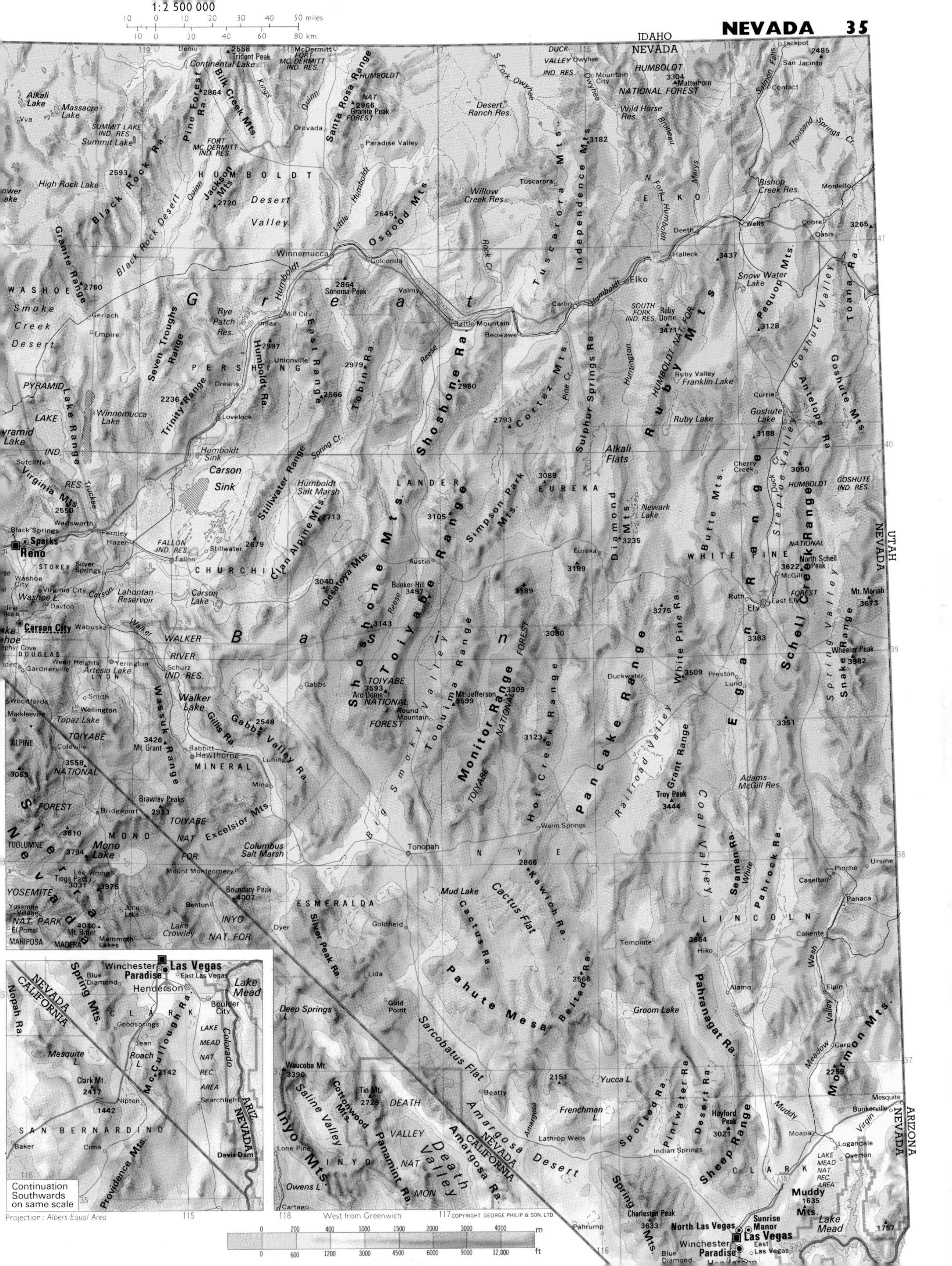

1:2 500 000

10 0 10 20 30 40 50 miles
10 0 20 40 60 80 km

IDAHO
NEVADA

Alkali Lake
Massacre Lake
Summit Lake IND. RES.
Summit Lake
High Rock Lake
Black Rock Desert
HUMBOLDT
Desert Valley
Granite Range
WASHOE
Smoke Creek Desert
Gerlach
Empire
PYRAMID LAKE
Pyramid Lake IND.
Virginia Mts.
Sparks
Reno
Carson City
Sierra Nevada
YOSEMITE NAT. PARK
Mono Lake
TOIYABE NATIONAL FOREST

Denio
Continental Lake
Trident Peak 2558
Kings
Pine Forest Ra.
2864
Blk Creek Mts.
Santa Rosa Range
Granite Peak 2966
Quinn
Orovada
Paradise Valley
Jackson Mts.
2720
2593
Desert Valley
Osgood Mts.
Little Humboldt
2645
Winnemucca
Golconda
Humboldt
Sonoma Peak 2864
Valmy
Battle Mountain
Beowawe
Mill City
Imlay
Rye Patch Res.
2997
Unionville
Oreana
2979
Lovelock
2236
Humboldt Ra.
Trinity Range
Tobin Ra.
2566
2950
Humboldt Sink
Carson Sink
Stillwater Range
Humboldt Salt Marsh
Clan Alpine Mts.
2713
2679
Stillwater
Fallon
CHURCHILL
Carson Lake
Lahontan Reservoir
Desatoya Mts.
3040
Austin
Bunker Hill 3497
Reese
3143
Shoshone Mts.
Toiyabe Range
Simpson Park Mts.
3105
3089
EUREKA
Eureka
3189
Newark Lake
Diamond Mts.
3235
WHITE PINE
3275
Ely
Ruth
East Ely
3383
Duckwater
White Pine Ra.
Hot Creek Range
Pancake Range
Railroad Valley
Grant Range
3509
Preston
Lund
Coal Valley
Troy Peak 3444
Warm Springs
Tonopah
NYE
2866
Kawich Ra.
Cactus Flat
Cactus Ra.
Belted Ra.
Pahute Mesa
Groom Lake
Sarcobatus Flat
Goldfield
Lida
Gold Point
Beatty
Yucca L.
Frenchman L.
Lathrop Wells
DEATH VALLEY
Amargosa Desert
Amargosa Ra.
Indian Springs
Spring Mts.
Charleston Peak 3633
North Las Vegas
Las Vegas
Winchester
Paradise
Henderson
Lake Mead
Boulder City
Colorado R.
ARIZONA
NEVADA

IDAHO NEVADA
Jackpot
San Jacinto 2485
Contact
Montello
HUMBOLDT NATIONAL FOREST
Matterhorn 3304
Wild Horse Res.
ELKO
Tuscarora
Independence Mts. 3182
Deeth
Wells
3437
Halleck
Elko
Carlin
Ruby Dome 3471
Ruby Valley
Franklin Lake
Ruby Lake
Ruby Mts.
Alkali Flats
3188
Goshute Lake
Goshute Mts.
Antelope Ra.
Cherry Creek
3050
Schell Creek Range
North Schell Peak 3622
McGill
Mt. Moriah 3673
Wheeler Peak 3982
Snake Range
Spring Valley
3351
Pioche
Panaca
Caliente
LINCOLN
Hiko 2664
Pahranagat Ra.
Seaman Ra.
Pahroc Ra.
Alamo
Elgin
Mormon Mts.
2259
Moapa
Overton
Sheep Range
LAKE MEAD NAT. REC. AREA
CLARK
Muddy Mts. 1635
Lake Mead
ARIZONA NEVADA
Bunkerville
Virgin R.

Continuation Southwards on same scale
Projection: Albers Equal Area
COPYRIGHT GEORGE PHILIP & SON LTD.
West from Greenwich

0 200 400 600 1000 1500 2000 3000 4000 m
0 600 1200 3000 4500 6000 9000 12,000 ft

1:1 250 000

10 0 10 20 miles
10 0 10 20 30 km

CANADA
UNITED STATES
QUEBEC
VERMONT
NEW HAMPSHIRE
MAINE
QUEBEC · MAINE

Major towns and cities: St-Jean, St-Luc, Ste-Brigide-d'Iberville, Ange-Gardien, Waterloo, Eastman, Sherbrooke, Lennoxville, Deauville, Sawyerville, La Patrie, Notre-Dame-des-Bois, Delson, Iberville, Bromont, Adamsville, L. Brome, Lac-Brome, Waterville, Compton, Napierville, Henryville, Farnham, East-Farnham, Cowansville, L. Massawippi, Magog, L. Magog, Coaticook, Barrington, Stanbridge-East, Bedford, Dunham, Ayer's-Cliff, Mt. Hereford 841, Mt. Megog, Lacolle, Pike River, Sutton Mts. 972, Mansonville, Beebe Plain, Rock Island, Salmon Mt. 1025, Rump Mt. 1112, Hemmingford, Philipsburg, Abercorn, QUEBEC, VERMONT, Derby Line, Stewartstown, Pittsburg, Second L.

Rouses Point, Highgate Center, Richford, North Troy, Derby, Norton, Beecher Falls, West Stewartstown, First Connecticut L., Kennebago L., FRANKLIN, Rangeley, Champlain, Alburg, Swanton, East Berkshire, Enosburg Falls, Jay Peak 1177, Newport, Troy, Clyde, Morgan, East Charleston, Gore Mt. 1015, Colebrook, Dixville Notch, Wilsons Mills, Oquossoc

Mooers, Montgomery Center, Lowell, Irasburg, Orleans, ORLEANS, Island Pond, Lemington, North Stratford, Aziscohos L., Mooselookmeguntic L.

West Chazy, Chazy, Isle La Motte, St. Albans, Bakersfield, Belvidere Mt. 1024, Eden, Albany, Glover, L. Willoughby, Westmore, Nulhegan R., Stratford, Errol, Upper Richardson L., Elephant Mt. 1150

Napierville, North Hero, GRAND ISLE, Georgia Center, Fairfax, Jeffersonville, Johnson, Greensboro, West Burke, ESSEX, Blue Mt. 1135, North Stratford, Lower Richardson L., OXFORD, Andover

Morrisonville, Plattsburg, South Hero, Milton, Cambridge, Hyde Park, Morrisville, Sutton, COOS, Umbagog L., Rumford

Peru, Port Kent, Keeseville, Winooski, Essex Jct., Williston, Mt. Mansfield 1339, Underhill Flats, Stowe, Hardwick, Lyndonville, CALEDONIA, Lunenburg, Concord, Stone Mt. 839, Mt. Cabot 1244, Groveton, West Milan, Milan, Berlin, Mt. Success 1094, Gorham, Gilead, Bethel

Clintonville, Burlington, South Burlington, Richmond, Waterbury Center 1083, Marshfield, Cabot, Danville, St. Johnsbury, Gilman, Whitefield, Meadows, WHITE MOUNTAIN NAT. FOR.

Lewis, Shelburne, Hinesburg, Huntington, Waterbury, Camels Hump 1244, WASHINGTON, Moore Res., Barnet, Littleton, Bethlehem, Twin Mountain, Mt. Washington 1917, Mt. Carrigain 1476, Jackson, North Waterford

Ferrisburg, Montpelier, Plainfield, Moore Res., Ammonoosuc R., Francona, White Mountains, Glen, Lovell

Westport, Vergennes, Bristol, Barre, Groton, Lisbon, Benton, Mt. Lafayette 1600, WHITE MOUNTAIN 1426, Bartlett, Intervale

Mineville, Witherbee, Addison, Waitsfield, Northfield, Wells R., Granbyville, West Topsham, Woodsville, GRAFTON, Lincoln, North Conway, Saco R., Fryeburg, Bridgton

Port Henry, Middlebury, GREEN MOUNTAIN NATIONAL FOREST, East Middlebury, Granville, Randolph Center, Chelsea, Bradford, Haverhill, East Haverhill, Mt. Moosilauke 1466, Woodstock, West Thornton, Mt. Tecumseh 1220, Waterville Valley 1059, Passaconaway, Conway, CARROLL, Denmark

Crown Point, Bridport, Cornwall, Salisbury, Hancock, Randolph, East Randolph, West Fairlee, Fairlee, Glencliff, Warren, Carr Mt. 1058, Stinson Lake, Sandwich Mt. 1217, Wonalancet, East Sebago

Chilson, Shoreham, Whiting, Leicester, Forest Dale, Rochester, Bethel, South Royalton, Sharon, South Strafford, Lyme, Smarts Mt. 988, Wentworth, Rumney, West Campton, Center Sandwich, West Ossipee, Kezar Falls, Sebago

Hague, Brandon, Stockbridge, Pittsfield, White R., Norwich, Dorchester, Plymouth, West Plymouth, Holderness, Squam L., Moultonboro, Ossipee L., Effingham Falls, Limerick

WARREN, L. George, Hubbardton, Benson, Chittenden, Sherburne, Woodstock, South Pomfret, Quechee, Wilder, West Canaan, Hebron, Mt. Cardigan 951, Ashland, Center Harbor, Melvin Village, Tuftonboro, Ossipee, West Newfield

Huletts Landing, L. Bomoseen, Castleton, Proctor, Mendon, White River Jct., Hanover, Canaan, Alexandria, Bristol, Meredith, Lake Winnipesaukee 154, Wolfeboro, North Shapleigh, Waterboro

Whitehall, Fair Haven, West Rutland, Rutland 1293, Bridgewater, Lebanon, Enfield, Enfield Center, Grafton, New Hampton, BELKNAP, Winnisquam, Laconia, Alton Bay, Sanbornville, YORK, Shapleigh, Springvale, Sanford

Fort Ann, Kingsbury, Poultney, Clarendon, Middletown Springs, Wells, Tinmouth, East Wallingford, Plymouth, South Woodstock, Hartland, Meriden, Plainfield 848, Grantham, Danbury, Andover, Franklin, Tilton, Salisbury Heights, Belmont, Gilmanton, Farmington, Milton

Granville, Wallingford, Tyson, Windsor, Ludlow, Healdville 1028, Ascutney, North Springfield, SULLIVAN, Croydon Flat, Sunapee L., Wendell, Sunapee, New London, Salisbury, Lower Gilmanton, Center Barnstead, Strafford, STRAFFORD, Rochester, North Berwick

South Hartford, Pawlet, East Wallingford, Danby, Proctorsville, Claremont, Sugar R., Newport, Mt. Sunapee, Mt. Kearsarge North 895, Sutton, MERRIMACK, Boscawen, Pittsfield, Loudon, Center Strafford, Somersworth

West Pawlet, East Rupert 1160, Dorset, Peru, Weston, Chester, Charlestown, Lempster, East Lempster, Washington, Warner, Penacook, North Chichester, Gossville, Northwood, East Barrington, Dover

WASHINGTON, Rupert, Equinox Mt. 1164, Manchester, GREEN, Londonderry, Grafton, South Charlestown, Newbury, Bradford, Henniker, Hopkinton, Concord, Suncook, Deerfield, Durham, Portsmouth, Kittery, Newmarket

Salem, Middle Falls, West Arlington, Arlington 1176, Rawsonville, Jamaica, Cambridgeport, Bellows Falls, Westminster, Townshend, Marlow, Hillsboro Upper Village, Weare, Bow, Dunbarton, Hooksett, South Deerfield, Raymond, Epping, Stratham, Greenland, Rye

Greenwich, Shushan, MOUNTAIN, Stratton, Somerset Res., West Dover, Putney, Westmoreland, Surry, South Stoddard, Nelson, Hancock, Francestown, New Boston, Bedford, Goffstown, Manchester, Massabesic L., Brentwood, Exeter, North Hampton, Hampton

Cambridge, BENNINGTON, Shaftsbury, Newfane, West Dummerston, Keene, Dublin, Mt. Monadnock 965, Peterborough, Mont Vernon, Amherst, Merrimack, Derry, Hampstead, Kingston, East Kingston, Amesbury, Salisbury

Hoosic R., North Hoosick, NATIONAL, Jamaica, Wilmington, Chesterfield, West Swanzey, Marlborough, HILLSBOROUGH, Wilton, Milford, South Merrimack, Canobie Lake, Salem, Plaistow, Seabrook

Hoosick Falls, Woodford, Bennington 839, The Dome 839, Searsburg, Brattleboro, West Chesterfield, Troy, Jaffrey, Temple, Greenville, Nashua, Hudson, Windham, Pelham, Dracut, West Newbury, Newburyport

RENSSELAER, Grafton, FOREST, Harriman Res., Readsboro, Hinsdale, Winchester, Richmond, West Rindge, New Ipswich, Mason, Brookline, Groveland, Byfield, PLUM I.

Petersburg, VERMONT, MASSACHUSETTS, NEW HAMPSHIRE, MASSACHUSETTS, Winchendon, Ashburnham, Townsend, Pepperell, Lowell, Lawrence, North Andover, Boxford, Topsfield, Ipswich B., Pigeon Cove

Berlin, Williamstown, Mt. Greylock 1064, North Adams, Adams, Pownal, Stamford, Deerfield, Charlemont, Colrain, Bernardston, Northfield, Warwick, Royalston, Millers R., Groton, Chelmsford, Georgetown, Rowley, South Hamilton, Gloucester, CAPE ANN, Rockport

Sand Lake

Physical features: Richelieu R., Missisquoi B., L. Champlain, Lake Champlain, Lamoille R., Winooski R., Green Mountains, Worcester Mts., Mad R., White R., Otter Cr., Omompanoosuc R., Ompompanoosuc R., Connecticut R., Passumpsic R., Moose R., Black R., Wells R., Waits R., Pemigewasset R., Androscoggin R., Saco R., Salmon Falls R., Merrimack R., Contoocook R., Ashuelot R., West R., Williams R., Hoosac Range, Taconic Range, Batten Kill, Champlain Canal, Hoosic R., Newfound L., L. Bomoseen, L. George, Squam L., Ossipee L., Lake Winnipesaukee, Lake Sunapee, Massabesic L., ATLANTIC OCEAN

Elevation scale (ft / m):
ft — 4500, 3000, 1200, 600, 0
m — 1500, 1000, 400, 200, 0

Projection: Lambert's Conformal Conic

West from Greenwich

73   72   71

COPYRIGHT GEORGE PHILIP & SON LTD.

1:1 250 000

10 0 10 20 miles
10 0 10 20 30 km

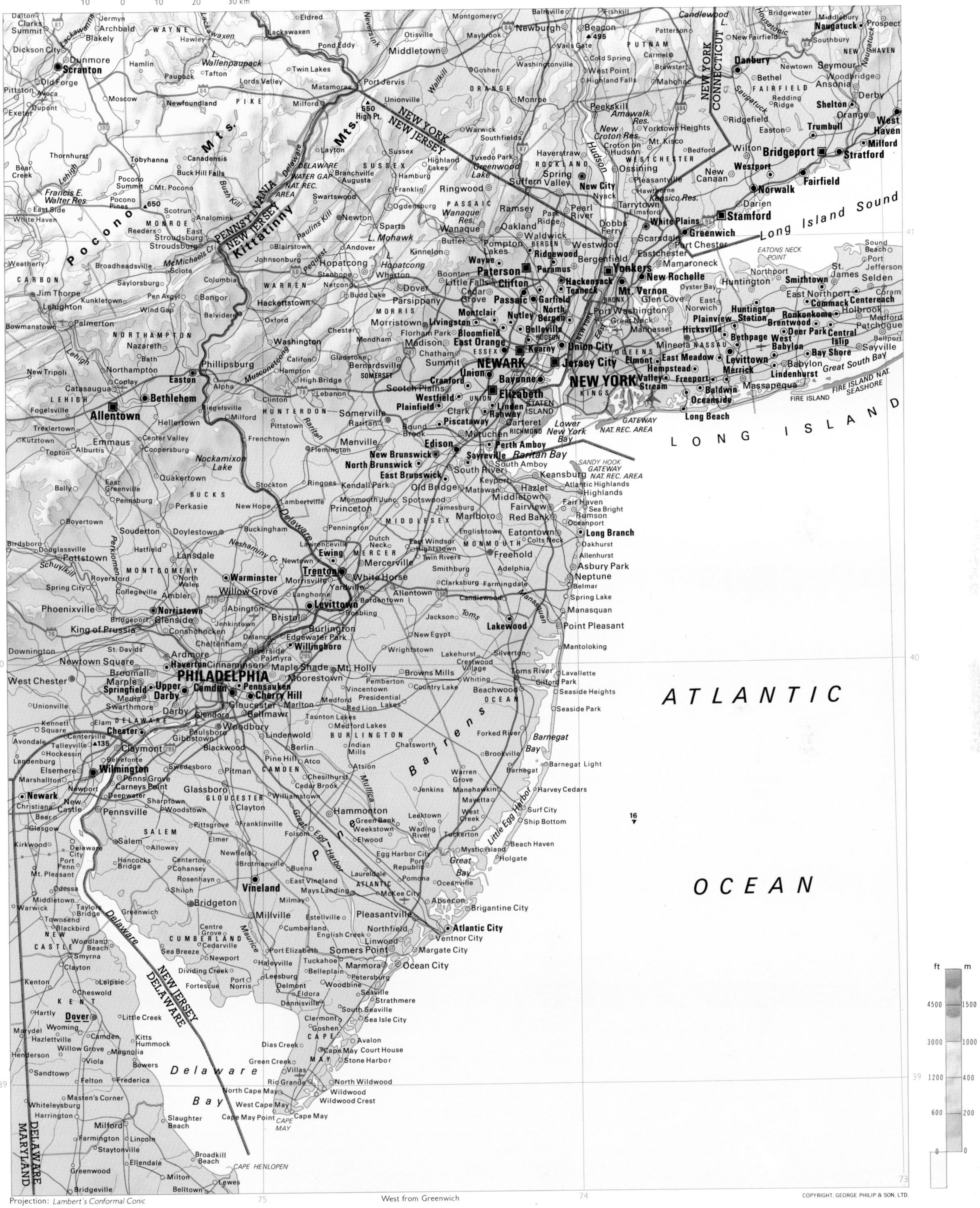

Projection: Lambert's Conformal Conic

West from Greenwich

COPYRIGHT. GEORGE. PHILIP & SON. LTD.

ATLANTIC

OCEAN

LONG ISLAND

Long Island Sound

NEW YORK

NEWARK

Jersey City

Elizabeth

Paterson

Trenton

PHILADELPHIA

Camden

Wilmington

Allentown

Bethlehem

Scranton

Atlantic City

Ocean City

Vineland

Dover

PENNSYLVANIA

NEW JERSEY

DELAWARE

MARYLAND

NEW YORK
CONNECTICUT

Delaware Bay

Pine Barrens

Raritan Bay

Barnegat Bay

Kittatinny Mts

Pocono Mts

ft m
4500 1500
3000 1000
1200 400
600 200
0 0

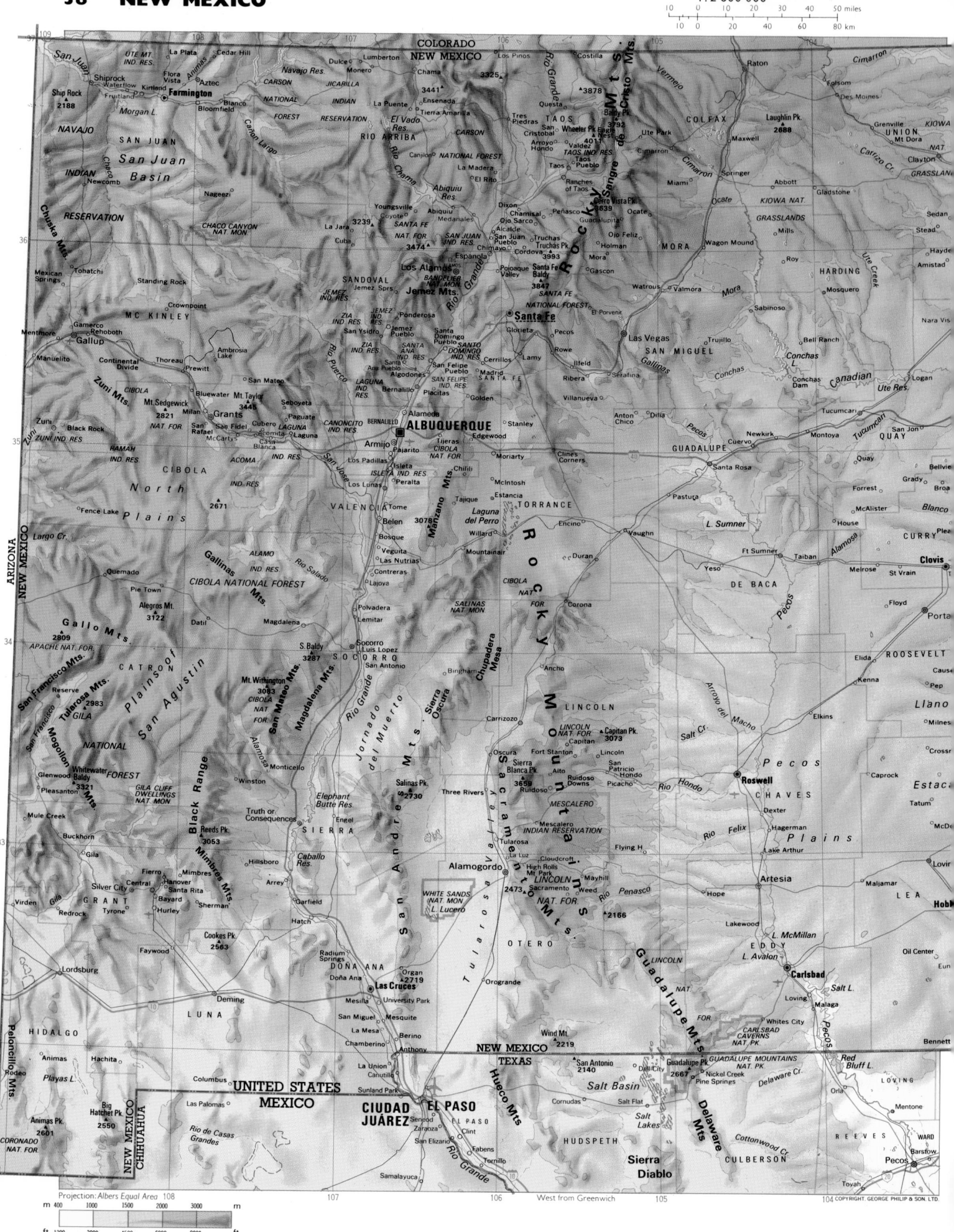

1 : 2 600 000

Projection: Albers Equal Area 108

West from Greenwich

COPYRIGHT. GEORGE PHILIP & SON. LTD.

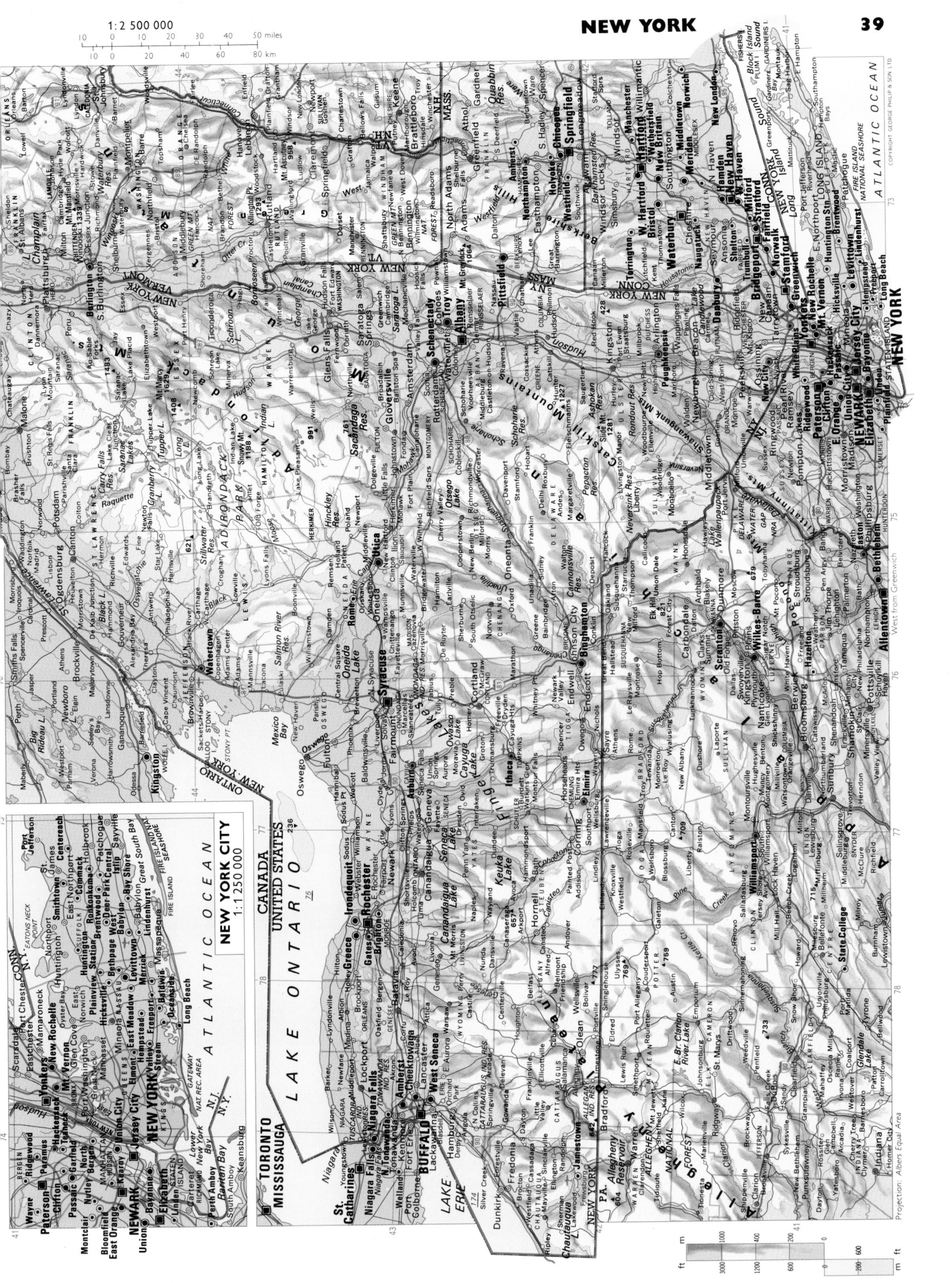

1 : 2 500 000

10   0   10   20   30   40   50 miles
10   0   20   40   60   80 km

ATLANTIC OCEAN

CANADA
UNITED STATES

NEW YORK CITY
1 : 1 250 000

ATLANTIC OCEAN

LAKE ONTARIO

TORONTO
MISSISSAUGA

St. Catharines

LAKE ERIE

NEW YORK

Projection: Albers Equal Area

West from Greenwich

COPYRIGHT GEORGE PHILIP & SON LTD

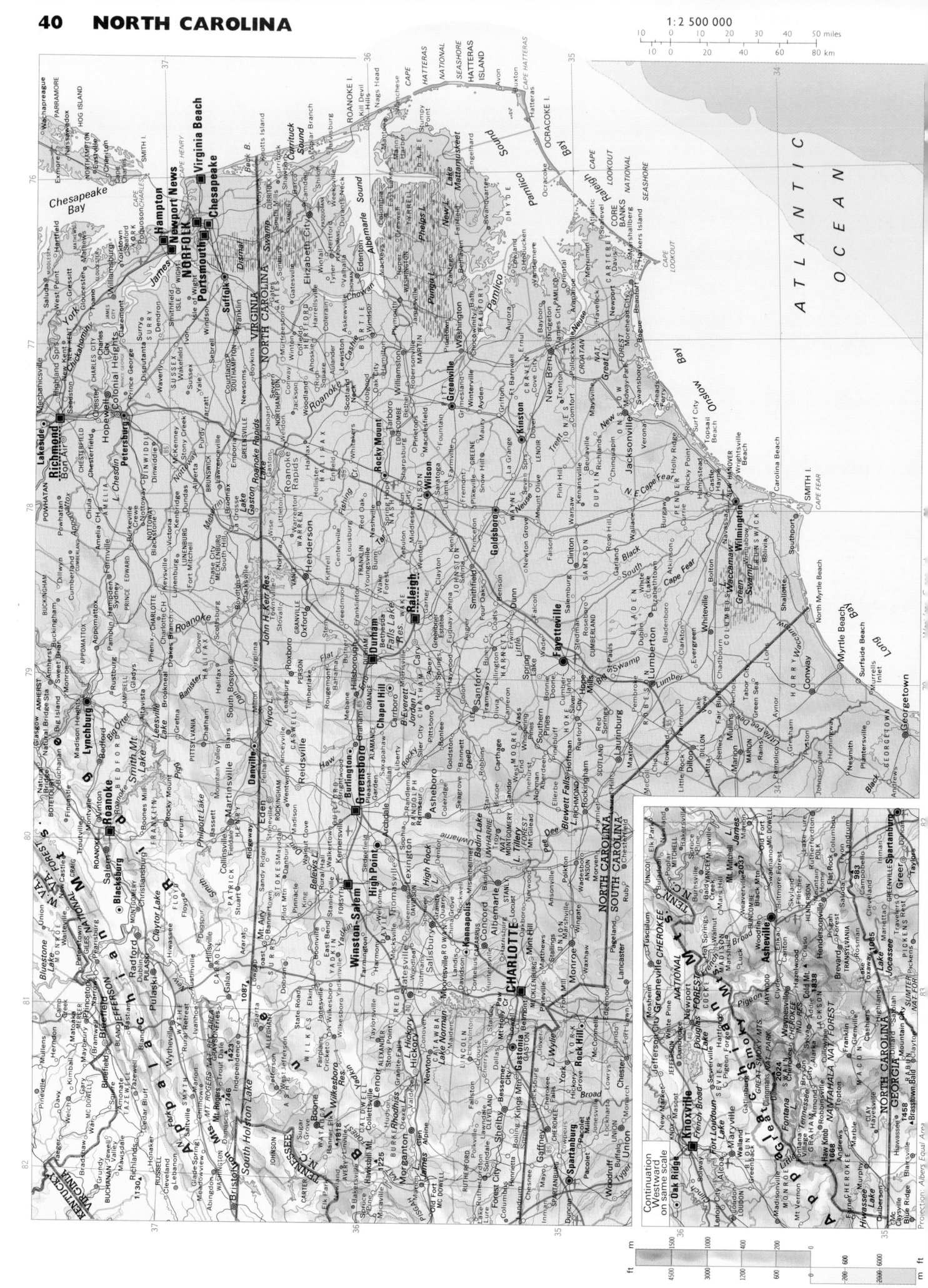

1 : 2 500 000

Continuation Westward on same scale

Projection: Albers Equal Area

1 : 2 500 000

10   0   10   20   30   40   50 miles
10   0   20   40   60   80 km

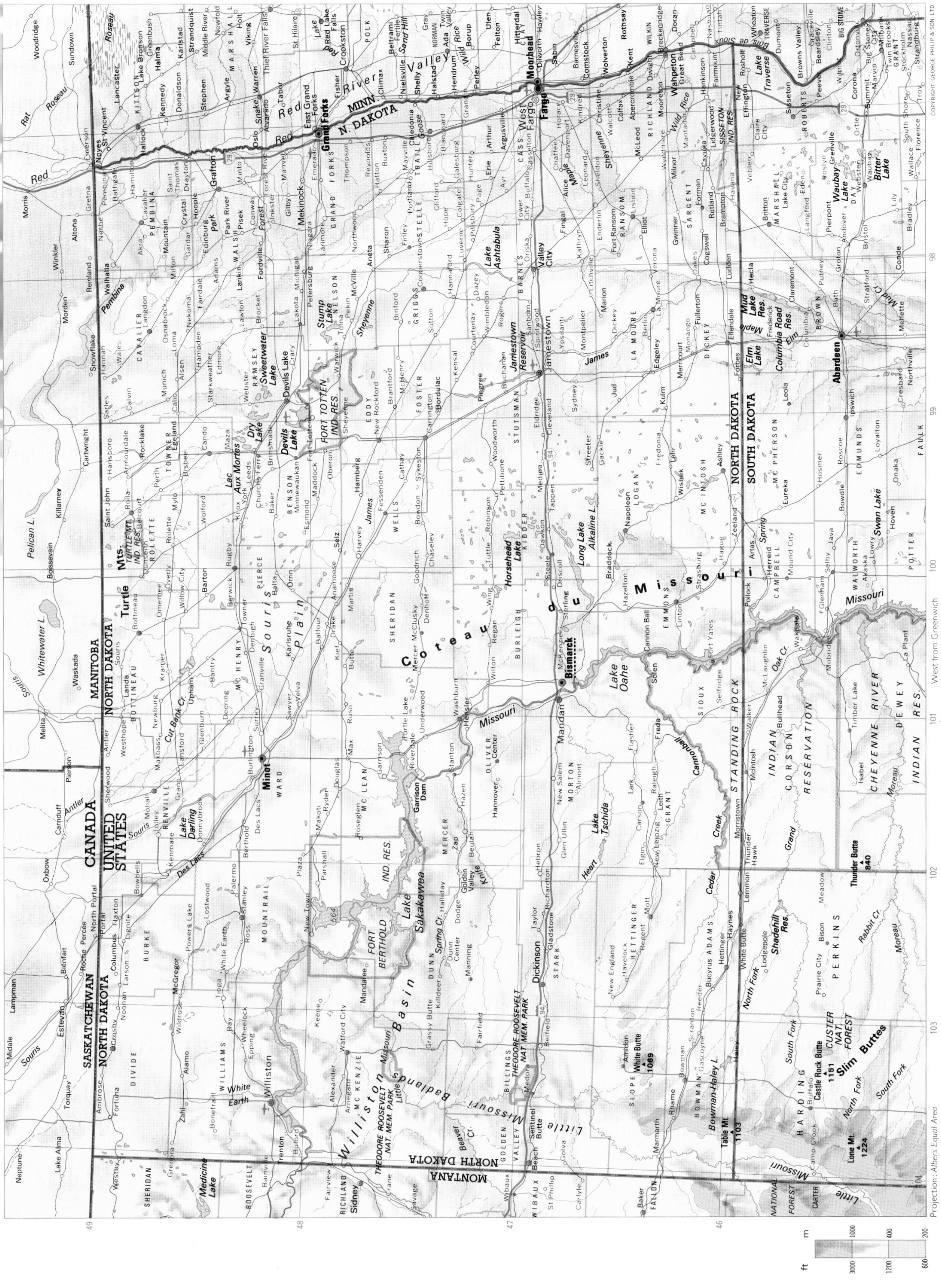

CANADA
UNITED STATES
SASKATCHEWAN
MANITOBA
NORTH DAKOTA
MINN.
N. DAKOTA
NORTH DAKOTA
SOUTH DAKOTA
MONTANA
NORTH DAKOTA

Missouri
Little Missouri
Red River
Souris
Cheyenne River
Moreau

Lake Sakakawea
Lake Oahe
Devils Lake
Lake Ashtabula
Jamestown Reservoir
Horsehead Lake
Long Lake
Lake Tschida
Lake Darling
Lac Aux Mortes
Sweetwater Lake
Stump Lake
Dry Lake
Mud Lake Res.
Elm Lake Res.
Swan Lake
Bitter Lake
Lake Traverse
Big Stone Lake
Medicine Lake
Whitewater L.
Pelican L.
Wild Rice

Williston Basin
Missouri Badlands
Coteau du Missouri
Turtle Plain
Souris Plain
Turtle Mts.
Red River Valley

THEODORE ROOSEVELT NAT. MEM. PARK
FORT BERTHOLD IND. RES.
FORT TOTTEN IND. RES.
TURTLE MT. IND. RES.
STANDING ROCK INDIAN RESERVATION
CHEYENNE RIVER INDIAN RES.
SISSETON IND. RES.
CUSTER NAT. FOREST
SHADEHILL RES.
Columbia Road Res.

Fargo
West Fargo
Moorhead
Grand Forks
East Grand Forks
Bismarck
Mandan
Minot
Jamestown
Valley City
Dickinson
Williston
Devils Lake
Wahpeton
Aberdeen

Garrison Dam

Thunder Butte ▲ 840
White Butte ▲ 1069
Castle Rock Butte ▲ 1151
Table Mt. ▲ 1103
Lone Mt. ▲ 1224
Slim Buttes

West from Greenwich
Projection: Albers Equal Area

m   3000   1200   1000   600   400   200
ft

1 : 2 500 000

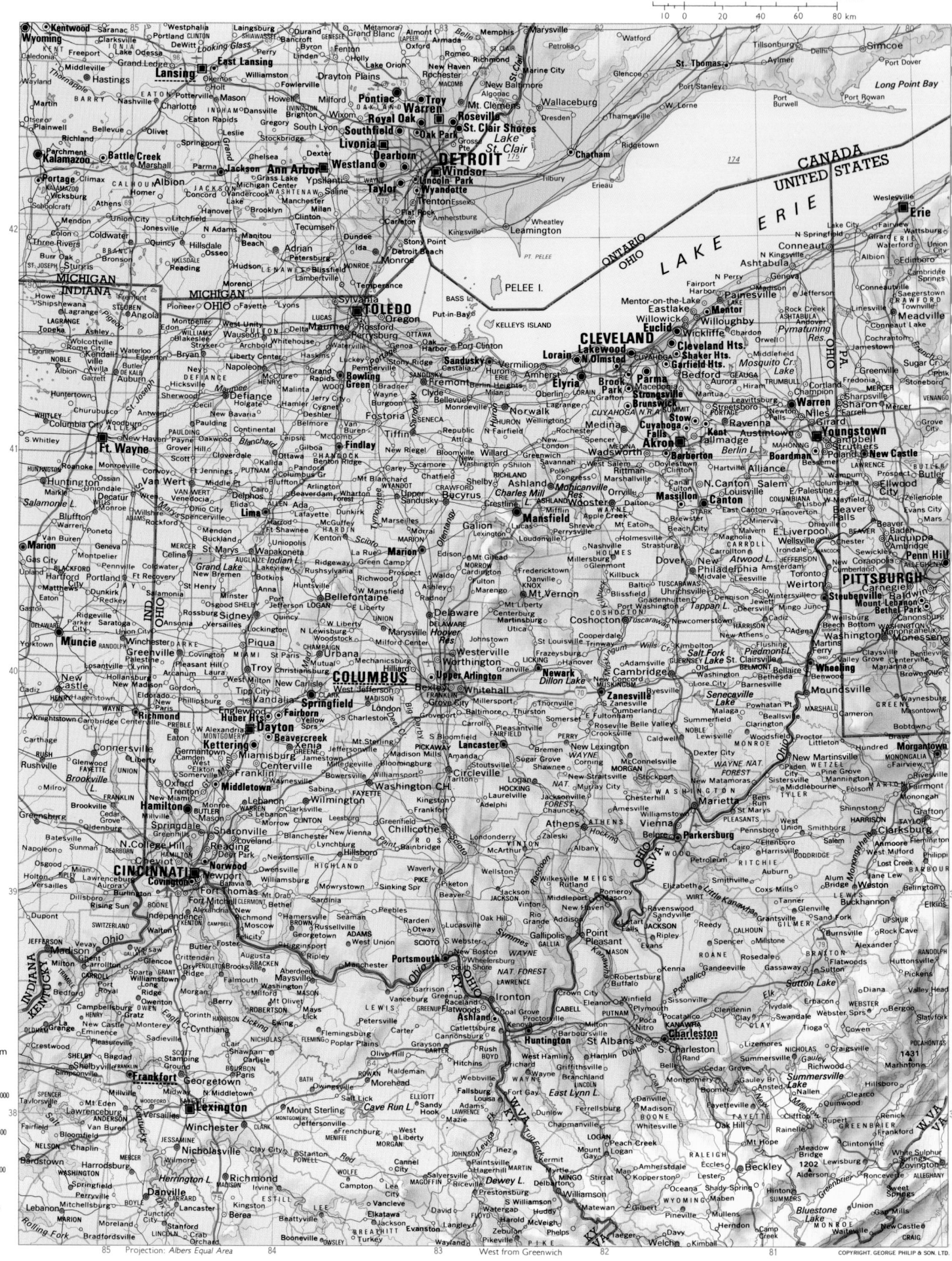

West from Greenwich

COPYRIGHT. GEORGE PHILIP & SON LTD.

1 : 2 500 000

Scale: 10 0 10 20 30 40 50 miles
10 0 20 40 60 80 km

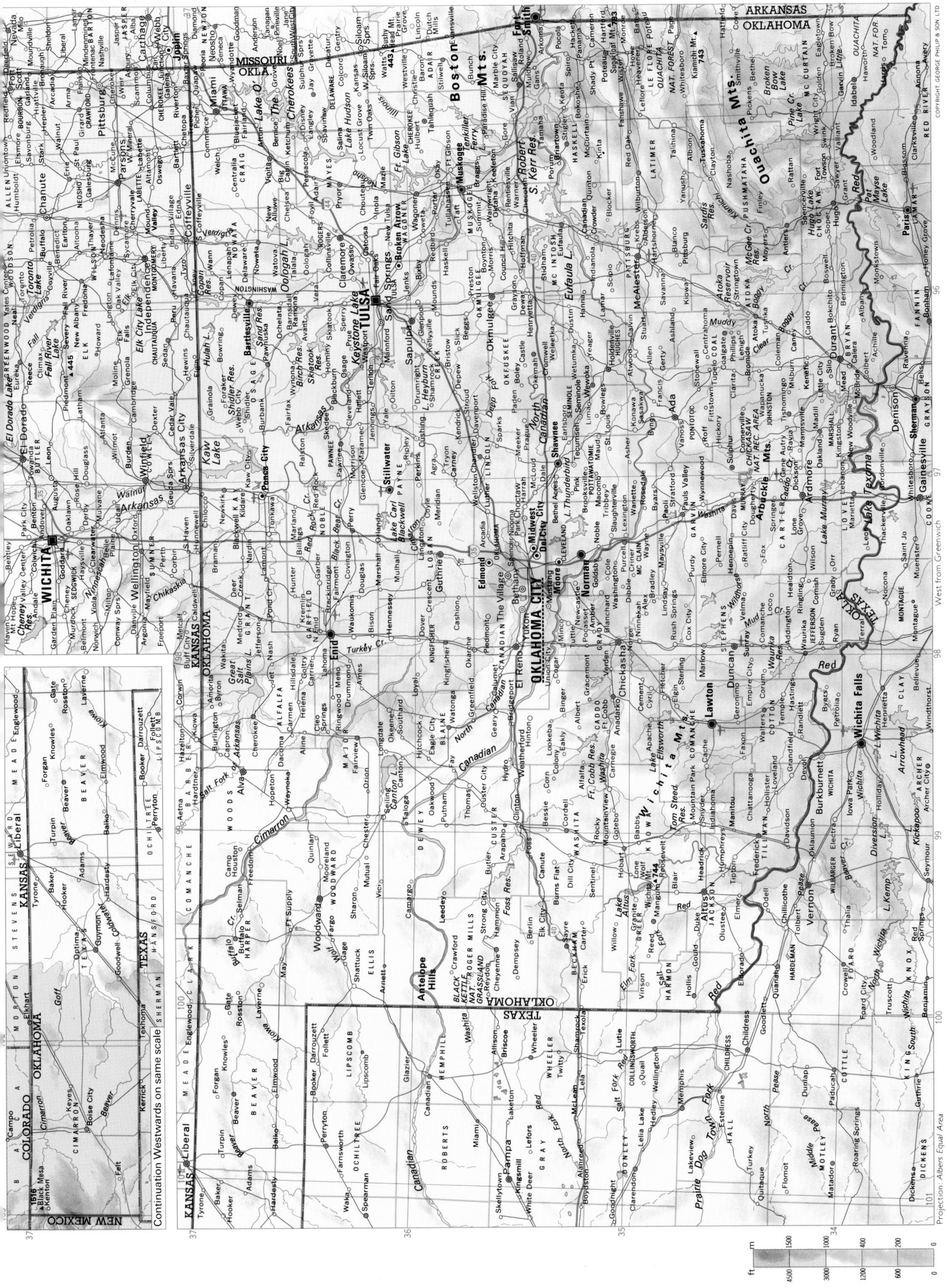

ARKANSAS
OKLAHOMA

MISSOURI
OKLA.

KANSAS
OKLAHOMA

OKLAHOMA CITY

TULSA

WICHITA

Wichita Falls

Denison

Sherman

Gainesville

Paris

Fort Smith

Boston Mts.

Ouachita Mts.

LE FLORE POTEAU
OUACHITA
NAT. FOREST

Lawton

Enid

Stillwater

Edmond

Norman

Moore

Midwest City
Del City

Shawnee

Muskogee

Sapulpa

Broken Arrow

Sand Springs

Bartlesville

McAlester

Ada

Ardmore

Duncan

Altus

Woodward

Wichita Mts.

Antelope Hills

BLACK KETTLE
NAT. GRASSLAND

Lake Texoma

Eufaula L.

Canadian

Red

Arkansas

Cimarron

NEW MEXICO

COLORADO
OKLAHOMA

TEXAS
OKLAHOMA

Continuation Westwards on same scale

West from Greenwich

Projection: Albers Equal Area

COPYRIGHT GEORGE PHILIP & SON LTD

m 1500 1000 400 200
ft 4500 3000 1200 600 0

1:2 500 000

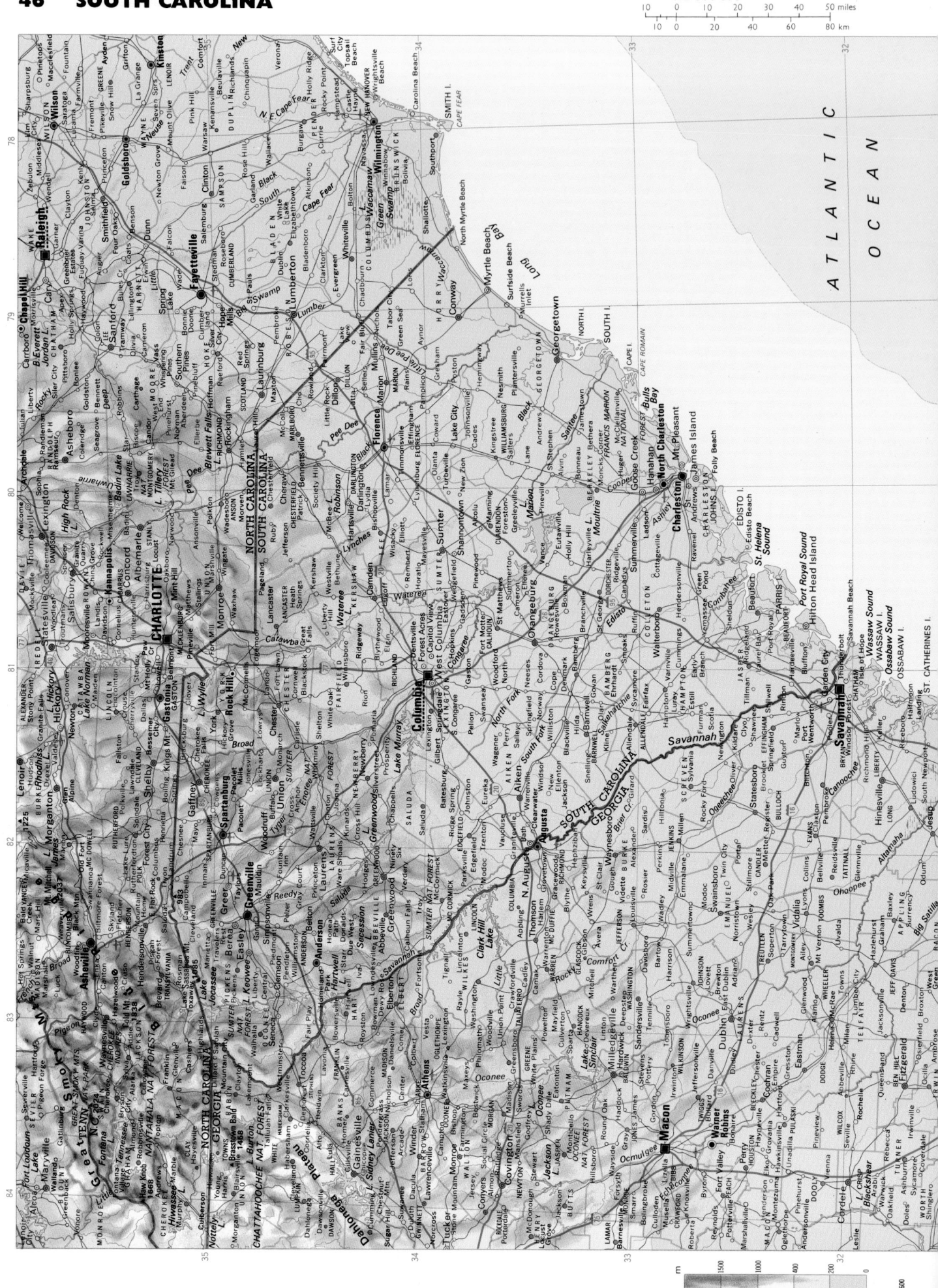

1:2 500 000

ATLANTIC OCEAN

1:2 500 000

MINN.

S. DAKOTA

NORTH DAKOTA
SOUTH DAKOTA

Aberdeen

Watertown

Brookings

Sioux Falls

Huron

James

Madison

Mitchell

Yankton

Pierre

Lake Oahe

Oahe Dam

Missouri

CHEYENNE RIVER INDIAN RESERVATION

STANDING ROCK INDIAN RESERVATION

Cheyenne

Missouri

LOWER BRULE INDIAN RES.

CROW CREEK IND. RES.

Big Bend Dam

Lake Sharpe

Lake Francis Case

Fort Randall Dam

Lake Andes

ROSEBUD INDIAN RESERVATION

PINE RIDGE INDIAN RESERVATION

BADLANDS NAT. PARK

Rapid City

BLACK HILLS

BLACK HILLS NATIONAL FOREST

CUSTER NAT. FOREST

CUSTER NATIONAL FOREST

WIND CAVE NAT. PK.

Harney Peak 2207

Mt. Rushmore 1745

Belle Fourche Reservoir

Sturgis

Spearfish

Lead

Deadwood

NEBRASKA

MONTANA

WYOMING

SOUTH DAKOTA

OGLALA NAT. GRASSLAND

SAMUEL R. McKELVIE NAT. FOR.

Sand Hills

CHERRY

Niobrara

AGATE FOSSIL BEDS NAT. MON.

FORT ROBINSON NEBRASKA NAT. FOR.

Chadron

Valentine

Coteau des Prairies

Coteau du Missouri

Turkey Ridge

Lewis and Clark Lake

WINNEBAGO IND. RES.

SANTEE IND. RES.

Lake Poinsett

Bitter Lake

Waubay Lake

Mud Lake Res.

Columbia Road Res.

Elm Lake

Swan Lake

Shadehill Res.

Angostura Res.

Merritt Res.

Thunder Butte 840

White Butte 1069

Castle Rock Butte 1151

Slim Buttes

Table Mt. 1103

Lone Mt. 1224

Eagle Nest Butte 1039

Keya Paha 741

1308

1036

1603

COPYRIGHT GEORGE PHILIP & SON LTD.

Projection: Albers Equal Area

West from Greenwich

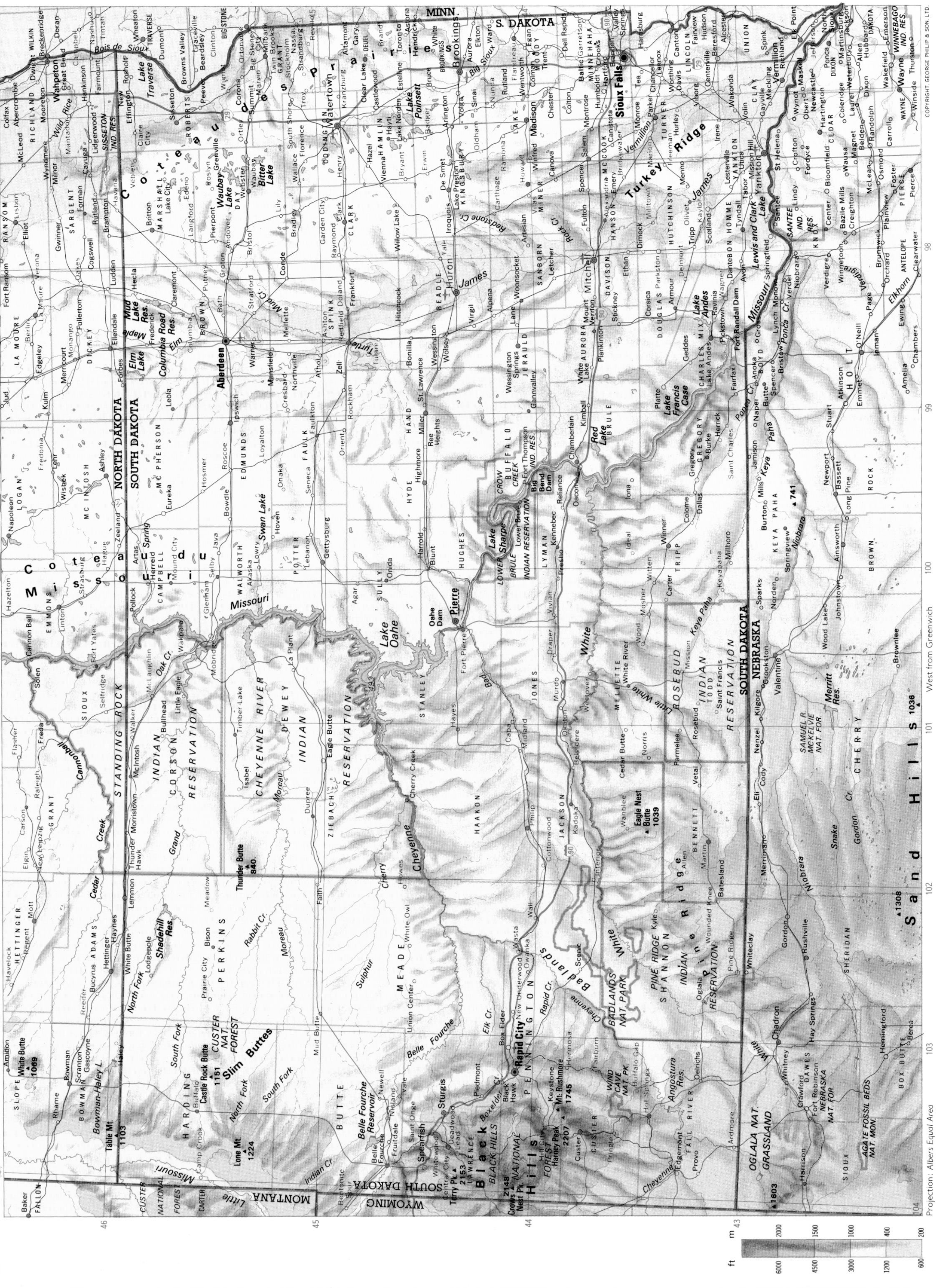

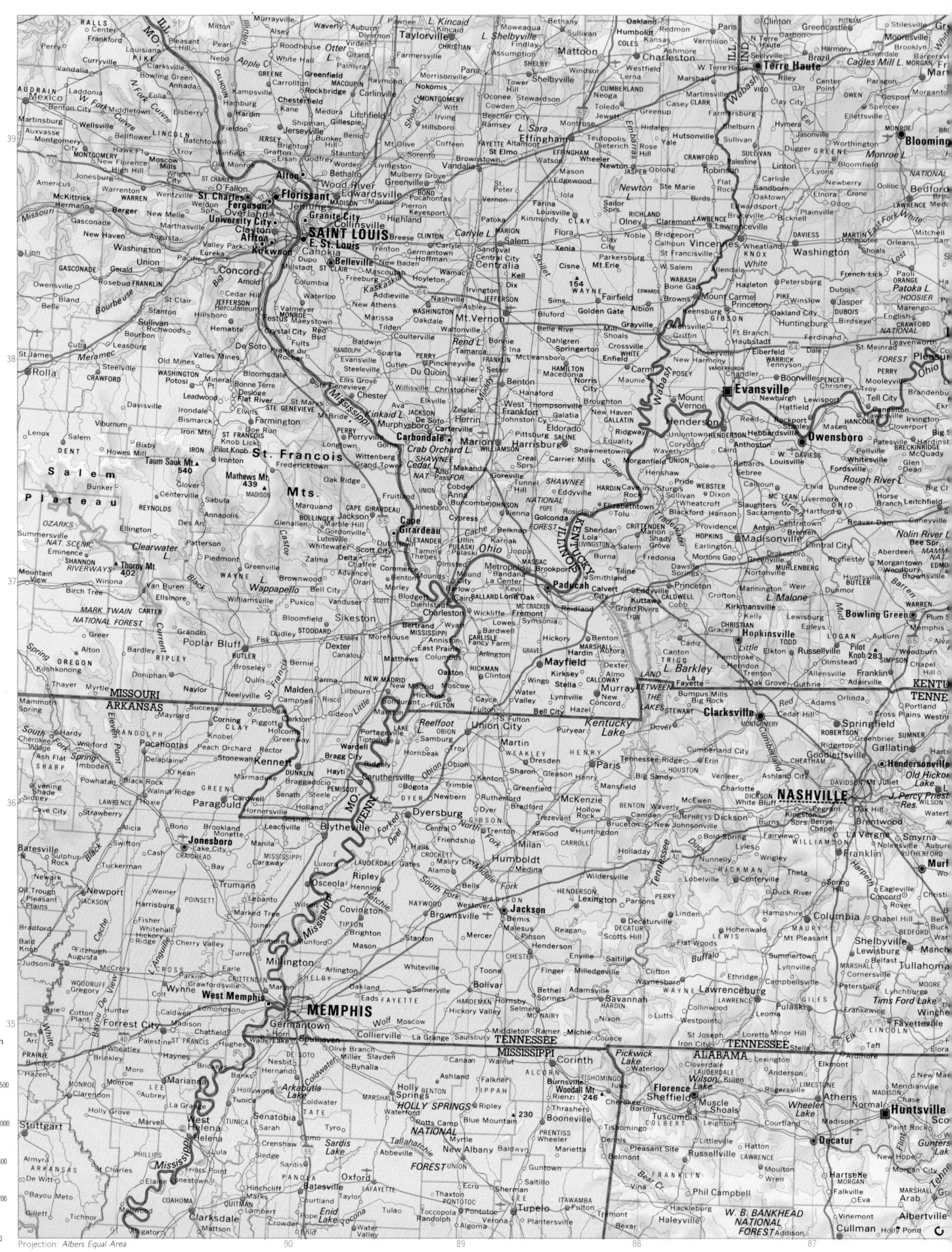

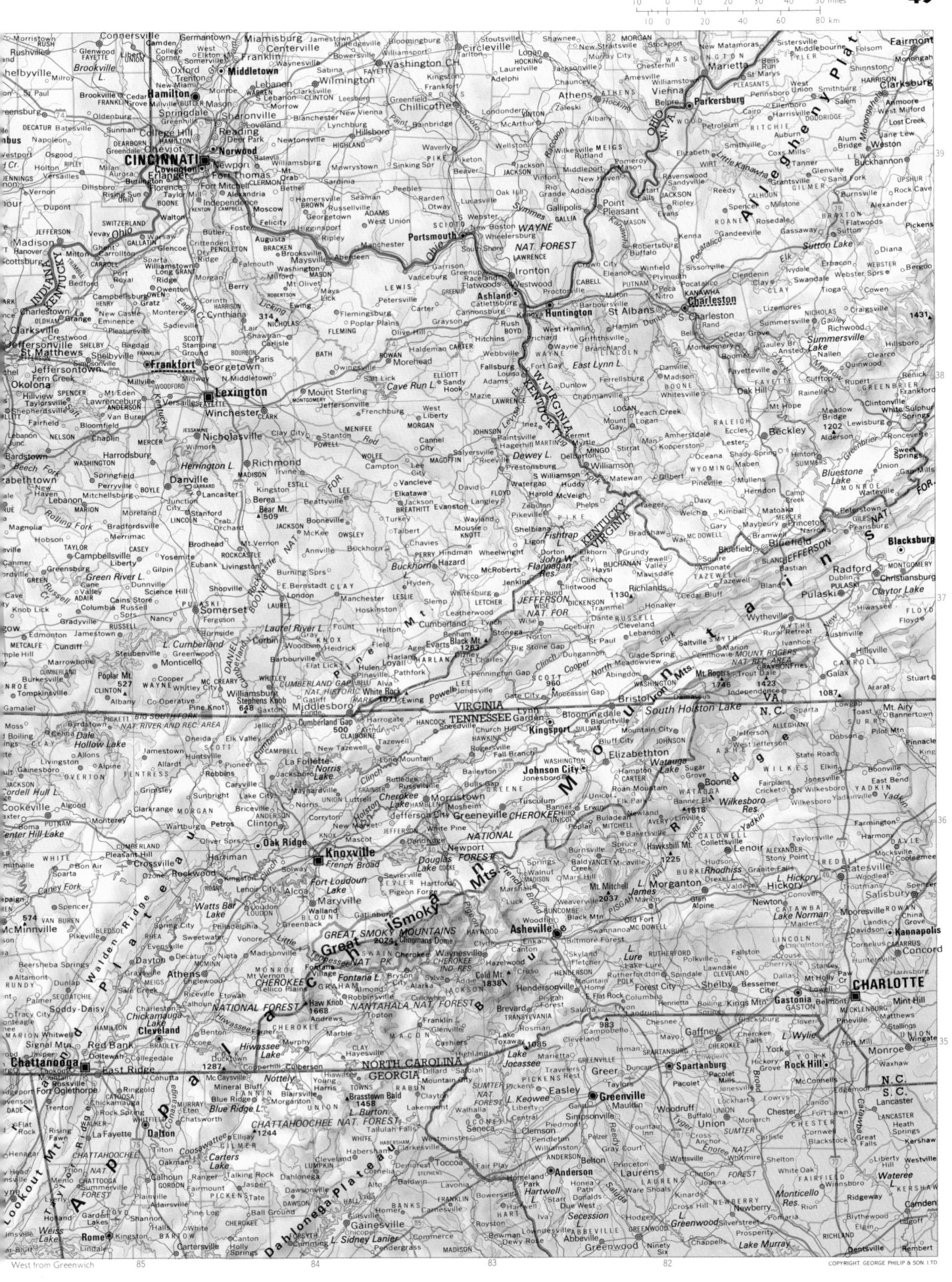

1 : 2 500 000

West from Greenwich

COPYRIGHT GEORGE PHILIP & SON LTD

Projection: Albers Equal Area

KEY TO MAP INSETS

Continuation Northwards

Continuation Southwards

T E X A S

West from Greenwich

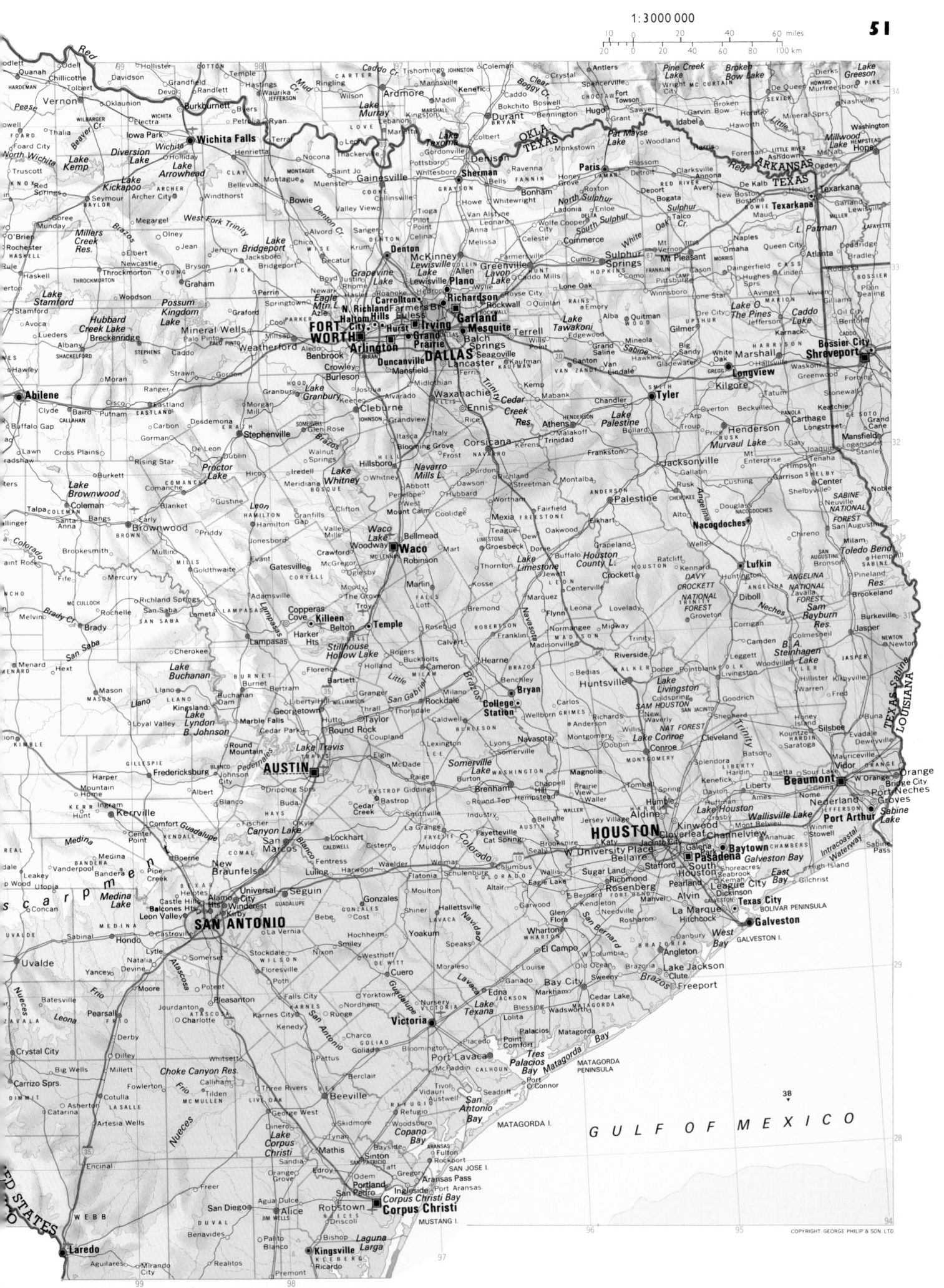

1:3 000 000

10   20   40   60 miles
20 40 60 80 100 km

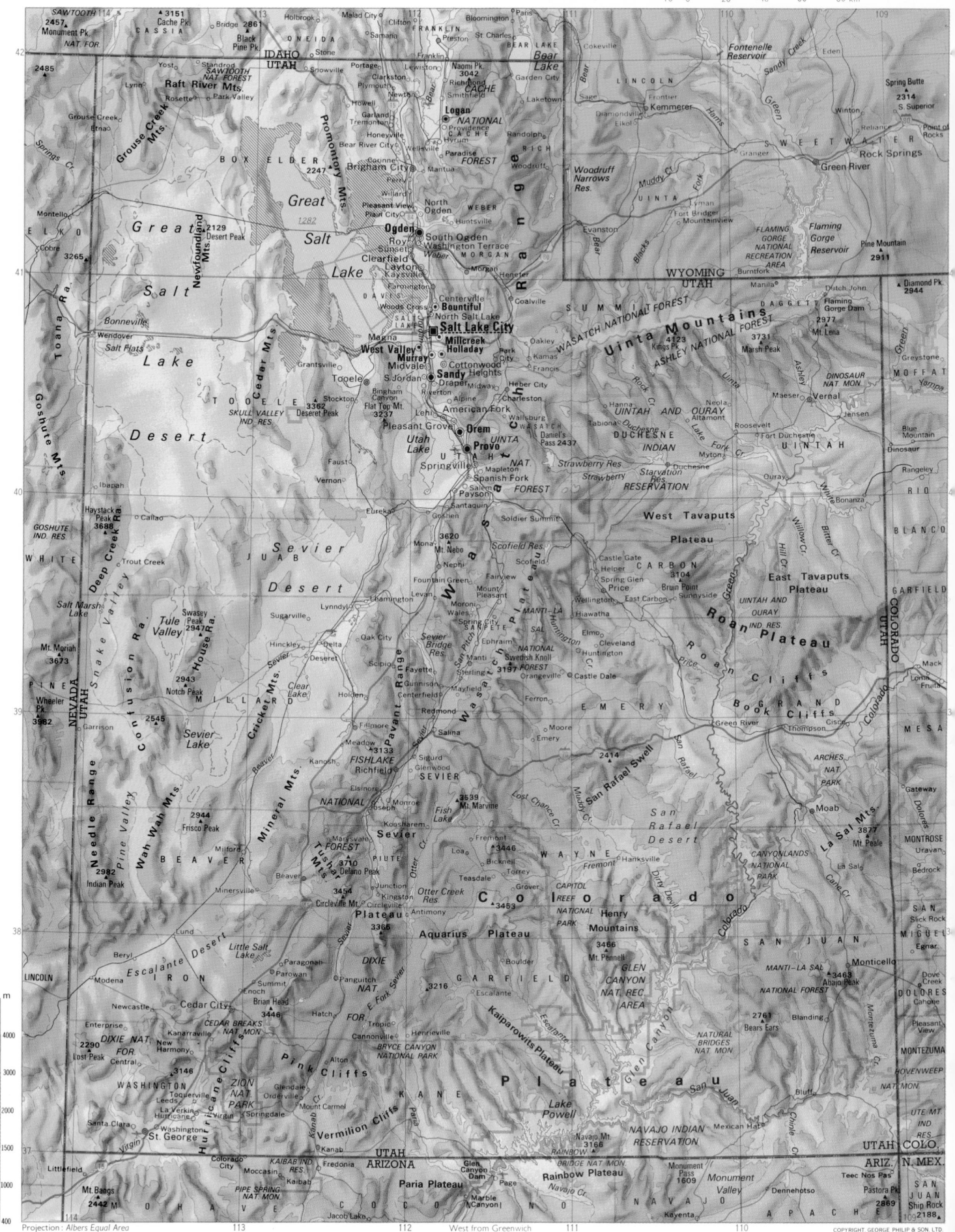

1 : 2 500 000

Projection: Albers Equal Area

West from Greenwich

COPYRIGHT GEORGE PHILIP & SON, LTD.

See page 54 for Virginia and page 36 for Vermont

1:2 500 000

PACIFIC OCEAN

Projection: Albers Equal Area

1 : 2 500 000

Continuation Westwards on same scale

1 : 2 500 000

10   0   10   20   30   40   50 miles
10   0   20   40   60   80 km

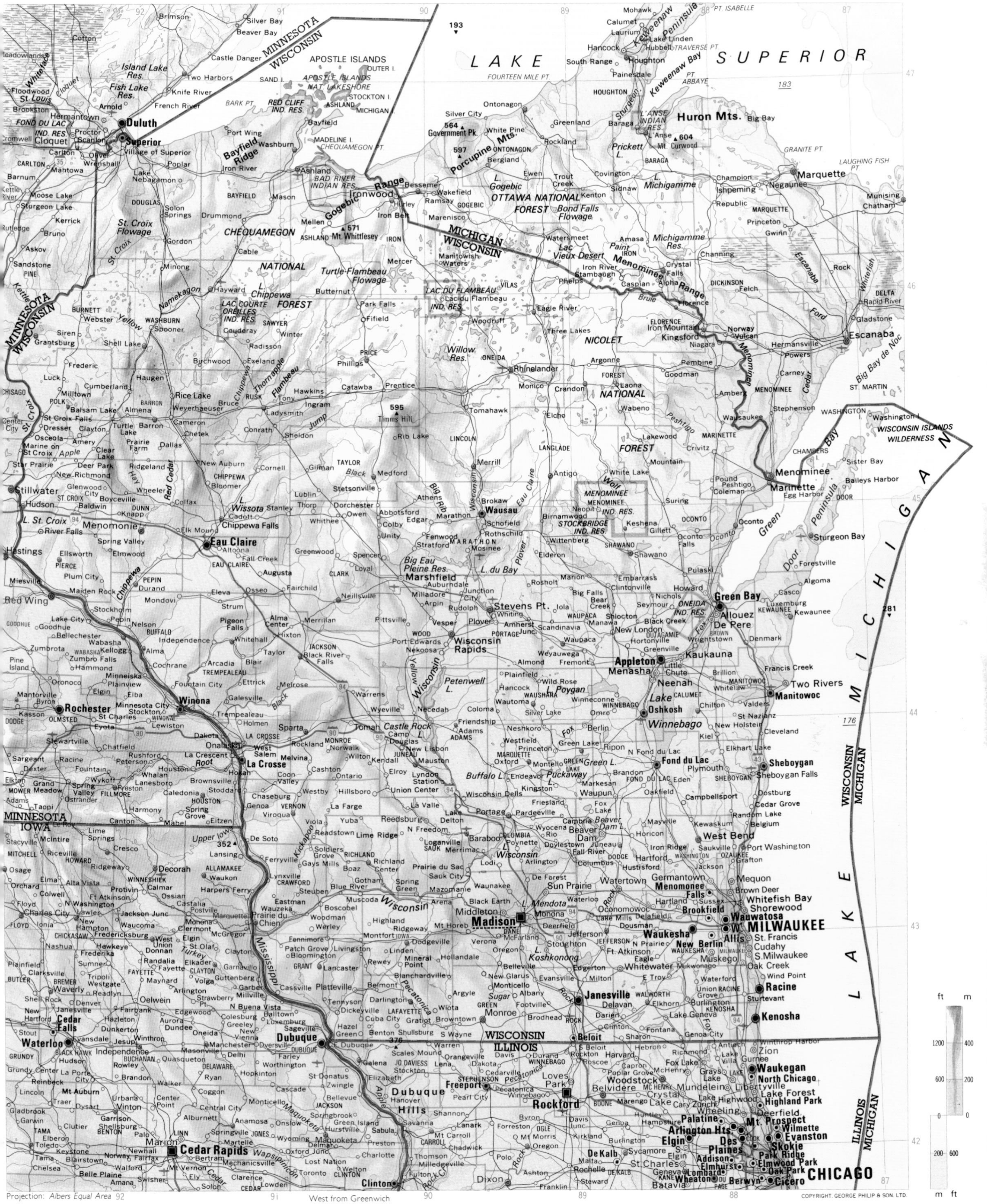

MINNESOTA
WISCONSIN

LAKE SUPERIOR

APOSTLE ISLANDS
APOSTLE ISLANDS NAT. LAKESHORE

Duluth
Superior

Marquette
Escanaba

MICHIGAN
WISCONSIN

CHEQUAMEGON
NATIONAL FOREST

NICOLET
NATIONAL FOREST

Eau Claire
Wausau

Green Bay
Appleton
Menasha
Neenah
Oshkosh

La Crosse
Winona

Wisconsin Rapids
Stevens Pt.

Marshfield

Manitowoc
Two Rivers

Sheboygan
Fond du Lac
Winnebago

Rochester

Madison
Middleton
Monona

MILWAUKEE
Wauwatosa
Waukesha
New Berlin

Janesville
Beloit

Racine
Kenosha

WISCONSIN
ILLINOIS

Dubuque

Cedar Rapids

Rockford
Freeport

Waukegan
North Chicago
Evanston
Skokie

CHICAGO

LAKE MICHIGAN

MINNESOTA
IOWA

MICHIGAN

ILLINOIS

Projection: Albers Equal Area 92

West from Greenwich

COPYRIGHT GEORGE PHILIP & SON LTD.

ft   m
1200 400
600   200
0   0
200   600
m   ft

1 : 2 500 000

10 0 10 20 30 40 50 miles
10 0 20 40 60 80 km

Black Hills / Northeast

Indian Cr. · CARTER · Belle Fourche · Belle Fourche Reservoir · Bellefield · Fruitdale · Aladdin · Alzada · Colony · Saint Onge · Spearfish · Deadwood · Central City · Lead · Terry Pk. 2148 · Lawrence · BLACK HILLS · BLACK HILLS FOREST · Cold Springs · Cheyenne · S.D. · SIOUX

NEBRASKA / WYOMING · Harrison · Henry · Mitchell · Scotts Bluff · KIMBALL · BANNER

Bentonite · Hulett · Carlile · Missouri Buttes 1637 · Warren Pks. 2029 · DEVILS TOWER NAT. MON. · Sundance · Crows NATIONAL Nest Pk. 2148 · CROOK

Little Powder · POWDER RIVER · Wyodak · Gillette · CAMPBELL · Belle Fourche · Keyhole Res. · Moorcroft · Upton · Newcastle · WESTON · Clareton · Beaver Cr. · NIOBRARA · Lance Creek · Lusk · Van Tassell · Node · GOSHEN · Lightning · Bill · THUNDER BASIN NATIONAL GRASSLAND · Cheyenne · Lost Springs · CONVERSE · Manville · Hartville · Guernsey · Sunrise · Fort Laramie · Hawk Springs · Albin · Burns · Carpenter · Hereford

North Butte 1850 · Edgerton · Midwest · Kaycee · Sussex · Linch · Glenrock · Orpha · Orin · Douglas · Glendo · Glendo Reservoir · Kortes Dam · PLATTE · Guernsey Res. · North Platte · Wheatland · Chugwater · Wheatland Res. No. 2 · Bosler · 2034 · Rock River · Laramie Peak 3131 · LARAMIE · ALBANY · Laramie Mts. Pole Mt. 2760 · LARAMIE · Cheyenne · Pine Bluffs · Grover · WELD · Orchard Valley · LEDGERPOLE CR · Horse Cr · Bear Cr · La Grange · Torrington · South Torrington · Lyman

Bighorn / Central

E. Pryor Mt. 2675 · BIGHORN CANYON NATIONAL RECREATION AREA · MONTANA / WYOMING · CROW INDIAN RESERVATION · Tongue River Reservoir · BIG HORN · Ranchester · Dayton · Sheridan · SHERIDAN · Wyarno · Story · Buffalo · JOHNSON · Clearmont · Arvada · Spotted Horse · Ucross · Clermont · Powder · Kaycee

Bighorn Lake · Lovell · Cowley · Byron · Deaver · Frannie · Powell · Cody · Ralston · Garland · Burlington · Otto · Basin · Greybull · Emblem · Manderson · Hyattville · Tensleep · Worland · Ten Sleep · Kirby · Thermopolis · Lucerne · Gebo · HOT SPRINGS · Hamilton Dome · Grass Creek

Cloud Peak 4013 · Hunt Mt. 2893 · BIGHORN MOUNTAINS · BIGHORN NATIONAL FOREST · Granite 2753 · Burgess Junction · Granite Pass 3097 · Hazelton Pk. 3211 · Guffy Peak 2452 · Gifty Peak · BIG HORN BASIN · Nowood Cr. · Nowater Creek · WASHAKIE

Shoshone R. · Owl Creek Mountains · Wind River · Boysen Reservoir · Pavillion · Ocean Lake · Riverton · Shoshoni · Lysite · Moneta · Hiland · Waltman · NATRONA · Casper · Evansville · Mills · Alcova · Pathfinder Reservoir · Independence Rock · SWEETWATER · Muddy Gap · 3059 · 2812 · Whiskey 2302 · Lamont · Bairoil

Yellowstone / West

Red Lodge · CUSTER NAT. FOREST · Cooke City · Granite Peak 3901 · Pilot Peak 3569 · CARBON · Bear Tooth Pass · 3337 · Trout Pk. 3732 · Saddle Mt. 3252 · Clarks Fork · GALLATIN NATIONAL FOREST · Gardiner · Mt. Holmes 3150 · Hot Springs · W. Yellowstone · Hebgen · YELLOWSTONE NATIONAL PARK · Canyon Village · Old Faithful · Yellowstone Lake · Frank's Peak 4009 · Carter Mt. 3794 · Mt. Crosby · 3724 · SHOSHONE NATIONAL FOREST · Wapiti · Buffalo Bill Reservoir · North Fork · South Fork

Lewis Lake 2518 · Shoshone Lake · Craig Pass 2518 · Heart Lake · Lewis Lake · Mt. Hancock · Coulter Peak 3256 · Fishing Bridge · PARK · ABSAROKA RANGE · Dubois · Togwotee Pass 2909 · Pinnacle Buttes 3610 · Union Pass · JOHN D. ROCKEFELLER JR. MEM. PARKWAY · GRAND TETON NATIONAL PARK · Grand Teton 4196 · Mt. Leidy · Mt. Moran · Jackson Lake · Colter Bay · Jenny Lake · TETON · TETON NATIONAL FOREST · Sheep Mt. 3426 · Pyramid Peak 3385 · Pinnacle Peak · Gros Ventre Range · Doubletop Pk. 3574

TARGHEE · Henrys Lake · Island Park · FREMONT · TETON NATIONAL FOREST · Felt · Tetonia · Driggs · Teton Pass 2570 · WYOMING / IDAHO · Victor · Wilson · Jackson · Hoback · Bondurant · Bald Knoll 3144 · WYOMING RANGE · Mt. McDougall 3281 · Wyoming Pk. 3463 · CARIBOU NAT. FOREST · Alpine · Etna · Thayne · Afton · Smoot · Cokeville · BONNEVILLE · Palisades Res. · Alta · 3035

Wind River / Southwest

ROCKY MOUNTAINS · Downs Mt. 4003 · Gannett Peak 4202 · Fremont Peak 3767 · Wolverine Peak 3278 · Bear Peak · Fort Washakie · WIND RIVER INDIAN RESERVATION · Lander · Atlantic City · South Pass 2301 · Bull Lake · Willow Lake · New Fork Lakes · Pinedale · Boulder · Boulder Lake · Fremont Lake · Daniel · SUBLETTE · Big Sandy · Eden · Eden Valley · Farson · La Barge · Marbleton · Big Piney · Opal · Kemmerer · Diamondville · LINCOLN · Fontenelle Reservoir · Green R. · FOSSIL BUTTE NAT. MON. · Frontier · Oakley · Mountainview · Fort Bridger · Lyman · Evanston · Bear · Woodruff Narrows Res. · UINTA · Uinta Mts. · SUMMIT · Carter · Granger · UTAH / WYOMING · COLORADO

Wild River Peak · Atlantic Pk. 3807 · Sweetwater · Wind River Range · GREEN MTS. · Jeffrey City · Antelope Hills · Crooks Mt. · Great Divide Basin · Continental Divide · Red Desert · Wamsutter · Bitter Creek · Point of Rocks · Rock Springs · Reliance · Superior · S. Superior · Winton · Green River · SWEETWATER · Spring Butte 2314 · Pine Mountain 2911 · 2944 · Flaming Gorge Reservoir · FLAMING GORGE NATIONAL RECREATION AREA · Flaming Gorge Dam · MOFFAT · ROUTT · DAGGETT · Manila

Medicine Bow / Southeast

MEDICINE BOW · MEDICINE BOW NATIONAL FOREST · Medicine Bow · Rock River · Mt. Arthur · Mt. Fadden · Hanna · Elk Mt. 3662 · Kennaday Pk. 3294 · 3400 · Centennial · Medicine Bow Pk. 3662 · MEDICINE BOW MTS. · Blackhall Mt. 3346 · Foxpark · JACKSON · Saratoga · Encampment · Riverside · Sierra Madre 3364 · Bridger Pk. · Battle Mt. 2776 · Baggs · Dixon · Savery · Muddy Cr. · ROUTT · CARBON · Rawlins · Creston · High Pt. 2231 · Wolcott · Walcott · Seminoe Reservoir · Shirley Basin · Medicine Bow · Mt. Steele 2302 · Granite Mountains · Rattlesnake Hills 2513 · Split Rock

m 4000 3000 2000 1500 1000 400
ft 12000 9000 6000 4500 3000 1200

1:1 000 000

10 5 0   10   20 miles
10 0 10 20 30 km

PUERTO RICO

VIRGIN IS.
On same scale

ST. CROIX I.
On same scale

ISLA MONA

PANAMA CANAL
On same scale

Projection: Modified Polyconic

Puerto Rico

ATLANTIC OCEAN

I. DE CULEBRA
Dewey
CULEBRITA
I. CULEBRA

Sonda de Vieques

I. DE VIEQUES
Isabel Segunda
Esperanza
Monte Pirata △ 301

1670 ▼
48 ▼
69 ▼

Fajardo
Pto. Medio Mundo
PTA. VACIA TALEGA
Pto. Puerca
PTA. PUERCA
PTA. ESTE
Ceiba
Naguabo
Playa de Humacao
Pto. Yabucoa
Playa de Guayanés
Pto. Mabo
PTA. LIMA
PTA. YEGUAS

SAN JUAN
Río Piedras
Carolina
Trujillo Alto
Bayamón
Cataño
Guaynabo
Caguas
Gurabo
Juncos
Las Piedras
Humacao
Yabucoa
Maunabo
El Toro △ 1074
El Yunque △ 1065
Sierra de Luquillo
HUMACAO
Luquillo
Mameyes
Palmer
Río Grande
Canóvanas
Loíza
Arecibo
Barceloneta
Manatí
Vega Baja
Vega Alta
Dorado
Toa Baja
Toa Alta
Bayamón
Corozal
Naranjito
Comerío
Barranquitas
Aibonito
Cidra
Cayey
Aguas Buenas
Lago Loíza
Lago de Cidra
Coamo
Santa Isabel
Juana Díaz
Villalba
Coto Laurel
Ponce
Peñuelas
Guayanilla
Yauco
Guánica
Sabana Grande
San Germán
Lajas
Cabo Rojo
Boquerón
Parguera
Guánica
Ensenada
Lajas
Mayagüez
Hormigueros
Cabo Rojo
Añasco
Rincón
Aguada
Aguadilla
Moca
Isabela
Quebradillas
Camuy
Hatillo
Arecibo
Utuado
Adjuntas
Jayuya
Lares
Las Marías
Maricao
San Sebastián
Las Tunas
Florida
Ciales
Morovis
Orocovis
Botijas
Corozal

Cordillera Central
△ 1338 Cerro Morales
△ 988
△ 1079 Cerro Doña Juana
△ 1205
△ 840
△ 903 Cerro la Santa
△ 764 Pico Fraile
△ 883

Cord. Jaicoa
Montañas de Uroyan
AGUADILLA
ARECIBO
MAYAGÜEZ
PONCE
GUAYAMA
SAN JUAN
Cerro Gordo

L. Caonillas
Lago de Guajataca
Grande de Arecibo
Grande de Manatí
Grande de Añasco
La Plata

Laguna Tortuguero
Laguna Las Tunas
Bahía de Anasco
Bahía de Mayagüez
Laguna de Guánica

Patillas
Arroyo
Guayama
Salinas
Aguirre
Jobos
Bahía de Jobos
Central Aguirre
Bahía de Rincón
Santa Isabel
Bahía de Guayanilla

Guayanés
Coquí
Bahía de Jobos

Arecibo
Camuy
Pueblo Nuevo
Dos Bocas
Esperanza
Villa Pérez
Monte Guilarte
Villalba
Canas
PTA. CUCHARA
PTA. AGUILA
PTA. SALINAS
PTA. VACIA TALEGA
PTA. PUERTO NUEVO
PTA. LAS TUNAS
PTA. HIGUERO
PTA. GUANAJIBO
PTA. ARENAS
PTA. AGUEREADA
CABO ROJO

I. CAJA DE MUERTOS

CARIBBEAN SEA

West from Greenwich

ISLA DESECHEO
ISLA MONITO
ISLA MONA
CABO NORTE
CABO ESTE
PTA. ARENAS

Virgin Is.

NECKER I.
Virgin Sound
VIRGIN GORDA (U.K.)
Spanish Town
GREAT CAMANOE
GUANA I.
SCRUB I.
BEEF I.
GINGER I.
COOPER I.
TORTOLA (U.K.)
Road Town
Drake Channel
PETER I.
NORMAN I.
SALT I.
JOST VAN DYKE I.
HANS LOLLIK I.
THATCH I.
Charlotte Amalie
ST. JOHN I. (U.S.)
Cruz Bay
Pillsbury Sd.
ST. THOMAS I. (U.S.)
BRASS I.
SAVANA I.
TOBAGO IS.

42 ▼
18° 30′
CARIBBEAN SEA
West from Greenwich

St. Croix I.

BUCK I.
EAST PT.
Christiansted
BARON BLUFF
Cane Bay
Mt. Eagle △ 353
Grove Place
Frederiksted
HAMS BLUFF
SOUTHWEST PT.
LONG PT.
4983 ▼
CARIBBEAN SEA
West from Greenwich

Panama Canal

PANAMA
Limón B.
Colón
Cristóbal
Fort Sherman
Coco Solo
Fort Davis
Gatún
Gatún Locks
Gatún Dam
Chagres
Madden L.
Madden Dam
Gatún Lake
Margarita
Salamanca
Puerto Pilón
ZORRA
El Limón
JUAN GALLEGOS
COLORADO
Escobal
Frijoles
Darién
Buenos Aires
Las Cascadas
The Gaillard Cut
Balboa Hill △ 350
Gamboa
Paraíso
Pedro Miguel
Pedro Miguel Locks
Miraflores Locks
Fort Clayton
Corozal
Fort Amador
BALBOA
PANAMA
Panama Bay
Gulf of Panama
Curundú
Arraiján
La Chorrera
Cárdenas
79° 45′

m
1000
400
200
0
ft
3000
1200
600
0
200
600
6000
12,000
ft
m

1:15 000 000

100   0   100   200   300   400 miles
100   0   100   200   300   400   500   600 km

Arctic Bay
Baffin Bay
Bylot I.
Pond Inlet
1890
C. Hewett
Svartenhuk Halvø
Disko (Qeqertarsuaq)
Disko B.
2136
Christianshåb (Qasigiannguit)
Angmagssalik
GREENLAND
Fury & Hecla Str.
Igloolik Island
Clyde
Home B.
Holsteinsborg (Sisimiut)
Søndre Strømfjord
Sukkertoppen (Manitsoq)
2850
Kong Frederik VI's Kyst
Melville Peninsula
Hall Lake
Prince Charles I.
C. Dyer
Cape Dyer
Broughton Island
Pangnirtung
2591
Cumberland Peninsula
Hoare B.
Sukkertoppen (Manitsoq)
Gotthåb (Nuuk)
Fiskenæsset (Qeqertarsuatsiaat)
Frederikshåb (Paamiut)
Ivigtut
Davis Strait
Kap Farvel
Julianehåb (Qaqortoq)
Sydprøven (Alluitsup Paa)
Nanortalik
ATLANTIC
Foxe Basin
Cumberland Sd.
C. Mercy
Foxe Channel
C. Dorchester
Amadjuak L.
Frobisher Bay
Committee B.
Repulse B.
Foxe Penin.
Amadjuak
Lake Harbour
Cape Dorset
Frobisher Bay
Resolution I.
Roes Welcome Str.
Southampton I.
Coral Harbour
Coats I.
Bell Pen.
Hudson Strait
C. Chidley
3809
Digges Is.
Mansel I.
Salluit (Sugluk)
Invujivik
Maricourt (Wakeham)
Koartac (Notre Dame de Koartac)
Akpatok
Port Nouveau-Quebec (George R.)
1676
Hebron
Hudson Bay
Ottawa Isl.
257
Ungava Peninsula
Portland Promontory
Inoucdjouac (Port Harrison)
Arnaud
Bellin (Payne Bay)
Payne L.
Feuilles
Ungava Bay
Koksoak
Ft. Chimo
George
Whale
Kaniapiskau
Nutak
Nain
Hopedale
Sleeper Is.
King George Is.
Baker's Dozen Is.
L. à L'Eau Claire
La L'Eau Claire
Lac Bienville
Scheffeville
North West R.
Smallwood Reservoir
Churchill Falls
Churchill
COAST OF LABRADOR
Indian Harbour
C. Harrison
L. Melville
Cartwright
Rigolet
Hamilton Inlet
Belle Isle
Battle Harb.
Belcher Is.
C. Henrietta Maria
King George Is.
Grand Baleine
Poste-de-la-Baleine (Great Whale River)
Kanaaupscow
Lobstick L.
Petitsikapau
Kaniapiskau
Natashquan
Str. of Belle Isle
Winisk
Pte. Louis-XIV
Ft. George
La Grande
N E W F O U N D L A N D
Twillingate
Lewisporte
Gander
Bonavista
DAY
Attawapiskat
Akimiski I.
Nouveau Comptoir (Paint Hills)
Eastmain
1128
Gagnon
Moisie
Ashuanipi
Romaine
Natashquan
St-Augustin
Saguenay
814
Buchans
Grand Falls
Harbour Grace
Trinity B.
Carbonear
St. John's
 O N T A R I O
James Bay
Charlton I.
Eastmain
Fort Rupert (Rupert House)
Rupert
Q U E B E C
Mistassini
L. Albanel
Péribonca
Mingan
Î. d'Anticosti
Placentia
Trepassey
C. Race
Ft. Albany
Albany
Moosonee
Nottaway
Harricana
Chibougamau
Baie-Comeau
Bétsiamites
Sept Îles
Port-Cartier
Îs. de la Madeleine
Placentia B.
Nakina
Kenogami
Missinaibi
Cochrane
Matagami
Res. de Gouin
Dolbeau
L. St-Jean
Manicouagan
R. St. Lawrence
Gaspé
Pén. de Gaspé
Gulf of St. Lawrence
Cabot Str.
P. aux Basques
Longlac
Heron Bay
Oba
Matagami
Taschereau
Senneterre
Val-d'Or
Roberval
Jonquière
Chicoutimi
1190
Matane
Combellton
Dalhousie
Cape Breton I.
C. North
Sydney
Glace Bay
Thunder Bay
Timmins
Noranda
Rouyn
La Tuque
Saguenay
Tadoussac
Rimouski
Gaspé
Bathurst
Chatham
Nigadan
Newcastle
Port Hawkesbury
Mulgrave
Michipicoten
Kirkland Lake
Cobalt
Haileybury
Témiscamingue
Rés. de Cabonga
Shawinigan
Trois-Rivières
Québec
Lévis
Thetford Mines
St-Léonard
Edmundston
PR. EDWARD I.
Summerside
Charlottetown
NOVA SCOTIA
Antigonish
New Glasgow
Pictou
Sault Ste. Marie
Sudbury
Copper Cliff
North Bay
Pembroke
Hull
Lachine
MONTRÉAL
St-Hyacinthe
Sorel
Granby
Sherbrooke
Woodstock
NEW BRUNSWICK
Fredericton
Moncton
Amherst
Springhill
Sackville
Truro
Windsor
Dartmouth
Sable I.
6309
Lake Superior
Calumet
Keweenaw Bay
Marquette
Sault Ste. Marie
North Chan.
Georgian Bay
Parry Sound
Pembroke
Arnprior
Ottawa
Cornwall
L. Champlain
Joliette
St-Jean
Magog
MAINE
Saint John
Bangor
B. of Fundy
Digby
Kentville
Bridgewater
Liverpool
Shelburne
C. Sable
Yarmouth
Halifax
Iron Mt.
Antigo
Menominee
Green Bay
Wausau
Appleton
Manistique
Cheboygan
Petoskey
Owen Sound
Orillia
Belleville
Kingston
Burlington
VERMONT
NEW HAMPSHIRE
Concord
Manchester
Lewiston
Portland
Augusta
Traverse City
Cadillac
Saginaw
Lake Huron
Collingwood
Oshawa
Lake Ontario
Watertown
Glens Falls
Lowell
Boston
C. Cod
Milwaukee
Ludington
Muskegon
TORONTO
Guelph
Kitchener
Stratford
Hamilton
St. Catharines
Niagara Falls
Rochester
Syracuse
Utica
Albany
Springfield
Worcester
MASS.
Providence
Racine
Kalamazoo
Grand Rapids
London
Brantford
Buffalo
NEW YORK
Binghamton
Scranton
Waterbury
Bridgeport
CONN.
New Haven
CHICAGO
Gary
Evanston
South Bend
DETROIT
Windsor
Toledo
Cleveland
Akron
Youngstown
Williamsport
PENNSYLVANIA
Allentown
Reading
Trenton
NEW YORK
Newark
Jersey City
NEW JERSEY
INDIANA
OHIO
Erie
Jamestown
Sarnia
Chatham
ILLINOIS

St-PIERRE & MIQUELON (Fr.)

West from Greenwich

N.W TERRITORIES

MANITOBA

HUDSON BAY

Belcher Islands

ONTARIO

JAMES BAY

QUÉBEC

LAKE SUPERIOR

Thunder Bay

Duluth
Superior

WISCONSIN

MICHIGAN

LAKE MICHIGAN

LAKE HURON

Sault Ste. Marie

Sudbury

North Bay

OTTAWA

Timmins

Kirkland Lake

Val-d'Or

Trois-Rivières

MILWAUKEE

CHICAGO

Grand Rapids

Flint

DETROIT

Windsor

TORONTO

HAMILTON

LAKE ONTARIO

Buffalo

Rochester

Syracuse

London

Cleveland

TOLEDO

OHIO

PENNSYLVANIA

INDIANA

NEW YORK

Adirondack Mountains

Lambert's Equivalent Azimuthal

ft   m
4500   1500
3000   1000
1200   400
600   200
0   0
200   600
2000   6000
4000   12 000
m   ft

50   0   50   100   150   200 miles
50   0   50 100 150 200 250 300 km

COAST OF LABRADOR

QUEBEC

NEWFOUNDLAND

South Aulatsivik I.
Paul I.
Nain
Voisey's B.
Kogaluk
Tunungayualok I.
Davis Inlet
Nunaksaluk I.
Big Bay
Hopedale
Kajvakok B.
Aillik
Adlavik Is.
Mokkovik
C. Harrison
Holton
Indian Harbour
Groswater B.
Rigolet
Cartwright
Island of Ponds
L. Melville
Mealy Mts.
Happy Valley-Goose Bay
Sandwich B.
Separation Point
Eagle
Paradise
St. Lewis
Alexis
Battle Harbour
Red Bay
St. Lunaire-Griquet
Str. of Belle Isle
Belle I.
St. Anthony
Hare B.
Flower's Cove
Groais I.
Bell I.
Conche
Englee
Roddickton
Horse Is.
C. St John
La Scie
Twillingate
Fogo I.
Carmanville
Notre Dame B.
Lewisporte
Botwood
Gander
Wesleyville
Bonavista
C. Bonavista
Catalina
Trinity
Bay de Verde
Conception B.
Carbonear
Harbour Grace
St. JOHN'S
Avalon Peninsula
Ferryland
Trepassey
C. Race

Fort McKenzie
Erlandson L.
Whale L.
Nachicapau L.
George L.
Champdoré L.
Fraser L.
Kogaluk
Séfrigny L.
Sandy L.
Chakonipau L.
Otelnuk L.
Wheeler L.
Champdoré L.
L. de la Hutte Sauvage
Mistastin L.
Kaniapiskau L.
Attikamagen L.
Tudor L.
Whitegull L.
Wakuach L.
610
Harp L.
Kanairiktok
Nasbaup L.
Seal L.
Nipishish
Lac Verneuil
Schefferville
Woods L.
Smallwood Reservoir
North-West River
Goose
Grand L.
Lac Petitsikapau
Clairambault
Lobstick L.
Churchill Falls
Kaniapiskau L.
Menihek Lakes
Churchill
Winokapau L.
Ossokmanuan
L. Bermen
Opiscoteo L.
Shabogamo
Opiskotish L.
Lac Joseph
Minipi L.
Little Mecatina
Ashuanipi L.
Labrador City
Waco L.
Atikonak L.
Burnt L.
a
Naococane L.
1128
Petit Lac Manicouagan
West Moine
St-Augustin Saguenay
St-Augustin
Ameé
Brador Bay
Lourdes-de-Blanc-Sablon
Fortead
St. Paul R.
Gagnon
Rés. Manicouagan
Nipissis L.
1048
St-Jean
Romaine
Nabisipi
Aguanus
Natashquan L.
Olomane
L. Musquaro
Outer I.
I. du Petit-Mécatina
Harrington Harbour
Daniel's Harbour
Gros Morne Nat. Park
Trout River
Port Saunders
White B.
Seal Cove
Baie Verte
Springdale
South Brook
Howley
Buchans
Red Indian
Grand Falls
Bishop's Falls
Dark Cove
Glenwood
Glovertown
Lac Allard
Gagnon
Walker L.
Clarke City
Sept-Îles
Moisie
Port-Cartier
Rivière-Pentecôte
Godbout
Baie-Trinité
Pte. des Monts
Mingan
Sheldrake
Havre-St-Pierre
Aguanish
Kegaska
Gethsémini
Etamamu
Natashquan
Pte. Ouest
Port-Menier
Î. d'Anticosti
Jupiter
Dét. de Jacques-Cartier
Det. Vallée
Grande-Vallée
Sud Ouest
Petit-Cap
Ste-Anne
Grande-Rivière
Mont-Louis
Pte. Sud
Heath Pt.
572
GULF OF ST. LAWRENCE
Long Range Mts.
Deer Lake
Corner Brook 814
Pasadena
Humber
Stephenville
Victoria Res.
Grey Res.
Salmon Res.
Port Blandford
Clarenville
381
Content
Trinity
Placentia
Baie d'Espoir
Bay of Islands
Long Pt.
Port au Port B.
St. George's B.
C. St.George
St. George's
St. David's
South Branch
Long Range Mts.
White Bear Res.
Burgeo
St. Alban's
Belleoram
Terrenceville
Fortune B.
Marystown
St. Lawrence
Placentia B.
Argentia
Holyrood
Spaniard's Bay
St. Mary's B.
C. St. Mary's
C. Pine

NEW BRUNSWICK
NOVA SCOTIA
PRINCE EDWARD ISLAND
MAINE

Forestville
Betsiamites
Hauterive
Baie-Comeau
Chicoutimi
Bagotville
Arvida
Jonquière
Saguenay
Tadoussac
Grandes-Bergeronnes
La Malbaie
Baie-St-Paul
St-Siméon
Rivière-du-Loup
Trois-Pistoles
Bic
Rimouski
Matane
Cap-Chat
Mt. Jacques-Cartier 1310
Ste-Anne
Parc Prov. de la Gaspésie
Mts. Chic-Chocs
Pén. de Gaspé
Gaspé
C. de Gaspé
Douglastown
Percé
Grande-Rivière
Chandler
Bonaventure
Pabos
Paspébiac
Port-Daniel
Chaleur Bay
New Carlisle
Miscou I.
Î. Brion
Grande-Entrée
Îs. de la Madeleine (Québec)
Cap-aux-Meules
Fatima
Amqui
Causapscal
Matapédia
Dalhousie
Campbellton
Atholville
Bathurst
Tracadie
Shippegan
Lamèque
Caraquet
Belledune
St-Léonard 819
Grand Falls
Plaster Rock
Edmundston
St. Leonard
Van Buren
Caribou
Presque Isle
Newcastle
Chatham
Collette
Richibucto
Blackville
Rogersville
Notre Dame
Buctouche
Shediac
Sackville
North Pt.
Tignish
Alberton
Summerside
Kensington
Malpeque
Cavendish
Charlottetown
Souris
East Pt.
St. Peters
Montague
Georgetown
Murray Hr.
Northumberland Strait
Borden
Cap-Pelé
Amherst
Cape Tormentine
Pictou
Parrsboro
Springhill
New Glasgow
Stellarton
Antigonish
Mulgrave
Canso
Chedabucto B.
Sherbrooke
Guysborough
C. North
St. Paul I.
Cabot Strait
Aspy B.
Pleasant Bay
Chéticamp
Cape Breton Nat. Park 532
Ingonish
Inverness
St. Anns B.
Sydney Mines
New Waterford
N. Sydney
North Sydney
Sydney
Glace Bay
Louisbourg
Bras d'Or
Baddeck
St. Peters
Port Hawkesbury
Cape Breton Island
I. Madame

Thetford Mines
Lac Mégantic
East Angus
Sherbrooke
Coaticook
Beauceville
St-Georges
Lac-Drolet
St-Joseph
Montmagny
Lauzon
Lévis
Ste-Marie
Beaupré
Plessisville
Armagh
St-Pacôme
St-Jean-Port-Joli
St-Pascal
Cabano
Eagle L.
Ashland
Houlton
Woodstock
Hartland
Florenceville
Grand Falls
Grand L.
Hartland
Fredericton Jc.
Fredericton
Gagetown
Chipman
Minto
Oromocto
Harcourt
Dorchester
Moncton
Riverside
Hillsborough
Petitcodiac
Sussex
Hampton
Elgin
Apohaqui
Saint John
Kennebecasis
Chignecto B.
Joggins
Maringouin
Minas Basin
Truro
Upper Musquodoboit
Stewiacke
Shubenacadie
Windsor
Kentville
Wolfville
Middleton
Bridgetown
Annapolis Royal
Digby
Weymouth
Yarmouth
Wedgeport
Clark's Harbour
C. Sable
Shelburne
Lockeport
Liverpool
Port Mouton
L. Rossignol Res.
Bridgewater
Lunenburg
Mahone Bay
Chester
Mahone Bay
St. Margarets Bay
Halifax
Dartmouth
Musquodoboit Hr.
Sheet Hr.
Ecum Secum
Sheet Harbour

Moosehead L.
Greenville
1606
Patten
Island Falls
Chesuncook L.
Millinocket
Mattawamkeag
Lincoln
Old Town
Brewer
Bangor
Brownville Jc.
Dover-Foxcroft
Guilford
Dexter
Newport
Waterville
Augusta
Gardiner
Skowhegan
Bingham
Moosehead
megantic L.
Rumford
Lewiston
Auburn
Brunswick
Bath
Freeport
Portland
Sanford
Saco
Biddeford
Berlin
Bethel
Rangeley
1917
Jackman
Kittery
Dover
Portsmouth
Rochester
Concord
Manchester
Nashua
Lawrence
Haverhill
Lowell
Lynn
Waltham
BOSTON
Brockton
Gloucester
Ann
Camden
Rockland
Belfast
Ellsworth
Bar Harbor
Mt. Desert I.
Machias
Jonesport
Eastport
Calais
Grand Manan I.
St. Croix
Stephen
Blacks Hr.
St. Andrews
Passamaquoddy Bay
Bay of Fundy
St. Martins

ATLANTIC OCEAN

Cabot Strait

Channel-Port aux Basques
Rose Blanche
Burgeo
Ramea
François
Harbour Breton
Grand Bank
Fortune
Lamaline
St. Lawrence
Miquelon
Langlade
SAINT-PIERRE ET MIQUELON (Fr.)
St. Pierre

Sable I. (Nova Scotia)

West from Greenwich

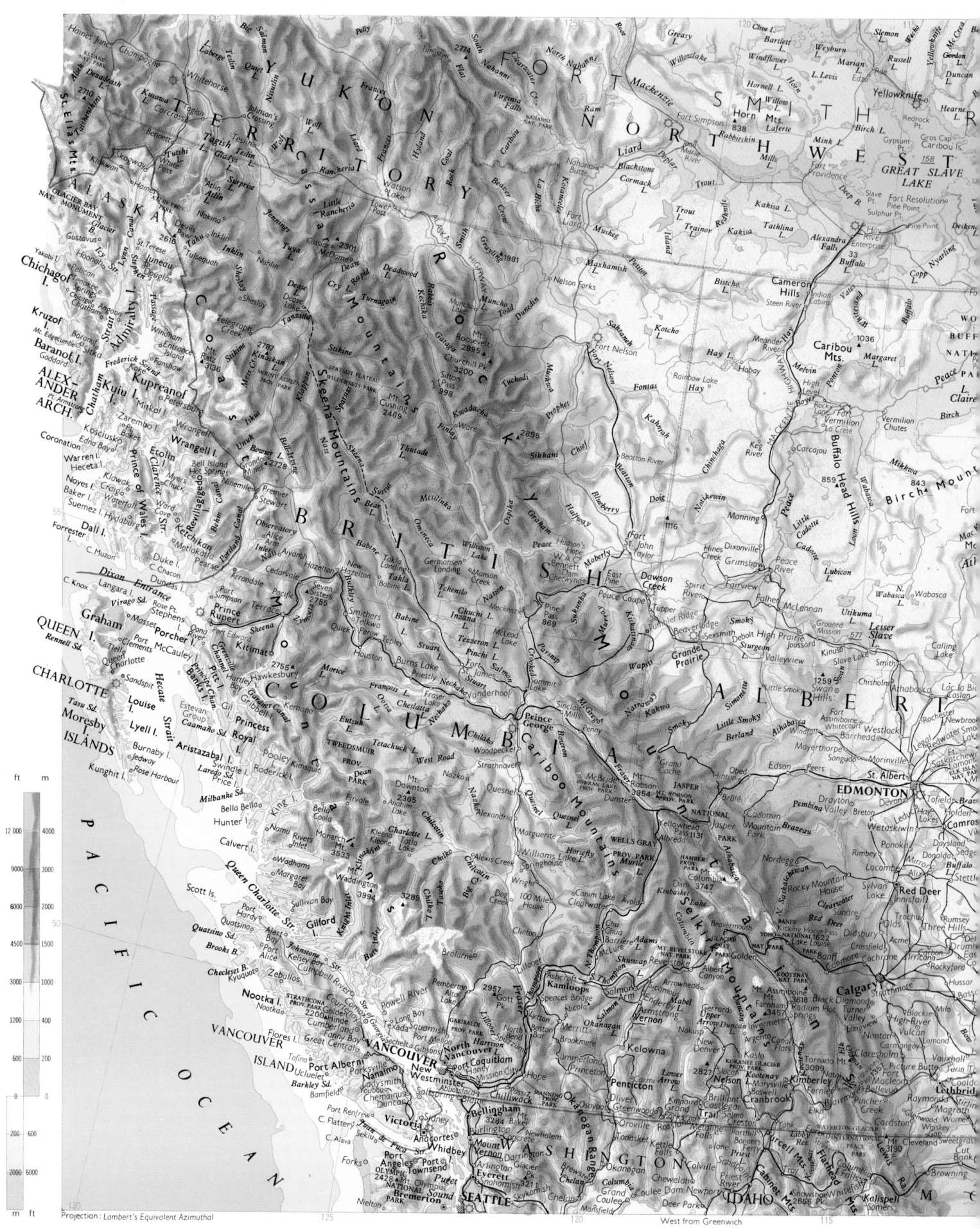

1:7 000 000

50   0   50   100   150   200 miles
50 0 50 100 150 200 250 300 km

HUDSON

BAY

NORTH WEST TERRITORIES   KEEWATIN REGION

SASKATCHEWAN

MANITOBA

ONTARIO

MINNESOTA

NORTH DAKOTA

MONTANA

Lake Athabasca

Reindeer L.

Lake Winnipeg

Lake Winnipegosis

Cedar Lake

Southern Indian L.

Wollaston L.

Cree L.

Prince Albert

North Battleford

Saskatoon

Regina

Moose Jaw

Swift Current

Yorkton

Dauphin

Brandon

WINNIPEG

Selkirk

Portage la Prairie

The Pas

Flin Flon

Churchill

Port Nelson

Thompson

Kenora

Fort Frances

Duluth

Grand Forks

Minot

Williston

Fort Peck Res.

RIDING MOUNTAIN NATIONAL PARK

PRINCE ALBERT NAT. PARK

MEADOW LAKE PROV. PARK

Lake of the Woods

COPYRIGHT. GEORGE PHILIP & SON. LTD.

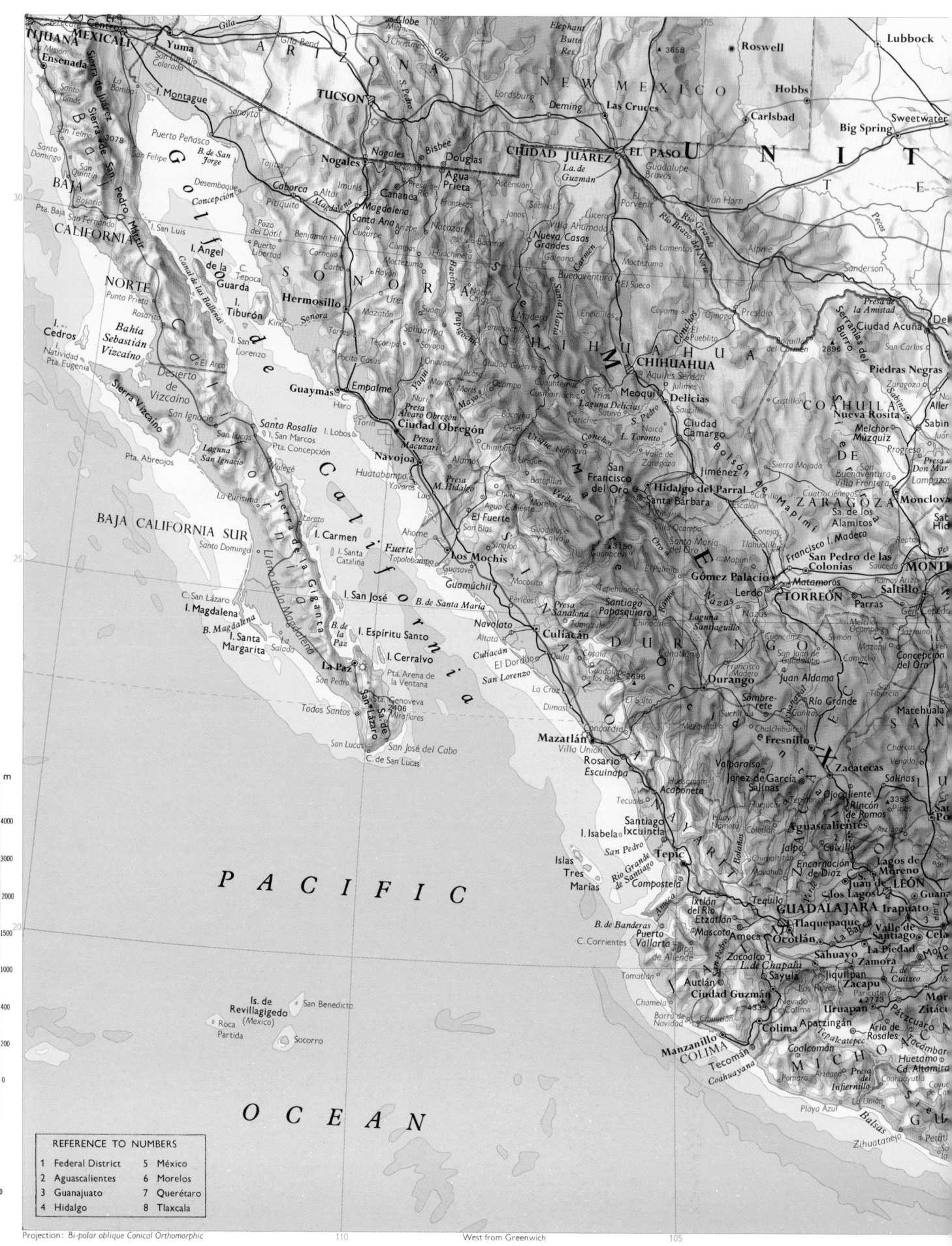

REFERENCE TO NUMBERS
1 Federal District   5 México
2 Aguascalientes   6 Morelos
3 Guanajuato   7 Querétaro
4 Hidalgo   8 Tlaxcala

Projection: Bi-polar oblique Conical Orthomorphic   West from Greenwich

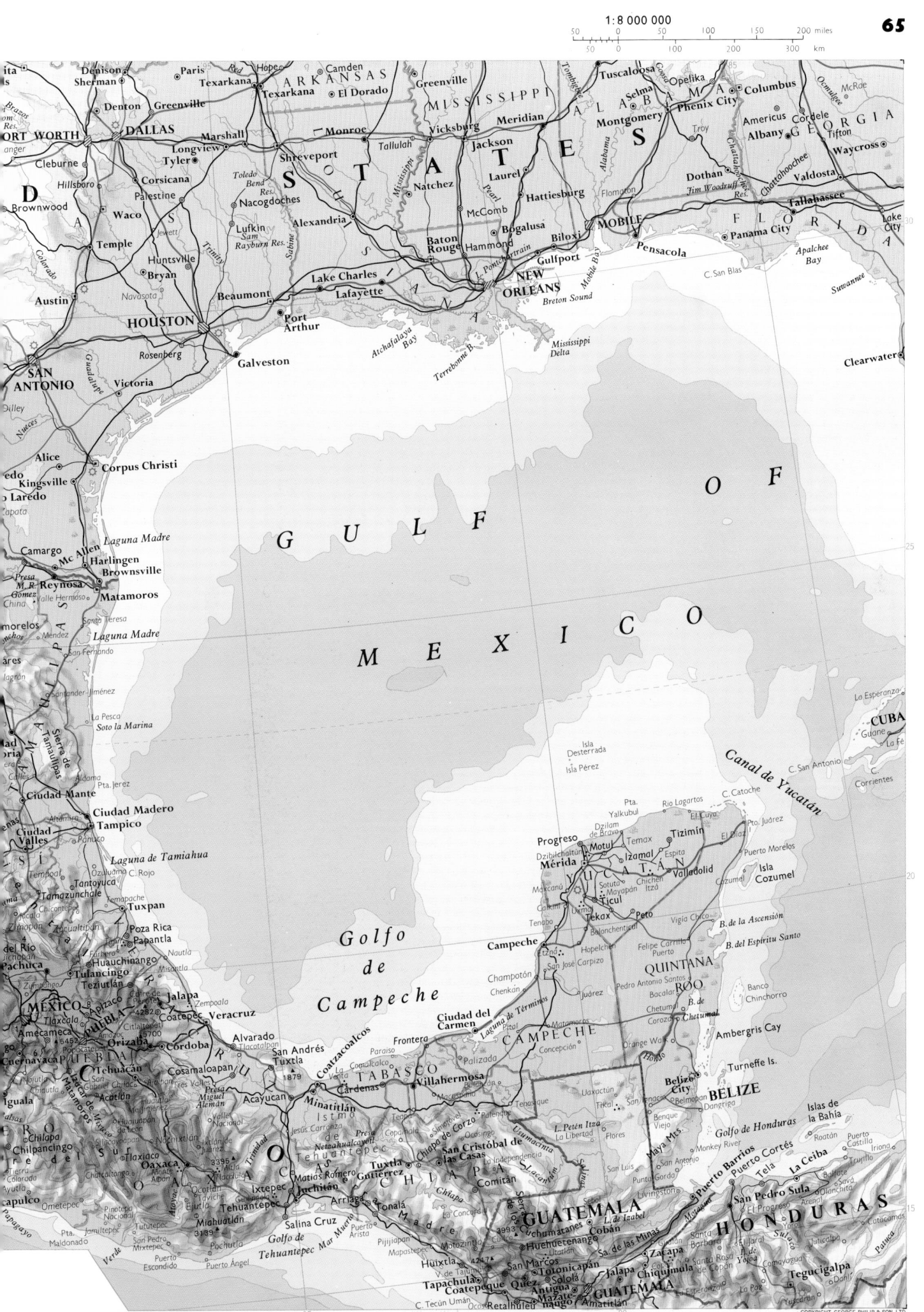

GULF OF MEXICO

GREATER

CARIBBEAN

Isla Desterrada
Isla Pérez

Progreso
Dzilam de Bravo
Mérida
YUCATAN
Campeche
CAMPECHE
Ciudad del Carmen
Laguna de Términos

QUINTANA ROO

BELIZE
Belize City
Turneffe Is.

GUATEMALA
HONDURAS
San Pedro Sula
Puerto Barrios
La Ceiba
Tegucigalpa

EL SALVADOR
SAN SALVADOR
San Miguel

NICARAGUA
MANAGUA
Granada
Lago de Nicaragua
Bluefields

COSTA RICA
San José
Cartago
Limón

PANAMÁ
Colón
David

Cayman Islands (Br.)

JAMAICA
Montego Bay
Kingston

La Habana
Pinar del Río
Matanzas
Santa Clara
Cienfuegos
Trinidad
Camagüey
Victoria de las Tunas

CUBA

Isla de la Juventud
Archipiélago de los Canarreos

Swan Islands (U.S.A. & Honduras)

I. de Providencia (Colombia)
I. de San Andrés (Colombia)

Islas del Maíz (Nicaragua, U.S.A.)

1 : 8 000 000

50   0   50   100   150   200 miles
50   0   50   100   200   300 km

A T L A N T I C

O C E A N

Tropic of Cancer

I.
San Salvador
(Watling I., Guanahani)
onception I.
Rum Cay
ong I.
Clarence
Town
Atwood or
Samana Cay
rde
Crooked I. Passage
Crooked I.
Richmond
Hill
Snug
Corner
Plana Cays
Albert
Town
Acklins I.
Mayaguana I.
Mira por vos Cay
Hogsty Reef
Caicos
Islands
(Br.)
Turks Islands
(Br.)
Little Inagua I.
Lake Rose
Great
Inagua I.
Matthew
Town
Moa
Baracoa
Pta. de
Maisí
I. de la
Tortue
Cap-Haïtien
Port-de-Paix
Monte Cristi
La Isabela
Puerto Plata
anamo
Paso de los
Vientos
(Windward Passage)
Jean-Rabel
Cap-à-Foux
Fort-Liberté
La Vega
C. Francés Viejo
San Francisco de Macorís
Nagua
Santiago de
Cabelleros
Cord.
Central
Sánchez
Sabana de La Mar
Bayamón
SAN JUAN
Virgin Gorda
Anegada
Virgin Is.
(Br.)
St. Thomas
Tortola
Road Town
Sombrero (Anguilla)
Jérémie
I. de la Gonâve
Gonaïves
Hinche
St-Marc
HAITI
DOMINICAN
3175
Arecibo
Aguadilla
Fajardo
Anguilla (Br.)
St.-Martin (Guad.)
Dame
Marie
PORT-
AU-PRINCE
San Juan
REP.
San Pedro
de Macorís
Hato Mayor
C. Engano
1338
Ponce
Caguas
Virgin Is.
(U.S.A.)
St-Barthélemy (Fr.)
Massif de la Hotte
Carcasse
Enriquillo
2280
Jacmel
Barahona
Higüey
La Romana
B. de
Yuma
Canal de la Mona
Mayagüez
Guayama
Charlotte Amalie
St. Croix
St. Maarten
(Neth.)
St. Eustatius
(Neth.)
Basseterre
Saba (Neth.)
ST.
Nevis
CHRISTOPHER-
NEVIS
Barbuda
St. Johns
Antigua
ANTIGUA
& BARBUDA
Les Cayes
Aquin
Pointe-à-Gravois
Pedernales
I. Beata
C. Beata
Isla
Mona
(U.S.A.)
PUERTO
RICO
(U.S.A.)
Frederiksted
Christiansted
Redonda
Montserrat
H I S P A N I O L A
A N T I L L E S
SANTO DOMINGO
L E S S E R
L E E W A R D   I S L A N D S
(Fr.)
GUADELOUPE
Basse-Terre
Moule
Désirade
Pointe-à-Pitre
Marie-Galante (Fr.)
Grand-Bourg
I. des Saintes
(Guad.)
Guadeloupe Passage
Dominica Passage
Portsmouth
DOMINICA
Roseau
B E A N   S E A
I. de Aves (Bird I.)
(Venezuela)
Martinique Passage
Mt. Pelée
1397
Ste-Marie
François
Rivière-Pilot
Fort-de-France
MARTINIQUE
St. Lucia Channel
(Fr.)
Castries
ST. LUCIA
Soufrière
St. Vincent Passage
Soufrière 1234
ST. VINCENT
Speightstown
Bridgetown
& THE BARBADOS
Kingstown
Hillsborough
The Grenadines
GRENADINES
St. George's
GRENADA
L E S S E R   A N T I L L E S
W I N D W A R D   I S L A N D S

ft   m
12.000   4000
9000   3000
6000   2000
4500   1500
3000   1000
1200   400
600   200
0   0
200   600
2000   6000
4000   12 000
6000   18 000
8000   24 000
m   ft

Aruba
(Neth.)
Curaçao
(Neth.)
Bonaire
(Neth.)
I. Blanquilla (Ven.)
Tobago
Scarborough
Pta. Gallinas
C. San Román
Pen. de la
Guajira
Pta.
Espada
Pen. de
Paraguaná
Willemstad
Neth.
Antilles
I. de Aves
(Ven.)
Is. Los Roques
(Ven.)
I. Orchila
(Ven.)
I. Los Hermanos
(Ven.)
Is. Los Testigos
(Ven.)
Pta. Peñas
Dragon's Mouth
Port of
Spain
Galera
Pt.
Punto Fijo
Puerto
Cumarebo
Maiquetía
La Guaira
I. La Tortuga
(Ven.)
I. Margarita
(Ven.)
La Asunción
NUEVA
ESPARTA
Porlamar
Pen. de Paria
Güiria
Arima
Trinidad
AN-
Marta
Santa
Ríohacha
Uribia
C. San Juan
de Guía
GUAJIRA
Golfo de
Venezuela
Coro
La Vela de Coro
FALCON
Tucacas
Puerto
Cabello
Macaray
CARACAS
DISTRITO
FEDERAL
Higuerote
Río Chico
Río
Caribe
Golfo de Paria
Carúpano
Cumaná
Río Claro
San Fernando
TRINIDAD
& TOBAGO
Serpent's Mouth
Cienaga
San
Rafael
Valencia
Los Teques
Puerto
La Cruz
SUCRE
Caripito
LA
Soledad
Sabanalarga
Punta
Cardón
Altagracia
Mene de Mauroa
Baragua
La Concepción
MARACAIBO
Santa Rita
Cabimas
Carora
San Felipe
YARACUY
Maracay
ARAGUA
MIRANDA
S. Juan de
los Morros
Villa
de Cura
Ocumare del Tuy
Altagracia de
Orituco
Aragua de
Barcelona
Barcelona
Cantaura
Maturín
MONAGAS
DELTA-
Tucupita
AMACUR
Fundación
Calamar
Agustín
Codazzi
Ciudad
Ojeda
Mene
Grande
Machiques
Lago de
Maracaibo
La Ceiba
El Tocuyo
Santiago de
los Morros
Maragua de
San Carlos
COJEDES
El Sombrero
Valle de la
Pascua
El Tigre
ANZOÁTEGUI
Anaco
Ciudad Guayana
Soledad
MAGDALENA
Plato
Zambrano
Valledupar
Villa del
Rosario
CÉSAR
ZULIA
Betijoque
TRUJILLO
Trujillo
Valera
Acarigua
PORTUGUESA
El Baúl
GUÁRICO
Calabozo
Santa María
de Ipire
El Pao
Sierra Imataca
Corozal
Magangué
Mompos
El Banco
Ocaña
Santander
SANTANDER
NORTE
MÉRIDA
Cord. de Mérida
Ciudad
Bolivia
BARINAS
Libertad
Barinas
Guanare
Portuguesa
San Fernando de
Apure
Ciudad
Bolívar
Ciudad Guayana
Upata
El Callao
Ayapel
Simití
BOLÍVAR
Cúcuta
Catatumbo
Encontrados
San Carlos
del Zulia
TÁCHIRA
Santa
Barbara
Achaguas
Mapire
Emb de Guri
Guasipati
Tumeremo
V E N E Z U E L A
Apure
Orinoco
Caicara

West from Greenwich   COPYRIGHT. GEORGE PHILIP & SON. LTD.

1:30 000 000

100 0 100 200 300 400 500 miles
100 0 200 400 600 800 km

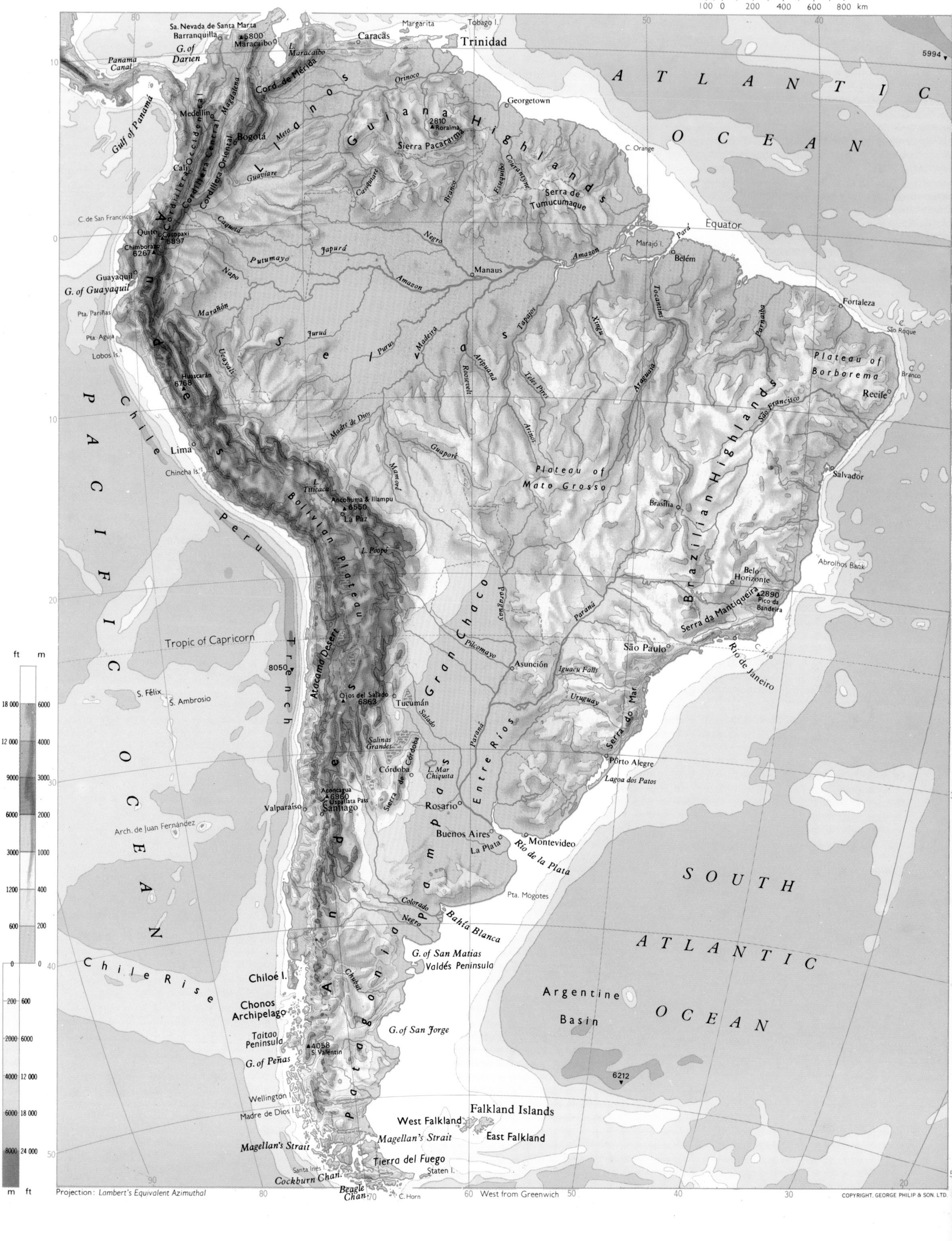

5994

Sa. Nevada de Santa Marta
Barranquilla ▲5800
G. of Darien
Maracaibo
L. Maracaibo
Caracas
Margarita
Tobago I.
Trinidad

ATLANTIC

Panama Canal
Cord. de Mérida
Orinoco
Georgetown
OCEAN

Medellín
Cali
Bogotá
Cordillera Occidental
Cordillera Central
Magdalena
Llanos
Guiana Highlands
Roraima ▲2810
Sierra Pacaraima
C. Orange

C. de San Francisco
Quito Cotopaxi ▲5897
Serra de Tumucumaque
Equator

Chimborazo 6267
Putumayo
Japurá
Negro
Branco
Essequibo
Corantijn
Pará
Belém

Guayaquil
G. of Guayaquil
Napo
Marañón
Amazon
Manaus
Amazon
Marajó I.

Pta. Parñas
Pta. Aguja
Lobos Is.
Ucayali
Juruá
Purus
Madeira
Tapajós
Xingu
Tocantins
Araguaia
Fortaleza
C. São Roque

Huascarán ▲6768
Selvas
Aripuaña
Teles Pires
Parnaíba
Plateau of Borborema
Recife
Branco

Chile
Peru
Lima
Chincha Is.
L. Titicaca
Bolivian Plateau
Guaporé
Mamoré
Madre de Dios
Roosevelt
Plateau of Mato Grosso
Brasília
Brazilian Highlands
São Francisco
Salvador
Abrolhos Bank

Ancohuma & Illampu ▲6550
La Paz
L. Poopó
Paraguay
Belo Horizonte
Serra da Mantiqueira ▲2890 Pico da Bandeira

PACIFIC
Tropic of Capricorn
Atacama Desert
▲8050
Ojos del Salado ▲6863
Tucumán
Gran Chaco
Pilcomayo
Paraná
Asunción
Iguaçu Falls
São Paulo
Serra do Mar
Pôrto Alegre

S. Félix
S. Ambrosio
Salinas Grandes
Salado
Entre Rios
Uruguay
Lagoa dos Patos

OCEAN
Andes
Córdoba
L. Mar Chiquita
Sierra de Córdoba
Pampas
Rio de Janeiro
C. Frio

Arch. de Juan Fernández
Aconcagua ▲6960
Uspallata Pass
Santiago
Valparaíso
Rosario
Buenos Aires
La Plata
Montevideo
Río de la Plata
Pta. Mogotes

Chile Rise
Chiloé I.
Chonos Archipelago
Taitao Peninsula
G. of Peñas
S. Valentin ▲4058
Patagonia
Chubut
Colorado
Negro
Bahía Blanca
G. of San Matias
Valdés Peninsula
G. of San Jorge

SOUTH

ATLANTIC

Argentine Basin

OCEAN

▼6212

Wellington
Madre de Dios
Santa Inés
Magellan's Strait
Magellan's Strait
Tierra del Fuego
Cockburn Chan.
Beagle Chan.
C. Horn
Staten I.

Falkland Islands
West Falkland
East Falkland

ft   m
18 000   6000
12 000   4000
9000   3000
6000   2000
3000   1000
1200   400
600   200
0   0
200   600
2000   6000
4000   12 000
6000   18 000
8000   24 000
m   ft

Projection: Lambert's Equivalent Azimuthal

90   80   70   West from Greenwich   60   50   40   30   20

COPYRIGHT. GEORGE PHILIP & SON, LTD.

1:30 000 000

100 0 100 200 300 400 500 miles
100 0 200 400 600 800 km

COSTA RICA

San José

PANAMA
Golfo de Panamá
S.F. 3227
Honolulu 4683

Barranquilla
Cartagena
Ciénaga
Golfo de Darién
Montería
San Cristóbal
Maracaibo
Cabimas
Barquisimeto
Valencia
Caracas
Cumaná
Maturín
Mérida

Punto Fijo
Isla de Margarita
Tobago
Port of Spain
TRINIDAD AND TOBAGO
Trinidad

VENEZUELA

Medellín
Manizales
Pereira
Ibagué
Buenaventura
Cali
Popayán
Bucaramanga
Cúcuta
Bogotá

Pto. Ayacucho
Ciudad Guayana
Ciudad Bolívar
San Fernando
Orinoco

Georgetown
New Amsterdam
Paramaribo
Cayenne
C. Orange

GUYANA SURINAM FRENCH GUIANA

COLOMBIA

Pasto
Quito
C. de San Francisco

ECUADOR
Guayaquil
Cuenca
G. de Guayaquil
Riobamba

Iquitos
Napo
Putumayo
Japurá
Negro

Manaus
Tefé
Santarem

Macapá
Ilha de Marajó
Belém (Pará)
Equator

Chiclayo
Trujillo
Pucallpa
Marañón
Cruzeiro do Sul

Pôrto Velho
Rio Branco
Guajará-Mirim
Madeira

São Luís
Bacabal
Teresina
Fortaleza (Ceara)
C. de São Roque
Natal
Juazeiro do Norte
Parnaiba
Recife (Pernambuco)
João Pessoa (Paraiba)
Maceió

PERU
Callao
Lima
Huancayo
Ayacucho
Cuzco

BRAZIL

Aracaju
São Francisco

Juliaca
Titicaca
La Paz
Arequipa
Mollendo
Tacna
Arica
Oruro
Sucre
Cochabamba
Santa Cruz

BOLIVIA

Cuiabá
Brasília
Goiânia
Jataí

Salvador (Bahia)

Iquique
Uyuni
Tarija
Corumbá

Campo Grande
Uberaba
Ribeirão Prêto
Montes Claros
Gov. Valadares

Belo Horizonte
Vitória

Antofagasta
Salta
San Miguel de Tucumán
Santiago del Estero

PARAGUAY
Pedro Juan Caballero
Asunción
Pilcomayo

Pres. Prudente
Bauru
Londrina
Campinas
SÃO PAULO
Santos
Campos
Niterói
RIO DE JANEIRO

Tropic of Capricorn

Resistencia
Corrientes

Curitiba
Ponta Grossa

ARGENTINA

Santiago del Estero
Salado
Uruguay
Uruguaiana

Florianópolis
Santa Maria
Pôrto Alegre

Córdoba
Santa Fe
Paraná
Rosario
URUGUAY

Pelotas
Lagoa dos Patos

Mendoza
Mercedes
La Plata
BUENOS AIRES
Montevideo

San Francisco
Valparaíso
Santiago
San Rafael
Talca
Concepción
Santa Rosa
Bahía Blanca
Colorado
Negro
Tandil
Mar del Plata

CHILE

Isla San Felix (Chile)
Isla San Ambrosio (Chile)
Arch. de Juan Fernández (Chile)
Coquimbo

PACIFIC OCEAN

SOUTH ATLANTIC OCEAN

Valdivia
Zapala
Viedma

Puerto Montt
Isla de Chiloé
San Carlos de Bariloche
Peninsula Valdés
Trelew
Chubut

Archipiélago de los Chonos

Golfo Comodoro Rivadavia
San Jorge

G. de Penas
I. Wellington
Santa Cruz
Río Gallegos
Estrecho de Magallanes
Strait of Magellan
Punta Arenas
Isla Grande de Tierra del Fuego
Cabo de Hornos (Cape Horn)

FALKLAND ISLANDS (ISLAS MALVINAS) (U.K.)
West Falkland
Stanley
East Falkland

NORTH ATLANTIC OCEAN

Projection : Lambert's Equivalent Azimuthal

West from Greenwich

COPYRIGHT. GEORGE PHILIP & SON. LTD.

CARIBBEAN   SEA

PANAMÁ

PACIFIC

OCEAN

COLOMBIA

VENEZUELA

ECUADOR

PERU

Projection: Lambert's Equivalent Azimuthal

ft   m
18 000   6000
12 000   4000
9000   3000
6000
4500   1500
3000
1200   400
600   200
0
0
200   600
2000   6000
4000   12 000
m   ft

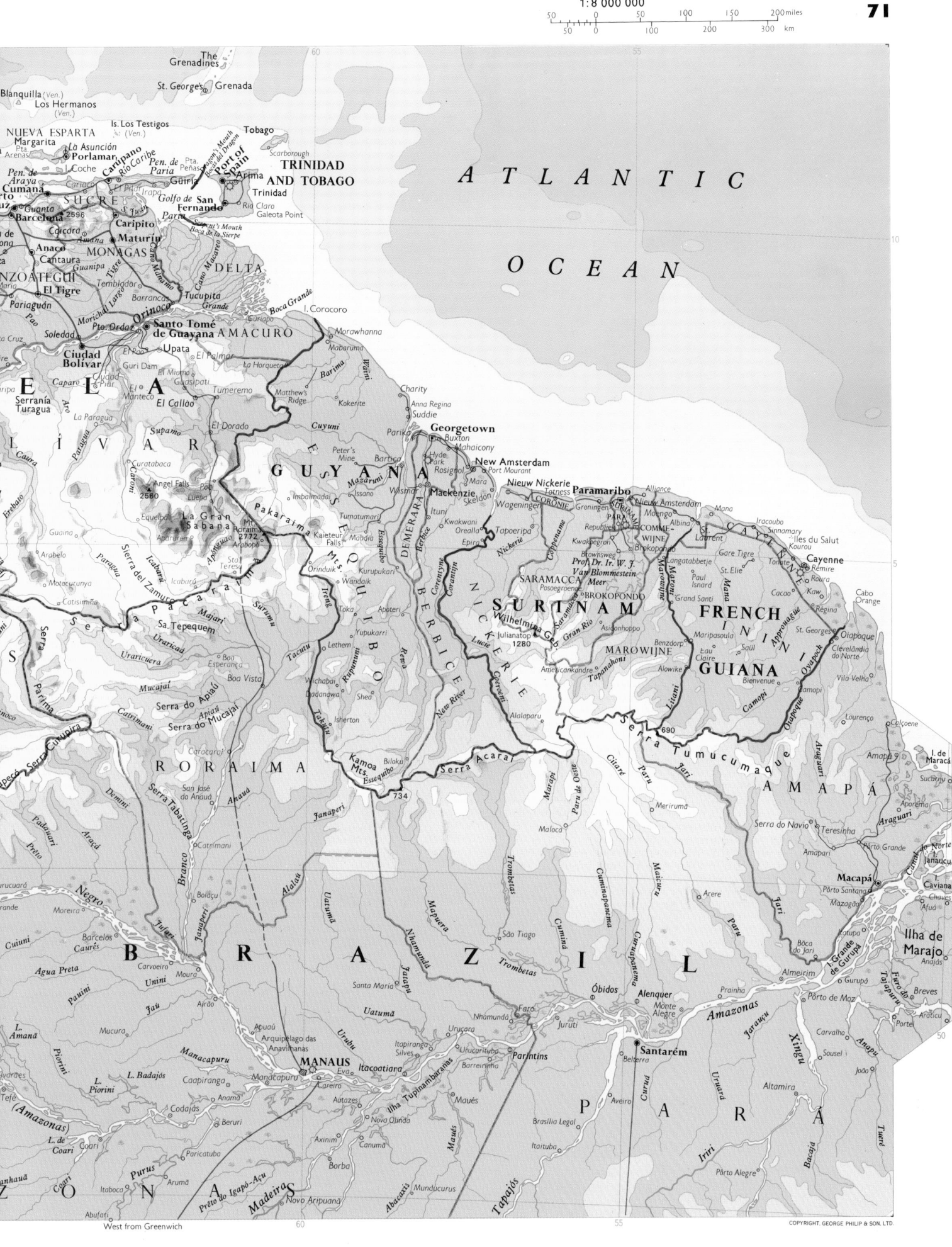

1:8 000 000

50   0   50   100   150   200miles
50   0   100   200   300   km

ATLANTIC

OCEAN

The
Grenadines
St. George's   Grenada
Blanquilla (Ven.)
Los Hermanos
(Ven.)
Is. Los Testigos
(Ven.)   Tobago
NUEVA ESPARTA   Scarborough
Margarita
La Asunción   TRINIDAD
Porlamar   Serpent's Mouth   AND TOBAGO
Coche   Carúpano   Boca del Dragon
Pen. de   Río Caribe   Port of
Araya   Güiria   Spain   Arima
Cumaná   Golfo de San   Trinidad
SUCRE   Fernando   Río Claro
Guanta   2596   Para   Galeota Point
Barcelona   San Juan
Caripito
Anaco   Maturín
Cantaura   MONAGAS
NZOÁTEGUI   Guanipa   Tucupita
El Tigre   Temblador   Cano Macareo   DELTA
Pariaguán   Tigre   Barrancas   AMACURO
Soledad   Pto. Ordaz   Orinoco   I. Corocoro
Santo Tomé   Morawhanna
Ciudad   de Guayana   Mabaruma
Bolívar   Upata   Barima
Guri Dam   Waini
El Palmar   Charity
La Horqueta   Anna Regina
Matthew's   Suddie
Ridge   Kokerite
Cuyuni   Parika   Georgetown
Peter's   Bartica   Buxton
Mine   Mahaicony
GUYANA   Hyde   New Amsterdam
Park   Port Mourant
Mackenzie   Nieuw Nickerie   Paramaribo
Skeldon   Totness   Nieuw Amsterdam
Wageningen   CORONIE   Mana
SURINAM   Moengo   Iracoubo
Prof. Dr. Ir. W. J.   COMME-   Sinnamary
Van Blommestein   WIJNE   CAYENNE
Meer   St.   Cayenne
SARAMACCA   Laurent   Rémire
BROKOPONDO   Roura
Wilhelmina Geb.   MAROWIJNE   FRENCH   Kaw
Julianatop   ININI
1280   GUIANA   Oiapoque

BRAZIL

PARÁ

West from Greenwich   COPYRIGHT. GEORGE PHILIP & SON. LTD.

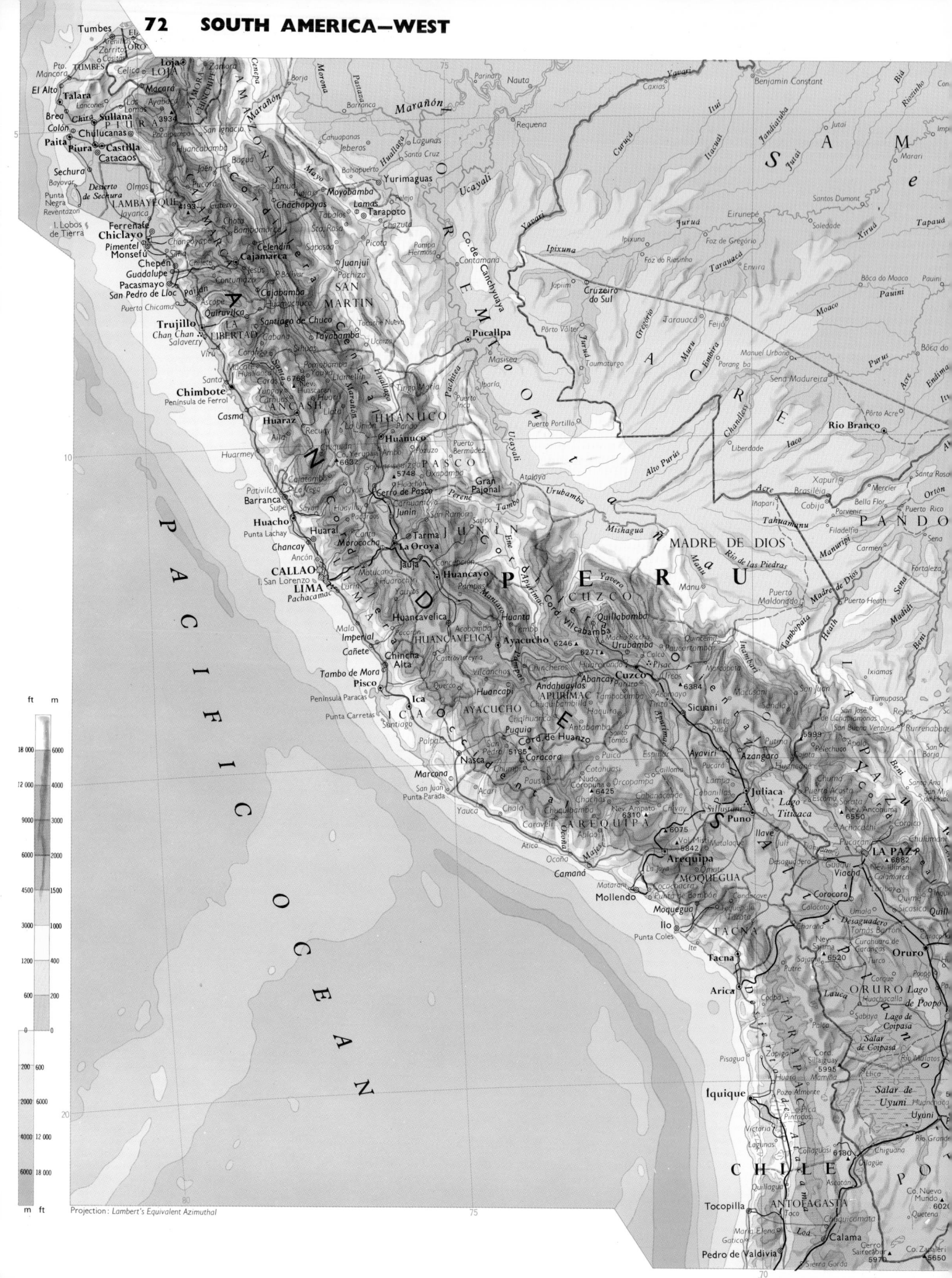

Tumbes
EL ORO
Arenillas
Zorritos
Pto. TUMBES
Santa Rosa
Pta. Mancora
Loja
Celica
Macará
Ayabaca
El Alto
Talara
Zamora
Brea
Chira
Sullana
Colón
Chulucanas
Paita
Piura
Castilla
Catacaos
Sechura
Bayovar
Punta Negra
Reventazón
LAMBAYEQUE
I. Lobos de Tierra
Ferreñafe
Chiclayo
Pimentel
Monsefú
Chepén
Guadalupe
Pacasmayo
San Pedro de Lloc
Trujillo
Chan Chan
Salaverry
Chimbote
Península de Ferrol
Casma
Huaraz
Huarmey

CAJAMARCA
Cajamarca
Jesús
Cajabamba
SAN MARTIN
Santiago de Chuco
LA LIBERTAD
Chota
Bambamarca
Celendín
Bolívar
Juanjui
Pachiza
Tayabamba

AMAZONAS
Loja
Jaén
Bagua
Moyobamba
Lamas
Tarapoto
Chachapoyas

Maranon

Yurimaguas

Contamana

Pucallpa

ANCASH
HUANUCO
Huánuco
PASCO
Cerro de Pasco
Oxapampa

JUNIN
La Oroya
Tarma
Jauja
Huancayo
Huancavelica
HUANCAVELICA

LIMA
CALLAO
Huaral
Huacho
Barranca
Supe
Chancay
Ancón

PERU

MADRE DE DIOS

CUZCO
Cuzco
Abancay
APURIMAC
Andahuaylas
Urubamba
Ayacucho
AYACUCHO
Puquio
Nasca
Marcona

AREQUIPA
Arequipa
MOQUEGUA
Moquegua
Mollendo
Ilo
TACNA
Tacna
Arica

Juliaca
PUNO
Puno
Lago Titicaca
LA PAZ
LA PAZ

ORURO
Oruro
Lago de Poopó

TARAPACA
Iquique
CHILE

ANTOFAGASTA
Tocopilla
Calama

PACIFIC

OCEAN

Projection: Lambert's Equivalent Azimuthal

Map labels

1:8 000 000

50   0   50   100   150   200 miles

50   0   50   100   200   300 km

73

Brazil / Amazonas region (north)

Z O N A S
Itanhauã   L. de Coari   Coari   Paricatuba   Axinim   Canumã   Itaituba   Pôrto Alegre   Bacajá
Purus   Aruma   Borba   Maués   Iriri
Canutama   Itaboca   Madeira   Munducurus   Abacaxis   Tapajós   Tucunaré   Entre Rios   Nazaré   São Félix
Jaburu   Itatuba   Prêto do Igapó-Açu   Manicoré   Novo Aripuanã   Capoeira   Sai-Cinza   Jamarixim   P A R Á
Santa Maria dos Marmeles   Miriti   Crepori   Curuá
B   R   A   Z
Axioma   Prainha   Canumã   S. Benedito   Cachimbo   Alto Iriri
Lábrea   Três Casas   Samaúma   Canudos   Serra do Cachimbo   Iriri   Riosinho
Majuriã   Muciura   Humaitá   Barracão do Barreto   Peixoto de Azevedo   Xingu   L
Calama   Aripuanã   Recreio   Manitsaud-Missu   Campo de Diauarum
Pôrto Velho   Jamari   Tipanirá   Aripuanã   Serra dos Apiacás   Pôrto Cajueiro   Suiá Missu   Liberdade
404   Jaciparaná   Caritianas   Presidente Hermes   Serra Formosa   Arraias   Pôrto dos Meinacos   Serra do Roncador
Abuná   Ariquemes   Rondônia   Jaru   Jaru   Pimenta Bueno   Barão de Melgaço   Nortelândia   Xingu   Romero   Culisen

Rondônia / Mato Grosso

Guajará-Mirim   Sa. dos Pacaás Novos   R O N D Ô N I A   Arinos   Diamantino   Cuiabá   P l a n a l t o   Aruanã
Guayaramerin   Versalles   Pedras Negras   663   Nhambiquara   Juruena   Utiariti   Arenápolis   Alto Paraguai   G R O S S O   Aragarças
Vilhena   Camararé   Tapirapuã   Rosário Oeste   Serra Azul   Chavantina   Araguaína
Príncipe da Beira   Mategua   Guaporé   Saturnina   M A T O   669   Barra do Bugres   Mato   915   Grosso   Barro do Garças
San Joaquín   Boures   Puerto Villazón   Mato Grosso   Guaporé   Acorizal   Chapada dos Guimarães   Mortes   Araguaína
Lago Rogoaguado   Lago de San Luis   El Carmen   Perseverancia   Serrania de Huanchaca   Várzea Grande   Cuiabá   Coronel Ponce   Poxoreu   Guiratinga   Baliza

Bolivia / Santa Cruz / Paraguay

B O L I V I A   Trinidad   San Javier   1995   Pôrto Esperidião   Cáceres   Santo Antônio do Levergér   Jaciara   Tesouro   Rio das Garças   Aragarças
San Ignacio   Concepción   Aguapei   Poconé   Barão de Melgaço   Rondonópolis   Ponte Branca   Ivolândia
S A N T A   C R U Z   San Ignacio   Santa Ana   San Matías   São Lourenço   Itiquira   Alto Garças   Araguaia   Caiapônia   Sa. das Divisões
Santa Cruz   Buena Vista   Laguna Concepción   Lagoa Uberaba   Pôrto Jofre   Correntes   Alto Araguaia   Santa Rita do Araguaia   Caiapó   Rio Verde
Montero Warnes   El Cerro   San José   Santo Corazón   Pantanal do São Lourenço   Baús   Jataí
Villegrande   Llanos de Chiquitos   1425   Serra de Santiago   La Cal   Lagoa Mandioré   Taquari   Itiquira   Verde
Bañados de Izozog   Raboré   Puerto Suárez   M A T O   G R O S S O   Coxim   Rio Verde de Mato Grosso   Claro   Ituruma
Santa Ana   Corumbá   Pantanal do Rio Negro   D O   S U L   Paranaíba
C H U Q U I S A C A   Portachuelo   Fortín General Pando   Ladário   Nhecolândia   Negro   Alto Sucurir   Cassilândia   Aporé
Charagua   Fortín Ingavi   Albuquerque   Corguinho   Rochedo   Sucuriú   Paranaíba
Camiri   Pôrto Esperança   Aquidauana   Aparecida do Taboado   Rubinéia
O L I M P O   Coimbra   Miranda   Terenos   Ribas do Rio Pardo   Pereira Barreto
Fortín Coronel Eugenio Garay   Bahía Negra   Aquidauana   Jango   Campo Grande   Água Clara   Três Lagoas   Andradina
C h a c o   B o r e a l   Fuerte Olimpo   Sa. da Bodoquena   Bonito   Sidrolândia   Garças   Lussanvira
PARAGUAY   Villa Montes   Fortín Garrapatal   Puerto Guaraní   Nioaque   Xavantina   Mirandópolis
B O Q U E R Ó N   Pôrto Murtinho   Jardim   Guia Lopes da Laguna   Maracaju   Anhanduí   Panorama   Aguapei
Tarija   Yacuiba   La Esperanza   Pôrto Murtinho   5663
S A L T A   Tartagal   West from Greenwich

5663

West from Greenwich

COPYRIGHT. GEORGE PHILIP & SON. LTD.

1:8 000 000

ATLANTIC OCEAN

ESPÍRITO SANTO

Tropic of Capricorn

SALVADOR (Bahia)

RIO DE JANEIRO

NITERÓI

CAMPOS

BELO HORIZONTE

BRASÍLIA

DISTRITO FEDERAL

GOIÂNIA

SÃO PAULO

SANTO ANDRÉ

SÃO VICENTE

SANTOS

CAMPINAS

CURITIBA

PARANÁ

Vitória

Vila Velha

West from Greenwich

Projection: Lambert's Equivalent Azimuthal

COPYRIGHT GEORGE PHILIP & SON LTD

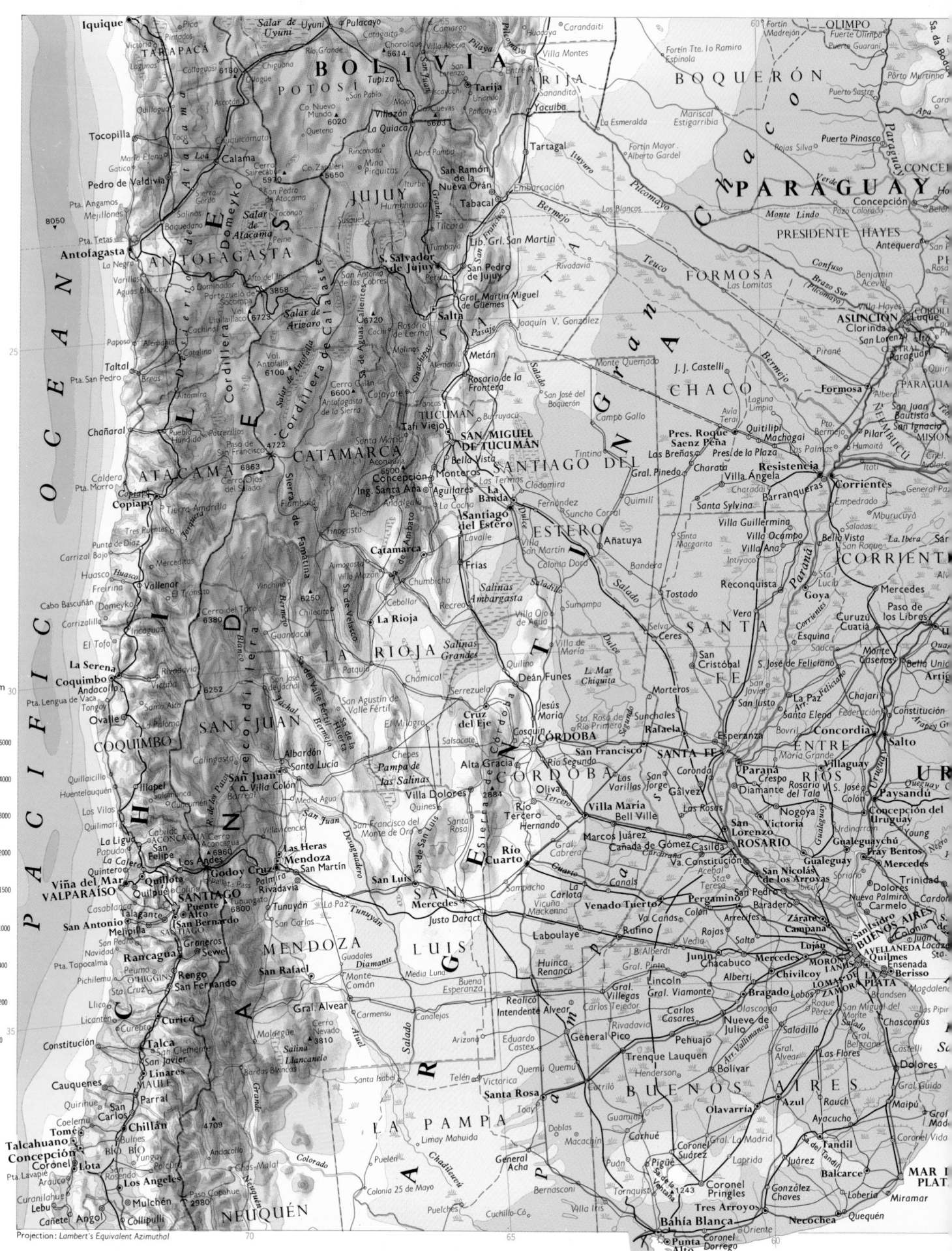

1:8 000 000

50   0   50   100   150 miles
50   0   50   100   150   200   km

BELO
HORIZONTE
N. Lima
Itabirito
VITÓRIA
Itaquari
Vila
Velha
Guaraparí

GROSSO

Três Lagoas   Andradina   Mirassol   S. José
Xavantina   Mirandópolis   do Rio Prêto   Olímpia
Araçatuba   Panorama   Bebedouro   Batatais   São Seb.
Birigui   Catanduva   Ribeirão   do Paraíso
Adamantina   Tupã   Penápolis   Jaboticabal   Prêto   Guaxupé
SÃO   Lins   Araraquara   Mococa   Alfenas
Pres.   PAULO   Bauru   São   Varginha
Epitácio   Martinópolis   Garça   Carlos   Poços de
Presidente   Marília   Jaú   Rio Claro   Caldas
Prudente   Rancharia   Limeira   Pinhal
Regente   Assis   Santa Cruz   Piracicaba   Americana
Paranaí   Londrina   do Rio Pardo   CAMPINAS   Mogi-Mirim
Nova   Rolândia   Ourinhos   Botucatu   Itu
Esperança   Cornélio   Jacarèzinho   Avaré   Jundiaí
Maringá   Procópio   Tatuí   Sorocaba
Apucarana   Itapetininga   SÃO PAULO
Mandaguari   SANTO ANDRÉ
Arapongas   Itararé   Paranapiacaba   São Vicente
Guaíra   PARANÁ   São Vicente   SANTOS
Cianorte   Ponta Grossa   Guarujá
Cruzeiro   BRAZIL   Itapeva   Ilha de São Sebastião
do Oeste   Guarapuava   Curitiba   Iguape   Pta. do Boi
Foz do Iguaçu   Palmeira   Lapa   Ilha Comprida
Iguaçú   União da   Antonina   Ilha do Cardoso
Falls   Vitória   Irati   Paranaguá
Bernardo   Rio Negro   Guaratuba
de Irigoyen   Mafra   São Francisco do Sul
Eldorado   Pto. União   Joinvile
San Pedro   Caçador   Blumenau   Itajaí
MISIONES   Santa Cecília   Brusque
Joaçaba   SANTA   Rio do Sul
Enechim   Campos Novos   CATARINA   Ilha de Santa Catarina
Carázinho   Lajes   Florianópolis
Cruz Alta   RIO GRANDE   Tubarão   Laguna
Passo Fundo   Vacaria   Cabo Santa Marta Grande
Santa Maria   Santa Cruz   Bento Gonçalves   Criciúma
do Sul   Caxias do Sul   Araranguá
Montenegro   Nôvo Hamburgo
Cachoeira do Sul   São   Taquara
Leopoldo   Osorio
DO SUL   PÔRTO ALEGRE
São   Encantadas
Gabriel
Santana do   Camaquã
Livramento   Camaquã
Bagé   Sa. do Canguçu
Canguçu   Lagoa dos Patos
Pelotas   Mostardas
Dom Pedrito
Santana
AY   Melo   Rio Grande
Gregorio   Jaguarão
Rio Branco   Mirim
José Batlle   Sta. Clara   Lagoa Mirim
y Ordóñez   de Olimar
Treinta y Tres   Lagoa Mangueira
Santa Vitória do Palmar
Minas   Rocha
San Carlos
Maldonado
EVIDEO

OLIVEIRA   Campo   Cons.
Belo   Lafaiete
Ouro   Ponte Nova
Prêto   Carangola
Lavras   Barbacena   Cataguases
Três   Santos   Leopoldina
Coroações   Dumont   Juiz de Fora
Pouso   São   Três   Além Paraíba
Alegre   Lourenço   Rios
Itajubá   Mantiqueira   Paraíba do   Guarus
Cruzeiro   Volta   Barra do Pirai   Nova Friburgo
Guaratinguetá   Redonda   RIO DE JANEIRO   Macaé
Paulista   Barra   NITERÓI
Taubaté   Mansa   SÃO GONÇALO   Cabo Frio
S. J. dos Campos   Angra dos Reis   DUQUE DE CAXIAS   La. de Araruama
Mogi das Cruzes   Ilha Grande   NOVA IGUAÇU
Baía da Ilha Grande   RIO DE JANEIRO
Pta. de Juatinga   Tropic of Capricorn

Vitória
Alegre
Castelo
Cachoeiro
de Itapemirim
Itaperuna
Campuá
CAMPOS
Cabo de
São Tomé

ATLANTIC

OCEAN

5304

25

30

35

55   West from Greenwich   50   45   40   COPYRIGHT. GEORGE PHILIP & SON. LTD

1:8 000 000

50 0 50 100 150 miles
50 0 100 200 km

Regions and Provinces

ARAUCANIA
NEUQUÉN
RÍO NEGRO
LA PAMPA
LOS LAGOS
CHUBUT
SANTA CRUZ
MAGALLANES
TIERRA DEL FUEGO

Oceans and Seas

PACIFIC OCEAN
SOUTH ATLANTIC OCEAN
Golfo San Matías
Golfo San Jorge
Bahía Grande
Strait of Magellan
Golfo de Penas

Places (north to south, Argentina)

Colonia 25 de Mayo, Bernasconi, Tornquist 1243, Coronel Pringles, González Chaves, Juárez, Balcarce, Loberia, Oquendo, Necochea, Bahía Blanca, Punta Alta, Coronel Dorrego, Oriente, BUENOS AIRES, Villa Iris, Cuchillo-Có, Puelches, Colorado, Barda del Medio, Anelo, Río Colorado, Choele Choel, Lamarque, Gral. Conesa, Stroeder, Carmen de Patagones, Viedma, Pta. Rasa, B. Anegada, Neuquén, Cipolletti, Allen, Gral. Roca, Negro, Río Colorado, Mayor Buratovich, I. Trinidad

El Cuy, La Esperanza, Sa. Colorada, Valcheta, Aguada Cecilio, San Antonio Oeste, Pta. Norte, Pen. Valdés, G. Nuevo, Puerto Pirámides, Punta Delgada, Puerto Madryn, Los Menucos, Maquinchao, Meseta de Somuncurá, Cona Niyeu, Sierra Grande, Puerto Lobos, G. San José

Ingeniero Jacobacci, El Caín, Quetrequile, Gan Gan, Telsen, Gaimán, Rawson, Trelew, Gualjaina, Chubut, Las Plumas, Perdido, C. Raso, Paso de Indios, José de San Martín, Gran Laguna Salada, Camarones, B. Camarones, B. Dos Bahías

Alto Río Senguer, Facundo, L. Musters, L. Colhué Huapi, Sarmiento, Holdich, B. Bustamante, Golfo San Jorge, Comodoro Rivadavia, Colonia Las Heras, Caleta Olivia, Pico Truncado, Mazarredo, C. Tres Puntas, C. Blanco, Fitz Roy, Jaramillo, Deseado, Puerto Deseado, Pta. Medanosa

L. Buenos Aires, Perito Moreno, Los Antiguos, Las Monos, Los Monos, 1335, Bahía Laura, Chile Chico, L. Gral. Carrera, Cochrane, L. Pueyrredón, Lago Posadas, Las Horquetas, Mt. Inés 1120, Gob. Gregores, San Julián, Gran Altiplanicie Central, San Martín, L. Cardiel, L. Viedma, Tres Lagos, Chico, Shehuen, Cmte. Luis Piedrabuena, Santa Cruz, Bahía Grande, Puerto Coig, Esperanza, Coig, Guer Aike, Río Gallegos, Monte Dinero, C. Vírgenes, El Turbio, Gallegos

Mte. Fitzroy 3375, Col. Muralión 3600, Lago Argentino, Calafate

Chile places

Mulchén, Collipulli, Victoria, Cañete, Angol, Capitán Pastene, Temuco, Lautaro, Curacautín, Cherquenco, Zapala, Valdivia, Corral, Pta. Galera, La Unión, Osorno, Río Bueno, Puerto Varas, Puerto Montt, Ancud, Isla de Chiloé, Castro, Achao, Puerto Quellón, C. Quilán, I. Guafo, Islas Guaitecas, Chaitén, Esquel, Palena, Río Pico, Magdalena, Coihaique, Puerto Aisén, Balmaceda, Mayo, Río Mayo, C. Taitao, Peninsula de Taitao, C. Tres Montes, I. Javier, Golfo de Penas, Archipiélago Guayaneco, I. Campana, I. Patricio Lynch, I. Esmeralda, I. Mornington, I. Madre de Dios, I. Duque de York, C. Santiago, B. Salvación, I. Hanover, Arch. Reina Adelaida, I. Desolación, Punta Arenas, Pen. Brunswick, Santa Inés, I. Riesco, Puerto Natales, Seno Skyring, Seno de Otway, Porvenir, Dawson, Clarence, Capt. Aracena, Pen. Brecknock, I. Stewart, I. Londonderry, B. Cook, Pen. Hardy, B. Nassau, Islas Wollaston, Is. Hermite, Cabo de Hornos (Cape Horn), Islas Diego Ramírez

Isla Grande de Tierra del Fuego, Cerro Sombrero, San Sebastián, Río Grande, Misión Fagnano, L. Fagnano, Ushuaia, Canal Beagle, I. Navarino, I. Picton, I. Nueva, I. Lennox, I. de los Estados (Staten I.), Est. de Le Maire, C. San Diego, Mte. Darwin 2469, I. Hoste, Gordon

FALKLAND ISLANDS (ISLAS MALVINAS)

Jason Is., Pebble I., C. Dolphin, King George B., Queen Charlotte B., Mt. Adam 700, Weddell I., Port Darwin, C. Meredith, West Falkland, East Falkland, Mt. Usborne 705, Stanley, Falkland Sound, Beauchêne I.

Elevation scale

ft — m
9000 — 3000
6000 — 2000
4500 — 1500
3000 — 1000
1200 — 400
600 — 200
0 — 0
200 — 600
2000 — 6000
4000 — 12 000
m — ft

Projection: Lambert's Equivalent Azimuthal

West from Greenwich

1:60 000 000

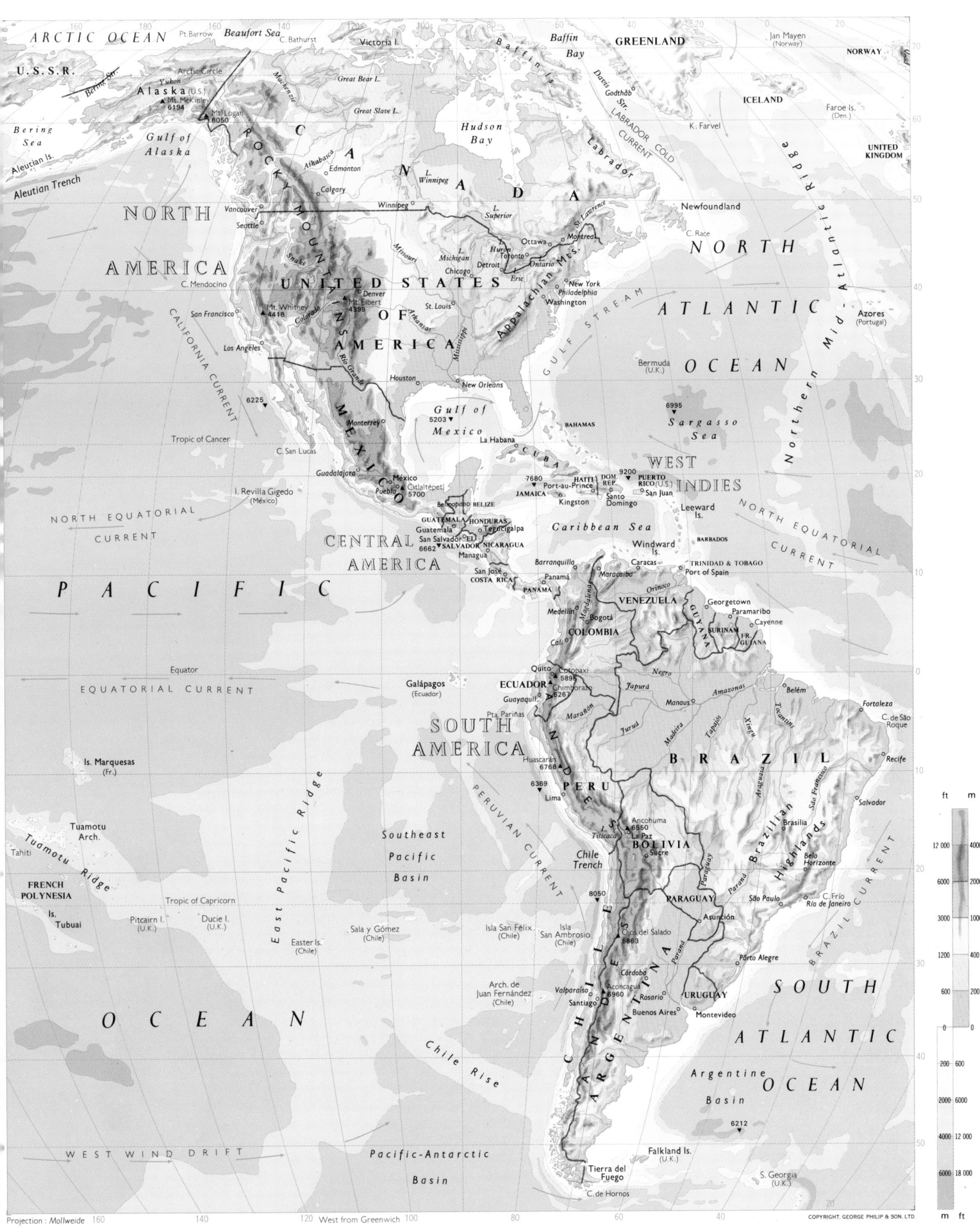

ARCTIC OCEAN
Pt.Barrow Beaufort Sea C. Bathurst Victoria I. Baffin Is. Baffin Bay GREENLAND Jan Mayen (Norway) NORWAY
U.S.S.R. Bering Str. Arctic Circle Yukon Alaska (U.S.) ▲Mt. McKinley 6194 Great Bear L. Mackenzie Great Slave L. Hudson Bay Godthåb LABRADOR COLD CURRENT K. Farvel ICELAND Faroe Is. (Den.)
Bering Sea Mt Logan 6050 Gulf of Alaska Athabasca Edmonton L. Winnipeg NORTH UNITED KINGDOM
Aleutian Is. Aleutian Trench Calgary Vancouver Seattle Winnipeg L. Superior St. Lawrence Newfoundland C. Race ATLANTIC
NORTH AMERICA C. Mendocino Snake Missouri L. Michigan Huron Toronto Ottawa Montreal NORTH
AMERICA San Francisco UNITED STATES Denver Mt. Elbert St. Louis Chicago Detroit Erie Ontario New York Philadelphia Washington ATLANTIC OCEAN Azores (Portugal)
Los Angeles Mt. Whitney 4418 Colorado OF 4395 Arkansas Appalachian Mts. GULF STREAM Bermuda (U.K.)
Tropic of Cancer 6225▼ AMERICA Rio Grande Mississippi Houston New Orleans 6995▼ Sargasso Sea
C. San Lucas MEXICO Monterrey Gulf of 5203▼ Mexico BAHAMAS WEST
Guadalajara México Citlaltépetl La Habana CUBA HAITI DOM. 9200 PUERTO INDIES
I. Revilla Gigedo (México) Pueblo 5700 Belmopan BELIZE 7680▼ Port-au-Prince REP. RICO (U.S.) Leeward NORTH EQUATORIAL
NORTH EQUATORIAL GUATEMALA HONDURAS JAMAICA Kingston Santo Domingo San Juan Is.
CURRENT CENTRAL Guatemala Tegucigalpa Caribbean Sea BARBADOS CURRENT
San Salvador EL SALVADOR NICARAGUA Windward Is. TRINIDAD & TOBAGO
AMERICA 6662 Managua Barranquilla Caracas Port of Spain
PACIFIC San José COSTA RICA Panamá Maracaibo Orinoco
PANAMA VENEZUELA Georgetown Paramaribo
Medellín Bogotá GUYANA SURINAM Cayenne FR. GUIANA
COLOMBIA Cali Negro Belém
Galápagos Quito Cotopaxi Japurá Manaus Amazonas Fortaleza C. de São
Equator (Ecuador) ECUADOR 5895 Marañón Madeira Roque
EQUATORIAL CURRENT Guayaquil Chimborazo 6267 Juruá Tapajós Xingu Recife
Pta. Pariñas SOUTH Huascarán Purus Tocantins BRAZIL
Is. Marquesas (Fr.) AMERICA 6768 Salvador
East Pacific Ridge 6369▼ PERU São Francisco Brazilian
Tuamotu Arch. Lima Ancohuma Highlands
Tahiti Southeast 6550 La Paz Brasilia
Tuamotu Ridge Pacific L. Titicaca BOLIVIA Sucre Belo Horizonte BRAZIL CURRENT
FRENCH Basin Chile Trench São Paulo C. Frio
POLYNESIA Tropic of Capricorn 8050▼ Rio de Janeiro
Is. Tubuai PARAGUAY Paraná Paraguay Paraná Pôrto Alegre
Pitcairn I. (U.K.) Ducie I. (U.K.) Sala y Gómez (Chile) Isla San Félix Isla Asunción
Easter Is. (Chile) (Chile) San Ambrosio Ojos del Salado Paraná
Arch. de (Chile) 6863 Córdoba SOUTH
Juan Fernández Córdoba Rosario Aconcagua URUGUAY
OCEAN (Chile) Valparaíso 6960 Buenos Aires Montevideo ATLANTIC
Santiago ANDES ARGENTINA Argentine OCEAN
WEST WIND DRIFT Chile Rise Basin 6212▼
Falkland Is. (U.K.) S. Georgia (U.K.)
Pacific-Antarctic Tierra del Fuego
Basin C. de Hornos

Projection : Mollweide 160 140 120 West from Greenwich 100 80 60 40 20

ft m
12 000 4000
6000 2000
3000 1000
1200 400
600 200
0
200 600
2000 6000
4000 12 000
6000 18 000
m ft

1:20 000 000

100 0 100 200 300 400 500 miles

100 0 200 400 600 800 km

ATLANTIC OCEAN

NORWEGIAN SEA

NORTH SEA

BALTIC SEA

BLACK SEA

CASPIAN SEA -28

ADRIATIC SEA

MEDITERRANEAN SEA

Tyrrhenian Sea

Ligurian Sea

Ionian Sea

Aegean Sea

Ural Mountains

Mt. 1617

Ob

Pechora

Kama

Obshchi Syrt

Volga Uplands

Volga

N. Dvina

Mezen

Onega

L. Onega

Ume

Kanin Peninsula

Kola Peninsula

White Sea

Tundra

Lapland

Finland

Scandinavia

L. Ladoga

L. Onega

Chudskoye

Neva

Central Russian Uplands

Don

Don

Volga

Oka

Kama

Manych

Tsimlyansk Res.

Rybinsk Res.

Ural

Sea of Azov

Kerch

Str. of Kerch

Crimea

Caucasus

5633

2211

Armenia

Kurdistan

5165

Anatolia

Taurus

3770

1766

Cyprus

5951

Euphrates

Rion

Terek

Kuban

Dnepr (Dnieper)

Ukraine

Pripyat Marshes

Pripyat

Bug

Dnestr (Dniester)

Prut

Danube

Wallachia

Transylvanian Alps

Balkans

Peloponnese

Pindus

Morea

Ionian Is.

5121

C. Matapan

Str. of Otranto

Dinaric Alps

2914

Saso

Apennines

4807

Etna

3263

Sicily

Str. of Messina

C. Bon

Malta

Corsica

Sardinia

C. Blanco

Str. of Bonifacio

Balearic Is.

Plain of Hungary

Carpathians

2655

Tatra

Tisza

Danube

Drava

Sava

Sudetes

Erz. Geb.

Moravian Heights

Bohemian For.

Bakony

Brenner P.

Elbe

Weser

Rhine

Meuse

Rhone

Saône

Jura

Vosges

Black For.

Main

Harz 1142

Weser

Danube

Neckar

Maas

Netherlands

Heligoland

Jutland

Kattegat

Skagerrak

Lindesnes

Gotland

Öland

Vänern

Vättern

Mälaren

Indals

Glommen

2469

Galdhöpiggen

2123

Kebnekaise

Vesterålen

Lofoten

North Cape

Nordkinn

Linaes

Stavanger

Dogger Bank

Fisher Bank

Shetland Is.

Orkney Is.

Hebrides

Faröe Is.

British Isles

Great Britain

Ireland

Snowdon 1085

Pennines

Thames

Land's End

English Channel

Irish Sea

Brittany

Seine

Loire

Garonne

Bay of Biscay

Gironde

Gulf of Bothnia

Gulf of Finland

Gulf of Riga

Niemen

Wisła (Vistula)

Odra (Oder)

Po

Iceland

1491

Hekla

2119

Vatnajökull

Arctic Circle

Rockall

Valentia

C. Clear

3734

ICELAND

Central Massif 1886

Mt. D'Or

Cévennes

Gulf of Lions

Pyrenees

4404

Pic de Nethou

Cantabrian Mts.

Old Castile

New Castile

Iberian Peninsula

Sierra Morena

Guadalquivir

Andalusia

Sa. Nevada

3478

Str. of Gibraltar

Maritime Atlas

Plateau of the Shotts

Sa. de Guadarrama

Sa. de Estrela

Ebro

Duero

Tagus

C. de Rocha

C. Finisterre

C. Trafalgar

C. Spartel

C. St. Vincent

4861

Picos de Europa

m 4000 2000 1000 600 200 0

ft 12000 6000 3000 1200 600 2000 4000 6000 12000

1:20 000 000

Projection Bonne   West from Greenwich 0 East from Greenwich

COPYRIGHT GEORGE PHILIP & SON, LTD.

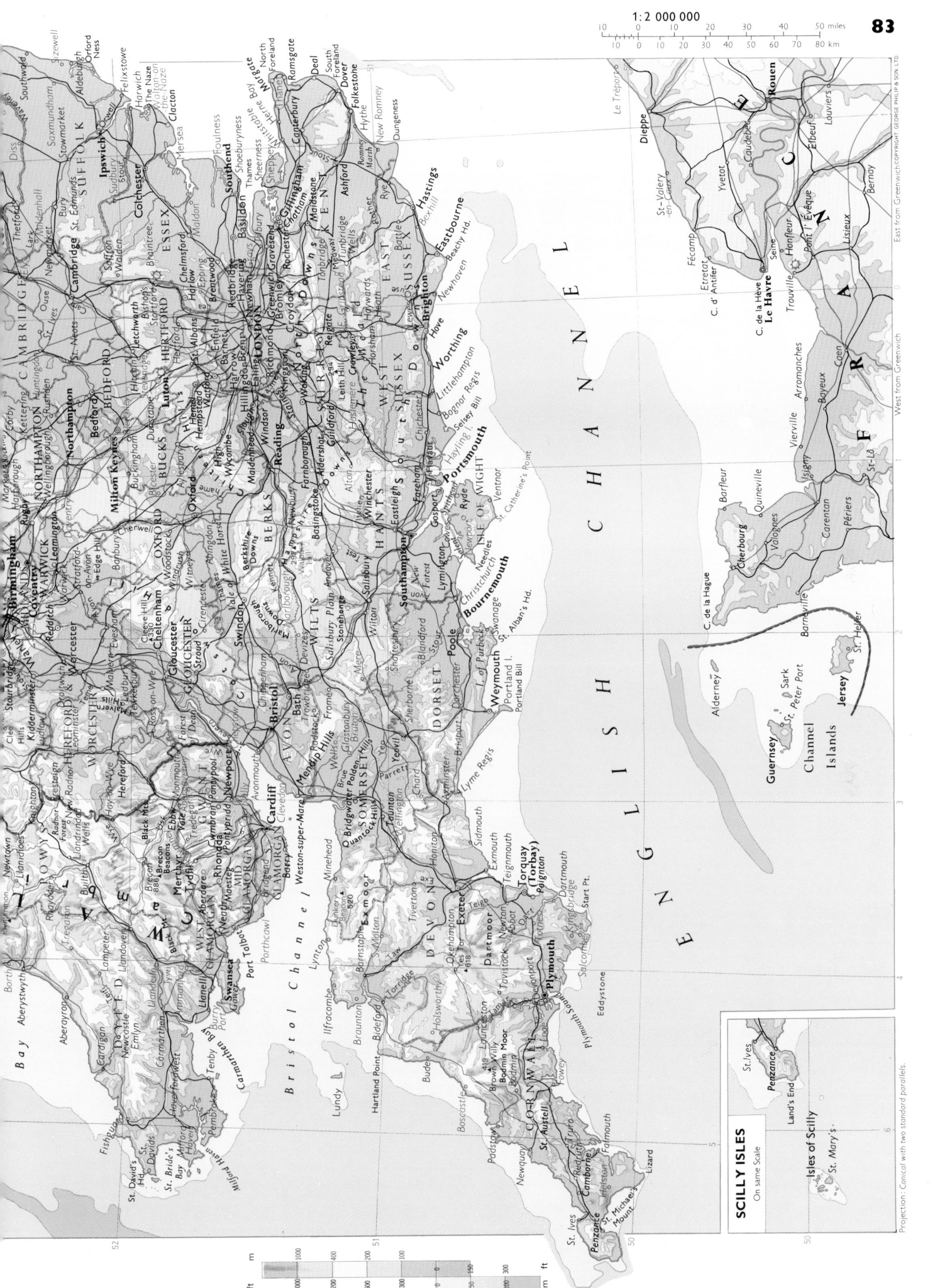

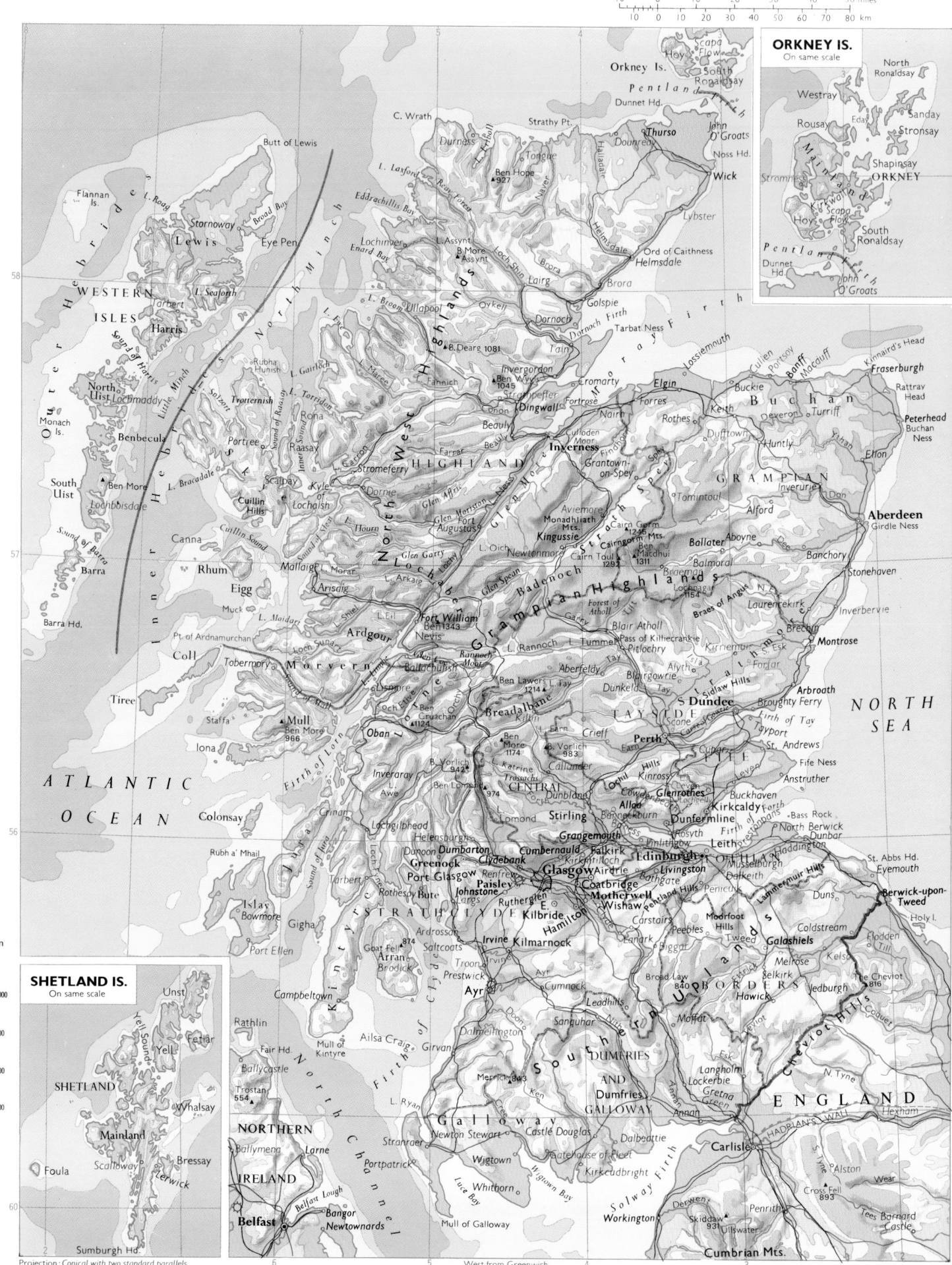

1 : 2 000 000

ORKNEY IS.
On same scale

SHETLAND IS.
On same scale

WESTERN ISLES

Outer Hebrides

Inner Hebrides

NORTH WEST HIGHLANDS

GRAMPIAN HIGHLANDS

ATLANTIC OCEAN

NORTH SEA

BUCHAN

GRAMPIAN

TAYSIDE

FIFE

CENTRAL

STRATHCLYDE

KINTYRE

South Uplands

BORDERS

DUMFRIES AND GALLOWAY

GALLOWAY

Cheviot Hills

ENGLAND

NORTHERN IRELAND

North Channel

Solway Firth

Cumbrian Mts.

Projection : Conical with two standard parallels.   West from Greenwich   COPYRIGHT. GEORGE PHILIP & SON. LTD.

ft   m
3000   1000
       400
1200
600   200
300   100
0   0
50   150
100   300
m   ft

1 : 2 000 000

Towns underlined in Northern Ireland give their
names to the Districts in which they stand

The remaining Districts are:—

1 Fermanagh	5 Castlereagh
2 Moyle	6 Ards
3 Newtownabbey	7 Down
4 North Down	8 Newry & Mourne

1:4 000 000

20   0   20   40   60   80   100 miles
20 0 20 40 60 80 100 120 140 160 km

Inset maps

Orkney Is.
Westray · N. Ronaldsay
Sanday
Rousay · Stronsay
Hoy · Kirkwall
Pentland Firth · South Ronaldsay
Thurso · Wick

Shetland Is.
Unst
Yell
Foula · Mainland · Lerwick
Fair I.

Scale (elevation)

ft   m
3000 1000
1800 600
1200 400
600   200
300   100
0   0
      100 · 300
      200 · 600
      400 · 1200
m   ft

Main map labels

ATLANTIC OCEAN

NORTH SEA

IRISH SEA

ENGLISH CHANNEL

St. George's Channel

North Channel

Bristol Channel

Cardigan Bay

Scotland

Pentland Firth · Thurso · Wick
Lairg · L. Shin · Golspie
Ullapool · Dingwall · Nairn · Elgin · Lossiemouth · Banff · Fraserburgh
Moray Firth · Peterhead
Inverness
Kingussie · Ballater · Balmoral · Stonehaven
SCOTLAND · Grampian Mts.
Fort William · Ben Nevis 1344 · Blair Atholl · Aberdeen
Mallaig · Forfar · Montrose · Arbroath
North West Highlands
Oban · Crieff · **Perth** · **Dundee** · Firth of Tay · St. Andrews
Stirling · Kinross · Cupar
Loch Lomond · Alloa · Dunfermline · Kirkcaldy · Forth
Greenock · Dumbarton · **Edinburgh** · Dunbar
Paisley · **Glasgow** · Falkirk · Firth of Forth · Haddington
Kilmarnock · Hamilton · Motherwell · Peebles · Galashiels · Berwick-on-Tweed
Saltcoats · Irvine · Prestwick · Selkirk · Jedburgh · Duns
Ayr · Sanquhar · Moffat · Hawick · Cheviot Hills · Alnwick
Dumfries · Wigtown · Kirkcudbright · Solway Firth

Lewis · Stornoway
Harris · North Minch
North Uist · Benbecula · South Uist · Barra
Outer Hebrides
Skye · Kyle of Lochalsh · Portree · Rhum · Eigg · Coll · Tiree
Inner Hebrides · Mull · Staffa · Iona · Colonsay · Jura · Islay · Campbeltown
St. Kilda · Firth of Lorn · Firth of Clyde · Arran

Malin Hd. · Tory I.

Northern Ireland / Ireland

Aran Is. · Coleraine · Portrush · Antrim Mts.
Derryveagh Mts. · Londonderry · Larne
Letterkenny · Lifford · Ballymena
Donegal · Omagh · NORTHERN IRELAND · Antrim · Bangor
Donegal Bay · Enniskillen · Armagh · Downpatrick · **Belfast** · Lisburn
Killala Bay · Sligo · Clones · Monaghan · Dundrum
Ballina · Leitrim · Cavan · Newry · Mourne Mts. · Greenore
Achill I. · Castlebar · L. Mask · Roscommon · Longford · Dundalk · Carlingford
Clare I. · Westport · Mullingar · Drogheda
Connemara · L. Corrib · Athlone · Balbriggan
Galway · **IRELAND** · Athenry · Tullamore · **Dublin** (Baile Átha Cliath)
Galway Bay · Birr · Kildare · Bray · Dun Laoghaire
Ennis · Nenagh · Port Laoise · Carlow · Wicklow Mts. · Wicklow
Loop Hd. · Kilrush · Thurles · Kilkenny · Arklow
Limerick · Tipperary · Golden Vale · Clonmel · Enniscorthy · New Ross · Wexford
Listowel · Mallow · Blackwater · Carrick-on-Suir · Waterford · Rosslare
Tralee · Fermoy · Dungarvan · Youghal · Carnsore Pt.
Macgillycuddy's Reeks 1040 · Killarney · **Cork** · Cobh · Cork Harbour
Cahirciveen · Blarney · Lee · Kinsale
Castletown Bere · Bandon · C. Clear · Bantry
St. David's Hd. · Fishguard

England & Wales

Isle of Man · Douglas
Whitehaven · St. Bee's Hd. · Carlisle · Appleby
Cumbrian Mts. · 978 Scafell · Kendal · Penrith
Barrow · Windermere · N York Moors · Whitby
Newcastle · Tynemouth · South Shields · Sunderland
Gateshead · Durham · Hartlepool
Stockton · Darlington · Middlesbrough
Pennine Range · Northallerton · Scarborough
Morecambe Bay · Lancaster · Ripon · York · Flamborough Hd.
Blackpool · Preston · Burnley · Keighley · Bradford · Leeds · Beverley · Hull
Blackburn · Bolton · Halifax · Wakefield · Barnsley · Scunthorpe · Grimsby · Spurn Hd.
Liverpool · St. Helens · Salford · Huddersfield · Oldham · Doncaster · Rotherham
Birkenhead · **Manchester** · Stockport · Sheffield · Lincoln · Skegness
Llandudno · Macclesfield · Chesterfield · The Wash
Rhyl · Chester · Crewe · Stoke-on-Trent · Derby · Nottingham · Grantham · Boston · Kings Lynn
Anglesey · Beaumaris · Denbigh · Ruthin · Wrexham · Mansfield · Sleaford
Holyhead · Caernarfon Bay · Cambrian Mts. · Snowdon 1085 · Shrewsbury · Stafford · Wolverhampton · Leicester · Oakham · Peterborough · **Norwich** · Gt. Yarmouth
Pwllheli · Dolgellau (Dolgelley) · Montgomery · Walsall · Rugby · Lowestoft
Cardigan Bay · Aberystwyth · Welshpool · **Birmingham** · Coventry · Northampton · Huntingdon · Bedford · Cambridge · Bury St. Edmunds · Ipswich
Cardigan · Rhayader · Llandrindod Wells · Presteigne · Kidderminster · Leamington · Stratford-on-Avon · Wellingborough · The Naze
Haverfordwest · Brecon · Hereford · Worcester · Warwick · Buckingham · Colchester
Milford Haven · Carmarthen · Merthyr Tydfil · Gloucester · Cheltenham · Oxford · Aylesbury · Hertford · Chiltern Hills · St. Albans · Watford · Chelmsford
Pembroke · Llanelli · Rhondda · Newport · Bristol · Bath · Swindon · Windsor · Reading · **LONDON** · Chatham · Southend · Thames · Margate
Swansea · Port Talbot · Cardiff · Weston-super-Mare · Wells · Trowbridge · Salisbury Plain · Aldershot · Guildford · Reigate · Maidstone · Canterbury · Dover · Folkestone
Lundy I. · Ilfracombe · Barnstaple · Exmoor · Taunton · Yeovil · Salisbury · Winchester · N. Downs · The Weald · Ashford · Hastings
Hartland Point · Bude · Southampton · Chichester · Portsmouth · South Downs · Brighton · Worthing · Eastbourne · Lewes · Newhaven
Dartmoor · Exeter · Dorchester · Weymouth · Bournemouth · Isle of Wight · Newport · Needles
Devonport · Plymouth · Torquay · Dartmouth · Poole
St. Austell · Truro · Camborne · Penzance · Falmouth · Land's End · Lizard · Start Pt.
Scilly Is.

Dieppe

West from Greenwich 0 East from Greenwich

COPYRIGHT. GEORGE PHILIP & SON, LTD.

1:2 500 000

10 0 10 20 30 40 50 miles
10 0 10 20 30 40 50 60 70 80 km

NORTH SEA

ENGLAND

N E T H E R L A N D S

B E L G I U M

G E R M A N Y

F R A N C E

LUXEMBOURG

AMSTERDAM
's-GRAVENHAGE (The Hague)
ROTTERDAM
Utrecht
Haarlem
Leiden
Groningen
Leeuwarden
Nijmegen
Arnhem
Eindhoven
Tilburg
Breda
Dordrecht
Antwerpen
BRUSSEL (Bruxelles)
Gent (Gand)
Brugge (Bruges)
Oostende (Ostend)
Liège
Namur
Charleroi
Mons
Hasselt
Maastricht
Luxembourg
DÜSSELDORF
KÖLN (Cologne)
DORTMUND
ESSEN
DUISBURG
Münster
Osnabrück
Bonn
Aachen
Bremerhaven
Oldenburg
Wiesbaden
Mainz
Saarbrücken
Trier
Koblenz
Metz
Nancy
Strasbourg
Reims
Amiens
Calais
Dunkerque
Lille
PARIS

Projection: Conical with two standard parallels

East from Greenwich

COPYRIGHT. GEORGE PHILIP & SON. LTD.

ft   m
1200 400
600 200
0
50 150
m   ft

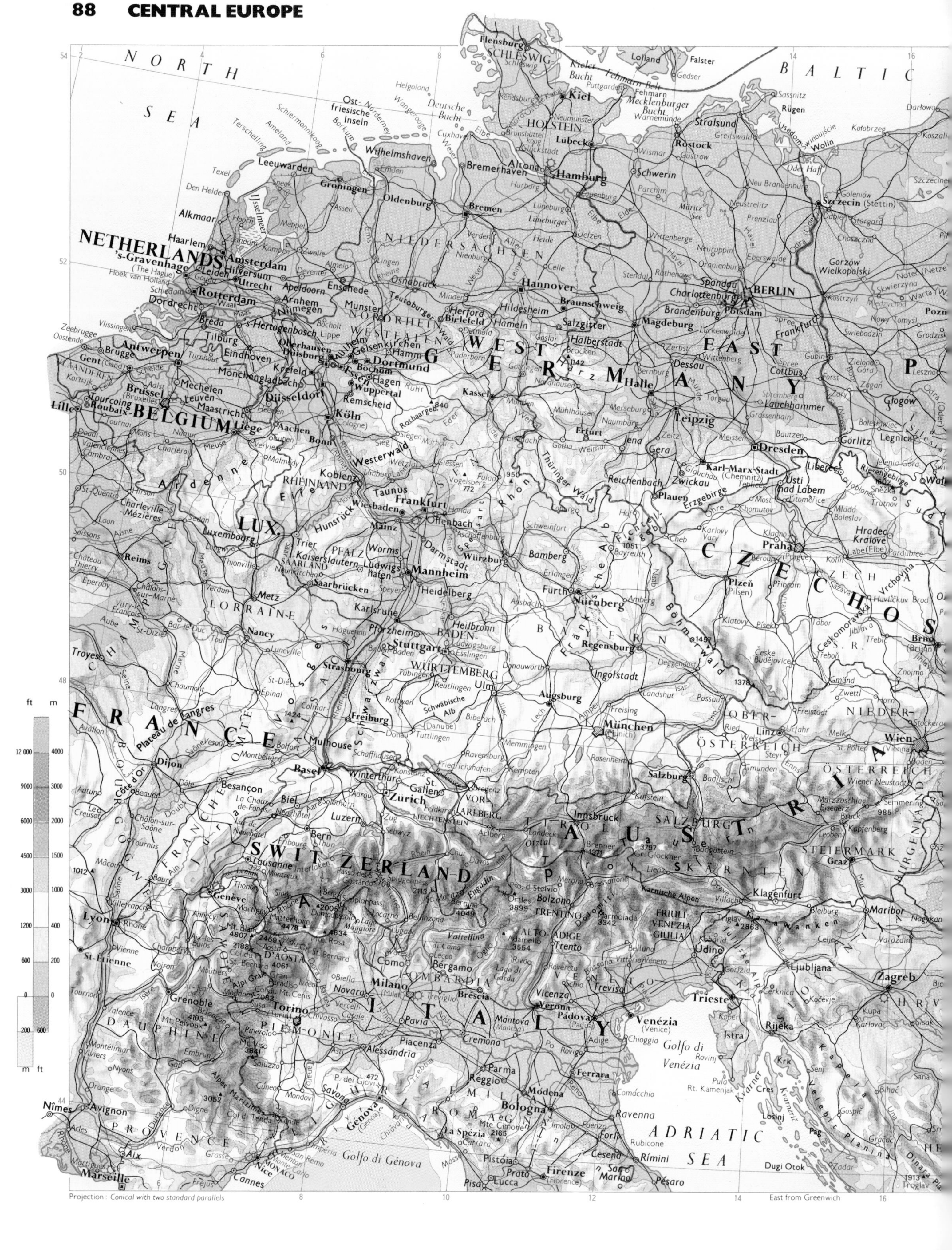

NORTH SEA

BALTIC

NETHERLANDS
's-Gravenhage (The Hague)
Hoek van Holland
Amsterdam
Haarlem
Leiden
Utrecht
Rotterdam
Dordrecht
Breda
Tilburg
's-Hertogenbosch
Eindhoven
Arnhem
Nijmegen
Groningen
Leeuwarden
Den Helder
Alkmaar
Hoorn
Zaandam
Hilversum
Apeldoorn
Deventer
Zwolle
Kampen
Assen
Meppel
Enschede
Almelo
Lingen
Oldenburg
Bremerhaven
Bremen
Wilhelmshaven
Emden

BELGIUM
Brussel (Bruxelles)
Antwerpen
Gent (Gand)
Brugge
Oostende
Zeebrugge
Vlissingen
Mechelen
Leuven
Maastricht
Liège
Namur
Charleroi
Mons
Tournai
Kortrijk
Aalst

Lille
Roubaix
Tourcoing

WEST GERMANY
Flensburg
SCHLESWIG
Kiel
HOLSTEIN
Neumünster
Lübeck
Hamburg
Altona
Harburg
Lüneburg
Celle
Hannover
Braunschweig
Hildesheim
Hameln
Herford
Bielefeld
Detmold
Paderborn
Osnabrück
Münster
NORDRHEIN WESTFALEN
NIEDERSACHSEN
Salzgitter
Goslar
Halberstadt
Kassel
Dortmund
Essen
Duisburg
Düsseldorf
Köln (Cologne)
Bonn
Aachen
Krefeld
Mönchengladbach
Oberhausen
Gelsenkirchen
Bochum
Hagen
Wuppertal
Remscheid
Solingen
Siegen
Koblenz
Wiesbaden
Frankfurt
Offenbach
Mainz
Darmstadt
Worms
Mannheim
Ludwigshafen
Heidelberg
Heilbronn
Würzburg
Schweinfurt
Bamberg
Erlangen
Fürth
Nürnberg
Regensburg
Ingolstadt
Augsburg
München (Munich)
Freising
Landshut
Ulm
Reutlingen
Tübingen
Stuttgart
Esslingen
Pforzheim
Karlsruhe
Baden
Freiburg
Rottweil
Trier
Kaiserslautern
Saarbrücken
Neunkirchen
Speyer

EAST GERMANY
Berlin
Potsdam
Spandau
Charlottenburg
Brandenburg
Magdeburg
Dessau
Halle
Leipzig
Erfurt
Weimar
Jena
Gera
Zwickau
Karl-Marx-Stadt (Chemnitz)
Plauen
Reichenbach
Dresden
Görlitz
Cottbus
Schwerin
Rostock
Stralsund
Greifswald
Neubrandenburg
Wismar
Güstrow
Parchim
Wittenberge
Stendal
Neuruppin
Oranienburg
Eberswalde
Frankfurt
Bautzen
Meissen
Bernburg
Zeitz
Naumburg
Merseburg
Torgau
Wittenberg

CZECHOSLOVAKIA
Praha (Prague)
Plzeň (Pilsen)
Ústí nad Labem
Teplice
Most
Cheb
Karlovy Vary
Litoměřice
Mladá Boleslav
Hradec Králové
Pardubice
Liberec
Jablonec
Trutnov
České Budějovice
Tábor
Jihlava
Třebíč
Brno (Brünn)
Znojmo
Gmünd

AUSTRIA / ÖSTERREICH
Wien (Vienna)
Linz
Salzburg
Innsbruck
Klagenfurt
Graz
Wiener Neustadt
St. Pölten
Villach
Bleiburg
Leoben
Bruck
Kapfenberg
Eisenerz
TIROL
SALZBURG
STEIERMARK
KÄRNTEN
BURGENLAND

SWITZERLAND
Zürich
Basel
Bern
Genève
Lausanne
Luzern
St. Gallen
Winterthur
Biel
Neuchâtel
Fribourg
Montreux
Interlaken
Davos
St. Moritz
Bellinzona
Locarno
Lugano
Chur
LIECHTENSTEIN
Vaduz

FRANCE
Lyon
St-Étienne
Grenoble
Valence
Metz
Nancy
Strasbourg
Mulhouse
Belfort
Besançon
Dijon
Colmar
Épinal
St-Dié
Reims
Troyes
Chaumont
Châlons-sur-Marne
Verdun
Thionville
Luxembourg
LUX
LORRAINE
CHAMPAGNE
BOURGOGNE
FRANCHE-COMTÉ
DAUPHINÉ
PROVENCE
SAVOIE
Chambéry
Annecy
Mont Blanc 4478
Matterhorn
Monte Rosa 4634
Nîmes
Avignon
Aix
Arles
Marseille
Cannes
Nice
MONACO
Monte-Carlo

ITALY
Milano
Torino
Genova
Bologna
Firenze (Florence)
Venezia (Venice)
Padova (Padua)
Verona
Vicenza
Brescia
Bergamo
Novara
Vercelli
Alessandria
Asti
Cuneo
Savona
Imperia
San Remo
Pavia
Cremona
Piacenza
Parma
Reggio
Modena
Ferrara
Ravenna
Rimini
Pesaro
Forlì
Cesena
Faenza
Imola
Mantova (Mantua)
Rovigo
Chioggia
Treviso
Vittorio Veneto
Belluno
Trento
Bolzano
Bressanone
Merano
Udine
Gorizia
Trieste
La Spézia
Carrara
Pisa
Lucca
Pistoia
Prato
Cremona
LOMBARDIA
PIEMONTE
LIGURIA
VENETO
TRENTINO
ALTO-ADIGE
FRIULI-VENEZIA GIULIA
EMILIA-ROMAGNA
VALLE D'AOSTA
Aosta

YUGOSLAVIA
Ljubljana
Zagreb
Maribor
Celje
Rijeka
Koper
Varaždin
Karlovac

ADRIATIC SEA
Golfo di Venezia
Golfo di Génova

Dugi Otok
Zadar

Projection: Conical with two standard parallels
East from Greenwich

ft m
12 000 4000
9000   3000
6000   2000
4500   1500
3000   1000
1200   400
600   200
0   0
200   600
m ft

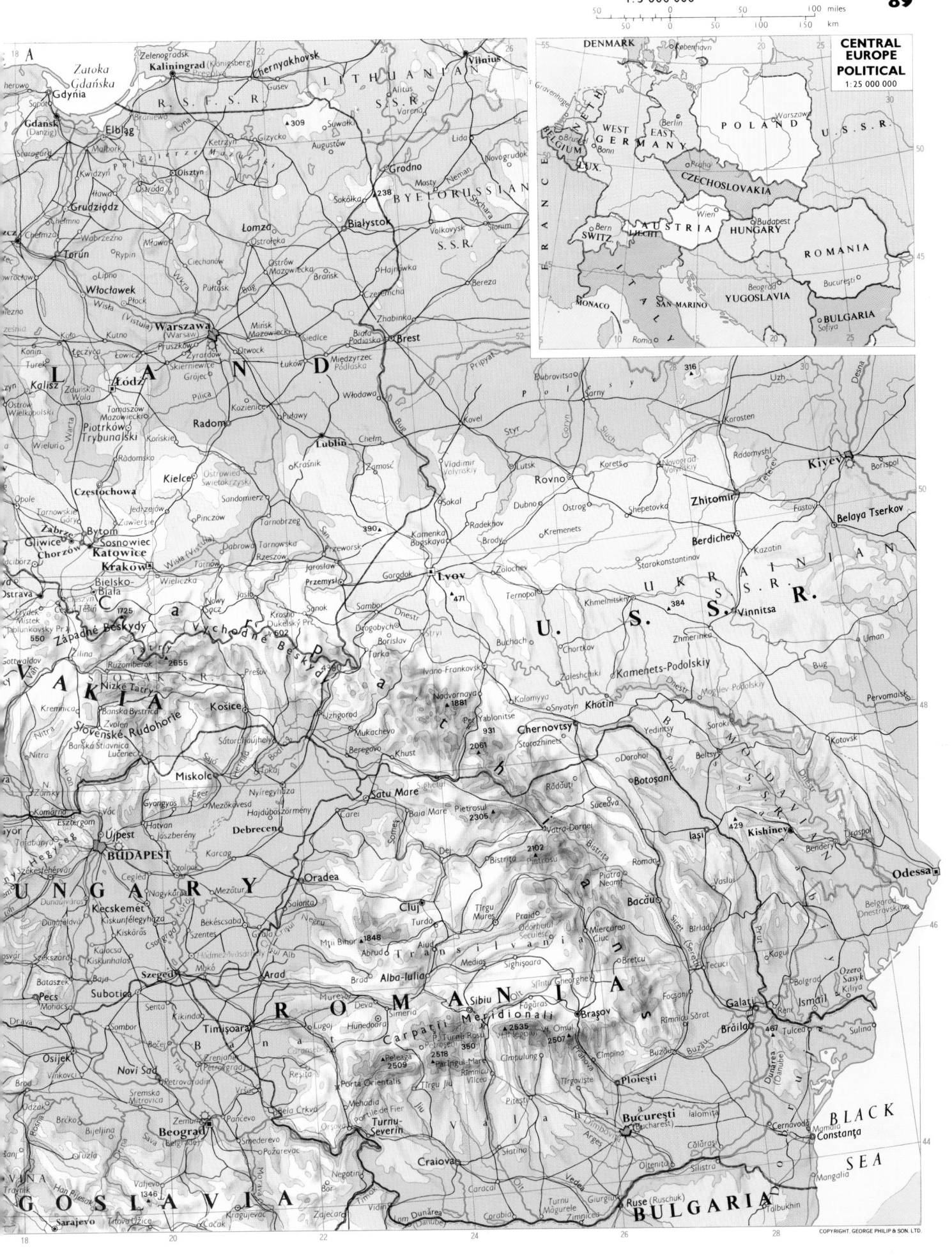

1 : 5 000 000

50   0   50   100 miles
50   0   50   100   150 km

DENMARK   København

WEST
GERMANY   EAST   Berlin   POLAND   U.S.S.R.
BELGIUM   Bonn   GERMANY   Warszawa
's Gravenhage   Brussel
LUX.   Praha
CZECHOSLOVAKIA

FRANCE   Bern   LIECHT.   Wien   Budapest
SWITZ.   AUSTRIA   HUNGARY   ROMANIA

ITALY   Beograd   Bucureşti

MONACO   SAN MARINO   YUGOSLAVIA
Roma   BULGARIA
Sofiya

COPYRIGHT. GEORGE PHILIP & SON. LTD.

Principal place names on main map

Zatoka Gdańska
Gdynia
Gdańsk (Danzig)
Elbląg
Kaliningrad (Königsberg)
Zelenogradsk
Chernyakhovsk
Gusev
LITHUANIAN S.S.R.
Vilnius

R.S.F.S.R.
Braniewo
Olsztyn
Grudziądz
Toruń
Włocławek
Łomża
Białystok
BYELORUSSIAN S.S.R.
Grodno
Suwałki
Augustów

Warszawa (Warsaw)
Łódź
Radom
Lublin
Kielce
Częstochowa
Kraków
Katowice
Przemyśl
Lvov
UKRAINIAN U.S.S.R.
Kiyev

SLOVAKIA
Košice
BUDAPEST
HUNGARY
Debrecen
Miskolc

ROMANIA
Oradea
Cluj
Satu Mare
Arad
Timişoara
Sibiu
Braşov
Bucureşti (Bucharest)
Ploieşti
Craiova
Galaţi
Constanţa

YUGOSLAVIA
Beograd
Novi Sad
Sarajevo

BULGARIA
Ruse (Ruschuk)
Sofiya

Odessa
Kishinev
MOLDAVIAN S.S.R.

BLACK SEA

1:5 000 000

50   0   50   100 miles
50   0   50   100   150 km

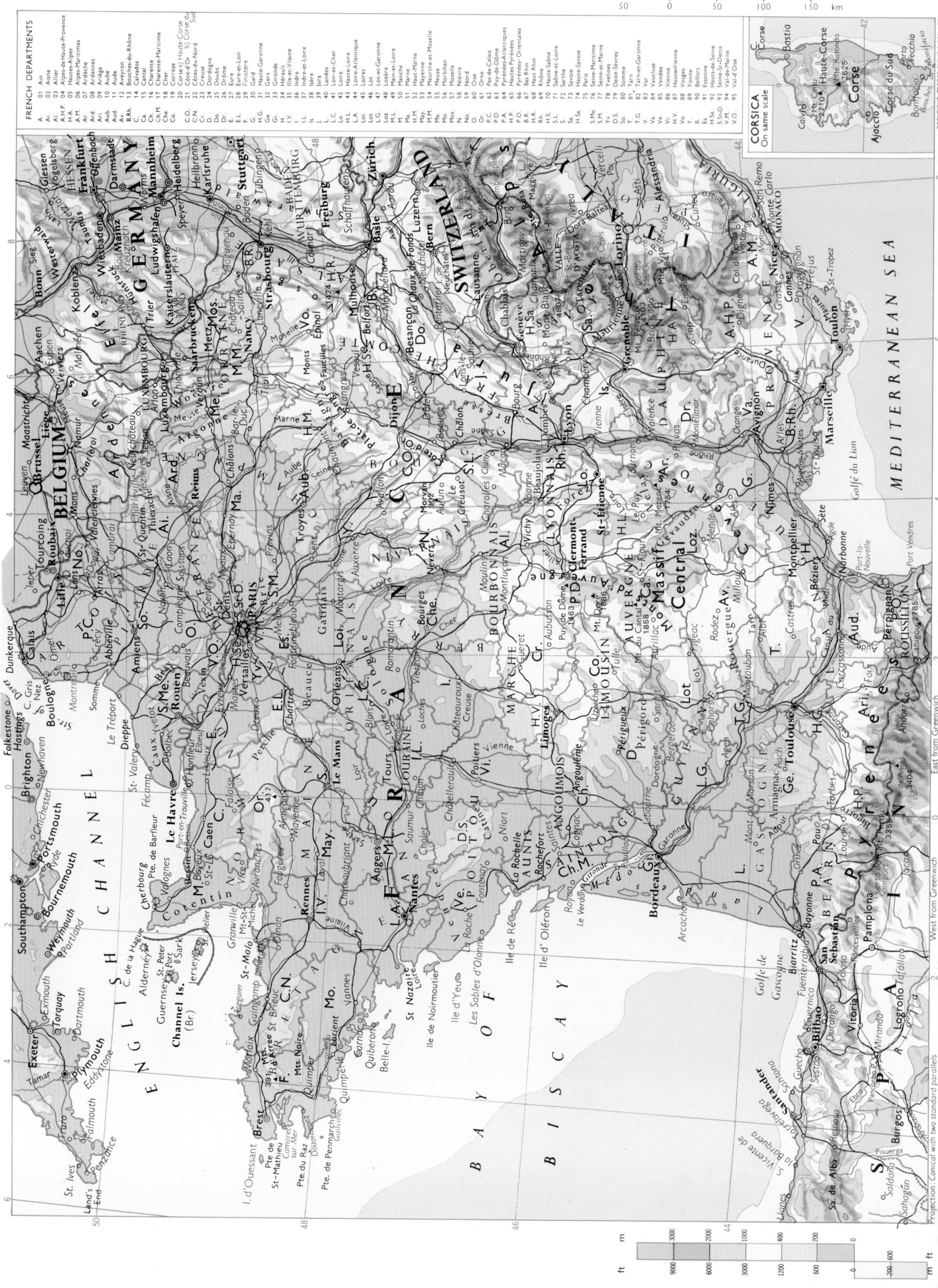

FRENCH DEPARTMENTS

		01	Ain
A.	Ai.	02	Aisne
Al.		03	Allier
H.A.		04	Alpes-de-Haute-Provence
H.-Alpes		05	Hautes-Alpes
A.M.		06	Alpes-Maritimes
Ard.		07	Ardèche
Ard.		08	Ardennes
Ar.		09	Ariège
Aud.		10	Aube
Aud.		11	Aude
Av.		12	Aveyron
B.Rh.		13	Bouches-du-Rhône
Ca.		14	Calvados
Ch.		15	Cantal
Ch.M.		16	Charente
Ch.		17	Charente-Maritime
Ch.		18	Cher
Co.		19	Corrèze
C.O.		20 a)	Haute-Corse
		20 b)	Corse du Sud
C.N.		21	Côte-d'Or
Cr.		22	Côtes-du-Nord
Cr.		23	Creuse
Do.		24	Dordogne
Do.		25	Doubs
Dr.		26	Drôme
E.L.		27	Eure
E.		28	Eure-et-Loir
Fi.		29	Finistère
G.		30	Gard
H.G.		31	Haute-Garonne
Ge.		32	Gers
Gi.		33	Gironde
H.		34	Hérault
I.V.		35	Ille-et-Vilaine
I.		36	Indre
I.L.		37	Indre-et-Loire
Is.		38	Isère
Ju.		39	Jura
L.		40	Landes
L.C.		41	Loir-et-Cher
Lo.		42	Loire
H.L.		43	Haute-Loire
L.A.		44	Loire-Atlantique
Loi.		45	Loiret
Lot		46	Lot
L.G.		47	Lot-et-Garonne
Loz.		48	Lozère
M.L.		49	Maine-et-Loire
Ma.		50	Manche
Mar.		51	Marne
H.Ma.		52	Haute-Marne
May.		53	Mayenne
M.M.		54	Meurthe-et-Moselle
Me.		55	Meuse
Mo.		56	Morbihan
Mos.		57	Moselle
		58	Nièvre
No.		59	Nord
O.		60	Oise
Or.		61	Orne
P.C.		62	Pas-de-Calais
P. de D.		63	Puy-de-Dôme
P.A.		64	Pyrénées-Atlantiques
H.P.		65	Hautes-Pyrénées
P.O.		66	Pyrénées-Orientales
B.Rh.		67	Bas-Rhin
H.R.		68	Haut-Rhin
Rh.		69	Rhône
H.Saône		70	Haute-Saône
S.L.		71	Saône-et-Loire
Sa.		72	Sarthe
Sav.		73	Savoie
H.Sa.		74	Haute-Savoie
		75	Paris
S.Me.		76	Seine-Maritime
S.M.		77	Seine-et-Marne
Y.		78	Yvelines
D.S.		79	Deux-Sèvres
So.		80	Somme
T.		81	Tarn
T.G.		82	Tarn-et-Garonne
Va.		83	Var
Va.		84	Vaucluse
V.		85	Vendée
Vi.		86	Vienne
H.V.		87	Haute-Vienne
Vo.		88	Vosges
Y.		89	Yonne
Be.		90	Belfort
E.		91	Essonne
H.Se.		92	Hauts-de-Seine
S.S-D.		93	Seine-St-Denis
V.M.		94	Val-de-Marne
V.O.		95	Val-d'Oise

CORSICA
On same scale

Corse
Bastia
Haute-Corse
Mte Rotondo 2625
Corse du Sud
Porto Vecchio
Bonifacio
Calvi
Ajaccio
Corse

COPYRIGHT GEORGE PHILIP & SON, LTD.

MEDITERRANEAN SEA

GERMANY

BELGIUM

SWITZERLAND

ENGLISH CHANNEL

BAY OF BISCAY

SPAIN

F R A N C E

MASSIF CENTRAL

P Y R É N É E S

A L P S

Paris
Lyon
Marseille
Bordeaux
Toulouse
Nantes
Rennes
Le Havre
Rouen
Brest
Lille
Strasbourg
Nancy
Dijon
Nice
Toulon
Perpignan
Clermont-Ferrand
St-Étienne
Grenoble
Limoges

Projection: Conical with two standard parallels

East from Greenwich   West from Greenwich

m   3000   2000   1000   400   200   0
ft   9000   6000   3000   1200 600   0   -600

1:5 000 000

100 miles

km

SPAIN

PORTUGAL

FRANCE

ALGERIA

MOROCCO

ANDORRE

MEDITERRANEAN SEA

ATLANTIC OCEAN

Bay of Biscay

ISLAS BALEARES

Mallorca · Menorca · Ibiza · Formentera · Cabrera

Palma · Sóller · Mahón

Madrid · Barcelona · Valencia · Sevilla · Málaga · Zaragoza · Bilbao · Lisboa · Porto · Cádiz · Granada · Córdoba · Murcia · Alicante · Cartagena · Almería · Albacete · Cuenca · Toledo · Salamanca · Valladolid · León · Oviedo · Gijón · Santander · San Sebastián · Pamplona · Logroño · Vitoria · Burgos · Palencia · Zamora · Cáceres · Badajoz · Huelva · Jerez · Ceuta · Tetouán · Tánger · Gibraltar · Alger · Blida · Oran · Mostaganem

Golfe du Lion · Golfo de Valencia · Golfo de Cádiz · Strait of Gibraltar

Montpellier · Béziers · Narbonne · Perpignan · Toulouse · Bayonne · Biarritz

GALICIA · ASTURIAS · CANTABRICA · NAVARRA · ARAGON · CATALUÑA · CASTILLA Y LEON · CASTILLA-LA MANCHA · EXTREMADURA · ANDALUCIA · MURCIA · PAIS VASCO

BEIRA ALTA · BEIRA BAIXA · BEIRA LITORAL · TRAS-OS-MONTES · ALTO ALENTEJO · BAIXO ALENTEJO · ALGARVE · ESTREMADURA · MINHO · DOURO LITORAL

Sierra Nevada · Sierra de Gredos · Sierra de Guadarrama · Montes de Toledo · Serranía de Cuenca · Sierra Morena

Projection : Conical with two standard parallels

COPYRIGHT GEORGE PHILIP & SON LTD.

West from Greenwich · East from Greenwich

m · ft
3000 · 2000 · 1500 · 1000 · 400 · 200 · 0
9000 · 6000 · 4500 · 3000 · 1200 · 600 · 0 · 600

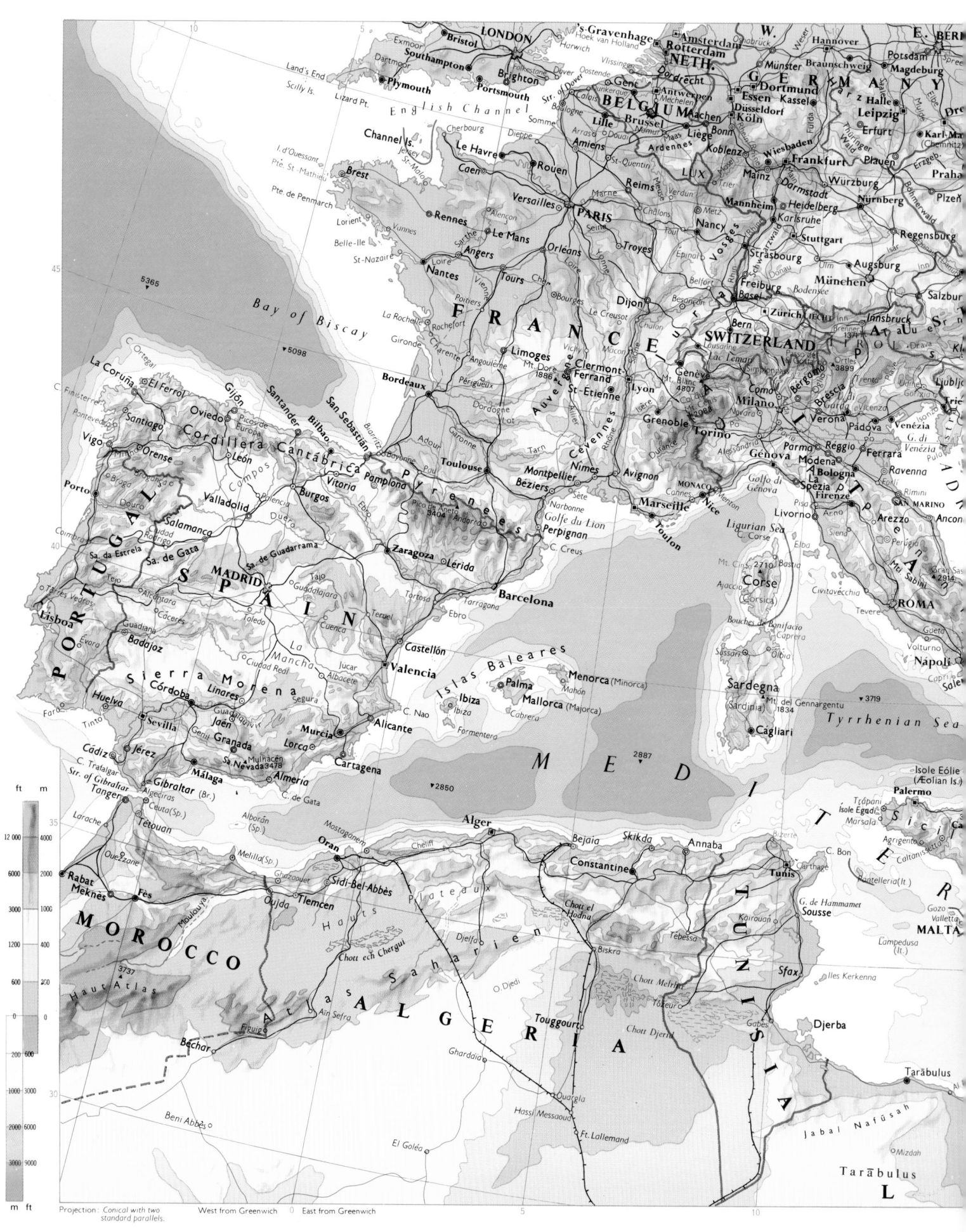

P O L A N D

Poznań   Płock   Warszawa   Brest   Pinsk   Polesye   Chernigov   Desna   Sumy   Belgorod   Kharkov   Volgograd

Łódź   Wisła (Vistula)

Wrocław   Radom   Lublin   Lutsk   Ровно   Zhitomir   Kiyev   Pereyaslav-Khmelnitskiy   Poltava   U. S. S. R.   Voroshilovgrad   Kamensk-Shakhtinskiy   Tsimlyanskoye Vdkhr.

Ostrava   Kielce   Tarnów   Przemyśl   Lvov   Vinnitsa   Belaya Tserkov   Kremenchug (Dnieper)   Pavlograd   Donets   Artemovsk   Shakhty   Novocherkassk

Bratislava   Kraków   Kamenets-Podol'skiy   Uman   Kirovograd   Dnepropetrovsk   Gorlovka   Makeyevka   Rostov   Manych

Miskolc   Košice   Chernovtsy   Mogilev-Podolskiy   Balta   Pervomaysk   Voznesensk   Krivoy Rog   Zaporozhye   Donetsk   Taganrog   Yeisk   Stavropol

HUNGARY   Debrecen   Iaşi   Kishinev   Nikolayev   Melitopol   Zhdanov (Mariupol)   Berdyansk   Tikhoretsk

BLACK SEA   MEDITERRANEAN SEA

TURKEY   GREECE   BULGARIA   ROMANIA   CYPRUS   SYRIA   EGYPT   ISRAEL   JORDAN   LEBANON

Division between Greeks
and Turks in Cyprus;
Turks to the north.

COPYRIGHT. GEORGE PHILIP & SON. LTD.

1:5 000 000

50   0   50   100 miles
50 0 50 100 150 km

U.S.S.R.

ROMANIA

Carpaţii Meridionali

Galaţi
Brăila
Buzău
Ploieşti
Bucureşti (Bucharest)
Constanţa
Mamaia
Mangalia

OSLAVIA

SERBIA

Beograd (Belgrade)

Craiova

BULGARIA

Sofiya (Sofia) 2198

BLACK SEA

Varna
Burgas

Stara Planina

Musala 2925

Plovdiv

Rhodopi Planina

TURKEY

Edirne

THRÁKI

İstanbul
Üsküdar

Marmara denizi

ALBANIA

MAKEDONIJA

Skopje

Bitola (Monastir)

Thessaloníki

Bursa

İzmir (Smyrna)

TURKEY
Anadolu

IONIAN SEA

GREECE

Thessalía

Lárisa

Vólos

Lésvos

Khíos

Sámos

Athínai (Athens)
Piraiévs (Piræus)

PELOPÓNNISOS

AEGEAN SEA

KIKLÁDHES

DHODEKÁNISOS

Ródhos
4486

MEDITERRANEAN SEA

KRITI

Iráklion

COPYRIGHT. GEORGE PHILIP & SON, LTD.

East from Greenwich

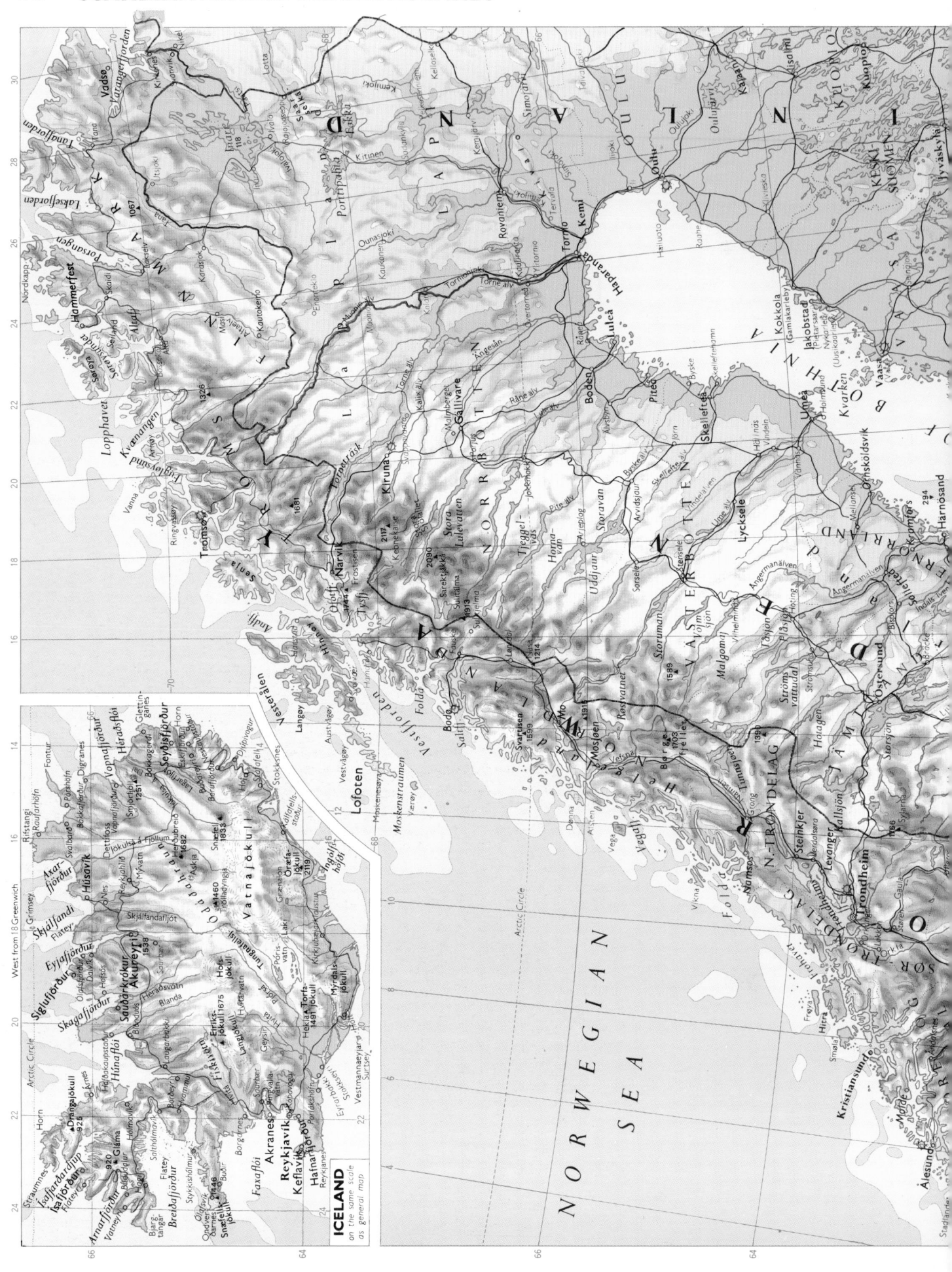

NORWEGIAN SEA

ICELAND
on the same scale
as general map

Lofoten

Arctic Circle

1:5 000 000

20 10 0 20 40 60 80 100 miles
40 20 0 40 80 120 160 km

Heinola
Kotka
Lovisa
Lahti
Porvoo
Hämeenlinna
HELSINKI (Helsingfors)
Hyvinkää
Rauma
Turku (Åbo)
Hangö (Hanko)

Rakvere
Kunda
Kärdla
ESTONIA S.S.R.
Valga
Viljandi
Tartu
Pärnu
Haapsalu
Hiiumaa (Dag)
Saaremaa (Ösel)
Kingisepp
Ruhnu

Valmiera
Cēsis
Riga
Rīgas Jūras
Līcis
(Gulf of Riga)
Ainaži
LATVIA S.S.R.
Jelgava
Bauska

Daugava
Krāslava

R.

S.

S.

R.

LITHUANIAN
S.S.R.
Kaunas
Vilnius

Grodno
Białystok
Łomża
Ostrołęka

POLAND

Ventspils
Liepāja
Klaipeda
Kaliningrad
Chernyakhovsk

Elbląg
Gdynia
Zatoka Gdańska
Gdańsk
Toruń
Grudziądz
Bydgoszcz

Szczecin (Stettin)

BALTIC SEA

Gotland
Visby

Öland
Kalmar
Karlskrona
Karlshamn
BLEKINGE
Bornholm
Rønne

STOCKHOLM
Uppsala
Västerås
Eskilstuna
Södertälje
Nyköping
Norrköping
Linköping
Örebro
Motala
Jönköping
Växjö
Kristianstad

Åland
(Ahvenanmaa)
Mariehamn
(Maarianhamina)

GÖTEBORG
Borås
Halmstad
Helsingborg
MALMÖ
KØBENHAVN
Trelleborg
Ystad

OSLO
Drammen
Skien
Larvik
Kristiansand

DENMARK

Ålborg
Århus
Odense
Randers
Horsens
Vejle
Kolding
Esbjerg
Flensburg

Rostock
Lübeck
Kiel
Hamburg
Schwerin

GERMANY

Bremerhaven
Bremen
Oldenburg
Groningen
Wilhelmshaven

NETHERLANDS

East from Greenwich

Projection: Conical with two standard parallels

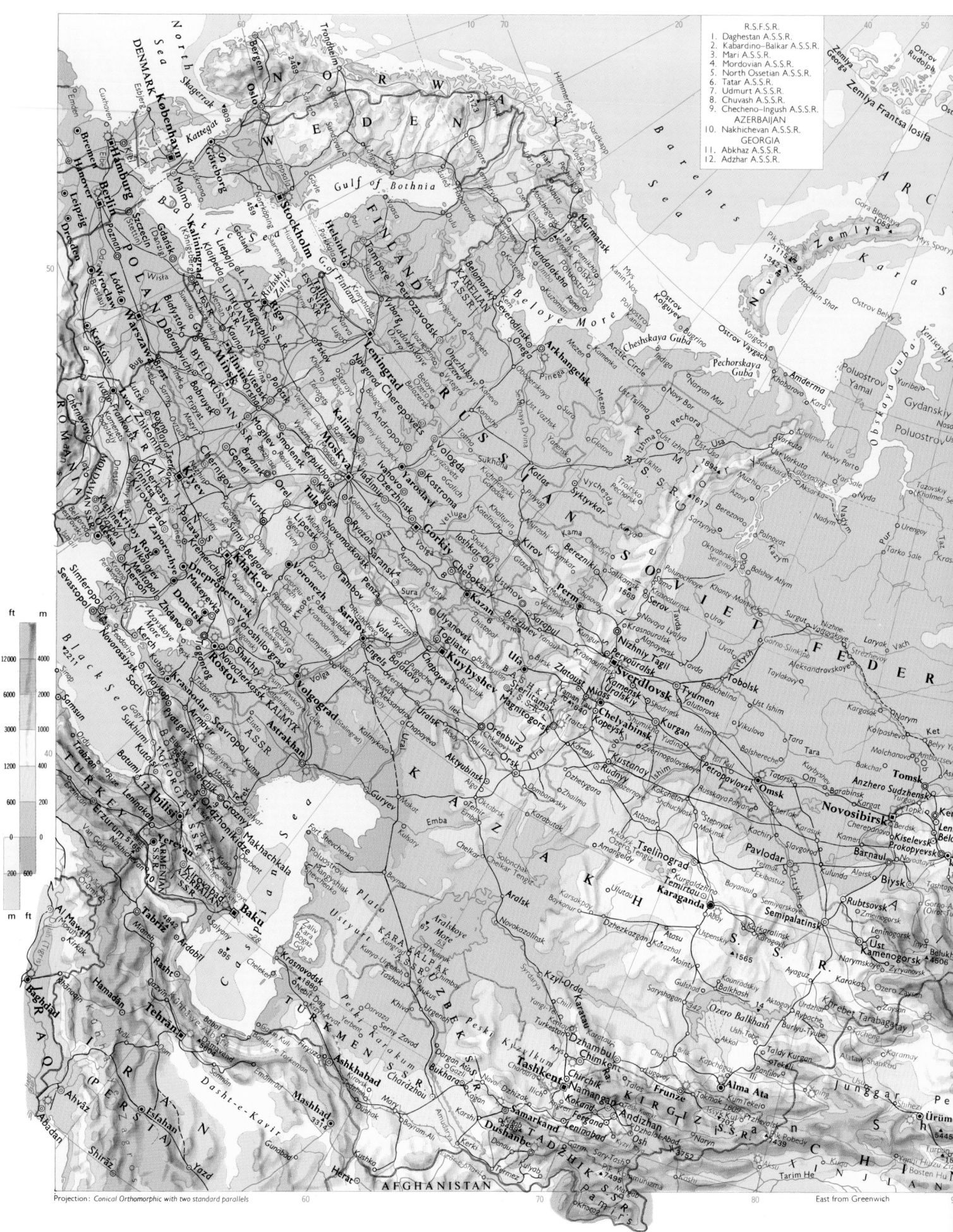

R.S.F.S.R.
1. Daghestan A.S.S.R.
2. Kabardino-Balkar A.S.S.R.
3. Mari A.S.S.R.
4. Mordovian A.S.S.R.
5. North Ossetian A.S.S.R.
6. Tatar A.S.S.R.
7. Udmurt A.S.S.R.
8. Chuvash A.S.S.R.
9. Checheno-Ingush A.S.S.R.
AZERBAIJAN
10. Nakhichevan A.S.S.R.
GEORGIA
11. Abkhaz A.S.S.R.
12. Adzhar A.S.S.R.

Projection: Conical Orthomorphic with two standard parallels   East from Greenwich

1:20 000 000

100   0   100   200   300   400   500 miles

100   0   200   400   600   800 km

101

OCEAN

Laptev Sea

East Siberian Sea

Chukotskoye More

Bering Sea

Severnaya Zemlya

Proliv Vilkitskogo

Ostrov Shmidt

Mys Arkticheskiy

Ostrov Komsomolets

Ostrov Oktyabrskoy Revolyutsii

Ostrov Pioner

965

Ostrov Bolshevik

Poluostrov Taymyr

Gory Byrranga

1146

Nordvik

Novorybnoye

Khatanga

Kheta

Olenyok

Tiksi

Ostrov Herrietta

Ostrova Delong

Ostrov Zhokhova

Novosibirskiye Ostrova

Ostrov Belkovskiy

Ostrov Kotelnyy

Ostrov Paddeyevskiy

Ostrov Novaya Sibir

Ostrova Medvezhi

Mys Dezhneva (East C.)

St. Lawrence (U.S.A.)

Anadyrskiy Zaliv

Chukotskiy Khrebet

2562

Koryakskiy Khrebet

60

Srednekolymsk

Verkhoyansk

Khrebet Cherskogo

Okhotsko Kolymskoye

Penzhinskaya Guba

Gizhiga

Sredinnyy Khrebet

Poluostrov Kamchatka

Petropavlovsk-Kamchatskiy

50

Sea of Okhotsk

Sakhalin

Komsomolsk

Nikolayevsk na-Am.

Khrebet Sikhote Alin

Yuzhno-Sakhalinsk

Kurilskiye Ostrova

Hokkaido

Sapporo

Hakodate

Krasnoyarsk

Nizhneudinsk

Bratsk

Kirensk

Stanovoy Khrebet

Khabarovsk

Cheremkhovo

Angarsk

Ulan Ude

Irkutsk

Chita

Blagoveshchensk

Birobidzhan

Jiamusi

Vladivostok

Ussuriysk

Nakhodka

JAPAN

Sea of Japan

Honshū

Niigata

Toyama

Kanazawa

MONGOLIA

Hangayn Nuruu

Ulaanbaatar (Ulan Bator)

GOBI

Hentiyn Nuruu

Qiqihar

Harbin

Jilin

Changchun

Fushun

Shenyang

Anshan

Jinzhou

Chongjin

Wŏnsan

NORTH

P'yŏngyang

Dalian

Yingkou

Beijing

Zhangjiakou

Baotou

Dandong

Inch'ŏn

Sŏul

South

Taejŏn

Pusan

Boundaries of U.S.S.R.

Boundaries of S.S.R.

Boundaries of A.S.S.R.

COPYRIGHT GEORGE PHILIP & SON LTD.

1:50 000 000

250 0 250 500 750 1000 miles
250 0 500 1000 1500 km

P A C I F I C   O C E A N

A R C T I C   O C E A N

I N D I A N   O C E A N

Aleutian Is.

C. Dezhnyova
Bering Str.
Kamchatka Peninsula
Klyuchevsk. Vol.
4750
Okhotsk
Sea of
Okhotsk
Sakhalin
Srednniy Ra.
Kurril Is.
Hokkaido
Honshu
Sea of Japan
Korea Str.
Shikoku
Kyushu
Ryukyu Is.
Tropic of Cancer
Formosa
Taiwan
Bonin Is.
10 556
Guam
Caroline Is.
Palau Is.
10 497
Mindanao
Philippine Is.
Luzon
New Guinea
Halmahera
Moluccas
Celebes Sea
Ceram
Banda Sea
Arafura Sea
Timor
Australia

Wrangel I.
7822
Gydan Ra. (Kolyma)
New Siberian Is.
Kolyma
Indigirka
Verkhoyansk Range
Stanovoy Ra.
Aldan
Lena
Yablonovyy Ra.
Amur
Sikhote Alin Ra.
Great Khingan Mts.
Manchurian Plain
Sungari
Yellow Sea
East China Sea
South China Sea
Hainan
Si-kiang
Hong Kong
G. of Tong-king
Mekong
Malay Peninsula
Str. of Malacca
Sumatra
Borneo
Palawan
Kinabalu 4101
Sulu Sea
Sunda Is.
Java
Java Sea
Bali
Flores
Makassar Strait
East Indies

Laptev Sea
Chelyuskin
Taimyr Peninsula
Severnaya Zemlya
Yenisei
Lower Tunguska
Kotuy
Angara
Central Siberian Plateau
Ob
Plateau of Mongolia
Altai
Selenga
Sayan Mts.
Tien Shan
Belukha 4506
Lop Nor
Koko Nor
Turfan Basin
Tarim Basin
Takla Makan
Kunlun Shan
Plateau of Tibet
Tsangpo
Brahmaputra
Salween
Irrawaddy
Chao Phraya
G. of Thailand
Andaman Is.
Nicobar Is.
Bay of Bengal

Novaya Zemlya
Kara Sea
Barents Sea
Kolguyev I.
Ob
Irtysh
West Siberian Plain
Tobol
Irtysh
Ishim
Narodnaya 1894
Ural Mountains
1640
Ural
L. Balkhash
Chu
Ili
Syr Darya
Aral Sea
Turanian Plain
Amu Darya
Hindu Kush
Pamir
Communism Pk. 7495
Karakoram Ra. 8611
Himalaya
Everest
India
Ganges
Yamuna
Sutlej
Thar
Sulaiman Ra.
Narmada
Godavari
Krishna
Deccan
Western Ghats
Eastern Ghats
Polk Strait
Ceylon
Equator
Chagos Arch.
Maldive Is.
Laccadive Is.
C. Comorin
Gulf of Mannar

Svalbard
Greenland
Iceland
North Cape
Kola Pen.
White Sea
Finland
N. Dvina
Volga
Dnepr
Baltic Sea
Scandinavia
North European Plain
Central Russian Uplands
Caspian Sea
Caucasus
Elbrus 5633
Ararat 5165
Black Sea
Elburz Mts.
Demavend 5604
Plateau of Iran
Dasht-i-Lut
Great Salt Desert
G. of Oman
The Gulf
Tigris
Euphrates
Mesopotamia
Helmand
Steppes

British Isles
North Sea
Rhine
Elbe
Oder
Vistula
Carpathians
Danube
Adriatic Sea
Mediterranean Sea
Cyprus
Taurus Mts.
Anatolia
Bosporus
Suez Canal
Dead Sea
Sinai Pen.
Nile
Syrian Desert
Arabia
Ar Rub' al Khali
G. of Aden
Socotra
Ras Asir (C. Guardafui)
Somali Peninsula
Red Sea
Libyan Desert
Lake Victoria
Seychelles
Amirantes

m   ft
6000 18 000
4000 12 000
2000 6000
1000 3000
400   1200
200   600
0   0
200   600
2000 6000
4000 12 000
6000 18 000
8000 24 000

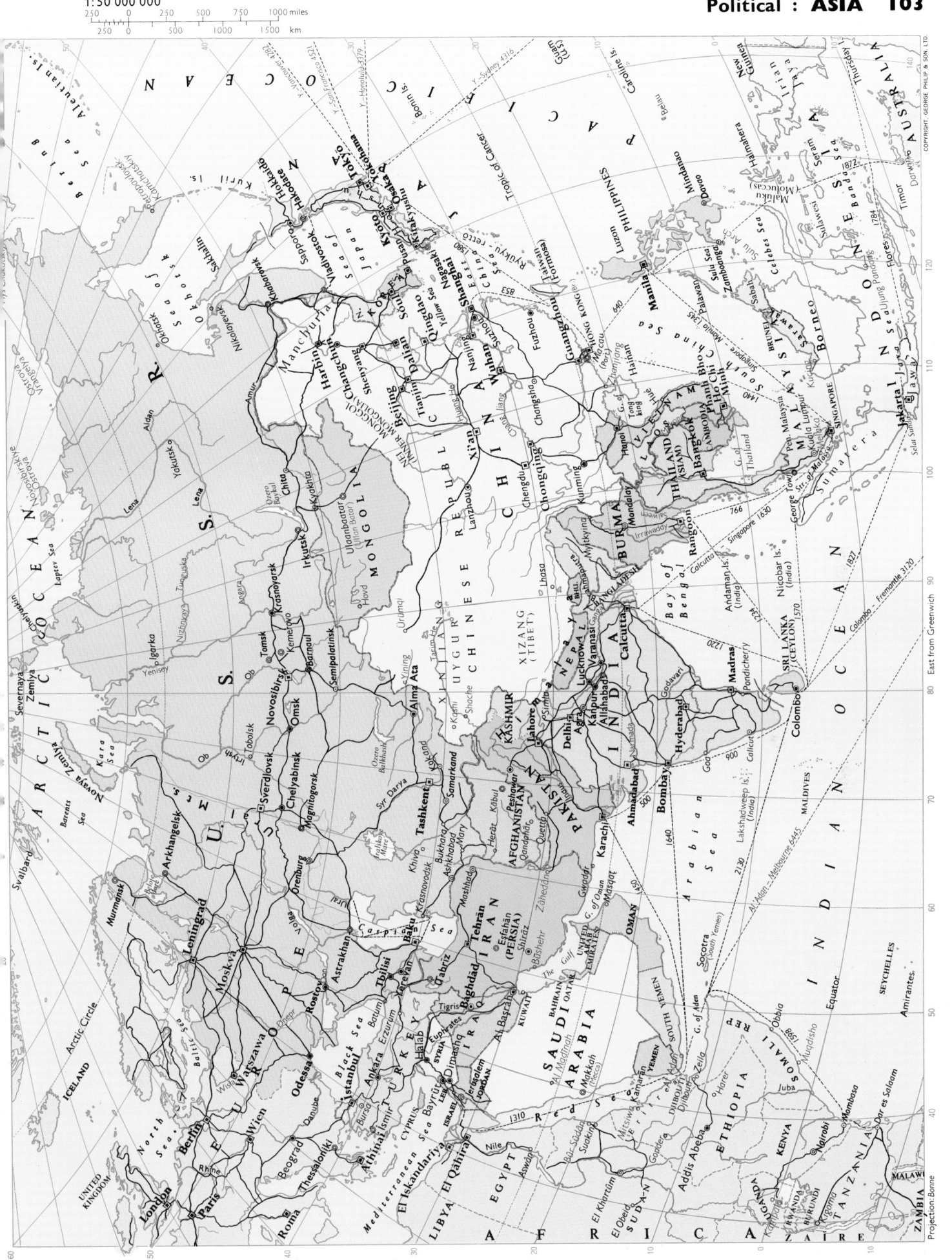

1:50 000 000

Projection: Bonne

1:1 000 000

10   5   0   20 miles
10   0   10   20   30 km

1949–1974 Armistice lines between
Israel and the Arab States.

MEDITERRANEAN SEA

LEBANON

SYRIA

JORDAN

ISRAEL

EGYPT

Şūr
(Tyre)

Qiryat Shemona

BIRKET RAM

Nahariyya

Al Qunayţirah

'Akko
(Acre)

HAZOR

Zefat

Yam Kinneret
(Sea of Galilee)

Hagalil
(Galilee)

KEFAR NAHUM
(CAPERNAUM)

Terverya
209

Qiryat Yam

HEFA
(Haifa)

Qiryat Ata

Tirat Karmel

Nazerat
(Nazareth)

'ATLIT

Dar'ā

Ar Ramthā

Irbid

TEL
MEGIDDO

'Afula

CAESAREA
Or 'Aqiva

Janin

Shōmrōn
(Samaria)

Hadera

Netanya

Tūlkarm

SAMARIA

Nablus
SHECHEM
JACOB'S WELL

Al Mafraq

TEL ARSHAF
Herzliyya
Ramat HaSharon

Qalqilya

Kefar Sava

Bene
Beraq

Petah Tiqwa

TEL AVIV
YAFO
(Jaffa)

Ramat
Gan
Or Yehuda

Bat Yam
Holon

As Salt

Az Zarqā'

Rishon le Ziyyon
Nes Ziyyona

Ramla
Rehovot

Lod
(Lydda)

Rām Allāh

Al Birah

'AMMAN

Ariha
(Jericho)

Ashdod

TEL
GEZER

JERUSALEM
(Yerushalayim, Al Quds)

QUMRĀN

Ashqelon

Qiryat Gat

BET GUVRIN
TEL
LAKHISH

Bayt Jālā
Bayt Lahm
(Bethlehem)
Bayt Şāhūr

BIRAK SULAYMĀN
(SOLOMON'S POOLS)

Gaza

Al Khalil
(Hebron)

En Gedi

MESADA

Gaza
Strip

Khān
Yūnis

Be'er Sheva

Newe Zohar

Projection: Conical with two standard parallels

East from Greenwich

COPYRIGHT. GEORGE PHILIP & SON LTD

Inset (Continuation Southwards):

Continuation
Southwards
1:2 500 000

0   10   20 miles
0   10 20 30 km

Gaza
Strip

Gaza
Ghazzah

Al Khalil
(Hebron)

Khān
Yūnis

Be'er Sheva

Dimona

ISRAEL

HORVOT
SHIVTA

Ha Negev

Mizpe Ramon

Makhtesh Ramon

PETRA

EGYPT

JORDAN

DEAD SEA

Elat
Al
'Aqabah

1:15 000 000

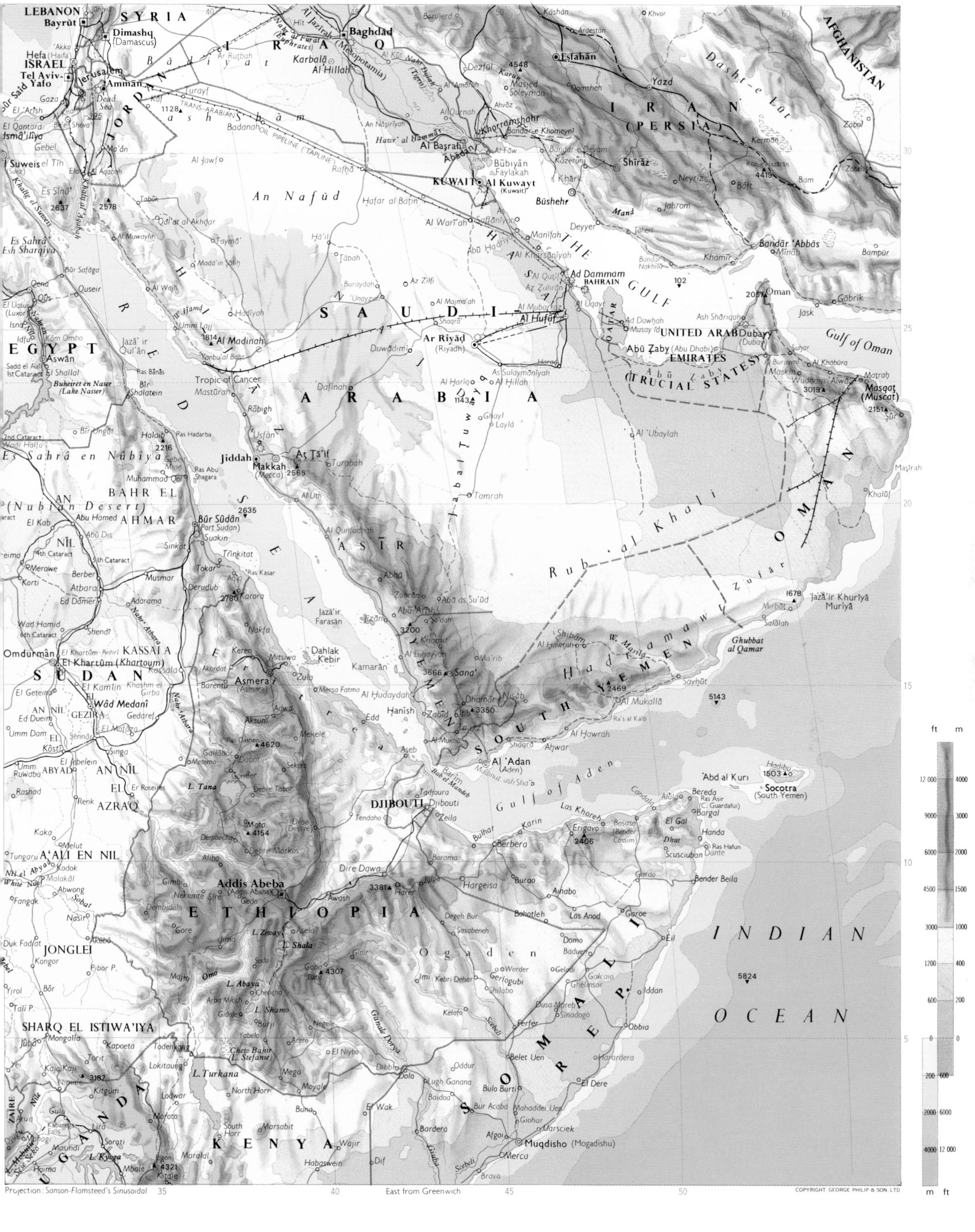

100 0 100 200 300 400 miles
100 0 100 200 300 400 500 600 km

LEBANON
Bayrût
Hefa (Haifa)
ISRAEL
Tel Aviv
Yafo
Jerusalem
Dimashq (Damascus)
SYRIA
IRAQ
Baghdâd
Al Jazîrah
Al Furât (Euphrates)
Karbalâ'
Al Hillah
Ar Rutbah
Hît
An Nâsirîyah
Al 'Amârah
Ahvâz
Khorramshahr
Abâdân
Al Başrah
Al Faw
Bandâr-e Deylam
Bûbiyân
Faylakah
KUWAIT
Al Kuwayt (Kuwait)
Bûshehr
Khârk
Deyyer
Tabrîz
Esfahân
Yazd
IRAN (PERSIA)
Dasht-e Lût
AFGHANISTAN
Zâbol
Kermân
Bam
Shîrâz
Neyrîz
Jahrom
Bandar 'Abbâs
Khamîr
Minâb
Bampûr
Gâbrik
Jask
Oman

JORDAN
Amman
Ma'ân
Dead Sea
Gaza
El 'Arîsh
El Qantara
Suweis (Suez)
Es Sînâ
Khalig el Suweis
Gebel et Tîh
Tabûk

An Nafûd
Hafar al Bâtin
Al Wârî'ah
Safânîyah
Manîfah
Al Khafjî
THE GULF
BAHRAIN
Ad Dammam
Az Zahrân
Al Qatîf
Ad Dawhah
QATAR
Abû Zaby (Abu Dhabi)
UNITED ARAB EMIRATES
(TRUCIAL STATES)
Dubayy (Dubai)
Ash Shâriqah
Buraymî
Al Khâbûra
Suhâr
Maskat
Masqat (Muscat)
Matrah
Gulf of Oman

EGYPT
Aswân
Asyût
Buheiret en Naser (Lake Nasser)
Es Sahrâ Esh Sharqîya
Quseir
Qena
Qûs
Bûr Safâga

SAUDI ARABIA
Al Madînah
Al Jawf
Taymâ'
Hâ'il
Az Zilfî
Unayzah
Buraydah
Ar Riyâd (Riyadh)
Al Hufûf
Al Majma'ah
Duwâdimî
Sulaymânîyah
Al Kharj
RUB' AL KHALI

Tropic of Cancer

RED SEA
Jiddah
Makkah (Mecca)
Aţ Ţâ'if
Yanbu' al Bahr
Râbigh
Al Qunfudhah
'ASÎR
Abhâ
Jîzân
Farasân
Jazâ'ir Farasân

BAHR EL AHMAR
(Nubian Desert)
Es Sahrâ en Nûbîya
Bûr Sûdân (Port Sudan)
Suakin
Tokar
Trinkitat

SUDAN
Omdurmân
El Khartûm (Khartoum)
Wâd Medanî
KASSALA
Kassala
Gedaref
GEZIRA
Sinnar
Kôsti
AN NIL EL AZRAQ
AN NIL EL ABYAD

Asmera (Asmara)
Keren
Mitsiwa
Eritrea
Dahlak Kebir
Kamaran
Al Hudaydah
YEMEN
Sana'
Dhamâr
Ta'izz
Zabîd
Al Mukhâ
SOUTH YEMEN
Al Mukallâ
HADRAMAWT
Shibâm
Ma'rib
Socotra (South Yemen)
'Abd al Kûrî
Zufâr
Salâlah
Mirbât
Ghubbat al Qamar
Jazâ'ir Khurîyâ Muriyâ

ETHIOPIA
Addis Abeba (Addis Ababa)
L. Tana
Gonder
Debre Markos
Dese (Dessye)
Mekele
Ras Dashen 4620
L. Zîway
L. Abaya
L. Shamo
L. Shala
Jima
Harer
Dire Dawa
Awash
Ogaden

DJIBOUTI
Djibouti
Zeila
Berbera
Hargeisa
Gulf of Aden
Al 'Adan (Aden)
Bab el Mandeb
SOMALI REP.
Muqdisho (Mogadishu)
Merca
Baidoa
Bur Acaba
Bosaso (Bender Cassim)
Erigavo
Bender Beila
Obbia
Garoe
Las Anod
Belet Uen

KENYA
L. Turkana
Marsabit
Wajir
Moyale
UGANDA
L. Kyoga
ZAIRE
JONGLEI
SHARQ EL ISTIWA'IYA
Jûba
A'ALI EN NIL
Malakâl
White Nile
Sobat

INDIAN OCEAN

ft	m
12 000	4000
9000	3000
6000	2000
4500	1500
3000	1000
1200	400
600	200
0	0
600	200
6000	2000
12 000	4000

m ft

Projection: Sanson-Flamsteed's Sinusoidal
East from Greenwich
COPYRIGHT GEORGE PHILIP & SON LTD.

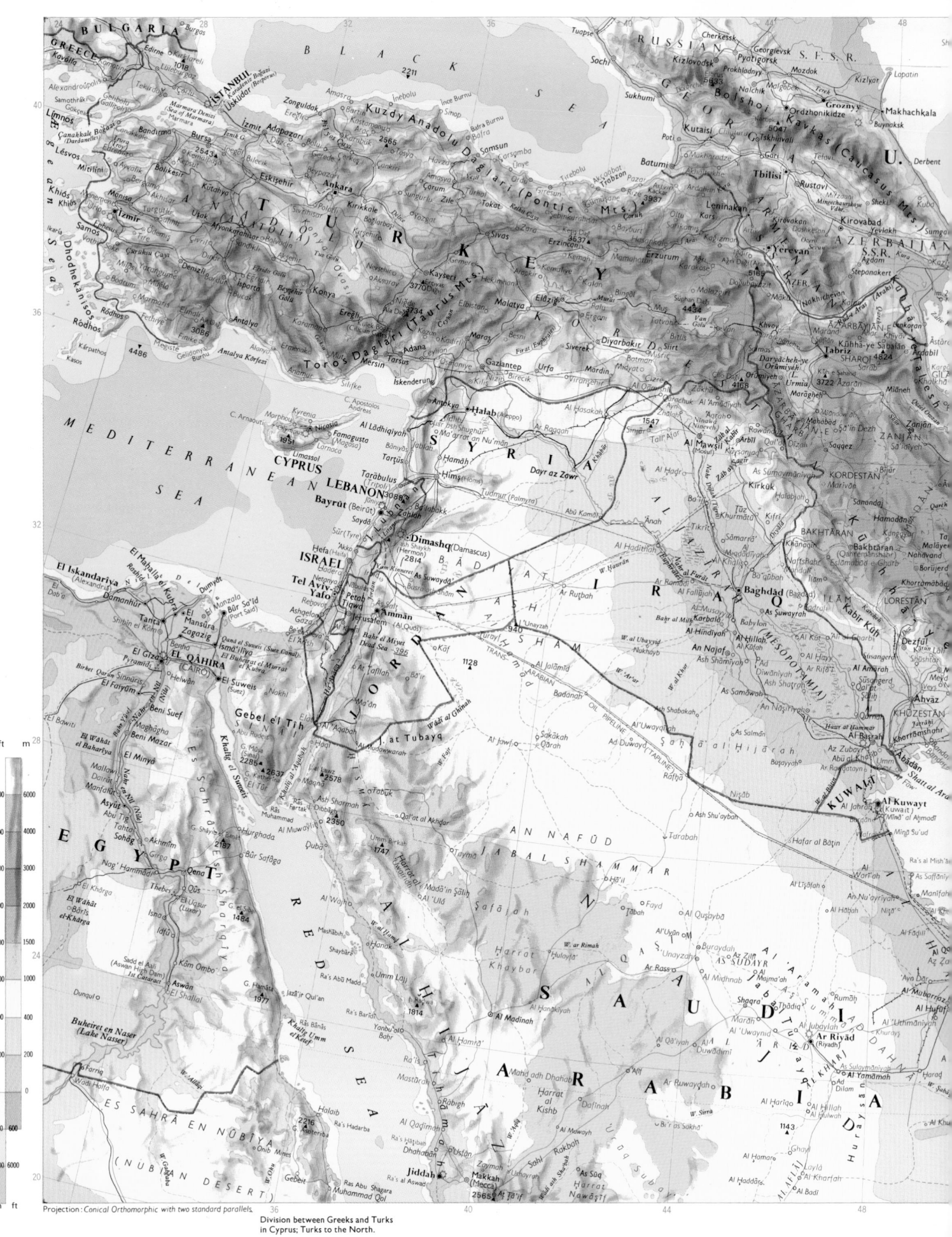

Projection: Conical Orthomorphic with two standard parallels

Division between Greeks and Turks in Cyprus; Turks to the North.

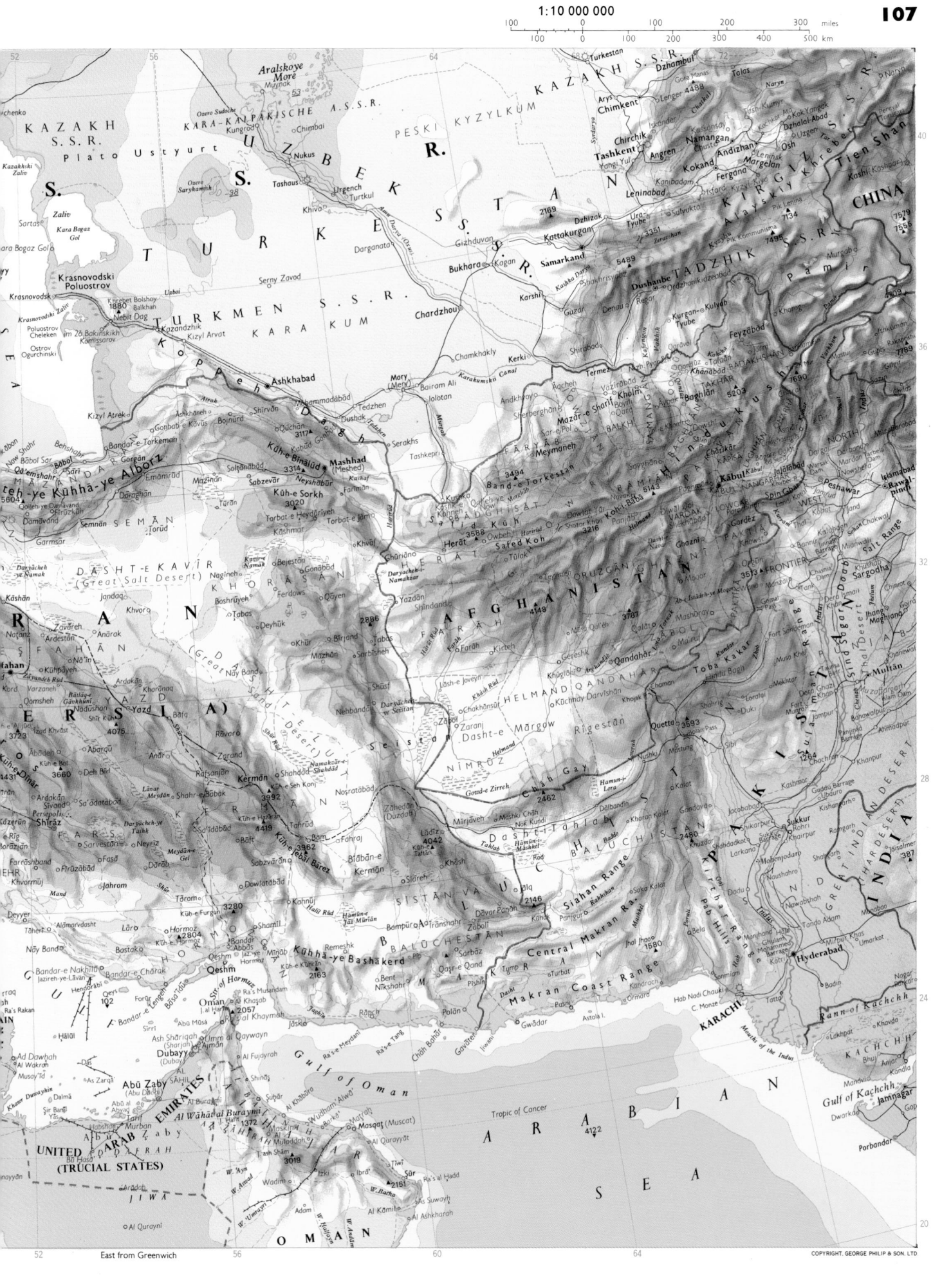

1:10 000 000

100   0   100   200   300 miles
100   0   100   200   300   400   500 km

KAZAKH S.S.R.

Aralskoye More

KARA-KALPAKISCHE A.S.S.R.

PESKI KYZYLKUM

KAZAKH
S.S.R.
Plato Ustyurt

Kazakhskiy Zaliv

Sartass

Zaliv

Krasnovodski Poluostrov
Krasnovodsk
Krasnovodskiy Zaliv

Kara Bogaz Gol

Kara Bogaz Gol

Muynak

Ozero Sudoche
Kungrad
Chimbai

Nukus

Ozero Sarykamish   -98

Khiva

Urgench
Turtkul

Darganata

Amu Darya (Oxus)

Tashaus

UZBEK S.S.R.

TURKMEN S.S.R.

KARA KUM

Chardzhou

Serny Zavod

Uzboi

Nebit Dag
Kazandzhik

Koppet Dagh

Ashkhabad

Mohammadabad

Tedzhen

KAZAKH S.S.R.

Turkestan

Dzhambul

Gora Manas

Talas

Naryn

Arys
Chimkent

Lenger 4488

Syrdarya

KIRGIZ
S.S.R.

Tien Shan

CHINA

7579
7555

Tashkent

Angren
Kokand
Fergana

Namangan
Andizhan
Margelan
Osh

Leninabad

Pik Lenina 7134
Pik Kommunizma 7495

TADZHIK

Dushanbe

Pamir

7789

Bukhara
Kagan

Samarkand

5489

Karshi

Guzar

Kerki

Termez

Mary (Merv)
Bairam Ali

Iolotan

Chamkhakly

Murgab

BADAKHSHAN

NORTH

7690

HINDU KUSH

HAZARAJAT

AFGHANISTAN

Kabul
Peshawar
Rawalpindi

WEST
PAKISTAN

INDIA

Herat

Mashhad (Meshed)

IRAN

DASHT-E KAVIR
(Great Salt Desert)

DASHT-E LUT (Great Sand Desert)

BALUCHISTAN

Quetta

Kandahar

Zahedan (Duzdab)

SISTAN VA BALUCHESTAN

Makran Coast Range

KARACHI

Gulf of Oman

OMAN

UNITED ARAB EMIRATES
(TRUCIAL STATES)

Abū Zaby (Abu Dhabi)

Dubayy (Dubai)

Masqat (Muscat)

ARABIAN

SEA

Tropic of Cancer

East from Greenwich

COPYRIGHT. GEORGE PHILIP & SON. LTD

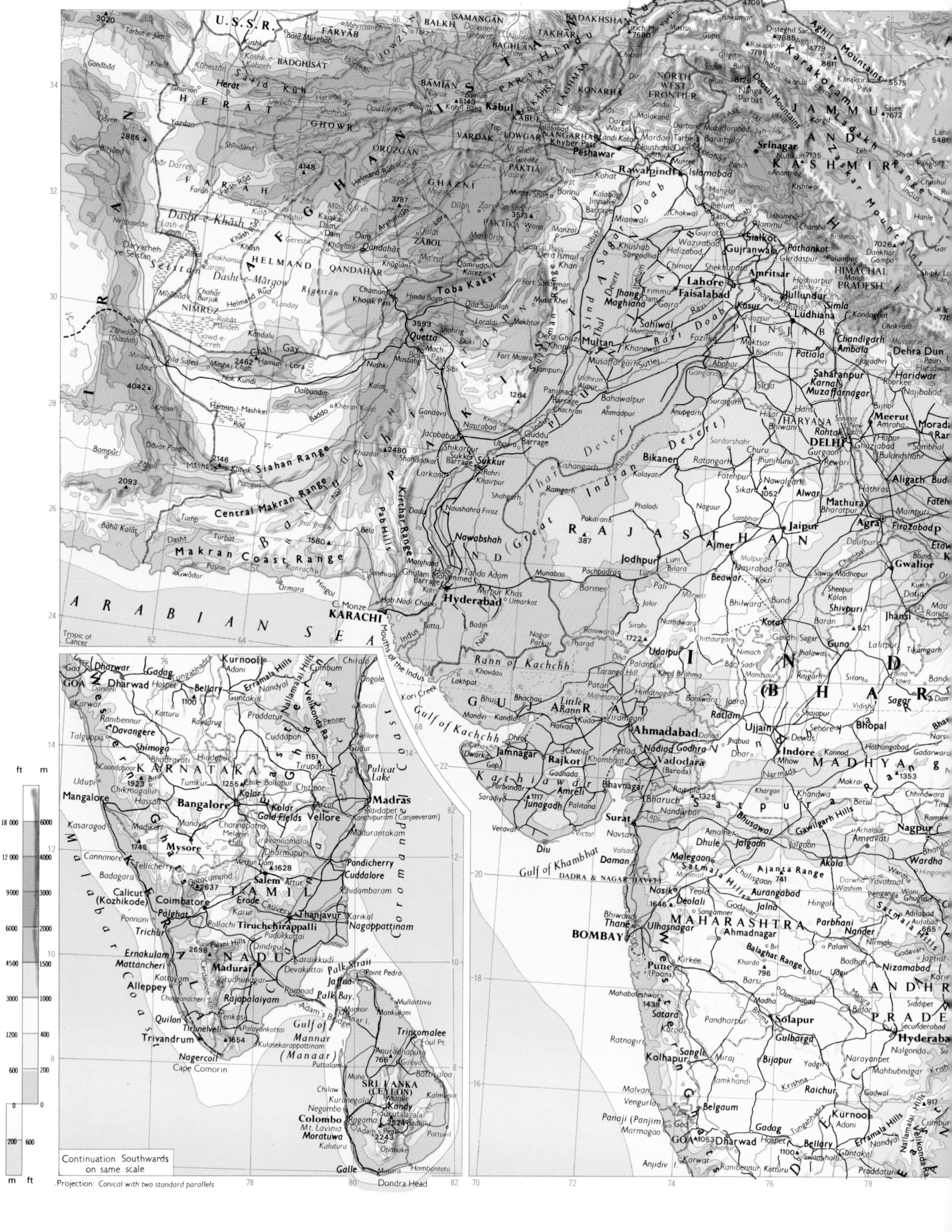

U.S.S.R.

AFGHANISTAN

IRAN

PAKISTAN

BALUCHISTAN

SIND

RAJASTHAN

GUJARAT

MAHARASHTRA

MADHYA PRADESH

ANDHRA PRADESH

KARNATAKA

TAMIL NADU

KERALA

HIMACHAL PRADESH

JAMMU AND KASHMIR

PUNJAB

HARYANA

HERĀT
GHOWR
FARĀH
HELMAND
NĪMRŪZ
ORŪZGĀN
GHAZNĪ
ZĀBOL
QANDAHĀR
PAKTIĀ
VARDAK
LOWGAR
NANGARHĀR
KONARHA
LAGHMAN
PARVĀN
BĀMIĀN
KĀBUL
BAGHLĀN
TAKHĀR
BADAKHSHĀN
SAMANGAN
BALKH
JOWZJĀN
FĀRYĀB
BĀDGHISĀT

Kabul
Herāt
Qandahār
Quetta
Peshawar
Rawalpindi
Islamabad
Lahore
Faisalabad
Multan
Hyderabad
KARACHI
Srinagar
Amritsar
Ludhiana
Chandigarh
Ambala
DELHI
Jaipur
Jodhpur
Ajmer
Udaipur
Ahmadabad
Vadodara (Baroda)
Rajkot
Jamnagar
Surat
Indore
Bhopal
Nagpur
Aurangabad
BOMBAY
Pune (Poona)
Solapur
Kolhapur
Hyderabad

ARABIAN SEA

Tropic of Cancer

Rann of Kachchh
Gulf of Kachchh
Gulf of Khambhat
Mouths of the Indus

KARNATAKA
Dharwar
Dharwad
GOA
Mangalore
Bangalore
Mysore
Calicut (Kozhikode)
Coimbatore
TAMIL NADU
Madras
Salem
Tiruchirappalli
Madurai
Trivandrum
Cape Comorin
Quilon
Alleppey
Ernakulam
Trichur
Pondicherry
Cuddalore
Thanjavur
Vellore

SRI LANKA (CEYLON)
Colombo
Kandy
Jaffna
Trincomalee
Moratuwa
Galle
Dondra Head

Gulf of Mannar (Manaar)
Palk Strait
Palk Bay
Adam's Bridge

Continuation Southwards on same scale

Projection: Conical with two standard parallels

ft m
18 000 6000
12 000 4000
9000 3000
6000 2000
4500 1500
3000 1000
1200 400
600 200
0 0
200 600
m ft

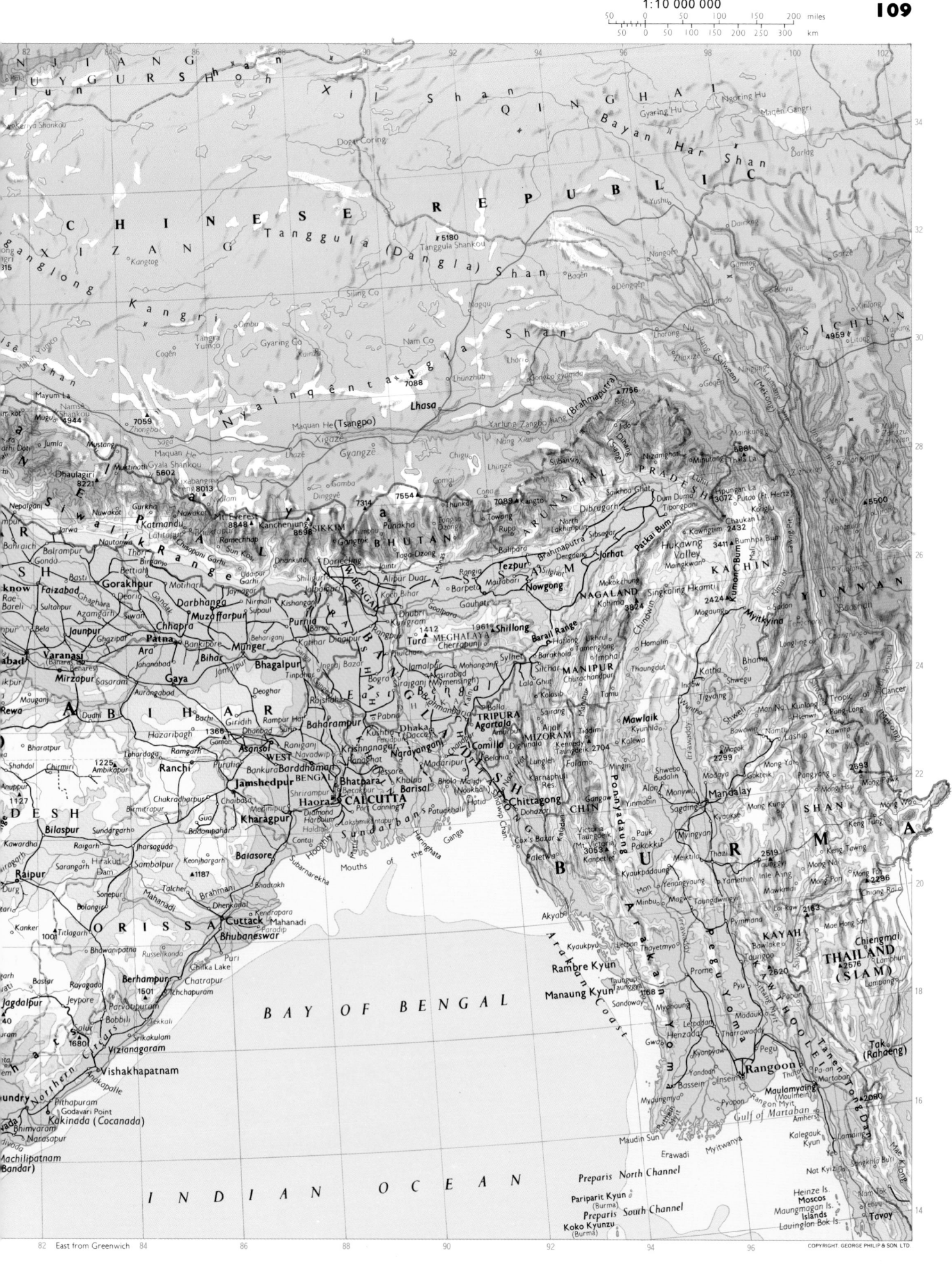

1:10 000 000

50   0   50   100   150   200 miles
50   0   50   100   150   200   250   300 km

N J I A N G

U I G U R S H

Qi-chan

Xil Shan

Q I N G H A I

Bayan Har Shan

Ngoring Hu

Maqên Gangri

Gyaring Hu

Dog-Coring

Darlag

C H I N E S E   R E P U B L I C

X I Z A N G   Tanggula   (Dangla) Shan

Siling Co

Yushu

S I C H U A N

4959

Litang

Ganze

Nam Co

N y a i n q ê n t a n g l h a   S h a n

7088

Lhasa

Yarlung Zangbo Jiang (Brahmaputra)

7756

A R U N A C H A L   P R A D E S H

6881

8500

Katmandu

Mt Everest
8848   Kanchenjunga
8598   S I K K I M   B H U T A N

A S S A M

K A C H I N

Y U N N A N

Myitkyina

N E P A L

Gorakhpur

Darjeeling

N A G A L A N D

Kohima
3824

Tezpur

Jorhat

Patna

Shillong

M E G H A L A Y A
Cherrapunji

M A N I P U R

Varanasi

B I H A R

Bhagalpur

B A N G L A D E S H

Dacca

T R I P U R A
Agartala

M I Z O R A M

C H I N

W E S T   B E N G A L

Calcutta

Chittagong

B U R M A

Mandalay

Kharagpur

S H A N

O R I S S A

Cuttack
Bhubaneswar

B A Y   O F   B E N G A L

K A Y A H

T H A I L A N D
(S I A M)

Chiengmai

Vishakhapatnam

Rangoon

Maulmyaing
(Moulmein)

Gulf of Martaban

I N D I A N   O C E A N

Preparis North Channel

Pariparit Kyun
(Burma)

Preparis South Channel

Koko Kyunzu
(Burma)

Heinze Is.

Moscos
Islands

Tavoy

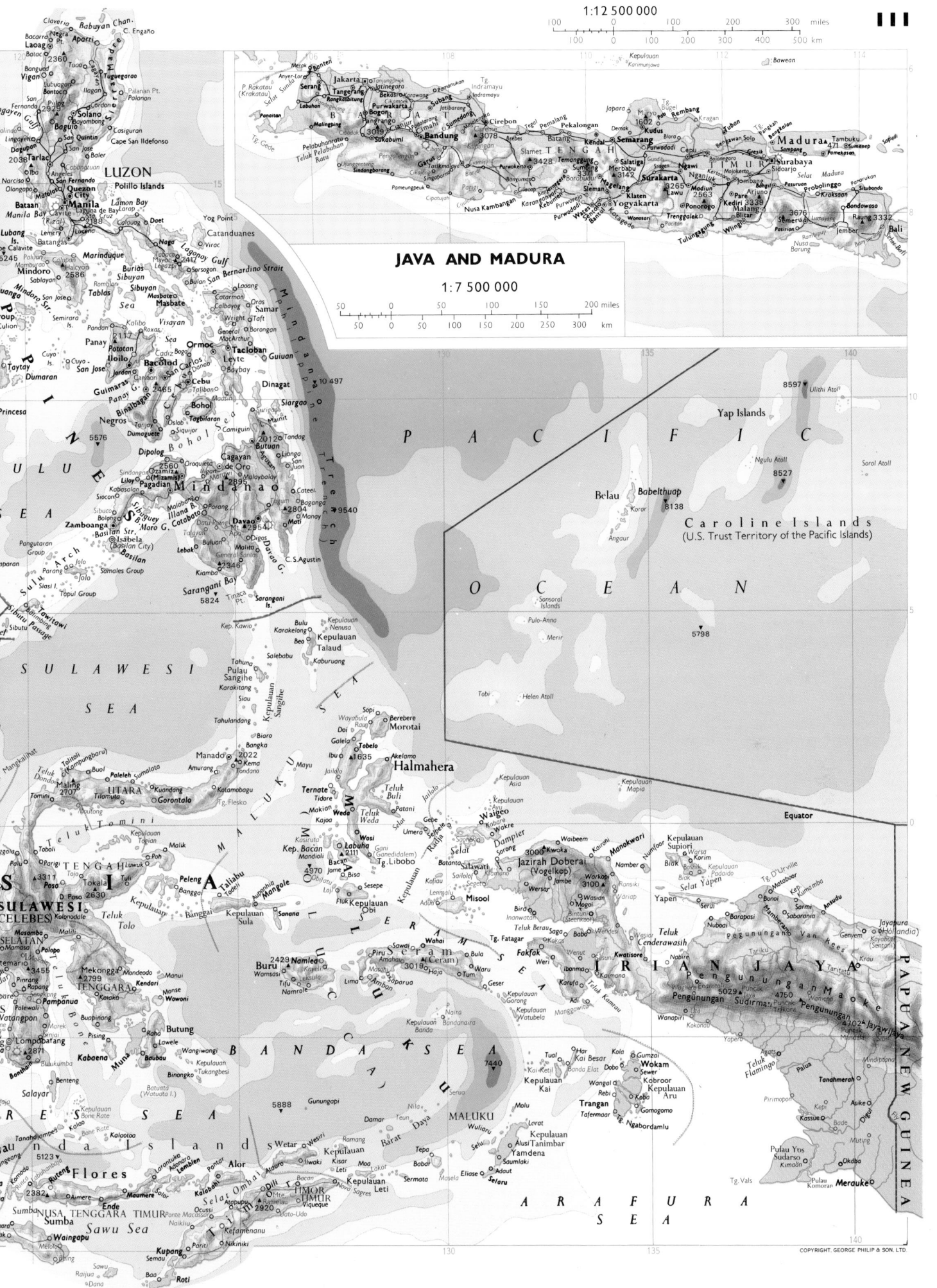

1:12 500 000

100   0   100   200   300 miles
100   0   100   200 300 400 500 km

JAVA AND MADURA

1:7 500 000

50   0   50   100   150   200 miles
50   0   50   100 150 200 250 300 km

P A C I F I C

O C E A N

Yap Islands

Belau   Babelthuap
8138

C a r o l i n e   I s l a n d s
(U.S. Trust Territory of the Pacific Islands)

Angaur

Sonsorol
Islands

Pulo-Anna

Merir   5798

Tobi   Helen Atoll

Ulithi Atoll
8597

Ngulu Atoll
8527

Sorol Atoll

Equator

LUZON

Manila

Mindoro

P
H
I
L
I
P
P
I
N
E

Panay

Negros

Cebu

Bohol

S U L U
S E A

Mindanao

Zamboanga

Davao

Sarangani Bay

Kepulauan
Talaud

S U L A W E S I

S E A

Pulau
Sangihe

Kepulauan
Sangihe

Manado

UTARA

Gorontalo

Ternate
Tidore

Halmahera

Morotai

Tobelo

Teluk
Weda

Waigeo

Teluk
Berau

Manokwari

Kepulauan
Asia

Kepulauan
Mapia

Biak

Yapen

Selat Yapen

Teluk
Cenderawasih

Jayapura
Hollandia

Jazirah Doberai
(Vogelkop)

Salawati

Misool

S E R A M

Fakfak

Weri

Teluk Kamrau

I R I A N   J A Y A

Pegunungan Maoke

Pengunungan
Sudirman

Jayawijaya

S U L A W E S I
(CELEBES)

SELATAN

TENGGARA

Teluk
Bone

Buton

Buru

Ceram
(Ceram)

C E R A M   S E A

M
A
L
U
K
U

Ambon

Kepulauan
Sula

Kepulauan
Obi

Bacan

B A N D A   S E A

Gunungapi
5888

Kepulauan
Banda

MALUKU

Kepulauan
Kai

Kai Besar

Wokam
Kepulauan
Aru

Trangan

Kepulauan
Tanimbar

Yamdena

Saumlaki

Kepulauan
Leti

Wetar

TIMOR
TIMUR

Dili

Flores

Sumba   NUSA TENGGARA TIMUR

Kupang

Sawu Sea

Roti

A R A F U R A

S E A

P A P U A   N E W   G U I N E A

Merauke

Pulau Yos
Sudarso

Tanahmerah

COPYRIGHT. GEORGE PHILIP & SON, LTD.

1:10 000 000

PENINSULAR MALAYSIA
AND SINGAPORE
1:6 000 000

Projection: Conical with two standard parallels

East from Greenwich

COPYRIGHT GEORGE PHILIP & SON LTD.

1:20 000 000

100 0 100 200 300 400 miles
100 0 100 200 300 400 500 600 km

COPYRIGHT GEORGE PHILIP & SON, LTD

U S S R

UNION OF SOVIET SOCIALIST REPUBLICS

KAZAKH S.S.R.

KIRGIZ S.S.R.

MONGOLIA

C H I N A

XIZANG (TIBET)

QINGHAI

XINJIANG UYGUR

NINGXIA HUI ZU

Tarim Pendi

Junggar Pendi

Qaidam Pendi

Kunlun Shan

Altun Shan

Qilian Shan

Tien Shan

Tannu Ola

Altai Shan

NORTH KOREA

SOUTH KOREA

JAPAN

TAIWAN (FORMOSA)

PHILIPPINES

VIETNAM

LAOS

THAILAND (SIAM)

BURMA

BANGLADESH

BHUTAN

NEPAL

INDIA

ASSAM

JAMMU & KASHMIR

Karakoram

Himalaya

YELLOW SEA

EAST CHINA SEA

SOUTH CHINA SEA

BAY OF BENGAL

Ryukyu-Retto

BEIJING

SHANGHAI

HARBIN

SHENYANG

TIANJIN

WUHAN

CHONGQING

CHENGDU

GUANGZHOU

Hong Kong

TAIYUAN

BAOTOU

QINGDAO

DALIAN

NANJING

Tropic of Cancer

East from Greenwich

Projection : Bonne

ft m 6000 4000 3000 2000 1500 1000 400 200 0
18 000 12 000 9000 6000 4500 3000 1200 600 0 200 600

ft 6000 12 000 18 000
m 2000 4000 6000

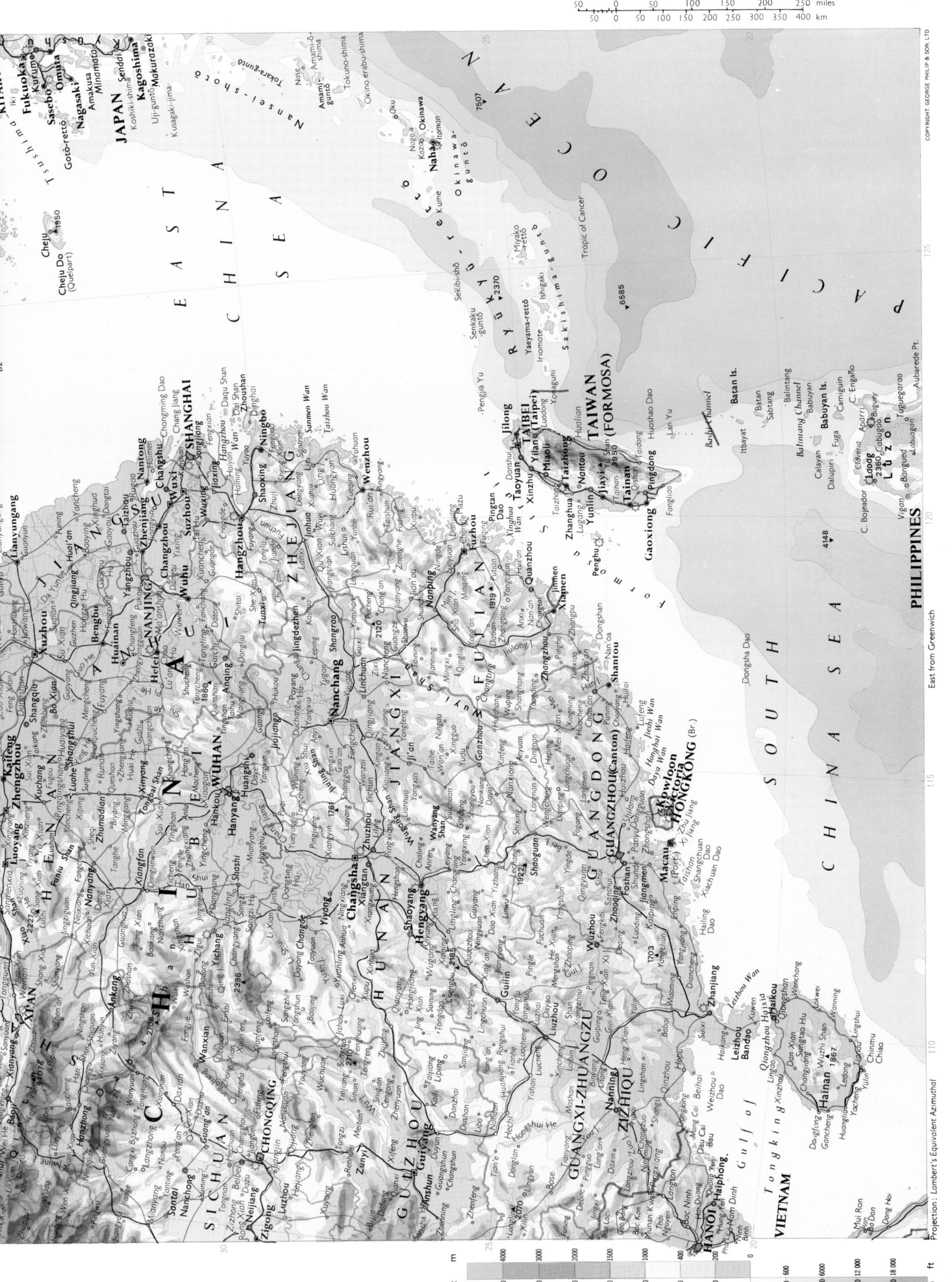

1:10 000 000

50   0   50   100   150   200   250 miles
50   0   50   100 150 200 250 300 350 400 km

JAPAN

Fukuoka
Kurume
Saseko
Nagasaki
Amakusa
Minamata
Kagoshima
Makurazaki
Iki
Sendai
Goto-retto

Tsushima

Koshiki-retto
Uji-gunto

Tanega-shima
Yaku-shima

Tokara-gunto

Nose.
Amami-o-shima
Amami-gunto
Tokuno-shima
Okino erabu-jima

Nansei-shoto

Oku
Tokuno-shima

Cheju
Cheju Do
(Quelpart)
1950

1907

Iheya
Naha
Okinawa
Okinawa-gunto
Kume
Sekibi-shō
Kerama-rettō
Senkaku-gunto
Miyako-rettō
2370
Miyako-shima
Ishigaki
Yaeyama-rettō
Iriomote
Sakishima-guntō
Yonaguni

RYUKYU

6585

PACIFIC OCEAN

Tropic of Cancer

EAST CHINA SEA

Chongming Dao
Daqu Shan
Zhoushan

Shanghai
Nantong
Changshu
Songjiang
Wuxi
Suzhou
Wuxing
Jiaxing
Hangzhou Wan
Ningbo

Hangzhou
Shaoxing
Sunmen Wan
Taizhou Wan

Wenzhou

Pengjia Yu

Peng-hu
Penghu

TAIWAN (FORMOSA)

Jilong
TAIBEI (Taipei)
Danshui
Xinzhu
Miaoli
Taizhong
Nantou
Jiayi
Tainan
Qishan
Gaoxiong
Pingdong

Huashan
Yilan
Taoyuan
Yunlin
3950
Taidong
Fangliao

Batan Is.
Batan
Sabtang

Balintang Channel
Babuyan Is.
Calayan
Dalupiri
Fuga
Camiguin

Bashi Channel

Luzon
2360
Aparri
Laoag
Vigan
C. Bojeador
C. Engaño
Buguey
Tuguegarao
Aubarede Pt.

4148

PHILIPPINES

JIANGSU
Lianyungang
Xuzhou
Huai'an
Yancheng
Yangzhou
NANJING
Zhenjiang
Changzhou
Wuhu

ANHUI
Bengbu
Huainan
Hefei

HENAN
Kaifeng
Zhengzhou
Luoyang

HUBEI
WUHAN
Hankou
Hanyang
Huangshi

Nanchang
Jingdezhen

ZHEJIANG

Fuzhou

FUJIAN
Nanping
Quanzhou
Xiamen
Zhangzhou

Jinmen

Shantou
Chaozhou
Jieshi Wan

GUANGDONG
GUANGZHOU (Canton)
Foshan
HONGKONG (Br.)
Kowloon
Victoria
Macau (Port.)
Zhu Jiang

XIAN

SHAANXI

HUNAN
Changsha
Xiangtan
Zhuzhou
Hengyang
Shaoyang

JIANGXI
Ganzhou

Shaoguan

SICHUAN
CHONGQING

GUIZHOU
Guiyang
Anshun

GUANGXI-ZHUANGZU
Nanning
Guilin
Liuzhou
Wuzhou

Zhanjiang
Leizhou Bandao

Hainan
Haikou
HAIZHOU

Gulf of Tongking

VIETNAM
HANOI
Haiphong

SOUTH CHINA SEA

Dongsha Dao

Zhongsha Dao

East from Greenwich

Projection: Lambert's Equivalent Azimuthal

ft   m
12 000 4000
9000   3000
6000   2000
4500   1500
3000   1000
1200   400
600   200
0   0
        200
        2000 600
        4000 1200 6000
        6000 2000 12 000
        m   ft   18 000

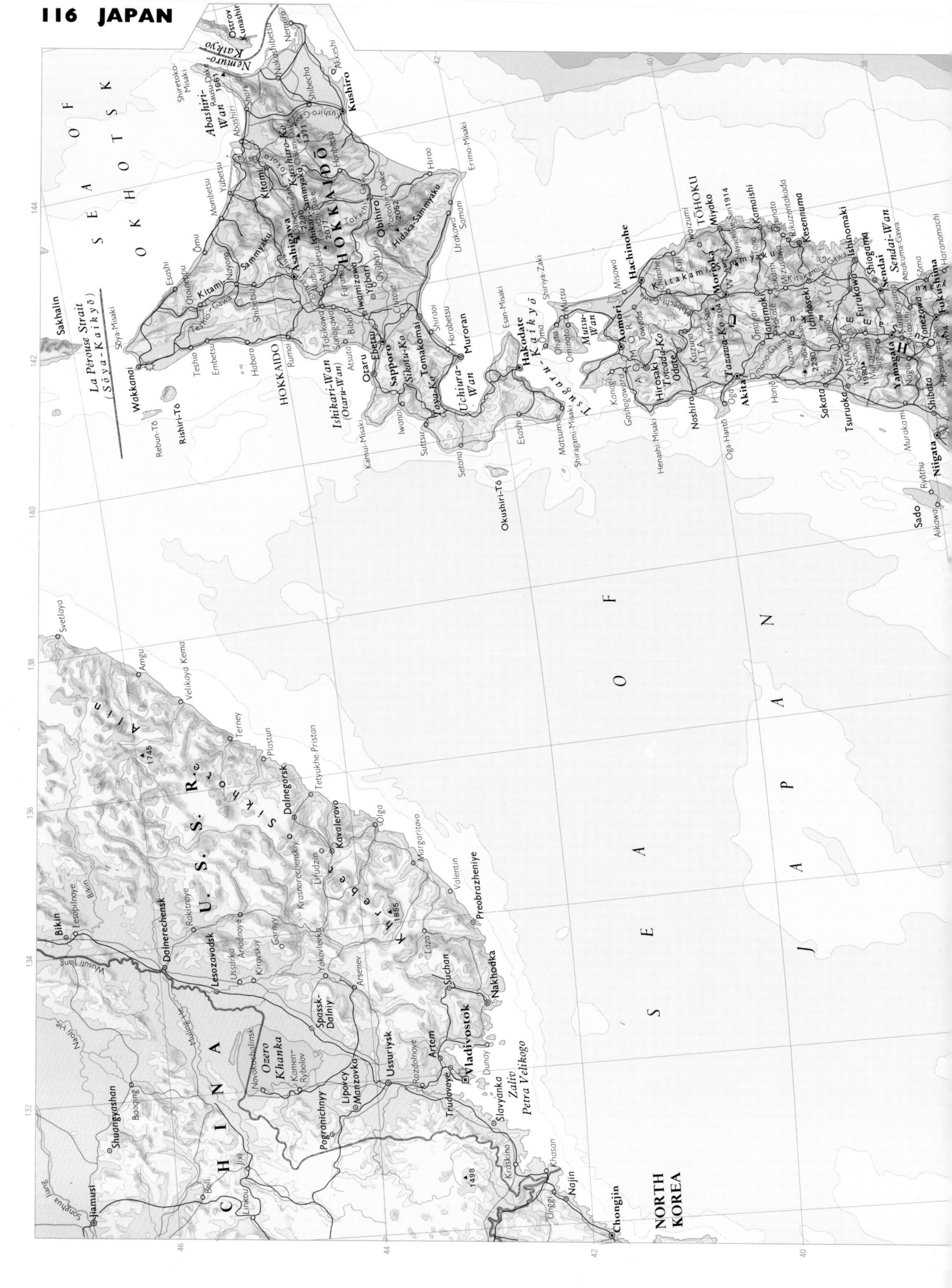

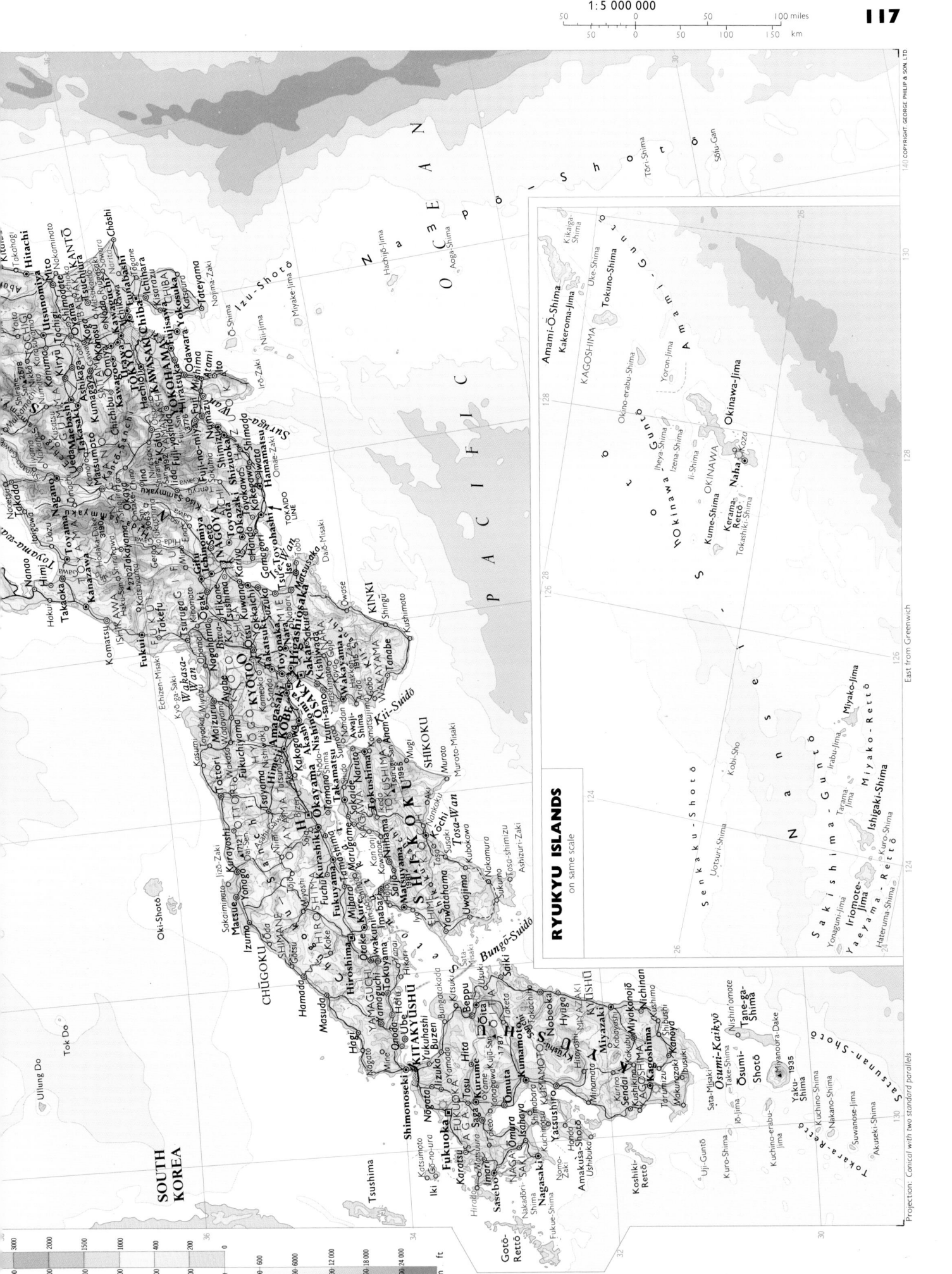

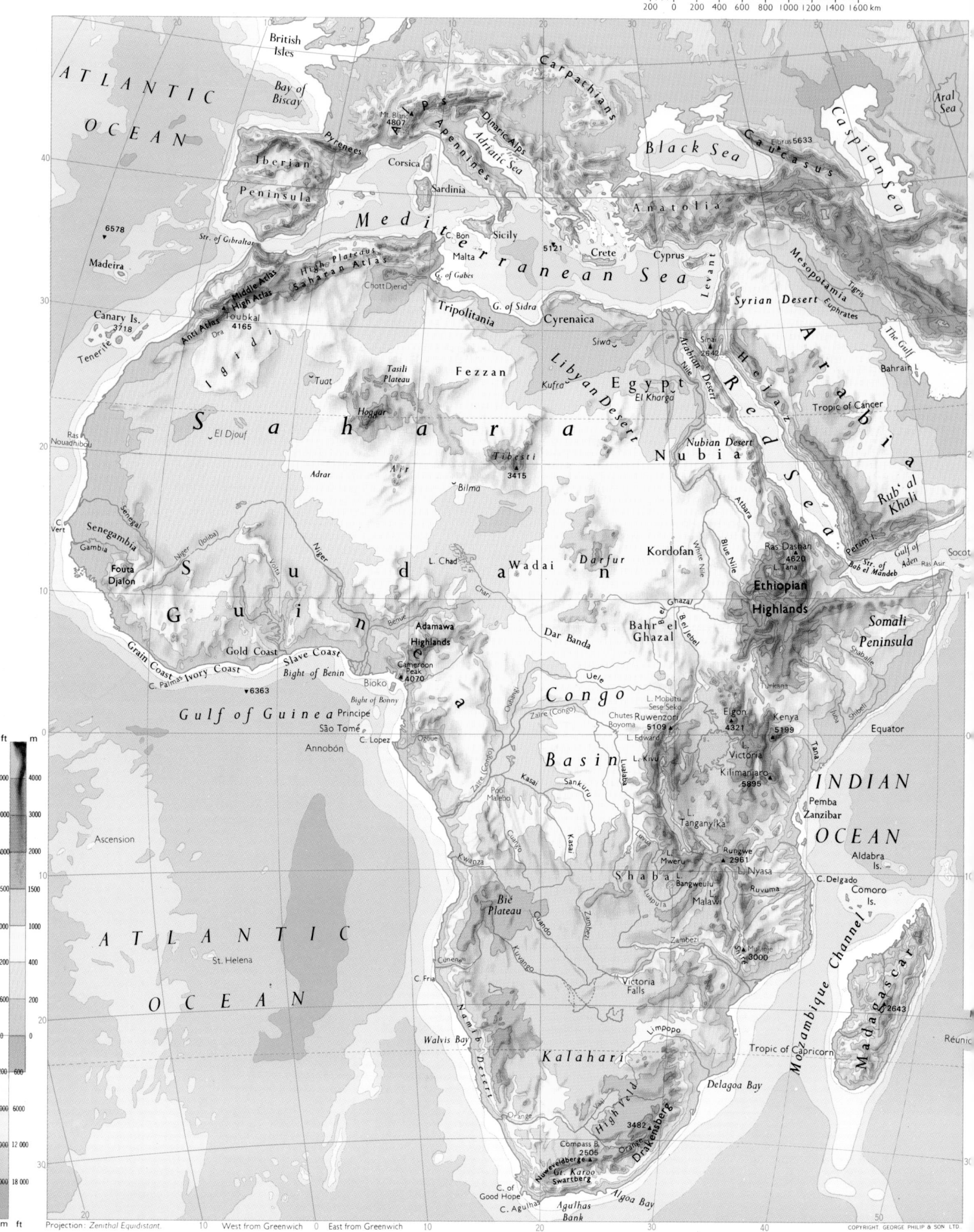

1:40 000 000

ATLANTIC OCEAN

British Isles

Bay of Biscay

Carpathians

Black Sea

Caucasus   Elbruz 5633

Aral Sea

Caspian Sea

Pyrenees   Mt. Blanc 4807   Alps   Apennines   Dinaric Alps   Adriatic Sea   Anatolia

Iberian Peninsula

Corsica

Sardinia

6578

Madeira

Str. of Gibraltar

Mediterranean Sea

Sicily   Malta   5121   Crete   Cyprus   Levant   Mesopotamia   Tigris   Euphrates   The Gulf

Canary Is.   3718

Tenerife

Middle Atlas   High Atlas   Toubkal 4165   Anti Atlas   Dra   Igidi   Saharan Atlas   High Plateaus   Chott Djerid   G. of Gabes   Tripolitania   G. of Sidra   Cyrenaica   Libyan Desert   Egypt   Arabian Desert   Sinai 2642   Red Sea   Hejaz   Arabia   Bahrain I.   Tropic of Cancer

Siwa   El Kharga   Nile   Nubian Desert   Nubia   Rub' al Khali   Perim I.   Str. of Bab el Mandeb   Gulf of Aden   Ras Asir   Socot

Ras Nouadhibou

Sahara

El Djouf   Tasili Plateau   Fezzan   Kufra

Tuat   Hoggar   Adrar   Aïr   Tibesti 3415   Bilma

C. Vert   Senegambia   Gambia   Fouta Djalon   Senegal   Niger (Joliba)   Niger   Volta   L. Chad   Chari   Wadai   Darfur   Kordofan   White Nile   Blue Nile   Atbara   Ras Dashan 4620   L. Tana   Ethiopian Highlands   Somali Peninsula

Sudan

Guinea

Grain Coast   Gold Coast   Ivory Coast   Slave Coast   Bight of Benin   C. Palmas   6363   Bioko   Benue   Adamawa Highlands   Cameroon Peak 4070   Dar Banda   Bahr el Ghazal   Bahr el Jebel   Shabelle

Gulf of Guinea   Príncipe   São Tomé   C. Lopez   Annobón   Ogôué   Uele   Ubangi   Congo Basin   Zaïre (Congo)   Chutes Boyoma   L. Mobutu Sese Seko   Ruwenzori 5109   L. Edward   Elgon 4321   Kenya 5199   Turkana   Equator

Ascension   St. Helena

ATLANTIC OCEAN

Kasai   Zaïre (Congo)   Pool Malebo   Kwango   Kasai   Sankuru   Lualaba   L. Kivu   Victoria   Kilimanjaro 5895   L. Tanganyika   Rungwe 2961   L. Mweru   Bangweulu   Luapula   Zambezi   L. Nyasa   Ruvuma   Mulanje 3000   INDIAN OCEAN   Pemba   Zanzibar   Aldabra Is.   C. Delgado   Comoro Is.

Bié Plateau   Cubango   Kwando   Kunene   Shaba   Malawi

Kalahari   Cunene   Kuvango   Namib Desert   Victoria Falls   Limpopo   Zambezi   Tropic of Capricorn   Mozambique Channel   Madagascar 2643   Réunic

Walvis Bay

High Veld   Drakensberg 3482   Compass B. 2505   Orange   Nuweveldberge   Gr. Karoo   Swartberg   C. of Good Hope   C. Agulhas   Agulhas Bank   Algoa Bay   Delagoa Bay

1:40 000 000

200   0   200   400   600   800   1000 miles
200   0   200   400   600   800   1000   1200   1400   1600 km

ATLANTIC OCEAN

UNITED KINGDOM · London · NETH. · GERMANY · POLAND · Warszawa
Paris · BELG. · E. · Praha · CZECHOSLOVAKIA · Kiyev
FRANCE · SWITZ · AUSTRIA · HUNGARY · Wien · ROMANIA · Odessa · Volgograd
Bay of Biscay · ITALY · YUGOSLAVIA · BULGARIA · Black Sea · U.   S.   S.   R.
PORTUGAL · SPAIN · Madrid · Roma · Adriatic Sea · ALB. · GREECE · Athínai · İstanbul · Ankara · TURKEY · Baku · Aral Sea
Lisboa · Corse · Sardegna · Kriti · CYPRUS · SYRIA · Halab · Al Mawşil · Tehrān · Caspian Sea
Madeira (Port.) · Tanger · Alger · Annaba · TUNIS · Sicilia · MALTA · Mediterranean Sea · Tel Aviv-Yafo · Dimashq · Baghdād · Eşfahān
Casablanca · Tétouan · Oran · Constantine · Sfax · Tarābulus · El Iskandarîya · Jerusalem · JORDAN · IRAN · Al Başrah
Rabat · Fès · MOROCCO · Marrakech · ALGERIA · Banghāzi · El Bayda · EL QAHIRA · El Suweis · KUWAIT · The Gulf · BAHRAIN
Essaouira · LIBYA · Sahra' el Libiya · EGYPT · El Faiyûm · SAUDI- ARABIA · QATAR
Islas Canarias · Tenerife · Ifni · Dra · Ghudāmis · In Salah · Ghat · Marzuq · Al Jawf · Aswân · Wadi Halfa · Es Sahrā en Nūbiya · Al Madīnah · Tropic of Cancer
El Aaiun · WESTERN SAHARA · Sahara · Dongola · Bûr Sûdân · Makkah · 'Asir
Dakhla · Fdérik · MAURITANIA · Agadez · Tombouctou · Gaò · NIGER · CHAD · Atbara · Kassala · Mitsiwa · YEMEN · SOUTH YEMEN · Socotra
Nouakchott · MALI · Niamey · Sokoto · Nguru · Lac Tchad · Abéché · Omdurmân · El Khartûm · Asmera · DJIBOUTI · G. of Aden · Berbera · Ras Asir · Dante
St. Louis · SENEGAL · Kayes · Bamako · BURKINA FASO · Ouagadougou · Kano · Maiduguri · Ndjamena (Ft.-Lamy) · Bousso · SUDAN · El Fasher · El Obeid · L. Tana · Addis Abeba · Harer · Hargeisa
Dakar · GAMBIA · Bissau · GUINEA · Kankan · NIGERIA · Kaduna · Bauchi · Sarh · ETHIOPIA · SOMALI REP.
Conakry · Freetown · SIERRA LEONE · LIBERIA · Bouake · Kumasi · Ibadan · Benue · Nggoundéré · CENTRAL AFRICAN REPUBLIC · Wâw · Mongalla · L. Turkana · Muqdisho
Monrovia · IVORY COAST · GHANA · Tamale · Lagos · Porto Novo · Enugu · CAMEROON · Bangui · Oubangui · KENYA · Equator · INDIAN
Abidjan · Accra · Lomé · Port Harcourt · Yaoundé · Malabo · Douala · EQUATORIAL GUINEA · Zaïre (Congo) · Kisangani · Kampala · UGANDA · L. Victoria · Nairobi
Sekondi-Takoradi · Bight of Benin · Bioko · SÃO TOMÉ & PRINCIPE · C. Lopez · GABON · Libreville · Mbandaka · L. Mobutu Sese Seko · RWANDA · Kisumu · Mombasa
Annobón · CONGO · ZAÏRE · L. Edward · L. Kivu · BURUNDI · Bujumbura · Kigoma · Tabora · Pemba · Zanzibar
Ascension · Brazzaville · Kinshasa · Ilebo · Mbuji-Mayi · L. Tanganyika · Dodoma · TANZANIA · Dar-es-Salaam
Pointe-Noire · Cabinda · Boma · Kananga · Kasai · Shaba · Kalemie · L. Mweru · Bukama · Likasi · Aldabra Is.
Luanda · ANGOLA · Lubumbashi · Kitwe · L. Nyasa · Ruvuma · Cabo Delgado · COMOROS · Antsiranana
Benguela · Lobito · Huambo · Namibe · ZAMBIA · Lilongwe · MALAWI · L. Malawi · Mozambique
Namib · Cunene · Kuvango · Kafue · Lusaka · Zambezi · Zomba · Blantyre · MOÇAMBIQUE · Quelimane · Mahajanga
Fria · Zambezi · Livingstone · ZIMBABWE · Harare · Chinde · Beira · MADAGASCAR · Toamasina · MAURITIUS
Swakopmund · Windhoek · NAMIBIA (SOUTH WEST AFRICA) · BOTSWANA · Bulawayo · Limpopo · Tropic of Capricorn · Antananarivo · Réunion (Fr.)
Walvis-baai · Kalahari · Gaborone · TRANSVAAL · Pretoria · Maputo (Lourenço Marques) · Fianarantsoa · Toliara
Lüderitz · Oranje · Kimberley · Bloem. · Johannesburg · SWAZ. · NATAL · Durban
Cape Town · Kaap die Goeie Hoop (Cape of Good Hope) · SOUTH AFRICA · CAPE PROVINCE · LES. · East London · Port Elizabeth

ATLANTIC OCEAN

Ascension (Br.) · St. Helena (Br.)

LES. = Lesotho
O. V. = Oranje-Vrystaat
SWAZ. = Swaziland

Projection: Zenithal Equidistant.   West from Greenwich   East from Greenwich   COPYRIGHT. GEORGE PHILIP & SON. LTD.

NORTH ATLANTIC

OCEAN

▼ 6578

SPAIN

Málaga • Almería

Cádiz
Str. of Gibraltar
Gibraltar (Br.)
Tanger
Ceuta (Sp.)
Tétouan
Larache
Al Hoceima
Melilla
Ksar el Kebir
Oujda
(Port Lyautey)
Kenitra
Quezzane
Tlemcen
Fès
Taza
Salé
Rabat
Meknès
Casablanca
El Jadida
Berrechid
Settat
Khouribga
Safi
Ras Beddouza
Marrakech
Essaouira
C. Rhir
4165
Agadir
Ifni

Oran
Sidi-Bel-Abbès
Mostaganem
Ech Cheliff
Blida
Algers (Algiers)
El Harrach
Tizi-Ouzou
Bejaïa
Skikda
Annaba
Médéa
2308
Constantine
Sétif
Batna
Biskra
Ghazaouet
Saïda
Tiaret
Bou Saâda
Hodna
Mecheria
Laghouat
Béchar
Abadla
Igli
Beni Ounif
El Goléa
Ghardaïa
Touggourt
El Oued
Chott el Djerid
Hassi el Rmel
Hassi Messaoud
Ft. Lallemand
Hassi el Gassi
Ghudāmis

Tindouf
Bir Mogrein

WESTERN SAHARA
Dakhla
Pta. Durnford
C. Barbas
Foûm el Hassane
Zouérate
Fdérik
Chār

MOROCCO
Moyen Atlas
Haut Atlas
Anti Atlas
Tiznit
Bou Izakarn
Dra
Mengoub

ALGERIA
Plateau du Tademaït
Adrar
In Belbel
Timimoun
Reggane
Aoulef el Arab
In Salah
Arak
Ouallene
Chech Erg
a Tanezrouft
Bidon 5 (Poste Maurice Cortier)
Tahat ▲ 2918
hbaggar
Tamanrasset
Idelès
Djanet
Illizi

Islas Canarias (Sp.)
La Palma
Tenerife
Gomera
Hierro
Lanzarote
Fuerteventura
Arrecife
Puerto del Rosario
Sta. Cruz
Las Palmas
Gran Canaria

El Aaiún
Semara
Bu Craa
Ain Ben Tili

MAURITANIA
Nouâdhibou (Port Étienne)
Ras La Güera
Nouâdhibou
Atâr
Chinguetti
Ouadâne
El Djouf
Terhazza
Taoudenni
Akjoujt
Tichît
Akreijit
Rachid
Tidjikja
Moudjeria
Togba
Nouakchott
Boutilimit
Mederdra
Aleg
Tâmchekket
Ouâlâta
Kiffa
Néma
Timbedgha
Bassikounou
Kaédi
Néma
Araouane
Bou Djébéha
Kidal

Poste Maurice Cortier
Adrar des Iforhas
Tessalit
Admer

Aïr (Azbine)
Monts Tamgak
Iférouâne
1800
In-Gall
Agadez

MALI
Tombouctou
Goundam
Diré
Kabara
Gourma-Rharous
Gao
Bourem
Bamba
Ansongo
Ménaka
Hombori
Douentza
Mopti

NIGER
Tahoua
Tamaské
Filingué
Birni Nkonni
Madaoua
Tanout
Tessaoua
Zinder
Kano
Maradi

St. Louis
Tivaouane
Rufisque
Thiès
Dakar
Kaolack

SENEGAL
Louga
Dahra
Linguère
Matam
Podor
Bogué
Dagana
Kayes
Bafoulabé
Nioro du Sahel
Nara
Yélimané
Sélibabi
Mbout

GAMBIA
Banjul
Georgetown

GUINEA-BISSAU
Bissau
Bafatá
Bolama
Gabú
Ziguinchor
Kolda
Sédhiou

Arquipélago dos Bijagós
C. Verga

GUINEA
Conakry
Dubréka
Boké
Fria
Kindia
Mamou
Dalaba
Labé
Fouta Djalon
Télimélé
Dinguiraye
Siguiri
Kankan
Kissidougou
Faranah
Kouroussa
Beyla
Nzérékoré

SIERRA LEONE
Freetown
Waterloo
Makeni
Bo
Kenema
Sherbro I.
Bonthe

LIBERIA
Monrovia
Marshall
Buchanan
River Cess
Greenville
Robertsport
Careysburg

IVORY COAST
Man
Daloa
Gagnoa
Bouaké
Séguéla
Korhogo
Katiola
Dimbokro
Abidjan
Grand Bassam
C. Palmas
San-Pédro
Sassandra
Tabou

Bamako
Koulikoro
Ségou
Sikasso
Bougouni
Kati
Kita
Bafing

BURKINA FASO
Ouagadougou
Ouahigouya
Kaya
Koudougou
Fada
Tenkodogo
Bobo-Dioulasso
Banfora
Diébougou
Gaoua
Léo
Djibo
Dori
Dédougou

Niamey
Say
Dosso
Birni N'Konni
Gaya

GHANA
Tamale
Yendi
Bolgatanga
Wa
Kumasi
Sunyani
Kintampo
Lake Volta
Koforidua
Accra
Cape Coast
Sekondi-Takoradi
Tema
Ho
Obuasi

TOGO
Lomé
Sokodé
Atakpamé
Sansanné-Mango
Kpalimé

BENIN
Porto-Novo
Cotonou
Abomey
Parakou
Djougou
Natitingou
Nikki
Kandi
Malanville
Savalou
Savé

NIGERIA
Lagos
Ibadan
Ibadan
Oyo
Oshogbo
Iwo
Ilorin
Ife
Ilesha
Ogbomosho
Abeokuta
Ondo
Akure
Benin City
Abuja
Kaduna
Zaria
Kano
Katsina
Gusau
Sokoto
Gumel
Hadejia
Potiskum
Bauchi
Jos
Makurdi
Enugu
Onitsha
Aba
Port-Harcourt
Calabar
Warri
Sapele
Lokoja
Minna
Lafia
Keffi
Shendam

CAMEROON
Douala
Bioko
Rey Malabo

Volta Noire
Black Volta
White Volta
Niger
Benue

Bight of Benin

Projection: Sanson Flamsteed's Sinusoidal
West from Greenwich
East from Greenwich

Pantelleria (It.)
C. Passero
Sicily
Ragusa
Lampedusa (It.)
Kerkenna
Djerba

TURKEY
Antalya
Antalya Körfezi
Ródhos
Karpathos
Iráklion
Kríti

CYPRUS
Limassol
Nicosia

Al Lādhiqīya
Hamāh
Hims
Tarābulus
Bayrūt
LEBANON
Dimashq (Damascus)

SYRIA
Halab
Al Mawşil (Mosul)
Nahr Dijlah (Tigris)
İskenderun
Antakya
Iskenderun Körfezi

IRAQ
Bādiyat ash Shām
Ar Rutbah

MEDITERRANEAN SEA

Tarābulus (Tripoli)
Al Khums
Zlītan
Misrātah
Banghāzī (Benghazi)
Banī Walīd
Gharyān
968
Mizdah
Tājūrā
Al Qawāḩah
Zuwārah
Khalīj Surt
Surt
Al Bu'ayrāt
Zueitina
Ajdābiyah
Marsa Brega
Ra's Al-Unuf
Al' Uqaylah

Tūkrah
Al Marj
Shaḩḩāt (Cyrene)
Apollonia
Zāwiyat al Bayḏā'
878
Darnah
Tulmaythah
Tubruq (Tobruk)
Khalīj Bunbah
Khalte el Salâm
Sîdi Barrâni
Barqūq
Salûm

5121

El Iskandarîya (Alexandria)
El 'Alamein
(Rosetta) Rashīd
Damanhûr
El Mahalla el Kubra
Dumyât
Port Saïd
El 'Arîsh
Gazaza
Rafaḩ
Beer Sheva
ISRAEL
Tel Aviv-Yafo
Jerusalem (Al Quds)
Dead Sea
'Ammān
JORDAN
Khalīj al 'Aqabah
Al Jawf
Ma'ān
Tabūk
An Nafūd
SAUDI ARABIA
Mada'in Salih
Taymā'
Al Muwayliḩ
'Aqaba
Elat
Tûr
Sinâi
Gebel

LIBYA
Tarâbulus
Hūn
Zillah
Marādah
Awjilah
Al 'Iraq
Cyrenaica
Sahrâ'
Al Jaghbūb
Qâra
Munkhafed el Qattâra (Qattâra Depression)
El 'Alamein
El Qâhira (Cairo)
El Gîza
Helwân
Ismā'īlīya
Buheirat-Murrat-el-Kubra
El Qantara
El Suweis (Suez)

Fezzan
Adri
Brach
Sabhā
Tmassah
Tasāwah
Marzūq
Al Qaţrūn
Wāw al Kabīr
Al Jazīrah
Al Jawf
Al Kufrah
Rebiana
Uweinat 1893
Ayn al 'Uwaynāt
Sadd el 'Ali (Aswân High Dam)
Buheiret en Naser (Lake Nasser)
Dunqul
Aswân
El Shallâl
1st Cataract
Bârîs
El Wâhât el-Khârga
El Khârga
El Qasr
El Wâhât el-Dakhla
Mūt
Qasr Farâfra
Es Sahrâ'
Asyūt
Qasr Qârûn
El Faiyûm
Beni Suef
Sinnuris
El Minyâ
Beni Mazâr
Mallawî
Manfalūt
Dairūt
Abu Tig
Akhmîm
Sohâg
Girga
Qena
Luxor (El Uqsur)
Qûs
Isnâ
Idfu
Edfu
Tahta
Esh Sharqîya
EGYPT
Lîbîya
Sahrâ'
El Bawiti

Tropic of Cancer

RED SEA
Quseir
Bûr Safâga
Umm Lajj
Al Wajh
Yanbu' al Bahr
Al Madīnah
Ras Bânâs
Bîr Shalatein
Rabigh Qasr
Halaib
Bîr Ungât
Ras Hadarba
Mersa
Jiddah
Makkah (Mecca)
Al Līth
At Ta'if
Muhammad Qôl
Ras Abu Shagara
2635
Bûr Sûdân (Port Sudan)
Sawâkin
Suakin
Sinkât
Haiya Junction
Trinkitat
Tokar
Aqîq
Ras Kasar
Karora
BAHR EL AHMAR

Tibesti
Emi Koussi 3415
Bardaï
3150
Tarso Emissi
Zouar
Aozou
Gouri
Toummo
Wour
Madama
Anaye
Bilma

ERITREA
Nakfa
Mitsiwa
Asmera
Zula
Keren
Akordat
Adi Ugri
Adi Keyih
Aksum
Adwa
Mekele
4620
Sekota
Lalibela

Borkou
Ounianga-Kébir
Ounianga-Sérir
Faya-Largeau
Ain Galakka
Fada
Ennedi
Djourab
Depression du Mourdi
Bahr el Ghazal (Soro)

CHAD
Zigey
Rig-Rig
Mao
Moussoro
Massaguet
Bokoro
Bol
Lac Tchad
Massakory
Yao
L. Fitri
Bitkine
Mongo
Massénya
Ati
Oum Hadjer
Am Dam
Ndjamena (Ft. Lamy)
Kousseri
Bongor
Melfi
Bousso
Kyabé
Am Timan
Lai
Kélo
Koumra
Goz Beïda
Moïssala
Moundou
Doba
Sarh
Mongororo

Nukheila
Laqiya Arba'in
Bir 'Atrun
Es Sahrâ en Nûbiya
Wadi Halfa
El Wâhât el Selîma
2nd Cataract
Kosha
Abri
Delgo
(Nubian Desert)
Abu Hamed
3rd Cataract
Dongola
Argo
Ed Debba
Kareima
Merowe
Korti
Old Dongola
El Khandaq
ESH SHAMÂLIYA
Karmakol
El Kab
Berber
Ed Dâmer
Atbara
Adarama
Musmar
Derudeb
AN NIL
4th Cataract
5th Cataract
6th Cataract
Shendî
Geili
El Khartûm Bahrî
Omdurmân
El Khartûm
Khartoum
Kassala
AN NKASSALA
Barentu

SHAMÂL DÂRFÛR
Tine
Kutum
Malha
Umm Keddada
Hamrat esh Sheykh
Sodiri
Kaga
Kagmar
El Wuza
Bara
SHAMÂL KORDOFAN
El Obeid
Umm Bel
Er Rahad
SUDAN
El Fâsher
Kabkabîya
El Junaynah
Zalingei
Marra 3088
DÂRFÛR
Nyālā
JANUB DÂRFÛR
Idd el Ghanam
Ghanam
Buram
Abu Matariq
Hajar Banga
Rahad al Bardi
GEZIRA
Wâd Medanî
El Mafâza
Ed Dueim
Umm Ruwaba
Ed Dâra
Rashad
Dilling
Kadugli
Talodi
Heiban
JANUB KORDOFAN
El Odaiya
Abū Zabad
En Nahud
Umm Dam
Wad Banda
Tandalti
Gedaref
Gallâbât
Rufa'a
Sennâr
Singa
Kôsti
Er Roseires
Renk
Melut
Kodok
Tungaru
A'ALI EN NIL
Malakal
Nasir
Abwong
Fangak
Bentiu
BUHEIRAT
Tonj
Yirol
Bôr
JONGLEI
Kongor
Pibor P.
Duk Fadiat
Akôbo
Gambela
ETHIOPIA
Addis Abeba (Addis Ababa)
Addis Alem
Nekemte
Dembidolo
Gore
Jima
Ziway
Asela
L. Shala
L. Abaya
L. Stefanie (L. Shamo)
4200
Sodo
Chencha
Gidole
Burji
Yabelo
Dilla
Chew Bahir (L. Stefanie)
Todenyang
Debre Markos
Debre Tabor
L. Tana
Gonder
Metema
Mota
Alibo

CENTRAL AFRICAN REPUBLIC
Bangui
Bozoum
Bossembélé
Bouca
Bossangoa
Batangafo
Markounda
Kaga Bandoro
Bria
Yalinga
Ippy
Grimari
Bambari
Bakouma
Rafaï
Zémio
Obo
GHARB EL ISTIWA'IYA
Maridi
Tambura
Amâdi
Yambio
SHARQ EL ISTIWA'IYA
Torit
Kapoeta
Juba
Mongalla
BAHR EL GHAZAL
Wâw
Deim Zubeir
Râga
Mvolo
Nyamlëll
Aweil
Gogrial
Mesha er Req
Rumbêk
EL BUHEIRAT
Tonj
Bentiu
Nil el Abyad (White Nile)
Jur
Bahr el 'Arab

ZAÏRE (CONGO)
Bondo
Uere
Bili
Ango
Faradje
Dungu
Niangara
Aba

KENYA
L. Turkana
Lokitaung
Moyale
Mega

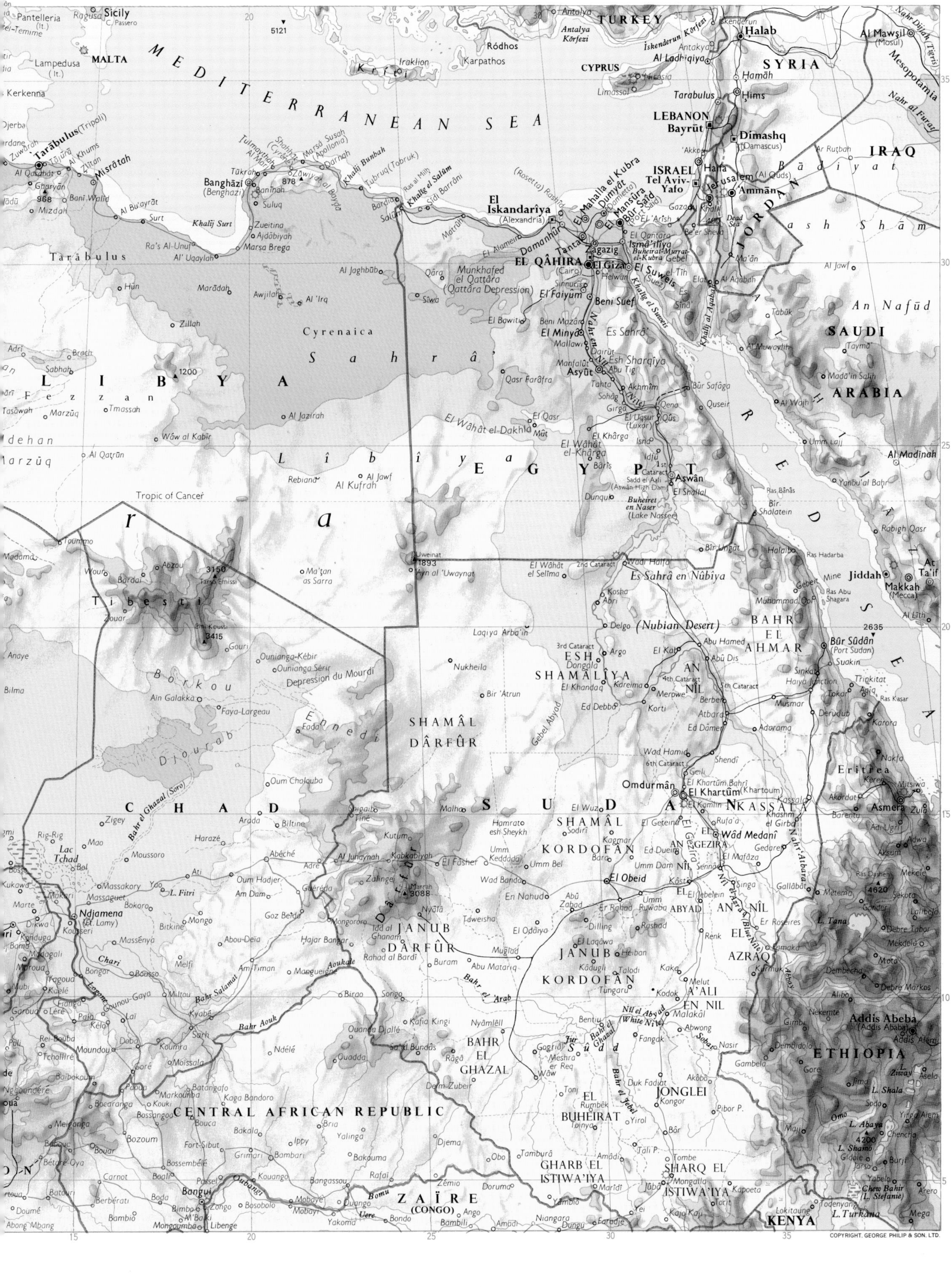

COPYRIGHT. GEORGE PHILIP & SON LTD.

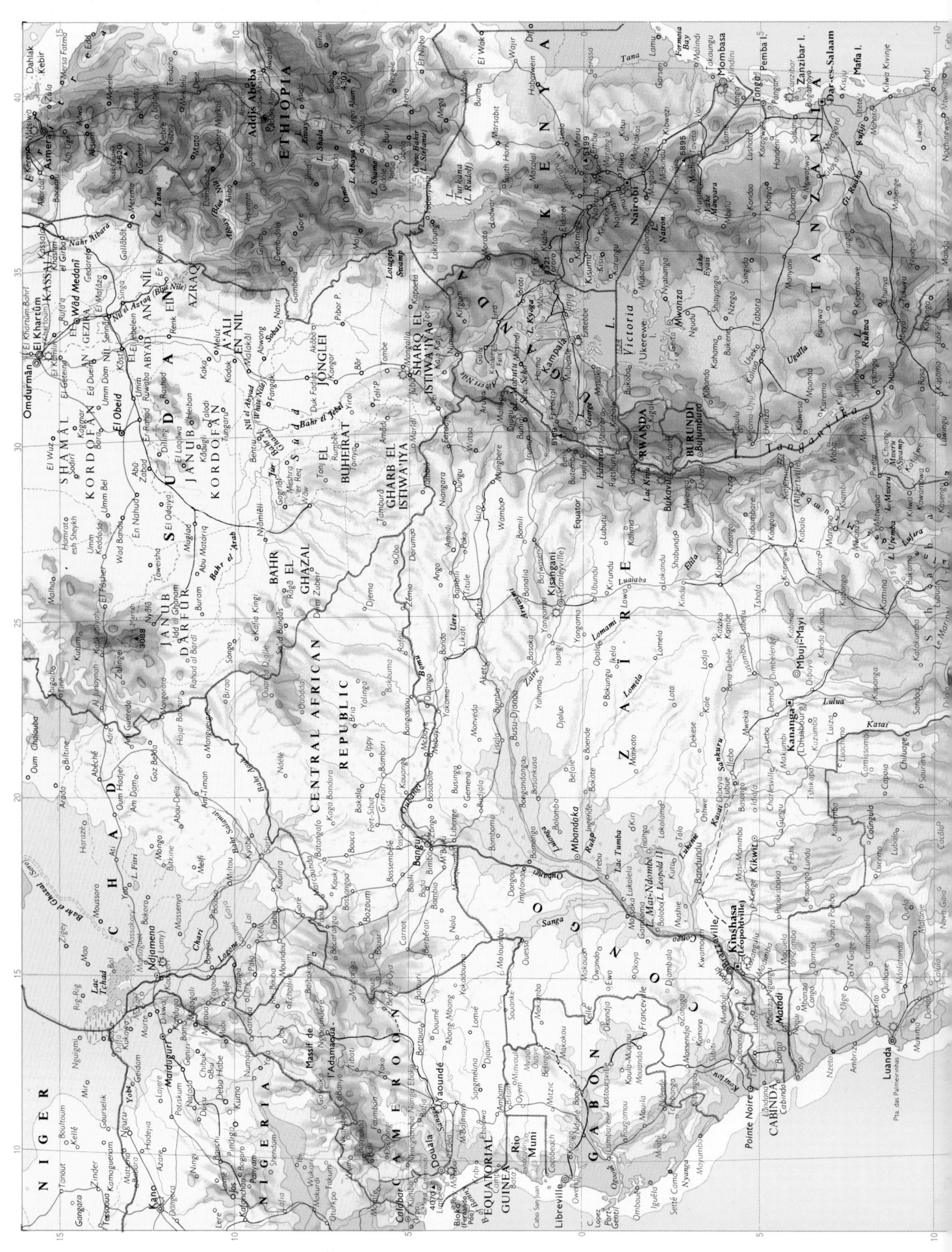

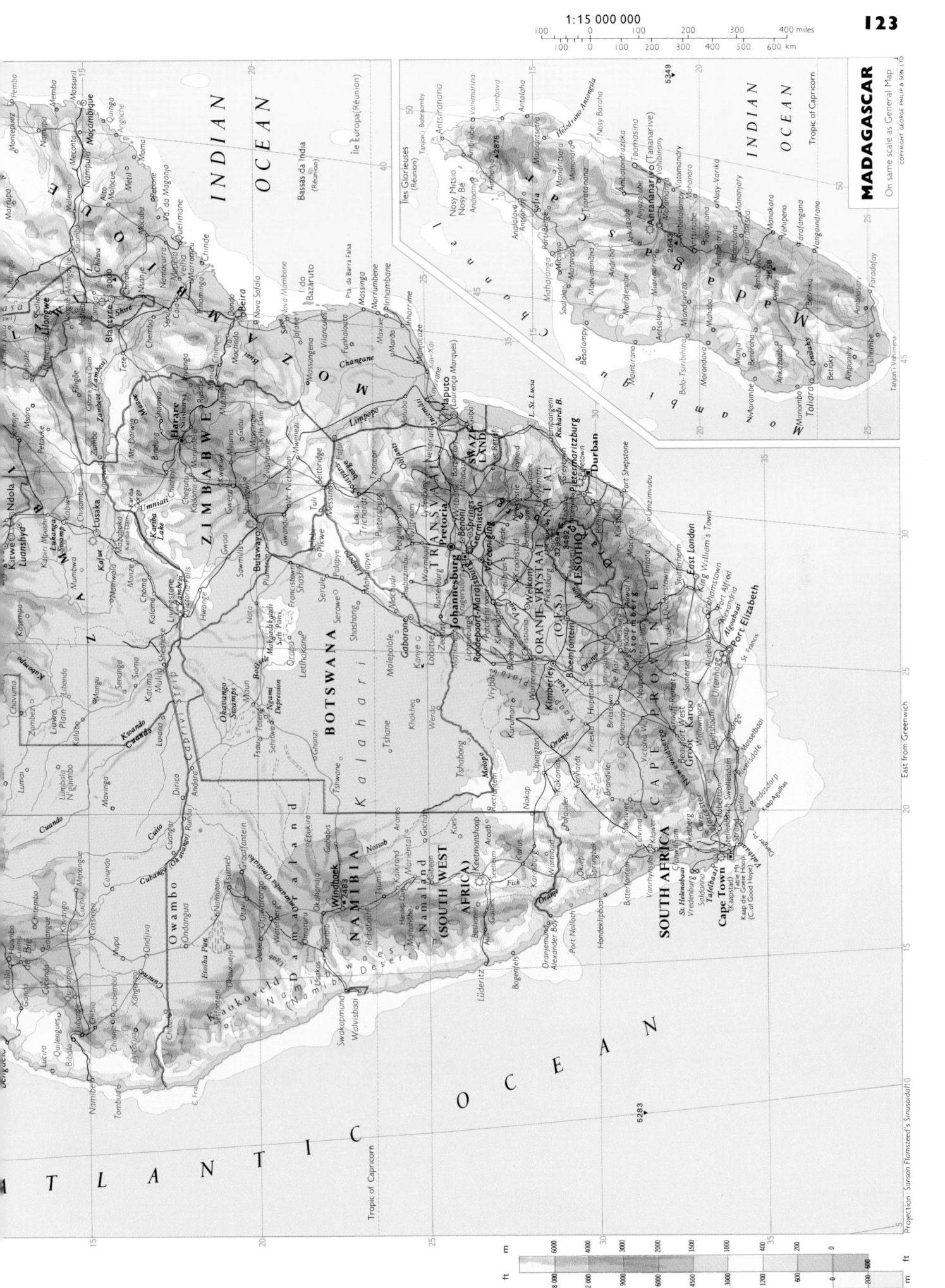

EUROPE

Leningrad

Moskva

U.S.S.R.

Sverdlovsk

Omsk

Tomsk

Ob

Novosibirsk

Barnaul

Irkutsk

Chita

Lena

Okhotsk

Kamchatka

Komandorskie Is. (U.S.S.R.)

Near I. 7822

Aleutian Is.

Aleutian Trench

Semipalatinsk

Yenisey

Ozero Baykal

Ulan Ude

Blagoveshchensk Amur

Khabarovsk

Sakhalin

Petropavlovsk

Karaganda

L. Balkhash

Hovd

Ulyasutay

Ulaanbaatar

MONGOLIA

Manchuria

Harbin

La Perouse Strait

Sea of Okhotsk

Kuril Is.

Kuril Trench

10,542

Yokohama - Vancouver 4280

KURO SIWO

Emperor Seamount Chain

7168

Aral Sea

Alma Ata

Ürümqi

Altai

Changchun

Shenyang

Vladivostok

Hakodate

3389

Tashkent

Samarkand

A   S   I   A

Beijing

Dandong

KOREA

Sea of Japan

Sendai

AFGHANISTAN

Kabul

Srinagar

Kunlun Shan

Lanzhou

Tianjin

Dalian

Sŏul

Pusan

JAPAN

Kyōto

TOKYO

Yokohama

Lahore

PAKISTAN

Mt. Everest 8848

XIZANG (TIBET)

Lhasa

Xi'an

Jinan

Qingdao

Kitakyūshū

Nagasaki

Ōsaka

Nagoya

Fuji-san 3776

Shikoku

Honshu Ridge

Japan Trench

Delhi

Agra

Himalaya

Nepal

CHINA

Nanjing

SHANGHAI

Yellow Sea

Kyūshū

1580

10,554

Kanpur

Brahmaputra

Chongqing

Wuhan

Hangzhou

1066

East China Sea

Ryūkyū Is.

KURO SIWO

Bonin Is.

Marcus I.

6603

INDIA

Calcutta

BANGLA- DESH

Chittagong

Ganges

Varanasi

Myitkyina

Kunming

Changsha

Chang Jiang

Wenzhou

Fuzhou

Xiamen

Taibei

Taiwan (Formosa)

Volcano Is.

Marcus

Necker Ridge

Wake I. (U.S.)

Cuttack

Mandalay

BURMA

Chiengmai

Guangzhou

MACAU (Port.)

HONG KONG

Hainan

6303

C. Engano

Northern Marianas

PA

Hyderabad

Bay of Bengal

Rangoon

THAILAND (SIAM)

Bangkok

VIETNAM

Hanoi

South China Sea

Manila

PHILIPPINES

Mariana Trench

Guam (U.S.)

U.S. TRUST TERR. OF THE PACIFIC ISLANDS

Bikini Atoll

Marshall Is.

Madras

Andaman Is.

Mergui Arch.

Isthmus of Kra

CAMBODIA

Phnom Penh

Ho Chi Minh (Saigon)

Mindoro

Samar

10,497

Palawan

Sulu Sea

11,022

Micronesia

Yap

Eniwetok Atoll

SRI LANKA

Colombo

Nicobar Is.

1567

Gulf of Thailand

C. Camau

1078

Kinabalu

Mindanao

Belau

Fed. States of Micronesia

Truk

Ponape

EQUATORIAL

Jaluit

1840

George Town

PENINSULAR MALAYSIA

Kuala Lumpur

Labuan

SABAH

4101

Celebes Sea

Mindanao Trench

Caroline Islands

Melanesia

O

Butaritari

SINGAPORE

Natuna

BRUNEI

SARAWAK

INDO

Borneo

Celebes

Moluccas

Halmahera

Dampier Strait

Admiralty Is.

New Ireland

NAURU

Banaba

Nias

Sunda

Bangka

Palembang

Sumatra

Buru

Ceram

Amboina

Irian Jaya

5029

PAPUA NEW GUINEA

Bismarck Arch.

Madang

Rabaul

New Britain

Gilbert Is.

Colombo - Fremantle 3100

Java Sea

Flores Sea

Ujung Pandang

Banda Sea

Aru Is.

NEW GUINEA

Lae

9103

SOLOMON ISLANDS

TUVALU (Ellice Is.)

Funafuti

Christmas I. (Austral.)

Jakarta

Semarang

Surabaya

Java

Bali

7440

Tanimbar Is.

Port Moresby

Honiara

Guadalcanal

Sta. Cruz I.

Cocos (Keeling) Is. (Austral.)

INDIAN

Sunda Strait

Java Trench

7450

Lombok

Sumbawa

Flores

Sumba

Timor

Arafura Sea

Torres Strait

Thursday I.

C. York

Louisiade Arch.

9165

Wallis & Futuna (Fr.)

Rotuma

1772

C. Arnhem

G. of Carpentaria

Coral Sea Islands Territory

VANUATU

Vanua Levu

FIJI

Vitu Levu

Suva

Darwin

Ashmore Is.

Larrimah

Coral Sea

Al 'Adan - Melbourne 6445

N.W. Cape

Onslow

Wyndham

NORTHERN TERRITORY

Newcastle Waters

Cairns

Townsville

Chesterfield Is.

New Caledonia (Fr.)

7570

Noumea

Loyalty Is.

OCEAN

Shark Bay

WESTERN AUSTRALIA

Alice Springs

Mt. Isa

AUSTRALIA

Great Divide

QUEENSLAND

Longreach

Rockhampton

Maryborough

Norfolk I. (Aust.)

Kermadec

Geraldton

Oodnadatta

L. Eyre

SOUTH AUSTRALIA

Brisbane

Ipswich

10,8

Perth

Fremantle

Kalgoorlie-Boulder

Darling

NEW SOUTH WALES

Lord Howe I. (Aust.)

Cape Town - Fremantle 5615

Geographe Bay

Albany

K. George Sd.

Great Australian Bight

F. - A. 1353

Murray

Sydney

Newcastle

Katoomba

Wollongong

S - A 1274

Kerr

10,047

South East Indian Ridge

Amsterdam I. (Fr.)

St. Paul I. (Fr.)

Encounter Bay

Adelaide

Ballarat

VICTORIA

Canberra

Mt. Kosciusko 2230

AUSTRALIAN CURRENT

Tasman Sea

Auckland

Hamilton

NEW ZEALAND

Crozet Is. (Fr.)

Cape Town - Melbourne 5814

Cape Town - Hobart 5838

Mid Oceanic

East Indian Ridge

Rise

Geelong

Bass Strait

Melbourne

Launceston

TASMANIA

Hobart

W. 1293

Mt. Cook 3764

Nelson

Wellington

Cook Strait

Palmerston N.

Kerguelen Is. (Fr.)

Indian-Antarctic Ridge

Christchurch

Oamaru

Dunedin

Invercargill

Stewart

Chath

Bounty Is.

Heard Is. (Aust.)

Auckland Is. (N.Z.)

Macquarie Is. (Austral.)

Campbell I. (N.Z.)

Antipode (N.

Pa

ft   m

18 000   6000

12 000   4000

6000   2000

3000   1000

600   200

0   0

200   600

2000   6000

4000   12 000

6000   18 000

8000   24 000

m   ft

ALASKA
Gulf of Alaska
Juneau
Prince of Wales
Sitka
Prince Rupert
Queen Charlotte Is.
Kitimat
Vancouver
Vancouver I.
Victoria
Seattle
Tacoma
Portland
C. Blanco
Mendocino Seascarp
C. Mendocino
Sacramento
Oakland
San Francisco
Los Angeles
San Diego
Hawaiian Is. (U.S.A.)
Oahu
Honolulu
Hawaii
(U.S.)

GREENLAND
C. Farewell
Hudson Bay
Churchill
Lynn Lake
Belcher Is.
Dawson Creek
L. Athabaska
Prince Albert
Edmonton
Saskatoon
Hamilton Inlet
Schefferville
Labrador
CANADA
NORTH AMERICA
Strait of Belle Isle
Newfoundland
NORTH
Winnipeg
L. Winnipeg
Regina
Medicine Hat
Spokane
Helena
Butte
Bismarck
Duluth
L. Superior
Ste. Marie
Montréal
Québec
Anticosti
G. of St. Lawrence
Pr. Edward I.
C. Race
C. Breton I.
Saint John
Sable I.
New York - Southampton
Boise
Cheyenne
Minneapolis
St. Paul
Milwaukee
CHICAGO
L. Michigan
L. Huron
Ottawa
Toronto
L. Erie
Buffalo
Detroit
Pittsburgh
Boston
C. Sable
ATLANTIC
Salt Lake City
Denver
Kansas
Des Moines
St. Louis
Cincinnati
Indianapolis
Philadelphia
NEW YORK
Baltimore
Washington
Richmond
Norfolk
OCEAN
UNITED STATES
Santa Fé
Oklahoma
Memphis
Little Rock
Atlanta
C. Hatteras
New York - Recife
Bermuda (U.K.)
Los Angeles
El Paso
Dallas
Mississippi
Appalachian Mts
Savannah
Jacksonville
Ciudad Juárez
Austin
San Antonio
Houston
New Orleans
Mobile
Tampa
Florida Strait
Miami
BAHAMAS
Guadalupe
Pto. Eugenia
CALIFORNIAN CURRENT
Sierra Madre
Gulf of California
Torreón
Monterrey
Tampico
San Luis Potosí
Gulf of Mexico
CUBA
La Habana
West Indies
Tropic of Cancer
C.S. Lucas
Revilla Gigedo Is. (Mexico)
Aguascalientes
Guadalajara
Mexico
Mérida
Yucatan Channel
Hispaniola
DOM. REP.
HAITI
JAMAICA
Kingston
PUERTO RICO (U.S.)
Leeward Is.
Clarion Fracture Zone
Puebla
Veracruz
Acapulco
BELIZE
GUATEMALA
HONDURAS
Tegucigalpa
Caribbean Sea
Santo Domingo
St. Thomas (U.S.)
Virgin Is.
Guadeloupe (Fr.)
Martinique (Fr.)
BARBADOS
Clipperton Fracture Zone
Clipperton I. (Fr.)
EL SALVADOR
NICARAGUA
Managua
CENTRAL AMERICA
COSTA RICA
PANAMA
San José
Barranquilla
Curaçao (Ne.)
Windward Is.
TRINIDAD & TOBAGO
Maracaibo
Caracas
VENEZUELA
Cocos I.
Panamá Canal
Medellín
Bogotá
Cali
COLOMBIA
Orinoco
Equator
Galápagos (Ecuador)
C.S. Francisco
Quito
ECUADOR
Chimborazo
Cuenca
Iquitos
Guayaquil
Amazon
Manaus
C. Pariñas
BRAZIL
SOUTH
PACIFIC OCEAN
Chiclayo
Trujillo
Lobos I.
PERU
Lima
Callao
AMERICA
Cuzco
L. Titicaca
Illampu & Ancohuma
La Paz
BOLIVIA
Arequipa
Arica
Iquique
Chile
PARAGUAY
Antofagasta Trench
Asunción
Tucumán
Corrientes
Tropic of Capricorn
Salta
Córdoba
Rosario
Santa Fé
URUGUAY
Aconcagua
Valparaíso
Santiago
Buenos Aires
La Plata
Montevideo
Rio de la Plata
ARGENTINA
Concepción
Neuquén
Mar del Plata
SOUTH
ATLANTIC
OCEAN
Chonos Arch.
Falkland Is. (U.K.)
Stanley
South Georgia
Wellington
Punta Arenas
Str. of Magellan
Tierra del Fuego
C. Horn

Boundaries of the artesian basins - - - - - - -

Projection: Bonne

East from Greenwich

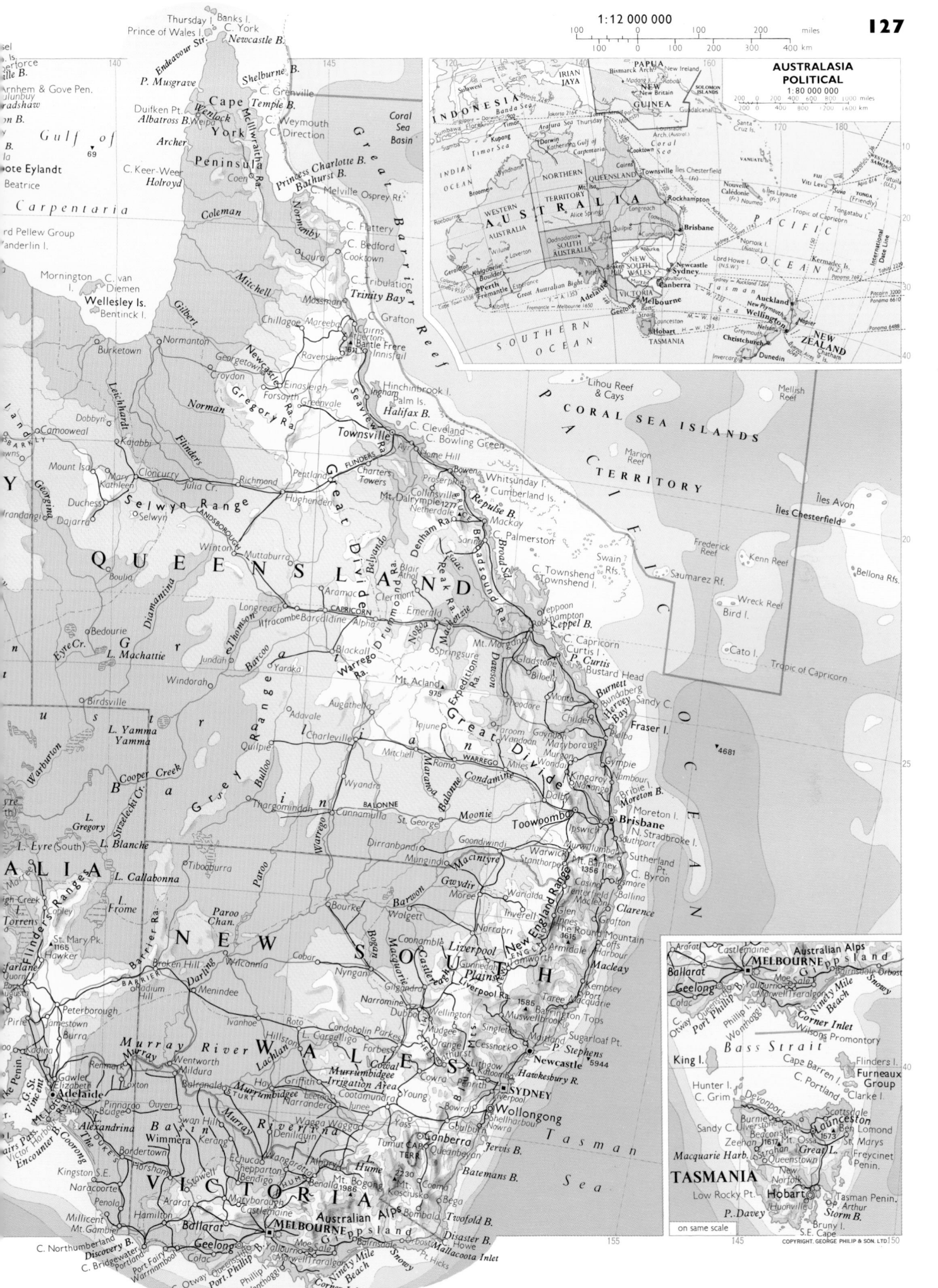

1:12 000 000

100   0   100   200   miles
100   0   100   200   300   400 km

AUSTRALASIA
POLITICAL
1:80 000 000

200   0   200   400   600   800   1000 miles
200   0   400   800   1200   1600 km

INDONESIA

PAPUA
NEW
GUINEA

Gulf of
Carpentaria

Coral
Sea
Basin

NORTHERN
TERRITORY

QUEENSLAND

WESTERN
AUSTRALIA

AUSTRALIA

SOUTH
AUSTRALIA

NEW
SOUTH
WALES

Sydney
Canberra
Adelaide   VICTORIA   Melbourne

SOUTHERN
OCEAN

TASMANIA
Hobart

PACIFIC
OCEAN

NEW
ZEALAND

Auckland
Wellington

Christchurch
Dunedin

Cape
York
Peninsula

QUEENSLAND

Gulf of
Carpentaria

Townsville

CORAL SEA ISLANDS
TERRITORY

Îles Chesterfield

Great Barrier Reef

Tropic of Capricorn

Rockhampton

Gladstone

Bundaberg
Hervey
Bay
Fraser I.

Brisbane

Toowoomba

PACIFIC

OCEAN

QUEENSLAND

Great Dividing Range

NEW   SOUTH   WALES

Newcastle

SYDNEY

Wollongong

Canberra
A.C.T.

Murray River

VICTORIA

MELBOURNE
Geelong

Australian Alps

Tasman
Sea

MELBOURNE
Ballarat
Geelong
Colac

Port Phillip

Bass Strait

King I.

Hunter I.
C. Grim

TASMANIA

Hobart

Gippsland

Ninety Mile
Beach
Corner Inlet
Wilsons Promontory

Cape Barren I.
Furneaux
Group
Flinders I.

Launceston

S.E. Cape

COPYRIGHT: GEORGE PHILIP & SON, LTD.

on same scale

1:6 000 000
20 0 20 40 60 80 100 miles
20 0 40 80 120 160 km

NEW ZEALAND & DEPENDENCIES
1:60 000 000
200 0 200 400 600 800 miles
200 0 400 800 1200 km
New Zealand Territory
Self-governing Territory

Tokelau or Union Group
WESTERN SAMOA
Rotuma (Fiji)
Vanua Levu
FIJI
Viti Levu
Fiji Is.
Lau or Eastern Group
TONGA (Friendly Is.)
Pukapuka (Danger)
Savai'i
Upolu
Tutuila (U.S.)
Rakahanga
Nassau
Suwarrow
Manihiki
Tongareva (Penrhyn) I.
Northern Group
Cook Is.
Niue
Palmerston Atoll
Lower Group
Rarotonga
Mitiaro
Atui
Mauke
Mangaia
Aitutaki
Îles de la Société

PACIFIC OCEAN
Tropic of Capricorn

Macauley
Raoul (Sunday) I.
Curtis
Kermadec Is.

Three Kings Is.
Auckland
NORTH I.
NEW ZEALAND
Cook Strait
Wellington
Christchurch
SOUTH I.
Tasman Sea
Dunedin
Stewart I.
Snares
Chatham I.
Chatham Is.
Pitt I.
Bounty Is.
Antipodes Is.
Campbell I.
Auckland Is.
Macquarie I. (Austr.)
SOUTHERN OCEAN

NORTH ISLAND

Three Kings Is.
North C.
C. Reinga
C. Maria van Diemen
Houhora
Ahipara B.
Kaitaia
Reef Pt.
Rawene
Hokianga Harb.
Donnelly's Crossing
Dargaville
Waipu
NORTHLAND
Rangaunu Bay
Doubtless Bay
Mangonui
Whangaroa Bay
B. of Islands
Opua
C. Brett
Kaikohe
Hikurangi
Whangarei
Whangarei Harb.
Bream Hd.
Bream Bay
Lit. Barrier I.
Gt. Barrier I.
Kaipara Harb.
Warkworth
Helensville
C. Rodney
C. Colville
Hauraki Gulf
Cuvier I.
Coromandel
Whitianga
Takapuna
Devonport
AUCKLAND
CENTRAL AUCKLAND
Onehunga
Manukau
Manukau Harb.
Papakura
Thames
Mayor I.
Waiuku
Waihi
Mercer
Tauranga Harb.
Waikato
Huntly
Paeroa
Te Aroha
Raglan
Morrinsville
Cambridge
Mt. Maunganui
Tauranga
White I.
C. Runaway
Bay of Plenty
Kawhia Harb.
Hamilton
SOUTH AUCKLAND
BAY OF PLENTY
Whakatane
Opotiki
Te Awamutu
Putaruru
Rotorua
Kawerau
Hikurangi
Otorohanga
Kinleith
Murupara
Te Kuiti
Makai
Waiotapu
Waira
EAST COAST
Tolaga Bay
Ormond
Gisborne
Poverty Bay
Mokau
North Taranaki Bight
Wairakei
Taupo
Mt. Taupo
Waikaremoana
Waikohu
New Plymouth
Inglewood
Whangamomona
Waitara
Mt. Egmont
C. Egmont
Opunake
Stratford
Eltham
Ruapehu
Raetihi
Waiouru
Mahia Peninsula
Wairoa
Waikokopu
Kapuni
Hawera
South Taranaki Bight
Waverley
Patea
Ohakune
Taihape
Mangaweka
Wanganui
Marton
Bulls
Hunterville
Feilding
Palmerston N.
Foxton
Dannevirke
Woodville
Pahiatua
Eketahuna
Waipawa
Waipukurau
Napier
Hastings
C. Kidnappers
Bay View
Hawke Bay
HAWKE'S BAY
C. Turnagain
Shannon
Levin
Otaki
Paraparaumu
Kapiti I.
Featherston
Carterton
Masterton
Greytown
Martinborough
Castle Pt.
WELLINGTON
Up. Hutt
Lr. Hutt
Petone
Eastbourne
PACIFIC OCEAN

SOUTH ISLAND

C. Farewell
Golden Bay
Collingwood
D'Urville I.
French Pass
Takaka
Tasman Bay
Te Hapu
Pelorus Sd.
Cook Strait
Tasman Mts.
Motueka
Picton
Havelock
Blenheim
Tory Channel
Nelson
Richmond
Wakefield
Renwick
MARLBOROUGH
Seddon
Ward
Karamea Bight
Tadmor
Murchison
Kaikoura
Seddonville
Granity
Inangahua Junction
Rotoroa
Tapuaenuku
Westport
Lyell
Reefton
Hanmer Springs
Clarence
Blackball
Greymouth
Runanga
Stillwater
L. Brunner
Jacksons
Otira Gorge
Spenser Mts.
Amuri
Hokitika
Ross
Arthur's Pass
Bealey
Culverden
Waiau
Waikari
Hurunui
Waipara
Amberley
Oxford
Rangiora
Kaiapoi
New Brighton
Christchurch
Riccarton
Lincoln
Lyttelton
Banks Peninsula
Akaroa
Little River
WESTLAND
Abut Hd.
Okarito
Coleridge
Springfield
Whitecliffs
Methven
Staveley
Rakaia
Southbridge
Ellesmere
Jackson B.
Okuru
Mt. Cook 3764
SOUTHERN ALPS
CANTERBURY
Haast
Mt. Aspiring 3027
Wanaka
Hawea
Pukaki
Tekapo
Fairlie
Temuka
Timaru
St. Andrews
Canterbury Bight
Ashburton
Rokaia
Milford Sd.
Mt. Earnslaw 2819
Bligh Sd.
George Sd.
Sutherland Falls
Kinloch
Arrowtown
Cromwell
Clyde
Alexandra
Naseby
Kyeburn
Ranfurly
OTAGO
Oamaru
Maheno
Hampden
Palmerston
Secretary I.
Doubtful Sd.
Queenstown
Wakatipu
Kingston
Roxburgh
Waikouaiti
Port Chalmers
Otago Harbour
Port Chalmers
Resolution I.
Dusky Sd.
Breaksea Sd.
Manapouri
Mossburn
Lumsden
Te Anau
SOUTHLAND
Nightcaps
Winton
Gore
Balclutha
Kaitangata
Nugget Pt.
Dunedin
Mosgiel
Lawrence
Fairfield
St. Kilda
C. Saunders
Chalky Inlet
Preservation Inlet
Tuatapere
Orepuki
Riverton
Otautau
Edendale
Kelso
Tapanui
Clinton
Milton
Owaka
Te Waewae B.
Wyndham
Mataura
Waikawa Harb.
Invercargill
Bluff
Ruapuke I.
Foveaux Str.
Halfmoon Bay
Stewart I.
S.W. Cape
Port Pegasus

TASMAN SEA
SOUTH ISLAND
Westland Bight

SAMOA ISLANDS
1:12 000 000
WESTERN SAMOA
Savai'i
Apia
Upolu
American Samoa
Pago Pago
Tutuila
Manua Is.
Rose I.

FIJI AND TONGA ISLANDS
1:12 000 000
50 0 50 100 150 miles
50 0 50 100 150 200 250 km

Futuna (Fr.)
Niuafo'ou (Tonga)
Thikombia
Lambasa
Vanua Levu
Taveuni
Vanua Balavu
FIJI
Yasawa Group
Kora
Lautoka
Nati 1323
Viti Levu
Levuka
Ovalau
Lau or Eastern Group
Suva
Koro Sea
Gau
Lakemba
Moala
Kandavu
Moala
Vatoa
Vava'u
TONGA
Tonga (Friendly) Is.
Tofua
Nuku'alofa
Tongatapu

Projection: Conical with two standard parallels

COPYRIGHT. GEORGE PHILIP & SON. LTD.

rt m
12 000 4000
9000 3000
6000 2000
3000 1000
1200 400
600 200
0 0
200 600
m ft

INDEX

Introduction to Index

The number in bold type which follows each name in the index refers to the number of the map-page where that feature or place will be found. This is usually the largest scale on which the place or feature appears. Names in the U.S. are indexed to their state, which is not necessarily the largest scale.

The geographical co-ordinates which follow the place name are sometimes only approximate but are close enough for the place name to be located.

A solid square ■ follows the name of a country while an open square □ refers to a first order administrative area (states in the U.S.) A diamond ◇ refers to counties in the U.S. (parishes in Louisiana, census areas in Alaska).

Rivers have been indexed to their mouth or to where they join another river. All river names are followed by the symbol ⌐▾.

Abbreviations used

A.S.S.R. – *Autonomous Soviet Socialist Republic*
Ala. – *Alabama*
Ang. – *Angola*
Arch. – *Archipelago*
Arg. – *Argentina*
Ariz. – *Arizona*
Ark. – *Arkansas*
B. – *Baie, Bahia, Bay, Boca, Bucht, Bugt*
B.C. – *British Columbia*
Br. – *British*
C. – *Cabo, Cap, Cape*
C.H. – *Court House*
C. Prov. – *Cape Province*
Calif. – *California*
Chan. – *Channel*
Col. – *Colombia*
Colo. – *Colorado*
Conn. – *Connecticut*
Cord. – *Cordillera*
D.C. – *District of Columbia*
Del. – *Delaware*
Dep. – *Dependency*
Des. – *Desert*
Dist. – *District*
Dom. Rep. – *Dominican Republic*
E. – *East*
Eng. – *England*
Fd. – *Fjord*
Fed. – *Federal, Federation*
Fla. – *Florida*
Fr. – *France, French*
G. – *Golfe, Golfo, Gulf, Guba*
Ga. – *Georgia*
Gt. – *Great*
Hd. – *Head*
Hts. – *Heights*

I.(s) – *Ile, Ilha, Insel, Isla, Island(s)*
Ill. – *Illinois*
Ind. – *Indiana*
Ind. Res. – *Indian Reservation*
K. – *Kap, Kapp*
Kans. – *Kansas*
Kep. – *Kepulauan*
Kól. – *Kólpos*
Ky. – *Kentucky*
L. – *Lac, Lacul, Lago, Lagoa, Lake, Limni, Loch, Lough*
La. – *Louisiana*
Ld. – *Land*
Mad. P. – *Madhya Pradesh*
Man. – *Manitoba*
Mass. – *Massachusetts*
Md. – *Maryland*
Mich. – *Michigan*
Minn. – *Minnesota*
Miss. – *Mississippi*
Mo. – *Missouri*
Mont. – *Montana*
Mt.(s) – *Mont, Monta, Monti, Muntii, Montaña, Mount, Mountain(s)*
Mys. – *Mysore*
N. – *North, Northern*
N.B. – *New Brunswick*
N.C. – *North Carolina*
N. Dak. – *North Dakota*
N.H. – *New Hampshire*
N.Ire. – *Northern Ireland*
N.J. – *New Jersey*
N. Mex. – *New Mexico*
N.S.W. – *New South Wales*
N.Y. – *New York*
N.Z. – *New Zealand*
Nat. For. – *National Forest*

Nat. Park – *National Park*
Nat. Rec. Area – *National Recreation Area*
Nebr. – *Nebraska*
Neth. – *Netherlands*
Nev. – *Nevada*
Newf. – *Newfoundland*
Nic. – *Nicaragua*
Nig. – *Nigeria*
O.F.S. – *Orange Free State*
Okla. – *Oklahoma*
Ont. – *Ontario*
Oreg. – *Oregon*
Oz. – *Ozero*
P. – *Pass, Passo, Pasul*
P.N.G. – *Papua New Guinea*
Pa. – *Pennsylvania*
Pak. – *Pakistan*
Pass. – *Passage*
Pen. – *Peninsula*
Pk. – *Peak*
Plat. – *Plateau*
Port. – *Portugal, Portuguese*
Prov. – *Province, Provincial*
Pt. – *Point*
Pta. – *Ponta, Punta*
Pte. – *Pointe*
Que. – *Quebec*
Queens. – *Queensland*
R. – *Rio, River*
R.I. – *Rhode Island*
R.S.F.S.R. – *Russian Soviet Federative Socialist Republic*
Ra.(s) – *Range(s)*
Reg. – *Region*
Rep. – *Republic*
Res. – *Reserve, Reservoir, Reservation*

S. – *South*
S. Africa – *South Africa*
S.C. – *South Carolina*
S. Dak – *South Dakota*
S. Leone – *Sierra Leone*
S.S.R. – *Soviet Socialist Republic*
Sa. – *Serra, Sierra*
Sask. – *Saskatchewan*
Scot. – *Scotland*
Sd. – *Sound*
Sp. – *Spain, Spanish*
Sprgs. – *Springs*
St. – *Saint*
Str. – *Strait, Stretto*
Switz. – *Switzerland*
Tanz. – *Tanzania*
Tas. – *Tasmania*
Tenn. – *Tennessee*
Terr. – *Territory*
Tex. – *Texas*
U.K. – *United Kingdom*
U.S.A. – *United States of America*
U.S.S.R. – *Union of Soviet Socialist Republics*
Ut. P. – *Uttar Pradesh*
Va. – *Virginia*
Ven. – *Venezuela*
Vic. – *Victoria*
Vt. – *Vermont*
Wash. – *Washington*
W. – *West*
W. Va. – *West Virginia*
Wis. – *Wisconsin*
Wyo. – *Wyoming*
Yug. – *Yugoslavia*

Alphabetical Order

The alphabetical order of names composed of two or more words is governed primarily by the first word and then by the second. This is an example of the rule:

East Tawas
Eastbourne
Easter Is.
Eastern Ghats
Eastmain ⤳

Physical features composed of a proper name (*Mexico*) and a description (*Gulf of*) are positioned alphabetically by the proper name. The description is positioned after the proper name and is usually abbreviated:

Mexico, G. of
Michigan, L.
Pacaraima, Sa.

Where a description forms part of a settlement or administrative name however it is always written in full and put in its true alphabetic position:

Lake Placid
Mount Vernon
Sturgeon Bay

Names composed of the definite article (*Le, La, Les, L'*) and a proper name are usually alphabetised by the proper name.

Havre, Le
Spezia, La
Wash, The

This rule does not apply where foreign definite articles have become part of U.S. town names. For example:

La Grange

Names beginning with M', Mc are all indexed as if they were spelled Mac. All names beginning St. are alphabetised under Saint, but Sankt, Sint, Sant', Santa and San are all spelt in full and are alphabetised accordingly.

If the same place name occurs two or more times in the index and all are in the same country, each is followed by the name of the administrative subdivision in which it is located. The names are placed in the alphabetical order of the subdivisions. For example:

Aberdeen, Ala.
Aberdeen, Idaho
Aberdeen, S. Dak.
Aberdeen, Wash.

If the same place name occurs twice or more in the index and the places are in different countries, they will be followed by the country names and the latter in alphabetical order.

Boston, U.K.
Boston, U.S.A.

If there is a mixture of these situations, the primary order is fixed by the alphabetical sequence of the countries and the secondary order by that of the country subdivisions. In the latter case the country names are omitted.

Bedford, Can.
Bedford, U.K.
Bedford, Ind., (U.S.A.)
Bedford, Pa., (U.S.A.)

Geographical Co-ordinates

In the index, each place name is followed by its geographical co-ordinates which allow the reader to find the place on the map. These co-ordinates give the latitude and the longitude of a particular place.

The unit of measurement for latitude and longitude is the degree, and it is subdivided into 60 minutes. An index entry states the position of a place in degrees and minutes, a space being left between the degrees and minutes. The latitude is followed by N(orth) or S(outh) and the longitude by E(ast) or W(est).

The diagrams below illustrate how the reader has to estimate the required distance from the nearest line of latitude or longitude. In the case of the first diagram, there is one degree, or 60 minutes between the lines and so to find the position of Newport an estimate has to be made. 28 parts of 60 north of the 41 degree latitude line and 19 parts of 60, or 19 minutes west of the 71 degree longitude line. In the case of the second diagram, it is a little more difficult to estimate since there are 10 degrees between the lines. In the example of Anchorage, the reader has to estimate 1 degree 13 minutes north of 60° and 9° 53 minutes west of 140°.

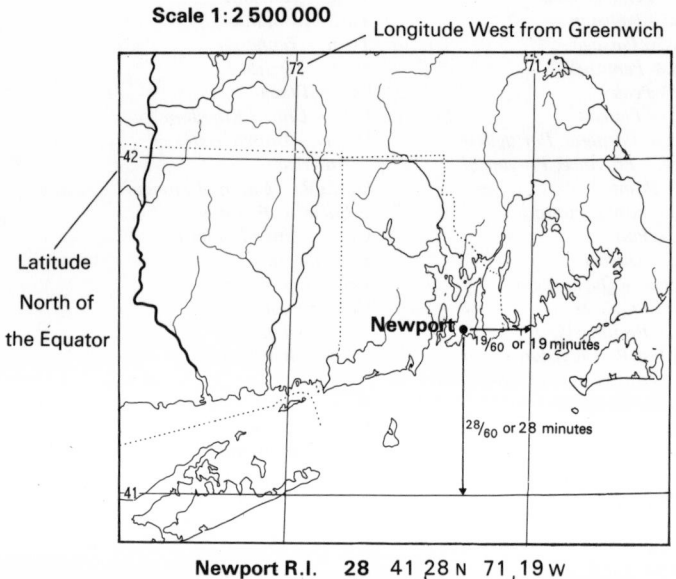

Newport R.I.   28   41 28 N 71 19 W

page latitude longitude

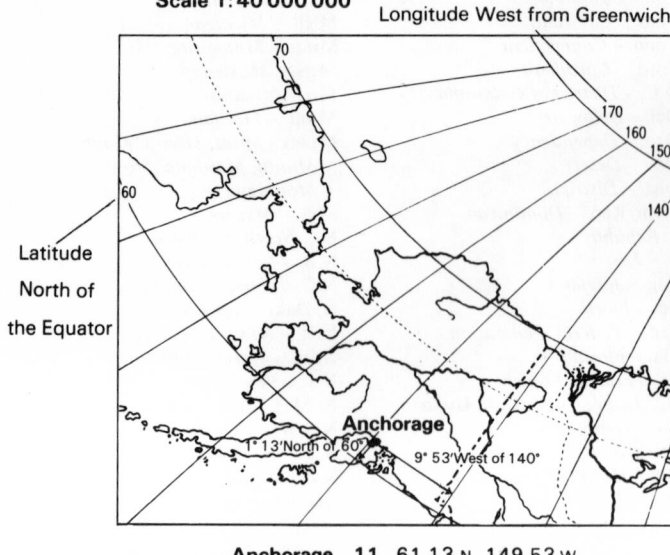

Anchorage 11 61 13 N 149 53 W

page latitude longitude

The latitude (or parallel) is the distance of a point north or south of the Equator measured as an angle with the center of the earth. The Equator is latitude 0°, the North Pole is 90°N, and the South Pole 90°S. On a globe, the lines could be drawn as concentric circles parallel to the Equator, decreasing in diameter from the Equator until they become a point at the poles. On the maps, these lines of latitude are usually represented as lines running across the map from East to West in smooth curves. They are numbered on the sides of the map. North of the Equator the numbers increase northwards, to the south they increase southwards. The degree interval between them depends on the scale of the map. On a large scale map (for example 1:2 500 000), the interval is one degree, but on a small scale map, (for example 1:40 000 000) the interval will be ten degrees.

Foreign Place Names

The atlas uses the local spellings for most place names, that is the name by which a place or feature is known within the country in which it occurs. For example:

Roma
's-Gravenhage

The English conventional form is usually added in brackets on the map thus:

Roma (Rome)
's-Gravenhage (The Hague)

In the index the English form is cross-referenced to the local spelling:

Rome = Roma
Hague, The = 's-Gravenhage

The Pronunciation of Foreign Place Names

English speaking people usually have no difficulty in reading and pronouncing correctly American and English place names. However, foreign place-name pronunciations may present many problems. Such problems can be minimised by following some simple rules. However, these rules cannot be applied to all situations, and there will be many exceptions.

1. In general, stress each syllable equally, unless your experience suggests otherwise.
2. Pronounce the letter 'a' as a broad 'a' as in 'arm'
3. Pronounce the letter 'e' as a short 'e' as in 'elm'
4. Pronounce the letter 'i' as a cross between a short 'i' and long 'e', as the two 'i's' in 'California'.
5. Pronounce the letter 'o' as an intermediate 'o' as in 'soft'
6. Pronounce the letter 'u' as an intermediate 'u' as in 'sure'
7. Pronounce consonants hard, except in the Romance-language areas where 'g's' are likely to be pronounced softly like 'j' in 'jam'; 'j' itself may be pronounced as 'y'; and 'x's' may be pronounced as 'h'.

Moreover, English has no diacritical marks (accent and pronunciation signs), although some languages do. The following is a brief and general guide to the pronunciation of those most frequently used in the Western European languages.

		Pronunciation as in
French	é	d*a*y and shows that the e is to be pronounced e.g. Orléans.
	è	m*a*re
	î	used over any vowel and does not affect pronunciation; shows contraction of the name, usually ommission of 's' following a vowel.
	ç	's' before 'a', 'o' and 'u'
	¨	over 'e', 'i', and 'u' when they are used with another vowel and shows that each is to be pronounced.
German	ä	f*a*t
	ö	f*u*r
	ü	no English equivalent; like French 't*u*'
Italian	à, é	over vowels and indicates stress.
Portuguese	ã, õ	vowels pronounced nasally.
	ç	bo*ss*
	á	shows stress.
	ô	shows that a vowel has an 'i' or 'u' sound combined with it.
Spanish	ñ	ca*ny*on
	ü	pronounced as *w* and separately from adjoining vowels.
	á	usually indicates that this is a stressed vowel

Lines of longitude (or meridians) cut the latitude lines at right angles on the globe and intersect with one another at the poles. Longitude is measured by an angle at the center of the earth between it and the meridian of origin which runs through Greenwich (0°). It may be a measurement East or West of this line from 0° to 180° in each direction. The longitude line of 180° runs North – South through the Pacific Ocean. On a particular map, the interval between the lines of longitude is always the same as that between the lines of latitude. Normally, the meridians are drawn vertically. They are numbered in the top and bottom margins and a note states East or West from Greenwich.

Spellings of names are in the form given in the latest official lists and generally agree with the rules of the Permanent Committee on Geographical Names and the U.S. Board on Geographic Names.

Where languages do not use Roman alphabets these rules are used to transcribe these languages into Roman alphabet. These rules are based largely on pronunciation.

Swedish	å	l*a*w
	ä	f*a*t
	ö	f*u*r

The problem of place-name pronunciation is more difficult where the written form of the name is a transliteration (changing of a letter or letters of one alphabet into corresponding characters of another alphabet or language) from a non-Roman alphabet. Early English-speaking travelers and traders to such countries as China, Japan, and U.S.S.R. prepared written forms of the names that they heard there. Although no based upon a formal system, many of these written forms have become conventional place-name spelling.

More advanced study of particular languages has produced complex transliteration rules. These attempt to retain the nuances of the language concerned. One of the more difficult languages from the standpoint of both transliteration and pronunciation, is Chinese. Following are four examples of place names in three commonly used transliteration systems.

Chinese Postal System	Wade-Giles (pronunciation)	Pinyin
Peking	Pei-ching (ba-jing)	Beijing
Shanghai	Shang-hai (shäng-hi)	Shanghai
Canton	Kuang-chou (gwäng-jo)	Guangzhou

The Pinyin system, as developed by the Peking government, is the most recent system. It is the one adopted by the U.S. Board on Geographic Names and is used in this atlas. The Postal system contains the conventional place-name spellings and does not require diacritical markings. It is listed by the U.S. Board on Geographic Names as an alternative to the Pinyin system for many place-names in China.

The Chinese place-name problem is complicated further by actual changes in place-names over the years. For example, Mukden is now known as Shenyang.

In contrast to Chinese, Japanese romanization commonly employs only one diacritical mark, a line over 'o's' and 'u's', which marks these as long vowels. Diacritical marks employed in the romanization of other languages not based on the Roman alphabet (such as Vietnamese and Hindi) are not commonly employed in general reference atlases as yet.

Aachen Ahome

A

Aachen 88 50 47N 6 4 E
A'âlâ en Nîl □ 121 8 50N 29 55 E
Aalsmeer 87 52 17N 4 43 E
Aalst, Belgium 87 50 56N 4 2 E
Aalst, Neth. 88 51 23N 5 29 E
Aalten 87 51 56N 6 35 E
Aarau 88 47 23N 8 4 E
Aare → 88 47 33N 8 14 E
Aarschot 87 50 59N 4 49 E
Aba 120 5 10N 7 19 E
Abacaxis → 71 3 54 S 58 47W
Ābādān 106 30 22N 48 20 E
Ābādeh 107 31 8N 52 40 E
Abadla 120 31 2N 2 45W
Abaeté 75 19 9 S 45 27W
Abaeté → 75 18 2 S 45 12W
Abaetetuba 74 1 40 S 48 50W
Abagnar Qi 114 43 52N 116 2 E
Abai 77 25 58 S 55 54W
Abajo Peak 52 37 51N 109 27W
Abakan 101 53 40N 91 10 E
Abancay 72 13 35 S 72 55W
Abapó 73 18 48 S 63 25W
Abariringa I. 124 2 50 S 171 40W
Abarqū 107 31 10N 53 20 E
'Abasān 104 31 19N 34 21 E
Abashiri 116 44 0N 144 15 E
Abashiri-Wan 116 44 0N 144 30 E
Abay 100 49 38N 72 53 E
Abaya, L. 121 6 30N 37 50 E
Abaza 100 52 39N 90 6 E
Abbay = Nîl el Azraq → 121 15 38N 32 31 E
Abbaye, Pt. 29 46 58N 88 8W
Abbeville, France 90 50 6N 1 49 E
Abbeville, Ala. 10 31 34N 85 15W
Abbeville, Ga. 18 31 59N 83 18W
Abbeville, La. 25 29 58N 92 8W
Abbeville, Miss. 31 34 30N 89 30W
Abbeville, S.C. 46 34 11N 82 23W
Abbeville County ◇ 46 34 15N 82 30W
Abbot Ice Shelf 5 73 0 S 92 0W
Abbotsford, Canada 62 49 5N 122 20W
Abbotsford, U.S.A. 55 44 57N 90 19W
Abbott, N. Mex. 38 36 18N 104 16W
Abbott, Tex. 51 31 53N 97 4W
Abbottabad 108 34 10N 73 15 E
Abd al Kūrī 105 12 5N 52 20 E
Abéché 121 13 50N 20 35 E
Åbenrå 97 55 3N 9 25 E
Abeokuta 120 7 3N 3 19 E
Aberaeron 83 52 15N 4 16W
Aberayron = Aberaeron 83 52 15N 4 16W
Abercorn = Mbala 122 8 46 S 31 24 E
Abercrombie 41 46 27N 96 44W
Aberdare 83 51 43N 3 27W
Aberdeen, Canada 63 52 20N 106 8W
Aberdeen, U.K. 84 57 9N 2 6W
Aberdeen, Idaho 20 42 57N 112 50W
Aberdeen, Ky. 48 37 15N 86 41W
Aberdeen, Md. 27 39 31N 76 10W
Aberdeen, Miss. 31 33 49N 88 33W
Aberdeen, N.C. 40 35 8N 79 26W
Aberdeen, S. Dak. 47 45 28N 98 29W
Aberdeen, Wash. 53 46 59N 123 50W
Aberdovey 83 52 33N 4 3W
Aberfeldy 84 56 37N 3 50W
Abergavenny 83 51 49N 3 1W
Abernant 10 33 17N 87 12W
Abernathy 50 33 50N 101 51W
Abert, L. 44 42 38N 120 14W
Aberystwyth 83 52 25N 4 6W
Abidjan 120 5 26N 3 58W
Abilene, Kans. 24 38 55N 97 13W
Abilene, Tex. 51 32 28N 99 43W
Abingdon, U.K. 83 51 40N 1 17W
Abingdon, Ill. 21 40 48N 90 24W
Abingdon, Va. 54 36 43N 81 59W
Abington, Conn. 28 41 52N 72 1W
Abington, Mass. 28 42 6N 70 57W
Abiquiu 38 36 13N 106 19W
Abiquiu Reservoir 38 36 16N 106 27W
Abita Springs 25 30 29N 90 2W
Abitau → 63 59 53N 109 3W
Abitau L. 63 60 27N 107 15W
Abitibi L. 60 48 40N 79 40W
Abkhaz A.S.S.R. □ 99 43 0N 41 0 E
Abkit 101 64 10N 157 10 E
Åbo 97 60 28N 22 15 E
Abohar 108 30 10N 74 10 E
Abomey 120 7 10N 2 5 E
Abong-Mbang 122 4 0N 13 8 E
Abou-Deïa 121 11 20N 19 20 E
Aboyne 84 57 4N 2 48W
Abra Pampa 76 22 43 S 65 42W
Abrantes 91 39 24N 8 7W
Abreojos, Pta. 64 26 50N 113 40W
Abri 121 20 50N 30 27 E
Abrolhos, Banka 75 18 0 S 38 0W
Abrud 89 46 19N 23 5 E
Abruzzi □ 94 42 15N 14 0 E
Absaroka Range 56 44 45N 109 50W
Absarokee 33 45 31N 109 27W
Absecon 37 39 26N 74 30W
Abū al Khaṣīb 106 30 25N 48 0 E
Abū 'Alī 106 27 20N 49 27 E
Abu 'Arīsh 105 16 53N 42 48 E
Abu Dhabi = Abū Ẓāby 107 24 28N 54 22 E
Abū Dīs, Jordan 104 31 47N 35 16 E
Abû Dis, Sudan 121 19 12N 33 38 E
Abū Ghaush 104 31 48N 35 6 E
Abu Hamed 121 19 32N 33 13 E
Abū Kamāl 106 34 30N 41 0 E
Abū Madd, Ra's 106 24 50N 37 7 E
Abu Matariq 121 10 59N 26 9 E
Abu Rudeis 106 28 54N 33 11 E
Abu Tig 121 27 4N 31 15 E
Abû Zabad 121 12 25N 29 10 E
Abū Ẓāby 107 24 28N 54 22 E
Abufari 73 5 25 S 62 59W
Abuja 120 9 16N 7 2 E
Abukuma-Gawa → 116 38 6N 140 52 E
Abukuma-Sammyaku 116 37 30N 140 45 E
Abunã 73 9 40 S 65 20W
Abunã → 73 9 41 S 65 20W
Abut Hd. 128 43 7 S 170 15 E
Abwong 121 9 2N 32 14 E
Acacías 70 3 59N 73 46W
Acadia National Park 26 44 20N 68 13W
Acadia Parish ◇ 25 30 13N 92 22W
Acajutla 66 13 36N 89 50W
Açailândia 74 5 0 S 47 50W
Acámbaro 64 20 0N 100 40W
Acaponeta 64 22 30N 105 20W
Acapulco 65 16 51N 99 56W
Acarai, Serra 71 1 50N 57 50W
Acaraú 74 2 53 S 40 7W
Acari, Brazil 74 6 31 S 36 38W
Acarí, Peru 72 15 25 S 74 36W
Acarigua 70 9 33N 69 12W
Acatlán 65 18 10N 98 3W
Acayucan 65 17 59N 94 58W
Accident 27 39 38N 79 19W
Accokeek 27 38 40N 77 2W
Accomac 54 37 43N 75 40W
Accomack County ◇ 54 37 45N 75 40W
Accra 120 5 35N 0 6W
Accrington 82 53 46N 2 22W
Acebal 76 33 20 S 60 50W
Aceh □ 110 4 15N 97 30 E
Achacachi 72 16 3 S 68 43W
Achaguas 70 7 46N 68 14W
Achalpur 108 21 22N 77 32 E
Achao 78 42 28 S 73 30W
Achill 85 53 56N 9 55W
Achill Hd. 85 53 59N 10 15W
Achill I. 85 53 58N 10 5W
Achill Sound 85 53 53N 9 55W
Achille 43 33 50N 96 23W
Achinsk 101 56 20N 90 20 E
Ackerman 31 33 19N 89 11W
Ackley 23 42 33N 93 3W
Acklins I. 67 22 30N 74 0W
Acland, Mt. 127 24 50 S 148 20 E
Acme, Canada 62 51 33N 113 30W
Acme, U.S.A. 25 31 17N 91 49W
Acobamba 72 12 52 S 74 35W
Acoma Indian Reservation 38 34 45N 107 30W
Acomayo 72 13 55 S 71 38W
Acomita 38 35 3N 107 34W
Aconcagua □, Argentina 76 32 50 S 70 0W
Aconcagua □, Chile 76 32 15 S 70 30W
Aconcagua, Cerro 76 32 39 S 70 0W
Aconquija, Mt. 76 27 0 S 66 0W
Acopiara 74 6 6 S 39 27W
Açores, Is. dos = Azores 2 38 44N 29 0W
Acorizal 73 15 12 S 56 22W
Acre = 'Akko 104 32 55N 35 4 E
Acre □ 72 9 1 S 71 0W
Acre → 72 8 45 S 67 22W
Açu 74 5 34 S 36 54W
Acushnet 28 41 41N 70 55W
Acworth 18 34 4N 84 41W
Ad Dahnā 106 24 30N 48 10 E
Ad Dammām 106 26 20N 50 5 E
Ad Dawhah 107 25 15N 51 35 E
Ad Dilam 106 23 55N 47 10 E
Ad Dīwānīyah 106 32 0N 45 0 E
Ada, Kans. 24 39 9N 97 53W
Ada, Minn. 30 47 18N 96 31W
Ada, Ohio 42 40 46N 83 49W
Ada, Okla. 43 34 46N 96 41W
Ada County ◇ 20 43 30N 116 15W
Adair, Iowa 23 41 30N 94 39W
Adair, Okla. 43 36 26N 95 16W
Adair County ◇, Iowa 23 41 20N 94 30W
Adair County ◇, Ky. 49 37 5N 85 20W
Adair County ◇, Mo. 32 40 10N 92 35W
Adair County ◇, Okla. 43 35 55N 94 45W
Adairsville 18 34 22N 84 56W
Adairville 48 36 40N 86 51W
Adaja → 91 41 32N 4 52W
Adak 11 51 45N 176 45W
Adak I. 11 51 45N 176 45W
Adam 107 22 15N 57 28 E
Adam, Mt. 78 51 34 S 60 4W
Adamantina 75 21 42 S 51 4W
Adamaoua, Massif de l' 121 7 20N 12 20 E
Adamawa Highlands =
Adamaoua, Massif de l' 121 7 20N 12 20 E
Adamello, Mt. 94 46 10N 10 34 E
Adams, Ky. 49 38 3N 82 43W
Adams, Mass. 28 42 38N 73 7W
Adams, Minn. 30 43 34N 92 43W
Adams, N. Dak. 41 48 25N 98 5W
Adams, N.Y. 39 43 49N 76 1W
Adams, Nebr. 34 40 28N 96 31W
Adams, Okla. 43 36 45N 101 5W
Adams, Tenn. 48 36 35N 87 4W
Adams, Wis. 55 43 57N 89 49W
Adam's Bridge 108 9 15N 79 40 E
Adams Center 39 43 52N 76 0W
Adams County ◇, Colo. 16 39 50N 104 10W
Adams County ◇, Idaho 20 45 0N 116 30W
Adams County ◇, Ill. 21 40 0N 90 10W
Adams County ◇, Ind. 22 40 45N 85 0W
Adams County ◇, Iowa 23 41 0N 94 40W
Adams County ◇, Miss. 31 31 23N 91 24W
Adams County ◇, N. Dak. 41 46 0N 102 30W
Adams County ◇, Nebr. 34 40 30N 98 30W
Adams County ◇, Ohio 42 38 48N 83 33W
Adams County ◇, Pa. 45 39 50N 77 14W
Adams County ◇, Wash. 53 47 0N 118 30W
Adams County ◇, Wis. 55 43 0N 89 50W
Adams L. 62 51 10N 119 40W
Adams-Mcgill Reservoir 35 38 22N 115 7W
Adams Mt. 53 46 12N 121 30W
Adam's Peak 108 6 48N 80 30 E
Adamstown 45 40 15N 76 3W
Adamsville, Ohio 42 40 4N 81 53W
Adamsville, R.I. 28 41 30N 71 10W
Adamsville, Tenn. 48 35 14N 88 23W
Adamsville, Tex. 51 31 18N 98 10W
Adana 106 37 0N 35 16 E
Adapazarı 106 40 48N 30 25 E
Adarama 121 17 10N 34 52 E
Adare, C. 5 71 0 S 171 0 E
Adaut 111 8 8 S 131 7 E
Adavale 127 25 52 S 144 32 E
Adda → 94 45 8N 9 53 E
Addie 40 35 24N 83 10W
Addieville 21 38 23N 89 29W
Addington 43 34 15N 97 58W
Addis 25 30 21N 91 16W
Addis Ababa = Addis
Abeba 121 9 2N 38 42 E
Addis Abeba 121 9 2N 38 42 E
Addis Alem 121 9 0N 38 17 E
Addison, Ala. 10 34 12N 87 11W
Addison, Ill. 21 41 55N 88 0W
Addison, N.Y. 39 42 1N 77 14W
Addison, Ohio 42 38 53N 82 9W
Addison, Vt. 36 44 8N 73 20W
Addison County ◇ 36 44 0N 73 15W
Addu Atoll 103 0 30 S 73 0 E
Addy 53 48 21N 117 50W
Adel, Ga. 18 31 8N 83 25W
Adel, Iowa 23 41 37N 94 1W
Adel, Oreg. 44 42 11N 119 54W
Adelaide, Australia 127 34 52 S 138 30 E
Adelaide, Bahamas 66 25 0N 77 31W
Adelaide I. 5 67 15 S 68 30W
Adelaide Pen. 58 68 15N 97 30W
Adelanto 15 34 35N 117 22W
Adélie, Terre 5 68 0 S 140 0 E
Adelphi 42 39 28N 82 45W
Adelphia 37 40 13N 74 15W
Aden = Al 'Adan 105 12 45N 45 0 E
Aden, G. of 105 13 0N 50 0 E
Adena 42 40 13N 80 53W
Adi 111 4 15 S 133 30 E
Adi Ugri 121 14 58N 38 48 E
Adieu, C. 126 32 0 S 132 10 E
Adige → 94 45 9N 12 20 E
Adilabad 108 19 33N 78 20 E
Adin 14 41 12N 120 57W
Adin Khel 107 32 45N 68 5 E
Adirondack Mts. 39 44 0N 74 0W
Adjud 95 46 7N 27 10 E
Adjuntas 57 18 10N 66 43W
Adlavik Is. 61 55 2N 57 45W
Admer 120 20 21N 5 27 E
Admiralty G. 126 14 20 S 125 55 E
Admiralty I. 11 57 30N 134 30W
Admiralty Inlet 53 48 8N 122 58W
Admiralty Is. 124 2 0 S 147 0 E
Adobe Creek Reservoir 16 38 14N 103 17W
Adonara 111 8 15 S 123 5 E
Adoni 108 15 33N 77 18W
Adour → 90 43 32N 1 32W
Adra 91 36 43N 3 3W
Adrano 94 37 40N 14 49 E
Adrar 120 27 51N 0 11W
Adré 121 13 40N 22 20 E
Adrī 121 27 32N 13 2 E
Adrian, Ga. 18 32 33N 82 35W
Adrian, Mich. 29 41 54N 84 2W
Adrian, Minn. 30 43 38N 95 56W
Adrian, Mo. 32 38 24N 94 21W
Adrian, Oreg. 44 43 45N 117 4W
Adrian, Tex. 50 35 16N 102 40W
Adriatic Sea 94 43 0N 16 0 E
Adua 111 1 45 S 129 50 E
Advance, Ind. 22 40 0N 86 40W
Advance, Mo. 32 37 6N 89 55W
Adwa 121 14 15N 38 52 E
Adzhar A.S.S.R. □ 99 42 0N 42 0 E
Ægean Sea 95 37 0N 25 0 E
Æolian Is. = Eólie, I. 94 38 30N 14 50 E
Aerht'ai Shan 113 46 40N 92 45 E
Aetna 24 37 5N 98 58W
Affton 32 38 33N 90 20W
Afghanistan ■ 107 33 0N 65 0 E
Afgoi 105 2 7N 44 59 E
'Afif 106 23 53N 42 56 E
Afogados da Ingàzeira 74 7 45 S 37 39W
Afognak I. 11 58 15N 152 30W
Africa 118 10 0N 20 0 E
Afton, Calif. 15 35 2N 116 23W
Afton, Iowa 23 41 2N 94 12W
Afton, N.Y. 39 42 14N 75 32W
Afton, Okla. 43 36 42N 94 58W
Afton, Wyo. 56 42 44N 110 56W
Afuá 74 0 15 S 50 20W
Afula 104 32 37N 35 17 E
Afyonkarahisar 106 38 45N 30 33 E
Agadès = Agadez 120 16 58N 7 59 E
Agadez 120 16 58N 7 59 E
Agadir 120 30 28N 9 35W
Agapa 101 71 27N 89 15 E
Agar 47 44 50N 100 5W
Agartala 109 23 50N 91 23 E
Ağaş 95 46 28N 26 15 E
Agassiz 62 49 14N 121 46W
Agassiz Pool 30 48 20N 95 59W
Agate 16 39 28N 103 57W
Agate Beach 44 44 41N 124 4W
Agate Fossil Beds National
Monument 34 42 20N 103 50W
Agats 111 5 33 S 138 0 E
Agattu I. 11 52 25N 173 35W
Agawam, Mass. 28 42 5N 72 37W
Agawam, Mont. 33 48 0N 112 10W
Agboville 120 5 55N 4 15W
Agde 90 43 19N 3 28 E
Agen 90 44 12N 0 38 E
Agency 23 41 0N 92 18W
Agency L. 44 42 33N 121 58W
Agenda 24 39 43N 97 26W
Ages 49 36 52N 83 21W
Aghil Mts. 108 36 0N 77 0 E
Aginskoye 101 51 6N 114 32 E
Agnita 95 45 59N 24 40 E
Agra, India 108 27 17N 77 58 E
Agra, Kans. 24 39 46N 99 7W
Agra, Okla. 43 35 54N 96 53W
Agri → 94 40 13N 16 44 E
Ağri Daği 106 39 50N 44 15 E
Ağri Karakose 106 39 44N 43 3 E
Agricola 31 30 48N 88 31W
Agrigento 94 37 19N 13 33 E
Agrinion 95 38 37N 21 27 E
Água Branca 74 5 50 S 42 40W
Agua Caliente 64 26 30N 108 20W
Água Clara 73 20 25 S 52 45W
Agua Dulce 51 27 47N 97 55W
Agua Fria → 12 33 23N 112 22W
Agua Nueva 50 26 54N 98 36W
Agua Preta → 71 1 41 S 63 48W
Agua Prieta 64 31 20N 109 32W
Aguachica 70 8 19N 73 38W
Aguada 57 18 23N 67 11W
Aguada Cecilio 78 40 51 S 65 51W
Aguadas 70 5 40N 75 38W
Aguadilla 57 18 26N 67 10W
Aguadilla ◇ 57 18 20N 67 0W
Aguadilla, Bahía de 57 18 25N 67 10W
Aguadulce 66 8 15N 80 32W
Aguanaval → 64 23 45N 103 10W
Aguanish 61 50 14N 62 2W
Aguanus → 61 50 13N 62 5W
Aguapeí 73 16 12 S 59 43W
Aguapeí → 75 21 0 S 51 0W
Aguapey → 76 29 7 S 56 36W
Aguaray Guazú → 76 24 47 S 57 19W
Aguarico → 70 0 59 S 75 11W
Aguas Blancas 76 24 15 S 69 55W
Aguas Buenas 57 18 16N 66 6W
Aguas Calientes, Sierra de 76 25 26 S 66 40W
Águas Formosas 75 17 5 S 40 57W
Aguascalientes 64 21 53N 102 12W
Aguascalientes □ 64 22 0N 102 20W
Aguila 12 33 57N 113 11W
Aguila, Punta 57 17 57N 67 13W
Aguilar 16 37 24N 104 39W
Aguilares, Argentina 76 27 26 S 65 35W
Aguilares, U.S.A. 50 27 27N 99 5W
Aguilas 91 37 23N 1 35W
Aguja, C. de la 70 11 18N 74 12W
Agujereada, Pta. 57 18 30N 67 8W
Agulhas, Kaap 123 34 52 S 20 0 E
Agung 110 8 20 S 115 28 E
'Agur 104 31 42N 34 55 E
Agusan → 111 9 0N 125 30 E
Agustín Codazzi 70 10 2N 73 14W
Ahaggar 120 23 0N 6 30 E
Ahar 106 38 35N 47 0 E
Ahipara B. 128 35 5 S 173 5 E
Ahiri 108 19 30N 80 0 E
Ahmadabad 108 23 0N 72 40 E
Ahmadnagar 108 19 7N 74 46 E
Ahmadpur 108 29 12N 71 10 E
Ahmedabad = Ahmadabad 108 23 0N 72 40 E
Ahmednagar = Ahmadnagar 108 19 7N 74 46 E
Ahome 64 25 55N 109 11W

Ahoskie **Aleutian Range**

Name	Page	Lat.	Long.
Ahoskie	**40**	36 17N	76 59W
Ahuachapán	**66**	13 54N	89 52W
Ahvāz	**106**	31 20N	48 40 E
Ahvenanmaa = Åland	**97**	60 15N	20 0 E
Ahwar	**105**	13 30N	46 40 E
Aiari →	**70**	1 22N	68 36W
Aibonito	**57**	18 9N	66 16W
Aichi □	**117**	35 0N	137 15 E
Aiea	**19**	21 23N	157 56W
Aigua	**77**	34 13 S	54 46W
Aigues-Mortes	**90**	43 35N	4 12 E
Aihui	**114**	50 10N	127 30 E
Aija	**72**	9 50 S	77 45W
Aikawa	**116**	38 2N	138 15 E
Aiken	**46**	33 34N	81 43W
Aiken County ◇	**46**	33 30N	81 40W
Ailey	**18**	32 11N	82 34W
Aillik	**61**	55 11N	59 18W
Ailsa Craig	**84**	55 15N	5 7W
'Ailūn	**104**	32 18N	35 47 E
Aim	**101**	59 0N	133 55 E
Aimere	**111**	8 45 S	121 3 E
Aimogasta	**76**	28 33 S	66 50W
Aimorés	**75**	19 30 S	41 4W
Ain □	**90**	46 5N	5 20 E
Ain Banaiyan	**107**	23 0N	51 0 E
Aïn Beïda	**120**	35 50N	7 29 E
Aïn Ben Tili	**120**	25 59N	9 27W
Aïn Galakka	**121**	18 10N	18 30 E
Aïn-Sefra	**120**	32 47N	0 37W
Ainabo	**105**	9 0N	46 25 E
Ainsworth, Iowa	**23**	41 17N	91 33W
Ainsworth, Nebr.	**34**	42 33N	99 52W
Aipe	**70**	3 13N	75 15W
Aiquile	**73**	18 10 S	65 10W
Aïr	**120**	18 30N	8 0 E
Airão	**71**	1 56 S	61 22W
Airdrie	**84**	55 53N	3 57W
Aire →	**82**	53 42N	0 55W
Aisen □	**78**	46 30 S	73 0W
Aisne □	**90**	49 42N	3 40 E
Aisne →	**90**	49 26N	2 50 E
Aitkin	**30**	46 32N	93 42W
Aitkin County ◇	**30**	46 30N	93 25W
Aiuaba	**74**	6 38 S	40 7W
Aiud	**89**	46 19N	23 44 E
Aix, Mt.	**53**	46 47N	121 15W
Aix-en-Provence	**90**	43 32N	5 27 E
Aix-la-Chapelle = Aachen	**88**	50 47N	6 4 E
Aiyansh	**62**	55 17N	129 2W
Áíyina	**95**	37 45N	23 26 E
Aiyion	**95**	38 15N	22 5 E
Aizawl	**109**	23 40N	92 44 E
Aizuwakamatsu	**116**	37 30N	139 56 E
Ajaccio	**94**	41 55N	8 40 E
Ajaju →	**70**	0 59N	72 20W
Ajalpan	**65**	18 22N	97 15W
Ajanta Ra.	**108**	20 28N	75 50 E
Ajdâbiyah	**121**	30 54N	20 4 E
'Ajmān	**107**	25 25N	55 30 E
Ajmer	**108**	26 28N	74 37 E
Ajo	**12**	32 22N	112 52W
Ak Dağ	**106**	36 30N	30 0 E
Akabira	**116**	43 33N	142 5 E
Akali L.	**44**	42 58N	120 2W
Akaroa	**128**	43 49 S	172 59 E
Akashi	**117**	34 45N	135 0 E
Akaska	**47**	45 20N	100 7W
Akelamo	**111**	1 35N	129 40 E
Akeley	**30**	47 0N	94 44W
Akershus fylke □	**97**	60 0N	11 10 E
Aketi	**122**	2 38N	23 47 E
Akhelóös →	**95**	38 36N	21 14 E
Akhiok	**11**	56 57N	154 10W
Akhisar	**106**	38 56N	27 48 E
Akhmîm	**121**	26 31N	31 47 E
Akhtopol	**95**	42 6N	27 56 E
Aki	**117**	33 30N	133 54 E
Akiachak	**11**	60 55N	161 26W
Akiak	**11**	60 55N	161 13W
Akimiski I.	**60**	52 50N	81 30W
Akita	**116**	39 45N	140 7 E
Akita □	**116**	39 40N	140 30 E
Akjoujt	**120**	19 45N	14 15W
Akkeshi	**116**	43 2N	144 51 E
'Akko	**104**	32 55N	35 4 E
Akkol	**100**	45 0N	75 39 E
Aklavik	**58**	68 12N	135 0W
Akō	**117**	34 45N	134 24 E
Akobo →	**121**	7 48N	33 3 E
Akola	**108**	20 42N	77 2 E
Akolmiut	**11**	60 55N	162 20W
Akordat	**121**	15 30N	37 40 E
Akpatok I.	**59**	60 25N	68 8W
Akra	**41**	48 47N	97 44W
Akranes	**96**	64 19N	21 58W
Akreïjit	**120**	18 19N	9 11W
Akron, Ala.	**10**	32 53N	87 45W
Akron, Colo.	**16**	40 10N	103 13W
Akron, Ind.	**22**	41 2N	86 1W
Akron, Iowa	**23**	42 50N	96 33W
Akron, N.Y.	**39**	43 1N	78 30W
Akron, Ohio	**42**	41 5N	81 31W
Akron, Pa.	**45**	40 9N	76 12W
Akrotíri, Ákra	**95**	40 26N	25 27 E
Aksai Chih	**108**	35 15N	79 55 E
Aksaray	**106**	38 25N	34 2 E
Aksarka	**100**	66 31N	67 50 E
Aksay	**98**	51 11N	53 0 E
Akşehir	**106**	38 18N	31 30 E
Aksenovo Zilovskoye	**101**	53 20N	117 40 E
Aksu	**113**	41 5N	80 10 E
Aksum	**121**	14 5N	38 40 E
Aktogay	**100**	46 57N	79 40 E
Aktyubinsk	**99**	50 17N	57 10 E
Aku	**120**	6 40N	7 18 E
Akun I.	**11**	54 11N	165 32W
Akure	**120**	7 15N	5 5 E
Akureyri	**96**	65 40N	18 6W
Akuseki-Shima	**117**	29 27N	129 37 E
Akutan	**11**	54 8N	165 46W
Akutan I.	**11**	54 7N	165 55W
Akutan Indian Reservation	**11**	54 10N	166 0W
Akyab = Sittwe	**109**	20 18N	92 45 E
Al 'Adan	**105**	12 45N	45 0 E
Al Aḩsā	**106**	25 50N	49 0 E
Al Amādīyah	**106**	37 5N	43 30 E
Al Amārah	**106**	31 55N	47 15 E
Al 'Aqabah	**104**	29 31N	35 0 E
Al 'Aramah	**106**	25 30N	46 0 E
Al Ashkhara	**107**	21 50N	59 30 E
Al 'Ayzarīyah	**104**	31 47N	35 15 E
Al Badī'	**106**	22 0N	46 35 E
Al Başrah	**106**	30 30N	47 50 E
Al Bāzūrīyah	**104**	33 15N	35 16 E
Al Bīrah	**104**	31 55N	35 12 E
Al Bu'ayrāt	**121**	31 24N	15 44 E
Al Buqay'ah	**104**	32 15N	35 30 E
Al Fallūjah	**106**	33 20N	43 55 E
Al Fāw	**106**	30 0N	48 30 E
Al Fujayrah	**107**	25 7N	56 18 E
Al Fuqaha	**121**	27 50N	16 22 E
Al Hābah	**106**	27 10N	47 0 E
Al Haddār	**106**	21 58N	45 57 E
Al Ḩadīthah	**106**	34 0N	41 13 E
Al Hāmad	**106**	31 30N	39 30 E
Al Ḩamar	**106**	22 23N	46 6 E
Al Ḩamrā'	**106**	24 2N	38 55 E
Al Ḩarīq	**106**	23 29N	46 27 E
Al Harīr, W. →	**104**	32 44N	35 59 E
Al Ḩasakah	**106**	36 35N	40 45 E
Al Ḩawrah	**105**	13 50N	47 35 E
Al Ḩawţah	**105**	16 5N	48 20 E
Al Ḩayy	**106**	32 5N	46 5 E
Al Ḩijāz	**106**	26 0N	37 30 E
Al Ḩillah, Iraq	**106**	32 30N	44 25 E
Al Ḩillah, Si. Arabia	**106**	23 35N	46 50 E
Al Hindīyah	**106**	32 30N	44 10 E
Al Ḩişnn	**104**	32 29N	35 52 E
Al Hoceïma	**120**	35 8N	3 58W
Al Ḩudaydah	**105**	14 50N	43 0 E
Al Hūfuf	**106**	25 25N	49 45 E
Al Ḩulwah	**106**	23 24N	46 48 E
Al Irq	**121**	29 5N	21 35 E
Al Ittihad = Madīnat ash Sha'b	**105**	12 50N	45 0 E
Al Jāfūrah	**106**	25 0N	50 15 E
Al Jaghbūb	**121**	29 42N	24 38 E
Al Jahrah	**106**	29 25N	47 40 E
Al Jalāmīd	**106**	31 20N	39 45 E
Al Jawf, Libya	**121**	24 10N	23 24 E
Al Jawf, Si. Arabia	**106**	29 55N	39 40 E
Al Jazirah, Asia	**106**	33 30N	44 0 E
Al Jazirah, Libya	**121**	26 10N	21 20 E
Al Jubayl	**106**	27 0N	49 50 E
Al Jubaylah	**106**	24 55N	46 25 E
Al Junaynah	**121**	13 27N	22 45 E
Al Khābūra	**107**	23 57N	57 5 E
Al Khalīl	**104**	31 32N	35 6 E
Al Khalūf	**105**	20 30N	58 13 E
Al Kharfah	**106**	22 0N	46 35 E
Al Kharj	**106**	24 0N	47 0 E
Al Kufrah	**121**	24 17N	23 15 E
Al Kūt	**106**	32 30N	46 0 E
Al Kuwayt	**106**	29 30N	47 30 E
Al Lādhiqīyah	**106**	35 30N	35 45 E
Al Lidām	**105**	20 33N	44 45 E
Al Lubban	**104**	32 9N	35 14 E
Al Luḩayyah	**105**	15 45N	42 40 E
Al Madīnah	**106**	24 35N	39 52 E
Al-Mafraq	**104**	32 17N	36 14 E
Al Majma'ah	**106**	25 57N	45 22 E
Al Manāmāh, Bahrain	**107**	26 10N	50 30 E
Al Marj	**121**	32 25N	20 30 E
Al Mawşil	**106**	36 15N	43 5 E
Al Mazra	**104**	31 16N	35 31 E
Al Midhnab	**106**	25 50N	44 18 E
Al Miqdādīyah	**106**	34 0N	45 0 E
Al Mish'āb	**106**	28 12N	48 36 E
Al Mubarraz	**106**	25 30N	49 40 E
Al Muḩarraq	**107**	26 15N	50 40 E
Al Mukallā	**105**	14 33N	49 2 E
Al Mukhā	**105**	13 18N	43 15 E
Al Musayyib	**106**	32 40N	44 25 E
Al Muwayliḩ	**106**	27 40N	35 30 E
Al Qaḑīmah	**106**	22 20N	39 13 E
Al Qāmishli	**106**	37 10N	41 10 E
Al Qaşabát	**121**	32 39N	14 1 E
Al Qaţīf	**106**	26 35N	50 0 E
Al Qaţrūn	**121**	24 56N	15 3 E
Al Quaisūmah	**106**	28 10N	46 20 E
Al Quds = Jerusalem	**104**	31 47N	35 10 E
Al Qurayyāt	**107**	23 17N	58 53 E
Al Qurnah	**106**	31 1N	47 25 E
Al 'Ulā	**106**	26 35N	38 0 E
Al Uqaylah ash Sharqigah	**121**	30 12N	19 10 E
Al Uqayr	**106**	25 40N	50 15 E
Al 'Uthmānīyah	**106**	25 5N	49 22 E
Al 'Uwaynid	**106**	24 50N	46 0 E
Al' 'Uwayqīlah	**106**	30 30N	42 10 E
Al 'Uyūn	**106**	26 30N	43 50 E
Al Wakrah	**107**	25 10N	51 40 E
Al Wari'āh	**106**	27 51N	47 25 E
Al Yamāmah	**106**	24 5N	47 30 E
Al Yāmūn	**104**	32 29N	35 14 E
Alabama □	**10**	33 0N	87 0W
Alabama →	**10**	31 8N	87 57W
Alabaster	**10**	33 15N	86 49W
Alachua	**17**	29 47N	82 30W
Alachua County ◇	**17**	29 45N	82 20W
Alagoa Grande	**74**	7 3 S	35 35W
Alagoas □	**74**	9 0 S	36 0W
Alagoinhas	**75**	12 7 S	38 20W
Alajuela	**66**	10 2N	84 8W
Alakunuk	**11**	62 41N	164 37W
Alakurtti	**98**	67 0N	30 30 E
Alalakeiki Channel	**19**	20 30N	156 30W
Alalapura	**71**	2 20N	56 25W
Alalaú →	**71**	0 30 S	61 9W
Alamance County ◇	**40**	36 0N	79 25W
Alameda, Calif.	**14**	37 46N	122 15W
Alameda, N. Mex.	**38**	35 11N	106 37W
Alameda County ◇	**14**	37 40N	121 50W
Alamito →	**50**	29 45N	104 18W
Alamitos, Sierra de los	**64**	37 21N	115 10W
Alamo, Ga.	**18**	32 9N	82 47W
Alamo, N. Dak.	**41**	48 35N	103 28W
Alamo, Nev.	**35**	37 22N	115 10W
Alamo, Tenn.	**48**	35 47N	89 7W
Alamo Heights	**51**	29 28N	98 28W
Alamo Ind. Res.	**38**	34 20N	107 30W
Alamo L.	**12**	34 10N	113 35W
Alamogordo	**38**	32 54N	105 57W
Alamos	**64**	27 0N	109 0W
Alamosa	**16**	37 28N	105 52W
Alamosa →	**16**	37 22N	105 46W
Alamosa County ◇	**16**	37 40N	105 40W
Åland	**97**	60 15N	20 0 E
Ålands hav	**97**	60 0N	19 30 E
Alandur	**108**	13 0N	80 15 E
Alanreed	**50**	35 13N	100 44W
Alanson	**29**	45 27N	84 47W
Alanya	**106**	36 38N	32 0 E
Alapaha	**18**	31 23N	83 13W
Alapayevsk	**100**	57 52N	61 42 E
Alarka	**40**	35 21N	83 27W
Alaşehir	**99**	38 23N	28 30 E
Alaska □	**11**	64 0N	154 0W
Alaska, Gulf of	**11**	59 0N	146 0W
Alaska Highway	**62**	60 0N	130 0W
Alaska Peninsula	**11**	56 0N	159 0W
Alaska Range	**11**	62 0N	149 0W
Alataw Shankou	**113**	45 5N	81 57 E
Alatyr	**98**	54 45N	46 35 E
Alausi	**70**	2 0 S	78 50W
Alava, C.	**53**	48 10N	124 44W
Alba, Italy	**94**	44 41N	8 1 E
Alba, Mo.	**32**	37 14N	94 25W
Alba, Tex.	**51**	32 48N	95 38W
Alba □	**95**	46 10N	23 30 E
Alba Iulia	**89**	46 8N	23 39 E
Albacete	**91**	39 0N	1 50W
Albania ■	**95**	41 0N	20 0 E
Albany, Australia	**126**	35 1 S	117 58 E
Albany, Ga.	**18**	31 35N	84 10W
Albany, Ind.	**22**	40 18N	85 14W
Albany, Ky.	**49**	36 42N	85 8W
Albany, La.	**25**	30 30N	90 35W
Albany, Minn.	**30**	45 38N	94 34W
Albany, Mo.	**32**	40 15N	94 20W
Albany, N.Y.	**39**	42 39N	73 45W
Albany, Ohio	**42**	39 14N	82 12W
Albany, Okla.	**43**	33 53N	96 10W
Albany, Oreg.	**44**	44 38N	123 6W
Albany, Tex.	**51**	32 44N	99 18W
Albany, Vt.	**36**	44 43N	72 23W
Albany →	**60**	52 17N	81 31W
Albany County ◇, N.Y.	**39**	42 30N	74 0W
Albany County ◇, Wyo.	**56**	41 50N	105 40W
Albardón	**76**	31 20 S	68 30W
Albarracín, Sierra de	**91**	40 30N	1 30W
Albatross B.	**127**	12 45 S	141 30 E
Albemarle	**40**	35 21N	80 11W
Albemarle County ◇	**54**	38 2N	78 30W
Albemarle Sd.	**40**	36 5N	76 0W
Alberche →	**91**	39 58N	4 46W
Alberdi	**76**	26 14 S	58 20W
Albert, Kans.	**24**	38 27N	99 1W
Albert, Okla.	**43**	35 14N	98 25W
Albert, Tex.	**51**	30 12N	98 36W
Albert, L. = Mobutu Sese Seko, L.	**122**	1 30N	31 0 E
Albert Canyon	**62**	51 8N	117 41W
Albert City	**23**	42 47N	94 57W
Albert Lea	**30**	43 39N	93 22W
Albert Nile →	**122**	3 36N	32 2 E
Albert Town	**67**	22 37N	74 33 E
Alberta, Ala.	**10**	32 14N	87 25W
Alberta, Va.	**54**	36 52N	77 53W
Alberta □	**62**	54 40N	115 0W
Alberti	**76**	35 1 S	60 16W
Alberton, Canada	**61**	46 50N	64 0W
Alberton, U.S.A.	**33**	47 0N	114 29W
Albertville = Kalemie	**122**	5 55 S	29 9 E
Albertville, Ala.	**10**	34 16N	86 13W
Albertville, Minn.	**30**	45 14N	93 39W
Albi	**90**	43 56N	2 9 E
Albia	**23**	41 2N	92 48W
Albin	**56**	41 25N	104 6W
Albina	**71**	5 37N	54 15W
Albion, Calif.	**14**	39 14N	123 46W
Albion, Idaho	**20**	42 25N	113 35W
Albion, Ill.	**21**	38 23N	88 4W
Albion, Ind.	**22**	41 24N	85 25W
Albion, Iowa	**23**	42 7N	92 59W
Albion, Maine	**26**	44 32N	69 27W
Albion, Mich.	**29**	42 15N	84 45W
Albion, N.Y.	**39**	43 15N	78 12W
Albion, Nebr.	**34**	41 42N	98 0W
Albion, Okla.	**43**	34 40N	95 6W
Albion, Pa.	**45**	41 53N	80 22W
Albion, Wash.	**53**	46 48N	117 15W
Ålborg	**97**	57 2N	9 54 E
Alborz, Reshteh-ye Kūhhā-ye	**107**	36 0N	52 0 E
Albreda	**62**	52 35N	119 10W
Albright	**54**	39 30N	79 39W
Albuquerque, Brazil	**73**	19 23 S	57 26W
Albuquerque, U.S.A.	**38**	35 5N	106 39W
Albuquerque, Cayos de	**66**	12 10N	81 50W
Alburg	**36**	44 59N	73 18W
Alburnett	**23**	42 9N	91 37W
Alburquerque	**91**	39 15N	6 59W
Albury	**127**	36 3 S	146 56 E
Alcalá de Henares	**91**	40 28N	3 22W
Alcalá la Real	**91**	37 27N	3 57W
Alcalde	**38**	36 5N	106 3W
Alcamo	**94**	37 59N	12 55 E
Alcaníz	**91**	41 2N	0 8W
Alcántara, Brazil	**74**	2 20 S	44 30W
Alcántara, Spain	**91**	39 41N	6 57W
Alcantara L.	**63**	60 57N	108 9W
Alcaraz, Sierra de	**91**	38 40N	2 20W
Alcaudete	**91**	37 35N	4 5W
Alcázar de San Juan	**91**	39 24N	3 12W
Alcester	**47**	43 1N	96 38W
Alcira	**91**	39 9N	0 30W
Alco	**13**	35 53N	92 22W
Alcoa	**49**	35 48N	83 59W
Alcobaça	**91**	39 32N	9 0W
Alcolu	**46**	33 45N	80 13W
Alcoma	**17**	27 54N	81 29W
Alcona County ◇	**29**	44 40N	83 40W
Alcorn	**31**	31 53N	91 8W
Alcorn County ◇	**31**	34 56N	88 31W
Alcova	**56**	42 34N	106 43W
Alcoy	**91**	38 43N	0 30W
Alda	**34**	40 52N	98 28W
Aldabra Is.	**3**	9 22 S	46 28 E
Aldama	**65**	23 0N	98 4W
Aldan	**101**	58 40N	125 30 E
Aldan →	**101**	63 28N	129 35 E
Aldeburgh	**83**	52 9N	1 35 E
Alden, Iowa	**23**	42 31N	93 23W
Alden, Kans.	**24**	38 15N	98 19W
Alden, Minn.	**30**	43 40N	93 34W
Alden, N.Y.	**39**	42 54N	78 30W
Alder	**33**	45 19N	112 6W
Alderney	**83**	49 42N	2 12W
Aldershot	**83**	51 15N	0 43W
Alderson	**54**	37 44N	80 38W
Aldersyde	**62**	50 40N	113 53W
Aldine	**51**	29 56N	95 23W
Aledo, Ill.	**21**	41 12N	90 45W
Aledo, Tex.	**51**	32 42N	97 36W
Aleg	**120**	17 3N	13 55W
Alegre	**75**	20 50 S	41 30W
Alegrete	**77**	29 40 S	56 0W
Alegros Mt.	**38**	34 9N	108 11W
Aleisk	**100**	52 40N	83 0 E
Alejandro Selkirk, I.	**125**	33 50 S	80 15W
Aleknagik	**11**	59 17N	158 36W
Aleksandrovo	**95**	43 14N	24 51 E
Aleksandrovsk-Sakhalinskiy	**101**	50 50N	142 20 E
Aleksandrovskiy Zavod	**101**	50 40N	117 50 E
Aleksandrovskoye	**100**	60 35N	77 50 E
Além Paraíba	**75**	21 52 S	42 41W
Alemania, Argentina	**76**	25 40 S	65 30W
Alemania, Chile	**76**	25 10 S	69 55W
Alençon	**90**	48 27N	0 4 E
Alentejo, Alto-	**91**	39 0N	7 40W
Alentejo, Baixo-	**91**	38 0N	8 30W
Alenuihaha Channel	**19**	20 30N	156 0W
Aleppo = Ḩalab	**106**	36 10N	37 15 E
Aléria	**94**	42 5N	9 26 E
Alert Bay	**62**	50 30N	126 55W
Alès	**90**	44 9N	4 5 E
Alesia	**27**	39 43N	76 51W
Alessándria	**94**	44 54N	8 37 E
Ålesund	**96**	62 28N	6 12 E
Aleutian Is.	**11**	52 0N	178 0W
Aleutian Islands ◇	**11**	53 0N	176 0W
Aleutian Range	**11**	60 0N	154 0W

Aleutian Trench **Amderma**

Aleutian Trench 124 48 0N 180 0 E
Alex 43 34 55N 97 47W
Alexander, Ga. 18 33 1N 81 53W
Alexander, Iowa 23 42 48N 93 29W
Alexander, Kans. 24 38 28N 99 33W
Alexander, N. Dak. 41 47 51N 103 39W
Alexander, W. Va. 54 38 47N 80 13W
Alexander Archipelago 11 56 0N 136 0W
Alexander B. 123 28 36 S 16 33 E
Alexander City 10 32 56N 85 58W
Alexander County ◇, Ill. 21 37 10N 89 20W
Alexander County ◇, N.C. 40 35 50N 81 10W
Alexander I. 5 69 0 S 70 0W
Alexandra 128 45 14 S 169 25 E
Alexandra Falls 62 60 29N 116 18W
Alexandretta = İskenderun 106 36 32N 36 10 E
Alexandria = El Iskandarîya 121 31 0N 30 0 E
Alexandria, B.C., Canada 62 52 35N 122 27W
Alexandria, Ont., Canada 60 45 19N 74 38W
Alexandria, Romania 95 43 57N 25 24 E
Alexandria, S. Africa 123 33 38 S 26 28 E
Alexandria, Ind. 22 40 16N 85 41W
Alexandria, Ky. 49 38 58N 84 23W
Alexandria, La. 25 31 18N 92 27W
Alexandria, Minn. 30 45 53N 95 22W
Alexandria, Mo. 32 40 27N 91 28W
Alexandria, N.H. 36 43 37N 71 47W
Alexandria, Nebr. 34 40 15N 97 23W
Alexandria, Pa. 45 40 34N 78 6W
Alexandria, S. Dak. 47 43 39N 97 47W
Alexandria, Tenn. 48 36 5N 86 2W
Alexandria, Va. 54 38 48N 77 3W
Alexandria Bay 39 44 20N 75 55W
Alexandrina, L. 127 35 25 S 139 10 E
Alexandroúpolis 95 40 50N 25 54 E
Alexis 21 41 4N 90 33W
Alexis → 61 52 33N 56 8W
Alexis Creek 62 52 10N 123 20W
Alfalfa 43 35 13N 98 36W
Alfalfa County ◇ 43 36 45N 98 15W
Alfatar 95 43 59N 27 13 E
Alfenas 77 21 20 S 46 10W
Alford, U.K. 84 57 13N 2 42W
Alford, U.S.A. 17 30 42N 85 24W
Alfred, Maine 26 43 29N 70 43W
Alfred, N.Y. 39 42 16N 77 48W
Alfreton 82 53 6N 1 22W
Alga 100 49 53N 57 20 E
Algarve 91 36 58N 8 20W
Algeciras 91 36 9N 5 28W
Algemesí 91 39 11N 0 27W
Alger 120 36 42N 3 8 E
Alger County ◇ 29 46 20N 86 50W
Algeria ■ 120 35 10N 3 11 E
Alghero 94 40 34N 8 20 E
Algiers = Alger 120 36 42N 3 8 E
Algoabaai 123 33 50 S 25 45 E
Algodones 38 35 23N 106 29W
Algoma, Miss. 31 34 11N 89 2W
Algoma, Wis. 55 44 36N 87 26W
Algona 23 43 4N 94 14W
Algonac 29 42 37N 82 32W
Algonquin 21 42 10N 88 18W
Algood 49 36 12N 85 27W
Alhama de Murcia 91 37 51N 1 25W
Alhambra 15 34 8N 118 6W
Alhucemas = Al Hoceïma 120 35 8N 3 58W
'Alī al Gharbī 106 32 30N 46 45 E
Ali Khel 108 33 56N 69 35 E
Aliákmon → 95 40 30N 22 36 E
Alibo 121 9 52N 37 5 E
Alicante 91 38 23N 0 30W
Alice, N. Dak. 41 46 46N 97 33W
Alice, Tex. 51 27 45N 98 5W
Alice Arm 62 55 29N 129 31W
Alice Springs 126 23 40 S 133 50 E
Aliceville, Ala. 10 33 8N 88 9W
Aliceville, Kans. 24 38 9N 95 33W
Alicia 13 35 54N 91 5W
Alida 63 49 25N 101 55W
Aligarh 108 27 55N 78 10 E
Alīgūdarz 106 33 25N 49 45 E
Aline 43 36 31N 98 27W
Alingsås 97 57 56N 12 31 E
Alipur 108 29 25N 70 55 E
Alipur Duar 109 26 30N 89 35 E
Aliquippa 45 40 37N 80 15W
Aliwal North 123 30 45 S 26 45 E
Alix 62 52 24N 113 11W
Aljustrel 91 37 55N 8 10W
Alkali Flats 35 40 0N 115 58W
Alkali L. 35 41 42N 119 51W
Alkaline L. 41 46 40N 99 34W
Alkmaar 87 52 37N 4 45 E
Allagash 26 47 5N 69 3W
Allagash → 26 47 5N 69 3W
Allagash L. 26 46 18N 69 35W
Allahabad 109 25 25N 81 58 E
Allakaket 11 66 34N 152 39W
Allakh-Yun 101 60 50N 137 5 E
Allamakee County ◇ 23 43 15N 91 20W
Allamoore 50 31 5N 105 0W
Allan 63 51 53N 106 4W
Allanmyo 109 19 30N 95 17 E
Allanwater 60 50 14N 90 10W
Allardt 49 36 23N 84 53W
Allatoona L. 18 34 10N 84 44W
Allegan 29 42 32N 85 51W
Allegan County ◇ 29 42 35N 85 50W
Allegany, N.Y. 39 42 6N 78 30W
Allegany, Oreg. 44 43 26N 124 2W
Allegany County ◇, Md. 27 39 40N 78 40W
Allegany County ◇, N.Y. 39 42 15N 78 0W
Allegany Indian Reservation 39 42 6N 78 55W
Alleghany County ◇, N.C. 40 36 25N 81 10W
Alleghany County ◇, Va. 54 37 50N 80 0W
Allegheny → 45 40 27N 80 1W
Allegheny County ◇ 45 40 25N 80 0W
Allegheny Mts. 54 38 15N 80 10W
Allegheny National Forest 45 41 45N 79 5W
Allegheny Reservoir 45 41 50N 79 0W
Allemands, L. des 25 29 55N 90 35W
Allen, Argentina 78 38 58 S 67 50W
Allen, Kans. 24 38 39N 96 10W
Allen, Md. 27 38 17N 75 42W
Allen, Nebr. 34 42 25N 96 51W
Allen, Okla. 43 34 53N 96 25W
Allen, S. Dak. 47 43 17N 101 56W
Allen, Tex. 51 33 6N 96 40W
Allen, Bog of 85 53 15N 7 0W
Allen, L. 85 54 12N 8 5W
Allen County ◇, Ind. 22 41 5N 85 5W
Allen County ◇, Kans. 24 37 50N 95 15W
Allen County ◇, Ky. 48 36 45N 86 10W
Allen County ◇, Ohio 42 40 44N 84 6W
Allen Parish ◇ 25 30 37N 92 46W
Allenby Br. = Jisr al Ḩusayn 104 31 53N 35 33 E
Allendale, Ill. 21 38 32N 87 43W
Allendale, S.C. 46 33 1N 81 18W
Allendale County ◇ 46 33 0N 81 20W
Allende 64 28 20N 100 50W
Allenhurst 37 40 15N 73 59W
Allenspark 16 40 12N 105 32W
Allensville 48 36 43N 87 4W
Allentown, N.J. 37 40 11N 74 35W
Allentown, Pa. 45 40 37N 75 29W
Alleppey 108 9 30N 76 28 E
Allerton, Ill. 21 39 55N 87 56W
Allerton, Iowa 23 40 42N 93 22W
Alliance, Surinam 71 5 50N 54 50W
Alliance, Nebr. 34 42 6N 102 52W
Alliance, Ohio 42 40 55N 81 6W
Allier □ 90 46 25N 3 0 E
Allier → 90 46 57N 3 4 E
Alligator 31 34 6N 90 43W
Allison, Colo. 16 37 2N 107 29W
Allison, Iowa 23 42 45N 92 48W
Allison, Tex. 50 35 36N 100 6W
Alliston 60 44 9N 79 52W
Alloa 84 56 7N 3 49W
Allons 49 36 27N 85 21W
Allouez 55 44 27N 88 4W
Alloway 37 39 34N 75 22W
Allyn 53 47 23N 122 50W
Alma, Canada 61 48 35N 71 40W
Alma, Ark. 13 35 29N 94 13W
Alma, Colo. 16 39 17N 106 4W
Alma, Ga. 18 31 33N 82 28W
Alma, Kans. 24 39 1N 96 17W
Alma, Mich. 29 43 23N 84 39W
Alma, Mo. 32 39 6N 93 33W
Alma, Nebr. 34 40 6N 99 22W
Alma, Wis. 55 44 20N 91 55W
'Almā ash Sha'b 104 33 7N 35 9 E
Alma Ata 100 43 15N 76 57 E
Alma Center 55 44 26N 90 55W
Almada 91 38 40N 9 9W
Almadén 91 38 49N 4 52W
Almanor, L. 14 40 14N 121 9W
Almansa 91 38 51N 1 5W
Almanzor, Pico de 91 40 15N 5 18W
Almanzora → 91 37 14N 1 46W
Almas 75 11 33 S 47 9W
Almaş, Mţii. 95 44 49N 22 12 E
Almazán 91 41 30N 2 30W
Almeirim 71 1 30 S 52 34W
Almelo 87 52 22N 6 42 E
Almena 24 39 54N 99 43W
Almenara 75 16 11 S 40 42W
Almendralejo 91 38 41N 6 26W
Almería, Spain 91 36 52N 2 27W
Almeria, U.S.A. 34 41 50N 99 31W
Almira 53 47 43N 118 56W
Almirante 66 9 10N 82 30W
Almirante Montt, G. 78 51 52 S 72 50W
Almo 48 36 42N 88 16W
Almon 18 33 37N 83 56W
Almond, N.C. 40 35 22N 83 34W
Almond, Wis. 55 44 16N 89 25W
Almont, Colo. 16 38 40N 106 51W
Almont, Mich. 29 42 55N 83 3W
Almont, N. Dak. 41 46 44N 101 30W
Almora 108 29 38N 79 40 E
Almyra 13 34 24N 91 25W
Alnwick 82 55 25N 1 42W
Aloha 44 45 29N 122 52W
Alon 109 22 12N 95 5 E
Alonsa 63 50 50N 99 0W
Alor 111 8 15 S 124 30 E
Alor Setar 112 6 7N 100 22 E
Alpaugh 15 35 53N 119 29W
Alpena, Ark. 13 36 18N 93 18W
Alpena, Mich. 29 45 4N 83 27W
Alpena, S. Dak. 47 44 11N 98 22W
Alpena County ◇ 29 45 0N 83 40W
Alpercatas → 74 6 2 S 44 19W
Alpes-de-Haute-Provence □ 90 44 8N 6 10 E
Alpes-Maritimes □ 90 43 55N 7 10 E
Alpha, Australia 127 23 39 S 146 37 E
Alpha, Ill. 21 41 12N 90 23W
Alpha, Mich. 29 46 3N 88 23W
Alpha, N.J. 37 40 40N 75 9W
Alpine, Ariz. 12 33 51N 109 9W
Alpine, Ark. 13 34 14N 93 23W
Alpine, Tenn. 49 36 24N 85 13W
Alpine, Tex. 50 30 22N 103 40W
Alpine, Utah 52 40 27N 111 47W
Alpine, Wyo. 56 43 11N 111 3W
Alpine County ◇ 14 38 40N 119 50W
Alps 88 47 0N 8 0 E
Alsace 90 48 15N 7 25 E
Alsask 63 51 21N 109 59W
Alsásua 91 42 54N 2 10W
Alsea → 44 44 26N 124 5W
Alsen 41 48 38N 98 42W
Alsey 21 39 34N 90 26W
Alstead 36 43 10N 72 30W
Alsten 96 65 58N 12 40 E
Alta, Norway 96 69 57N 23 10 E
Alta, U.S.A. 23 42 40N 95 18W
Alta Gracia 76 31 40 S 64 30W
Alta Lake 62 50 10N 123 0W
Alta Vista, Iowa 23 43 12N 92 25W
Alta Vista, Kans. 24 38 52N 96 29W
Altaelva → 96 69 46N 23 45 E
Altafjorden 96 70 5N 23 5 E
Altagracia 70 10 45N 71 30W
Altagracia de Orituco 70 9 52N 66 23W
Altai = Aerht'ai Shan 113 46 40N 92 45 E
Altai Mts. 102 46 40N 92 45 E
Altair 51 29 34N 96 27W
Altamachi → 72 16 8 S 66 50W
Altamaha → 18 31 20N 81 20W
Altamira, Brazil 71 3 12 S 52 10W
Altamira, Chile 76 25 47 S 69 51W
Altamira, Colombia 70 2 3N 75 47W
Altamira, Mexico 65 22 24N 97 55W
Altamont, Ill. 21 39 4N 88 45W
Altamont, Kans. 24 37 12N 95 18W
Altamont, Mo. 32 39 53N 94 5W
Altamont, Oreg. 44 42 12N 121 44W
Altamont, S. Dak. 47 44 50N 96 42W
Altamont, Tenn. 49 35 26N 85 44W
Altamont, Utah 52 40 22N 110 17W
Altanbulag 113 50 16N 106 30 E
Altar 64 30 40N 111 50W
Altata 64 24 30N 108 0W
Altavista 54 37 6N 79 17W
Altay 113 47 48N 88 10 E
Altha 17 30 34N 85 8W
Altheimer 13 34 19N 91 51W
Altiplano 72 17 0 S 68 0W
Alto, Ga. 18 34 28N 83 35W
Alto, La. 25 32 22N 91 52W
Alto, N. Mex. 38 33 23N 105 41W
Alto, Tex. 51 31 39N 95 4W
Alto Adige = Trentino-Alto Adige □ 94 46 30N 11 0 E
Alto Araguaia 73 17 15 S 53 20W
Alto Cuchumatanes = Cuchumatanes, Sierra de los 66 15 35N 91 25W
Alto del Inca 76 24 10 S 68 10W
Alto Garças 73 16 56 S 53 32W
Alto Iriri → 73 8 50 S 53 25W
Alto Molocue 123 15 50 S 37 35 E
Alto Paraguai 73 14 30 S 56 31W
Alto Paraná □ 77 25 0 S 54 50W
Alto Parnaíba 74 9 6 S 45 57W
Alto Purús → 72 9 12 S 70 28W
Alto Río Senguerr 78 45 2 S 70 50W
Alto Santo 74 5 31 S 38 15W
Alto Sucuriú 73 19 19 S 52 47W
Alto Turi 74 2 54 S 45 38W
Alton, Ill. 21 38 53N 90 11W
Alton, Iowa 23 42 59N 96 1W
Alton, Kans. 24 39 28N 98 57W
Alton, Mo. 32 36 42N 91 24W
Alton, Utah 52 37 26N 112 29W
Alton Bay 36 43 27N 71 13W
Altona 88 53 32N 9 56 E
Altoona, Ala. 10 34 2N 86 20W
Altoona, Iowa 23 41 39N 93 28W
Altoona, Kans. 24 37 32N 95 40W
Altoona, Pa. 45 40 31N 78 24W
Altoona, Wis. 55 44 48N 91 26W
Altos 74 5 3 S 42 28W
Altun Shan 113 38 30N 88 0 E
Alturas 14 41 29N 120 32W
Altus 43 34 38N 99 20W
Altus, L. 43 34 53N 99 18W
Alùla 105 11 50N 50 45 E
Alum Bridge 54 39 2N 80 40W
Alusi 111 7 35 S 131 40 E
Alva, Ky. 49 36 44N 83 25W
Alva, Okla. 43 36 48N 98 40W
Alvarado, Mexico 65 18 40N 95 50W
Alvarado, Minn. 30 48 10N 97 0W
Alvarado, Tex. 51 32 24N 97 13W
Alvarães 71 3 12 S 64 50W
Alvaro Obregón, Presa 64 27 55N 109 52W
Alvaton 48 36 53N 86 21W
Alvear 76 29 5 S 56 30W
Alvesta 97 56 54N 14 35 E
Alvin, S.C. 46 33 22N 79 48W
Alvin, Tex. 51 29 26N 95 15W
Älvkarleby 97 60 34N 17 26 E
Alvo 34 40 52N 96 23W
Alvord, Iowa 23 43 21N 96 18W
Alvord, Tex. 51 33 22N 97 42W
Alvord Desert 44 42 30N 118 25W
Alvord L. 44 42 23N 118 36W
Älvsborgs län □ 97 58 30N 12 30 E
Älvsbyn 96 65 40N 21 0 E
Alwar 108 27 38N 76 34 E
Alxa Zuoqi 114 38 50N 105 40 E
Alyangula 127 13 55 S 136 30 E
Alyaskitovyy 101 64 45N 141 30 E
Alyata 99 39 58N 49 25 E
Alyth 84 56 38N 3 15W
Alzada 33 45 2N 104 25W
Am Dam 121 12 40N 20 35 E
Am Géréda 121 12 53N 21 14 E
Am-Timan 121 11 0N 20 10 E
Amacuro □ 71 8 50N 61 5W
Amadeus, L. 126 24 54 S 131 0 E
Amâdi, Sudan 121 5 29N 30 25 E
Amadi, Zaïre 122 3 40N 26 40 E
Amadjuak 59 64 0N 72 39W
Amadjuak L. 59 65 0N 71 8W
Amador County ◇ 14 38 25N 120 45W
Amagansett 39 40 59N 72 9W
Amagasaki 117 34 42N 135 20 E
Amakusa-Shotō 117 32 15N 130 10 E
Amalfi 70 6 55N 75 4W
Amalner 108 21 5N 75 5 E
Amambaí 77 23 5 S 55 13W
Amambaí → 77 23 22 S 53 56W
Amambay □ 77 23 0 S 56 0W
Amambay, Cordillera de 77 23 0 S 55 45W
Amami-Guntō 117 28 16N 129 21 E
Amami-Ō-Shima 117 28 0N 129 0 E
Amana 23 41 48N 91 52W
Amana → 71 9 45N 62 39W
Amaná, Lago 71 2 35 S 64 40W
Amanda 42 39 39N 82 45W
Amangeldy 100 50 10N 65 10 E
Amapá 74 2 5N 50 50W
Amapá □ 74 1 40N 52 0W
Amapari 71 0 37N 51 39W
Amarante 74 6 14 S 42 50W
Amarante do Maranhão 74 5 36 S 46 45W
Amaranth 63 50 36N 98 43W
Amargosa 75 13 2 S 39 36W
Amargosa → 15 36 14N 116 51W
Amargosa Range 15 36 20N 116 45W
Amarillo 50 35 13N 101 50W
Amaro, Mt. 94 42 5N 14 6 E
Amaro Leite 75 13 58 S 49 9W
Amasa 29 46 14N 88 27W
Amasra 106 41 45N 32 30 E
Amasya 106 40 40N 35 50 E
Amataurá 70 3 29 S 68 6W
Amatignak I. 11 51 16N 179 6W
Amatitlán 66 14 29N 90 38W
Amazon = Amazonas → 71 0 5 S 50 0W
Amazonas □, Brazil 72 4 0 S 62 0W
Amazonas □, Peru 72 5 0 S 78 0W
Amazonas □, Venezuela 70 3 30N 66 0W
Amazonas → 71 0 5 S 50 0W
Amazonia 32 39 53N 94 54W
Ambala 108 30 23N 76 56 E
Ambalavao 123 21 50 S 46 56 E
Ambam 122 2 20N 11 15 E
Ambanja 123 13 40 S 48 27 E
Ambarchik 101 69 40N 162 20 E
Ambartsevo 100 57 30N 83 52 E
Ambato 70 1 5 S 78 42W
Ambato, Sierra de 76 28 25 S 66 10W
Ambatolampy 123 19 20 S 47 35 E
Ambatondrazaka 123 17 55 S 48 28 E
Amber 43 35 10N 97 53W
Amberg 88 49 25N 11 52 E
Ambergris Cay 65 18 0N 88 0W
Amberley 128 43 9 S 172 44 E
Ambikapur 109 23 15N 83 15 E
Ambilobé 123 13 10 S 49 3 E
Ambler 11 67 5N 157 52W
Ambleside 82 54 26N 2 58W
Ambo 72 10 5 S 76 10W
Ambohitra 123 12 30 S 49 10 E
Ambon 111 3 35 S 128 20 E
Ambositra 123 20 31 S 47 25 E
Amboy, Calif. 15 34 33N 115 45W
Amboy, Ill. 21 41 44N 89 20W
Amboy, Minn. 30 43 53N 94 10W
Amboyna I. 110 7 50N 112 50 E
Ambridge 45 40 36N 80 14W
Ambriz 122 7 48 S 13 8 E
Ambrose, Ga. 18 31 36N 83 1W
Ambrose, N. Dak. 41 48 57N 103 29W
Ambrosia Lake 38 35 26N 107 54W
Amchitka I. 11 51 32N 179 0 E
Amderma 100 69 45N 61 30 E

Ameca Antigo

Ameca 64 20 30N 104 0W
Ameca → 64 20 40N 105 15W
Amecameca 65 19 7N 98 46W
Ameland 87 53 27N 5 45 E
Amelia, La. 25 29 40N 91 6W
Amelia, Nebr. 34 42 14N 98 55W
Amelia City 17 30 35N 81 28W
Amelia County ◇ 54 37 21N 77 59W
Amelia Court House 54 37 21N 77 59W
Amelia I. 17 30 40N 81 25W
Amen 101 68 45N 180 0 E
American Corners 27 38 47N 75 51W
American Falls 20 42 47N 112 51W
American Falls Dam 20 43 0N 113 0W
American Falls Reservoir 20 42 47N 112 52W
American Fork 52 40 23N 111 48W
American Highland 5 73 0 S 75 0 E
American Samoa ■ 128 14 20 S 170 40W
Americana 77 22 45 S 47 20W
Americus, Ga. 18 32 4N 84 14W
Americus, Kans. 24 38 30N 96 16W
Americus, Mo. 32 38 47N 91 34W
Amersfoort 87 52 9N 5 23 E
Amery, Canada 63 56 34N 94 3W
Amery, U.S.A. 55 45 19N 92 22W
Amery Ice Shelf 5 69 30 S 72 0 E
Ames, Iowa 23 42 2N 93 37W
Ames, Okla. 43 36 15N 98 11W
Ames, Tex. 51 30 3N 94 45W
Amesbury 28 42 51N 70 56W
Amesdale 63 50 2N 92 55W
Amesville 42 39 24N 81 57W
Amga 101 60 50N 132 0 E
Amga → 101 62 38N 134 32 E
Amgu 101 45 45N 137 15 E
Amgun → 101 52 56N 139 38 E
Amherst, Burma 109 16 2N 97 20 E
Amherst, Canada 61 45 48N 64 8W
Amherst, Colo. 16 40 41N 102 10W
Amherst, Maine 26 44 50N 68 22W
Amherst, Mass. 28 42 23N 72 31W
Amherst, N.H. 36 42 52N 71 38W
Amherst, N.Y. 39 42 59N 78 48W
Amherst, Ohio 42 41 24N 82 14W
Amherst, Tex. 50 34 1N 102 25W
Amherst, Va. 54 37 35N 79 3W
Amherst County ◇ 54 37 38N 79 5W
Amherst Junction 55 44 28N 89 19W
Amherstburg 60 42 6N 83 6W
Amherstdale 54 37 47N 81 49W
Amiata, Mte. 94 42 54N 11 40 E
Amidon 41 46 29N 103 19W
Amiens 90 49 54N 2 16 E
Amirante Is. 3 6 0 S 53 0 E
Amisk L. 63 54 35N 102 15W
Amistad 38 35 55N 103 9W
Amistad, Presa de la 64 29 24N 101 0W
Amistad National Recreation Area 50 29 32N 101 12W
Amistad Reservoir 50 29 28N 101 4W
Amite 25 30 44N 90 30W
Amite → 25 30 18N 90 34W
Amite County ◇ 31 31 10N 90 49W
Amity, Ark. 13 34 16N 93 28W
Amity, Ind. 22 39 26N 86 0W
Amity, Oreg. 44 45 7N 123 12W
Amlia I. 11 52 4N 173 30W
Amlwch 82 53 24N 4 21W
'Ammān 104 31 57N 35 52 E
Ammanford 83 51 48N 4 0W
Ammi'ad 104 32 55N 35 32 E
Ammon 20 43 28N 111 58W
Ammonoosuc → 36 44 10N 72 2W
Amonate 54 37 12N 81 38W
Amoret 32 38 15N 94 35W
Amorgós 95 36 50N 25 57 E
Amorita 43 36 56N 98 18W
Amory 31 33 59N 88 29W
Amos 60 48 35N 78 5W
Amozoc 65 19 2N 98 3W
Ampanihy 123 24 40 S 44 45 E
Ampato, Nevado 72 15 40 S 71 56W
Ampenan 110 8 35 S 116 13 E
Amqa 104 32 59N 35 10 E
Amqui 61 48 28N 67 27W
Amraoti 108 20 55N 77 45 E
Amreli 108 21 35N 71 17 E
Amritsar 108 31 35N 74 57 E
Amroha 108 28 53N 78 30 E
Amsden 36 43 25N 72 30W
Amsterdam, Neth. 87 52 23N 4 54 E
Amsterdam, N.Y. 39 42 56N 74 11W
Amsterdam, Ohio 42 40 29N 80 56W
Amsterdam, I. 3 37 30 S 77 30 E
Amudarya → 100 43 40N 59 0 E
Amukta I. 11 52 30N 171 16W
Amukta Pass 11 52 0N 171 0W
Amund Ringnes I. 4 78 20N 96 25W
Amundsen Gulf 58 71 0N 124 0W
Amundsen Sea 5 72 0 S 115 0W
Amuntai 110 2 28 S 115 25 E
Amur → 101 52 56N 141 10 E
Amurang 111 1 5N 124 40 E
Amuri Pass 128 42 31 S 172 11 E
Amursk 101 50 14N 136 54 E
Amurzet 101 47 50N 131 5 E
Amy 13 33 44N 92 49W
An Nafūd 106 28 15N 41 0 E
An Najaf 106 32 3N 44 15 E
An Nāqūrah 104 33 7N 35 8 E
An Nāṣirīyah 106 31 0N 46 15 E
An Nhon 112 13 55N 109 7 E
An Nîl □ 121 19 30N 33 0 E
An Nîl el Abyad □ 121 14 0N 32 15 E
An Nîl el Azraq □ 121 12 30N 34 30 E
An Nu'ayrīyah 106 27 30N 48 30 E
An Uaimh 85 53 39N 6 40W
Anabar → 101 73 8N 113 36 E
'Anabtā 104 32 19N 35 7 E
Anacapa I. 15 34 1N 119 26W
Anaco 71 9 27N 64 28W
Anacoco 25 31 15N 93 21W
Anaconda 33 46 8N 112 57W
Anaconda Ra. 33 45 30N 113 30W
Anacortes 53 48 30N 122 37W
Anadarko 43 35 4N 98 15W
Anadia 74 9 42 S 36 18W
Anadolu 106 38 0N 30 0 E
Anadyr 101 64 35N 177 20 E
Anadyr → 101 64 55N 176 5 E
Anadyrskiy Zaliv 101 64 0N 180 0 E
'Ānah 106 34 25N 42 0 E
Anahalu → 19 21 37N 158 6W
Anaheim 15 33 50N 117 55W
Anahim Lake 62 52 28N 125 18W
Anahola 19 22 9N 159 19W
Anáhuac, Mexico 64 27 14N 100 9W
Anahuac, U.S.A. 51 29 46N 94 41W
Anajás 74 0 59 S 49 57W
Anajatuba 74 3 16 S 44 37W
Anakapalle 109 17 42N 83 6 E
Anaktuvuk Pass 11 68 8N 151 45W
Analalava 123 14 35 S 48 0 E
Anamã 71 3 35 S 61 22W
Anambas, Kepulauan 110 3 20N 106 30 E
Anamoose 41 47 53N 100 15W
Anamosa 23 42 7N 91 17W
Anamur 106 36 8N 32 58 E
Anan 117 33 54N 134 40 E
Anandale 25 31 16N 92 27W
Anantnag 108 33 45N 75 10 E
Anápolis 75 16 15 S 48 50W
Anapu → 71 1 53 S 50 53W
Anār 107 30 55N 55 13 E
Anārak 107 33 25N 53 40 E
Anasco 57 18 17N 67 8W
Anatolia = Anadolu 106 38 0N 30 0 E
Anatone 53 46 8N 117 8W
Añatuya 76 28 20 S 62 50W
Anauá → 71 0 58N 61 21W
Anaunethad L. 63 60 55N 104 25W
Anavilhanas, Arquipélago das 71 2 42 S 60 45W
Anaye 121 19 15N 12 50 E
Ancash □ 72 9 30 S 77 45W
Anceney 33 45 39N 111 21W
Ancho 38 33 56N 105 45W
Ancho, Canal 78 50 0 S 74 20W
Anchor 21 40 34N 88 32W
Anchorage 11 61 13N 149 54W
Anchorage ◇ 11 61 0N 150 0W
Ancohuma, Nevada 72 16 0 S 68 50W
Ancon, Panama 57 8 56N 79 38W
Ancón, Peru 72 11 50 S 77 10W
Ancona 94 43 37N 13 30 E
Ancud 78 42 0 S 73 50W
Ancud, G. de 78 42 0 S 73 0W
Anda 114 46 24N 125 19 E
Andacollo, Argentina 76 37 10 S 70 42W
Andacollo, Chile 76 30 5 S 71 10W
Andahuaylas 72 13 40 S 73 25W
Andale 24 37 48N 97 38W
Andalgalá 76 27 40 S 66 30W
Åndalsnes 96 62 35N 7 43 E
Andalucía □ 91 37 35N 5 0W
Andalusia, Ala. 10 31 18N 86 29W
Andalusia, Ill. 21 41 26N 90 43W
Andalusia □ = Andalucía □ 91 37 35N 5 0W
Andaman Is. 112 12 30N 92 30 E
Andaman Sea 112 13 0N 96 0 E
Andaman Str. 112 12 15N 92 20 E
Andara 123 18 2 S 21 9 E
Andaraí 75 12 48 S 41 20W
Andenne 87 50 30N 5 5 E
Anderson, Ala. 10 34 55N 87 16W
Anderson, Alaska 11 64 25N 149 15W
Anderson, Calif. 14 40 27N 122 18W
Anderson, Ind. 22 40 10N 85 41W
Anderson, Mo. 32 36 39N 94 27W
Anderson, S.C. 46 34 31N 82 39W
Anderson, Tex. 51 30 29N 95 59W
Anderson → 58 69 42N 129 0W
Anderson County ◇, Kans. 24 38 15N 95 15W
Anderson County ◇, Ky. 49 38 0N 85 0W
Anderson County ◇, S.C. 46 34 30N 82 40W
Anderson County ◇, Tenn. 49 36 6N 84 8W
Anderson County ◇, Tex. 51 31 46N 95 38W
Anderson Ranch Reservoir 20 43 22N 115 27W
Anderson Reservoir 14 37 10N 121 38W
Andersonville 18 32 12N 84 9W
Andes, Colombia 72 5 40N 75 53W
Andes, U.S.A. 39 42 12N 74 47W
Andes, Cord de los 72 20 0 S 68 0W
Andes, L. 47 43 11N 98 27W
Andfjorden 96 69 10N 16 20 E
Andhra Pradesh □ 108 16 0N 79 0 E
Andikíthira 95 35 52N 23 15 E
Andizhan 100 41 10N 72 0 E
Andkhvoy 107 36 52N 65 8 E
Andoany 123 13 25 S 48 16 E
Andoas 70 2 55 S 76 25W
Andong 114 36 40N 128 43 E
Andorra ■ 91 42 30N 1 30 E
Andorra La Vella 91 42 31N 1 32 E
Andover, U.K. 83 51 13N 1 29W
Andover, Conn. 28 41 44N 72 23W
Andover, Kans. 24 37 43N 97 7W
Andover, Maine 26 44 38N 70 45W
Andover, Mass. 28 42 40N 71 8W
Andover, Minn. 30 45 17N 93 21W
Andover, N.H. 36 43 26N 71 49W
Andover, N.J. 37 40 59N 74 45W
Andover, N.Y. 39 42 10N 77 48W
Andover, Ohio 42 41 36N 80 34W
Andover, S. Dak. 47 45 25N 97 54W
Andradina 75 20 54 S 51 23W
Andreanof Is. 11 51 30N 176 0W
Andrew County ◇ 32 40 0N 94 45W
Andrews, Ind. 22 40 52N 85 36W
Andrews, Md. 27 38 20N 76 10W
Andrews, N.C. 40 35 12N 83 49W
Andrews, S.C. 46 33 27N 79 34W
Andrews, Tex. 50 32 19N 102 33W
Andrews County ◇ 50 32 19N 102 33W
Ándria 94 41 13N 16 17 E
Andriba 123 17 30 S 46 58 E
Androka 123 24 58 S 44 2 E
Andropov 98 58 5N 38 50E
Andros 95 37 50N 24 57E
Andros I. 66 24 43N 77 47W
Androscoggin → 26 43 58N 69 52W
Androscoggin County ◇ 26 44 5N 70 10W
Andújar 91 38 3N 4 5W
Anegada, Bahía 78 40 20 S 62 20W
Anegada Passage 67 18 15N 63 45W
Anegam 12 32 22N 112 2W
Aného 120 6 12N 1 34 E
Añelo 78 38 20 S 68 45W
Aneta 41 47 41N 97 59W
Aneto, Pico de 91 42 37N 0 40 E
Añez 73 15 40 S 63 10W
Ang Thong 112 14 35N 100 31 E
Angamos, Punta 76 23 1 S 70 32W
Ang'angxi 114 47 10N 123 48 E
Angara → 101 58 30N 97 0 E
Angarsk 101 52 30N 104 0 E
Ånge 96 62 31N 15 35 E
Angel de la Guarda 64 29 30N 113 30W
Angel Falls 71 5 57N 62 30W
Angeles 111 15 9N 120 33 E
Angeles National Forest 15 33 15N 118 0W
Ängelholm 97 56 15N 12 58 E
Angelina → 51 30 54N 94 12W
Angelina County ◇ 51 31 21N 94 44W
Angelina National Forest 51 31 7N 94 15W
Angels Camp 14 38 4N 120 32W
Angelus 24 39 11N 100 41W
Ångermanälven → 96 62 40N 18 0 E
Angers 90 47 30N 0 35W
Ängesån → 96 66 50N 22 15 E
Angical 75 12 0 S 44 42W
Angie 25 30 58N 89 49W
Angier 40 35 31N 78 44W
Angikuni L. 63 62 0N 100 0W
Angkor 112 13 22N 103 50 E
Angle Inlet 30 49 21N 95 4W
Anglesey 82 53 17N 4 20W
Angleton 51 29 10N 95 26W
Angmagssalik 4 65 40N 37 20W
Ango 122 4 10N 26 5 E
Angoche, I. 123 16 20 S 39 50 E
Angol 76 37 56 S 72 45W
Angola, Del. 27 38 40N 75 10W
Angola, Ind. 22 41 38N 85 0W
Angola, N.Y. 39 42 38N 79 2W
Angola ■ 123 12 0 S 18 0 E
Angoon 11 57 30N 134 35W
Angora 34 41 51N 103 8W
Angostura Reservoir 47 43 21N 103 26W
Angoulême 90 45 39N 0 10 E
Angoumois 90 45 50N 0 25 E
Angra dos Reis 77 23 0 S 44 10W
Angren 100 41 1N 70 12 E
Anguilla, U.S.A. 31 32 59N 90 50W
Anguilla, W. Indies 67 18 14N 63 5W
Angus, Braes of 84 56 51N 3 10W
Angwin 14 38 34N 122 26W
Anhanduí → 77 21 46 S 52 9W
Anholt 97 56 42N 11 33 E
Anhua 115 28 23N 111 12 E
Anhui □ 115 32 0N 117 0 E
Anhwei □ = Anhui □ 115 32 0N 117 0 E
Aniak 11 61 35N 159 32W
Anicuns 75 16 28 S 49 58W
Animas 38 31 57N 108 48W
Animas → 38 36 43N 108 13W
Animas Peak 38 31 35N 108 47W
Anin 112 15 36N 97 50 E
Anita 23 41 27N 94 46W
Anjidiv I. 108 14 40N 74 10 E
Anjou 90 47 20N 0 15W
Anjozorobe 123 18 22 S 47 52 E
Anju 114 39 36N 125 40 E
Anka 120 12 13N 5 58 E
Ankaboa, Tanjona 123 21 58 S 43 20 E
Ankang 115 32 40N 109 1 E
Ankara 106 40 0N 32 54 E
Ankazoabo 123 22 18 S 44 31 E
Ankazobe 123 18 20 S 47 10 E
Ankeny 23 41 44N 93 36W
Ankona 17 27 21N 80 17W
Ankoro 122 6 45 S 26 55 E
Anlu 115 31 15N 113 45 E
Anmoore 54 39 16N 80 18W
Ann, C. 28 42 38N 70 35W
Ann Arbor 29 42 17N 83 45W
Anna, Ill. 21 37 28N 89 15W
Anna, Ohio 42 40 24N 84 11W
Anna, Tex. 51 33 21N 96 33W
Anna, L. 54 38 4N 77 45W
Anna Regina 71 7 10N 58 30W
Annaba 120 36 50N 7 46 E
Annada 32 39 16N 90 50W
Annalee → 85 54 3N 7 15W
Annam = Trung-Phan 110 16 0N 108 0 E
Annamitique, Chaîne 112 17 0N 106 0 E
Annan 84 55 0N 3 17W
Annan → 84 54 58N 3 18W
Annandale, Minn. 30 45 16N 94 8W
Annandale, Va. 54 38 50N 77 12W
Annapolis, Md. 27 38 59N 76 30W
Annapolis, Mo. 32 37 22N 90 42W
Annapolis Royal 61 44 44N 65 32W
Annawan 21 41 24N 89 55W
Anne Arundel County ◇ 27 39 0N 76 40W
Annecy 90 45 55N 6 8 E
Annette I. 11 55 9N 131 28W
Annette Island Indian Reservation 11 55 5N 131 30W
Anning 113 24 55N 102 26 E
Anniston, Ala. 10 33 39N 85 50W
Anniston, Mo. 32 36 50N 89 20W
Annobón = Pagalu 119 1 25 S 5 36 E
Annona 51 33 35N 94 55W
Annonciation, L' 60 46 25N 74 55W
Annotto Bay 66 18 17N 77 3W
Annville, Ky. 49 37 19N 83 58W
Annville, Pa. 45 40 20N 76 31W
Año Nuevo, Pt. 14 37 7N 122 19W
Anoka, Minn. 30 45 12N 93 23W
Anoka, Nebr. 34 42 57N 98 50W
Anoka County ◇ 30 45 15N 93 15W
Anqing 115 30 30N 117 3 E
Anren 115 26 43N 113 18 E
Ansāb 106 29 11N 44 43 E
Ansai 114 36 50N 109 20 E
Ansbach 88 49 17N 10 34 E
Anse au Loup, L' 61 51 32N 56 50W
Anselmo 34 41 37N 99 52W
Anserma 70 5 13N 75 48W
Anshan 114 41 5N 122 58 E
Anshun 115 26 18N 105 57 E
Ansirabe 123 19 55 S 47 2 E
Ansley, La. 25 32 24N 92 42W
Ansley, Nebr. 34 41 18N 99 23W
Anson 51 32 45N 99 54W
Anson B. 126 13 20 S 130 6 E
Anson County ◇ 40 35 0N 80 0W
Ansongo 120 15 25N 0 35 E
Ansonia, Conn. 28 41 21N 73 5W
Ansonia, Ohio 42 40 13N 84 38W
Ansonville 40 35 6N 80 7W
Ansted 54 38 8N 81 6W
Anstruther 84 56 14N 2 40W
Ansudu 111 2 11 S 139 22 E
Antabamba 72 14 40 S 73 0W
Antakya 106 36 14N 36 10 E
Antalaha 123 14 57 S 50 20 E
Antalya 106 36 52N 30 45 E
Antalya Körfezi 106 36 15N 31 30 E
Antananarivo 123 18 55 S 47 31 E
Antarctic Pen. 5 67 0 S 60 0W
Antarctica 5 90 0 S 0 0 E
Antelope, Kans. 24 38 26N 96 59W
Antelope, Oreg. 44 44 55N 120 43W
Antelope County ◇ 34 42 15N 98 0W
Antelope Cr. → 44 42 28N 117 13W
Antelope Hills, Okla. 43 35 55N 99 50W
Antelope Hills, Wyo. 56 42 20N 108 25W
Antelope Range 35 40 10N 114 30W
Antelope Reservoir 44 42 54N 117 14W
Antenor Navarro 74 6 44 S 38 27W
Antequera, Paraguay 76 24 8 S 57 7W
Antequera, Spain 91 37 5N 4 33W
Antero, Mt. 16 38 41N 106 15W
Antero Reservoir 16 38 50N 105 55W
Anthon 23 42 23N 95 52W
Anthony, Fla. 17 29 18N 82 7W
Anthony, Kans. 24 37 9N 98 2W
Anthony, N. Mex. 38 32 0N 106 36W
Anthoston 48 37 46N 87 32W
Anti Atlas 120 30 0N 8 30W
Anticosti, Î. d' 61 49 30N 63 0W
Antigo 55 45 9N 89 9W

Antigonish **Arklow**

Antigonish **61** 45 38N 61 58W
Antigua, Guat. **66** 14 34N 90 41W
Antigua, W. Indies **67** 17 0N 61 50W
Antigua and Barbuda ■ **67** 17 20N 61 48W
Antilla **66** 20 40N 75 50W
Antimony **52** 38 7N 112 0W
Antioch, Calif. **14** 38 1N 121 48W
Antioch, Ill. **21** 42 29N 88 6W
Antioch, Nebr. **34** 42 4N 102 35W
Antioquia **70** 6 40N 75 55W
Antioquia □ **70** 7 0N 75 30W
Antipodes Is. **124** 49 45 S 178 40 E
Antler **41** 48 59N 101 17W
Antler → **63** 49 8N 101 0W
Antlers **43** 34 14N 95 37W
Antofagasta **76** 23 50 S 70 30W
Antofagasta □ **76** 24 0 S 69 0W
Antofagasta de la Sierra **76** 26 5 S 67 20W
Antofalla **76** 25 30 S 68 5W
Antofalla, Salar de **76** 25 40 S 67 45W
Antoine **13** 34 2N 93 25W
Anton, Colo. **16** 39 45N 103 13W
Anton, Ky. **48** 37 21N 87 24W
Anton, Tex. **50** 33 49N 102 10W
Anton Chico **38** 35 12N 105 9W
Antongila, Helodrano **123** 15 30 S 49 50 E
Antonina **77** 25 26 S 48 42W
Antonino **24** 38 47N 99 24W
Antonito **16** 37 5N 106 0W
Antrim **85** 54 43N 6 13W
Antrim □ **85** 54 55N 6 20W
Antrim, Mts. of **85** 54 57N 6 8W
Antrim County ◇ **29** 45 0N 85 10W
Antsalova **123** 18 40 S 44 37 E
Antsiranana **123** 12 25 S 49 20 E
Antsohihy **123** 14 50 S 47 59 E
Antwerp = Antwerpen **87** 51 13N 4 25 E
Antwerp, N.Y. **39** 44 12N 75 37W
Antwerp, Ohio **42** 41 11N 84 45W
Antwerpen **87** 51 13N 4 25 E
Antwerpen □ **87** 51 15N 4 40 E
Anupgarh **108** 29 10N 73 10 E
Anuradhapura **108** 8 22N 80 28 E
Anvers = Antwerpen **87** 51 13N 4 25 E
Anvers I. **5** 64 30 S 63 40W
Anvik **11** 62 39N 160 13W
Anxi, Fujian, China **115** 25 2N 118 12 E
Anxi, Gansu, China **113** 40 30N 95 43 E
Anxious B. **126** 33 24 S 134 45 E
Anyang **114** 36 5N 114 21 E
Anyi, Jiangxi, China **115** 28 49N 115 25 E
Anyi, Shanxi, China **115** 35 2N 111 2 E
Anyuan **115** 25 9N 115 21 E
Anza Borrego Desert State Park **15** 33 0N 116 26W
'Anzah **104** 32 22N 35 12 E
Anzhero-Sudzhensk **100** 56 10N 86 0 E
Ánzio **94** 41 28N 12 37 E
Anzoátegui □ **71** 9 0N 64 30W
Aoga-Shima **117** 32 28N 139 46 E
Aomori **116** 40 45N 140 45 E
Aomori □ **116** 40 45N 140 40 E
Aosta **94** 45 43N 7 20 E
Aoudéras **120** 17 45N 8 20 E
Aoulef el Arab **120** 26 55N 1 2 E
Aozi **121** 21 11N 18 34 E
Apa → **76** 22 6 S 58 2W
Apache **43** 34 54N 98 22W
Apache County ◇ **12** 35 0N 109 30W
Apache Junction **12** 33 25N 111 33W
Apache L. **12** 33 36N 111 21W
Apache Mts. **50** 31 12N 104 35W
Apache National Forest **12** 33 30N 109 10W
Apache Sitgreaves National Forest **12** 34 30N 110 30W
Apalachee B. **17** 30 0N 84 0W
Apalachicola **17** 29 43N 84 59W
Apalachicola → **17** 29 43N 84 58W
Apalachicola B. **17** 29 40N 85 0W
Apalachicola National Forest **17** 30 10N 85 0W
Apaporis → **70** 1 23 S 69 25W
Aparecida do Taboado **75** 20 5 S 51 5W
Aparri **111** 18 22N 121 38 E
Aparurén **71** 5 6N 62 8W
Apàtity **98** 67 34N 33 22 E
Apatzingán **64** 19 0N 102 20W
Apeldoorn **87** 52 13N 5 57 E
Apennines **80** 44 20N 10 20 E
Apere → **73** 13 44 S 65 18W
Apex **40** 35 44N 78 51W
Apia **128** 13 50 S 171 50W
Apiacás, Serra dos **73** 9 50 S 57 0W
Apiaú → **71** 2 39N 61 12W
Apiaú, Serra do **71** 2 30N 62 0W
Apidiá → **73** 11 39 S 61 11W
Apinajé **75** 11 31 S 48 18W
Apishapa → **16** 38 8N 103 57W
Apizaco **65** 19 26N 98 9W
Aplao **72** 16 0 S 72 40W
Apo, Mt. **111** 6 53N 125 14 E
Apodi **74** 5 39 S 37 48W
Apollonia = Marsá Susah **121** 32 52N 21 59 E
Apolo **72** 14 30 S 68 30W
Apónguao → **71** 4 48N 61 36W
Apopka **17** 28 40N 81 31W
Apopka L. **17** 28 38N 81 38W
Aporé **73** 18 58 S 52 1W
Aporé → **75** 19 27 S 50 57W
Aporema **74** 1 14N 50 49W
Apostle Is. **55** 47 0N 90 40W
Apostle Islands Nat. Lakeshore **55** 46 55N 91 0W
Apóstoles **77** 28 0 S 56 0W
Apoteri **71** 4 2N 58 32W
Appalachia **54** 36 54N 82 47W
Appalachian Mts. **54** 36 40N 81 45W
Appanoose County ◇ **23** 40 45N 92 50W
Appennini **94** 41 0N 15 0 E
Apple →, Ill. **21** 42 11N 90 14W
Apple →, Wis. **55** 45 9N 92 45W
Apple Creek **42** 40 45N 81 51W
Apple Creek → **21** 39 22N 90 37W
Apple Hill **83** 45 13N 74 46W
Apple Valley **15** 34 32N 117 14W
Appleby **82** 54 35N 2 29W
Applegate, Mich. **29** 43 21N 82 38W
Applegate, Oreg. **44** 42 16N 123 10W
Appleton, Minn. **30** 45 12N 96 1W
Appleton, Wis. **55** 44 16N 88 25W
Appleton City **32** 38 11N 94 2W
Appling **18** 33 33N 82 19W
Appling County ◇ **18** 31 45N 82 15W
Appomattox **54** 37 21N 78 50W
Appomattox → **54** 37 19N 77 17W
Appomattox County ◇ **54** 37 21N 78 50W
Approuague **71** 4 20N 52 0W
Approuague → **71** 4 30N 51 57W
Apuaú **71** 2 25 S 60 53W
Apucarana **77** 23 55 S 51 33W
Apulia = Púglia □ **94** 41 0N 16 30 E
Apure □ **70** 7 10N 68 50W
Apure → **70** 7 37N 66 25W
Apurímac □ **72** 14 0 S 73 0W
Apurimac → **72** 12 17 S 73 56W
Aqabah = Al 'Aqabah **104** 29 31N 35 0 E
'Aqabah, Khalīj al **106** 28 15N 33 20 E
Āqcheh **107** 37 0N 66 5 E
Aqīq **121** 18 14N 38 12 E
Aqrabā **104** 32 9N 35 20 E
Aqrah **106** 36 46N 43 45 E
Aquarius Mts. **12** 34 45N 113 20W
Aquarius Plateau **52** 38 0N 111 40W
Aquasco **27** 38 35N 76 43W
Aquidauana **73** 20 30 S 55 50W
Aquidauana → **73** 19 44 S 56 50W
Áquila, L' **94** 42 21N 13 24 E
Aquiles Serdán **64** 28 37N 105 54W
Aquin **67** 18 16N 73 24W
Ar Rachidiya **120** 31 58N 4 20W
Ar Rafid **104** 32 57N 35 52 E
Ar Ramādī **106** 33 25N 43 20 E
Ar Ramthā **104** 32 34N 36 0 E
Ar Raqqah **106** 36 0N 38 55 E
Ar Rass **106** 25 50N 43 40 E
Ar Rifā'ī **106** 31 50N 46 10 E
Ar Riyāḑ **106** 24 41N 46 42 E
Ar Rummān **104** 32 9N 35 48 E
Ar Ruţbah **106** 33 0N 40 15 E
Ar Ruwaydah **106** 23 40N 44 40 E
Ara **109** 25 35N 84 32 E
Arab **10** 34 19N 86 30W
'Arab, Bahr el → **121** 18 0N 36 30 E
Arab, Shatt al **106** 30 0N 48 31 E
Arabelo **71** 4 55N 64 13W
Arabi **18** 31 50N 83 44W
Arabia **102** 25 0N 45 0 E
Arabian Gulf = The Gulf **107** 27 0N 50 0 E
Arabian Sea **102** 16 0N 65 0 E
Arac **106** 41 15N 33 21 E
Aracaju **74** 10 55 S 37 4W
Aracataca **70** 10 38N 74 9W
Aracati **74** 4 30 S 37 44W
Araçatuba **75** 21 10 S 50 30W
Aracena **91** 37 53N 6 38W
Araçuaí **75** 16 52 S 42 4W
Araçuaí → **75** 16 46 S 42 2W
'Arad, Israel **104** 31 15N 35 12 E
Arad, Romania **89** 46 10N 21 20 E
Arada **121** 15 0N 20 20 E
Arafura Sea **111** 9 0 S 135 0 E
Aragarças **73** 15 55 S 52 15W
Aragon **18** 34 2N 85 3W
Aragón □ **91** 41 25N 1 0W
Aragón → **91** 42 13N 1 44W
Aragua □ **70** 10 0N 67 10W
Aragua de Barcelona **71** 9 28N 64 49W
Araguacema **74** 8 50 S 49 20W
Araguaçu **75** 12 49 S 49 51W
Araguaia → **75** 5 21 S 48 41W
Araguaiana **73** 15 43 S 51 51W
Araguaína **74** 7 12 S 48 12W
Araguari **75** 18 38 S 48 11W
Araguari → **74** 1 15N 49 55W
Araguatins **74** 5 38 S 48 7W
Araioses **74** 2 53 S 41 55W
Arak, Algeria **120** 25 20N 3 45 E
Arāk, Iran **106** 34 0N 49 40 E
Arakan Coast **109** 19 0N 94 0 E
Arakan Yoma **109** 20 0N 94 40 E
Araks = Aras, Rūd-e → **106** 39 10N 47 10 E
Aral Sea = Aralskoye More **100** 44 30N 60 0 E
Aralsk **100** 46 50N 61 20 E
Aralskoye More **100** 44 30N 60 0 E
Aramac **127** 22 58 S 145 14 E
Aran I. **85** 55 0N 8 30W
Aran Is. **85** 53 5N 9 42W
Aranjuez **91** 40 1N 3 40W
Aranos **123** 24 9 S 19 7 E
Aransas County ◇ **51** 28 5N 96 28W
Aransas Pass **51** 27 55N 97 9W
Aranzazu **70** 5 16N 75 30W
Araouane **120** 18 55N 3 30W
Arapaho **43** 35 34N 98 58W
Arapaho National Forest **16** 39 30N 106 15W
Arapahoe, Colo. **16** 38 51N 102 11W
Arapahoe, N.C. **40** 35 2N 76 49W
Arapahoe, Nebr. **34** 40 18N 99 54W
Arapahoe County ◇ **16** 39 40N 104 15W
Arapari **74** 5 34 S 49 15W
Arapey Grande → **76** 30 55 S 57 49W
Arapiraca **74** 9 45 S 36 39W
Arapkir **106** 39 5N 38 30 E
Arapongas **77** 23 29 S 51 28W
Araracuara **70** 0 24 S 72 17W
Araranguá **77** 29 0 S 49 30W
Araraquara **75** 21 50 S 48 0W
Ararás, Serra das **77** 25 0 S 53 10W
Ararat, Australia **127** 37 16 S 143 0 E
Ararat, U.S.A. **54** 36 36N 80 31W
Ararat, Mt. = Ağri Daği **106** 39 50N 44 15 E
Arari **74** 3 28 S 44 47W
Araripe, Chapada do **74** 7 20 S 40 0W
Araripina **74** 7 33 S 40 34W
Araruama, Lagoa de **75** 22 53 S 42 12W
Araruna **74** 6 52 S 35 44W
Aras, Rūd-e → **106** 39 10N 47 10 E
Araticu **74** 1 58 S 49 51W
Arauca **70** 7 0N 70 40W
Arauca □ **70** 6 40N 71 0W
Arauca → **70** 7 24N 66 35W
Arauco **76** 37 16 S 73 25W
Arauco □ **76** 37 40 S 73 25W
Araújos **75** 19 56 S 45 14W
Arauquita **70** 7 2N 71 25W
Araure **70** 9 34N 69 13W
Araxá **75** 19 35 S 46 55W
Araya, Pen. de **71** 10 40N 64 0W
Arbatax **94** 39 57N 9 42 E
Arbaza **101** 52 40N 92 30 E
Arbīl **106** 36 15N 44 5 E
Arboletes **70** 8 51N 76 26W
Arbon **20** 42 27N 112 34W
Arborfield **63** 53 6N 103 39W
Arborg **63** 50 54N 97 13W
Arbroath **84** 56 34N 2 35W
Arbuckle **14** 39 1N 122 3W
Arbuckle L. **17** 27 42N 81 24W
Arbuckle Mts. **43** 34 20N 97 10W
Arc Dome **35** 38 51N 117 22W
Arcachon **90** 44 40N 1 10W
Arcade, Calif. **15** 34 2N 118 15W
Arcade, Ga. **18** 34 5N 83 34W
Arcade, N.Y. **39** 42 32N 78 25W
Arcadia, Fla. **17** 27 13N 81 52W
Arcadia, Ind. **22** 40 11N 86 1W
Arcadia, Iowa **23** 42 5N 95 3W
Arcadia, Kans. **24** 37 38N 94 37W
Arcadia, La. **25** 32 33N 92 55W
Arcadia, Mich. **29** 44 30N 86 14W
Arcadia, Nebr. **34** 41 25N 99 8W
Arcadia, Okla. **43** 35 40N 97 20W
Arcadia, Pa. **45** 40 47N 78 51W
Arcadia, Wis. **55** 44 15N 91 30W
Arcanum **42** 39 59N 84 33W
Arcata **14** 40 52N 124 5W
Arcata B. **14** 40 52N 124 5W
Archangel = Arkhangelsk **98** 64 40N 41 0 E
Archbald **45** 41 30N 75 32W
Archbold **42** 41 31N 84 18W
Archdale **40** 35 56N 79 57W
Archer, Fla. **17** 29 32N 82 32W
Archer, Iowa **23** 43 7N 95 45W
Archer, Nebr. **34** 41 10N 98 8W
Archer → **127** 13 28 S 141 41 E
Archer City **51** 33 36N 98 38W
Archer County ◇ **51** 33 35N 98 40W
Arches National Monument **52** 38 45N 109 25W
Archibald **25** 32 21N 91 47W
Archie, La. **25** 31 35N 91 58W
Archie, Mo. **32** 38 29N 94 21W
Archuleta County ◇ **16** 37 10N 107 0W
Arcila = Asilah **120** 35 29N 6 0W
Arco, Idaho **20** 43 38N 113 18W
Arco, Minn. **30** 44 23N 96 11W
Arcola, Canada **63** 49 40N 102 30W
Arcola, Ill. **21** 39 41N 88 19W
Arcola, Miss. **31** 33 16N 90 53W
Arcola, Mo. **32** 37 33N 93 53W
Arcos **91** 41 12N 2 16W
Arcot **108** 12 53N 79 20 E
Arcoverde **74** 8 25 S 37 4W
Arctic Bay **59** 73 1N 85 7W
Arctic Ocean **4** 78 0N 160 0W
Arctic Red River **58** 67 15N 134 0W
Arctic Village **11** 68 8N 145 32W
Arda → **95** 41 40N 26 29 E
Ardabīl **106** 38 15N 48 18 E
Ardahan **106** 41 7N 42 41 E
Ardakān = Sepīdān **107** 30 20N 52 5 E
Ardèche □ **90** 44 42N 4 16 E
Ardee **85** 53 51N 6 32W
Arden **14** 38 36N 121 33W
Ardennes **87** 50 0N 5 10 E
Ardennes □ **90** 49 35N 4 40 E
Ardenvoir **53** 47 44N 120 22W
Ardestān **107** 33 20N 52 25 E
Ardgour **84** 56 45N 5 25W
Ardino **95** 41 34N 25 9 E
Ardjuno **111** 7 49 S 112 34 E
Ardmore, Ala. **10** 34 59N 86 52W
Ardmore, Okla. **43** 34 10N 97 8W
Ardmore, S. Dak. **47** 43 1N 103 40W
Ardnacrusha **85** 52 43N 8 38W
Ardnamurchan, Pt. of **84** 56 44N 6 14W
Ardrossan **84** 55 39N 4 50W
Ards □ **85** 54 35N 5 30W
Ards Pen. **85** 54 30N 5 25W
Arecibo **57** 18 29N 66 43W
Arecibo ◇ **57** 18 20N 66 35W
Aredale **23** 42 50N 93 0W
Areia Branca **74** 5 0 S 37 0W
Arena **55** 43 10N 89 55W
Arena, Pt. **14** 38 57N 123 44W
Arena de la Ventana, Punta **64** 24 4N 109 52W
Arenac County ◇ **29** 44 0N 83 55W
Arenales, Cerro **78** 47 5 S 73 40W
Arenápolis **73** 14 26 S 56 49W
Arendal **97** 58 28N 8 46 E
Arenillas **70** 3 33 S 80 10W
Arenzville **21** 39 53N 90 22W
Arequipa **72** 16 20 S 71 30W
Arequipa □ **72** 16 0 S 72 50W
Arere **71** 0 16 S 53 52W
Arero **121** 4 41N 38 50 E
Arévalo **91** 41 3N 4 43W
Arezzo **94** 43 28N 11 50 E
Argenta, Canada **62** 50 20N 116 55W
Argenta, U.S.A. **21** 39 59N 88 49W
Argentário, Mte. **94** 42 23N 11 11 E
Argentia **61** 47 18N 53 58W
Argentina ■ **78** 35 0 S 66 0W
Argentina Is. **5** 66 0 S 64 0W
Argentino, L. **78** 50 10 S 73 0W
Argeş □ **95** 45 0N 24 45 E
Argeş → **89** 44 30N 25 50 E
Arghandab → **108** 31 30N 64 15 E
Argo **121** 19 28N 30 30 E
Argolikós Kólpos **95** 37 20N 22 52 E
Argonia **24** 37 16N 97 46W
Argonne, France **90** 49 0N 5 20 E
Argonne, U.S.A. **55** 45 40N 88 53W
Árgos, Greece **95** 37 40N 22 43 E
Argos, U.S.A. **22** 41 14N 86 15W
Argostólion **95** 38 12N 20 33 E
Arguello, Pt. **15** 34 35N 120 39W
Argun → **101** 53 20N 121 28 E
Argungu **120** 12 40N 4 31 E
Argus Range **15** 36 10N 117 40W
Argusville **41** 47 3N 96 56W
Argyle, Minn. **30** 48 20N 96 49W
Argyle, Wis. **55** 42 42N 89 52W
Århus **97** 56 8N 10 11 E
Ariadnoye **116** 45 8N 134 25 E
Ariari → **70** 2 35N 72 47W
Arica, Chile **72** 18 32 S 70 20W
Arica, Colombia **70** 2 0 S 71 50W
Arid, C. **126** 34 1 S 123 10 E
Arida **117** 34 5N 135 8 E
Aridh **106** 25 0N 46 0 E
Ariège □ **90** 42 56N 1 30 E
Ariel **53** 45 57N 122 34W
Arieş → **95** 46 24N 23 20 E
Arikaree → **34** 40 1N 101 56W
Arima **67** 10 38N 61 17W
Arimo **20** 42 34N 112 10W
Arinos → **73** 10 25 S 58 20W
Ario de Rosales **64** 19 12N 102 0W
Arion **23** 41 57N 95 27W
Aripuanã **73** 9 25 S 60 30W
Aripuanã → **73** 5 7 S 60 25W
Ariquemes **73** 9 55 S 63 6W
Arisaig **84** 56 55N 5 50W
Arismendi **70** 8 29N 68 22W
Arispe **23** 40 57N 94 13W
Aristazabal I. **62** 52 40N 129 10W
Ariton **10** 31 36N 85 43W
Arizaro, Salar de **76** 24 40 S 67 50W
Arizona **76** 35 45 S 65 25W
Arizona □ **12** 34 0N 112 0W
Arizpe **64** 30 20N 110 11W
Arjeplog **96** 66 3N 18 2 E
Arjona **70** 10 14N 75 22W
Arka **101** 60 15N 142 0 E
Arkabutla L. **31** 34 46N 90 8W
Arkadelphia **13** 34 7N 93 4W
Arkaig, L. **84** 56 58N 5 10W
Arkalyk **100** 50 13N 66 50 E
Arkansas □ **13** 35 0N 92 0W
Arkansas → **13** 33 47N 91 4W
Arkansas City, Ark. **13** 33 37N 91 12W
Arkansas City, Kans. **24** 37 4N 97 2W
Arkansas County ◇ **13** 34 18N 91 20W
Arkhangelsk **98** 64 40N 41 0 E
Arklow **85** 52 48N 6 10W

Arkoma **Atlantic Highlands**

Arkoma 43 35 21N 94 26W
Arkport 39 42 24N 77 42W
Arkticheskiy, Mys 101 81 10N 95 0 E
Arlanzón ➝ 91 42 3N 4 17W
Arlberg Pass 88 47 9N 10 12 E
Arlee 33 47 10N 114 5W
Arles 90 43 41N 4 40 E
Arley 10 34 4N 87 13W
Arlington, Ariz. 12 33 20N 112 46W
Arlington, Colo. 16 38 20N 103 21W
Arlington, Ga. 18 31 26N 84 44W
Arlington, Ill. 21 41 29N 89 15W
Arlington, Iowa 23 42 45N 91 40W
Arlington, Kans. 24 37 54N 98 11W
Arlington, Ky. 48 36 47N 89 1W
Arlington, Mass. 28 42 25N 71 9W
Arlington, Minn. 30 44 36N 94 5W
Arlington, N.Y. 39 41 42N 73 54W
Arlington, Nebr. 34 41 27N 96 21W
Arlington, Ohio 42 40 54N 83 39W
Arlington, Oreg. 44 45 43N 120 12W
Arlington, S. Dak. 47 44 22N 97 8W
Arlington, Tenn. 48 35 18N 89 40W
Arlington, Tex. 51 32 44N 97 7W
Arlington, Va. 54 38 53N 77 7W
Arlington, Vt. 36 43 5N 73 9W
Arlington, Wash. 53 48 12N 122 8W
Arlington, Wis. 55 43 20N 89 23W
Arlington Heights 21 42 5N 87 59W
Arlon 87 49 42N 5 49 E
Arm 31 31 30N 90 1W
Arma 24 37 33N 94 42W
Armada 29 42 51N 82 53W
Armagh 85 54 22N 6 40W
Armagh □ 85 54 18N 6 37W
Armagnac 90 43 44N 0 10 E
Armavir 99 45 2N 41 7 E
Armenia 70 4 35N 75 45W
Armenian S.S.R. □ 99 40 0N 44 0 E
Armidale 127 30 30 S 151 40 E
Armijo 38 35 4N 106 39W
Armona 15 36 19N 119 42W
Armour 47 43 19N 98 21W
Armourdale 41 48 52N 99 23W
Armstrong, B.C., Canada 62 50 25N 119 10W
Armstrong, Ont., Canada 60 50 18N 89 4W
Armstrong, Iowa 23 43 24N 94 29W
Armstrong, Mo. 32 39 16N 92 42W
Armstrong, Tex. 50 26 56N 97 47W
Armstrong County ◇, Pa. 45 40 45N 79 25W
Armstrong County ◇, Tex. 50 35 0N 101 20W
Arnaouti, C. 106 35 6N 32 17 E
Arnarfjörður 96 65 48N 23 40W
Arnaud ➝ 59 60 0N 70 0W
Arnaudville 25 30 24N 91 56W
Arnegard 41 47 49N 103 27W
Árnes 96 66 1N 21 31W
Arnett 43 36 8N 99 46W
Arnhem 87 51 58N 5 55 E
Arnhem, C. 127 12 20 S 137 30 E
Arnhem B. 126 12 20 S 136 10 E
Arnhem Land 126 13 10 S 134 30 E
Arno ➝ 94 43 41N 10 17 E
Arnold, Md. 27 39 2N 76 30W
Arnold, Minn. 30 46 53N 92 5W
Arnold, Mo. 32 38 26N 90 23W
Arnold, Nebr. 34 41 26N 100 12W
Arnolds Park 23 43 22N 95 8W
Arnot 63 55 56N 96 41W
Arnøy 96 70 9N 20 40 E
Arnprior 60 45 26N 76 21W
Aro ➝ 71 8 1N 64 11W
Aroab 123 26 41 S 19 39 E
Arock 44 42 55N 117 32W
Aroeiras 74 7 31 S 35 41W
Aroma Park 21 41 5N 87 48W
Aroostook ➝ 26 45 48N 67 45W
Aroostook County ◇ 26 47 0N 69 0W
Arp 51 32 14N 95 4W
Arpin 55 44 33N 90 2W
Arque 72 17 48 S 66 23W
Arraias 75 12 56 S 46 57W
Arraias ➝, Mato Grosso, Brazil 73 11 10 S 53 35W
Arraias ➝, Pará, Brazil 74 7 30 S 49 20W
Arraijan 57 8 56N 79 36W
Arran 84 55 34N 5 12W
Arrandale 62 54 57N 130 0W
Arras 90 50 17N 2 46 E
Arrecife 120 28 57N 13 37W
Arrecifes 76 34 6 S 60 9W
Arrée, Mts. d' 90 48 26N 3 55W
Arrey 38 32 48N 107 19W
Arriaga, Chiapas, Mexico 65 16 15N 93 52W
Arriaga, San Luis Potosí, Mexico 64 21 55N 101 23W
Arriba 16 39 17N 103 17W
Arrington 24 39 28N 95 32W
Arrojado ➝ 75 13 24 S 44 20W
Arrow, L. 85 54 3N 8 20W
Arrow Cr. ➝ 33 47 43N 109 50W
Arrow Rock 32 39 4N 92 57W
Arrowhead 62 50 40N 117 55W
Arrowhead, L. 51 33 45N 98 25W
Arrowrock Reservoir 20 43 36N 115 56W
Arrowsmith 21 40 27N 88 38W
Arrowtown 128 44 57 S 168 50 E
Arroyo 57 17 58N 66 4W
Arroyo del Macho ➝ 38 33 49N 104 7W
Arroyo Grande 15 35 7N 120 35W
Arroyo Hondo 38 36 32N 105 40W
Arsenault L. 63 55 6N 108 32W
Arsenev 116 44 10N 133 15 E
Árta 95 39 8N 21 2 E
Artas 47 45 53N 99 49W
Arteaga 64 18 50N 102 20W
Artemovsk, R.S.F.S.R., U.S.S.R. 101 54 45N 93 35 E
Artemovsk, Ukraine S.S.R., U.S.S.R. 99 48 35N 38 0 E
Arten 116 43 22N 132 13 E
Artesia, Miss. 31 33 25N 88 39W
Artesia, N. Mex. 38 32 51N 104 24W
Artesia L. 35 38 56N 119 22W
Artesia Wells 51 28 17N 99 17W
Artesian 47 44 1N 97 55W
Arthur, Ill. 21 39 43N 88 28W
Arthur, N. Dak. 41 47 6N 97 13W
Arthur, Nebr. 34 41 35N 101 41W
Arthur, Tenn. 49 36 33N 83 40W
Arthur County ◇ 34 41 30N 101 40W
Arthur's Pass 128 42 54 S 171 35 E
Arthur's Town 67 24 38N 75 42W
Artigas 76 30 20 S 56 30W
Artillery L. 63 63 9N 107 52W
Artois, France 90 50 20N 2 30 E
Artois, U.S.A. 14 39 37N 122 12W
Artvin 106 41 14N 41 44 E
Aru, Kepulauan 111 6 0 S 134 30 E
Arua 122 3 1N 30 58 E
Aruanã 75 14 54 S 51 10W
Aruba 67 12 30N 70 0W
Arumã 71 4 44 S 62 8W
Arunachal Pradesh □ 109 28 0N 95 0 E
Arusha 122 3 20 S 36 40 E
Aruwimi ➝ 122 1 13N 23 36 E
Arvada, Colo. 16 39 48N 105 5W
Arvada, Wyo. 56 44 39N 106 8W
Arvayheer 113 46 15N 102 48 E
Arvida 61 48 25N 71 14W
Arvidsjaur 96 65 35N 19 10 E
Arvika 97 59 40N 12 36 E
Arvin 15 35 12N 118 50W
Arxan 114 47 11N 119 57 E
Arys 100 42 26N 68 48 E
Arzamas 98 55 27N 43 55 E
Arzew 120 35 50N 0 23W
'As Saffānīyah 106 28 5N 48 50 E
Aş Şāfī 104 31 2N 35 28 E
As Salt 104 32 2N 35 43 E
As Samāwah 106 31 15N 45 15 E
As Samū' 104 31 24N 35 4 E
As Sanamayn 104 33 3N 36 10 E
As Sulaymānīyah 106 24 9N 47 18 E
As Sumaymānīyah 106 35 35N 45 29 E
As Summān 106 25 0N 47 0 E
As Sūq 106 21 58N 42 3 E
As Suwaydā' 106 32 40N 36 30 E
As Suwayh 107 22 10N 59 33 E
As Şuwayrah 106 32 55N 45 0 E
Asahi-Gawa ➝ 117 34 36N 133 58 E
Asahigawa 116 43 46N 142 22 E
Asansol 109 23 40N 87 1 E
Asbestos 61 45 47N 71 58W
Asbury 32 37 16N 94 36W
Asbury Park 37 40 13N 74 1W
Ascensión 64 31 6N 107 59W
Ascensión, B. de la 65 19 50N 87 20W
Ascension I. 2 8 0 S 14 15W
Ascension Parish ◇ 25 30 14N 90 55W
Aschaffenburg 88 49 58N 9 8 E
Áscoli Piceno 94 42 51N 13 34 E
Ascope 72 7 46 S 79 8W
Ascotán 76 21 45 S 68 17W
Ascutney 36 43 24N 72 25W
Aseb 105 13 0N 42 40 E
Asela 121 8 0N 39 0 E
Asenovgrad 95 42 1N 24 51 E
Ash Flat 13 36 13N 91 37W
Ash Fork 12 35 13N 112 29W
Ash Grove 32 37 19N 93 35W
Ash Shām, Bādiyat 106 32 0N 40 0 E
Ash Shāmīyah 106 31 55N 44 35 E
Ash Shāriqah 107 25 23N 55 26 E
Ash Shaţrah 106 31 30N 46 10 E
Ash Shaykh, J. 106 33 25N 35 50 E
Ash Shu'aybah 106 27 53N 44 43 E
Ash Shu'bah 106 28 54N 44 44 E
Ash Shūnah ash Shamālīyah 104 32 37N 35 34 E
Asha 98 55 0N 57 16 E
Ashaway 28 41 25N 71 47W
Ashburn 18 31 43N 83 39W
Ashburnham 28 42 38N 71 55W
Ashburton 128 43 53 S 171 48 E
Ashburton ➝ 126 21 40 S 114 56 E
Ashby, Minn. 30 46 6N 95 49W
Ashby, Nebr. 34 42 1N 101 56W
Ashby-de-la-Zouch 82 52 45N 1 29W
Ashcroft 62 50 40N 121 20W
Ashdod 104 31 49N 34 35 E
Ashdot Yaaqov 104 32 39N 35 35 E
Ashdown 13 33 40N 94 8W
Ashe County ◇ 40 36 25N 81 30W
Asheboro 40 35 43N 79 49W
Asher 43 34 59N 96 56W
Asherton 51 28 27N 99 46W
Asherville 24 39 24N 97 59W
Asheville 40 35 36N 82 33W
Asheweig ➝ 60 54 17N 87 12W
Ashfield 28 42 32N 72 48W
Ashford, U.K. 83 51 8N 0 53 E
Ashford, Ala. 10 31 11N 85 14W
Ashford, Wash. 53 46 46N 122 2W
Ashibetsu 116 43 31N 142 11 E
Ashikaga 117 36 28N 139 29 E
Ashizuri-Zaki 117 32 44N 133 0 E
Ashkhabad 100 38 0N 57 50 E
Ashkum 21 40 53N 87 57W
Ashland, Ala. 10 33 16N 85 50W
Ashland, Ill. 21 39 53N 90 1W
Ashland, Kans. 24 37 11N 99 46W
Ashland, Ky. 49 38 28N 82 38W
Ashland, La. 25 32 9N 93 6W
Ashland, Maine 26 46 38N 68 24W
Ashland, Miss. 31 34 50N 89 11W
Ashland, Mo. 32 38 47N 92 16W
Ashland, Mont. 33 45 36N 106 16W
Ashland, N.H. 36 43 42N 71 38W
Ashland, Nebr. 34 41 3N 96 23W
Ashland, Ohio 42 40 52N 82 19W
Ashland, Okla. 43 34 46N 96 4W
Ashland, Oreg. 44 42 12N 122 43W
Ashland, Va. 54 37 46N 77 29W
Ashland, Wis. 55 46 35N 90 53W
Ashland City 48 36 17N 87 4W
Ashland County ◇, Ohio 42 40 52N 82 19W
Ashland County ◇, Wis. 55 46 35N 90 45W
Ashley, Ill. 21 38 20N 89 11W
Ashley, Ind. 22 41 32N 85 4W
Ashley, Mich. 29 43 11N 84 29W
Ashley, N. Dak. 41 46 2N 99 22W
Ashley, Ohio 42 40 25N 82 57W
Ashley ➝ 52 40 20N 109 17W
Ashley County ◇ 13 33 14N 91 48W
Ashley National Forest 52 40 55N 110 0W
Ashmont 62 54 7N 111 35W
Ashmore 21 39 32N 88 1W
Ashmore Reef 126 12 14 S 123 5 E
Ashokan Reservoir 39 41 56N 74 13W
Ashq'elon 104 31 42N 34 35 E
Ashtabula 42 41 52N 80 47W
Ashtabula County ◇ 42 41 40N 80 52W
Ashtabula L. 41 47 2N 98 5W
Ashton, Idaho 20 44 4N 111 27W
Ashton, Ill. 21 41 52N 89 13W
Ashton, Iowa 23 43 19N 95 47W
Ashton, Nebr. 34 41 15N 98 48W
Ashton, R.I. 28 41 56N 71 26W
Ashton, S. Dak. 47 44 59N 98 31W
Ashton-under-Lyne 82 53 30N 2 8W
Ashuanipi, L. 61 52 45N 66 15W
Ashuelot ➝ 36 43 0N 72 29W
Ashville, Ala. 10 33 50N 86 15W
Ashville, Fla. 17 30 37N 83 39W
Ashville, Pa. 45 40 34N 78 33W
Ashwood 44 44 44N 120 45W
Asia 102 45 0N 75 0 E
Asia, Kepulauan 111 1 0N 131 13 E
Asidonhoppo 71 3 50N 55 30W
Asifabad 108 19 20N 79 24 E
Asike 111 6 39 S 140 24 E
Asilah 120 35 29N 6 0W
Asinara, G. dell' 94 41 0N 8 30 E
Asinara I. 94 41 5N 8 15 E
Asino 100 57 0N 86 0 E
'Asīr □ 105 18 40N 42 30 E
Asir, Ras 105 11 55N 51 10 E
Askersund 97 58 53N 14 55 E
Askewville 40 36 7N 76 57W
Askja 96 65 3N 16 48W
Askov 30 46 12N 92 47W
Āsmār 107 35 10N 71 27 E
Asmara = Asmera 121 15 19N 38 55 E
Asmera 121 15 19N 38 55 E
Asotin 53 46 20N 117 3W
Asotin County ◇ 53 46 8N 117 8W
Aspen 16 39 11N 106 49W
Aspen Hill 27 39 5N 77 5W
Aspermont 50 33 8N 100 14W
Aspiring, Mt. 128 44 23 S 168 46 E
Asquith 63 52 8N 107 13W
Assam □ 109 26 0N 93 0 E
Assaria 24 38 41N 97 36W
Assateague I. 27 38 15N 75 10W
Assateague Island National Seashore 27 38 15N 75 10W
Assawompset Pond 28 41 50N 70 55W
Asse 87 50 24N 4 10 E
Assen 87 53 0N 6 35 E
Assini 120 5 9N 3 17W
Assiniboia 63 49 40N 105 59W
Assiniboine ➝ 63 49 53N 97 8W
Assinippi 28 42 10N 70 51W
Assis 77 22 40 S 50 20W
Assisi 94 43 4N 12 36 E
Assonet 28 41 48N 71 4W
Assumption 21 39 31N 89 3W
Assumption Parish ◇ 25 30 0N 91 0W
Assynt, L. 84 58 25N 5 15W
Astara 99 38 30N 48 50 E
Astatula 17 28 43N 81 44W
Asti 94 44 54N 8 11 E
Astipálaia 95 36 32N 26 22 E
Astorga 91 42 29N 6 8W
Astoria, Ill. 21 40 14N 90 21W
Astoria, Oreg. 44 46 11N 123 50W
Astoria, S. Dak. 47 44 34N 96 33W
Astrakhan 99 46 25N 48 5 E
Astrakhan-Bazàr 99 39 14N 48 30 E
Asturias □ 91 43 15N 6 0W
Asunción 76 25 10 S 57 30W
Asunción, La 71 11 2N 63 53W
Aswân 121 24 4N 32 57 E
Aswân High Dam = Sadd el Aali 121 23 54N 32 54 E
Asyût 121 27 11N 31 4 E
At Ţafilah 106 30 45N 35 30 E
At Ta'if 105 21 5N 40 27 E
Aţ Ţur 104 31 47N 35 14 E
Aţ Ţurrah 104 32 39N 35 59 E
Atacama □ 76 27 30 S 70 0W
Atacama, Desierto de 76 24 0 S 69 20W
Atacama, Salar de 76 23 30 S 68 20W
Ataco 70 3 35N 75 23W
Atakpamé 120 7 31N 1 13 E
Atalaya 72 10 45 S 73 50W
Ataléia 75 18 3 S 41 6W
Atami 117 35 5N 139 4 E
Atapupu 111 9 0 S 124 51 E
Atâr 120 20 30N 13 5W
Atara 101 63 10N 129 10 E
Atascadero 15 35 29N 120 40W
Atascosa County ◇ 51 28 55N 98 33W
Atasu 100 48 30N 71 0 E
Atauro 111 8 10 S 125 30 E
Atbara 121 17 42N 33 59 E
'Atbara ➝ 121 17 40N 33 56 E
Atbasar 100 51 48N 68 20 E
Atchafalaya ➝ 25 29 53N 91 28W
Atchafalaya B. 25 29 25N 91 25W
Atchison 24 39 34N 95 7W
Atchison County ◇, Kans. 24 39 30N 95 15W
Atchison County ◇, Mo. 32 40 25N 95 25W
Atco 37 39 46N 74 53W
Ath 87 50 38N 3 47 E
Athabasca 62 54 45N 113 20W
Athabasca ➝ 63 58 40N 110 50W
Athabasca, L. 63 59 15N 109 15W
Athboy 85 53 37N 6 55W
Athena, Fla. 17 29 59N 83 30W
Athena, Oreg. 44 45 49N 118 30W
Athenry 85 53 18N 8 45W
Athens = Athínai 95 37 58N 23 46 E
Athens, Ala. 10 34 48N 86 58W
Athens, Ga. 18 33 57N 83 23W
Athens, Ill. 21 39 58N 89 44W
Athens, La. 25 32 39N 93 1W
Athens, Mich. 29 42 5N 85 14W
Athens, N.Y. 39 42 16N 73 49W
Athens, Ohio 42 39 20N 82 6W
Athens, Pa. 45 41 57N 76 31W
Athens, Tenn. 49 35 27N 84 36W
Athens, Tex. 51 32 12N 95 51W
Athens, Wis. 55 45 2N 90 5W
Athens County ◇ 42 39 20N 82 6W
Atherton 127 17 17 S 145 30 E
Athínai 95 37 58N 23 46 E
Athlone 85 53 26N 7 57W
Athol, Idaho 20 47 57N 116 42W
Athol, Mass. 28 42 36N 72 14W
Athol, S. Dak. 47 45 1N 98 36W
Atholl, Forest of 84 56 51N 3 50W
Atholville 61 47 59N 66 43W
Áthos 95 40 9N 24 22 E
Athy 85 53 0N 7 0W
Ati 121 13 13N 18 20 E
Atico 72 16 14 S 73 40W
Atikokan 60 48 45N 91 37W
Atikonak L. 61 52 40N 64 32W
Atka, U.S.A. 11 52 12N 174 12W
Atka, U.S.S.R. 101 60 50N 151 48 E
Atka I. 11 52 7N 174 30W
Atkins 13 35 14N 92 56W
Atkinson, Ga. 18 31 13N 81 47W
Atkinson, Ill. 21 41 25N 90 1W
Atkinson, N.C. 40 34 32N 78 10W
Atkinson, Nebr. 34 42 32N 98 59W
Atkinson County ◇ 18 31 15N 82 50W
Atlanta, Ga. 18 33 45N 84 23W
Atlanta, Idaho 20 43 48N 115 8W
Atlanta, Ill. 21 40 16N 89 14W
Atlanta, Ind. 22 40 13N 86 2W
Atlanta, Kans. 24 37 26N 96 46W
Atlanta, La. 25 31 48N 92 45W
Atlanta, Mich. 29 45 0N 84 9W
Atlanta, Mo. 32 39 54N 92 29W
Atlanta, Nebr. 34 40 22N 99 28W
Atlanta, Tex. 51 33 7N 94 10W
Atlantic, Iowa 23 41 24N 95 1W
Atlantic, N.C. 40 34 54N 76 20W
Atlantic Beach 17 30 20N 81 24W
Atlantic City 37 39 21N 74 27W
Atlantic County ◇ 37 39 30N 74 40W
Atlantic Highlands 37 40 25N 74 3W

Atlantic Ocean Baffin I.

Atlantic Ocean 2 0 0 20 0W
Atlantic Pk. 56 42 37N 109 0W
Atlántico □ 70 10 45N 75 0W
Atlin 62 59 31N 133 41W
Atlin, L. 62 59 26N 133 45W
'Atlit 104 32 42N 34 56 E
Atmore 10 31 2N 87 29W
Atoka 43 34 23N 96 8W
Atoka County ◇ 43 34 25N 96 0W
Atoka Reservoir 43 34 27N 96 5W
Atomic City 20 43 27N 112 49W
Atoyac → 65 16 30N 97 31W
Atrak → 107 37 50N 57 0 E
Atrato → 70 8 17N 76 58W
Atsion 37 39 44N 74 44W
Atsuta 116 43 24N 141 26 E
Attala County ◇ 31 33 4N 89 35W
Attalla 10 34 1N 86 6W
Attapulgus 18 30 45N 84 29W
Attawapiskat 60 52 56N 82 24W
Attawapiskat → 60 52 57N 82 18W
Attawapiskat, L. 60 52 18N 87 54W
Attica, Ind. 22 40 18N 87 15W
Attica, Kans. 24 37 15N 98 13W
Attica, N.Y. 39 42 52N 78 17W
Attica, Ohio 42 41 4N 82 53W
Attikamagen L. 61 55 0N 66 30W
'Attīl 104 32 23N 35 4 E
Attleboro 28 41 57N 71 17W
Attock 108 33 52N 72 20 E
Attopeu 112 14 48N 106 50 E
Attu 11 52 56N 173 15 E
Attu I. 11 52 55N 172 55 E
Attur 108 11 35N 78 30 E
Atuel → 76 36 17 S 66 50W
Åtvidaberg 97 58 12N 16 0 E
Atwater, Calif. 14 37 21N 120 37W
Atwater, Minn. 30 45 8N 94 47W
Atwood, Colo. 16 40 33N 103 16W
Atwood, Ill. 21 39 48N 88 28W
Atwood, Kans. 24 39 48N 101 3W
Atwood, Okla. 43 34 57N 96 20W
Atwood, Tenn. 48 35 59N 88 41W
Atwood L. 42 40 33N 81 13W
Au Gres 29 44 3N 83 42W
Au Sable 29 44 25N 83 20W
Au Sable → 29 44 25N 83 20W
Au Sable Forks 39 44 27N 73 41W
Au Sable Pt., Mich. 29 46 40N 86 8W
Au Sable Pt., Mich. 29 44 20N 83 20W
Auau Channel 19 20 50N 156 45W
Aube □ 90 48 15N 4 0 E
Aube → 90 48 34N 3 43 E
Aubrey 13 34 43N 90 54W
Aubrey Cliffs 12 35 45N 113 0W
Auburn, Ala. 10 32 36N 85 29W
Auburn, Calif. 14 38 54N 121 4W
Auburn, Ill. 21 39 36N 89 45W
Auburn, Ind. 22 41 22N 85 4W
Auburn, Iowa 23 42 15N 94 53W
Auburn, Kans. 24 38 54N 95 49W
Auburn, Ky. 48 36 52N 86 43W
Auburn, Maine 26 44 6N 70 14W
Auburn, Mass. 28 42 12N 71 50W
Auburn, Mich. 29 43 36N 84 4W
Auburn, Miss. 31 31 22N 90 37W
Auburn, N.Y. 39 42 56N 76 34W
Auburn, Nebr. 34 40 23N 95 51W
Auburn, W. Va. 54 39 6N 80 51W
Auburn, Wash. 53 47 18N 122 14W
Auburndale, Fla. 17 28 4N 81 48W
Auburndale, Wis. 55 44 38N 90 0W
Auburntown 48 35 57N 86 5W
Aubusson 90 45 57N 2 11 E
Auch 90 43 39N 0 36 E
Aucilla → 17 30 5N 83 59W
Auckland 128 36 52 S 174 46 E
Auckland Is. 124 50 40 S 166 5 E
Aude □ 90 43 8N 2 28 E
Aude → 90 43 13N 3 14 E
Auden 60 50 14N 87 53W
Audrain County ◇ 32 39 10N 91 50W
Audubon, Iowa 23 41 43N 94 56W
Audubon, Minn. 30 46 52N 95 59W
Audubon County ◇ 23 41 40N 94 50W
Aueti Paraná → 70 1 51 S 65 37W
Augathella 127 25 48 S 146 35 E
Auglaize County ◇ 42 40 34N 84 12W
Augsburg 88 48 22N 10 54 E
Augusta, Italy 94 37 14N 15 12 E
Augusta, Ark. 13 35 17N 91 22W
Augusta, Ga. 18 33 28N 81 58W
Augusta, Ill. 21 40 14N 90 57W
Augusta, Kans. 24 37 41N 96 59W
Augusta, Ky. 49 38 47N 84 0W
Augusta, Maine 26 44 19N 69 47W
Augusta, Mo. 32 38 34N 90 53W
Augusta, Mont. 33 47 30N 112 24W
Augusta, N.J. 37 41 8N 74 44W
Augusta, W. Va. 54 39 18N 78 38W
Augusta, Wis. 55 44 41N 91 7W
Augusta County ◇ 54 38 9N 79 4W
Augustine I. 11 59 22N 153 26W
Augustów 89 53 51N 23 0 E
Augustus, Mt. 126 24 20 S 116 50 E
Aulander 40 36 14N 77 6W
Aullville 32 39 1N 93 41W
Ault 16 40 35N 104 44W
Aunis 90 46 5N 0 50W
Auponhia 111 1 58 S 125 27 E
Aurangabad, Bihar, India 109 24 45N 84 18 E
Aurangabad, Maharashtra, India 108 19 50N 75 23 E
Aurelia 23 42 43N 95 26W
Aurilândia 75 16 44 S 50 28W
Aurillac 90 44 55N 2 26 E
Aurora, Colo. 16 39 44N 104 52W
Aurora, Ill. 21 41 45N 88 19W
Aurora, Ind. 22 39 4N 84 54W
Aurora, Iowa 23 42 37N 91 44W
Aurora, Kans. 24 39 27N 97 32W
Aurora, Ky. 48 36 47N 88 9W
Aurora, Maine 26 44 51N 68 20W
Aurora, Minn. 30 47 32N 92 14W
Aurora, Mo. 32 36 58N 93 43W
Aurora, N.C. 40 35 18N 76 47W
Aurora, N.Y. 39 42 45N 76 42W
Aurora, Nebr. 34 40 52N 98 0W
Aurora, S. Dak. 47 44 17N 96 41W
Aurora, W. Va. 54 39 19N 79 33W
Aurora County ◇ 47 43 43N 98 29W
Aus 123 26 35 S 16 12 E
Aust-Agder fylke □ 97 58 55N 7 40 E
Austerlitz = Slavkov 88 49 10N 16 52 E
Austin, Ark. 13 35 0N 92 0W
Austin, Ind. 22 38 45N 85 49W
Austin, Minn. 30 43 40N 92 58W
Austin, Mont. 33 46 39N 112 15W
Austin, Nev. 35 39 30N 117 4W
Austin, Pa. 45 41 38N 78 6W
Austin, Tex. 51 30 17N 97 45W
Austin, L. 126 27 40 S 118 0 E
Austin County ◇ 51 29 57N 96 15W
Austintown 42 41 6N 80 48W
Austinville 54 36 51N 80 55W
Austral Downs 127 20 30 S 137 45 E
Austral Is. = Tubuai Is. 125 25 0 S 150 0W
Austral Seamount Chain 125 24 0 S 150 0W
Australia ■ 124 23 0 S 135 0 E
Australian Alps 127 36 30 S 148 30 E
Australian Cap. Terr. □ 127 35 30 S 149 0 E
Australian Dependency □ 5 73 0 S 90 0 E
Austria ■ 88 47 0N 14 0 E
Austvågøy 96 68 20N 14 40 E
Austwell 51 28 23N 96 51W
Autauga County ◇ 10 32 26N 86 39W
Autaugaville 10 32 26N 86 39W
Autazes 71 3 35 S 59 8W
Autlán 64 19 40N 104 30W
Autun 90 46 58N 4 17 E
Auvergne 90 45 20N 3 15 E
Auxerre 90 47 48N 3 32 E
Auxvasse 32 39 1N 91 54W
Auxvasse → 32 38 41N 91 49W
Ava, Ill. 21 37 53N 89 30W
Ava, Mo. 32 36 57N 92 40W
Avallon 90 47 30N 3 53 E
Avalon, Calif. 15 33 21N 118 20W
Avalon, Miss. 31 33 39N 90 5W
Avalon, N.J. 37 39 6N 74 43W
Avalon, L. 38 32 27N 104 15W
Avalon Pen. 61 47 30N 53 20W
Avant 43 36 29N 96 4W
Avaré 77 23 4 S 48 58W
Avawatz Mts. 15 35 40N 116 30W
Aveiro, Brazil 71 3 10 S 55 5W
Aveiro, Portugal 91 40 37N 8 38W
Āvej 106 35 40N 49 15 E
Avellaneda 76 34 50 S 58 10W
Avellino 94 40 54N 14 46 E
Avenal 15 36 0N 120 8W
Avenue 27 38 16N 76 46W
Avera 18 33 12N 82 32W
Aversa 94 40 58N 14 11 E
Avery, Idaho 20 47 15N 115 49W
Avery, Tex. 51 33 33N 94 47W
Avery County ◇ 40 36 5N 82 0W
Avery Island 25 29 55N 91 54W
Aves, I. de 67 15 45N 63 55W
Aves, Is. de 67 12 0N 67 30W
Avesta 97 60 9N 16 10 E
Aveyron □ 90 44 22N 2 45 E
Aviá Terai 76 26 45 S 60 50W
Avignon 90 43 57N 4 50 E
Ávila 91 40 39N 4 43W
Avilés 91 43 35N 5 57W
Avilla, Ind. 22 41 22N 85 14W
Avilla, Mo. 32 37 8N 94 8W
Avinger 51 32 54N 94 33W
Avis 45 41 11N 77 19W
Avoca, Ireland 85 52 52N 6 13W
Avoca, Iowa 23 41 29N 95 20W
Avoca, Minn. 30 43 57N 95 39W
Avoca, N.Y. 39 42 25N 77 25W
Avoca, Nebr. 34 40 48N 96 7W
Avoca, Tex. 51 32 52N 99 43W
Avola 62 51 45N 119 19W
Avon, Colo. 16 39 38N 106 31W
Avon, Conn. 28 41 49N 72 50W
Avon, Ill. 21 40 40N 90 26W
Avon, Mont. 33 46 36N 112 36W
Avon, N.C. 40 35 21N 75 30W
Avon, N.Y. 39 42 55N 77 45W
Avon, S. Dak. 47 43 0N 98 4W
Avon □ 83 51 30N 2 40W
Avon →, Avon, U.K. 83 51 30N 2 43W
Avon →, Hants., U.K. 83 50 44N 1 45W
Avon →, Warwick, U.K. 83 52 0N 2 9W
Avon, Îles 127 19 37 S 158 17 E
Avon Park 17 27 36N 81 31W
Avondale, Ariz. 12 33 26N 112 21W
Avondale, Colo. 16 38 14N 104 21W
Avondale, Pa. 45 39 50N 75 47W
Avonlea 63 50 0N 105 0W
Avonmore 45 40 32N 79 28W
Avonmouth 83 51 30N 2 42W
Avoyelles Parish ◇ 25 31 0N 92 0W
Avramov 95 42 45N 26 38 E
Avranches 90 48 40N 1 20W
Avrig 95 45 43N 24 21 E
Awaji-Shima 117 34 30N 134 50 E
'Awālī 107 26 0N 50 30 E
'Awartā 104 32 10N 35 17 E
Awash 105 9 1N 40 10 E
Awatere → 128 41 37 S 174 10 E
Awbārī 121 26 46N 12 57 E
Awe, L. 84 56 15N 5 15W
Awjilah 121 29 8N 21 7 E
Axarfjörður 96 66 15N 16 45W
Axel Heiberg I. 4 80 0N 90 0W
Axial 16 40 17N 107 47W
Axim 120 4 51N 2 15W
Axinim 71 4 2 S 59 22W
Axintele 95 44 37N 26 47 E
Axioma 73 6 45 S 64 31W
Axminster 83 50 47N 3 1W
Axson 18 31 17N 82 44W
Axtell, Kans. 24 39 52N 96 15W
Axtell, Nebr. 34 40 29N 99 8W
Ayabaca 72 4 40 S 79 53W
Ayabe 117 35 20N 135 20 E
Ayacucho, Argentina 76 37 5 S 58 20W
Ayacucho, Peru 72 13 0 S 74 0W
Ayaguz 100 48 10N 80 0 E
Ayamonte 91 37 12N 7 24W
Ayan 101 56 30N 138 16 E
Ayapel 70 8 19N 75 9W
Ayaviri 72 14 50 S 70 35W
Āybak 107 36 15N 68 5 E
Ayden 40 35 28N 77 20W
Ayer 28 42 34N 71 35W
Ayeritam 112 5 24N 100 15 E
Ayers Rock 126 25 23 S 131 5 E
Ayíos Evstrátios 95 39 34N 24 58 E
Aykin 98 62 15N 49 56 E
Aylesbury 83 51 48N 0 49W
Aylmer L. 58 64 0N 110 8W
'Ayn 'Arīk 104 31 54N 35 8 E
Ayn Dār 106 25 55N 49 10 E
Ayn Zālah 106 36 45N 42 35 E
Aynor 46 34 0N 79 12W
Ayolas 76 27 10 S 56 59W
Ayon, Ostrov 101 69 50N 169 0 E
Ayr, Australia 127 19 35 S 147 25 E
Ayr, U.K. 84 55 28N 4 37W
Ayr, N. Dak. 41 47 3N 97 29W
Ayr, Nebr. 34 40 26N 98 26W
Ayr → 84 55 29N 4 40W
Ayre, Pt. of 82 54 27N 4 21W
Ayshire 23 43 2N 94 50W
Aytos 95 42 42N 27 16 E
Aytoska Planina 95 42 45N 27 30 E
Ayu, Kepulauan 111 0 35N 131 5 E
Ayutla, Guat. 66 14 40N 92 10W
Ayutla, Mexico 65 16 58N 99 17W
Ayvalık 106 39 20N 26 46 E
Az Zahrān 106 26 10N 50 7 E
Az Zarqā 104 32 5N 36 4 E
Az-Zilfī 106 26 12N 44 52 E
Az Zubayr 106 30 20N 47 50 E
Azamgarh 109 26 5N 83 13 E
Azangaro 72 14 55 S 70 13W
Āzarbāyjān-e Gharbī □ 106 37 0N 44 30 E
Āzarbāyjān-e Sharqī □ 106 37 20N 47 0 E
Azare 120 11 55N 10 10 E
Azbine = Aïr 120 18 30N 8 0 E
Azerbaijan S.S.R. □ 99 40 20N 48 0 E
Aziscohos L. 26 45 0N 71 0W
Azle 51 32 54N 97 32W
Azogues 70 2 35 S 78 0W
Azor 104 32 2N 34 48 E
Azores 2 38 44N 29 0W
Azov 99 47 3N 39 25 E
Azov Sea = Azovskoye More 99 46 0N 36 30 E
Azovskoye More 99 46 0N 36 30 E
Azovy 100 64 55N 64 35 E
Aztec, Ariz. 12 32 49N 113 27W
Aztec, N. Mex. 38 36 49N 107 59W
Aztec Peak 12 33 49N 110 54W
Azúa de Compostela 67 18 25N 70 44W
Azuaga 91 38 16N 5 39W
Azuay □ 70 2 55 S 79 0W
Azuero, Pen. de 66 7 30N 80 30W
Azul 76 36 42 S 59 43W
Azul, Serra 73 14 50 S 54 50W
Azurduy 73 19 59 S 64 29W
Azusa 15 34 8N 117 52W

B

B. A. Steinhagen L. 51 30 50N 94 15W
B. Everett Jordan L. 40 35 30N 79 0W
Ba Don 112 17 45N 106 26 E
Ba Ngoi = Cam Lam 112 11 54N 109 10 E
Ba Ria 112 10 30N 107 10 E
Ba Xian 114 39 8N 116 22 E
Baa 111 10 50 S 123 0 E
Baarle Nassau 87 51 27N 4 56 E
Baarn 87 52 12N 5 17 E
Bāb el Māndeb 105 12 35N 43 25 E
Baba 95 42 44N 23 59 E
Babaçulândia 74 7 13 S 47 46W
Babadag 95 44 53N 28 44 E
Babaeski 95 41 26N 27 6 E
Babahoyo 70 1 40 S 79 30W
Babana 120 10 31N 3 46 E
Babar 111 8 0 S 129 30 E
Babb 33 48 51N 113 27W
Babbitt, Minn. 30 47 43N 91 54W
Babbitt, Nev. 35 38 32N 118 39W
Babbs 43 34 57N 99 3W
Babine 62 55 22N 126 37W
Babine → 62 55 45N 127 44W
Babine L. 62 54 48N 126 0W
Babo 111 2 30 S 133 30 E
Bābol 107 36 40N 52 50 E
Bābol Sar 107 36 45N 52 45 E
Baboquivari Peak 12 31 46N 111 36W
Baboua 122 5 49N 14 58 E
Babson Park 17 27 49N 81 32W
Babura 120 12 51N 8 59 E
Babuyan Chan. 111 18 40N 121 30 E
Babylon, Iraq 106 32 40N 44 30 E
Babylon, U.S.A. 39 40 42N 73 19W
Bac Kan 112 22 5N 105 50 E
Bac Ninh 112 21 13N 106 4 E
Bac Phan 112 22 0N 105 0 E
Bac Quang 112 22 30N 104 48 E
Baca County ◇ 16 37 15N 102 30W
Bacabal 74 4 15 S 44 45W
Bacajá → 71 3 25 S 51 50W
Bacalar 65 18 50N 87 27W
Bacan 111 8 27 S 126 27 E
Bacan, Kepulauan 111 0 35 S 127 30 E
Bacan, Pulau 111 0 50 S 127 30 E
Bacarra 111 18 15N 120 37 E
Bacău 89 46 35N 26 55 E
Bacău □ 95 46 30N 26 45 E
Bacerac 64 30 18N 108 50W
Bachaquero 70 9 56N 71 8W
Bachelina 100 57 45N 67 20 E
Back → 58 65 10N 104 0W
Back B. 54 36 35N 75 57W
Backbone Mt. 27 39 12N 79 28W
Backstairs Passage 127 35 40 S 138 5 E
Backus 30 46 49N 94 31W
Bacolod 111 10 40N 122 57 E
Bacon County ◇ 18 31 30N 82 30W
Baconton 18 31 23N 84 10W
Bad → 47 44 21N 100 22W
Bad Axe 29 43 48N 83 0W
Bad Ischl 88 47 44N 13 38 E
Bad River Indian Reservation 55 46 30N 90 45W
Badagara 108 11 35N 75 40 E
Badajós, L. 71 3 15 S 62 50W
Badajoz 91 38 50N 6 59W
Badakhshān □ 107 36 30N 71 0 E
Badalona 91 41 26N 2 15 E
Badalzai 108 29 50N 65 35 E
Badampahar 109 22 10N 86 10 E
Badanah 106 30 58N 41 30 E
Badarinath 108 30 45N 79 30 E
Badas 110 4 33N 114 25 E
Badas, Kepulauan 110 0 45N 107 5 E
Baddo → 107 28 0N 64 20 E
Bade 111 7 10 S 139 35 E
Baden, Austria 88 48 1N 16 13 E
Baden, U.S.A. 45 40 38N 80 14W
Baden-Baden 88 48 45N 8 15 E
Baden-Württemberg □ 88 48 40N 9 0 E
Badgastein 88 47 7N 13 9 E
Badger, Canada 61 49 0N 56 4W
Badger, Iowa 23 42 37N 94 9W
Badger, Minn. 30 48 47N 96 1W
Badger → 16 40 17N 103 42W
Bādghīsāt □ 107 35 0N 63 0 E
Badin, Pakistan 108 24 38N 68 54 E
Badin, U.S.A. 40 35 24N 80 6W
Badin L. 40 35 25N 80 6W
Badlands 47 43 55N 102 30W
Badlands National Park 47 43 38N 102 56W
Badong 115 31 1N 110 23 E
Baduen 105 7 15N 47 40 E
Badulla 108 7 1N 81 7 E
Badwater Cr. → 56 43 17N 108 8W
Baeza, Ecuador 70 0 25 S 77 53W
Baeza, Spain 91 37 57N 3 25W
Bafatá 120 12 8N 14 40W
Baffin B., Canada 4 72 0N 64 0W
Baffin B., U.S.A. 50 27 18N 97 30W
Baffin I. 59 68 0N 75 0W

Bafia Banyo

Bafia 122 4 40N 11 10 E
Bafing → 120 13 49N 10 50W
Bafoulabé 120 13 50N 10 55W
Bāfq 107 31 40N 55 25 E
Bafra 106 41 34N 35 54 E
Bāft 107 29 15N 56 38 E
Bafwasende 122 1 3N 27 5 E
Bagamoyo 122 6 28 S 38 55 E
Baganga 111 7 34N 126 33 E
Bagansiapiapi 110 2 12N 100 50 E
Bagdad, Ariz. 12 34 34N 113 11W
Bagdad, Fla. 17 30 36N 87 2W
Bagdad, Ky. 49 38 16N 85 3W
Bagdarin 101 54 26N 113 36 E
Bagé 77 31 20 S 54 15W
Bagenalstown = Muine Bheag 85 52 42N 6 57W
Baggs 56 41 2N 107 39W
Baghdād 106 33 20N 44 30 E
Baghlān 107 36 12N 69 0 E
Baghlān □ 107 36 0N 68 30 E
Bagley 30 47 32N 95 24W
Bagotville 61 48 22N 70 54W
Bagua 72 5 35 S 78 22W
Baguio 111 16 26N 120 34 E
Bahama 40 36 10N 78 53W
Bahama, Canal Viejo de 66 22 10N 77 30W
Bahamas ■ 67 24 0N 75 0W
Baharampur 109 24 2N 88 27 E
Bahau 112 2 48N 102 26 E
Bahawalpur 108 29 24N 71 40 E
Bahía = Salvador 75 13 0 S 38 30W
Bahía □ 75 12 0 S 42 0W
Bahía, Islas de la 66 16 45N 86 15W
Bahía Blanca 76 38 35 S 62 13W
Bahía de Caráquez 70 0 40 S 80 27W
Bahía Honda 66 22 54N 83 10W
Bahía Laura 78 48 10 S 66 30W
Bahía Negra 73 20 5 S 58 5W
Bahr Aouk → 122 8 40N 19 0 E
Bahr el Ahmar □ 121 20 0N 35 0 E
Bahr el Ghazāl □ 121 7 0N 28 0 E
Bahr el Jebel → 121 7 30N 30 30 E
Bahr Salamat → 121 9 20N 18 0 E
Bahraich 109 27 38N 81 37 E
Bahrain ■ 107 26 0N 50 35 E
Bai Bung, Mui 112 8 38N 104 44 E
Baia Mare 89 47 40N 23 35 E
Baião 74 2 40 S 49 40W
Baïbokoum 121 7 46N 15 43 E
Baicheng 114 45 38N 122 42 E
Băicoi 95 45 3N 25 52 E
Baidoa 105 3 8N 43 30 E
Baie Comeau 61 49 12N 68 10W
Baie-St-Paul 61 47 28N 70 32W
Baie Trinité 61 49 25N 67 20W
Baie Verte 61 49 55N 56 12W
Ba'ījī 106 35 0N 43 30 E
Baikal, L. = Baykal, Oz. 101 53 0N 108 0 E
Baile Atha Cliath = Dublin 85 53 20N 6 18W
Băileşti 95 44 1N 23 20 E
Bailey 16 39 25N 105 29W
Bailey County ◇ 50 34 0N 102 55W
Baileys Harbor 55 45 4N 87 8W
Baileyton 49 36 20N 82 50W
Baileyville 24 39 51N 96 11W
Bailique, Ilha 74 1 2N 49 58W
Bailundo 123 12 10 S 15 50 E
Bainbridge, Ga. 18 30 55N 84 35W
Bainbridge, Ind. 22 39 46N 86 49W
Bainbridge, N.Y. 39 42 18N 75 29W
Bainbridge, Ohio 42 39 14N 83 16W
Baing 111 10 14 S 120 34 E
Bainville 33 48 8N 104 13W
Bā'ir 106 30 45N 36 55 E
Baird 51 32 24N 99 24W
Baird Mts. 11 67 0N 160 0W
Bairin Youqi 114 43 30N 118 35 E
Bairin Zuoqi 114 43 58N 119 15 E
Bairnsdale 127 37 48 S 147 36 E
Bairoil 56 42 15N 107 33W
Baitadi 109 29 35N 80 25 E
Baixa Grande 75 11 57 S 40 11W
Baiyin 114 36 45N 104 14 E
Baiyu Shan 114 37 15N 107 30 E
Baja 89 46 12N 18 59 E
Baja, Pta. 64 29 50N 116 0W
Baja California 64 31 10N 115 12W
Bajo Nuevo 66 15 40N 78 50W
Bakala 122 6 15N 20 20 E
Bakchav 100 57 1N 82 5 E
Bakel 120 14 56N 12 20W
Baker, Calif. 15 35 16N 116 4W
Baker, Fla. 17 30 48N 86 41W
Baker, Idaho 20 45 6N 113 44W
Baker, La. 25 30 35N 91 10W
Baker, Mont. 33 46 22N 104 17W
Baker, N. Dak. 41 48 10N 99 39W
Baker, Okla. 43 36 52N 101 1W
Baker, Oreg. 44 44 47N 117 50W
Baker, Canal 78 47 45 S 74 45W
Baker, L. 58 64 0N 96 0W
Baker, Mt. 53 48 47N 121 49W
Baker Butte 12 34 27N 111 22W
Baker County ◇, Fla. 17 30 20N 82 15W
Baker County ◇, Ga. 18 31 20N 84 30W
Baker County ◇, Oreg. 44 44 40N 117 50W
Baker Hill 10 31 47N 85 18W
Baker I. 124 0 10N 176 35W
Baker Lake 58 64 20N 96 3W
Baker's Dozen Is. 60 56 45N 78 45W
Bakersfield, Calif. 15 35 23N 119 1W
Bakersfield, Tex. 50 30 54N 102 18W
Bakersfield, Vt. 36 44 45N 72 48W
Bakhtārān 106 34 23N 47 30E
Bakinskikh Komissarov, im. 26 106 39 20N 49 15 E
Bakırköy 95 40 59N 28 53 E
Bakkafjörður 96 66 2N 14 48W
Bakkagerði 96 65 31N 13 49W
Bakony Forest = Bakony Hegység 89 47 10N 17 30 E
Bakony Hegység 89 47 10N 17 30 E
Bakouma 122 5 40N 22 56 E
Baku 99 40 25N 49 45 E
Bakutis Coast 5 74 0 S 120 0W
Bal'ā, Jordan 104 32 20N 35 6 E
Bala, U.S.A. 24 39 19N 96 57W
Bala, L. = Tegid, L. 82 52 53N 3 38W
Balabac, Str. 110 7 53N 117 5 E
Balabac I. 110 8 0N 117 0 E
Balabakk 106 34 0N 36 10 E
Balabalangan, Kepulauan 110 2 20 S 117 30 E
Bălăciţa 95 44 23N 23 8 E
Balaghat 108 21 49N 80 12 E
Balaghat Ra. 108 18 50N 76 30 E
Balaguer 91 41 50N 0 50 E
Balaklava 99 44 30N 33 30 E
Balakovo 98 52 4N 47 55 E
Balancán 65 17 48N 91 32W
Balashov 98 51 30N 43 10 E
Balasore = Baleshwar 109 21 35N 87 3 E
Balaton, Hungary 89 46 50N 17 40 E
Balaton, U.S.A. 30 44 14N 95 52W
Balboa, Panama 57 8 57N 79 34W
Balboa Hill 57 9 6N 79 44W
Balbriggan 85 53 35N 6 10W
Balcarce 76 38 0 S 58 10W
Balcarres 63 50 50N 103 35W
Balch Springs 51 32 43N 96 38W
Balchik 95 43 28N 28 11 E
Balclutha 128 46 15 S 169 45 E
Balcones Escarpment 50 29 30N 99 15W
Balcones Heights 51 29 26N 98 36W
Bald Creek 40 35 55N 82 25W
Bald Knob, Ark. 13 35 19N 91 34W
Bald Knob, Va. 54 37 56N 79 51W
Bald Knoll 56 42 22N 110 28W
Bald Mt. 44 43 16N 121 21W
Baldock L. 63 56 33N 97 57W
Baldwin, Fla. 17 30 18N 81 59W
Baldwin, Ga. 18 34 30N 83 32W
Baldwin, Ill. 21 38 11N 89 51W
Baldwin, La. 25 29 50N 91 33W
Baldwin, Mich. 29 43 54N 85 51W
Baldwin, N. Dak. 41 47 2N 100 45W
Baldwin, N.Y. 39 40 39N 73 36W
Baldwin, Pa. 45 40 23N 79 59W
Baldwin, Wis. 55 44 58N 92 22W
Baldwin City 24 38 47N 95 11W
Baldwin County ◇, Ala. 10 30 53N 87 46W
Baldwin County ◇, Ga. 18 33 5N 83 10W
Baldwinsville 39 43 10N 76 20W
Baldwinville 28 42 37N 72 5W
Baldwyn 31 34 31N 88 38W
Baldy Peak 12 33 54N 109 34W
Baldy Pk. 38 36 38N 105 13W
Baleares, Islas 91 39 30N 3 0 E
Balearic Is. = Baleares, Islas 91 39 30N 3 0 E
Baleia, Punta da 75 17 40 S 39 7W
Băleni 95 45 48N 27 51 E
Baler 111 15 46N 121 34 E
Baleshwar 109 21 35N 87 3 E
Balfate 66 15 48N 86 25W
Balfour 41 47 57N 100 32W
Balfouriyya 104 32 38N 35 18 E
Bali, Cameroon 120 5 54N 10 0 E
Bali, Indonesia 110 8 20 S 115 0 E
Bali □ 110 8 20 S 115 0 E
Bali, Selat 111 8 18 S 114 25 E
Balikesir 106 39 35N 27 58 E
Balikpapan 110 1 10 S 116 55 E
Balimbing 111 5 5N 119 58 E
Baling 112 5 41N 100 55 E
Balipara 109 26 50N 92 45 E
Baliza 73 16 0 S 52 20W
Balkan Mts. = Stara Planina 95 43 15N 23 0 E
Balkan Pen. 80 42 0N 22 0 E
Balkh 107 36 44N 66 47 E
Balkh □ 107 36 30N 67 0 E
Balkhash 100 46 50N 74 50 E
Balkhash, Ozero 100 46 0N 74 50 E
Balko 43 36 38N 100 41W
Ball 25 31 25N 92 25W
Ball Ground 18 34 20N 84 23W
Balla 109 24 10N 91 35 E
Ballachulish 84 56 40N 5 10W
Ballantine 33 45 57N 108 9W
Ballarat 127 37 33 S 143 50 E
Ballard, L. 126 29 20 S 120 10 E
Ballard County ◇ 48 37 0N 89 0W
Ballater 84 57 2N 3 2W
Ballenas, Canal de las 64 29 10N 113 45W
Balleny Is. 5 66 30 S 163 0 E
Ballina, Australia 127 28 50 S 153 31 E
Ballina, Mayo, Ireland 85 54 7N 9 10W
Ballina, Tipp., Ireland 85 52 49N 8 27W
Ballinasloe 85 53 20N 8 12W
Ballinger 51 31 45N 99 57W
Ballinrobe 85 53 36N 9 13W
Ballinskelligs B. 85 51 46N 10 11W
Ballston Spa 39 43 0N 73 51W
Balltown 23 42 38N 90 51W
Bally 45 40 24N 75 35W
Ballycastle 85 55 12N 6 15W
Ballymena 85 54 53N 6 18W
Ballymena □ 85 54 53N 6 18W
Ballymoney 85 55 5N 6 30W
Ballymoney □ 85 55 5N 6 23W
Ballyshannon 85 54 30N 8 10W
Balmaceda 78 46 0 S 71 50W
Balmoral 84 57 3N 3 13W
Balmorhea 50 30 59N 103 45W
Balonne → 127 28 47 S 147 56 E
Balrampur 109 27 30N 82 20 E
Balranald 127 34 38 S 143 33 E
Balş 95 44 22N 24 5 E
Balsam Lake 55 45 27N 92 27W
Balsapuerto 72 5 48 S 76 33W
Balsas 65 18 0N 99 40W
Balsas →, Goiás, Brazil 74 9 58 S 47 52W
Balsas →, Maranhão, Brazil 74 7 15 S 44 35W
Balsas →, Mexico 64 17 55N 102 10W
Balta, Romania 95 44 54N 22 38 E
Balta, U.S.A. 41 48 10N 100 2W
Balta, U.S.S.R. 99 48 2N 29 45 E
Baltic, Conn. 28 41 37N 72 5W
Baltic, Ohio 42 40 26N 81 42W
Baltic, S. Dak. 47 43 46N 96 44W
Baltic Sea 97 56 0N 20 0 E
Baltimore, Ireland 85 51 29N 9 22W
Baltimore, Md. 27 39 17N 76 37W
Baltimore, Ohio 42 39 51N 82 36W
Baltimore County ◇ 27 39 20N 76 40W
Baluchistan □ 107 27 30N 65 0 E
Balygychan 101 63 56N 154 12 E
Balzar 70 2 2 S 79 54W
Bam 107 29 7N 58 14 E
Bama 121 11 33N 13 41 E
Bamako 120 12 34N 7 55W
Bamba 120 17 5N 1 24W
Bambamarca 72 6 36 S 78 32W
Bambari 122 5 40N 20 35 E
Bamberg, Germany 88 49 54N 10 53 E
Bamberg, U.S.A. 46 33 18N 81 2W
Bamberg County ◇ 46 33 10N 81 0W
Bambili 122 3 40N 26 0 E
Bambuí 75 20 1 S 45 58W
Bamenda 120 5 57N 10 11 E
Bamfield 62 48 45N 125 10W
Bāmīān □ 107 35 0N 67 0 E
Bamiancheng 114 43 15N 124 2 E
Bampūr 107 27 15N 60 21 E
Ban Aranyaprathet 112 13 41N 102 30 E
Ban Ban 112 19 31N 103 30 E
Ban Bua Chum 112 15 11N 101 12 E
Ban Don = Surat Thani 112 9 6N 99 20 E
Ban Houei Sai 112 20 22N 100 32 E
Ban Khe Bo 112 19 10N 104 39 E
Ban Khun Yuam 112 18 49N 97 57 E
Ban Phai 112 16 4N 102 44 E
Ban Thateng 112 15 25N 106 27 E
Banaba 124 0 45 S 169 50 E
Banalia 122 1 32N 25 5 E
Banam 112 11 20N 105 17 E
Banamba 120 13 29N 7 22W
Bananal, I. do 75 11 30 S 50 30W
Banaras = Varanasi 109 25 22N 83 0 E
Banbridge 85 54 21N 6 17W
Banbridge □ 85 54 21N 6 16W
Banbury 83 52 4N 1 21W
Banchory 84 57 3N 2 30W
Bancroft, Canada 60 45 3N 77 51W
Bancroft, Idaho 20 42 43N 111 53W
Bancroft, Iowa 23 43 18N 94 13W
Bancroft, La. 25 30 34N 93 41W
Bancroft, Mich. 29 42 53N 84 4W
Bancroft, Nebr. 34 42 1N 96 34W
Band 95 46 30N 24 25 E
Band-e Torkestān 107 35 30N 64 0 E
Banda 108 25 30N 80 26 E
Banda, Kepulauan 111 4 37 S 129 50 E
Banda, La 76 27 45 S 64 10W
Banda Aceh 110 5 35N 95 20 E
Banda Elat 111 5 40 S 133 5 E
Banda Sea 111 6 0 S 130 0 E
Bandai-San 116 37 36N 140 4 E
Bandana 48 37 9N 88 56W
Bandanaira 111 4 32 S 129 54 E
Bandar = Machilipatnam 109 16 12N 81 8 E
Bandār 'Abbās 107 27 15N 56 15 E
Bandar-e Anzalī 106 37 30N 49 30 E
Bandar-e Chārak 107 26 45N 54 20 E
Bandar-e Deylam 106 30 5N 50 10 E
Bandar-e Khomeyni 106 30 30N 49 5 E
Bandar-e Lengeh 107 26 35N 54 58 E
Bandar-e Ma'shur 106 30 35N 49 10 E
Bandar-e Nakhīlū 107 26 58N 53 30 E
Bandar-e Rīg 107 29 29N 50 38 E
Bandar-e Torkeman 107 37 0N 54 10 E
Bandar Maharani 112 2 3N 102 34 E
Bandar Penggaram 110 1 50N 102 56 E
Bandar Seri Begawan 110 4 52N 115 0 E
Bandawe 123 11 58 S 34 5 E
Bandeira, Pico da 75 20 26 S 41 47W
Bandeirante 75 13 41 S 50 48W
Bandelier National Monument 38 35 50N 106 25W
Bandera, Argentina 76 28 55 S 62 20W
Bandera, U.S.A. 51 29 44N 99 5W
Bandera County ◇ 51 29 48N 99 15W
Banderas, Bahía de 64 20 40N 105 30W
Bandiagara 120 14 12N 3 29W
Bandırma 106 40 20N 28 0 E
Bandon, Ireland 85 51 44N 8 45W
Bandon, U.S.A. 44 43 7N 124 25W
Bandon → 85 51 40N 8 41W
Bandundu 122 3 15 S 17 22 E
Bandung 111 6 54 S 107 36 E
Băneasa 95 45 56N 27 55 E
Banes 67 21 0N 75 42W
Banff, Canada 62 51 10N 115 34W
Banff, U.K. 84 57 40N 2 32W
Banff Nat. Park 62 51 30N 116 15W
Banfora 120 10 40N 4 40W
Bang Hieng → 112 16 10N 105 10 E
Bang Lamung 112 13 3N 100 56 E
Bang Saphan 112 11 14N 99 28 E
Bangala Dam 123 21 7 S 31 25 E
Bangalore 108 12 59N 77 40 E
Bangassou 122 4 55N 23 7 E
Banggai 111 1 40 S 123 30 E
Banggi, P. 110 7 17N 117 12 E
Banghāzī 121 32 11N 20 3 E
Bangil 111 7 36 S 112 50 E
Bangka, Pulau, Sulawesi, Indonesia 111 1 50N 125 5 E
Bangka, Pulau, Sumatera, Indonesia 110 2 0 S 105 50 E
Bangka, Selat 110 2 30 S 105 30 E
Bangkalan 111 7 2 S 112 46 E
Bangkinang 110 0 18N 101 5 E
Bangko 110 2 5 S 102 9 E
Bangkok 112 13 45N 100 35 E
Bangladesh ■ 109 24 0N 90 0 E
Bangor, N. Ireland, U.K. 85 54 40N 5 40W
Bangor, Wales, U.K. 82 53 13N 4 9W
Bangor, Maine 26 44 48N 68 46W
Bangor, Mich. 29 42 18N 86 7W
Bangor, Pa. 45 40 52N 75 13W
Bangs 51 31 43N 99 8W
Bangs Mt. 12 36 48N 113 51W
Bangued 111 17 40N 120 37 E
Bangui 122 4 23N 18 35 E
Bangweulu, L. 122 11 0 S 30 0 E
Bani 67 18 16N 70 22W
Banī Na'īm 104 31 31N 35 10 E
Banī Suhaylah 104 31 21N 34 19 E
Banīnah 121 32 0N 20 12 E
Banister → 54 36 42N 78 48W
Bāniyās 106 35 10N 36 0 E
Banja Luka 94 44 49N 17 11 E
Banjar 111 7 24 S 108 30 E
Banjarmasin 110 3 20 S 114 35 E
Banjarnegara 111 7 24 S 109 42 E
Banjul 120 13 28N 16 40W
Bankipore 109 25 35N 85 10 E
Banks, Ala. 10 31 49N 85 51W
Banks, Ark. 13 33 35N 92 16W
Banks, Idaho 20 44 5N 116 8W
Banks, Miss. 31 34 50N 90 14W
Banks County ◇ 18 34 30N 83 30W
Banks I., B.C., Canada 62 53 20N 130 0W
Banks I., N.W.T., Canada 4 73 15N 121 30W
Banks I., Papua N. G. 127 10 10 S 142 15 E
Banks L., Ga. 18 31 2N 83 6W
Banks L., Wash. 53 47 47N 119 19W
Banks Pen. 128 43 45 S 173 15 E
Bankura 109 23 11N 87 18 E
Bann →, Down, U.K. 85 54 30N 6 31W
Bann →, Londonderry, U.K. 85 55 10N 6 34W
Bannack 33 45 10N 112 59W
Banner County ◇ 34 41 30N 103 40W
Banner Elk 40 36 10N 81 52W
Banner Hill 49 36 8N 82 25W
Bannertown 40 36 29N 80 35W
Banning 15 33 56N 116 53W
Banningville = Bandundu 122 3 15 S 17 22 E
Bannock County ◇ 20 42 30N 112 10W
Bannock Cr. → 20 42 53N 112 40W
Bannock Range 20 42 40N 112 30W
Bannockburn 84 56 5N 3 55W
Bannu 108 33 0N 70 18 E
Banská Bystrica 89 48 46N 19 14 E
Banská Štiavnica 89 48 25N 18 55 E
Bansko 95 41 52N 23 28 E
Banswara 108 23 32N 74 24 E
Banten 111 6 5 S 106 8 E
Bantry, Ireland 85 51 40N 9 28W
Bantry, U.S.A. 41 48 30N 100 37W
Bantry, B. 85 51 35N 9 50W
Bantul 111 7 55 S 110 19 E
Banu 108 35 35N 69 5 E
Banya 95 42 33N 24 50 E
Banyak, Kepulauan 110 2 10N 97 10 E
Banyo 120 6 52N 11 45 E

Banyumas

Baxley

Banyumas 111 7 32 S 109 18 E
Banyuwangi 111 8 13 S 114 21 E
Banzare Coast 5 68 0 S 125 0 E
Banzyville = Mobayi 122 4 15N 21 8 E
Baocheng 115 33 12N 106 56 E
Baode 114 39 1N 111 5 E
Baoding 114 38 50N 115 28 E
Baoji 115 34 20N 107 5 E
Baojing 115 28 45N 109 41 E
Baokang 115 31 54N 111 12 E
Baoshan 113 25 10N 99 5 E
Baotou 114 40 32N 110 2 E
Baoying 115 33 17N 119 20 E
Bapatla 109 15 55N 80 30 E
Bapchule 12 33 12N 111 50W
Bâqa el Gharbîyya 104 32 25N 35 2 E
Ba'qūbah 106 33 45N 44 50 E
Baquedano 76 23 20 S 69 52W
Bar 95 42 8N 19 8 E
Bar Harbor 26 44 23N 68 13W
Bar-le-Duc 90 48 47N 5 10 E
Barabai 110 2 32 S 115 34 E
Barabinsk 100 55 20N 78 20 E
Baraboo 55 43 28N 89 45W
Baracoa 67 20 20N 74 30W
Barada 34 40 13N 95 35W
Baradero 76 33 52 S 59 29W
Baraga 29 46 47N 88 30W
Baraga County ◇ 29 46 40N 88 20W
Barahona 67 18 13N 71 7W
Barail Range 109 25 15N 93 20 E
Barakhola 109 25 0N 92 45 E
Barakpur 109 22 44N 88 30 E
Baralzon L. 63 60 0N 98 3W
Baramula 108 34 15N 74 20 E
Baran 108 25 9N 76 40 E
Baranoa 70 10 48N 74 55W
Baranof 11 57 5N 134 50W
Baranof I. 11 57 0N 135 0W
Baranovichi 98 53 10N 26 0 E
Barão de Cocais 75 19 56 S 43 28W
Barão de Grajaú 74 6 45 S 43 1W
Barão de Melgaço,
Mato Grosso, Brazil 73 16 14 S 55 52W
Barão de Melgaço,
Rondônia, Brazil 73 11 50 S 60 45W
Baraolt 95 46 5N 25 34 E
Barapasi 111 2 15 S 137 5 E
Barat Daya, Kepulauan 111 7 30 S 128 0 E
Barataria 25 29 44N 90 8W
Barataria B. 25 29 20N 89 55W
Baraya 70 3 10N 75 4W
Barbacena 75 21 15 S 43 56W
Barbacoas, Colombia 70 1 45N 78 0W
Barbacoas, Venezuela 70 9 29N 66 58W
Barbados ■ 67 13 0N 59 30W
Barbalha 74 7 19 S 39 17W
Barber County ◇ 24 37 15N 98 40W
Barbers Pt. 19 21 18N 158 7W
Barberton, S. Africa 123 25 42 S 31 2 E
Barberton, U.S.A. 42 41 0N 81 39W
Barberville 17 29 11N 81 26W
Barbosa 70 5 57N 73 37W
Barbour County ◇, Ala. 10 31 53N 85 27W
Barbour County ◇, W. Va. 54 39 9N 80 3W
Barboursville 54 38 24N 82 18W
Barbourville 49 36 52N 83 53W
Barbuda I. 67 17 30N 61 40W
Barca, La 64 20 20N 102 40W
Barcaldine 127 23 43 S 145 6 E
Barcelona, Spain 91 41 21N 2 10 E
Barcelona, Venezuela 71 10 10N 64 40W
Barceloneta 57 18 27N 66 32W
Barcelos 71 1 0 S 63 0W
Barclay 27 39 9N 75 52W
Barco 40 36 24N 75 59W
Barcoo → 127 25 30 S 142 50 E
Barda del Medio 78 38 45 S 68 11W
Bardas Blancas 76 35 49 S 69 45W
Barddhaman 109 23 14N 87 39 E
Bardera 105 2 20N 42 27 E
Bardi, Ra's 106 24 17N 37 31 E
Bardia 121 31 45N 25 0 E
Bardley 32 36 42N 91 7W
Bardsey I. 82 52 46N 4 47W
Bardstown 49 37 49N 85 28W
Bardwell 48 36 52N 89 1W
Bare Mt. 53 45 55N 122 4W
Bareilly 108 28 22N 79 27 E
Barents Sea 4 73 0N 39 0 E
Barentu 121 15 2N 37 35 E
Barga 113 30 40N 81 20 E
Bargal 105 11 25N 51 0 E
Bargersville 22 39 31N 86 10W
Barguzin 101 53 37N 109 37 E
Barhi 109 24 15N 85 25 E
Bari 94 41 6N 16 52 E
Bari Doab 108 30 20N 73 0 E
Barīm 105 12 39N 43 25 E
Barima → 71 8 33N 60 25W
Barinas 70 8 36N 70 15W
Barinas □ 70 8 10N 69 50W
Baring 32 40 15N 92 12W
Baring, C. 58 70 0N 117 30W
Baringo 122 0 47N 36 16 E
Baringo, L. 122 0 47N 36 16 E
Barinitas 70 8 45N 70 25W
Bariri 75 22 4 S 48 44W
Bârîs 121 24 42N 30 31 E
Barisal 109 22 45N 90 20 E
Barisan, Bukit 110 3 30 S 102 15 E
Barito → 110 4 0 S 114 50 E
Bark Pt. 55 46 53N 91 11W
Barkā' 107 23 40N 58 0 E
Barker 39 43 20N 78 33W
Barkhamsted Reservoir 28 41 53N 72 58W
Barkley, L. 48 37 1N 88 14W
Barkley Sound 62 48 50N 125 10W
Barkly Tableland 127 17 50 S 136 40 E
Barksdale 51 29 44N 100 2W
Barlee, L. 126 29 15 S 119 30 E
Barletta 94 41 20N 16 17 E
Barling 13 35 20N 94 18W
Barlow 48 37 3N 89 3W
Barlow L. 63 62 0N 103 0W
Barmer 108 25 45N 71 20 E
Barmouth 82 52 44N 4 3W
Barnard, Kans. 24 39 11N 98 3W
Barnard, Mo. 32 40 10N 94 50W
Barnard, Vt. 36 43 43N 72 38W
Barnard Castle 82 54 33N 1 55W
Barnaul 100 53 20N 83 40 E
Barnegat 37 39 45N 74 14W
Barnegat Bay 37 39 45N 74 10W
Barnegat Light 37 39 46N 74 6W
Barnes 24 39 43N 96 52W
Barnes City 23 41 31N 92 27W
Barnes County ◇ 41 47 0N 98 0W
Barnesboro 45 40 40N 78 47W
Barneston 34 40 5N 96 38W
Barnesville, Ga. 18 33 3N 84 9W
Barnesville, Md. 27 39 13N 77 23W
Barnesville, Minn. 30 46 39N 96 25W
Barnesville, Ohio 42 39 59N 81 11W
Barnet, U.K. 83 51 37N 0 15W
Barnet, U.S.A. 36 44 18N 72 3W
Barnett 32 38 23N 92 41W
Barneveld 87 52 7N 5 36 E
Barney 18 31 1N 83 31W
Barney, Mt. 127 28 17 S 152 44 E
Barnhart 50 31 8N 101 10W
Barnsdall 43 36 34N 96 10W
Barnsley 82 53 33N 1 29W
Barnstable 28 41 42N 70 18W
Barnstable County ◇ 28 41 40N 70 15W
Barnstaple 83 51 5N 4 3W
Barnstaple Harbor 28 41 43N 70 18W
Barnum 30 46 30N 92 42W
Barnwell 46 33 15N 81 23W
Barnwell County ◇ 46 33 15N 81 30W
Baro 120 8 35N 6 18 E
Baroda = Vadodara 108 22 20N 73 10 E
Baron 43 35 55N 94 36W
Barpeta 109 26 20N 91 10 E
Barques, Pt. Aux, Mich. 29 44 4N 82 58W
Barques, Pt. Aux, Mich. 29 45 48N 86 21W
Barquísimeto 70 10 4N 69 19W
Barra, Brazil 74 11 5 S 43 10W
Barra, U.K. 84 57 0N 7 30W
Barra, Sd. of 84 57 4N 7 25W
Barra da Estiva 75 13 38 S 41 19W
Barra de Navidad 64 19 12N 104 41W
Barra do Corda 74 5 30 S 45 10W
Barra do Mendes 75 11 43 S 42 4W
Barra do Piraí 75 22 30 S 43 50W
Barra Falsa, Pta. da 123 22 58 S 35 37 E
Barra Hd. 84 56 47N 7 40W
Barra Mansa 77 22 35 S 44 12W
Barracão do Barreto 73 8 48 S 58 24W
Barrackpur = Barakpur 109 22 44N 88 30 E
Barranca, Lima, Peru 72 10 45 S 77 50W
Barranca, Loreto, Peru 70 4 50 S 76 50W
Barrancabermeja 70 7 0N 73 50W
Barrancas, Colombia 70 10 57N 72 50W
Barrancas, Venezuela 71 8 55N 62 5W
Barrancos 91 38 10N 6 58W
Barranqueras 76 27 30 S 59 0W
Barranquilla 70 11 0N 74 50W
Barranquitas 57 18 11N 66 19W
Barras, Brazil 74 4 15 S 42 18W
Barras, Colombia 70 1 45 S 73 13W
Barraute 60 48 26N 77 38W
Barre, Mass. 28 42 25N 72 6W
Barre, Vt. 36 44 12N 72 30W
Barre do Bugres 73 15 0 S 57 11W
Barreal 76 31 33 S 69 28W
Barreiras 75 12 8 S 45 0W
Barreirinha 71 2 30 S 62 50W
Barreirinhas 74 2 30 S 42 50W
Barreiro 91 38 40N 9 6W
Barreiros 74 8 49 S 35 12W
Barren → 48 37 11N 86 37W
Barren County ◇ 48 37 0N 86 0W
Barren I., India 112 12 17N 93 50 E
Barren I., U.S.A. 11 58 55N 152 15W
Barren River L. 48 36 54N 86 8W
Barretos 75 20 30 S 48 35W
Barrett 30 45 55N 95 53W
Barrhead 62 54 10N 114 24W
Barrie 60 44 24N 79 40W
Barrier Ra. 127 31 0 S 141 30 E
Barrière 62 51 12N 120 7W
Barrineau Park 17 30 42N 87 26W
Barrington 28 41 44N 71 18W
Barrington L. 63 56 55N 100 15W
Barrington Tops 127 32 6 S 151 28 E
Barro do Garças 73 15 54 S 52 16W
Barron 55 45 24N 91 51W
Barron County ◇ 55 45 25N 91 50W
Barrow 11 71 18N 156 47W
Barrow → 85 52 10N 6 57W
Barrow County ◇ 18 34 0N 83 40W
Barrow Creek 126 21 30 S 133 55 E
Barrow I. 126 20 45 S 115 20 E
Barrow-in-Furness 82 54 8N 3 15W
Barrow Pt. 11 71 24N 156 29W
Barrow Ra. 126 26 0 S 127 40 E
Barrow Str. 4 74 20N 95 0W
Barry, U.K. 83 51 23N 3 19W
Barry, U.S.A. 21 39 42N 91 2W
Barry County ◇, Mich. 29 42 35N 85 25W
Barry County ◇, Mo. 32 36 45N 93 45W
Barry's Bay 60 45 29N 77 41W
Barryton 29 43 45N 85 9W
Barsi 108 18 10N 75 50 E
Barsoi 109 25 48N 87 57 E
Barstow, Calif. 15 34 54N 117 1W
Barstow, Tex. 50 31 28N 103 24W
Bartholomew County ◇ 22 39 10N 85 55W
Bartica 71 6 25N 58 40W
Bartin 106 41 38N 32 21 E
Bartle Frere, Mt. 127 17 27 S 145 50 E
Bartlesville 43 36 45N 95 59W
Bartlett, Kans. 24 37 3N 95 13W
Bartlett, N.H. 36 44 5N 71 17W
Bartlett, Nebr. 34 41 53N 98 33W
Bartlett, Tex. 51 30 48N 97 26W
Bartlett, L. 62 63 5N 118 20W
Bartlett Reservoir 12 33 49N 111 38W
Bartley 34 40 15N 100 18W
Barton, Ala. 10 34 44N 87 54W
Barton, Md. 27 39 34N 79 2W
Barton, N. Dak. 41 48 30N 100 11W
Barton, Vt. 36 44 45N 72 11W
Barton → 36 44 53N 72 13W
Barton County ◇, Kans. 24 38 30N 98 40W
Barton County ◇, Mo. 32 37 30N 94 20W
Barton-upon-Humber 82 53 41N 0 27W
Bartonville 21 40 39N 89 39W
Bartow, Fla. 17 27 54N 81 50W
Bartow, Ga. 18 32 53N 82 29W
Bartow County ◇ 18 34 20N 84 50W
Barú, I. de 70 10 15N 75 35W
Barú, Volcan 66 8 55N 82 35W
Barwick 18 30 54N 83 44W
Bas-Rhin □ 90 48 40N 7 30 E
Bāsa'idū 107 26 35N 55 20 E
Basalt, Colo. 16 39 22N 107 2W
Basalt, Idaho 20 43 19N 112 10W
Basankusa 122 1 5N 19 50 E
Basco 21 40 20N 91 12W
Bascuñán, C. 76 28 52 S 71 35W
Basel 88 47 35N 7 35 E
Bashkir A.S.S.R. □ 98 54 0N 57 0 E
Basilan 111 6 35N 122 0 E
Basilan Str. 111 6 50N 122 0 E
Basildon 83 51 34N 0 29 E
Basile 25 30 29N 92 36W
Basilicata □ 94 40 30N 16 0 E
Basim = Washim 108 20 3N 77 0 E
Basin, Mont. 33 46 16N 112 16W
Basin, Wyo. 56 44 23N 108 2W
Basinger 17 27 23N 81 2W
Basingstoke 83 51 15N 1 5W
Baskahegan L. 26 45 30N 67 48W
Baskatong, Rés. 60 46 46N 75 50W
Baskerville C. 126 17 10 S 122 15 E
Baskin 25 32 16N 91 45W
Basle = Basel 88 47 35N 7 35 E
Basoka 122 1 16N 23 40 E
Basongo 122 4 15 S 20 20 E
Basque Provinces =
Vascongadas 91 42 50N 2 45W
Basra = Al Başrah 106 30 30N 47 50 E
Bass I. 42 41 40N 82 56W
Bass Lake 14 37 19N 119 33W
Bass Rock 84 56 5N 2 40W
Bass Str. 127 39 15 S 146 30 E
Bassano 62 50 48N 112 20W
Bassano del Grappa 94 45 45N 11 45 E
Bassas da India 123 22 0S 39 0 E
Basse-Terre 67 16 0N 61 40W
Bassein 109 16 45N 94 30 E
Basseterre 67 17 17N 62 43W
Bassett, Nebr. 34 42 35N 99 32W
Bassett, Va. 54 36 46N 79 59W
Bassfield 31 31 30N 89 45W
Bassigny 90 48 0N 5 10 E
Bassikounou 120 15 55N 6 1W
Basswood L. 30 48 7N 91 34W
Bastain 54 37 9N 81 9W
Bastak 107 27 15N 54 25 E
Bastar 109 19 15N 81 40 E
Basti 109 26 52N 82 55 E
Bastia 94 42 40N 9 30 E
Bastogne 87 50 1N 5 43 E
Bastrop, La. 25 32 47N 91 55W
Bastrop, Tex. 51 30 7N 97 19W
Bastrop County ◇ 51 30 10N 97 20W
Bat Yam 104 32 2N 34 44 E
Bata 122 1 57N 9 50 E
Bataan 111 14 40N 120 25 E
Batabanó 66 22 40N 82 20W
Batabanó, G. de 66 22 30N 82 30W
Batac 111 18 3N 120 34 E
Batagoy 101 67 38N 134 38 E
Batak 95 41 57N 24 12 E
Batakan 110 4 5 S 114 38 E
Batalha 91 39 40N 8 50W
Batamay 101 63 30N 129 15 E
Batang, China 113 30 1N 99 0 E
Batang, Indonesia 111 6 55 S 109 45 E
Batangafo 122 7 25N 18 20 E
Batangas 111 13 35N 121 10 E
Batanta 111 0 55 S 130 40 E
Batatais 77 20 54 S 47 37W
Batavia, Ill. 21 41 51N 88 19W
Batavia, Iowa 23 41 0N 92 10W
Batavia, N.Y. 39 43 0N 78 11W
Batavia, Ohio 42 39 5N 84 11W
Batchelor 126 13 4 S 131 1 E
Batchtown 21 39 2N 90 43W
Bateman's B. 127 35 40 S 150 12 E
Bates, Ark. 13 34 55N 94 23W
Bates, Oreg. 44 44 36N 118 30W
Bates County ◇ 32 38 15N 94 20W
Batesburg 46 33 54N 81 33W
Batesland 47 43 8N 102 6W
Batesville, Ark. 13 35 46N 91 39W
Batesville, Ind. 22 39 18N 85 13W
Batesville, Miss. 31 34 19N 89 57W
Batesville, Tex. 51 28 58N 99 37W
Bath, U.K. 83 51 22N 2 22W
Bath, Ill. 21 40 11N 90 8W
Bath, Maine 26 43 55N 69 49W
Bath, N.C. 40 35 29N 76 49W
Bath, N.Y. 39 42 20N 77 19W
Bath, Pa. 45 40 44N 75 24W
Bath, S.C. 46 33 31N 81 51W
Bath, S. Dak. 47 45 28N 98 20W
Bath County ◇, Ky. 49 38 10N 83 45W
Bath County ◇, Va. 54 38 0N 79 50W
Bathgate, U.K. 84 55 54N 3 38W
Bathgate, U.S.A. 41 48 53N 97 29W
Bathurst = Banjul 120 13 28N 16 40W
Bathurst, Australia 127 33 25 S 149 31 E
Bathurst, Canada 61 47 37N 65 43W
Bathurst, C. 58 70 34N 128 0W
Bathurst B. 127 14 16 S 144 25 E
Bathurst I., Australia 126 11 30 S 130 10 E
Bathurst I., Canada 4 76 0N 100 30W
Bathurst In. 58 68 10N 108 50W
Bathurst Inlet 58 66 50N 108 1W
Batinah 107 24 0N 56 0 E
Batman 106 37 55N 41 5 E
Batna 120 35 34N 6 15 E
Baton Rouge 25 30 27N 91 11W
Batopilas 64 27 0N 107 45W
Batouri 122 4 30N 14 25 E
Batson 51 30 15N 94 40W
Battambang 112 13 7N 103 12 E
Batten Kill → 36 43 6N 73 35W
Batticaloa 108 7 43N 81 45 E
Battīr 104 31 44N 35 8 E
Battle, Canada 63 52 58N 110 52W
Battle, U.K. 83 50 55N 0 30 E
Battle →, Canada 63 52 43N 108 15W
Battle →, U.S.A. 14 40 21N 122 11W
Battle Creek, Iowa 23 42 19N 95 36W
Battle Creek, Mich. 29 42 19N 85 11W
Battle Creek, Nebr. 34 42 0N 97 36W
Battle Ground, Ind. 22 40 31N 86 50W
Battle Ground, Wash. 53 45 47N 122 32W
Battle Harbour 61 52 16N 55 35W
Battle Lake 30 46 17N 95 43W
Battle Mountain 35 40 38N 116 56W
Battle Mt. 56 41 2N 107 16W
Battleford 63 52 45N 108 15W
Batu 105 6 55N 39 45 E
Batu, Kepulauan 110 0 30 S 98 25 E
Batu Gajah 112 4 28N 101 3 E
Batu Pahat = Bandar
Penggaram 110 1 50N 102 56 E
Batuata 111 6 12 S 122 42 E
Batumi 99 41 30N 41 30 E
Baturaja 110 4 11 S 104 15 E
Baturité 74 4 28 S 38 45W
Bau 110 1 25N 110 9 E
Baubau 111 5 25 S 122 38 E
Bauchi 120 10 22N 9 48 E
Baudette 30 48 43N 94 36W
Baures 73 13 35 S 63 35W
Bauru 75 22 10 S 49 0W
Baús 73 18 22 S 52 47W
Bautzen 88 51 11N 14 25 E
Bauxite 13 34 33N 92 30W
Bavaria = Bayern □ 88 49 7N 11 30 E
Bavaria 24 38 48N 97 45W
Bavispe → 64 29 30N 109 11W
Bawdwin 109 23 5N 97 20 E
Bawean 110 5 46 S 112 35 E
Bawku 120 11 3N 0 19W
Bawlake 109 19 11N 97 21 E
Baxley 18 31 47N 82 21W

Baxter Bellevue

Baxter, Iowa **23** 41 49N 93 9W
Baxter, Minn. **30** 46 21N 94 17W
Baxter, Tenn. **49** 36 9N 85 38W
Baxter County ◇ **13** 36 20N 92 23W
Baxter Springs **24** 37 2N 94 44W
Baxterville **31** 31 5N 89 36W
Bay **13** 35 45N 90 34W
Bay, Laguna de **111** 14 20N 121 11 E
Bay Bulls **61** 47 19N 52 50W
Bay City, Mich. **29** 43 36N 83 54W
Bay City, Oreg. **44** 45 31N 123 53W
Bay City, Tex. **51** 28 59N 95 58W
Bay County ◇, Fla. **17** 30 20N 85 45W
Bay County ◇, Mich. **29** 43 45N 84 5W
Bay de Verde **61** 48 5N 52 54W
Bay Mills Indian Reservation **29** 46 25N 84 15W
Bay Minette **10** 30 53N 87 46W
Bay Port **29** 43 51N 83 23W
Bay St. Louis **31** 30 19N 89 20W
Bay Shore **39** 40 43N 73 15W
Bay Springs **31** 31 59N 89 17W
Bay View, N.Z. **128** 39 25 S 176 50 E
Bay View, U.S.A. **27** 39 39N 75 58W
Bayamo **66** 20 20N 76 40W
Bayamon **57** 18 24N 66 10W
Bayamon → **57** 18 24N 66 9W
Bayan **114** 46 5N 127 24 E
Bayan Har Shan **113** 34 0N 98 0 E
Bayan Hot = Alxa Zuoqi **114** 38 50N 105 40 E
Bayan Obo **114** 41 52N 109 59 E
Bayanaul **100** 50 45N 75 45 E
Bayanhongor **113** 46 8N 102 43 E
Bayard, Iowa **23** 41 51N 94 33W
Bayard, N. Mex. **38** 32 46N 108 8W
Bayard, Nebr. **34** 41 45N 103 20W
Bayard, W. Va. **54** 39 16N 79 22W
Bayázeh **107** 33 30N 54 40 E
Baybay **111** 10 40N 124 55 E
Bayboro **40** 35 9N 76 46W
Bayburt **106** 40 15N 40 20 E
Bayern □ **88** 49 7N 11 30 E
Bayeux **90** 49 17N 0 42W
Bayfield, Colo. **16** 37 14N 107 36W
Bayfield, Wis. **55** 46 49N 90 49W
Bayfield County ◇ **55** 46 25N 91 15W
Bayfield Ridge **55** 46 45N 91 25W
Baykal, Oz. **101** 53 0N 108 0 E
Baykit **101** 61 50N 95 50 E
Baykonur **100** 47 48N 65 50 E
Baylor County ◇ **51** 33 35N 99 16W
Baymak **98** 52 36N 58 19 E
Bayombong **111** 16 30N 121 10 E
Bayonne, France **90** 43 30N 1 28W
Bayonne, U.S.A. **37** 40 40N 74 7W
Bayou Bartholomew → **25** 32 43N 92 4W
Bayou Bodcau → **25** 32 13N 93 30W
Bayou Cane **25** 29 37N 90 45W
Bayou D'Arbonne L. **25** 32 43N 92 21W
Bayou De View → **13** 34 48N 91 18W
Bayou Dorcheat → **25** 32 10N 93 25W
Bayou George **17** 30 16N 85 33W
Bayou La Batre **10** 30 24N 88 15W
Bayou Lafourche → **25** 29 5N 90 14W
Bayou Macon → **25** 31 55N 91 33W
Bayou Meto **13** 34 13N 91 31W
Bayou Nepique → **25** 30 11N 92 34W
Bayou Pierre → **31** 31 55N 91 11W
Bayou Vista **25** 29 41N 90 13W
Bayovar **72** 5 50 S 81 0W
Bayport **17** 28 32N 82 39W
Bayram-Ali **100** 37 37N 62 10 E
Bayreuth **88** 49 56N 11 35 E
Bayrūt **106** 33 53N 35 31 E
Bayshore **17** 26 43N 81 50W
Bayside **51** 28 6N 97 13W
Bayside Beach **27** 39 8N 76 27W
Bayt Awlá **104** 31 37N 35 2 E
Bayt Fajjār **104** 31 38N 35 9 E
Bayt Fūrīk **104** 32 11N 35 20 E
Bayt Ḩānūn **104** 31 32N 34 32 E
Bayt Jālā **104** 31 43N 35 11 E
Bayt Lahm **104** 31 43N 35 12 E
Bayt Rīma **104** 32 2N 35 6 E
Bayt Sāḩūr **104** 31 42N 35 13 E
Bayt Ummar **104** 31 38N 35 7 E
Bayt 'ūr al Taḩtā **104** 31 54N 35 5 E
Baytīn **104** 31 56N 35 14 E
Baytown **51** 29 43N 94 59W
Baytūniyā **104** 31 54N 35 10 E
Bayview **20** 47 59N 116 34W
Baza **91** 37 30N 2 47W
Bazaar **24** 38 16N 96 32W
Bazaruto, I. do **123** 21 40 S 35 28 E
Bazhong **115** 31 52N 106 46 E
Bazile Mills **34** 42 31N 97 53W
Bazine **24** 38 27N 99 42W
Beach **41** 46 58N 104 0W
Beach City **42** 40 39N 81 35W
Beach Haven **37** 39 34N 74 14W
Beachville **27** 38 8N 76 24W
Beachwood **37** 39 56N 74 12W
Beachy Head **83** 50 44N 0 16 E
Beacon, Iowa **23** 41 17N 92 41W
Beacon, N.Y. **39** 41 30N 73 58W
Beacon Hill **17** 29 55N 85 23W
Beaconia **63** 50 25N 96 31W
Beaconsfield **127** 41 11 S 146 48 E
Beadle County ◇ **47** 44 22N 98 13W
Beagle **24** 38 25N 94 57W
Beagle, Canal **78** 55 0 S 68 30W
Beallsville **42** 39 51N 81 2W
Beals Branch → **50** 32 10N 101 51W
Bear **27** 39 38N 75 39W
Bear → **52** 41 30N 112 8W
Bear Cr. →, Ala. **10** 33 11N 88 5W
Bear Cr. →, Wyo. **56** 41 41N 104 13W
Bear Creek **55** 44 32N 88 44W
Bear I. **85** 51 38N 9 50W
Bear L., B.C., Canada **62** 56 10N 126 52W
Bear L., Man., Canada **63** 55 8N 96 0W
Bear L., U.S.A. **52** 41 59N 111 21W
Bear Lake **29** 44 25N 86 9W
Bear Lake County ◇ **20** 42 10N 111 15W
Bear Mt. **49** 37 32N 84 16W
Bear Peak **56** 43 4N 109 13W
Bear River City **52** 41 37N 112 8W
Bear Tooth Pass **56** 44 58N 109 28W
Bearden **13** 33 43N 92 37W
Beardmore **60** 49 36N 87 57W
Beardmore Glacier **5** 84 30 S 170 0 E
Beardsley, Kans. **24** 39 49N 101 14W
Beardsley, Minn. **30** 45 33N 96 43W
Beardstown **21** 40 1N 90 26W
Bearmouth **33** 46 48N 113 20W
Béarn **90** 43 8N 0 36W
Bearpaw Mts. **33** 48 12N 109 30W
Bears Ears **52** 37 38N 109 51W
Bearskin Lake **60** 53 58N 91 2W
Beartooth Ra. **33** 45 5N 109 40W
Beata, C. **67** 17 40N 71 30W
Beata, I. **67** 17 34N 71 31W
Beatrice, Ala. **10** 31 44N 87 13W
Beatrice, Nebr. **34** 40 16N 96 45W
Beatrice, C. **127** 14 20 S 136 55 E
Beattie **24** 39 52N 96 25W
Beatton → **62** 56 15N 120 45W
Beatton River **62** 57 26N 121 20W
Beatty, Nev. **35** 36 54N 116 46W
Beatty, Oreg. **44** 42 27N 121 16W
Beattyville **49** 37 35N 83 42W
Beauce, Plaine de la **90** 48 10N 1 45 E
Beauceville **61** 46 13N 70 46W
Beauchêne, I. **78** 52 55 S 59 15W
Beaufort, Malaysia **110** 5 30N 115 40 E
Beaufort, N.C. **40** 34 43N 76 40W
Beaufort, S.C. **46** 32 26N 80 40W
Beaufort County ◇, N.C. **40** 35 30N 76 50W
Beaufort County ◇, S.C. **46** 32 20N 80 50W
Beaufort Sea **4** 72 0N 140 0W
Beaufort West **123** 32 18 S 22 36 E
Beauharnois **60** 45 20N 73 52W
Beaulieu → **62** 62 3N 113 11W
Beauly **84** 57 29N 4 27W
Beauly → **84** 57 26N 4 28W
Beaumaris **82** 53 16N 4 7W
Beaumont, Calif. **15** 33 56N 116 58W
Beaumont, Miss. **31** 31 10N 88 55W
Beaumont, Tex. **51** 30 5N 94 6W
Beaune **90** 47 2N 4 50 E
Beauregard Parish ◇ **25** 30 39N 93 25W
Beauséjour **63** 50 5N 96 35W
Beauvais **90** 49 25N 2 8 E
Beauval **63** 55 9N 107 37W
Beaver, Alaska **11** 66 22N 147 24W
Beaver, Kans. **24** 38 38N 98 40W
Beaver, Ohio **42** 39 2N 82 50W
Beaver, Okla. **43** 36 49N 100 31W
Beaver, Oreg. **44** 45 17N 123 49W
Beaver, Pa. **45** 40 42N 80 19W
Beaver, Utah **52** 38 17N 112 38W
Beaver, Wis. **55** 45 8N 88 1W
Beaver →, B.C., Canada **62** 59 52N 124 20W
Beaver →, Ont., Canada **60** 55 55N 87 48W
Beaver →, Sask., Canada **63** 55 26N 107 45W
Beaver →, U.S.A. **52** 39 10N 112 57W
Beaver Bay **30** 47 16N 91 18W
Beaver City **34** 40 8N 99 50W
Beaver County ◇, Okla. **43** 36 45N 100 25W
Beaver County ◇, Pa. **45** 40 45N 80 20W
Beaver County ◇, Utah **52** 38 20N 113 10W
Beaver Cr. →, Colo. **16** 40 20N 103 34W
Beaver Cr. →, Mont. **33** 48 27N 107 18W
Beaver Cr. →, N. Dak. **41** 47 20N 103 39W
Beaver Cr. →, Nebr. **34** 40 7N 99 29W
Beaver Cr. →, Tex. **51** 33 53N 98 49W
Beaver Cr. →, Wyo. **56** 42 58N 108 26W
Beaver Creek **30** 43 37N 96 22W
Beaver Crossing **34** 40 47N 97 17W
Beaver Dam, Ky. **48** 37 24N 86 52W
Beaver Dam, Wis. **55** 43 28N 88 50W
Beaver Dam L. **55** 43 31N 88 53W
Beaver Falls **45** 40 46N 80 20W
Beaver I. **29** 45 40N 85 33W
Beaver L. **13** 36 25N 93 51W
Beaverdam **42** 40 50N 83 59W
Beaverhead → **33** 45 31N 112 21W
Beaverhead County ◇ **33** 45 5N 113 10W
Beaverhead Mts. **20** 45 0N 113 20W
Beaverhill L., Alta., Canada **62** 53 27N 112 32W
Beaverhill L., Man., Canada **63** 54 5N 94 50W
Beaverhill L., N.W.T., Canada **63** 63 2N 104 22W
Beaverlodge **62** 55 11N 119 29W
Beavermouth **62** 51 32N 117 23W
Beaverstone → **60** 54 59N 89 25W
Beaverton, Mich. **29** 43 53N 84 29W
Beaverton, Mont. **33** 48 26N 107 15W
Beaverton, Oreg. **44** 45 29N 122 48W
Beawar **108** 26 3N 74 18 E
Bebe **51** 29 25N 97 38W
Bebedouro **77** 21 0 S 48 25W
Beccles **83** 52 27N 1 33 E
Bečej **95** 45 36N 20 3 E
Beceni **95** 45 23N 26 48 E
Béchar **120** 31 38N 2 18W
Becharof L. **11** 57 56N 156 23W
Bechyn **30** 44 39N 95 5W
Becker County ◇ **30** 46 50N 95 50W
Beckham County ◇ **43** 35 15N 99 40W
Beckley **54** 37 47N 81 11W
Beckville **51** 32 15N 92 27W
Beckwith Cr. → **25** 30 13N 93 13W
Bedford, Canada **60** 45 7N 72 59W
Bedford, S. Africa **123** 32 40 S 26 10 E
Bedford, U.K. **83** 52 8N 0 29W
Bedford, Ind. **22** 38 52N 86 29W
Bedford, Iowa **23** 40 40N 94 44W
Bedford, Ky. **49** 38 36N 85 19W
Bedford, Mass. **28** 42 29N 71 17W
Bedford, N.H. **36** 42 55N 71 32W
Bedford, Ohio **42** 41 23N 81 32W
Bedford, Pa. **45** 40 1N 78 30W
Bedford, Va. **54** 37 20N 79 31W
Bedford □ **83** 52 4N 0 28W
Bedford, C. **127** 15 14 S 145 21 E
Bedford County ◇, Pa. **45** 40 0N 78 30W
Bedford County ◇, Tenn. **48** 35 29N 86 28W
Bedford County ◇, Va. **54** 37 20N 79 31W
Bedias **51** 30 47N 95 57W
Bedourie **127** 24 30 S 139 30 E
Bedrock **16** 38 19N 108 54W
Bee **34** 41 0N 97 4W
Bee County ◇ **51** 28 24N 97 45W
Bee Ridge **17** 27 17N 82 29W
Bee Springs **48** 37 17N 86 17W
Beebe **13** 35 4N 91 53W
Beech Bottom **54** 40 14N 80 39W
Beech Creek **45** 41 5N 77 36W
Beech Fork → **49** 37 46N 85 41W
Beech Grove **22** 39 44N 86 3W
Beecher **21** 41 21N 87 38W
Beecher City **21** 39 11N 88 47W
Beecher Falls **36** 45 1N 71 31W
Beechgrove **48** 35 38N 86 14W
Beechy **63** 50 53N 107 24W
Beeler **24** 38 26N 100 12W
Beemer **34** 41 56N 96 48W
Be'er Sheva' **104** 31 15N 34 48 E
Be'er Sheva' → **104** 31 12N 34 40 E
Be'er Toviyya **104** 31 44N 34 42 E
Be'eri **104** 31 25N 34 30 E
Be'erotayim **104** 32 19N 34 59 E
Beersheba = Be'er Sheva' **104** 31 15N 34 48 E
Beersheba Springs **49** 35 28N 85 39W
Beeston **82** 52 55N 1 11W
Beeville **51** 28 24N 97 45W
Befale **122** 0 25N 20 45 E
Befandriana **123** 21 55 S 44 0 E
Bega **127** 36 41 S 149 51 E
Beggs **43** 35 45N 96 4W
Behara **123** 24 55 S 46 20 E
Behbehān **106** 30 30N 50 15 E
Behshahr **107** 36 45N 53 35 E
Bei Jiang → **115** 23 2N 112 58 E
Bei'an **114** 48 10N 126 20 E
Beibei **115** 29 47N 106 22 E
Beihai **115** 21 28N 109 6 E
Beijing **114** 39 55N 116 20 E
Beijing □ **114** 39 55N 116 20 E
Beilen **87** 52 52N 6 27 E
Beira **123** 19 50 S 34 52 E
Beira-Alta **91** 40 35N 7 35W
Beira-Baixa **91** 40 2N 7 30W
Beira-Litoral **91** 40 5N 8 30W
Beirut = Bayrūt **106** 33 53N 35 31 E
Beit Lāhiyah **104** 31 32N 34 30 E
Beitaolaizhao **114** 44 58N 125 58 E
Beitbridge **123** 22 12 S 30 0 E
Beizhen **114** 37 20N 118 2 E
Beja, Portugal **91** 38 2N 7 53W
Béja, Tunisia **120** 36 43N 9 12 E
Bejaia **120** 36 42N 5 2 E
Bejestān **107** 34 30N 58 5 E
Bekasi **111** 6 14 S 106 59 E
Békéscsaba **89** 46 40N 21 5 E
Bekok **112** 2 20N 103 7 E
Bel Air **27** 39 32N 76 21W
Bel Alton **27** 38 28N 76 59W
Bela, India **109** 25 50N 82 0 E
Bela, Pakistan **108** 26 12N 66 20 E
Bela Crkva **95** 44 55N 21 27 E
Bela Vista, Brazil **76** 22 12 S 56 20W
Bela Vista, Mozam. **123** 26 10 S 32 44 E
Belau Is. **124** 7 30N 134 30 E
Belawan **110** 3 33N 98 32 E
Belaya → **98** 56 0N 54 32 E
Belaya Tserkov **99** 49 45N 30 10 E
Belcamp **27** 39 28N 76 14W
Belcher Is. **60** 56 15N 78 45W
Belchertown **28** 42 17N 72 24W
Belcourt **41** 48 50N 99 45W
Belden **34** 42 25N 97 13W
Belding **29** 43 6N 85 14W
Belebey **98** 54 7N 54 7 E
Belém **74** 1 20 S 48 30W
Belém de São Francisco **74** 8 46 S 38 58W
Belén, Argentina **76** 27 40 S 67 5W
Belén, Colombia **70** 1 26N 75 56W
Belén, Paraguay **76** 23 30 S 57 6W
Belen, U.S.A. **38** 34 40N 106 46W
Belene **95** 43 39N 25 10 E
Belet Uen **105** 4 30N 45 5 E
Belev **98** 53 50N 36 5 E
Belews L. **40** 36 15N 80 5W
Belfair **53** 47 27N 122 50W
Belfast, S. Africa **123** 25 42 S 30 2 E
Belfast, U.K. **85** 54 35N 5 56W
Belfast, Maine **26** 44 26N 69 1W
Belfast, N.Y. **39** 42 21N 78 7W
Belfast, Tenn. **48** 35 25N 86 42W
Belfast □ **85** 54 35N 5 56W
Belfast, L. **85** 54 40N 5 50W
Belfield **41** 46 53N 103 12W
Belfort **90** 47 38N 6 50 E
Belfort □ **90** 47 38N 6 52 E
Belfry **33** 45 9N 109 1W
Belgaum **108** 15 55N 74 35 E
Belgium **55** 43 30N 87 51W
Belgium ■ **87** 50 30N 5 0 E
Belgorod **99** 50 35N 36 35 E
Belgorod-Dnestrovskiy **99** 46 11N 30 23 E
Belgrade = Beograd **95** 44 50N 20 37 E
Belgrade, Maine **26** 44 27N 69 50W
Belgrade, Minn. **30** 45 27N 95 0W
Belgrade, Mont. **33** 45 47N 111 11W
Belgrade, Nebr. **34** 41 28N 98 4W
Belhaven **40** 35 33N 76 37W
Beli Drim → **95** 42 6N 20 25 E
Belinga **122** 1 10N 13 2 E
Belington **54** 39 2N 79 56W
Belinyu **110** 1 35 S 105 50 E
Belitung **110** 3 10 S 107 50 E
Belize ■ **65** 17 0N 88 30W
Belize City **65** 17 25N 88 0W
Belknap **21** 37 19N 88 56W
Belknap County ◇ **36** 43 30N 71 30W
Belkovskiy, Ostrov **101** 75 32N 135 44 E
Bell **17** 29 45N 82 52W
Bell → **60** 49 48N 77 38W
Bell Buckle **48** 35 35N 86 21W
Bell City, Ky. **48** 36 31N 88 30W
Bell City, Mo. **32** 37 1N 89 49W
Bell County ◇, Ky. **49** 36 45N 83 40W
Bell County ◇, Tex. **51** 31 3N 97 28W
Bell I. **61** 50 46N 55 35W
Bell-Irving → **62** 56 12N 129 5W
Bell Peninsula **59** 63 50N 82 0W
Bell Ranch **38** 35 32N 104 6W
Bell Ville **76** 32 40 S 62 40W
Bella Bella **62** 52 10N 128 10W
Bella Coola **62** 52 25N 126 40W
Bella Flor **72** 11 9 S 67 49W
Bella Unión **76** 30 15 S 57 40W
Bella Vista, Corrientes, Argentina **76** 28 33 S 59 0W
Bella Vista, Tucuman, Argentina **76** 27 10 S 65 25W
Bellaire, Mich. **29** 44 59N 85 13W
Bellaire, Ohio **42** 40 1N 80 45W
Bellaire, Tex. **51** 29 42N 95 28W
Bellamy **10** 32 27N 88 8W
Bellary **108** 15 10N 76 56 E
Belle, Mo. **32** 38 17N 91 43W
Belle, W. Va. **54** 38 14N 81 33W
Belle → **29** 42 43N 82 30W
Belle Fourche **47** 44 40N 103 51W
Belle Fourche → **47** 44 26N 102 18W
Belle Fourche Reservoir **47** 44 44N 103 41W
Belle Glade **17** 26 41N 80 40W
Belle-Île **90** 47 20N 3 10W
Belle Isle, Canada **61** 51 57N 55 25W
Belle Isle, U.S.A. **17** 28 27N 81 21W
Belle Isle, Str. of **61** 51 30N 56 30W
Belle Plaine, Iowa **23** 41 54N 92 17W
Belle Plaine, Kans. **24** 37 24N 97 17W
Belle Plaine, Minn. **30** 44 37N 93 46W
Belle Rive **21** 38 14N 88 45W
Belle Valley **42** 39 47N 81 33W
Bellechester **30** 44 22N 92 31W
Belledune **61** 47 55N 65 50W
Bellefontaine **42** 40 22N 83 46W
Bellefonte, Del. **27** 39 47N 75 30W
Bellefonte, Pa. **45** 40 55N 77 47W
Bellemont **12** 35 14N 111 50W
Belleoram **61** 47 31N 55 25W
Belleplain **37** 39 11N 74 46W
Belleview **17** 29 4N 82 3W
Belleville, Canada **60** 44 10N 77 23W
Belleville, Ill. **21** 38 31N 89 59W
Belleville, Kans. **24** 39 50N 97 38W
Belleville, N.J. **37** 40 47N 74 9W
Belleville, Wis. **55** 42 52N 89 32W
Bellevue, Canada **62** 49 35N 114 22W
Bellevue, Idaho **20** 43 28N 114 16W

Bellevue Bethpage

Bellevue, Iowa 23 42 16N 90 26W
Bellevue, Md. 27 38 42N 76 11W
Bellevue, Mich. 29 42 27N 85 1W
Bellevue, Nebr. 34 41 9N 95 54W
Bellevue, Ohio 42 41 17N 82 51W
Bellevue, Tex. 51 33 38N 98 1W
Bellevue, Wash. 53 47 37N 122 12W
Bellflower, Ill. 21 40 20N 88 32W
Bellflower, Mo. 32 39 0N 91 21W
Bellin 59 60 0N 70 0W
Bellingham, Mass. 28 42 5N 71 28W
Bellingham, Minn. 30 45 8N 96 17W
Bellingham, Wash. 53 48 46N 122 29W
Bellingshausen 5 62 0S 59 0W
Bellingshausen Sea 5 66 0S 80 0W
Bellinzona 88 46 11N 9 1E
Bellmawr 37 39 52N 75 5W
Bellmead 51 31 35N 97 6W
Bello 70 6 20N 75 33W
Bellona Reefs 127 21 26S 159 0E
Bellows Falls 36 43 8N 72 27W
Bellport 39 40 46N 72 56W
Bells, Tenn. 48 35 43N 89 5W
Bells, Tex. 51 33 37N 96 25W
Belltown 27 38 45N 75 11W
Belluno 94 46 8N 12 13E
Bellview 38 34 49N 103 7W
Bellville, Ga. 18 32 9N 81 59W
Bellville, Tex. 51 29 57N 96 15W
Bellvue 16 40 38N 105 10W
Bellwood, La. 25 31 32N 93 12W
Bellwood, Nebr. 34 41 21N 97 14W
Bellwood, Pa. 45 40 36N 78 20W
Belmar 37 40 11N 74 2W
Bélmez 91 38 17N 5 17W
Belmond 23 42 51N 93 37W
Belmont, Kans. 24 37 32N 97 56W
Belmont, Miss. 31 34 31N 88 13W
Belmont, N.C. 40 35 14N 81 2W
Belmont, N.H. 36 43 27N 71 29W
Belmont, N.Y. 39 42 14N 78 2W
Belmont, Wis. 55 42 44N 90 20W
Belmont County ◇ 42 40 1N 81 4W
Belmonte 75 16 0S 39 0W
Belmopan 65 17 18N 88 30W
Belmore 42 41 9N 83 56W
Belmullet 85 54 13N 9 58W
Belo Horizonte 75 19 55S 43 56W
Belo Jardim 74 8 20S 36 26W
Belo-Tsiribihina 123 19 40S 44 30E
Belogorsk 101 51 0N 128 20E
Belogradets 95 43 22N 27 18E
Beloit, Kans. 24 39 28N 98 6W
Beloit, Wis. 55 42 31N 89 2W
Belomorsk 98 64 35N 34 30E
Belonia 109 23 15N 91 30E
Beloretsk 98 53 58N 58 24E
Belovo 100 54 30N 86 0E
Beloye, Oz. 98 60 10N 37 35E
Beloye More 98 66 30N 38 0E
Belozem 95 42 12N 25 2E
Belozersk 98 60 0N 37 30E
Belpre, Kans. 24 37 57N 99 6W
Belpre, Ohio 42 39 17N 81 34W
Belt 33 47 23N 110 55W
Belterra 71 2 45S 55 0W
Belton, Mo. 32 38 49N 94 32W
Belton, S.C. 46 34 31N 82 30W
Belton, Tex. 51 31 3N 97 28W
Beltrami 30 47 33N 96 32W
Beltrami County ◇ 30 47 45N 94 50W
Beltsville 27 39 2N 76 54W
Beltsy 99 47 48N 28 0E
Belturbet 85 54 6N 7 28W
Belukha 100 49 50N 86 50E
Beluran 110 5 48N 117 35E
Belvidere, Ill. 21 42 15N 88 50W
Belvidere, N.J. 37 40 50N 75 5W
Belvidere, Nebr. 34 40 15N 97 33W
Belvidere, S. Dak. 47 43 50N 101 16W
Belvidere Mt. 36 44 46N 72 33W
Belview 30 44 36N 95 20W
Belvue 24 39 13N 96 11W
Belyando → 127 21 38S 146 50E
Belyy, Ostrov 100 73 30N 71 0E
Belyy Yar 100 58 26N 84 39E
Belzoni 31 33 11N 90 29W
Bembéréke 120 10 11N 2 43E
Bement 21 39 55N 88 34W
Bemidji 30 47 28N 94 53W
Bemis, Tenn. 48 35 35N 88 49W
Bemis, W. Va. 54 38 49N 79 45W
Ben 'Ammi 104 33 0N 35 7E
Ben Cruachan 84 56 26N 5 8W
Ben Dearg 84 57 47N 4 58W
Ben Gardane 121 33 11N 11 11E
Ben Hill County ◇ 18 31 45N 83 10W
Ben Hope 84 58 24N 4 36W
Ben Lawers 84 56 33N 4 13W
Ben Lomond, Australia 127 41 38S 147 42E
Ben Lomond, U.K. 84 56 12N 4 39W
Ben Lomond, Ark. 13 33 50N 94 7W
Ben Lomond, Calif. 14 37 5N 122 5W
Ben Macdhui 84 57 4N 3 40W
Ben Mhor 84 57 16N 7 21W
Ben More, Central, U.K. 84 56 23N 4 31W
Ben More, Strathclyde, U.K. 84 56 26N 6 2W
Ben More Assynt 84 58 7N 4 51W
Ben Nevis 84 56 48N 5 0W
Ben Vorlich 84 56 22N 4 15W
Ben Wyvis 84 57 40N 4 35W
Bena, Nigeria 120 11 20N 5 50E
Bena, U.S.A. 30 47 21N 94 12W
Bena Dibele 122 4 4S 22 50E
Benalla 127 36 30S 146 0E
Benavides 50 27 36N 98 25W
Benbecula 84 57 26N 7 21W
Benbrook 51 32 41N 97 28W
Benchley 51 30 45N 96 27W
Bencubbin 126 30 48S 117 52E
Bend 44 44 4N 121 19W
Bender Beila 105 9 30N 50 48E
Bendery 99 46 50N 29 30E
Bendigo 127 36 40S 144 15E
Benē Beraq 104 32 6N 34 51E
Benedict, Kans. 24 37 38N 95 45W
Benedict, Md. 27 38 31N 76 41W
Benedict, Nebr. 34 41 0N 97 36W
Beneditinos 74 5 27S 42 22W
Benedito Leite 74 7 13S 44 34W
Benevento 94 41 7N 14 45E
Benevolence 18 31 53N 84 44W
Benewah County ◇ 20 47 5N 116 35W
Bengal, Bay of 109 15 0N 90 0E
Bengbu 115 32 58N 117 20E
Benghazi = Banghāzī 121 32 11N 20 3E
Bengkalis 110 1 30N 102 10E
Bengkulu 110 3 50S 102 12E
Bengkulu □ 110 3 48S 102 16E
Bengough 63 49 25N 105 10W
Benguela 123 12 37S 13 25E
Benham 49 36 58N 82 57W
Beni 122 0 30N 29 27E
Beni □ 73 14 0S 65 0W
Beni → 73 10 23S 65 24W
Beni Abbès 120 30 5N 2 5W
Beni Mazâr 121 28 32N 30 44E
Beni Mellal 120 32 21N 6 21W
Beni Ounif 120 32 0N 1 10W
Beni Suef 121 29 5N 31 6E
Beni Ulid 121 31 36N 13 53E
Beniah L. 62 63 23N 112 17W
Benidorm 91 38 33N 0 9W
Benin ■ 120 10 0N 2 0E
Benin, Bight of 120 5 0N 3 0E
Benin City 120 6 20N 5 31E
Benjamin 51 33 35N 99 48W
Benjamin Aceval 76 24 58S 57 34W
Benjamin Constant 70 4 40S 70 15W
Benjamin Hill 64 30 10N 111 10W
Benkelman 34 40 3N 101 32W
Benld 21 39 6N 89 48W
Bennet 34 40 41N 96 30W
Bennett, Canada 62 59 56N 134 53W
Bennett, Colo. 16 39 46N 104 26W
Bennett, Iowa 23 41 43N 90 59W
Bennett, N.C. 40 35 34N 79 33W
Bennett, N. Mex. 38 32 4N 103 12W
Bennett, Ostrov 101 76 21N 148 56E
Bennett County ◇ 47 43 5N 101 45W
Bennettsville 46 34 37N 79 41W
Bennington, Idaho 20 42 24N 111 19W
Bennington, Kans. 24 39 2N 97 36W
Bennington, N.H. 36 43 0N 71 55W
Bennington, Nebr. 34 41 22N 96 9W
Bennington, Okla. 43 34 0N 96 2W
Bennington, Vt. 36 42 53N 73 12W
Bennington County ◇ 36 43 0N 73 10W
Benoa 110 8 50S 115 20E
Benoit 31 33 39N 91 1W
Benoni 123 26 11S 28 18E
Benque Viejo 65 17 5N 89 8W
Bens Run 54 39 28N 81 6W
Benson, Ariz. 12 31 58N 110 18W
Benson, Ill. 21 40 51N 89 7W
Benson, La. 25 31 52N 93 42W
Benson, Minn. 30 45 19N 95 36W
Benson, N.C. 40 35 23N 78 33W
Benson, Vt. 36 43 42N 73 18W
Benson County ◇ 41 48 5N 99 25W
Bent 107 26 20N 59 31E
Bent County ◇ 16 38 0N 103 0W
Benteng 111 6 10S 120 30E
Bentinck I. 127 17 3S 139 35E
Bentley 24 37 54N 97 31W
Bentleyville 45 40 7N 80 1W
Bento Gonçalves 77 29 10S 51 31W
Benton, Ark. 13 34 34N 92 35W
Benton, Calif. 14 37 48N 118 32W
Benton, Ill. 21 38 0N 88 55W
Benton, Iowa 23 40 42N 94 22W
Benton, Kans. 24 37 47N 97 6W
Benton, Ky. 48 36 52N 88 21W
Benton, La. 25 32 42N 93 44W
Benton, Miss. 31 32 50N 90 16W
Benton, Mo. 32 37 6N 89 34W
Benton, N.H. 36 44 8N 71 55W
Benton, Pa. 45 41 12N 76 23W
Benton, Tenn. 49 35 10N 84 39W
Benton, Wis. 55 42 34N 90 23W
Benton City, Mo. 32 39 8N 91 46W
Benton City, Wash. 53 46 16N 119 29W
Benton County ◇, Ark. 13 36 22N 94 13W
Benton County ◇, Ind. 22 40 35N 87 20W
Benton County ◇, Iowa 23 42 0N 92 0W
Benton County ◇, Minn. 30 45 45N 94 0W
Benton County ◇, Miss. 31 34 50N 89 11W
Benton County ◇, Mo. 32 38 20N 93 15W
Benton County ◇, Oreg. 44 44 30N 123 20W
Benton County ◇, Tenn. 48 36 4N 88 6W
Benton County ◇, Wash. 53 46 25N 119 25W
Benton Harbor 29 42 6N 86 27W
Benton Heights 29 42 7N 86 24W
Benton L. 33 47 40N 111 20W
Benton Ridge 42 41 0N 83 48W
Bentonia 31 32 38N 90 22W
Bentonite Spur 56 44 52N 104 9W
Bentonville, Ark. 13 36 22N 94 13W
Bentonville, Va. 54 38 50N 78 19W
Bentung 112 3 31N 101 55E
Benue → 120 7 48N 6 46E
Benwood 54 40 1N 80 44W
Benxi 114 41 20N 123 48E
Benzdorp 71 3 44N 54 5W
Benzie County ◇ 29 44 40N 86 0W
Beo 111 4 25N 126 50E
Beograd 95 44 50N 20 37E
Beowawe 35 40 35N 116 29W
Beppu 117 33 15N 131 30E
Berau, Teluk 111 2 30S 132 30E
Berber 121 18 0N 34 0E
Berbera 105 10 30N 45 2E
Berbérati 122 4 15N 15 40E
Berbice □ 71 4 0N 58 0W
Berbice → 71 6 20N 57 32W
Berclair 51 28 32N 97 36W
Berdichev 99 49 57N 28 30E
Berdsk 100 54 47N 83 2E
Berdyansk 99 46 45N 36 50E
Berea, Ky. 49 37 34N 84 17W
Berea, Nebr. 34 42 13N 102 59W
Berebere 111 2 25N 128 45E
Bereda 105 11 45N 51 0E
Berekum 120 7 29N 2 34W
Berens → 63 52 25N 97 2W
Berens I. 63 52 18N 97 18W
Berens River 63 52 25N 97 0W
Beresford 47 43 5N 96 47W
Bereşti 95 46 6N 27 50E
Berezina → 98 52 33N 30 14E
Berezniki 100 59 24N 56 46E
Berezovo 100 64 0N 65 0E
Bergama 106 39 8N 27 15E
Bérgamo 94 45 42N 9 40E
Bergen, Neth. 87 52 40N 4 43E
Bergen, Norway 97 60 23N 5 20E
Bergen, U.S.A. 39 43 5N 77 57W
Bergen County ◇ 37 41 0N 74 10W
Bergen-op-Zoom 87 51 30N 4 18E
Bergenfield 37 40 54N 73 58W
Berger 32 38 41N 91 20W
Bergerac 90 44 51N 0 30E
Bergland 29 46 36N 89 34W
Bergoo 54 38 29N 80 18W
Bergum 87 53 13N 5 59E
Berhala, Selat 110 1 0S 104 15E
Berhampore = Baharampur 109 24 2N 88 27E
Berhampur 109 19 15N 84 54E
Berheci → 95 46 7N 27 19E
Bering Glacier 11 60 20N 143 30W
Bering Sea 11 60 0N 175 0W
Bering Strait 11 65 30N 169 0W
Beringen 87 51 3N 5 14E
Beringovskiy 101 63 3N 179 19E
Berino 38 32 4N 106 37W
Berisso 76 34 56S 57 50W
Berja 91 36 50N 2 56W
Berkeley, U.K. 83 51 41N 2 28W
Berkeley, U.S.A. 14 37 52N 122 16W
Berkeley County ◇, S.C. 46 33 15N 80 0W
Berkeley County ◇, W. Va. 54 39 27N 77 58W
Berkeley Springs 54 39 38N 78 14W
Berkner I. 5 79 30S 50 0W
Berkovitsa 95 43 16N 23 8E
Berks County ◇ 45 40 25N 76 0W
Berkshire □ 83 51 30N 1 20W
Berkshire County ◇ 28 42 25N 73 15W
Berkshire Hills 28 42 20N 73 10W
Berland → 62 54 0N 116 50W
Berlin, Germany 88 52 32N 13 24E
Berlin, Ga. 18 31 4N 83 37W
Berlin, Md. 27 38 20N 75 13W
Berlin, N. Dak. 41 46 23N 98 29W
Berlin, N.H. 36 44 28N 71 11W
Berlin, N.J. 37 39 48N 74 56W
Berlin, Okla. 43 35 27N 99 36W
Berlin, Pa. 45 39 55N 78 57W
Berlin, Wis. 55 43 58N 88 57W
Berlin Heights 42 41 20N 82 30W
Berlin L. 42 41 3N 81 0W
Bermejo →, Formosa, Argentina 76 26 51S 58 23W
Bermejo →, San Juan, Argentina 76 32 30S 67 30W
Bermuda ■ 2 32 45N 65 0W
Bern, Switz. 88 46 57N 7 28E
Bern, U.S.A. 24 39 58N 95 58W
Bernalillo 38 35 18N 106 33W
Bernalillo County ◇ 38 35 0N 106 45W
Bernam → 112 3 45N 101 5E
Bernardo de Irigoyen 77 26 15S 53 40W
Bernardo O'Higgins □ 76 34 15S 70 45W
Bernardston 28 42 40N 72 33W
Bernardsville 37 40 43N 74 34W
Bernasconi 76 37 55S 63 44W
Bernburg 88 51 40N 11 42E
Berne = Bern 88 46 57N 7 28E
Berne 22 40 39N 84 57W
Bernice, La. 25 32 49N 92 39W
Bernice, Okla. 43 36 34N 94 57W
Bernie 32 36 40N 89 58W
Bernier I. 126 24 50S 113 12E
Beror Hayil 104 31 34N 34 38E
Beroroha 123 21 40S 45 10E
Beroun 88 49 57N 14 5E
Berrechid 120 33 18N 7 36W
Berrien County ◇, Ga. 18 31 15N 83 10W
Berrien County ◇, Mich. 29 42 0N 86 25W
Berrien Springs 29 41 57N 86 20W
Berry, France 90 47 0N 2 0E
Berry, Ala. 10 33 40N 87 36W
Berry, Ky. 49 38 31N 84 23W
Berry Is. 66 25 40N 77 50W
Berrydale 17 30 53N 87 3W
Berryessa L. 14 38 31N 122 6W
Berryville, Ark. 13 36 22N 93 34W
Berryville, Va. 54 39 9N 77 59W
Bertha 30 46 16N 95 4W
Berthold 41 48 19N 101 44W
Berthoud 16 40 19N 105 5W
Berthoud Pass 16 39 48N 105 47W
Bertie County ◇ 40 36 0N 77 0W
Bertoua 122 4 30N 13 45E
Bertram, Iowa 23 41 57N 91 32W
Bertram, Tex. 51 30 45N 98 3W
Bertrand, Mich. 29 41 47N 86 16W
Bertrand, Mo. 32 36 55N 89 27W
Bertrand, Nebr. 34 40 32N 99 38W
Berufjörður 96 64 48N 14 29W
Beruri 71 3 54S 61 22W
Berwick, Maine 26 43 16N 70 52W
Berwick, N. Dak. 41 48 22N 100 15W
Berwick, Pa. 45 41 3N 76 14W
Berwick-upon-Tweed 82 55 47N 2 0W
Berwyn, Ill. 21 41 51N 87 47W
Berwyn, Nebr. 34 41 21N 99 30W
Berwyn Mts. 82 52 54N 3 26W
Beryl 52 37 54N 113 40W
Besalampy 123 16 43S 44 29E
Besançon 90 47 15N 6 0E
Besar 110 2 40S 116 0E
Beserah 112 3 50N 103 21E
Besnard L. 63 55 25N 106 0W
Besni 106 37 41N 37 52E
Besor, N. → 104 31 28N 34 22E
Bessemer, Ala. 10 33 24N 86 58W
Bessemer, Mich. 29 46 29N 90 3W
Bessemer, Pa. 45 40 59N 80 30W
Bessemer City 40 35 17N 81 17W
Bessie 43 35 23N 98 59W
Best 50 31 13N 101 37W
Bet Alfa 104 32 31N 35 25E
Bet Dagan 104 32 1N 34 49E
Bet Guvrin 104 31 37N 34 54E
Bet Ha'Emeq 104 32 58N 35 8E
Bet Hashitta 104 32 31N 35 27E
Bet Qeshet 104 32 41N 35 21E
Bet She'an 104 32 30N 35 30E
Bet Shemesh 104 31 44N 35 0E
Bet Yosef 104 32 34N 35 33E
Betanzos 73 19 34S 65 27W
Bétaré Oya 122 5 40N 14 5E
Bethalto 21 38 55N 90 2W
Bethanien 123 26 31S 17 8E
Bethany = Al 'Ayzarīyah 104 31 47N 35 15E
Bethany, Ill. 21 39 39N 88 45W
Bethany, Mo. 32 40 16N 94 2W
Bethany, Okla. 43 35 31N 97 38W
Bethany Beach 27 38 32N 75 5W
Bethel, Alaska 11 60 48N 161 45W
Bethel, Conn. 28 41 22N 73 25W
Bethel, Maine 26 44 25N 70 47W
Bethel, Minn. 30 45 24N 93 16W
Bethel, N.C. 40 35 48N 77 22W
Bethel, Ohio 42 38 58N 84 5W
Bethel, Okla. 43 34 22N 94 51W
Bethel, Pa. 45 40 28N 76 18W
Bethel, Vt. 36 43 50N 72 38W
Bethel ◇ 11 60 15N 163 0W
Bethel Acres 43 35 22N 97 3W
Bethel Park 45 40 20N 80 1W
Bethel Springs 48 35 14N 88 36W
Bethera 46 33 12N 79 47W
Bethesda, Md. 27 38 59N 77 6W
Bethesda, N.C. 40 35 57N 78 50W
Bethesda, Ohio 42 40 1N 81 4W
Bethlehem = Bayt Lahm 104 31 43N 35 12E
Bethlehem, S. Africa 123 28 14S 28 18E
Bethlehem, Conn. 28 41 38N 73 13W
Bethlehem, Md. 27 38 45N 75 57W
Bethlehem, N.H. 36 44 17N 71 41W
Bethlehem, Pa. 45 40 37N 75 23W
Bethpage 39 40 44N 73 30W

Bethulie Bjargtangar

Bethulie **123** 30 30 S 25 59 E
Bethune, Colo. **16** 39 18N 102 26W
Bethune, S.C. **46** 34 25N 80 21W
Betijoque **70** 9 23N 70 44W
Betim **75** 19 58 S 44 7W
Betioky **123** 23 48 S 44 20 E
Betong **112** 5 45N 101 5 E
Betroka **123** 23 16 S 46 0 E
Betsiamites **61** 48 56N 68 40W
Betsiamites → **61** 48 56N 68 38W
Bettendorf **23** 41 32N 90 30W
Betterton **27** 39 22N 76 4W
Bettiah **109** 26 48N 84 33 E
Betul **108** 21 58N 77 59 E
Betung **110** 1 24N 111 31 E
Beuca **95** 44 14N 24 56 E
Beulah, Colo. **16** 38 5N 104 59W
Beulah, Mich. **29** 44 38N 86 6W
Beulah, N. Dak. **41** 47 16N 101 47W
Beulahville **40** 34 55N 77 46W
Beverley, Australia **126** 32 9 S 116 56 E
Beverley, U.K. **82** 53 52N 0 26W
Beverly, Kans. **24** 39 1N 97 58W
Beverly, Mass. **28** 42 33N 70 53W
Beverly, W. Va. **54** 38 51N 79 53W
Beverly, Wash. **53** 46 50N 119 56W
Beverly Beach **27** 38 53N 76 31W
Beverly Hills **15** 34 4N 118 25W
Beverwijk **87** 52 28N 4 38 E
Bevier **32** 39 45N 92 34W
Bexar **10** 34 11N 88 9W
Bexar County ◇ **51** 29 25N 98 30W
Bexley **42** 39 58N 82 56W
Beykoz **95** 41 8N 29 7 E
Beyla **120** 8 30N 8 38W
Beyneu **100** 45 10N 55 3 E
Beypazarı **106** 40 10N 31 56 E
Beyşehir Gölü **106** 37 40N 31 45 E
Bezet **104** 33 4N 35 8 E
Bezhitsa **98** 53 19N 34 17 E
Béziers **90** 43 20N 3 12 E
Bezwada = Vijayawada **109** 16 31N 80 39 E
Bhachau **108** 23 20N 70 16 E
Bhadrakh **109** 21 10N 86 30 E
Bhadravati **108** 13 49N 75 40 E
Bhagalpur **109** 25 10N 87 0 E
Bhakra Dam **108** 31 30N 76 45 E
Bhamo **109** 24 15N 97 15 E
Bhandara **108** 21 5N 79 42 E
Bhanrer Ra. **108** 23 40N 79 45 E
Bharat = India ■ **103** 20 0N 78 0 E
Bharatpur **108** 27 15N 77 30 E
Bhatpara **109** 22 50N 88 25 E
Bhaunagar = Bhavnagar **108** 21 45N 72 10 E
Bhavnagar **108** 21 45N 72 10 E
Bhawanipatna **109** 19 55N 80 10 E
Bhilsa = Vidisha **108** 23 28N 77 53 E
Bhilwara **108** 25 25N 74 38 E
Bhima → **108** 16 25N 77 17 E
Bhimavaram **109** 16 30N 81 30 E
Bhind **108** 26 30N 78 46 E
Bhiwandi **108** 19 20N 73 0 E
Bhiwani **108** 28 50N 76 9 E
Bhola **109** 22 45N 90 35 E
Bhopal **108** 23 20N 77 30 E
Bhubaneshwar **109** 20 15N 85 50 E
Bhuj **108** 23 15N 69 49 E
Bhumibol Dam **110** 17 15N 98 58 E
Bhusaval **108** 21 3N 75 46 E
Bhutan ■ **109** 27 25N 90 30 E
Biá → **70** 3 28 S 67 23W
Biafra, B. of = Bonny, Bight of **122** 3 30N 9 20 E
Biak **111** 1 10 S 136 6 E
Biała Podlaska **89** 52 4N 23 6 E
Białystok **89** 53 10N 23 10 E
Biaro **111** 2 5N 125 26 E
Biarritz **90** 43 29N 1 33W
Bibai **116** 43 19N 141 52 E
Bibala **123** 14 44 S 13 24 E
Bibb County ◇, Ala. **10** 32 57N 87 8W
Bibb County ◇, Ga. **18** 32 50N 83 45W
Bibby I. **63** 61 55N 93 0W
Biberach **88** 48 5N 9 49 E
Bibiani **120** 6 30N 2 8W
Bic **61** 48 20N 68 41W
Biche, La → **62** 59 57N 123 50W
Bicknell, Ind. **22** 38 47N 87 19W
Bicknell, Utah **52** 38 20N 111 33W
Bida **120** 9 3N 5 58 E
Bidar **108** 17 55N 77 35 E
Biddeford **26** 43 30N 70 28W
Biddiyā **104** 32 7N 35 4 E
Biddū **104** 31 50N 35 8 E
Bideford **83** 51 1N 4 13W
Bidon 5 = Poste Maurice Cortier **120** 22 14N 1 2 E
Bidor **112** 4 6N 101 15 E
Bié, Planalto de **123** 12 0 S 16 0 E
Bieber **14** 41 7N 121 8W
Biel **88** 47 8N 7 14 E
Bielé Karpaty **89** 49 5N 18 0 E
Bielefeld **88** 52 2N 8 31 E
Biella **94** 45 33N 8 3 E
Bielsko-Biała **89** 49 50N 19 2 E
Bien Hoa **112** 10 57N 106 49 E
Bienfait **63** 49 10N 102 50W
Bienne = Biel **88** 47 8N 7 14 E
Bienvenue **71** 3 0N 52 30W
Bienville **25** 32 22N 92 59W
Bienville, L. **60** 55 5N 72 40W
Bienville National Forest **31** 32 10N 89 25W
Bienville Parish ◇ **25** 32 20N 93 0W
Big →, Canada **61** 54 50N 58 55W
Big →, U.S.A. **32** 38 28N 90 37W
Big B. **61** 55 43N 60 35W
Big Baldy **20** 44 47N 115 13W
Big Bar **14** 40 45N 123 15W
Big Bay **29** 46 49N 87 44W
Big Bay de Noc **29** 45 45N 86 40W
Big Bear City **15** 34 16N 116 51W
Big Bear Lake **15** 34 15N 116 56W
Big Beaver **63** 49 10N 105 10W
Big Belt Mts. **33** 46 30N 111 25W
Big Bend, Calif. **14** 41 1N 121 55W
Big Bend, La. **25** 31 5N 91 48W
Big Bend Dam **47** 44 1N 99 23W
Big Bend National Park **50** 29 20N 103 5W
Big Black → **31** 32 3N 91 4W
Big Blue → **24** 39 35N 96 34W
Big Bow **24** 37 34N 101 34W
Big Cabin **43** 36 32N 95 14W
Big Canyon → **50** 29 45N 101 48W
Big Chino Wash → **12** 34 52N 112 28W
Big Clifty **48** 37 33N 86 9W
Big Cr. →, Canada **62** 51 42N 122 41W
Big Cr. →, U.S.A. **25** 32 10N 91 53W
Big Creek **20** 45 8N 115 20W
Big Creek L. **10** 30 43N 88 20W
Big Cypress Indian Reservation **17** 26 20N 81 10W
Big Cypress National Preserve **17** 26 0N 81 10W
Big Cypress Swamp **17** 26 15N 81 30W
Big Darby → **42** 39 37N 82 58W
Big Delta **11** 64 10N 145 51W
Big Eau Pleine Reservoir **55** 44 44N 89 46W
Big Falls, Minn. **30** 48 12N 93 48W
Big Falls, Wis. **55** 44 37N 89 1W
Big Flat **13** 36 1N 92 24W
Big Fork → **30** 48 31N 93 43W
Big Hatchet Peak **38** 31 38N 108 24W
Big Hole → **33** 45 34N 112 20W
Big Horn Basin **56** 44 15N 108 0W
Big Horn County ◇, Mont. **33** 45 25N 107 45W
Big Horn County ◇, Wyo. **56** 44 45N 108 0W
Big Island **54** 37 32N 79 22W
Big L., Calif. **14** 41 7N 121 25W
Big L., Maine **26** 45 11N 67 41W
Big L., Oreg. **44** 42 8N 120 2W
Big Lake, Alaska **11** 67 30N 149 27W
Big Lake, Minn. **30** 45 20N 93 45W
Big Lake, Tex. **50** 31 12N 101 28W
Big Lookout Mt. **44** 44 36N 117 17W
Big Lost → **20** 43 50N 112 44W
Big Muddy Cr. → **33** 48 8N 104 36W
Big Nemaha → **34** 40 1N 95 32W
Big Otter → **54** 37 7N 79 23W
Big Pine, Calif. **15** 37 10N 118 17W
Big Pine, Fla. **17** 24 40N 81 21W
Big Piney **56** 42 32N 110 7W
Big Quill L. **63** 51 55N 104 50W
Big Rapids **29** 43 42N 85 29W
Big Rib → **55** 44 56N 89 41W
Big River **63** 53 50N 107 0W
Big Rock **48** 36 35N 87 46W
Big Sable Pt. **29** 44 3N 86 1W
Big Sage Reservoir **14** 41 35N 120 38W
Big Sand L. **63** 57 45N 99 45W
Big Sandy, Mont. **33** 48 11N 110 7W
Big Sandy, Tenn. **48** 36 14N 88 5W
Big Sandy, Tex. **51** 32 35N 95 7W
Big Sandy → **12** 34 19N 113 31W
Big Sandy Cr. →, Colo. **16** 38 7N 102 29W
Big Sandy Cr. →, Mont. **33** 48 34N 109 48W
Big Sandy Cr. →, Nebr. **34** 40 13N 97 18W
Big Sandy L. **30** 46 46N 93 17W
Big Sandy Reservoir **56** 42 15N 109 26W
Big Satilla → **18** 31 27N 82 3W
Big Sheep Mt. **33** 47 10N 105 40W
Big Sioux → **47** 42 29N 96 27W
Big Smoky Valley **35** 38 40N 117 10W
Big Snowy Mts. **33** 46 45N 109 30W
Big Southern Butte **20** 43 23N 113 1W
Big Spring, Ky. **48** 37 48N 86 9W
Big Spring, Tex. **50** 32 15N 101 28W
Big Springs **34** 41 4N 102 5W
Big Stone City **47** 45 18N 96 28W
Big Stone County ◇ **30** 45 25N 96 15W
Big Stone Gap **54** 36 52N 82 47W
Big Sur **14** 36 15N 121 48W
Big Swamp → **40** 34 28N 78 57W
Big Timber **33** 45 50N 109 57W
Big Trout L. **60** 53 40N 90 0W
Big Wells **51** 28 34N 99 34W
Big Wood → **20** 42 52N 114 54W
Bigelow, Ark. **13** 35 0N 92 38W
Bigelow, Minn. **30** 43 30N 95 42W
Bigfork, Minn. **30** 47 45N 93 39W
Bigfork, Mont. **33** 48 4N 114 4W
Biggar, Canada **63** 52 4N 108 0W
Biggar, U.K. **84** 55 38N 3 31W
Biggs, Calif. **14** 39 25N 121 43W
Biggs, Oreg. **44** 45 40N 120 50W
Biggsville **21** 40 51N 90 52W
Bighorn **33** 46 10N 107 27W
Bighorn → **33** 46 10N 107 28W
Bighorn Canyon Nat. Rec. Area **33** 45 10N 108 0W
Bighorn L. **56** 44 55N 108 15W
Bighorn Mts. **56** 44 25N 107 0W
Bighorn National Forest **56** 44 50N 107 25W
Biglerville **45** 39 56N 77 15W
Bigorre **90** 43 6N 0 5 E
Bigpoint **31** 30 35N 88 29W
Bigstone L. **63** 53 42N 95 44W
Bihać **94** 44 49N 15 57 E
Bihar **109** 25 5N 85 40 E
Bihar □ **109** 25 0N 86 0 E
Bijagós, Arquipélago dos **120** 11 15N 16 10W
Bijapur, Karnataka, India **108** 16 50N 75 55 E
Bijapur, Mad. P., India **109** 18 50N 80 50 E
Bījār **106** 35 52N 47 35 E
Bijeljina **95** 44 46N 19 17 E
Bijie **115** 27 20N 105 16 E
Bijnor **108** 29 27N 78 11 E
Bijou Cr. → **16** 40 17N 104 0W
Bikaner **108** 28 2N 73 18 E
Bikin **101** 46 50N 134 20 E
Bikin → **116** 46 51N 134 2 E
Bikini Atoll **124** 12 0N 167 30 E
Bilara **108** 26 14N 73 53 E
Bilaspur **109** 22 2N 82 15 E
Bilauk Taung dan **112** 13 0N 99 0 E
Bilbao **91** 43 16N 2 56W
Bíldudalur **96** 65 41N 23 36W
Bilecik **106** 40 5N 30 5 E
Bilibino **101** 68 3N 166 20 E
Bilir **101** 65 40N 131 20 E
Bilk Creek Mts. **35** 41 50N 118 27W
Bill **56** 43 14N 105 16W
Bill Williams → **12** 34 18N 114 4W
Bill Williams Mts. **12** 35 12N 112 12W
Billerica **28** 42 34N 71 16W
Billingham **82** 54 36N 1 18W
Billings, Mo. **32** 37 4N 93 33W
Billings, Mont. **33** 45 47N 108 30W
Billings, Okla. **43** 36 32N 97 27W
Billings County ◇ **41** 47 0N 103 15W
Billiton Is = Belitung **110** 3 10 S 107 50 E
Billy Chinook, L. **44** 44 33N 121 20W
Bilma **121** 18 50N 13 30 E
Biloela **127** 24 24 S 150 31 E
Biloku **71** 1 50N 58 25W
Biloxi **31** 30 24N 88 53W
Biltine **121** 14 40N 20 50 E
Biltmore Forest **40** 35 34N 82 33W
Bima **111** 8 22 S 118 49 E
Bimbo **122** 4 15N 18 33 E
Bimini Is. **66** 25 42N 79 25W
Bin Xian **115** 35 2N 108 4 E
Bina-Etawah **108** 24 13N 78 14 E
Binalbagan **111** 10 12N 122 50 E
Bīnālūd, Kūh-e **107** 36 30N 58 30 E
Binatang **110** 2 10N 111 40 E
Binche **87** 50 26N 4 10 E
Bindura **123** 17 18 S 31 18 E
Binford **41** 47 34N 98 21W
Binger **43** 35 18N 98 21W
Bingham, Maine **26** 45 3N 69 53W
Bingham, N. Mex. **38** 33 55N 106 21W
Bingham, Nebr. **34** 42 1N 102 5W
Bingham Canyon **52** 40 32N 112 9W
Bingham County ◇ **20** 43 15N 112 30W
Binghamton **39** 42 6N 75 55W
Bingöl **106** 38 53N 40 29 E
Binh Dinh = An Nhon **112** 13 55N 109 7 E
Binh Son **112** 15 20N 108 40 E
Binjai **110** 3 20N 98 30 E
Binongko **111** 5 55 S 123 55 E
Binscarth **63** 50 37N 101 17W
Bint Jubayl **104** 33 8N 35 25 E
Bintan **110** 1 0N 104 0 E
Bintulu **110** 3 10N 113 0 E
Bintuni **111** 2 7 S 133 32 E
Binyamina **104** 32 32N 34 56 E
Binyang **115** 23 12N 108 47 E
Binzert = Bizerte **120** 37 15N 9 50 E
Bío Bío □ **76** 37 35 S 72 0W
Bioko **122** 3 30N 8 40 E
Biola **15** 36 48N 120 1W
Biq'at Bet Netofa **104** 32 49N 35 22 E
Bir **108** 19 0N 75 54 E
Bir Autrun **121** 18 15N 26 40 E
Bir Mogrein **120** 25 10N 11 25W
Bi'r Nabālā **104** 31 52N 35 12 E
Bîr Ungât **121** 22 8N 33 48 E
Bi'r Zayt **104** 31 59N 35 11 E
Bira **111** 2 3 S 132 2 E
Birak Sulaymān **104** 31 42N 35 7 E
Birao **121** 10 20N 22 47 E
Bîrca **95** 43 59N 23 36 E
Birch → **20** 43 51N 112 43W
Birch Hills **63** 52 59N 105 25W
Birch I. **63** 52 26N 99 54W
Birch L., N.W.T., Canada **62** 62 4N 116 33W
Birch L., Ont., Canada **60** 51 23N 92 18W
Birch L., U.S.A. **30** 47 45N 91 51W
Birch Mts. **62** 57 30N 113 10W
Birch Res. **43** 36 30N 96 27W
Birch River **63** 52 24N 101 6W
Birch Run **29** 43 15N 83 48W
Birch Tree **32** 36 59N 91 30W
Birchwood **55** 45 40N 91 33W
Bird **63** 56 30N 94 13W
Bird City **24** 39 45N 101 32W
Bird I. = Aves, I. de **67** 15 45N 63 55W
Bird I. **127** 22 10 S 155 28 E
Bird Island **30** 44 46N 94 54W
Birdlip **83** 51 50N 2 7W
Birds **21** 38 50N 87 40W
Birdseye **22** 38 19N 86 42W
Birdsville, Australia **127** 25 51 S 139 20 E
Birdsville, U.S.A. **27** 38 54N 76 36W
Birdum **126** 15 39 S 133 13 E
Birecik **106** 37 0N 38 0 E
Bireuen **110** 5 14N 96 39 E
Birigui **77** 21 18 S 50 16W
Birkenhead **82** 53 24N 3 1W
Bîrlad **89** 46 15N 27 38 E
Birmingham, U.K. **83** 52 30N 1 55W
Birmingham, Ala. **10** 33 31N 86 48W
Birmingham, Iowa **23** 40 53N 91 57W
Birmingham, Mich. **29** 42 33N 83 13W
Birmitrapur **109** 22 24N 84 46 E
Birnamwood **55** 44 56N 89 13W
Birni Nkonni **120** 13 55N 5 15 E
Birnin Kebbi **120** 12 32N 4 12 E
Birobidzhan **101** 48 50N 132 50 E
Birqīn **104** 32 27N 35 15 E
Birr **85** 53 7N 7 55W
Birsk **98** 55 25N 55 30 E
Birtle **63** 50 30N 101 5W
Birur **108** 13 30N 75 55 E
Bisa **111** 1 15 S 127 28 E
Bisbee, Ariz. **12** 31 27N 109 55W
Bisbee, N. Dak. **41** 48 37N 99 23W
Biscay **30** 44 50N 94 16W
Biscay, B. of **92** 45 0N 2 0W
Biscayne National Park **17** 25 25N 80 12W
Biscoe, Ark. **13** 34 49N 91 25W
Biscoe, N.C. **40** 35 22N 79 47W
Biscoe Bay **5** 77 0 S 152 0W
Biscoe I. **5** 66 0 S 67 0W
Biscostasing **60** 47 18N 82 9W
Biscucuy **70** 9 22N 69 59W
Bishop, Calif. **15** 37 22N 118 24W
Bishop, Ga. **18** 33 49N 83 26W
Bishop, Tex. **50** 27 35N 97 48W
Bishop Auckland **82** 54 40N 1 40W
Bishop Creek Reservoir **35** 41 15N 114 55W
Bishop's Falls **61** 49 2N 55 30W
Bishops Head **27** 38 16N 76 5W
Bishop's Stortford **83** 51 52N 0 11 E
Bishopville, Md. **27** 38 22N 75 12W
Bishopville, S.C. **46** 34 13N 80 15W
Biskra **120** 34 50N 5 44 E
Bislig **111** 8 15N 126 27 E
Bismarck, Ark. **13** 34 19N 93 10W
Bismarck, Ill. **21** 40 16N 87 37W
Bismarck, Mo. **32** 37 46N 90 38W
Bismarck, N. Dak. **41** 46 48N 100 47W
Bismarck Arch. **124** 2 30 S 150 0 E
Bison, Kans. **24** 38 31N 99 12W
Bison, Okla. **43** 36 12N 97 53W
Bison, S. Dak. **47** 45 31N 102 28W
Bispfors **96** 63 1N 16 37 E
Bissagos = Bijagós, Arquipélago dos **120** 11 15N 16 10W
Bissau **120** 11 45N 15 45W
Bissett **63** 51 2N 95 41W
Bistcho L. **62** 59 45N 118 50W
Bistineau, L. **25** 32 20N 93 25W
Bistreţu **95** 43 54N 23 23 E
Bistriţa **89** 47 9N 24 35 E
Bistriţa → **89** 46 30N 26 57 E
Bitam **122** 2 5N 11 25 E
Bitely **29** 43 45N 85 52W
Bithlo **17** 28 33N 81 6W
Bitkine **121** 11 59N 18 13 E
Bitlis **106** 38 20N 42 3 E
Bitola **95** 41 5N 21 10 E
Bitolj = Bitola **95** 41 5N 21 10 E
Bitter Cr. →, Utah **52** 39 59N 109 19W
Bitter Cr. →, Wyo. **56** 41 31N 109 27W
Bitter Creek **56** 41 33N 108 33W
Bitter L. = Buheirat-Murrat-el-Kubra **121** 30 15N 32 40 E
Bitter L. **47** 45 17N 97 19W
Bitterfontein **123** 31 0 S 18 32 E
Bitterroot → **33** 46 52N 114 7W
Bitterroot National Forest **20** 45 40N 114 30W
Bitterroot Range **20** 46 0N 114 20W
Bittinger **27** 39 37N 79 14W
Biu **121** 10 40N 12 3 E
Biwa-Ko **117** 35 15N 136 10 E
Biwabik **30** 47 32N 92 21W
Bixby, Mo. **32** 37 40N 91 7W
Bixby, Okla. **43** 35 57N 95 53W
Biyang **115** 32 38N 113 21 E
Biysk **100** 52 40N 85 0 E
Bizen **117** 34 43N 134 8 E
Bizerte **120** 37 15N 9 50 E
Bjargtangar **96** 65 30N 24 30W

Bjelovar Bojnūrd

Bjelovar 94 45 56N 16 49 E
Bjørnøya 4 74 30N 19 0 E
Black → = Da → 112 21 15N 105 20 E
Black →, Alaska 11 66 42N 144 42W
Black →, Ariz. 12 33 44N 110 13W
Black →, Ark. 13 35 38N 91 20W
Black →, La. 25 31 16N 91 50W
Black →, N.C. 40 34 35N 78 16W
Black →, N.Y. 39 43 59N 76 4W
Black →, S.C. 46 33 24N 79 15W
Black →, Wis. 55 43 57N 91 22W
Black →, Caledonia, Vt. 36 44 55N 72 13W
Black →, Mich. 29 45 39N 84 31W
Black →, Mich. 29 42 59N 82 27W
Black →, Windsor, Vt. 36 43 16N 72 27W
Black Bear Cr. → 43 36 25N 96 38W
Black Butte Reservoir 14 39 49N 122 20W
Black Canyon City 12 34 3N 112 5W
Black Canyon of the Gunnison National Monument 16 38 40N 107 35W
Black Cr. →, Ariz. 12 35 16N 109 14W
Black Cr. →, Miss. 31 30 39N 88 39W
Black Creek 55 44 29N 88 27W
Black Diamond, Canada 62 50 45N 114 14W
Black Diamond, U.S.A. 53 47 19N 122 0W
Black Earth 55 43 8N 89 45W
Black Forest = Schwarzwald 88 48 0N 8 0 E
Black Forest 16 39 0N 104 43W
Black Hawk 47 44 9N 103 19W
Black Hawk County ◇ 23 42 25N 92 20W
Black Hills 47 44 0N 103 45W
Black Hills National Forest 47 44 10N 103 50W
Black I. 63 51 12N 96 30W
Black Kettle National Grassland 43 35 45N 99 45W
Black L., Canada 63 59 12N 105 15W
Black L., Mich. 29 45 28N 84 16W
Black L., N.Y. 39 44 31N 75 36W
Black Mesa, Ariz. 12 36 30N 110 15W
Black Mesa, Okla. 43 36 58N 102 58W
Black Mt. = Mynydd Du 83 51 45N 3 45W
Black Mountain 40 35 37N 82 19W
Black Mt., Ky. 49 36 54N 82 54W
Black Mt., Oreg. 44 45 13N 119 17W
Black Mt., Tex. 50 29 38N 100 20W
Black Mts., U.K. 83 51 52N 3 5W
Black Mts., U.S.A. 12 35 30N 114 30W
Black Pine Pk. 20 42 8N 113 8W
Black Range 38 33 15N 107 50W
Black River, Jamaica 66 18 0N 77 50W
Black River, U.S.A. 39 44 1N 75 48W
Black River Falls 55 44 18N 90 51W
Black Rock, Ark. 13 36 7N 91 6W
Black Rock, N. Mex. 38 35 5N 108 47W
Black Rock Desert 35 41 10N 118 50W
Black Rock Range 35 41 20N 119 8W
Black Sea 93 43 30N 35 0 E
Black Springs 35 39 37N 119 51W
Black Squirrel Cr. → 16 38 14N 104 21W
Black Volta → 120 8 41N 1 33W
Black Warrior → 10 32 32N 87 51W
Blackall 127 24 25 S 145 45 E
Blackball 128 42 22 S 171 26 E
Blackbird 27 39 21N 75 40W
Blackburn, U.K. 82 53 44N 2 30W
Blackburn, Mo. 32 39 6N 93 29W
Blackburn, Okla. 43 36 23N 96 38W
Blackburn, Mt. 11 61 44N 143 26W
Blackduck 30 47 44N 94 33W
Blackfeet Indian Reservation 33 48 45N 113 0W
Blackfoot 20 43 11N 112 21W
Blackfoot →, Idaho 20 43 8N 112 30W
Blackfoot →, Mont. 33 46 52N 113 53W
Blackfoot River Reservoir 20 43 0N 111 43W
Blackford 48 37 27N 87 56W
Blackford County ◇ 22 40 30N 85 20W
Blackhall Mt. 56 41 2N 106 41W
Blackie 62 50 36N 113 37W
Blackman 17 30 56N 86 38W
Blackpool 82 53 48N 3 3W
Blacks Fork → 56 41 25N 109 37W
Blacks Harbour 61 45 3N 66 49W
Blacksburg, S.C. 46 35 7N 81 31W
Blacksburg, Va. 54 37 14N 80 25W
Blackshear 18 31 18N 82 14W
Blackshear L. 18 31 51N 83 56W
Blacksod B. 85 54 6N 10 0W
Blackstock 46 34 34N 81 8W
Blackstone, Mass. 28 42 1N 71 30W
Blackstone, Va. 54 37 4N 78 0W
Blackstone → 62 61 5N 122 55W
Blackstone Ra. 126 26 0 S 129 0 E
Blackville, Canada 61 46 44N 65 50W
Blackville, U.S.A. 46 33 22N 81 16W
Blackwater 32 38 59N 92 59W
Blackwater →, Ireland 85 51 55N 7 50W
Blackwater →, U.K. 85 54 31N 6 35W
Blackwater →, Fla. 17 30 36N 87 2W
Blackwater →, Md. 27 38 21N 76 1W
Blackwater →, Tex. 50 33 40N 100 47W
Blackwell, Okla. 43 36 48N 97 17W
Blackwell, Tex. 50 32 5N 100 19W
Blackwood 37 39 48N 75 4W
Bladen 34 40 19N 98 36W
Bladen County ◇ 40 34 30N 78 30W
Bladenboro 40 34 33N 78 48W
Bladsell 39 42 48N 78 50W
Blaenau Ffestiniog 82 53 0N 3 57W
Blagodarnoye 99 45 7N 43 37 E
Blagoveshchensk 101 50 20N 127 30 E
Blain 45 40 20N 77 31W
Blaine, Minn. 30 45 10N 93 13W
Blaine, Wash. 53 48 59N 122 45W
Blaine County ◇, Idaho 20 43 30N 114 0W
Blaine County ◇, Mont. 33 48 20N 109 0W
Blaine County ◇, Nebr. 34 42 0N 100 0W
Blaine County ◇, Okla. 43 35 50N 98 25W
Blaine Lake 63 52 51N 106 52W
Blair, Nebr. 34 41 33N 96 8W
Blair, Okla. 43 34 47N 99 20W
Blair, Wis. 55 44 18N 91 14W
Blair Athol 127 22 42 S 147 31 E
Blair Atholl 84 56 46N 3 50W
Blair County ◇ 45 40 30N 78 20W
Blairgowrie 84 56 36N 3 20W
Blairmore 62 49 40N 114 25W
Blairs 54 36 41N 79 23W
Blairsburg 23 42 29N 93 39W
Blairsden 14 39 47N 120 37W
Blairstown, Iowa 23 41 55N 92 5W
Blairstown, Mo. 32 38 34N 93 58W
Blairstown, N.J. 37 40 59N 74 57W
Blairsville, Ga. 18 34 53N 83 58W
Blairsville, Pa. 45 40 26N 79 16W
Blaj 95 46 10N 23 57 E
Blake Pt. 29 48 11N 88 25W
Blakely, Ga. 18 31 23N 84 56W
Blakely, Pa. 45 41 28N 75 37W
Blakeman 24 39 49N 101 7W
Blakesburg 23 40 58N 92 38W
Blakeslee 42 41 32N 84 44W
Blalock 44 45 42N 120 22W
Blanc, Mont 90 45 48N 6 50 E
Blanca 16 37 27N 105 31W
Blanca, Bahía 78 39 10 S 61 30W
Blanca, Sierra 50 31 15N 105 26W
Blanca Peak 16 37 35N 105 29W
Blanchard, Idaho 20 48 1N 116 59W
Blanchard, Iowa 23 40 35N 95 13W
Blanchard, N. Dak. 41 47 21N 97 13W
Blanchard, Okla. 43 35 8N 97 39W
Blanchard, Wash. 53 48 36N 122 25W
Blanchard → 42 41 2N 84 18W
Blanchardville 55 42 49N 89 52W
Blanche L., S. Austral., Australia 127 29 15 S 139 40 E
Blanche L., W. Austral., Australia 126 22 25 S 123 17 E
Blanchester 42 39 17N 83 59W
Blanco, N. Mex. 38 36 43N 107 50W
Blanco, Okla. 43 34 45N 95 46W
Blanco, Tex. 51 30 6N 98 25W
Blanco →, Argentina 76 30 20 S 68 42W
Blanco →, U.S.A. 51 29 51N 97 55W
Blanco, C., U.S.A. 44 42 51N 124 34W
Blanco, C., C. Rica 66 9 34N 85 8W
Blanco County ◇ 51 30 17N 98 25W
Bland, Mo. 32 38 18N 91 38W
Bland, Va. 54 37 6N 81 7W
Bland County ◇ 54 37 6N 81 7W
Blanda → 96 65 20N 19 40W
Blandford 28 42 11N 72 56W
Blandford Forum 83 50 52N 2 10W
Blanding 52 37 37N 109 29W
Blandinsville 21 40 33N 90 52W
Blaney Park 29 46 9N 85 55W
Blankenberge 87 51 20N 3 9 E
Blanket 51 31 49N 98 47W
Blanquilla, La 71 11 51N 64 37W
Blanquillo 77 32 53 S 55 37W
Blantyre 123 15 45 S 35 0 E
Blarney 85 51 57N 8 35W
Blatnitsa 95 43 41N 28 32 E
Blåvands Huk 97 55 33N 8 4 E
Blaydon 82 54 56N 1 47W
Blaze, Pt. 126 12 56 S 130 11 E
Bleckley County ◇ 18 32 25N 83 15W
Blednaya, Gora 100 76 20N 65 0 E
Bledsoe 50 33 38N 103 1W
Bledsoe County ◇ 49 35 36N 85 11W
Bleiburg 88 46 35N 14 49 E
Blejeşti 95 44 19N 25 27 E
Blekinge län □ 97 56 20N 15 20 E
Blencoe 23 41 56N 96 5W
Blenheim 128 41 38 S 173 57 E
Bletchley 83 51 59N 0 44W
Blewett Falls L. 40 35 3N 79 54W
Blida 120 36 30N 2 49 E
Bligh Sound 128 44 47 S 167 32 E
Blind River 60 46 10N 82 58W
Bliss 20 42 56N 114 57W
Blissfield, Mich. 29 41 50N 83 52W
Blissfield, Ohio 42 40 24N 81 58W
Blitar 111 8 5 S 112 11 E
Blitchton 18 32 12N 81 26W
Blitta 120 8 23N 1 6 E
Block I. 28 41 11N 71 35W
Block Island Sd. 28 41 15N 71 40W
Blocker 43 35 4N 95 34W
Blockton 23 40 37N 94 29W
Blodgett 32 37 0N 89 32W
Blodgett Iceberg Tongue 5 66 8 S 130 35 E
Bloemfontein 123 29 6 S 26 14 E
Bloemhof 123 27 38 S 25 32 E
Blois 90 47 35N 1 20 E
Blönduós 96 65 40N 20 12W
Bloodsworth I. 27 38 10N 76 3W
Bloodvein → 63 51 47N 96 43W
Bloody Foreland 85 55 10N 8 18W
Bloomer 55 45 6N 91 29W
Bloomfield, Ind. 22 39 1N 86 57W
Bloomfield, Iowa 23 40 45N 92 25W
Bloomfield, Ky. 49 37 55N 85 19W
Bloomfield, Mo. 32 36 53N 89 56W
Bloomfield, N.J. 37 40 48N 74 12W
Bloomfield, N. Mex. 38 36 43N 107 59W
Bloomfield, Nebr. 34 42 36N 97 39W
Blooming Grove 51 32 6N 96 43W
Blooming Prairie 30 43 52N 93 3W
Bloomingburg 42 39 36N 83 24W
Bloomingdale 49 36 34N 82 32W
Bloomington, Idaho 20 42 11N 111 24W
Bloomington, Ill. 21 40 28N 89 0W
Bloomington, Ind. 22 39 10N 86 32W
Bloomington, Minn. 30 44 50N 93 17W
Bloomington, Tex. 51 28 39N 96 54W
Bloomington, Wis. 55 42 53N 90 55W
Bloomsburg 45 41 0N 76 27W
Bloomsdale 32 38 1N 90 13W
Bloomville 42 41 3N 83 1W
Blora 111 6 57 S 111 25 E
Blossburg 45 41 41N 77 4W
Blossom 51 33 40N 95 23W
Blount County ◇, Ala. 10 33 57N 86 28W
Blount County ◇, Tenn. 49 35 46N 83 58W
Blountstown 17 30 27N 85 3W
Blountsville 10 34 5N 86 35W
Blountville 49 36 32N 82 19W
Bloxom 54 37 50N 75 38W
Blue → 22 38 11N 86 19W
Blue Cypress L. 17 27 44N 80 45W
Blue Diamond 35 36 3N 115 24W
Blue Earth 30 43 38N 94 6W
Blue Earth County ◇ 30 44 5N 94 0W
Blue Eye 32 36 30N 93 24W
Blue Hill, Maine 26 44 25N 68 35W
Blue Hill, Nebr. 34 40 20N 98 27W
Blue Knob 45 40 17N 78 34W
Blue Lake 14 40 53N 123 59W
Blue Mesa Reservoir 16 38 28N 107 20W
Blue Mound, Ill. 21 39 42N 89 7W
Blue Mound, Kans. 24 38 5N 95 0W
Blue Mountain, Colo. 16 40 15N 108 52W
Blue Mountain, Miss. 31 34 40N 89 2W
Blue Mountain L. 13 35 2N 93 53W
Blue Mts. 127 33 40 S 150 0 E
Blue Mt., Ark. 13 34 41N 94 3W
Blue Mt., N.H. 36 44 47N 71 28W
Blue Mt., Pa. 45 40 30N 76 20W
Blue Mts., Maine 26 44 50N 70 35W
Blue Mts., Oreg. 44 45 0N 118 20W
Blue Mud B. 127 13 30 S 136 0 E
Blue Nile = An Nîl el Azraq □ 121 12 30N 34 30 E
Blue Nile = Nîl el Azraq → 121 15 38N 32 31 E
Blue Rapids 24 39 41N 96 39W
Blue Ridge, Ga. 18 34 52N 84 20W
Blue Ridge, Va. 54 36 40N 80 50W
Blue Ridge L. 18 34 53N 84 17W
Blue River, Oreg. 44 44 9N 122 20W
Blue River, Wis. 55 43 11N 90 34W
Blue Springs, Mo. 32 39 1N 94 17W
Blue Springs, Nebr. 34 40 9N 96 40W
Blue Stack Mts. 85 54 46N 8 5W
Blueberry 55 46 35N 91 55W
Blueberry → 62 56 45N 120 49W
Bluefield, Va. 54 37 15N 81 17W
Bluefield, W. Va. 54 37 16N 81 13W
Bluefields 66 12 20N 83 50W
Bluejacket 43 36 48N 95 4W
Bluejoint L. 44 42 42N 119 38W
Bluestone L. 54 37 38N 80 53W
Bluewater 38 35 15N 107 59W
Bluff, N.Z. 128 46 37 S 168 20 E
Bluff, U.S.A. 52 37 17N 109 33W
Bluff City, Ark. 13 33 43N 93 8W
Bluff City, Kans. 24 37 5N 97 53W
Bluff City, Tenn. 49 36 28N 82 16W
Bluff Park 10 33 27N 86 47W
Bluffs 21 39 45N 90 32W
Bluffton, Ark. 13 34 54N 93 36W
Bluffton, Ga. 18 31 31N 84 52W
Bluffton, Ind. 22 40 44N 85 11W
Bluffton, Minn. 30 46 28N 95 14W
Bluffton, Ohio 42 40 54N 83 54W
Bluffton, S.C. 46 32 14N 80 52W
Bluford 21 38 20N 88 45W
Blumenau 77 27 0 S 49 0W
Blunt 47 44 31N 99 59W
Bly 44 42 24N 121 3W
Blyn 53 48 1N 123 0W
Blyth 82 55 8N 1 32W
Blythe, Calif. 15 33 37N 114 36W
Blythe, Ga. 18 33 17N 82 12W
Blytheville 13 35 56N 89 55W
Blythewood 46 34 13N 80 58W
Bo 120 7 55N 11 50W
Bo Duc 112 11 58N 106 50 E
Bo Hai 114 39 0N 120 0 E
Bo Xian 115 33 50N 115 45 E
Boa Esperança 71 3 21N 61 23W
Boa Nova 75 14 22 S 40 10W
Boa Viagem 74 5 7 S 39 44W
Boa Vista 71 2 48N 60 30W
Boaco 66 12 29N 85 35W
Boardman, Ohio 42 41 2N 80 40W
Boardman, Oreg. 44 45 51N 119 43W
Boaz, Ala. 10 34 12N 86 10W
Boaz, Wis. 55 43 20N 90 32W
Bobai 115 22 17N 109 59 E
Bobbili 109 18 35N 83 30 E
Bobcaygeon 60 44 33N 78 33W
Bobo-Dioulasso 120 11 8N 4 13W
Boboc 95 45 13N 26 59 E
Bobonaza → 70 2 36 S 76 38W
Bóbr → 88 52 4N 15 4 E
Bobraomby, Tanjon' i 123 12 40 S 49 10 E
Bobruysk 98 53 10N 29 15 E
Bobtown 45 39 46N 79 59W
Bobures 70 9 15N 71 11W
Boca de Drago 71 11 0N 61 50W
Boca de Uracoa 70 9 8N 62 20W
Bôca do Acre 72 8 50 S 67 27W
Bôca do Jari 71 1 7 S 51 58W
Bôca do Moaco 72 7 41 S 68 17W
Boca Grande, U.S.A. 17 26 45N 82 16W
Boca Grande, Venezuela 71 8 40N 60 40W
Boca Raton 17 26 21N 80 5W
Bocaiúva 75 17 7 S 43 49W
Bocanda 120 7 5N 4 31W
Bocaranga 122 7 0N 15 35 E
Bocas del Toro 66 9 15N 82 20W
Bocholt 88 51 50N 6 35 E
Bochum 88 51 28N 7 12 E
Bock 30 45 47N 93 33W
Boconó 70 9 15N 70 16W
Boconó → 70 8 43N 69 34W
Bocoyna 64 27 52N 107 35W
Boda 122 4 19N 17 26 E
Bodaybo 101 57 50N 114 0 E
Bodcaw 13 33 33N 93 25W
Bode 23 42 52N 94 17W
Bodega Bay 14 38 20N 123 3W
Boden 96 65 50N 21 42 E
Bodensee 88 47 35N 9 25 E
Bodhan 108 18 40N 77 44 E
Bodmin 83 50 28N 4 44W
Bodmin Moor 83 50 33N 4 36W
Bodoquena, Serra da 73 21 0 S 56 50W
Bodrog → 89 48 15N 21 35 E
Bodrum 106 37 5N 27 30 E
Boelus 34 41 5N 98 43W
Boende 122 0 24 S 21 12 E
Boerne 51 29 47N 98 44W
Boeuf → 25 30 36N 92 3W
Boffa 120 10 16N 14 3W
Bogalusa 25 30 47N 89 52W
Bogan → 127 29 59 S 146 17 E
Bogard 32 39 27N 93 32W
Bogata 51 33 28N 95 13W
Bogenfels 123 27 25 S 15 25 E
Boggeragh Mts. 85 52 2N 8 55W
Bognor Regis 83 50 47N 0 40W
Bogo 111 11 3N 124 0 E
Bogong, Mt. 127 36 47 S 147 17 E
Bogor 111 6 36 S 106 48 E
Bogorodskoye 101 52 22N 140 30 E
Bogota, Colombia 70 4 34N 74 0W
Bogota, U.S.A. 48 36 10N 89 26W
Bogotol 100 56 15N 89 50 E
Bogra 109 24 51N 89 22 E
Boguchany 101 58 40N 97 30 E
Bogué, Maurit. 120 16 45N 14 10W
Bogue, Kans. 24 39 22N 99 41W
Bogue, N.C. 40 34 42N 77 2W
Bogue Chitto 31 31 26N 90 27W
Bogue Chitto → 25 30 34N 89 50W
Bogue Hama Cr. → 31 31 10N 88 55W
Bohemian Forest = Böhmerwald 88 49 30N 12 40 E
Böhmerwald 88 49 30N 12 40 E
Bohol 111 9 50N 124 10 E
Bohol Sea 111 9 0N 124 0 E
Bohotleh 105 8 20N 46 25 E
Boi, Pta. de 77 23 55 S 45 15W
Boiaçu 71 0 27 S 61 46W
Boileau, C. 126 17 40 S 122 7 E
Boiling Springs 40 35 15N 81 40W
Boipeba, I. de 75 13 39 S 38 55W
Bois → 75 18 35 S 50 2W
Bois Blanc I. 29 45 46N 84 27W
Bois D'Arc 32 37 16N 93 30W
Bois de Sioux → 41 46 16N 96 36W
Boise 20 43 37N 116 13W
Boise → 20 43 49N 117 1W
Boise City 43 36 44N 102 31W
Boise County ◇ 20 44 0N 115 45W
Boise National Forest 20 44 5N 115 30W
Boissevain 63 49 15N 100 5W
Boistfort Pk. 53 46 29N 123 12W
Bojador C. 120 26 0N 14 30W
Bojana → 95 41 52N 19 22 E
Bojnūrd 107 37 30N 57 20 E

Boyes Hot Springs Brodhead

Boyes Hot Springs 14 38 19N 122 29W
Boykin 18 31 6N 84 41W
Boykins 54 36 35N 77 12W
Boyle, Ireland 85 53 58N 8 19W
Boyle, U.S.A. 31 33 42N 90 44W
Boyle County ◇ 49 37 35N 84 55W
Boyne → 85 53 43N 6 15W
Boyne City 29 45 13N 85 1W
Boyne Falls 29 45 10N 84 55W
Boyni Qara 107 36 20N 67 0 E
Boynton 43 35 39N 95 39W
Boynton Beach 17 26 32N 80 4W
Boyoma, Chutes 118 0 35N 25 23 E
Boys Town 34 41 16N 96 8W
Boysen Reservoir 56 43 25N 108 11W
Bozeman 33 45 41N 111 2W
Bozen = Bolzano 94 46 30N 11 20 E
Bozman 27 38 46N 76 16W
Bozoum 122 6 25N 16 35 E
Bozovici 95 44 56N 22 1 E
Brabant □ 87 50 46N 4 30 E
Brabant L. 63 55 58N 103 43W
Brač 94 43 20N 16 40 E
Bracadale, L. 84 57 20N 6 30W
Bracciano, L. di 94 42 8N 12 11 E
Bracebridge 60 45 2N 79 19W
Brach 121 27 31N 14 20 E
Bräcke 96 62 45N 15 26 E
Bracken County ◇ 49 38 40N 84 5W
Brackettville 50 29 19N 100 25W
Brad 89 46 10N 22 50 E
Braddock 41 46 34N 100 6W
Braddock Heights 27 39 25N 77 30W
Braddyville 23 40 35N 95 2W
Bradenton 17 27 30N 82 34W
Bradford, U.K. 82 53 47N 1 45W
Bradford, Ark. 13 35 25N 91 27W
Bradford, Ill. 21 41 11N 89 39W
Bradford, N.H. 36 43 17N 71 56W
Bradford, Pa. 45 41 58N 78 38W
Bradford, R.I. 28 41 24N 71 45W
Bradford, Tenn. 48 36 5N 88 49W
Bradford, Vt. 36 43 59N 72 9W
Bradford County ◇, Fla. 17 30 0N 82 15W
Bradford County ◇, Pa. 45 41 50N 76 30W
Bradford Mt. 28 41 59N 73 18W
Bradfordsville 49 37 30N 85 9W
Bradgate 23 42 48N 94 25W
Bradley, Ark. 13 33 6N 93 39W
Bradley, Calif. 15 35 52N 120 48W
Bradley, Fla. 17 27 48N 81 59W
Bradley, Ill. 21 41 9N 87 52W
Bradley, Okla. 43 34 53N 97 42W
Bradley, S. Dak. 47 45 5N 97 39W
Bradley County ◇, Ark. 13 33 27N 92 10W
Bradley County ◇, Tenn. 49 35 10N 84 53W
Bradner 42 41 20N 83 26W
Bradore Bay 61 51 27N 57 18W
Bradshaw, Australia 127 15 21 S 130 16 E
Bradshaw, Nebr. 34 40 53N 97 45W
Bradshaw, Tex. 51 32 6N 99 54W
Bradshaw, W. Va. 54 37 21N 81 48W
Brady, Mont. 33 48 2N 111 51W
Brady, Nebr. 34 41 1N 100 22W
Brady, Tex. 51 31 9N 99 20W
Brady Cr. → 51 31 8N 98 59W
Braga 91 41 35N 8 25W
Bragado 76 35 2 S 60 27W
Bragança, Brazil 74 1 0 S 47 2W
Bragança, Portugal 91 41 48N 6 50W
Bragança Paulista 77 22 55 S 46 32W
Bragg City 32 36 16N 89 55W
Braggadocio 32 36 11N 89 50W
Braggs 43 35 40N 95 12W
Braham 30 45 44N 93 10W
Brahmanbaria 109 23 58N 91 15 E
Brahmani → 109 20 39N 86 46 E
Brahmaputra → 109 24 2N 90 59 E
Brahmaur 108 32 28N 76 32 E
Braich-y-pwll 82 52 47N 4 46W
Braidwood 21 41 16N 88 13W
Brăila 89 45 19N 27 59 E
Brăila □ 95 45 5N 27 30 E
Brainard 34 41 11N 97 0W
Brainerd 30 46 22N 94 12W
Braintree, U.K. 83 51 53N 0 34 E
Braintree, U.S.A. 28 42 13N 71 0W
Bralorne 62 50 50N 123 45W
Braman 43 36 56N 97 20W
Brampton, Canada 60 43 45N 79 45W
Brampton, U.S.A. 41 46 0N 97 52W
Bramwell 54 37 20N 81 19W
Branch 13 35 18N 93 57W
Branch County ◇ 29 41 50N 85 5W
Branchland 54 38 13N 82 12W
Branchville, N.J. 37 41 9N 74 45W
Branchville, S.C. 46 33 15N 80 49W
Branco → 71 1 20 S 61 50W
Branco, Cabo 74 7 9 S 34 47W
Brandenburg, Germany 88 52 24N 12 33 E
Brandenburg, U.S.A. 48 38 0N 86 10W
Brandon, Canada 63 49 50N 99 57W
Brandon, Colo. 16 38 27N 102 26W
Brandon, Fla. 17 27 56N 82 17W
Brandon, Iowa 23 42 19N 92 0W
Brandon, Minn. 30 45 58N 95 36W
Brandon, Miss. 31 32 16N 89 59W
Brandon, Nebr. 34 40 48N 101 55W
Brandon, S. Dak. 47 43 35N 96 35W
Brandon, Vt. 36 43 48N 73 6W
Brandon, Wis. 55 43 44N 88 47W
Brandon, Mt. 85 52 15N 10 15W
Brandon B. 85 52 17N 10 8W
Brandonville 54 39 40N 79 37W
Brandreth 39 43 56N 74 51W
Brandsen 76 35 10 S 58 15W
Brandsville 32 36 39N 91 42W
Brandt 47 44 40N 96 38W
Brandvlei 123 30 25 S 20 30 E
Brandy Pk. 44 42 36N 123 53W
Brandywine, Md. 27 38 42N 76 51W
Brandywine, W. Va. 54 38 38N 79 15W
Branford, Conn. 28 41 17N 72 49W
Branford, Fla. 17 29 58N 82 56W
Braniewo 89 54 25N 19 50 E
Bransfield Str. 5 63 0 S 59 0W
Brańsk 89 52 45N 22 50 E
Branson, Colo. 16 37 1N 103 53W
Branson, Mo. 32 36 39N 93 13W
Brantford, Canada 60 43 10N 80 15W
Brantford, U.S.A. 41 47 36N 98 55W
Brantley 10 31 35N 86 16W
Brantley County ◇ 18 31 10N 82 0W
Bras d'Or, L. 61 45 50N 60 50W
Brashear 32 40 9N 92 23W
Brasher Falls 39 44 49N 74 47W
Brasil, Planalto 68 18 0 S 46 30W
Brasiléia 72 11 0 S 68 45W
Brasília 75 15 47 S 47 55 E
Brasília Legal 71 3 49 S 55 36W
Braşov 89 45 38N 25 35 E
Braşov □ 95 45 45N 25 15 E
Brasschaat 87 51 19N 4 27 E
Brassey, Banjaran 110 5 0N 117 15 E
Brasstown Bald 18 34 53N 83 49W
Brassua L. 26 45 40N 69 55W
Bratan = Morozov 95 42 30N 25 10 E
Bratislava 88 48 10N 17 7 E
Bratsigovo 95 42 1N 24 22 E
Bratsk 101 56 10N 101 30 E
Bratt 17 30 58N 87 26W
Brattleboro 36 42 51N 72 34W
Braţul Chilia → 95 45 25N 29 20 E
Bratul Sfîntu Gheorghe → 95 45 0N 29 20 E
Braţul Sulina → 95 45 10N 29 20 E
Braunschweig 88 52 17N 10 28 E
Braunton 83 51 6N 4 9W
Brava 105 1 20N 44 8 E
Brave 45 39 44N 80 16W
Bravo del Norte → 64 25 57N 97 9W
Bravo del Norte, R. → = Grande, R. → 50 25 57N 97 9W
Brawley 15 32 59N 115 31W
Brawley Peaks 35 38 15N 118 55W
Brawley Wash → 12 32 34N 111 26W
Braxton 31 32 1N 89 58W
Braxton County ◇ 54 38 43N 80 39W
Bray 85 53 12N 6 6W
Bray-sur-Seine 90 48 25N 3 14 E
Braymer 32 39 35N 93 48W
Brayton 23 41 33N 94 56W
Brazeau → 62 52 55N 115 14W
Brazil 22 39 32N 87 8W
Brazil ■ 75 10 0 S 50 0W
Brazilian Highlands = Brasil, Planalto 68 18 0 S 46 30W
Brazo Sur → 76 25 21 S 57 42W
Brazoria 51 29 3N 95 34W
Brazoria County ◇ 51 29 10N 95 26W
Brazos → 51 28 53N 95 23W
Brazos County ◇ 51 30 40N 96 22W
Brazzaville 122 4 9 S 15 12 E
Brčko 95 44 54N 18 46 E
Brea 72 4 40 S 81 7W
Breadalbane 84 56 30N 4 15W
Breaksea Sd. 128 45 35 S 166 35 E
Bream Bay 128 35 56 S 174 28 E
Bream Head 128 35 51 S 174 36 E
Breas 76 25 29 S 70 24W
Breathitt County ◇ 49 37 30N 83 20W
Breaux Bridge 25 30 16N 91 54W
Brebes 111 6 52 S 109 3 E
Brechin 84 56 44N 2 40W
Breckenridge, Colo. 16 39 29N 106 3W
Breckenridge, Mich. 29 43 24N 84 29W
Breckenridge, Minn. 30 46 16N 96 35W
Breckenridge, Mo. 32 39 46N 93 48W
Breckenridge, Tex. 51 32 45N 98 54W
Breckinridge 43 36 26N 97 44W
Breckinridge County ◇ 48 37 45N 86 25W
Brecknock, Pen. 78 54 35 S 71 30W
Brecon 83 51 57N 3 23W
Brecon Beacons 83 51 53N 3 27W
Breda, Neth. 87 51 35N 4 45 E
Breda, U.S.A. 23 42 11N 94 59W
Bredasdorp 123 34 33 S 20 2 E
Breese 21 38 37N 89 32W
Bregenz 88 47 30N 9 45 E
Breiðafjörður 96 65 15N 23 15W
Brejinho de Nazaré 74 11 1 S 48 34W
Brejo 74 3 41 S 42 47W
Bremen, Germany 88 53 4N 8 47 E
Bremen, Ala. 10 33 59N 86 58W
Bremen, Ga. 18 33 43N 85 9W
Bremen, Ind. 22 41 27N 86 9W
Bremen, Ky. 48 37 22N 87 13W
Bremen, Ohio 42 39 42N 82 26W
Bremer County ◇ 23 42 50N 92 20W
Bremerhaven 88 53 34N 8 35 E
Bremerton 53 47 34N 122 38W
Bremond 51 31 10N 96 41W
Brenham 51 30 10N 96 24W
Brenner Pass 88 47 0N 11 30 E
Brent, Canada 60 46 2N 78 29W
Brent, U.K. 83 51 33N 0 18W
Brent, U.S.A. 10 32 56N 87 10W
Brentwood, U.K. 83 51 37N 0 19 E
Brentwood, Calif. 14 37 56N 121 42W
Brentwood, N.H. 36 42 58N 71 6W
Brentwood, N.Y. 39 40 47N 73 15W
Brentwood, Tenn. 48 36 2N 86 47W
Bréscia 94 45 33N 10 13 E
Breskens 87 51 23N 3 33 E
Breslau = Wrocław 88 51 5N 17 5 E
Bressanone 94 46 43N 11 40 E
Bressay I. 84 60 10N 1 5W
Bresse, Plaine de 90 46 50N 5 10 E
Brest, France 90 48 24N 4 31W
Brest, U.S.S.R. 98 52 10N 23 40 E
Bretagne 90 48 0N 3 0W
Bretçu 89 46 7N 26 18 E
Breton 62 53 7N 114 28W
Breton I. 25 29 13N 89 12W
Breton Sd. 25 29 35N 89 15W
Brett, C. 128 35 10 S 174 20 E
Brevard 40 35 14N 82 44W
Brevard County ◇ 17 28 20N 80 45W
Breves 74 1 40 S 50 29W
Brevig Mission 11 65 20N 166 29W
Brevort 29 46 1N 85 2W
Brewer 26 44 48N 68 46W
Brewerton 39 43 14N 76 9W
Brewster, Kans. 24 39 22N 101 23W
Brewster, Mass. 28 41 46N 70 5W
Brewster, Minn. 30 43 42N 95 28W
Brewster, Nebr. 34 41 56N 99 52W
Brewster, Ohio 42 40 43N 81 36W
Brewster, Wash. 53 48 6N 119 47W
Brewster, Kap 4 70 7N 22 0W
Brewster County ◇ 50 30 0N 103 0W
Brewton, Ala. 10 31 7N 87 4W
Brewton, Ga. 18 32 36N 82 48W
Brezhnev 100 55 42N 52 19 E
Brezovo 95 42 21N 25 5 E
Bria 122 6 30N 21 58 E
Brian Head 52 37 41N 112 50W
Briançon 90 44 54N 6 39 E
Briartown 43 35 18N 95 14W
Bribie I. 127 27 0 S 152 58 E
Briceland 14 40 7N 123 54W
Bricelyn 30 43 34N 93 49W
Briceville 49 36 11N 84 11W
Brickeys 13 34 52N 90 36W
Bridge, Idaho 20 42 8N 113 20W
Bridge, Oreg. 44 43 1N 124 0W
Bridge City 51 30 1N 93 51W
Bridgeboro 18 31 24N 83 59W
Bridgend 83 51 30N 3 35W
Bridgeport, Ala. 10 34 57N 85 43W
Bridgeport, Calif. 14 38 15N 119 14W
Bridgeport, Conn. 28 41 11N 73 12W
Bridgeport, Ill. 21 38 43N 87 46W
Bridgeport, Mich. 29 43 22N 83 53W
Bridgeport, Nebr. 34 41 40N 103 6W
Bridgeport, Okla. 43 35 33N 98 23W
Bridgeport, Tex. 51 33 13N 97 45W
Bridgeport, Wash. 53 48 0N 119 40W
Bridgeport, L. 51 33 13N 97 50W
Bridger 33 45 18N 108 55W
Bridger Peak 56 41 11N 107 2W
Bridger-Teton National Forest 56 43 5N 110 5W
Bridgeton, N.C. 40 35 7N 77 1W
Bridgeton, N.J. 37 39 26N 75 14W
Bridgetown, Australia 126 33 58 S 116 7 E
Bridgetown, Barbados 67 13 0N 59 30W
Bridgetown, Canada 61 44 55N 65 18W
Bridgetown, U.S.A. 27 39 2N 75 53W
Bridgeville, Calif. 14 40 25N 123 50W
Bridgeville, Del. 27 38 45N 75 36W
Bridgewater, Canada 61 44 25N 64 31W
Bridgewater, Conn. 28 41 32N 73 22W
Bridgewater, Iowa 23 41 15N 94 40W
Bridgewater, Maine 26 46 25N 67 51W
Bridgewater, Mass. 28 41 59N 70 58W
Bridgewater, N.Y. 39 42 53N 75 15W
Bridgewater, S. Dak. 47 43 33N 97 30W
Bridgewater, Va. 54 38 23N 78 59W
Bridgewater, Vt. 36 43 35N 72 38W
Bridgewater, C. 127 38 23 S 141 23 E
Bridgman 29 41 57N 86 33W
Bridgnorth 83 52 33N 2 25W
Bridgton 26 44 3N 70 42W
Bridgwater 83 51 7N 3 0W
Bridlington 82 54 6N 0 11W
Bridport, U.K. 83 50 43N 2 45W
Bridport, U.S.A. 36 43 58N 73 20W
Brie, Plaine de la 90 48 35N 3 10 E
Brier Cr. → 18 32 44N 81 26W
Brig 88 46 18N 7 59 E
Brigantine City 37 39 24N 74 22W
Brigg 82 53 33N 0 30W
Briggsdale 16 40 38N 104 20W
Briggsville 13 34 56N 93 30W
Brigham City 52 41 31N 112 1W
Brighton, Canada 60 44 2N 77 44W
Brighton, U.K. 83 50 50N 0 9W
Brighton, Colo. 16 39 59N 104 49W
Brighton, Fla. 17 27 14N 81 6W
Brighton, Ill. 21 39 2N 90 8W
Brighton, Iowa 23 41 10N 91 49W
Brighton, Mich. 29 42 32N 83 47W
Brighton, N.Y. 39 43 8N 77 34W
Brighton, Tenn. 48 35 29N 89 43W
Brighton Indian Reservation 17 27 0N 81 15W
Brightwood 40 36 10N 79 45W
Brilliant, Canada 62 49 19N 117 38W
Brilliant, U.S.A. 10 34 1N 87 46W
Brillion 55 44 11N 88 4W
Brimfield, Ill. 21 40 50N 89 53W
Brimfield, Mass. 28 42 7N 72 12W
Brimley 29 46 24N 84 34W
Bríndisi 95 40 39N 17 55 E
Brinkley 13 34 53N 91 12W
Brinnon 53 47 41N 122 54W
Brinsmade 41 48 11N 99 19W
Brinson 18 30 59N 84 44W
Brion, Î. 61 47 46N 61 26W
Brisbane 127 27 25 S 153 2 E
Briscoe 50 35 35N 100 17W
Briscoe County ◇ 50 34 28N 101 19W
Bristol, U.K. 83 51 26N 2 35W
Bristol, Colo. 16 38 7N 102 19W
Bristol, Conn. 28 41 40N 72 57W
Bristol, Fla. 17 30 26N 84 59W
Bristol, Ind. 22 41 43N 85 49W
Bristol, Md. 27 38 47N 76 40W
Bristol, N.H. 36 43 36N 71 44W
Bristol, Pa. 45 40 6N 74 51W
Bristol, R.I. 28 41 40N 71 16W
Bristol, S. Dak. 47 45 21N 97 45W
Bristol, Tenn. 49 36 36N 82 11W
Bristol, Va. 54 36 36N 82 11W
Bristol, Vt. 36 44 8N 73 5W
Bristol Bay 11 58 0N 159 0W
Bristol Bay ◇ 11 59 0N 156 30W
Bristol Channel 83 51 18N 4 30W
Bristol County ◇, Mass. 28 41 45N 71 0W
Bristol County ◇, R.I. 28 41 40N 71 20W
Bristol I. 5 58 45 S 28 0W
Bristol L. 15 34 28N 115 41W
Bristol Mts. 15 34 30N 115 50W
Bristow, Nebr. 34 42 51N 98 35W
Bristow, Okla. 43 35 50N 96 23W
British Antarctic Territory □ 5 66 0 S 45 0W
British Columbia □ 62 55 0N 125 15W
British Guiana = Guyana ■ 71 5 0N 59 0W
British Honduras = Belize ■ 65 17 0N 88 30W
British Isles 80 55 0N 4 0W
Britstown 123 30 37 S 23 30 E
Britt, Canada 60 45 46N 80 34W
Britt, U.S.A. 23 43 6N 93 48W
Brittany = Bretagne 90 48 0N 3 0W
Britton 47 45 48N 97 45W
Brlik 100 44 0N 74 5 E
Brno 88 49 10N 16 35 E
Broad →, Ga. 18 33 59N 82 39W
Broad →, S.C. 46 34 1N 81 4W
Broad B. 84 58 14N 6 16W
Broad Haven 85 54 20N 9 55W
Broad Law 84 55 30N 3 22W
Broad Sd. 127 22 0 S 149 45 E
Broadalbin 39 43 4N 74 12W
Broadbent 44 43 1N 124 0W
Broadhurst 18 31 28N 81 55W
Broadkill Beach 27 38 47N 75 10W
Broadmoor 16 38 50N 104 50W
Broads, The 82 52 45N 1 30 E
Broadsound Ra. 127 22 50 S 149 30 E
Broadus 33 45 27N 105 25W
Broadview, Canada 63 50 22N 102 35W
Broadview, Mont. 33 46 6N 108 53W
Broadview, N. Mex. 38 34 49N 103 13W
Broadwater 34 41 36N 102 51W
Broadwater County ◇ 33 46 25N 111 30W
Broadway 54 38 37N 78 48W
Broadwell 21 40 4N 89 27W
Brochet 63 57 53N 101 40W
Brochet, L. 63 58 36N 101 35W
Brock, Canada 63 51 26N 108 43W
Brock, U.S.A. 34 40 29N 95 58W
Brocken 88 51 48N 10 40 E
Brocket 41 48 13N 98 21W
Brockport 39 43 13N 77 56W
Brockton, Mass. 28 42 5N 71 1W
Brockton, Mont. 33 48 9N 104 55W
Brockville 60 44 35N 75 41W
Brockway, Mont. 33 47 18N 105 45W
Brockway, Pa. 45 41 15N 78 47W
Brocton, Ill. 21 39 43N 87 56W
Brocton, N.Y. 39 42 23N 79 26W
Brod 95 41 35N 21 17 E
Brodeur Pen. 59 72 30N 88 10W
Brodhead, Ky. 49 37 24N 84 25W

Brodhead Bunker Hill

Brodhead, Wis. 55 42 37N 89 22W
Brodick 84 55 34N 5 9W
Brodnax 54 36 43N 78 2W
Brogan 44 44 15N 117 31W
Brokaw 55 45 2N 89 39W
Broken Arrow 43 36 3N 95 48W
Broken Bow, Nebr. 34 41 24N 99 38W
Broken Bow, Okla. 43 34 2N 94 44W
Broken Bow Lake 43 34 9N 94 40W
Broken Hill = Kabwe 123 14 30 S 28 29 E
Broken Hill 127 31 58 S 141 29 E
Brokopondo 71 5 3N 54 59W
Brokopondo □ 71 4 30N 55 30W
Bromfield 83 52 25N 2 45W
Bromide 43 34 24N 96 31W
Bromley 83 51 20N 0 5 E
Bronaugh 32 37 41N 94 28W
Brønderslev 97 57 16N 9 57 E
Bronson, Fla. 17 29 27N 82 39W
Bronson, Kans. 24 37 54N 95 4W
Bronson, Mich. 29 41 52N 85 12W
Bronson, Tex. 51 31 21N 94 1W
Bronte 50 31 53N 100 18W
Bronwood 18 31 50N 84 22W
Bronx County ◇ 39 40 50N 73 52W
Brook 22 40 52N 87 22W
Brook Park 42 41 24N 80 51W
Brooke County ◇ 54 40 16N 80 37W
Brookeland 51 31 10N 94 0W
Brookesmith 51 31 33N 99 7W
Brookfield, Mass. 28 42 13N 72 6W
Brookfield, Mo. 32 39 47N 93 4W
Brookfield, Vt. 36 44 4N 72 38W
Brookfield, Wis. 55 43 4N 88 9W
Brookhaven 31 31 35N 90 26W
Brookings, Oreg. 44 42 3N 124 17W
Brookings, S. Dak. 47 44 19N 96 48W
Brookings County ◇ 47 44 19N 96 48W
Brookland 13 35 54N 90 35W
Brooklet 18 32 23N 81 40W
Brookline, Mass. 28 42 20N 71 7W
Brookline, N.H. 36 42 44N 71 40W
Brooklyn, Ala. 10 31 16N 86 46W
Brooklyn, Conn. 28 41 47N 71 57W
Brooklyn, Ind. 22 39 32N 86 22W
Brooklyn, Iowa 23 41 44N 92 27W
Brooklyn, Mich. 29 42 7N 84 15W
Brooklyn, Miss. 31 31 3N 89 11W
Brooklyn, Wash. 53 46 47N 123 31W
Brooklyn Park, Md. 27 39 14N 76 37W
Brooklyn Park, Minn. 30 45 6N 93 23W
Brookmere 62 49 52N 120 53W
Brookneal 54 37 3N 78 57W
Brookport 21 37 8N 88 38W
Brooks, Canada 62 50 35N 111 55W
Brooks, Ky. 49 38 4N 85 43W
Brooks, Minn. 30 47 49N 96 0W
Brooks B. 62 50 15N 127 55W
Brooks County ◇, Ga. 18 30 50N 83 45W
Brooks County ◇, Tex. 50 27 0N 98 5W
Brooks L. 63 61 55N 106 35W
Brooks Range 11 68 0N 152 0W
Brookshire 51 29 47N 95 57W
Brookston, Ind. 22 40 36N 86 52W
Brookston, Minn. 30 46 52N 92 36W
Brooksville, Fla. 17 28 33N 82 23W
Brooksville, Ky. 49 38 41N 84 4W
Brooksville, Miss. 31 33 14N 88 35W
Brooksville, Okla. 43 35 12N 96 58W
Brookvale 16 39 38N 105 26W
Brookview 27 38 35N 75 48W
Brookville, Ind. 22 39 25N 85 1W
Brookville, Kans. 24 38 46N 97 52W
Brookville, N.J. 37 39 44N 74 18W
Brookville, Pa. 45 41 10N 79 5W
Brookville L. 22 39 28N 85 0W
Brookwood 10 33 17N 87 18W
Broom, L. 84 57 55N 5 15W
Broome 126 18 0 S 122 15 E
Broome County ◇ 39 42 5N 75 45W
Broomes Island 27 38 25N 76 33W
Broomfield 16 39 55N 105 5W
Brooten 30 45 30N 95 8W
Brora 84 58 0N 3 50W
Brora → 84 58 4N 3 52W
Broseley 32 36 40N 90 15W
Brosna → 85 53 8N 8 0W
Brotas de Macaúbas 75 12 0 S 42 38W
Brothers 44 43 49N 120 36W
Brotmanville 37 39 33N 75 3W
Broughton, Ill. 21 37 56N 88 27W
Broughton, Kans. 24 39 19N 97 3W
Broughton Island 59 67 33N 63 0W
Broughty Ferry 84 56 29N 2 50W
Broussard 25 30 9N 91 58W
Brouwershaven 87 51 45N 3 55 E
Broward County ◇ 17 26 15N 80 30W
Browerville 30 46 5N 94 52W
Brown City 29 43 13N 82 59W
Brown County ◇, Ill. 21 39 55N 90 45W
Brown County ◇, Ind. 22 39 10N 86 15W
Brown County ◇, Kans. 24 39 45N 95 30W
Brown County ◇, Minn. 30 44 10N 94 50W
Brown County ◇, Nebr. 34 42 30N 100 0W
Brown County ◇, Ohio 42 38 55N 83 59W
Brown County ◇, S. Dak. 47 45 37N 98 19W
Brown County ◇, Tex. 51 31 43N 98 59W
Brown County ◇, Wis. 55 44 30N 88 0W
Brown Deer 55 43 10N 87 58W
Brown Willy 83 50 35N 4 34W
Brownell 24 38 38N 99 45W
Brownfield 50 33 11N 102 17W
Browning, Ill. 21 40 8N 90 22W
Browning, Mont. 33 48 34N 113 1W
Brownlee, Canada 63 50 43N 106 1W
Brownlee, U.S.A. 34 42 17N 100 37W
Brownlee Reservoir 20 44 50N 116 54W
Browns 21 38 23N 87 59W
Browns Mills 37 39 58N 74 34W
Browns Valley 30 45 36N 96 50W
Brownsburg 22 39 51N 86 24W
Brownsdale 30 43 45N 92 52W
Brownstown, Ill. 21 39 0N 88 57W
Brownstown, Ind. 22 38 53N 86 3W
Brownsville, Ky. 48 37 12N 86 16W
Brownsville, La. 25 32 29N 92 9W
Brownsville, Minn. 30 43 42N 91 17W
Brownsville, Oreg. 44 44 24N 122 59W
Brownsville, Pa. 45 40 1N 79 53W
Brownsville, Tenn. 48 35 36N 89 16W
Brownsville, Tex. 50 25 54N 97 30W
Brownsweg 71 5 5N 55 15W
Browntown 55 42 35N 89 48W
Brownville, Ala. 10 33 24N 87 52W
Brownville, Maine 26 45 18N 69 2W
Brownville, N.Y. 39 44 0N 75 59W
Brownville, Nebr. 34 40 24N 95 40W
Brownville Junction 26 45 21N 69 3W
Brownwood, Mo. 32 37 5N 89 57W
Brownwood, Tex. 51 31 43N 98 59W
Brownwood, L. 51 31 50N 99 0W
Broxton 18 31 38N 82 53W
Bruas 112 4 31N 100 46 E
Bruce, Fla. 17 30 28N 85 58W
Bruce, Miss. 31 33 59N 89 21W
Bruce, S. Dak. 47 44 26N 96 54W
Bruce, Wis. 55 45 28N 91 16W
Bruce, Mt. 126 22 37 S 118 8 E
Bruceton 48 36 3N 88 15W
Bruceton Mills 54 39 40N 79 38W
Bruceville, Ind. 22 38 46N 87 25W
Bruceville, Md. 27 38 40N 75 59W
Bruck an der Leitha 88 48 1N 16 47 E
Brue → 83 51 10N 2 59W
Bruges = Brugge 87 51 13N 3 13 E
Brugge 87 51 13N 3 13 E
Bruin Pt. 52 39 39N 110 21W
Brûlé, Canada 62 53 15N 117 58W
Brule, U.S.A. 34 41 6N 101 53W
Brule → 55 45 57N 88 12W
Brule County ◇ 47 43 45N 99 0W
Brule L. 30 46 58N 90 50W
Brumado 75 14 14 S 41 40W
Brumado → 75 14 13 S 41 40W
Brumley 32 38 5N 92 29W
Brundidge 10 31 43N 85 49W
Bruneau 20 42 53N 115 48W
Bruneau → 20 42 56N 115 57W
Brunei = Bandar Seri Begawan 110 4 52N 115 0 E
Brunei ■ 110 4 50N 115 0 E
Bruning 34 40 20N 97 34W
Brunner, L. 128 42 37 S 171 27 E
Bruno, Canada 63 52 20N 105 30W
Bruno, Minn. 30 46 17N 92 40W
Bruno, Nebr. 34 41 17N 96 58W
Brunsbüttelkoog 88 53 52N 9 13 E
Brunsville 23 42 49N 96 16W
Brunswick = Braunschweig 88 52 17N 10 28 E
Brunswick, Ga. 18 31 10N 81 30W
Brunswick, Maine 26 43 55N 69 58W
Brunswick, Md. 27 39 19N 77 38W
Brunswick, Mo. 32 39 26N 93 8W
Brunswick, Nebr. 34 42 20N 97 58W
Brunswick, Ohio 42 41 14N 81 51W
Brunswick, Pen. de 78 53 30 S 71 30W
Brunswick B. 126 15 15 S 124 50 E
Brunswick County ◇, N.C. 40 34 0N 78 20W
Brunswick County ◇, Va. 54 36 46N 77 51W
Bruny I. 127 43 20 S 147 15 E
Brus Laguna 66 15 47N 84 35W
Brush 16 40 15N 103 37W
Brush Creek 48 36 7N 86 2W
Brushton 39 44 50N 74 31W
Brusly 25 30 23N 91 14W
Brusque 77 27 5 S 49 0W
Brussel 87 50 51N 4 21 E
Brussels = Bruxelles 87 50 51N 4 21 E
Brussels 55 44 44N 87 37W
Bruxelles 87 50 51N 4 21 E
Bryagovo 95 41 58N 25 8 E
Bryan, Ohio 42 41 28N 84 33W
Bryan, Tex. 51 30 40N 96 22W
Bryan County ◇, Ga. 18 32 0N 81 30W
Bryan County ◇, Okla. 43 34 0N 96 15W
Bryans Road 27 38 38N 77 4W
Bryansk 98 53 13N 34 25 E
Bryant, Ark. 13 34 36N 92 29W
Bryant, Ind. 22 40 32N 84 58W
Bryant, S. Dak. 47 44 35N 97 28W
Bryant Cr. → 32 36 36N 92 17W
Bryantown 27 38 36N 76 52W
Bryce Canyon National Park 52 37 30N 112 10W
Bryne 97 58 44N 5 38 E
Bryson 51 33 10N 98 23W
Bryson City 40 35 26N 83 27W
Bu Craa 120 26 45N 12 50W
Bua Yai 112 15 33N 102 26 E
Buabuq 121 31 29N 25 29 E
Buapinang 111 4 40 S 121 30 E
Buayan 111 6 3N 125 6 E
Bucak 106 37 28N 30 36 E
Bucaramanga 70 7 0N 73 0W
Buchan 84 57 32N 2 8W
Buchan Ness 84 57 29N 1 48W
Buchanan, Canada 63 51 40N 102 45W
Buchanan, Liberia 120 5 57N 10 2W
Buchanan, Ga. 18 33 48N 85 11W
Buchanan, Mich. 29 41 50N 86 22W
Buchanan, N. Dak. 41 47 4N 98 50W
Buchanan, Va. 54 37 32N 79 41W
Buchanan, L., Australia 126 25 33 S 123 2 E
Buchanan, L., U.S.A. 51 30 45N 98 25W
Buchanan County ◇, Iowa 23 42 30N 91 50W
Buchanan County ◇, Mo. 32 39 40N 94 50W
Buchanan County ◇, Va. 54 37 17N 82 6W
Buchanan Dam 51 30 45N 98 25W
Buchans 61 48 50N 56 52W
Bucharest = Bucureşti 89 44 27N 26 10 E
Buchon, Pt. 15 35 15N 120 54W
Buck Grove 23 41 55N 95 23W
Buck I. 57 17 46N 64 37W
Buckatunna 31 31 32N 88 32W
Buckeye, Ariz. 12 33 22N 112 35W
Buckeye, Iowa 23 42 25N 93 23W
Buckeystown 27 39 20N 77 26W
Buckfield 26 44 17N 70 22W
Buckhannon 54 39 0N 80 8W
Buckhaven 84 56 10N 3 2W
Buckholts 51 30 52N 97 7W
Buckhorn, Ky. 49 37 21N 83 28W
Buckhorn, N. Mex. 38 33 2N 108 42W
Buckhorn L. 49 37 21N 83 28W
Buckie 84 57 40N 2 58W
Buckingham, Canada 60 45 37N 75 24W
Buckingham, U.K. 83 52 0N 0 59W
Buckingham, Colo. 16 40 37N 103 58W
Buckingham, Va. 54 37 33N 78 33W
Buckingham □ 83 51 50N 0 55W
Buckingham B. 127 12 10 S 135 40 E
Buckingham County ◇ 54 37 40N 78 40W
Buckland, Alaska 11 65 59N 161 8W
Buckland, Ohio 42 40 37N 84 16W
Buckland Newton 83 50 45N 2 25W
Buckley, Ill. 21 40 36N 88 2W
Buckley, Mich. 29 44 30N 85 41W
Buckley, Wash. 53 47 10N 122 2W
Bucklin, Kans. 24 37 33N 99 38W
Bucklin, Mo. 32 39 47N 92 53W
Buckman 30 45 54N 94 6W
Bucks County ◇ 45 40 15N 75 10W
Bucks L. 14 39 54N 121 12W
Bucksport 26 44 34N 68 47W
Bucktown 27 38 25N 76 3W
Bucoda 53 46 48N 122 52W
Buctouche 61 46 30N 64 45W
Bucureşti 89 44 27N 26 10 E
Bucyrus, Kans. 24 38 44N 94 44W
Bucyrus, N. Dak. 41 46 4N 102 47W
Bucyrus, Ohio 42 40 48N 82 59W
Buda, Ill. 21 41 20N 89 41W
Buda, Tex. 51 30 5N 97 51W
Budalin 109 22 20N 95 10 E
Budapest 89 47 29N 19 5 E
Budaun 108 28 5N 79 10 E
Budd Coast 5 68 0 S 112 0 E
Budd Lake 37 40 52N 74 44W
Budds Creek 27 38 23N 76 51W
Bude, U.K. 83 50 49N 4 33W
Bude, U.S.A. 31 31 28N 90 51W
Budeşti 95 44 13N 26 30 E
Búðareyri 96 65 2N 14 13W
Búðir 96 64 49N 23 23W
Budjala 122 2 50N 19 40 E
Buechel 49 38 12N 85 39W
Buena 37 39 31N 74 56W
Buena Vista, Bolivia 73 17 27 S 63 40W
Buena Vista, Colo. 16 38 51N 106 8W
Buena Vista, Ga. 18 32 19N 84 31W
Buena Vista, Va. 54 37 44N 79 21W
Buena Vista County ◇ 23 42 45N 95 10W
Buena Vista L. 15 35 12N 119 18W
Buenaventura, Colombia 70 3 53N 77 4W
Buenaventura, Mexico 64 29 50N 107 30W
Buenaventura, B. de 70 3 48N 77 17W
Buenópolis 75 17 54 S 44 11W
Buenos Aires, Argentina 76 34 30 S 58 20W
Buenos Aires, Colombia 70 1 36N 73 18W
Buenos Aires, C. Rica 66 9 10N 83 20W
Buenos Aires □ 76 36 30 S 60 0W
Buenos Aires, Lago 78 46 35 S 72 30W
Buesaco 70 1 23N 77 9W
Buffalo, Kans. 24 37 42N 95 42W
Buffalo, Minn. 30 45 10N 93 53W
Buffalo, Mo. 32 37 39N 93 6W
Buffalo, N. Dak. 41 46 55N 97 33W
Buffalo, N.Y. 39 42 53N 78 53W
Buffalo, Okla. 43 36 50N 99 38W
Buffalo, S.C. 46 34 43N 81 41W
Buffalo, S. Dak. 47 45 35N 103 33W
Buffalo, Tex. 51 31 28N 96 4W
Buffalo, W. Va. 54 38 37N 81 59W
Buffalo, Wyo. 56 44 21N 106 42W
Buffalo →, Canada 62 60 5N 115 5W
Buffalo →, Ark. 13 36 10N 92 26W
Buffalo →, Minn. 30 47 6N 96 49W
Buffalo →, Tenn. 48 36 0N 87 50W
Buffalo Bill Reservoir 56 44 30N 109 11W
Buffalo Center 23 43 23N 93 57W
Buffalo County ◇, Nebr. 34 40 50N 99 0W
Buffalo County ◇, S. Dak. 47 44 0N 99 5W
Buffalo County ◇, Wis. 55 44 20N 91 50W
Buffalo Cr. →, Okla. 43 36 47N 99 15W
Buffalo Cr. →, Wyo. 56 43 40N 106 30W
Buffalo Creek 16 39 23N 105 17W
Buffalo Gap, S. Dak. 47 43 30N 103 19W
Buffalo Gap, Tex. 51 32 17N 99 50W
Buffalo Head Hills 62 57 25N 115 55W
Buffalo L., Canada 62 52 27N 112 54W
Buffalo L., Tex. 50 34 52N 102 12W
Buffalo L., Wis. 55 43 47N 89 25W
Buffalo Narrows 63 55 51N 108 29W
Buffalo River National Park 13 36 14N 92 36W
Buford 41 48 0N 103 59W
Bug →, Poland 99 52 31N 21 5 E
Bug →, U.S.S.R. 99 46 59N 31 58 E
Buga 70 4 0N 76 15W
Bugel, Tanjung 110 6 26 S 111 3 E
Bugsuk 110 8 15N 117 15 E
Bugt 114 48 47N 121 56 E
Bugulma 98 54 33N 52 48 E
Buguruslan 98 53 39N 52 26 E
Buheirat-Murrat-el-Kubra 121 30 15N 32 40 E
Buhl 20 42 36N 114 46W
Buhler 24 38 8N 97 46W
Buies Creek 40 35 25N 78 44W
Builth Wells 83 52 10N 3 26W
Buíque 74 8 37 S 37 9W
Buir Nur 113 47 50N 117 42 E
Bujumbura 122 3 16 S 29 18 E
Bukachacha 101 52 55N 116 50 E
Bukama 122 9 10 S 25 50 E
Bukavu 122 2 20 S 28 52 E
Bukene 122 4 15 S 32 48 E
Bukhara 100 39 48N 64 25 E
Bukittinggi 110 0 20 S 100 20 E
Bukoba 122 1 20 S 31 49 E
Bula 111 3 6 S 130 30 E
Buladean 40 36 7N 82 12W
Bulan 111 12 40N 123 52 E
Bulandshahr 108 28 28N 77 51 E
Bulawayo 123 20 7 S 28 32 E
Buldir I. 11 52 21N 175 56 E
Bulgan 113 48 45N 103 34 E
Bulgaria ■ 95 42 35N 25 30 E
Bulhar 105 10 25N 44 30 E
Buli, Teluk 111 1 5N 128 25 E
Buliluyan, C. 110 8 20N 117 15 E
Bulkley → 62 55 15N 127 40W
Bull L. 56 43 13N 109 3W
Bull Mts. 33 46 8N 109 0W
Bull Shoals L. 13 36 22N 92 35W
Bullard, Ga. 18 32 38N 83 30W
Bullard, Tex. 51 32 8N 95 19W
Buller → 128 41 44 S 171 36 E
Bullfinch 126 30 58 S 119 3 E
Bullhead 47 45 46N 101 5W
Bullion Mts. 15 34 40N 116 10W
Bullitt County ◇ 49 38 0N 85 40W
Bulloch County ◇ 18 32 20N 81 45W
Bullock County ◇ 10 32 9N 85 43W
Bulloo → 127 28 43 S 142 30 E
Bulls 128 40 10 S 175 24 E
Bulls B. 46 32 59N 79 35W
Bulls Gap 49 36 15N 83 5W
Bulnes 76 36 42 S 72 19W
Bulo Burti 105 3 50N 45 33 E
Bulsar = Valsad 108 20 40N 72 58 E
Bulu Karakelong 111 4 35N 126 50 E
Bulukumba 111 5 33 S 120 11 E
Bulun 101 70 37N 127 30 E
Bumba 122 2 13N 22 30 E
Bumhpa Bum 109 26 51N 97 14 E
Bumpus Mills 48 36 36N 87 50W
Buna, Kenya 122 2 58N 39 30 E
Buna, U.S.A. 51 30 26N 93 58W
Bunbah, Khalij 121 32 20N 23 15 E
Bunbury 126 33 20 S 115 35 E
Bunceton 32 38 47N 92 48W
Bunch 43 35 41N 94 46W
Buncombe 21 37 27N 88 58W
Buncombe County ◇ 40 35 30N 82 30W
Buncrana 85 55 8N 7 28W
Bundaberg 127 24 54 S 152 22 E
Bundi 108 25 30N 75 35 E
Bundlicks Cr. → 25 30 36N 92 57W
Bundoran 85 54 24N 8 17W
Bungatakada 117 33 35N 131 25 E
Bungo-Suidō 117 33 0N 132 15 E
Bungun Shara 113 49 0N 104 0 E
Bunia 122 1 35N 30 20 E
Bunji 108 35 45N 74 40 E
Bunker 32 37 27N 91 13W
Bunker Hill, Ill. 21 39 3N 89 57W

Bunker Hill Caicó

Bunker Hill, Ind. 22 40 40N 86 6W
Bunker Hill, Kans. 24 38 53N 98 42W
Bunker Hill, Nev. 35 39 15N 117 8W
Bunker Hill, Oreg. 44 43 22N 124 12W
Bunkerville 35 36 46N 114 8W
Bunkie 25 30 57N 92 11W
Bunn 40 35 58N 78 15W
Bunnell 17 29 28N 81 16W
Buntok 110 1 40 S 114 58 E
Bunyu 110 3 35N 117 50 E
Buol 111 1 15N 121 32 E
Buon Me Thuot 112 12 40N 108 3 E
Buorkhaya, Mys 101 71 50N 132 40 E
Buqayq 106 26 0N 49 45 E
Buqei'a 104 32 58N 35 20 E
Bur Acaba 105 3 12N 44 20 E
Bûr Safâga 121 26 43N 33 57 E
Bûr Sa'îd 121 31 16N 32 18 E
Bûr Sûdân 121 19 32N 37 9 E
Bura 122 1 4 S 39 58 E
Burao 105 9 32N 45 32 E
Buras 25 29 22N 89 32W
Buraydah 106 26 20N 44 8 E
Buraymī, Al Wāhāt al 107 24 10N 55 43 E
Burbank, Calif. 15 34 11N 118 19W
Burbank, Okla. 43 36 42N 96 44W
Burbank, Wash. 53 46 12N 119 1W
Burchard 34 40 9N 96 21W
Burden 24 37 19N 96 45W
Burdett, Canada 62 49 50N 111 32W
Burdett, Kans. 24 38 12N 99 32W
Burdett, N.Y. 39 42 25N 76 51W
Burdick 24 38 34N 96 51W
Burdur 106 37 45N 30 22 E
Burdwan = Barddhaman 109 23 14N 87 39 E
Bure → 82 52 38N 1 45 E
Bureau County ◇ 21 41 25N 89 30W
Bureya → 101 49 27N 129 30 E
Burgas 95 42 33N 27 29 E
Burgaski Zaliv 95 42 30N 27 39 E
Burgaw 40 34 33N 77 56W
Burgenland □ 88 47 20N 16 20 E
Burgeo 61 47 37N 57 38W
Burgersdorp 123 31 0 S 26 20 E
Burgess Junction 56 44 46N 107 32W
Burgoon 42 41 16N 83 15W
Burgos 91 42 21N 3 41W
Burgsvik 97 57 3N 18 19 E
Burgundy = Bourgogne 90 47 0N 4 30 E
Burias 111 12 55N 123 5 E
Burica, Pta. 66 8 3N 82 51W
Burien 53 47 28N 122 21W
Burin, Canada 61 47 1N 55 14W
Būrīn, Jordan 104 32 11N 35 15 E
Buriram 112 15 0N 103 0 E
Buriti Alegre 75 18 9 S 49 3W
Buriti Bravo 74 5 50 S 43 50W
Buriti dos Lopes 74 3 10 S 41 52W
Burji 121 5 29N 37 51 E
Burkburnett 51 34 6N 98 34W
Burke, Idaho 20 47 31N 115 49W
Burke, S. Dak. 47 43 11N 99 18W
Burke County ◇, Ga. 18 33 0N 82 0W
Burke County ◇, N.C. 40 35 45N 81 40W
Burke County ◇, N. Dak. 41 48 55N 102 30W
Burkesville 49 36 48N 85 22W
Burketown 127 17 45 S 139 33 E
Burkett 51 32 0N 99 8W
Burkettsville 42 40 21N 84 39W
Burkeville, Tex. 51 31 0N 93 40W
Burkeville, Va. 54 37 11N 78 12W
Burkina Faso ■ 120 12 0N 1 0W
Burk's Falls 60 45 37N 79 24W
Burleigh County ◇ 41 47 0N 100 30W
Burleson 51 32 33N 97 19W
Burleson County ◇ 51 30 32N 96 42W
Burley 20 42 32N 113 48W
Burlingame, Calif. 14 37 35N 122 21W
Burlingame, Kans. 24 38 45N 95 50W
Burlington, Colo. 16 39 18N 102 16W
Burlington, Ill. 21 42 3N 88 33W
Burlington, Ind. 22 40 29N 86 24W
Burlington, Iowa 23 40 49N 91 14W
Burlington, Kans. 24 38 12N 95 45W
Burlington, Ky. 49 39 2N 84 43W
Burlington, Mass. 28 42 30N 71 12W
Burlington, N.C. 40 36 6N 79 26W
Burlington, N. Dak. 41 48 17N 101 26W
Burlington, N.J. 37 40 4N 74 51W
Burlington, Okla. 43 36 54N 98 25W
Burlington, Vt. 36 44 29N 73 12W
Burlington, Wash. 53 48 28N 122 20W
Burlington, Wis. 55 42 41N 88 17W
Burlington, Wyo. 56 44 27N 108 26W
Burlington County ◇ 37 39 50N 74 45W
Burlington Junction 32 40 27N 95 4W
Burlyu-Tyube 100 46 30N 79 10 E
Burma ■ 109 21 0N 96 30 E
Burna 48 37 15N 88 22W
Burnaby I. 62 52 25N 131 19W
Burnet 51 30 45N 98 14W
Burnet County ◇ 51 30 45N 98 15W
Burnett → 127 24 45 S 152 23 E
Burnett County ◇ 55 45 50N 92 20W
Burnettsville 22 40 46N 86 36W
Burney 14 40 53N 121 40W
Burnham, Maine 26 44 42N 69 26W
Burnham, Pa. 45 40 38N 77 34W
Burnie 127 41 4 S 145 56 E
Burning Springs 49 37 15N 83 49W
Burnley 82 53 47N 2 15W
Burns, Colo. 16 39 52N 106 53W
Burns, Kans. 24 38 5N 96 53W
Burns, Oreg. 44 43 35N 119 3W
Burns, Tenn. 48 36 3N 87 19W
Burns, Wyo. 56 41 12N 104 21W
Burns Flat 43 35 21N 99 10W
Burns Lake 62 54 20N 125 45W
Burnside 49 36 59N 84 36W
Burnside → 58 66 51N 108 4W
Burnsville, Ala. 10 32 28N 86 53W
Burnsville, Minn. 30 44 47N 93 17W
Burnsville, Miss. 31 34 51N 88 19W
Burnsville, N.C. 40 35 55N 82 18W
Burnsville, W. Va. 54 38 52N 80 40W
Burnt → 44 44 22N 117 14W
Burnt Corn 10 31 33N 87 10W
Burntfork 56 41 2N 109 59W
Burntwood → 63 56 8N 96 34W
Burntwood L. 63 55 22N 100 26W
Burqā 104 32 18N 35 11 E
Burqān 106 29 0N 47 57 E
Burqin 113 47 43N 87 0 E
Burr 34 40 33N 96 19W
Burr Oak, Kans. 24 39 52N 98 18W
Burr Oak, Mich. 29 41 51N 85 19W
Burra 127 33 40 S 138 55 E
Burro, Serranías del 64 29 0N 102 0W
Burrton 24 38 2N 97 41W
Burruyacú 76 26 30 S 64 40W
Burry Port 83 51 41N 4 17W
Bursa 106 40 15N 29 5 E
Burstall 63 50 39N 109 54W
Burt 23 43 12N 94 13W
Burt County ◇ 34 41 50N 96 15W
Burt L. 29 45 28N 84 40W
Burton, Nebr. 34 42 55N 99 35W
Burton, Tex. 51 30 11N 96 42W
Burton, L. 18 34 50N 83 33W
Burton L. 60 54 45N 78 20W
Burton-upon-Trent 82 52 48N 1 39W
Burtrum 30 45 52N 94 41W
Buru 111 3 30 S 126 30 E
Burundi ■ 122 3 15 S 30 0 E
Burung 110 0 24N 103 33 E
Burutu 120 5 20N 5 29 E
Burwell 34 41 47N 99 8W
Bury 82 53 36N 2 19W
Bury St. Edmunds 83 52 15N 0 42 E
Buryat A.S.S.R. □ 101 53 0N 110 0 E
Buşayyah 106 30 0N 46 10 E
Bush 25 30 36N 89 54W
Bush City 24 38 13N 95 9W
Būshehr 107 28 55N 50 55 E
Būshehr □ 107 28 20N 51 45 E
Bushell 63 59 31N 108 45W
Bushire = Būshehr 107 28 55N 50 55 E
Bushland 50 35 11N 102 4W
Bushnell, Fla. 17 28 40N 82 7W
Bushnell, Ill. 21 40 33N 90 31W
Bushnell, Nebr. 34 41 14N 103 54W
Bushong 24 38 39N 96 15W
Bushton 24 38 31N 98 24W
Bushwood 27 38 18N 76 47W
Bushy Head Mt. 43 36 2N 94 35W
Businga 122 3 16N 20 59 E
Buskerud fylke □ 97 60 13N 9 0 E
Busra ash Shām 106 32 30N 36 25 E
Busselton 126 33 42 S 115 15 E
Bussey 23 41 12N 92 53W
Bussum 87 52 16N 5 10 E
Bustamante, B. 78 45 5 S 66 18W
Bustard Hd. 127 24 0 S 151 48 E
Busto Arsizio 94 45 40N 8 50 E
Busu-Djanoa 122 1 43N 21 23 E
Busuanga 111 12 10N 120 0 E
Buta 122 2 50N 24 53 E
Butare 122 2 31 S 29 52 E
Butaritari 124 3 30N 174 0 E
Bute 84 55 48N 5 2W
Bute Inlet 62 50 40N 124 53W
Butembo 122 0 9N 29 18 E
Butha Qi 114 48 0N 122 32 E
Butiaba 122 1 50N 31 20 E
Butler, Ala. 10 32 5N 88 13W
Butler, Ga. 18 32 33N 84 14W
Butler, Ind. 22 41 26N 84 52W
Butler, Ky. 49 38 47N 84 22W
Butler, Md. 27 39 35N 76 45W
Butler, Mo. 32 38 16N 94 20W
Butler, N.J. 37 41 0N 74 20W
Butler, Okla. 43 35 38N 99 11W
Butler, Pa. 45 40 52N 79 54W
Butler County ◇, Ala. 10 31 50N 86 38W
Butler County ◇, Iowa 23 42 45N 92 45W
Butler County ◇, Kans. 24 37 45N 96 45W
Butler County ◇, Ky. 48 37 10N 86 45W
Butler County ◇, Mo. 32 36 45N 90 25W
Butler County ◇, Nebr. 34 41 15N 97 0W
Butler County ◇, Ohio 42 39 24N 84 34W
Butler County ◇, Pa. 45 41 0N 80 0W
Butner 40 36 8N 78 45W
Butte, Mont. 33 46 0N 112 32W
Butte, N. Dak. 41 47 50N 100 40W
Butte, Nebr. 34 42 58N 98 51W
Butte County ◇, Calif. 14 39 40N 121 45W
Butte County ◇, Idaho 20 43 50N 113 0W
Butte County ◇, S. Dak. 47 45 0N 103 30W
Butte Falls 44 42 33N 122 34W
Butte Mts. 35 39 50N 115 5W
Butterfield, Minn. 30 43 58N 94 48W
Butterfield, Mo. 32 36 45N 93 54W
Butternut 55 46 1N 90 30W
Butterworth 112 5 24N 100 23 E
Button B. 63 58 45N 94 23W
Buttonwillow 15 35 24N 119 28W
Butts County ◇ 18 33 20N 84 0W
Butuan 111 8 57N 125 33 E
Butung 111 5 0 S 122 45 E
Buturlinovka 99 50 50N 40 35 E
Buxton, Guyana 71 6 48N 58 2W
Buxton, U.K. 82 53 16N 1 54W
Buxton, N.C. 40 35 16N 75 32W
Buxton, N. Dak. 41 47 36N 97 6W
Buy 98 58 28N 41 28 E
Buyaga 101 59 50N 127 0 E
Büyük Çekmece 95 41 2N 28 35 E
Buzău 89 45 10N 26 50 E
Buzău □ 95 45 20N 26 30 E
Buzău → 89 45 10N 27 20 E
Buzău, Pasul 95 45 35N 26 12 E
Buzaymah 121 24 50N 22 2 E
Buzen 117 33 35N 131 5 E
Buzi → 123 19 50 S 34 43 E
Buzuluk 98 52 48N 52 12 E
Buzzards B. 28 41 30N 70 45W
Buzzards Bay 28 41 45N 70 37W
Byala, Ruse, Bulgaria 95 43 28N 25 44 E
Byala, Varna, Bulgaria 95 42 53N 27 55 E
Byala Slatina 95 43 26N 23 55 E
Byars 43 34 53N 97 3W
Bydgoszcz 89 53 10N 18 0 E
Byelorussian S.S.R. □ 98 53 30N 27 0 E
Byers, Colo. 16 39 43N 104 14W
Byers, Kans. 24 37 48N 98 52W
Byers, Tex. 51 34 4N 98 11W
Byesville 42 39 58N 81 32W
Byfield 28 42 46N 70 57W
Byhalia 31 34 52N 89 41W
Bylas 12 33 8N 110 7W
Bylot I. 59 73 13N 78 34W
Byng 43 34 50N 96 42W
Bynum 33 47 59N 112 19W
Byram 31 32 11N 90 15W
Byrd, C. 5 69 38 S 76 7W
Byrd Land 5 79 30 S 125 0W
Byrd Sub-Glacial Basin 5 82 0 S 120 0W
Byrdstown 49 36 34N 85 8W
Byron, Ga. 18 32 39N 83 46W
Byron, Ill. 21 42 8N 89 15W
Byron, Maine 26 44 43N 70 38W
Byron, Mich. 29 42 49N 83 57W
Byron, Minn. 30 44 2N 92 41W
Byron, Nebr. 34 40 0N 97 46W
Byron, Okla. 43 36 54N 98 19W
Byron, Wyo. 56 44 48N 108 30W
Byron, C. 127 28 38 S 153 40 E
Byrranga, Gory 101 75 0N 100 0 E
Byske 96 64 57N 21 11 E
Byske älv → 96 64 57N 21 13 E
Bytom 89 50 25N 18 54 E

C

C. J. Strike Reservoir 20 42 59N 115 58W
Ca Mau = Quan Long 112 9 7N 105 8 E
Ca Mau, Mui = Bai Bung, Mui 112 8 38N 104 44 E
Caacupé 76 25 23 S 57 5W
Caála 123 12 46 S 15 30 E
Caamano Sd. 62 52 55N 129 25W
Caapiranga 71 3 18 S 61 13W
Caazapá 76 26 8 S 56 19W
Caazapá □ 77 26 10 S 56 0W
Caballo Reservoir 38 32 54N 107 18W
Cabana 72 8 25 S 78 5W
Cabanaconde 72 15 38 S 71 58W
Cabanatuan 111 15 30N 120 58 E
Cabanillas 72 15 36 S 70 28W
Cabano 61 47 40N 68 56W
Cabarrus County ◇ 40 35 20N 80 30W
Cabazon 15 33 55N 116 47W
Cabedelo 74 7 0 S 34 50W
Cabell County ◇ 54 38 26N 82 8W
Cabery 21 41 0N 88 12W
Cabildo 76 32 30 S 71 5W
Cabimas 70 10 23N 71 25W
Cabinda 122 5 33 S 12 11 E
Cabinda □ 122 5 0 S 12 30 E
Cabinet Mts. 33 45 30N 115 0W
Cable 55 46 13N 91 17W
Cabo Blanco 78 47 15 S 65 47W
Cabo Frio 75 22 51 S 42 3W
Cabo Pantoja 70 1 0 S 75 10W
Cabo Raso 78 44 20 S 65 15W
Cabo Rojo 57 18 5N 67 9W
Cabonga, Réservoir 60 47 20N 76 40W
Cabool 32 37 7N 92 6W
Cabora Bassa Dam 123 15 20 S 32 50 E
Caborca 64 30 40N 112 10W
Cabot, Ark. 13 34 59N 92 1W
Cabot, Vt. 36 44 23N 72 18W
Cabot, Mt. 36 44 30N 71 25W
Cabot Strait 61 47 15N 59 40W
Cabrera, I. 91 39 8N 2 57 E
Cabri 63 50 35N 108 25W
Cabriel → 91 39 14N 1 3W
Cabrillo, Pt. 14 39 21N 123 50W
Cabruta 70 7 50N 66 10W
Çabuyaro 70 4 18N 72 49W
Čačak 95 43 54N 20 20 E
Cacao 71 4 33N 52 26W
Cacapon → 54 39 37N 78 16W
Cáceres, Brazil 73 16 5 S 57 40W
Cáceres, Colombia 70 7 35N 75 20W
Cáceres, Spain 91 39 26N 6 23W
Cache 43 34 38N 98 38W
Cache →, Ark. 13 34 43N 91 20W
Cache →, Ill. 21 37 4N 89 10W
Cache Bay 60 46 22N 80 0W
Cache County ◇ 52 41 40N 111 45W
Cache Cr. → 14 38 42N 121 42W
Cache la Poudre → 16 40 25N 104 36W
Cache National Forest 52 41 45N 111 29W
Cache Peak 20 42 11N 113 40W
Cachi 76 25 5 S 66 10W
Cachimbo 73 8 57 S 54 54W
Cachimbo, Serra do 73 9 30 S 55 0W
Cachoeira 75 12 30 S 39 0W
Cachoeira Alta 75 18 48 S 50 58W
Cachoeira de Itapemirim 75 20 51 S 41 7W
Cachoeira do Sul 77 30 3 S 52 53W
Cachoeiro do Arari 74 1 5 S 48 58W
Cachuela Esperanza 73 10 32 S 65 38W
Cacólo 122 10 9 S 19 21 E
Caconda 123 13 48 S 15 8 E
Cactus 50 36 4N 101 59W
Caçu 75 18 37 S 51 4W
Caculé 75 14 30 S 42 13W
Caddo, Okla. 43 34 7N 96 16W
Caddo, Tex. 51 32 43N 98 40W
Caddo → 13 34 10N 93 3W
Caddo County ◇ 43 35 10N 98 20W
Caddo Cr. → 43 34 14N 96 59W
Caddo Gap 13 34 24N 93 37W
Caddo L. 25 32 43N 93 55W
Caddo Mills 51 33 4N 96 14W
Caddo Parish ◇ 25 32 45N 93 58W
Caddoa 16 38 4N 102 56W
Cader Idris 82 52 43N 3 56W
Cades 46 33 47N 79 47W
Cadillac, Canada 60 48 14N 78 23W
Cadillac, U.S.A. 29 44 15N 85 24W
Cadiz, Phil. 111 10 57N 123 15 E
Cádiz, Spain 91 36 30N 6 20W
Cadiz, Ind. 22 39 57N 85 29W
Cadiz, Ky. 48 36 52N 87 50W
Cadiz, Ohio 42 40 22N 81 0W
Cádiz, G. de 91 36 40N 7 0W
Cadiz L. 15 34 18N 115 24W
Cadley 18 33 32N 82 40W
Cadomin 62 53 2N 117 20W
Cadott 55 44 57N 91 9W
Cadotte → 62 56 43N 117 10W
Cadwell 18 32 20N 83 3W
Caen 90 49 10N 0 22W
Caernarfon 82 53 8N 4 17W
Caernarfon B. 82 53 4N 4 40W
Caernarvon = Caernarfon 82 53 8N 4 17W
Caerphilly 83 51 34N 3 13W
Caesarea 104 32 30N 34 53 E
Caeté 75 19 55 S 43 40W
Caetité 75 13 50 S 42 32W
Cafayate 76 26 2 S 66 0W
Cafifi 70 5 13N 71 4W
Cagayan → 111 18 25N 121 42 E
Cagayan de Oro 111 8 30N 124 40 E
Cagles Mill L. 22 39 30N 86 53W
Cágliari 94 39 15N 9 6 E
Cágliari, G. di 94 39 8N 9 10 E
Caguán → 70 0 8 S 74 18W
Caguas 57 18 14N 66 2W
Caha Mts. 85 51 45N 9 40W
Cahaba → 10 32 20N 87 5W
Caher 85 52 23N 7 56W
Cahersiveen 85 51 57N 10 13W
Cahokia 21 38 34N 90 11W
Cahone 16 37 39N 108 49W
Cahore Pt. 85 52 34N 6 11W
Cahors 90 44 27N 1 27 E
Cahuapanas 72 5 15 S 77 0W
Cahuinari → 70 1 21 S 70 44W
Caia 123 17 51 S 35 24 E
Caiabis, Serra dos 73 11 30 S 56 30W
Caiapó, Serra do 73 17 0 S 52 0W
Caiapônia 73 16 57 S 51 49W
Caibarién 66 22 30N 79 30W
Caicara, Bolívar, Venezuela 70 7 38N 66 10W
Caicara, Monagas, Venezuela 71 9 52N 63 38W
Caicó 74 6 20 S 37 0W

Caicos Is. **Candlemas I.**

Caicos Is. 67 21 40N 71 40W
Caicos Passage 67 22 45N 72 45W
Cailloma 72 15 9 S 71 45W
Caillou B. 25 29 3N 91 0W
Caine → 73 18 23 S 65 21W
Cains Store 49 37 8N 84 50W
Cainsville 32 40 26N 93 47W
Caird Coast 5 75 0 S 25 0W
Cairn Gorm 84 57 7N 3 40W
Cairn Toul 84 57 3N 3 44W
Cairngorm Mts. 84 57 6N 3 42W
Cairns 127 16 57 S 145 45 E
Cairo = El Qâhira 121 30 1N 31 14 E
Cairo, Ga. 18 30 52N 84 13W
Cairo, Ill. 21 37 0N 89 11W
Cairo, Ky. 48 37 42N 87 39W
Cairo, Mo. 32 39 31N 92 27W
Cairo, Nebr. 34 41 0N 98 36W
Cairo, Ohio 42 40 50N 84 5W
Cairo, W. Va. 54 39 13N 81 9W
Caithness, Ord of 84 58 9N 3 37W
Caiundo 123 15 50 S 17 28 E
Caiza 73 20 2 S 65 40W
Caja de Muertos, Isla 57 17 54N 66 31W
Cajabamba 72 7 38 S 78 4W
Cajamarca 72 7 5 S 78 28W
Cajamarca □ 72 6 15 S 78 50W
Cajapió 74 2 58 S 44 48W
Cajatambo 72 10 30 S 77 2W
Cajàzeiras 74 6 52 S 38 30W
Cajon Summit 15 34 21N 117 27W
Cal, La → 73 17 27 S 58 15W
Calabar 120 4 57N 8 20 E
Calabozo 70 9 0N 67 28W
Calábria □ 94 39 24N 16 30 E
Calacota 72 17 16 S 68 38W
Calafate 78 50 19 S 72 15W
Calahorra 91 42 18N 1 59W
Calais, France 90 50 57N 1 56 E
Calais, U.S.A. 26 45 11N 67 17W
Calalaste, Cord. de 76 25 0 S 67 0W
Calama, Brazil 73 8 0 S 62 50W
Calama, Chile 76 22 30 S 68 55W
Calamar, Bolívar, Colombia 70 10 15N 74 55W
Calamar, Vaupés, Colombia 70 1 58N 72 32W
Calamarca 72 16 55 S 68 9W
Calamian Group 111 11 50N 119 55 E
Calamocha 91 40 50N 1 17W
Calamus → 34 41 48N 99 9W
Calang 110 4 37N 95 37 E
Calapan 111 13 25N 121 7 E
Calapooia → 44 44 38N 123 8W
Călăraşi 95 44 12N 27 20 E
Călăraşi □ 95 44 10N 27 0 E
Calatayud 91 41 20N 1 40W
Calauag 111 13 55N 122 15 E
Calaveras County ◇ 14 38 15N 120 40W
Calavite, Cape 111 13 26N 120 20 E
Calbayog 111 12 4N 124 38 E
Calca 72 13 22 S 72 0W
Calcasieu → 25 30 5N 93 20W
Calcasieu L. 25 29 55N 93 18W
Calcasieu Parish ◇ 25 30 14N 93 23W
Calcutta 109 22 36N 88 24 E
Caldas □ 70 5 15N 75 30W
Caldas Novas 75 17 45 S 48 38W
Calder → 82 53 44N 1 21W
Caldera 76 27 5 S 70 55W
Caldwell, Ark. 13 35 5N 90 49W
Caldwell, Idaho 20 43 40N 116 41W
Caldwell, Kans. 24 37 2N 97 37W
Caldwell, Ohio 42 39 45N 81 31W
Caldwell, Tex. 51 30 32N 96 42W
Caldwell County ◇, Ky. 48 37 10N 87 50W
Caldwell County ◇, Mo. 32 39 40N 94 0W
Caldwell County ◇, N.C. 40 36 0N 81 30W
Caldwell County ◇, Tex. 51 29 53N 97 40W
Caldwell Parish ◇ 25 32 0N 92 0W
Caledon 123 34 14 S 19 26 E
Caledon → 123 30 31 S 26 5 E
Caledon B. 127 12 45 S 137 0 E
Caledonia, Mich. 29 42 47N 85 31W
Caledonia, Minn. 30 43 38N 91 30W
Caledonia, Miss. 31 33 41N 88 20W
Caledonia, N. Dak. 41 47 28N 96 53W
Caledonia, N.Y. 39 42 58N 77 51W
Caledonia County ◇ 36 44 30N 72 10W
Calella 91 41 37N 2 40 E
Calera, Ala. 10 33 6N 86 45W
Calera, Okla. 43 33 52N 96 29W
Calera, La 76 32 50 S 71 10W
Caleta Olivia 78 46 25 S 67 25W
Calexico 15 32 40N 115 30W
Calf of Man 82 54 4N 4 48W
Calgary 62 51 0N 114 10W
Calhan 16 39 2N 104 18W
Calhoun, Ga. 18 34 30N 84 57W
Calhoun, Ill. 21 38 39N 88 3W
Calhoun, Ky. 48 37 32N 87 16W
Calhoun, Mo. 32 38 28N 93 38W
Calhoun, Tenn. 49 35 18N 84 45W
Calhoun City 31 33 51N 89 19W
Calhoun County ◇, Ala. 10 33 47N 86 0W
Calhoun County ◇, Ark. 13 33 35N 92 31W
Calhoun County ◇, Fla. 17 30 30N 85 15W
Calhoun County ◇, Ga. 18 31 30N 84 35W
Calhoun County ◇, Ill. 21 39 10N 90 40W
Calhoun County ◇, Iowa 23 42 25N 94 40W
Calhoun County ◇, Mich. 29 42 15N 85 0W
Calhoun County ◇, Miss. 31 33 56N 89 20W
Calhoun County ◇, S.C. 46 33 45N 80 50W
Calhoun County ◇, Tex. 51 28 37N 96 38W
Calhoun County ◇, W. Va. 54 38 55N 81 6W
Calhoun Falls 46 34 6N 82 36W
Cali 70 3 25N 76 35W
Calico Rock 13 36 7N 92 9W
Calicut 108 11 15N 75 43 E
Caliente, Calif. 15 35 17N 118 38W
Caliente, Nev. 35 37 37N 114 31W
Califon 37 40 42N 74 50W
California, Md. 27 38 18N 76 32W
California, Mo. 32 38 38N 92 34W
California, Pa. 45 40 4N 79 54W
California □ 14 37 30N 119 30W
California, Baja 64 32 10N 115 12W
California, Baja, T.N. □ 64 30 0N 115 0W
California, Baja, T.S. □ 64 25 50N 111 50W
California, Golfo de 64 27 0N 111 0W
California, Lr. = California, Baja 64 32 10N 115 12W
California Aqueduct 15 33 52N 117 12W
Călimăneşti 95 45 14N 24 20 E
Călineşti 95 45 21N 24 18 E
Calingasta 76 31 15 S 69 30W
Calio 41 48 38N 98 56W
Calion 13 33 20N 92 32W
Calipatria 15 33 8N 115 31W
Calistoga 14 38 35N 122 35W
Calkiní 65 20 21N 90 3W
Callabonna, L. 127 29 40 S 140 5 E
Callahan, Calif. 14 41 18N 122 48W
Callahan, Fla. 17 30 34N 81 50W
Callahan County ◇ 51 32 24N 99 24W
Callan 85 52 33N 7 25W
Callander 84 56 15N 4 14W
Callao, Peru 72 12 0 S 77 0W
Callao, U.S.A. 52 39 54N 113 43W
Callaway, Fla. 17 30 8N 85 36W
Callaway, Minn. 30 46 59N 95 54W
Callaway, Nebr. 34 41 18N 99 56W
Callaway County ◇ 32 38 50N 91 50W
Callender 23 42 22N 94 17W
Calles 65 23 2N 98 42W
Callicoon 39 41 46N 75 3W
Calliham 51 28 29N 98 21W
Calling Lake 62 55 15N 113 12W
Calloway County ◇ 48 36 40N 88 15W
Calmar 23 43 11N 91 52W
Calne 82 51 26N 2 0W
Caloosahatchee → 17 26 31N 82 1W
Calpella 14 39 14N 123 12W
Calpine 14 39 40N 120 27W
Calstock 60 49 47N 84 9W
Caltagirone 94 37 13N 14 30 E
Caltanissetta 94 37 30N 14 3 E
Calulo 122 10 1 S 14 56 E
Calumet, Iowa 23 42 57N 95 33W
Calumet, Mich. 29 47 14N 88 27W
Calumet, Minn. 30 47 19N 93 17W
Calumet, Okla. 43 35 36N 98 7W
Calumet City 21 41 37N 87 32W
Calumet County ◇ 55 44 5N 88 10W
Calunda 123 12 7 S 23 36 E
Calvados □ 90 49 5N 0 15W
Calvert, Md. 27 39 42N 75 58W
Calvert, Tex. 51 30 59N 96 40W
Calvert City 48 37 2N 88 21W
Calvert County ◇ 27 38 30N 76 35W
Calvert I. 62 51 30N 128 0W
Calverton 27 39 3N 76 56W
Calvi 90 42 34N 8 45 E
Calvillo 64 21 51N 102 43W
Calvin, La. 25 31 58N 92 47W
Calvin, N. Dak. 41 48 51N 98 56W
Calvin, Okla. 43 34 58N 96 15W
Calvinia 123 31 28 S 19 45 E
Calwa 15 36 42N 119 46W
Cam → 83 52 21N 0 16 E
Cam Lam 112 11 54N 109 10 E
Cam Ranh 112 11 54N 109 12 E
Camabatela 122 8 20 S 15 26 E
Camacã 75 15 24 S 39 30W
Camaçari 75 12 41 S 38 18W
Camacho 64 24 25N 102 18W
Camacupa 123 11 58 S 17 22 E
Camaguán 70 8 6N 67 36W
Camagüey 66 21 20N 78 0W
Camak 18 33 27N 82 39W
Camamu 75 13 57 S 39 7W
Camaná 72 16 30 S 72 50W
Camanche 23 41 47N 90 15W
Camanche Reservoir 14 38 14N 121 1W
Camano I. 53 48 0N 122 30W
Camaquã → 77 31 17 S 51 47W
Camararé → 73 12 15 S 58 55W
Camaret 90 48 16N 4 37W
Camargo, Bolivia 73 20 38 S 65 15 E
Camargo, U.S.A. 43 36 1N 99 17W
Camarillo 15 34 13N 119 2W
Camarón, C. 66 16 0N 85 0W
Camarones 78 44 50 S 65 40W
Camarones, B. 78 44 45 S 65 35W
Camas, Idaho 20 44 0N 112 13W
Camas, Wash. 53 45 35N 122 24W
Camas County ◇ 20 43 30N 114 50W
Camas Valley 44 43 2N 123 40W
Cambará 77 23 2 S 50 5W
Cambay = Khambhat 108 22 23N 72 33 E
Cambay, G. of 108 20 45N 72 30 E
Cambodia ■ 112 12 15N 105 0 E
Camborne 83 50 13N 5 18W
Cambrai 90 50 11N 3 14 E
Cambria, Calif. 15 35 34N 121 5W
Cambria, Wis. 55 43 33N 89 7W
Cambria County ◇ 45 40 30N 78 52W
Cambrian Mts. 83 52 25N 3 52W
Cambridge, Canada 60 43 23N 80 15W
Cambridge, Jamaica 66 18 18N 77 54W
Cambridge, N.Z. 128 37 54 S 175 29 E
Cambridge, U.K. 83 52 13N 0 8 E
Cambridge, Idaho 20 44 34N 116 41W
Cambridge, Ill. 21 41 18N 90 12W
Cambridge, Iowa 23 41 54N 93 32W
Cambridge, Kans. 24 37 19N 96 40W
Cambridge, Mass. 28 42 22N 71 6W
Cambridge, Md. 27 38 34N 76 5W
Cambridge, Minn. 30 45 34N 93 13W
Cambridge, N.Y. 39 43 2N 73 22W
Cambridge, Nebr. 34 40 17N 100 10W
Cambridge, Ohio 42 40 2N 81 35W
Cambridge, Vt. 36 44 39N 72 53W
Cambridge Bay 58 69 10N 105 0W
Cambridge City 22 39 49N 85 10W
Cambridge Gulf 126 14 55 S 128 15 E
Cambridge Springs 45 41 48N 80 4W
Cambridgeport 36 43 10N 72 35W
Cambridgeshire □ 83 52 12N 0 7 E
Cambuci 75 21 35 S 41 55W
Camden, Ala. 10 31 59N 87 17W
Camden, Ark. 13 33 35N 92 50W
Camden, Del. 27 39 7N 75 33W
Camden, Ill. 21 40 9N 90 46W
Camden, Maine 26 44 13N 69 4W
Camden, Miss. 31 32 47N 89 50W
Camden, N.C. 40 36 20N 76 10W
Camden, N.J. 37 39 56N 75 7W
Camden, N.Y. 39 43 20N 75 45W
Camden, Ohio 42 39 38N 84 39W
Camden, S.C. 46 34 16N 80 36W
Camden, Tenn. 48 36 4N 88 6W
Camden, Tex. 51 30 55N 94 44W
Camden Bay 11 70 10N 145 15W
Camden County ◇, Ga. 18 31 0N 81 45W
Camden County ◇, Mo. 32 38 0N 92 45W
Camden County ◇, N.C. 40 36 20N 76 15W
Camden County ◇, N.J. 37 39 45N 75 0W
Camdenton 32 38 1N 92 45W
Camels Hump 36 44 19N 72 53W
Cameron, Ariz. 12 35 53N 111 25W
Cameron, La. 25 29 48N 93 20W
Cameron, Mo. 32 39 44N 94 14W
Cameron, Mont. 33 45 13N 111 41W
Cameron, N.C. 40 35 20N 79 15W
Cameron, Okla. 43 35 8N 94 32W
Cameron, S.C. 46 33 34N 80 43W
Cameron, Tex. 51 30 51N 96 59W
Cameron, W. Va. 54 39 50N 80 34W
Cameron, Wis. 55 45 25N 91 44W
Cameron County ◇, Pa. 45 41 30N 78 5W
Cameron County ◇, Tex. 50 26 12N 97 42W
Cameron Falls 60 49 8N 88 19W
Cameron Highlands 112 4 27N 101 22 E
Cameron Hills 62 59 48N 118 0W
Cameron Parish ◇ 25 29 58N 93 10W
Cameroon ■ 122 6 0N 12 30 E
Cameroun, Mt. 122 4 13N 9 10 E
Cametá 74 2 12 S 49 30W
Camiguin, I. 111 8 55N 124 45 E
Camilla 18 31 14N 84 12W
Caminha 91 41 50N 8 50W
Camino 14 38 44N 120 41W
Camiranga 74 1 48 S 46 17W
Camiri 73 20 3 S 63 31W
Camissombo 122 8 7 S 20 38 E
Camoa Mts. 71 1 30N 58 50W
Camocim 74 2 55 S 40 50W
Camooweal 127 19 56 S 138 7 E
Camopi 71 3 12N 52 17W
Camopi → 71 3 10N 52 20W
Camp County ◇ 51 33 0N 94 59W
Camp Creek 54 37 30N 81 6W
Camp Crook 47 45 33N 103 59W
Camp Douglas 55 43 55N 90 16W
Camp Hill, Ala. 10 32 48N 85 39W
Camp Hill, Pa. 45 40 14N 76 55W
Camp Houston 43 36 49N 99 7W
Camp Point 21 40 3N 91 4W
Camp Springs 27 38 48N 76 55W
Camp Verde 12 34 34N 111 51W
Camp Wood 51 29 40N 100 1W
Campagna 94 40 40N 15 5 E
Campaign 49 35 46N 85 38W
Campana 76 34 10 S 58 55W
Campana, I. 78 48 20 S 75 20W
Campania □ 94 40 50N 14 45 E
Campbell, Ala. 10 31 55N 87 59W
Campbell, Calif. 14 37 17N 121 57W
Campbell, Minn. 30 46 6N 96 24W
Campbell, Mo. 32 36 30N 90 4W
Campbell, Nebr. 34 40 18N 98 44W
Campbell, Ohio 42 41 5N 80 37W
Campbell County ◇, Ky. 49 38 55N 84 20W
Campbell County ◇, S. Dak. 47 45 55N 100 0W
Campbell County ◇, Tenn. 49 36 23N 84 7W
Campbell County ◇, Va. 54 37 15N 79 5W
Campbell County ◇, Wyo. 56 44 15N 105 30W
Campbell I. 124 52 30 S 169 0 E
Campbell L. 63 63 14N 106 55W
Campbell River 62 50 5N 125 20W
Campbellsburg, Ind. 22 38 39N 86 16W
Campbellsburg, Ky. 49 38 31N 85 12W
Campbellsport 55 43 36N 88 17W
Campbellsville, Ky. 49 37 21N 85 20W
Campbellsville, Tenn. 48 35 20N 87 8W
Campbellton, Canada 61 47 57N 66 43W
Campbellton, U.S.A. 17 30 57N 85 24W
Campbeltown 84 55 25N 5 36W
Campeche 65 19 50N 90 32W
Campeche □ 65 19 50N 90 32W
Campeche, Bahía de 65 19 30N 93 0W
Camperville 63 51 59N 100 9W
Campina Grande 74 7 20 S 35 47W
Campina Verde 75 19 31 S 49 28W
Campinas 77 22 50 S 47 0W
Campion 16 40 21N 105 5W
Campo, Cameroon 122 2 22N 9 50 E
Campo, U.S.A. 16 37 6N 102 35W
Campo Belo 75 20 52 S 45 16W
Campo de Diauarum 73 11 12 S 53 14W
Campo Flórido 75 19 47 S 48 35W
Campo Formoso 74 10 30 S 40 20W
Campo Grande 73 20 25 S 54 40W
Campo Maíor 74 4 50 S 42 12W
Campo Mourão 75 24 3 S 52 22W
Campoalegre 70 2 41N 75 20W
Campobasso 94 41 34N 14 40 E
Campobello 46 35 7N 82 9W
Campos 75 21 50 S 41 20W
Campos Altos 75 19 47 S 46 10W
Campos Belos 75 13 10 S 47 3W
Campos Novos 77 27 21 S 51 50W
Campos Sales 74 7 4 S 40 23W
Campti 25 31 54N 93 7W
Campton, Fla. 17 30 53N 86 31W
Campton, Ga. 18 33 52N 83 43W
Campton, Ky. 49 37 44N 83 33W
Camptonville 14 39 27N 121 3W
Campuya → 70 1 40 S 73 30W
Campville 17 29 40N 82 7W
Camrose 62 53 0N 112 50W
Camsell Portage 63 59 37N 109 15W
Camuy 57 18 29N 66 51W
Camuy → 57 18 29N 66 51W
Can Tho 112 10 2N 105 46 E
Canaan, Conn. 28 42 2N 73 20W
Canaan, Miss. 31 34 56N 89 8W
Canaan, N.H. 36 43 40N 72 1W
Canada ■ 58 60 0N 100 0W
Cañada de Gómez 76 32 40 S 61 30W
Canadian, Okla. 43 35 11N 95 39W
Canadian, Tex. 50 35 55N 100 23W
Canadian → 43 35 28N 95 3W
Canadian County ◇ 43 35 35N 98 0W
Canadys 46 33 3N 80 37W
Canajoharie 39 42 54N 74 35W
Çanakkale 106 40 8N 26 30 E
Çanakkale Boğazi 106 40 0N 26 0 E
Canal Flats 62 50 10N 115 48W
Canal Fulton 42 40 53N 81 36W
Canal Point 17 26 52N 80 38W
Canalejas 76 35 15 S 66 34W
Canalou 32 36 46N 89 41W
Canals 76 33 35 S 62 53W
Canandaigua 39 42 54N 77 17W
Canandaigua L. 39 42 47N 77 19W
Cananea 64 31 0N 110 20W
Cañar 70 2 33 S 78 56W
Cañar □ 70 2 30 S 79 0W
Canarias, Islas 120 28 30N 16 0W
Canarreos, Arch. de los 66 21 35N 81 40W
Canary Is. = Canarias, Islas 120 28 30N 16 0W
Canas, Rio → 57 18 3N 66 26W
Canaseraga 39 42 27N 77 45W
Canastra, Serra da 75 20 0 S 46 20W
Canatlán 64 24 31N 104 47W
Canaveral, C. 17 28 27N 80 32W
Canaveral National Seashore 17 28 28N 80 34W
Canavieiras 75 15 39 S 39 0W
Canberra 127 35 15 S 149 8 E
Canby, Calif. 14 41 27N 120 52W
Canby, Minn. 30 44 43N 96 16W
Canby, Oreg. 44 45 16N 122 42W
Canchyuaya, Cordillera de 72 7 30 S 74 0W
Candala 105 11 30N 49 58 E
Candarave 72 17 15 S 70 13W
Candeias → 73 8 39 S 63 31W
Candelaria, Argentina 77 27 29 S 55 44W
Candelaria, U.S.A. 50 30 8N 104 41W
Candia = Iráklion 95 35 20N 25 12 E
Cândido de Abreu 75 24 35 S 51 20W
Cândido Mendes 74 1 27 S 45 43W
Candle 11 65 55N 161 56W
Candle L. 63 53 50N 105 18W
Candlemas I. 5 57 3 S 26 40W

Candler County Carrauntoohill, Mt.

Candler County ◇ **18** 32 30N 82 0W
Candlewood **37** 40 9N 74 10W
Candlewood, L. **28** 41 30N 73 27W
Cando **41** 48 32N 99 12W
Candor **40** 35 18N 79 45W
Candy Res. **43** 36 32N 96 1W
Cane Bay **57** 17 40N 64 50W
Cane Cr. → **52** 38 35N 109 35W
Cane Valley **49** 37 11N 85 19W
Canea = Khaniá **95** 35 30N 24 4 E
Canela **74** 10 15 S 48 25W
Canelones **77** 34 32 S 56 17W
Cañete, Chile **76** 37 50 S 73 30W
Cañete, Peru **72** 13 8 S 76 30W
Caney, Kans. **24** 37 1N 95 56W
Caney, Okla. **43** 34 14N 96 13W
Caney Fork → **49** 36 15N 85 57W
Caneyville **48** 37 26N 86 29W
Canfield **13** 33 11N 93 38W
Cangas **91** 42 16N 8 47W
Canguaretama **74** 6 20 S 35 5W
Canguçu **77** 31 22 S 52 43W
Cangxi **115** 31 47N 105 59 E
Cangzhou **114** 38 19N 116 52 E
Canicado **123** 24 2 S 33 2 E
Canim Lake **62** 51 47N 120 54W
Canindé **74** 4 22 S 39 19W
Canindé → **74** 6 15 S 42 52W
Canipaan **110** 8 33N 117 15 E
Canisteo **39** 42 16N 77 36W
Canisteo → **39** 42 7N 77 8W
Canistota **47** 43 36N 97 18W
Cañitas **64** 23 36N 102 43W
Canjilon **38** 36 29N 106 26W
Çankırı **106** 40 40N 33 37 E
Canmer **49** 37 17N 85 46W
Canmore **62** 51 7N 115 18W
Canna **84** 57 3N 6 33W
Cannanore **108** 11 53N 75 27 E
Cannel City **49** 37 47N 83 17W
Cannelton **22** 37 55N 86 45W
Cannes **90** 43 32N 7 0 E
Canning Basin **126** 19 50 S 124 0 E
Cannock **82** 52 42N 2 2W
Cannon → **30** 44 35N 92 33W
Cannon Ball **41** 46 26N 100 38W
Cannon Beach **44** 45 54N 123 58W
Cannon County ◇ **48** 35 50N 86 4W
Cannon Falls **30** 44 31N 92 54W
Cannonball → **41** 46 26N 100 35W
Cannonsburg **49** 38 23N 82 42W
Cannonsville Reservoir **39** 42 4N 75 22W
Cannonville **52** 37 34N 112 3W
Caño Colorado **70** 2 18N 68 22W
Canobie Lake **36** 42 49N 71 15W
Canoe L. **63** 55 10N 108 15W
Canon **18** 34 21N 83 7W
Canon City **16** 38 27N 105 14W
Canon Largo → **38** 36 43N 107 49W
Canoncito Indian Reservation **38** 35 10N 107 0W
Canonsburg **45** 40 16N 80 11W
Canoochee → **18** 31 59N 81 19W
Canora **63** 51 40N 102 30W
Canova **47** 43 53N 97 30W
Canovanas **57** 18 23N 65 54W
Canso **61** 45 20N 61 0W
Canta **72** 11 29 S 76 37W
Cantabria □ **91** 43 10N 4 0W
Cantabrian Mts. = Cantábrica, Cordillera **91** 43 0N 5 10W
Cantábrica, Cordillera **91** 43 0N 5 10W
Cantal □ **90** 45 4N 2 45 E
Cantaura **71** 9 19N 64 21W
Canterbury, U.K. **83** 51 17N 1 5 E
Canterbury, U.S.A. **28** 41 41N 71 57W
Canterbury □ **128** 43 45 S 171 19 E
Canterbury Bight **128** 44 16 S 171 55 E
Canterbury Plains **128** 43 55 S 171 22 E
Canto do Buriti **74** 8 7 S 42 58W
Canton = Guangzhou, Guangdong, China **115** 23 5N 113 10 E
Canton = Guangzhou, Guangdong, China **115** 23 5N 113 10 E
Canton, Conn. **28** 41 49N 72 54W
Canton, Ga. **18** 34 14N 84 29W
Canton, Ill. **21** 40 33N 90 2W
Canton, Kans. **24** 38 23N 97 26W
Canton, Ky. **48** 36 48N 87 58W
Canton, Mass. **28** 42 9N 71 9W
Canton, Minn. **30** 43 32N 91 56W
Canton, Miss. **31** 32 37N 90 2W
Canton, Mo. **32** 40 8N 91 32W
Canton, N.C. **40** 35 32N 82 50W
Canton, N.Y. **39** 44 36N 75 10W
Canton, Ohio **42** 40 48N 81 23W
Canton, Okla. **43** 36 3N 98 35W
Canton, Pa. **45** 41 39N 76 51W
Canton, S. Dak. **47** 43 18N 96 35W
Canton, Tex. **51** 32 33N 95 52W
Canton L. **43** 36 6N 98 35W
Cantonment **17** 30 37N 87 20W
Cantril **23** 40 39N 92 4W
Cantwell **11** 63 24N 148 57W
Canudos **73** 7 13 S 58 5W
Canumã, Amazonas, Brazil **71** 4 2 S 59 4W
Canumã, Amazonas, Brazil **73** 6 8 S 60 10W
Canumã → **73** 3 55 S 59 10W
Canutama **73** 6 30 S 64 20W
Canute **43** 35 25N 99 17W
Canutillo **50** 31 55N 106 36W
Canyon **50** 34 59N 101 55W
Canyon City **44** 44 23N 118 57W
Canyon County ◇ **20** 43 35N 116 50W
Canyon Creek **33** 46 49N 112 16W
Canyon De Chelly National Monument **12** 36 10N 109 20W
Canyon Ferry L. **33** 46 39N 111 44W
Canyon L. **51** 29 52N 98 12W
Canyon Village **56** 44 46N 110 32W
Canyonlands National Park **52** 38 15N 110 0W
Canyonville **44** 42 56N 123 17W
Cao Xian **115** 34 50N 115 35 E
Caonillas, Lago **57** 18 17N 66 39W
Cap-aux-Meules **61** 47 23N 61 52W
Cap-Chat **61** 49 6N 66 40W
Cap-de-la-Madeleine **60** 46 22N 72 31W
Cap-Haïtien **67** 19 40N 72 20W
Cap St.-Jacques = Vung Tau **112** 10 21N 107 4 E
Capa **47** 44 7N 100 59W
Capac **29** 43 1N 82 56W
Capaia **122** 8 27 S 20 13 E
Capanaparo → **70** 7 1N 67 7W
Capanema **74** 1 12 S 47 11W
Caparo →, Barinas, Venezuela **70** 7 46N 70 23W
Caparo →, Bolívar, Venezuela **71** 7 30N 64 0W
Capatárida **70** 11 11N 70 37W
Cape Barren I. **127** 40 25 S 148 15 E
Cape Breton Highlands Nat. Park **61** 46 50N 60 40W
Cape Breton I. **61** 46 0N 60 30W
Cape Canaveral **17** 28 24N 80 36W
Cape Charles **54** 37 16N 76 1W
Cape Coast **120** 5 5N 1 15W
Cape Cod B. **28** 41 50N 70 20W
Cape Cod National Seashore **28** 41 56N 70 6W
Cape Coral **17** 26 33N 81 57W
Cape Dorset **59** 64 14N 76 32W
Cape Dyer **59** 66 30N 61 22W
Cape Elizabeth **26** 43 34N 70 12W
Cape Fear → **40** 33 53N 78 1W
Cape Girardeau **32** 37 19N 89 32W
Cape Girardeau County ◇ **32** 37 25N 89 40W
Cape Hatteras National Seashore **40** 35 30N 75 28W
Cape I. **46** 33 2N 79 21W
Cape Lookout National Seashore **40** 35 45N 76 25W
Cape May **37** 38 56N 74 56W
Cape May County ◇ **37** 39 10N 74 45W
Cape May Court House **37** 39 5N 74 50W
Cape May Point **37** 38 56N 74 58W
Cape Montague **61** 46 5N 62 25W
Cape Pole **11** 55 58N 133 48W
Cape Province □ **123** 32 0 S 23 0 E
Cape St. Claire **27** 39 3N 76 25W
Cape Tormentine **61** 46 8N 63 47W
Cape Town **123** 33 55 S 18 22 E
Cape Verde Is. ■ **2** 17 10N 25 20W
Cape Vincent **39** 44 8N 76 20W
Cape Yakataga **11** 60 4N 142 26W
Cape York Peninsula **127** 12 0 S 142 30 E
Capela **74** 10 30 S 37 0W
Capela de Campo **74** 4 40 S 41 55W
Capelinha **75** 17 42 S 42 31W
Capernaum = Kefar Naḥum **104** 32 54N 35 34 E
Capim **74** 1 41 S 47 47W
Capim → **74** 1 40 S 47 47W
Capinópolis **75** 18 41 S 49 35W
Capinota **72** 17 43 S 66 14W
Capitan **38** 33 35N 105 35W
Capitán Aracena, I. **78** 54 10 S 71 20W
Capitan Arturo Prat **5** 63 0 S 60 15W
Capitán Pastene **78** 38 13 S 73 1W
Capitan Pk. **38** 33 36N 105 16W
Capitol Reef National Monument **52** 38 15N 111 10W
Capitola **17** 30 27N 84 5W
Capivara, Serra da **75** 14 35 S 45 0W
Capoeira **73** 5 37 S 59 33W
Capon Bridge **54** 39 18N 78 26W
Capraia **94** 43 2N 9 50 E
Capreol **60** 46 43N 80 56W
Caprera **94** 41 12N 9 28 E
Capri **94** 40 34N 14 15 E
Capricorn, C. **127** 23 30 S 151 13 E
Caprivi Strip **123** 18 0 S 23 0 E
Caprock **38** 33 24N 103 43W
Capron, Ill. **21** 42 24N 88 44W
Capron, Okla. **43** 36 54N 98 35W
Captain Cook **19** 19 30N 155 55W
Captiva **17** 26 31N 82 11W
Caquetá □ **70** 1 0N 74 0W
Caquetá → **70** 1 15 S 69 15W
Carabobo **70** 10 2N 68 5W
Carabobo □ **70** 10 10N 68 5W
Caracal **89** 44 8N 24 22 E
Caracaraí **71** 1 50N 61 8W
Caracas **70** 10 30N 66 55W
Caracol **74** 9 15 S 43 22W
Caracollo **72** 17 39 S 67 10W
Carahue **78** 38 43 S 73 12W
Caraí **75** 17 12 S 41 42W
Carajás, Serra dos **74** 6 0 S 51 30W
Caranapatuba **73** 6 38 S 62 34W
Carandaiti **73** 20 45 S 63 4W
Carangola **75** 20 44 S 42 5W
Caransebeş **89** 45 28N 22 18 E
Caraparaná → **70** 1 45 S 73 13W
Caras **72** 9 3 S 77 47W
Caratasca, Laguna **66** 15 20N 83 40W
Caratinga **75** 19 50 S 42 10W
Caratunk **26** 45 8N 69 59W
Caraúbas **74** 5 43 S 37 33W
Caravaca **91** 38 8N 1 52W
Caravelas **75** 17 45 S 39 15W
Caraveli **72** 15 45 S 73 25W
Caraway **13** 35 46N 90 19W
Caràzinho **77** 28 16 S 52 46W
Carballo **91** 43 13N 8 41W
Carberry **63** 49 50N 99 25W
Carbó **64** 29 42N 110 58W
Carbon, Canada **62** 51 30N 113 9W
Carbon, Ind. **22** 39 36N 87 6W
Carbon, Iowa **23** 41 3N 94 50W
Carbon, Tex. **51** 32 16N 98 50W
Carbon County ◇, Mont. **33** 45 10N 109 0W
Carbon County ◇, Pa. **45** 41 0N 75 50W
Carbon County ◇, Utah **52** 39 40N 110 30W
Carbon County ◇, Wyo. **56** 42 0N 107 0W
Carbon Hill **10** 33 53N 87 32W
Carbonado **53** 47 5N 122 3W
Carbonara, C. **94** 39 8N 9 30 E
Carbondale, Colo. **16** 39 24N 107 13W
Carbondale, Ill. **21** 37 44N 89 13W
Carbondale, Kans. **24** 38 49N 95 41W
Carbondale, Pa. **45** 41 35N 75 30W
Carbonear **61** 47 42N 53 13W
Carbonia **94** 39 10N 8 30 E
Carcajou **62** 57 47N 117 6W
Carcasse, C. **67** 18 30N 74 28W
Carcassonne **90** 43 13N 2 20 E
Carchi □ **70** 0 45N 78 0W
Cardamom Hills **108** 9 30N 77 15 E
Cárdenas, Cuba **66** 23 0N 81 30W
Cárdenas, San Luis Potosí, Mexico **65** 22 0N 99 41W
Cárdenas, Tabasco, Mexico **65** 17 59N 93 21W
Cardiel, L. **78** 48 55 S 71 10W
Cardiff, U.K. **83** 51 28N 3 11W
Cardiff, U.S.A. **16** 39 31N 107 19W
Cardigan **83** 52 6N 4 41W
Cardigan, Mt. **36** 43 40N 71 54W
Cardigan B. **83** 52 30N 4 30W
Cardington **42** 40 30N 82 54W
Cardón, Punta **70** 11 37N 70 14W
Cardona, Spain **91** 41 56N 1 40 E
Cardona, Uruguay **76** 33 53 S 57 18W
Cardross **63** 49 50N 105 40W
Cardston **62** 49 15N 113 20W
Cardwell **32** 36 3N 90 17W
Careen L. **63** 57 0N 108 11W
Carefree **12** 33 50N 111 55W
Carei **89** 47 40N 22 29 E
Careiro **71** 3 12 S 59 45W
Careme **111** 6 55 S 108 27 E
Carencro **25** 30 19N 92 3W
Carey, Idaho **20** 43 19N 113 57W
Carey, Ohio **42** 40 57N 83 23W
Carey, L. **126** 29 0 S 122 15 E
Carey L. **63** 62 12N 102 55W
Careysburg **120** 6 34N 10 30W
Cargados Garajos **3** 17 0 S 59 0 E
Carhuamayo **72** 10 51 S 76 4W
Carhuas **72** 9 15 S 77 39W
Carhué **76** 37 10 S 62 50W
Caribbean Sea **67** 15 0N 75 0W
Cariboo Mts. **62** 53 0N 121 0W
Caribou **26** 46 52N 68 1W
Caribou →, Man., Canada **63** 59 20N 94 44W
Caribou →, N.W.T., Canada **62** 61 27N 125 45W
Caribou County ◇ **20** 42 50N 111 30W
Caribou I. **60** 47 22N 85 49W
Caribou Is. **62** 61 55N 113 15W
Caribou L., Man., Canada **63** 59 21N 96 10W
Caribou L., Ont., Canada **60** 50 25N 89 5W
Caribou Mts. **62** 59 12N 115 40W
Caribou Nat. Forest **20** 42 50N 111 5W
Caribou National Forest **20** 42 40N 111 10W
Caribou Range **20** 43 10N 111 15W
Carichic **64** 27 56N 107 3W
Carillo **64** 26 50N 103 55W
Carinhanha **75** 14 15 S 44 46W
Carinhanha → **75** 14 20 S 43 47W
Carinthia □ = Kärnten □ **88** 46 52N 13 30 E
Caripito **71** 10 8N 63 6W
Carite, Lago **57** 18 5N 66 6W
Caritianas **73** 9 20 S 63 6W
Carl Blackwell, L. **43** 36 8N 97 11W
Carl Junction **32** 37 11N 94 34W
Carleton, Mich. **29** 42 4N 83 24W
Carleton, Nebr. **34** 40 18N 97 41W
Carleton Place **60** 45 8N 76 9W
Carlin **35** 40 43N 116 7W
Carlingford, L. **85** 54 0N 6 5W
Carlinville **21** 39 17N 89 53W
Carlisle, U.K. **82** 54 54N 2 55W
Carlisle, Ark. **13** 34 47N 91 45W
Carlisle, Ind. **22** 38 58N 87 24W
Carlisle, Iowa **23** 41 30N 93 29W
Carlisle, Ky. **49** 38 19N 84 1W
Carlisle, Pa. **45** 40 12N 77 12W
Carlisle, S.C. **46** 34 36N 81 28W
Carlisle, Wash. **53** 47 10N 124 6W
Carlisle County ◇ **48** 36 50N 89 0W
Carlock **21** 40 35N 89 8W
Carlos, Minn. **30** 45 58N 95 18W
Carlos, Tex. **51** 30 36N 96 5W
Carlos Casares **76** 35 32 S 61 20W
Carlos Chagas **75** 17 43 S 40 45W
Carlos Tejedor **76** 35 25 S 62 25W
Carlota, La **76** 33 30 S 63 20W
Carlow **85** 52 50N 6 58W
Carlow □ **85** 52 43N 6 50W
Carlsbad, Calif. **15** 33 10N 117 21W
Carlsbad, N. Mex. **38** 32 25N 104 14W
Carlsbad, Tex. **50** 31 36N 100 38W
Carlsbad Caverns National Park **38** 32 10N 104 35W
Carlton, Minn. **30** 46 40N 92 25W
Carlton, Oreg. **44** 45 18N 123 11W
Carlton County ◇ **30** 46 35N 92 50W
Carlyle, Canada **63** 49 40N 102 20W
Carlyle, Ill. **21** 38 37N 89 22W
Carlyle, Mont. **33** 46 40N 104 4W
Carlyle L. **21** 38 37N 89 21W
Carmacks **58** 62 5N 136 16W
Carman **63** 49 30N 98 0W
Carmangay **62** 50 10N 113 10W
Carmanville **61** 49 23N 54 19W
Carmarthen **83** 51 52N 4 20W
Carmarthen B. **83** 51 40N 4 30W
Carmel, Ind. **22** 39 59N 86 8W
Carmel, N.Y. **39** 41 26N 73 41W
Carmel-by-the-Sea **14** 36 33N 121 55W
Carmel Mt. **104** 32 45N 35 3 E
Carmel Valley **14** 36 29N 121 43W
Carmelo **76** 34 0 S 58 20W
Carmen, Bolivia **72** 11 40 S 67 51W
Carmen, Colombia **70** 9 43N 75 8W
Carmen, Paraguay **77** 27 13 S 56 12W
Carmen, Idaho **20** 45 15N 113 54W
Carmen, Okla. **43** 36 35N 98 28W
Carmen → **64** 30 42N 106 29W
Carmen, I. **64** 26 0N 111 20W
Carmen de Patagones **78** 40 50 S 63 0W
Carmensa **76** 35 15 S 67 40W
Carmi **21** 38 5N 88 10W
Carmichael **14** 38 38N 121 19W
Carmona **91** 37 28N 5 42W
Carnarvon, Australia **126** 24 51 S 113 42 E
Carnarvon, S. Africa **123** 30 56 S 22 8 E
Carnation **53** 47 39N 121 55W
Carndonagh **85** 55 15N 7 16W
Carnduff **63** 49 10N 101 50W
Carnegie, Ga. **18** 31 39N 84 47W
Carnegie, Okla. **43** 35 6N 98 36W
Carnegie, Pa. **45** 40 24N 80 5W
Carnegie, L. **126** 26 5 S 122 30 E
Carneiro **24** 38 44N 98 2W
Carnesville **18** 34 22N 83 14W
Carney, Mich. **29** 45 35N 87 34W
Carney, Okla. **43** 35 48N 97 1W
Carneys Point **37** 39 43N 75 28W
Carnic Alps = Karnische Alpen **88** 46 36N 13 0 E
Carniche, Alpi **94** 46 36N 13 0 E
Carnot **122** 4 59N 15 56 E
Carnot B. **126** 17 20 S 121 30 E
Carnsore Pt. **85** 52 10N 6 20W
Caro **29** 43 29N 83 24W
Carol City **17** 25 56N 80 16W
Caroleen **40** 35 17N 81 48W
Carolina, Brazil **74** 7 10 S 47 30W
Carolina, Puerto Rico **57** 18 23N 65 58W
Carolina, U.S.A. **28** 41 28N 71 40W
Carolina, La **91** 38 17N 3 38W
Carolina Beach **40** 34 2N 77 54W
Caroline County ◇, Md. **27** 38 50N 75 50W
Caroline County ◇, Va. **54** 38 3N 77 21W
Caroline I. **125** 9 15 S 150 3W
Caroline Is. **124** 8 0N 150 0 E
Carollton **29** 43 28N 83 55W
Caron **63** 50 30N 105 50W
Caroni → **71** 8 21N 62 43W
Carora **70** 10 11N 70 5W
Carp **35** 37 7N 114 29W
Carpathians, Mts. **89** 49 50N 21 0 E
Carpaţii Meridionali **89** 45 30N 25 0 E
Carpentaria, G. of **127** 14 0 S 139 0 E
Carpenter, Iowa **23** 43 25N 93 1W
Carpenter, Wyo. **56** 41 3N 104 22W
Carpenterville **44** 42 13N 124 17W
Carpina **74** 7 51 S 35 15W
Carpinteria **15** 34 24N 119 31W
Carr **16** 40 54N 104 53W
Carr Mt. **36** 43 52N 71 50W
Carrabassett **26** 45 5N 70 13W
Carrabelle **17** 29 51N 84 40W
Carrara **94** 44 5N 10 7 E
Carrauntoohill, Mt. **85** 52 0N 9 49W

Carretas, Punta **Cedar L.**

Carretas, Punta **72** 14 12 S 76 17W
Carrick-on-Shannon **85** 53 57N 8 7W
Carrick-on-Suir **85** 52 22N 7 30W
Carrickfergus **85** 54 43N 5 50W
Carrickfergus □ **85** 54 43N 5 49W
Carrickmacross **85** 54 0N 6 43W
Carrier **43** 36 29N 98 2W
Carrier Mills **21** 37 41N 88 38W
Carriere **31** 30 37N 89 39W
Carrigain, Mt. **36** 44 6N 71 26W
Carrington **41** 47 27N 99 8W
Carrizal Bajo **76** 28 5 S 71 20W
Carrizalillo **76** 29 5 S 71 30W
Carrizo Springs **51** 28 31N 99 52W
Carrizozo **38** 33 38N 105 53W
Carroll, Iowa **23** 42 4N 94 52W
Carroll, Nebr. **34** 42 17N 97 12W
Carroll, Ohio **42** 39 48N 82 43W
Carroll County ◇, Ark. **13** 36 22N 93 34W
Carroll County ◇, Ga. **18** 33 30N 85 10W
Carroll County ◇, Ill. **21** 42 0N 90 0W
Carroll County ◇, Ind. **22** 40 35N 86 35W
Carroll County ◇, Iowa **23** 42 0N 94 50W
Carroll County ◇, Ky. **49** 38 40N 85 5W
Carroll County ◇, Md. **27** 39 30N 77 0W
Carroll County ◇, Miss. **31** 33 30N 89 55W
Carroll County ◇, Mo. **32** 39 25N 93 30W
Carroll County ◇, N.H. **36** 43 50N 71 45W
Carroll County ◇, Ohio **42** 40 34N 81 5W
Carroll County ◇, Tenn. **48** 36 0N 88 26W
Carroll County ◇, Va. **54** 36 55N 80 50W
Carrolls **53** 46 4N 122 52W
Carrollton, Ala. **10** 33 16N 88 6W
Carrollton, Ga. **18** 33 35N 85 5W
Carrollton, Ill. **21** 39 18N 90 24W
Carrollton, Ky. **49** 38 41N 85 11W
Carrollton, Miss. **31** 33 30N 89 55W
Carrollton, Mo. **32** 39 22N 93 30W
Carrollton, Ohio **42** 40 34N 81 5W
Carrollton, Tex. **51** 32 57N 96 55W
Carrolltown **45** 40 36N 78 43W
Carron → **84** 57 30N 5 30W
Carron, L. **84** 57 22N 5 35W
Carrot → **63** 53 50N 101 17W
Carrot River **63** 53 17N 103 35W
Carruthers **63** 52 52N 109 16W
Carry Falls Reservoir **39** 44 31N 74 45W
Çarşamba **106** 41 15N 36 45 E
Carse of Gowrie **84** 56 30N 3 10W
Carson, Calif. **15** 33 48N 118 17W
Carson, Iowa **23** 41 14N 95 25W
Carson, N. Dak. **41** 46 25N 101 34W
Carson, Wash. **53** 45 44N 121 49W
Carson → **35** 39 45N 118 40W
Carson City **35** 39 10N 119 46W
Carson County ◇ **50** 35 20N 101 25W
Carson L. **35** 39 18N 118 43W
Carson National Forest **38** 36 30N 106 15W
Carson Sink **35** 39 50N 118 25W
Carstairs **84** 55 42N 3 41W
Carta Valley **50** 29 48N 100 41W
Cartagena, Colombia **70** 10 25N 75 33W
Cartagena, Spain **91** 37 38N 0 59W
Cartago, Colombia **70** 4 45N 75 55W
Cartago, C. Rica **66** 9 50N 85 52W
Cartago, U.S.A. **15** 36 19N 118 2W
Carter, Ky. **49** 38 26N 83 8W
Carter, Okla. **43** 35 13N 99 30W
Carter, S. Dak. **47** 43 23N 100 12W
Carter County ◇, Ky. **49** 38 20N 83 0W
Carter County ◇, Mo. **32** 37 0N 91 0W
Carter County ◇, Mont. **33** 45 30N 104 30W
Carter County ◇, Okla. **43** 34 15N 97 15W
Carter County ◇, Tenn. **49** 36 17N 82 10W
Carter Lake **23** 41 18N 95 54W
Carter Lake Reservoir **16** 40 20N 105 13W
Carter Mt. **56** 44 12N 109 25W
Carteret **37** 40 34N 74 13W
Carteret County ◇ **40** 34 50N 76 30W
Carters L. **18** 34 37N 84 40W
Cartersville, Ga. **18** 34 10N 84 48W
Cartersville, Va. **54** 37 40N 78 6W
Carterton **128** 41 2 S 175 31 E
Carterville **21** 37 46N 89 5W
Carthage, Ark. **13** 34 4N 92 33W
Carthage, Ill. **21** 40 25N 91 8W
Carthage, Ind. **22** 39 44N 85 34W
Carthage, Miss. **31** 32 44N 89 32W
Carthage, Mo. **32** 37 11N 94 19W
Carthage, N.C. **40** 35 21N 79 25W
Carthage, N.Y. **39** 43 59N 75 37W
Carthage, S. Dak. **47** 44 10N 97 43W
Carthage, Tenn. **49** 36 15N 85 57W
Carthage, Tex. **51** 32 9N 94 20W
Cartier I. **126** 12 31 S 123 29 E
Cartwright **61** 53 41N 56 58W
Caruaru **74** 8 15 S 35 55W
Carúpano **71** 10 39N 63 15W
Carutapera **74** 1 13 S 46 1W
Caruthersville **32** 36 11N 89 39W
Carvalho **71** 2 16 S 51 29W
Carver County ◇ **30** 44 50N 93 45W
Carville **25** 30 13N 91 6W
Carvoeiro **71** 1 30 S 61 59W
Cary, Ill. **21** 42 13N 88 14W
Cary, Miss. **31** 32 49N 90 56W
Cary, N.C. **40** 35 47N 78 46W
Caryville **49** 36 18N 84 13W
Casa **13** 35 2N 93 3W
Casa Blanca **38** 35 3N 107 28W
Casa Branca **75** 21 46 S 47 4W
Casa Grande **12** 32 53N 111 45W
Casa Grande Ruins National Monument **12** 33 0N 111 30W
Casa Nova **74** 9 25 S 41 5W
Casablanca, Chile **76** 33 20 S 71 25W
Casablanca, Morocco **120** 33 36N 7 36W
Casale Monferrato **94** 45 8N 8 28 E
Casanare → **70** 6 2N 69 51W
Casas Grandes **64** 30 22N 108 0W
Cascade, Colo. **16** 38 54N 104 58W
Cascade, Idaho **20** 44 31N 116 2W
Cascade, Iowa **23** 42 18N 91 1W
Cascade, Mont. **33** 47 16N 111 42W
Cascade County ◇ **33** 47 20N 111 30W
Cascade Head **44** 45 3N 124 1W
Cascade Locks **44** 45 40N 121 54W
Cascade Range **44** 45 0N 121 30W
Cascade Reservoir **20** 44 32N 116 3W
Cascadia **44** 44 24N 122 29W
Casco, Maine **26** 44 0N 70 31W
Casco, Wis. **55** 44 34N 87 37W
Casco B. **26** 43 45N 70 0W
Caserta **94** 41 5N 14 20 E
Caseville **29** 43 56N 83 16W
Casey, Ill. **21** 39 18N 87 59W
Casey, Iowa **23** 41 31N 94 32W
Casey County ◇ **49** 37 20N 85 0W
Cash **13** 35 48N 90 56W
Cashel **85** 52 31N 7 53W
Cashie → **40** 35 53N 76 49W
Cashiers **40** 35 6N 83 6W
Cashion **43** 35 48N 97 41W
Cashmere **53** 47 31N 120 28W
Cashton **55** 43 43N 90 47W
Casibare → **70** 3 48N 72 18W
Casiguran **111** 16 22N 122 7 E
Casilda **76** 33 10 S 61 10W
Casimcea **95** 44 45N 28 23 E
Casino **127** 28 52 S 153 3 E
Casiquiare → **70** 2 1N 67 7W
Casitas **72** 3 54 S 80 39W
Caslan **62** 54 38N 112 31W
Casma **72** 9 30 S 78 20W
Casmalia **15** 34 50N 120 32W
Casnovia **29** 43 14N 85 48W
Cason **51** 33 2N 94 49W
Caspe **91** 41 14N 0 1W
Casper **56** 42 51N 106 19W
Caspian **29** 46 4N 88 38W
Caspian Sea **99** 43 0N 50 0 E
Caspiana **25** 32 17N 93 33W
Cass **54** 38 24N 79 55W
Cass → **29** 43 23N 83 59W
Cass City **29** 43 36N 83 11W
Cass County ◇, Ill. **21** 40 0N 90 15W
Cass County ◇, Ind. **22** 40 45N 86 20W
Cass County ◇, Iowa **23** 41 20N 94 55W
Cass County ◇, Mich. **29** 41 50N 86 0W
Cass County ◇, Minn. **30** 47 0N 94 10W
Cass County ◇, Mo. **32** 38 40N 94 20W
Cass County ◇, N. Dak. **41** 47 0N 97 0W
Cass County ◇, Nebr. **34** 40 50N 96 10W
Cass County ◇, Tex. **51** 33 1N 94 22W
Cass Lake **30** 47 23N 94 37W
Cassadaga **39** 42 20N 79 19W
Casselton **41** 46 54N 97 13W
Cassia County ◇ **20** 42 20N 113 30W
Cassiar **62** 59 16N 129 40W
Cassiar Mts. **62** 59 30N 130 30W
Cassilândia **73** 19 9 S 51 45W
Cassinga **123** 15 5 S 16 4 E
Cassoday **24** 38 3N 96 38W
Cassopolis **29** 41 55N 86 1W
Cassville, Mo. **32** 36 41N 93 52W
Cassville, Pa. **45** 40 18N 78 2W
Cassville, Wis. **55** 42 43N 90 59W
Castaic L. **15** 34 32N 118 37W
Castalia, Iowa **23** 43 7N 91 41W
Castalia, Ohio **42** 41 24N 82 49W
Castana **23** 42 4N 95 55W
Castanhal **74** 1 18 S 47 55W
Castella **14** 41 9N 122 19W
Castellammare del Golfo **94** 38 2N 12 53 E
Castellammare di Stábia **94** 40 47N 14 29 E
Castelli **76** 36 7 S 57 47W
Castellón de la Plana **91** 39 58N 0 3W
Castelo **75** 20 33 S 41 14 E
Castelo Branco **91** 39 50N 7 31W
Castelo do Piauí **74** 5 20 S 41 33W
Castelvetrano **94** 37 40N 12 46 E
Castile **39** 42 38N 78 3W
Castilla **72** 5 12 S 80 38W
Castilla La Mancha **91** 39 30N 3 30W
Castilla La Nueva **91** 39 45N 3 20W
Castilla La Vieja **91** 41 55N 4 0W
Castilla y Leon **91** 42 0N 5 0 E
Castillón **64** 28 20N 103 38W
Castillos **77** 34 12 S 53 52W
Castle **43** 35 28N 96 23W
Castle Dale **52** 39 13N 111 1W
Castle Dome Peak **12** 33 5N 114 9W
Castle Douglas **84** 54 57N 3 57W
Castle Gate **52** 39 44N 110 52W
Castle Hayne **40** 34 21N 77 54W
Castle Hills **51** 29 32N 98 31W
Castle Peak **16** 39 1N 106 52W
Castle Pk. **20** 44 1N 114 42W
Castle Point **128** 40 54 S 176 15 E
Castle Rock, Colo. **16** 39 22N 104 51W
Castle Rock, Wash. **53** 46 17N 122 54W
Castle Rock Butte **47** 45 0N 103 27W
Castle Rock L. **55** 43 52N 89 57W
Castlebar **85** 53 52N 9 17W
Castleberry **10** 31 18N 87 1W
Castleblaney **85** 54 7N 6 44W
Castleford **20** 42 31N 114 52W
Castlegar **62** 49 20N 117 40W
Castlemaine **127** 37 2 S 144 12 E
Castlereagh **85** 53 47N 8 30W
Castlereagh □ **85** 54 33N 5 53W
Castlereagh → **127** 30 12 S 147 32 E
Castlereagh B. **126** 12 10 S 135 10 E
Castleton **36** 43 37N 73 11W
Castleton-on-Hudson **39** 42 32N 73 45W
Castletown **82** 54 4N 4 40W
Castletown Bearhaven **85** 51 40N 9 54W
Castlewood **47** 44 44N 97 2W
Castolon **50** 29 8N 103 31W
Castor, Canada **62** 52 15N 111 50W
Castor, U.S.A. **25** 32 15N 93 10W
Castor → **32** 36 51N 89 44W
Castor Bayou → **25** 31 47N 99 22W
Castres **90** 43 37N 2 13 E
Castries **67** 14 0N 60 50W
Castro, Brazil **77** 24 45 S 50 0W
Castro, Chile **78** 42 30 S 73 50W
Castro Alves **75** 12 46 S 39 33W
Castro County ◇ **50** 34 33N 102 19W
Castro del Río **91** 37 41N 4 29W
Castro Valley **14** 37 42N 122 4W
Castroville, Calif. **14** 36 46N 121 45W
Castroville, Tex. **51** 29 21N 98 53W
Castrovirreyna **72** 13 20 S 75 18W
Casummit Lake **60** 51 29N 92 22W
Caswell County ◇ **40** 36 20N 79 15W
Cat Head Pt. **29** 45 11N 85 37W
Cat I., Bahamas **67** 24 30N 75 30W
Cat I., U.S.A. **31** 30 14N 89 6W
Cat L. **60** 51 40N 91 50W
Cat Spring **51** 29 51N 96 20W
Catacamas **66** 14 54N 85 56W
Catacáos **72** 5 20 S 80 45W
Cataguases **75** 21 23 S 42 39W
Catahoula L. **25** 31 31N 92 7W
Catahoula Parish ◇ **25** 31 35N 91 58W
Catalão **75** 18 10 S 47 57W
Catalina, Canada **61** 48 31N 53 4W
Catalina, U.S.A. **12** 32 30N 110 50W
Catalonia = Cataluña □ **91** 41 40N 1 15 E
Cataluña □ **91** 41 40N 1 15 E
Catamarca **76** 28 30 S 65 50W
Catamarca □ **76** 27 0 S 65 50W
Catanduanes **111** 13 50N 124 20 E
Catanduva **75** 21 5 S 48 58W
Catánia **94** 37 31N 15 4 E
Catano **57** 18 27N 66 7W
Catanzaro **94** 38 54N 16 38 E
Cataract L. **22** 39 29N 86 55W
Catarina **51** 28 21N 99 37W
Catarman **111** 12 28N 124 35 E
Catastrophe C. **126** 34 59 S 136 0 E
Cataula **18** 32 39N 84 52W
Catawba **55** 45 32N 90 32W
Catawba → **46** 34 28N 80 53W
Catawba County ◇ **40** 35 40N 81 10W
Catawissa **45** 40 57N 76 28W
Cateel **111** 7 47N 126 24 E
Catende **74** 8 40 S 35 43W
Cathay **41** 47 33N 99 25W
Cathedral City **15** 33 47N 116 28W
Cathedral Mt. **50** 30 11N 103 40W
Catherine, Ala. **10** 32 11N 87 28W
Catherine, Kans. **24** 38 56N 99 13W
Cathlamet **53** 46 12N 123 23W
Catismiña **71** 4 5N 63 40W
Catita **74** 9 31 S 43 1W
Catlettsburg **49** 38 25N 82 36W
Catlin **21** 40 4N 87 42W
Catlow Valley **44** 42 20N 119 5W
Cato I. **127** 23 15 S 155 32 E
Catoche, C. **65** 21 40N 87 8W
Catoctin Mts. **27** 39 35N 77 30W
Catolé do Rocha **74** 6 21 S 37 45W
Catonsville **27** 39 17N 76 44W
Catoosa **43** 36 11N 95 45W
Catoosa County ◇ **18** 34 50N 85 10W
Catrima **51** 28 21N 99 37W
Catrimani **71** 0 27N 61 41W
Catrimani → **71** 0 28N 61 44W
Catron County ◇ **38** 34 0N 108 15W
Catskill **39** 42 14N 73 52W
Catskill Mts. **39** 42 10N 74 25W
Cattaraugus County ◇ **39** 42 30N 78 45W
Cattaraugus Indian Reservation **39** 42 30N 79 0W
Catu **75** 12 21 S 38 23W
Cauca □ **70** 2 30N 76 50W
Cauca → **70** 8 54N 74 28W
Caucaia **74** 3 40 S 38 35W
Caucasia **70** 8 0N 75 12W
Caucasus Mts. = Bolshoi Kavkas **99** 42 50N 44 0 E
Caucomgomoc L. **26** 46 13N 69 36W
Caúngula **122** 8 26 S 18 38 E
Cauquenes **76** 36 0 S 72 22W
Caura → **71** 7 38N 64 53W
Caurés → **71** 1 21 S 62 20W
Causapscal **61** 48 19N 67 12W
Causey **38** 33 53N 103 8W
Cauthron **13** 34 55N 94 18W
Cautín □ **78** 39 0 S 72 30W
Cauvery → **108** 11 9N 78 52 E
Caux, Pays de **90** 49 38N 0 35 E
Cavalcante **75** 13 48 S 47 30W
Cavalier **41** 48 48N 97 37W
Cavalier County ◇ **41** 48 55N 97 30W
Cavan **85** 54 0N 7 22W
Cavan □ **85** 53 58N 7 10W
Cave City, Ark. **13** 35 57N 91 33W
Cave City, Ky. **49** 37 8N 85 58W
Cave Creek **12** 33 50N 111 57W
Cave in Rock **21** 37 28N 88 10W
Cave Junction **44** 42 10N 123 39W
Cave Run L. **49** 38 5N 83 25W
Cave Spring **18** 34 6N 85 20W
Caviana, I. **74** 0 10N 50 10W
Cavite **111** 14 29N 120 55 E
Cawker City **24** 39 31N 98 26W
Cawnpore = Kanpur **108** 26 28N 80 20 E
Caxias **74** 4 55 S 43 20W
Caxias do Sul **77** 29 10 S 51 10W
Caxito **122** 8 30 S 13 30 E
Cay Sal Bank **66** 23 45N 80 0W
Cayambe **70** 0 3N 78 8W
Cayambe, Vol. **70** 0 2N 77 59W
Cayce, Ky. **48** 36 33N 89 2W
Cayce, S.C. **46** 33 59N 81 4W
Cayenne **71** 5 0N 52 18W
Cayenne □ **71** 4 0N 53 0W
Cayes, Les **67** 18 15N 73 46W
Cayey **57** 18 7N 66 10W
Cayman Brac **66** 19 43N 79 49W
Cayman Is. **66** 19 40N 80 30W
Cayo Romano **67** 22 0N 78 0W
Cayucos **15** 35 27N 120 54W
Cayuga, Ind. **22** 39 57N 87 28W
Cayuga, N. Dak. **41** 46 4N 97 23W
Cayuga County ◇ **39** 43 0N 76 35W
Cayuga Heights **39** 42 28N 76 30W
Cayuga L. **39** 42 41N 76 41W
Cayuse **44** 45 41N 118 33W
Căzănești **95** 44 36N 27 3 E
Cazenovia **39** 42 56N 75 51W
Cazombo **123** 11 54 S 22 56 E
Cazorla **70** 8 1N 67 0W
Ceamurlia de Jos **95** 44 43N 28 47 E
Ceanannus Mor **85** 53 42N 6 53W
Ceará = Fortaleza **74** 3 45 S 38 35W
Ceará □ **74** 5 0 S 40 0W
Ceará Mirim **74** 5 38 S 35 25W
Cearfoss **27** 39 0N 77 0W
Ceauru, L. **95** 44 58N 23 11 E
Cebaco, I. de **66** 7 33N 81 9W
Cebollar **76** 29 10 S 66 35W
Cebu **111** 10 18N 123 54 E
Cecil, Ga. **18** 31 3N 83 24W
Cecil, Oreg. **44** 45 37N 119 58W
Cecil County ◇ **27** 39 30N 76 0W
Cecilia **49** 37 40N 85 57W
Cecilton **27** 39 24N 75 52W
Cecilville **14** 41 9N 123 8W
Cedar →, Iowa **23** 41 17N 91 21W
Cedar →, Mich. **29** 45 25N 87 26W
Cedar →, Nebr. **34** 41 22N 97 56W
Cedar Bluff, Ala. **10** 34 13N 85 37W
Cedar Bluff, Va. **54** 37 5N 81 46W
Cedar Bluff Reservoir **24** 38 47N 99 43W
Cedar Bluffs, Kans. **24** 39 59N 100 34W
Cedar Bluffs, Nebr. **34** 41 24N 96 37W
Cedar Breaks National Monument **52** 37 40N 112 50W
Cedar Brook **37** 39 43N 74 54W
Cedar Butte **47** 43 35N 101 1W
Cedar City, Mo. **32** 38 36N 92 11W
Cedar City, Utah **52** 37 41N 113 4W
Cedar County ◇, Iowa **23** 41 45N 91 10W
Cedar County ◇, Mo. **32** 37 45N 93 50W
Cedar County ◇, Nebr. **34** 42 40N 97 15W
Cedar Cr. → **41** 46 8N 101 19W
Cedar Creek, Ark. **13** 34 47N 93 51W
Cedar Creek, Nebr. **34** 41 2N 96 6W
Cedar Creek, Tex. **51** 30 5N 97 30W
Cedar Creek Reservoir **51** 32 11N 96 4W
Cedar Falls **23** 42 32N 92 27W
Cedar Grove, Ind. **22** 39 22N 84 56W
Cedar Grove, N.J. **37** 40 51N 74 14W
Cedar Grove, W. Va. **54** 38 13N 81 26W
Cedar Grove, Wis. **55** 43 34N 87 49W
Cedar Hill, Mo. **32** 38 21N 90 39W
Cedar Hill, N. Mex. **38** 36 56N 107 53W
Cedar Hill, Tenn. **48** 36 33N 87 0W
Cedar Key **17** 29 8N 83 2W
Cedar L., Canada **63** 53 10N 100 0W

Cedar L. Charlevoix, L.

Cedar L., Ill. **21** 37 37N 89 18W
Cedar L., Tex. **50** 32 49N 102 17W
Cedar Lake, Ind. **22** 41 22N 87 26W
Cedar Lake, Tex. **51** 28 54N 95 38W
Cedar Mills **30** 44 57N 94 31W
Cedar Mts. **52** 40 10N 112 30W
Cedar Park **51** 30 30N 97 49W
Cedar Point **24** 38 16N 96 49W
Cedar Rapids, Iowa **23** 41 59N 91 40W
Cedar Rapids, Nebr. **34** 41 34N 98 9W
Cedar Springs **29** 43 13N 85 33W
Cedar Vale **24** 37 6N 96 30W
Cedaredge **16** 38 54N 107 56W
Cedartown **18** 34 1N 85 15W
Cedarvale **62** 55 1N 128 22W
Cedarville, Calif. **14** 41 32N 120 10W
Cedarville, Ill. **21** 42 23N 89 38W
Cedarville, Md. **27** 38 40N 76 47W
Cedarville, N.J. **37** 39 18N 75 12W
Cedarville, Ohio **42** 39 44N 83 49W
Cedarwood **16** 37 57N 104 37W
Cedral **64** 23 50N 100 42W
Cedro **74** 6 34 S 39 3W
Cedros, I. de **64** 28 10N 115 20W
Ceduna **126** 32 7 S 133 46 E
Cefalù **94** 38 3N 14 1 E
Cegléd **89** 47 11N 19 47 E
Cehegín **91** 38 6N 1 48W
Ceiba **57** 18 16N 65 39W
Ceiba, La **66** 15 40N 86 50W
Celaya **64** 20 31N 100 37W
Celbridge **85** 53 20N 6 33W
Celebes = Sulawesi □ **111** 2 0 S 120 0 E
Celebes Sea **111** 3 0N 123 0 E
Celendín **72** 6 52 S 78 10W
Celeste **51** 33 18N 96 12W
Celica **70** 4 7 S 79 59W
Celina, Ohio **42** 40 33N 84 35W
Celina, Tenn. **49** 36 33N 85 30W
Celina, Tex. **51** 33 19N 96 47W
Celje **94** 46 16N 15 18 E
Celle **88** 52 37N 10 4 E
Cement **43** 34 56N 98 8W
Cenepa → **70** 4 40 S 78 10W
Cengong **115** 27 13N 108 44 E
Centenário do Sul **75** 22 48 S 51 36W
Centenary **46** 34 2N 79 21W
Centennial Mts. **20** 44 35N 111 55W
Centennial Wash → **12** 33 17N 112 48W
Center, Colo. **16** 37 45N 106 6W
Center, Ga. **18** 34 3N 83 25W
Center, Mo. **32** 39 30N 91 32W
Center, N. Dak. **41** 47 7N 101 18W
Center, Nebr. **34** 42 37N 97 53W
Center, Tex. **51** 31 48N 94 11W
Center Barnstead **36** 43 19N 71 15W
Center City **30** 45 24N 92 49W
Center Cross **54** 37 48N 76 47W
Center Harbor **36** 43 42N 71 27W
Center Hill **17** 28 38N 82 3W
Center Hill L. **49** 36 6N 85 50W
Center Ossipee **36** 43 45N 71 9W
Center Point, Ala. **10** 33 38N 86 41W
Center Point, Ind. **22** 39 25N 87 4W
Center Point, Iowa **23** 42 12N 91 46W
Center Point, La. **25** 31 15N 92 13W
Center Point, Tex. **51** 29 57N 99 2W
Center Sandwich **36** 43 39N 71 25W
Center Strafford **34** 43 17N 71 10W
Centerburg **42** 40 18N 82 42W
Centereach **39** 40 52N 73 6W
Centerfield **52** 39 8N 111 49W
Centerton **37** 39 59N 75 0W
Centertown **32** 38 38N 92 25W
Centerville, Ark. **13** 35 7N 93 10W
Centerville, Calif. **15** 36 44N 119 30W
Centerville, Del. **27** 39 49N 75 37W
Centerville, Ind. **22** 39 49N 85 0W
Centerville, Iowa **23** 40 44N 92 52W
Centerville, Kans. **24** 38 13N 95 1W
Centerville, La. **25** 29 46N 91 26W
Centerville, Mo. **32** 37 26N 90 58W
Centerville, N.C. **40** 36 11N 78 6W
Centerville, N.Y. **39** 42 29N 78 15W
Centerville, Ohio **42** 39 38N 84 8W
Centerville, S. Dak. **47** 43 7N 96 58W
Centerville, Tenn. **48** 35 47N 87 28W
Centerville, Tex. **51** 31 16N 95 59W
Centerville, Utah **52** 40 55N 111 52W
Centerville, Pa. **45** 41 44N 79 46W
Centerville, Pa. **45** 40 3N 79 59W
Centrahoma **43** 34 37N 96 21W
Central, Brazil **74** 11 8 S 42 8W
Central, Alaska **11** 65 35N 144 48W
Central, Mich. **29** 47 25N 88 12W
Central, N. Mex. **38** 32 47N 108 9W
Central, S.C. **46** 34 44N 82 47W
Central, Utah **52** 37 25N 113 38W
Central □ **84** 56 10N 4 30W
Central, Cordillera, Bolivia **73** 18 30 S 64 55W
Central, Cordillera, Colombia **70** 5 0N 75 0W
Central, Cordillera, C. Rica **66** 10 10N 84 5W
Central, Cordillera, Dom. Rep. **67** 19 15N 71 0W
Central, Cordillera, Peru **72** 7 0 S 77 30W
Central, Cordillera, Puerto Rico **57** 18 8N 66 35W
Central African Republic ■ **122** 7 0N 20 0 E
Central Aguirre **57** 17 58N 66 14W
Central City, Colo. **16** 39 48N 105 31W
Central City, Ill. **21** 38 33N 89 8W
Central City, Iowa **23** 42 12N 91 32W
Central City, Ky. **48** 37 18N 87 7W
Central City, Nebr. **34** 41 7N 98 0W
Central City, Pa. **45** 40 7N 78 49W
Central City, S. Dak. **47** 44 22N 103 46W
Central Falls **28** 41 54N 71 23W
Central Islip **39** 40 47N 73 12W
Central Lake **29** 45 4N 85 16W
Central Makran Range **107** 26 30N 64 15 E
Central Patricia **60** 51 30N 90 9W
Central Point **44** 42 23N 122 55W
Central Russian Uplands **80** 54 0N 36 0 E
Central Siberian Plateau **101** 65 0N 105 0 E
Central Square **39** 43 17N 76 9W
Central Valley **14** 40 41N 122 22W
Centralhatchee **18** 33 22N 85 6W
Centralia, Ill. **21** 38 32N 89 8W
Centralia, Kans. **24** 39 44N 96 8W
Centralia, Mo. **32** 39 13N 92 8W
Centralia, Okla. **43** 36 48N 95 21W
Centralia, Wash. **53** 46 43N 122 58W
Centre **10** 34 9N 85 41W
Centre County ◇ **45** 41 0N 78 0W
Centre Grove **37** 39 20N 75 8W
Centreville, Ala. **10** 32 57N 87 8W
Centreville, Md. **27** 39 3N 76 4W
Centreville, Mich. **29** 41 55N 85 32W
Centreville, Miss. **31** 31 5N 91 4W
Century **17** 30 58N 87 16W
Cephalonia = Kefallinía **95** 38 20N 20 30 E
Ceptura **95** 45 1N 26 21 E
Cepu **111** 7 9 S 111 35 E
Ceram = Seram **111** 3 10 S 129 0 E
Ceram Sea = Seram Sea **111** 2 30 S 128 30 E
Cerbu **95** 44 46N 24 46 E
Ceres, Argentina **76** 29 55 S 61 55W
Ceres, Brazil **75** 15 17 S 49 35W
Ceres, S. Africa **123** 33 21 S 19 18 E
Ceres, U.S.A. **14** 37 35N 120 57W
Ceresco **34** 41 3N 96 39W
Cereté **70** 8 53N 75 48W
Cerignola **94** 41 17N 15 53 E
Cerigo = Kíthira **95** 36 9N 23 0 E
Çerkeş **106** 40 49N 32 52 E
Cerknica **94** 45 48N 14 21 E
Cerna **95** 45 4N 28 17 E
Cerna → **95** 44 45N 24 0 E
Cernavodă **89** 44 22N 28 3 E
Cerralvo **64** 24 20N 109 45 E
Cerrillos **38** 35 26N 106 8W
Cerritos **64** 22 27N 100 20W
Cerro Gordo **21** 39 53N 88 44W
Cerro Gordo County ◇ **23** 43 5N 93 15W
Cerro Sombrero **78** 52 45 S 69 15W
Cerro Vista Peak **38** 36 14N 105 25W
Cervera **91** 41 40N 1 16 E
Cervera del Río Alhama **91** 42 2N 1 58W
César □ **70** 9 0N 73 30W
Çesena **94** 44 9N 12 14 E
České Budějovice **88** 48 55N 14 25 E
Çeskomoravská Vrchovina **88** 49 30N 15 40 E
Český Těšin **89** 49 45N 18 39 E
Cessnock **127** 32 50 S 151 21 E
Cetinje **95** 42 23N 18 59 E
Ceuta **120** 35 52N 5 18W
Cévennes **90** 44 10N 3 50 E
Ceyhan **106** 37 4N 35 47 E
Ceylon = Sri Lanka ■ **108** 7 30N 80 50 E
Ceylon **30** 43 32N 94 38W
Cha Pa **112** 22 20N 103 47 E
Chablais **90** 46 20N 6 36 E
Chacabuco **76** 34 40 S 60 27W
Chachapoyas **72** 6 15 S 77 50W
Chachasp **72** 15 30 S 72 15W
Chachran **108** 28 55N 70 30 E
Chaco □ **76** 26 30 S 61 0W
Chaco → **38** 36 46N 108 39W
Chaco Canyon National Monument **38** 36 6N 108 0W
Chacuaco → **16** 37 34N 103 38W
Chad ■ **121** 15 0N 17 15 E
Chad, L. = Tchad, L. **121** 13 30N 14 30 E
Chadan **101** 51 17N 91 35 E
Chadbourn **40** 34 19N 78 50W
Chadileuvú → **76** 37 46 S 66 0W
Chadron **34** 42 50N 103 0W
Chadwick **21** 42 1N 89 53W
Chaffee, Mo. **32** 37 11N 89 40W
Chaffee, N. Dak. **41** 46 46N 97 21W
Chaffee County ◇ **16** 38 45N 106 10W
Chagai Hills **108** 29 30N 63 0 E
Chagda **101** 58 45N 130 38 E
Chagos Arch. **102** 6 0 S 72 0 E
Chagres → **57** 9 10N 79 40W
Chāh Bahār **107** 25 20N 60 40 E
Chāh Gay Hills **107** 29 30N 64 0 E
Chahar Burjak **108** 30 15N 62 0 E
Chahār Mahāll va Bakhtīarī □ **106** 32 0N 49 0 E
Chaibasa **109** 22 42N 85 49 E
Chaires **17** 30 26N 84 7W
Chaitén **78** 42 55 S 72 43W
Chajari **76** 30 42 S 58 0W
Chakhānsūr **107** 31 10N 62 0 E
Chakonipau, L. **61** 56 18N 68 30W
Chakradharpur **109** 22 45N 85 40 E
Chakwal **108** 32 56N 72 53 E
Chala **72** 15 48 S 74 20W
Chalcatongo **65** 17 4N 97 34W
Chalchihuites **64** 23 29N 103 53W
Chalcis = Khalkís **95** 38 27N 23 42 E
Chaleur B. **61** 47 55N 65 30W
Chalhuanca **72** 14 15 S 73 15W
Chaling **115** 26 58N 113 30 E
Chalisgaon **108** 20 30N 75 10 E
Chalk Mts. **50** 29 30N 103 18W
Chalky Inlet **128** 46 3 S 166 31 E
Chalkyitsik **11** 66 39N 143 43W
Challapata **72** 18 53 S 66 50W
Challis **20** 44 30N 114 14W
Challis National Forest **20** 44 0N 113 40W
Chalmers **22** 40 40N 86 52W
Chalmette **25** 29 56N 89 58W
Châlons-sur-Marne **90** 48 58N 4 20 E
Chama, Colo. **16** 37 10N 105 23W
Chama, N. Mex. **38** 36 54N 106 35W
Chaman **107** 30 58N 66 25 E
Chamba, India **108** 32 35N 76 10 E
Chamba, Tanzania **123** 11 37 S 37 0 E
Chambal → **108** 26 29N 79 15 E
Chamberino **38** 32 3N 106 41W
Chamberlain **47** 43 49N 99 20W
Chamberlain L. **26** 46 14N 69 19W
Chambers, Ariz. **12** 35 11N 109 26W
Chambers, Nebr. **34** 42 12N 98 45W
Chambers County ◇, Ala. **10** 32 54N 85 24W
Chambers County ◇, Tex. **51** 29 47N 94 35W
Chambers I. **55** 45 11N 87 22W
Chambersburg **45** 39 56N 77 40W
Chambéry **90** 45 34N 5 55 E
Chamblee **18** 33 53N 84 18W
Chambord **61** 48 25N 72 6W
Chamela **64** 19 32N 105 5W
Chamical **76** 30 22 S 66 27W
Chamisal **38** 36 10N 105 44W
Chamois **32** 38 41N 91 46W
Chamonix **90** 45 55N 6 51 E
Champagne **62** 60 49N 136 30W
Champagne, Plaine de **90** 49 0N 4 30 E
Champaign **21** 40 7N 88 15W
Champaign County ◇, Ill. **21** 40 10N 88 10W
Champaign County ◇, Ohio **42** 40 7N 83 45W
Champion, Mich. **29** 46 31N 87 58W
Champion, Ohio **42** 41 19N 80 51W
Champion B. **126** 28 44 S 114 36 E
Champion Creek Reservoir **50** 32 17N 100 52W
Champlain, Canada **60** 46 27N 72 24W
Champlain, U.S.A. **39** 44 59N 73 27W
Champlain, L. **39** 44 40N 73 20W
Champlain Canal **39** 43 30N 73 27W
Champotón **65** 19 20N 90 50W
Chan Chan **72** 8 7 S 79 0W
Chañaral **76** 26 23 S 70 40W
Chancay **72** 11 32 S 77 25W
Chancellor **47** 43 22N 96 59W
Chandalar → **11** 66 37N 146 0W
Chandeleur Is. **25** 29 55N 88 57W
Chandeleur Sd. **25** 29 55N 89 0W
Chandigarh **108** 30 43N 76 47 E
Chandler, Canada **61** 48 18N 64 46W
Chandler, Ariz. **12** 33 18N 111 50W
Chandler, Ind. **22** 38 3N 87 22W
Chandler, Minn. **30** 43 56N 95 57W
Chandler, Okla. **43** 35 42N 96 53W
Chandler, Tex. **51** 32 18N 95 29W
Chandlerville **21** 40 3N 90 9W
Chandless → **72** 9 8 S 69 51W
Chandmani **113** 45 22N 98 2 E
Chandpur **109** 23 8N 90 45 E
Chandrapur **108** 19 57N 79 25 E
Chang Jiang → **115** 31 48N 121 10 E
Changanacheri **108** 9 25N 76 31 E
Changane → **123** 23 30 S 33 50 E
Changbai **114** 41 25N 128 5 E
Changbai Shan **114** 42 20N 129 0 E
Ch'angchou = Changzhou **115** 31 47N 119 58 E
Changchun **114** 43 57N 125 17 E
Changde **115** 29 4N 111 35 E
Changfeng **115** 32 28N 117 10 E
Changhai = Shanghai **115** 31 15N 121 26 E
Changjiang **115** 19 20N 108 55 E
Changjin-chŏsuji **114** 40 30N 127 15 E
Changle **115** 25 59N 119 27 E
Changli **114** 39 40N 119 13 E
Changning **115** 26 28N 112 22 E
Changping **114** 40 14N 116 12 E
Changsha **115** 28 12N 113 0 E
Changshou **115** 29 51N 107 8 E
Changshu **115** 31 38N 120 43 E
Changshun **115** 26 3N 106 25 E
Changtai **115** 24 35N 117 42 E
Changting **115** 25 50N 116 22 E
Changyang **115** 30 30N 111 10 E
Changzhi **114** 36 10N 113 6 E
Changzhou **115** 31 47N 119 58 E
Chanhassen **30** 44 55N 93 32W
Channahon **21** 41 26N 88 14W
Channapatna **108** 12 40N 77 15 E
Channel Is., U.K. **83** 49 30N 2 40W
Channel Is., U.S.A. **15** 33 40N 119 15W
Channel Islands National Park **15** 33 30N 119 0W
Channel-Port aux Basques **61** 47 30N 59 9W
Channelview **51** 29 47N 95 8W
Channing, Mich. **29** 46 9N 88 5W
Channing, Tex. **50** 35 41N 102 20W
Chantada **91** 42 36N 7 46W
Chanthaburi **112** 12 38N 102 12 E
Chantrey Inlet **58** 67 48N 96 20W
Chanute **24** 37 41N 95 27W
Chao Hu **115** 31 30N 117 30 E
Chao Phraya → **112** 13 32N 100 36 E
Chao'an **115** 23 42N 116 32 E
Chaoyang, Guangdong, China **115** 23 17N 116 30 E
Chaoyang, Liaoning, China **114** 41 35N 120 22 E
Chapada dos Guimarães **73** 15 26 S 55 45W
Chapala, Lago de **64** 20 10N 103 20W
Chaparé → **73** 15 58 S 64 42W
Chaparral **70** 3 43N 75 28W
Chapayevo **99** 50 25N 51 10 E
Chapayevsk **98** 53 0N 49 40 E
Chapecó **77** 27 14 S 52 41W
Chapel Hill, Ky. **48** 36 43N 86 18W
Chapel Hill, N.C. **40** 35 55N 79 4W
Chapel Hill, Tenn. **48** 35 38N 86 41W
Chapin **21** 39 46N 90 24W
Chapleau **60** 47 50N 83 24W
Chaplin, Canada **63** 50 28N 106 40W
Chaplin, U.S.A. **49** 37 54N 85 13W
Chapman, Ala. **10** 31 40N 86 43W
Chapman, Kans. **24** 38 58N 97 1W
Chapman, Nebr. **34** 41 2N 98 10W
Chapmanville **54** 37 59N 82 1W
Chappaquiddick Island **28** 41 23N 70 30W
Chappell **34** 41 6N 102 28W
Chappell Hill **51** 30 9N 96 15W
Chappells **46** 34 11N 81 52W
Chaptico **27** 38 21N 76 49W
Châr **120** 21 32N 12 45 E
Chara **101** 56 54N 118 20 E
Charadai **76** 27 35 S 60 0W
Charagua **73** 19 45 S 63 10W
Charalá **70** 6 17N 73 10W
Charambirá, Punta **70** 4 16N 77 32W
Charaña **72** 17 30 S 69 25W
Charapita **70** 0 37 S 74 21W
Charata **76** 27 13 S 61 14W
Charcas **64** 23 10N 101 20W
Charco **51** 28 44N 97 37W
Charcoal L. **63** 58 49N 102 22W
Chard **83** 50 52N 2 59W
Chardara **100** 41 16N 67 59 E
Chardon **42** 41 35N 81 12W
Chardzhou **100** 39 6N 63 34 E
Charente □ **90** 45 50N 0 16 E
Charente-Maritime □ **90** 45 30N 0 35W
Charenton **25** 29 53N 91 32W
Chari → **121** 12 58N 14 31 E
Chārīkār **107** 35 0N 69 10 E
Charing **18** 32 28N 84 22W
Chariton **23** 41 1N 93 19W
Chariton → **32** 39 19N 92 58W
Chariton County ◇ **32** 39 30N 93 0W
Charity, Guyana **71** 7 24N 58 36W
Charity, U.S.A. **32** 37 31N 93 1W
Charity I. **29** 44 2N 83 26W
Charlemont **28** 42 38N 72 52W
Charleroi, Belgium **87** 50 24N 4 27 E
Charleroi, U.S.A. **45** 40 9N 79 57W
Charles **18** 32 8N 84 50W
Charles → **28** 42 22N 71 3W
Charles, C. **54** 37 7N 75 58W
Charles City, Iowa **23** 43 4N 92 41W
Charles City, Va. **54** 37 21N 77 4W
Charles City County ◇ **54** 37 21N 77 4W
Charles County ◇ **27** 38 30N 77 0W
Charles L. **63** 59 50N 110 33W
Charles M. Russell National Wildlife Refuge **33** 47 45N 107 0W
Charles Mill L. **42** 40 45N 82 22W
Charles Mix County ◇ **47** 43 15N 98 42W
Charles Town **54** 39 17N 77 52W
Charleston, Ark. **13** 35 18N 94 5W
Charleston, Ill. **21** 39 30N 88 10W
Charleston, Miss. **31** 34 1N 90 4W
Charleston, Mo. **32** 36 55N 89 21W
Charleston, S.C. **46** 32 46N 79 56W
Charleston, Tenn. **49** 35 17N 84 45W
Charleston, Utah **52** 40 39N 111 28W
Charleston, W. Va. **54** 38 21N 81 38W
Charleston County ◇ **46** 32 50N 80 0W
Charleston Peak **35** 36 16N 115 42W
Charlestown, Ind. **22** 38 27N 85 40W
Charlestown, Md. **27** 39 35N 75 59W
Charlestown, N.H. **36** 43 14N 72 25W
Charlestown, R.I. **28** 41 23N 71 45W
Charlesville **122** 5 27 S 20 59 E
Charleville = Rath Luirc **85** 52 21N 8 40W
Charleville **127** 26 24 S 146 15 E
Charleville-Mézières **90** 49 44N 4 40 E
Charlevoix **29** 45 19N 85 16W
Charlevoix, L. **29** 45 16N 85 8W

Charlevoix County

Chilmark

Charlevoix County ◇ 29 45 15N 85 10W
Charlo 33 47 26N 114 10W
Charlotte, Iowa 23 41 58N 90 28W
Charlotte, Mich. 29 42 34N 84 50W
Charlotte, N.C. 40 35 13N 80 51W
Charlotte, Tenn. 48 36 11N 87 21W
Charlotte, Tex. 51 28 52N 98 43W
Charlotte Amalie, Virgin Is. 57 18 21N 64 56W
Charlotte County ◇, Fla. 17 26 50N 82 0W
Charlotte County ◇, Va. 54 37 0N 78 55W
Charlotte Court House 54 37 3N 78 39W
Charlotte Hall 27 38 28N 76 45W
Charlotte Harbor 17 26 50N 82 10W
Charlotte Waters 126 25 56 S 134 54 E
Charlottesville 54 38 2N 78 30W
Charlottetown 61 46 14N 63 8W
Charlton City 28 42 9N 71 58W
Charlton County ◇ 18 30 50N 82 10W
Charlton I. 60 52 0N 79 20W
Charny 61 46 43N 71 15W
Charolles 90 46 27N 4 16 E
Charouine 120 29 0N 0 15W
Charter Oak 23 42 4N 95 36W
Charters Towers 127 20 5 S 146 13 E
Chartres 90 48 29N 1 30 E
Chascomús 76 35 30 S 58 0W
Chase, Ala. 10 34 47N 86 33W
Chase, Kans. 24 38 21N 98 21W
Chase, Md. 27 39 22N 76 22W
Chase, Mich. 29 43 53N 85 38W
Chase City 54 36 48N 78 28W
Chase County ◇, Kans. 24 38 15N 96 45W
Chase County ◇, Nebr. 34 40 30N 101 40W
Chaseburg 55 43 40N 91 6W
Chaseley 41 47 27N 99 49W
Chasovnya-Uchurskaya 101 57 15N 132 50 E
Chataignier 25 30 34N 92 19W
Chatal Balkan = Udvoy Balkan 95 42 50N 26 50 E
Chatanika 11 65 7N 147 28W
Château-Salins 90 48 50N 6 30 E
Châteaubriant 90 47 43N 1 23W
Chateaugay 39 44 56N 74 5W
Châteauroux 90 46 50N 1 40 E
Châtellerault 90 46 50N 0 30 E
Chatfield, Ark. 13 35 0N 90 24W
Chatfield, Minn. 30 43 51N 92 11W
Chatfield, Ohio 42 40 57N 82 57W
Chatham, N.B., Canada 61 47 2N 65 28W
Chatham, Ont., Canada 60 42 24N 82 11W
Chatham, U.K. 83 51 22N 0 32 E
Chatham, Ill. 21 39 40N 89 42W
Chatham, La. 25 32 18N 92 27W
Chatham, Mass. 28 41 41N 69 58W
Chatham, Mich. 29 46 21N 86 56W
Chatham, N.J. 37 40 44N 74 23W
Chatham, N.Y. 39 42 21N 73 36W
Chatham, Va. 54 36 50N 79 24W
Chatham, I. 78 50 40 S 74 25W
Chatham County ◇, Ga. 18 32 0N 81 10W
Chatham County ◇, N.C. 40 35 45N 79 10W
Chatham Is. 124 44 0 S 176 40W
Chatom 10 31 28N 88 16W
Chatrapur 109 19 22N 85 2 E
Chatsworth, Ga. 18 34 46N 84 46W
Chatsworth, Ill. 21 40 45N 88 18W
Chatsworth, Iowa 23 42 55N 96 31W
Chatsworth, N.J. 37 39 49N 74 32W
Chattahoochee 17 30 42N 84 51W
Chattahoochee → 18 30 54N 84 57W
Chattahoochee County ◇ 18 32 20N 84 50W
Chattahoochee National Forest 18 34 50N 84 0W
Chattanooga, Okla. 43 34 25N 98 39W
Chattanooga, Tenn. 49 35 3N 85 19W
Chattaroy 53 47 53N 117 21W
Chattooga County ◇ 18 34 30N 85 15W
Chauk 109 20 53N 94 49 E
Chaukan La 109 27 0N 97 15 E
Chaumont, France 90 48 7N 5 8 E
Chaumont, U.S.A. 39 44 4N 76 8W
Chauncey 42 39 24N 82 8W
Chautauqua 24 37 1N 96 11W
Chautauqua County ◇, Kans. 24 37 15N 96 15W
Chautauqua County ◇, N.Y. 39 42 20N 79 15W
Chautauqua L. 39 42 10N 79 24W
Chauvin, Canada 63 52 45N 110 10W
Chauvin, U.S.A. 25 29 26N 90 36W
Chaux-de-Fonds, La 88 47 7N 6 50 E
Chavantina 73 14 40 S 52 21W
Chaves, Brazil 74 0 15 S 49 55W
Chaves, Portugal 91 41 45N 7 32W
Chaves County ◇ 38 33 15N 104 30W
Chavies 49 37 21N 83 21W
Chavuma 123 13 4 S 22 40 E
Chaykovskiy 98 56 47N 54 9 E
Chazuta 72 6 30 S 76 0W
Chazy 39 44 53N 73 26W
Cheaha Mt. 10 33 29N 85 49W
Cheatham County ◇ 48 36 17N 87 4W
Cheb 88 50 9N 12 28 E
Chebanse 21 41 0N 87 54W
Cheboksary 98 56 8N 47 12 E
Cheboygan 29 45 39N 84 29W
Cheboygan County ◇ 29 45 20N 84 30W
Chech, Erg 120 25 0N 2 15W
Checheno-Ingush A.S.S.R. □ 99 43 30N 45 29 E
Checleset B. 62 50 5N 127 35W
Checotah 43 35 28N 95 31W
Chedabucto B. 61 45 25N 61 8W
Cheduba I. 109 18 45N 93 40 E
Cheektowaga 39 42 54N 78 45W
Cheesman L. 16 39 13N 105 16W
Chefornak 11 60 13N 164 12W
Chegdomyn 101 51 7N 133 1 E
Chegga 120 25 27N 5 40W
Chehalis 53 46 40N 122 58W
Chehalis → 53 46 57N 123 50W
Cheju Do 115 33 29N 126 34 E
Chekiang = Zhejiang □ 115 29 0N 120 0 E
Chelan 53 47 51N 120 1W
Chelan, L. 53 48 11N 120 30W
Chelan County ◇ 53 48 0N 120 30W
Chelan Falls 53 47 48N 119 59W
Chelatchie 53 45 55N 122 25W
Cheleken 99 39 26N 53 7 E
Chelforó 78 39 0 S 66 33W
Chelkar 100 47 48N 59 39 E
Chelkar Tengiz, Solonchak 100 48 0N 62 30 E
Chełm 89 51 8N 23 30 E
Chełmno 89 53 20N 18 30 E
Chelmsford, U.K. 83 51 44N 0 29 E
Chelmsford, U.S.A. 28 42 36N 71 21W
Chełmża 89 53 10N 18 39 E
Chelsea, Iowa 23 41 55N 92 24W
Chelsea, Mich. 29 42 19N 84 1W
Chelsea, Okla. 43 36 32N 95 26W
Chelsea, Vt. 36 43 59N 72 27W
Cheltenham, U.K. 83 51 55N 2 5W
Cheltenham, U.S.A. 27 38 42N 76 50W
Chelyabinsk 100 55 10N 61 24 E
Chelyuskin, C. 102 77 30N 103 0 E
Chemainus 62 48 55N 123 42W
Chemehuevi Indian Reservation 15 34 30N 114 25W
Chemnitz = Karl-Marx-Stadt 88 50 50N 12 55 E
Chemquasabamticook L. 26 46 30N 69 37W
Chemung County ◇ 39 42 10N 76 45W
Chen, Gora 101 65 16N 141 50 E
Chen Xian 115 25 47N 113 1 E
Chenab → 108 30 23N 71 2 E
Chenango → 39 42 6N 75 55W
Chenango County ◇ 39 42 30N 75 40W
Chencha 121 6 15N 37 32 E
Chenchiang = Zhenjiang 115 32 11N 119 26 E
Chenes, Pointe aux 29 45 55N 84 54W
Cheney, Kans. 24 37 38N 97 47W
Cheney, Wash. 53 47 30N 117 35W
Cheney Reservoir 24 37 43N 97 48W
Cheneyville 25 31 1N 92 17W
Chengbu 115 26 18N 110 16 E
Chengcheng 115 35 8N 109 56 E
Chengchou = Zhengzhou 115 34 45N 113 34 E
Chengde 114 40 59N 117 58 E
Chengdu 113 30 38N 104 2 E
Chenggu 115 33 10N 107 21 E
Chengjiang 113 24 39N 103 0 E
Chengyang 114 36 18N 120 21 E
Chenkán 65 19 8N 90 58W
Chenoa 21 40 45N 88 43W
Chenoweth 44 45 37N 121 13W
Chenxi 115 28 2N 110 12 E
Cheo Reo 112 13 25N 108 28 E
Cheom Ksan 112 14 13N 104 56 E
Chepachet 28 41 55N 71 40W
Chepelare 95 41 44N 24 40 E
Chepén 72 7 15 S 79 23W
Chepes 76 31 20 S 66 35W
Chepo 66 9 10N 79 6W
Chequamegon National Forest 55 46 10N 91 0W
Chequamegon Pt. 55 46 42N 90 45W
Cher □ 90 47 10N 2 30 E
Cher → 90 47 21N 0 29 E
Cheraw, Colo. 16 38 6N 103 31W
Cheraw, S.C. 46 34 42N 79 53W
Cherbourg 90 49 39N 1 40W
Cherchell 120 36 35N 2 12 E
Cherdyn 98 60 24N 56 29 E
Cheremkhovo 101 53 8N 103 1 E
Cherepanovo 100 54 15N 83 30 E
Cherepovets 98 59 5N 37 55 E
Chergui, Chott ech 120 34 21N 0 25 E
Cheriton 54 37 17N 75 58W
Cherkassy 99 49 27N 32 4 E
Cherlak 100 54 15N 74 55 E
Cherni 95 42 35N 23 18 E
Chernigov 98 51 28N 31 20 E
Chernikovsk 98 54 48N 56 8 E
Chernogorsk 101 53 49N 91 18 E
Chernovtsy 99 48 15N 25 52 E
Chernoye 101 70 30N 89 10 E
Chernyshovskiy 101 63 0N 112 30 E
Cherokee, Ala. 10 34 45N 87 58W
Cherokee, Iowa 23 42 45N 95 33W
Cherokee, Kans. 24 37 21N 94 49W
Cherokee, N.C. 40 35 29N 83 19W
Cherokee, Okla. 43 36 45N 98 21W
Cherokee, Tex. 51 30 59N 98 43W
Cherokee County ◇, Ala. 10 34 9N 85 41W
Cherokee County ◇, Ga. 18 34 20N 84 20W
Cherokee County ◇, Iowa 23 42 45N 95 35W
Cherokee County ◇, Kans. 24 37 15N 94 45W
Cherokee County ◇, N.C. 40 35 10N 84 10W
Cherokee County ◇, Okla. 43 36 0N 95 0W
Cherokee County ◇, S.C. 46 35 0N 81 40W
Cherokee County ◇, Tex. 51 31 58N 95 17W
Cherokee Falls 46 35 4N 81 32W
Cherokee Indian Reservation 40 35 30N 83 20W
Cherokee L. 49 36 10N 83 30W
Cherokee National Forest 49 36 0N 82 40W
Cherokees, Lake O' The 43 36 28N 95 2W
Cherquenco 78 38 35 S 72 0W
Cherrapunji 109 25 17N 91 47 E
Cherry → 47 44 36N 101 30W
Cherry County ◇ 34 42 30N 101 0W
Cherry Cr. → 16 39 45N 104 1W
Cherry Creek, Nev. 35 39 54N 114 53W
Cherry Creek, S. Dak. 47 44 36N 101 30W
Cherry Creek Lake 16 39 39N 104 52W
Cherry Hill 37 39 56N 75 2W
Cherry L. 14 37 59N 119 55W
Cherry Tree 45 40 44N 78 48W
Cherry Valley, Ark. 13 35 24N 90 45W
Cherry Valley, N.Y. 39 42 48N 74 45W
Cherryfield 26 44 36N 67 56W
Cherryvale 24 37 16N 95 33W
Cherryville 40 35 23N 81 23W
Cherskiy 101 68 45N 161 18 E
Cherskogo Khrebet 101 65 0N 143 0 E
Cherven-Bryag 95 43 17N 24 7 E
Cherwell → 83 51 46N 1 18W
Chesaning 29 43 11N 84 7W
Chesapeake 54 36 50N 76 17W
Chesapeake B. 54 38 0N 76 10W
Chesapeake Beach 27 38 41N 76 32W
Chesapeake City 27 39 32N 75 49W
Chesaw 53 48 57N 119 3W
Chesdin, L. 54 37 20N 77 40W
Cheshire, Conn. 28 41 30N 72 54W
Cheshire, Mass. 28 42 34N 73 10W
Cheshire □ 82 53 14N 2 30W
Cheshire County ◇ 36 43 0N 72 15W
Cheshskaya Guba 98 67 20N 47 0 E
Chesilhurst 37 39 44N 74 52W
Cheslatta L. 62 53 49N 125 20W
Chesnee 46 35 9N 81 52W
Chester, U.K. 82 53 12N 2 53W
Chester, Ark. 13 35 41N 94 11W
Chester, Calif. 14 40 19N 121 14W
Chester, Ga. 18 32 24N 83 9W
Chester, Ill. 21 37 55N 89 49W
Chester, Mass. 28 42 17N 72 59W
Chester, Mont. 33 48 31N 110 58W
Chester, N.H. 36 42 55N 71 15W
Chester, N.J. 37 40 47N 74 42W
Chester, Okla. 43 36 13N 98 55W
Chester, Pa. 45 39 51N 75 22W
Chester, S.C. 46 34 43N 81 12W
Chester, S. Dak. 47 43 54N 96 56W
Chester, Va. 54 37 21N 77 27W
Chester, Vt. 36 43 16N 72 36W
Chester, W. Va. 54 40 37N 80 34W
Chester → 27 39 3N 76 16W
Chester County ◇, Pa. 45 39 59N 75 50W
Chester County ◇, S.C. 46 34 30N 81 10W
Chester County ◇, Tenn. 48 35 20N 88 45W
Chesterfield, U.K. 82 53 14N 1 26W
Chesterfield, Ill. 21 39 15N 90 4W
Chesterfield, N.H. 36 42 52N 72 28W
Chesterfield, S.C. 46 34 44N 80 5W
Chesterfield, Va. 54 37 23N 77 31W
Chesterfield, Îles 124 19 52 S 158 15 E
Chesterfield County ◇, S.C. 46 34 30N 80 10W
Chesterfield County ◇, Va. 54 37 23N 77 31W
Chesterfield In. 58 63 25N 90 45W
Chesterfield Inlet 58 63 30N 90 45W
Chesterhill 42 39 29N 81 52W
Chestertown 27 39 13N 76 4W
Chesterville 27 39 17N 75 55W
Chestnut 25 32 3N 93 1W
Chestnut Mountain 18 34 10N 83 50W
Chesuncook L. 26 46 0N 69 21W
Cheswold 27 39 13N 75 35W
Chetco → 44 42 3N 124 16W
Chetek 55 45 19N 91 39W
Chéticamp 61 46 37N 60 59W
Chetopa 24 37 2N 95 5W
Chetumal 65 18 30N 88 20W
Chetumal, Bahía de 65 18 40N 88 10W
Chetwynd 62 55 45N 121 36W
Chevak 11 61 32N 165 35W
Cheviot 42 39 10N 84 37W
Cheviot, The 82 55 29N 2 8W
Cheviot Hills 82 55 20N 2 30W
Chevy Chase 27 38 59N 77 5W
Chew Bahir 121 4 40N 36 50 E
Chewelah 53 48 17N 117 43W
Cheyenne, Okla. 43 35 37N 99 40W
Cheyenne, Wyo. 56 41 8N 104 49W
Cheyenne → 47 44 41N 101 18W
Cheyenne Bottoms 24 38 27N 98 40W
Cheyenne County ◇, Colo. 16 38 50N 102 35W
Cheyenne County ◇, Kans. 24 39 45N 101 45W
Cheyenne County ◇, Nebr. 34 41 15N 103 0W
Cheyenne River Indian Reservation 47 45 0N 101 0W
Cheyenne Wells 16 38 49N 102 21W
Chhapra 109 25 48N 84 44 E
Chhatarpur 108 24 55N 79 35 E
Chhindwara 108 22 2N 78 59 E
Chhlong 112 12 15N 105 58 E
Chi → 112 15 11N 104 43 E
Chiamis 111 7 20 S 108 21 E
Chiamussu = Jiamusi 114 46 40N 130 26 E
Chiang Mai 112 18 47N 98 59 E
Chiange 123 15 35 S 13 40 E
Chiapa → 65 16 42N 93 0W
Chiapa de Corzo 65 16 42N 93 0W
Chiapas □ 65 17 0N 92 45W
Chiautla 65 18 18N 98 34W
Chiba 117 35 30N 140 7 E
Chibatu 111 7 6 S 107 59 E
Chibemba 123 15 48 S 14 8 E
Chibia 123 15 10 S 13 42 E
Chibougamau 60 49 56N 74 24W
Chibougamau L. 60 49 50N 74 20W
Chibuk 121 10 52N 12 50 E
Chic-Chocs, Mts. 61 48 55N 66 0W
Chicacole = Srikakulam 109 18 14N 83 58 E
Chicago 21 41 53N 87 38W
Chicago Heights 21 41 30N 87 38W
Chicamuxen 27 38 33N 77 15W
Chichagof I. 11 57 30N 135 30W
Chichén Itzá 65 20 40N 88 32W
Chichester 83 50 50N 0 47W
Chichibu 117 36 5N 139 10 E
Ch'ich'ihaerh = Qiqihar 114 47 26N 124 0 E
Chickahominy → 54 37 14N 76 53W
Chickamauga 18 34 52N 85 18W
Chickamauga L. 49 35 6N 85 14W
Chickasaw 10 30 46N 88 5W
Chickasaw County ◇, Iowa 23 43 5N 92 20W
Chickasaw County ◇, Miss. 31 33 54N 89 0W
Chickasaw Nat. Rec. Area 43 34 26N 97 0W
Chickasawhay → 31 30 59N 88 44W
Chickasha 43 35 3N 97 58W
Chicken 11 64 5N 141 56W
Chiclana de la Frontera 91 36 26N 6 9W
Chiclayo 72 6 42 S 79 50W
Chico, Calif. 14 39 44N 121 50W
Chico, Tex. 51 33 16N 97 48W
Chico → 78 50 0 S 68 30W
Chicoa 123 15 35 S 32 20 E
Chicontepec 65 20 58N 98 10W
Chicopee, Ga. 18 34 15N 83 51W
Chicopee, Mass. 28 42 9N 72 37W
Chicopee → 28 42 9N 72 37W
Chicora 31 31 34N 88 34W
Chicot 13 33 12N 91 17W
Chicot County ◇ 13 33 12N 91 17W
Chicoutimi 61 48 28N 71 5W
Chidambaram 108 11 20N 79 45 E
Chidester 13 33 42N 93 1W
Chidley C. 59 60 23N 64 26W
Chiefland 17 29 29N 82 52W
Chiengi 122 8 45 S 29 10 E
Chiese → 94 45 8N 10 25 E
Chieti 94 42 22N 14 10 E
Chifeng 114 42 18N 118 58 E
Chignecto B. 61 45 30N 64 40W
Chignik 11 56 18N 158 24W
Chigorodó 70 7 41N 76 42W
Chiguana 76 21 0 S 67 58W
Chihuahua 64 28 40N 106 3W
Chihuahua □ 64 28 40N 106 3W
Chiili 100 44 20N 66 15 E
Chik Bollapur 108 13 25N 77 45 E
Chikaskia → 43 36 37N 97 15W
Chikmagalur 108 13 15N 75 45 E
Chilac 65 18 20N 97 24W
Chilako → 62 53 53N 122 57W
Chilapa 65 17 40N 99 11W
Chilas 108 35 25N 74 5 E
Chilaw 108 7 30N 79 50 E
Chilcotin → 62 51 44N 122 23W
Childers 127 25 15 S 152 17 E
Childersburg 10 33 16N 86 21W
Childress 50 34 25N 100 13W
Childress County ◇ 50 34 25N 100 15W
Chile ■ 78 35 0 S 72 0W
Chile Chico 78 46 33 S 71 44W
Chile Rise 125 38 0 S 92 0W
Chilecito 76 29 10 S 67 30W
Chilete 72 7 10 S 78 50W
Chilhowee 32 38 36N 93 51W
Chilhowie 54 36 48N 81 41W
Chililabombwe 123 12 18 S 27 43 E
Chilili 38 34 53N 106 14W
Chilka L. 109 19 40N 85 25 E
Chilko → 62 52 0N 123 40W
Chilko, L. 62 51 20N 124 10W
Chillagoe 127 17 7 S 144 33 E
Chillán 76 36 40 S 72 10W
Chillicothe, Ill. 21 40 55N 89 29W
Chillicothe, Iowa 23 41 5N 92 32W
Chillicothe, Mo. 32 39 48N 93 33W
Chillicothe, Ohio 42 39 20N 82 59W
Chillicothe, Tex. 51 34 15N 99 31W
Chilliwack 62 49 10N 121 54W
Chillum 27 38 56N 76 58W
Chilmark 28 41 21N 70 45W

Chilocco Claremont

Chilocco 43 36 59N 97 4W
Chiloé □ 78 43 0S 73 0W
Chiloé, I. de 78 42 30S 73 50W
Chiloquin 44 42 35N 121 52W
Chilpancingo 65 17 30N 99 30W
Chiltern Hills 83 51 44N 0 42W
Chilton 55 44 2N 88 10W
Chilton County ◇ 10 32 51N 86 38W
Chiluage 122 9 30S 21 50E
Chilwa, L. 123 15 15S 35 40E
Chimaltitán 64 21 46N 103 50W
Chimán 66 8 45N 78 40W
Chimay 87 50 3N 4 20E
Chimayo 38 36 0N 105 56W
Chimbay 100 42 57N 59 47E
Chimborazo 70 1 29S 78 55W
Chimborazo □ 70 1 0S 78 40W
Chimbote 72 9 0S 78 35W
Chimishliya 95 46 34N 28 44E
Chimkent 100 42 18N 69 36E
Chimney Rock 16 37 13N 107 18W
Chimoio 123 19 4S 33 30E
Chin □ 109 22 0N 93 0E
China, Mexico 65 25 40N 99 20W
China, U.S.A. 51 30 3N 94 20W
China ■ 113 30 0N 110 0E
China Grove 40 35 34N 80 35W
Chinacates 64 25 0N 105 14W
Chinacota 70 7 37N 72 36W
Chinandega 66 12 35N 87 12W
Chinati Mts. 50 29 55N 104 30W
Chinati Peak 50 29 57N 104 29W
Chincha Alta 72 13 25S 76 7W
Chinchón 91 40 9N 3 26W
Chinchorro, Banco 65 18 35N 87 20W
Chinchou = Jinzhou 114 41 5N 121 3E
Chincoteague 54 37 56N 75 23W
Chincoteague Bay 27 38 15N 75 15W
Chinde 123 18 35S 36 30E
Chindwin → 109 21 26N 95 15E
Chingola 123 12 31S 27 53E
Chinguetti 120 20 25N 12 24W
Chinhae 114 35 9N 128 47E
Chinhoyi 123 17 20S 30 8E
Chiniot 108 31 45N 73 0E
Chinipas 64 27 22N 108 32W
Chinju 114 35 12N 128 2E
Chinle 12 36 9N 109 33W
Chinle Cr. → 52 37 12N 109 43W
Chinnampo 114 38 52N 125 10E
Chino, Japan 117 35 59N 138 9E
Chino, U.S.A. 15 34 1N 117 41W
Chino Valley 12 34 45N 112 27W
Chinon 90 47 10N 0 15E
Chinook, Canada 63 51 28N 110 59W
Chinook, Mont. 33 48 35N 109 14W
Chinook, Wash. 53 46 16N 123 57W
Chinook Pass 53 46 52N 121 32W
Chinquapin 40 34 50N 77 49W
Chinsali 122 10 30S 32 2E
Chióggia 94 45 13N 12 15E
Chíos = Khíos 95 38 27N 26 9E
Chipata 123 13 38S 32 28E
Chipatujah 111 7 45S 108 0E
Chipewyan L. 63 58 0N 98 27W
Chipley 17 30 47N 85 32W
Chipman 61 46 6N 65 53W
Chipola → 17 30 1N 85 5W
Chippenham 83 51 27N 2 7W
Chippewa →, Mich. 29 43 35N 84 17W
Chippewa →, Minn. 30 44 56N 95 44W
Chippewa →, Wis. 55 44 25N 92 5W
Chippewa, L. 55 45 57N 91 12W
Chippewa County ◇, Mich. 29 46 20N 84 40W
Chippewa County ◇, Minn. 30 45 0N 95 35W
Chippewa County ◇, Wis. 55 45 5N 91 20W
Chippewa Falls 55 44 56N 91 24W
Chippewa National Forest 30 47 45N 94 0W
Chiputneticook Lakes, Maine 26 45 35N 67 35W
Chiputneticook Lakes, Maine 26 45 43N 67 50W
Chiquián 72 10 10S 77 0W
Chiquimula 66 14 51N 89 37W
Chiquinquira 70 5 37N 73 50W
Chiquitos, Llanos de 73 18 0S 61 30W
Chirala 108 15 50N 80 26E
Chirchik 100 41 29N 69 35E
Chireno 51 31 30N 94 21W
Chirgua → 70 8 54N 67 58W
Chiricahua Mts. 12 32 0N 109 15W
Chiricahua National Monument 12 32 0N 109 20W
Chiricahua Peak 12 31 51N 109 18W
Chiriquí, Golfo de 66 8 0N 82 10W
Chiriquí, Lago de 66 9 10N 82 0W
Chirmiri 109 23 15N 82 20E
Chirnogi 95 44 7N 26 32E
Chiromo 123 16 30S 35 7E
Chirpan 95 42 10N 25 19E
Chirripó Grande, Cerro 66 9 29N 83 29W
Chisago County ◇ 30 45 30N 92 55W
Chisamba 123 14 55S 28 20E
Chisapani Garhi 109 27 30N 84 2E
Chisholm, Canada 62 54 55N 114 10W
Chisholm, Maine 26 44 29N 70 12W
Chisholm, Minn. 30 47 29N 92 53W
Chisimaio 119 0 22S 42 32E
Chisos Mts. 50 29 5N 103 15W
Chistochina 11 62 34N 144 40W
Chistopol 98 55 25N 50 38E
Chita, Colombia 70 6 11N 72 28W
Chita, U.S.S.R. 101 52 0N 113 35E
Chitado 123 17 10S 14 8E
Chitembo 123 13 30S 16 50E
Chitina 11 61 31N 144 26W
Chitokoloki 123 13 50S 23 13E
Chitose 116 42 49N 141 39E
Chitral 107 35 50N 71 56E
Chitré 66 7 59N 80 27W
Chittagong 109 22 19N 91 48E
Chittagong □ 109 24 5N 91 0E
Chittaurgarh 108 24 52N 74 38E
Chittenango 39 43 3N 75 52W
Chittenden 36 43 42N 72 55W
Chittenden County ◇ 36 44 30N 73 10W
Chittoor 108 13 15N 79 5E
Chiusi 94 43 1N 11 58E
Chivacoa 70 10 10N 68 54W
Chivasso 94 45 10N 7 52E
Chivay 72 15 40S 71 35W
Chivilcoy 76 34 55S 60 0W
Chivington 16 38 26N 102 32W
Chkalov = Orenburg 98 51 45N 55 6E
Chloride 12 35 25N 114 12W
Chocó □ 70 6 0N 77 0W
Chocolate Mts., Ariz. 12 33 15N 114 30W
Chocolate Mts., Calif. 15 33 15N 115 15W
Chocontá 70 5 9N 73 41W
Chocowinity 40 35 31N 77 6W
Choctaw 43 35 31N 97 17W
Choctaw Bluff 10 31 22N 87 46W
Choctaw County ◇, Ala. 10 32 0N 88 10W
Choctaw County ◇, Miss. 31 33 19N 89 11W
Choctaw County ◇, Okla. 43 34 0N 95 30W
Choctaw Indian Reservation 31 32 48N 89 7W
Choctawatchee → 17 30 25N 86 8W
Choctawhatchee B. 17 30 20N 86 20W
Choele Choel 78 39 11S 65 40W
Choix 64 26 40N 108 23W
Chojnice 89 53 42N 17 32E
Chōkai-San 116 39 6N 140 3E
Choke Canyon Res. 51 28 30N 98 20W
Chokio 30 45 34N 96 10W
Chokoloskee 17 25 49N 81 22W
Chokurdakh 101 70 38N 147 55E
Cholet 90 47 4N 0 52W
Choluteca 66 13 20N 87 14W
Choluteca → 66 13 0N 87 20W
Choma 123 16 48S 26 59E
Chomutov 88 50 28N 13 23E
Chon Buri 112 13 21N 101 1E
Chonan 114 36 48N 127 9E
Chone 70 0 40S 80 0W
Chong'an 115 27 45N 118 0E
Chongde 115 30 32N 120 26E
Chongjin 114 41 47N 129 50E
Chŏngju, N. Korea 114 39 40N 125 5E
Chŏngju, S. Korea 114 36 39N 127 27E
Chongli 114 40 58N 115 15E
Chongoyape 72 6 35S 79 25W
Chongqing 115 29 35N 106 25E
Chongzuo 115 22 23N 107 20E
Chŏnju 114 35 50N 127 4E
Chonming Dao 115 31 40N 121 30E
Chonos, Arch. de los 78 45 0S 75 0W
Chopim → 77 25 35S 53 5W
Choptank 27 38 41N 75 57W
Choptank → 27 38 38N 76 13W
Chorley 82 53 39N 2 39W
Chorolque, Cerro 76 20 59S 66 5W
Chorrera, La 70 0 44S 73 1W
Chŏrwŏn 114 38 15N 127 10E
Chorzów 89 50 18N 18 57E
Chos-Malal 76 37 20S 70 15W
Chosan 114 40 50N 125 47E
Choszczno 88 53 7N 15 25E
Chota 72 6 33S 78 39W
Choteau 33 47 49N 112 11W
Chotila 108 22 23N 71 15E
Chouteau 43 36 11N 95 21W
Chouteau County ◇ 33 47 55N 110 30W
Chowan → 40 36 1N 76 40W
Chowan County ◇ 40 36 10N 76 40W
Chowchilla 14 37 7N 120 16W
Choybalsan 113 48 4N 114 30E
Chrisman 21 39 48N 87 41W
Chrisney 22 38 1N 87 2W
Christchurch, N.Z. 128 43 33S 172 47E
Christchurch, U.K. 83 50 44N 1 33W
Christian County ◇, Ill. 21 39 30N 89 15W
Christian County ◇, Ky. 48 36 50N 87 30W
Christian County ◇, Mo. 32 37 0N 93 10W
Christian Sd. 11 55 56N 134 40W
Christiana, S. Africa 123 27 52S 25 8E
Christiana, Del. 27 39 40N 75 40W
Christiana, Tenn. 48 35 43N 86 24W
Christiansburg, Ohio 42 40 3N 84 2W
Christiansburg, Va. 54 37 8N 80 25W
Christiansted, Virgin Is. 57 17 45N 64 42W
Christie 43 35 57N 94 42W
Christie B. 63 62 32N 111 10W
Christina → 63 56 40N 111 3W
Christine 41 46 35N 96 48W
Christmas I. = Kiritimati, Pac. Oc. 125 1 58N 157 27W
Christmas I. = Kiritimati, Pac. Oc. 125 1 58N 157 27W
Christmas I. 124 10 30S 105 40E
Christopher 21 37 59N 89 3W
Christoval 50 31 12N 100 30W
Chromo 16 37 2N 106 50W
Chrysler 10 31 18N 87 42W
Chu 100 43 36N 73 42E
Chu → 112 19 53N 105 45E
Chu Chua 62 51 22N 120 10W
Chualar 14 36 34N 121 31W
Ch'uanchou = Quanzhou 115 24 55N 118 34E
Chuathbaluk 11 61 40N 159 15W
Chubbuck 20 42 55N 112 28W
Chūbu □ 117 36 45N 137 30E
Chubut □ 78 43 30S 69 0W
Chubut → 78 43 20S 65 5W
Chuchi L. 62 55 12N 124 30W
Chuckawalla Mts. 15 33 30N 115 20W
Chudskoye, Oz. 98 58 13N 27 30E
Chugach Mts. 11 60 45N 147 0W
Chugach National Forest 11 58 15N 152 45W
Chugiak 11 61 24N 149 29W
Chuginadak I. 11 52 50N 169 45W
Chūgoku □ 117 35 0N 133 0E
Chūgoku-Sanchi 117 35 0N 133 0E
Chugwater 56 41 46N 104 50W
Chukotskiy Khrebet 101 68 0N 175 0E
Chukotskoye More 101 68 0N 175 0W
Chula, Ga. 18 31 33N 83 32W
Chula, Mo. 32 39 55N 93 29W
Chula, Va. 54 37 23N 77 54W
Chula Vista 15 32 39N 117 5W
Chulman 101 56 52N 124 52E
Chulucanas 72 5 8S 80 10W
Chulumani 72 16 24S 67 31W
Chulym → 100 57 43N 83 51E
Chuma 72 15 24S 68 56W
Chumbicha 76 29 0S 66 10W
Chumerna 95 42 45N 25 55E
Chumikan 101 54 40N 135 10E
Chumphon 112 10 35N 99 14E
Chumpi 72 15 4S 73 46W
Chuna → 101 57 47N 94 37E
Chun'an 115 29 35N 119 3E
Chunchŏn 114 37 58N 127 44E
Chunchula 10 30 55N 88 12W
Chunky 31 32 20N 88 56W
Chunya 122 8 30S 33 27E
Chupadera Mesa 38 34 0N 106 0W
Chuquibamba 72 15 47S 72 44W
Chuquibambilla 72 14 7S 72 41W
Chuquicamata 76 22 15S 69 0W
Chuquisaca □ 73 23 30S 63 30W
Chur 88 46 52N 9 32E
Churachandpur 109 24 20N 93 40E
Church Creek 27 38 30N 76 10W
Church Hill, Md. 27 39 9N 75 59W
Church Hill, Tenn. 49 36 31N 82 43W
Church Point 25 30 24N 92 13W
Churchill 63 58 47N 94 11W
Churchill →, Man., Canada 63 58 47N 94 12W
Churchill →, Newf., Canada 61 53 19N 60 10W
Churchill, C. 63 58 46N 93 12W
Churchill County ◇ 35 39 30N 118 20W
Churchill Falls 61 53 36N 64 19W
Churchill L. 63 55 55N 108 20W
Churchill Pk. 62 58 10N 125 10W
Churchs Ferry 41 48 16N 99 12W
Churchville 27 39 34N 76 15W
Churdan 23 42 9N 94 29W
Churu 108 28 20N 74 50E
Churubusco 22 41 14N 85 19W
Chushal 108 33 40N 78 40E
Chuska Mts. 38 36 15N 108 50W
Chusovoy 98 58 15N 57 40E
Chuvash A.S.S.R. □ 98 55 30N 47 0E
Ci Xian 114 36 20N 114 25E
Ciales 57 18 20N 66 28W
Cianjur 111 6 49S 107 8E
Cibadok 111 6 53S 106 47E
Cibatu 111 7 8S 107 59E
Cibola County ◇ 38 35 0N 108 0W
Cibola National Forest 38 35 10N 108 15W
Cicero, Ill. 21 41 51N 87 45W
Cicero, Ind. 22 40 8N 86 1W
Cícero Dantas 74 10 36S 38 23W
Cidra 57 18 11N 66 10W
Cidra, Lago de 57 18 12N 66 8W
Ciechanów 89 52 52N 20 38E
Ciego de Avila 66 21 50N 78 50W
Ciénaga 70 11 1N 74 15W
Ciénaga de Oro 70 8 53N 75 37W
Cienfuegos 66 22 10N 80 30W
Cieszyn 89 49 45N 18 35E
Cieza 91 38 17N 1 23W
Cihuatlán 64 19 14N 104 35W
Cijulang 111 7 42S 108 27E
Cikajang 111 7 25S 107 48E
Cikampek 111 6 23S 107 28E
Cilacap 111 7 43S 109 0E
Cilician Gates P. 106 37 20N 34 52E
Cîlnicu 95 44 54N 23 4E
Cima 15 35 14N 115 30W
Cimahi 111 6 53S 107 33E
Cimarron, Kans. 24 37 48N 100 21W
Cimarron, N. Mex. 38 36 31N 104 55W
Cimarron → 43 36 10N 96 17W
Cimarron County ◇ 43 36 45N 102 30W
Cimone, Mte. 94 44 10N 10 40E
Cîmpic Turzii 95 46 34N 23 53E
Cîmpina 89 45 10N 25 45E
Cîmpulung 89 45 17N 25 3E
Cîmpuri 95 46 0N 26 50E
Cinca → 91 41 26N 0 21E
Cincinnati, Iowa 23 40 38N 92 56W
Cincinnati, Ohio 42 39 6N 84 31W
Cîndeşti 95 45 15N 26 42E
Ciney 87 50 18N 5 5E
Cinto, Mt. 94 42 24N 8 54E
Ciorani 95 44 45N 26 25E
Cipó 74 11 6S 38 31W
Circle, Alaska 11 65 50N 144 4W
Circle, Mont. 33 47 25N 105 35W
Circleville, Kans. 24 39 31N 95 52W
Circleville, Ohio 42 39 36N 82 57W
Circleville, Utah 52 38 10N 112 16W
Circleville, W. Va. 54 38 40N 79 30W
Circleville Mt. 52 38 12N 112 24W
Cirebon 111 6 45S 108 32E
Cirencester 83 51 43N 1 59W
Cireşu 95 44 47N 22 31E
Cisco, Ill. 21 40 1N 88 44W
Cisco, Tex. 51 32 23N 98 59W
Cisco, Utah 52 38 58N 109 19W
Cislău 95 45 14N 26 20E
Cisnădie 95 45 42N 24 9E
Cisne 21 38 31N 88 26W
Cisneros 70 6 33N 75 4W
Cissna Park 21 40 34N 87 54W
Cistern 51 29 49N 97 13W
Citaré → 71 1 11N 54 41W
Citlaltépetl 65 19 0N 97 20W
Citra 17 29 25N 82 7W
Citronelle 10 31 6N 88 14W
Citrus County ◇ 17 28 45N 82 30W
Citrus Heights 14 38 42N 121 17W
Citrus Springs 17 29 2N 82 27W
Ciuc, Munţii 95 46 25N 26 5E
Ciucaş 95 45 31N 25 56E
Ciudad Acuña 64 29 20N 100 58W
Ciudad Altamirano 64 18 20N 100 40W
Ciudad Bolívar 71 8 5N 63 36W
Ciudad Camargo 64 27 41N 105 10W
Ciudad de Valles 65 22 0N 99 0W
Ciudad del Carmen 65 18 38N 91 50W
Ciudad Delicias = Delicias 64 28 10N 105 30W
Ciudad Guayana 71 8 0N 62 30W
Ciudad Guerrero 64 28 33N 107 28W
Ciudad Guzmán 64 19 40N 103 30W
Ciudad Juárez 64 31 40N 106 28W
Ciudad Madero 65 22 19N 97 50W
Ciudad Mante 65 22 50N 99 0W
Ciudad Obregón 64 27 28N 109 59W
Ciudad Ojeda 70 10 12N 71 19W
Ciudad Real 91 38 59N 3 55W
Ciudad Rodrigo 91 40 35N 6 32W
Ciudad Trujillo = Santo Domingo 67 18 30N 64 54W
Ciudad Victoria 65 23 41N 99 9W
Ciulniţa 95 44 26N 27 22E
Civitanova Marche 94 43 18N 13 41E
Civitavécchia 94 42 6N 11 46E
Çivril 106 38 20N 29 43E
Cizre 106 37 19N 42 10E
Clackamas → 44 45 22N 122 36W
Clackamas County ◇ 44 45 15N 122 15W
Clacton-on-Sea 83 51 47N 1 10E
Claflin 24 38 31N 98 32W
Claiborne, Ala. 10 31 33N 87 31W
Claiborne, Md. 27 38 50N 76 17W
Claiborne County ◇, Miss. 31 31 58N 90 59W
Claiborne County ◇, Tenn. 49 36 27N 83 34W
Claiborne Parish ◇ 25 32 48N 93 4W
Clair Engle L. 14 40 48N 122 46W
Clair Haven 29 42 36N 82 49W
Claire, L. 62 58 35N 112 5W
Claire City 47 45 52N 97 6W
Clairton 45 40 18N 79 53W
Clallam Bay 53 48 15N 124 16W
Clallam County ◇ 53 48 0N 124 0W
Clam Gulch 11 60 15N 151 23W
Clan Alpine Mts. 35 39 40N 117 55W
Clancy 33 46 28N 111 59W
Clanton 10 32 51N 86 38W
Clanwilliam 123 32 11S 18 52E
Clara, Ireland 85 53 20N 7 38W
Clara, U.S.A. 31 31 35N 88 42W
Clara City 30 44 57N 95 22W
Clare, Iowa 23 42 35N 94 21W
Clare, Mich. 29 43 49N 84 46W
Clare □ 85 52 20N 9 0W
Clare → 85 53 22N 9 5W
Clare County ◇ 29 44 0N 84 50W
Clare I. 85 53 48N 10 0W
Claremont, Calif. 15 34 6N 117 43W
Claremont, Ill. 21 38 43N 87 58W
Claremont, N.H. 36 43 23N 72 20W

Claremont Cobre

Claremont, S. Dak. 47 45 40N 98 1W
Claremont, Va. 54 37 14N 76 58W
Claremore 43 36 19N 95 36W
Claremorris 85 53 45N 9 0W
Clarence, Iowa 23 41 53N 91 4W
Clarence, La. 25 31 49N 93 2W
Clarence, Mo. 32 39 45N 92 16W
Clarence →, Australia 127 29 25 S 153 22 E
Clarence →, N.Z. 128 42 10 S 173 56 E
Clarence, I. 78 54 0 S 72 0W
Clarence, Port 11 65 15N 166 40W
*Clarence Cannon L. 32 39 28N 91 55W
Clarence I. 5 61 10 S 54 0W
Clarence Str. 126 12 0 S 131 0 E
Clarence Town 67 23 6N 74 59W
Clarendon, Ark. 13 34 42N 91 19W
Clarendon, Pa. 45 41 47N 79 6W
Clarendon, Tex. 50 34 56N 100 53W
Clarendon County ◇ 46 33 45N 80 10W
Clarenville 61 48 10N 54 1W
Claresholm 62 50 0N 113 33W
Clareton 56 43 42N 104 42W
Clarie Coast 5 68 0 S 135 0 E
Clarinda 23 40 44N 95 2W
Clarington 42 39 46N 80 52W
Clarion, Iowa 23 42 44N 93 44W
Clarion, Pa. 45 41 13N 79 23W
Clarion → 45 41 7N 79 41W
Clarion County ◇ 45 41 5N 79 40W
Clarion Fracture Zone 125 20 0N 120 0W
Clarissa 30 46 8N 94 57W
Clarita 43 34 29N 96 26W
Clark, Mo. 32 39 17N 92 21W
Clark, N.J. 37 40 38N 74 18W
Clark, S. Dak. 47 44 53N 97 44W
Clark County ◇, Ark. 13 33 55N 93 9W
Clark County ◇, Idaho 20 44 15N 112 30W
Clark County ◇, Ill. 21 39 20N 87 45W
Clark County ◇, Ind. 22 38 30N 85 40W
Clark County ◇, Kans. 24 37 15N 99 45W
Clark County ◇, Ky. 49 38 0N 84 10W
Clark County ◇, Mo. 32 40 25N 91 40W
Clark County ◇, Nev. 35 36 10N 115 10W
Clark County ◇, Ohio 42 39 55N 83 49W
Clark County ◇, S. Dak. 47 44 50N 97 44W
Clark County ◇, Wash. 53 45 55N 122 25W
Clark County ◇, Wis. 55 44 40N 90 40W
Clark Fork 20 48 9N 116 11W
Clark Fork → 20 48 9N 116 15W
Clark Hill L. 18 33 40N 82 12W
Clark Mt. 15 35 32N 115 35W
†Clark National Forest 32 37 40N 92 10W
Clarkdale 12 34 46N 112 3W
Clarke, I. 127 40 32 S 148 10 E
Clarke City 61 50 12N 66 38W
Clarke County ◇, Ala. 10 31 42N 87 47W
Clarke County ◇, Ga. 18 34 0N 83 15W
Clarke County ◇, Iowa 23 41 0N 93 45W
Clarke County ◇, Miss. 31 32 2N 88 44W
Clarke County ◇, Va. 54 39 0N 77 59W
Clarke L. 63 54 24N 106 54W
Clarkesville 18 34 37N 83 31W
Clarkfield 30 44 48N 95 48W
Clarkia 20 47 1N 116 15W
Clarkrange 49 36 11N 85 1W
Clarks, La. 25 32 2N 92 8W
Clarks, Nebr. 34 41 13N 97 50W
Clarks Fork → 33 45 32N 108 50W
Clarks Grove 30 43 46N 93 20W
Clark's Harbour 61 43 25N 65 38W
Clarks Hill 22 40 15N 86 43W
Clarks Point 11 58 51N 158 33W
Clarks Summit 45 41 30N 75 42W
Clarksburg, Calif. 14 38 25N 121 32W
Clarksburg, Mo. 32 38 40N 92 40W
Clarksburg, N.J. 37 40 12N 74 27W
Clarksburg, W. Va. 54 39 17N 80 30W
Clarksdale, Miss. 31 34 12N 90 35W
Clarksdale, Mo. 32 39 49N 94 33W
Clarkson, Ky. 48 37 30N 86 13W
Clarkson, Nebr. 34 41 43N 97 7W
Clarkston, Utah 52 41 55N 112 3W
Clarkston, Wash. 53 46 25N 117 3W
Clarksville, Ark. 13 35 28N 93 28W
Clarksville, Ind. 22 38 17N 85 45W
Clarksville, Iowa 23 42 47N 92 40W
Clarksville, Md. 27 39 12N 76 57W
Clarksville, Mich. 29 42 50N 85 15W
Clarksville, Mo. 32 39 22N 90 54W
Clarksville, Ohio 42 39 24N 83 59W
Clarksville, Tenn. 48 36 32N 87 21W
Clarksville, Tex. 51 33 37N 95 3W
Clarksville, Va. 54 36 37N 78 34W
Clarkton 40 34 29N 78 39W
Claro → 75 19 8 S 50 40W
Clatonia 34 40 28N 96 51W
Clatskanie 44 46 6N 123 12W
Clatsop County ◇ 44 46 0N 123 40W
Claude 50 35 7N 101 22W
Claveria 111 18 37N 121 4 E
Claxton 18 32 10N 81 55W
Clay 54 38 28N 81 5W
Clay Center, Kans. 24 39 23N 97 8W
Clay Center, Nebr. 34 40 32N 98 3W
Clay City, Ill. 21 38 41N 88 21W
Clay City, Ind. 22 39 17N 87 7W
Clay City, Ky. 49 37 52N 83 55W
Clay County ◇, Ala. 10 33 16N 85 50W
Clay County ◇, Ark. 13 36 19N 90 36W
Clay County ◇, Fla. 17 30 0N 81 45W
Clay County ◇, Ga. 18 31 30N 85 0W
Clay County ◇, Ill. 21 38 45N 88 30W
Clay County ◇, Ind. 22 39 20N 87 10W
Clay County ◇, Iowa 23 43 5N 95 10W
Clay County ◇, Kans. 24 39 20N 97 10W
Clay County ◇, Ky. 49 37 10N 83 45W
Clay County ◇, Minn. 30 46 50N 96 30W
Clay County ◇, Miss. 31 33 36N 88 39W
Clay County ◇, Mo. 32 39 20N 94 20W
Clay County ◇, N.C. 40 35 5N 83 45W
Clay County ◇, Nebr. 34 40 30N 98 0W
Clay County ◇, S. Dak. 47 43 0N 97 0W
Clay County ◇, Tenn. 49 36 33N 85 30W
Clay County ◇, Tex. 51 33 49N 98 12W
Clay County ◇, W. Va. 54 38 28N 81 5W
Clay Springs 12 34 22N 110 18W
Claymont 27 39 48N 75 27W
Claypool, Ariz. 12 33 25N 110 51W
Claypool, Ind. 22 41 8N 85 53W
Claysville 45 40 7N 80 25W
Clayton, Ala. 10 31 53N 85 27W
Clayton, Del. 27 39 17N 75 38W
Clayton, Ga. 18 34 53N 83 23W
Clayton, Idaho 20 44 16N 114 24W
Clayton, Ill. 21 40 2N 90 54W
Clayton, Ind. 22 39 41N 86 31W
Clayton, Iowa 23 42 54N 91 9W
Clayton, Kans. 24 39 44N 100 11W
Clayton, La. 25 31 43N 91 33W
Clayton, Mo. 32 38 39N 90 20W
Clayton, N.C. 40 35 39N 78 28W
Clayton, N.J. 37 39 40N 75 6W
Clayton, N. Mex. 38 36 27N 103 11W
Clayton, N.Y. 39 44 14N 76 5W
Clayton, Okla. 43 34 35N 95 21W
Clayton, Wis. 55 45 20N 92 10W
Clayton County ◇, Ga. 18 33 30N 84 20W
Clayton County ◇, Iowa 23 42 50N 91 20W
Clayton Lake 26 46 36N 69 32W
Claytor L. 54 37 5N 80 35W
Cle Elum 53 47 12N 120 56W
Clear → 12 34 59N 110 38W
Clear, C. 85 51 26N 9 30W
Clear Boggy Cr. → 43 34 3N 95 47W
Clear Cr. → 56 44 53N 106 4W
Clear Creek County ◇ 16 39 40N 105 40W
Clear I. 85 51 26N 9 30W
Clear L., Calif. 14 39 2N 122 47W
Clear L., Iowa 23 43 8N 93 26W
Clear L., La. 25 31 53N 93 0W
Clear L., Utah 52 39 7N 112 38W
Clear Lake, Iowa 23 43 8N 93 23W
Clear Lake, Minn. 30 45 27N 94 0W
Clear Lake, Okla. 43 36 41N 100 16W
Clear Lake, S. Dak. 47 44 45N 96 41W
Clear Lake, Wis. 55 45 15N 92 16W
Clear Lake Reservoir 14 41 56N 121 5W
Clear Spring 27 39 39N 77 56W
Clearbrook 30 47 42N 95 26W
Clearco 54 38 6N 80 34W
Clearfield, Iowa 23 40 48N 94 29W
Clearfield, Pa. 45 41 2N 78 27W
Clearfield, Utah 52 41 7N 112 2W
Clearfield County ◇ 45 41 0N 78 35W
Clearlake Highlands 14 38 57N 122 38W
Clearmont, Mo. 32 40 31N 95 2W
Clearmont, Wyo. 56 44 38N 106 23W
Clearwater, Canada 62 51 38N 120 2W
Clearwater, Fla. 17 27 58N 82 48W
Clearwater, Kans. 24 37 30N 97 30W
Clearwater, Nebr. 34 42 10N 98 11W
Clearwater →, Alta., Canada 62 52 22N 114 57W
Clearwater →, Alta., Canada 63 56 44N 111 23W
Clearwater →, Idaho 20 46 31N 116 33W
Clearwater →, Minn. 30 47 54N 96 16W
Clearwater County ◇, Idaho 20 46 50N 115 30W
Clearwater County ◇, Minn. 30 47 30N 95 20W
Clearwater Cr. 62 61 36N 125 30W
Clearwater L. 32 37 8N 90 47W
Clearwater Mts. 20 46 5N 115 20W
Clearwater National Forest 20 46 40N 115 5W
Clearwater Prov. Park 63 54 0N 101 0W
Cleburne 51 32 21N 97 23W
Cleburne County ◇, Ala. 10 33 39N 85 35W
Cleburne County ◇, Ark. 13 35 30N 92 2W
Cleethorpes 82 53 33N 0 2W
Cleeve Cloud 83 51 56N 2 0W
Clem 18 33 32N 85 1W
Clements, Kans. 24 38 18N 96 44W
Clements, Md. 27 38 18N 76 43W
Clements, Minn. 30 44 23N 95 3W
Clemson 46 34 41N 82 50W
Clendenin 54 38 29N 81 21W
Cleo Springs 43 36 26N 98 29W
Clerks Rocks 5 56 0 S 34 30W
Clermont, Australia 127 22 49 S 147 39 E
Clermont, Fla. 17 28 33N 81 46W
Clermont, Iowa 23 43 0N 91 39W
Clermont, N.J. 37 39 59N 74 48W
Clermont County ◇ 42 39 5N 84 11W
Clermont-Ferrand 90 45 46N 3 4 E
Clervaux 87 50 4N 6 2 E
Cleveland, Ga. 18 34 36N 83 46W
Cleveland, Minn. 30 44 19N 93 50W
Cleveland, Miss. 31 33 45N 90 43W
Cleveland, N. Dak. 41 46 54N 99 6W
Cleveland, Ohio 42 41 30N 81 42W
Cleveland, Okla. 43 36 19N 96 28W
Cleveland, S.C. 46 35 4N 82 31W
Cleveland, Tenn. 49 35 10N 84 53W
Cleveland, Tex. 51 30 21N 95 5W
Cleveland, Utah 52 39 21N 110 51W
Cleveland, Va. 54 36 57N 82 9W
Cleveland, Wis. 55 43 55N 87 45W
Cleveland □ 82 54 35N 1 8 E
Cleveland, C. 127 19 11 S 147 1 E
Cleveland, Mt. 33 48 56N 113 51W
Cleveland County ◇, Ark. 13 33 58N 92 11W
Cleveland County ◇, N.C. 40 35 20N 81 40W
Cleveland County ◇, Okla. 43 35 10N 97 20W
Cleveland Heights 42 41 30N 81 34W
Cleveland National Forest 15 32 45N 116 40W
Clevelândia 77 26 24 S 52 23W
Clevelândia do Norte 71 3 49N 51 52W
Clever 32 37 2N 93 28W
Clew B. 85 53 54N 9 50W
Clewiston 17 26 45N 80 56W
Clifden, Ireland 85 53 30N 10 2W
Clifden, N.Z. 128 46 1 S 167 42 E
Clifford, Mich. 29 43 19N 83 11W
Clifford, N. Dak. 41 47 21N 97 24W
Cliffside 40 35 14N 81 46W
Clifftop 54 38 0N 80 56W
Clifton, Ariz. 12 33 3N 109 18W
Clifton, Colo. 16 39 7N 108 25W
Clifton, Idaho 20 42 11N 112 0W
Clifton, Ill. 21 40 56N 87 56W
Clifton, Kans. 24 39 34N 97 17W
Clifton, N.J. 37 40 53N 74 9W
Clifton, Tenn. 48 35 18N 88 1W
Clifton, Tex. 51 31 47N 97 35W
Clifton Forge 54 37 49N 79 50W
Clifton Springs 39 42 58N 77 8W
Clifty 13 36 14N 93 48W
Climax, Canada 63 49 10N 108 20W
Climax, Colo. 16 39 22N 106 11W
Climax, Ga. 18 30 53N 84 26W
Climax, Kans. 24 37 43N 96 13W
Climax, Mich. 29 42 14N 85 20W
Climax, Minn. 30 47 37N 96 49W
Clinch → 49 35 53N 84 29W
Clinch County ◇ 18 31 0N 82 45W
Clinchco 54 37 10N 82 22W
Cline 51 29 15N 100 5W
Clines Corners 38 35 1N 105 40W
Clingmans Dome 49 35 34N 83 30W
Clint 50 31 35N 106 14W
Clinton, B.C., Canada 62 51 6N 121 35W
Clinton, Ont., Canada 60 43 37N 81 32W
Clinton, N.Z. 128 46 12 S 169 23 E
Clinton, Ala. 10 32 58N 88 0W
Clinton, Ark. 13 35 36N 92 28W
Clinton, Conn. 28 41 17N 72 32W
Clinton, Ill. 21 40 9N 88 57W
Clinton, Ind. 22 39 40N 87 24W
Clinton, Iowa 23 41 51N 90 12W
Clinton, Ky. 48 36 40N 89 0W
Clinton, La. 25 30 52N 91 1W
Clinton, Maine 26 44 38N 69 30W
Clinton, Mass. 28 42 25N 71 41W
Clinton, Md. 27 38 46N 76 54W
Clinton, Mich. 29 42 4N 83 58W
Clinton, Minn. 30 45 28N 96 26W
Clinton, Miss. 31 32 20N 90 20W
Clinton, Mo. 32 38 22N 93 46W
Clinton, Mont. 33 46 46N 113 43W
Clinton, N.C. 40 35 0N 78 22W
Clinton, N.J. 37 40 38N 74 55W
Clinton, N.Y. 39 43 3N 75 23W
Clinton, Ohio 42 40 56N 81 38W
Clinton, Okla. 43 35 31N 98 58W
Clinton, S.C. 46 34 29N 81 53W
Clinton, Tenn. 49 36 6N 84 8W
Clinton, Wash. 53 47 59N 122 21W
Clinton, Wis. 55 42 34N 88 52W
Clinton Colden L. 58 63 58N 107 27W
Clinton County ◇, Ill. 21 38 35N 89 25W
Clinton County ◇, Ind. 22 40 20N 86 30W
Clinton County ◇, Iowa 23 41 55N 90 30W
Clinton County ◇, Ky. 49 36 45N 85 10W
Clinton County ◇, Mich. 29 42 55N 84 40W
Clinton County ◇, Mo. 32 39 35N 94 25W
Clinton County ◇, N.Y. 39 44 50N 73 40W
Clinton County ◇, Ohio 42 39 27N 83 50W
Clinton County ◇, Pa. 45 41 10N 77 50W
Clinton L. 21 40 15N 88 45W
Clintonville, W. Va. 54 37 54N 80 36W
Clintonville, Wis. 55 44 37N 88 46W
Clintwood 54 37 9N 82 28W
Clio, Ala. 10 31 43N 85 37W
Clio, Iowa 23 40 38N 93 27W
Clio, Mich. 29 43 11N 83 44W
Clio, S.C. 46 34 35N 79 33W
Clipperton, I. 125 10 18N 109 13W
Clipperton Fracture Zone 125 19 0N 122 0W
Clive L. 62 63 13N 118 54W
Cliza 73 17 36 S 65 56W
Cloates, Pt. 126 22 43 S 113 40 E
Clodomira 76 27 35 S 64 14W
Clonakilty 85 51 37N 8 53W
Clonakilty B. 85 51 33N 8 50W
Cloncurry 127 20 40 S 140 28 E
Clones 85 54 10N 7 13W
Clonmel 85 52 22N 7 42W
Clontarf 30 45 23N 95 40W
Cloquet 30 46 43N 92 28W
Cloquet → 30 46 52N 92 35W
Clorinda 76 25 16 S 57 45W
Cloud County ◇ 24 39 30N 97 45W
Cloud Peak 56 44 23N 107 11W
Cloudcroft 38 32 58N 105 45W
Clover, S.C. 46 35 7N 81 14W
Clover, Va. 54 36 50N 78 44W
Cloverdale, Ala. 10 34 56N 87 46W
Cloverdale, Calif. 14 38 48N 123 1W
Cloverdale, Ind. 22 39 31N 86 48W
Cloverdale, Ohio 42 41 1N 84 18W
Cloverleaf 51 29 46N 95 10W
Cloverport 48 37 50N 86 38W
Clovis, Calif. 15 36 49N 119 42W
Clovis, N. Mex. 38 34 24N 103 12W
Cluj-Napoca 89 46 47N 23 38 E
Cluny 90 46 26N 4 38 E
Clute 51 29 1N 95 24W
Clutha → 128 46 20 S 169 49 E
Clutier 23 42 4N 92 24W
Clwyd □ 82 53 5N 3 20W
Clwyd → 82 53 20N 3 30W
Clyattville 18 30 42N 83 19W
Clyde, N.Z. 128 45 12 S 169 20 E
Clyde, Kans. 24 39 36N 97 24W
Clyde, N.C. 40 35 32N 82 55W
Clyde, N.Y. 39 43 5N 76 52W
Clyde, Ohio 42 41 18N 82 59W
Clyde, Tex. 51 32 24N 99 30W
Clyde, Vt. 36 44 56N 73 0W
Clyde → 84 55 56N 4 29W
Clyde, Firth of 84 55 20N 5 0W
Clyde River 59 70 30N 68 30W
Clydebank 84 55 54N 4 25W
Clymer 45 40 40N 79 1W
Clyo 18 32 29N 81 16W
Co-Operative 49 36 42N 84 37W
Coachella 15 33 41N 116 10W
Coachella Canal 15 32 43N 114 57W
Coahoma 50 32 18N 101 18W
Coahoma County ◇ 31 34 12N 90 35W
Coahuayana → 64 18 41N 103 45W
Coahuayutla 64 18 19N 101 42W
Coahuila de Zaragoza □ 64 27 0N 103 0W
Coal → 62 59 39N 126 57W
Coal City 21 41 17N 88 17W
Coal County ◇ 43 34 40N 96 15W
Coal Grove 42 38 30N 82 39W
Coal Hill 13 35 26N 93 40W
Coalcomán 64 18 40N 103 10W
Coaldale, Canada 62 49 45N 112 35W
Coaldale, U.S.A. 16 38 22N 105 45W
Coalgate 43 34 32N 96 13W
Coaling 10 33 10N 87 20W
Coalinga 15 36 9N 120 21W
Coalmont, Colo. 16 40 34N 106 27W
Coalmont, Tenn. 49 35 20N 85 42W
Coalport 45 40 45N 78 32W
Coalville, U.K. 82 52 43N 1 21W
Coalville, U.S.A. 52 40 55N 111 24W
Coamo 57 18 5N 66 22W
Coaraci 75 14 38 S 39 32W
Coari 71 4 8 S 63 7W
Coari → 71 4 30 S 63 33W
Coari, L. de 71 4 15 S 63 22W
Coarsegold 14 37 16N 119 42W
Coast Mts. 62 55 0N 129 0W
Coast Ranges 44 44 0N 123 40W
Coastal Plains Basin 126 30 10 S 115 30 E
Coatbridge 84 55 52N 4 2W
Coatepec 65 19 27N 96 58W
Coatepeque 66 14 46N 91 55W
Coates 30 44 43N 93 2W
Coatesville 45 39 59N 75 50W
Coaticook 61 45 10N 71 46W
Coats, Kans. 24 37 31N 98 50W
Coats, N.C. 40 35 25N 78 40W
Coats I. 59 62 30N 83 0W
Coats Land 5 77 0 S 25 0W
Coatzacoalcos 65 18 7N 94 25W
Cobadin 95 44 5N 28 13 E
Cobalt, Canada 60 47 25N 79 42W
Cobalt, U.S.A. 20 45 6N 114 14W
Cobán 66 15 30N 90 21W
Cobar 127 31 27 S 145 48 E
Cobb 48 36 59N 87 47W
Cobb County ◇ 18 33 50N 84 40W
Cobb Island 27 38 16N 76 51W
Cobden, Ill. 21 37 32N 89 15W
Cobden, Minn. 30 44 17N 94 51W
Cóbh 85 51 50N 8 18W
Cobija 72 11 0 S 68 50W
Cobleskill 39 42 41N 74 29W
Cobourg 60 43 58N 78 10W
Cobourg Pen. 126 11 20 S 132 15 E
Cobre 35 41 7N 114 24W

*Renamed Mark Twain Lake
† Now part of Mark Twain Nat. Forest

Concepción **Corumbá**

Concepción, Chile **76** 36 50 S 73 0W
Concepción, Mexico **65** 18 15N 90 5W
Concepción, Paraguay **76** 23 22 S 57 26W
Concepción, Peru **72** 11 54 S 75 19W
Concepción □ **76** 37 0 S 72 30W
Concepción → **64** 30 32N 113 2W
Concepción, Est. de **78** 50 30 S 74 55W
Concepción, L. **73** 17 20 S 61 20W
Concepción, La **70** 10 30N 71 50W
Concepción, Punta **64** 26 55N 111 59W
Concepción del Oro **64** 24 40N 101 30W
Concepción del Uruguay **76** 32 35 S 58 20W
Conception, Pt. **15** 34 27N 120 28W
Conception B. **123** 23 55 S 14 22 E
Conception I. **67** 23 52N 75 9W
Conception Junction **32** 40 16N 94 42W
Conchas → **38** 35 23N 104 18W
Conchas Dam **38** 35 22N 104 11W
Conchas Lake **38** 35 23N 104 11W
Conche **61** 50 55N 55 58W
Concho **12** 34 28N 109 36W
Concho → **51** 31 34N 99 43W
Concho County ◇ **51** 31 13N 99 51W
Conchos →, Chihuahua, Mexico **64** 29 32N 104 25W
Conchos →, Tamaulipas, Mexico **65** 25 9N 98 35W
Conconully **53** 48 34N 119 45W
Concord, Calif. **14** 37 59N 122 2W
Concord, Ga. **18** 33 5N 84 27W
Concord, Mass. **28** 42 28N 71 21W
Concord, Md. **27** 38 38N 75 48W
Concord, Mich. **29** 42 11N 84 38W
Concord, Mo. **32** 38 28N 90 23W
Concord, N.C. **40** 35 25N 80 35W
Concord, N.H. **36** 43 12N 71 32W
Concord, Tenn. **49** 35 52N 84 8W
Concord, Vt. **36** 44 26N 71 53W
Concordia, Argentina **76** 31 20 S 58 2W
Concórdia, Brazil **70** 4 36 S 66 36W
Concordia, Mexico **64** 23 18N 106 2W
Concordia, Kans. **24** 39 34N 97 40W
Concordia, Mo. **32** 38 59N 93 34W
Concordia, La **65** 16 8N 92 38W
Concordia Parish ◇ **25** 31 38N 91 33W
Concrete **53** 48 32N 121 45W
Conda **20** 42 44N 111 32W
Condamine → **127** 27 7 S 149 48 E
Conde, Brazil **75** 11 49 S 37 37W
Conde, U.S.A. **47** 45 9N 98 6W
Condeúba **75** 14 52 S 42 0W
Condon, Mont. **33** 47 34N 113 45W
Condon, Oreg. **44** 45 14N 120 11W
Conecuh → **17** 30 58N 87 13W
Conecuh County ◇ **10** 31 26N 86 57W
Conecuh National Forest **10** 31 2N 86 45W
Conejos, Mexico **64** 26 14N 103 53W
Conejos, U.S.A. **16** 37 5N 106 1W
Conejos → **16** 37 18N 105 44W
Conejos County ◇ **16** 37 10N 106 10W
Conesville **23** 41 23N 91 21W
Confluence **45** 39 49N 79 21W
Confusion Range **52** 39 20N 113 40W
Confuso → **76** 25 9 S 57 34W
Congaree → **46** 33 44N 80 38W
Conger **30** 43 37N 93 32W
Congleton **82** 53 10N 2 12W
Congo = Zaïre → **122** 6 4 S 12 24 E
Congo **74** 7 48 S 36 40W
Congo (Kinshasa) ■ = Zaïre ■ **122** 3 0 S 23 0 E
Congo ■ **122** 1 0 S 16 0 E
Congo Basin **118** 0 10 S 24 30 E
Congonhas **75** 20 30 S 43 52W
Congress, Ariz. **12** 34 9N 112 51W
Congress, Ohio **42** 40 56N 82 3W
Conifer **16** 39 31N 105 18W
Coniston **60** 46 29N 80 51W
Conjeeveram = Kanchipuram **108** 12 52N 79 45 E
Conklin, Canada **63** 55 38N 111 5W
Conklin, U.S.A. **39** 42 2N 75 49W
Conlen **50** 36 14N 102 15W
Conn, L. **85** 54 3N 9 15W
Connacht **85** 53 23N 8 40W
Conneaut **42** 41 57N 80 34W
Conneaut Lake **45** 41 36N 80 18W
Conneautville **45** 41 45N 80 22W
Connecticut □ **28** 41 30N 72 45W
Connecticut → **28** 41 16N 72 20W
Connell **53** 46 40N 118 52W
Connellsville **45** 40 1N 79 35W
Connemara **85** 53 29N 9 45W
Connemaugh → **45** 40 28N 79 19W
Conner **33** 45 56N 114 7W
Connersville **22** 39 39N 85 8W
Connerville **43** 34 27N 96 38W
Conon → **84** 57 33N 4 28W
Cononaco → **70** 1 32 S 75 35W
Cononbridge **84** 57 32N 4 30W
Conover **40** 35 42N 81 13W
Conowingo **27** 39 40N 76 11W
Conquest **63** 51 32N 107 14W
Conrad, Iowa **23** 42 14N 92 52W
Conrad, Mont. **33** 48 10N 111 57W
Conrath **55** 45 22N 91 2W
Conroe **51** 30 19N 95 27W
Conselheiro Lafaiete **75** 20 40 S 43 48W
Conselheiro Pena **75** 19 10 S 41 30W
Consort **63** 52 1N 110 46W
Constance = Konstanz **88** 47 39N 9 10 E
Constance, L. = Bodensee **88** 47 35N 9 25 E
Constanţa **89** 44 14N 28 38 E
Constanţa □ **95** 44 15N 28 15 E
Constantina **91** 37 51N 5 40W
Constantine, Algeria **120** 36 25N 6 42 E
Constantine, U.S.A. **29** 41 50N 85 40W
Constantine, C. **11** 58 24N 158 54W
Constitución, Chile **76** 35 20 S 72 30W
Constitución, Uruguay **76** 42 0 S 57 50W
Consul **63** 49 20N 109 30W
Contact **35** 41 46N 114 45W
Contai **109** 21 54N 87 46 E
Contamana **72** 7 19 S 74 55W
Contas → **75** 14 17 S 39 1W
Continental **42** 41 6N 84 16W
Continental Divide **38** 35 25N 108 19W
Continental L. **35** 41 54N 118 43W
Contoocook → **36** 43 27N 71 35W
Contra Costa County ◇ **14** 37 50N 121 50W
Contreras **38** 34 23N 106 49W
Controller B. **11** 60 7N 144 15W
Contumaza **72** 7 23 S 78 57W
Convención **70** 8 28N 73 21W
Convent **25** 30 1N 90 50W
Converse, Ind. **22** 40 35N 85 52W
Converse, La. **25** 31 47N 93 42W
Converse County ◇ **56** 43 0N 105 45W
Convoy **42** 40 55N 84 43W
Conway = Conwy **82** 53 17N 3 50W
Conway = Conwy → **82** 53 18N 3 50W
Conway, Ark. **13** 35 5N 92 26W
Conway, Kans. **24** 38 22N 97 47W
Conway, Mo. **32** 37 30N 92 49W
Conway, N.C. **40** 36 26N 77 14W
Conway, N. Dak. **41** 48 14N 97 41W
Conway, N.H. **36** 43 59N 71 7W
Conway, S.C. **46** 33 51N 79 3W
Conway, Tex. **50** 35 13N 101 23W
Conway County ◇ **13** 35 10N 92 38W
Conway L. **13** 34 58N 92 25W
Conway Springs **24** 37 24N 97 39W
Conwy **82** 53 17N 3 50W
Conwy → **82** 53 18N 3 50W
Conyers **18** 33 40N 84 1W
Coober Pedy **126** 29 1 S 134 43 E
Cooch Behar = Koch Bihar **109** 26 22N 89 29 E
Cook **34** 40 31N 96 10W
Cook, Bahía **78** 55 10 S 70 0W
Cook, Mt. **128** 43 36 S 170 9 E
Cook County ◇, Ga. **18** 31 10N 83 30W
Cook County ◇, Ill. **21** 41 50N 87 45W
Cook County ◇, Minn. **30** 47 50N 90 30W
Cook Inlet **11** 60 0N 152 0W
Cook Is. **125** 17 0 S 160 0W
Cook Strait **128** 41 15 S 174 29 E
Cooke City **33** 45 1N 109 56W
Cooke County ◇ **51** 33 38N 97 8W
Cookes Peak **38** 32 32N 107 44W
Cookeville **49** 36 10N 85 30W
Cooks Hammock **17** 29 56N 83 17W
Cookstown **85** 54 40N 6 43W
Cookstown □ **85** 54 40N 6 43W
Cooksville **21** 40 33N 88 43W
Cooktown **127** 15 30 S 145 16 E
Cool **51** 32 49N 98 1W
Cooleemee **40** 35 49N 80 33W
Coolgardie **126** 30 55 S 121 8 E
Coolidge, Ariz. **12** 32 59N 111 31W
Coolidge, Ga. **18** 31 1N 83 52W
Coolidge, Kans. **24** 38 3N 102 1W
Coolidge, Tex. **51** 31 45N 96 39W
Coolidge Dam **12** 33 0N 110 20W
Coolin **20** 48 29N 116 51W
Cooma **127** 36 12 S 149 8 E
Coon Rapids, Iowa **23** 41 53N 94 41W
Coon Rapids, Minn. **30** 45 9N 93 19W
Coon Valley **55** 43 42N 91 1W
Coonamble **127** 30 56 S 148 27 E
Coondapoor **108** 13 42N 74 40 E
Cooper, Ky. **49** 36 46N 84 52W
Cooper, Tex. **51** 33 23N 95 42W
Cooper →, S.C. **46** 32 50N 79 56W
Cooper →, Va. **54** 36 40N 82 44W
Cooper County ◇ **32** 38 50N 92 45W
Cooperdale **42** 40 13N 82 4W
Coopers Cr. → **127** 28 29 S 137 46 E
Coopersburg **45** 40 31N 75 23W
Cooperstown, N. Dak. **41** 47 27N 98 8W
Cooperstown, N.Y. **39** 42 42N 74 56W
Coopersville **29** 43 4N 85 57W
Coorong, The **127** 35 50 S 139 20 E
Coos Bay **44** 43 22N 124 13W
Coos County ◇, N.H. **36** 44 40N 71 15W
Coos County ◇, Oreg. **44** 43 15N 124 0W
Coosa → **10** 32 30N 86 16W
Coosa County ◇ **10** 32 53N 86 13W
Coosawattee → **18** 34 35N 84 55W
Cootamundra **127** 34 36 S 148 1 E
Cootehill **85** 54 5N 7 5W
Copahue Paso **76** 37 49 S 71 8W
Copainalá **65** 17 8N 93 11W
Copalis Beach **53** 47 7N 124 10W
Copán, Hond. **66** 14 50N 89 9W
Copan, U.S.A. **43** 36 54N 95 56W
Copan Res. **43** 36 58N 95 57W
Copano B. **51** 28 5N 97 5W
Copatana **70** 2 48 S 67 4W
Copco L. **14** 41 59N 122 20W
Cope, Colo. **16** 39 40N 102 51W
Cope, S.C. **46** 33 23N 81 0W
Copeland, Fla. **17** 25 57N 81 22W
Copeland, Idaho **20** 48 54N 116 23W
Copeland, Kans. **24** 37 33N 100 38W
Copenhagen = København **97** 55 41N 12 34 E
Copenhagen **39** 43 54N 75 41W
Copiague **39** 40 41N 73 24W
Copiah County ◇ **31** 31 52N 90 24W
Copiapó **76** 27 30 S 70 20W
Copiapó → **76** 27 19 S 70 56W
Copp L. **62** 60 14N 114 40W
Coppename → **71** 5 48N 55 55W
Copper → **11** 60 18N 145 3W
Copper Butte **53** 48 42N 118 28W
Copper Center **11** 61 58N 145 18W
Copper Cliff **60** 46 28N 81 4W
Copper Harbor **29** 47 28N 87 53W
Copperas Cove **51** 31 8N 97 54W
Copperhill **49** 35 0N 84 15W
Coppermine **58** 67 50N 115 5W
Coppermine → **58** 67 49N 116 4W
Coquet → **82** 55 18N 1 45W
Coqui **57** 17 59N 66 14W
Coquilhatville = Mbandaka **122** 0 1N 18 18 E
Coquille **44** 43 11N 124 11W
Coquille → **44** 43 7N 124 26W
Coquimbo **76** 30 0 S 71 20W
Coquimbo □ **76** 31 0 S 71 0W
Corabia **89** 43 48N 24 30 E
Coração de Jesus **75** 16 43 S 44 22W
Coracora **72** 15 5 S 73 45W
Coral Gables **17** 25 45N 80 16W
Coral Harbour **59** 64 8N 83 10W
Coral Sea **124** 15 0 S 150 0 E
Coral Sea Islands Terr. **127** 20 0 S 155 0 E
Coralville **23** 41 40N 91 35W
Coralville L. **23** 41 42N 91 33W
Coram, Mont. **33** 48 25N 114 3W
Coram, N.Y. **39** 40 52N 73 0W
Corantijn → **71** 5 50N 57 8W
Coraopolis **45** 40 31N 80 10W
Corato **94** 41 12N 16 22 E
Corbin, Kans. **24** 37 8N 97 33W
Corbin, Ky. **49** 36 57N 84 6W
Corbin, Mont. **33** 46 23N 112 4W
Corby, Lincs., U.K. **83** 52 49N 0 31W
Corby, Northants., U.K. **86** 52 29N 0 41W
Corcoran **15** 36 6N 119 33W
Corcubión **91** 42 56N 9 12W
Cordele **18** 31 58N 83 47W
Cordell **43** 35 17N 98 59W
Cordisburgo **75** 19 7 S 44 21W
Córdoba, Argentina **76** 31 20 S 64 10W
Córdoba, Mexico **65** 18 50N 97 0W
Córdoba, Spain **91** 37 50N 4 50W
Córdoba □, Argentina **76** 31 22 S 64 15W
Córdoba □, Colombia **70** 8 20N 75 40W
Córdoba, Sierra de **76** 31 10 S 64 25W
Cordon **111** 16 42N 121 32 E
Cordova, Ala. **10** 33 46N 87 11W
Cordova, Alaska **11** 60 33N 145 45W
Cordova, Ill. **21** 41 41N 90 19W
Cordova, N. Mex. **38** 36 1N 105 52W
Cordova, Nebr. **34** 40 43N 97 21W
Cordova, S.C. **46** 33 26N 80 55W
Core Banks **40** 34 45N 76 15W
Coremas **74** 7 1 S 37 58W
Corentyne → **71** 5 50N 57 8W
Corfu = Kérkira **95** 39 38N 19 50 E
Corfu **39** 42 58N 78 24W
Corguinho **73** 19 53 S 54 52W
Corigliano Cálabro **94** 39 36N 16 31 E
Corinna **26** 44 55N 69 16W
Corinne **52** 41 33N 112 7W
Corinth = Kórinthos **95** 37 56N 22 55 E
Corinth, Ga. **18** 33 14N 84 57W
Corinth, Ky. **49** 38 30N 84 34W
Corinth, Miss. **31** 34 56N 88 31W
Corinth, N.Y. **39** 43 15N 73 49W
Corinth, W. Va. **54** 39 25N 79 30W
Corinth, G. of = Korinthiakós Kólpos **95** 38 16N 22 30 E
Corinto, Brazil **75** 18 20 S 44 30W
Corinto, Nic. **66** 12 30N 87 10W
Corj □ **95** 45 5N 23 25 E
Cork **85** 51 54N 8 30W
Cork □ **85** 51 50N 8 50W
Cork Harbour **85** 51 46N 8 16W
Çorlu **95** 41 11N 27 49 E
Cormack L. **62** 60 56N 121 37W
Cormorant **63** 54 14N 100 35W
Cormorant L. **63** 54 15N 100 50W
Corn **43** 35 24N 98 48W
Corn Is. = Maiz, Islas del **66** 12 15N 83 4W
Cornelia **18** 34 31N 83 32W
Cornelio **64** 29 55N 111 8W
Cornélio Procópio **77** 23 7 S 50 40W
Cornelius **40** 35 29N 80 52W
Cornell, Ill. **21** 41 0N 88 44W
Cornell, Wis. **55** 45 10N 91 9W
Corner Brook **61** 48 57N 57 58W
Corner Inlet **127** 38 45 S 146 20 E
Cornersville **48** 35 22N 86 50W
Cornerville **13** 33 51N 91 56W
Corning, Ark. **13** 36 25N 90 35W
Corning, Calif. **14** 39 56N 122 11W
Corning, Iowa **23** 40 59N 94 44W
Corning, Kans. **24** 39 40N 96 2W
Corning, N.Y. **39** 42 9N 77 3W
Corning, Ohio **42** 39 36N 82 5W
Cornish **43** 34 9N 97 36W
Cornlea **34** 41 41N 97 34W
Cornucopia **44** 45 0N 117 12W
Cornudas **50** 31 47N 105 28W
Cornville **12** 34 43N 111 55W
Cornwall, Canada **60** 45 2N 74 44W
Cornwall, Conn. **28** 41 50N 73 20W
Cornwall, Pa. **45** 40 17N 76 25W
Cornwall, Vt. **36** 43 56N 73 13W
Cornwall □ **83** 50 26N 4 40W
Cornwall Bridge **28** 41 49N 73 22W
Cornwallis I. **4** 75 8N 95 0W
Cornwell, Fla. **17** 27 23N 81 6W
Cornwell, S.C. **46** 34 37N 81 10W
Coro **70** 11 25N 69 41W
Coroaci **75** 18 35 S 42 17W
Coroatá **74** 4 8 S 44 0W
Corocoro **72** 17 15 S 68 28W
Corocoro, I. **71** 8 30N 60 10W
Coroico **72** 16 0 S 67 50W
Coromandel, Brazil **75** 18 28 S 47 13W
Coromandel, N.Z. **128** 36 45 S 175 31 E
Coromandel Coast **108** 12 30N 81 0 E
Corona, Calif. **15** 33 53N 117 34W
Corona, N. Mex. **38** 34 15N 105 36W
Corona, S. Dak. **47** 45 20N 96 46W
Coronado **15** 32 41N 117 11W
Coronado, Bahía de **66** 9 0N 83 40W
Coronado Nat. Forest **12** 32 10N 110 20W
Coronados, G. de los **78** 41 40 S 74 0W
Coronation **62** 52 5N 111 27W
Coronation Gulf **58** 68 25N 110 0W
Coronation I. **5** 60 45 S 46 0W
Coronda **76** 31 58 S 60 56W
Coronel **76** 37 0 S 73 10W
Coronel Bogado **76** 27 11 S 56 18W
Coronel Dorrego **76** 38 40 S 61 10W
Coronel Fabriciano **75** 19 31 S 42 38W
Coronel Murta **75** 16 37 S 42 11W
Coronel Oviedo **76** 25 24 S 56 30W
Coronel Ponce **73** 15 34 S 55 1W
Coronel Pringles **76** 38 0 S 61 30W
Coronel Suárez **76** 37 30 S 61 52W
Coronel Vidal **76** 37 28 S 57 45W
Corongo **72** 8 30 S 77 53W
Coronie □ **71** 5 55N 56 20W
Coropuna, Nevado **72** 15 30 S 72 41W
Corozal, Belize **65** 18 23N 88 23W
Corozal, Colombia **70** 9 19N 75 18W
Corozal, Panama **57** 8 59N 79 34W
Corozal, Puerto Rico **57** 18 21N 66 19W
Corpus **77** 27 10 S 55 30W
Corpus Christi **51** 27 47N 97 24W
Corpus Christi, L. **51** 28 2N 97 52W
Corpus Christi B. **51** 27 47N 97 22W
Corque **72** 18 20 S 67 41W
Corral, Chile **78** 39 52 S 73 26W
Corral, U.S.A. **20** 43 21N 114 57W
Correctionville **23** 42 29N 95 47W
Correll **30** 45 14N 96 10W
Corrente **74** 10 27 S 45 10W
Corrente → **75** 13 8 S 43 28W
Correntes → **73** 17 38 S 55 8W
Correntina **75** 13 20 S 44 39W
Corrèze □ **90** 45 20N 1 45 E
Corrib, L. **85** 53 5N 9 10W
Corrientes **76** 27 30 S 58 45W
Corrientes □ **76** 28 0 S 57 0W
Corrientes →, Argentina **76** 30 42 S 59 38W
Corrientes →, Peru **72** 3 43 S 74 35W
Corrientes, C., Colombia **70** 5 30N 77 34W
Corrientes, C., Cuba **66** 21 43N 84 30W
Corrientes, C., Mexico **64** 20 25N 105 42W
Corrigan **51** 31 0N 94 52W
Corriganville **27** 39 45N 78 17W
Corry **45** 41 55N 79 39W
Corryton **49** 36 9N 83 47W
Corse **90** 42 0N 9 0 E
Corse, C. **94** 43 1N 9 25 E
Corse-du-Sud □ **90** 41 45N 9 0 E
Corsica = Corse **90** 42 0N 9 0 E
Corsica **47** 43 25N 98 24W
Corsicana **51** 32 6N 96 28W
Corson County ◇ **47** 45 55N 101 0W
Cortez **16** 37 21N 108 35W
Cortez Mts. **35** 40 20N 116 20W
Cortland, N.Y. **39** 42 36N 76 11W
Cortland, Nebr. **34** 40 30N 96 42W
Cortland, Ohio **42** 41 20N 80 44W
Cortland County ◇ **39** 42 35N 76 5W
Cortona **94** 43 16N 12 0 E
Çorum, Turkey **106** 40 30N 34 57 E
Corum, U.S.A. **43** 34 22N 98 6W
Corumbá **73** 19 0 S 57 30W

Corumbá Crown City

Corumbá → **75** 18 19 S 48 55W
Corumbá de Goiás **75** 16 0 S 48 50W
Corumbaíba **75** 18 9 S 48 34W
Coruña, La **91** 43 20N 8 25W
Corund **95** 46 30N 25 13 E
Corunna = Coruña, La **91** 43 20N 8 25W
Corunna **29** 42 59N 84 7W
Corvallis, Mont. **33** 46 19N 114 7W
Corvallis, Oreg. **44** 44 34N 123 16W
Corvette, L. de la **60** 53 25N 74 3W
Corwin **24** 37 5N 98 18W
Corwith **23** 42 59N 93 57W
Corydon, Ind. **22** 38 13N 86 7W
Corydon, Iowa **23** 40 46N 93 19W
Corydon, Ky. **48** 37 44N 87 43W
Coryell County ◇ **51** 31 26N 97 45W
Cosalá **64** 24 28N 106 40W
Cosamaloapan **65** 18 23N 95 50W
Cosenza **94** 39 17N 16 14 E
Coşereni **95** 44 38N 26 35 E
Coshocton **42** 40 16N 81 51W
Coshocton County ◇ **42** 40 16N 81 51W
Cosmopolis **53** 46 57N 123 46W
Cosquín **76** 31 15 S 64 30W
Cossatot → **13** 33 48N 94 9W
Cost **51** 29 26N 97 32W
Costa Blanca **91** 38 25N 0 10W
Costa Brava **91** 41 30N 3 0 E
Costa del Sol **91** 36 30N 4 30W
Costa Dorada **91** 40 45N 1 15 E
Costa Mesa **15** 33 38N 117 55W
Costa Rica ■ **66** 10 0N 84 0W
Costilla **38** 36 59N 105 32W
Costilla County ◇ **16** 37 15N 105 30W
Cosumnes → **14** 38 16N 121 26W
Cotabato **111** 7 14N 124 15 E
Cotacajes → **72** 16 0 S 67 1W
Cotagaita **76** 20 45 S 65 40W
Cotahuasi **72** 15 12 S 72 50W
Cotati **14** 38 20N 122 42W
Côte-d'Or □ **90** 47 30N 4 50 E
Coteau des Prairies **47** 44 20N 96 0W
Coteau du Missouri **41** 47 0N 100 0W
Cotegipe **75** 12 2 S 44 15W
Cotentin **90** 49 30N 1 30W
Côtes-du-Nord □ **90** 48 25N 2 40W
Cotesfield **34** 41 22N 98 38W
Coto Laurel **57** 18 3N 66 33W
Cotoca **73** 17 49 S 63 3W
Cotonou **120** 6 20N 2 25 E
Cotopaxi **16** 38 22N 105 41W
Cotopaxi □ **70** 0 5 S 78 55W
Cotopaxi, Vol. **72** 0 40 S 78 30W
Cotswold Hills **83** 51 42N 2 10W
Cottage Grove **44** 43 48N 123 3W
Cottageville **46** 32 56N 80 29W
Cottbus **88** 51 44N 14 20 E
Cottle County ◇ **50** 34 0N 100 18W
Cotton, Ga. **18** 31 10N 84 4W
Cotton, Minn. **30** 47 10N 92 28W
Cotton County ◇ **43** 34 15N 98 20W
Cotton Plant **13** 35 0N 91 15W
Cotton Valley **25** 32 49N 93 25W
Cottondale, Ala. **10** 33 11N 87 27W
Cottondale, Fla. **17** 30 48N 85 23W
Cottonport **25** 30 59N 92 3W
Cottonwood, Ala. **10** 31 3N 85 18W
Cottonwood, Ariz. **12** 34 45N 112 1W
Cottonwood, Calif. **14** 40 23N 122 17W
Cottonwood, Idaho **20** 46 3N 116 21W
Cottonwood, Minn. **30** 44 37N 95 41W
Cottonwood, S. Dak. **47** 43 58N 101 54W
Cottonwood → **30** 44 17N 94 25W
Cottonwood County ◇ **30** 44 0N 95 10W
Cottonwood Cr. → **50** 31 23N 103 46W
Cottonwood Falls **24** 38 22N 96 32W
Cottonwood Heights **52** 40 38N 111 49W
Cottonwood Mts. **15** 36 50N 117 40W
Cotuit **28** 41 37N 70 26W
Cotulla **51** 28 26N 99 14W
Couchwood **25** 32 46N 93 23W
Couderay **55** 45 48N 91 18W
Coudersport **45** 41 46N 78 1W
Cougar **53** 46 3N 122 18W
Coulee City **53** 47 37N 119 17W
Coulee Dam **53** 47 58N 118 58W
Coulee Dam Nat. Rec. Area **53** 47 48N 119 45W
Coulman I. **5** 73 35 S 170 0 E
Coulonge → **60** 45 52N 76 46W
Coulterville, Calif. **14** 37 43N 120 12W
Coulterville, Ill. **21** 38 11N 89 36W
Counce **48** 35 3N 88 16W
Council, Ga. **18** 30 37N 82 31W
Council, Idaho **20** 44 44N 116 26W
Council Bluffs **23** 41 16N 95 52W
Council Grove **24** 38 40N 96 29W
Council Grove Lake **24** 38 41N 96 33W
Council Hill **43** 35 31N 95 42W
Country Lake **37** 39 55N 74 32W
Coupeville **53** 48 13N 122 41W
Coupland **51** 30 28N 97 23W
Courantyne → **72** 5 55N 57 5W
Courtenay, Canada **62** 49 45N 125 0W
Courtenay, U.S.A. **41** 47 13N 98 34W
Courtland, Ala. **10** 34 40N 87 19W
Courtland, Calif. **14** 38 20N 121 34W
Courtland, Kans. **24** 39 47N 97 54W
Courtland, Minn. **30** 44 16N 94 20W
Courtland, Miss. **31** 34 14N 89 57W
Courtland, Va. **54** 36 43N 77 4W
Courtrai = Kortrijk **87** 50 50N 3 17 E
Courtright Reservoir **15** 37 5N 118 58W
Coushatta **25** 32 1N 93 21W
Coutts **62** 49 0N 111 57W
Covasna **95** 45 50N 26 10 E
Covasna □ **95** 45 50N 26 0 E
Cove, Ark. **13** 34 26N 94 25W
Cove, Oreg. **44** 45 18N 117 49W
Cove City **40** 35 13N 77 19W
Cove Point **27** 38 23N 76 24W
Covelo **14** 39 48N 123 15W
Coveñas **70** 9 24N 75 44W
Coventry, U.K. **83** 52 25N 1 31W
Coventry, Conn. **28** 41 48N 72 23W
Coventry, R.I. **28** 41 41N 71 34W
Coventry L. **63** 61 15N 106 15W
Coverdale **18** 31 38N 83 58W
Covilhã **91** 40 17N 7 31W
Covington, Ga. **18** 33 36N 83 51W
Covington, Ind. **22** 40 9N 87 24W
Covington, Ky. **49** 39 5N 84 31W
Covington, La. **25** 30 29N 90 6W
Covington, Mich. **29** 46 33N 88 32W
Covington, Ohio **42** 40 7N 84 21W
Covington, Okla. **43** 36 18N 97 35W
Covington, Tenn. **48** 35 34N 89 39W
Covington, Va. **54** 37 47N 79 59W
Covington County ◇, Ala. **10** 31 18N 86 29W
Covington County ◇, Miss. **31** 31 39N 89 33W
Cow Cr. → **44** 42 57N 123 22W
Cow Head L. **14** 41 55N 120 2W
Cowal, L. **127** 33 40 S 147 25 E
Cowan, Canada **63** 52 5N 100 45W
Cowan, U.S.A. **48** 35 10N 86 1W
Cowan, L. **126** 31 45 S 121 45 E
Cowan L. **63** 54 0N 107 15W
Coward **46** 33 58N 79 45W
Cowden **21** 39 15N 88 52W
Cowdenbeath **84** 56 7N 3 20W
Cowdrey **16** 40 52N 106 19W
Cowen **54** 38 25N 80 34W
Cowes **83** 50 45N 1 18W
Coweta **43** 35 57N 95 39W
Coweta County ◇ **18** 33 20N 84 50W
Cowles **34** 40 10N 98 27W
Cowley **56** 44 53N 108 28W
Cowley County ◇ **24** 37 15N 96 45W
Cowlic **12** 31 48N 111 59W
Cowlitz → **53** 46 6N 122 55W
Cowlitz County ◇ **53** 46 5N 122 50W
Cowpens **46** 35 1N 81 48W
Cowra **127** 33 49 S 148 42 E
Cox **18** 31 27N 81 34W
Cox City **43** 34 43N 97 44W
Coxim **73** 18 30 S 54 55W
Coxim → **73** 18 34 S 54 46W
Cox's Bazar **109** 21 26N 91 59 E
Cox's Cove **61** 49 7N 58 5W
Coxs Mills **54** 39 3N 80 50W
Coxsackie **39** 42 21N 73 48W
Coy **13** 34 32N 91 53W
Coyame **64** 29 28N 105 6W
Coyanosa Draw → **50** 31 18N 103 6W
Coyle **43** 35 57N 97 14W
Coyote **38** 36 10N 106 37W
Coyote L. **15** 35 4N 116 46W
Coyote Reservoir **14** 37 7N 121 33W
Coyuca de Benítez **65** 17 1N 100 8W
Coyuca de Catalan **64** 18 18N 100 41W
Coyville **24** 37 41N 95 54W
Cozad **34** 40 52N 99 59W
Cozumel **65** 20 31N 86 55W
Cozumel, Isla de **65** 20 30N 86 40W
Crab Cr. → **53** 46 49N 119 55W
Crab Orchard, Ky. **49** 37 28N 84 30W
Crab Orchard, Nebr. **34** 40 20N 96 25W
Crab Orchard L. **21** 37 43N 89 9W
Crabtree **44** 44 38N 122 54W
Cracow = Kraków **89** 50 4N 19 57 E
Cradock **123** 32 8 S 25 36 E
Craig, Alaska **11** 55 29N 133 9W
Craig, Colo. **16** 40 31N 107 33W
Craig, Iowa **23** 42 54N 96 19W
Craig, Mo. **32** 40 12N 95 23W
Craig, Mont. **33** 47 5N 111 58W
Craig, Nebr. **34** 41 47N 96 22W
Craig County ◇, Okla. **43** 36 45N 95 10W
Craig County ◇, Va. **54** 37 25N 80 5W
Craig Pass **56** 44 26N 110 43W
Craigavon = Lurgan **85** 54 28N 6 20W
Craighead County ◇ **13** 35 50N 90 42W
Craigmont **20** 46 15N 116 29W
Craigsville, Va. **54** 38 5N 79 23W
Craigsville, W. Va. **54** 38 20N 80 39W
Craiova **89** 44 21N 23 48 E
Cranberry L. **39** 44 11N 74 50W
Cranberry Portage **63** 54 35N 101 23W
Cranbrook **62** 49 30N 115 46W
Crandall **31** 31 58N 88 32W
Crandon **55** 45 34N 88 54W
Crane, Ind. **22** 38 54N 86 54W
Crane, Mo. **32** 36 54N 93 34W
Crane, Mont. **33** 47 35N 104 16W
Crane, Oreg. **44** 43 25N 118 35W
Crane, Tex. **50** 31 24N 102 21W
Crane County ◇ **50** 31 24N 102 21W
Crane Mt. **44** 42 4N 120 13W
Cranfills Gap **51** 31 46N 97 50W
Cranford **37** 40 40N 74 18W
Cranston **28** 41 47N 71 26W
Crapo **27** 38 18N 76 9W
Crary **41** 48 4N 98 38W
Crasna **95** 46 32N 27 51 E
Crater L. **44** 42 56N 122 6W
Crater Lake **44** 42 54N 122 8W
Crater Lake National Park **44** 42 55N 122 10W
Craters of the Moon National Monument **20** 43 25N 113 30W
Crateús **74** 5 10 S 40 39W
Crato **74** 7 10 S 39 25W
Craven County ◇ **40** 35 15N 77 10W
Cravo Norte **70** 6 18N 70 12W
Cravo Norte → **70** 6 18N 70 12W
Crawford, Ala. **10** 32 27N 85 11W
Crawford, Colo. **16** 38 42N 107 37W
Crawford, Miss. **31** 33 18N 88 37W
Crawford, Nebr. **34** 42 41N 103 25W
Crawford, Okla. **43** 35 50N 99 48W
Crawford, Tex. **51** 31 32N 97 27W
Crawford County ◇, Ark. **13** 35 20N 94 18W
Crawford County ◇, Ga. **18** 32 50N 84 0W
Crawford County ◇, Ill. **21** 39 0N 87 45W
Crawford County ◇, Ind. **22** 38 15N 86 25W
Crawford County ◇, Iowa **23** 42 0N 95 20W
Crawford County ◇, Kans. **24** 37 30N 94 45W
Crawford County ◇, Mich. **29** 44 45N 84 40W
Crawford County ◇, Mo. **32** 38 0N 91 20W
Crawford County ◇, Ohio **42** 40 48N 82 59W
Crawford County ◇, Pa. **45** 41 45N 80 0W
Crawford County ◇, Wis. **55** 43 15N 90 50W
Crawfordsville, Ark. **13** 35 14N 90 20W
Crawfordsville, Ind. **22** 40 2N 86 54W
Crawfordsville, Iowa **23** 41 12N 91 32W
Crawfordville, Fla. **17** 30 11N 84 23W
Crawfordville, Ga. **18** 33 33N 82 54W
Crawley **83** 51 7N 0 10W
Crazy Mts. **33** 46 12N 110 20W
Crazy Woman Cr. → **56** 44 29N 106 8W
Creagerstown **27** 39 37N 77 22W
Creal Springs **21** 37 37N 88 50W
Crean L. **63** 54 5N 106 9W
Crécy-en-Ponthieu **90** 50 15N 1 53 E
Cree →, Canada **63** 58 57N 105 47W
Cree →, U.K. **84** 54 51N 4 24W
Cree L. **63** 57 30N 106 30W
Creede **16** 37 51N 106 56W
Creedmoor **40** 36 7N 78 41W
Creek County ◇ **43** 35 50N 96 20W
Creel **64** 27 45N 107 38W
Creighton, Mo. **32** 38 30N 94 4W
Creighton, Nebr. **34** 42 28N 97 54W
Crellin **27** 39 25N 79 25W
Cremona **94** 45 8N 10 2 E
Crenshaw **31** 34 30N 90 12W
Crenshaw County ◇ **10** 31 43N 86 16W
Creole **25** 29 49N 93 7W
Crepori → **73** 5 42 S 57 8W
Cres **94** 44 58N 14 25 E
Cresaptown **27** 39 36N 78 50W
Cresbard **47** 45 10N 98 57W
Crescent, Okla. **43** 35 57N 97 36W
Crescent, Oreg. **44** 43 28N 121 42W
Crescent Beach **17** 29 46N 81 15W
Crescent City, Calif. **14** 41 45N 124 12W
Crescent City, Fla. **17** 29 26N 81 31W
Crescent L. **17** 29 28N 81 30W
Cresco **23** 43 22N 92 7W
Crespo **76** 32 2 S 60 19W
Cresson **45** 40 28N 78 36W
Crested Butte **16** 38 52N 106 59W
Crestline, Calif. **15** 34 14N 117 18W
Crestline, Ohio **42** 40 47N 82 44W
Creston, Canada **62** 49 10N 116 31W
Creston, Iowa **23** 41 4N 94 22W
Creston, Wash. **53** 47 46N 118 31W
Creston, Wyo. **56** 41 42N 107 45W
Crestone **16** 37 56N 105 47W
Crestview **17** 30 46N 86 34W
Crestwood **49** 38 19N 85 28W
Crestwood Village **37** 39 56N 74 20W
Creswell, N.C. **40** 35 53N 76 24W
Creswell, Oreg. **44** 43 55N 123 1W
Crete = Kríti **95** 35 15N 25 0 E
Crete, Ill. **21** 41 27N 87 38W
Crete, Nebr. **34** 40 38N 96 58W
Crete, I. **95** 35 15N 25 0 E
Crete, La **62** 58 11N 116 24W
Creus, C. **91** 42 20N 3 19 E
Creuse □ **90** 46 0N 2 0 E
Creuse → **90** 47 0N 0 34 E
Creusot, Le **90** 46 50N 4 24 E
Creve Coeur **21** 40 39N 89 35W
Crewe, U.K. **82** 53 6N 2 28W
Crewe, U.S.A. **54** 37 10N 78 8W
Criciúma **77** 28 40 S 49 23W
Cricket **40** 36 11N 81 12W
Cricket Mts. **52** 39 0N 112 0W
Crieff **84** 56 22N 3 50W
Crimea = Krymskiy P-ov. **99** 45 0N 34 0 E
Crinan **84** 56 6N 5 34W
Criner **43** 34 58N 97 34W
Cripple Creek **16** 38 45N 105 11W
Crisfield **27** 37 59N 75 51W
Crisp County ◇ **18** 31 50N 83 50W
Crisp Pt. **29** 46 45N 85 16W
Cristalândia **74** 10 36 S 49 11W
Cristino Castro **74** 8 49 S 44 13W
Cristobal **57** 9 21N 79 55W
Crişul Alb → **89** 46 42N 21 17 E
Crişul Negru → **89** 46 38N 22 26 E
Crittenden **49** 38 47N 84 36W
Crittenden County ◇, Ark. **13** 35 14N 90 20W
Crittenden County ◇, Ky. **48** 37 20N 88 5W
Crivitz **55** 45 14N 88 1W
Crixás **75** 14 27 S 49 58W
Crna Gora **95** 42 10N 21 30 E
Crna Gora □ **95** 42 40N 19 20 E
Crna Reka → **95** 41 33N 21 59 E
Croaghpatrick **85** 53 46N 9 40W
Croatan National Forest **40** 34 50N 77 5W
Crocheron **27** 38 15N 76 3W
Crocker **32** 37 57N 92 16W
Crocker, Banjaran **110** 5 40N 116 30 E
Crocker I. **126** 11 12 S 132 32 E
Crockett **51** 31 19N 95 27W
Crockett County ◇, Tenn. **48** 35 49N 89 14W
Crockett County ◇, Tex. **50** 30 45N 101 30W
Crocodile Is. **126** 12 3 S 134 58 E
Crofton, Ky. **48** 37 3N 87 29W
Crofton, Md. **27** 39 1N 76 42W
Crofton, Nebr. **34** 42 44N 97 30W
Croghan **39** 43 54N 75 24W
Croix, La, L. **60** 48 20N 92 15W
Cromarty, Canada **63** 58 3N 94 9W
Cromarty, U.K. **84** 57 40N 4 2W
Cromer **82** 52 56N 1 18 E
Cromwell, N.Z. **128** 45 3 S 169 14 E
Cromwell, Ala. **10** 32 14N 88 17W
Cromwell, Minn. **30** 46 41N 92 53W
Cromwell, Okla. **43** 35 22N 96 29W
Crook **16** 40 52N 102 48W
Crook County ◇, Oreg. **44** 44 10N 120 20W
Crook County ◇, Wyo. **56** 44 44N 104 30W
Crooked →, Canada **62** 54 50N 122 54W
Crooked →, U.S.A. **44** 44 32N 121 16W
Crooked Creek **11** 61 52N 158 7W
Crooked I. **67** 22 50N 74 10W
Crooked Island Passage **67** 23 0N 74 30W
Crooked L. **17** 27 48N 81 35W
Crooks **47** 43 40N 96 49W
Crookston, Minn. **30** 47 47N 96 37W
Crookston, Nebr. **34** 42 56N 100 45W
Crooksville **42** 39 46N 82 6W
Croom **27** 38 45N 76 46W
Cropsey **21** 40 37N 88 29W
Crosby, Minn. **30** 46 29N 93 58W
Crosby, Miss. **31** 31 17N 91 4W
Crosby, N. Dak. **41** 48 55N 103 18W
Crosby, Tex. **51** 29 55N 95 4W
Crosby, Mt. **56** 43 52N 109 20W
Crosby County ◇ **50** 33 40N 101 14W
Crosbyton **50** 33 40N 101 14W
Cross Anchor **46** 34 39N 81 51W
Cross City **17** 29 38N 83 7W
Cross County ◇ **13** 35 14N 90 47W
Cross Fell **82** 54 44N 2 29W
Cross Hill **46** 34 18N 81 59W
Cross L., Canada **63** 54 45N 97 30W
Cross L., U.S.A. **26** 47 7N 68 20W
Cross Lake **30** 46 40N 94 7W
Cross Plains, Tenn. **48** 36 33N 86 42W
Cross Plains, Tex. **51** 32 8N 99 11W
Cross Sound **11** 56 0N 135 0W
Cross Timbers **32** 38 1N 93 14W
Crossett **13** 33 8N 91 58W
Crossfield **62** 51 25N 114 0W
Crosshaven **85** 51 48N 8 19W
Crossroads **38** 33 31N 103 20W
Crossville, Ill. **21** 38 10N 88 4W
Crossville, Tenn. **49** 35 57N 85 2W
Croswell **29** 43 16N 82 37W
Crothersville **22** 38 48N 85 50W
Crotone **94** 39 5N 17 6 E
Crouch **20** 44 7N 115 58W
Crouse **40** 35 25N 81 18W
Crow →, Canada **62** 59 41N 124 20W
Crow →, U.S.A. **16** 40 23N 104 29W
Crow Agency **33** 45 36N 107 28W
Crow Creek Indian Reservation **47** 44 3N 99 25W
Crow Hd. **85** 51 34N 10 9W
Crow Indian Reservation **33** 45 25N 108 0W
Crow Wing → **30** 46 19N 94 20W
Crow Wing County ◇ **30** 46 30N 94 0W
Crowder, Miss. **31** 34 11N 90 8W
Crowder, Okla. **43** 35 7N 95 40W
Crowell **51** 33 59N 99 43W
Crowley, Colo. **16** 38 12N 103 51W
Crowley, La. **25** 30 13N 92 22W
Crowley, Tex. **51** 32 35N 97 22W
Crowley, L. **14** 37 35N 118 42W
Crowley County ◇ **16** 38 15N 103 45W
Crowley Ridge **13** 35 45N 90 45W
Crown City **42** 38 36N 82 17W

Crown Point
Dalmatia

Crown Point 22 41 25N 87 22W
Crownpoint 38 35 41N 108 9W
Crows Nest Pk. 47 44 3N 103 58W
Crowsnest Pass 62 49 40N 114 40W
Croydon, Australia 127 18 13 S 142 14 E
Croydon, U.K. 83 51 18N 0 5W
Croydon Flat 36 43 25N 72 12W
Crozet 54 38 4N 78 42W
Crozet Is. 3 46 27 S 52 0 E
Cruger 31 33 19N 90 14W
Crump L. 44 42 17N 119 50W
Crumpton 27 39 14N 75 55W
Cruz, C. 66 19 50N 77 50W
Cruz, La, C. Rica 66 11 4N 85 39W
Cruz, La, Mexico 64 23 55N 106 54W
Cruz Alta 77 28 45 S 53 40W
Cruz Bay 57 18 20N 64 48W
Cruz das Almas 75 12 0 S 39 6W
Cruz de Malta 74 8 15 S 40 20W
Cruz del Eje 76 30 45 S 64 50W
Cruzeiro 75 22 33 S 45 0W
Cruzeiro do Oeste 77 23 46 S 53 4W
Cruzeiro do Sul 72 7 35 S 72 35W
Cry L. 62 58 45N 129 0W
Crystal, Minn. 30 45 3N 93 22W
Crystal, N. Dak. 41 48 36N 97 40W
Crystal → 16 39 25N 107 14W
Crystal B. 17 28 50N 82 45W
Crystal Bay 35 39 15N 120 0W
Crystal Beach, Fla. 17 28 5N 82 47W
Crystal Beach, Md. 27 39 26N 75 59W
Crystal City, Mo. 32 38 13N 90 23W
Crystal City, Tex. 51 28 41N 99 50W
Crystal Falls 29 46 5N 88 20W
Crystal L. 29 44 40N 86 10W
Crystal Lake, Ill. 21 42 14N 88 19W
Crystal Lake, Iowa 23 43 13N 93 47W
Crystal River 17 28 54N 82 35W
Crystal Springs 31 31 59N 90 21W
Csongrád 89 46 43N 20 12 E
Cu Lao Hon 112 10 54N 108 18 E
Cuamba 123 14 45 S 36 22 E
Cuando → 123 14 0 S 19 30 E
Cuanza → 118 9 2 S 13 30 E
Cuarto → 76 33 25 S 63 2W
Cuatrociénegas 64 26 59N 102 5W
Cuauhtémoc 64 28 25N 106 52W
Cuba, Ala. 10 32 26N 88 23W
Cuba, Ill. 21 40 30N 90 12W
Cuba, Kans. 24 39 48N 97 27W
Cuba, Mo. 32 38 4N 91 24W
Cuba, N. Mex. 38 36 1N 107 4W
Cuba, N.Y. 39 42 13N 78 17W
Cuba ■ 66 22 0N 79 0W
Cuba City 55 42 36N 90 26W
Cubango → 123 18 50 S 22 25 E
Cubero 38 35 5N 107 31W
Cuchara, Pta. 57 17 57N 66 42W
Cucharas → 16 37 55N 104 32W
Cuchi 123 14 37 S 16 58 E
Cuchillo-Có 78 38 20 S 64 37W
Cuchivero → 70 7 40N 65 57W
Cuchumatanes, Sierra de los 66 15 35N 91 25W
Cucuí 70 1 12N 66 50W
Cucurpe 64 30 20N 110 43W
Cucurrupí 70 4 23N 76 56W
Cúcuta 70 7 54N 72 31W
Cudahy 55 42 58N 87 52W
Cudalbi 95 45 46N 27 41 E
Cuddalore 108 11 46N 79 45 E
Cuddapah 108 14 30N 78 47 E
Cuddeback L. 15 35 18N 117 29W
Cue 126 27 25 S 117 54 E
Cuenca, Ecuador 70 2 50 S 79 9W
Cuenca, Spain 91 40 5N 2 10W
Cuenca, Serranía de 91 39 55N 1 50W
Cuencamé 64 24 53N 103 41W
Cuernavaca 65 18 50N 99 20W
Cuero 51 29 6N 97 17W
Cuervo 38 35 2N 104 25W
Cuevas, Cerro 73 22 0 S 65 12W
Cuevas del Almanzora 91 37 18N 1 58W
Cuevo 72 20 15 S 63 30W
Cugir 95 45 48N 23 25 E
Cuiabá 73 15 30 S 56 0W
Cuiabá → 73 17 5 S 56 36W
Cuilco 66 15 24N 91 58W
Cuillin Hills 84 57 14N 6 15W
Cuillin Sd. 84 57 4N 6 20W
Cuiluan 114 47 51N 128 32 E
Cuima 123 13 25 S 15 45 E
Cuité 74 6 29 S 36 9W
Cuito → 123 18 1 S 20 48 E
Cuitzeo, L. de 64 19 55N 101 5W
Cuiuni → 71 0 45 S 63 7W
Cukai 110 4 13N 103 25 E
Culberson 40 35 0N 84 9W
Culberson County ◇ 50 31 30N 104 30W
Culbertson, Mont. 33 48 9N 104 31W
Culbertson, Nebr. 34 40 14N 100 50W
Culdesac 20 46 23N 116 40W
Culebra, Isla de 57 18 19N 65 18W
Culebra, Sierra de la 91 41 55N 6 20W
Culebrita, Isla 57 18 19N 65 14W
Culiacán 64 24 50N 107 23W
Culiacán → 64 24 30N 107 42W
Culion 111 11 54N 120 1 E
Culiseu → 73 12 14 S 53 17W
Cullen, U.K. 84 57 45N 2 50W
Cullen, U.S.A. 25 32 58N 93 27W
Cullera 91 39 9N 0 17W
Cullison 24 37 38N 98 54W
Cullman 10 34 11N 86 51W
Cullman County ◇ 10 34 11N 86 51W
Culloden 18 32 52N 84 6W
Culloden Moor 84 57 29N 4 7W
Cullom 21 40 53N 88 16W
Cullomburg 10 31 43N 88 18W
Cullowhee 40 35 19N 83 11W
Culp Creek 44 43 42N 122 50W
Culpeper 54 38 30N 78 0W
Culpeper County ◇ 54 38 28N 78 0W
Culuene → 73 12 56 S 52 51W
Culver, Ind. 22 41 13N 86 25W
Culver, Kans. 24 38 58N 97 46W
Culver, Oreg. 44 44 32N 121 13W
Culver, Pt. 126 32 54 S 124 43 E
Culverden 128 42 47 S 172 49 E
Culverton 18 33 19N 82 54W
Cumaná 71 10 30N 64 5W
Cumare 70 0 49N 72 32W
Cumari 75 18 16 S 48 11W
Cumberland, Canada 62 49 40N 125 0W
Cumberland, Iowa 23 41 16N 94 52W
Cumberland, Ky. 49 36 59N 82 59W
Cumberland, Md. 27 39 39N 78 46W
Cumberland, N.C. 40 35 0N 78 59W
Cumberland, N.J. 37 39 26N 75 14W
Cumberland, Ohio 42 39 51N 81 40W
Cumberland, Va. 54 37 30N 78 15W
Cumberland, Wis. 55 45 32N 92 1W
Cumberland → 48 37 9N 88 25W
Cumberland, L. 49 36 52N 85 9W
Cumberland City 48 36 23N 87 38W
Cumberland County ◇, Ill. 21 39 15N 88 15W
Cumberland County ◇, Ky. 49 36 45N 85 25W
Cumberland County ◇, Maine 26 43 50N 70 30W
Cumberland County ◇, N.C. 40 35 0N 78 45W
Cumberland County ◇, N.J. 37 39 20N 75 10W
Cumberland County ◇, Pa. 45 40 5N 77 10W
Cumberland County ◇, Tenn. 49 36 0N 85 0W
Cumberland County ◇, Va. 54 37 30N 78 15W
Cumberland Gap 49 36 36N 83 41W
Cumberland Gap Nat. Historic Park 49 36 36N 83 40W
Cumberland Hill 28 41 59N 71 28W
Cumberland I. 18 30 50N 81 25W
Cumberland I. Nat. Seashore 18 30 12N 81 24W
Cumberland Is. 127 20 35 S 149 10 E
Cumberland L. 63 54 3N 102 18W
Cumberland Pen. 59 67 0N 64 0W
Cumberland Plateau 49 36 0N 85 0W
Cumberland Pt. 29 47 51N 89 14W
Cumberland Sd. 59 65 30N 66 0W
Cumbria □ 82 54 35N 2 55W
Cumbrian Mts. 82 54 30N 3 0W
Cumbum 108 15 40N 79 10 E
Cumby 51 33 8N 95 50W
Cuminá → 71 1 30 S 56 0W
Cuminapanema → 71 1 9 S 54 54W
Cuming County ◇ 34 41 50N 96 40W
Cumming 18 34 12N 84 9W
Cummings 46 32 47N 80 59W
Cumnock 84 55 27N 4 18W
Cumpas 64 30 0N 109 48W
Cuncumén 76 31 53 S 70 38W
Cundiff 49 36 57N 85 15W
Cundinamarca □ 70 5 0N 74 0W
Cunene → 123 17 20 S 11 50 E
Cúneo 94 44 23N 7 31 E
Cunnamulla 127 28 2 S 145 38 E
Cunningham 24 37 39N 98 26W
Cupar, Canada 63 50 57N 104 10W
Cupar, U.K. 84 56 20N 3 0W
Cupertino 14 37 19N 122 2W
Cupica, Golfo de 70 6 25N 77 30W
Cuprum 20 45 5N 116 41W
Curaçá 74 8 59 S 39 54W
Curaçao 67 12 10N 69 0W
Curacautín 78 38 26 S 71 53W
Curahuara de Carangas 72 17 52 S 68 26W
Curanilahue 76 37 29 S 73 28W
Curaray → 70 2 20 S 74 5W
Curatabaca 71 6 19N 62 51W
Curecanti Nat. Rec. Area 16 38 24N 107 25W
Curepto 76 35 8 S 72 1W
Curiapo 72 8 33N 61 5W
Curicó 76 34 55 S 71 20W
Curicó □ 76 34 50 S 71 15W
Curicuriari → 70 0 14 S 66 48W
Curimatá 74 10 2 S 44 17W
Curiplaya 70 0 16N 74 52W
Curitiba 77 25 20 S 49 10W
Curlew, Iowa 23 42 59N 94 44W
Curlew, Wash. 53 48 53N 118 36W
Currais Novos 74 6 13 S 36 30W
Curralinho 74 1 45 S 49 46W
Current → 13 36 15N 90 55W
Currie, Minn. 30 44 3N 95 40W
Currie, N.C. 40 34 28N 78 6W
Currie, Nev. 35 40 16N 114 45W
Currituck 40 36 27N 76 1W
Currituck County ◇ 40 36 20N 76 0W
Currituck Sd. 40 36 20N 75 52W
Curry County ◇, N. Mex. 38 34 30N 103 15W
Curry County ◇, Oreg. 44 42 20N 124 20W
Curryville 32 39 21N 91 21W
Curtea de Argeş 95 45 12N 24 42 E
Curtin 44 43 43N 123 12W
Curtis, Ark. 13 34 0N 93 2W
Curtis, Nebr. 34 40 38N 100 31W
Curtis I. 127 23 35 S 151 10 E
Curuá →, Pará, Brazil 71 2 24 S 54 5W
Curuá →, Pará, Brazil 73 5 23 S 54 22W
Curuá, I. 74 0 48N 50 10W
Curuaés → 73 7 30 S 54 45W
Curuápanema → 71 2 25 S 55 2W
Curuçá 74 0 43 S 47 50W
Curuguaty 77 24 31 S 55 42W
Çürüksu Çayi → 99 37 27N 27 11 E
Curundu 57 8 59N 79 38W
Curup 110 4 26 S 102 13 E
Curupira, Serra 71 1 25N 64 30W
Cururu → 73 7 12 S 58 3W
Cururupu 74 1 50 S 44 50W
Curuzú Cuatiá 76 29 50 S 58 5W
Curvelo 75 18 45 S 44 27W
Cushing, Iowa 23 42 28N 95 41W
Cushing, Nebr. 34 41 19N 98 22W
Cushing, Okla. 43 35 59N 96 46W
Cushing, Tex. 51 31 49N 94 51W
Cushing, Mt. 62 57 35N 126 57W
Cushman, Ark. 13 35 53N 91 45W
Cushman, Oreg. 44 43 59N 124 3W
Cusick 53 48 20N 117 18W
Cusihuiriáchic 64 28 10N 106 50W
Cusseta 18 32 18N 84 47W
Custer, Mont. 33 46 8N 107 33W
Custer, S. Dak. 47 43 46N 103 36W
Custer, Wash. 53 48 55N 122 38W
Custer City 43 35 40N 98 53W
Custer County ◇, Colo. 16 38 10N 105 20W
Custer County ◇, Idaho 20 44 0N 114 0W
Custer County ◇, Mont. 33 46 25N 105 30W
Custer County ◇, Nebr. 34 41 30N 99 40W
Custer County ◇, Okla. 43 35 40N 99 0W
Custer County ◇, S. Dak. 47 43 50N 103 30W
Custer National Forest 33 45 15N 109 50W
Cut Bank 33 48 38N 112 20W
Cut Bank Cr. →, Mont. 33 48 29N 112 14W
Cut Bank Cr. →, N. Dak. 41 48 10N 100 45W
Cut Off 25 29 33N 90 20W
Cutervo 72 6 25 S 78 55W
Cuthbert 18 31 46N 84 48W
Cutler, Calif. 15 36 31N 119 17W
Cutler, Ill. 21 38 2N 89 34W
Cutler, Maine 26 44 40N 67 12W
Cutler Ridge 17 25 35N 80 20W
Cutlerville 29 42 50N 85 40W
Cutral-Có 78 38 58 S 69 15W
Cuttack 109 20 25N 85 57 E
Cuttyhunk I. 28 41 25N 70 56W
Cuvier, C. 126 23 14 S 113 22 E
Cuvier I. 128 36 27 S 175 50 E
Cuxhaven 88 53 51N 8 41 E
Cuyabeno 70 0 16 S 75 53W
Cuyahoga County ◇ 42 41 23N 81 43W
Cuyahoga Falls 42 41 8N 81 29W
Cuyo 111 10 50N 121 5 E
Cuyuma → 15 34 58N 120 38W
Cuyuna Range 30 46 25N 93 30W
Cuyuni → 71 6 23N 58 41W
Cuzco, Bolivia 72 20 0 S 66 50W
Cuzco, Peru 72 13 32 S 72 0W
Cuzco □ 72 13 31 S 71 59W
Cwmbran 83 51 39N 3 0W
Cyclades = Kikládhes 95 37 20N 24 30 E
Cyclone 45 41 50N 78 35W
Cygnes → 32 38 3N 94 17W
Cygnet 42 41 14N 83 39W
Cylinder 23 43 5N 94 33W
Cynthiana 49 38 23N 84 18W
Cypress 21 37 22N 89 1W
Cypress Hills 63 49 40N 109 30W
Cyprus ■ 106 35 0N 33 0 E
Cyrenaica 121 27 0N 23 0 E
Cyrene = Shaḥḥāt 121 32 48N 21 54 E
Cyril 43 34 54N 98 12W
Cyrus 30 45 37N 95 44W
Czar 63 52 27N 110 50W
Czechoslovakia ■ 88 49 0N 17 0 E
Czeremcha 89 52 32N 23 20 E
Częstochowa 89 50 49N 19 7 E

D

Da → 112 21 15N 105 20 E
Da Hinggan Ling 114 48 0N 121 0 E
Da Lat 112 11 56N 108 25 E
Da Nang 112 16 4N 108 13 E
Da Qaidam 113 37 50N 95 15 E
Da Yunhe, Jiangsu, China 115 34 25N 120 5 E
Da Yunhe, Zhejiang, China 115 30 45N 120 35 E
Da'an 114 45 30N 124 7 E
Daba Shan 115 32 0N 109 0 E
Dabajuro 70 11 2N 70 40W
Dabakala 120 8 15N 4 20W
Dabbūrīya 104 32 42N 35 22 E
Dabeiba 70 7 1N 76 16W
Dąbie 88 53 27N 14 45 E
Dabo 110 0 30 S 104 33 E
Dabola 120 10 50N 11 5W
Daboya 120 9 30N 1 20W
Dabrowa Tarnówska 89 50 10N 20 59 E
Dacca = Dhaka 109 23 43N 90 26 E
Dacca = Dhaka □ 109 24 25N 90 25 E
Dacoma 43 36 40N 98 34W
Dacula 18 33 59N 83 54W
Dadanawa 71 2 50N 59 30W
Dade City 17 28 22N 82 11W
Dade County ◇, Fla. 17 25 30N 80 30W
Dade County ◇, Ga. 18 35 30N 84 30W
Dade County ◇, Mo. 32 37 25N 93 50W
Dadeville, Ala. 10 32 50N 85 46W
Dadeville, Mo. 32 37 29N 93 41W
Dadra and Nagar Haveli □ 108 20 5N 73 0 E
Dadu 108 26 45N 67 45 E
Dăeni 95 44 51N 28 10 E
Daet 111 14 2N 122 55 E
Dafang 115 27 9N 105 39 E
Dagana 120 16 30N 15 35W
Dagestan A.S.S.R. □ 99 42 30N 47 0 E
Daggett County ◇ 52 40 55N 109 30W
Dagsboro 27 38 33N 75 15W
Dagupan 111 16 3N 120 20 E
Dahlak Kebir 105 15 50N 40 10 E
Dahlgren 21 38 12N 88 41W
Dahlonega 18 34 32N 83 59W
Dahlonega Plat. 18 34 10N 84 20W
Dahod 108 22 50N 74 15 E
Dahomey = Benin ■ 120 10 0N 2 0 E
Dahra 120 15 22N 15 30W
Dai-Sen 117 35 22N 133 32 E
Dai Shan 115 30 25N 122 10 E
Dai Xian 114 39 4N 112 58 E
Dailey 54 38 48N 79 54W
Daingean 85 53 18N 7 15W
Daingerfield 51 33 2N 94 44W
Daiō-Misaki 117 34 15N 136 45 E
Dairût 121 27 34N 30 43 E
Dairy 44 42 14N 121 31W
Daisetsu-Zan 116 43 30N 142 57 E
Daisetta 51 30 7N 94 39W
Daisy, Ark. 13 34 14N 93 45W
Daisy, Wash. 53 48 22N 118 10W
Dajarra 127 21 42 S 139 30 E
Dakar 120 14 34N 17 29W
Dakhla 120 23 50N 15 53W
Dakhla, El Wâhât el- 121 25 30N 28 50 E
Dakhovskaya 99 44 13N 40 13 E
Dakota, Ill. 21 42 23N 89 32W
Dakota, Minn. 30 43 55N 91 22W
Dakota City, Iowa 23 42 43N 94 12W
Dakota City, Nebr. 34 42 25N 96 25W
Dakota County ◇, Minn. 30 44 45N 93 0W
Dakota County ◇, Nebr. 34 42 30N 96 30W
Đakovica 95 42 22N 20 26 E
Dalachi 114 36 48N 105 0 E
Dalai Nur 114 43 20N 116 45 E
Dalälven 97 60 12N 16 43 E
Dalandzadgad 113 43 27N 104 30 E
Dalark 13 34 2N 92 53W
Dalarö 97 59 8N 18 24 E
Dālbandīn 107 29 0N 64 23 E
Dalbeattie 84 54 55N 3 50W
Dalby 127 27 10 S 151 17 E
Dale, Ind. 22 38 10N 86 59W
Dale, Okla. 43 35 24N 97 3W
Dale County ◇ 10 31 28N 85 39W
Dale Hollow L. 49 36 32N 85 27W
Daleville, Ala. 10 31 19N 85 43W
Daleville, Ind. 22 40 7N 85 33W
Daleville, Miss. 31 32 34N 88 41W
Dalhart 50 36 4N 102 31W
Dalhousie 61 48 5N 66 26W
Dali, Shaanxi, China 115 34 48N 109 58 E
Dali, Yunnan, China 113 25 40N 100 10 E
Dalian 114 38 50N 121 40 E
Dāliyat el Karmel 104 32 43N 35 2 E
Dalkeith, U.K. 84 55 54N 3 5W
Dalkeith, U.S.A. 17 30 0N 85 9W
Dallam County ◇ 50 36 15N 102 30W
Dallas, Ga. 18 33 55N 84 51W
Dallas, N.C. 40 35 19N 81 11W
Dallas, Oreg. 44 44 55N 123 19W
Dallas, Pa. 45 41 20N 75 58W
Dallas, S. Dak. 47 43 14N 99 31W
Dallas, Tex. 51 32 47N 96 49W
Dallas, Wis. 55 45 16N 91 51W
Dallas Center 23 41 41N 93 58W
Dallas City 21 40 38N 91 10W
Dallas County ◇, Ala. 10 32 25N 87 1W
Dallas County ◇, Ark. 13 33 59N 92 38W
Dallas County ◇, Iowa 23 41 40N 94 0W
Dallas County ◇, Mo. 32 37 40N 93 0W
Dallas County ◇, Tex. 51 32 50N 96 50W
Dalmacija □ 94 43 20N 17 0 E
Dalmatia = Dalmacija □ 94 43 20N 17 0 E

Dalmellington Dedéagach

Dalmellington **84** 55 20N 4 25W
Dalnegorsk **116** 44 32N 135 33 E
Dalneretchensk **101** 45 50N 133 40 E
Daloa **120** 7 0N 6 30W
Dalrymple, Mt. **127** 21 1 S 148 39 E
Dalton, Canada **60** 48 11N 84 1W
Dalton, Ga. **18** 34 46N 84 58W
Dalton, Mass. **28** 42 28N 73 11W
Dalton, Minn. **30** 46 10N 95 55W
Dalton, Nebr. **34** 41 25N 102 58W
Dalton, Ohio **42** 40 48N 81 42W
Dalton, Pa. **45** 41 32N 75 44W
Dalton Iceberg Tongue **5** 66 15 S 121 30 E
Dalvík **96** 65 58N 18 32W
Daly → **126** 13 35 S 130 19 E
Daly City **14** 37 42N 122 28W
Daly L. **63** 56 32N 105 39W
Daly Waters **126** 16 15 S 133 24 E
Daman **108** 20 25N 72 57 E
Damanhûr **121** 31 0N 30 30 E
Damar, Indonesia **111** 7 7 S 128 40 E
Damar, U.S.A. **24** 39 19N 99 35W
Damaraland **123** 21 0 S 17 0 E
Damascus = Dimashq **106** 33 30N 36 18 E
Damascus, Ark. **13** 35 22N 92 25W
Damascus, Ga. **18** 31 18N 84 43W
Damascus, Md. **27** 39 17N 77 12W
Damascus, Va. **54** 36 38N 81 47W
Damāvand **107** 35 47N 52 0 E
Damāvand, Qolleh-ye **107** 35 56N 52 10 E
Damba **122** 6 44 S 15 20 E
Dâmboviţa → **89** 44 40N 26 0 E
Dame Marie **67** 18 36N 74 26W
Dameron **27** 38 10N 76 22W
Dames Quarter **27** 38 11N 75 54W
Dāmghān **107** 36 10N 54 17 E
Damietta = Dumyât **121** 31 24N 31 48 E
Daming **114** 36 15N 115 6 E
Dāmīya **104** 32 6N 35 34 E
Damoh **108** 23 50N 79 28 E
Dampier **126** 20 41 S 116 42 E
Dampier, Selat **111** 0 40 S 131 0 E
Dampier Arch. **126** 20 38 S 116 32 E
Dampier Downs **126** 18 24 S 123 5 E
Dan → **54** 36 42N 78 50W
Dan Xian **115** 19 31N 109 33 E
Dana, Indonesia **111** 11 0 S 122 52 E
Dana, Ind. **22** 39 48N 87 30W
Dana, Iowa **23** 42 6N 94 14W
Dana, Lac **60** 50 53N 77 20W
Dana Point **15** 33 28N 117 42W
Danao **111** 10 31N 124 1 E
Danbury, Conn. **28** 41 24N 73 28W
Danbury, Iowa **23** 42 14N 95 43W
Danbury, N.C. **40** 36 25N 80 12W
Danbury, N.H. **36** 43 32N 71 52W
Danbury, Nebr. **34** 40 3N 100 25W
Danbury, Tex. **51** 29 14N 95 21W
Danby **36** 43 20N 72 59W
Danby L. **15** 34 13N 115 5W
Dandeldhura **109** 29 20N 80 35 E
Dandeli **108** 15 5N 74 30 E
Dandong **114** 40 10N 124 20 E
Dandridge **49** 36 1N 83 25W
Dane County ◊ **55** 43 0N 89 29W
Danforth, Ill. **21** 40 49N 87 59W
Danforth, Maine **26** 45 40N 67 52W
Danforth Hills **16** 40 15N 108 0W
Danger Pt. **123** 34 40 S 19 17 E
Dangora **120** 11 30N 8 7 E
Dangriga **65** 17 0N 88 13W
Dangshan **115** 34 27N 116 22 E
Dangtu **115** 31 32N 118 25 E
Dangyang **115** 30 52N 111 44 E
Daniel **56** 42 52N 110 4W
Daniel Boone National Forest **49** 37 30N 84 0W
Daniels County ◊ **33** 48 40N 105 20W
Daniel's Harbour **61** 50 13N 57 35W
Daniel's Pass **52** 40 18N 111 10W
Danielson **28** 41 48N 71 53W
Danielsville **18** 34 8N 83 13W
Danilov **98** 58 16N 40 13 E
Dankhar Gompa **108** 32 10N 78 10 E
Danlí **66** 14 4N 86 35W
Dannebrog **34** 41 7N 98 33W
Dannemora, Sweden **97** 60 12N 17 51 E
Dannemora, U.S.A. **39** 44 43N 73 44W
Dannevirke **128** 40 12 S 176 8 E
Danshui **115** 25 12N 121 25 E
Dansville, Mich. **29** 42 34N 84 19W
Dansville, N.Y. **39** 42 34N 77 42W
Dante, Somalia **105** 10 25N 51 26 E
Dante, S. Dak. **47** 43 2N 98 11W
Dante, Va. **54** 36 59N 82 18W
Danube → = Donau → **88** 48 10N 17 0 E
Danube → **95** 45 20N 29 40 E
Danvers, Ill. **21** 40 32N 89 11W
Danvers, Mass. **28** 42 34N 70 56W
Danville, Ark. **13** 35 3N 93 24W
Danville, Calif. **14** 37 49N 122 0W
Danville, Ga. **18** 32 37N 83 15W
Danville, Ill. **21** 40 8N 87 37W
Danville, Ind. **22** 39 46N 86 32W
Danville, Iowa **23** 40 52N 91 19W
Danville, Kans. **24** 37 17N 97 54W
Danville, Ky. **49** 37 39N 84 46W
Danville, Ohio **42** 40 27N 82 16W
Danville, Pa. **45** 40 58N 76 37W
Danville, Va. **54** 36 36N 79 23W
Danville, Vt. **36** 44 25N 72 9W
Danville, W. Va. **54** 38 5N 81 50W
Danville, Wash. **53** 48 59N 118 30W
Danzhai **115** 26 11N 107 48 E
Danzig = Gdańsk **89** 54 22N 18 40 E
Dao **111** 10 30N 121 57 E
Dao Xian **115** 25 36N 111 31 E
Daoud = Aïn Beïda **120** 35 50N 7 29 E
Daphne **10** 30 36N 87 54W
Daqing Shan **114** 40 40N 111 0 E
Daqu Shan **115** 30 25N 122 20 E
Dar al Hamrā, Ad **106** 27 22N 37 43 E
Dar es Salaam **122** 6 50 S 39 12 E
Dar'ā **104** 32 36N 36 7 E
Dārāb **107** 28 50N 54 30 E
Daraj **120** 30 10N 10 28 E
Darband **108** 34 20N 72 50 E
Darbhanga **109** 26 15N 85 55 E
Darby **33** 46 1N 114 11W
Darby, C. **11** 64 19N 162 47W
Dardanelle, Ark. **13** 35 13N 93 9W
Dardanelle, Calif. **14** 38 20N 119 50W
Dardanelle L. **13** 35 14N 93 10W
Dardanelles = Çanakkale Boğazi **106** 40 0N 26 0 E
Dare County ◊ **40** 35 45N 75 40W
Dârfûr, Sudan **121** 13 40N 24 0 E
Darfur, U.S.A. **30** 44 3N 94 50W
Dargai **108** 34 25N 71 55 E
Dargan Ata **100** 40 29N 62 10 E
Dargaville **128** 35 57 S 173 52 E
Darhan Muminggan Lianheqi **114** 41 40N 110 28 E
Darien, Panama **57** 9 7N 79 46W
Darien, Conn. **28** 41 5N 73 28W
Darien, Ga. **18** 31 23N 81 26W
Darien, Wis. **55** 42 36N 88 43W
Darién, G. del **70** 9 0N 77 0W
Darién, Serranía del **70** 8 30N 77 30W
Darjeeling = Darjiling **109** 27 3N 88 18 E
Darjiling **109** 27 3N 88 18 E
Dark Cove **61** 48 47N 54 13W
Darke County ◊ **42** 40 6N 84 38W
Darling → **127** 34 4 S 141 54 E
Darling, L. **41** 48 27N 101 35W
Darling Ra. **126** 32 30 S 116 0 E
Darlington, U.K. **82** 54 33N 1 33W
Darlington, Fla. **17** 30 57N 86 3W
Darlington, Ind. **22** 40 6N 86 47W
Darlington, La. **25** 30 53N 90 47W
Darlington, Md. **27** 39 38N 76 12W
Darlington, S.C. **46** 34 18N 79 52W
Darlington, Wis. **55** 42 41N 90 7W
Darlington County ◊ **46** 34 20N 80 0W
Darłowo **88** 54 25N 16 25 E
Dărmăneşti **95** 46 21N 26 33 E
Darmstadt **88** 49 51N 8 40 E
Darnah **121** 32 40N 22 35 E
Darnestown **27** 39 6N 77 18W
Darnley, C. **5** 68 0 S 69 0 E
Darnley B. **58** 69 30N 123 30W
Darr **34** 40 49N 99 53W
Darrington **53** 48 15N 121 36W
Darror → **105** 10 30N 50 0 E
Darrouzett **50** 36 27N 100 20W
Dart → **83** 50 24N 3 36W
Dart, C. **5** 73 6 S 126 20W
Dartmoor **83** 50 36N 4 0W
Dartmouth, Canada **61** 44 40N 63 30W
Dartmouth, U.K. **83** 50 21N 3 35W
Darvaza **100** 40 11N 58 24 E
Darvel, Teluk **111** 4 50N 118 20 E
Darwha **108** 20 15N 77 45 E
Darwin **126** 12 25 S 130 51 E
Darwin, Mt. **78** 0 10 S 69 55W
Dās **107** 25 20N 53 30 E
Dasher **18** 30 45N 83 13W
Dasht → **107** 25 10N 61 40 E
Dasht-e Kavīr **107** 34 30N 55 0 E
Dasht-e Lūt **107** 31 30N 58 0 E
Dasht-e Mārgow **107** 30 40N 62 30 E
Dassel **30** 45 5N 94 19W
Dateland **12** 32 48N 113 33W
Datia **108** 25 39N 78 27 E
Datian **115** 25 40N 117 50 E
Datil **38** 34 9N 107 51W
Datong, Anhui, China **115** 30 48N 117 44 E
Datong, Shanxi, China **114** 40 6N 113 18 E
Datu, Tanjung **110** 2 5N 109 39 E
Datu Piang **111** 7 2N 124 30 E
Daugava → **98** 57 4N 24 3 E
Daugavpils **98** 55 53N 26 32 E
Daule **70** 1 56 S 79 56W
Daule → **70** 2 10 S 79 52W
Daulpur **108** 26 45N 77 59 E
Dauphin, Canada **63** 51 9N 100 5W
Dauphin, U.S.A. **45** 40 22N 76 56W
Dauphin County ◊ **45** 40 20N 76 55W
Dauphin I. **10** 30 15N 88 11W
Dauphin Island **10** 30 15N 88 7W
Dauphin L. **63** 51 20N 99 45W
Dauphiné **90** 45 15N 5 25 E
Davangere **108** 14 25N 75 55 E
Davao **111** 7 0N 125 40 E
Davao, G. of **111** 6 30N 125 48 E
Dāvar Panāh **107** 27 25N 62 15 E
Davenport, Calif. **14** 37 1N 122 12W
Davenport, Fla. **17** 28 10N 81 36W
Davenport, Iowa **23** 41 32N 90 35W
Davenport, N. Dak. **41** 46 43N 97 4W
Davenport, N.Y. **39** 42 28N 74 51W
Davenport, Nebr. **34** 40 19N 97 49W
Davenport, Okla. **43** 35 42N 96 46W
Davenport, Wash. **53** 47 39N 118 9W
Davenport Ra. **126** 20 28 S 134 0 E
Davey **34** 40 59N 96 40W
David, Panama **66** 8 30N 82 30W
David, U.S.A. **49** 37 36N 82 54W
David City **34** 41 15N 97 8W
Davidson, Canada **63** 51 16N 105 59W
Davidson, N.C. **40** 35 30N 80 51W
Davidson, Okla. **43** 34 14N 99 5W
Davidson County ◊, N.C. **40** 35 45N 80 10W
Davidson County ◊, Tenn. **48** 36 10N 86 47W
Davidsonville **27** 38 55N 76 38W
Davie County ◊ **40** 35 50N 80 30W
Daviess County ◊, Ind. **22** 38 40N 87 5W
Daviess County ◊, Ky. **48** 38 40N 87 5W
Daviess County ◊, Mo. **32** 40 0N 94 0W
Davis, Antarct. **5** 68 34 S 17 55 E
Davis, Calif. **14** 38 33N 121 44W
Davis, Ill. **21** 42 25N 89 25W
Davis, N.C. **40** 34 48N 76 28W
Davis, Okla. **43** 34 30N 97 7W
Davis, S. Dak. **47** 43 16N 96 59W
Davis, W. Va. **54** 39 8N 79 28W
Davis, Mt. **45** 39 48N 79 10W
Davis City **23** 40 38N 93 49W
Davis County ◊, Iowa **23** 40 45N 92 25W
Davis County ◊, Utah **52** 41 0N 112 5W
Davis Creek **14** 41 44N 120 22W
Davis Dam **12** 35 11N 114 34W
Davis Inlet **61** 55 50N 60 59W
Davis Junction **21** 42 6N 89 6W
Davis Mts. **50** 30 50N 103 55W
Davis Sea **5** 66 0 S 92 0 E
Davis Str. **59** 65 0N 58 0W
Davisboro **18** 32 59N 82 36W
Davison **29** 43 2N 83 31W
Davison County ◊ **47** 43 43N 98 2W
Davisville **32** 37 49N 91 11W
Davos **88** 46 48N 9 49 E
Davy **54** 37 29N 81 39W
Davy Crockett National Forest **51** 31 12N 95 2W
Davy L. **63** 58 53N 108 18W
Dawes County ◊ **34** 42 45N 103 0W
Dawn **50** 34 55N 102 12W
Dawson, Canada **58** 64 10N 139 30W
Dawson, Ga. **18** 31 46N 84 27W
Dawson, Minn. **30** 44 56N 96 3W
Dawson, N. Dak. **41** 46 52N 99 45W
Dawson, Nebr. **34** 40 8N 95 50W
Dawson, Oreg. **44** 44 22N 123 25W
Dawson, Tex. **51** 31 54N 96 43W
Dawson → **127** 23 25 S 149 45 E
Dawson, I. **78** 53 50 S 70 50W
Dawson County ◊, Ga. **18** 34 25N 84 10W
Dawson County ◊, Mont. **33** 47 15N 105 0W
Dawson County ◊, Nebr. **34** 40 50N 99 50W
Dawson County ◊, Tex. **50** 32 44N 101 58W
Dawson Creek **62** 55 45N 120 15W
Dawson Inlet **63** 61 50N 93 25W
Dawson Springs **48** 37 10N 87 41W
Dawsonville **18** 34 25N 84 7W
Daxian **115** 31 15N 107 23 E
Daxin **115** 22 50N 107 11 E
Daxue Shan **113** 30 30N 101 30 E
Day **17** 30 12N 83 17W
Day County ◊ **47** 45 20N 97 31W
Daye **115** 30 6N 114 58 E
Daykin **34** 40 21N 97 18W
Dayong **115** 29 11N 110 30 E
Dayr Abū Sa'īd **104** 32 30N 35 42 E
Dayr al-Ghuşūn **104** 32 21N 35 4 E
Dayr az Zawr **106** 35 20N 40 5 E
Dayr Dirwān **104** 31 55N 35 15 E
Daysland **62** 52 50N 112 20W
Dayton, Ala. **10** 32 21N 87 38W
Dayton, Mont. **33** 47 52N 114 17W
Dayton, Nev. **35** 39 14N 119 36W
Dayton, Ohio **42** 39 45N 84 12W
Dayton, Pa. **45** 40 53N 79 15W
Dayton, Tenn. **49** 35 30N 85 1W
Dayton, Tex. **51** 30 3N 94 54W
Dayton, Va. **54** 38 25N 78 56W
Dayton, Wash. **53** 46 19N 117 59W
Dayton, Wyo. **56** 44 53N 107 16W
Daytona Beach **17** 29 13N 81 1W
Dayu **115** 25 24N 114 22 E
Dayville **44** 44 28N 119 32W
Dazey **41** 47 11N 98 12W
Dazhu **115** 30 41N 107 15 E
Dazu **115** 29 40N 105 42 E
De Aar **123** 30 39 S 24 0 E
De Armanville **10** 33 38N 85 45W
De Baca County ◊ **38** 34 15N 104 30W
De Bary **17** 28 54N 81 18W
De Beque **16** 39 20N 108 13W
De Forest **55** 43 15N 89 20W
De Funiak Springs **17** 30 43N 86 7W
De Graff **30** 45 16N 95 28W
De Gray L. **13** 34 13N 93 7W
De Grey **126** 20 12 S 119 12 E
De Kalb, Ill. **21** 41 56N 88 46W
De Kalb, Miss. **31** 32 46N 88 39W
De Kalb, Tex. **51** 33 31N 94 37W
De Kalb County ◊, Ala. **10** 34 26N 85 43W
De Kalb County ◊, Ga. **18** 33 40N 84 10W
De Kalb County ◊, Ill. **21** 41 50N 88 45W
De Kalb County ◊, Ind. **22** 41 25N 85 0W
De Kalb County ◊, Mo. **32** 39 50N 94 25W
De Kalb County ◊, Tenn. **48** 36 0N 86 0W
De Kalb Junction **39** 44 30N 75 17W
De Land **17** 29 2N 81 18W
De Leon **51** 32 7N 98 32W
De Leon Springs **17** 29 7N 81 21W
De Long Mts. **11** 68 30N 163 0W
De Pere **55** 44 27N 88 4W
De Queen **13** 34 2N 94 21W
De Quincy **25** 30 27N 93 26W
De Ridder **25** 30 51N 93 17W
De Ruyter **39** 42 46N 75 53W
De Smet **47** 44 23N 97 33W
De Smet, L. **56** 44 29N 106 45W
De Soto, Ill. **21** 37 49N 89 14W
De Soto, Kans. **24** 38 59N 94 58W
De Soto, Miss. **31** 31 58N 88 43W
De Soto, Mo. **32** 38 8N 90 34W
De Soto, Wis. **55** 43 25N 91 12W
De Soto City **17** 27 27N 81 24W
De Soto County ◊, Fla. **17** 27 15N 81 45W
De Soto County ◊, Miss. **31** 34 53N 90 1W
De Soto National Forest **31** 31 0N 89 0W
De Soto Parish ◊ **25** 32 2N 93 43W
De Tour Village **29** 46 0N 83 56W
De Witt, Ark. **13** 34 18N 91 20W
De Witt, Ill. **21** 40 11N 88 47W
De Witt, Iowa **23** 41 49N 90 33W
De Witt, Mich. **29** 42 51N 84 34W
De Witt, Nebr. **34** 40 24N 96 55W
De Witt County ◊, Ill. **21** 40 10N 88 55W
De Witt County ◊, Tex. **51** 29 6N 97 17W
Dead L. **17** 30 10N 85 10W
Dead Sea **106** 31 30N 35 30 E
Deadhorse **11** 70 11N 148 27W
Deadman B. **17** 29 30N 83 30W
Deadwood **47** 44 23N 103 44W
Deadwood L. **62** 59 10N 128 30W
Deaf Smith County ◊ **50** 35 0N 102 30W
Deakin **126** 30 46 S 128 0 E
Deal **83** 51 13N 1 25 E
Deale **27** 38 47N 76 33W
Dean, Forest of **83** 51 50N 2 35W
Deán Funes **76** 30 20 S 64 20W
Dearborn, Mich. **29** 42 19N 83 11W
Dearborn, Mo. **32** 39 32N 94 46W
Dearborn County ◊ **22** 39 10N 85 0W
Deary **20** 46 48N 116 32W
Dease → **62** 59 56N 128 32W
Dease Inlet **11** 70 30N 155 0W
Dease L. **62** 58 40N 130 5W
Dease Lake **62** 58 25N 130 6W
Death Valley **15** 36 15N 116 50W
Death Valley Junction **14** 36 20N 110 25W
Death Valley National Monument **15** 36 45N 117 15W
Deatsville **10** 32 37N 86 24W
Deaver **56** 44 54N 108 36W
Deba Habe **120** 10 14N 11 20 E
Debao **115** 23 21N 106 46 E
Debar **95** 41 31N 20 30 E
Debden **63** 53 30N 106 50W
Deblois **26** 44 45N 68 1W
Debolt **62** 55 12N 118 1W
Debre Markos **120** 10 20N 37 40 E
Debre Tabor **121** 11 50N 38 26 E
Debrecen **89** 47 33N 21 42 E
Decatur, Ala. **10** 34 36N 86 59W
Decatur, Ark. **13** 36 20N 94 28W
Decatur, Ga. **18** 33 47N 84 18W
Decatur, Ill. **21** 39 51N 88 57W
Decatur, Ind. **22** 40 50N 84 56W
Decatur, Mich. **29** 42 7N 85 58W
Decatur, Miss. **31** 32 26N 89 7W
Decatur, Nebr. **34** 42 0N 96 15W
Decatur, Tenn. **49** 35 31N 84 47W
Decatur, Tex. **51** 33 14N 97 35W
Decatur City **23** 40 45N 93 50W
Decatur County ◊, Ga. **18** 31 0N 84 30W
Decatur County ◊, Ind. **22** 39 15N 85 30W
Decatur County ◊, Iowa **23** 40 45N 93 45W
Decatur County ◊, Kans. **24** 39 45N 100 20W
Decatur County ◊, Tenn. **48** 35 35N 88 7W
Decaturville **48** 35 35N 88 7W
Deccan **108** 18 0N 79 0 E
Deception, Mt. **53** 47 49N 123 14W
Deception I. **5** 63 0 S 60 15W
Deception L. **63** 56 33N 104 13W
Decherd **48** 35 13N 86 5W
Deckerville **29** 43 32N 82 44W
Declo **20** 42 32N 113 40W
Decorah **23** 43 18N 91 48W
Dedéagach = Alexandroúpolis **95** 40 50N 25 54 E

Dedham
Diamond Head

Dedham, Iowa 23 41 55N 94 49W
Dedham, Mass. 28 42 15N 71 10W
Dédougou 120 12 30N 3 25W
Dee →, Scotland, U.K. 84 57 4N 2 7W
Dee →, Wales, U.K. 82 53 15N 3 7W
Deefield 55 43 3N 89 5W
Deep → 40 35 36N 79 3W
Deep B. 62 61 15N 116 35W
Deep Cr. → 42 39 27N 83 0W
Deep Creek L. 27 39 31N 79 24W
Deep Creek Range 52 39 50N 113 50W
Deep Fork Canadian → 43 35 28N 95 50W
Deep River, Conn. 28 41 23N 72 26W
Deep River, Iowa 23 41 35N 92 22W
Deep Springs L. 15 37 20N 118 0W
Deepdale 126 21 42 S 116 10 E
Deepstep 18 33 1N 82 58W
Deepwater, Mo. 32 38 16N 93 47W
Deepwater, N.J. 37 39 41N 75 29W
Deer 13 35 50N 93 13W
Deer → 63 58 23N 94 13W
Deer Cr. →, Ind. 22 40 34N 86 41W
Deer Cr. →, Md. 27 39 40N 76 10W
Deer Creek, Ill. 21 40 38N 89 20W
Deer Creek, Okla. 43 36 48N 97 31W
Deer Grove 21 41 37N 89 42W
Deer I., Alaska 11 54 55N 162 18W
Deer I., Maine 26 44 13N 68 41W
Deer Isle 26 44 14N 68 41W
Deer Lake, Newf., Canada 61 49 11N 57 27W
Deer Lake, Ont., Canada 63 52 36N 94 20W
Deer Lodge 33 46 24N 112 44W
Deer Lodge County ◇ 33 46 0N 113 0W
Deer Park, Ala. 10 31 13N 88 19W
Deer Park, Fla. 17 28 6N 80 54W
Deer Park, Md. 27 39 25N 79 18W
Deer Park, N.Y. 39 40 46N 73 20W
Deer Park, Ohio 42 39 13N 84 23W
Deer Park, Wash. 53 47 57N 117 28W
Deer Park, Wis. 55 45 11N 92 23W
Deer River 30 47 20N 93 48W
Deer Trail 16 39 37N 104 2W
Deerfield, Ill. 21 42 10N 87 51W
Deerfield, Kans. 24 37 59N 101 8W
Deerfield, Mo. 32 37 50N 94 30W
Deerfield → 28 42 35N 72 35W
Deerfield Beach 17 26 19N 80 6W
Deering, Alaska 11 66 4N 162 42W
Deering, N. Dak. 41 48 24N 101 3W
Deerlodge National Forest 33 46 20N 113 30W
Deersville 42 40 18N 81 11W
Deerwood 30 46 29N 93 54W
Deeth 35 41 4N 115 17W
Defiance, Iowa 23 41 49N 95 20W
Defiance, Ohio 42 41 17N 84 22W
Defiance County ◇ 42 41 23N 84 32W
Deganya 104 32 43N 35 34 E
Degeh Bur 105 8 11N 43 31 E
Deggendorf 88 48 49N 12 59 E
Deh Bīd 107 30 39N 53 11 E
Dehi Titan 108 33 45N 63 50 E
Dehibat 120 32 0N 10 47 E
Dehkareqan 106 37 43N 45 55 E
Dehra Dun 108 30 20N 78 4 E
Dehui 114 44 30N 125 40 E
Deinze 87 50 59N 3 32 E
Dej 89 47 10N 23 52 E
Dekese 122 3 24 S 21 24 E
Del City 43 35 26N 97 26W
Del Mar 15 32 58N 117 16W
Del Norte 16 37 41N 106 21W
Del Norte County ◇ 14 41 40N 124 0W
Del Rio 50 29 22N 100 54W
Delacroix 25 29 46N 89 45W
Delafield 55 43 4N 88 24W
Delanco 37 40 3N 74 57W
Delano, Calif. 15 35 46N 119 15W
Delano, Minn. 30 45 2N 93 47W
Delano Peak 52 38 22N 112 22W
Delaplaine 13 36 14N 90 44W
Delavan, Ill. 21 40 22N 89 33W
Delavan, Kans. 24 38 40N 96 49W
Delavan, Wis. 55 42 38N 88 39W
Delaware, Ark. 13 35 17N 93 19W
Delaware, Ohio 42 40 18N 83 4W
Delaware, Okla. 43 36 47N 95 39W
Delaware □ 27 39 0N 75 20W
Delaware → 27 39 15N 75 20W
Delaware B. 27 39 0N 75 10W
Delaware City 27 39 35N 75 36W
Delaware County ◇, Ind. 22 40 15N 85 25W
Delaware County ◇, Iowa 23 42 30N 91 20W
Delaware County ◇, N.Y. 39 42 15N 75 0W
Delaware County ◇, Ohio 42 40 18N 83 4W
Delaware County ◇, Okla. 43 36 25N 94 50W
Delaware County ◇, Pa. 45 39 55N 75 23W
Delaware Cr. → 50 32 2N 104 0W
Delaware Mts. 50 31 45N 104 50W
Delaware Water Gap Nat. Rec. Area 37 41 10N 74 55W
Delbarton 54 37 43N 82 11W
Delcambre 25 29 57N 91 58W
Delevan 39 42 29N 78 29W
Delft 87 52 1N 4 22 E
Delfzijl 87 53 20N 6 55 E
Delgada, Pt. 14 40 2N 124 5W
Delgado, C. 122 10 45 S 40 40 E
Delgo 121 20 6N 30 40 E
Delhi, India 108 28 38N 77 17 E
Delhi, Calif. 14 37 26N 120 46W
Delhi, Iowa 23 42 26N 91 20W
Delhi, La. 25 32 28N 91 30W
Delhi, N.Y. 39 42 17N 74 55W
Delia, Canada 62 51 38N 112 23W
Delia, U.S.A. 24 39 15N 95 59W
Delice → 106 39 45N 34 15 E
Delicias 64 28 10N 105 30W
Delicias, Laguna 64 28 7N 105 40W
Delight 13 34 2N 93 31W
Dell 33 44 44N 112 42W
Dell City 50 31 56N 105 12W
Dell Rapids 47 43 50N 96 43W
Delmar, Del. 27 38 27N 75 35W
Delmar, Iowa 23 42 0N 90 37W
Delmar, N.Y. 39 42 37N 73 50W
Delmarva Peninsula 27 38 45N 75 45W
Delmiro Gouveia 74 9 24 S 38 6W
Delmont, N.J. 37 39 13N 74 57W
Delmont, S. Dak. 47 43 16N 98 10W
Deloit 23 42 6N 95 19W
Delong, Ostrova 101 76 40N 149 20 E
Deloraine 63 49 15N 100 29W
Delorme, L. 61 54 31N 69 52W
Delphi 22 40 36N 86 41W
Delphos, Kans. 24 39 17N 97 46W
Delphos, Ohio 42 40 51N 84 21W
Delray Beach 17 26 28N 80 4W
Delta, Ala. 10 33 26N 85 42W
Delta, Colo. 16 38 44N 108 4W
Delta, Mo. 32 37 12N 89 44W
Delta, Ohio 42 41 34N 84 0W
Delta, Utah 52 39 21N 112 35W
Delta Amacuro □ 71 8 30N 61 30W
Delta County ◇, Colo. 16 38 50N 107 50W
Delta County ◇, Mich. 29 46 0N 87 0W
Delta County ◇, Tex. 51 33 23N 95 42W
Delta Junction 11 64 2N 145 44W
Delta National Forest 31 32 50N 90 55W
Deltona 17 28 54N 81 16W
Demanda, Sierra de la 91 42 15N 3 0W
Demba 122 5 28 S 22 15 E
Dembecha 121 10 32N 37 30 E
Dembidolo 121 8 34N 34 50 E
Demer → 87 50 57N 4 42 E
Demerara □ 71 6 0N 58 30W
Deming, N. Mex. 38 32 16N 107 46W
Deming, Wash. 53 48 50N 122 13W
Demini → 71 0 46 S 62 56W
Demopolis 10 32 31N 87 50W
Demorest 18 34 34N 83 33W
Demotte 22 41 12N 87 12W
Dempo, Mt. 110 4 2 S 103 15 E
Dempsey 43 35 31N 99 49W
Den Burg 87 53 3N 4 47 E
Den Haag = 's-Gravenhage 87 52 7N 4 17 E
Den Helder 87 52 57N 4 45 E
Den Oever 87 52 56N 5 2 E
Denair 14 37 32N 120 48W
Denau 100 38 16N 67 54 E
Denbigh, U.K. 82 53 12N 3 26W
Denbigh, U.S.A. 41 48 19N 100 35W
Denbigh, C. 11 64 23N 161 32W
Dendang 110 3 7 S 107 56 E
Dendermonde 87 51 2N 4 5 E
Dendron 54 37 3N 76 56W
Deng Xian 115 32 34N 112 4 E
Denham, Australia 126 25 56 S 113 31 E
Denham, U.S.A. 30 46 22N 92 57W
Denham Ra. 127 21 55 S 147 46 E
Denham Springs 25 30 29N 90 57W
Denhoff 41 47 29N 100 16W
Denia 91 38 49N 0 8 E
Deniliquin 127 35 30 S 144 58 E
Denio 35 41 59N 118 38W
Denison, Iowa 23 42 1N 95 21W
Denison, Kans. 24 39 24N 95 38W
Denison, Tex. 51 33 45N 96 33W
Denison Range 127 28 30 S 136 5 E
Denizli 106 37 42N 29 2 E
Denman Glacier 5 66 45 S 99 25 E
Denmark, Australia 126 34 59 S 117 25 E
Denmark, Kans. 24 39 5N 98 17W
Denmark, S.C. 46 33 19N 81 9W
Denmark, Wis. 55 44 21N 87 50W
Denmark ■ 97 55 30N 9 0 E
Denmark Str. 4 66 0N 30 0W
Dennard 13 35 46N 92 31W
Dennehotso 12 36 51N 109 51W
Dennis, Kans. 24 37 21N 95 25W
Dennis, Miss. 31 34 34N 88 14W
Dennis Port 28 41 39N 70 8W
Dennison, Minn. 30 44 25N 93 2W
Dennison, Ohio 42 40 24N 81 19W
Dennisville 37 39 12N 74 49W
Denpasar 110 8 45 S 115 14 E
Dent 30 46 33N 95 43W
Dent County ◇ 32 37 35N 91 30W
Denton, Ga. 18 31 44N 82 42W
Denton, Kans. 24 39 44N 95 16W
Denton, Md. 27 38 53N 75 50W
Denton, Mont. 33 47 19N 109 57W
Denton, N.C. 40 35 38N 80 6W
Denton, Nebr. 34 40 44N 96 51W
Denton, Tex. 51 33 13N 97 8W
Denton County ◇ 51 33 15N 97 10W
Denton Cr. → 51 32 58N 96 57W
D'Entrecasteaux Pt. 126 34 50 S 115 57 E
Dentsville, Md. 27 38 28N 76 51W
Dentsville, S.C. 46 34 4N 80 58W
Denver, Colo. 16 39 44N 104 59W
Denver, Ind. 22 40 52N 86 5W
Denver, Iowa 23 42 40N 92 20W
Denver, Pa. 45 40 14N 76 8W
Denver City 50 32 58N 102 50W
Denver County ◇ 16 39 45N 105 0W
Deoghar 109 24 30N 86 42 E
Deolali 108 19 58N 73 50 E
Deora 16 37 38N 102 56W
Deoria 109 26 31N 83 48 E
Deosai Mts. 108 35 40N 75 0 E
Depew 43 35 48N 96 31W
Deping 114 37 25N 116 58 E
Depoe Bay 44 44 49N 124 4W
Deport 51 33 32N 95 19W
Deposit 39 42 4N 75 25W
Depue 21 41 19N 89 19W
Deputatskiy 101 69 18N 139 54 E
Dêqên 113 28 34N 98 51 E
Deqing 115 23 8N 111 42 E
Dera Ghazi Khan 108 30 5N 70 43 E
Dera Ismail Khan 108 31 50N 70 50 E
Derbent 99 42 5N 48 15 E
Derby, Australia 126 17 18 S 123 38 E
Derby, U.K. 82 52 55N 1 28W
Derby, Conn. 28 41 19N 73 5W
Derby, Iowa 23 40 56N 93 27W
Derby, Kans. 24 37 33N 97 16W
Derby, N.Y. 39 42 41N 78 58W
Derby, Tex. 51 28 46N 99 8W
Derby, Vt. 36 44 57N 72 8W
Derby □ 82 52 55N 1 28W
Derby Line 36 45 0N 72 6W
Derg → 85 54 42N 7 26W
Derg, L. 85 53 0N 8 20W
Dergaon 109 26 45N 94 0 E
Derma 31 33 51N 89 17W
Dermantsi 95 43 8N 24 17 E
Dermott, Ark. 13 33 32N 91 26W
Dermott, Tex. 50 32 51N 101 1W
Dernieres, Isles 25 29 2N 90 50W
Derry = Londonderry 85 55 0N 7 20W
Derry 36 42 53N 71 19W
Derryveagh Mts. 85 55 0N 8 40W
Derudub 121 17 31N 36 7 E
Derwent 63 53 41N 110 58W
Derwent →, Derby, U.K. 82 52 53N 1 17W
Derwent →, N. Yorks., U.K. 82 53 45N 0 57W
Derwentwater, L. 82 54 35N 3 9W
Des Allemands 25 29 49N 90 28W
Des Arc, Ark. 13 34 58N 91 30W
Des Arc, Mo. 32 37 17N 90 38W
Des Lacs 41 48 16N 101 34W
Des Lacs → 41 48 17N 100 20W
Des Moines, Iowa 23 41 35N 93 37W
Des Moines, N. Mex. 38 36 46N 103 50W
Des Moines → 23 40 23N 91 25W
Des Moines County ◇ 23 40 55N 91 10W
Des Plaines 21 42 3N 87 52W
Des Plaines → 21 41 23N 88 15W
Desaguadero →, Argentina 76 34 30 S 66 46W
Desaguadero →, Bolivia 72 18 24 S 67 5W
Desaguadero →, Peru 72 16 35 S 69 5W
Desatoya Mts. 35 39 20N 117 40W
Descanso 15 32 51N 116 37W
Deschaillons 61 46 32N 72 7W
Descharme → 63 56 51N 109 13W
Deschutes → 44 45 38N 120 55W
Deschutes County ◇ 44 44 0N 121 30W
Deschutes National Forest 44 43 40N 121 20W
Deschutes-Umatilla Plat. 44 45 0N 119 40W
Desdemona 51 32 16N 98 33W
Dese 105 11 5N 39 40 E
Deseado, C. 78 52 45 S 74 42W
Desecheo, Isla 57 18 23N 67 29W
Desemboque 64 30 30N 112 57W
Deseret 52 39 17N 112 39W
Deseret Peak 52 40 28N 112 38W
Desert Center 15 33 43N 115 24W
Desert Hot Springs 15 33 58N 116 30W
Desert Peak 52 41 11N 113 22W
Desert Ranch Reservoir 35 41 42N 116 33W
Desert Valley 35 41 10N 118 5W
Desha 13 35 44N 91 41W
Desha County ◇ 13 33 48N 91 16W
Deshler, Nebr. 34 40 9N 97 44W
Deshler, Ohio 42 41 13N 83 54W
Désirade, I. 67 16 18N 61 3W
Deskenatlata L. 62 60 55N 112 3W
Desloge 32 37 51N 90 32W
Desna → 98 50 33N 30 32 E
Desnătui → 95 44 15N 23 27 E
Desolación, I. 78 53 0 S 74 0W
Despeñaperros, Paso 91 38 24N 3 30W
Dessau 88 51 49N 12 15 E
Dessye = Dese 105 11 5N 39 40 E
Destin 17 30 24N 86 30W
Detmold 88 51 55N 8 50 E
Detroit, Mich. 29 42 20N 83 3W
Detroit, Oreg. 44 44 44N 122 9W
Detroit, Tex. 51 33 40N 95 16W
Detroit → 29 42 3N 83 9W
Detroit Beach 29 41 56N 83 19W
Detroit Lakes 30 46 49N 95 51W
Deuel County ◇, Nebr. 34 41 10N 102 20W
Deuel County ◇, S. Dak. 47 44 45N 96 41W
Deurne, Belgium 87 51 12N 4 24 E
Deurne, Neth. 87 51 27N 5 49 E
Deutsche Bucht 88 54 10N 7 51 E
Deux-Sèvres □ 90 46 35N 0 20W
Deva 89 45 53N 22 55 E
Devakottai 108 9 55N 78 45 E
Deventer 87 52 15N 6 10 E
Devereux 18 33 13N 83 5W
Deveron → 84 57 40N 2 31W
Devesel 95 44 28N 22 41 E
Devils Den 15 35 46N 119 58W
Devils L., N. Dak. 41 48 2N 98 58W
Devils L., Tex. 50 29 34N 100 59W
Devils Lake 41 48 7N 98 52W
Devils Paw 62 58 47N 134 0W
Devils Playground 15 35 0N 115 50W
Devils Tower National Monument 56 44 48N 104 55W
Devin 95 41 44N 24 24 E
Devine 51 29 8N 98 54W
Devizes 83 51 21N 2 0W
Devnya 95 43 13N 27 33 E
Devol 43 34 11N 98 35W
Devon, Canada 62 53 24N 113 44W
Devon, Kans. 24 37 55N 94 49W
Devon, Mont. 33 48 28N 111 29W
Devon I. 4 75 10N 85 0W
Devonport, Australia 127 41 10 S 146 22 E
Devonport, N.Z. 128 36 49 S 174 49 E
Devonport, U.K. 83 50 23N 4 11W
Devonshire □ 83 50 50N 3 40W
Dew 51 31 36N 96 9W
Dewar 43 35 28N 95 56W
Dewas 108 22 59N 76 3 E
Deweese 34 40 21N 98 8W
Dewey, Puerto Rico 57 18 18N 65 18W
Dewey, Ariz. 12 34 32N 112 15W
Dewey, Okla. 43 36 48N 95 56W
Dewey Beach 27 38 42N 75 5W
Dewey County ◇, Okla. 43 36 0N 99 0W
Dewey County ◇, S. Dak. 47 45 0N 101 0W
Dewey L. 49 37 44N 82 44W
Deweyville 51 30 18N 93 45W
Dewsbury 82 53 42N 1 38W
Dewy Rose 18 34 10N 82 57W
Dexter, Ga. 18 32 27N 83 4W
Dexter, Kans. 24 37 11N 96 43W
Dexter, Ky. 48 36 44N 88 17W
Dexter, Maine 26 45 1N 69 18W
Dexter, Mich. 29 42 20N 83 53W
Dexter, Minn. 30 43 43N 92 42W
Dexter, Mo. 32 36 48N 89 57W
Dexter, N. Mex. 38 33 12N 104 22W
Dexter City 42 39 39N 81 28W
Deyhūk 107 33 15N 57 30 E
Deyyer 107 27 55N 51 55 E
Dezadeash L. 62 60 28N 136 58W
Dezfūl 106 32 20N 48 30 E
Dezhneva, Mys 101 66 5N 169 40W
Dezhou 114 37 26N 116 18 E
Dhafra 107 23 20N 54 0 E
Dhahira 107 23 40N 57 0 E
Dhahran = Aẓ Ẓahrān 106 26 10N 50 7 E
Dhaka 109 23 43N 90 26 E
Dhamtari 109 20 42N 81 35 E
Dhanbad 109 23 50N 86 30 E
Dhangarhi 109 28 55N 80 40 E
Dhankuta 109 26 55N 87 40 E
Dhar 108 22 35N 75 26 E
Dharmapuri 108 12 10N 78 10 E
Dharwad 108 15 22N 75 15 E
Dharwar 108 15 43N 75 1 E
Dhaulagiri 109 28 39N 83 28 E
Dhenkanal 109 20 45N 85 35 E
Dhidhimótikhon 95 41 22N 26 29 E
Dhikti 95 35 8N 25 22 E
Dhírfis 95 38 40N 23 54 E
Dhodhekánisos 95 36 35N 27 0 E
Dhrol 108 22 33N 70 25 E
Dhubaibah 107 23 25N 54 35 E
Dhuburi 109 26 2N 89 59 E
Dhula 105 15 10N 47 30 E
Dhule 108 20 58N 74 50 E
Di Linh, Cao Nguyen 112 11 30N 108 0 E
Diablo 53 48 58N 121 8W
Diablo, Sierra 50 31 15N 105 0W
Diablo Range 14 37 20N 121 25W
Diafarabé 120 14 9N 4 57W
Diagonal 23 40 49N 94 20W
Diamante 76 32 5 S 60 40W
Diamante → 76 34 30 S 66 46W
Diamantina 75 18 17 S 43 40W
Diamantina → 127 26 45 S 139 10 E
Diamantino 73 14 30 S 56 30W
Diamond 32 36 59N 94 19W
Diamond, L. 44 43 10N 122 9W
Diamond Harbour 109 22 11N 88 14 E
Diamond Head 19 21 16N 157 49W

Diamond Mts. Dot Lake

Diamond Mts. 35 39 50N 115 30W
Diamond Pk., Colo. 16 40 59N 108 50W
Diamond Pk., Idaho 20 44 9N 113 5W
Diamond Springs 14 38 42N 120 49W
Diamondville 56 41 47N 110 32W
Diana 54 38 34N 80 27W
Diancheng 115 21 30N 111 4 E
Dianópolis 75 11 38 S 46 50W
Diapaga 120 12 5N 1 46 E
Dias Creek 37 39 8N 74 53W
Dībā 107 25 45N 56 16 E
Dibaya 122 6 30 S 22 57 E
Dibaya-Lubue 122 4 12 S 19 54 E
Dibbi 105 4 10N 41 52 E
Dibble 43 35 2N 97 38W
Dibble Glacier Tongue 5 66 8 S 134 32 E
D'Iberville 31 30 26N 88 54W
Diboll 51 31 11N 94 47W
Dibrugarh 109 27 29N 94 55 E
Dickens, Nebr. 34 40 49N 101 2W
Dickens, Tex. 50 33 37N 100 50W
Dickens County ◇ 50 33 40N 100 50W
Dickenson County ◇ 54 37 10N 82 22W
Dickey 41 46 32N 98 27W
Dickey County ◇ 41 46 2N 98 30W
Dickeyville 55 42 38N 90 36W
Dickinson, N. Dak. 41 46 53N 102 47W
Dickinson, Tex. 51 29 28N 95 3W
Dickinson County ◇, Iowa 23 43 20N 95 10W
Dickinson County ◇, Kans. 24 38 50N 97 10W
Dickinson County ◇, Mich. 29 46 0N 87 50W
Dickson, Okla. 43 34 11N 96 59W
Dickson, Tenn. 48 36 5N 87 23W
Dickson, U.S.S.R. 100 73 40N 80 5 E
Dickson County ◇ 48 36 11N 87 21W
Didiéni 120 13 53N 8 6W
Didsbury 62 51 35N 114 10W
Diébougou 120 11 0N 3 15W
Diefenbaker L. 63 51 0N 106 55W
Diego Garcia 3 7 50 S 72 50 E
Diehlstadt 32 36 58N 89 26W
Diekirch 87 49 52N 6 10 E
Dien Bien 112 21 20N 103 0 E
Dieppe 90 49 54N 1 4 E
Dieren 87 52 3N 6 6 E
Dierks 13 34 7N 94 1W
Diest 87 50 58N 5 4 E
Dieterich 21 39 4N 88 23W
Dietrich 20 42 55N 114 16W
Differdange 87 49 31N 5 54 E
Difficult 49 36 22N 85 54W
Digby 61 44 38N 65 50W
Digges 63 58 40N 94 0W
Digges Is. 59 62 40N 77 50W
Dighinala 109 23 15N 92 5 E
Dighton 24 38 29N 100 28W
Digne 90 44 5N 6 12 E
Digos 111 6 45N 125 20 E
Digranes 96 66 4N 14 44 E
Digul → 111 7 7 S 138 42 E
Dihang → 109 27 48N 95 30 E
Dijlah, Nahr → 106 31 0N 47 25 E
Dijon 90 47 20N 5 0 E
Diksmuide 87 51 2N 2 52 E
Dikson = Dickson 100 73 40N 80 5 E
Dikwa 121 12 4N 13 30 E
Dili 111 8 39 S 125 34 E
Dilia 38 35 12N 105 4W
Dill City 43 35 17N 99 8W
Dillard 18 34 58N 83 23W
Diller 34 40 7N 96 56W
Dilley 51 28 40N 99 10W
Dilling 121 12 3N 29 35 E
Dillingham 11 59 3N 158 28W
Dillingham ◇ 11 58 0N 157 0W
Dillon, Canada 63 55 56N 108 35W
Dillon, Colo. 16 39 37N 106 4W
Dillon, Mont. 33 45 13N 112 38W
Dillon, S.C. 46 34 25N 79 22W
Dillon → 63 55 56N 108 56W
Dillon County ◇ 46 34 20N 79 20W
Dillon L. 42 40 1N 80 4W
Dillon Reservoir 16 39 37N 106 3W
Dillsboro 22 39 1N 85 4W
Dillsburg 45 40 7N 77 2W
Dillwyn 54 37 32N 78 27W
Dilolo 122 10 28 S 22 18 E
Dimas 64 23 43N 106 47W
Dimashq 106 33 30N 36 18 E
Dimbokro 120 6 45N 4 46W
Dîmbovița □ 95 45 0N 25 30 E
Dîmbovița → 95 44 14N 26 13 E
Dîmbovnic → 95 44 28N 25 18 E
Dimitrovgrad, Bulgaria 95 42 5N 25 35 E
Dimitrovgrad, U.S.S.R. 98 54 14N 49 39 E
Dimmit County ◇ 51 28 27N 99 46W
Dimmitt 50 34 33N 102 19W
Dimock 47 43 29N 97 59W
Dimona 104 31 2N 35 1 E
Dinagat 111 10 10N 125 40 E
Dinajpur 109 25 33N 88 43 E
Dinan 90 48 28N 2 2W
Dinant 87 50 16N 4 55 E
Dinar 106 38 5N 30 15 E
Dinara Planina 94 44 0N 16 30 E
Dinard 90 48 38N 2 6W
Dinaric Alps = Dinara Planina 94 44 0N 16 30 E
Dindigul 108 10 25N 78 0 E
Dinero 51 28 14N 97 58W
Ding Xian 114 38 30N 114 59 E
Dingbian 114 37 35N 107 32 E
Dinghai 115 30 1N 122 6 E
Dingle 85 52 9N 10 17W
Dingle B. 85 52 3N 10 20W
Dingnan 115 24 45N 115 0 E
Dingtao 115 35 5N 115 35 E
Dinguiraye 120 11 18N 10 49W
Dingwall 84 57 36N 4 26W
Dingxi 114 35 30N 104 33 E
Dingxiang 114 38 30N 112 58 E
Dinnebito Wash → 12 35 29N 111 14W
Dinosaur 16 40 15N 109 1W
Dinosaur National Monument 16 40 30N 108 45W
Dinuba 15 36 32N 119 23W
Dinwiddie 54 37 5N 77 35W
Dinwiddie County ◇ 54 37 5N 77 35W
Diomede 11 65 47N 169 0W
Diourbel 120 14 39N 16 12W
Dipolog 111 8 36N 123 20 E
Dir 107 35 8N 71 59 E
Diré 120 16 20N 3 25W
Dire Dawa 105 9 35N 41 45 E
Diriamba 66 11 51N 86 19W
Dirico 123 17 50 S 20 42 E
Dirk Hartog I. 126 25 50 S 113 5 E
Dirranbandi 127 28 33 S 148 17 E
Dirty Devil → 52 37 58N 110 24W
Disa 108 24 18N 72 10 E
Disappointment, C. 53 46 18N 124 5W
Disappointment L. 126 23 20 S 122 40 E
Disaster B. 127 37 15 S 150 0 E
Disautel 53 48 22N 119 14W
Discovery B. 127 38 10 S 140 40 E
Dishman 53 47 39N 117 17W
Disko 4 69 45N 53 30W
Disko Bugt 4 69 10N 52 0W
Dismal → 34 41 50N 100 5W
Dismal Swamp 54 36 40N 76 20W
Disney 43 36 29N 95 1W
Disputanta 54 37 8N 77 14W
Disteghil Sar 108 36 20N 75 12 E
District of Columbia □ 27 38 54N 77 1W
Distrito Federal □, Brazil 75 15 45 S 47 45W
Distrito Federal □, Venezuela 70 10 30N 66 55W
Diu 108 20 45N 70 58 E
Divernon 21 39 34N 89 39W
Diversion L. 51 33 49N 98 56W
Divide 33 45 45N 112 45W
Divide County ◇ 41 48 55N 103 30W
Dividing Creek 37 39 16N 75 6W
Divinópolis 75 20 10 S 44 54W
Divisões, Serra dos 75 17 0 S 51 0W
Divnoye 99 45 55N 43 21 E
Dīwāl Kol 108 34 23N 67 52 E
Dix, Ill. 21 38 27N 88 56W
Dix, Nebr. 34 41 14N 103 29W
Dix → 49 37 49N 84 43W
Dix Hills 39 40 49N 73 22W
Dixfield 26 44 32N 70 28W
Dixie, Ala. 10 31 9N 86 44W
Dixie, Ark. 13 35 5N 91 22W
Dixie, Wash. 53 46 8N 118 9W
Dixie County ◇ 17 29 30N 83 15W
Dixie National Forest 52 37 45N 112 15W
Dixie Union 18 31 20N 82 28W
Dixmont 26 44 41N 69 10W
Dixon, Calif. 14 38 27N 121 49W
Dixon, Ill. 21 41 50N 89 29W
Dixon, Iowa 23 41 45N 90 47W
Dixon, Ky. 48 37 31N 87 41W
Dixon, Mo. 32 37 59N 92 6W
Dixon, Mont. 33 47 19N 114 19W
Dixon, N. Mex. 38 36 12N 105 53W
Dixon, Nebr. 34 42 24N 97 2W
Dixon, Wyo. 56 41 2N 107 32W
Dixon County ◇ 34 42 30N 96 50W
Dixons Mills 10 32 4N 87 47W
Dixonville 62 56 32N 117 40W
Dixville Notch 36 44 50N 71 18W
Diyarbakir 106 37 55N 40 18 E
Diz Chah 107 35 30N 55 30 E
Dizney 49 36 51N 83 7W
Djado 121 21 4N 12 14 E
Djakarta = Jakarta 111 6 9 S 106 49 E
Djambala 122 2 32 S 14 30 E
Djanet 120 24 35N 9 32 E
Djawa = Jawa 111 7 0 S 110 0 E
Djelfa 120 34 40N 3 15 E
Djema 122 6 3N 25 15 E
Djenné 120 14 0N 4 30W
Djerid, Chott 120 33 42N 8 30 E
Djibo 120 14 9N 1 35W
Djibouti 105 11 30N 43 5 E
Djibouti ■ 105 12 0N 43 0 E
Djolu 122 0 35N 22 5 E
Djougou 120 9 40N 1 45 E
Djoum 122 2 41N 12 35 E
Djourab 121 16 40N 18 50 E
Djugu 122 1 55N 30 35 E
Djúpivogur 96 64 39N 14 17W
Dmitriya Lapteva, Proliv 101 73 0N 140 0 E
Dneiper = Dnepr → 99 46 30N 32 18 E
Dnepr → 99 46 30N 32 18 E
Dneprodzerzhinsk 99 48 32N 34 37 E
Dnepropetrovsk 99 48 30N 35 0 E
Dnestr → 99 46 18N 30 17 E
Dnestrovski = Belgorod 99 50 35N 36 35 E
Dniester = Dnestr → 99 46 18N 30 17 E
Doba 121 8 40N 16 50 E
Dobbin 51 30 22N 95 46W
Dobbs Ferry 39 41 1N 73 52W
Dobbyn 127 19 44 S 139 59 E
Doberai, Jazirah 111 1 25 S 133 0 E
Doblas 76 37 5 S 64 0W
Dobo 111 5 45 S 134 15 E
Dobra 95 44 52N 25 40 E
Dobrinishta 95 41 49N 23 34 E
Dobruja 95 44 30N 28 15 E
Dobson 40 36 24N 80 43W
Doce → 75 19 37 S 39 49W
Doctors Inlet 17 30 6N 81 47W
Doddridge 13 33 6N 93 55W
Doddridge County ◇ 54 39 17N 80 44W
Dodecanese = Dhodhekánisos 95 36 35N 27 0 E
Dodge, N. Dak. 41 47 18N 102 12W
Dodge, Nebr. 34 41 43N 96 53W
Dodge, Tex. 51 30 45N 95 24W
Dodge Center 30 44 2N 92 52W
Dodge City 24 37 45N 100 1W
Dodge County ◇, Ga. 18 33 10N 83 10W
Dodge County ◇, Minn. 30 44 0N 92 50W
Dodge County ◇, Nebr. 34 41 30N 96 40W
Dodge County ◇, Wis. 55 43 20N 88 45W
Dodge L. 63 59 50N 105 36W
Dodgeville 55 42 58N 90 8W
Dodoma 122 6 8 S 35 45 E
Dodsland 63 51 50N 108 45W
Dodson, La. 25 32 5N 92 39W
Dodson, Mont. 33 48 24N 108 15W
Doe Run 32 37 45N 90 30W
Doerun 18 31 19N 83 55W
Doetinchem 87 51 59N 6 18 E
Doftana 95 45 11N 25 45 E
Dog Creek 62 51 35N 122 14W
Dog I. 17 29 48N 84 36W
Dog L., Man., Canada 63 51 2N 98 31W
Dog L., Ont., Canada 60 48 18N 89 30W
Dogger Bank 80 54 50N 2 0 E
Dogi 108 32 20N 62 50 E
Dohazari 109 22 10N 92 5 E
Doi 111 2 14N 127 49 E
Doi Luang 112 18 30N 101 0 E
Doig → 62 56 25N 120 40W
Dois Irmãos, Sa. 74 9 0 S 42 30W
Dojran 95 41 10N 22 45 E
Dokka 97 60 49N 10 7 E
Dokkum 87 53 20N 5 59 E
Doland 47 44 54N 98 6W
Dolbeau 61 48 53N 72 18W
Dole 90 47 7N 5 31 E
Doles 18 31 42N 83 53W
Dolgellau 82 52 44N 3 53W
Dolgelley = Dolgellau 82 52 44N 3 53W
Dolgeville 39 43 6N 74 46W
Dolj □ 95 44 10N 23 30 E
Dollart 87 53 20N 7 10 E
Dolliver 23 43 28N 94 37W
Dolna Banya 95 42 18N 23 44 E
Dolni Dŭbnik 95 43 24N 24 26 E
Dolomites = Dolomiti 94 46 30N 11 40 E
Dolomiti 94 46 30N 11 40 E
Dolores, Argentina 76 36 20 S 57 40W
Dolores, Uruguay 76 33 34 S 58 15W
Dolores, U.S.A. 16 37 28N 108 30W
Dolores → 52 38 49N 109 17W
Dolores County ◇ 16 37 45N 108 30W
Dolphin and Union Str. 58 69 5N 114 45W
Dolphin C. 78 51 10 S 59 0W
Dolton 21 41 38N 87 36W
Dom Joaquim 75 18 57 S 43 16W
Dom Pedrito 77 31 0 S 54 40W
Dom Pedro 74 4 59 S 44 27W
Dombarovskiy 100 50 46N 59 32 E
Dombås 97 62 4N 9 8 E
Dombes 90 46 3N 5 0 E
Domburg 87 51 34N 3 30 E
Dome, The 36 42 45N 73 12W
Domel I. = Letsôk-aw Kyun 112 11 30N 98 25 E
Domeyko 76 29 0 S 71 0W
Domeyko, Cordillera 76 24 30 S 69 0W
Dominador 76 24 21 S 69 20W
Dominica ■ 67 15 20N 61 20W
Dominica Passage 67 15 10N 61 20W
Dominican Rep. ■ 67 19 0N 70 30W
Domo 105 7 50N 47 10 E
Domodóssola 88 46 6N 8 19 E
Don →, England, U.K. 82 53 41N 0 51W
Don →, Scotland, U.K. 84 57 14N 2 5W
Don →, U.S.S.R. 99 47 4N 39 18 E
Don Benito 91 38 53N 5 51W
Don Martín, Presa de 64 27 30N 100 50W
Dona Ana 38 32 23N 106 49W
Dona Ana County ◇ 38 32 20N 107 0W
Dona Juana, Cerro 57 18 0N 66 0W
Donaghadee 85 54 38N 5 32W
Donahue 23 41 42N 90 41W
Donalda 62 52 35N 112 34W
Donalds 46 34 23N 82 21W
Donaldson, Ark. 13 34 14N 92 55W
Donaldson, Minn. 30 48 35N 96 53W
Donaldsonville 25 30 6N 90 59W
Donalsonville 18 31 3N 84 53W
Donau → 88 48 10N 17 0 E
Donauwörth 88 48 42N 10 47 E
Doncaster, U.K. 82 53 31N 1 9W
Doncaster, U.S.A. 27 38 30N 77 15W
Dondo, Angola 122 9 45 S 14 25 E
Dondo, Mozam. 123 19 33 S 34 46 E
Dondo, Teluk 111 0 29N 120 30 E
Dondra Head 108 5 55N 80 40 E
Donegal 85 54 39N 8 8W
Donegal □ 85 54 53N 8 0W
Donegal B. 85 54 30N 8 35W
Donets → 99 47 33N 40 55 E
Donetsk 99 48 0N 37 45 E
Dongara 126 29 14 S 114 57 E
Dongfang 115 18 50N 108 33 E
Donggala 111 0 30 S 119 40 E
Donggou 114 39 52N 124 10 E
Dongguan 115 22 58N 113 44 E
Dongguang 114 37 50N 116 30 E
Dongjingcheng 114 44 0N 129 10 E
Donglan 115 24 30N 107 21 E
Dongliu 115 30 13N 116 55 E
Dongola 121 19 9N 30 22 E
Dongou 122 2 0N 18 5 E
Dongping 114 35 55N 116 20 E
Dongshan 115 23 43N 117 30 E
Dongsheng 114 39 50N 110 0 E
Dongtai 115 32 51N 120 21 E
Dongting Hu 113 29 18N 112 45 E
Dongxing 115 21 34N 108 0 E
Dongyang 115 29 13N 120 15 E
Donie 51 31 29N 96 13W
Doniphan, Kans. 24 39 38N 95 5W
Doniphan, Mo. 32 36 37N 90 50W
Doniphan, Nebr. 34 40 46N 98 22W
Doniphan County ◇ 24 39 45N 95 0W
Donley County ◇ 50 35 0N 100 45W
Dønna, Norway 96 66 6N 12 30 E
Donna, U.S.A. 50 26 9N 98 4W
Donnaconna 61 46 41N 71 41W
Donnan 23 42 54N 91 53W
Donnelly, Idaho 20 44 44N 116 5W
Donnelly, Minn. 30 45 42N 96 1W
Donnelly's Crossing 128 35 42 S 173 38 E
Donner Pass 14 39 19N 120 20W
Donner und Blitzen → 44 43 17N 118 49W
Donnybrook 41 48 31N 101 53W
Donora 45 40 11N 79 52W
Donovan 21 40 53N 87 37W
Dooly County ◇ 18 32 10N 83 50W
Doon 23 43 17N 96 14W
Doon → 84 55 26N 4 41W
Door County ◇ 55 45 0N 87 15W
Door Peninsula 55 44 45N 87 25W
Dor 104 32 37N 34 55 E
Dora, Ala. 10 33 44N 87 5W
Dora, Oreg. 44 43 10N 123 59W
Dora, L. 126 22 0 S 123 0 E
Dora Báltea → 94 45 11N 8 5 E
Dorada, La 70 5 30N 74 40W
Dorado 57 18 28N 66 16W
Doran 30 46 11N 96 29W
Doran L. 63 61 13N 108 6W
Doraville 18 33 54N 84 17W
Dorchester, U.K. 83 50 42N 2 28W
Dorchester, N.H. 36 43 44N 71 56W
Dorchester, Nebr. 34 40 39N 97 7W
Dorchester, Wis. 55 45 0N 90 20W
Dorchester, C. 59 65 27N 77 27W
Dorchester County ◇, Md. 27 38 20N 76 0W
Dorchester County ◇, S.C. 46 33 10N 80 30W
Dordogne □ 90 45 5N 0 40 E
Dordogne → 90 45 2N 0 36W
Dordrecht 87 51 48N 4 39 E
Dore, Mt. 90 45 32N 2 50 E
Doré L. 63 54 46N 107 17W
Doré Lake 63 54 38N 107 36W
Dorena 44 43 43N 122 52W
Dores do Indaiá 75 19 27 S 45 36W
Dori 120 14 3N 0 2W
Dorion 60 45 23N 74 3W
Dornoch 84 57 52N 4 0W
Dornoch Firth 84 57 52N 4 0W
Dorohoi 89 47 56N 26 30 E
Döröö Nuur 113 48 0N 93 0 E
Dorrance 24 38 51N 98 35W
Dorre I. 126 25 13 S 113 12 E
Dorris 14 41 58N 121 55W
Dorset 36 43 15N 73 6W
Dorset □ 83 50 48N 2 25W
Dortmund 88 51 32N 7 28 E
Dorton 49 37 17N 82 35W
Doruma 122 4 42N 27 33 E
Dos Bahías, C. 78 44 58 S 65 32W
Dos Bocas 57 18 20N 66 40W
Dos Palos 14 36 59N 120 37W
Dosso 120 13 0N 3 13 E
Dot Lake 11 63 40N 144 4W

Dothan **Dusty**

Dothan **10** 31 13N 85 24W
Doty **53** 46 38N 123 17W
Douai **90** 50 21N 3 4 E
Douala **122** 4 0N 9 45 E
Douarnenez **90** 48 6N 4 21W
Douăzeci Şi Trei August **95** 43 55N 28 40 E
Double Mountain Fork
Brazos → **50** 33 16N 100 0W
Double Springs **10** 34 9N 87 24W
Doubletop Pk. **56** 43 21N 110 17W
Doubs □ **90** 47 10N 6 20 E
Doubs → **90** 46 53N 5 1 E
Doubtful Sd. **128** 45 20 S 166 49 E
Doubtless B. **128** 34 55 S 173 26 E
Douentza **120** 14 58N 2 48W
Dougherty, Iowa **23** 42 55N 93 3W
Dougherty, Okla. **43** 34 24N 97 3W
Dougherty County ◇ **18** 31 30N 84 15W
Douglas, U.K. **82** 54 9N 4 29W
Douglas, Alaska **11** 58 17N 134 24W
Douglas, Ariz. **12** 31 21N 109 33W
Douglas, Ga. **18** 31 31N 82 51W
Douglas, Mass. **28** 42 6N 71 45W
Douglas, N. Dak. **41** 47 51N 101 30W
Douglas, Nebr. **34** 40 36N 96 23W
Douglas, Okla. **43** 36 16N 97 40W
Douglas, Wyo. **56** 42 45N 105 24W
Douglas C. **11** 58 51N 153 15W
Douglas City **14** 40 39N 122 57W
Douglas County ◇, Colo. **16** 39 15N 105 0W
Douglas County ◇, Ga. **18** 33 40N 84 45W
Douglas County ◇, Ill. **21** 39 45N 88 15W
Douglas County ◇, Kans. **24** 38 50N 95 15W
Douglas County ◇, Minn. **30** 45 50N 95 20W
Douglas County ◇, Mo. **32** 36 55N 92 30W
Douglas County ◇, Nebr. **34** 41 15N 96 10W
Douglas County ◇, Nev. **35** 38 55N 119 45W
Douglas County ◇, Oreg. **44** 43 15N 123 0W
Douglas County ◇, S. Dak. **47** 43 25N 98 24W
Douglas County ◇, Wash. **53** 47 50N 119 45W
Douglas County ◇, Wis. **55** 46 25N 91 55W
Douglas L. **49** 35 58N 83 32W
Douglass, Kans. **24** 37 31N 97 1W
Douglass, Tex. **51** 31 40N 94 53W
Douglastown **61** 48 46N 64 24W
Douglasville **18** 33 45N 84 45W
Doumé **122** 4 15N 13 25 E
Dounreay **84** 58 34N 3 44W
Dourada, Serra **75** 13 10 S 48 45W
Dourados **77** 22 9 S 54 50W
Dourados → **77** 21 58 S 54 18W
Douro → **91** 41 8N 8 40W
Douro Litoral □ **91** 41 10N 8 20W
Dousman **55** 43 1N 88 29W
Dove → **82** 52 51N 1 36W
Dove Creek **16** 37 46N 108 54W
Dover, U.K. **83** 51 7N 1 19 E
Dover, Ark. **13** 35 24N 93 7W
Dover, Del. **27** 39 10N 75 32W
Dover, Idaho **20** 48 15N 116 36W
Dover, N.H. **36** 43 12N 70 56W
Dover, N.J. **37** 40 53N 74 34W
Dover, Ohio **42** 40 32N 81 29W
Dover, Okla. **43** 35 59N 97 55W
Dover, Tenn. **48** 36 29N 87 50W
Dover, Pt. **126** 32 32 S 125 32 E
Dover, Str. of **90** 51 0N 1 30 E
Dover-Foxcroft **26** 45 11N 69 13W
Dovey → **83** 52 32N 4 0W
Dovrefjell **96** 62 15N 9 33 E
Dow City **23** 41 56N 95 30W
Dowa **123** 13 38 S 33 58 E
Dowagiac **29** 41 59N 86 6W
Dowlat Yār **107** 34 30N 65 45 E
Dowlatābād **107** 28 20N 56 40W
Dowling Park **17** 30 15N 83 15W
Down □ **85** 54 20N 6 0W
Downers Grove **21** 41 48N 88 1W
Downey **20** 42 26N 112 7W
Downham Market **83** 52 36N 0 22 E
Downieville **14** 39 34N 102 50W
Downing **32** 40 29N 92 22W
Downpatrick **85** 54 20N 5 43W
Downpatrick Hd. **85** 54 20N 9 21W
Downs **21** 40 24N 88 52W
Downs Mt. **56** 43 18N 109 40W
Downsville **27** 39 35N 77 48W
Dows **23** 42 39N 93 30W
Dowshī **107** 35 35N 68 43 E
Doylestown **55** 43 25N 89 10W
Doyleville **16** 38 25N 106 35W
Doyline **25** 32 32N 93 25W
Dozier **10** 31 10N 86 28W
Draa, Oued → **120** 30 29N 6 1W
Drachten **87** 53 7N 6 5 E
Dracut **28** 42 40N 71 18W
Drăgăneşti **95** 44 9N 24 32 E
Drăgăneşti-Viaşca **95** 44 5N 25 33 E
Drăgăsani **95** 44 39N 24 17 E
Dragerton **52** 39 33N 110 25W
Dragoman, Prokhod **95** 43 0N 22 53 E
Dragoon **12** 32 2N 110 2W
Draguignan **90** 43 30N 6 27 E
Drain **44** 43 40N 123 19W
Drake, Ariz. **12** 35 0N 112 20W
Drake, Colo. **16** 40 40N 105 20W
Drake, N. Dak. **41** 47 55N 100 23W
Drake Passage **5** 58 0 S 68 0W
Drake Pk. **44** 42 19N 120 7W
Drakensberg **123** 31 0 S 28 0 E
Drakes Branch **54** 36 59N 78 36W
Drakesboro **48** 37 13N 87 3W
Drakesville **23** 40 47N 92 31W
Dráma **95** 41 9N 24 10 E
Drammen **97** 59 42N 10 12 E
Drangajökull **96** 66 9N 22 15W
Dranov, Ostrov **95** 44 55N 29 30 E
Draper, S. Dak. **47** 43 52N 100 30W
Draper, Utah **52** 40 32N 111 52W
Drau = Drava → **89** 45 33N 18 55 E
Drava → **89** 45 33N 18 55 E
Drayden **27** 38 11N 76 28W
Drayton Valley **62** 53 12N 114 58W
Drenthe □ **87** 52 52N 6 40 E
Dresden, Germany **88** 51 2N 13 45 E
Dresden, Kans. **24** 39 38N 100 26W
Dresden, N.Y. **39** 42 41N 76 58W
Dresden, Tenn. **48** 36 18N 88 42W
Dresser **55** 45 20N 92 38W
Dreux **90** 48 44N 1 23 E
Drew County ◇ **13** 33 35N 91 40W
Drews Reservoir **44** 42 7N 120 37W
Drexel, Mo. **32** 38 29N 94 37W
Drexel, N.C. **40** 35 45N 81 36W
Driffield **82** 54 0N 0 25W
Driftwood **45** 41 20N 78 8W
Driggs, Ark. **13** 35 14N 93 46W
Driggs, Idaho **20** 43 44N 111 6W
Drina → **95** 44 53N 19 21 E
Drincea → **95** 44 20N 22 55 E
Dripping Springs **51** 30 12N 98 5W
Driscoll, N. Dak. **41** 46 51N 100 9W
Driscoll, Tex. **50** 27 41N 97 45W
Driskill Mt. **25** 32 25N 92 54W
Drøbak **97** 59 39N 10 39 E
Drogheda **85** 53 45N 6 20W
Drogobych **99** 49 20N 23 30 E
Droichead Nua **85** 53 11N 6 50W
Droitwich **83** 52 16N 2 10W
Drôme □ **90** 44 38N 5 15 E
Dronning Maud Land **5** 72 30 S 12 0 E
Drouzhba **95** 43 15N 28 0 E
Drumheller **62** 51 25N 112 40W
Drummond, Idaho **20** 43 59N 111 20W
Drummond, Mont. **33** 46 40N 113 9W
Drummond, Okla. **43** 36 18N 98 2W
Drummond, Wis. **55** 46 20N 91 15W
Drummond, L. **54** 36 36N 76 28W
Drummond I. **29** 46 1N 83 39W
Drummond Ra. **127** 23 45 S 147 10 E
Drummondville **60** 45 55N 72 25W
Drumright **43** 35 59N 96 36W
Drury **27** 38 48N 76 42W
Druzhina **101** 68 14N 145 18 E
Dry Cr. → **56** 44 31N 108 3W
Dry Creek **25** 30 40N 93 3W
Dry Devils → **50** 29 47N 100 59W
Dry Falls Dam **53** 47 37N 119 19W
Dry L. **41** 48 16N 98 59W
Dry Prong **25** 31 35N 92 32W
Dry Ridge **49** 38 41N 84 35W
Dryanovo **95** 42 59N 25 28 E
Dryden, Canada **63** 49 47N 92 50W
Dryden, N.Y. **39** 42 30N 76 18W
Dryden, Tex. **50** 30 3N 102 7W
Drygalski I. **5** 66 0 S 92 0 E
Drysdale → **126** 13 59 S 126 51 E
Dschang **120** 5 32N 10 3 E
Du Bay, L. **55** 44 40N 89 39W
Du Bois **34** 40 2N 96 4W
Du Page County ◇ **21** 41 50N 88 5W
Du Quoin **21** 38 1N 89 14W
Ḑubā **106** 27 10N 35 40 E
Dubach **25** 32 42N 92 39W
Dubai = Dubayy **107** 25 18N 55 20 E
Dubawnt → **63** 64 33N 100 6W
Dubawnt, L. **63** 63 4N 101 42W
Dubayy **107** 25 18N 55 20 E
Dubbo **127** 32 11 S 148 35 E
Dublin, Ireland **85** 53 20N 6 18W
Dublin, Ga. **18** 32 32N 82 54W
Dublin, Md. **27** 39 39N 76 16W
Dublin, Miss. **31** 34 4N 90 30W
Dublin, N.C. **40** 34 39N 78 43W
Dublin, N.H. **36** 42 52N 72 5W
Dublin, Tex. **51** 32 5N 98 21W
Dublin, Va. **54** 37 6N 80 41W
Dublin □ **85** 53 24N 6 20W
Dublin B. **85** 53 18N 6 5W
Dubois, Idaho **20** 44 10N 112 14W
Dubois, Ind. **22** 38 27N 86 48W
Dubois, Pa. **45** 41 7N 78 46W
Dubois, Wyo. **56** 43 33N 109 38W
Dubois County ◇ **22** 38 20N 86 50W
Dubovka **99** 49 5N 44 50 E
Dubréka **120** 9 46N 13 31W
Dubrovnik **95** 42 39N 18 6 E
Dubrovskoye **101** 58 55N 111 10 E
Dubuque **23** 42 30N 90 41W
Dubuque County ◇ **23** 42 30N 90 50W
Dubuque Hills **21** 42 15N 90 0W
Duchang **115** 29 18N 116 12 E
Duchesne **52** 40 10N 110 24W
Duchesne → **52** 40 5N 109 41W
Duchesne County ◇ **52** 40 20N 110 30W
Duchess **127** 21 20 S 139 50 E
Ducie I. **125** 24 40 S 124 48W
Duck → **48** 36 2N 87 52W
Duck Hill **31** 33 38N 89 43W
Duck Lake **63** 52 50N 106 16W
Duck Mt. Prov. Parks **63** 51 45N 101 0W
Duck River **48** 35 43N 87 16W
Duck Valley Indian
Reservation **35** 42 0N 116 10W
Ducktown **49** 35 3N 84 23W
Duckwater **35** 38 55N 115 40W
Dudhi **109** 24 15N 83 10 E
Dudinka **101** 69 30N 86 13 E
Dudley, U.K. **83** 52 30N 2 5W
Dudley, Ga. **18** 32 32N 83 5W
Dudley, Mo. **32** 36 46N 90 8W
Dudley, Pa. **45** 40 12N 78 10W
Dudleyville **12** 32 54N 110 42W
Due West **46** 34 20N 82 23W
Dueré **75** 11 20 S 49 17W
Duero → **91** 41 8N 8 40W
Duff Is. **124** 9 53 S 167 8 E
Dufftown **84** 57 26N 3 9W
Dufur **44** 45 27N 121 8W
Dugdemona → **25** 31 47N 92 22W
Dugger **22** 39 4N 87 18W
Dugi Otok **94** 44 0N 15 0 E
Duifken Pt. **127** 12 33 S 141 38 E
Duisburg **88** 51 27N 6 42 E
Duitama **70** 5 50N 73 2W
Duke **43** 34 40N 99 34W
Dukes County ◇ **28** 41 23N 70 31W
Dukhān **107** 25 25N 50 50 E
Duki **108** 30 14N 68 25 E
Duku **120** 10 43N 10 43 E
Dulac **25** 29 23N 90 42W
Dulce **38** 36 56N 107 0W
Dulce → **76** 30 32 S 62 33W
Dulce, Golfo **66** 8 40N 83 20W
Dŭlgopol **95** 43 3N 27 22 E
Dulit, Banjaran **110** 3 15N 114 30 E
Dulovo **95** 43 48N 27 9 E
Duluth, Ga. **18** 34 0N 84 9W
Duluth, Minn. **30** 46 47N 92 6W
Dum Duma **109** 27 40N 95 40 E
Dum Hadjer **121** 13 18N 19 41 E
Dumaguete **111** 9 17N 123 15 E
Dumai **110** 1 35N 101 28 E
Dumaran **111** 10 33N 119 50 E
Dumaring **111** 1 46N 118 10 E
Dumas, Ark. **13** 33 53N 91 29W
Dumas, Tex. **50** 35 52N 101 58W
Dumbarton **84** 55 58N 4 35W
Dumbrăveni **95** 46 14N 24 34 E
Dumfries **84** 55 4N 3 37W
Dumfries & Galloway □ **84** 55 0N 4 0W
Dumoine → **60** 46 13N 77 51W
Dumoine L. **60** 46 55N 77 55W
Dumont **23** 42 45N 92 58W
Dumyât **121** 31 24N 31 48 E
Dun Laoghaire **85** 53 17N 6 9W
Dunaföldvár **89** 46 50N 18 57 E
Dunărea → **89** 45 30N 8 15 E
Dunay **116** 42 52N 132 22 E
Dunback **128** 45 23 S 170 36 E
Dunbar, U.K. **84** 56 0N 2 32W
Dunbar, Nebr. **34** 40 38N 96 1W
Dunbar, Pa. **45** 39 58N 79 37W
Dunbar, W. Va. **54** 38 22N 81 45W
Dunbarton **36** 43 8N 71 38W
Dunblane **84** 56 10N 3 58W
Duncan, Canada **62** 48 45N 123 40W
Duncan, Ariz. **12** 32 43N 109 6W
Duncan, Nebr. **34** 41 25N 97 30W
Duncan, Okla. **43** 34 30N 97 57W
Duncan, L. **60** 53 29N 77 58W
Duncan L. **62** 62 51N 113 58W
Duncan Pass. **112** 11 0N 92 30 E
Duncan Town **66** 22 15N 75 45W
Duncannon **45** 40 23N 77 2W
Duncanville **51** 32 39N 96 55W
Duncombe **23** 42 28N 94 0W
Dundalk, Ireland **85** 54 1N 6 25W
Dundalk, U.S.A. **27** 39 16N 76 32W
Dundalk Bay **85** 53 55N 6 15W
Dundas, Canada **60** 43 17N 79 59W
Dundas, Minn. **30** 44 26N 93 12W
Dundas, Va. **54** 36 55N 78 1W
Dundas, L. **126** 32 35 S 121 50 E
Dundas I. **62** 54 30N 130 50W
Dundas Str. **126** 11 15 S 131 35 E
Dundee, S. Africa **123** 28 11 S 30 15 E
Dundee, U.K. **84** 56 29N 3 0W
Dundee, Iowa **23** 42 35N 91 33W
Dundee, Ky. **48** 37 34N 86 46W
Dundee, Mich. **29** 41 57N 83 40W
Dundee, Minn. **30** 43 51N 95 28W
Dundee, N.Y. **39** 42 32N 76 59W
Dundrum **85** 54 17N 5 50W
Dundrum B. **85** 54 12N 5 40W
Dundy County ◇ **34** 40 15N 101 45W
Dunedin, N.Z. **128** 45 50 S 170 33 E
Dunedin, U.S.A. **17** 28 1N 82 47W
Dunedin → **62** 59 30N 124 5W
Dunfermline **84** 56 5N 3 28W
Dungannon, U.K. **85** 54 30N 6 47W
Dungannon, U.S.A. **54** 36 50N 82 28W
Dungannon □ **85** 54 30N 6 55W
Dungarvan **85** 52 6N 7 40W
Dungarvan Bay **85** 52 5N 7 35W
Dungeness, U.K. **83** 50 54N 0 59 E
Dungeness, U.S.A. **53** 48 9N 123 7W
Dungu **122** 3 40N 28 32 E
Dunhua **114** 43 20N 128 14 E
Dunhuang **113** 40 8N 94 36 E
Dunkeld **84** 56 34N 3 36W
Dunkerque **90** 51 2N 2 20 E
Dunkerton **23** 42 34N 92 10W
Dunkery Beacon **83** 51 15N 3 37W
Dunkirk = Dunkerque **90** 51 2N 2 20 E
Dunkirk, Ind. **22** 40 23N 85 13W
Dunkirk, Mont. **33** 48 29N 111 40W
Dunkirk, N.Y. **39** 42 29N 79 20W
Dunkirk, Ohio **42** 40 48N 83 39W
Dunklin County ◇ **32** 36 20N 90 0W
Dunkwa **120** 6 0N 1 47W
Dunlap, Ill. **21** 40 52N 89 40W
Dunlap, Ind. **22** 41 39N 85 56W
Dunlap, Iowa **23** 41 51N 95 36W
Dunlap, Kans. **24** 38 35N 96 22W
Dunlap, Tenn. **49** 35 23N 85 23W
Dunlap, Tex. **50** 34 8N 100 18W
Dúnleary = Dun Laoghaire **85** 53 17N 6 9W
Dunlow **54** 38 1N 82 26W
Dunmanus B. **85** 51 31N 9 50W
Dunmor **48** 37 4N 86 59W
Dunmore **45** 41 25N 75 38W
Dunmore Hd. **85** 52 10N 10 35W
Dunmore Town **66** 25 30N 76 39W
Dunn, La. **25** 32 28N 91 35W
Dunn, N.C. **40** 35 19N 78 37W
Dunn Center **41** 47 21N 102 37W
Dunn County ◇, N. Dak. **41** 47 15N 102 35W
Dunn County ◇, Wis. **55** 44 55N 91 50W
Dunnell **30** 43 34N 94 47W
Dunnellon **17** 29 3N 82 28W
Dunnet Hd. **84** 58 38N 3 22W
Dunning **34** 41 50N 100 6W
Dunnville **49** 37 12N 85 1W
Dunoon **84** 55 57N 4 56W
Dunqul **121** 23 26N 31 37 E
Duns **84** 55 47N 2 20W
Dunseith **41** 48 50N 100 3W
Dunsmuir **14** 41 13N 122 16W
Dunstable **83** 51 53N 0 31W
Dunstan Mts. **128** 44 53 S 169 35 E
Dunster **62** 53 8N 119 50W
Dunvegan L. **63** 60 8N 107 10W
Duolun **114** 42 12N 116 28 E
Duplin County ◇ **40** 34 50N 78 0W
Dupo **21** 38 31N 90 13W
Dupont **22** 38 53N 85 31W
Dupuyer **33** 48 13N 112 30W
Duque de Caxias **75** 22 45 S 43 19W
Duque de York, I. **78** 50 37 S 75 25W
Dūrā **104** 31 31N 35 1 E
Durack Range **126** 16 50 S 127 40 E
Duran **38** 34 28N 105 24W
Durance → **90** 43 55N 4 45 E
Durand, Ga. **18** 32 54N 84 51W
Durand, Ill. **21** 42 26N 89 20W
Durand, Mich. **29** 42 55N 83 59W
Durand, Wis. **55** 44 38N 91 58W
Durango, Mexico **64** 24 3N 104 39W
Durango, Spain **91** 43 13N 2 40W
Durango, U.S.A. **16** 37 16N 107 53W
Durango □ **64** 25 0N 105 0W
Durant, Iowa **23** 41 36N 90 54W
Durant, Miss. **31** 33 4N 89 51W
Durant, Okla. **43** 33 59N 96 25W
Durants Neck **40** 36 8N 76 18W
Durazno **76** 33 25 S 56 31W
Durazzo = Durrësi **95** 41 19N 19 28 E
Durban **123** 29 49 S 31 1 E
Durbin **54** 38 33N 79 50W
Durg **109** 21 15N 81 22 E
Durham, Canada **60** 44 10N 80 49W
Durham, U.K. **82** 54 47N 1 34W
Durham, Conn. **28** 41 29N 72 41W
Durham, Kans. **24** 38 30N 97 15W
Durham, N.C. **40** 35 59N 78 54W
Durham, N.H. **36** 43 8N 70 56W
Durham □ **82** 54 42N 1 45W
Durham County ◇ **40** 36 0N 78 55W
Durkee **44** 44 35N 117 30W
Durmitor **92** 43 10N 19 0 E
Durness **84** 58 34N 4 45W
Durrësi **95** 41 19N 19 28 E
D'Urville, Tanjung **111** 1 28 S 137 54 E
D'Urville I. **128** 40 50 S 173 55 E
Dusa Mareb **105** 5 30N 46 15 E
Dushak **100** 37 13N 60 1 E
Dushan **115** 25 48N 107 30 E
Dushanbe **100** 38 33N 68 48 E
Dushore **45** 41 31N 76 24W
Dusky Sd. **128** 45 47 S 166 30 E
Düsseldorf **88** 51 15N 6 46 E
Dustin **43** 35 12N 96 1W
Dusty **53** 46 51N 117 38W

Dutch Harbor Edmonton

Dutch Harbor **11** 53 53N 166 32W
Dutch John **52** 40 55N 109 24W
Dutch Mills **13** 35 52N 94 29W
Dutch Neck **37** 40 17N 74 40W
Dutchess County ◇ **39** 41 45N 73 45W
Dutchtown **32** 37 18N 89 42W
Dutton **33** 47 51N 111 43W
Duval County ◇, Fla. **17** 30 30N 81 30W
Duval County ◇, Tex. **51** 27 50N 98 30W
Duwādimi **106** 24 35N 44 15 E
Duxbury **28** 42 2N 70 40W
Duyun **115** 26 18N 107 29 E
Duzce **106** 40 50N 31 10 E
Duzdab = Zāhedān **107** 29 30N 60 50 E
Dve Mogili **95** 43 35N 25 55 E
Dvina, Sev. → **98** 64 32N 40 30 E
Dvinsk = Daugavpils **98** 55 53N 26 32 E
Dvinskaya Guba **98** 65 0N 39 0 E
Dwarka **108** 22 18N 69 8 E
Dwight, Ill. **21** 41 5N 88 26W
Dwight, Kans. **24** 38 50N 96 38W
Dwight, Nebr. **34** 41 5N 97 1W
Dworshak Reservoir **20** 46 48N 116 0W
Dyer **48** 36 4N 88 59W
Dyer, C. **59** 66 40N 61 0W
Dyer County ◇ **48** 36 0N 89 25W
Dyer Plateau **5** 70 45 S 65 30W
Dyersburg **48** 36 3N 89 23W
Dyersville **23** 42 29N 91 8W
Dyfed □ **83** 52 0N 4 30W
Dysart, Canada **63** 50 57N 104 2W
Dysart, U.S.A. **23** 42 10N 92 18W
Dzamin Üüd **113** 43 50N 111 58 E
Dzerzhinsk, Byelorussian S.S.R., U.S.S.R. **98** 53 40N 27 1 E
Dzerzhinsk, R.S.F.S.R., U.S.S.R. **98** 56 14N 43 30 E
Dzhalal-Abad **100** 40 56N 73 0 E
Dzhalinda **101** 53 26N 124 0 E
Dzhambul **100** 42 54N 71 22 E
Dzhankoi **99** 45 40N 34 20 E
Dzhardzhan **101** 68 10N 124 10 E
Dzhelinde **101** 70 0N 114 20 E
Dzhetygara **100** 52 11N 61 12 E
Dzhezkazgan **100** 47 44N 67 40 E
Dzhikimde **101** 59 1N 121 47 E
Dzhizak **100** 40 6N 67 50 E
Dzhugdzur, Khrebet **101** 57 30N 138 0 E
Dzhungarskiye Vorota **100** 45 0N 82 0 E
Dzibilchaltún **65** 21 5N 89 36W
Dzilam de Bravo **65** 21 24N 88 53W
Dzungarian Gates = Dzhungarskiye Vorota **100** 45 0N 82 0 E
Dzuumod **113** 47 45N 106 58 E

E

E. V. Spence Reservoir **50** 31 58N 100 40W
Eabamet, L. **60** 51 30N 87 46W
Eads, Colo. **16** 38 29N 102 47W
Eads, Tenn. **48** 35 12N 89 39W
Eagar **12** 34 6N 109 17W
Eagle, Alaska **11** 64 47N 141 12W
Eagle, Colo. **16** 39 39N 106 50W
Eagle, Idaho **20** 43 42N 116 21W
Eagle, Nebr. **34** 40 49N 96 26W
Eagle, Wis. **55** 42 53N 88 29W
Eagle →, Canada **61** 53 36N 57 26W
Eagle →, U.S.A. **16** 39 39N 107 4W
Eagle, Mt. **57** 17 46N 64 49W
Eagle Bend **30** 46 10N 95 2W
Eagle Butte **47** 45 0N 101 10W
Eagle City **43** 35 56N 98 35W
Eagle County ◇ **16** 39 40N 106 50W
Eagle Cr. → **49** 38 36N 85 4W
Eagle Grove **23** 42 40N 93 54W
Eagle Harbor **27** 38 35N 76 40W
Eagle L., Calif. **14** 40 39N 120 45W
Eagle L., Maine **26** 46 20N 69 22W
Eagle Lake, Maine **26** 47 3N 68 36W
Eagle Lake, Minn. **30** 44 10N 93 53W
Eagle Lake, Tex. **51** 29 35N 96 20W
Eagle Mills **13** 33 41N 92 43W
Eagle Mountain **15** 33 49N 115 27W
Eagle Mountain L. **51** 32 53N 97 28W
Eagle Nest **38** 36 33N 105 16W
Eagle Nest Butte **47** 43 27N 101 39W
Eagle Pass **50** 28 43N 100 30W
Eagle Peak **14** 41 17N 120 12W
Eagle Point **44** 42 28N 122 48W
Eagle River **55** 45 55N 89 15W
Eagle Rock **54** 37 38N 79 48W
Eagletail Mts. **12** 33 20N 113 30W
Eagletown **43** 34 2N 94 34W
Eagleville, Calif. **14** 41 19N 120 7W
Eagleville, Mo. **32** 40 28N 93 59W
Eagleville, Tenn. **48** 35 45N 86 39W
Eakly **43** 35 18N 98 34W
Ealing **83** 51 30N 0 19W
Earl, L. **14** 41 50N 124 11W
Earl Grey **63** 50 57N 104 43W
Earl Park **22** 40 42N 87 25W
Earle **13** 35 16N 90 28W
Earleville **27** 39 24N 75 54W
Earlham **23** 41 30N 94 7W
Earlimart **15** 35 53N 119 16W
Earling **23** 41 28N 95 46W
Earlington **48** 37 16N 87 30W
Earlsboro **43** 35 19N 96 47W
Earlville, Ill. **21** 41 35N 88 55W
Earlville, N.Y. **39** 42 44N 75 33W
Early, Iowa **23** 42 28N 95 9W
Early, Tex. **51** 31 46N 98 58W
Early Branch **46** 32 45N 80 55W
Early County ◇ **18** 31 20N 84 50W
Earn → **84** 56 20N 3 19W
Earn, L. **84** 56 23N 4 14W
Earnslaw, Mt. **128** 44 32 S 168 27 E
Earth **50** 34 14N 102 24W
Easley **46** 34 50N 82 36W
East → **39** 40 48N 73 48W
East Angus **61** 45 30N 71 40W
East Arm Grand Traverse B. **29** 44 50N 85 30W
East Aurora **39** 42 46N 78 37W
East B., Fla. **17** 30 5N 85 32W
East B., La. **25** 29 0N 89 15W
East B., Tex. **51** 29 30N 94 35W
East Barrington **36** 43 12N 70 59W
East Baton Rouge Parish ◇ **25** 30 30N 91 20W
East Bend **40** 36 13N 80 31W
East Bengal **109** 24 0N 90 0 E
East Berkshire **36** 44 56N 72 42W
East Berlin **45** 39 56N 76 59W
East Bernard **51** 29 32N 96 4W
East Bernstadt **49** 37 9N 84 12W
East Beskids = Vychodné Beskydy **89** 49 30N 22 0 E
East Branch Clarion River L. **45** 41 35N 78 35W
East Brewton **10** 31 5N 87 4W
East Bridgewater **28** 42 2N 70 58W
East Brunswick **37** 40 25N 74 23W
East Canton **42** 40 47N 81 17W
East C. **128** 37 42 S 178 35 E
East Carbon **52** 39 35N 110 25W
East Carroll Parish ◇ **25** 32 45N 91 15W
East Charleston **36** 44 49N 72 0W
East Chicago **22** 41 38N 87 27W
East China Sea **113** 30 5N 126 0 E
East Corinth **36** 44 5N 72 12W
East Coulee **62** 51 23N 112 27W
East Dorset **36** 43 13N 73 0W
East Douglas **28** 42 4N 71 43W
East Dublin **18** 32 32N 82 52W
East Dubuque **21** 42 30N 90 39W
East Ely **35** 39 15N 114 53W
East Fairfield **36** 44 47N 72 51W
East Falkland **78** 51 30 S 58 30W
East Feliciana Parish ◇ **25** 30 47N 91 8W
East Fork Bruneau → **20** 42 34N 115 38W
East Fork Sevier → **52** 38 14N 112 12W
East Fork White → **22** 38 33N 87 14W
East Fultonham **42** 39 51N 82 8W
East Germany ■ **88** 52 0N 12 0 E
East Glacier Park **33** 48 27N 113 13W
East Granby **28** 41 57N 72 44W
East Grand Forks **30** 47 56N 97 1W
East Grand Rapids **29** 42 58N 85 37W
East Greenwich **28** 41 40N 71 27W
East Haddam **28** 41 27N 72 28W
East Hampton, Conn. **28** 41 35N 72 31W
East Hampton, N.Y. **39** 40 58N 72 11W
East Hartford **28** 41 46N 72 39W
East Haven **28** 41 17N 72 52W
East Haverhill **36** 44 3N 71 58W
East Helena **33** 46 35N 111 56W
East Holden **26** 44 44N 68 38W
East Hope **20** 48 14N 116 17W
East Indies **110** 0 0 120 0 E
East Jordan **29** 45 10N 85 7W
East Kilbride **84** 55 46N 4 10W
East Kingston **36** 42 54N 71 2W
East Lake, Mich. **29** 44 15N 86 18W
East Lake, N.C. **40** 35 53N 75 58W
East Lansing **29** 42 44N 84 29W
East Las Vegas **35** 36 6N 115 3W
East Lempster **36** 43 13N 72 13W
East Liberty **42** 40 20N 83 35W
East Liverpool **42** 40 37N 80 35W
East London **123** 33 0 S 27 55 E
East Longmeadow **28** 42 4N 72 31W
East Lyme **28** 41 22N 72 13W
East Lynn L. **54** 38 10N 82 23W
East Lynne **32** 38 40N 94 14W
East Main = Eastmain **60** 52 10N 78 30W
East Meadow **39** 40 43N 73 34W
East Middlebury **36** 43 58N 73 6W
East Millinocket **26** 45 38N 68 35W
East Moline **21** 41 32N 90 26W
East Naples **17** 26 8N 81 46W
East New Market **27** 38 36N 75 56W
East Nishnabotna → **23** 40 39N 95 38W
East Northport **39** 40 53N 73 20W
East Norwich **39** 40 51N 73 32W
East Olympia **53** 46 58N 122 50W
East Orange **37** 40 46N 74 13W
East Pacific Ridge **125** 15 0 S 110 0W
East Pakistan = Bangladesh ■ **109** 24 0N 90 0 E
East Palatka **17** 29 39N 81 36W
East Palestine **42** 40 50N 80 33W
East Park Reservoir **14** 39 37N 122 31W
East Peoria **21** 40 40N 89 34W
East Peru **23** 41 14N 93 56W
East Petersburg **45** 40 6N 76 21W
East Pine **62** 55 48N 120 12W
East Pt. **61** 46 27N 61 58W
East Point **18** 33 41N 84 27W
East Portal **16** 39 54N 105 39W
East Prairie **32** 36 47N 89 23W
East Prospect **45** 39 58N 76 32W
East Providence **28** 41 49N 71 23W
East Pt. **57** 17 45N 64 34W
East Randolph **36** 43 57N 72 33W
East Range **35** 40 30N 117 57W
East Retford **82** 53 19N 0 55W
East Ridge **49** 34 59N 85 13W
East Rochester **39** 43 7N 77 29W
East Rupert **36** 43 16N 73 8W
East St. Louis **21** 38 37N 90 9W
East Schelde → = Oosterschelde **87** 51 33N 4 0 E
East Siberian Sea **101** 73 0N 160 0 E
East Spring Cr. → **16** 39 30N 102 30W
East Sussex □ **83** 51 0N 0 20 E
East Tavaputs Plateau **52** 39 40N 109 40W
East Tawas **29** 44 17N 83 29W
East Tohopekaliga Lake **17** 28 18N 81 15W
East Troy **55** 42 47N 88 24W
East Vineland **37** 39 30N 74 55W
East Wallingford **36** 43 25N 72 54W
East Wareham **28** 41 46N 70 40W
East Wenatchee **53** 47 25N 120 18W
Eastbourne, N.Z. **128** 41 19 S 174 55 E
Eastbourne, U.K. **83** 50 46N 0 18 E
Eastchester **39** 40 57N 73 49W
Eastend **63** 49 32N 108 50W
Easter Islands **125** 27 0 S 109 0W
Eastern Bay **27** 38 50N 76 15W
Eastern Ghats **108** 14 0N 78 50 E
Eastern Group = Lau **128** 17 0 S 178 30W
Eastern Shore **27** 38 30N 75 50W
Easterville **63** 53 8N 99 49W
Eastham **28** 41 50N 69 58W
Easthampton **28** 42 16N 72 40W
Eastlake **42** 41 40N 81 26W
Eastland **51** 32 24N 98 49W
Eastland County ◇ **51** 32 25N 98 50W
Eastleigh **83** 50 58N 1 21W
Eastmain **60** 52 10N 78 30W
Eastmain → **60** 52 27N 78 26W
Eastman, Ga. **18** 32 12N 83 11W
Eastman, Wis. **55** 43 10N 91 1W
Easton, Calif. **15** 36 39N 119 47W
Easton, Conn. **28** 41 15N 73 18W
Easton, Ill. **21** 40 14N 89 50W
Easton, Kans. **24** 39 21N 95 7W
Easton, Md. **27** 38 47N 76 5W
Easton, Minn. **30** 43 46N 93 54W
Easton, Mo. **32** 39 43N 94 39W
Easton, Pa. **45** 40 41N 75 13W
Easton, Wash. **53** 47 14N 121 11W
Eastover **46** 33 52N 80 41W
Eastpoint **17** 29 44N 84 53W
Eastport, Idaho **20** 48 59N 116 10W
Eastport, Maine **26** 44 56N 67 0W
Eastsound **53** 48 42N 122 55W
Eastville **54** 37 21N 75 57W
Eaton, Colo. **16** 40 32N 104 42W
Eaton, Ind. **22** 40 21N 85 21W
Eaton, Ohio **42** 39 45N 84 38W
Eaton County ◇ **29** 42 35N 84 50W
Eaton Rapids **29** 42 31N 84 39W
Eatonia **63** 51 13N 109 25W
Eatons Neck Pt. **39** 40 57N 73 24W
Eatonton **18** 33 20N 83 23W
Eatontown **37** 40 19N 74 4W
Eatonville **53** 46 52N 122 16W
Eau Claire, Fr. Gui. **71** 3 30N 53 40W
Eau Claire, Mich. **29** 41 59N 86 18W
Eau Claire, Wis. **55** 44 49N 91 30W
Eau Claire → **55** 44 55N 89 35W
Eau Claire County ◇ **55** 44 45N 91 20W
Eau Galle **55** 44 42N 92 1W
Ebbw Vale **83** 51 47N 3 12W
Ebeltoft **97** 56 12N 10 41 E
Ebensburg **45** 40 29N 78 44W
Eberswalde **88** 52 49N 13 50 E
Ebetsu **116** 43 7N 141 34 E
Eboli **94** 40 39N 15 2 E
Ebolowa **122** 2 55N 11 10 E
Ebony **54** 36 37N 77 59W
Ebro → **91** 40 43N 0 54 E
Eccles **54** 37 47N 81 16W
Ech Cheliff **120** 36 10N 1 20 E
Echechonnee → **18** 32 39N 83 36W
Echigo-Sammyaku **117** 36 50N 139 50 E
Echizen-Misaki **117** 35 59N 135 57 E
Echo, Ala. **10** 31 29N 85 28W
Echo, Minn. **30** 44 37N 95 25W
Echo, Oreg. **44** 45 45N 119 12W
Echo Bay, N.W.T., Canada **58** 66 5N 117 55W
Echo Bay, Ont., Canada **60** 46 29N 84 4W
Echo Cliffs **12** 36 40N 111 35W
Echoing → **63** 55 51N 92 5W
Echols County ◇ **18** 30 45N 83 0W
Echternach **87** 49 49N 6 25 E
Echuca **126** 36 10 S 144 20 E
Ecija **91** 37 30N 5 10W
Eckley **16** 40 7N 102 29W
Eclectic **10** 32 38N 86 2W
Econfina **17** 30 22N 85 35W
Economy **22** 39 59N 85 5W
Ecoporanga **75** 18 23 S 40 50W
Ecru **31** 34 21N 89 2W
Ector County ◇ **50** 31 46N 102 31W
Ecuador ■ **70** 2 0 S 78 0W
Ed Dâmer **121** 17 27N 34 0 E
Ed Debba **121** 18 0N 30 51 E
Ed Dueim **121** 14 0N 32 10 E
Edam, Canada **63** 53 11N 108 46W
Edam, Neth. **87** 52 31N 5 3 E
Eday **84** 59 11N 2 47W
Edcouch **50** 26 18N 97 58W
Edd **105** 14 0N 41 38 E
Eddiceton **31** 31 30N 90 48W
Eddrachillis B. **84** 58 16N 5 10W
Eddy County ◇, N. Dak. **41** 47 50N 99 0W
Eddy County ◇, N. Mex. **38** 32 30N 104 20W
Eddystone **83** 50 11N 4 16W
Eddyville, Ill. **21** 37 30N 88 35W
Eddyville, Iowa **23** 41 9N 92 38W
Eddyville, Ky. **48** 37 3N 88 4W
Eddyville, Nebr. **34** 41 1N 99 38W
Ede **87** 52 4N 5 40 E
Édea **122** 3 51N 10 9 E
Edehon L. **63** 60 25N 97 15W
Eden, Miss. **31** 32 59N 90 20W
Eden, N.C. **40** 36 29N 79 53W
Eden, S. Dak. **47** 45 37N 97 25W
Eden, Tex. **51** 31 13N 99 51W
Eden, Vt. **36** 44 42N 72 33W
Eden, Wis. **55** 43 42N 88 22W
Eden, Wyo. **56** 42 3N 109 26W
Eden → **82** 54 57N 3 2W
Eden L. **63** 56 38N 100 15W
Eden Valley **30** 45 19N 94 33W
Eden Valley Reservoir **56** 42 14N 109 21W
Edenderry **85** 53 21N 7 3W
Edenton **40** 36 4N 76 39W
Edesville **27** 39 9N 76 13W
Edgar, Nebr. **34** 40 22N 97 58W
Edgar, Wis. **55** 44 55N 89 59W
Edgar County ◇ **21** 39 40N 87 45W
Edgar Springs **32** 37 42N 91 52W
Edgard **25** 30 3N 90 34W
Edgartown **28** 41 23N 70 31W
Edge Hill **83** 52 7N 1 28W
Edgecombe County ◇ **40** 35 50N 77 30W
Edgefield **46** 33 47N 81 56W
Edgefield County ◇ **46** 33 50N 82 0W
Edgeley **41** 46 22N 98 43W
Edgemere **27** 39 14N 76 27W
Edgemont, Colo. **16** 39 44N 105 8W
Edgemont, S. Dak. **47** 43 18N 103 50W
Edgemoor **46** 34 48N 81 1W
Edgeøya **4** 77 45N 22 30 E
Edgerton, Kans. **24** 38 46N 95 1W
Edgerton, Minn. **30** 43 53N 96 8W
Edgerton, Mo. **32** 39 30N 94 38W
Edgerton, Ohio **42** 41 27N 84 45W
Edgerton, Wis. **55** 42 50N 89 4W
Edgerton, Wyo. **56** 43 25N 106 15W
Edgewater **17** 28 59N 80 54W
Edgewater Park **37** 40 4N 74 54W
Edgewood, Ill. **21** 38 55N 88 40W
Edgewood, Ind. **22** 39 41N 86 8W
Edgewood, Iowa **23** 42 39N 91 24W
Edgewood, Md. **27** 39 25N 76 18W
Edgewood, N. Mex. **38** 35 4N 106 11W
Edgewood, Tex. **51** 32 42N 95 53W
Edhessa **95** 40 48N 22 5 E
Edievale **128** 45 49 S 169 22 E
Edina, Minn. **30** 44 53N 93 21W
Edina, Mo. **32** 40 10N 92 11W
Edinboro **45** 41 52N 80 8W
Edinburg, Ill. **21** 39 39N 89 23W
Edinburg, Ind. **22** 39 21N 85 58W
Edinburg, Miss. **31** 32 48N 89 20W
Edinburg, N. Dak. **41** 48 30N 97 52W
Edinburg, Tex. **50** 26 18N 98 10W
Edinburg, Va. **54** 38 49N 78 34W
Edinburgh **84** 55 57N 3 12W
Edirne **95** 41 40N 26 34 E
Edison, Ga. **18** 31 34N 84 44W
Edison, N.J. **37** 40 31N 74 25W
Edison, Nebr. **34** 40 17N 99 47W
Edison, Ohio **42** 40 33N 82 52W
Edisto → **46** 32 29N 80 21W
Edisto Beach **46** 32 29N 80 20W
Edisto I. **46** 32 35N 80 20W
Edith **50** 31 54N 100 37W
Edmond, Kans. **24** 39 37N 99 50W
Edmond, Okla. **43** 35 39N 97 29W
Edmonds **53** 47 49N 122 23W
Edmondson **13** 35 6N 90 19W
Edmonson **50** 34 17N 101 54W
Edmonson County ◇ **48** 37 10N 86 15W
Edmonton, Canada **62** 53 30N 113 30W

Edmonton Elliott

Edmonton, U.S.A. 49 36 59N 85 37W
Edmore, Mich. 29 43 25N 85 3W
Edmore, N. Dak. 41 48 25N 98 27W
Edmund L. 63 54 45N 93 17W
Edmunds County ◇ 47 45 27N 99 20W
Edmundston 61 47 23N 68 20W
Edna, Kans. 24 37 4N 95 22W
Edna, Tex. 51 28 59N 96 39W
Edon 42 41 33N 84 46W
Edremit 106 39 34N 27 0 E
Edroy 51 27 59N 97 41W
Edsel Ford Ra. 5 77 0 S 143 0W
Edson, Canada 62 53 35N 116 28W
Edson, U.S.A. 24 39 20N 101 33W
Eduardo Castex 76 35 50 S 64 18W
Edwall 53 47 30N 117 57W
Edward, L. 122 0 25 S 29 40 E
Edward I. 60 48 22N 88 37W
Edward VII Pen. 5 80 0 S 150 0W
Edwards, Colo. 16 39 39N 106 36W
Edwards, Miss. 31 32 20N 90 36W
Edwards, N.Y. 39 44 20N 75 15W
Edwards → 21 41 9N 90 59W
Edwards County ◇, Ill. 21 38 25N 88 5W
Edwards County ◇, Kans. 24 37 50N 99 15W
Edwards County ◇, Tex. 50 30 10N 100 13W
Edwards Plateau 50 30 45N 101 20W
Edwardsburg 29 41 48N 86 6W
Edwardsport 22 38 49N 87 15W
Edwardsville 21 38 49N 89 58W
Edzo 62 62 49N 116 4W
Eek 11 60 14N 162 2W
Eekloo 87 51 11N 3 33 E
Eel →, Calif. 14 40 38N 124 20W
Eel →, Ind. 22 40 45N 86 22W
Eel →, Ind. 22 39 7N 86 57W
Ef'e, Nahal 104 31 9N 35 13 E
Effie 30 47 50N 93 38W
Effingham, Ill. 21 39 7N 88 33W
Effingham, Kans. 24 39 31N 95 24W
Effingham, S.C. 46 34 5N 79 46W
Effingham County ◇, Ga. 18 32 20N 81 15W
Effingham County ◇, Ill. 21 39 5N 88 35W
Effingham Falls 36 43 47N 71 5W
Eforie Sud 95 44 1N 28 37 E
Égadi, Ísole 94 37 55N 12 16 E
Egan 47 44 0N 96 37W
Egan Range 35 39 35N 114 55W
Eganville 60 45 32N 77 5W
Egegik 11 58 13N 157 22W
Egeland 41 48 38N 99 6W
Egenolf L. 63 59 3N 100 0W
Eger = Cheb 88 50 9N 12 28 E
Eger 89 47 53N 20 27 E
Egersund 97 58 26N 6 1 E
Egg Harbor 55 45 3N 87 17W
Egg Harbor City 37 39 32N 74 39W
Egg L. 63 55 5N 105 30W
Egmont, C. 128 39 16 S 173 45 E
Egmont, Mt. 128 39 17 S 174 5 E
Egnar 16 37 55N 108 56W
Eğridir 106 37 52N 30 51 E
Eğridir Gölü 106 37 53N 30 50 E
Éguas → 75 13 26 S 44 14W
Egvekinot 101 66 19N 179 50W
Egypt 31 33 54N 88 44W
Egypt ■ 121 28 0N 31 0 E
Ehime □ 117 33 30N 132 40 E
Ehrenberg 12 33 36N 114 31W
Ehrhardt 46 33 6N 81 1W
Eidsvoll 97 60 19N 11 14 E
Eifel 88 50 10N 6 45 E
Eigg 84 56 54N 6 10W
Eighty Mile Beach 126 19 30 S 120 40 E
Eil 105 8 0N 49 50 E
Eil, L. 84 56 50N 5 15W
Eileen L. 63 62 16N 107 37W
Einasleigh 127 18 32 S 144 5 E
Eindhoven 87 51 26N 5 30 E
Eire ■ 85 53 0N 8 0W
Eiríksjökull 96 64 46N 20 24W
Eirunepé 72 6 35 S 69 53W
Eisenach 88 50 58N 10 18 E
Eisenerz 88 47 32N 14 54 E
Eitzen 30 43 31N 91 28W
Ejutla 65 16 34N 96 44W
Ekalaka 33 45 53N 104 33W
Eketahuna 128 40 38 S 175 43 E
Ekibastuz 100 51 50N 75 10 E
Ekimchan 101 53 0N 133 0W
Ekron 48 37 56N 86 11W
Ekwan → 60 53 12N 82 15W
Ekwan Pt. 60 53 16N 82 7W
Ekwok 11 59 22N 157 30W
El Aaiún 120 27 9N 13 12W
El Aat 104 32 50N 35 45 E
El Alamein 121 30 48N 28 58 E
El Alto 72 4 15 S 81 14W
El Aricha 120 34 13N 1 10W
El Arīhā 104 31 52N 35 27 E
El 'Arîsh 121 31 8N 33 50 E
El Asnam = Ech Cheliff 120 36 10N 1 20 E
El Banco 70 9 0N 73 58W
El Baúl 70 8 57N 68 17W
El Bawiti 121 28 25N 28 45 E
El Bayadh 120 33 40N 1 1 E
El Bluff 66 11 59N 83 40W
El Bolsón 78 41 55 S 71 30W
El Buheirat □ 121 7 0N 30 0 E
El Caín 78 41 38 S 68 19W
El Cajon 15 32 48N 116 58W
El Callao 71 7 18N 61 50W
El Campo 51 29 12N 96 16W
El Capitan 33 46 1N 114 23W
El Capitan Reservoir 15 32 53N 116 49W
El Carmen, Bolivia 73 13 40 S 63 55W
El Carmen, Venezuela 70 1 16N 66 52W
El Centro 15 32 48N 115 34W
El Cerrito 14 37 55N 122 19W
El Cerro 73 17 30 S 61 40W
El Cocuy 70 6 25N 72 27W
El Corcovado 78 43 25 S 71 35W
El Cuy 78 39 55 S 68 25W
El Cuyo 65 21 30N 87 40W
El Dere 105 3 50N 47 8 E
El Díaz 65 21 1N 87 17W
El Diviso 70 1 22N 78 14W
El Djouf 120 20 0N 11 30 E
El Dorado, Ark. 13 33 12N 92 40W
El Dorado, Kans. 24 37 49N 96 52W
El Dorado, Venezuela 71 6 55N 61 37W
El Dorado County ◇ 14 38 45N 120 40W
El Escorial 91 40 35N 4 7W
El Faiyûm 121 29 19N 30 50 E
El Fâsher 121 13 33N 25 26 E
El Ferrol 91 43 29N 8 15W
El Fuerte 64 26 30N 108 40W
El Gal 105 10 58N 50 20 E
El Geteina 121 14 50N 32 27 E
El Gezira □ 121 15 0N 33 0 E
El Gîza 121 30 0N 31 10 E
El Goléa 120 30 30N 2 50 E
El Harrache 120 36 45N 3 5 E
El Indio 50 28 31N 100 19W
El Iskandarîya 121 31 0N 30 0 E
El Jadida 120 33 11N 8 17W
El Jebelein 121 12 40N 32 55 E
El Kab 121 19 27N 32 46 E
El Kala 120 36 50N 8 30 E
El Kamlin 121 15 3N 33 11 E
El Kef 120 36 12N 8 47 E
El Khandaq 121 18 30N 30 30 E
El Khârga 121 25 30N 30 33 E
El Khartûm 121 15 31N 32 35 E
El Khartûm Bahrî 121 15 40N 32 31 E
El Laqâwa 121 11 25N 29 1 E
El Mafâza 121 13 38N 34 30 E
El Mahalla el Kubra 121 31 0N 31 0 E
El Maitén 78 42 3 S 71 10W
El Mansûra 121 31 0N 31 19 E
El Mantico 71 7 38N 62 45W
El Miamo 71 7 39N 61 46W
El Milagro 76 30 59 S 65 59W
El Minyâ 121 28 7N 30 33 E
El Mirage 12 33 36N 112 19W
El Mirage L. 15 34 39N 117 37W
El Nido 14 37 8N 120 29W
El Obeid 121 13 8N 30 10 E
El Odaiya 121 12 8N 28 12 E
El Oro = Santa María del Oro 64 25 58N 105 20W
El Oro 65 19 48N 100 8W
El Oro □ 70 3 30 S 79 50W
El Oued 120 33 20N 6 58 E
El Palmar, Bolivia 73 17 50 S 63 9W
El Palmar, Venezuela 71 7 58N 61 53W
El Palmito, Presa 64 25 40N 105 30W
El Paso, Ill. 21 40 44N 89 1W
El Paso, Tex. 50 31 45N 106 29W
El Paso County ◇, Colo. 16 38 50N 104 30W
El Paso County ◇, Tex. 50 31 55N 106 5W
El Portal 14 37 41N 119 47W
El Porvenir, Mexico 64 31 15N 105 51W
El Porvenir, U.S.A. 38 35 43N 105 25W
El Progreso 66 15 26N 87 51W
El Pueblito 64 29 3N 105 4W
El Qâhira 121 30 1N 31 14 E
El Qantara 121 30 51N 32 20 E
El Qasr 120 25 44N 28 42 E
El Reno 43 35 32N 97 57W
El Rio 15 34 14N 119 10W
El Rito 38 36 21N 106 11W
El Salto 64 23 47N 105 22W
El Salvador ■ 66 13 50N 89 0W
El Sauce 66 13 0N 86 40W
El Shallal 121 24 0N 32 53 E
El Sombrero 70 9 23N 67 3W
El Suweis 121 29 58N 32 31 E
El Tigre 71 8 44N 64 15W
El Tocuyo 70 9 47N 69 48W
El Tofo 76 29 22 S 71 18W
El Toro 57 18 17N 65 50W
El Tránsito 76 28 52 S 70 17W
El Turbio 78 51 45 S 72 5W
El Uqsur 121 25 41N 32 38 E
El Vado Reservoir 38 36 36N 106 44W
El Vigía 70 8 38N 71 39W
El Wak 122 2 49N 40 56 E
El Wuz 121 15 0N 30 7 E
El Yunque 57 18 19N 65 50W
Elaine 13 34 19N 90 51W
Elat 104 29 30N 34 56 E
Elâzığ 106 38 37N 39 14 E
Elba, Italy 94 42 48N 10 15 E
Elba, Ala. 10 31 25N 86 4W
Elba, Minn. 30 44 5N 92 1W
Elba, Nebr. 34 41 17N 98 34W
Elbasani 95 41 9N 20 9 E
Elbe → 88 53 50N 9 0 E
Elberfeld 22 38 10N 87 27W
Elberon 23 42 0N 92 19W
Elbert, Colo. 16 39 13N 104 32W
Elbert, Tex. 51 33 15N 99 0W
Elbert, Mt. 16 39 7N 106 27W
Elbert County ◇, Colo. 16 39 20N 104 15W
Elbert County ◇, Ga. 18 34 10N 82 50W
Elberta 29 44 37N 86 14W
Elberton 18 34 7N 82 52W
Elbeuf 90 49 17N 1 2 E
Elbidtan 106 38 13N 37 12 E
Elbing = Elbląg 89 54 10N 19 25 E
Elbing 24 38 3N 97 8W
Elbląg 89 54 10N 19 25 E
Elbow 63 51 7N 106 35W
Elbow Lake 30 45 59N 95 58W
Elbrus 99 43 21N 42 30 E
Elburg 87 52 26N 5 50 E
Elburz Mts. = Alborz, Reshteh-ye Kūhhā-ye 107 36 0N 52 0 E
Elche 91 38 15N 0 42W
Elcho 55 45 26N 89 11W
Elcho I. 127 11 55 S 135 45 E
Elderon 55 44 47N 89 15W
Eldersburg 27 39 24N 76 57W
Eldon, Iowa 23 40 55N 92 13W
Eldon, Mo. 32 38 21N 92 35W
Eldon, Wash. 53 47 33N 123 3W
Eldora, Iowa 23 42 22N 93 5W
Eldora, N.J. 37 39 12N 74 52W
Eldorado, Argentina 77 26 28 S 54 43W
Eldorado, Canada 63 59 35N 108 30W
Eldorado, Mexico 64 24 20N 107 22W
Eldorado, Ill. 21 37 49N 88 26W
Eldorado, Md. 27 38 37N 75 48W
Eldorado, Ohio 42 39 54N 84 41W
Eldorado, Okla. 43 34 28N 99 39W
Eldorado, Tex. 50 30 52N 100 36W
Eldorado National Forest 35 38 50N 120 20W
Eldorado Springs 32 37 52N 94 1W
Eldorendo 18 31 3N 84 39W
Eldoret 122 0 30N 35 17 E
Eldred 45 41 58N 78 23W
Eldridge, Ala. 10 33 55N 87 37W
Eldridge, Iowa 23 41 39N 90 35W
Eldridge, Mo. 32 37 50N 92 45W
Eldridge, N. Dak. 41 46 54N 98 51W
Eleanor 54 38 32N 81 56W
Eleanor, L. 14 37 59N 119 53W
Electra 51 34 2N 98 55W
Electra L. 16 37 33N 107 48W
Electric Mills 31 32 46N 88 28W
Elefantes, G. 78 46 28 S 73 49W
Elena 95 42 55N 25 53 E
Elephant Butte Reservoir 38 33 9N 107 11W
Elephant I. 5 61 0 S 55 0W
Elesbão Veloso 74 6 13 S 42 8W
Eleshnitsa 95 41 52N 23 36 E
Eleuthera 66 25 0N 76 20W
Eleva 55 44 35N 91 28W
Eleven Point → 13 36 9N 91 5W
Elevenmile Canyon Reservoir 16 38 54N 105 29W
Elfers 17 28 13N 82 43W
Elfin Cove 11 58 12N 136 22W
Elfrida 12 31 41N 109 41W
Elgin, Canada 61 45 48N 65 10W
Elgin, U.K. 84 57 39N 3 20W
Elgin, Ill. 21 42 2N 88 17W
Elgin, Iowa 23 42 57N 91 38W
Elgin, Kans. 24 37 0N 96 17W
Elgin, Minn. 30 44 8N 92 15W
Elgin, N. Dak. 41 46 24N 101 51W
Elgin, Nebr. 34 41 59N 98 5W
Elgin, Nev. 35 37 21N 114 32W
Elgin, Okla. 43 34 47N 98 18W
Elgin, Oreg. 44 45 34N 117 55W
Elgin, S.C. 46 34 10N 80 48W
Elgin, Tex. 51 30 21N 97 22W
Elgon, Mt. 122 1 10N 34 30 E
Eli 34 42 57N 101 29W
Eliase 111 8 21 S 130 48 E
Elida, N. Mex. 38 33 57N 103 39W
Elida, Ohio 42 40 47N 84 12W
Elim 11 64 37N 162 15W
Elim Indian Reservation 11 64 40N 162 0W
Elin Pelin 95 42 40N 23 36 E
Eliot 26 43 7N 70 47W
Elisabethville = Lubumbashi 123 11 40 S 27 28 E
Eliseu Martins 74 8 13 S 43 42W
Elista 99 46 16N 44 14 E
Elizabeth, Australia 127 34 42 S 138 41 E
Elizabeth, Colo. 16 39 22N 104 36W
Elizabeth, Ill. 21 42 19N 90 13W
Elizabeth, La. 25 30 52N 92 48W
Elizabeth, Minn. 30 46 23N 96 8W
Elizabeth, N.J. 37 40 40N 74 13W
Elizabeth, W. Va. 54 39 4N 81 24W
Elizabeth, C. 53 47 21N 124 19W
Elizabeth City 40 36 18N 76 14W
Elizabeth Islands 28 41 27N 70 47W
Elizabethton 49 36 21N 82 13W
Elizabethtown, Ill. 21 37 27N 88 18W
Elizabethtown, Ky. 49 37 42N 85 52W
Elizabethtown, N.C. 40 34 38N 78 37W
Elizabethtown, N.Y. 39 44 13N 73 36W
Elizabethtown, Pa. 45 40 9N 76 36W
Elizabethville 45 40 33N 76 49W
Elk 14 39 8N 123 43W
Elk →, Ala. 10 34 46N 87 16W
Elk →, Kans. 24 37 15N 95 41W
Elk →, Md. 27 39 26N 76 1W
Elk →, W. Va. 54 38 21N 81 38W
Elk City, Idaho 20 45 50N 115 26W
Elk City, Kans. 24 37 18N 95 55W
Elk City, Okla. 43 35 25N 99 25W
Elk City Lake 24 37 17N 95 47W
Elk County ◇, Kans. 24 37 30N 96 15W
Elk County ◇, Pa. 45 41 35N 78 45W
Elk Cr. → 47 44 15N 102 22W
Elk Creek, Calif. 14 39 36N 122 32W
Elk Creek, Nebr. 34 40 17N 96 8W
Elk Falls 24 37 22N 96 11W
Elk Garden 54 39 23N 79 9W
Elk Grove 14 38 25N 121 22W
Elk Hill 45 41 42N 75 32W
Elk Horn 23 41 36N 95 3W
Elk Island Nat. Park 62 53 35N 112 59W
Elk L. 29 44 50N 85 20W
Elk Lake 60 47 40N 80 25W
Elk Mound 55 44 52N 91 42W
Elk Mountain 56 41 41N 106 25W
Elk Mt. 56 41 38N 106 32W
Elk Neck 27 39 31N 75 57W
Elk Park 40 36 10N 81 59W
Elk Point, Canada 63 53 54N 110 55W
Elk Point, U.S.A. 47 42 41N 96 41W
Elk Rapids 29 44 54N 85 25W
Elk River, Idaho 20 46 47N 116 11W
Elk River, Minn. 30 45 18N 93 35W
Elk Springs 16 40 21N 108 27W
Elk Valley 49 36 29N 84 15W
Elkader 23 42 51N 91 24W
Elkatawa 49 37 34N 83 25W
Elkhart, Ill. 21 40 1N 89 29W
Elkhart, Ind. 22 41 41N 85 58W
Elkhart, Iowa 23 41 48N 93 31W
Elkhart, Kans. 24 37 0N 101 54W
Elkhart, Tex. 51 31 38N 95 35W
Elkhart County ◇ 22 41 35N 85 50W
Elkhart Lake 55 43 50N 88 1W
Elkhorn, Canada 63 49 59N 101 14W
Elkhorn, U.S.A. 55 42 40N 88 33W
Elkhorn → 34 41 8N 96 19W
Elkhorn City 49 37 18N 82 21W
Elkhovo 95 42 10N 26 40 E
Elkin 40 36 15N 80 51W
Elkins, N. Mex. 38 33 42N 104 4W
Elkins, W. Va. 54 38 55N 79 51W
Elkland, Mo. 32 37 27N 93 2W
Elkland, Pa. 45 41 59N 77 19W
Elkmont 10 34 56N 86 58W
Elko, Canada 62 49 20N 115 10W
Elko, Ga. 18 32 20N 83 42W
Elko, Minn. 30 44 34N 93 19W
Elko, Nev. 35 40 50N 115 46W
Elko County ◇ 35 41 10N 115 20W
Elkol 56 41 43N 110 37W
Elkridge 27 39 13N 76 43W
Elkton, Ky. 48 36 49N 87 9W
Elkton, Md. 27 39 36N 75 50W
Elkton, Mich. 29 43 49N 83 11W
Elkton, Minn. 30 43 40N 92 42W
Elkton, Oreg. 44 43 38N 123 34W
Elkton, S. Dak. 47 44 14N 96 29W
Elkton, Va. 54 38 25N 78 37W
Elkville 21 37 55N 89 14W
Ella 55 44 32N 92 3W
Ellaville 18 32 14N 84 19W
Ellef Ringnes I. 4 78 30N 102 2W
Ellenboro 54 39 16N 81 3W
Ellenburg 39 44 54N 73 48W
Ellendale, Del. 27 38 48N 75 26W
Ellendale, Minn. 30 43 52N 93 18W
Ellendale, N. Dak. 41 46 0N 98 32W
Ellensburg 53 46 59N 120 34W
Ellenton 18 31 11N 83 35W
Ellenville 39 41 43N 74 24W
Ellerbe 40 35 4N 79 46W
Ellesmere I. 4 79 30N 80 0W
Ellesworth Land 5 76 0 S 89 0W
Ellettsville 22 39 14N 86 38W
Ellice Is. = Tuvalu ■ 124 8 0 S 178 0 E
Ellicott City 27 39 16N 76 48W
Ellicottville 39 42 17N 78 40W
Ellijay 18 34 42N 84 29W
Ellington, Conn. 28 41 54N 72 28W
Ellington, Mo. 32 37 14N 90 58W
Ellington, N.Y. 39 42 13N 79 7W
Ellinwood 24 38 21N 98 35W
Elliot Lake 60 46 25N 82 35W
Elliott, Iowa 23 41 9N 95 10W
Elliott, Md. 27 38 38N 75 59W
Elliott, Miss. 31 33 11N 89 45W
Elliott, N. Dak. 41 46 24N 97 49W

Elliott
Escoma

Elliott, S.C. 46 34 6N 80 10W
Elliott County ◇ 49 38 5N 83 5W
Elliott Key 17 25 27N 80 12W
Elliott Knob 54 38 10N 79 19W
Ellis, Idaho 20 44 42N 114 3W
Ellis, Kans. 24 38 56N 99 34W
Ellis, Nebr. 34 40 13N 96 53W
Ellis County ◇, Kans. 24 38 45N 99 15W
Ellis County ◇, Okla. 43 36 20N 99 50W
Ellis County ◇, Tex. 51 32 24N 96 51W
Ellis Grove 21 38 1N 89 55W
Elliston 33 46 33N 112 26W
Ellisville 31 31 36N 89 12W
Ellon 84 57 21N 2 5W
Ellore = Eluru 109 16 48N 81 8 E
Elloree 46 33 32N 80 34W
Ells → 62 57 18N 111 40W
Ellsinore 32 36 56N 90 45W
Ellston 23 40 51N 94 7W
Ellsworth, Kans. 24 38 44N 98 14W
Ellsworth, Maine 26 44 33N 68 25W
Ellsworth, Mich. 29 45 10N 85 15W
Ellsworth, Minn. 30 43 31N 96 1W
Ellsworth, Nebr. 34 42 4N 102 17W
Ellsworth, Wis. 55 44 44N 92 29W
Ellsworth County ◇ 24 38 45N 98 15W
Ellsworth Land 5 76 0 S 89 0W
Ellsworth Mts. 5 78 30 S 85 0W
Ellwood City 45 40 52N 80 17W
Ellzey 17 29 19N 82 48W
Elm → 47 44 21N 102 42W
Elm City 40 35 48N 77 52W
Elm Cr. → 51 28 42N 99 59W
Elm Creek 34 40 43N 99 22W
Elm Fork 43 34 53N 99 19W
Elm L. 47 45 51N 98 42W
Elma, Canada 63 49 52N 95 55W
Elma, Iowa 23 43 15N 92 26W
Elma, Wash. 53 47 0N 123 25W
Elmalı 106 36 44N 29 56 E
Elmdale 24 38 22N 96 39W
Elmer, Mo. 32 39 57N 92 39W
Elmer, N.J. 37 39 36N 75 10W
Elmer, Okla. 43 34 29N 99 21W
Elmer City 53 48 0N 118 58W
Elmhurst 21 41 53N 87 56W
Elmira, Idaho 20 48 29N 116 27W
Elmira, N.Y. 39 42 6N 76 48W
Elmira Heights 39 42 8N 76 50W
Elmo, Kans. 24 38 41N 97 14W
Elmo, Mont. 33 47 50N 114 21W
Elmo, Utah 52 39 23N 110 49W
Elmodel 18 31 21N 84 29W
Elmont 39 40 43N 73 43W
Elmore, Ala. 10 32 32N 86 19W
Elmore, Minn. 30 43 30N 94 5W
Elmore City 43 34 37N 97 24W
Elmore County ◇, Ala. 10 32 32N 86 13W
Elmore County ◇, Idaho 20 43 30N 115 30W
Elmwood, Ill. 21 40 47N 89 58W
Elmwood, Nebr. 34 40 50N 96 18W
Elmwood, Wis. 55 44 47N 92 9W
Elmwood Park 21 41 56N 87 49W
Elnora 22 38 53N 87 5W
Elora 48 35 1N 86 21W
Elorza 70 7 3N 69 31W
Eloy 12 32 45N 111 33W
Elrosa 30 45 34N 94 57W
Elrose 63 51 12N 108 0W
Elroy 55 43 45N 90 16W
Elsa 50 26 18N 97 59W
Elsah 21 38 57N 90 22W
Elsas 60 48 32N 82 55W
Elsberry 32 39 10N 90 47W
Elsie, Mich. 29 43 5N 84 23W
Elsie, Nebr. 34 40 51N 101 23W
Elsie, Oreg. 44 45 52N 123 36W
Elsinore = Helsingør 97 56 2N 12 35 E
Elsinore 52 38 41N 112 9W
Elsinore L. 15 33 40N 117 21W
Elsinore Lake 15 33 40N 117 20W
Elsmere, Del. 27 39 44N 75 35W
Elsmere, Nebr. 34 42 10N 100 11W
Elsmore 24 37 48N 95 9W
Elsworth, L. 43 34 49N 98 22W
Eltham 128 39 26 S 174 19 E
Eltopia 53 46 27N 119 1W
Eluru 109 16 48N 81 8 E
Elvas 91 38 50N 7 10W
Elverson 45 40 9N 75 50W
Elverum 97 60 53N 11 34 E
Elvins 32 37 50N 90 32W
Elwood, Ill. 21 41 24N 88 7W
Elwood, Ind. 22 40 17N 85 50W
Elwood, Kans. 24 39 45N 94 52W
Elwood, N.J. 37 39 35N 74 43W
Elwood, Nebr. 34 40 36N 99 52W
Elwood Reservoir 34 40 42N 99 55W
Ely, U.K. 83 52 24N 0 16 E
Ely, Iowa 23 41 52N 91 35W
Ely, Minn. 30 47 55N 91 51W
Ely, Nev. 35 39 15N 114 54W
Elyashiv 104 32 23N 34 55 E
Elyria, Kans. 24 38 17N 97 38W
Elyria, Nebr. 34 41 41N 99 0W
Elyria, Ohio 42 41 22N 82 7W
Emāmrūd 107 36 30N 55 0 E
Emanuel County ◇ 18 32 40N 82 20W
Emba 100 48 50N 58 8 E
Emba → 100 46 38N 53 14 E
Embarcación 76 23 10 S 64 0W
Embarras → 21 38 39N 87 37W
Embarras Portage 63 58 27N 111 28W
Embarrass 55 44 40N 88 42W
Embetsu 116 44 44N 141 47 E
Embira → 72 7 19 S 70 15W
Embrun 90 44 34N 6 30 E
Embu 122 0 32 S 37 38 E
Emden, Germany 88 53 22N 7 12 E
Emden, U.S.A. 21 40 18N 89 29W
Emelle 10 32 44N 88 19W
'Emeq Yizre'el 104 32 35N 35 12 E
Emerado 41 47 55N 97 22W
Emerald 127 23 32 S 148 10 E
Emerson, Canada 63 49 0N 97 10W
Emerson, Ark. 13 33 6N 93 11W
Emerson, Ga. 18 34 8N 84 45W
Emerson, Nebr. 34 42 17N 96 44W
Emerson L. 15 34 27N 116 23W
Emery, S. Dak. 47 43 36N 97 37W
Emery, Utah 52 38 55N 111 15W
Emery County ◇ 52 39 0N 110 45W
Emigrant Gap 14 39 19N 120 38W
Emilia-Romagna □ 94 44 33N 10 40 E
Emily 30 46 44N 93 58W
Emine, Nos 95 42 40N 27 56 E
Eminece 32 37 9N 91 21W
Eminence 49 38 22N 85 11W
Emlenton 45 41 11N 79 43W
Emmalane 18 32 46N 82 0W
Emmaus 45 40 32N 75 30W
Emmeloord 87 52 44N 5 46 E
Emmen 87 52 48N 6 57 E
Emmet, Ark. 13 33 44N 93 28W
Emmet, Nebr. 34 42 29N 98 49W
Emmet County ◇, Iowa 23 43 20N 94 40W
Emmet County ◇, Mich. 29 45 30N 84 55W
Emmetsburg 23 43 7N 94 41W
Emmett, Idaho 20 43 52N 116 30W
Emmett, Kans. 24 39 19N 96 3W
Emmett, Mich. 29 42 59N 82 46W
Emmitsburg 27 39 42N 77 20W
Emmonak 11 62 46N 164 30W
Emmons 30 43 30N 93 29W
Emmons County ◇ 41 46 20N 100 10W
Emmorton 27 39 30N 76 20W
Emona 95 42 43N 27 53 E
Emory 51 32 52N 95 46W
Emory Peak 50 29 15N 103 18W
Empalme 64 28 1N 110 49W
Empangeni 123 28 50 S 31 52 E
Empedrado 76 28 0 S 58 46W
Emperor Seamount Chain 124 40 0N 170 0 E
Empire, Calif. 14 37 38N 120 54W
Empire, Colo. 16 39 46N 105 41W
Empire, Ga. 18 32 21N 83 18W
Empire, La. 25 29 23N 89 36W
Empire, Mich. 29 44 49N 86 4W
Empire, Nev. 35 40 35N 119 21W
Empire City 43 34 25N 98 2W
Empire Reservoir 16 40 16N 104 12W
Emporia, Kans. 24 38 25N 96 11W
Emporia, Va. 54 36 42N 77 32W
Emporium 45 41 31N 78 14W
Empress 63 50 57N 110 0W
Ems → 88 52 37N 9 26 E
Emu 114 43 40N 128 6 E
En Gedi 104 31 28N 35 25 E
En Gev 104 32 47N 35 38 E
En Harod 104 32 33N 35 22 E
'En Kerem 104 31 47N 35 6 E
En Nahud 121 12 45N 28 25 E
Ena 117 35 25N 137 25 E
Enambú 70 1 1N 70 17W
Enaratoli 111 3 55 S 136 21 E
Enard B. 84 58 5N 5 20W
Encampment 56 41 12N 106 47W
Encantadas, Serra 77 30 40 S 53 0W
Encanto, C. 111 15 45N 121 38 E
Encarnación 77 27 15 S 55 50W
Encarnación de Diaz 64 21 30N 102 13W
Encinal 51 28 2N 99 21W
Encinillas 64 29 14N 106 18W
Encinitas 15 33 3N 117 17W
Encino, N. Mex. 38 34 39N 105 28W
Encino, Tex. 50 26 56N 98 8W
Encontrados 70 9 3N 72 14W
Encounter B. 127 35 45 S 138 45 E
Encruzilhada 75 15 31 S 40 54W
Endau 112 2 40N 103 38 E
Endau → 112 2 30N 103 30 E
Ende 111 8 45 S 121 40 E
Endeavour 63 52 10N 102 39W
Endeavour Str. 127 10 45 S 142 0 E
Enderbury I. 124 3 8 S 171 5W
Enderby 62 50 35N 119 10W
Enderby Land 5 66 0 S 53 0 E
Enderlin 41 46 38N 97 36W
Enders 34 40 27N 101 32W
Enders Reservoir 34 40 25N 101 31W
Endicott, N.Y. 39 42 6N 76 4W
Endicott, Nebr. 34 40 5N 97 6W
Endicott, Wash. 53 46 56N 117 41W
Endicott Mts. 11 68 0N 152 0W
Endimari → 72 8 46 S 66 7W
Endwell 39 42 6N 76 2W
Ene → 72 11 10 S 74 18W
Enez 99 40 45N 26 5 E
Enfield, U.K. 83 51 39N 0 4W
Enfield, Conn. 28 41 58N 72 36W
Enfield, Ill. 21 38 6N 88 20W
Enfield, N.C. 40 36 11N 77 41W
Enfield, N.H. 36 43 39N 72 9W
Enfield Center 36 43 38N 72 8W
Engadin 88 46 45N 10 10 E
Engaño, C., Dom. Rep. 67 18 30N 68 20W
Engaño, C., Phil. 111 18 35N 122 23 E
Engel 38 33 4N 107 2W
Engelhard 40 35 30N 75 58W
Engels 98 51 28N 46 6 E
Engemann L. 63 58 0N 106 55W
Enggano 110 5 20 S 102 40 E
Enghien 87 50 37N 4 2 E
Engkilili 110 1 3N 111 42 E
England 13 34 33N 91 58W
England □ 86 53 0N 2 0W
Englebright L. 14 39 14N 121 16W
Englee 61 50 45N 56 5W
Englehart 60 47 49N 79 52W
Engler L. 63 59 8N 106 52W
Englewood, Colo. 16 39 39N 104 59W
Englewood, Fla. 17 26 58N 82 21W
Englewood, Kans. 24 37 2N 99 59W
Englewood, Ohio 42 39 53N 84 18W
Englewood, Tenn. 49 35 26N 84 29W
English 22 38 20N 86 28W
English → 63 50 35N 93 30W
English Bazar = Ingraj Bazar 109 24 58N 88 10 E
English Channel 86 50 0N 2 0W
English Creek 37 39 20N 74 42W
English River 60 49 14N 91 0W
Englishtown 37 40 18N 74 22W
Enid, Miss. 31 34 7N 89 56W
Enid, Okla. 43 36 24N 97 53W
Enid L. 31 34 9N 89 54W
Eniwetok 124 11 30N 162 15 E
Enka 40 35 33N 82 39W
Enkhuizen 87 52 42N 5 17 E
Enloe 51 33 26N 95 39W
Enna 94 37 34N 14 15 E
Ennadai 63 61 8N 100 53W
Ennadai L. 63 61 0N 101 0W
Ennedi 121 17 15N 22 0 E
Ennis, Ireland 85 52 51N 8 59W
Ennis, Mont. 33 45 21N 111 44W
Ennis, Tex. 51 32 20N 96 38W
Enniscorthy 85 52 30N 6 35W
Enniskillen 85 54 20N 7 40W
Ennistimon 85 52 56N 9 18W
Enns → 88 48 14N 14 32 E
Eno → 40 36 5N 78 50W
Enoch 52 37 47N 113 2W
Enochs 50 33 52N 102 46W
Enola 34 41 54N 97 28W
Enontekiö 96 68 23N 23 37 E
Enoree → 46 34 26N 81 25W
Enosburg Falls 36 44 55N 72 48W
Enping 115 22 16N 112 21 E
Enriquillo, L. 67 18 20N 72 5W
Enschede 87 52 13N 6 53 E
Ensenada, Argentina 76 34 55 S 57 55W
Ensenada, Mexico 64 31 50N 116 50W
Ensenada, Puerto Rico 57 17 58N 66 56W
Ensenada, U.S.A. 38 36 44N 106 32W
Ensenada, La 78 41 12 S 72 33W
Enshi 115 30 18N 109 29 E
Ensign 24 37 39N 100 14W
Ensley 17 30 31N 87 16W
Entebbe 122 0 4N 32 28 E
Enterprise, Canada 62 60 47N 115 45W
Enterprise, Ala. 10 31 19N 85 51W
Enterprise, Calif. 14 40 30N 122 22W
Enterprise, Kans. 24 38 54N 97 7W
Enterprise, La. 25 31 54N 91 53W
Enterprise, Miss. 31 32 10N 88 49W
Enterprise, Oreg. 44 45 25N 117 17W
Enterprise, Utah 52 37 34N 113 43W
Entiat 53 47 40N 120 13W
Entre Ríos, Bolivia 76 21 30 S 64 25W
Entre Rios, Bahia, Brazil 75 11 56 S 38 5W
Entre Rios, Pará, Brazil 73 5 24 S 54 21W
Entre Ríos □ 76 30 30 S 58 30W
Entrecasteaux, Pt. d' 128 34 50 S 115 56 E
Enugu 120 6 20N 7 30 E
Enugu Ezike 120 7 0N 7 29 E
Enumclaw 53 47 12N 121 59W
Envigado 70 6 10N 75 35W
Enville 48 35 23N 88 26W
Envira 72 7 18 S 70 13W
Eolia 32 39 14N 91 1W
Eólie, I. 94 38 30N 14 50 E
Eoline 10 32 59N 87 8W
Epe 87 52 21N 5 59 E
Épernay 90 49 3N 3 56 E
Epes 10 32 42N 88 7W
Ephesus 106 37 50N 27 33 E
Ephraim 52 39 22N 111 35W
Ephrata, Pa. 45 40 11N 76 11W
Ephrata, Wash. 53 47 19N 119 33W
Épinal 90 48 10N 6 27 E
Epira 71 5 5N 57 20W
Epleys 48 36 56N 86 56W
Epping, U.K. 83 51 42N 0 8 E
Epping, N. Dak. 41 48 17N 103 21W
Epping, N.H. 36 43 2N 71 4W
Epps 25 32 36N 91 29W
Epukiro 123 21 40 S 19 9 E
Equality 21 37 44N 88 20W
Equatorial Guinea ■ 122 2 0 S 8 0 E
Equeipa 71 5 22N 62 43W
Equinox Mt. 36 43 11N 73 9W
Er Rahad 121 12 45N 30 32 E
Er Rif 120 35 1N 4 1W
Er Roseires 121 11 55N 34 30 E
Erath 25 29 58N 92 2W
Erath County ◇ 51 32 13N 98 12W
Erāwadī Myit → =
Irrawaddy → 109 15 50N 95 6 E
Erbacon 54 38 31N 80 35W
Ercha 101 69 45N 147 20 E
Erciyaş Dağı 106 38 30N 35 30 E
Erdao Jiang → 114 43 0N 127 0 E
Erebato → 71 5 54N 64 16W
Erebus, Mt. 5 77 35 S 167 0 E
Erechim 77 27 35 S 52 15W
Ereğli, Turkey 106 41 15N 31 30 E
Ereğli, Turkey 106 37 31N 34 4 E
Erenhot 114 43 48N 111 59 E
Eresma → 91 41 26N 40 45W
Erewadi Myitwanya 109 15 30N 95 0 E
Erfurt 88 50 58N 11 2 E
Ergani 106 38 17N 39 49 E
Ergene → 95 41 1N 26 22 E
Ergeni Vozyshennost 99 47 0N 44 0 E
Ergun Zuoqi 114 50 47N 121 31 E
Erhard 30 46 29N 96 6W
Eriboll, L. 84 58 28N 4 41W
Érice 94 38 4N 12 34 E
Erick 43 35 13N 99 52W
Ericson 34 41 47N 98 41W
Eridu 17 30 18N 83 45W
Erie, Colo. 16 40 3N 105 3W
Erie, Ill. 21 41 39N 90 5W
Erie, Kans. 24 37 34N 95 15W
Erie, N. Dak. 41 47 7N 97 23W
Erie, Pa. 45 42 8N 80 5W
Erie Canal 39 43 5N 78 43W
Erie County ◇, N.Y. 39 42 50N 78 45W
Erie County ◇, Ohio 42 41 24N 82 33W
Erie County ◇, Pa. 45 42 0N 80 0W
Erie L. 42 41 50N 82 0W
Erigavo 105 10 35N 47 20 E
Eriksdale 63 50 52N 98 7W
Erímanthos 95 37 57N 21 50 E
Erimo-misaki 116 41 50N 143 15 E
Erin 48 36 19N 87 42W
Eritrea □ 121 14 0N 41 0 E
Erlangen 88 49 35N 11 0 E
Erlanger 49 39 1N 84 36W
Erling, L. 13 33 3N 93 32W
Ermelo 87 52 18N 5 35 E
Ermenak 106 36 38N 33 0 E
Ermoúpolis = Síros 95 37 28N 24 57 E
Ernakulam = Cochin 108 9 59N 76 22 E
Erne → 85 54 30N 8 16W
Erne, Lough 85 54 26N 7 46W
Ernul 40 35 15N 77 4W
Erode 108 11 24N 77 45 E
Erramala Hills 108 15 30N 78 15 E
Errigal, Mt. 85 55 2N 8 8W
Erris Hd. 85 54 19N 10 0W
Errol 36 44 47N 71 8W
Erskine 30 47 40N 96 0W
Erwin, N.C. 40 35 20N 78 41W
Erwin, S. Dak. 47 44 29N 97 27W
Erwin, Tenn. 49 36 9N 82 25W
Erwinville 25 30 32N 91 24W
Erzgebirge 88 50 25N 13 0 E
Erzin 101 50 15N 95 10 E
Erzincan 106 39 46N 39 30 E
Erzurum 106 39 57N 41 15 E
Es Sahrâ' Esh Sharqîya 121 26 0N 33 30 E
Es Sînâ' 121 29 0N 34 0 E
Esan-Misaki 116 41 40N 141 10 E
Esashi, Hokkaidō, Japan 116 44 56N 142 35 E
Esashi, Hokkaidō, Japan 116 41 52N 140 7 E
Esbjerg 97 55 29N 8 29 E
Esbon 24 39 49N 98 26W
Escada 74 8 22 S 35 8W
Escalante 52 37 47N 111 36W
Escalante → 52 37 24N 110 57W
Escalante Desert 52 37 50N 113 20W
Escalón, Mexico 64 26 46N 104 20W
Escalon, U.S.A. 14 37 48N 121 0W
Escambia → 17 30 32N 87 11W
Escambia County ◇, Ala. 10 31 7N 87 4W
Escambia County ◇, Fla. 17 30 30N 87 30W
Escanaba 29 45 45N 87 4W
Escanaba → 29 45 47N 87 3W
Escatawpa → 31 30 26N 88 33W
Escatawpu → 31 30 25N 88 35W
Esch-sur-Alzette 87 49 32N 6 0 E
Escobal 57 9 9N 79 58W
Escoma 72 15 40 S 69 8W

Fisher County Fort Oglethorpe

Fisher County ◇ 50 32 45N 100 23W
Fishers 22 39 57N 86 1W
Fishers I. 39 41 15N 72 0W
Fishers Peak 16 37 6N 104 28W
Fishguard 83 51 59N 4 59W
Fishing Bridge 56 44 29N 110 22W
Fishing Creek 27 38 20N 76 14W
Fishing L. 63 52 10N 95 24W
Fishlake National Forest 52 38 40N 112 20W
Fishtrap L. 49 37 25N 82 26W
Fisk 32 36 47N 90 12W
Fiskdale 28 42 7N 72 7W
Fitchburg 28 42 35N 71 48W
Fitri, L. 121 12 50N 17 28 E
Fittstown 43 34 37N 96 38W
Fitz Roy 78 47 0 S 67 0W
Fitzgerald, Canada 62 59 51N 111 36W
Fitzgerald, U.S.A. 18 31 43N 83 15W
Fitzhugh 13 35 22N 91 19W
Fitzroy → 126 17 31 S 123 35 E
Fitzroy Crossing 126 18 9 S 125 38 E
Fiume = Rijeka 94 45 20N 14 21 E
Fizi 122 4 17 S 28 55 E
Flagler 16 39 18N 103 4W
Flagler Beach 17 29 29N 81 8W
Flagler County ◇ 17 29 30N 81 20W
Flagstaff 12 35 12N 111 39W
Flagstaff L., Maine 26 45 12N 70 19W
Flagstaff L., Oreg. 44 42 35N 119 45W
Flaherty 48 37 50N 86 4W
Flaherty I. 60 56 15N 79 15W
Flåm 97 60 50N 7 7 E
Flambeau → 55 45 18N 91 14W
Flamborough Hd. 82 54 8N 0 4W
Flaming Gorge Dam 52 40 55N 109 25W
Flaming Gorge National Recreation Area 56 41 10N 109 25W
Flaming Gorge Reservoir 56 41 10N 109 25W
Flamingo 17 25 8N 80 57W
Flamingo, Teluk 111 5 30 S 138 0 E
Flanagan 21 40 53N 88 52W
Flanders = Flandres 87 51 10N 3 15 E
Flandre Occidental □ 87 51 0N 3 0 E
Flandre Orientale □ 87 51 0N 4 0 E
Flandreau 47 44 3N 96 36W
Flandres 87 51 10N 3 15 E
Flandres, Plaines des 87 51 10N 3 15 E
Flannan Is. 86 58 9N 7 52W
Flasher 41 46 27N 101 14W
Flåsjön 96 64 5N 15 40 E
Flat 11 62 28N 158 1W
Flat →, Canada 62 61 51N 128 0W
Flat →, Mich. 29 42 56N 85 20W
Flat →, N.C. 40 36 5N 78 49W
Flat Lick 49 36 50N 83 46W
Flat River 32 37 51N 90 31W
Flat River Res. 28 41 42N 71 37W
Flat Rock, Ala. 10 34 46N 85 42W
Flat Rock, Ill. 21 38 54N 87 40W
Flat Rock, Mich. 29 42 6N 83 17W
Flat Top Mt. 52 40 22N 112 11W
Flat Woods 48 35 29N 87 50W
Flatey, Barðastrandarsýsla, Iceland 96 66 10N 17 52W
Flatey, Suður-Þingeyjarsýsla, Iceland 96 65 22N 22 56W
Flathead → 33 47 22N 114 47W
Flathead County ◇ 33 48 15N 113 30W
Flathead Indian Reservation 33 47 35N 114 30W
Flathead L. 33 47 51N 114 8W
Flathead National Forest 33 47 45N 113 10W
Flatonia 51 29 41N 97 7W
Flatrock → 22 39 12N 85 56W
Flattery, C. 53 48 23N 124 29W
Flatwillow Cr. → 33 46 56N 107 55W
Flatwoods, Ky. 48 38 31N 82 43W
Flatwoods, La. 25 31 24N 92 52W
Flatwoods, W. Va. 54 38 43N 80 39W
Flaxton 41 48 54N 102 24W
Flaxville 33 48 48N 105 11W
Fleetwood, U.K. 82 53 55N 3 1W
Fleetwood, U.S.A. 45 40 27N 75 49W
Fleischmanns 39 42 10N 74 32W
Flekkefjord 97 58 18N 6 39 E
Fleming 16 40 41N 102 50W
Fleming County ◇ 49 38 20N 83 40W
Flemingsburg 49 38 25N 83 45W
Flemington, N.J. 37 40 31N 74 52W
Flemington, W. Va. 54 39 16N 80 8W
Flensburg 30 45 57N 94 32W
Flesko, Tanjung 111 0 29N 124 30 E
Fletcher, N.C. 40 35 26N 82 30W
Fletcher, Okla. 43 34 50N 98 15W
Fletcher Pond 29 45 1N 83 47W
Fletton 83 52 34N 0 13W
Flin Flon 63 54 46N 101 53W
Flinders → 127 17 36 S 140 36 E
Flinders B. 126 34 19 S 115 19 E
Flinders I. 127 40 0 S 148 0 E
Flinders Ranges 127 31 30 S 138 30 E
Flint, U.K. 82 53 15N 3 7W
Flint, U.S.A. 29 43 1N 83 41W
Flint →, Ala. 10 34 30N 86 30W
Flint →, Ga. 18 30 57N 84 34W
Flint, I. 125 11 26 S 151 48W
Flint Hills 24 38 0N 96 40W
Flintstone 27 39 42N 78 34W
Flippin 13 36 17N 92 36W
Flodden 82 55 37N 2 8W
Flomaton 10 31 0N 87 16W
Flomot 50 34 14N 100 59W
Flora, Ill. 21 38 40N 88 29W
Flora, Ind. 22 40 33N 86 31W
Flora, Miss. 31 32 33N 90 19W
Flora, Oreg. 44 45 54N 117 19W
Flora Vista 38 36 48N 108 3W
Florahome 17 29 44N 81 54W
Floral 13 35 36N 91 45W
Floral City 17 28 45N 82 17W
Florala 10 31 0N 86 20W
Florânia 74 6 8 S 36 49W
Florence = Firenze 94 43 47N 11 15 E
Florence, Ala. 10 34 48N 87 41W
Florence, Ariz. 12 33 2N 111 23W
Florence, Ark. 13 33 46N 91 39W
Florence, Colo. 16 38 23N 105 8W
Florence, Kans. 24 38 15N 96 56W
Florence, Ky. 49 39 0N 84 38W
Florence, Md. 27 39 20N 77 8W
Florence, Miss. 31 32 9N 90 8W
Florence, Mo. 32 38 35N 92 59W
Florence, Mont. 33 46 38N 114 5W
Florence, Oreg. 44 43 58N 124 7W
Florence, S.C. 46 34 12N 79 46W
Florence, S. Dak. 47 45 3N 97 20W
Florence, Tex. 51 30 51N 97 48W
Florence, Wis. 55 45 56N 88 15W
Florence County ◇, S.C. 46 34 0N 79 45W
Florence County ◇, Wis. 55 45 50N 88 20W
Florennes 87 50 15N 4 35 E
Florenville 87 49 40N 5 19 E
Flores, Brazil 74 7 51 S 37 59W
Flores, Guat. 66 16 59N 89 50W
Flores, Indonesia 111 8 35 S 121 0 E
Flores I. 62 49 20N 126 10W
Flores Sea 110 6 30 S 124 0 E
Floresta 74 8 40 S 37 26W
Floresville 51 29 8N 98 10W
Florey 50 32 27N 102 36W
Florham Park 37 40 47N 74 23W
Floriano 74 6 50 S 43 0W
Florianópolis 77 27 30 S 48 30W
Florida, Cuba 66 21 32N 78 14W
Florida, Puerto Rico 57 18 22N 66 34W
Florida, Uruguay 77 34 7 S 56 10W
Florida □ 17 28 0N 82 0W
Florida B. 17 25 0N 80 45W
Florida City 17 25 27N 80 29W
Florida Keys 17 24 40N 81 0W
Florida Ridge 17 27 38N 80 24W
Florien 25 31 27N 93 28W
Floris 23 40 52N 92 20W
Florissant, Colo. 16 38 57N 105 17W
Florissant, Mo. 32 38 48N 90 20W
Florissant National Monument 16 38 54N 105 17W
Florø 97 61 35N 5 1 E
Flower's Cove 61 51 14N 56 46W
Floyd, Iowa 23 43 8N 92 44W
Floyd, N. Mex. 38 34 13N 103 35W
Floyd, Va. 54 36 55N 80 19W
Floyd → 23 42 29N 96 23W
Floyd County ◇, Ga. 18 34 15N 85 10W
Floyd County ◇, Ind. 22 38 20N 85 55W
Floyd County ◇, Iowa 23 43 5N 92 45W
Floyd County ◇, Ky. 49 37 30N 82 45W
Floyd County ◇, Tex. 50 34 0N 101 15W
Floyd County ◇, Va. 54 36 58N 80 25W
Floydada 50 33 59N 101 20W
Fluk 111 1 42 S 127 44 E
Flushing = Vlissingen 87 51 26N 3 34 E
Flushing, Mich. 29 43 4N 83 51W
Flushing, Ohio 42 40 9N 81 4W
Fluvanna County ◇ 54 37 52N 78 16W
Fly → 124 8 25 S 143 0 E
Flying Fish, C. 5 72 6 S 102 29W
Flying H 38 33 2N 105 8W
Flynn 51 31 9N 96 8W
Foam Lake 63 51 40N 103 32W
Foard City 51 33 53N 99 48W
Foard County ◇ 51 33 59N 99 43W
Focşani 95 45 41N 27 15 E
Fogang 115 23 52N 113 30 E
Fóggia 94 41 28N 15 31 E
Fogo 61 49 43N 54 17W
Fogo I. 61 49 40N 54 5W
Foix 90 42 58N 1 38 E
Folda, Nord-Trøndelag, Norway 96 64 41N 10 50 E
Folda, Nordland, Norway 96 67 38N 14 50 E
Foley, Ala. 10 30 24N 87 41W
Foley, Fla. 17 30 4N 83 32W
Foley, Minn. 30 45 40N 93 55W
Foleyet 60 48 15N 82 25W
Folgefonn 97 60 3N 6 23 E
Folkestone 83 51 5N 1 11 E
Folkston 18 30 50N 82 0W
Follett 50 36 26N 100 8W
Folsom, La. 25 30 38N 90 11W
Folsom, N.J. 37 39 38N 74 51W
Folsom, N. Mex. 38 36 51N 103 55W
Folsom, W. Va. 54 39 28N 80 31W
Folsom L. 14 38 42N 121 9W
Fond-du-Lac, Canada 63 59 19N 107 12W
Fond du Lac, U.S.A. 55 43 47N 88 27W
Fond-du-Lac → 63 59 17N 106 0W
Fond du Lac County ◇ 55 43 40N 88 30W
Fond du Lac Indian Reservation 30 46 45N 92 40W
Fonda, Iowa 23 42 35N 94 51W
Fonda, N.Y. 39 42 57N 74 22W
Fonde 49 36 36N 83 53W
Fonseca, G. de 66 13 10N 87 40W
Fontainebleau 90 48 24N 2 40 E
Fontana, Calif. 15 34 6N 117 26W
Fontana, Kans. 24 38 25N 94 51W
Fontana, Wis. 55 42 33N 88 35W
Fontana, L. 78 44 55 S 71 30W
Fontana L. 40 35 27N 83 48W
Fontana Village 40 35 26N 83 50W
Fontanelle 23 41 17N 94 34W
Fontas → 62 58 14N 121 48W
Fonte Boa 70 2 33 S 66 0W
Fontenay-le-Comte 90 46 28N 0 48W
Fontenelle Reservoir 56 42 1N 110 3W
Fontur 96 66 23N 14 32W
Foochow = Fuzhou 115 26 5N 119 16 E
Foosland 21 40 22N 88 26W
Footville 55 42 40N 89 12W
Foping 115 33 41N 108 0 E
Forada 30 45 48N 95 21W
Foraker 43 36 52N 96 34W
Foraker, Mt. 11 62 58N 151 24W
Forbes, Australia 127 33 22 S 148 0 E
Forbes, U.S.A. 41 45 57N 98 47W
Forbing 25 32 24N 93 44W
Ford 24 37 38N 99 45W
Ford → 29 45 41N 87 9W
Ford City, Calif. 15 35 9N 119 27W
Ford City, Pa. 45 40 46N 79 32W
Ford County ◇, Ill. 21 40 30N 88 10W
Ford County ◇, Kans. 24 37 45N 100 0W
Ford Dry L. 15 33 37N 114 59W
Ford I. 19 21 22N 157 58W
Fordland 32 37 9N 92 57W
Fordoche 25 30 36N 91 37W
Fordsville 48 37 38N 86 43W
Fordville 41 48 13N 97 48W
Fordyce, Ark. 13 33 49N 92 25W
Fordyce, Nebr. 34 42 42N 97 22W
Forécariah 120 9 28N 13 10W
Forel, Mt. 4 66 52N 36 55W
Foreman 13 33 43N 94 24W
Foremost 62 49 26N 111 34W
Forest, La. 25 32 47N 91 25W
Forest, Miss. 31 32 22N 89 29W
Forest, Ohio 42 40 48N 83 31W
Forest → 41 48 21N 97 9W
Forest Acres 46 34 1N 80 58W
Forest Center 30 47 48N 91 19W
Forest City, Iowa 23 43 16N 93 39W
Forest City, N.C. 40 35 20N 81 52W
Forest City, Pa. 45 41 39N 75 28W
Forest County ◇, Pa. 45 41 30N 79 10W
Forest County ◇, Wis. 55 45 35N 88 45W
Forest Dale 36 43 48N 73 4W
Forest Grove 44 45 31N 123 7W
Forest Hill, La. 25 31 3N 92 32W
Forest Hill, Md. 27 39 35N 76 23W
Forest Home 10 31 52N 86 50W
Forest Lake 30 45 17N 92 59W
Forest Park 18 33 37N 84 22W
Forest River 41 48 13N 97 28W
Forestburg 62 52 35N 112 1W
Foresthill 14 39 1N 120 49W
Foreston, Minn. 30 45 44N 93 43W
Foreston, S.C. 46 33 38N 80 4W
Forestville, Canada 61 48 48N 69 2W
Forestville, Md. 27 38 51N 76 52W
Forestville, Mich. 29 43 40N 82 37W
Forestville, N.Y. 39 42 28N 79 10W
Forestville, Wis. 55 44 41N 87 29W
Forez, Mts. du 90 45 40N 3 50 E
Forfar 84 56 40N 2 53W
Forgan 43 36 54N 100 32W
Forge Village 28 42 35N 71 29W
Fork Union 54 37 46N 78 16W
Forked Deer → 48 35 56N 89 35W
Forked River 37 39 50N 74 12W
Forkland 10 32 39N 87 53W
Forks 53 47 57N 124 23W
Forks of Salmon 14 41 16N 123 19W
Forkville 31 32 28N 89 40W
Forlì 94 44 14N 12 2 E
Forman 41 46 7N 97 38W
Formby Pt. 82 53 33N 3 7W
Formentera 91 38 43N 1 27 E
Formiga 75 20 27 S 45 25W
Formosa = Taiwan ■ 115 23 30N 121 0 E
Formosa, Argentina 76 26 15 S 58 10W
Formosa, Brazil 75 15 32 S 47 20W
Formosa □ 76 25 0 S 60 0W
Formosa, Serra 73 12 0 S 55 0W
Formosa Bay 122 2 40 S 40 20 E
Formoso → 75 10 34 S 49 56W
Forres 84 57 37N 3 38W
Forrest, Ill. 21 40 45N 88 25W
Forrest, N. Mex. 38 34 48N 103 36W
Forrest City 13 35 1N 90 47W
Forrest County ◇ 31 31 10N 89 13W
Forreston 21 42 8N 89 35W
Forsayth 127 18 33 S 143 34 E
Forsyth, Ga. 18 33 2N 83 56W
Forsyth, Mo. 32 36 41N 93 6W
Forsyth, Mont. 33 46 16N 106 41W
Forsyth County ◇, Ga. 18 34 15N 84 5W
Forsyth County ◇, N.C. 40 36 10N 80 15W
Fort Adams 31 31 5N 91 33W
Fort Albany 60 52 15N 81 35W
Fort Amador 57 8 56N 79 32W
Fort Apache Indian Reservation 12 33 45N 110 0W
Fort Assiniboine 62 54 20N 114 45W
Fort Atkinson, Iowa 23 43 9N 91 56W
Fort Atkinson, Wis. 55 42 56N 88 50W
Fort Augustus 84 57 9N 4 40W
Fort Barnwell 40 35 18N 77 20W
Fort Belknap Agency 33 48 29N 108 45W
Fort Belknap Indian Reservation 33 48 20N 108 40W
Fort Bend County ◇ 51 29 34N 95 49W
Fort Benton 33 47 49N 110 40W
Fort Berthold Indian Reservation 41 47 45N 102 15W
Fort Bidwell 14 41 52N 120 9W
Fort Bragg 14 39 26N 123 48W
Fort Branch 22 38 15N 87 35W
Fort Bridger 56 41 19N 110 23W
Fort Calhoun 34 41 27N 96 2W
Fort Chimo 59 58 6N 68 15W
Fort Chipewyan 63 58 42N 111 8W
Fort Clayton 57 9 0N 79 35W
Fort Cobb 43 35 6N 98 26W
Fort Cobb Reservoir 43 35 10N 98 27W
Fort Collins 16 40 35N 105 5W
Fort-Coulonge 60 45 50N 76 45W
Fort Davis, Panama 57 9 17N 79 56W
Fort Davis, Ala. 10 32 15N 85 43W
Fort Davis, Tex. 50 30 35N 103 54W
Fort-de-France 67 14 36N 61 2W
Fort de Possel = Possel 122 5 5N 19 10 E
Fort Defiance 12 35 45N 109 5W
Fort Deposit 10 31 59N 86 35W
Fort Dick 14 41 52N 124 9W
Fort Dodge 23 42 30N 94 11W
Fort Drum 17 27 32N 80 48W
Fort Duchesne 52 40 17N 109 52W
Fort Edward 39 43 16N 73 35W
Fort Fairfield 26 46 46N 67 50W
Fort Frances 63 48 36N 93 24W
Fort Franklin 58 65 10N 123 30W
Fort Gaines 18 31 36N 85 3W
Fort Garland 16 37 26N 105 26W
Fort Gay 54 38 7N 82 36W
Fort George 60 53 50N 79 0W
Fort Gibson 43 35 48N 95 15W
Fort Gibson L. 43 35 52N 95 14W
Fort Good-Hope 58 66 14N 128 40W
Fort Hall 20 43 2N 112 26W
Fort Hall Indian Reservation 20 43 2N 112 5W
Fort Hancock 50 31 18N 105 51W
Fort Hertz = Putao 109 27 28N 97 30 E
Fort Hope 60 51 30N 88 0W
Fort Jameson = Chipata 123 13 38 S 32 28 E
Fort Jennings 42 40 54N 84 18W
Fort Jesup 25 31 37N 93 24W
Fort Jones 14 41 36N 122 51W
Fort Kent 26 47 15N 68 36W
Fort Klamath 44 42 42N 122 0W
Fort Knox 49 37 54N 85 57W
Fort Lallemand 120 31 13N 6 17 E
Fort-Lamy = Ndjamena 121 12 10N 14 59 E
Fort Laramie 56 42 13N 104 31W
Fort Lauderdale 17 26 7N 80 8W
Fort Lawn 46 34 42N 80 54W
Fort Liard 62 60 14N 123 30W
Fort Liberté 67 19 42N 71 51W
Fort Loudoun L. 49 35 47N 84 15W
Fort Lupton 16 40 5N 104 49W
Fort McDermitt Ind. Res. 44 42 0N 117 42W
Fort McDowell Indian Reservation 12 33 40N 111 50W
Fort Mackay 62 57 12N 111 41W
Fort McKenzie 61 57 20N 69 0W
Fort Macleod 62 49 45N 113 30W
Fort MacMahon 120 29 43N 1 45 E
Fort McMurray 62 56 44N 111 7W
Fort McPherson 58 67 30N 134 55W
Fort Madison 23 40 38N 91 27W
Fort Meade 17 27 45N 81 48W
Fort Mill 46 35 2N 80 57W
Fort Miribel 120 29 25N 2 55 E
Fort Mitchell, Ala. 10 32 20N 85 1W
Fort Mitchell, Ky. 49 39 2N 84 34W
Fort Mitchell, Va. 54 36 55N 78 29W
Fort Mohave Ind. Res. 12 34 55N 114 35W
Fort Morgan 16 40 15N 103 48W
Fort Motte 46 33 44N 80 42W
Fort Myers 17 26 39N 81 52W
Fort Myers Villas 17 26 34N 81 52W
Fort Nelson 62 58 50N 122 44W
Fort Nelson → 62 59 32N 124 0W
Fort Norman 58 64 57N 125 30W
Fort Oglethorpe 18 34 57N 85 16W

Fort Payne Friesland

Fort Payne 10 34 26N 85 43W
Fort Peck 33 48 1N 106 27W
Fort Peck Dam 33 48 0N 106 26W
Fort Peck Indian Reservation 33 48 30N 105 30W
Fort Peck L. 33 48 0N 106 26W
Fort Pierce 17 27 27N 80 20W
Fort Pierre 47 44 21N 100 22W
Fort Plain 39 42 56N 74 37W
Fort Portal 122 0 40N 30 20 E
Fort Providence 62 61 3N 117 40W
Fort Qu'Appelle 63 50 45N 103 50W
Fort Randall Dam 47 43 4N 98 34W
Fort Ransom 41 46 31N 97 56W
Fort Recovery 42 40 25N 84 47W
Fort Resolution 62 61 10N 113 40W
Fort Ripley 30 46 10N 94 22W
Fort Robinson 34 42 40N 103 28W
Fort Roseberry = Mansa 122 11 13 S 28 55 E
Fort Rupert 60 51 30N 78 40W
Fort St. James 62 54 30N 124 10W
Fort St. John 62 56 15N 120 50W
Fort Sandeman 108 31 20N 69 31 E
Fort Saskatchewan 62 53 40N 113 15W
Fort Scott 24 37 50N 94 42W
Fort Severn 60 56 0N 87 40W
Fort Shawnee 42 40 42N 84 7W
Fort Sherman 57 9 22N 79 56W
Fort Shevchenko 99 43 40N 51 20 E
Fort-Sibut 122 5 46N 19 10 E
Fort Simpson 62 61 45N 121 15W
Fort Smith, Canada 62 60 0N 111 51W
Fort Smith, U.S.A. 13 35 23N 94 25W
Fort Stanton 38 33 30N 105 31W
Fort Stockton 50 30 53N 102 53W
Fort Sumner 38 34 28N 104 15W
Fort Supply 43 36 35N 99 35W
Fort Thomas 49 39 5N 84 27W
Fort Thompson 47 44 3N 99 26W
Fort Totten 41 47 59N 99 0W
Fort Totten Indian Reservation 41 47 58N 99 0W
Fort Towson 43 34 0N 95 10W
Fort Trinquet = Bir Mogrein 120 25 10N 11 25W
Fort Valley 18 32 33N 83 53W
Fort Vermilion 62 58 24N 116 0W
Fort Walton Beach 17 30 25N 86 36W
Fort Washakie 56 43 0N 108 53W
Fort Washington 27 38 42N 77 3W
Fort Wayne 22 41 4N 85 9W
Fort White 17 29 55N 82 43W
Fort William 84 56 48N 5 8W
Fort Worth 51 32 45N 97 18W
Fort Yates 41 46 5N 100 38W
Fort Yukon 11 66 34N 145 16W
Fort Yuma Indian Reservation 15 32 45N 114 35W
Fortaleza, Bolivia 72 12 6 S 66 49W
Fortaleza, Brazil 74 3 45 S 38 35W
Forteau 61 51 28N 56 58W
Fortescue 37 39 12N 75 12W
Forth, Firth of 84 56 5N 2 55W
Fortín Coronel Eugenio Garay 73 20 31 S 62 8W
Fortín Garrapatal 73 21 27 S 61 30W
Fortín General Pando 73 19 45 S 59 47W
Fortín Madrejón 73 20 45 S 59 52W
Fortín Uno 78 38 50 S 65 18W
Fortine 33 48 46N 114 54W
Fortrose 84 57 35N 4 10W
Fortsonia 18 34 1N 82 47W
Fortuna, Calif. 14 40 36N 124 9W
Fortuna, Mo. 32 38 34N 92 48W
Fortuna, N. Dak. 41 48 55N 103 47W
Fortuna Ledge 11 61 53N 162 5W
Fortune B. 61 47 30N 55 22W
Fortville 22 39 56N 85 51W
Forūr 107 26 20N 54 30 E
Foshan 115 23 4N 113 5 E
Foss Reservoir 43 35 33N 99 11W
Fossil 44 45 0N 120 9W
Fossil Butte Nat. Mon. 56 41 50N 110 27W
Fossil L. 44 43 19N 120 25W
Fosston 30 47 35N 95 45W
Foster, Ky. 49 38 48N 84 13W
Foster, Nebr. 34 42 16N 97 40W
Foster, Oreg. 44 44 25N 122 40W
Foster, R.I. 28 41 47N 71 44W
Foster → 63 55 47N 105 49W
Foster County ◇ 41 47 30N 99 0W
Foster L. 44 42 59N 119 15W
Fosters 10 33 6N 87 41W
Fostoria, Iowa 23 43 15N 95 9W
Fostoria, Kans. 24 39 26N 96 30W
Fostoria, Ohio 42 41 10N 83 25W
Fougamou 122 1 16 S 10 30 E
Fougères 90 48 21N 1 14W
Fouke 13 33 16N 93 53W
Foul Pt. 108 8 35N 81 18 E
Foula, I. 86 60 10N 2 5W
Foulness I. 83 51 36N 0 55 E
Foulness Pt. 83 51 36N 0 59 E
Foumban 120 5 45N 10 50 E
Fount 49 36 59N 83 50W
Fountain, Colo. 16 38 41N 104 42W
Fountain, Fla. 17 30 29N 85 25W
Fountain, Mich. 29 44 3N 86 11W
Fountain, Minn. 30 43 45N 92 8W
Fountain, N.C. 40 35 41N 77 38W
Fountain City, Ind. 22 39 57N 84 55W
Fountain City, Wis. 55 44 8N 91 43W
Fountain County ◇ 22 40 5N 87 15W
Fountain Cr. → 16 38 15N 104 36W
Fountain Green 52 39 38N 111 38W
Fountain Head 27 39 42N 77 42W
Fountain Hill 13 33 21N 91 51W
Fountain Inn 46 34 42N 82 12W
Fountain Run 48 36 18N 85 56W
Four Mountains, Is. of 11 53 0N 170 0W
Four Oaks 40 35 27N 78 26W
Four Town 30 48 17N 95 20W
Fourchu 61 45 43N 60 17W
Fourteen Mile Pt. 29 47 0N 89 10W
Fouta Djalon 120 11 20N 12 10W
Foux, Cap-à- 67 19 43N 73 27W
Foveaux Str. 128 46 42 S 168 10 E
Fowblesburg 27 39 34N 76 50W
Fowey 83 50 20N 4 39W
Fowler, Calif. 15 36 38N 119 41W
Fowler, Colo. 16 38 8N 104 2W
Fowler, Ind. 22 40 37N 87 19W
Fowler, Kans. 24 37 23N 100 12W
Fowler, Mich. 29 43 0N 84 45W
Fowlerton, Ind. 22 40 25N 85 34W
Fowlerton, Tex. 51 28 28N 98 48W
Fowlerville 29 42 40N 84 4W
Fowlstown 18 30 48N 84 33W
Fownhope 83 52 0N 2 37W
Fox 43 34 22N 97 30W
Fox →, Canada 63 56 3N 93 18W
Fox →, Ill. 21 41 21N 88 50W
Fox →, Wis. 55 44 32N 88 0W
Fox Is. 11 54 0N 168 0W
Fox Lake, Ill. 21 42 24N 88 11W
Fox Lake, Wis. 55 43 34N 88 55W
Fox Valley 63 50 30N 109 25W
Foxboro 28 42 4N 71 16W
Foxe Basin 59 66 0N 77 0W
Foxe Chan. 59 65 0N 80 0W
Foxe Pen. 59 65 0N 76 0W
Foxpark 56 41 5N 106 9W
Foxton 128 40 29 S 175 18 E
Foyil 43 36 26N 95 31W
Foyle, Lough 85 55 6N 7 8W
Foynes 85 52 37N 9 5W
Foz do Gregório 72 6 47 S 70 44W
Foz do Iguaçu 77 25 30 S 54 30W
Foz do Riosinho 72 7 11 S 71 50W
Frackville 45 40 47N 76 14W
Framingham 28 42 17N 71 25W
Franca 75 20 33 S 47 30W
Francavilla Fontana 95 40 32N 17 35 E
France ■ 90 47 0N 3 0 E
Frances 53 46 33N 123 30W
Frances → 62 60 16N 129 10W
Frances, L. 33 48 16N 112 13W
Frances L. 62 61 23N 129 30W
Francés Viejo, C. 67 19 40N 70 0W
Francestown 36 42 58N 71 48W
Francesville 22 40 59N 86 53W
Franceville 122 1 40 S 13 32 E
Franche-Comté 90 46 30N 5 50 E
Francis, Mont. 33 46 9N 111 5W
Francis, Okla. 43 34 52N 96 36W
Francis, Utah 52 40 37N 111 17W
Francis, L. 36 45 2N 71 20W
Francis Case, L. 47 43 4N 98 34W
Francis Creek 55 44 12N 87 44W
Francis Marion National Forest 46 33 10N 79 40W
Francisco de Orellana 70 0 28 S 76 58W
Francisco I. Madero, Coahuila, Mexico 64 25 48N 103 18W
Francisco I. Madero, Durango, Mexico 64 24 32N 104 22W
Francisco Sáo 75 16 28 S 43 30W
Francistown 123 21 7 S 27 33 E
François, Canada 61 47 35N 56 45W
François, Mart. 67 14 38N 60 57W
François L. 62 54 0N 125 30W
Franconia, Ariz. 12 34 44N 114 17W
Franconia, N.H. 36 44 14N 71 44W
Francs Pk. 56 43 58N 109 18W
Franeker 87 53 12N 5 33 E
Frankenmuth 29 43 20N 83 44W
Frankewing 48 35 12N 86 51W
Frankford, Del. 27 38 31N 75 14W
Frankford, Mo. 32 39 29N 91 19W
Frankford, W. Va. 54 37 56N 80 23W
Frankfort, Ind. 22 40 17N 86 31W
Frankfort, Kans. 24 39 42N 96 25W
Frankfort, Ky. 49 38 12N 84 52W
Frankfort, Maine 26 44 37N 68 53W
Frankfort, Mich. 29 44 38N 86 14W
Frankfort, Ohio 42 39 24N 83 11W
Frankfort, S. Dak. 47 44 53N 98 18W
Frankfurt am Main 88 50 7N 8 40 E
Frankfurt an der Oder 88 52 50N 14 31 E
Fränkische Alb 88 49 20N 11 30 E
Franklin, Ariz. 12 32 41N 109 5W
Franklin, Ga. 18 33 17N 85 6W
Franklin, Idaho 20 42 1N 111 48W
Franklin, Ill. 21 39 37N 90 3W
Franklin, Ind. 22 39 29N 86 3W
Franklin, Kans. 24 37 32N 94 42W
Franklin, Ky. 48 36 43N 86 35W
Franklin, La. 25 29 48N 91 30W
Franklin, Maine 26 44 35N 68 14W
Franklin, Mass. 28 42 5N 71 24W
Franklin, Minn. 30 47 32N 92 32W
Franklin, N.C. 40 35 11N 83 23W
Franklin, N.H. 36 43 27N 71 39W
Franklin, N.J. 37 41 7N 74 35W
Franklin, N.Y. 39 42 21N 75 10W
Franklin, Nebr. 34 40 6N 98 57W
Franklin, Ohio 42 39 34N 84 18W
Franklin, Pa. 45 41 24N 79 50W
Franklin, Tenn. 48 35 55N 86 52W
Franklin, Tex. 51 31 2N 96 29W
Franklin, Va. 54 36 41N 76 56W
Franklin, W. Va. 54 38 39N 79 20W
Franklin, Pt. 11 70 55N 158 48W
Franklin B. 58 69 45N 126 0W
Franklin County ◇, Ala. 10 34 21N 87 42W
Franklin County ◇, Ark. 13 35 29N 93 50W
Franklin County ◇, Fla. 17 29 50N 84 45W
Franklin County ◇, Ga. 18 34 20N 83 10W
Franklin County ◇, Idaho 20 42 10N 111 50W
Franklin County ◇, Ill. 21 38 0N 89 0W
Franklin County ◇, Ind. 22 39 25N 85 5W
Franklin County ◇, Iowa 23 42 45N 93 25W
Franklin County ◇, Kans. 24 38 30N 95 15W
Franklin County ◇, Ky. 49 38 15N 84 55W
Franklin County ◇, Maine 26 45 0N 70 30W
Franklin County ◇, Mass. 28 42 30N 72 35W
Franklin County ◇, Miss. 31 31 28N 90 54W
Franklin County ◇, Mo. 32 38 25N 91 0W
Franklin County ◇, N.C. 40 36 0N 78 20W
Franklin County ◇, N.Y. 39 44 30N 74 15W
Franklin County ◇, Nebr. 34 40 15N 99 0W
Franklin County ◇, Ohio 42 40 0N 83 4W
Franklin County ◇, Pa. 45 39 56N 77 40W
Franklin County ◇, Tenn. 48 35 10N 86 1W
Franklin County ◇, Tex. 51 33 11N 95 13W
Franklin County ◇, Va. 54 37 0N 80 0W
Franklin County ◇, Vt. 36 44 50N 72 50W
Franklin County ◇, Wash. 53 46 30N 119 0W
Franklin D. Roosevelt L. 53 48 18N 118 9W
Franklin Grove 21 41 51N 89 18W
Franklin I. 5 76 10 S 168 30 E
Franklin L. 35 40 25N 115 22W
Franklin Mts. 58 65 0N 125 0W
Franklin Parish ◇ 25 32 10N 91 43W
Franklin Square 39 40 43N 73 41W
Franklin Str. 58 72 0N 96 0W
Franklinton, La. 25 30 51N 90 9W
Franklinton, N.C. 40 36 6N 78 27W
Franklinville, N.J. 37 39 37N 75 5W
Franklinville, N.Y. 39 42 20N 78 27W
Frankston 51 32 3N 95 30W
Frankton 22 40 13N 85 46W
Frankville 10 31 39N 88 9W
Frannie 56 44 58N 108 37W
Frantsa Iosifa, Zemlya 100 82 0N 55 0 E
Franz 60 48 25N 84 30W
Franz Josef Land = Frantsa Iosifa, Zemlya 100 82 0N 55 0 E
Fraser 16 39 57N 105 49W
Fraser →, B.C., Canada 62 49 7N 123 11W
Fraser →, Newf., Canada 61 56 39N 62 10W
Fraser I. 127 25 15 S 153 10 E
Fraser Lake 62 54 0N 124 50W
Fraserburgh 84 57 41N 2 0W
Fraserdale 60 49 55N 81 37W
Fray Bentos 76 33 10 S 58 15W
Frazee 30 46 44N 95 42W
Frazer 33 48 3N 106 2W
Frazeysburg 42 40 7N 82 7W
Frazier Park 15 34 49N 118 56W
Fred 51 30 34N 94 10W
Freda 41 46 21N 101 10W
Frederic, Mich. 29 44 47N 84 45W
Frederic, Wis. 55 45 40N 92 28W
Frederica 27 39 1N 75 28W
Fredericia 97 55 34N 9 45 E
Frederick, Colo. 16 40 6N 104 56W
Frederick, Md. 27 39 25N 77 25W
Frederick, Okla. 43 34 23N 99 1W
Frederick, S. Dak. 47 45 50N 98 31W
Frederick County ◇, Md. 27 39 30N 77 25W
Frederick County ◇, Va. 54 39 5N 78 13W
Frederick Reef 127 20 58 S 154 23 E
Fredericksburg, Iowa 23 42 58N 92 12W
Fredericksburg, Tex. 51 30 16N 98 52W
Fredericksburg, Va. 54 38 18N 77 28W
Fredericktown, Mo. 32 37 34N 90 18W
Fredericktown, Ohio 42 40 29N 82 33W
Fredericton 61 45 57N 66 40W
Fredericton Junc. 61 45 41N 66 40W
Frederika 23 42 53N 92 19W
Frederikshavn 97 57 28N 10 31 E
Frederiksted, Virgin Is. 57 17 43N 64 53W
Fredonia, Ariz. 12 36 57N 112 32W
Fredonia, Kans. 24 37 32N 95 49W
Fredonia, Ky. 48 37 12N 88 4W
Fredonia, N. Dak. 41 46 20N 99 6W
Fredonia, N.Y. 39 42 26N 79 20W
Fredonia, Pa. 45 41 19N 80 16W
Fredrikstad 97 59 13N 10 57 E
Freeborn County ◇ 30 43 40N 93 15W
Freeburg, Ill. 21 38 26N 89 55W
Freeburg, Mo. 32 38 19N 91 56W
Freedom 43 36 46N 99 7W
Freehold 37 40 16N 74 17W
Freel Peak 35 38 52N 119 54W
Freeland 45 41 1N 75 54W
Freeling, Mt. 126 22 35 S 133 6 E
Freels, C. 61 49 15N 53 30W
Freeman, Mo. 32 38 37N 94 30W
Freeman, S. Dak. 47 43 21N 97 26W
Freeman L. 22 40 42N 86 45W
Freeport, Bahamas 66 26 30N 78 47W
Freeport, Canada 61 44 15N 66 20W
Freeport, Fla. 17 30 30N 86 8W
Freeport, Ill. 21 42 17N 89 36W
Freeport, Kans. 24 37 12N 97 51W
Freeport, Maine 26 43 52N 70 6W
Freeport, Mich. 29 42 46N 85 19W
Freeport, Minn. 30 45 40N 94 42W
Freeport, N.Y. 39 40 39N 73 35W
Freeport, Pa. 45 40 41N 79 41W
Freeport, Tex. 51 28 57N 95 21W
Freer 51 27 53N 98 37W
Freesoil 29 44 7N 86 14W
Freestone County ◇ 51 31 44N 96 10W
Freetown 120 8 30N 13 17W
Freeville 39 42 31N 76 21W
Frégate, L. 60 53 15N 74 45W
Freiberg 88 50 55N 13 20 E
Freire 78 38 54 S 72 38W
Freirina 76 28 30 S 71 10W
Freising 88 48 24N 11 47 E
Freistadt 88 48 30N 14 30 E
Freistatt 32 37 1N 93 54W
Fréjus 90 43 25N 6 44 E
Fremantle 126 32 7 S 115 47 E
Fremont, Calif. 14 37 32N 121 57W
Fremont, Ind. 22 41 44N 84 56W
Fremont, Iowa 23 41 13N 92 26W
Fremont, Ky. 48 36 58N 88 37W
Fremont, Mich. 29 43 28N 85 57W
Fremont, N.C. 40 35 33N 77 58W
Fremont, Nebr. 34 41 26N 96 30W
Fremont, Ohio 42 41 21N 83 7W
Fremont, Utah 52 38 27N 111 37W
Fremont, Wis. 55 44 16N 88 52W
Fremont → 52 38 24N 110 42W
Fremont County ◇, Colo. 16 38 30N 105 30W
Fremont County ◇, Idaho 20 44 15N 111 20W
Fremont County ◇, Iowa 23 40 45N 95 35W
Fremont County ◇, Wyo. 56 43 0N 108 30W
Fremont L. 56 42 57N 109 48W
Fremont National Forest 44 42 20N 120 50W
French → 45 45 56N 80 54W
French Broad →, N.C. 40 35 57N 83 51W
French Broad →, Tenn. 49 35 58N 83 51W
French Camp, Calif. 14 37 53N 121 16W
French Camp, Miss. 31 33 18N 89 24W
French Frigate Shoals 19 23 45N 166 10W
French Guiana ■ 71 4 0N 53 0W
French Gulch 14 40 42N 122 38W
French Lick 22 38 33N 86 37W
French Meadows Res. 14 39 10N 120 40W
French River 30 46 54N 91 54W
French Terr. of Afars & Issas = Djibouti ■ 105 12 0N 43 0 E
Frenchboro 26 44 7N 68 22W
Frenchburg 49 37 57N 83 38W
Frenchglen 44 42 50N 118 55W
Frenchman Butte 63 53 35N 109 38W
Frenchman Cr. →, Mont. 33 48 31N 107 10W
Frenchman Cr. →, Nebr. 34 40 14N 100 50W
Frenchman L., Calif. 14 39 54N 120 11W
Frenchman L., Nev. 35 36 48N 115 56W
Frenchtown, Mont. 33 47 1N 114 14W
Frenchtown, N.J. 37 40 32N 75 4W
Frenchville 26 47 17N 68 23W
Fresco → 73 7 15 S 51 30W
Freshfield, C. 5 68 25 S 151 10 E
Fresnillo 64 23 10N 103 0W
Fresno 15 36 44N 119 47W
Fresno County ◇ 15 36 40N 120 0W
Fresno Reservoir 33 48 36N 109 57W
Frewsburg 39 42 3N 79 10W
Freycinet Pen. 127 42 10 S 148 25 E
Fria, C. 123 18 0 S 12 0 E
Fría, La 70 8 13N 72 15W
Friant 15 36 59N 119 43W
Friars Point 31 34 22N 90 38W
Frías 76 28 40 S 65 5W
Fribourg 88 48 0N 7 52 E
Friday Harbor 53 48 32N 123 1W
Fridley 30 45 5N 93 16W
Friedrichshafen 88 47 39N 9 29 E
Friend, Kans. 24 38 16N 100 55W
Friend, Nebr. 34 40 38N 97 17W
Friendly 27 38 42N 76 59W
Friendly, Is. = Tonga ■ 128 19 50 S 174 30W
Friendship, N.Y. 39 42 12N 78 8W
Friendship, Tenn. 48 35 55N 89 14W
Friendship, Wis. 55 43 58N 89 49W
Friendsville 27 39 40N 79 24W
Fries 54 36 43N 80 59W
Friesland 55 43 35N 89 4W

Friesland Garfield County

Friesland □ 87 53 5N 5 50 E
Frijoles 57 9 11N 79 48W
Frio ⟶ 51 28 26N 98 11W
Frio County ◇ 51 28 54N 99 6W
Frio Draw ⟶ 50 34 50N 102 19W
Friona 50 34 38N 102 43W
Frisco 16 39 35N 106 6W
Frisco City 10 31 26N 87 24W
Frisco Peak 52 38 31N 113 17W
Frissell, Mt. 28 42 3N 73 28W
Fritch 50 35 38N 101 36W
Friuli-Venezia Giulia □ 94 46 0N 13 0 E
Frobisher B. 59 62 30N 66 0W
Frobisher Bay 59 63 44N 68 31W
Frobisher L. 63 56 20N 108 15W
Frohavet 96 63 50N 9 35 E
Froid 33 48 20N 104 30W
Fromberg 33 45 24N 108 54W
Frome 83 51 16N 2 17W
Frome, L. 127 30 45 S 139 45 E
Front Range 16 40 25N 105 45W
Front Royal 54 38 55N 78 12W
Fronteiras 74 7 5 S 40 37W
Frontenac 24 37 27N 94 42W
Frontera 65 18 30N 92 40W
Frontier 56 41 49N 110 32W
Frontier County ◇ 34 40 30N 100 30W
Frosinone 94 41 38N 13 20 E
Frost, Minn. 30 43 35N 93 56W
Frost, Tex. 51 32 5N 96 49W
Frostburg 27 39 39N 78 56W
Frostisen 96 68 14N 17 10 E
Frostproof 17 27 45N 81 32W
Frøya 96 63 43N 8 40 E
Fruita 16 39 9N 108 44W
Fruitdale, Ala. 10 31 21N 88 25W
Fruitdale, S. Dak. 47 44 40N 103 42W
Fruithurst 10 33 44N 85 26W
Fruitland, Idaho 20 44 0N 116 55W
Fruitland, Iowa 23 41 21N 91 8W
Fruitland, Md. 27 38 19N 75 37W
Fruitland, Mo. 32 37 27N 89 38W
Fruitland, N. Mex. 38 36 44N 108 24W
Fruitland Park 17 28 51N 81 54W
Fruitport 29 43 7N 86 9W
Fruitvale, Colo. 16 39 5N 108 30W
Fruitvale, Idaho 20 44 49N 116 26W
Fruitvale, Wash. 53 46 37N 120 33W
Frumoasa 95 46 28N 25 48 E
Frunze 100 42 54N 74 46 E
Frutal 75 20 0 S 49 0W
Frýdek-Místek 89 49 40N 18 20 E
Fryeburg 26 44 1N 70 59W
Fu Xian, Liaoning, China 114 39 38N 121 58 E
Fu Xian, Shaanxi, China 114 36 0N 109 20 E
Fucheng 114 37 50N 116 10 E
Fuchū 117 34 34N 133 14 E
Fuchuan 115 24 50N 111 5 E
Fuchun Jiang ⟶ 115 30 5N 120 5 E
Fuding 115 27 20N 120 12 E
Fuente Ovejuna 91 38 15N 5 25W
Fuentes de Oñoro 91 40 33N 6 52W
Fuerte ⟶ 64 25 50N 109 25W
Fuerte Olimpo 76 21 0 S 57 51W
Fuerteventura 120 28 30N 14 0W
Fugløysund 96 70 15N 20 20 E
Fugou 115 34 3N 114 25 E
Fuhai 113 47 2N 87 25 E
Fuji 117 35 9N 138 39 E
Fuji-no-miya 117 35 10N 138 40 E
Fuji-San 117 35 22N 138 44 E
Fuji-yoshida 117 35 30N 138 46 E
Fujian □ 115 26 0N 118 0 E
Fujin 114 47 16N 132 1 E
Fujisawa 117 35 22N 139 29 E
Fukien = Fujian □ 115 26 0N 118 0 E
Fukuchiyama 117 35 19N 135 9 E
Fukue-Shima 117 32 40N 128 45 E
Fukui 117 36 0N 136 10 E
Fukui □ 117 36 0N 136 12 E
Fukuoka 117 33 39N 130 21 E
Fukuoka □ 117 33 30N 131 0 E
Fukushima, Japan 116 37 44N 140 28 E
Fukushima, Japan 116 37 45N 140 28 E
Fukushima □ 116 37 30N 140 15 E
Fukuyama 117 34 35N 133 20 E
Fulda, Germany 88 50 32N 9 41 E
Fulda, U.S.A. 30 43 53N 95 36W
Fulda ⟶ 88 51 27N 9 40 E
Fuling 115 29 40N 107 20 E
Fullerton, Calif. 15 33 53N 117 56W
Fullerton, N. Dak. 41 46 10N 98 26W
Fullerton, Nebr. 34 41 22N 97 58W
Fulton, Ala. 10 31 47N 87 44W
Fulton, Ark. 13 33 37N 93 49W
Fulton, Ill. 21 41 52N 90 11W
Fulton, Kans. 24 38 1N 94 43W
Fulton, Ky. 48 36 30N 88 53W
Fulton, Miss. 31 34 16N 88 25W
Fulton, Mo. 32 38 52N 91 57W
Fulton, N.Y. 39 43 19N 76 25W
Fulton, Ohio 42 40 28N 82 50W
Fulton, S. Dak. 47 43 44N 97 49W
Fulton, Tex. 51 28 4N 97 2W
Fulton County ◇, Ark. 13 36 22N 91 50W
Fulton County ◇, Ga. 18 33 40N 84 40W
Fulton County ◇, Ill. 21 40 30N 90 10W
Fulton County ◇, Ind. 22 41 5N 86 15W
Fulton County ◇, Ky. 48 36 32N 89 10W
Fulton County ◇, N.Y. 39 43 10N 74 30W
Fulton County ◇, Ohio 42 41 33N 84 8W
Fulton County ◇, Pa. 45 39 55N 78 5W
Fultondale 10 33 37N 86 48W
Fults 21 38 10N 90 13W
Funabashi 117 35 45N 140 0 E
Funafuti 124 8 30 S 179 0 E
Funchal 120 32 38N 16 54W
Fundación 70 10 31N 74 11W
Fundão, Brazil 75 19 55 S 40 24W
Fundão, Portugal 91 40 8N 7 30W
Fundy, B. of, Canada 61 45 0N 66 0W
Fundy, B. of, U.S.A. 26 44 30N 66 30W
Funing, Jiangsu, China 115 33 45N 119 50 E
Funing, Yunnan, China 115 23 35N 105 45 E
Funiu Shan 115 33 30N 112 20 E
Funk 34 40 28N 99 15W
Funston 18 31 12N 83 52W
Funtua 120 11 30N 7 18 E
Fuping 114 38 48N 114 12 E
Fuqing 115 25 41N 119 21 E
Fuquay-Varina 40 35 35N 78 48W
Furano 116 43 21N 142 23 E
Furāt, Nahr al ⟶ 106 31 0N 47 25 E
Furbero 65 20 22N 97 31W
Furman 46 32 41N 81 11W
Furnas, Represa de 75 20 50 S 45 0W
Furnas County ◇ 34 40 15N 100 0W
Furneaux Group 127 40 10 S 147 50 E
Furness, Pen. 82 54 12N 3 10W
Fürth 88 49 29N 11 0 E
Furukawa 116 38 34N 140 58 E
Fury and Hecla Str. 59 69 56N 84 0W
Fusagasuga 70 4 21N 74 22W
Fushan 114 37 30N 121 15 E
Fushun 114 41 50N 123 56 E
Fusong 114 42 20N 127 15 E
Fusui 115 22 40N 107 56 E
Futrono 78 40 8 S 72 24W
Futuna 124 14 25 S 178 20 E
Fuxin 114 42 5N 121 48 E
Fuyang, Anhui, China 115 33 0N 115 48 E
Fuyang, Zhejiang, China 115 30 5N 119 57 E
Fuyu 114 45 12N 124 43 E
Fuyuan 114 48 20N 134 5 E
Fuzhou 115 26 5N 119 16 E
Fwaka 123 12 5 S 29 25 E
Fylde 82 53 50N 2 58W
Fyn 97 55 20N 10 30 E
Fyne, L. 84 56 0N 5 20W

G

Gabbettville 18 32 57N 85 8W
Gabbs 35 38 52N 117 55W
Gabbs Valley Range 35 38 34N 118 0W
Gabela 122 11 0 S 14 24 E
Gabès 120 33 53N 10 2 E
Gabès, Golfe de 121 34 0N 10 30 E
Gabilan Range 15 36 30N 121 15W
Gabon ■ 122 0 10 S 10 0 E
Gaborone 123 24 45 S 25 57 E
Gabrovo 95 42 52N 25 19 E
Gachsārān 107 30 15N 50 45 E
Gackle 41 46 38N 99 9W
Gadag 108 15 30N 75 45 E
Gadarwara 108 22 50N 78 50 E
Gadhada 108 22 0N 71 35 E
Gadsden, Ala. 10 34 1N 86 1W
Gadsden, Ariz. 12 32 33N 114 47W
Gadsden, S.C. 46 33 51N 80 46W
Gadsden County ◇ 17 30 30N 84 45W
Gadwal 108 16 10N 77 50 E
Găeşti 95 44 48N 25 19 E
Gaffney 46 35 5N 81 39W
Gafsa 120 32 24N 8 43 E
Gage 43 36 19N 99 45W
Gage County ◇ 34 40 20N 96 45W
Gagetown 61 45 46N 66 10W
Gagnoa 120 6 56N 5 16W
Gagnon 61 51 50N 68 5W
Gagnon, L. 63 62 3N 110 27W
Gai Xian 114 40 22N 122 20 E
Gail 50 32 46N 101 27W
Gaillard, L. 28 41 21N 72 46W
Gaimán 78 43 10 S 65 25W
Gaines County ◇ 50 32 43N 102 39W
Gainesboro 49 36 21N 85 39W
Gainesville, Fla. 17 29 40N 82 20W
Gainesville, Ga. 18 34 18N 83 50W
Gainesville, Mo. 32 36 36N 92 26W
Gainesville, Tex. 51 33 38N 97 8W
Gainsborough 82 53 23N 0 46W
Gairdner L. 126 31 30 S 136 0 E
Gairloch, L. 84 57 43N 5 45W
Gaithersburg 27 39 8N 77 12W
Gakona 11 62 18N 145 18W
Galán, Cerro 76 25 55 S 66 52W
Galangue 123 13 42 S 16 9 E
Galápagos 125 0 0 89 0W
Galas ⟶ 112 4 55N 101 57 E
Galashiels 84 55 37N 2 50W
Galaţi 89 45 27N 28 2 E
Galaţi □ 95 45 45N 27 30 E
Galatia, Ill. 21 37 51N 88 37W
Galatia, Kans. 24 38 38N 98 58W
Galatina 95 40 10N 18 10 E
Galax 54 36 40N 80 56W
Galcaio 105 6 30N 47 30 E
Galdhøpiggen 97 61 38N 8 18 E
Galeana 64 24 50N 100 4W
Galela 111 1 50N 127 49 E
Galena, Alaska 11 64 44N 156 56W
Galena, Ill. 21 42 25N 90 26W
Galena, Kans. 24 37 4N 94 38W
Galena, Md. 27 39 21N 75 53W
Galena, Mo. 32 36 48N 93 28W
Galena Park 51 29 44N 95 14W
Galera, Pta. 78 39 59 S 73 43W
Galera Point 67 10 8N 61 0W
Galesburg, Ill. 21 40 57N 90 22W
Galesburg, Kans. 24 37 28N 95 21W
Galesburg, Mich. 29 42 17N 85 26W
Galesburg, N. Dak. 41 47 16N 97 24W
Galestown 27 38 35N 75 42W
Galesville 55 44 5N 91 21W
Galeton, Colo. 16 40 31N 104 35W
Galeton, Pa. 45 41 44N 77 39W
Galheirão ⟶ 75 12 23 S 45 5W
Galheiros 75 13 18 S 46 25W
Galicea Mare 95 44 4N 23 19 E
Galich 98 58 23N 42 12 E
Galiche 95 43 34N 23 50 E
Galicia □ 91 42 43N 7 45W
Galilee = Hagalil 104 32 53N 35 18 E
Galion 42 40 44N 82 47W
Galiuro Mts. 12 32 30N 110 20W
Gallabat 121 12 58N 36 11 E
Gallatin, Mo. 32 39 55N 93 58W
Gallatin, Tenn. 48 36 24N 86 27W
Gallatin, Tex. 51 31 54N 95 9W
Gallatin ⟶ 33 45 56N 111 30W
Gallatin County ◇, Ill. 21 37 45N 88 15W
Gallatin County ◇, Ky. 49 38 45N 84 55W
Gallatin County ◇, Mont. 33 45 55N 111 15W
Gallatin Gateway 33 45 35N 111 12W
Gallatin National Forest 33 45 15N 111 15W
Galle 108 6 5N 80 10 E
Gállego ⟶ 91 41 39N 0 51W
Gallegos ⟶ 78 51 35 S 69 0W
Galley Hd. 85 51 32N 8 56W
Gallia County ◇ 42 38 49N 82 12W
Galliano 25 29 26N 90 18W
Gallinas, Pta. 70 12 28N 71 40W
Gallion 10 32 30N 87 43W
Gallipoli = Gelibolu 95 40 28N 26 43 E
Gallípoli 95 40 8N 18 0 E
Gallipolis 42 38 49N 82 12W
Gällivare 96 67 9N 20 40 E
Gallman 31 31 56N 90 23W
Gallo Mts. 38 34 5N 108 35W
Galloo I. 39 43 55N 76 25W
Galloway 84 55 0N 4 25W
Galloway, Mull of 84 54 38N 4 50W
Gallup 38 35 32N 108 45W
Gal'on 104 31 38N 34 51 E
Galoya 108 8 10N 80 55 E
Galt, Calif. 14 38 15N 121 18W
Galt, Iowa 23 42 42N 93 36W
Galt, Mo. 32 40 8N 93 23W
Galty Mts. 85 52 22N 8 10W
Galtymore 85 52 22N 8 12W
Galva, Ill. 21 41 10N 90 3W
Galva, Iowa 23 42 30N 95 25W
Galvarino 78 38 24 S 72 47W
Galveston, Ind. 22 40 35N 86 11W
Galveston, Tex. 51 29 18N 94 48W
Galveston B. 51 29 36N 94 50W
Galveston County ◇ 51 29 28N 95 5W
Galveston I. 51 29 16N 94 51W
Gálvez 76 32 0 S 61 14W
Galway 85 53 16N 9 4W
Galway □ 85 53 16N 9 3W
Galway B. 85 53 10N 9 20W
Gamagori 117 34 50N 137 14 E
Gamaliel, Ark. 13 36 27N 92 14W
Gamaliel, Ky. 49 36 38N 85 48W
Gambaga 120 10 30N 0 28W
Gambela 121 8 14N 34 38 E
Gambell 11 63 47N 171 45W
Gamber 27 39 28N 76 56W
Gambia ■ 120 13 25N 16 0W
Gambia ⟶ 120 13 28N 16 34W
Gamboa 57 9 7N 79 42W
Gamboma 122 1 55 S 15 52 E
Gamerco 38 35 34N 108 46W
Gamlakarleby = Kokkola 96 63 50N 23 8 E
Gammon ⟶ 63 51 24N 95 44W
Gan Gan 78 42 30 S 68 10W
Gan Jiang ⟶ 113 29 15N 116 0 E
Gan Shemu'el 104 32 28N 34 56 E
Gan Yavne 104 31 48N 34 42 E
Ganado, Ariz. 12 35 43N 109 33W
Ganado, Tex. 51 29 2N 96 31W
Gananoque 60 44 20N 76 10W
Ganaveh 107 29 35N 50 35 E
Gancheng 115 18 51N 108 37 E
Gand = Gent 87 51 2N 3 42 E
Ganda 123 13 3 S 14 35 E
Gandak ⟶ 109 25 39N 85 13 E
Gandava 108 28 32N 67 32 E
Gandeeville 54 38 42N 81 25W
Gander 61 48 58N 54 35W
Gander L. 61 48 58N 54 35W
Gandhi Sagar 108 24 40N 75 40 E
Gandi 120 12 55N 5 49 E
Gandu 75 13 45 S 39 30W
Ganedidalem = Gani 111 0 48 S 128 14 E
Ganga ⟶ 109 23 20N 90 30 E
Ganganagar 108 29 56N 73 56 E
Gangara 120 14 35N 8 29 E
Gangaw 109 22 5N 94 5 E
Gangdisê Shan 109 31 20N 81 0 E
Ganges = Ganga ⟶ 109 23 20N 90 30 E
Gangtok 109 27 20N 88 37 E
Gani 111 0 48 S 128 14 E
Gannett 20 43 22N 114 11W
Gannett Peak 56 43 11N 109 39W
Gannvalley 47 44 2N 98 59W
Ganquan 114 36 20N 109 20 E
Gans 43 35 23N 94 42W
Gansu □ 114 36 0N 104 0 E
Ganta 120 7 15N 8 59W
Gantheaume B. 126 27 40 S 114 10 E
Gantt 10 31 25N 86 29W
Ganyem 111 2 46 S 140 12 E
Ganyu 115 34 50N 119 8 E
Ganzhou 115 25 51N 114 56 E
Gao Bang 112 22 37N 106 18 E
Gao'an 115 28 26N 115 17 E
Gaomi 114 36 20N 119 42 E
Gaoping 114 35 45N 112 55 E
Gaoua 120 10 20N 3 8W
Gaoual 120 11 45N 13 25W
Gaoxiong 115 22 38N 120 18 E
Gaoyou 115 32 47N 119 26 E
Gaoyou Hu 115 32 45N 119 20 E
Gaoyuan 114 37 8N 117 58 E
Gap 90 44 33N 6 5 E
Gar 113 32 10N 79 58 E
Gar Dzong 108 32 20N 79 55 E
Garachiné 66 8 0N 78 12W
Garanhuns 74 8 50 S 36 30W
Garawe 120 4 35N 8 0W
Garber 43 36 26N 97 35W
Garberville 14 40 6N 123 48W
Garça 75 22 14 S 49 37W
Garças ⟶ 74 8 43 S 39 41W
Garças, Rio das ⟶ 73 15 54 S 52 16W
Garcia 16 37 0N 105 32W
Garcias 73 20 34 S 52 13W
Gard 105 9 30N 49 6 E
Gard □ 90 44 2N 4 10 E
Garda, L. di 94 45 40N 10 40 E
Gardala 121 5 40N 37 25 E
Gardar 41 48 35N 97 53W
Garde L. 63 62 50N 106 13W
Garden 29 45 47N 86 33W
Garden City, Ala. 10 34 1N 86 45W
Garden City, Ga. 18 32 6N 81 9W
Garden City, Idaho 20 43 38N 116 16W
Garden City, Kans. 24 37 58N 100 53W
Garden City, Mo. 32 38 34N 94 12W
Garden City, S. Dak. 47 44 57N 97 35W
Garden City, Tex. 50 31 52N 101 29W
Garden City, Utah 52 41 57N 111 24W
Garden County ◇ 34 41 30N 102 15W
Garden Grove, Calif. 15 33 47N 117 55W
Garden Grove, Iowa 23 40 50N 93 36W
Garden I. 29 45 49N 85 30W
Garden Island B. 25 29 0N 89 0W
Garden Lakes 18 34 19N 85 17W
Garden Plain 24 37 40N 97 41W
Garden Valley 20 44 6N 115 57W
Gardena 20 43 58N 116 12W
Gardendale 10 33 39N 86 49W
Gardēz 107 33 37N 69 9 E
Gardi 18 31 32N 81 48W
Gardiner, Maine 26 44 14N 69 47W
Gardiner, Oreg. 44 43 44N 124 7W
Gardiners B. 39 41 5N 72 5W
Gardiners I. 39 41 6N 72 6W
Gardner, Colo. 16 37 47N 105 10W
Gardner, Fla. 17 27 21N 81 48W
Gardner, Kans. 24 38 49N 94 56W
Gardner, Mass. 28 42 34N 71 59W
Gardner Canal 62 53 27N 128 8W
Gardner L. 26 44 45N 67 20W
Gardner Pinnacles 19 25 0N 167 55W
Gardnerville 35 38 56N 119 45W
Gare Tigre 71 4 58N 53 9W
Gareloi I. 11 51 48N 178 48W
Garfield, Ark. 13 36 27N 93 58W
Garfield, Kans. 24 38 5N 99 14W
Garfield, Minn. 30 45 56N 95 30W
Garfield, N.J. 37 40 52N 74 6W
Garfield, N. Mex. 38 32 46N 107 16W
Garfield, Wash. 53 47 1N 117 9W
Garfield County ◇, Colo. 16 39 30N 108 0W

Garfield County
Gifu

Garfield County ◇, Mont. 33 47 15N 107 0W
Garfield County ◇, Nebr. 34 41 50N 99 0W
Garfield County ◇, Okla. 43 36 20N 97 45W
Garfield County ◇, Utah 52 37 50N 111 20W
Garfield County ◇, Wash. 53 46 28N 117 36W
Garfield Heights 42 41 26N 81 37W
Garfield Mt. 33 44 31N 112 37W
Gargano, Mte. 94 41 43N 15 43 E
Garibaldi 44 45 34N 123 55W
Garibaldi Prov. Park 62 49 50N 122 40W
Garies 123 30 32 S 17 59 E
Garigliano —► 94 41 13N 13 44 E
Garland, Ala. 10 31 33N 86 50W
Garland, Ark. 13 33 22N 93 43W
Garland, Kans. 24 37 44N 94 37W
Garland, N.C. 40 34 47N 78 24W
Garland, Nebr. 34 40 57N 96 59W
Garland, Tex. 51 32 55N 96 38W
Garland, Utah 52 41 45N 112 10W
Garland County ◇ 13 34 34N 93 10W
Garm 100 39 0N 70 20 E
Garmsār 107 35 20N 52 25 E
Garnavillo 23 42 52N 91 14W
Garner, Iowa 23 43 6N 93 36W
Garner, N.C. 40 35 43N 78 37W
Garnett 24 38 17N 95 14W
Garoe 105 8 25N 48 33 E
Garonne —► 90 45 2N 0 36W
Garoua 121 9 19N 13 21 E
Garrard County ◇ 49 37 35N 84 30W
Garretson 47 43 43N 96 30W
Garrett 22 41 21N 85 8W
Garrett County ◇ 27 39 30N 79 20W
Garrison, Iowa 23 42 9N 92 8W
Garrison, Ky. 49 38 36N 83 10W
Garrison, Minn. 30 46 18N 93 50W
Garrison, Mont. 33 46 31N 112 49W
Garrison, N. Dak. 41 47 40N 101 25W
Garrison, Nebr. 34 41 11N 97 10W
Garrison, Tex. 51 31 49N 94 30W
Garrison, Utah 52 38 56N 114 2W
Garrison Dam 41 47 30N 101 25W
Garry —► 84 56 47N 3 47W
Garry L. 58 65 58N 100 18W
Garsen 122 2 20 S 40 5 E
Garson —► 63 56 20N 110 1W
Garson L. 63 56 19N 110 2W
Garut 111 7 14 S 107 53 E
Garvie Mts. 128 45 30 S 168 50 E
Garvin 43 33 57N 94 56W
Garvin County ◇ 43 34 45N 97 20W
Garwa = Garoua 121 9 19N 13 21 E
Garwin 23 42 6N 92 41W
Garwood 51 29 27N 96 24W
Gary, Ind. 22 41 36N 87 20W
Gary, Minn. 30 47 22N 96 16W
Gary, S. Dak. 47 44 48N 96 27W
Gary, Tex. 51 32 2N 94 22W
Gary, W. Va. 54 37 22N 81 33W
Garza County ◇ 50 33 12N 101 23W
Garza-Little Elm Reservoir 51 33 4N 96 59W
Garzê 113 31 39N 99 58 E
Garzón 70 2 10N 75 40W
Gas City 22 40 29N 85 37W
Gas-San 116 38 32N 140 1 E
Gasan Kuli 100 37 40N 54 20 E
Gascogne 90 43 45N 0 20 E
Gascogne, G. de 90 44 0N 2 0W
Gascon 38 35 53N 105 27W
Gasconade 32 38 40N 91 34W
Gasconade —► 32 38 41N 91 33W
Gasconade County ◇ 32 38 25N 91 30W
Gascony = Gascogne 90 43 45N 0 20 E
Gascoyne 41 46 7N 103 5W
Gascoyne —► 126 24 52 S 113 37 E
Gashaka 120 7 20N 11 29 E
Gasparilla I. 17 26 46N 82 16W
Gaspé 61 48 52N 64 30W
Gaspé, C. 61 48 48N 64 7W
Gaspé, Pén. de 61 48 45N 65 40W
Gaspésie, Parc Prov. de la 61 48 55N 65 50W
Gasquet 14 41 51N 123 58W
Gassaway 54 38 41N 80 47W
Gaston, Ind. 22 40 19N 85 31W
Gaston, N.C. 40 36 30N 77 39W
Gaston, S.C. 46 33 49N 81 5W
Gaston, L. 40 36 30N 77 49W
Gaston County ◇ 40 31 15N 81 10W
Gastonia 40 35 16N 81 11W
Gastre 78 42 20 S 69 15W
Gata, C. de 91 36 41N 2 13W
Gata, Sierra de 91 40 20N 6 45W
Gataga —► 62 58 35N 126 59W
Gate 43 36 51N 100 4W
Gate City 54 36 38N 82 35W
Gates, N.C. 40 36 30N 76 46W
Gates, N.Y. 39 43 9N 77 42W
Gates, Oreg. 44 44 45N 122 25W
Gates, Tenn. 48 35 50N 89 24W
Gates County ◇ 40 36 25N 76 40W
Gateshead 82 54 57N 1 37W
Gatesville, N.C. 40 36 24N 76 45W
Gatesville, Tex. 51 31 26N 97 45W
Gateway 16 38 41N 108 59W
Gatico 76 22 29 S 70 20W
Gâtinais 90 48 5N 2 40 E
Gatineau —► 60 45 27N 75 42W
Gatineau, Parc de la 60 45 40N 76 0W
Gatliff 49 36 41N 84 1W
Gatlinburg 49 35 43N 83 31W
Gato 16 37 3N 107 12W
Gatooma 123 18 20 S 29 52 E
Gatun 57 9 16N 79 55W
Gatun, L. 66 9 7N 79 56W
Gatun Dam 57 9 16N 79 55W
Gatun Locks 57 9 16N 79 55W
Gau 128 18 2 S 179 18 E
Gauer L. 63 57 0N 97 50W
Gauhati 109 26 10N 91 45 E
Gaula —► 96 63 21N 10 14 E
Gauley —► 54 38 10N 81 12W
Gauley Bridge 54 38 10N 81 12W
Gausta, Mt. 97 59 48N 8 40 E
Gautier 31 30 23N 88 37W
Gavāter 107 25 10N 61 31 E
Gavins Point Dam 47 42 51N 97 29W
Gaviota 15 34 29N 120 13W
Gävleborgs län □ 97 61 30N 16 15 E
Gawilgarh Hills 108 21 15N 76 45 E
Gawler 127 34 30 S 138 42 E
Gawler Ranges 126 32 30 S 135 45 E
Gaxun Nur 113 42 22N 100 30 E
Gay, Ga. 18 33 6N 84 35W
Gay, Mich. 29 47 14N 88 10W
Gay, U.S.S.R. 98 51 27N 58 27 E
Gaya, India 109 24 47N 85 4 E
Gaya, Niger 120 11 52N 3 28 E
Gaylord, Kans. 24 39 39N 98 51W
Gaylord, Mich. 29 45 2N 84 41W
Gaylord, Minn. 30 44 33N 94 13W
Gaylordsville 28 41 39N 73 29W
Gayndah 127 25 35 S 151 32 E
Gays Mills 55 43 19N 90 51W
Gayville 47 42 53N 97 10W
Gaza 104 31 30N 34 28 E
Gaza Strip 104 31 29N 34 25 E
Gazelle 14 41 31N 122 31W
Gaziantep 106 37 6N 37 23 E
Gazli 100 40 14N 63 24 E
Gdańsk 89 54 22N 18 40 E
Gdańska, Zatoka 89 54 30N 19 20 E
Gdov 98 58 48N 27 55 E
Gdynia 89 54 35N 18 33 E
Ge'a 104 31 38N 34 37 E
Gearhart 44 46 1N 123 55W
Gearhart Mt. 44 42 30N 120 53W
Geary 43 35 38N 98 19W
Geary County ◇ 24 39 0N 96 45W
Geauga County ◇ 42 41 35N 81 12W
Gebe 111 0 5N 129 25 E
Gebeit Mine 121 21 3N 36 29 E
Gebel Mûsa 106 28 32N 33 59 E
Gedaref 121 14 2N 35 28 E
Geddes 47 43 15N 98 42W
Gede, Tanjung 110 6 46 S 105 12 E
Gedera 104 31 49N 34 46 E
Gedser 97 54 35N 11 55 E
Geelong 127 38 10 S 144 22 E
Geidam 121 12 57N 11 57 E
Geiger 10 32 52N 88 18W
Geikie —► 63 57 45N 103 52W
Geili 121 16 1N 32 37 E
Geistown 45 40 18N 78 52W
Geita 122 2 48 S 32 12 E
Gejiu 113 23 20N 103 10 E
Gela 94 37 6N 14 18 E
Geladi 105 6 59N 46 30 E
Gelderland □ 87 52 5N 6 10 E
Geldermalsen 87 51 53N 5 17 E
Geldrop 87 51 25N 5 32 E
Geleen 87 50 57N 5 49 E
Gelehun 120 8 20N 11 40W
Gelibolu 95 40 28N 26 43 E
Gelsenkirchen 88 51 30N 7 5 E
Gem 24 39 26N 100 54W
Gem County ◇ 20 44 0N 116 25W
Gemas 112 2 37N 102 36 E
Gembloux 87 50 34N 4 43 E
Gemena 122 3 13N 19 48 E
Gemerek 106 39 15N 36 10 E
Gen He —► 114 50 16N 119 32 E
Gendringen 87 51 52N 6 21 E
Gene Autry 43 34 19N 97 2W
General Acha 76 37 20 S 64 38W
General Alvear, Buenos Aires, Argentina 76 36 0 S 60 0W
General Alvear, Mendoza, Argentina 76 35 0 S 67 40W
General Artigas 76 26 52 S 56 16W
General Belgrano 76 36 35 S 58 47W
General Cabrera 76 32 53 S 63 52W
General Carrera, L. 78 46 35 S 72 0W
General Cepeda 64 25 23N 101 27W
General Conesa 78 40 6 S 64 25W
General Guido 76 36 40 S 57 50W
General Juan Madariaga 76 37 0 S 57 0W
General La Madrid 76 37 17 S 61 20W
General Lorenzo Vintter 78 40 45 S 64 26W
General MacArthur 111 11 18N 125 28 E
General Martin Miguel de Güemes 76 24 35 S 65 0W
General Paz 76 27 45 S 57 36W
General Pico 76 35 45 S 63 50W
General Pinedo 76 27 15 S 61 20W
General Pinto 76 34 45 S 61 50W
General Sampaio 74 4 2 S 39 29W
General Santos 111 6 5N 125 14 E
General Toshevo 95 43 42N 28 6 E
General Trevino 65 26 14N 99 29W
General Trías 64 28 21N 106 22W
General Viamonte 76 35 1 S 61 3W
General Villegas 76 35 0 S 63 0W
General Vintter, L. 78 43 55 S 71 40W
Genesee 20 46 33N 116 56W
Genesee —► 39 43 16N 77 36W
Genesee County ◇, Mich. 29 43 0N 83 40W
Genesee County ◇, N.Y. 39 43 0N 78 10W
Geneseo, Ill. 21 41 27N 90 9W
Geneseo, Kans. 24 38 31N 98 10W
Geneseo, N.Y. 39 42 48N 77 49W
Geneva = Genève 88 46 12N 6 9 E
Geneva, Ala. 10 31 2N 85 52W
Geneva, Ga. 18 32 35N 84 33W
Geneva, Ill. 21 41 53N 88 18W
Geneva, Ind. 22 40 36N 84 58W
Geneva, Iowa 23 42 41N 93 8W
Geneva, Minn. 30 43 49N 93 16W
Geneva, N.Y. 39 42 52N 76 59W
Geneva, Nebr. 34 40 32N 97 36W
Geneva, Ohio 42 41 48N 80 57W
Geneva, L. = Léman, Lac 88 46 26N 6 30 E
Geneva County ◇ 10 31 6N 85 42W
Genève 88 46 12N 6 9 E
Genil —► 91 37 42N 5 19W
Genk 87 50 58N 5 32 E
Gennargentu, Mti. del 94 40 0N 9 10 E
Gennep 87 51 41N 5 59 E
Genoa = Génova 94 44 24N 8 56 E
Genoa, Colo. 16 39 17N 103 30W
Genoa, Ill. 21 42 6N 88 42W
Genoa, Nebr. 34 41 27N 97 44W
Genoa, Ohio 42 41 31N 83 22W
Genoa, Wis. 55 43 35N 91 13W
Genoa —► 78 44 55 S 70 5W
Genoa City 55 42 30N 88 20W
Genola 30 45 58N 94 7W
Génova 94 44 24N 8 56 E
Génova, Golfo di 94 44 0N 9 0 E
Gent 87 51 2N 3 42 E
Gentio do Ouro 74 11 25 S 42 30W
Gentry, Ark. 13 36 16N 94 29W
Gentry, Mo. 32 40 20N 94 25W
Gentry County ◇ 32 40 10N 94 25W
Geographe B. 126 33 30 S 115 15 E
Geographe Chan. 126 24 30 S 113 0 E
Georga, Zemlya 100 80 30N 49 0 E
George, S. Africa 123 33 58 S 22 29 E
George, Iowa 23 43 21N 96 0W
George, Wash. 53 47 5N 119 53W
George —► 61 58 49N 66 10W
George, L., Uganda 122 0 5N 30 10 E
George, L., Fla. 17 29 17N 81 36W
George, L., Mich. 29 46 27N 84 8W
George, L., N.Y. 39 43 37N 73 33W
George County ◇ 31 30 56N 88 35W
George River = Port Nouveau-Québec 59 58 30N 65 59W
George Sound 128 44 52 S 167 25 E
George Town, Bahamas 66 23 33N 75 47W
George Town, Malaysia 112 5 25N 100 15 E
George V Coast 5 69 0 S 148 0 E
George VI Sound 5 71 0 S 68 0W
George Washington National Forest 54 38 0N 79 50W
George West 51 28 20N 98 7W
Georgetown, Australia 127 18 17 S 143 33 E
Georgetown, Ont., Canada 60 43 40N 79 56W
Georgetown, P.E.I., Canada 61 46 13N 62 24W
Georgetown, Cayman Is. 66 19 20N 81 24W
Georgetown, Gambia 120 13 30N 14 47W
Georgetown, Guyana 71 6 50N 58 12W
Georgetown, Calif. 14 38 54N 120 50W
Georgetown, Colo. 16 39 42N 105 42W
Georgetown, Del. 27 38 41N 75 23W
Georgetown, Fla. 17 29 23N 81 38W
Georgetown, Ga. 18 31 53N 85 6W
Georgetown, Idaho 20 42 29N 111 22W
Georgetown, Ill. 21 39 59N 87 38W
Georgetown, Ky. 49 38 13N 84 33W
Georgetown, La. 25 31 46N 92 23W
Georgetown, Mass. 28 42 44N 70 59W
Georgetown, Miss. 31 31 52N 90 10W
Georgetown, Ohio 42 38 52N 83 54W
Georgetown, S.C. 46 33 23N 79 17W
Georgetown, Tex. 51 30 38N 97 41W
Georgetown County ◇ 46 33 30N 79 15W
Georgi Dimitrov 95 42 15N 23 54 E
Georgi Dimitrov, Yazovir 95 42 37N 25 18 E
Georgia □ 18 32 50N 83 15W
Georgia, Str. of 62 49 25N 124 0W
Georgia, Strait of 53 49 20N 124 0W
Georgia Center 36 44 42N 73 9W
Georgian B. 60 45 15N 81 0W
Georgian S.S.R. □ 99 42 0N 43 0 E
Georgiana 10 31 38N 86 44W
Georgievsk 99 44 12N 43 28 E
Georgina —► 127 23 30 S 139 47 E
Georgiu-Dezh 99 51 3N 39 30 E
Gera 88 50 53N 12 11 E
Geraardsbergen 87 50 45N 3 53 E
Geral, Serra, Bahia, Brazil 75 14 0 S 41 0W
Geral, Serra, Goiás, Brazil 74 11 15 S 46 30W
Geral, Serra, Sta. Catarina, Brazil 77 26 25 S 50 0W
Geral de Goiás, Serra 75 12 0 S 46 0W
Geral do Paranã Serra 75 15 0 S 47 30W
Gerald 32 38 24N 91 20W
Geraldine 33 47 36N 110 16W
Geraldton, Australia 126 28 48 S 114 32 E
Geraldton, Canada 60 49 44N 86 59W
Gerber 14 40 4N 122 9W
Gerber Reservoir 44 42 12N 121 8W
Gerdine, Mt. 11 61 35N 152 27W
Gerede 106 40 45N 32 10 E
Gereshk 107 31 47N 64 35 E
Gerik 112 5 25N 101 0 E
Gering 34 41 50N 103 40W
Gerizim 104 32 13N 35 15 E
Gerlach 35 40 39N 119 21W
Gerlogubi 105 6 53N 45 3 E
Germansen Landing 62 55 43N 124 40W
Germantown, Ill. 21 38 33N 89 32W
Germantown, Ohio 42 39 38N 84 22W
Germantown, Tenn. 48 35 5N 89 49W
Germantown, Wis. 55 43 14N 88 6W
Germany, East ■ 88 52 0N 12 0 E
Germany, West ■ 88 52 0N 9 0 E
Germiston 123 26 15 S 28 10 E
Gero 117 35 48N 137 14 E
Gerona 91 41 58N 2 46 E
Geronimo 43 34 29N 98 23W
Gerrard 62 50 30N 117 17W
Gers □ 90 43 35N 0 38 E
Gerty 43 34 50N 96 17W
Geser 111 3 50 S 130 54 E
Gethsémani 61 50 13N 60 40W
Gettysburg, Pa. 45 39 50N 77 14W
Gettysburg, S. Dak. 47 45 1N 99 57W
Getz Ice Shelf 5 75 0 S 130 0W
Geuda Springs 24 37 7N 97 9W
Gévaudan 90 44 40N 3 40 E
Geyser 33 47 16N 110 30W
Geyserville 14 38 42N 122 54W
Geysir 96 64 19N 20 18W
Ghaghara —► 109 25 45N 84 40 E
Ghana ■ 120 6 0N 1 0W
Ghanzi 123 21 50 S 21 34 E
Gharb el Istiwa'iya □ 121 5 0N 30 0 E
Ghardaïa 120 32 20N 3 37 E
Gharyān 121 32 10N 13 0 E
Ghat 120 24 59N 10 11 E
Ghawdex = Gozo 94 36 0N 14 13 E
Ghayl 106 21 40N 46 20 E
Ghazal, Bahr el —►, Chad 121 15 0N 17 0 E
Ghazâl, Bahr el —►, Sudan 121 9 31N 30 25 E
Ghazaouet 120 35 8N 1 50W
Ghaziabad 108 28 42N 77 26 E
Ghazipur 109 25 38N 83 35 E
Ghaznī 108 33 30N 68 28 E
Ghaznī □ 107 32 10N 68 20 E
Ghèlinsor 105 6 28N 46 39 E
Ghent = Gent 87 51 2N 3 42 E
Ghent, Ky. 49 38 44N 85 4W
Ghent, Minn. 30 44 31N 95 54W
Gheorghe Gheorghiu-Dej 95 46 17N 26 47 E
Ghergani 95 44 37N 25 37 E
Ghizao 108 33 20N 65 44 E
Ghowr □ 107 34 0N 64 20 E
Ghugus 108 19 58N 79 12 E
Ghūrīān 107 34 17N 61 25 E
Gia Lai = Pleiku 112 13 57N 108 0 E
Gia Nghia 112 12 0N 107 42 E
Gian 111 5 45N 125 20 E
Giant's Causeway 85 55 15N 6 30W
Giarabub = Al Jaghbūb 121 29 42N 24 38 E
Giarre 94 37 44N 15 10 E
Gibara 66 21 9N 76 11W
Gibbon, Nebr. 34 40 45N 98 51W
Gibbon, Oreg. 44 45 42N 118 21W
Gibbonsville 20 45 33N 113 56W
Gibbstown 37 39 50N 75 18W
Gibeon 123 25 7 S 17 45 E
Gibraltar 91 36 7N 5 22W
Gibraltar, Str. of 91 35 55N 5 40W
Gibsland 25 32 33N 93 3W
Gibson, Ga. 18 33 14N 82 36W
Gibson, La. 25 29 41N 90 59W
Gibson City 21 40 28N 88 22W
Gibson County ◇, Ind. 22 38 20N 87 35W
Gibson County ◇, Tenn. 48 36 0N 89 0W
Gibson Des. 126 24 0 S 126 0 E
Gibsons 62 49 24N 123 32W
Gibsonton 17 27 51N 82 23W
Giddings 51 30 11N 96 56W
Gideon 32 36 27N 89 55W
Giessen 88 50 34N 8 40 E
Gifford, Fla. 17 27 40N 80 25W
Gifford, Iowa 23 42 17N 93 5W
Gifford, Wash. 53 48 18N 118 9W
Gifford Pinchot National Forest 53 46 15N 121 55W
Gifu 117 35 30N 136 45 E
Gifu □ 117 35 40N 137 0 E

Goodman Grass

Goodman, Miss. 31 32 58N 89 55W
Goodman, Mo. 32 36 44N 94 25W
Goodman, Wis. 55 45 38N 88 21W
Goodnews Bay 11 59 7N 161 35W
Goodnight 50 35 2N 101 11W
Goodrich, Colo. 16 40 20N 104 7W
Goodrich, N. Dak. 41 47 29N 100 8W
Goodrich, Tex. 51 30 36N 94 57W
Goodridge 30 48 9N 95 48W
Goodsoil 63 54 24N 109 13W
Goodsprings 35 35 50N 115 26W
Goodwater 10 33 4N 86 3W
Goodwell 43 36 36N 101 38W
Goodyear 12 33 26N 112 21W
Goole 82 53 42N 0 52W
Goondiwindi 127 28 30 S 150 21 E
Goor 87 52 13N 6 33 E
Goose →, Canada 61 53 20N 60 35W
Goose →, U.S.A. 41 47 28N 96 52W
Goose Bay 61 53 15N 60 20W
Goose Creek 46 32 59N 80 2W
Goose L. 14 41 56N 120 26W
Gop 108 22 5N 69 50 E
Gorakhpur 109 26 47N 83 23 E
Gorda, Punta, Nic. 66 14 20N 83 10W
Gorda, Punta, U.S.A. 14 40 16N 124 22W
Gordo 10 33 19N 87 54W
Gordon, Ga. 18 32 54N 83 20W
Gordon, Nebr. 34 42 48N 102 12W
Gordon, Ohio 42 39 56N 84 31W
Gordon, Tex. 51 32 33N 98 22W
Gordon, Wis. 55 46 15N 91 48W
Gordon, I. 78 54 55 S 69 30W
Gordon County 18 34 30N 84 50W
Gordon Cr. → 34 42 49N 100 40W
Gordon Downs 126 18 48 S 128 33 E
Gordon L., Alta., Canada 63 56 30N 110 25W
Gordon L., N.W.T., Canada 62 63 5N 113 11W
Gordonsville 54 38 9N 78 11W
Gordonville, Mo. 32 37 19N 89 41W
Gordonville, Tex. 51 33 48N 96 51W
Goré, Chad 121 7 59N 16 31 E
Gore, Ethiopia 121 8 12N 35 32 E
Gore, N.Z. 128 46 5 S 168 58 E
Gore, U.S.A. 43 35 32N 95 7W
Gore Bay 60 45 57N 82 28W
Gore Mt. 36 44 55N 71 48W
Goree 51 33 28N 99 31W
Goreville 21 37 33N 88 58W
Gorey 85 52 41N 6 18W
Gorgān 107 36 55N 54 30 E
Gorgona, I. 72 3 0N 78 10W
Gorham, Ill. 21 37 43N 89 29W
Gorham, Kans. 24 38 53N 99 1W
Gorham, Maine 26 43 41N 70 26W
Gorham, N.H. 36 44 23N 71 10W
Gorin 32 40 22N 92 1W
Gorinchem 87 51 50N 4 59 E
Gorinhatã 75 19 15 S 49 45W
Gorízia 94 45 56N 13 37 E
Gorki = Gorkiy 98 56 20N 44 0 E
Gorkiy 98 56 20N 44 0 E
Gorkovskoye Vdkhr. 98 57 2N 43 4 E
Görlitz 88 51 10N 14 59 E
Gorlovka 99 48 19N 38 5 E
Gorman 51 32 12N 98 41W
Gorna Oryakhovitsa 95 43 7N 25 40 E
Gorno Ablanovo 95 43 37N 25 43 E
Gorno-Altaysk 100 51 50N 86 5 E
Gorno Slinkino 100 60 5N 70 0 E
Gornyatski 98 67 32N 64 3 E
Gornyi 116 44 57N 133 59 E
Gorontalo 111 0 35N 123 5 E
Gort 85 53 4N 8 50W
Gortner 27 39 20N 79 24W
Gorum 25 31 26N 92 56W
Gorzów Wielkopolski 88 52 43N 15 15 E
Goshen, Calif. 15 36 21N 119 25W
Goshen, Conn. 28 41 50N 73 14W
Goshen, Ind. 22 41 35N 85 50W
Goshen, N.J. 37 39 8N 74 51W
Goshen, N.Y. 39 41 24N 74 20W
Goshen, Oreg. 44 43 58N 123 2W
Goshen, Utah 52 39 57N 111 54W
Goshen County ◇ 56 42 0N 104 10W
Goshogawara 116 40 48N 140 27 E
Goshute Indian Reservation 35 39 50N 114 5W
Goshute L. 35 40 9N 114 42W
Goshute Mts. 35 40 15N 114 19W
Goshute Valley 35 40 45N 114 20W
Goslar 88 51 55N 10 23 E
Gosnell 13 35 58N 89 58W
Gosper County ◇ 34 40 30N 99 50W
Gospič 94 44 35N 15 23 E
Gosport, U.K. 83 50 48N 1 8W
Gosport, U.S.A. 22 39 21N 86 40W
Goss 31 31 21N 89 53W
Gossville 36 43 12N 71 22W
Göta kanal 97 58 50N 13 58 E
Gotebo 43 35 4N 98 53W
Göteborg 97 57 43N 11 59 E
Göteborgs och Bohus län □ 97 58 30N 11 30 E
Gotha 88 50 56N 10 42 E
Gotham 55 43 13N 90 18W
Gothenburg 34 40 56N 100 10W
Gotland 97 57 30N 18 33 E
Gotse Delchev 95 41 43N 23 46 E
Gotska Sandön 97 58 24N 19 15 E
Gōtsu 117 35 0N 132 14 E
Göttingen 88 51 31N 9 55 E
Gottwaldov 89 49 14N 17 40 E
Goubangzi 114 41 20N 121 52 E
Gouda 87 52 1N 4 42 E
Gough 18 33 6N 82 14W
Gough I. 2 40 10 S 9 45W
Gouin Rés. 60 48 35N 74 40W
Goulburn 127 34 44 S 149 44 E
Goulburn Is. 126 11 40 S 133 20 E
Gould, Ark. 13 33 59N 91 34W
Gould, Okla. 43 34 40N 99 47W
Gould City 29 46 6N 85 42W
Goulds 17 25 33N 80 23W
Gounou-Gaya 121 9 38N 15 31 E
Gouri 121 19 36N 19 36 E
Gourma Rharous 120 16 55N 1 50W
Gouvêa 75 18 27 S 43 44W
Gouverneur 39 44 20N 75 28W
Govan, Canada 63 51 20N 105 0W
Govan, U.S.A. 46 33 13N 81 11W
Gove, Australia 127 12 25 S 136 55 E
Gove, U.S.A. 24 38 58N 100 29W
Gove County ◇ 24 38 50N 100 30W
Governador Valadares 75 18 15 S 41 57W
Governor's Harbour 66 25 10N 76 14W
Gowanda 39 42 28N 78 56W
Gowd-e Zirreh 107 29 45N 62 0 E
Gower 32 39 37N 94 36W
Gower, The 83 51 35N 4 10W
Gowna, L. 85 53 52N 7 35W
Gowrie 23 42 17N 94 17W
Gowrie, Carse of 84 56 30N 3 10W
Goya 76 29 10 S 59 10W
Goyllarisquisga 72 10 31 S 76 24W
Goz Beîda 121 12 10N 21 20 E
Gozo 94 36 0N 14 13 E
Graaff-Reinet 123 32 13 S 24 32 E
Gračac 94 44 18N 15 57 E
Grace 20 42 35N 111 44W
Gracemont 43 35 11N 98 16W
Graceville, Fla. 17 30 58N 85 31W
Graceville, Minn. 30 45 34N 96 26W
Gracewood 18 33 22N 82 2W
Gracey 48 36 53N 87 40W
Gracias a Dios, C. 66 15 0N 83 10W
Gradaús 74 7 43 S 51 11W
Gradaús, Serra dos 74 8 0 S 50 45W
Gradets 95 42 46N 26 30 E
Grado 91 43 23N 6 4W
Grady, Ala. 10 31 59N 86 3W
Grady, Ark. 13 34 5N 91 42W
Grady, N. Mex. 38 34 49N 103 19W
Grady County ◇, Ga. 18 30 50N 84 15W
Grady County ◇, Okla. 43 35 0N 97 50W
Gradyville 49 37 4N 85 25W
Graeca, Lacul 95 44 5N 26 10 E
Graénalon, L. 96 64 10N 17 20W
Graettinger 23 43 14N 94 45W
Graford 51 32 56N 98 14W
Grafton, Australia 127 29 38 S 152 58 E
Grafton, Ill. 21 38 58N 90 26W
Grafton, Iowa 23 43 20N 93 4W
Grafton, Mass. 28 42 12N 71 41W
Grafton, N. Dak. 41 48 25N 97 25W
Grafton, N.H. 36 43 34N 71 57W
Grafton, Ohio 42 41 16N 82 4W
Grafton, Vt. 36 43 10N 72 37W
Grafton, W. Va. 54 39 21N 80 2W
Grafton, Wis. 55 43 19N 87 57W
Grafton, C. 127 16 51 S 146 0 E
Grafton County ◇ 36 43 50N 71 45W
Graham, Canada 60 49 20N 90 30W
Graham, Ga. 18 31 50N 82 30W
Graham, N.C. 40 36 5N 79 25W
Graham, Tex. 51 33 6N 98 35W
Graham → 62 56 31N 122 17W
Graham, Mt. 12 32 42N 109 52W
Graham Bell, Os. 100 80 5N 70 0 E
Graham County ◇, Ariz. 12 33 0N 110 0W
Graham County ◇, Kans. 24 39 20N 99 45W
Graham County ◇, N.C. 40 35 20N 83 50W
Graham I. 62 53 40N 132 30W
Graham L. 26 44 39N 68 24W
Graham Land 5 65 0 S 64 0W
Grahamdale 63 51 23N 98 30W
Grahamstown 123 33 19 S 26 31 E
Grain Coast 118 4 20N 10 0W
Grainfield 24 39 7N 100 28W
Grainger County ◇ 49 36 17N 83 31W
Grainola 43 36 57N 96 39W
Grajaú 74 5 50 S 46 4W
Grajaú → 74 3 41 S 44 48W
Grambling 25 32 32N 92 43W
Gramercy 25 30 4N 90 42W
Grampian 45 40 58N 78 37W
Grampian □ 84 57 0N 3 0W
Grampian Mts. 84 56 50N 4 0W
Gran → 71 4 1N 55 30W
Gran Altiplanicie Central 78 49 0 S 69 30W
Gran Canaria 120 27 55N 15 35W
Gran Chaco 76 25 0 S 61 0W
Gran Paradiso 94 45 33N 7 17 E
Gran Sabana, La 71 5 30N 61 30W
Gran Sasso d'Italia 94 42 25N 13 30 E
Granada, Nic. 66 11 58N 86 0W
Granada, Spain 91 37 10N 3 35W
Granada, Colo. 16 38 4N 102 19W
Granada, Minn. 30 43 42N 94 21W
Granard 85 53 47N 7 30W
Granbury 51 32 27N 97 47W
Granby, Canada 60 45 25N 72 45W
Granby, Colo. 16 40 5N 105 56W
Granby, Conn. 28 41 57N 72 47W
Granby, Mo. 32 36 55N 94 15W
Granby, L. 16 40 9N 105 52W
Grand →, Mich. 29 43 4N 86 15W
Grand →, Mo. 32 39 23N 93 7W
Grand →, S. Dak. 47 45 40N 100 45W
Grand Bahama 66 26 40N 78 30W
Grand Bank 61 47 6N 55 48W
Grand Bassam 120 5 10N 3 49W
Grand Bay 10 30 29N 88 21W
Grand Blanc 29 42 56N 83 38W
Grand-Bourge 67 15 53N 61 19W
Grand Cane 25 32 5N 93 49W
Grand Canyon 12 36 3N 112 9W
Grand Canyon National Park 12 36 15N 112 30W
Grand Cayman 66 19 20N 81 20W
Grand Chenier 25 29 46N 92 58W
Grand Coulee 53 47 57N 119 0W
Grand Coulee Dam 53 47 57N 118 59W
Grand County ◇, Colo. 16 40 10N 106 15W
Grand County ◇, Utah 52 39 0N 109 30W
Grand Falls 61 48 56N 55 40W
Grand Forks, Canada 62 49 0N 118 30W
Grand Forks, U.S.A. 41 47 55N 97 3W
Grand Forks County ◇ 41 47 55N 97 22W
Grand Haven 29 43 4N 86 13W
Grand I., La. 25 29 10N 90 0W
Grand I., Mich. 29 46 31N 86 40W
Grand Island 34 40 55N 98 21W
Grand Isle, La. 25 29 14N 90 0W
Grand Isle, Vt. 36 44 43N 73 18W
Grand Isle County ◇ 36 44 57N 73 17W
Grand Junction, Colo. 16 39 4N 108 33W
Grand Junction, Iowa 23 42 2N 94 14W
Grand L., N.B., Canada 61 45 57N 66 7W
Grand L., Newf., Canada 61 49 0N 57 30W
Grand L., Newf., Canada 61 53 40N 60 30W
Grand L., La. 25 29 55N 92 47W
Grand L., Maine 26 45 40N 67 50W
Grand L., Ohio 42 40 32N 84 25W
Grand Lac Victoria 60 47 35N 77 35W
Grand Lahou 120 5 10N 5 0W
Grand Lake, Colo. 16 40 15N 105 49W
Grand Lake, La. 25 30 2N 93 17W
Grand Lake Matagamon 26 46 12N 68 47W
Grand Lake Seboeis 26 46 18N 68 39W
Grand Ledge 29 42 45N 84 45W
Grand Manan Channel 26 44 40N 67 0W
Grand Manan I. 61 44 45N 66 52W
Grand Marais, Canada 60 47 45N 90 25W
Grand Marais, Mich. 29 46 40N 85 59W
Grand Marais, Minn. 30 47 45N 90 20W
Grand Meadow 30 43 42N 92 34W
Grand Mère 60 46 36N 72 40W
Grand Mesa 16 39 0N 108 15W
Grand Mesa National Forest 16 39 20N 107 50W
Grand Portage 30 47 58N 89 41W
Grand Portage Indian Reservation 30 47 55N 89 50W
Grand Prairie 51 32 47N 97 0W
Grand Rapids, Canada 63 53 12N 99 19W
Grand Rapids, Mich. 29 42 58N 85 40W
Grand Rapids, Minn. 30 47 14N 93 31W
Grand Rapids, Ohio 42 41 25N 83 52W
Grand Ridge, Fla. 17 30 43N 85 1W
Grand Ridge, Ill. 21 41 14N 88 50W
Grand River 23 40 49N 93 58W
Grand Rivers 48 37 1N 88 14W
Grand Ronde 44 45 4N 123 37W
Grand Rounde → 53 46 5N 116 59W
Grand Saline 51 32 41N 95 43W
Grand Santi 71 4 20N 54 24W
Grand Teton Mt. 56 43 44N 110 48W
Grand Teton National Park 56 43 50N 110 50W
Grand Tower 21 37 38N 89 30W
Grand Traverse B. 29 45 5N 85 35W
Grand Traverse County ◇ 29 44 40N 85 35W
Grand Valley 16 39 27N 108 3W
Grand View, Canada 63 51 10N 100 42W
Grand View, U.S.A. 20 42 59N 116 6W
Grand Wash Cliffs 12 36 0N 113 50W
Grande →, Jujuy, Argentina 76 24 20 S 65 2W
Grande →, Mendoza, Argentina 76 36 52 S 69 45W
Grande →, Bolivia 73 15 51 S 64 39W
Grande →, Bahia, Brazil 74 11 30 S 44 30W
Grande →, Minas Gerais, Brazil 75 20 6 S 51 4W
Grande →, Venezuela 71 8 36N 61 39W
Grande, B. 78 50 30 S 68 20W
Grande, Coxilha 77 28 18 S 51 30W
Grande, I. 75 23 9 S 44 14W
Grande, Rio → 50 25 58N 97 9W
Grande, Serra, Goiás, Brazil 74 11 15 S 46 30W
Grande, Serra, Piauí, Brazil 74 8 0 S 45 0W
Grande Baie 61 48 19N 70 52W
Grande Baleine, R. de la → 60 55 16N 77 47W
Grande Cache 62 53 53N 119 8W
Grande de Anasco, Rio → 57 18 16N 67 11W
Grande de Arecibo, Rio → 57 18 29N 66 43W
Grande de Loiza, Rio → 57 18 26N 65 53W
Grande de Manati, Rio → 57 18 29N 66 32W
Grande de Santiago → 64 21 20N 105 50W
Grande-Entrée 61 47 30N 61 40W
Grande Prairie 62 55 10N 118 50W
Grande-Rivière 61 48 26N 64 30W
Grande Ronde → 44 46 5N 116 59W
Grande-Vallée 61 49 14N 65 8W
Grandes-Bergeronnes 61 48 16N 69 35W
Grandfalls 50 31 20N 102 51W
Grandfield 43 34 14N 98 41W
Grandin, Mo. 32 36 50N 90 50W
Grandin, N. Dak. 41 47 14N 97 0W
Grandoe Mines 62 56 29N 129 54W
Grandview, Iowa 23 41 16N 91 11W
Grandview, Mo. 32 38 53N 94 32W
Grandview, Tex. 51 32 16N 97 11W
Grandview, Wash. 53 46 15N 119 54W
Grandville 29 42 54N 85 46W
Graneros 76 34 5 S 70 45W
Grangemouth 84 56 1N 3 43W
Granger, Iowa 23 41 46N 93 49W
Granger, Tex. 51 30 43N 97 26W
Granger, Wash. 53 46 21N 120 11W
Granger, Wyo. 56 41 35N 109 58W
Grangeville 20 45 56N 116 7W
Granite, Colo. 16 39 3N 106 16W
Granite, Okla. 43 34 58N 99 23W
Granite City 21 38 42N 90 9W
Granite County ◇ 33 46 25N 113 30W
Granite Falls, Minn. 30 44 49N 95 33W
Granite Falls, N.C. 40 35 48N 81 26W
Granite Falls, Wash. 53 48 5N 121 58W
Granite Mts., Ariz. 12 32 20N 113 20W
Granite Mts., Wyo. 56 42 45N 107 40W
Granite Pass 56 44 38N 107 30W
Granite Peak, Mont. 33 45 10N 109 48W
Granite Peak, Nev. 35 41 40N 117 35W
Granite Pt. 29 46 47N 87 36W
Granite Quarry 40 35 37N 80 26W
Granite Range 35 40 15N 119 25W
Graniteville, S.C. 46 33 34N 81 49W
Graniteville, Vt. 36 44 8N 72 29W
Granity 128 41 39 S 171 51 E
Granja 74 3 7 S 40 50W
Granja de Torrehermosa 91 38 19N 5 35W
Grannis 13 34 14N 94 20W
Grano 41 48 37N 101 35W
Granollers 91 41 39N 2 18 E
Grant, Colo. 16 39 28N 105 40W
Grant, Fla. 17 27 56N 80 32W
Grant, Iowa 23 41 9N 94 59W
Grant, La. 25 30 47N 92 57W
Grant, Mich. 29 43 20N 85 51W
Grant, Mont. 33 45 1N 113 4W
Grant, Nebr. 34 40 50N 101 43W
Grant, Okla. 43 33 57N 95 31W
Grant, Mt. 35 38 34N 118 48W
Grant City 32 40 29N 94 25W
Grant County ◇, Ark. 13 34 19N 92 24W
Grant County ◇, Ind. 22 40 30N 85 40W
Grant County ◇, Kans. 24 37 30N 101 15W
Grant County ◇, Ky. 49 38 35N 84 35W
Grant County ◇, Minn. 30 45 55N 96 0W
Grant County ◇, N. Dak. 41 46 15N 101 30W
Grant County ◇, N. Mex. 38 33 0N 108 30W
Grant County ◇, Nebr. 34 41 50N 101 45W
Grant County ◇, Okla. 43 36 50N 97 45W
Grant County ◇, Oreg. 44 44 30N 119 0W
Grant County ◇, S. Dak. 47 45 12N 96 47W
Grant County ◇, W. Va. 54 39 4N 79 4W
Grant County ◇, Wash. 53 47 10N 119 30W
Grant County ◇, Wis. 55 42 50N 90 45W
Grant Parish ◇ 25 31 32N 92 25W
Grant Park 21 41 14N 87 39W
Grant Range 35 38 30N 115 25W
Grantham, U.K. 82 52 55N 0 39W
Grantham, U.S.A. 36 43 29N 72 8W
Grantown-on-Spey 84 57 19N 3 36W
Grants 38 35 9N 107 52W
Grants Pass 44 42 26N 123 19W
Grantsburg 55 45 47N 92 41W
Grantsdale 33 46 12N 114 9W
Grantsville, Md. 27 39 42N 79 12W
Grantsville, Utah 52 40 36N 112 28W
Grantsville, W. Va. 54 38 55N 81 6W
Grantville 18 33 14N 84 50W
Granville, France 90 48 50N 1 35W
Granville, Ill. 21 41 16N 89 14W
Granville, Mass. 28 42 4N 72 52W
Granville, N. Dak. 41 48 16N 100 47W
Granville, N.Y. 39 43 24N 73 16W
Granville, Ohio 42 40 4N 82 31W
Granville, Vt. 36 43 58N 72 51W
Granville County ◇ 40 36 20N 78 40W
Granville L. 63 56 18N 100 30W
Grapeland 51 31 30N 95 29W
Grapevine L. 51 32 58N 97 4W
Gras, L. de 58 64 30N 110 30W
Grasmere 20 42 23N 115 53W
Grasonville 27 38 57N 76 13W
Grass → 63 56 3N 96 33W

Grundy Center Hajdúböszörmény

Grundy Center 23 42 22N 92 47W
Grundy County ◇, Ill. 21 41 20N 88 25W
Grundy County ◇, Iowa 23 42 25N 92 45W
Grundy County ◇, Mo. 32 40 5N 93 30W
Grundy County ◇, Tenn. 49 35 26N 85 44W
Gruver, Iowa 23 43 24N 94 42W
Gruver, Tex. 50 36 16N 101 24W
Gryazi 98 52 30N 39 58 E
Grygla 30 48 18N 95 37W
Grytviken 5 53 50 S 37 10W
Gu Achi 12 32 20N 112 2W
Gua 109 22 18N 85 20 E
Guacanayabo, G. de 66 20 40N 77 20W
Guacara 70 10 14N 67 53W
Guachípas → 76 25 40 S 65 30W
Guachiría → 70 5 27N 70 36W
Guadalajara, Mexico 64 20 40N 103 20W
Guadalajara, Spain 91 40 37N 3 12W
Guadalcanal 124 9 32 S 160 12 E
Guadales 76 34 30 S 67 55W
Guadalete → 91 36 35N 6 13W
Guadalhorce → 91 36 41N 4 27W
Guadalquivir → 91 36 47N 6 22W
Guadalupe = Guadeloupe ■ 67 16 20N 61 40W
Guadalupe, Brazil 74 6 44 S 43 47W
Guadalupe, U.S.A. 12 33 25N 111 55W
Guadalupe → 51 28 27N 96 47W
Guadalupe, Sierra de 91 39 28N 5 30W
Guadalupe Bravos 64 31 20N 106 10W
Guadalupe County ◇, N. Mex. 38 35 0N 104 45W
Guadalupe County ◇, Tex. 51 29 34N 97 58W
Guadalupe de los Reyes 64 24 10N 106 0W
Guadalupe I. 125 29 0N 118 50W
Guadalupe Mts. 38 32 15N 105 0W
Guadalupe Mts. Nat. Pk. 50 32 0N 104 30W
Guadalupe Peak 50 31 50N 104 52W
Guadalupe y Calvo 64 26 6N 106 58W
Guadalupita 38 36 8N 105 14W
Guadarrama, Sierra de 91 41 0N 4 0W
Guadeloupe ■ 67 16 20N 61 40W
Guadeloupe Passage 67 16 50N 62 15W
Guadiana → 91 37 14N 7 22W
Guadix 91 37 18N 3 11W
Guafo, Boca del 78 43 35 S 74 0W
Guafo, I. 78 43 35 S 74 50W
Guainía □ 70 2 30N 69 0W
Guainía → 70 2 1N 67 7W
Guaíra 77 24 5 S 54 10W
Guaira, La 70 10 36N 66 56W
Guaitecas, Islas 78 44 0 S 74 30W
Guajará-Mirim 73 10 50 S 65 20W
Guajataca, Lago de 57 18 24N 66 56W
Guajira □ 70 11 30N 72 30W
Guajira, La □ 70 11 30N 72 30W
Guajira, Pen. de la 70 12 0N 72 0W
Gualaceo 70 2 54 S 78 47W
Gualala 14 38 46N 123 32W
Gualán 66 15 8N 89 22W
Gualeguay 76 33 10 S 59 14W
Gualeguaychú 76 33 3 S 59 31W
Gualicho, Salina 78 40 25 S 65 20W
Gualjaina 78 42 45 S 70 30W
Guam 124 13 27N 144 45 E
Guamá 74 1 37 S 47 29W
Guamá → 74 1 29 S 48 30W
Guamblin, I. 78 44 50 S 75 0W
Guaminí 76 37 1 S 62 28W
Guamote 70 1 56 S 78 43W
Guampí, Sierra de 71 6 0N 65 35W
Guamúchil 64 25 25N 108 3W
Guan Xian 113 31 2N 103 38 E
Guanabacoa 66 23 8N 82 18W
Guanacaste, Cordillera del 66 10 40N 85 4W
Guanaceví 64 25 40N 106 0W
Guanahani = San Salvador 67 24 0N 74 40W
Guanajay 66 22 56N 82 42W
Guanajibo, Punta 57 18 10N 67 11W
Guanajuato 64 21 0N 101 20W
Guanajuato □ 64 20 40N 101 20W
Guanambi 75 14 13 S 42 47W
Guanare 70 8 42N 69 12W
Guanare → 70 8 13N 67 46W
Guandacol 76 29 30 S 68 40W
Guane 66 22 10N 84 7W
Guang'an 115 30 28N 106 35 E
Guangde 115 30 54N 119 25 E
Guangdong □ 115 23 0N 113 0 E
Guanghua 115 32 22N 111 38 E
Guangshun 115 26 8N 106 21 E
Guangxi Zhuangzu Zizhiqu □ 115 24 0N 109 0 E
Guangyuan 115 32 26N 105 51 E
Guangze 115 27 30N 117 12 E
Guangzhou 115 23 5N 113 10 E
Guanhães 75 18 47 S 42 57W
Guanica 57 17 59N 66 55W
Guanica, Laguna de 57 17 58N 66 0W
Guanipa → 71 9 56N 62 26W
Guano L. 44 42 11N 119 32W
Guanta 71 10 14N 64 36W
Guantánamo 67 20 10N 75 14W
Guantao 114 36 42N 115 25 E
Guanyun 115 34 20N 119 18 E
Guapí 70 2 36N 77 54W
Guápiles 66 10 10N 83 46W
Guaporé → 73 11 55 S 65 4W
Guaqui 72 16 41 S 68 54W
Guarabira 74 6 51 S 35 29W
Guaranda 70 1 36 S 79 0W
Guarapari 75 20 40 S 40 30W
Guarapuava 77 25 20 S 51 30W
Guaratinguetá 77 22 49 S 45 9W
Guaratuba 77 25 53 S 48 38W
Guarda 91 40 32N 7 20W
Guardafui, C. = Asir, Ras 105 11 55N 51 10 E
Guaria □ 76 25 45 S 56 30W
Guárico □ 70 8 40N 66 35W
Guarrojo → 70 4 6N 70 42W
Guarujá 77 24 2 S 46 25W
Guarus 75 21 44 S 41 20W
Guasave 64 25 34N 108 27W
Guascama, Pta. 70 2 32N 8 24W
Guasdualito 70 7 15N 70 44W
Guasipati 71 7 28N 61 54W
Guatemala 66 14 40N 90 22W
Guatemala ■ 66 15 40N 90 30W
Guatire 70 10 28N 66 32W
Guaviare → 70 4 3N 67 44W
Guaxupé 75 21 10 S 47 5W
Guayabero → 70 2 36N 72 47W
Guayama 57 17 59N 66 7W
Guayama ◇ 57 18 10N 66 15W
Guayaneco, Arch. 78 47 45 S 75 10W
Guayanilla 57 18 1N 66 47W
Guayanilla, Bahia de 57 17 55N 66 50W
Guayaquil 70 2 15 S 79 52W
Guayaquil, G. de 70 3 10 S 81 0W
Guayaramerín 73 10 48 S 65 23W
Guayas → 70 1 23N 74 50W
Guaymas 64 27 59N 110 54W
Guaynabo 57 18 22N 66 7W
Guazhou 115 32 17N 119 21 E
Guchil 112 5 35N 102 10 E
Gudbrandsdalen 97 61 33N 10 0 E
Guddu Barrage 108 28 30N 69 50 E
Gudivada 109 16 30N 81 3 E
Gudur 108 14 12N 79 55 E
Guecho 91 43 21N 2 59W
Guékédou 120 8 40N 10 5W
Guelma 120 36 25N 7 29 E
Guelph 60 43 35N 80 20W
Güepi 70 0 9 S 75 10W
Güer Aike 78 51 39 S 69 35W
Güera, La 120 20 51N 17 0W
Guéréda 121 14 31N 22 5 E
Guéret 90 46 11N 1 51 E
Guerneville 14 38 30N 123 0W
Guernica 91 43 19N 2 40W
Guernsey, Chan. Is. 83 49 30N 2 35W
Guernsey, Iowa 23 41 39N 92 21W
Guernsey, Wyo. 56 42 16N 104 45W
Guernsey County ◇ 42 40 2N 81 35W
Guernsey Reservoir 56 42 17N 104 46W
Guerra 50 26 53N 98 54W
Guerrero □ 65 17 30N 100 0W
Gueydan 25 30 2N 92 31W
Guffey 16 38 45N 105 31W
Guffy Peak 56 43 29N 107 54W
Gui Jiang → 115 23 30N 111 15 E
Gui Xian 115 23 8N 109 35 E
Guia Lopes da Laguna 77 21 26 S 56 7W
Guichi 115 30 39N 117 27 E
Guide Rock 34 40 4N 98 20W
Guidong 115 26 7N 113 57 E
Guiglo 120 6 45N 7 30W
Guilarte, Monte 57 18 9N 66 46W
Guildford 83 51 14N 0 34W
Guildhall 36 44 34N 71 34W
Guilford, Conn. 28 41 17N 72 41W
Guilford, Maine 26 45 10N 69 23W
Guilford County ◇ 40 36 10N 79 45W
Guilin 115 25 18N 110 15 E
Guilvinec 90 47 48N 4 17W
Guimarães 74 2 9 S 44 42W
Guimaras 111 10 35N 122 37 E
Guin 10 33 58N 87 55W
Guinda 14 38 50N 122 12W
Guinea ■ 120 10 20N 10 0W
Guinea, Gulf of 118 3 0N 2 30 E
Guinea-Bissau ■ 120 12 0N 15 0W
Güines 66 22 50N 82 0W
Guingamp 90 48 34N 3 10W
Guion 13 35 56N 91 57W
Guiping 115 23 21N 110 2 E
Guiratinga 73 16 21 S 53 45W
Güiria 71 10 32N 62 18W
Guiuan 111 11 5N 125 55 E
Guixi 115 28 16N 117 15 E
Guiyang, Guizhou, China 115 26 32N 106 40 E
Guiyang, Hunan, China 115 25 46N 112 42 E
Guizhou □ 115 27 0N 107 0 E
Gujarat □ 108 23 20N 71 0 E
Gujranwala 108 32 10N 74 12 E
Gujrat 108 32 40N 74 2 E
Gulbarga 108 17 20N 76 50 E
Gulf Basin 126 15 20 S 129 0 E
Gulf Breeze 17 30 22N 87 9W
Gulf County ◇ 17 29 50N 85 15W
Gulf Hammock 17 29 15N 82 43W
Gulf Islands National Seashore 17 30 10N 87 10W
Gulf Shores 10 30 17N 87 41W
Gulfport, Fla. 17 27 44N 82 43W
Gulfport, Miss. 31 30 22N 89 6W
Gulkana 11 62 16N 145 23W
Gull L. 30 46 25N 94 21W
Gull Lake 63 50 10N 108 29W
Gullivan B. 17 25 45N 81 40W
Gulshad 100 46 45N 74 25 E
Gulu 122 2 48N 32 17 E
Gumboro 27 38 28N 75 22W
Gumma □ 117 36 30N 138 20 E
Gummi 120 12 4N 5 9 E
Gümüsane 106 40 30N 39 30 E
Gumzai 111 5 28 S 134 42 E
Gun L. 29 42 36N 85 31W
Guna 108 24 40N 77 19 E
Gundih 111 7 10 S 110 56 E
Gungu 122 5 43 S 19 20 E
Gunisao → 63 53 56N 97 53W
Gunisao L. 63 53 33N 96 15W
Gunnedah 127 30 59 S 150 15 E
Gunnison, Colo. 16 38 33N 106 56W
Gunnison, Miss. 31 33 57N 90 57W
Gunnison, Utah 52 39 9N 111 49W
Gunnison → 16 39 4N 108 35W
Gunnison County ◇ 16 38 40N 107 0W
Gunnison National Forest 16 38 30N 107 0W
Gunnison Peak 16 38 49N 107 23W
Gunpowder → 27 39 20N 76 20W
Guntakal 108 15 11N 77 27 E
Guntersville 10 34 21N 86 18W
Guntersville L. 10 34 25N 86 23W
Guntown 31 34 27N 88 40W
Guntur 109 16 23N 80 30 E
Gunungapi 111 6 45 S 126 30 E
Gunungsitoli 110 1 15N 97 30 E
Gunza 122 10 50 S 13 50 E
Guo He → 115 32 59N 117 10 E
Guoyang 115 33 32N 116 12 E
Gupis 108 36 15N 73 20 E
Gura-Teghii 95 45 30N 26 25 E
Gurabo 57 18 16N 65 58W
Gūrchañ 106 34 55N 49 25 E
Gurdaspur 108 32 5N 75 31 E
Gurdon 13 33 55N 93 9W
Gurgaon 108 28 27N 77 1 E
Gurguéia → 74 6 50 S 43 24W
Guri Dam 71 7 50N 62 52W
Gurkha 109 28 5N 84 40 E
Gurley 34 41 19N 102 58W
Gurnee 21 42 22N 87 55W
Gurnet Point 28 42 1N 70 34W
Gurun 112 5 49N 100 27 E
Gurupá 74 1 25 S 51 35W
Gurupá, I. Grande de 71 1 25 S 51 45W
Gurupi 75 11 43 S 49 4W
Gurupi → 74 1 13 S 46 6W
Gurupi, Serra do 74 5 0 S 47 30W
Guryev 99 47 5N 52 0 E
Gusau 120 12 12N 6 40 E
Gushan 114 39 50N 123 35 E
Gushi 115 32 11N 115 41 E
Gustavus 11 58 25N 135 44W
Gustine, Calif. 14 37 16N 121 0W
Gustine, Tex. 51 31 51N 98 24W
Güstrow 88 53 47N 12 12 E
Guthrie, Ky. 48 36 39N 87 10W
Guthrie, Okla. 43 35 53N 97 25W
Guthrie, Tex. 50 33 37N 100 19W
Guthrie Center 23 41 41N 94 30W
Guthrie County ◇ 23 41 40N 94 30W
Gutiérrez 73 19 25 S 63 34W
Guttenberg 23 42 47N 91 6W
Guyana ■ 71 5 0N 59 0W
Guyandotte → 54 38 25N 82 25W
Guyanes → 57 18 6N 65 50W
Guyang 114 41 0N 110 5 E
Guyenne 90 44 30N 0 40 E
Guymon 43 36 41N 101 29W
Guyton 18 32 20N 81 24W
Guyuan 114 36 0N 106 20 E
Guzhen 115 33 22N 117 18 E
Guzmán, Laguna de 64 31 25N 107 25W
Gwa 109 17 36N 94 34 E
Gwaai 123 19 15 S 27 45 E
Gwādar 107 25 10N 62 18 E
Gwalior 108 26 12N 78 10 E
Gwanda 123 20 55 S 29 0 E
Gweebarra B. 85 54 52N 8 21W
Gweedore 85 55 4N 8 15W
Gwent □ 83 51 45N 2 55W
Gweru 123 19 28 S 29 45 E
Gwinn 29 46 19N 87 27W
Gwinner 41 46 14N 97 40W
Gwinnett County ◇ 18 34 0N 84 0W
Gwydir → 127 29 27 S 149 48 E
Gwynedd □ 82 53 0N 4 0W
Gyaring Hu 113 34 50N 97 40 E
Gydanskiy P-ov. 100 70 0N 78 0 E
Gympie 127 26 11 S 152 38 E
Gyöngyös 89 47 48N 20 0 E
Györ 89 47 41N 17 40 E
Gypsum, Colo. 16 39 39N 106 57W
Gypsum, Kans. 24 38 42N 97 26W
Gypsum Pt. 62 61 53N 114 35W
Gypsumville 63 51 45N 98 40W

H

Ha 'Arava 104 30 50N 35 20 E
Haakon County ◇ 47 44 25N 101 35W
Haapamäki 96 62 18N 24 28 E
Haarlem 87 52 23N 4 39 E
Haast → 128 43 50 S 169 2 E
Hab Nadi Chauki 108 25 0N 66 50 E
Habana, La 66 23 8N 82 22W
Habaswein 122 1 2N 39 30 E
Habay 62 58 50N 118 44W
Habersham 18 34 36N 83 34W
Habersham County ◇ 18 34 40N 83 30W
Haboro 116 44 22N 141 42 E
Hachijō-Jima 117 33 5N 139 45 E
Hachinohe 116 40 30N 141 29 E
Hachiōji 117 35 40N 139 20 E
Hachita 38 31 55N 108 19W
Hackberry, Ariz. 12 35 22N 113 44W
Hackberry, La. 25 30 0N 93 17W
Hackensack, Minn. 30 46 56N 94 31W
Hackensack, N.J. 37 40 53N 74 3W
Hackett 13 35 11N 94 25W
Hackettstown 37 40 51N 74 50W
Hackleburg 10 34 17N 87 50W
Hadarba, Ras 121 22 4N 36 51 E
Hadd, Ras al 107 22 35N 59 50 E
Haddam 24 39 52N 97 18W
Haddington 84 55 57N 2 48W
Haddock 18 33 2N 83 26W
Hadejia 120 12 30N 10 5 E
Ḥadera 104 32 27N 34 55 E
Ḥadera, N. → 104 32 28N 34 52 E
Hadhramaut = Haḑramawt 105 15 30N 49 30 E
Hadlock 53 48 2N 122 45W
Hadlyme 28 41 25N 72 25W
Haḑramawt 105 15 30N 49 30 E
Hadrians Wall 82 55 0N 2 30W
Haeju 114 38 3N 125 45 E
Haena 19 22 14N 159 34W
Haerhpin = Harbin 114 45 48N 126 40 E
Hafar al Bāţin 106 28 25N 46 0 E
Hafizabad 108 32 5N 73 40 E
Haflong 109 25 10N 93 5 E
Hafnarfjörður 96 64 4N 21 57W
Haft-Gel 106 31 30N 49 32 E
Hafun, Ras 105 10 29N 51 30 E
Hagalil 104 32 53N 35 18 E
Hagemeister I. 11 58 39N 160 54W
Hagen 88 51 21N 7 29 E
Hagerhill 49 37 42N 82 48W
Hagerman, Idaho 20 42 49N 114 54W
Hagerman, N. Mex. 38 33 7N 104 20W
Hagerstown, Ind. 22 39 55N 85 10W
Hagerstown, Md. 27 39 39N 77 43W
Hagfors 97 60 3N 13 45 E
Hagi, Iceland 96 65 28N 23 25W
Hagi, Japan 117 34 30N 131 22 E
Hagolan 104 33 0N 35 45 E
Hags Hd. 85 52 57N 9 30W
Hague, N. Dak. 41 46 2N 99 59W
Hague, N.Y. 39 43 45N 73 30W
Hague, C. de la 90 49 44N 1 56W
Hague, The = 's-Gravenhage 87 52 7N 4 17 E
Haguenau 90 48 49N 7 47 E
Hahira 18 30 59N 83 22W
Hahnville 25 29 59N 90 25W
Haicheng 114 40 50N 122 45 E
Haifa = Ḥefa 104 32 46N 35 0 E
Haifeng 115 22 58N 115 10 E
Haig 34 41 53N 103 45W
Haigler 34 40 1N 101 56W
Haikang 115 20 52N 110 8 E
Haikou 115 20 1N 110 16 E
Ḩā'il 106 27 28N 41 45 E
Hailar 114 49 10N 119 38 E
Hailar He → 114 49 30N 117 50 E
Hailey 20 43 31N 114 19W
Haileybury 60 47 30N 79 38W
Hailin 114 44 37N 129 30 E
Hailing Dao 115 21 35N 111 47 E
Hailong 114 42 32N 125 40 E
Hailun 114 47 28N 126 50 E
Hailuoto 96 65 3N 24 45 E
Haimen 115 31 52N 121 10 E
Hainan 115 19 0N 110 0 E
Hainan Dao 115 19 0N 109 30 E
Hainaut □ 87 50 30N 4 0 E
Haines, Alaska 11 59 14N 135 26W
Haines, Oreg. 44 44 55N 117 56W
Haines ◇ 11 57 0N 135 30W
Haines City 17 28 7N 81 38W
Haines Junction 62 60 45N 137 30W
Hainesport 37 39 59N 74 50W
Haining 115 30 28N 120 40 E
Haiphong 112 20 47N 106 41 E
Haiti ■ 67 19 0N 72 30W
Haiwee Reservoir 15 36 8N 117 57W
Haiya Junction 121 18 20N 36 21 E
Haiyan 115 30 28N 120 58 E
Haiyang 114 36 47N 121 9 E
Haiyuan 114 36 35N 105 52 E
Haja 111 3 19 S 129 37 E
Hajar Bangar 121 10 40N 22 45 E
Hajdúböszörmény 89 47 40N 21 30 E

Hajnówka Harman

Hajnówka 89 52 45N 23 32 E
Hajr 107 24 0N 56 34 E
Hakken-Zan 117 34 10N 135 54 E
Hakodate 116 41 45N 140 44 E
Haku-San 117 36 9N 136 46 E
Hakui 117 36 53N 136 47 E
Hala 108 25 43N 68 20 E
Ḥalab 106 36 10N 37 15 E
Ḥalabjah 106 35 10N 45 58 E
Ḥalaib 121 22 12N 36 30 E
Halalii L. 19 21 52N 160 11W
Halawa, C. 19 21 10N 156 43W
Halawa Heights 19 21 23N 157 55W
Halberstadt 88 51 53N 11 2 E
Halbur 23 42 0N 94 59W
Halcombe 128 40 8 S 175 30 E
Halcon, Mt. 111 13 0N 121 30 E
Haldeman 49 38 15N 83 19W
Halden 97 59 9N 11 23 E
Haldia 109 22 5N 88 3 E
Haldwani 108 29 31N 79 30 E
Hale, Colo. 16 39 38N 102 9W
Hale, Mo. 32 39 36N 93 20W
Hale Center 50 34 4N 101 51W
Hale County ◇, Ala. 10 32 42N 87 36W
Hale County ◇, Tex. 50 34 0N 101 55W
Haleakala Crater 19 20 43N 156 16W
Haleakala National Park 19 20 40N 156 15W
Haleiwa 19 21 36N 158 6W
Halethorpe 27 39 15N 76 42W
Haley 41 45 58N 103 7W
Haleyville, Ala. 10 34 14N 87 37W
Haleyville, N.J. 37 39 17N 75 2W
Half Way 32 37 37N 93 15W
Halfmoon Landing 18 31 42N 81 16W
Halfway 27 39 37N 77 46W
Halfway → 62 56 12N 121 32W
Ḥalḥul 104 31 35N 35 7 E
Ḥali 105 18 30N 41 30 E
Haliburton 60 45 3N 78 30W
Halifax, Canada 61 44 38N 63 35W
Halifax, U.K. 82 53 43N 1 51W
Halifax, Mass. 28 41 59N 70 52W
Halifax, N.C. 40 36 20N 77 35W
Halifax, Va. 54 36 46N 78 56W
Halifax B. 127 18 50 S 147 0 E
Halifax County ◇, N.C. 40 36 15N 77 40W
Halifax County ◇, Va. 54 36 55N 79 0W
Ḥalīl → 107 27 40N 58 30 E
Halkett, C. 11 70 48N 152 11W
Hall 33 46 35N 113 12W
Hall Beach 59 68 46N 81 12W
Hall County ◇, Ga. 18 34 15N 83 50W
Hall County ◇, Nebr. 34 40 45N 98 30W
Hall County ◇, Tex. 50 34 30N 100 35W
Hall I. 11 60 40N 173 6W
Hall Summit 25 32 11N 93 18W
Hallam 34 40 32N 96 47W
Hallandale 17 25 59N 80 8W
Hallands län □ 97 56 50N 12 50 E
Halle, Belgium 87 50 44N 4 13 E
Halle, Germany 88 51 29N 12 0 E
Halleck 35 40 57N 115 27W
Hällefors 97 59 47N 14 31 E
Hallett 43 36 19N 96 35W
Hallettsville 51 29 27N 96 57W
Halley 13 33 32N 91 20W
Halley Bay 5 75 31 S 26 36W
Halliday 41 47 21N 102 20W
Halliday L. 63 61 21N 108 56W
Halligan Reservoir 16 40 53N 105 20W
Hallingdal → 97 60 34N 9 12 E
Hällnäs 96 64 19N 19 36 E
Hallock 30 48 47N 96 57W
Halls, Ga. 18 34 18N 84 56W
Halls, Tenn. 48 35 53N 89 24W
Halls Creek 126 18 16 S 127 38 E
Halls Summit 24 38 21N 95 41W
Hallstead 45 41 58N 75 45W
Hallsville, Mo. 32 39 7N 92 13W
Hallsville, Tex. 51 32 30N 94 35W
Halltown 32 37 12N 93 38W
Hallwood 54 37 53N 75 36W
Halma 30 48 40N 96 36W
Halmahera 111 0 40N 128 0 E
Halmstad 97 56 41N 12 52 E
Halq el Oued 121 36 53N 10 18 E
Hals 97 56 59N 10 18 E
Halsey, Nebr. 34 41 54N 100 16W
Halsey, Oreg. 44 44 23N 123 7W
Hälsingborg = Helsingborg 97 56 3N 12 42 E
Halstad 30 47 21N 96 50W
Halstead 24 38 0N 97 31W
Haltom City 51 32 48N 97 16W
Halul 107 25 40N 52 40 E
Hamada 117 34 56N 132 4 E
Hamadān 106 34 52N 48 32 E
Hamadān □ 106 35 0N 49 0 E
Hamāh 106 35 5N 36 40 E
Hamamatsu 117 34 45N 137 45 E
Hamar 97 60 48N 11 7 E
Hamarøy 96 68 5N 15 38 E
Hambantota 108 6 10N 81 10 E
Hamber Prov. Park 62 52 20N 118 0W
Hamberg 41 47 46N 99 31W
Hamblen County ◇ 49 36 13N 83 18W
Hambleton 54 39 5N 79 39W
Hamburg, Germany 88 53 32N 9 59 E
Hamburg, Ark. 13 33 14N 91 48W
Hamburg, Calif. 14 41 47N 123 4W
Hamburg, Conn. 28 41 23N 72 21W
Hamburg, Ill. 21 39 14N 90 43W
Hamburg, Iowa 23 40 36N 95 39W
Hamburg, Minn. 30 44 44N 93 58W
Hamburg, Miss. 31 31 35N 91 4W
Hamburg, N.J. 37 41 9N 74 35W
Hamburg, N.Y. 39 42 43N 78 50W
Hamburg, Pa. 45 40 33N 75 59W
Hamden 28 41 23N 72 54W
Hame 97 61 30N 24 0 E
Hämeenlinna 96 61 0N 24 28 E
Hameln 88 52 7N 9 24 E
Hamer 20 43 56N 112 12W
Hamersley Ra. 126 22 0 S 117 45 E
Hamersville 42 38 55N 83 59W
Hamhung 114 39 54N 127 30 E
Hami 113 42 55N 93 25 E
Hamilton, Australia 127 37 45 S 142 2 E
Hamilton, Canada 60 43 15N 79 50W
Hamilton, N.Z. 128 37 47 S 175 19 E
Hamilton, U.K. 84 55 47N 4 2W
Hamilton, Ala. 10 34 9N 87 59W
Hamilton, Alaska 11 62 54N 163 53W
Hamilton, Colo. 16 40 22N 107 37W
Hamilton, Ga. 18 32 45N 84 53W
Hamilton, Ill. 21 40 24N 91 21W
Hamilton, Kans. 24 37 59N 96 10W
Hamilton, Mich. 29 42 41N 86 0W
Hamilton, Mo. 32 39 45N 94 0W
Hamilton, Mont. 33 46 15N 114 10W
Hamilton, N.C. 40 35 57N 77 12W
Hamilton, N. Dak. 41 48 48N 97 24W
Hamilton, N.Y. 39 42 50N 75 33W
Hamilton, Ohio 42 39 24N 84 34W
Hamilton, Oreg. 44 44 44N 119 18W
Hamilton, Tex. 51 31 42N 98 7W
Hamilton, L. 13 34 26N 93 2W
Hamilton City 14 39 45N 122 1W
Hamilton County ◇, Fla. 17 30 30N 83 0W
Hamilton County ◇, Ill. 21 38 5N 88 30W
Hamilton County ◇, Ind. 22 40 5N 86 5W
Hamilton County ◇, Iowa 23 42 20N 93 40W
Hamilton County ◇, Kans. 24 38 0N 101 45W
Hamilton County ◇, N.Y. 39 43 30N 74 30W
Hamilton County ◇, Nebr. 34 40 45N 98 0W
Hamilton County ◇, Ohio 42 39 13N 84 33W
Hamilton County ◇, Tenn. 49 35 17N 85 10W
Hamilton County ◇, Tex. 51 31 40N 98 8W
Hamilton Dome 56 43 46N 108 35W
Hamilton Inlet 61 54 0N 57 30W
Hamiota 63 50 11N 100 38W
Hamler 42 41 14N 84 2W
Hamlet, Ind. 22 41 23N 86 35W
Hamlet, N.C. 40 34 53N 79 42W
Hamlet, Nebr. 34 40 23N 101 14W
Hamlin, Tex. 50 32 53N 100 8W
Hamlin, W. Va. 54 38 17N 82 6W
Hamlin County ◇ 47 44 40N 97 13W
Hamlin L. 29 44 3N 86 28W
Hamm 88 51 40N 7 49 E
Hammerfest 96 70 39N 23 41 E
Hammon 43 35 38N 99 23W
Hammond, Ill. 21 39 48N 88 36W
Hammond, Ind. 22 41 38N 87 30W
Hammond, La. 25 30 30N 90 28W
Hammond, Minn. 30 44 13N 92 23W
Hammond, N.Y. 39 44 27N 75 42W
Hammond, Oreg. 44 46 12N 123 57W
Hammondsport 39 42 25N 77 13W
Hammonton 37 39 39N 74 48W
Hampden, N.Z. 128 45 18 S 170 50 E
Hampden, Maine 26 44 44N 68 51W
Hampden, N. Dak. 41 48 32N 98 40W
Hampden County ◇ 28 42 10N 72 35W
Hampden Sydney 54 37 14N 78 28W
Hampshire, Ill. 21 42 6N 88 32W
Hampshire, Tenn. 48 35 36N 87 18W
Hampshire □ 83 51 3N 1 20W
Hampshire County ◇, Mass. 28 42 15N 72 35W
Hampshire County ◇, W. Va. 54 39 18N 78 38W
Hampshire Downs 83 51 10N 1 10W
Hampstead, Md. 27 39 37N 76 51W
Hampstead, N.C. 40 34 22N 77 44W
Hampstead, N.H. 36 42 51N 71 10W
Hampton, Ark. 13 33 32N 92 28W
Hampton, Conn. 28 41 47N 72 3W
Hampton, Fla. 17 29 52N 82 8W
Hampton, Ga. 18 33 23N 84 17W
Hampton, Iowa 23 42 45N 93 13W
Hampton, Minn. 30 44 37N 93 0W
Hampton, N.H. 36 42 57N 70 50W
Hampton, N.J. 37 40 42N 74 58W
Hampton, Nebr. 34 40 53N 97 53W
Hampton, Oreg. 44 43 40N 120 14W
Hampton, S.C. 46 32 52N 81 7W
Hampton, Tenn. 49 36 17N 82 10W
Hampton, Va. 54 37 2N 76 21W
Hampton Bays 39 40 53N 72 30W
Hampton County ◇ 46 32 50N 81 10W
Hampton Harbour 126 20 30 S 116 30 E
Hampton Springs 17 30 5N 83 40W
Hampton Tableland 126 32 0 S 127 0 E
Hamrat esh Sheykh 121 14 38N 27 55 E
Hams → 56 41 35N 109 57W
Hams Bluff 57 17 46N 64 52W
Han Jiang → 115 23 25N 116 40 E
Han Pijesak 95 44 0N 19 0 E
Han Shui → 115 30 35N 114 18 E
Hana 19 20 45N 155 59W
Hanaford 21 37 57N 88 50W
Hanahan 46 32 55N 80 0W
Hanalei 19 22 12N 159 30W
Hanamaki 116 39 23N 141 7 E
Hanamaulu 19 21 59N 159 22W
Hanapepe 19 21 55N 159 35W
Hanau 88 50 8N 8 56 E
Hanauma B. 19 21 15N 157 40W
Hanceville 10 34 4N 86 46W
Hancheng 114 35 31N 110 25 E
Hancock, Iowa 23 41 24N 95 21W
Hancock, Md. 27 39 42N 78 11W
Hancock, Mich. 29 47 8N 88 35W
Hancock, Minn. 30 45 30N 95 48W
Hancock, N.H. 36 42 57N 71 58W
Hancock, N.Y. 39 41 57N 75 17W
Hancock, Vt. 36 43 56N 72 51W
Hancock, Wis. 55 44 8N 89 31W
Hancock, Mt. 56 44 9N 110 25W
Hancock County ◇, Ga. 18 33 20N 83 0W
Hancock County ◇, Ill. 21 40 25N 91 10W
Hancock County ◇, Ind. 22 39 50N 85 45W
Hancock County ◇, Iowa 23 43 5N 93 45W
Hancock County ◇, Ky. 48 37 50N 86 45W
Hancock County ◇, Maine 26 44 30N 68 30W
Hancock County ◇, Miss. 31 30 17N 89 23W
Hancock County ◇, Ohio 42 41 2N 83 39W
Hancock County ◇, Tenn. 49 36 32N 83 13W
Hancock County ◇, W. Va. 54 40 30N 80 35W
Hancocks Bridge 37 39 31N 75 28W
Hand County ◇ 47 44 31N 98 59W
Handa, Japan 117 34 53N 137 0 E
Handa, Somalia 105 10 37N 51 2 E
Handan 114 36 35N 114 28 E
Handeni 122 5 25 S 38 2 E
Hanegev 104 30 50N 35 0 E
Haney 62 49 12N 122 40W
Hanford, Calif. 15 36 20N 119 39W
Hanford, Wash. 53 46 37N 119 19W
Hangang → 114 37 50N 126 30 E
Hangayn Nuruu 113 47 30N 100 0 E
Hangchou = Hangzhou 115 30 18N 120 11 E
Hanggin Houqi 114 40 58N 107 4 E
Hangö 97 59 50N 22 57 E
Hangu 114 39 18N 117 53 E
Hangzhou 115 30 18N 120 11 E
Hangzhou Wan 115 30 15N 120 45 E
Ḥanīsh J. 105 13 45N 42 46 E
Ḥanita 104 33 5N 35 10 E
Hankinson 41 46 4N 96 54W
Hanko 97 59 59N 22 57 E
Hankou 115 30 35N 114 30 E
Hanksville 52 38 22N 110 43W
Hanle 108 32 42N 79 4 E
Hanley Falls 30 44 42N 95 37W
Hanmer Springs 128 42 32 S 172 50 E
Hann, Mt. 126 16 0 S 126 0 E
Hanna, Canada 62 51 40N 111 54W
Hanna, Ind. 22 41 25N 86 47W
Hanna, La. 25 31 58N 93 21W
Hanna, Okla. 43 35 12N 95 53W
Hanna, Utah 52 40 26N 110 48W
Hanna, Wyo. 56 41 52N 106 34W
Hanna City 21 40 42N 89 48W
Hannaford 41 47 19N 98 11W
Hannah 41 48 58N 98 42W
Hannah B. 60 51 40N 80 0W
Hannibal, Mo. 32 39 42N 91 22W
Hannibal, N.Y. 39 43 19N 76 35W
Hannover, Germany 88 52 23N 9 43 E
Hannover, U.S.A. 41 47 7N 101 26W
Hanoi 112 21 5N 105 55 E
Hanover = Hannover 88 52 23N 9 43 E
Hanover, Ill. 21 42 15N 90 17W
Hanover, Ind. 22 38 43N 85 28W
Hanover, Kans. 24 39 54N 96 53W
Hanover, Mass. 28 42 7N 70 49W
Hanover, Mich. 29 42 6N 84 33W
Hanover, Minn. 30 45 10N 93 40W
Hanover, Mont. 33 47 7N 109 33W
Hanover, N.H. 36 43 42N 72 17W
Hanover, N. Mex. 38 32 48N 108 6W
Hanover, Ohio 42 40 4N 82 16W
Hanover, Pa. 45 39 48N 76 59W
Hanover, Va. 54 37 46N 77 22W
Hanover, I. 78 51 0 S 74 50W
Hanover County ◇ 54 37 46N 77 29W
Hanoverton 42 40 45N 80 56W
Hans Lollik I. 57 18 24N 64 53W
Hansboro 41 48 57N 99 23W
Hansen 20 42 32N 114 18W
Hansford County ◇ 50 36 10N 101 30W
Hansi 108 29 10N 75 57 E
Hanska 30 44 9N 94 30W
Hanson, Fla. 17 30 34N 83 21W
Hanson, Ky. 48 37 25N 87 29W
Hanson County ◇ 47 43 39N 97 47W
Hanson Range 126 27 0 S 136 30 E
Hanston 24 38 7N 99 43W
Hanyang 115 30 35N 114 2 E
Hanyin 115 32 54N 108 28 E
Hanzhong 115 33 10N 107 1 E
Hanzhuang 115 34 33N 117 23 E
Haora 109 22 37N 88 20 E
Haparanda 96 65 52N 24 8 E
Hapeville 18 33 40N 84 25W
Happy 50 34 45N 101 52W
Happy Camp 14 41 48N 123 23W
Happy Jack 12 34 45N 111 24W
Happy Valley 61 53 15N 60 20W
Hapur 108 28 45N 77 45 E
Ḥaql 106 29 10N 35 0 E
Haquira 72 14 14 S 72 12W
Har 111 5 16 S 133 14 E
Har Hu 113 38 20N 97 38 E
Har Us Nuur 113 48 0N 92 0 E
Har Yehuda 104 31 35N 34 57 E
Ḥaraḍ 106 24 22N 49 0 E
Harahan 25 29 56N 90 11W
Haraisan Plateau 106 23 0N 47 40 E
Haralson 18 33 14N 84 34W
Haralson County ◇ 18 33 45N 85 10W
Haranomachi 116 37 38N 140 58 E
Harardera 105 4 33N 47 38 E
Harare 123 17 43 S 31 2 E
Harazé 121 14 20N 19 12 E
Harbeson 27 38 43N 75 17W
Harbin 114 45 48N 126 40 E
Harbor Beach 29 43 51N 82 39W
Harbor Springs 29 45 26N 85 0W
Harbour Breton 61 47 29N 55 50W
Harbour Grace 61 47 40N 53 22W
Harburg 88 53 27N 9 58 E
Harcourt 23 42 16N 94 11W
Harcuvar Mts. 12 34 0N 113 30W
Hardangerfjorden 97 60 15N 6 0 E
Hardap Dam 123 24 32 S 17 50 E
Hardee County ◇ 17 27 30N 81 45W
Hardeeville 46 32 17N 81 5W
Hardeman County ◇, Tenn. 48 35 6N 89 0W
Hardeman County ◇, Tex. 51 34 20N 99 50W
Hardenberg 87 52 34N 6 37 E
Harderwijk 87 52 21N 5 38 E
Hardesty 43 36 37N 101 12W
Hardin, Ill. 21 39 10N 90 37W
Hardin, Ky. 48 36 46N 88 18W
Hardin, Mo. 32 39 16N 93 50W
Hardin, Mont. 33 45 44N 107 37W
Hardin, Tex. 51 30 9N 94 44W
Hardin County ◇, Ill. 21 37 30N 88 15W
Hardin County ◇, Iowa 23 42 25N 93 15W
Hardin County ◇, Ky. 48 37 40N 86 0W
Hardin County ◇, Ohio 42 40 42N 83 47W
Hardin County ◇, Tenn. 48 35 14N 88 15W
Hardin County ◇, Tex. 51 30 22N 94 19W
Harding, S. Africa 123 30 35 S 29 55 E
Harding, U.S.A. 30 46 7N 94 2W
Harding, L. 10 32 40N 85 5W
Harding County ◇, N. Mex. 38 36 0N 104 0W
Harding County ◇, S. Dak. 47 45 30N 103 30W
Hardinsburg, Ind. 22 38 28N 86 17W
Hardinsburg, Ky. 48 37 47N 86 28W
Hardisty 62 52 40N 111 18W
Hardman 44 45 10N 119 41W
Hardoi 108 27 26N 80 6 E
Hardtner 24 37 1N 98 39W
Hardwar = Haridwar 108 29 58N 78 9 E
Hardwick, Ga. 18 33 4N 83 14W
Hardwick, Mass. 28 42 21N 72 12W
Hardwick, Minn. 30 43 47N 96 12W
Hardwick, Vt. 36 44 30N 72 22W
Hardy, Ark. 13 36 19N 91 29W
Hardy, Mont. 33 47 12N 111 47W
Hardy, Nebr. 34 40 1N 97 56W
Hardy, Pen. 78 55 30 S 68 20W
Hardy County ◇ 54 39 0N 78 50W
Hardy Dam Pond 29 43 30N 85 37W
Hare B. 61 51 15N 55 45W
Hare Gilboa 104 32 31N 35 25 E
Hare Meron 104 32 59N 35 24 E
Harer 105 9 20N 42 8 E
Harford County ◇ 27 39 35N 76 25W
Hargeisa 105 9 30N 44 2 E
Harghita □ 95 46 30N 25 30 E
Harghita, Mții 95 46 25N 25 35 E
Hargill 50 26 27N 98 1W
Hargshamn 97 60 12N 18 30 E
Hari → 110 1 16 S 104 5 E
Haridwar 108 29 58N 78 9 E
Haringhata → 109 22 0N 89 58 E
Harīrūd 107 35 0N 61 0 E
Harīrūd → 107 34 20N 62 30 E
Harker Heights 51 31 5N 97 40W
Harkers Island 40 34 42N 76 34W
Harlan, Iowa 23 41 39N 95 19W
Harlan, Kans. 24 39 36N 98 46W
Harlan, Ky. 49 36 51N 83 19W
Harlan County ◇, Ky. 49 36 50N 83 15W
Harlan County ◇, Nebr. 34 40 15N 99 30W
Harlan County Lake 34 40 4N 99 13W
Harlech 82 52 52N 4 7W
Harlem, Ga. 18 33 25N 82 19W
Harlem, Mont. 33 48 32N 108 47W
Harleyville 46 33 13N 80 27W
Harlingen, Neth. 87 53 11N 5 25 E
Harlingen, U.S.A. 50 26 12N 97 42W
Harlowton 33 46 26N 109 50W
Harman 54 38 55N 79 32W

Harmon Heber

Harmon 21 41 43N 89 33W
Harmon County ◇ 43 34 45N 99 50W
Harmony, Ind. 22 39 32N 87 4W
Harmony, Maine 26 44 58N 69 33W
Harmony, Md. 27 38 47N 75 53W
Harmony, Minn. 30 43 33N 92 1W
Harmony, N.C. 40 35 58N 80 46W
Harnett County ◇ 40 35 20N 78 50W
Harney 27 39 44N 77 13W
Harney, L. 17 28 45N 81 3W
Harney Basin 44 43 0N 119 30W
Harney County ◇ 44 45 0N 119 0W
Harney L. 44 43 14N 119 8W
Harney Peak 47 43 52N 103 32W
Härnösand 96 62 38N 18 0 E
Haro, C. 64 27 50N 110 55W
Harold, Fla. 17 30 40N 86 53W
Harold, Ky. 49 37 32N 82 38W
Harp L. 61 55 5N 61 50W
Harper, Iowa 23 41 22N 92 3W
Harper, Kans. 24 37 17N 98 1W
Harper, Oreg. 44 43 52N 117 37W
Harper, Tex. 51 30 18N 99 15W
Harper, Mt. 11 64 14N 143 51W
Harper County ◇, Kans. 24 37 15N 98 0W
Harper County ◇, Okla. 43 36 50N 99 40W
Harper L. 15 35 2N 117 17W
Harpers Ferry, Iowa 23 43 12N 91 9W
Harpers Ferry, W. Va. 54 39 20N 77 44W
Harpersville 10 33 21N 86 26W
Harpeth → 48 36 18N 87 10W
Harqualala Mts. 12 33 45N 113 20W
Harrah, Okla. 43 35 29N 97 10W
Harrah, Wash. 53 46 24N 120 33W
Ḩarrat al Kishb 106 22 30N 40 15 E
Ḩarrat al 'Uwairidh 106 26 50N 38 0 E
Harrell 13 33 31N 92 24W
Harrellsville 40 36 18N 76 48W
Harriman 49 35 56N 84 33W
Harriman Reservoir 36 42 48N 72 55W
Harrington, Del. 27 38 56N 75 35W
Harrington, Maine 26 44 37N 67 49W
Harrington, Wash. 53 47 29N 118 15W
Harrington Harbour 61 50 31N 59 30W
Harris, U.K. 84 57 50N 6 55W
Harris, Kans. 24 38 19N 95 26W
Harris, Minn. 30 45 35N 92 58W
Harris, Mo. 32 40 18N 93 21W
Harris, Okla. 43 33 45N 94 44W
Harris, L. 17 28 47N 81 49W
Harris, Sd. of 84 57 44N 7 6W
Harris County ◇, Ga. 18 32 40N 84 50W
Harris County ◇, Tex. 51 29 46N 95 22W
Harris L. 126 31 10 S 135 10 E
Harrisburg, Ark. 13 35 34N 90 43W
Harrisburg, Ill. 21 37 44N 88 32W
Harrisburg, Mo. 32 39 9N 92 28W
Harrisburg, N.C. 40 35 19N 80 39W
Harrisburg, Nebr. 34 41 33N 103 44W
Harrisburg, Oreg. 44 44 16N 123 10W
Harrisburg, Pa. 45 40 16N 76 53W
Harrisburg, S. Dak. 47 43 26N 96 42W
Harrison, Ark. 13 36 14N 93 7W
Harrison, Ga. 18 32 50N 82 43W
Harrison, Idaho 20 47 27N 116 47W
Harrison, Mich. 29 44 1N 84 48W
Harrison, Mont. 33 45 42N 111 47W
Harrison, Nebr. 34 42 41N 103 53W
Harrison, C. 61 54 55N 57 55W
Harrison Bay 11 70 40N 151 0W
Harrison County ◇, Ind. 22 38 10N 86 10W
Harrison County ◇, Iowa 23 41 40N 95 50W
Harrison County ◇, Ky. 49 38 25N 84 20W
Harrison County ◇, Miss. 31 30 30N 89 7W
Harrison County ◇, Mo. 32 40 20N 94 0W
Harrison County ◇, Ohio 42 40 18N 81 11W
Harrison County ◇, Tex. 51 32 33N 94 23W
Harrison County ◇, W. Va. 54 39 17N 80 30W
Harrison L. 62 49 33N 121 50W
Harrisonburg, La. 25 31 46N 91 49W
Harrisonburg, Va. 54 38 27N 78 52W
Harrisonville 32 38 39N 94 21W
Harriston, Canada 60 43 57N 80 53W
Harriston, U.S.A. 31 31 44N 91 2W
Harrisville, Mich. 29 44 39N 83 17W
Harrisville, N.Y. 39 44 9N 75 19W
Harrisville, R.I. 28 41 58N 71 41W
Harrisville, W. Va. 54 39 13N 81 3W
Harrod 42 40 43N 83 56W
Harrodsburg 49 37 46N 84 51W
Harrogate, U.K. 82 53 59N 1 32W
Harrogate, U.S.A. 49 36 35N 83 40W
Harrold 47 44 31N 99 44W
Harrow 83 51 35N 0 15W
Harry S. Truman Reservoir 32 38 16N 93 24W
Harry Strunk L. 34 40 23N 100 13W
Harstad 96 68 48N 16 30 E
Hart, Mich. 29 43 42N 86 22W
Hart, Tex. 50 34 23N 102 7W
Hart County ◇, Ga. 18 34 15N 83 0W
Hart County ◇, Ky. 49 37 20N 85 50W
Hart L. 44 42 25N 119 51W
Hart Mt. 44 42 23N 119 53W
Hartfield 54 37 33N 76 27W
Hartford, Ala. 10 31 6N 85 42W
Hartford, Ark. 13 35 1N 94 23W
Hartford, Conn. 28 41 46N 72 41W
Hartford, Ga. 18 32 17N 83 28W
Hartford, Iowa 23 41 28N 93 24W
Hartford, Ky. 48 37 27N 86 55W
Hartford, Mich. 29 42 13N 86 10W
Hartford, S. Dak. 47 43 38N 96 57W
Hartford, Tenn. 49 35 49N 83 9W
Hartford, Wis. 55 43 19N 88 22W
Hartford City 22 40 27N 85 22W
Hartford County ◇ 28 41 45N 72 45W
Hartington 34 42 37N 97 16W
Hartland, Canada 61 46 20N 67 32W
Hartland, Maine 26 44 53N 69 27W
Hartland, Minn. 30 43 48N 93 29W
Hartland, Vt. 36 43 32N 72 24W
Hartland, Wis. 55 43 6N 88 21W
Hartland Pt. 83 51 2N 4 32W
Hartlepool 82 54 42N 1 11W
Hartley, Iowa 23 43 11N 95 29W
Hartley, Tex. 50 35 53N 102 24W
Hartley, Zimbabwe 123 18 10 S 30 14 E
Hartley Bay 62 53 25N 129 15W
Hartley County ◇ 50 35 50N 102 30W
Hartline 53 47 41N 119 6W
Hartly 27 39 10N 75 43W
Hartman 16 38 7N 102 13W
Hartney 63 49 30N 100 35W
Hartsburg 32 38 42N 92 19W
Hartsel 16 39 1N 105 48W
Hartselle 10 34 27N 86 56W
Hartshorne 43 34 51N 95 34W
Hartsville, S.C. 46 34 23N 80 4W
Hartsville, Tenn. 48 36 24N 86 10W
Hartville, Mo. 32 37 15N 92 31W
Hartville, Ohio 42 40 58N 81 20W
Hartville, Wyo. 56 42 20N 104 44W
Hartwell 18 34 21N 82 56W
Hartwell L. 46 34 21N 82 49W
Hartwick 23 41 47N 92 21W
Harvard, Idaho 20 46 55N 116 44W
Harvard, Ill. 21 42 25N 88 37W
Harvard, Nebr. 34 40 37N 98 6W
Harvard, Mt. 16 38 56N 106 19W
Harvey, Ark. 13 34 51N 93 47W
Harvey, Ill. 21 41 36N 87 50W
Harvey, N. Dak. 41 47 47N 99 56W
Harvey Cedars 37 39 43N 74 11W
Harvey County ◇ 24 38 0N 97 30W
Harveyville 24 38 47N 95 58W
Harwich, U.K. 83 51 56N 1 18 E
Harwich, U.S.A. 28 41 41N 70 5W
Harwinton 28 41 46N 73 4W
Harwood, Mo. 32 37 57N 94 9W
Harwood, Tex. 51 29 40N 97 30W
Haryana □ 108 29 0N 76 10 E
Harz 88 51 40N 10 40 E
Hasa 106 26 0N 49 0 E
Hasharon 104 32 12N 34 49 E
Hashefela 104 31 30N 34 43 E
Hashimoto 117 34 19N 135 37 E
Haskell, Ark. 13 34 30N 92 38W
Haskell, Okla. 43 35 50N 95 40W
Haskell, Tex. 51 33 10N 99 44W
Haskell County ◇, Kans. 24 37 30N 100 45W
Haskell County ◇, Okla. 43 35 10N 95 10W
Haskell County ◇, Tex. 51 33 12N 99 45W
Haskins 42 41 28N 83 42W
Haslet 51 32 59N 97 21W
Hassayampa → 12 33 19N 112 42W
Hasselt 87 50 56N 5 21 E
Hassi Inifel 120 29 50N 3 41 E
Hassi Messaoud 120 31 43N 6 8 E
Hastings, N.Z. 128 39 39 S 176 52 E
Hastings, U.K. 83 50 51N 0 36 E
Hastings, Fla. 17 29 43N 81 31W
Hastings, Iowa 23 41 1N 95 30W
Hastings, Mich. 29 42 39N 85 17W
Hastings, Minn. 30 44 44N 92 51W
Hastings, Nebr. 34 40 35N 98 23W
Hastings, Okla. 43 34 14N 98 7W
Hasty 16 38 7N 102 58W
Haswell 16 38 27N 103 10W
Hat Nhao 112 14 46N 106 32 E
Hatch, N. Mex. 38 32 40N 107 9W
Hatch, Utah 52 37 39N 112 26W
Hatches Creek 126 20 56 S 135 12 E
Hatchet L. 63 58 36N 103 40W
Hatchie → 48 35 35N 89 53W
Hatchineha, L. 17 28 2N 81 25W
Haţeg, Mţii. 95 45 25N 23 0 E
Hateruma-Shima 117 24 3N 123 47 E
Hatfield, Ark. 13 34 29N 94 23W
Hatfield, Ind. 22 37 54N 87 14W
Hatfield, Mass. 28 42 22N 72 36W
Hatfield, Minn. 30 43 58N 96 12W
Hatfield, Pa. 45 40 17N 75 18W
Hatgal 113 50 26N 100 9 E
Hathras 108 27 36N 78 6 E
Hatia 109 22 30N 91 5 E
Hatillo 57 18 29N 66 50W
Hato de Corozal 70 6 11N 71 45W
Hato Mayor 67 18 46N 69 15W
Hatteras 40 35 13N 75 42W
Hatteras, C. 40 35 14N 75 32W
Hatteras I. 40 35 30N 75 28W
Hattiesburg 31 31 20N 89 17W
Hatton, Ala. 10 34 34N 87 25W
Hatton, N. Dak. 41 47 38N 97 27W
Hatton, Wash. 53 46 47N 118 50W
Hatvan 89 47 40N 19 45 E
Hau Bon = Cheo Reo 112 13 25N 108 28 E
Haubstadt 22 38 12N 87 34W
Haugan 33 47 23N 115 24W
Haugen 55 45 37N 91 46W
Haugesund 97 59 23N 5 13 E
Haultain → 63 55 51N 106 46W
Hauppauge 39 40 50N 73 12W
Hauraki Gulf 128 36 35 S 175 5 E
Hauran 104 32 50N 36 15 E
Hauser 44 43 30N 124 13W
Haut, I. au 26 44 3N 68 38W
Haut Atlas 120 32 30N 5 0W
Haut-Rhin □ 90 48 0N 7 15 E
Hautah, Wahãt al 106 23 40N 47 0 E
Haute-Corse □ 90 42 30N 9 30 E
Haute-Garonne □ 90 43 28N 1 30 E
Haute-Loire □ 90 45 5N 3 50 E
Haute-Marne □ 90 48 10N 5 20 E
Haute-Saône □ 90 47 45N 6 10 E
Haute-Savoie □ 90 46 0N 6 20 E
Haute-Vienne □ 90 45 50N 1 10 E
Hauterive 61 49 10N 68 16W
Hautes-Alpes □ 90 44 42N 6 20 E
Hautes-Pyrénées □ 90 43 0N 0 10 E
Hauts-de-Seine □ 90 48 52N 2 15 E
Hauts Plateaux 120 34 14N 1 0 E
Hauula 19 21 37N 157 55W
Havana = Habana, La 66 23 8N 82 22W
Havana, Ark. 13 35 7N 93 32W
Havana, Fla. 17 30 37N 84 25W
Havana, Ill. 21 40 18N 90 4W
Havana, Kans. 24 37 6N 95 57W
Havana, N. Dak. 41 45 57N 97 37W
Havant 86 50 51N 0 59W
Havasu Cr. → 12 36 19N 112 46W
Havasu L. 12 34 18N 114 8W
Havasupai Indian
Reservation 12 36 15N 112 35W
Havel → 88 52 40N 12 15 E
Havelange 87 50 23N 5 15 E
Havelock, N.B., Canada 61 46 2N 65 24W
Havelock, Ont., Canada 60 44 26N 77 53W
Havelock, N.Z. 128 41 17 S 173 48 E
Havelock, N.C. 40 34 53N 76 54W
Havelock, N. Dak. 41 46 29N 102 45W
Havelock I. 112 11 55N 93 2 E
Haven 24 37 54N 97 47W
Havensville 24 39 31N 96 5W
Haverfordwest 83 51 48N 4 59W
Haverhill, Fla. 17 26 42N 80 7W
Haverhill, Mass. 28 42 47N 71 5W
Haverhill, N.H. 36 44 3N 72 4W
Havering 83 51 33N 0 20 E
Havertown 45 39 58N 75 18W
Haviland 24 37 37N 99 6W
Havlíčkův Brod 88 49 36N 15 33 E
Havre 33 48 33N 109 41W
Havre, Le 90 49 30N 0 5 E
Havre-Aubert 61 47 12N 61 56W
Havre de Grace 27 39 33N 76 6W
Havre-St.-Pierre 61 50 18N 63 33W
Havza 106 41 0N 35 35 E
Haw → 40 35 36N 79 3W
Haw Knob 40 35 19N 84 2W
Hawaii 19 19 30N 155 30W
Hawaii □ 19 20 0N 157 45W
Hawaii County ◇ 19 19 30N 155 30W
Hawaii Volcanoes National
Park 19 19 23N 155 17W
Hawaiian Is. 125 20 30N 156 0W
Hawaiian Ridge 125 24 0N 165 0W
Hawarden, Canada 63 51 25N 106 36W
Hawarden, U.S.A. 23 43 0N 96 29W
Hawea Lake 128 44 28 S 169 19 E
Hawera 128 39 35 S 174 19 E
Hawesville 48 37 54N 86 45W
Hawi 19 20 14N 155 50W
Hawick 84 55 25N 2 48W
Hawk Junction 60 48 5N 84 38W
Hawk Point 32 38 58N 91 8W
Hawk Springs 56 41 47N 104 16W
Hawke B. 128 39 25 S 177 20 E
Hawker 127 31 59 S 138 22 E
Hawke's Bay □ 128 39 45 S 176 35 E
Hawkesbury 60 45 37N 74 37W
Hawkesbury → 127 33 30 S 151 10 E
Hawkesbury I. 62 53 37N 129 3W
Hawkeye 23 42 56N 91 57W
Hawkins, Tex. 51 32 35N 95 12W
Hawkins, Wis. 55 45 31N 90 43W
Hawkins County ◇ 49 36 24N 83 1W
Hawkinsville 18 32 17N 83 28W
Hawks 29 45 18N 83 53W
Hawksbill 54 38 34N 78 27W
Hawksbill Mt. 40 35 55N 81 53W
Hawley, Minn. 30 46 53N 96 19W
Hawley, Pa. 45 41 28N 75 11W
Hawley, Tex. 51 32 37N 99 49W
Haworth 43 33 51N 94 39W
Hawrān 104 32 45N 36 15 E
Hawthorne, Fla. 17 29 36N 82 5W
Hawthorne, Nev. 35 38 32N 118 38W
Haxtun 16 40 39N 102 38W
Hay, Australia 127 34 30 S 144 51 E
Hay, U.K. 83 52 4N 3 9W
Hay, U.S.A. 53 46 41N 117 55W
Hay →, Australia 127 25 14 S 138 0 E
Hay →, Canada 62 60 50N 116 26W
Hay →, U.S.A. 55 44 59N 91 51W
Hay L. 62 58 50N 118 50W
Hay Lakes 62 53 12N 113 2W
Hay River 62 60 51N 115 44W
Hay Springs 34 42 41N 102 41W
Hayachine-San 116 39 34N 141 29 E
Hayden, Ariz. 12 33 0N 110 47W
Hayden, Colo. 16 40 30N 107 16W
Hayden, Idaho 20 47 46N 116 47W
Hayden, N. Mex. 38 35 59N 103 16W
Hayden Peak 20 42 59N 116 40W
Hayes, La. 25 30 7N 92 55W
Hayes, S. Dak. 47 44 23N 101 1W
Hayes → 63 57 3N 92 12W
Hayes, Mt. 11 63 37N 146 43W
Hayes Center 34 40 31N 101 1W
Hayes County ◇ 34 40 30N 101 0W
Hayesville, Iowa 23 41 16N 92 15W
Hayesville, N.C. 40 35 3N 83 49W
Hayfield 30 43 53N 92 51W
Hayfork 14 40 33N 123 11W
Haylow 18 30 50N 82 54W
Haymarket 54 38 49N 77 38W
Haynes, Ark. 13 34 54N 90 47W
Haynes, N. Dak. 41 45 59N 102 28W
Haynesville, La. 25 32 58N 93 8W
Haynesville, Maine 26 45 50N 67 59W
Hayneville, Ala. 10 32 11N 86 35W
Hayneville, Ga. 18 32 23N 83 37W
Hays, Canada 62 50 6N 111 48W
Hays, U.S.A. 24 38 53N 99 20W
Hays County ◇ 51 29 59N 97 53W
Haysi 54 37 12N 82 18W
Haystack Peak 52 39 50N 113 55W
Haysville 24 37 34N 97 21W
Hayti, Mo. 32 36 14N 89 44W
Hayti, S. Dak. 47 44 40N 97 13W
Hayward, Calif. 14 37 40N 122 5W
Hayward, Minn. 30 43 39N 93 15W
Hayward, Wis. 55 46 1N 91 29W
Hayward's Heath 83 51 0N 0 5W
Haywood 40 35 37N 79 4W
Haywood County ◇, N.C. 40 35 30N 83 0W
Haywood County ◇, Tenn. 48 35 36N 89 16W
Hazard, Ky. 49 37 15N 83 12W
Hazard, Nebr. 34 41 6N 99 9W
Hazaribag 109 23 58N 85 26 E
Hazel, Ky. 48 36 30N 88 20W
Hazel, S. Dak. 47 44 46N 97 23W
Hazel → 54 38 33N 77 51W
Hazel Green 55 42 32N 90 26W
Hazel Run 30 44 45N 95 43W
Hazelton, Canada 62 55 20N 127 42W
Hazelton, Idaho 20 42 36N 114 8W
Hazelton, Kans. 24 37 5N 98 24W
Hazelton, N. Dak. 41 46 29N 100 17W
Hazelton Peak 56 44 6N 107 3W
Hazelwood 40 35 28N 83 0W
Hazen, Ark. 13 34 47N 91 35W
Hazen, N. Dak. 41 47 18N 101 38W
Hazen, Nev. 35 39 34N 119 3W
Hazlehurst, Ga. 18 31 52N 82 36W
Hazlehurst, Miss. 31 31 52N 90 24W
Hazlet 37 40 25N 74 12W
Hazleton, Ind. 22 38 29N 87 33W
Hazleton, Iowa 23 42 37N 91 54W
Hazleton, Pa. 45 40 57N 75 59W
Hazlettville 27 39 9N 75 40W
Ḩazor 104 33 2N 35 32 E
He Devil 20 45 21N 116 33W
He Xian 115 24 27N 111 30 E
Head of Bight 126 31 30 S 131 25 E
Headland 10 31 21N 85 21W
Headquarters 20 46 38N 115 48W
Headrick 43 34 38N 99 9W
Healdsburg 14 38 37N 122 52W
Healdton 43 34 14N 97 29W
Healdville 36 43 25N 72 45W
Healy, Alaska 11 63 52N 148 58W
Healy, Kans. 24 38 36N 100 37W
Heanor 82 53 1N 1 20W
Heard County ◇ 18 33 15N 85 0W
Heard I. 3 53 0 S 74 0 E
Hearne 51 30 53N 96 36W
Hearne B. 63 60 10N 99 10W
Hearne L. 62 62 20N 113 10W
Hearst 60 49 40N 83 41W
Heart → 41 46 46N 100 50W
Heart L. 56 44 16N 110 29W
Heart's Content 61 47 54N 53 27W
Heartwell 34 40 34N 98 47W
Heath → 72 12 31 S 68 38W
Heath Pt. 61 49 8N 61 40W
Heath Springs 46 34 36N 80 40W
Heath Steele 61 47 17N 66 5W
Heathsville 54 37 55N 76 29W
Heavener 43 34 53N 94 36W
Hebbardsville 48 37 47N 87 23W
Hebbronville 50 27 18N 98 41W
Hebei □ 114 39 0N 116 0 E
Heber, Ariz. 12 34 26N 110 36W
Heber, Calif. 15 32 44N 115 32W

Heber City Hillsboro

Heber City 52 40 31N 111 25W
Heber Springs 13 35 30N 92 2W
Hebert 63 50 30N 107 10W
Hebgen L. 33 44 52N 111 20W
Hebi 114 35 57N 114 7 E
Hebo 44 45 14N 123 52W
Hebrides 84 57 30N 7 0W
Hebrides, Inner Is. 84 57 20N 6 40W
Hebrides, Outer Is. 84 57 30N 7 40W
Hebron = Al Khalīl 104 31 32N 35 6 E
Hebron, Canada 59 58 5N 62 30W
Hebron, Conn. 28 41 39N 72 22W
Hebron, Ill. 21 42 28N 88 26W
Hebron, Ind. 22 41 19N 87 12W
Hebron, Md. 27 38 25N 75 41W
Hebron, N. Dak. 41 46 54N 102 3W
Hebron, N.H. 36 43 42N 71 48W
Hebron, Nebr. 34 40 10N 97 35W
Hebron, Tex. 51 33 2N 96 52W
Hecate Str. 62 53 10N 130 30W
Hechi 115 24 40N 108 2 E
Hechuan 115 30 2N 106 12 E
Hecla 47 45 53N 98 9W
Hecla I. 63 51 10N 96 43W
Hector, Ark. 13 35 28N 92 59W
Hector, Minn. 30 44 45N 94 43W
Hede 96 62 23N 13 30 E
Hedemora 97 60 18N 15 58 E
Hedgesville 54 39 31N 77 58W
Hedley 50 34 52N 100 39W
Hedrick 23 41 11N 92 19W
Heemstede 87 52 22N 4 37 E
Heerde 87 52 24N 6 2 E
Heerenveen 87 52 57N 5 55 E
Heerlen 87 50 55N 6 0 E
Ḥefa 104 32 46N 35 0 E
Hefei 115 31 52N 117 18 E
Heflin 10 33 39N 85 35W
Hefner, L. 43 35 35N 97 36W
Hegang 114 47 20N 130 19 E
Heiberger 10 32 46N 87 17W
Heidelberg, Germany 88 49 23N 8 41 E
Heidelberg, Minn. 30 44 30N 93 38W
Heidelberg, Miss. 31 31 53N 88 59W
Heidrick 49 36 52N 83 54W
Heilbron 123 27 16 S 27 59 E
Heilbronn 88 49 8N 9 13 E
Heilongjiang □ 114 48 0N 126 0 E
Heilunkiang =
Heilongjiang □ 114 48 0N 126 0 E
Heinola 97 61 13N 26 2 E
Heinze Is. 112 14 25N 97 45 E
Heizer 24 38 25N 98 53W
Hejaz = Al Ḥijāz 106 26 0N 37 30 E
Hejian 114 38 25N 116 5 E
Hejiang 115 28 43N 105 46 E
Hekimhan 106 38 50N 38 0 E
Hekla 96 63 56N 19 35W
Hekou 113 22 30N 103 59 E
Helan Shan 114 39 0N 105 55 E
Helemano → 19 21 35N 158 7W
Helen 27 38 22N 76 42W
Helena, Ala. 10 33 18N 86 51W
Helena, Ark. 13 34 32N 90 36W
Helena, Calif. 14 40 47N 123 8W
Helena, Ga. 18 32 5N 82 55W
Helena, Mont. 33 46 36N 112 2W
Helena National Forest 33 46 30N 111 30W
Helensburgh 84 56 0N 4 44W
Helensville 128 36 41 S 174 29 E
Ḥelez 104 31 36N 34 39 E
Helgoland 88 54 10N 7 51 E
Heligoland = Helgoland 88 54 10N 7 51 E
Helix 44 45 51N 118 39W
Hell Cr. → 16 39 30N 102 30W
Hellendoorn 87 52 24N 6 27 E
Hellertown 45 40 35N 75 21W
Hellevoetsluis 87 51 50N 4 8 E
Hellín 91 38 31N 1 40W
Hells Canyon 44 45 10N 116 50W
Hells Canyon Nat. Rec. Area 44 45 30N 117 45W
Helmand □ 107 31 20N 64 0 E
Helmand → 107 31 12N 61 34 E
Helmand, Hamun 107 31 15N 61 15 E
Helmond 87 51 29N 5 41 E
Helmsdale 84 58 7N 3 40W
Helmville 33 46 52N 112 58W
Helotes 51 29 35N 98 41W
Helper 52 39 41N 110 51W
Helsingborg 97 56 3N 12 42 E
Helsingfors 97 60 15N 25 3 E
Helsingør 97 56 2N 12 35 E
Helsinki 97 60 15N 25 3 E
Helston 83 50 7N 5 17W
Helton 49 36 58N 83 24W
Helvellyn 82 54 31N 3 1W
Helwân 121 29 50N 31 20 E
Hematite 32 38 12N 90 29W
Hemet 15 33 45N 116 58W
Hemingford 34 42 19N 103 4W
Hemingway 46 33 45N 79 27W
Hemphill 51 31 20N 93 51W
Hemphill County ◇ 50 35 55N 100 15W
Hempstead, N.Y. 39 40 43N 73 38W
Hempstead, Tex. 51 30 6N 96 5W
Hempstead County ◇ 13 33 40N 93 36W
Hemse 97 57 15N 18 22 E
Henagar 10 34 38N 85 46W
Henan □ 115 34 0N 114 0 E
Henares → 91 40 24N 3 30W
Henashi-Misaki 116 40 37N 139 51 E
Henderson, Argentina 76 36 18 S 61 43W
Henderson, Ga. 18 32 21N 83 47W
Henderson, Iowa 23 41 8N 95 26W
Henderson, Ky. 48 37 50N 87 35W
Henderson, Md. 27 39 6N 75 47W
Henderson, N.C. 40 36 20N 78 25W
Henderson, Nebr. 34 40 47N 97 49W
Henderson, Nev. 35 36 2N 114 59W
Henderson, Tenn. 48 35 26N 88 38W
Henderson, Tex. 51 32 9N 94 48W
Henderson County ◇, Ill. 21 40 50N 90 55W
Henderson County ◇, Ky. 48 37 45N 87 35W
Henderson County ◇, N.C. 40 35 15N 82 30W
Henderson County ◇, Tenn. 48 35 39N 88 24W
Henderson County ◇, Tex. 50 32 12N 95 51W
Hendersonville, N.C. 40 35 19N 82 28W
Hendersonville, S.C. 46 32 48N 80 43W
Hendersonville, Tenn. 48 36 18N 86 37W
Hendley 34 40 8N 99 58W
Hendorf 95 46 4N 24 55 E
Hendricks 30 44 30N 96 25W
Hendricks County ◇ 22 39 45N 86 30W
Hendrum 30 47 16N 96 49W
Hendry County ◇ 17 26 30N 81 20W
Henefer 52 41 1N 111 30W
Heng Xian 115 22 40N 109 17 E
Hengdaohezi 114 44 52N 129 0 E
Hengelo 87 52 3N 6 19 E
Hengshan, Hunan, China 115 27 16N 112 45 E
Hengshan, Shaanxi, China 114 37 58N 109 5 E
Hengshui 114 37 41N 115 40 E
Hengyang 115 26 52N 112 33 E
Henlopen, C. 27 38 48N 75 6W
Hennepin, Ill. 21 41 15N 89 21W
Hennepin, Okla. 43 34 31N 97 21W
Hennepin County ◇ 30 45 0N 93 30W
Hennessey 43 36 6N 97 54W
Henniker 36 43 11N 71 50W
Henning, Ill. 21 40 18N 87 42W
Henning, Minn. 30 46 19N 95 27W
Henning, Tenn. 48 35 41N 89 34W
Henrico County ◇ 54 37 33N 77 20W
Henrietta 51 33 49N 98 12W
Henrietta, Ostrov 101 77 6N 156 30 E
Henrietta Maria C. 60 55 9N 82 20W
Henriette 30 45 53N 93 7W
Henrieville 52 37 30N 112 0W
Henry, Ill. 21 41 7N 89 22W
Henry, Nebr. 34 41 58N 104 4W
Henry, S. Dak. 47 44 53N 97 28W
Henry, Tenn. 48 36 12N 88 25W
Henry, C. 54 36 56N 76 1W
Henry County ◇, Ala. 10 31 34N 85 15W
Henry County ◇, Ga. 18 33 25N 84 5W
Henry County ◇, Ill. 21 41 20N 90 10W
Henry County ◇, Ind. 22 39 55N 85 25W
Henry County ◇, Iowa 23 41 0N 91 30W
Henry County ◇, Ky. 49 38 25N 85 10W
Henry County ◇, Mo. 32 38 25N 93 45W
Henry County ◇, Ohio 42 41 19N 84 2W
Henry County ◇, Tenn. 48 36 18N 88 19W
Henry County ◇, Va. 54 36 50N 79 56W
Henry Mts. 52 38 0N 110 50W
Henryetta 43 35 27N 95 59W
Henrys Fork → 20 41 0N 109 39W
Henrys Lake 20 44 36N 111 21W
Henshaw 48 37 37N 88 3W
Henshaw L. 15 33 15N 116 46W
Hensler 41 47 16N 101 5W
Hentiyn Nuruu 113 48 30N 108 30 E
Henzada 109 17 38N 95 26 E
Hepburn 23 40 51N 95 1W
Hephzibah 18 33 19N 82 6W
Heping 115 24 29N 115 0 E
Hepler 24 37 40N 94 58W
Heppner 44 45 21N 119 33W
Hepu 115 21 40N 109 12 E
Héraðsflói 96 65 42N 14 12W
Héraðsvötn → 96 65 45N 19 25W
Herāt 107 34 20N 62 7 E
Herāt □ 107 35 0N 62 0 E
Hérault □ 90 43 34N 3 15 E
Herbert I. 11 52 45N 170 7W
Hercegnovi 95 42 30N 18 33 E
Hercegovina = Bosna i
Hercegovina □ 94 44 0N 18 0 E
Herculaneum 32 38 16N 90 23W
Herðubreið 96 65 11N 16 21W
Hereford, U.K. 83 52 4N 2 42W
Hereford, Ariz. 12 31 26N 110 6W
Hereford, Colo. 16 40 57N 104 18W
Hereford, Md. 27 39 35N 76 40W
Hereford, Tex. 50 34 49N 102 24W
Hereford and Worcester □ 83 52 10N 2 30W
Herentals 87 51 12N 4 51 E
Herford 88 52 7N 8 40 E
Herington 24 38 40N 96 57W
Herjehogna 97 61 43N 12 7 E
Herkimer, Kans. 24 39 54N 96 43W
Herkimer, N.Y. 39 43 2N 74 59W
Herkimer County ◇ 39 43 0N 75 0W
Herman, Minn. 30 45 49N 96 9W
Herman, Nebr. 34 41 40N 96 13W
Hermann 32 38 42N 91 27W
Hermansville 29 45 42N 87 36W
Hermantown 30 46 50N 92 15W
Hermanville 31 31 58N 90 50W
Hermiston 44 45 51N 119 17W
Hermitage, N.Z. 128 43 44 S 170 5 E
Hermitage, Ark. 13 33 27N 92 10W
Hermitage, Mo. 32 37 56N 93 19W
Hermite, I. 78 55 50 S 68 0W
Hermleigh 50 32 38N 100 46W
Hermon 39 44 28N 75 14W
Hermon, Mt. = Ash Shaykh,
J. 106 33 25N 35 50 E
Hermosa 47 43 50N 103 12W
Hermosillo 64 29 10N 111 0W
Hernad → 89 47 56N 21 8 E
Hernandarias 77 25 20 S 54 40W
Hernando, Argentina 76 32 28 S 63 40W
Hernando, Fla. 17 28 54N 82 23W
Hernando, Miss. 31 34 50N 90 0W
Hernando County ◇ 17 28 35N 82 30W
Herndon, Kans. 24 39 55N 100 47W
Herndon, Ky. 48 36 44N 87 34W
Herndon, Pa. 45 40 43N 76 51W
Herndon, Va. 54 38 58N 77 23W
Herne Bay 83 51 22N 1 8 E
Herning 97 56 8N 8 58 E
Herod 18 31 42N 84 26W
Heroica = Caborca 64 30 40N 112 10W
Heroica Nogales = Nogales 64 31 20N 110 56W
Heron 33 48 3N 115 57W
Heron Bay 60 48 40N 86 25W
Heron Lake 30 43 48N 95 19W
Herreid 47 45 50N 100 4W
Herrera 91 37 26N 4 55W
Herrick 47 43 7N 99 11W
Herrin 21 37 48N 89 2W
Herrington L. 49 37 45N 84 44W
Herscher 21 41 3N 88 6W
Hersey 29 43 51N 85 27W
Hershey 34 41 10N 101 0W
Herstal 87 50 40N 5 38 E
Hertford, U.K. 83 51 47N 0 4W
Hertford, U.S.A. 40 36 11N 76 28W
Hertford □ 83 51 51N 0 5W
Hertford County ◇ 40 36 20N 77 0W
's-Hertogenbosch 87 51 42N 5 17 E
Hervey B. 127 25 0 S 152 52 E
Herzliyya 104 32 10N 34 50 E
Hesperia, Calif. 15 34 25N 117 18W
Hesperia, Mich. 29 43 34N 86 3W
Hesperus 16 37 17N 108 2W
Hesse = Hessen □ 88 50 40N 9 20 E
Hessel 29 46 0N 84 26W
Hessen □ 88 50 40N 9 20 E
Hessmer 25 31 3N 92 8W
Hesston 24 38 8N 97 26W
Hetch Hetchy Aqueduct 14 37 29N 122 19W
Hetch Hetchy Reservoir 14 37 57N 119 47W
Hettinger 41 46 0N 102 42W
Hettinger County ◇ 41 46 25N 102 30W
Heuvelton 39 44 37N 75 25W
Hevron → 104 31 12N 34 42 E
Hewett, C. 59 70 16N 67 45W
Hewins 24 37 3N 96 25W
Hewitt 30 46 20N 95 5W
Hewlett 54 37 55N 77 35W
Hexham 82 54 58N 2 7W
Hexigten Qi 114 43 18N 117 30 E
Hext 51 30 52N 99 32W
Heyburn, L. 43 35 57N 96 18W
Heysham 82 54 5N 2 53W
Heyworth 21 40 19N 88 59W
Hialeah 17 25 50N 80 17W
Hiattville 24 37 43N 94 52W
Hiawassee 18 34 58N 83 46W
Hiawatha, Kans. 24 39 51N 95 32W
Hiawatha, Utah 52 39 29N 111 1W
Hiawatha National Forest 29 46 15N 86 40W
Hibbing 30 47 25N 92 56W
Hickman, Del. 27 38 50N 75 42W
Hickman, Ky. 48 36 34N 89 11W
Hickman, Nebr. 34 40 37N 96 38W
Hickman County ◇, Ky. 48 36 40N 89 0W
Hickman County ◇, Tenn. 48 35 47N 87 28W
Hickok 24 37 34N 101 14W
Hickory, Ky. 48 36 48N 88 40W
Hickory, N.C. 40 35 44N 81 21W
Hickory, L. 40 35 49N 81 12W
Hickory County ◇ 32 37 55N 93 15W
Hickory Grove 46 34 59N 81 25W
Hickory Plains 13 34 59N 91 44W
Hickory Ridge 13 35 24N 90 58W
Hickory Valley 48 35 9N 89 8W
Hicks Pt. 127 37 49 S 149 17 E
Hicksville, N.Y. 39 40 46N 73 32W
Hicksville, Ohio 42 41 18N 84 46W
Hico 51 31 59N 98 2W
Hida-Gawa → 117 35 26N 137 3 E
Hida-Sammyaku 117 36 30N 137 40 E
Hidaka-Sammyaku 116 42 35N 142 45 E
Hidalgo, Mexico 65 24 15N 99 26W
Hidalgo, Ill. 21 39 9N 88 9W
Hidalgo, Tex. 50 26 6N 98 16W
Hidalgo □ 65 20 30N 99 10W
Hidalgo, Presa M. 64 26 30N 108 35W
Hidalgo County ◇, N. Mex. 38 32 0N 108 45W
Hidalgo County ◇, Tex. 50 26 25N 98 10W
Hidalgo del Parral 64 26 58N 105 40W
Hidrolândia 75 17 0 S 49 15W
Hierro 120 27 44N 18 0 E
Higashiajima-San 116 37 40N 140 10 E
Higashiōsaka 117 34 40N 135 37 E
Higbee 32 39 19N 92 31W
Higgins 50 36 7N 100 2W
Higgins L. 29 44 29N 84 43W
Higginsport 42 38 47N 83 58W
Higginsville 32 39 4N 93 43W
High Atlas = Haut Atlas 120 32 30N 5 0W
High Bridge 37 40 40N 74 54W
High Hill 32 38 53N 91 23W
High I., Canada 61 56 40N 61 10W
High I., U.S.A. 29 45 44N 85 41W
High Island 51 29 34N 94 24W
High Level 62 58 31N 117 8W
High Point 40 35 57N 80 0W
High Prairie 62 55 30N 116 30W
High Pt., N.J. 37 41 19N 74 40W
High Pt., Wyo. 56 41 37N 107 43W
High River 62 50 30N 113 50W
High Rock L., N.C. 40 35 36N 80 14W
High Rock L., Nev. 35 41 17N 119 17W
High Rolls 38 32 57N 105 50W
High Springs 17 29 50N 82 36W
High Wycombe 83 51 37N 0 45W
Highgate Center 36 44 56N 73 3W
Highland, Calif. 15 34 8N 117 13W
Highland, Ill. 21 38 44N 89 41W
Highland, Ind. 22 41 33N 87 28W
Highland, Kans. 24 39 52N 95 16W
Highland, N.Y. 39 41 43N 73 58W
Highland, Wis. 55 43 5N 90 22W
Highland □ 84 57 30N 5 0W
Highland Beach 27 38 56N 76 28W
Highland City 17 27 58N 81 53W
Highland County ◇, Ohio 42 39 12N 83 37W
Highland County ◇, Va. 54 38 25N 79 35W
Highland Hills 21 41 51N 88 1W
Highland Home 10 31 57N 86 19W
Highland Lakes 37 41 11N 74 28W
Highland Mills 18 33 17N 84 17W
Highland Park 21 42 11N 87 48W
Highland Springs 54 37 33N 77 20W
Highland View 17 29 50N 85 19W
Highlands, N.C. 40 35 3N 83 12W
Highlands, N.J. 37 40 24N 73 59W
Highlands County ◇ 17 27 20N 81 20W
Highmore 47 44 31N 99 27W
Highpoint 31 33 11N 89 9W
Highrock L. 63 57 5N 105 32W
Hightstown 37 40 16N 74 31W
Highwood 21 42 12N 87 48W
Highwood Mts. 33 47 30N 110 30W
Higüay 67 18 37N 68 42W
Higuero, Punta 57 18 22N 67 16W
Hiiumaa 98 58 50N 22 45 E
Ḥijārah, Ṣaḥrā' al 106 30 25N 44 30 E
Hijo = Tagum 111 7 33N 125 53 E
Hikari 117 33 58N 131 58 E
Hiko 35 37 32N 115 14W
Hikone 117 35 15N 136 10 E
Hiland 56 43 7N 107 21W
Hilda 46 33 16N 81 15W
Hildesheim 88 52 9N 9 55 E
Hildreth 34 40 20N 99 3W
Hilgard 44 45 21N 118 14W
Hill City, Idaho 20 43 18N 115 3W
Hill City, Kans. 24 39 22N 99 51W
Hill City, Minn. 30 46 59N 93 36W
Hill City, S. Dak. 47 43 56N 103 35W
Hill County ◇, Mont. 33 48 40N 110 0W
Hill County ◇, Tex. 51 32 1N 97 8W
Hill Cr. → 52 39 55N 109 40W
Hill Island L. 63 60 30N 109 50W
Hillcrest Center 15 35 23N 118 57W
Hillcrest Heights 27 38 50N 76 57W
Hillegom 87 52 18N 4 35 E
Hilliard, Fla. 17 30 41N 81 55W
Hilliard, Ohio 42 40 2N 83 10W
Hilliards 45 41 5N 79 50W
Hillingdon 83 51 33N 0 29W
Hillister 51 30 40N 94 23W
Hillman, Mich. 29 45 4N 83 54W
Hillman, Minn. 30 46 0N 93 53W
Hillmond 63 53 26N 109 41W
Hillrose 16 40 20N 103 31W
Hills, Iowa 23 41 33N 91 32W
Hills, Minn. 30 43 32N 96 21W
Hills Creek L. 44 43 43N 122 26W
Hillsboro, Ga. 18 33 11N 83 38W
Hillsboro, Ill. 21 39 9N 89 29W
Hillsboro, Kans. 24 38 21N 97 12W
Hillsboro, Md. 27 38 55N 75 50W
Hillsboro, Mo. 32 38 14N 90 34W
Hillsboro, N. Dak. 41 47 26N 97 3W
Hillsboro, N.H. 36 43 7N 71 54W
Hillsboro, N. Mex. 38 32 55N 107 34W
Hillsboro, Ohio 42 39 12N 83 37W
Hillsboro, Oreg. 44 45 31N 122 59W
Hillsboro, Tex. 51 32 1N 97 8W

Hillsboro Hopkins

Hillsboro, W. Va. 54 38 8N 80 13W
Hillsboro, Wis. 55 43 39N 90 21W
Hillsboro Canal 17 26 30N 80 15W
Hillsboro Upper Village 36 43 9N 71 58W
Hillsborough, U.S.A. 40 36 5N 79 7W
Hillsborough, W. Indies 67 12 28N 61 28W
Hillsborough County ◇, Fla. 17 27 50N 82 20W
Hillsborough County ◇, N.H. 36 42 50N 71 45W
Hillsdale, Ill. 21 41 37N 90 11W
Hillsdale, Kans. 24 38 40N 94 51W
Hillsdale, Mich. 29 41 56N 84 38W
Hillsdale, Okla. 43 36 34N 97 59W
Hillsdale County ◇ 29 41 50N 84 40W
Hillside, Ariz. 12 34 25N 112 55W
Hillside, N.J. 37 40 42N 74 13W
Hillsmere Shore 27 38 56N 76 32W
Hillsport 60 49 27N 85 34W
Hillston 127 33 30S 145 31 E
Hillsville 54 36 46N 80 44W
Hilltonia 18 32 53N 81 40W
Hillview 49 38 5N 85 49W
Hilo 19 19 44N 155 5W
Hilo B. 19 19 45N 155 5W
Hilt 14 41 50N 122 37W
Hilton 39 43 17N 77 48W
Hilton Head I. 46 32 13N 80 45W
Hilversum 87 52 14N 5 10 E
Himachal Pradesh □ 108 31 30N 77 0 E
Himalaya, Mts. 109 29 0N 84 0 E
Himatnagar 108 23 37N 72 57 E
Himeji 117 34 50N 134 40 E
Himi 117 36 50N 137 0 E
Ḥimş 106 34 40N 36 45 E
Hinako, Kepulauan 110 0 50N 97 20 E
Hinchcliff 31 34 19N 90 17W
Hinche 67 19 9N 72 1W
Hinchinbrook I. 127 18 20S 146 15 E
Hinckley, U.K. 83 52 33N 1 21W
Hinckley, Ill. 21 41 46N 88 38W
Hinckley, Minn. 30 46 1N 92 56W
Hinckley, Utah 52 39 20N 112 40W
Hinckley Reservoir 39 43 19N 75 7W
Hindman 49 37 20N 82 59W
Hinds County ◇ 31 32 16N 90 25W
Hindsboro 21 39 41N 88 8W
Hindu Kush 107 36 0N 71 0 E
Hindubagh 108 30 56N 67 57 E
Hindupur 108 13 49N 77 32 E
Hines, Fla. 17 29 45N 83 14W
Hines, Oreg. 44 43 34N 119 5W
Hines Creek 62 56 20N 118 40W
Hinesburg 36 44 18N 73 6W
Hineston 25 31 9N 92 46W
Hinesville 18 31 51N 81 36W
Hinganghat 108 20 30N 78 52 E
Hingham, Mass. 28 42 15N 70 53W
Hingham, Mont. 33 48 33N 110 25W
Hingoli 108 19 41N 77 15 E
Hinlopenstretet 4 79 35N 18 40 E
Hinna = Imi 105 6 28N 42 10 E
Hinsdale, Md. 27 42 26N 73 8W
Hinsdale, Mont. 33 48 24N 107 5W
Hinsdale, N.H. 36 42 47N 72 29W
Hinsdale County ◇ 16 37 50N 107 20W
Hinson 17 30 39N 84 25W
Hinton, Canada 62 53 26N 117 34W
Hinton, Iowa 23 42 38N 96 18W
Hinton, Okla. 43 35 28N 98 21W
Hinton, W. Va. 54 37 40N 80 54W
Hippolytushoef 87 52 54N 4 58 E
Hirado 117 33 22N 129 33 E
Hirakud Dam 109 21 32N 83 45 E
Hiram 42 41 19N 81 9W
Hiratsuka 117 35 19N 139 21 E
Hiroo 116 42 17N 143 19 E
Hirosaki 116 40 34N 140 28 E
Hiroshima 117 34 24N 132 30 E
Hiroshima □ 117 34 50N 133 0 E
Hîrşova 95 44 40N 27 59 E
Hisar 108 29 12N 75 45 E
Hispaniola 67 19 0N 71 0W
Hita 117 33 20N 130 58 E
Hitachi 117 36 36N 140 39 E
Hitchcock, Okla. 43 35 58N 98 21W
Hitchcock, S. Dak. 47 44 38N 98 25W
Hitchcock, Tex. 51 29 21N 95 1W
Hitchcock County ◇ 34 40 15N 101 0W
Hitchin 83 51 57N 0 16W
Hitchins 49 38 17N 82 55W
Hitchita 43 35 31N 95 44W
Hitoyoshi 117 32 13N 130 45 E
Hitra 96 63 30N 8 45 E
Hitterdal 30 46 59N 96 16W
Hiwannee 31 31 49N 88 41W
Hiwassee 54 36 58N 80 43W
Hiwassee → 49 35 19N 84 47W
Hiwassee L. 40 35 9N 84 11W
Hixton 55 44 23N 91 1W
Ḥiyyon, N. → 104 30 25N 35 10 E
Hjalmar L. 63 61 33N 109 25W
Hjälmaren 97 59 18N 15 40 E
Hjørring 97 57 29N 9 59 E
Hńak 4 70 40N 52 10W
Ho 120 6 37N 0 27 E
Ho Chi Minh, Phanh Bho 112 10 58N 106 40 E
Ho Chi Minh City = Phanh Bho Ho Chi Minh, Vietnam 112 10 58N 106 40 E
Ho Chi Minh City = Phanh Bho Ho Chi Minh, Vietnam 112 10 58N 106 40 E
Hoa Binh 112 20 50N 105 20 E
Hoai Nhon 112 14 28N 109 1 E
Hoare B. 59 65 17N 62 30W
Hobart, Australia 127 42 50S 147 21 E
Hobart, Ind. 22 41 32N 87 15W
Hobart, N.Y. 39 42 22N 74 40W
Hobart, Okla. 43 35 1N 99 6W
Hobbs 38 32 42N 103 8W
Hobbs Coast 5 74 50S 131 0W
Hobe Sound 17 27 4N 80 8W
Hoberg 32 37 4N 93 51W
Hobgood 40 36 2N 77 24W
Hobo 70 2 35N 75 30W
Hoboken, Belgium 87 51 11N 4 21 E
Hoboken, U.S.A. 18 31 11N 82 8W
Hobro 97 56 39N 9 46 E
Hobson, Ky. 49 37 25N 85 22W
Hobson, Mont. 33 47 0N 109 52W
Hobucken 40 35 15N 76 34W
Hoburgen 97 56 55N 18 7 E
Hochheim 51 29 19N 97 17W
Hockessin 27 39 47N 75 42W
Hocking 42 39 12N 81 45W
Hocking County ◇ 42 39 32N 82 25W
Hockley County ◇ 50 33 35N 102 23W
Hodaka-Dake 117 36 17N 137 39 E
Hodge 25 32 17N 92 43W
Hodgeman County ◇ 24 38 0N 100 0W
Hodgenville 49 37 34N 85 44W
Hodges 46 34 17N 82 15W
Hodgson 63 51 13N 97 36W
Hódmezővásárhely 89 46 28N 20 22 E
Hodna, Chott el 120 35 30N 5 0 E
Hodonín 88 48 50N 17 10 E
Hoehne 16 37 17N 104 23W
Hoek van Holland 87 52 0N 4 7 E
Hof, Germany 88 50 18N 11 55 E
Hof, Iceland 96 64 33N 14 40W
Höfðakaupstaður 96 65 50N 20 19W
Hoffman, Ill. 21 38 32N 89 16W
Hoffman, Minn. 30 45 50N 95 48W
Hoffman, N.C. 40 35 2N 79 33W
Hoffman, Okla. 43 35 29N 95 51W
Hofsjökull 96 64 49N 18 48W
Hofsós 96 65 53N 19 26W
Hōfu 117 34 3N 131 34 E
Hog I., Mich. 29 45 48N 85 22W
Hog I., Va. 54 37 26N 75 42W
Hogansville 18 33 10N 84 55W
Hogback Mt., Mont. 33 44 54N 112 7W
Hogback Mt., Nebr. 34 41 44N 103 42W
Hogeland 33 48 51N 108 40W
Hogsty Reef 67 21 41N 73 48W
Hoh → 53 47 45N 124 29W
Hoh Xil Shan 113 35 0N 89 0 E
Hohe Venn 87 50 30N 6 5 E
Hohenwald 48 35 33N 87 33W
Hohhot 114 40 52N 111 40 E
Hoi An 112 15 30N 108 19 E
Hoi Xuan 112 20 25N 105 9 E
Hoisington 24 38 31N 98 47W
Hōjō 117 33 58N 132 46 E
Hokah 30 43 46N 91 21W
Hoke County ◇ 40 35 0N 79 15W
Hokianga Harbour 128 35 31S 173 22 E
Hokitika 128 42 42S 171 0 E
Hokkaidō □ 116 43 30N 143 0 E
Holbrook, Ariz. 12 34 54N 110 10W
Holbrook, Idaho 20 42 10N 112 39W
Holbrook, Mass. 28 42 9N 71 1W
Holbrook, N.Y. 39 40 49N 73 5W
Holbrook, Nebr. 34 40 18N 100 1W
Holcomb, Kans. 24 37 59N 100 59W
Holcomb, Mo. 32 36 24N 90 2W
Holcomb, N.Y. 39 42 54N 77 25W
Holden, Canada 62 53 13N 112 11W
Holden, Mass. 28 42 21N 71 52W
Holden, Mo. 32 38 43N 94 1W
Holden, Utah 52 39 6N 112 16W
Holdenville 43 35 5N 96 24W
Holder 17 28 58N 82 25W
Holderness, U.K. 82 53 45N 0 5W
Holderness, U.S.A. 36 43 43N 71 37W
Holdfast 63 50 58N 105 25W
Holdich 78 45 57S 68 13W
Holdingford 30 45 44N 94 28W
Holdrege 34 40 26N 99 23W
Holgate, N.J. 37 39 33N 74 15W
Holgate, Ohio 42 41 15N 84 8W
Holguín 66 20 50N 76 20W
Holladay, Tenn. 48 35 52N 88 9W
Holladay, Utah 52 40 40N 111 50W
Hollams Bird I. 123 24 40S 14 30 E
Holland, Ark. 13 35 10N 92 16W
Holland, Ga. 18 34 21N 85 22W
Holland, Iowa 23 42 24N 92 48W
Holland, Mich. 29 42 47N 86 7W
Holland, Minn. 30 44 6N 96 11W
Holland, Mo. 32 36 3N 89 52W
Holland, Tex. 51 30 53N 97 24W
Holland Patent 39 43 15N 75 15W
Hollandale, Minn. 30 43 46N 93 12W
Hollandale, Miss. 31 33 10N 90 51W
Hollandale, Wis. 55 42 53N 89 56W
Hollansburg 42 39 59N 84 50W
Hollenberg 24 39 58N 96 59W
Holley, Fla. 17 30 27N 86 54W
Holley, N.Y. 39 43 14N 78 2W
Holley, Oreg. 44 44 21N 122 47W
Hollick Kenyon Plateau 5 82 0S 110 0W
Holliday 51 33 49N 98 42W
Hollidaysburg 45 40 26N 78 24W
Hollis, Ark. 13 34 52N 93 7W
Hollis, Kans. 24 39 38N 97 33W
Hollis, Okla. 43 34 41N 99 55W
Hollister, Calif. 14 36 51N 121 24W
Hollister, Idaho 20 42 21N 114 35W
Hollister, Mo. 32 36 38N 93 12W
Hollister, N.C. 40 36 15N 77 56W
Hollister, Okla. 43 34 21N 98 52W
Holliston 28 42 12N 71 26W
Hollow Rock 48 36 2N 88 16W
Holloway 30 45 15N 95 55W
Holly, Colo. 16 38 3N 102 7W
Holly, Mich. 29 42 48N 83 38W
Holly Grove 13 34 36N 91 12W
Holly Hill, Fla. 17 29 16N 81 3W
Holly Hill, S.C. 46 33 19N 80 25W
Holly Pond 10 34 10N 86 37W
Holly Ridge 40 34 30N 77 33W
Holly Springs, Ga. 18 34 10N 84 30W
Holly Springs, Miss. 31 34 46N 89 27W
Holly Springs, N.C. 40 35 39N 78 50W
Holly Springs National Forest 31 34 40N 89 5W
Hollywood, Ala. 10 34 44N 85 59W
Hollywood, Fla. 17 26 1N 80 9W
Hollywood, Md. 27 38 21N 76 34W
Hollywood, Miss. 31 34 45N 90 22W
Holman 38 36 2N 105 23W
Holman Island 58 70 42N 117 41W
Hólmavík 96 65 42N 21 40W
Holmen 55 43 58N 91 15W
Holmes → 17 30 30N 85 50W
Holmes, Mt. 56 44 49N 110 51W
Holmes Beach 17 27 31N 82 43W
Holmes County ◇, Fla. 17 30 50N 85 45W
Holmes County ◇, Miss. 31 33 7N 90 3W
Holmes County ◇, Ohio 42 40 33N 81 55W
Holmesville 42 40 38N 81 56W
Holmsund 96 63 41N 20 20 E
Holon 104 32 2N 34 47 E
Holopaw 17 28 8N 81 5W
Holroyd → 127 14 10S 141 36 E
Holstebro 97 56 22N 8 37 E
Holstein, Iowa 23 42 29N 95 33W
Holstein, Nebr. 34 40 28N 98 39W
Holston → 49 35 58N 83 51W
Holsworthy 83 50 48N 4 21W
Holt, Iceland 96 63 33N 19 48W
Holt, Fla. 17 30 43N 86 45W
Holt, Mich. 29 42 39N 84 31W
Holt, Minn. 30 48 18N 96 11W
Holt, Mo. 32 39 27N 94 21W
Holt County ◇, Mo. 32 40 5N 95 10W
Holt County ◇, Nebr. 34 42 30N 98 45W
Holton, Canada 61 54 31N 57 12W
Holton, Ind. 22 39 5N 85 23W
Holton, Kans. 24 39 28N 95 44W
Holtville 15 32 49N 115 23W
Holualoa 19 19 37N 155 57W
Holwerd 87 53 22N 5 54 E
Holy Cross 11 62 12N 159 46W
Holy I., England, U.K. 82 55 42N 1 48W
Holy I., Wales, U.K. 82 53 17N 4 37W
Holyhead 82 53 18N 4 38W
Holyoke, Colo. 16 40 35N 102 18W
Holyoke, Mass. 28 42 12N 72 37W
Holyrood, Canada 61 47 27N 53 8W
Holyrood, U.S.A. 24 38 35N 98 25W
Homalin 109 24 55N 95 0 E
Hombori 120 15 20N 1 38W
Home 24 39 51N 96 31W
Home B. 59 68 40N 67 10W
Home Hill 127 19 43S 147 25 E
Homedale 20 43 37N 116 56W
Homeland 18 30 51N 82 1W
Homer, Alaska 11 59 39N 151 33W
Homer, Ga. 18 34 20N 83 30W
Homer, La. 25 32 48N 93 4W
Homer, Mich. 29 42 9N 84 49W
Homer, N.Y. 39 42 38N 76 11W
Homer, Nebr. 34 42 19N 96 29W
Homer City 45 40 32N 79 10W
Homer Youngs Pk. 33 45 19N 113 41W
Homerville 18 31 2N 82 45W
Homestead, Fla. 17 25 28N 80 29W
Homestead, Oreg. 44 45 2N 116 51W
Homewood, Ala. 10 33 29N 86 47W
Homewood, Ill. 21 41 34N 87 40W
Hominy 43 36 25N 96 24W
Homochitto National Forest 31 31 15N 31 20W
Homorod 95 46 5N 25 15 E
Homosassa Springs 17 28 48N 82 35W
Homs = Ḥimş 106 34 40N 36 45 E
Hon 13 34 56N 94 11W
Hon Chong 112 10 25N 104 30 E
Honaker 54 37 1N 81 59W
Honan = Henan □ 115 34 0N 114 0 E
Honaunau 19 19 26N 155 55W
Honbetsu 116 43 7N 143 37 E
Honda 70 5 12N 74 45W
Hondeklipbaai 123 30 19S 17 17 E
Hondo, Japan 117 32 27N 130 12 E
Hondo, N. Mex. 38 33 24N 105 16W
Hondo, Tex. 51 29 21N 99 9W
Hondo → 65 18 25N 88 21W
Honduras ■ 66 14 40N 86 30W
Honduras, Golfo de 66 16 50N 87 0W
Honea Path 46 34 27N 82 24W
Hønefoss 97 60 10N 10 18 E
Honesdale 45 41 34N 75 16W
Honey Grove 51 33 35N 95 55W
Honey Island 51 30 24N 94 27W
Honey L. 14 40 15N 120 19W
Honeyville, Fla. 17 30 3N 85 11W
Honeyville, Utah 52 41 38N 112 4W
Honfleur 90 49 25N 0 13 E
Hong Kong ■ 115 22 11N 114 14 E
Honga 27 38 19N 76 14W
Hong'an 115 31 20N 114 40 E
Hongha → 112 22 0N 104 0 E
Honghai Wan 115 22 40N 115 0 E
Honghu 115 29 50N 113 30 E
Hongjiang 115 27 7N 109 59 E
Hongshui He → 115 23 48N 109 30 E
Hongtong 114 36 16N 111 40 E
Honguedo, Détroit d' 61 49 15N 64 0W
Hongze Hu 115 33 15N 118 35 E
Honiara 124 9 27S 159 57 E
Honiton 83 50 48N 3 11W
Honjō 116 39 23N 140 3 E
Honokaa 19 20 5N 155 28W
Honokahua 19 21 0N 156 40W
Honolulu 19 21 19N 157 52W
Honolulu County ◇ 19 21 25N 157 50W
Honomu 19 19 52N 155 7W
Honor 29 44 40N 86 1W
Honouliuli 19 21 22N 158 2W
Honshū 117 36 0N 138 0 E
Honuapo B. 19 19 5N 155 33W
Hood, Mt. 44 45 23N 121 42W
Hood, Pt. 126 34 23S 119 34 E
Hood Canal 53 47 35N 123 0W
Hood County ◇ 51 32 27N 97 47W
Hood River 44 45 43N 121 31W
Hood River County ◇ 44 45 30N 121 20W
Hoodoo Peak 53 48 15N 120 19W
Hoodsport 53 47 24N 123 9W
Hoogeveen 87 52 44N 6 30 E
Hoogezand 87 53 11N 6 45 E
Hooghly → = Hughli → 109 21 56N 88 4 E
Hook Hd. 85 52 8N 6 57W
Hook of Holland = Hoek van Holland 87 52 0N 4 7 E
Hooker 43 36 52N 101 13W
Hooker County ◇ 34 41 50N 101 0W
Hooks 51 33 28N 94 16W
Hoolehua 19 21 10N 157 5W
Hoonah 11 58 7N 135 27W
Hoopa 14 41 3N 123 41W
Hoopa Valley Indian Reservation 14 41 10N 123 45W
Hooper, Colo. 16 37 45N 105 53W
Hooper, Nebr. 34 41 37N 96 33W
Hooper, Wash. 53 46 45N 118 9W
Hooper Bay 11 61 32N 166 6W
Hooper Str. 27 38 15N 76 5W
Hoopersville 27 38 16N 76 11W
Hoopeston 21 40 28N 87 40W
Hoople 41 48 32N 97 38W
Hoorn 87 52 38N 5 4 E
Hoosac Range 28 42 45N 73 2W
Hoosick Falls 39 42 54N 73 21W
Hoosier National Forest, Ind. 22 38 30N 86 35W
Hoosier National Forest, Ind. 22 39 0N 86 10W
Hoover Dam 12 36 1N 114 44W
Hoover Reservoir 42 40 7N 82 53W
Hooversville 45 40 9N 78 55W
Hop Bottom 45 41 42N 75 46W
Hopatcong 37 40 55N 74 40W
Hopatcong, L. 37 40 57N 74 38W
Hope, Canada 62 49 25N 121 25 E
Hope, Ark. 13 33 40N 93 36W
Hope, Ind. 22 39 18N 85 46W
Hope, Kans. 24 38 41N 97 5W
Hope, N. Dak. 41 47 19N 97 43W
Hope, N. Mex. 38 32 49N 104 44W
Hope, R.I. 28 41 44N 71 34W
Hope Mills 40 34 59N 78 57W
Hope Town 66 26 35N 76 57W
Hope Valley 28 41 30N 71 43W
Hopedale, Canada 61 55 28N 60 13W
Hopedale, U.S.A. 21 40 25N 89 25W
Hopei = Hebei □ 114 39 0N 116 0 E
Hopelchén 65 19 46N 89 50W
Hopeton 43 36 41N 98 40W
Hopetoun 126 33 57S 120 7 E
Hopetown 123 29 34S 24 3 E
Hopewell, Miss. 31 31 57N 90 13W
Hopewell, Va. 54 37 18N 77 17W
Hopi Indian Reservation 12 36 15N 110 30W
Hopkins, Mich. 29 42 37N 85 46W

Hopkins
Hungry Horse Reservoir

Hopkins, Mo. 32 40 33N 94 49W
Hopkins, S.C. 46 33 54N 80 53W
Hopkins County ◇, Ky. 48 37 20N 87 30W
Hopkins County ◇, Tex. 51 33 8N 95 36W
Hopkinsville 48 36 52N 87 29W
Hopkinton, Iowa 23 42 21N 91 15W
Hopkinton, Mass. 28 42 14N 71 31W
Hopkinton, N.H. 36 43 12N 71 41W
Hopkinton, R.I. 28 41 28N 71 48W
Hopland 14 38 58N 123 7W
Hoquiam 53 46 59N 123 53W
Horace, Kans. 24 38 29N 101 47W
Horace, N. Dak. 41 46 45N 96 54W
Horatio, Ark. 13 33 56N 94 21W
Horatio, S.C. 46 34 1N 80 33W
Hordaland fylke □ 97 60 25N 6 15 E
Horden Hills 126 20 40 S 130 20 E
Hordville 34 41 5N 97 53W
Horezu 95 45 6N 24 0 E
Horicon 55 43 27N 88 38W
Horlick Mts. 5 84 0 S 102 0W
Hormigueros 57 18 8N 67 8W
Hormoz 107 27 35N 55 0 E
Hormoz, Jaz. ye 107 27 8N 56 28 E
Hormozgān □ 107 27 30N 56 0 E
Hormuz Str. 107 26 30N 56 30 E
Horn, Austria 88 48 39N 15 40 E
Horn, Ísafjarðarsýsla, Iceland 96 66 28N 22 28W
Horn, Suður-Múlasýsla, Iceland 96 65 10N 13 31W
Horn → 62 61 30N 118 1W
Horn, Cape = Hornos, Cabo de 78 55 50 S 67 30W
Horn Head 85 55 13N 8 0W
Horn I. 31 30 14N 88 39W
Horn Lake 31 34 58N 90 2W
Horn Mts. 62 62 15N 119 15W
Hornavan 96 66 15N 17 30 E
Hornbeak 48 36 20N 89 18W
Hornbeck 25 31 20N 93 24W
Hornbrook 14 41 55N 122 33W
Horncastle 82 53 13N 0 8W
Hornell 39 42 20N 77 40W
Hornell L. 62 62 20N 119 25W
Hornepayne 60 49 14N 84 48W
Hornersville 32 36 3N 90 7W
Hornick 23 42 14N 96 6W
Hornitos 14 37 30N 120 14W
Hornos, Cabo de 78 55 50 S 67 30W
Hornsby 48 35 14N 88 50W
Hornsea 82 53 55N 0 10W
Horobetsu 116 42 24N 141 6 E
Horqin Youyi Qianqi 114 46 5N 122 3 E
Horqueta 76 23 15 S 56 55W
Horqueta, La 71 7 55N 60 20W
Horry County ◇ 46 33 50N 79 0W
Horse → 16 38 5N 103 19W
Horse Branch 48 37 28N 86 41W
Horse Cave 49 37 11N 85 54W
Horse Cr. →, Fla. 17 27 6N 81 58W
Horse Cr. →, Mo. 32 37 46N 93 53W
Horse Cr. →, Wyo. 56 41 57N 103 58W
Horse Creek 56 41 25N 105 11W
Horse Creek Reservoir 16 38 10N 103 24W
Horse Heaven Hills 53 46 3N 119 30W
Horse Is. 61 50 15N 55 50W
Horse L. 14 40 40N 120 31W
Horsefly L. 62 52 25N 121 0W
Horsehead L. 41 47 3N 99 47W
Horseheads 39 42 10N 76 49W
Horsens 97 55 52N 9 51 E
Horseshoe Bend 20 43 55N 116 12W
Horseshoe Reservoir 12 33 59N 111 42W
Horsetooth Reservoir 16 40 36N 105 10W
Horsham, Australia 127 36 44 S 142 13 E
Horsham, U.K. 83 51 4N 0 20W
Horten 97 59 25N 10 32 E
Hortense 18 31 20N 81 57W
Horton 24 39 40N 95 32W
Horton → 58 69 56N 126 52W
Hortonville 55 44 20N 88 38W
Horwood, L. 60 48 5N 82 20W
Hose, Gunung-Gunung 110 2 5N 114 6 E
Hosford 17 30 23N 84 48W
Hoshangabad 108 22 45N 77 45 E
Hoshiarpur 108 31 30N 75 58 E
Hoskins, Nebr. 34 42 7N 97 18W
Hoskins, Oreg. 44 44 41N 123 28W
Hoskinston 49 37 5N 83 24W
Hosmer 47 45 34N 99 28W
Hospers 23 43 4N 95 54W
Hospet 108 15 15N 76 20 E
Hospitalet de Llobregat 91 41 21N 2 6 E
Hoste, I. 78 55 0 S 69 0W
Hot 112 18 8N 98 29 E
Hot Creek Range 35 38 40N 116 20W
Hot Spring County ◇ 13 34 14N 92 55W
Hot Springs, Ark. 13 34 31N 93 3W
Hot Springs, Mont. 33 47 37N 114 40W
Hot Springs, N.C. 40 35 54N 82 50W
Hot Springs, S. Dak. 47 43 26N 103 29W
Hot Springs, Va. 54 38 0N 79 50W
Hot Springs County ◇ 56 43 55N 108 30W
Hot Sulphur Springs 16 40 4N 106 6W
Hotagen 96 63 50N 14 30 E
Hotan 113 37 25N 79 55 E
Hotchkiss 16 38 48N 107 43W
Hotevilla 12 35 56N 110 41W
Hoting 96 64 8N 16 15 E
Hotte, Massif de la 67 18 30N 73 45W
Houck 12 35 20N 109 10W
Houffalize 87 50 8N 5 48 E
Houghton, Mich. 29 47 7N 88 34W
Houghton, N.Y. 39 42 25N 78 10W
Houghton County ◇ 29 47 0N 88 45W
Houghton L. 29 44 21N 84 44W
Houghton Lake 29 44 18N 84 45W
Houghton-le-Spring 82 54 51N 1 28W
Houhora 128 34 49 S 173 9 E
Houlka 31 34 2N 89 1W
Houlton 26 46 8N 67 51W
Houma 25 29 36N 90 43W
Housatonic 28 42 16N 73 22W
Housatonic → 28 41 10N 73 7W
House 38 34 39N 103 54W
House Range 52 39 30N 113 20W
Houston, Canada 62 54 25N 126 39W
Houston, Ark. 13 35 2N 92 42W
Houston, Fla. 17 30 15N 82 54W
Houston, Minn. 30 43 46N 91 34W
Houston, Miss. 31 33 54N 89 0W
Houston, Mo. 32 37 22N 91 58W
Houston, Tex. 51 29 46N 95 22W
Houston → 25 30 16N 93 13W
Houston, L. 51 29 55N 95 8W
Houston County ◇, Ala. 10 31 11N 85 14W
Houston County ◇, Ga. 18 32 20N 83 45W
Houston County ◇, Minn. 30 43 35N 91 30W
Houston County ◇, Tenn. 48 36 19N 87 42W
Houston County ◇, Tex. 51 31 19N 95 27W
Houston County L. 51 31 25N 95 35W
Houstonia 32 38 54N 93 22W
Houtman Abrolhos 126 28 43 S 113 48 E
Hovd 113 48 2N 91 37 E
Hove 83 50 50N 0 10W
Hoven 47 45 15N 99 47W
Hovenweep National Monument 16 37 20N 109 0W
Hovland 30 47 51N 89 58W
Hövsgöl Nuur 113 51 0N 100 30 E
Howard, Colo. 16 38 27N 105 50W
Howard, Ga. 18 32 36N 84 23W
Howard, Kans. 24 37 28N 96 16W
Howard, Pa. 45 41 1N 77 40W
Howard, S. Dak. 47 44 1N 97 32W
Howard, Wis. 55 44 33N 88 4W
Howard City 29 43 24N 85 28W
Howard County ◇, Ark. 13 34 7N 94 1W
Howard County ◇, Ind. 22 40 30N 86 10W
Howard County ◇, Iowa 23 43 20N 92 20W
Howard County ◇, Md. 27 39 15N 77 0W
Howard County ◇, Mo. 32 39 10N 92 40W
Howard County ◇, Nebr. 34 41 15N 98 30W
Howard County ◇, Tex. 50 32 15N 101 28W
Howard Draw → 50 30 10N 101 35W
Howard Hanson Reservoir 53 47 17N 121 47W
Howard L. 63 62 15N 105 57W
Howard Lake 30 45 4N 94 4W
Howe, Idaho 20 43 48N 113 0W
Howe, Ind. 22 41 43N 85 25W
Howe, Okla. 43 34 57N 94 38W
Howe, Tex. 51 33 30N 96 37W
Howe, C. 127 37 30 S 150 0 E
Howell, Mich. 29 42 36N 83 56W
Howell, Utah 52 41 48N 112 27W
Howell County ◇ 32 36 45N 91 50W
Howes 47 44 37N 102 3W
Howes Mill 32 37 38N 91 16W
Howison 31 30 40N 89 8W
Howland 26 45 14N 68 40W
Howley 61 49 12N 57 2W
Howrah = Haora 109 22 37N 88 20 E
Howth Hd. 85 53 21N 6 0W
Hoxie, Ark. 13 36 3N 90 59W
Hoxie, Kans. 24 39 21N 100 26W
Hoy I. 84 58 50N 3 15W
Høyanger 97 61 13N 6 4 E
Hoyleton 21 38 27N 89 16W
Hoyt, Colo. 16 40 1N 104 5W
Hoyt, Kans. 24 39 15N 95 43W
Hpungan Pass 109 27 30N 96 55 E
Hrádec Králové 88 50 15N 15 50 E
Hron → 89 47 49N 18 45 E
Hrvatska 94 45 20N 16 0 E
Hsenwi 109 23 22N 97 55 E
Hsiamen = Xiamen 114 24 25N 118 4 E
Hua Hin 112 12 34N 99 58 E
Hua Xian, Henan, China 115 35 30N 114 30 E
Hua Xian, Shaanxi, China 115 34 30N 109 48 E
Huacaya 73 20 45 S 63 43W
Huacheng 115 24 4N 115 37 E
Huachinera 64 30 9N 108 55W
Huacho 72 11 10 S 77 35W
Huachón 72 10 35 S 76 0W
Huachuan 114 46 50N 130 21 E
Huachuca City 12 31 34N 110 21W
Huade 114 41 55N 113 59 E
Huadian 114 43 0N 126 40 E
Huai He → 115 33 0N 118 30 E
Huai'an 115 33 30N 119 10 E
Huaide 114 43 30N 124 40 E
Huainan 115 32 38N 116 58 E
Huaiyang 115 33 40N 114 52 E
Huaiyuan 115 24 31N 108 22 E
Huajianzi 114 41 23N 125 20 E
Huajuapan de Leon 65 17 50N 97 48W
Hualalai 19 19 42N 155 52W
Hualapai Indian Reservation 12 35 45N 113 20W
Hualapai Mts. 12 34 45N 113 45W
Hualapai Peak 12 35 5N 113 54W
Hualian 115 23 59N 121 37 E
Huallaga → 72 5 0 S 75 30W
Huallanca 72 8 50 S 77 56W
Huamachuco 72 7 50 S 78 5W
Huambo 123 12 42 S 15 54 E
Huan Jiang → 114 34 28N 109 0 E
Huan Xian 114 36 33N 107 7 E
Huancabamba 72 5 10 S 79 15W
Huancane 72 15 10 S 69 44W
Huancapi 72 13 40 S 74 0W
Huancavelica 72 12 50 S 75 5W
Huancavelica □ 72 13 0 S 75 0W
Huancayo 72 12 5 S 75 12W
Huanchaca 72 20 15 S 66 40W
Huanchaca, Serranía de 73 14 30 S 60 39W
Huang He → 114 37 55N 118 50 E
Huangchuan 115 32 15N 115 10 E
Huangliu 115 18 20N 108 50 E
Huanglong 114 35 30N 109 59 E
Huangshi 115 30 10N 115 3 E
Huangyan 115 28 38N 121 19 E
Huanta 72 12 55 S 74 20W
Huánuco 72 9 55 S 76 15W
Huánuco □ 72 9 55 S 76 14W
Huanuni 72 18 16 S 66 51W
Huanzo, Cordillera de 72 14 35 S 73 20W
Huaral 72 11 32 S 77 13W
Huaraz 72 9 30 S 77 32W
Huari 72 9 14 S 77 14W
Huarmey 72 10 5 S 78 5W
Huarochiri 72 12 9 S 76 15W
Huarocondo 72 13 26 S 72 14W
Huasamota 64 22 30N 104 30W
Huascarán 72 9 8 S 77 36W
Huascarán, Nevado 72 9 7 S 77 37W
Huasco 76 28 30 S 71 15W
Huasco → 76 28 27 S 71 13W
Huatabampo 64 26 50N 109 50W
Huauchinango 65 20 11N 98 3W
Huautla de Jiménez 65 18 8N 96 51W
Huay Namota 64 21 56N 104 30W
Huayllay 72 11 3 S 76 21W
Hubbard, Iowa 23 42 18N 93 18W
Hubbard, Nebr. 34 42 23N 96 36W
Hubbard, Oreg. 44 45 11N 122 48W
Hubbard, Tex. 51 31 51N 96 48W
Hubbard County ◇ 30 47 10N 94 50W
Hubbard Creek L. 51 32 50N 98 58W
Hubbard L. 29 44 48N 83 34W
Hubbardton 36 43 42N 73 12W
Hubbart Pt. 63 59 21N 94 41W
Hubbell, Mich. 29 47 11N 88 26W
Hubbell, Nebr. 34 40 1N 97 29W
Hubei □ 115 31 0N 112 0 E
Hubli-Dharwad = Dharwad 108 15 22N 75 15 E
Huddersfield 82 53 38N 1 49W
Huddy 49 37 36N 82 17W
Hudiksvall 97 61 43N 17 10 E
Hudson, Canada 63 50 6N 92 9W
Hudson, Colo. 16 40 4N 104 39W
Hudson, Fla. 17 28 22N 82 42W
Hudson, Iowa 23 42 24N 92 28W
Hudson, Kans. 24 38 6N 98 40W
Hudson, Maine 26 45 0N 68 53W
Hudson, Mass. 28 42 23N 71 34W
Hudson, Md. 27 38 36N 76 15W
Hudson, Mich. 29 41 51N 84 21W
Hudson, N.C. 40 35 51N 81 30W
Hudson, N.H. 36 42 46N 71 26W
Hudson, N.Y. 39 42 15N 73 46W
Hudson, S. Dak. 47 43 8N 96 27W
Hudson, Wis. 55 44 58N 92 45W
Hudson, Wyo. 56 42 54N 108 35W
Hudson → 39 40 42N 74 2W
Hudson, L. 43 36 14N 95 11W
Hudson Bay 59 52 51N 102 23W
Hudson County ◇ 37 40 45N 74 5W
Hudson Falls 39 43 18N 73 35W
Hudson Hope 62 56 0N 121 54W
Hudson Mts. 5 74 32 S 99 20W
Hudson Str. 59 62 0N 70 0W
Hudsonville 29 42 52N 85 52W
Hudspeth County ◇ 50 31 30N 105 30W
Hue 112 16 30N 107 35 E
Huechucuicui, Pta. 78 41 48 S 74 2W
Hueco Mts. 50 31 53N 105 58W
Huehuetenango 66 15 20N 91 28W
Huejúcar 64 22 21N 103 13W
Huelva 91 37 18N 6 57W
Huentelauquén 76 31 38 S 71 33W
Huerfano → 16 38 14N 104 15W
Huerfano County ◇ 16 37 40N 104 50W
Huerta, Sa. de la 76 31 10 S 67 30W
Huesca 91 42 8N 0 25W
Huetamo 64 18 36N 100 54W
Huffman 51 30 1N 95 6W
Huger 46 33 6N 79 48W
Hugh → 126 25 1 S 134 1 E
Hugh Butler L. 34 40 21N 100 39W
Hughenden 127 20 52 S 144 10 E
Hughes, Alaska 11 66 3N 154 15W
Hughes, Ark. 13 34 57N 90 28W
Hughes County ◇, Okla. 43 35 0N 96 15W
Hughes County ◇, S. Dak. 47 44 30N 100 0W
Hughes Springs 51 33 0N 94 38W
Hughesville, Md. 27 38 32N 76 47W
Hughesville, Mo. 32 38 50N 93 18W
Hughesville, Pa. 45 41 14N 76 44W
Hughli → 109 21 56N 88 4 E
Hughson 14 37 36N 120 52W
Hugo, Colo. 16 39 8N 103 28W
Hugo, Okla. 43 34 1N 95 31W
Hugo L. 43 34 3N 95 27W
Hugoton 24 37 11N 101 21W
Hui Xian 114 35 27N 113 12 E
Hui'an 115 25 1N 118 43 E
Huichang 115 25 32N 115 45 E
Huichapán 65 20 24N 99 40W
Huihe 114 48 12N 119 17 E
Huila □ 70 2 30N 75 45W
Huila, Nevado del 70 3 0N 76 0W
Huilai 115 23 0N 116 18 E
Huimin 114 37 27N 117 28 E
Huinan 114 42 40N 126 2 E
Huinca Renancó 76 34 51 S 64 22W
Huining 114 35 38N 105 0 E
Huinong 114 39 5N 106 35 E
Huixtla 65 15 9N 92 28W
Huize 113 26 24N 103 15 E
Huizhou 115 23 0N 114 23 E
Hukawng Valley 109 26 30N 96 30 E
Hukou 115 29 45N 116 21 E
Hulah L. 43 36 56N 96 5W
Hulan 114 46 1N 126 37 E
Ḩulayfā' 106 25 58N 40 45 E
Hulbert, Mich. 29 46 21N 85 9W
Hulbert, Okla. 43 35 56N 95 9W
Huld 113 45 5N 105 30 E
Ḩulda 104 31 50N 34 51 E
Hulen 49 36 47N 83 31W
Hulett 56 44 41N 104 36W
Hulin 114 45 48N 132 59 E
Hull, Canada 60 45 25N 75 44W
Hull, U.K. 82 53 45N 0 20W
Hull, Fla. 17 27 7N 81 56W
Hull, Ill. 21 39 43N 91 13W
Hull, Iowa 23 43 11N 96 8W
Hull, Mass. 28 42 18N 70 55W
Hull → 82 53 43N 0 25W
Hulst 87 51 17N 4 2 E
Hulun Nur 114 49 0N 117 30 E
Huma 114 51 43N 126 38 E
Huma He → 114 51 42N 126 42 E
Humacao 57 18 9N 65 50W
Humacao ◇ 57 18 15N 65 45W
Humahuaca 76 23 10 S 65 25W
Humaitá, Brazil 73 7 35 S 63 1W
Humaitá, Paraguay 76 27 2 S 58 31W
Humansville 32 37 48N 93 35W
Humber → 82 53 40N 0 10W
Humberside □ 82 53 50N 0 30W
Humble 51 30 0N 95 18W
Humboldt, Canada 63 52 15N 105 9W
Humboldt, Ariz. 12 34 30N 112 14W
Humboldt, Ill. 21 39 36N 88 19W
Humboldt, Iowa 23 42 44N 94 13W
Humboldt, Kans. 24 37 49N 95 26W
Humboldt, Nebr. 34 40 10N 95 57W
Humboldt, S. Dak. 47 43 39N 97 5W
Humboldt, Tenn. 48 35 50N 88 55W
Humboldt → 35 39 59N 118 36W
Humboldt B. 14 40 45N 124 10W
Humboldt County ◇, Calif. 14 40 50N 124 0W
Humboldt County ◇, Iowa 23 42 50N 94 10W
Humboldt County ◇, Nev. 35 41 20N 118 10W
Humboldt Gletscher 4 79 30N 62 0W
Humboldt National Forest 35 41 45N 115 30W
Humboldt Peak 16 37 59N 105 33W
Humboldt Range 35 40 20N 118 10W
Humboldt Sink 35 40 1N 118 38W
Humbolt Salt Marsh 35 39 50N 117 55W
Hume 32 38 6N 94 34W
Hume, L. 127 36 0 S 147 0 E
Humeston 23 40 52N 93 30W
Humnoke 13 34 33N 91 45W
Humphrey, Ark. 13 34 25N 91 43W
Humphrey, Nebr. 34 41 42N 97 29W
Humphreys 43 34 33N 99 14W
Humphreys, Mt. 15 37 17N 118 40W
Humphreys County ◇, Miss. 31 33 6N 90 30W
Humphreys County ◇, Tenn. 48 36 5N 87 48W
Humphreys Peak 12 35 21N 111 41W
Hūn 121 29 2N 16 0 E
Húnaflói 96 65 50N 20 50W
Hunan □ 115 27 30N 112 0 E
Hunchun 114 42 52N 130 28 E
Hundred 54 39 41N 80 28W
Hundred Mile House 62 51 38N 121 18W
Hunedoara 89 45 40N 22 50 E
Hungary ■ 89 47 20N 19 20 E
Hungary, Plain of 80 47 0N 20 0 E
Hŭngnam 114 39 49N 127 45 E
Hungry Horse 33 48 23N 114 4W
Hungry Horse Reservoir 33 48 21N 114 1W

Hunnewell   Indian Cr.

Hunnewell, Kans. 24 37 1N 97 25W
Hunnewell, Mo. 32 39 40N 91 52W
Hunsrück 88 49 30N 7 0 E
Hunstanton 82 52 57N 0 30 E
Hunt 51 30 4N 99 20W
Hunt County ◇ 51 33 8N 96 7W
Hunt Mt. 56 44 55N 107 59W
Hunter, Ark. 13 35 3N 91 8W
Hunter, Kans. 24 39 14N 98 24W
Hunter, N. Dak. 41 47 12N 97 13W
Hunter, N.Y. 39 42 13N 74 13W
Hunter, Okla. 43 36 34N 97 40W
Hunter I., Australia 127 40 30 S 144 45 E
Hunter I., Canada 62 51 55N 128 0W
Hunterdon County ◇ 37 40 30N 75 0W
Hunters 53 48 7N 118 12W
Huntersville 40 35 25N 80 51W
Huntertown 22 41 14N 85 10W
Hunterville 128 39 56 S 175 35 E
Huntingburg 22 38 18N 86 57W
Huntingdon, Canada 60 45 6N 74 10W
Huntingdon, U.K. 83 52 20N 0 11W
Huntingdon, Pa. 45 40 30N 78 1W
Huntingdon, Tenn. 48 36 0N 88 26W
Huntingdon County ◇ 45 40 15N 78 0W
Huntington, Ark. 13 35 5N 94 16W
Huntington, Ind. 22 40 53N 85 30W
Huntington, Mass. 28 42 14N 72 53W
Huntington, N.Y. 39 40 52N 73 26W
Huntington, Oreg. 44 44 21N 117 16W
Huntington, Tex. 51 31 17N 94 34W
Huntington, Utah 52 39 20N 110 58W
Huntington, Vt. 36 44 22N 72 58W
Huntington, W. Va. 54 38 25N 82 27W
Huntington →, Nev. 35 40 37N 115 43W
Huntington →, Utah 52 39 9N 110 55W
Huntington Beach 15 33 40N 118 5W
Huntington County ◇ 22 40 50N 85 30W
Huntington Station 39 40 51N 73 25W
Huntingtown 27 38 37N 76 37W
Huntland 48 35 3N 86 16W
Huntley, Ill. 21 42 10N 88 26W
Huntley, Mont. 33 45 54N 108 19W
Huntley, Nebr. 34 40 13N 99 18W
Huntly, N.Z. 128 37 34 S 175 11 E
Huntly, U.K. 84 57 27N 2 48W
Huntsville, Canada 60 45 20N 79 14W
Huntsville, Ala. 10 34 44N 86 35W
Huntsville, Ark. 13 36 5N 93 44W
Huntsville, Ky. 48 37 10N 86 53W
Huntsville, Mo. 32 39 26N 92 33W
Huntsville, Ohio 42 40 26N 83 48W
Huntsville, Tenn. 49 36 25N 84 29W
Huntsville, Tex. 51 30 43N 95 33W
Huntsville, Utah 52 41 16N 111 46W
Huo Xian 114 36 36N 111 42 E
Huonville 127 43 0 S 147 5 E
Huoqiu 115 32 20N 116 12 E
Huoshao Dao 115 22 40N 121 30 E
Hupeh □ = Hubei □ 115 31 0N 112 0 E
Hure Qi 114 42 45N 121 45 E
Hurezani 95 44 49N 23 40 E
Hurley, Miss. 31 30 40N 88 30W
Hurley, Mo. 32 36 56N 93 30W
Hurley, N. Mex. 38 32 42N 108 8W
Hurley, N.Y. 39 41 55N 74 4W
Hurley, S. Dak. 47 43 17N 97 5W
Hurley, Wis. 55 46 27N 90 11W
Hurlock 27 38 38N 75 52W
Huron, Calif. 15 36 12N 120 6W
Huron, Kans. 24 39 38N 95 21W
Huron, Ohio 42 41 24N 82 33W
Huron, S. Dak. 47 44 22N 98 13W
Huron → 29 42 2N 83 11W
Huron, L. 29 44 30N 82 40W
Huron Beach 29 45 30N 84 6W
Huron County ◇, Mich. 29 43 50N 83 0W
Huron County ◇, Ohio 42 41 15N 82 37W
Huron Mts. 29 46 50N 88 0W
Huron National Forest 29 44 30N 84 0W
Hurricane 52 37 11N 113 17W
Hurricane Cliffs 12 36 45N 113 20W
Hurst 51 32 49N 97 9W
Hurstboro 10 32 15N 85 25W
Hurstville 23 42 6N 90 41W
Hurunui → 128 42 54 S 173 18 E
Húsavík 96 66 3N 17 21W
Huskvarna 97 57 47N 14 15 E
Huslia 11 65 41N 156 24W
Hussar 62 51 3N 112 41W
Hustisford 55 43 21N 88 36W
Husum 53 45 48N 121 29W
Hutch Mt. 12 34 47N 111 22W
Hutchinson, Kans. 24 38 5N 97 56W
Hutchinson, Minn. 30 44 54N 94 22W
Hutchinson County ◇, S. Dak. 47 43 25N 97 48W
Hutchinson County ◇, Tex. 50 35 50N 101 30W
Hutou 114 45 58N 133 38 E
Hutsonville 21 39 7N 87 40W
Huttig 13 33 2N 92 11W
Hutto 51 30 33N 97 33W
Hutton 27 39 25N 79 28W
Huttonsville 54 38 43N 79 59W
Ḩuwwārah 104 32 9N 35 15 E
Huxford 10 31 13N 87 28W
Huxley 23 41 54N 93 36W
Huy 87 50 31N 5 15 E
Huyett 27 39 40N 77 20W
Hvammur 96 65 13N 21 49W
Hvar 94 43 11N 16 28 E
Hvítá 96 64 40N 21 5W
Hvítá → 96 64 0N 20 58W
Hvítárvatn 96 64 37N 19 50W
Hwang Ho = Huang He → 114 37 55N 118 50 E
Hwange 123 18 18 S 26 30 E
Hyak 53 47 24N 121 24W
Hyannis, Mass. 28 41 39N 70 17W
Hyannis, Nebr. 34 42 0N 101 46W
Hyargas Nuur 113 49 0N 93 0 E
Hyattsville 27 38 57N 76 56W
Hyattville 56 44 15N 107 36W
Hybart 10 31 50N 87 23W
Hyco L. 40 36 31N 79 3W
Hydaburg 11 55 12N 132 50W
Hyde County ◇, N.C. 40 35 30N 76 20W
Hyde County ◇, S. Dak. 47 44 31N 99 27W
Hyde Park, Guyana 71 6 30N 58 16W
Hyde Park, U.S.A. 36 44 36N 72 37W
Hyden 49 37 10N 83 22W
Hyderabad, India 108 17 22N 78 29 E
Hyderabad, Pakistan 108 25 23N 68 24 E
Hydes 27 39 30N 76 29W
Hydro 43 35 33N 98 39W
Hyères 90 43 8N 6 9 E
Hyesan 114 41 20N 128 10 E
Hygiene 16 40 11N 105 11W
Hyland → 62 59 52N 128 12W
Hymera 22 39 11N 87 18W
Hyndman 45 39 49N 78 43W
Hyndman Peak 20 43 45N 114 8W
Hyōgo □ 117 35 15N 135 0 E
Hyrum 52 41 38N 111 51W
Hysham 33 46 18N 107 14W
Hythe 83 51 4N 1 5 E
Hyūga 117 32 25N 131 35 E
Hyvinge = Hyvinkää 97 60 38N 24 50 E
Hyvinkää 97 60 38N 24 50 E

I

I-n-Gall 120 16 51N 7 1 E
Iaco → 72 9 3 S 68 34W
Iaçu 75 12 45 S 40 13W
Iaeger 54 37 28N 81 49W
Ialomiţa □ 95 44 30N 27 30 E
Ialomiţa → 95 44 42N 27 51 E
Iamonia L. 17 30 38N 84 14W
Ianca 95 45 6N 27 29 E
Iara 95 46 31N 23 35 E
Iaşi 89 47 10N 27 40 E
Iatan 32 39 29N 94 59W
Iatt L. 25 31 35N 92 40W
Iauaretê 70 0 36N 69 12W
Iba 111 15 22N 120 0 E
Ibadan 120 7 22N 3 58 E
Ibagué 70 4 20N 75 20W
Ibaiti 75 23 50 S 50 10W
Ibapah 52 40 2N 113 59W
Ibar → 95 43 43N 20 45 E
Ibaraki □ 117 36 10N 140 10 E
Ibarra 70 0 21N 78 7W
Ibera, Laguna 76 28 30 S 57 9W
Iberia 32 38 5N 92 18W
Iberia Parish ◇ 25 30 1N 91 49W
Iberian Peninsula 80 40 0N 5 0W
Iberville 60 45 19N 73 17W
Iberville, Lac d' 60 55 55N 73 15W
Iberville Parish ◇ 25 30 17N 91 14W
Ibi 120 8 15N 9 44 E
Ibiá 75 19 30 S 46 30W
Ibicaraí 75 14 51 S 39 36W
Ibicuí 75 14 51 S 39 59W
Ibicuy 76 33 55 S 59 10W
Ibioapaba, Sa. da 74 4 0 S 41 30W
Ibipetuba 74 11 0 S 44 32W
Ibitiara 75 12 39 S 42 13W
Ibiza 91 38 54N 1 26 E
Ibo 123 12 22 S 40 40 E
Ibonma 111 3 29 S 133 31 E
Ibotirama 75 12 13 S 43 12W
Ibu 111 1 35N 127 33 E
Ibusuki 117 31 12N 130 40 E
Icá 72 14 0 S 75 48W
Ica □ 72 14 20 S 75 30W
Içá → 72 2 55 S 67 58W
Icabarú 71 4 20N 61 45W
Icabarú → 71 4 45N 62 15W
Içana 70 0 21N 67 19W
Içana → 70 0 26N 67 19W
Icatu 74 2 46 S 44 4W
Ice Harbor Dam 53 46 15N 118 53W
Iceland ■ 96 65 0N 19 0W
Icha 101 55 30N 156 0 E
Ich'ang = Yichang 115 30 40N 111 20 E
Ichchapuram 109 19 10N 84 40 E
Ichihara 117 35 28N 140 5 E
Ichikawa 117 35 44N 139 55 E
Ichilo → 73 15 57 S 64 50W
Ichinohe 116 40 13N 141 17 E
Ichinomiya 117 35 18N 136 48 E
Ichinoseki 116 38 55N 141 8 E
Icó 74 6 24 S 38 51W
Icoraci 74 1 18 S 48 28W
Icy C. 11 70 20N 161 52W
Ida 29 41 55N 83 34W
Ida County ◇ 23 42 25N 95 30W
Ida Grove 23 42 21N 95 28W
Idabel 43 33 54N 94 50W
Idaho □ 20 45 0N 115 0W
Idaho City 20 43 50N 115 50W
Idaho County ◇ 20 45 35N 115 30W
Idaho Falls 20 43 30N 112 2W
Idaho Springs 16 39 45N 105 31W
Idalia 16 39 42N 102 18W
Idalou 50 33 40N 101 41W
Idana 24 39 22N 97 16W
Idanha 44 44 42N 122 5W
Idd el Ghanam 121 11 30N 24 19 E
Iddan 105 6 10N 48 55 E
Ideal 47 43 33N 99 54W
Idehan 121 27 10N 11 30 E
Idehan Marzūq 121 24 50N 13 51 E
Idelès 120 23 50N 5 53 E
Idfû 121 25 0N 32 49 E
Ídhi Óros 95 35 15N 24 45 E
Ídhra 95 37 20N 23 28 E
Idi 110 5 2N 97 37 E
Idiofa 122 4 55 S 19 42 E
Idlip 106 35 55N 36 38 E
Idna 104 31 34N 34 58 E
Idria 15 36 25N 120 41W
Idutywa 123 32 8 S 28 18 E
Ieper 87 50 51N 2 53 E
Ierápetra 95 35 0N 25 44 E
Ierzu 94 39 48N 9 32 E
Ifanadiana 123 21 19 S 47 39 E
Ife 120 7 30N 4 31 E
Ifni 120 29 29N 10 12W
Iforas, Adrar des 120 19 40N 1 40 E
Igara Paraná → 70 2 9 S 71 47W
Igarapava 75 20 3 S 47 47W
Igarapé Açu 74 1 4 S 47 33W
Igarapé-Mirim 74 1 59 S 48 58W
Igarka 101 67 30N 86 33 E
Igatimi 77 24 5 S 55 40W
Igbetti 120 8 44N 4 8 E
Iggesund 97 61 39N 17 10 E
Igiugig 11 59 20N 155 55W
Iglésias 94 39 19N 8 27 E
Igli 120 30 25N 2 19W
Igloolik 59 69 20N 81 49W
Ignace 60 49 30N 91 40W
Ignacio 16 37 7N 107 38W
Iguaçu → 77 25 36 S 54 36W
Iguaçu, Cat. del 77 25 41 S 54 26W
Iguala 65 18 20N 99 40W
Igualada 91 41 37N 1 37 E
Iguape 75 24 43 S 47 33W
Iguassu = Iguaçu → 77 25 36 S 54 36W
Iguatu 74 6 20 S 39 18W
Iguéla 122 2 0 S 9 16 E
Iheya-Shima 117 27 4N 127 58 E
Ihlen 30 43 55N 96 22W
Ihosy 123 22 24 S 46 8 E
Ii 96 65 19N 25 22 E
Ii-Shima 117 26 43N 127 47 E
Iida 117 35 35N 137 50 E
Iijoki → 96 65 20N 25 20 E
Iisalmi 96 63 32N 27 10 E
Iiyama 117 36 51N 138 22 E
Iizuka 117 33 38N 130 42 E
Ijebu-Ode 120 6 47N 3 58 E
IJmuiden 87 52 28N 4 35 E
IJssel → 87 52 35N 5 50 E
IJsselmeer 87 52 45N 5 20 E
Ijuí → 77 27 58 S 55 20W
Ikaría 95 37 35N 26 10 E
Ikeda 117 34 1N 133 48 E
Ikela 122 1 6 S 23 6 E
Ikhtiman 95 42 27N 23 48 E
Iki 117 33 45N 129 42 E
Ilagan 111 17 7N 121 53 E
Īlām 106 33 0N 46 0 E
Ilanskiy 101 56 14N 96 3 E
Île-à-la Crosse 63 55 27N 107 53W
Île-à-la-Crosse, Lac 63 55 40N 107 45W
Île-de-France 90 49 0N 2 20 E
Ilebo 122 4 17 S 20 55 E
Ilek 100 51 32N 53 21 E
Ilek → 98 51 30N 53 22 E
Ilfeld 38 35 25N 105 34W
Ilford 63 56 4N 95 35W
Ilfov □ 95 44 20N 26 0 E
Ilfracombe, Australia 127 23 30 S 144 30 E
Ilfracombe, U.K. 83 51 13N 4 8W
Ilha Grande 71 0 27 S 65 2W
Ilha Grande, Baía da 75 23 9 S 44 30W
Ilhéus 75 14 49 S 39 2W
Iliamna 11 59 45N 154 55W
Iliamna L. 11 59 30N 155 0W
Ilich 100 40 50N 68 27 E
Iliff 16 40 45N 103 4W
Iligan 111 8 12N 124 13 E
Ilio Pt. 19 21 13N 157 16W
Iliodhrómia 95 39 12N 23 50 E
Ilion 39 43 1N 75 2W
Ilkeston 82 52 59N 1 19W
Illana B. 111 7 35N 123 45 E
Illapel 76 32 0 S 71 10W
'Illâr 104 32 23N 35 7 E
Ille-et-Vilaine □ 90 48 10N 1 30W
Iller → 88 48 23N 9 58 E
Illimani 72 16 30 S 67 50W
Illinois □ 21 41 0N 89 0W
Illinois →, Ark. 13 35 30N 95 5W
Illinois →, Ill. 21 38 58N 90 28W
Illinois →, Oreg. 44 42 33N 124 3W
Illiopolis 21 39 51N 89 15W
Illium = Troy 106 39 57N 26 12 E
Illmo 32 37 13N 89 30W
Ilmen, Oz. 98 58 15N 31 10 E
Ilo 72 17 40 S 71 20W
Iloilo 111 10 45N 122 33 E
Ilorin 120 8 30N 4 35 E
Ilwaco 53 46 19N 124 3W
Ilwaki 111 7 55 S 126 30 E
Imabari 117 34 4N 133 0 E
Imandra, Oz. 98 67 30N 33 0 E
Imari 117 33 15N 129 52 E
Imbabura □ 70 0 30N 78 45W
Imbaimadai 71 5 44N 60 17W
Imbler 44 45 28N 117 58W
Imboden 13 36 12N 91 11W
imeni 26 Bakinskikh Komissarov, Azerbaijan, U.S.S.R. 99 39 19N 49 12 E
imeni 26 Bakinskikh Komissarov, Turkmen S.S.R., U.S.S.R. 99 39 22N 54 10 E
Imeni Poliny Osipenko 101 52 30N 136 29 E
Imeri, Serra 70 0 50N 65 25W
Imi 105 6 28N 42 10 E
Imlay 35 40 40N 118 9W
Imlay City 29 43 2N 83 5W
Immingham 82 53 37N 0 12W
Immokalee 17 26 25N 81 25W
Imnaha → 44 45 49N 116 46W
Imogene 23 40 53N 95 29W
Imola 94 44 20N 11 42 E
Imperatriz, Amazonas, Brazil 72 5 18 S 67 11W
Imperatriz, Maranhão, Brazil 74 5 30 S 47 29W
Impéria 94 43 52N 8 0 E
Imperial, Canada 63 51 21N 105 28W
Imperial, Peru 72 13 4 S 76 21W
Imperial, Calif. 15 32 51N 115 34W
Imperial, Nebr. 34 40 31N 101 39W
Imperial, Pt. 12 36 15N 111 57W
Imperial Beach 15 32 35N 117 8W
Imperial County ◇ 15 33 0N 115 20W
Imperial Dam 12 32 55N 114 25W
Imperial Reservoir 12 32 53N 114 28W
Imperial Valley 15 33 0N 115 30W
Impfondo 122 1 40N 18 0 E
Imphal 109 24 48N 93 56 E
Imuruan B. 111 10 40N 119 10 E
In Belbel 120 27 55N 1 12 E
In Salah 120 27 10N 2 32 E
Ina, Japan 117 35 50N 138 0 E
Ina, U.S.A. 21 38 9N 88 54W
Inajá 74 8 54 S 37 49W
Inangahua Junc. 128 41 52 S 171 59 E
Inanwatan 111 2 10 S 132 14 E
Iñapari 72 11 0 S 69 40W
Inari 96 68 54N 27 5 E
Inarijärvi 96 69 0N 28 0 E
Inawashiro-Ko 116 37 29N 140 6 E
Inca 91 39 43N 2 54 E
Incaguasi 76 29 12 S 71 5W
İnce-Burnu 106 42 7N 34 56 E
Inchon 114 37 27N 126 40 E
Incline Village 35 39 10N 119 58W
Incomáti → 123 25 46 S 32 43 E
Indalsälven → 96 62 36N 17 30 E
Indaw 109 24 15N 96 5 E
Independence, Calif. 15 36 48N 118 12W
Independence, Iowa 23 42 28N 91 54W
Independence, Kans. 24 37 14N 95 42W
Independence, Ky. 49 38 57N 84 33W
Independence, La. 25 30 38N 90 30W
Independence, Mo. 32 39 6N 94 25W
Independence, Oreg. 44 44 51N 123 11W
Independence, Va. 54 36 37N 81 9W
Independence, Wis. 55 44 22N 91 25W
Independence County ◇ 13 35 46N 91 39W
Independence Cr. → 50 30 27N 101 44W
Independence Fjord 4 82 10N 29 0W
Independence Mts. 35 41 20N 116 0W
Independence Pass 16 39 7N 106 33W
Independência 74 5 23 S 40 19W
Independencia, La 65 16 31N 91 47W
Independenţa 95 45 25N 27 42 E
Index 53 47 50N 121 33W
India ■ 103 20 0N 78 0 E
Indiahoma 43 34 37N 98 45W
Indialantic 17 28 6N 80 34W
Indian → 17 27 10N 80 10W
Indian-Antarctic Ridge 124 49 0 S 120 0 E
Indian Cabins 62 59 52N 117 40W
Indian Cr. → 47 44 39N 103 19W

Indian Harbour **Itajubá**

Indian Harbour **61** 54 27N 57 13W
Indian Harbour Beach **17** 28 10N 80 35W
Indian Head, Canada **63** 50 30N 103 41W
Indian Head, U.S.A. **27** 38 38N 77 12W
Indian Heights **22** 40 26N 86 10W
Indian L., Mich. **29** 45 59N 86 20W
Indian L., N.Y. **39** 43 42N 74 19W
Indian L., Ohio **42** 40 30N 83 53W
Indian Lake **39** 43 47N 74 16W
Indian Mills **37** 39 48N 74 46W
Indian Ocean **3** 5 0S 75 0E
Indian Peak **52** 38 16N 113 53W
Indian River **29** 45 25N 84 37W
Indian River Bay **27** 38 36N 75 4W
Indian River County ◇ **17** 27 40N 80 45W
Indian Rock **53** 45 59N 120 49W
Indian Rocks Beach **17** 27 53N 82 51W
Indian Springs **35** 36 35N 115 40W
Indian Village **24** 37 5N 95 38W
Indiana **45** 40 37N 79 9W
Indiana □ **22** 40 0N 86 0W
Indiana County ◇ **45** 40 45N 79 0W
Indiana Dunes Nat. Lakeshore **22** 41 40N 87 0W
Indianapolis **22** 39 46N 86 9W
Indianola, Iowa **23** 41 22N 93 34W
Indianola, Miss. **31** 33 27N 90 39W
Indianola, Nebr. **34** 40 14N 100 25W
Indianola, Okla. **43** 35 10N 95 46W
Indiantown **17** 27 1N 80 28W
Indiapora **75** 19 57S 50 17W
Indiga **98** 67 50N 48 50E
Indigirka → **101** 70 48N 148 54E
Indio **15** 33 43N 116 13W
Indonesia ■ **110** 5 0S 115 0E
Indore **108** 22 42N 75 53E
Indramayu **111** 6 20S 108 19E
Indravati → **109** 19 20N 80 20E
Indre □ **90** 46 50N 1 39E
Indre-et-Loire □ **90** 47 12N 0 40E
Indrio **17** 27 31N 80 21W
Indus → **108** 24 20N 67 47E
Industry, Ill. **21** 40 20N 90 36W
Industry, Kans. **24** 39 8N 97 10W
Industry, Tex. **51** 29 58N 96 30W
İnebolu **106** 41 55N 33 40E
İnegöl **106** 40 5N 29 31E
Inés, Mt. **78** 48 30S 69 40W
Inez **49** 37 52N 82 32W
Infiernillo, Presa del **64** 18 9N 102 0W
Ingalls, Ark. **13** 33 23N 92 9W
Ingalls, Kans. **24** 37 50N 100 27W
Ingapirca **70** 2 38S 78 56W
Ingende **122** 0 12S 18 57E
Ingeniero Jacobacci **78** 41 20S 69 36W
Ingenio Santa Ana **76** 27 25S 65 40W
Ingham **127** 18 43S 146 10E
Ingham County ◇ **29** 42 35N 84 30W
Ingleborough **82** 54 11N 2 23W
Ingleside, Md. **27** 39 6N 75 53W
Ingleside, Tex. **51** 27 53N 97 13W
Inglewood, N.Z. **128** 39 9S 174 14E
Inglewood, U.S.A. **15** 33 58N 118 21W
Inglis **17** 29 2N 82 40W
Ingólfshöfði **96** 63 48N 16 39W
Ingolstadt **88** 48 45N 11 26E
Ingomar **33** 46 35N 107 23W
Ingonish **61** 46 42N 60 18W
Ingraj Bazar **109** 24 58N 88 10E
Ingram, Tex. **51** 30 5N 99 14W
Ingram, Wis. **55** 45 31N 90 49W
Ingrid Christensen Coast **5** 69 30S 76 0E
Ingulec **99** 47 42N 33 14E
Inhambane **123** 23 54S 35 30E
Inhambupe **75** 11 47S 38 21W
Inhaminga **123** 18 26S 35 0E
Inharrime **123** 24 30S 35 0E
Inhuma **74** 6 40S 41 42W
Inhumas **75** 16 22S 49 30W
Inini □ **71** 4 0N 53 0W
Inírida → **70** 3 55N 67 52W
Inishbofin **85** 53 35N 10 12W
Inishmore **85** 53 8N 9 45W
Inishowen **85** 55 14N 7 15W
Injune **127** 25 53S 148 32E
Inklin **62** 58 56N 133 5W
Inklin → **62** 58 50N 133 10W
Inkom **20** 42 48N 112 15W
Inkster, Mich. **29** 42 18N 83 19W
Inkster, N. Dak. **41** 48 9N 97 39W
Inland L. **10** 33 50N 86 30W
Inle L. **109** 20 30N 96 58E
Inlet **39** 43 45N 74 48W
Inman, Kans. **24** 38 14N 97 47W
Inman, Nebr. **34** 42 23N 98 32W
Inman, S.C. **46** 35 3N 82 5W
Inn → **88** 48 35N 13 28E
Inner Hebrides **84** 57 0N 6 30W
Inner Mongolia = Nei Monggol Zizhiqu □ **114** 42 0N 112 0E
Inner Sound **84** 57 30N 5 55W
Innetalling I. **60** 56 0N 79 0W
Innisfail, Australia **127** 17 33S 146 5E
Innisfail, Canada **62** 52 0N 113 57W
In'no-shima **117** 34 19N 133 10E
Innsbruck **88** 47 16N 11 23E
Inny → **85** 53 30N 7 50W
Inocência **75** 19 47S 51 48W
Inola **43** 36 9N 95 31W
Inongo **122** 1 55S 18 30E
Inoucdjouac **59** 58 25N 78 15W
Inowrocław **89** 52 50N 18 12E
Inquisivi **72** 16 50S 67 10W
Insein **109** 16 50N 96 5E
Însurăţei **95** 44 50N 27 40E
Inta **98** 66 5N 60 8E
Intendente Alvear **76** 35 12S 63 32W
Intercession City **17** 28 16N 81 31W
Interior **47** 43 44N 101 59W
Interlachen **17** 29 37N 81 53W
Interlaken **39** 42 37N 76 44W
International Falls **30** 48 36N 93 25W
Intervale **36** 44 6N 71 8W
Interview I. **112** 12 55N 92 42E
Inthanon, Doi **112** 18 35N 98 29E
Intiyaco **76** 28 43S 60 5W
Intracoastal City **25** 29 47N 92 9W
Intutu **70** 3 32S 74 48W
Inútil, B. **78** 53 30S 70 15W
Inuvik **58** 68 16N 133 40W
Inver Grove Heights **30** 44 51N 93 1W
Inveraray **84** 56 13N 5 5W
Inverbervie **84** 56 50N 2 17W
Invercargill **128** 46 24S 168 24E
Inverell **127** 29 45S 151 8E
Invergordon **84** 57 41N 4 10W
Invermere **62** 50 30N 116 2W
Inverness, Canada **61** 46 15N 61 19W
Inverness, U.K. **84** 57 29N 4 12W
Inverness, Ala. **10** 32 1N 85 45W
Inverness, Calif. **14** 38 6N 122 51W
Inverness, Fla. **17** 28 50N 82 20W
Inverness, Miss. **31** 33 21N 90 35W
Inverurie **84** 57 15N 2 21W
Investigator Group **126** 34 45S 134 20E
Investigator Str. **127** 35 30S 137 0E
Inwood **23** 43 19N 96 26W
Inya **100** 50 28N 86 37E
Inyo County ◇ **15** 36 30N 117 40W
Inyo Mts. **15** 36 40N 118 0W
Inyo National Forest **15** 37 30N 118 15W
Inyokern **15** 35 39N 117 49W
Inza **98** 53 55N 46 25E
Iō-Jima **117** 30 48N 130 18E
Ioánnina □ **95** 39 39N 20 57E
Iola, Ill. **21** 38 50N 88 38W
Iola, Kans. **24** 37 55N 95 24W
Iola, Wis. **55** 44 30N 89 8W
Ion Corvin **95** 44 7N 27 50E
Iona, U.K. **84** 56 20N 6 25W
Iona, Idaho **20** 43 32N 111 56W
Iona, Minn. **30** 43 55N 95 47W
Iona, S. Dak. **47** 43 33N 99 26W
Ione, Calif. **14** 38 21N 120 56W
Ione, Oreg. **44** 45 30N 119 50W
Ione, Wash. **53** 48 45N 117 25W
Ionia, Iowa **23** 43 2N 92 27W
Ionia, Kans. **24** 39 40N 98 21W
Ionia, Mich. **29** 42 59N 85 4W
Ionia, Mo. **32** 38 30N 93 19W
Ionia County ◇ **29** 42 55N 85 5W
Ionian Is. = Iónioi Nísoi **95** 38 40N 20 0E
Ionian Sea **95** 37 30N 17 30E
Iónioi Nísoi **95** 38 40N 20 0E
Íos **95** 36 41N 25 20E
Iosco County ◇ **29** 44 20N 83 40W
Iota **25** 30 20N 92 30W
Iowa **25** 30 14N 93 1W
Iowa □ **23** 42 15N 93 15W
Iowa → **23** 41 10N 91 1W
Iowa City **23** 41 40N 91 32W
Iowa County ◇, Iowa **23** 41 40N 92 0W
Iowa County ◇, Wis. **55** 43 0N 90 10W
Iowa Falls **23** 42 31N 93 16W
Iowa Park **51** 33 57N 98 40W
Ipameri **75** 17 44S 48 9W
Iparía **72** 9 17S 74 29W
Ipava **21** 40 21N 90 19W
Ipiales **70** 0 50N 77 37W
Ipiaú **75** 14 8S 39 44W
Ipin = Yibin **113** 28 45N 104 32E
Ipirá **75** 12 10S 39 44W
Ipiranga **70** 3 13S 65 57W
Ípiros □ **95** 39 30N 20 30E
Ipixuna **72** 7 0S 71 40W
Ipixuna →, Amazonas, Brazil **72** 7 11S 71 51W
Ipixuna →, Amazonas, Brazil **73** 5 45S 63 2W
Ipoh **112** 4 35N 101 5E
Iporá **75** 11 23S 50 40W
Ippy **122** 6 5N 21 7E
Ipswich, Australia **127** 27 35S 152 40E
Ipswich, U.K. **83** 52 4N 1 9E
Ipswich, Mass. **28** 42 41N 70 50W
Ipswich, S. Dak. **47** 45 27N 99 2W
Ipswich B. **28** 42 41N 70 42W
Ipu **74** 4 23S 40 44W
Ipueiras **74** 4 33S 40 43W
Ipupiara **75** 11 49S 42 37W
Iquique **72** 20 19S 70 5W
Iquitos **70** 3 45S 73 10W
Ira **50** 32 35N 101 0W
Iraan **50** 30 55N 101 54W
Irabu-Jima **117** 24 50N 125 10E
Iracoubo **71** 5 30N 53 10W
Iráklion **95** 35 20N 25 12E
Irala **77** 25 55S 54 35W
Iran ■ **107** 33 0N 53 0E
Iran, Gunung-Gunung **110** 2 20N 114 50E
Īrānshahr **107** 27 15N 60 40E
Irapa **71** 10 34N 62 35W
Irapuato **64** 20 40N 101 30W
Iraq ■ **106** 33 0N 44 0E
Irasburg **36** 44 18N 73 47W
Irati **77** 25 25S 50 38W
Irbid **104** 32 35N 35 48E
Irebu **122** 0 40S 17 46E
Irecê **74** 11 18S 41 52W
Iredell **51** 31 59N 97 52W
Iredell County ◇ **40** 35 45N 80 50W
Ireland ■ **85** 53 0N 8 0W
Ireland's Eye **85** 53 25N 6 4W
Ireng → **71** 3 33N 59 51W
Iret **101** 60 3N 154 20E
Ireton **23** 42 58N 96 19W
Iri **114** 35 59N 127 0E
Irian Jaya □ **111** 4 0S 137 0E
Iringa **122** 7 48S 35 43E
Iriomote-Jima **117** 24 19N 123 48E
Irion County ◇ **50** 31 15N 101 0W
Iriona **66** 15 57N 85 11W
Iriri → **71** 3 52S 52 37W
Iriri Novo → **73** 8 46S 53 22W
Irish Sea **82** 54 0N 5 0W
Irkineyeva **101** 58 30N 96 49E
Irkutsk **101** 52 18N 104 20E
Irma **63** 52 55N 111 14W
Irō-Zaki **117** 34 36N 138 51E
Iron Belt **55** 46 24N 90 19W
Iron City, Ga. **18** 31 1N 84 49W
Iron City, Tenn. **48** 35 1N 87 35W
Iron County ◇, Mich. **29** 46 15N 88 35W
Iron County ◇, Mo. **32** 37 30N 90 40W
Iron County ◇, Utah **52** 37 50N 113 20W
Iron County ◇, Wis. **55** 46 15N 90 15W
Iron Gate = Portile de Fier **89** 44 42N 22 30E
Iron Junction **30** 47 25N 92 36W
Iron Knob **127** 32 46S 137 8E
Iron Mountain, Mich. **29** 45 49N 88 4W
Iron Mountain, Mo. **32** 37 42N 90 39W
Iron Mts. **54** 36 40N 81 45W
Iron Ridge **55** 43 24N 88 32W
Iron River, Mich. **29** 46 6N 88 39W
Iron River, Wis. **55** 46 34N 91 24W
Ironbridge **83** 52 38N 2 29W
Irondale, Ala. **10** 33 32N 86 42W
Irondale, Mo. **32** 37 50N 90 41W
Irondale, Ohio **42** 40 34N 80 44W
Irondequoit **39** 43 13N 77 35W
Ironside **44** 44 19N 117 57W
Ironsides **27** 38 30N 77 12W
Ironton, Minn. **30** 46 28N 93 59W
Ironton, Mo. **32** 37 36N 90 38W
Ironton, Ohio **42** 38 32N 82 41W
Ironwood **29** 46 27N 90 9W
Iroquois, Ill. **21** 40 50N 87 35W
Iroquois, S. Dak. **47** 44 22N 97 51W
Iroquois → **22** 41 5N 87 49W
Iroquois County ◇ **21** 40 45N 87 50W
Iroquois Falls **60** 48 46N 80 41W
Irrawaddy □ **109** 17 0N 95 0E
Irrawaddy → **109** 15 50N 95 6E
Irrigon **44** 45 54N 119 30W
Irtysh → **100** 61 4N 68 52E
Irumu **122** 1 32N 29 53E
Irún **91** 43 20N 1 52W
Irvine, Canada **63** 49 57N 110 16W
Irvine, U.K. **84** 55 37N 4 40W
Irvine, Calif. **15** 33 41N 117 46W
Irvine, Ky. **49** 37 42N 83 58W
Irvinestown **85** 54 28N 7 38W
Irving, Ill. **21** 39 12N 89 24W
Irving, Tex. **51** 32 49N 96 56W
Irvington, Ill. **21** 38 26N 89 10W
Irvington, Ky. **48** 37 53N 86 17W
Irvona **45** 40 46N 78 33W
Irwin **23** 41 47N 95 12W
Irwin County ◇ **18** 31 40N 83 15W
Irwinton **18** 32 49N 83 10W
Irwinville **18** 31 39N 83 23W
Isaac → **127** 22 55S 149 20E
Isabel, Kans. **24** 37 28N 98 33W
Isabel, S. Dak. **47** 45 24N 101 26W
Isabel Segunda **57** 18 9N 65 27W
Isabela, Phil. **111** 6 40N 122 10E
Isabela, Puerto Rico **57** 18 30N 67 2W
Isabela, I. **64** 21 51N 105 55W
Isabela, La **67** 19 58N 71 2W
Isabella, Cord. **66** 13 30N 85 25W
Isabella County ◇ **29** 43 40N 84 50W
Isabella L. **15** 35 39N 118 28W
Isabelle, Pt. **29** 47 21N 87 56W
Ísafjarðardjúp **96** 66 10N 23 0W
Ísafjörður **96** 66 5N 23 9W
Isahaya **117** 32 52N 130 2E
Isana → **70** 0 26N 67 19W
Isangi **122** 0 52N 24 10E
Isanti **30** 45 29N 93 15W
Isanti County ◇ **30** 45 30N 93 15W
Isaquah **53** 47 32N 122 2W
Isar → **88** 48 49N 12 58E
Isbiceni **95** 43 45N 24 40E
Iscayachi **73** 21 31S 65 3W
Íschia **94** 40 45N 13 51E
Iscuandé **70** 2 28N 77 59W
Ise **117** 34 25N 136 45E
Ise-Wan **117** 34 43N 136 43E
Isère □ **90** 45 15N 5 40E
Isère → **90** 44 59N 4 51E
Isherton **71** 2 20N 59 25W
Ishigaki-Shima **117** 24 20N 124 10E
Ishikari-Gawa → **116** 43 15N 141 23E
Ishikari-Sammyaku **116** 43 30N 143 0E
Ishikari-Wan **116** 43 25N 141 1E
Ishikawa □ **117** 36 30N 136 30E
Ishim **100** 56 10N 69 30E
Ishim → **100** 57 45N 71 10E
Ishinomaki **116** 38 32N 141 20E
Ishioka **117** 36 11N 140 16E
Ishkuman **108** 36 30N 73 50E
Ishpeming **29** 46 29N 87 40W
Isil Kul **100** 54 55N 71 16E
Isiolo **122** 0 24N 37 33E
Isiro **122** 2 53N 27 40E
İskenderun **106** 36 32N 36 10E
İskenderun Körfezi **99** 36 40N 35 50E
Iskŭr → **95** 43 45N 24 25E
Iskŭr, Yazovir **95** 42 23N 23 30E
Iskut → **62** 56 45N 131 49W
Isla → **84** 56 32N 3 20W
Isla Vista **15** 34 25N 119 53W
Islamabad **108** 33 40N 73 10E
Islamorada **17** 24 56N 80 37W
Island → **62** 60 25N 121 12W
Island County ◇ **53** 48 10N 122 35W
Island Creek **27** 38 27N 76 35W
Island Falls, Canada **60** 49 35N 81 20W
Island Falls, U.S.A. **26** 46 1N 68 16W
Island Heights **37** 39 57N 74 9W
Island L. **63** 53 47N 94 25W
Island Lake Res. **30** 47 48N 94 19W
Island Park **20** 44 24N 111 19W
Island Park Reservoir **20** 44 25N 111 24W
Island Pond **36** 44 49N 71 53W
Islands, B. of **61** 49 11N 58 15W
Islay **84** 55 46N 6 10W
Isle **30** 46 8N 93 28W
Isle aux Morts **61** 47 35N 59 0W
Isle La Motte **36** 44 52N 73 18W
Isle of Hope **18** 31 58N 81 5W
Isle of Wight **54** 36 54N 76 43W
Isle of Wight □ **83** 50 40N 1 20W
Isle of Wight Bay **27** 38 22N 75 6W
Isle of Wight County ◇ **54** 36 54N 76 43W
Isle Royale **29** 48 0N 88 54W
Isle Royale National Park **29** 48 0N 88 55W
Islesboro I. **26** 44 19N 68 54W
Isleta **38** 34 55N 106 42W
Isleta Indian Reservation **38** 34 55N 106 45W
Isleton **14** 38 10N 121 37W
Ismail **99** 45 22N 28 46E
Ismâ'ilîya **121** 30 37N 32 18E
Ismay **33** 46 30N 104 48W
Isna **121** 25 17N 32 30E
Isola **31** 33 16N 90 35W
İsparta **106** 37 47N 30 30E
Isperikh **95** 43 43N 26 50E
Íspica **94** 36 47N 14 53E
Israel ■ **104** 32 0N 34 50E
Israel → **36** 44 29N 71 35W
Issano **71** 5 49N 59 26W
Issaquena County ◇ **31** 32 54N 91 3W
Issue **27** 38 16N 76 53W
Issyk-Kul, Ozero **100** 42 25N 77 15E
İstanbul **106** 41 0N 29 0E
Istmina **70** 5 10N 76 39W
Isto, Mt. **11** 69 12N 143 48W
Istokpoga, L. **17** 27 23N 81 17W
Istra **94** 45 10N 14 0E
Istranca Dağları **95** 41 48N 27 30E
Istria = Istra **94** 45 10N 14 0E
Itá **76** 25 29S 57 21W
Itabaiana, Paraíba, Brazil **74** 7 18S 35 19W
Itabaiana, Sergipe, Brazil **74** 10 41S 37 37W
Itabaianinha **74** 11 16S 37 47W
Itaberaba **75** 12 32S 40 18W
Itaberaí **75** 16 2S 49 48W
Itabira **75** 19 37S 43 13W
Itabirito **75** 20 15S 43 48W
Itaboca **71** 4 50S 62 40W
Itabuna **75** 14 48S 39 16W
Itacajá **74** 8 19S 47 46W
Itacaunas → **74** 5 21S 49 8W
Itacoatiara **71** 3 8S 58 25W
Itacuaí → **72** 4 20S 70 12W
Itaguaçu **75** 19 48S 40 51W
Itaguari → **75** 14 11S 44 40W
Itaguatins **74** 5 47S 47 29W
Itaim → **74** 7 2S 42 2W
Itainópolis **74** 7 24S 41 31W
Itaituba **71** 4 10S 55 50W
Itajaí **77** 27 50S 48 39W
Itajubá **75** 22 24S 45 30W

Itajuípe Javier, I.

Itajuípe 75 14 41 S 39 22W
Italy 51 32 11N 96 53W
Italy ■ 94 42 0N 13 0 E
Itamataré 74 2 16 S 46 24W
Itambacuri 75 18 1 S 41 42W
Itambé 75 15 15 S 40 37W
Itanhauã → 71 4 45 S 63 48W
Itanhém 75 17 9 S 40 20W
Itapaci 75 14 57 S 49 34W
Itapagé 74 3 41 S 39 34W
Itaparica, I. de 75 12 54 S 38 42W
Itapebi 75 15 56 S 39 32W
Itapecuru-Mirim 74 3 24 S 44 20W
Itaperuna 75 21 10 S 41 54W
Itapetinga 75 15 15 S 40 15W
Itapetininga 77 23 36 S 48 7W
Itapeva 77 23 59 S 48 59W
Itapicuru →, Bahia, Brazil 74 11 47 S 37 32W
Itapicuru →, Maranhão, Brazil 74 2 52 S 44 12W
Itapinima 73 5 25 S 60 44W
Itapipoca 74 3 30 S 39 35W
Itapiranga 71 2 45 S 58 1W
Itapiúna 74 4 33 S 38 57W
Itaporanga 74 7 18 S 38 0W
Itapuá □ 77 26 40 S 55 40W
Itapuranga 75 15 40 S 49 59W
Itaquari 75 20 20 S 40 25W
Itaquatiara 72 2 58 S 58 30W
Itaquí 76 29 8 S 56 30W
Itararé 77 24 6 S 49 23W
Itarumã 75 18 42 S 51 25W
Itasca 51 32 10N 97 9W
Itasca County ◇ 30 47 25N 93 25W
Itatí 76 27 16 S 58 15W
Itatira 74 4 30 S 39 37W
Itatuba 73 5 46 S 63 20W
Itatupa 71 0 37 S 51 12W
Itaueira 74 7 36 S 43 2W
Itaueira → 74 6 41 S 42 55W
Itaúna 75 20 4 S 44 34W
Itawamba County ◇ 31 34 16N 88 25W
Itchen → 83 50 57N 1 20W
Ite 72 17 55 S 70 57W
Ithaca = Itháki 88 38 25N 20 40 E
Ithaca, Mich. 29 43 18N 84 36W
Ithaca, N.Y. 39 42 27N 76 30W
Ithaca, Nebr. 34 41 10N 96 33W
Itháki 88 38 25N 20 40 E
Itinga 75 16 36 S 41 47W
Itiquira 73 17 12 S 54 7W
Itiquira → 73 17 18 S 56 44W
Itiruçu 75 13 31 S 40 9W
Itiúba 74 10 43 S 39 51W
Itkilik → 11 70 9N 150 56W
Ito 117 34 58N 139 5 E
Itoigawa 117 37 2N 137 51 E
Itonamas → 72 12 28 S 64 24W
Itta Bena 31 33 30N 90 20W
Itu 77 23 17 S 47 15W
Ituaçu 75 13 50 S 41 18W
Ituango 70 7 4N 75 45W
Ituiutaba 75 19 0 S 49 25W
Itumbiara 75 18 20 S 49 10W
Ituna 63 51 10N 103 24W
Ituni 71 5 28N 58 15W
Itupiranga 74 5 9 S 49 20W
Iturama 75 19 44 S 50 11W
Iturbe 76 23 0 S 65 25W
Iturup, Ostrov 101 45 0N 148 0 E
Ituverava 75 20 20 S 47 47W
Ituxi → 73 7 18 S 64 51W
Ituyuro → 76 22 40 S 63 50W
Iuka, Kans. 24 37 44N 98 44W
Iuka, Miss. 31 34 49N 88 12W
Iva 46 34 19N 82 40W
Ivaí → 77 23 18 S 53 42W
Ivalo 96 68 38N 27 35 E
Ivalojoki → 96 68 40N 27 40 E
Ivan 13 33 55N 92 26W
Ivanhoe, Australia 127 32 56 S 144 20 E
Ivanhoe, Calif. 15 36 23N 119 13W
Ivanhoe, Minn. 30 44 28N 96 15W
Ivanhoe, Va. 54 36 50N 80 58W
Ivanhoe L. 63 60 25N 106 30W
Ivano-Frankovsk 99 48 40N 24 40 E
Ivanof Bay 11 55 54N 159 29W
Ivanovo 98 57 5N 41 0 E
Ivaylovgrad 95 41 32N 26 8 E
Ivdel 98 60 42N 60 24 E
Ivesdale 21 39 57N 88 28W
Ivinheima → 77 23 14 S 53 42W
Iviza = Ibiza 91 38 54N 1 26 E
Ivolândia 75 16 34 S 50 51W
Ivor 54 36 54N 76 54W
Ivory Coast ■ 120 7 30N 5 0W
Ivrea 94 45 30N 7 52 E
Ivugivik 59 62 24N 77 55W
Ivydale 54 38 32N 81 2W
Ivywild 16 38 49N 104 51W
Iwahig 110 8 36N 117 32 E
Iwaizumi 116 39 50N 141 45 E
Iwaki 117 37 4N 140 55 E
Iwakuni 117 34 15N 132 8 E
Iwamizawa 116 43 12N 141 46 E
Iwanai 116 42 58N 140 30 E
Iwata 117 34 42N 137 51 E
Iwate □ 116 39 30N 141 30 E
Iwate-San 116 39 51N 141 0 E
Iwo 120 7 39N 4 9 E
Ixiamas 72 13 50 S 68 5W
Ixtepec 65 16 32N 95 10W
Ixtlán de Juárez 65 17 23N 96 28W
Ixtlán del Río 64 21 5N 104 21W
Iyo 117 33 45N 132 45 E
Izabel, L. de 66 15 30N 89 10W
Izamal 65 20 56N 89 1W
Izard County ◇ 13 36 4N 91 54W
Izegem 87 50 55N 3 12 E
Izena-Shima 117 26 56N 127 56 E
Izgrev 95 43 36N 26 58 E
Izhevsk = Ustinov 98 56 51N 53 14 E
Izmir 99 38 25N 27 8 E
Izmit 106 40 45N 29 50 E
Izozog, Bañados de 73 18 48 S 62 10W
Izra 104 32 51N 36 15 E
Iztochni Rodopi 95 41 45N 25 30 E
Izu-Shotō 117 34 30N 140 0 E
Izumi-sano 117 34 23N 135 18 E
Izumo 117 35 20N 132 46 E

J

J. B. Thomas, L. 50 32 36N 101 8W
J.F. Rodrigues 74 2 55 S 50 20W
J. Percy Priest Reservoir 48 36 9N 86 37W
Jaba' 104 32 20N 35 13 E
Jabalpur 108 23 9N 79 58 E
Jabālyah 104 31 32N 34 27 E
Jablah 106 35 20N 36 0 E
Jablanica 95 41 20N 20 30 E
Jablonec 88 50 43N 15 10 E
Jaboatão 74 8 7 S 35 1W
Jaboticabal 77 21 15 S 48 17W
Jaburu 73 5 30 S 64 0W
Jaca 91 42 35N 0 33W
Jacala 65 21 1N 99 11W
Jacaré → 74 10 3 S 42 13W
Jacareí 77 23 20 S 46 0W
Jacarèzinho 77 23 5 S 50 0W
Jaciara 73 15 59 S 54 57W
Jacinto 75 16 10 S 40 17W
Jacinto City 51 29 46N 95 13W
Jaciparaná 73 9 15 S 64 23W
Jack County ◇ 51 33 13N 98 10W
Jackman Station 26 45 37N 70 15W
Jackpot 35 41 59N 114 40W
Jacks Fork → 32 37 12N 91 18W
Jacksboro, Tenn. 49 36 20N 84 11W
Jacksboro, Tex. 51 33 13N 98 10W
Jackson, Ala. 10 31 31N 87 53W
Jackson, Calif. 14 38 21N 120 46W
Jackson, Ga. 18 33 20N 83 57W
Jackson, Ky. 49 37 33N 83 23W
Jackson, La. 25 30 50N 91 13W
Jackson, Mich. 29 42 15N 84 24W
Jackson, Minn. 30 43 37N 95 1W
Jackson, Miss. 31 32 18N 90 12W
Jackson, Mo. 32 37 23N 89 40W
Jackson, Mont. 33 45 23N 113 28W
Jackson, N.C. 40 36 23N 77 25W
Jackson, N.H. 36 44 10N 71 11W
Jackson, N.J. 37 40 6N 74 23W
Jackson, Nebr. 34 42 27N 96 34W
Jackson, Ohio 42 39 3N 82 39W
Jackson, S.C. 46 33 20N 81 47W
Jackson, Tenn. 48 35 37N 88 49W
Jackson, Wis. 55 43 19N 88 10W
Jackson, Wyo. 56 43 29N 110 46W
Jackson Bay 128 43 58 S 168 42 E
Jackson County ◇, Ala. 10 34 40N 86 2W
Jackson County ◇, Ark. 13 35 37N 91 16W
Jackson County ◇, Colo. 16 40 45N 106 20W
Jackson County ◇, Fla. 17 30 45N 85 15W
Jackson County ◇, Ga. 18 34 10N 83 30W
Jackson County ◇, Ill. 21 37 45N 89 25W
Jackson County ◇, Ind. 22 38 55N 86 0W
Jackson County ◇, Iowa 23 42 10N 90 35W
Jackson County ◇, Kans. 24 39 20N 95 45W
Jackson County ◇, Ky. 49 37 25N 84 0W
Jackson County ◇, Mich. 29 42 15N 84 30W
Jackson County ◇, Minn. 30 43 40N 95 10W
Jackson County ◇, Miss. 31 30 32N 88 42W
Jackson County ◇, Mo. 32 39 0N 94 20W
Jackson County ◇, N.C. 40 35 20N 83 10W
Jackson County ◇, Ohio 42 39 3N 82 39W
Jackson County ◇, Okla. 43 34 30N 99 25W
Jackson County ◇, Oreg. 44 42 20N 122 45W
Jackson County ◇, S. Dak. 47 43 45N 101 45W
Jackson County ◇, Tenn. 49 36 21N 85 39W
Jackson County ◇, Tex. 51 28 59N 96 39W
Jackson County ◇, W. Va. 54 38 49N 81 43W
Jackson County ◇, Wis. 55 44 20N 90 45W
Jackson Junction 23 43 7N 92 2W
Jackson L., Fla. 17 30 30N 84 17W
Jackson L., Ga. 18 33 19N 83 50W
Jackson L., Wyo. 56 43 52N 110 36W
Jackson Mts. 35 41 10N 118 30W
Jackson Parish ◇ 25 32 15N 92 43W
Jackson Reservoir 16 40 22N 104 6W
Jacksons 128 42 46 S 171 32 E
Jacksonville, Ala. 10 33 49N 85 46W
Jacksonville, Ark. 13 34 52N 92 7W
Jacksonville, Fla. 17 30 20N 81 39W
Jacksonville, Ga. 18 31 49N 82 59W
Jacksonville, Ill. 21 39 44N 90 14W
Jacksonville, N.C. 40 34 45N 77 26W
Jacksonville, Ohio 42 39 29N 82 5W
Jacksonville, Oreg. 44 42 19N 122 57W
Jacksonville, Tex. 51 31 58N 95 17W
Jacksonville, Vt. 36 42 47N 72 49W
Jacksonville Beach 17 30 17N 81 24W
Jacmel 67 18 14N 72 32W
Jacob Lake 12 36 43N 112 13W
Jacobabad 108 28 20N 68 29 E
Jacobina 74 11 11 S 40 30W
Jacob's Well 104 32 13N 35 13 E
Jacobsville 27 39 7N 76 31W
Jacques-Cartier, Mt. 61 48 57N 66 0W
Jacuí → 77 30 2 S 51 15W
Jacumba 15 32 37N 116 11W
Jacundá → 74 1 57 S 50 26W
Jadotville = Likasi 122 10 55 S 26 48 E
Jādū 121 32 0N 12 0 E
Jaén, Peru 72 5 25 S 78 40W
Jaén, Spain 91 37 44N 3 43W
Jaffa = Tel Aviv-Yafo 104 32 4N 34 48 E
Jaffna 108 9 45N 80 2 E
Jaffrey 36 42 49N 72 2W
Jagadhri 108 30 10N 77 20 E
Jagdalpur 109 19 3N 82 0 E
Jagersfontein 123 29 44 S 25 27 E
Jagraon 108 30 50N 75 25 E
Jagtial 108 18 50N 79 0 E
Jaguaquara 75 13 32 S 39 58W
Jaguariaíva 77 24 10 S 49 50W
Jaguaribe 74 5 53 S 38 37W
Jaguaribe → 74 4 25 S 37 45W
Jaguaruana 74 4 50 S 37 47W
Jagüey Grande 66 22 35N 81 7W
Jahrom 107 28 30N 53 31 E
Jaicoa, Cord. 57 18 25N 67 5W
Jaicós 74 7 21 S 41 8W
Jailolo 111 1 5N 127 30 E
Jailolo, Selat 111 0 5N 129 5 E
Jaipur 108 27 0N 75 50 E
Jakarta 111 6 9 S 106 49 E
Jakin 18 31 6N 84 59W
Jakobstad 96 63 40N 22 43 E
Jal 38 32 7N 103 12W
Jalai Nur 114 49 27N 117 42 E
Jalalabad 108 34 30N 70 29 E
Jalapa, Guat. 66 14 39N 89 59W
Jalapa, Mexico 65 19 30N 96 56W
Jalas, Jabal al 106 27 30N 36 30 E
Jales 75 20 10 S 50 33W
Jalgaon, Maharashtra, India 108 21 2N 76 31 E
Jalgaon, Maharashtra, India 108 21 0N 75 42 E
Jalisco □ 64 20 0N 104 0W
Jalna 108 19 48N 75 38 E
Jalón → 91 41 47N 1 4W
Jalpa 64 21 38N 102 58W
Jalpaiguri 109 26 32N 88 46 E
Jalq 107 27 35N 62 46 E
Jaluit I. 124 6 0N 169 30 E
Jamaica, Iowa 23 41 51N 94 18W
Jamaica, Vt. 36 43 13N 72 46W
Jamaica ■ 66 18 10N 77 30W
Jamalpur, Bangla. 109 24 52N 89 56 E
Jamalpur, India 109 25 18N 86 28 E
Jamanxim → 73 4 43 S 56 18W
Jamari 73 8 45 S 63 27W
Jamari → 73 8 27 S 63 30W
Jambe 111 1 15 S 132 10 E
Jambi 110 1 38 S 103 30 E
Jambi □ 110 1 30 S 102 30 E
James 18 32 58N 83 29W
James →, Mo. 32 36 45N 93 30W
James →, S. Dak. 47 42 52N 97 18W
James →, Va. 54 36 56N 76 27W
James, L. 40 35 44N 81 54W
James B. 60 51 30N 80 0W
James City 40 35 5N 77 2W
James City County ◇ 54 37 16N 76 40W
James Range 126 24 10 S 132 30 E
James Ross I. 5 63 58 S 57 50W
Jamesburg 37 40 21N 74 27W
Jamesport 32 39 58N 93 48W
Jamestown, Australia 127 33 10 S 138 32 E
Jamestown, Calif. 14 37 57N 120 25W
Jamestown, Ind. 22 39 56N 86 38W
Jamestown, Kans. 24 39 36N 97 52W
Jamestown, Ky. 49 36 59N 85 4W
Jamestown, La. 25 32 21N 93 13W
Jamestown, N. Dak. 41 46 54N 98 42W
Jamestown, N.Y. 39 42 6N 79 14W
Jamestown, Ohio 42 39 39N 83 33W
Jamestown, Pa. 45 41 29N 80 27W
Jamestown, R.I. 28 41 30N 71 22W
Jamestown, S.C. 46 33 17N 79 42W
Jamestown, Tenn. 49 36 26N 84 56W
Jamestown, Va. 54 37 13N 76 47W
Jamestown Reservoir 41 46 56N 98 43W
Jamesville 40 35 49N 76 54W
Jamieson 44 44 11N 117 26W
Jamiltepec 65 16 17N 97 49W
Jamison 34 43 0N 99 18W
Jamkhaudi 108 16 30N 75 15 E
Jammā'īn 104 32 8N 35 12 E
Jammu 108 32 43N 74 54 E
Jammu & Kashmir □ 108 34 25N 77 0 E
Jamnagar 108 22 30N 70 6 E
Jamrud 108 33 59N 71 24 E
Jamshedpur 109 22 44N 86 12 E
Jämtlands län □ 96 62 40N 13 50 E
Jan L. 63 54 56N 102 55W
Jan Mayen Is. 4 71 0N 9 0W
Janaúba 75 15 48 S 43 19W
Janaucu, I. 74 0 30N 50 10W
Jand 108 33 30N 72 6 E
Jandaia 75 17 6 S 50 7W
Jandaq 107 34 3N 54 22 E
Jandiatuba → 70 3 28 S 68 42W
Jane 32 36 33N 94 18W
Jane Lew 54 39 7N 80 25W
Janesville, Calif. 14 40 18N 120 32W
Janesville, Iowa 23 42 39N 92 28W
Janesville, Minn. 30 44 7N 93 42W
Janesville, Wis. 55 42 41N 89 1W
Jangeru 110 2 20 S 116 29 E
Jango 73 20 27 S 55 29W
Janīn 104 32 28N 35 18 E
Janinà = Ioánnina □ 95 39 39N 20 57 E
Janos 64 30 45N 108 10W
Jansen, Colo. 16 37 9N 104 32W
Jansen, Nebr. 34 40 11N 97 5W
Januária 75 15 25 S 44 25W
Janub Dârfûr □ 121 11 0N 25 0 E
Janub Kordofân □ 121 12 0N 30 0 E
Jaora 108 23 40N 75 10 E
Japan ■ 117 36 0N 136 0 E
Japan, Sea of 116 40 0N 135 0 E
Japan Trench 124 32 0N 142 0 E
Japen = Yapen 111 1 50 S 136 0 E
Japurá → 70 3 8 S 64 46W
Jaque 70 7 27N 78 8W
Jaraguá 75 15 45 S 49 20W
Jaraguari 73 20 9 S 54 35W
Jarama → 91 40 2N 3 39W
Jaramillo 78 47 10 S 67 7W
Jarash 104 32 17N 35 54 E
Jarauçu → 71 1 48 S 52 22W
Jardim 76 21 28 S 56 2W
Jardines de la Reina, Is. 66 20 50N 78 50W
Jargalant = Hovd 113 48 2N 91 37 E
Jari → 71 1 9 S 51 54W
Jarosław 89 50 2N 22 42 E
Jarratt 54 36 48N 77 28W
Jarrettsville 27 39 36N 76 29W
Jarso 121 5 15N 37 30 E
Jaru 73 10 26 S 62 27W
Jaru → 73 10 5 S 61 59W
Jarvis I. 125 0 15 S 159 55W
Jarvisburg 40 36 9N 75 52W
Jarwa 109 27 38N 82 30 E
Jasin 112 2 20N 102 26 E
Jāsk 107 25 38N 57 45 E
Jasło 89 49 45N 21 30 E
Jason, Is. 78 51 0 S 61 0W
Jasonville 22 39 10N 87 12W
Jasper, Canada 62 52 55N 118 5W
Jasper, Ala. 10 33 50N 87 17W
Jasper, Ark. 13 36 1N 93 11W
Jasper, Fla. 17 30 31N 82 57W
Jasper, Ga. 18 34 28N 84 26W
Jasper, Ind. 22 38 24N 86 56W
Jasper, Minn. 30 43 51N 96 24W
Jasper, Mo. 32 37 20N 94 18W
Jasper, Tenn. 49 35 5N 85 38W
Jasper, Tex. 51 30 56N 94 1W
Jasper County ◇, Ga. 18 33 20N 83 45W
Jasper County ◇, Ill. 21 39 0N 88 10W
Jasper County ◇, Ind. 22 41 0N 87 5W
Jasper County ◇, Iowa 23 41 40N 93 0W
Jasper County ◇, Miss. 31 32 2N 89 2W
Jasper County ◇, Mo. 32 37 10N 94 20W
Jasper County ◇, S.C. 46 32 30N 81 0W
Jasper County ◇, Tex. 51 30 40N 93 54W
Jasper Nat. Park 62 52 50N 118 8W
Jassy = Iaşi 89 47 10N 27 40 E
Jászberény 89 47 30N 19 55 E
Jataí 75 17 58 S 51 48W
Jatapu → 71 2 13 S 58 17W
Jatibarang 111 6 28 S 108 18 E
Jatinegara 111 6 13 S 106 52 E
Játiva 91 39 0N 0 32W
Jatobal 74 4 35 S 49 33W
Jatt 104 32 24N 35 2 E
Jaú 75 22 10 S 48 30W
Jaú → 71 1 54 S 61 26W
Jauaperí → 71 1 26 S 61 35W
Jauja 72 11 45 S 75 15W
Jaunpur 109 25 46N 82 44 E
Jauru → 73 16 22 S 57 46W
Java = Jawa 111 7 0 S 110 0 E
Java 47 45 30N 99 53W
Java Sea 110 4 35 S 107 15 E
Java Trench 124 10 0 S 110 0W
Javhlant = Ulyasutay 113 47 56N 97 28 E
Javier, I. 78 47 5 S 74 25W

Jawa Joseph

Jawa **111** 7 0 S 110 0 E
Jay, Fla. **17** 30 57N 87 9W
Jay, Maine **26** 44 30N 70 13W
Jay, N.Y. **39** 44 20N 73 45W
Jay, Okla. **43** 36 25N 94 48W
Jay County ◇ **22** 40 25N 85 0W
Jay Peak **36** 44 55N 72 32W
Jaya, Puncak **111** 3 57 S 137 17 E
Jayanca **72** 6 24 S 79 50W
Jayanti **109** 26 45N 89 40 E
Jayapura **111** 2 28 S 140 38 E
Jayawijaya, Pegunungan **111** 5 0 S 139 0 E
Jaynagar **109** 26 43N 86 9 E
Jayton **50** 33 15N 100 34W
Jayuya **57** 18 14N 66 36W
Jazminal **64** 24 56N 101 25W
Jean, Nev. **35** 35 47N 115 20W
Jean, Tex. **51** 33 18N 98 37W
Jean Marie River **58** 61 32N 120 38W
Jean Rabel **67** 19 50N 73 5W
Jeanerette **25** 29 55N 91 40W
Jeanette, Ostrov **101** 76 43N 158 0 E
Jebba **120** 9 9N 4 48 E
Jebel, Bahr el → **121** 15 38N 32 31 E
Jeberos **72** 5 15 S 76 10W
Jedburgh **84** 55 28N 2 33W
Jędrzejów **89** 50 35N 20 15 E
Jedway **62** 52 17N 131 14W
Jeff Davis County ◇, Ga. **18** 31 50N 82 45W
Jeff Davis County ◇, Tex. **50** 30 55N 104 5W
Jeffers **30** 44 3N 95 12W
Jefferson, Colo. **16** 39 23N 105 48W
Jefferson, Ga. **18** 34 7N 83 35W
Jefferson, Iowa **23** 42 1N 94 23W
Jefferson, Maine **26** 44 13N 69 27W
Jefferson, Md. **27** 39 22N 77 32W
Jefferson, N.C. **40** 36 25N 81 28W
Jefferson, Ohio **42** 41 44N 80 46W
Jefferson, Okla. **43** 36 43N 97 48W
Jefferson, Oreg. **44** 44 43N 123 1W
Jefferson, S.C. **46** 34 39N 80 23W
Jefferson, S. Dak. **47** 42 36N 96 34W
Jefferson, Tex. **51** 32 46N 94 21W
Jefferson, Wis. **55** 43 0N 88 48W
Jefferson → **33** 45 56N 111 31W
Jefferson, Mt. **44** 44 41N 121 48W
Jefferson City, Mo. **32** 38 34N 92 10W
Jefferson City, Tenn. **49** 36 7N 83 30W
Jefferson County ◇, Ala. **10** 33 31N 86 48W
Jefferson County ◇, Ark. **13** 34 13N 92 1W
Jefferson County ◇, Colo. **16** 39 40N 105 15W
Jefferson County ◇, Fla. **17** 30 20N 84 0W
Jefferson County ◇, Ga. **18** 33 10N 82 25W
Jefferson County ◇, Idaho **20** 43 50N 112 20W
Jefferson County ◇, Ill. **21** 38 20N 88 55W
Jefferson County ◇, Ind. **22** 43 50N 85 25W
Jefferson County ◇, Iowa **23** 41 0N 92 0W
Jefferson County ◇, Kans. **24** 39 15N 95 30W
Jefferson County ◇, Ky. **49** 38 10N 85 40W
Jefferson County ◇, Miss. **31** 31 43N 91 4W
Jefferson County ◇, Mo. **32** 38 15N 90 30W
Jefferson County ◇, Mont. **33** 46 8N 112 0W
Jefferson County ◇, N.Y. **39** 44 0N 76 0W
Jefferson County ◇, Nebr. **34** 40 15N 97 10W
Jefferson County ◇, Ohio **42** 40 25N 80 54W
Jefferson County ◇, Okla. **43** 34 10N 97 50W
Jefferson County ◇, Oreg. **44** 44 40N 121 10W
Jefferson County ◇, Pa. **45** 41 5N 79 0W
Jefferson County ◇, Tenn. **49** 36 7N 83 30W
Jefferson County ◇, Tex. **51** 29 55N 94 15W
Jefferson County ◇, W. Va. **54** 39 17N 77 52W
Jefferson County ◇, Wash. **53** 47 50N 123 45W
Jefferson County ◇, Wis. **55** 43 0N 88 45W
Jefferson Davis County ◇ **31** 31 36N 89 52W
Jefferson Davis Parish ◇ **25** 30 14N 92 49W
Jefferson Mt. **35** 38 46N 116 55W
Jefferson National Forest **54** 37 10N 81 15W
Jefferson Parish ◇ **25** 29 44N 90 8W
Jeffersonton **54** 38 38N 77 55W
Jeffersontown **49** 38 12N 85 35W
Jeffersonville, Ga. **18** 32 41N 83 20W
Jeffersonville, Ind. **22** 38 17N 85 44W
Jeffersonville, Ky. **49** 37 59N 83 51W
Jeffersonville, Ohio **42** 39 39N 83 34W
Jeffersonville, Vt. **36** 44 40N 72 50W
Jeffrey City **56** 42 30N 107 49W
Jeffrey Reservoir **34** 40 58N 100 24W
Jega **120** 12 15N 4 23 E
Jekyll I. **18** 31 4N 81 25W
Jelenia Góra **88** 50 50N 15 45 E
Jelgava **98** 56 41N 23 49 E
Jellico **49** 36 35N 84 8W
Jellicoe **60** 49 40N 87 30W
Jemaja **110** 3 5N 105 45 E
Jember **111** 8 11 S 113 41 E
Jembongan **110** 6 45N 117 20 E
Jemeppe **87** 50 37N 5 30 E
Jemez Indian Reservation **38** 35 40N 106 50W
Jemez Mts. **38** 35 45N 106 30W
Jemez Pueblo **38** 35 37N 106 44W
Jemez Springs **38** 35 46N 106 42W
Jemison **10** 32 58N 86 45W
Jena, Germany **88** 50 56N 11 33 E
Jena, Fla. **17** 29 40N 83 22W
Jena, La. **25** 31 41N 92 8W
Jenison **29** 42 54N 85 47W
Jenkins, Ky. **49** 37 10N 82 38W
Jenkins, Minn. **30** 46 39N 94 20W
Jenkins, N.J. **37** 39 42N 74 32W
Jenkins County ◇ **18** 32 45N 82 0W
Jenks **43** 36 1N 95 58W
Jenner **14** 38 27N 123 7W
Jennings, Fla. **17** 30 36N 83 6W
Jennings, Kans. **24** 39 41N 100 18W
Jennings, La. **25** 30 13N 92 40W
Jennings, Mo. **32** 38 43N 90 16W
Jennings, Okla. **43** 36 11N 96 34W
Jennings → **62** 59 38N 132 5W
Jennings County ◇ **22** 39 0N 85 40W
Jensen **52** 40 22N 109 20W
Jensen Beach **17** 27 15N 80 14W
Jequié **75** 13 51 S 40 5W
Jequitaí → **75** 17 4 S 44 50W
Jequitinhonha **75** 16 30 S 41 0W
Jequitinhonha → **75** 15 51 S 38 53W
Jerada **120** 34 17N 2 10W
Jerantut **112** 3 56N 102 22 E
Jerauld County ◇ **47** 44 0N 98 45W
Jérémie **67** 18 40N 74 10W
Jeremoabo **74** 10 4 S 38 21W
Jeremy Point **28** 41 53N 70 4W
Jerez, Punta **65** 22 58N 97 40W
Jerez de García Salinas **64** 22 39N 103 0W
Jerez de la Frontera **91** 36 41N 6 7W
Jerez de los Caballeros **91** 38 20N 6 45W
Jericho = El Arīhā **104** 31 52N 35 27 E
Jerico Springs **32** 37 37N 94 1W
Jerimoth Hill **28** 41 51N 71 47W
Jermyn **51** 33 16N 98 23W
Jerome, Ariz. **12** 34 45N 112 7W
Jerome, Ark. **13** 33 24N 91 28W
Jerome, Idaho **20** 42 44N 114 31W
Jerome County ◇ **20** 42 42N 114 15W
Jerrobert **63** 51 56N 109 8W
Jerry City **42** 41 15N 83 36W
Jersey, Ark. **13** 33 26N 92 19W
Jersey, Ga. **18** 33 43N 83 47W
Jersey, I. **83** 49 13N 2 7W
Jersey City **37** 40 44N 74 4W
Jersey County ◇ **21** 39 5N 90 20W
Jersey Shore **45** 41 12N 77 15W
Jersey Village **51** 29 53N 95 34W
Jerseyville **21** 39 7N 90 20W
Jerusalem, Asia **104** 31 47N 35 10 E
Jerusalem, U.S.A. **18** 30 58N 81 50W
Jervis B. **127** 35 8 S 150 46 E
Jessamine County ◇ **49** 37 50N 84 35W
Jesselton = Kota Kinabalu **110** 6 0N 116 4 E
Jessieville **13** 34 42N 93 4W
Jessore **109** 23 10N 89 10 E
Jessup L. **17** 28 43N 81 14W
Jesup, Ga. **18** 31 36N 81 53W
Jesup, Iowa **23** 42 29N 92 4W
Jesús **72** 7 15 S 78 25W
Jesús Carranza **65** 17 28N 95 1W
Jesús María **76** 30 59 S 64 5W
Jet **43** 36 40N 98 11W
Jetmore **24** 38 4N 99 54W
Jewell, Iowa **23** 42 20N 93 39W
Jewell, Kans. **24** 39 40N 98 10W
Jewell County ◇ **24** 39 45N 98 10W
Jewell Valley **54** 37 15N 81 48W
Jewett, Ill. **21** 39 13N 88 15W
Jewett, Ohio **42** 40 22N 81 2W
Jewett, Tex. **51** 31 22N 96 9W
Jewett City **28** 41 36N 72 0W
Jeypore **109** 18 50N 82 38 E
Jhal Jhao **107** 26 20N 65 35 E
Jhalawar **108** 24 40N 76 10 E
Jhang Maghiana **108** 31 15N 72 22 E
Jhansi **108** 25 30N 78 36 E
Jharsaguda **109** 21 50N 84 5 E
Jhelum **108** 33 0N 73 45 E
Jhelum → **108** 31 20N 72 10 E
Jhunjhunu **108** 28 10N 75 30 E
Ji Xian **114** 36 7N 110 40 E
Jia Xian **114** 38 12N 110 28 E
Jiamusi **114** 46 40N 130 26 E
Ji'an **115** 27 6N 114 59 E
Jianchuan **113** 26 38N 99 55 E
Jiande **115** 29 23N 119 15 E
Jiangbei **115** 29 40N 106 34 E
Jiange **115** 32 4N 105 32 E
Jiangjin **115** 29 14N 106 14 E
Jiangling **115** 30 25N 112 12 E
Jiangmen **115** 22 32N 113 0 E
Jiangshan **115** 28 40N 118 37 E
Jiangsu □ **115** 33 0N 120 0 E
Jiangxi □ **115** 27 30N 116 0 E
Jiangyin **115** 31 54N 120 17 E
Jiangyong **115** 25 20N 111 22 E
Jiangyou **115** 31 44N 104 43 E
Jianning **115** 26 50N 116 50 E
Jian'ou **115** 27 3N 118 17 E
Jianshi **115** 30 37N 109 38 E
Jianshui **113** 23 36N 102 43 E
Jianyang **115** 27 20N 118 5 E
Jiao Xian **114** 36 18N 120 1 E
Jiaohe **114** 38 2N 116 20 E
Jiaozhou Wan **114** 36 5N 120 10 E
Jiaozuo **115** 35 16N 113 12 E
Jiawang **115** 34 28N 117 26 E
Jiaxing **115** 30 49N 120 45 E
Jiayi **115** 23 30N 120 24 E
Jibão, Serra do **75** 14 48 S 45 0W
Jibuti = Djibouti ■ **105** 12 0N 43 0 E
Jicarilla Indian Reservation **38** 36 45N 107 0W
Jicarón, I. **66** 7 10N 81 50W
Jiddah **105** 21 29N 39 10 E
Jido **109** 29 2N 94 58 E
Jifnā **104** 31 58N 35 13 E
Jigger **25** 32 2N 91 45W
Jihlava **88** 49 28N 15 35 E
Jihlava → **88** 48 55N 16 36 E
Jijel **120** 36 52N 5 50 E
Jijiga **105** 9 20N 42 50 E
Jilin **114** 43 44N 126 30 E
Jilin □ **114** 44 0N 124 0 E
Jiloca → **91** 41 21N 1 39W
Jilong **115** 25 8N 121 42 E
Jim Hogg County ◇ **50** 27 0N 98 45W
Jim Thorpe **45** 40 52N 75 44W
Jim Wells County ◇ **51** 28 0N 98 0W
Jima **121** 7 40N 36 47 E
Jiménez **64** 27 10N 104 54W
Jimo **114** 36 23N 120 30 E
Jin Xian **114** 38 55N 121 42 E
Jinan **114** 36 38N 117 1 E
Jincheng **114** 35 29N 112 50 E
Jing He → **115** 34 27N 109 4 E
Jing Xian **115** 26 33N 109 40 E
Jingchuan **114** 35 20N 107 20 E
Jingdezhen **115** 29 20N 117 11 E
Jinggu **113** 23 35N 100 41 E
Jinghai **114** 38 55N 116 55 E
Jingle **114** 38 20N 111 55 E
Jingmen **115** 31 0N 112 10 E
Jingning **114** 35 30N 105 43 E
Jingshan **115** 31 1N 113 7 E
Jingtai **114** 37 10N 104 6 E
Jingxi **115** 23 8N 106 27 E
Jingyu **114** 42 25N 126 45 E
Jingyuan **114** 36 30N 104 40 E
Jingziguan **115** 33 15N 111 0 E
Jinhe **114** 51 18N 121 32 E
Jinhua **115** 29 8N 119 38 E
Jining, Nei Mongol Zizhiqu, China **114** 41 5N 113 0 E
Jining, Shandong, China **115** 35 22N 116 34 E
Jinja **122** 0 25N 33 12 E
Jinmen Dao **115** 24 25N 118 25 E
Jinnah Barrage **107** 32 58N 71 33 E
Jinotega **66** 13 6N 85 59W
Jinotepe **66** 11 50N 86 10W
Jinshi **115** 29 40N 111 50 E
Jinxiang **115** 35 5N 116 22 E
Jinzhou **114** 41 5N 121 3 E
Jiparaná → **73** 8 3 S 62 52W
Jipijapa **70** 1 0 S 80 40W
Jiquilpan **64** 19 57N 102 42W
Jishou **115** 28 21N 109 43 E
Jisr al Ḩusayn **104** 31 53N 35 33 E
Jisr ash Shughūr **106** 35 49N 36 18 E
Jitra **112** 6 16N 100 25 E
Jiu → **89** 44 40N 23 25 E
Jiudengkou **114** 39 56N 106 40 E
Jiujiang **115** 29 42N 115 58 E
Jiuling Shan **115** 28 40N 114 40 E
Jiuquan **113** 39 50N 98 20 E
Jixi **114** 45 20N 130 50 E
Jizō-Zaki **117** 35 34N 133 20 E
Jo Daviess County ◇ **21** 42 20N 90 10W
Joaçaba **77** 27 5 S 51 31W
Joaíma **75** 16 39 S 41 2W
Joanna **46** 34 25N 81 49W
João **74** 2 46 S 50 59W
João Amaro **75** 12 46 S 40 22W
João Câmara **74** 5 32 S 35 48W
João Pessoa **74** 7 10 S 34 52W
João Pinheiro **75** 17 45 S 46 10W
Joaquim Távora **75** 23 30 S 49 58W
Joaquin **51** 31 58N 94 3W
Joaquín V. González **76** 25 10 S 64 0W
Jobos **57** 17 58N 66 10W
Jobos, Bahía de **57** 17 59N 66 14W
Jocassee, L. **46** 34 58N 82 56W
Jodhpur **108** 26 23N 73 8 E
Joensuu **98** 62 37N 29 49 E
Joes **16** 39 39N 102 41W
Jofane **123** 21 15 S 34 18 E
Joggins **61** 45 42N 64 27W
Jogjakarta = Yogyakarta **111** 7 49 S 110 22 E
Johannesburg, S. Africa **123** 26 10 S 28 2 E
Johannesburg, U.S.A. **15** 35 22N 117 38W
John Day **44** 44 25N 118 57W
John Day → **44** 45 44N 120 39W
John Day Dam **53** 45 43N 120 41W
John Day Fossil Buttes Nat. Mon. **44** 44 43N 120 21W
John H. Kerr Reservoir **40** 36 36N 78 18W
John Martin Reservoir **16** 38 4N 102 56W
John o' Groats **84** 58 39N 3 3W
John Redmond Reservoir **24** 38 14N 95 46W
John W. Flanagan Reservoir **54** 37 15N 82 22W
Johns I. **46** 32 40N 80 10W
Johns Island **46** 32 47N 80 7W
Johnson, Kans. **24** 37 34N 101 45W
Johnson, Vt. **36** 44 38N 72 41W
Johnson City, N.Y. **39** 42 7N 75 58W
Johnson City, Tenn. **49** 36 19N 82 21W
Johnson City, Tex. **51** 30 17N 98 25W
Johnson County ◇, Ark. **13** 35 28N 93 28W
Johnson County ◇, Ga. **18** 32 45N 82 40W
Johnson County ◇, Ill. **21** 37 30N 88 50W
Johnson County ◇, Ind. **22** 39 30N 86 5W
Johnson County ◇, Iowa **23** 41 40N 91 35W
Johnson County ◇, Kans. **24** 38 45N 94 45W
Johnson County ◇, Ky. **49** 37 50N 82 50W
Johnson County ◇, Mo. **32** 38 45N 93 45W
Johnson County ◇, Nebr. **34** 40 20N 96 15W
Johnson County ◇, Tenn. **49** 36 29N 81 48W
Johnson County ◇, Tex. **51** 32 21N 97 23W
Johnson County ◇, Wyo. **56** 44 0N 106 35W
Johnson Draw → **50** 30 8N 101 7W
Johnson Reservoir **34** 40 42N 99 49W
Johnsonburg, N.J. **37** 40 58N 74 53W
Johnsonburg, Pa. **45** 41 29N 78 41W
Johnsondale **15** 35 58N 118 32W
Johnson's Crossing **62** 60 29N 133 18W
Johnsonville **46** 33 49N 79 27W
Johnston, R.I. **28** 41 50N 71 30W
Johnston, S.C. **46** 33 50N 81 48W
Johnston, L. **126** 32 25 S 120 30 E
Johnston City **21** 37 49N 88 56W
Johnston County ◇, N.C. **40** 35 30N 78 20W
Johnston County ◇, Okla. **43** 34 20N 96 40W
Johnston Falls = Mambilima Falls **122** 10 31 S 28 45 E
Johnston I. **125** 17 10N 169 8W
Johnstone Str. **62** 50 28N 126 0W
Johnstown, Colo. **16** 40 20N 104 54W
Johnstown, N.Y. **39** 43 0N 74 22W
Johnstown, Nebr. **34** 42 34N 100 3W
Johnstown, Ohio **42** 40 9N 82 41W
Johnstown, Pa. **45** 40 20N 78 55W
Johor □ **112** 2 5N 103 20 E
Johor Baharu **112** 1 28N 103 46 E
Joice **23** 43 22N 93 27W
Joiner **13** 35 31N 90 9W
Joinvile **77** 26 15 S 48 55 E
Joinville I. **5** 65 0 S 55 30W
Jojutla **65** 18 37N 99 11W
Jokkmokk **96** 66 35N 19 50 E
Jökulsá á Dal → **96** 65 40N 14 16W
Jökulsá Fjöllum → **96** 66 10N 16 30W
Joliet, Ill. **21** 41 32N 88 5W
Joliet, Mont. **33** 45 29N 108 58W
Joliette **60** 46 3N 73 24W
Jolley **23** 42 29N 94 43W
Jolo **111** 6 0N 121 0 E
Jombang **111** 7 33 S 112 14 E
Jome **111** 1 16 S 127 30 E
Jones **25** 32 58N 91 39W
Jones County ◇, Ga. **18** 33 0N 83 30W
Jones County ◇, Iowa **23** 42 5N 91 5W
Jones County ◇, Miss. **31** 31 36N 89 12W
Jones County ◇, N.C. **40** 35 0N 77 30W
Jones County ◇, S. Dak. **47** 44 0N 100 50W
Jones County ◇, Tex. **51** 32 45N 99 54W
Jones Sound **4** 76 0N 85 0W
Jonesboro, Ark. **13** 35 50N 90 42W
Jonesboro, Ga. **18** 33 31N 84 22W
Jonesboro, Ill. **21** 37 27N 89 16W
Jonesboro, Ind. **22** 40 29N 85 38W
Jonesboro, La. **25** 32 15N 92 43W
Jonesboro, Tenn. **49** 36 18N 82 29W
Jonesboro, Tex. **51** 31 37N 97 53W
Jonesburg **32** 38 51N 91 18W
Jonesport **26** 44 32N 67 37W
Jonestown, Miss. **31** 34 19N 90 27W
Jonestown, Pa. **45** 40 25N 76 29W
Jonesville, La. **25** 31 38N 91 49W
Jonesville, Mich. **29** 41 59N 84 40W
Jonesville, N.C. **40** 36 14N 80 51W
Jonesville, S.C. **46** 34 50N 81 41W
Jonesville, Va. **54** 36 41N 83 7W
Jonglei □ **121** 7 30N 32 30 E
Jönköping **97** 57 45N 14 10 E
Jönköpings län □ **97** 57 30N 14 30 E
Jonquière **61** 48 27N 71 14W
Joplin, Mo. **32** 37 6N 94 31W
Joplin, Mont. **33** 48 34N 110 46W
Joppa **21** 37 12N 88 51W
Jordan, Phil. **111** 10 41N 122 38 E
Jordan, Minn. **30** 44 40N 93 38W
Jordan, Mont. **33** 47 19N 106 55W
Jordan, N.Y. **39** 43 4N 76 29W
Jordan ■ **106** 31 0N 36 0 E
Jordan →, Asia **104** 31 48N 35 32 E
Jordan →, U.S.A. **52** 40 49N 112 8W
Jordan Valley **44** 42 59N 117 3W
Jordânia **75** 15 55 S 40 11W
Jorge, C. **78** 51 40 S 75 35W
Jorhat **109** 26 45N 94 12 E
Jorm **107** 36 50N 70 52 E
Jörn **96** 65 4N 20 1 E
Jornado del Muerto **38** 33 15N 106 50W
Jorong **110** 3 58 S 114 56 E
Jorquera → **76** 28 3 S 69 58W
Jos **120** 9 53N 8 51 E
José Batlle y Ordóñez **77** 33 20 S 55 10W
José de San Martín **78** 44 4 S 70 26W
Joseph, Oreg. **44** 45 21N 117 14W
Joseph, Utah **52** 38 38N 112 13W

Joseph Kanawha County

Joseph → 53 46 3N 117 1W
Joseph, L. 61 52 45N 65 18W
Joseph Bonaparte G. 126 14 35 S 128 50 E
Joseph City 12 34 57N 110 20W
Josephine County ◇ 44 42 20N 123 40W
Joshua 51 32 28N 97 23W
Joshua Tree 15 34 8N 116 19W
Joshua Tree National Monument 15 33 55N 116 0W
Jostedal 97 61 35N 7 15 E
Jotunheimen 97 61 35N 8 25 E
Jourdanton 51 28 55N 98 33W
Joussard 62 55 22N 115 50W
Jovellanos 66 22 40N 81 10W
Jowzjān □ 107 36 10N 66 0 E
Joy 21 41 12N 90 53W
Joya, La 72 16 43 S 71 52W
Joyce 53 48 8N 123 44W
Ju Xian 115 36 35N 118 20 E
Juab County ◇ 52 39 40N 113 0W
Juan Aldama 64 24 20N 103 23W
Juan Bautista Alberdi 76 34 26 S 61 48W
Juan de Fuca, Str of 53 48 18N 124 0W
Juan de Nova 123 17 3 S 43 45 E
Juan Fernández, Arch. de 125 33 50 S 80 0W
Juan José Castelli 76 25 27 S 60 57W
Juan L. Lacaze 76 34 26 S 57 25W
Juana Diaz 57 18 3N 66 31W
Juanjuí 72 7 10 S 76 45W
Juárez, Argentina 76 37 40 S 59 43W
Juárez, Mexico 64 27 37N 100 44W
Juárez, Sierra de 64 32 0N 116 0W
Juatinga, Ponta de 75 23 17 S 44 30W
Juàzeiro 74 9 30 S 40 30W
Juàzeiro do Norte 74 7 10 S 39 18W
Jubbulpore = Jabalpur 108 23 9N 79 58 E
Juby, C. 120 28 0N 12 59W
Júcar → 91 39 5N 0 10W
Júcaro 66 21 37N 78 51W
Juchitán 65 16 27N 95 5W
Jud 41 46 32N 98 54W
Judaea = Har Yehuda 104 31 35N 34 57 E
Judith → 33 47 44N 109 39W
Judith, Pt. 28 41 22N 71 29W
Judith Basin County ◇ 33 46 55N 110 10W
Judith Gap 33 46 41N 109 45W
Judith Mts. 33 47 15N 109 20W
Judsonia 13 35 16N 91 38W
Jufari → 71 1 13 S 62 0W
Jugoslavia = Yugoslavia ■ 95 44 0N 20 0 E
Juigalpa 66 12 6N 85 26W
Juiz de Fora 75 21 43 S 43 19W
Jujuy □ 76 23 20 S 65 40W
Julesburg 16 40 59N 102 16W
Julesburg Reservoir 16 40 56N 102 38W
Juli 72 16 10 S 69 25W
Julia Creek 127 20 39 S 141 44 E
Juliaca 72 15 25 S 70 10W
Julian, N.C. 40 35 54N 79 39W
Julian, Nebr. 34 40 31N 95 52W
Julianatop 71 3 40N 56 30W
Julianehåb 4 60 43N 46 0W
Juliette, L 18 33 2N 83 50W
Julimes 64 28 25N 105 27W
Jullundur 108 31 20N 75 40 E
Julu 114 37 15N 115 2 E
Jumentos Cays 67 23 0N 75 40 E
Jumet 87 50 27N 4 25 E
Jumilla 91 38 28N 1 19W
Jumla 109 29 15N 82 13 E
Jumna = Yamuna → 109 25 30N 81 53 E
Jump → 55 45 17N 91 5W
Junagadh 108 21 30N 70 30 E
Juncos 57 18 14N 65 55W
Junction, Tex. 51 30 29N 99 46W
Junction, Utah 52 38 14N 112 13W
Junction B. 126 11 52 S 133 55 E
Junction City, Ga. 18 32 36N 84 28W
Junction City, Kans. 24 39 2N 96 50W
Junction City, Ky. 49 37 35N 84 48W
Junction City, La. 25 33 0N 92 43W
Junction City, Oreg. 44 44 13N 123 12W
Junction City, Wis. 55 44 35N 89 46W
Jundah 127 24 46 S 143 2 E
Jundiaí 77 24 30 S 47 0W
June Lake 14 37 47N 119 4W
Juneau, Alaska 11 58 18N 134 25W
Juneau, Wis. 55 43 24N 88 42W
Juneau ◇ 11 58 30N 134 0W
Juneau County ◇ 55 43 50N 90 10W
Junee 127 34 53 S 147 35 E
Junggar Pendi 113 44 30N 86 0 E
Juniata 34 40 35N 98 30W
Juniata → 45 40 24N 77 1W
Juniata County ◇ 45 40 45N 77 5W
Junín, Argentina 76 34 33 S 60 57W
Junín, Peru 72 11 12 S 76 0W
Junín □ 72 11 30 S 75 0W
Junín de los Andes 78 39 45 S 71 0W
Junior 54 38 59N 79 57W
Juniper 18 32 32N 84 36W
Juniper Mts. 12 35 10N 113 0W
Jūniyah 106 33 59N 35 38 E
Juno 50 30 9N 101 7W
Juno Beach 17 26 52N 80 3W
Juntura 44 43 45N 118 5W
Juparanã, Lagoa 75 19 16 S 40 8W
Jupiter 17 26 57N 80 6W
Jupiter → 61 49 29N 63 37W
Juquiá 75 24 19 S 47 38W
Jur, Nahr el → 121 8 45N 29 15 E
Jura 84 56 0N 5 50W
Jura □ 90 46 47N 5 45 E
Jura, Mts. 90 46 40N 6 5 E
Jura, Sd. of 84 55 57N 5 45W
Jurado 70 7 7N 77 46W
Jurilovca 95 44 46N 28 52 E
Juruá → 70 2 37 S 65 44W
Juruena 73 13 0 S 58 10W
Juruena → 73 7 20 S 58 3W
Juruti 71 2 9 S 56 4W
Justice 54 37 35N 81 50W
Justin 51 33 5N 97 18W
Justo Daract 76 33 52 S 65 12W
Jutaí 72 5 11 S 68 54W
Jutaí → 70 2 43 S 66 57W
Juticalpa 66 14 40N 86 12W
Jutland = Jylland 97 56 25N 9 30 E
Juventud, I. de la 66 21 40N 82 40W
Juwain 107 31 45N 61 30 E
Jylland 97 56 25N 9 30 E
Jyväskylä 110 62 14N 25 50 E

K

K2 108 35 58N 76 32 E
Ka Lae 19 18 55N 155 41W
Kaaawa 19 21 33N 157 51W
Kaala 19 21 31N 158 9W
Kaalasin 112 16 26N 103 30 E
Kaalualu B. 19 18 58N 155 37W
Kaap die Goeie Hoop 123 34 24 S 18 30 E
Kaap Plato 123 28 30 S 24 0 E
Kaapkruis 123 21 43 S 14 0 E
Kaapstad = Cape Town 123 33 55 S 18 22 E
Kabaena 111 5 15 S 122 0 E
Kabala 120 9 38N 11 37W
Kabale 122 1 15 S 30 0 E
Kabalo 122 6 0 S 27 0 E
Kabambare 122 4 41 S 27 39 E
Kabanjahe 110 3 6N 98 30 E
Kabara 120 16 40N 2 50W
Kabardino-Balkar-A.S.S.R. □ 99 43 30N 43 30 E
Kabare 111 0 4 S 130 58 E
Kabarega Falls 122 2 15N 31 30 E
Kabasalan 111 7 47N 122 44 E
Kabba 120 7 50N 6 3 E
Kabetogama L. 30 48 28N 93 1W
Kabi 121 13 30N 12 35 E
Kabinakagami L. 60 48 54N 84 25W
Kabīr, Zab al 106 36 0N 43 0 E
Kabīr Kūh 106 33 0N 47 30 E
Kabkabīyah 121 13 50N 24 0 E
Kabompo → 123 14 10 S 23 11 E
Kabongo 122 7 22 S 25 33 E
Kabūd Gonbad 107 37 5N 59 45 E
Kābul 107 34 28N 69 11 E
Kābul □ 107 34 30N 69 0 E
Kabul → 108 33 55N 72 14 E
Kaburuang 111 3 50N 126 30 E
Kabwe 123 14 30 S 28 29 E
Kachchh, Gulf of 108 22 50N 69 15 E
Kachchh, Rann of 108 24 0N 70 0 E
Kachin □ 109 26 0N 97 30 E
Kachiry 100 53 10N 75 50 E
Kackar 106 40 45N 41 10 E
Kackley 24 39 42N 97 51W
Kadan Kyun 110 12 30N 98 20 E
Kadina 127 34 0 S 137 43 E
Kadirli 106 37 23N 36 5 E
Kadiyevka = Stakhanov 99 48 35N 38 40 E
Kadoka 47 43 50N 101 31W
Kādugli 121 11 0N 29 45 E
Kaduna 120 10 30N 7 21 E
Kaédi 120 16 9N 13 28W
Kaelé 121 10 7N 14 27 E
Kaena Pt. 19 21 35N 158 17W
Kaesŏng 114 37 58N 126 35 E
Kāf 106 31 25N 37 29 E
Kafakumba 122 9 38 S 23 46 E
Kafan 99 39 18N 46 15 E
Kafanchan 120 9 40N 8 20 E
Kaffrine 120 14 8N 15 36W
Kafia Kingi 121 9 20N 24 25 E
Kafirévs, Ákra 95 38 9N 24 38 E
Kafr 'Ayn 104 32 3N 35 7 E
Kafr Kammā 104 32 44N 35 26 E
Kafr Kannā 104 32 45N 35 20 E
Kafr Mālik 104 32 0N 35 18 E
Kafr Mandā 104 32 49N 35 15 E
Kafr Quaddūm 104 32 14N 35 7 E
Kafr Rā'ī 104 32 23N 35 9 E
Kafr Şīr 104 33 19N 35 23 E
Kafr Yāsīf 104 32 58N 35 10 E
Kafue → 123 15 30 S 29 0 E
Kafulwe 122 9 0 S 29 1 E
Kaga Bandoro 122 7 0N 19 10 E
Kagamil I. 11 53 0N 169 43W
Kagan 100 39 43N 64 33 E
Kagawa □ 117 34 15N 134 0 E
Kağizman 106 40 5N 43 10 E
Kagoshima 117 31 35N 130 33 E
Kagoshima □ 117 31 30N 130 30 E
Kahaluu 19 21 28N 157 50W
Kahama 122 4 8 S 32 30 E
Kahana 19 21 34N 157 53W
Kahana B. 19 21 35N 157 50W
Kahayan → 110 3 40 S 114 0 E
Kahemba 122 7 18 S 18 55 E
Kahlotus 53 46 39N 118 33W
Kahniah → 62 58 15N 120 55W
Kahnūj 107 27 55N 57 40 E
Kahoka 32 40 25N 91 44W
Kahoolawe 19 20 33N 156 37W
Kahuku 19 21 41N 157 57W
Kahuku Pt. 19 21 43N 157 59W
Kahului 19 20 54N 156 28W
Kai, Kepulauan 111 5 55 S 132 45W
Kai Besar 111 5 35 S 133 0 E
Kai-Ketil 111 5 45 S 132 40 E
Kaiama 120 9 36N 4 1 E
Kaiapoi 128 42 24 S 172 40 E
Kaibab 12 36 54N 112 44W
Kaibab Indian Reservation 12 36 55N 112 40W
Kaibab National Forest 12 36 35N 112 15W
Kaibab Plateau 12 36 45N 112 15W
Kaibito Plateau 12 36 30N 111 15W
Kaieteur Falls 71 5 1N 59 10W
Kaifeng 115 34 48N 114 21 E
Kaihua 115 29 12N 118 20 E
Kaikohe 128 35 25 S 173 49 E
Kaikoura 128 42 25 S 173 43 E
Kaikoura Pen. 128 42 25 S 173 43 E
Kaikoura Ra. 128 41 59 S 173 41 E
Kaili 115 26 33N 107 59 E
Kailu 114 43 38N 121 18 E
Kailua, Hawaii 19 21 24N 157 44W
Kailua, Hawaii 19 21 24N 157 45W
Kailua B. 19 21 25N 157 40W
Kailua Kona 19 19 39N 155 59W
Kaimana 111 3 39 S 133 45 E
Kaimanawa Mts. 128 39 15 S 175 56 E
Kaimuki 19 21 17N 157 48W
Kaingaroa Forest 128 38 24 S 176 30 E
Kainji Res. 120 10 1N 4 40 E
Kaipara Harbour 128 36 25 S 174 14 E
Kaiparowits Plateau 52 37 30N 111 20W
Kaiping 115 22 23N 112 42 E
Kaipokok B. 61 54 54N 59 47W
Kaironi 111 0 47 S 133 40 E
Kairouan 120 35 45N 10 5 E
Kaiserslautern 88 49 30N 7 43 E
Kaitaia 128 35 8 S 173 17 E
Kaitangata 128 46 17 S 169 51 E
Kaiwi Channel 19 21 15N 157 30W
Kaiyuan 114 42 28N 124 1 E
Kaiyuh Mts. 11 64 30N 158 0W
Kajaani 96 64 17N 27 46 E
Kajabbi 127 20 0 S 140 1 E
Kajana = Kajaani 96 64 17N 27 46 E
Kajang 112 2 59N 101 48 E
Kajo Kaji 122 3 58N 31 40 E
Kaka 121 10 38N 32 10 E
Kaka Pt. 19 20 31N 156 33W
Kakabeka Falls 60 48 24N 89 37W
Kakamas 123 28 45 S 20 33 E
Kakamega 122 0 20N 34 46 E
Kakanui Mts. 128 45 10 S 170 30 E
Kake, Japan 117 34 36N 132 19 E
Kake, U.S.A. 11 56 59N 133 57W
Kakegawa 117 34 45N 138 1 E
Kakeroma-Jima 117 28 8N 129 14 E
Kakhonak 11 59 26N 154 51W
Kakhovka 99 46 40N 33 15 E
Kakhovskoye Vdkhr. 99 47 5N 34 16 E
Kakinada 109 16 57N 82 11 E
Kakisa → 62 61 3N 118 10W
Kakisa L. 62 60 56N 117 43W
Kakogawa 117 34 46N 134 51 E
Kaktovik 11 70 8N 143 38W
Kakwa → 62 54 37N 118 28W
Kalabagh 108 33 0N 71 28 E
Kalabahi 111 8 13 S 124 31 E
Kalabáka 95 39 42N 21 39 E
Kalabo 123 14 58 S 22 40 E
Kalach 99 50 22N 41 0 E
Kaladan → 109 20 20N 93 5 E
Kalahari 123 24 0 S 21 30 E
Kalaheo 19 21 56N 159 32W
Kalakan 101 55 15N 116 45 E
Kalama 53 46 1N 122 51W
Kalamata 95 37 3N 22 10 E
Kalamazoo 29 42 17N 85 35W
Kalamazoo → 29 42 40N 86 10W
Kalamazoo County ◇ 29 42 15N 85 30W
Kalan 106 39 7N 39 32 E
Kalao 111 7 21 S 121 0 E
Kalaotoa 111 7 20 S 121 50 E
Kalapana 19 19 21N 154 59W
Kalasin 112 16 26N 103 30 E
Kalat 107 29 8N 66 31 E
Kalaupapa 19 21 12N 156 59W
Kalegauk Kyun 109 15 33N 97 35 E
Kalemie 122 5 55 S 29 9 E
Kaleva 29 44 22N 86 1W
Kalewa 109 23 10N 94 15 E
Kálfafellsstaður 96 64 11N 15 53W
Kalgan = Zhangjiakou 114 40 48N 114 55 E
Kalgoorlie-Boulder 126 30 40 S 121 22 E
Kaliakra, Nos 95 43 21N 28 30 E
Kalianda 110 5 50 S 105 45 E
Kalibo 111 11 43N 122 22 E
Kalida 42 40 59N 84 12W
Kalihi 19 21 20N 157 53W
Kalima 122 2 33 S 26 32 E
Kalimantan Barat □ 110 0 0 110 30 E
Kalimantan Selatan □ 110 2 30 S 115 30 E
Kalimantan Tengah □ 110 2 0 S 113 30 E
Kalimantan Timur □ 110 1 30N 116 30 E
Kálimnos 95 37 0N 27 0 E
Kalinin 98 56 55N 35 55 E
Kaliningrad 98 54 42N 20 32 E
Kalipetrovo 95 44 5N 27 14 E
Kalispell 33 48 12N 114 19W
Kalisz 89 51 45N 18 8 E
Kaliua 122 5 5 S 31 48 E
Kalix → 96 65 50N 23 11 E
Kalkaska 29 44 44N 85 11W
Kalkaska County ◇ 29 44 45N 85 5W
Kalkrand 123 24 1 S 17 35 E
Kallia 104 31 46N 35 30 E
Kallsjön 96 63 38N 13 0 E
Kalmar 97 56 40N 16 20 E
Kalmyk A.S.S.R. □ 99 46 5N 46 1 E
Kalmykovo 99 49 0N 51 47 E
Kalocsa 89 46 32N 19 0 E
Kalofer 95 42 37N 24 59 E
Kalohi Channel 19 21 0N 157 0W
Kalomo 123 17 0 S 26 30 E
Kalona 23 41 29N 91 43W
Kaltag 11 64 20N 158 43W
Kaluga 98 54 35N 36 10 E
Kalundborg 97 55 41N 11 5 E
Kalutara 108 6 35N 80 0 E
Kalvesta 24 38 4N 100 18W
Kalya 98 60 15N 59 59 E
Kam Keut 112 18 20N 104 48 E
Kama → 98 55 45N 52 0 E
Kamaishi 116 39 16N 141 53 E
Kamakou 19 21 7N 156 52W
Kamananui → 19 21 38N 158 4W
Kamandorskiye Ostrava 101 55 0N 167 0 E
Kamaran 105 15 21N 42 35 E
Kamas 52 40 38N 111 17W
Kambarka 98 56 15N 54 11 E
Kamchatka, P-ov. 101 57 0N 160 0 E
Kamehameha Heights 19 21 20N 157 52W
Kamela 44 45 26N 118 24W
Kamen 100 53 50N 81 30 E
Kamen-Rybolov 116 44 46N 132 2 E
Kamenets-Podolskiy 99 48 45N 26 10 E
Kamenjak, Rt. 94 44 47N 13 55 E
Kamenka 98 65 58N 44 0 E
Kameno 95 42 34N 27 18 E
Kamensk-Shakhtinskiy 99 48 23N 40 20 E
Kamensk Uralskiy 100 56 25N 62 2 E
Kamenskoye 101 62 45N 165 30 E
Kamenyak 95 43 24N 26 57 E
Kameoka 117 35 0N 135 35 E
Kamiah 20 46 14N 116 2W
Kamilukuak, L. 63 62 22N 101 40W
Kamina 122 8 45 S 25 0 E
Kaminak L. 63 62 10N 95 0W
Kaminoyama 116 38 9N 140 17 E
Kamishak Bay 11 59 15N 153 45W
Kamloops 62 50 40N 120 20W
Kamloops L. 62 50 45N 120 40W
Kamo 116 37 39N 139 3 E
Kamooloa 19 21 34N 158 7W
Kampala 122 0 20N 32 30 E
Kampar 112 4 18N 101 9 E
Kampar → 110 0 30N 103 8 E
Kampen 87 52 33N 5 53 E
Kampot 112 10 36N 104 10 E
Kampsville 21 39 18N 90 37W
Kampuchea = Cambodia ■ 112 12 15N 105 0 E
Kampung → 111 5 44 S 138 24 E
Kampungbaru = Tolitoli 111 1 5N 120 50 E
Kamrar 23 42 23N 93 44W
Kamrau, Teluk 111 3 30 S 133 36 E
Kamsack 63 51 34N 101 54W
Kamskoye Vdkhr. 98 58 0N 56 0 E
Kamuchawie L. 63 56 18N 101 59W
Kamuela 19 20 1N 155 41W
Kamui-Misaki 116 43 20N 140 21 E
Kamyshin 99 50 10N 45 24 E
Kanaaupscow 60 54 2N 76 30W
Kanab 52 37 3N 112 32W
Kanab → 12 36 24N 112 38W
Kanabec County ◇ 30 45 55N 93 20W
Kanaga I. 11 51 45N 177 22W
Kanagi 116 40 54N 140 27 E
Kanairiktok → 61 55 2N 60 18W
Kananga 122 5 55 S 22 18 E
Kanarraville 52 37 32N 113 11W
Kanash 98 55 30N 47 32 E
Kanawha 23 42 56N 93 48W
Kanawha → 54 38 50N 82 9W
Kanawha County ◇ 54 38 21N 81 38W

Kanazawa Kelibia

Kanazawa **117** 36 30N 136 38 E
Kanchanaburi **112** 14 2N 99 31 E
Kanchenjunga **109** 27 50N 88 10 E
Kanchipuram **108** 12 52N 79 45 E
Kanda Kanda **122** 6 52 S 23 48 E
Kandalaksha **98** 67 9N 32 30 E
Kandalakshkiy Zaliv **98** 66 0N 35 0 E
Kandalu **108** 29 55N 63 20 E
Kandangan **110** 2 50 S 115 20 E
Kandi **120** 11 7N 2 55 E
Kandiyohi County ◇ **30** 45 10N 95 0W
Kandla **108** 23 0N 70 10 E
Kandy **108** 7 18N 80 43 E
Kane, Ill. **21** 39 11N 90 21W
Kane, Pa. **45** 41 40N 78 49W
Kane, Wyo. **56** 44 51N 108 12W
Kane Bassin **4** 79 30N 68 0W
Kane County ◇, Ill. **21** 41 50N 88 25W
Kane County ◇, Utah **52** 37 15N 112 0W
Kaneilio Pt. **19** 21 27N 158 12W
Kaneohe **19** 21 25N 157 48W
Kaneohe B. **19** 21 30N 157 50W
Kangar **112** 6 27N 100 12 E
Kangaroo I. **127** 35 45 S 137 0 E
Kangavar **106** 34 40N 48 0 E
Kangean, Kepulauan **110** 6 55 S 115 23 E
Kangerdlugsuak **4** 68 10N 32 20W
Kanggyee **114** 41 0N 126 35 E
Kangnŭng **114** 37 45N 128 54 E
Kango **122** 0 11N 10 5 E
Kangto **109** 27 50N 92 35 E
Kaniapiskau → **61** 56 40N 69 30W
Kaniapiskau L. **61** 54 10N 69 55W
Kaniksu National Forest **20** 48 50N 116 30W
Kanin, P-ov. **98** 68 0N 45 0 E
Kanin Nos, Mys **98** 68 45N 43 20 E
Kankakee **21** 41 7N 87 52W
Kankakee → **21** 41 23N 88 15W
Kankakee County ◇ **21** 41 10N 87 50W
Kankan **120** 10 23N 9 15W
Kanker **109** 20 10N 81 40 E
Kankunskiy **101** 57 37N 126 8 E
Kannapolis **40** 35 30N 80 37W
Kannauj **108** 27 3N 79 56 E
Kannod **108** 22 45N 76 40 E
Kano **120** 12 2N 8 30 E
Kan'onji **117** 34 7N 133 39 E
Kanopolis **24** 38 43N 98 9W
Kanopolis Lake **24** 38 37N 97 58W
Kanorado **24** 39 20N 102 2W
Kanosh **52** 38 48N 112 26W
Kanowit **110** 2 14N 112 20 E
Kanowna **126** 30 32 S 121 31 E
Kanoya **117** 31 25N 130 50 E
Kanpetlet **109** 21 10N 93 59 E
Kanpur **108** 26 28N 80 20 E
Kansas, Ill. **21** 39 33N 87 56W
Kansas, Okla. **43** 36 12N 94 48W
Kansas □ **24** 38 30N 99 0W
Kansas → **24** 39 7N 94 37W
Kansas City, Kans. **24** 39 7N 94 38W
Kansas City, Mo. **32** 39 6N 94 35W
Kansk **101** 56 20N 95 37 E
Kansu = Gansu □ **114** 36 0N 104 0 E
Kantang **112** 7 25N 99 31 E
Kantishna → **11** 64 45N 149 58W
Kantō □ **117** 36 15N 139 30 E
Kantō-Sanchi **117** 35 59N 138 50 E
Kanturk **85** 52 10N 8 55W
Kanuma **117** 36 34N 139 42 E
Kanye **123** 25 0 S 25 28 E
Kaohsiung = Gaoxiong **115** 22 38N 120 18 E
Kaoko Otavi **123** 18 12 S 13 45 E
Kaolack **120** 14 5N 16 8W
Kapaa **19** 22 5N 159 19W
Kapahulu **19** 21 0N 157 0W
Kapanga **122** 8 30 S 22 40 E
Kapapa I. **19** 21 29N 157 48W
Kapchagai **100** 43 50N 77 10 E
Kapela **94** 44 40N 15 40 E
Kapfenberg **88** 47 26N 15 18 E
Kapiri Mposhi **123** 13 59 S 28 43 E
Kāpīsā □ **107** 35 0N 69 20 E
Kapiskau → **60** 52 47N 81 55W
Kapit **110** 2 0N 112 55 E
Kapiti I. **128** 40 50 S 174 56 E
Kaplan **25** 30 0N 92 17W
Kapoeta **121** 4 50N 33 35 E
Kaposvár **89** 46 25N 17 47 E
Kapowsin **53** 46 59N 122 13W
Kapuas → **110** 0 25 S 109 20 E
Kapuas Hulu, Pegunungan **110** 1 30N 113 30 E
Kapuskasing **60** 49 25N 82 30W
Kapuskasing → **60** 49 49N 82 0W
Kaputir **122** 2 5N 35 28 E
Kara **100** 69 10N 65 0 E
Kara Bogaz Gol, Zaliv **99** 41 0N 53 30 E
Kara Kalpak A.S.S.R. □ **100** 43 0N 60 0 E
Kara Sea **100** 75 0N 70 0 E
Karabük **106** 41 12N 32 37 E
Karabutak **100** 49 59N 60 14 E
Karachi **108** 24 53N 67 0 E
Karad **108** 17 15N 74 10 E
Karadeniz Boğazı **106** 41 10N 29 10 E
Karaganda **100** 49 50N 73 10 E
Karagayly **100** 49 26N 76 0 E
Karaginskiy, Ostrov **101** 58 45N 164 0 E
Karagiye Depression **99** 43 27N 51 45 E
Karaikal **108** 10 59N 79 50 E
Karaikkudi **108** 10 0N 78 45 E
Karaj **107** 35 48N 51 0 E
Karakas **100** 48 20N 83 30 E
Karakitang **111** 3 14N 125 28 E
Karakoram Pass **108** 35 33N 77 50 E
Karakoram Ra. **108** 35 30N 77 0 E
Karakum, Peski **100** 39 30N 60 0 E
Karalon **101** 57 5N 115 50 E
Karaman **106** 37 14N 33 13 E
Karamay **113** 45 30N 84 58 E
Karambu **110** 3 53 S 116 6 E
Karamea Bight **128** 41 22 S 171 40 E
Karanganyar **111** 7 38 S 109 37 E
Karasburg **123** 28 0 S 18 44 E
Karasino **100** 66 50N 86 50 E
Karasjok **96** 69 27N 25 30 E
Karasuk **100** 53 44N 78 2 E
Karasuyama **117** 36 39N 140 9 E
Karatau **100** 43 10N 70 28 E
Karatau, Khrebet **100** 43 30N 69 30 E
Karawanken **94** 46 30N 14 40 E
Karazhal **100** 48 2N 70 49 E
Karbalā **106** 32 36N 44 3 E
Karcag **89** 47 19N 20 57 E
Karda **101** 55 0N 103 16 E
Kardhítsa **95** 39 23N 21 54 E
Kareeberge **123** 30 50 S 22 0 E
Karelian A.S.S.R. □ **98** 65 30N 32 30 E
Karen **112** 12 49N 92 53 E
Kargānrūd **106** 37 55N 49 0 E
Kargasok **100** 59 3N 80 53 E
Kargat **100** 55 10N 80 15 E
Kargil **108** 34 32N 76 12 E
Kargopol **98** 61 30N 38 58 E
Kariba Dam **123** 16 30 S 28 35 E
Kariba Gorge **123** 16 30 S 28 50 E
Kariba Lake **123** 16 40 S 28 25 E
Karibib **123** 21 0 S 15 56 E
Karimata, Kepulauan **110** 1 25 S 109 0 E
Karimata, Selat **110** 2 0 S 108 40 E
Karimnagar **108** 18 26N 79 10 E
Karimunjawa, Kepulauan **110** 5 50 S 110 30 E
Karin **105** 10 50N 45 52 E
Kariya **117** 34 58N 137 1 E
Karkaralinsk **100** 49 26N 75 30 E
Karkinitskiy Zaliv **99** 45 56N 33 0 E
Karkur **104** 32 29N 34 57 E
Karl-Marx-Stadt **88** 50 50N 12 55 E
Karlovac **94** 45 31N 15 36 E
Karlovy Vary **88** 50 13N 12 51 E
Karlsborg **97** 58 33N 14 33 E
Karlshamn **97** 56 10N 14 51 E
Karlskoga **97** 59 22N 14 33 E
Karlskrona **97** 56 10N 15 35 E
Karlsruhe, Germany **88** 49 3N 8 23 E
Karlsruhe, U.S.A. **41** 48 6N 100 37W
Karlstad, Sweden **97** 59 23N 13 30 E
Karlstad, U.S.A. **30** 48 35N 96 31W
Karluk **11** 57 34N 154 28W
Karluk Indian Reservation **11** 57 35N 154 20W
Karnack **51** 32 40N 94 10W
Karnak **21** 37 18N 88 58W
Karnal **108** 29 42N 77 2 E
Karnali → **109** 29 0N 83 20 E
Karnaphuli Res. **109** 22 40N 92 20 E
Karnataka □ **108** 13 15N 77 0 E
Karnes City **51** 28 53N 97 54W
Karnes County ◇ **51** 28 49N 97 51W
Karnische Alpen **88** 46 36N 13 0 E
Kärnten □ **88** 46 52N 13 30 E
Karonga **122** 9 57 S 33 55 E
Karora **121** 17 44N 38 15 E
Kárpathos **95** 35 37N 27 10 E
Karpinsk **98** 59 45N 60 1 E
Karpogory **98** 63 59N 44 27 E
Kars **106** 40 40N 43 5 E
Karsakpay **100** 47 55N 66 40 E
Karshi **100** 38 53N 65 48 E
Karsun **98** 54 14N 46 57 E
Kartaly **100** 53 3N 60 40 E
Karufa **111** 3 50 S 133 20 E
Karungu **122** 0 50 S 34 10 E
Karur **108** 10 59N 78 2 E
Karval **16** 38 44N 103 32W
Karwar **108** 14 55N 74 13 E
Kas Kong **112** 11 27N 102 12 E
Kasaan **11** 55 32N 132 24W
Kasai → **122** 3 30 S 16 10 E
Kasama **122** 10 16 S 31 9 E
Kasanga **122** 8 30 S 31 10 E
Kasangulu **122** 4 33 S 15 15 E
Kasaragod **108** 12 30N 74 58 E
Kasba L. **63** 60 20N 102 10W
Kasempa **123** 13 30 S 25 44 E
Kasenga **122** 10 20 S 28 45 E
Kashabowie **60** 48 40N 90 26W
Kāshān **107** 34 5N 51 30 E
Kashi **113** 39 30N 76 2 E
Kashiwazaki **117** 37 22N 138 33 E
Kashk-e Kohneh **107** 34 55N 62 30 E
Kāshmar **107** 35 16N 58 26 E
Kashmir **108** 34 0N 76 0 E
Kashun Noerh = Gaxun Nur **113** 42 22N 100 30 E
Kasilof **11** 60 23N 151 18W
Kasimov **98** 54 55N 41 20 E
Kasiruta **111** 0 25 S 127 12 E
Kaskaskia → **21** 37 58N 89 57W
Kaskattama → **63** 57 3N 90 4W
Kaskinen **96** 62 22N 21 15 E
Kaskö **96** 62 22N 21 15 E
Kaslo **62** 49 55N 116 55W
Kasmere L. **63** 59 34N 101 10W
Kasongo **122** 4 30 S 26 33 E
Kasongo Lunda **122** 6 35 S 16 49 E
Kásos **95** 35 20N 26 55 E
Kaspichan **95** 43 18N 27 11 E
Kassala **121** 16 0N 36 0 E
Kassalā □ **121** 15 20N 36 26 E
Kassel **88** 51 19N 9 32 E
Kasson **30** 44 2N 92 45W
Kassue **111** 6 58 S 139 21 E
Kastamonu **106** 41 25N 33 43 E
Kastellorizon = Megiste **93** 36 8N 29 34 E
Kastoría **95** 40 30N 21 19 E
Kasulu **122** 4 37 S 30 5 E
Kasumi **117** 35 38N 134 38 E
Kasur **108** 31 5N 74 25 E
Kata **101** 58 46N 102 40 E
Katahdin, Mt. **26** 45 54N 68 56W
Katako Kombe **122** 3 25 S 24 20 E
Katalla **11** 60 12N 144 31W
Katangi **108** 21 56N 79 50 E
Katangli **101** 51 42N 143 14 E
Katanning **126** 33 40 S 117 33 E
Katha **109** 24 10N 96 30 E
Katherine **126** 14 27 S 132 20 E
Kathiawar **108** 22 20N 71 0 E
Kathleen **17** 28 7N 82 2W
Kathryn **41** 46 41N 97 58W
Katiet **110** 2 21 S 99 54 E
Katihar **109** 25 34N 87 36 E
Katima Mulilo **123** 17 28 S 24 13 E
Katingan = Mendawai → **110** 3 30 S 113 0 E
Katiola **120** 8 10N 5 10W
Katmai National Monument **11** 58 20N 155 0W
Katmandu **109** 27 45N 85 20 E
Katompe **122** 6 2 S 26 23 E
Katoomba **127** 33 41 S 150 19 E
Katowice **89** 50 17N 19 5 E
Katrine, L. **84** 56 15N 4 30W
Katrineholm **97** 59 9N 16 12 E
Katsumoto **117** 33 51N 129 42 E
Katsuura **117** 35 10N 140 20 E
Katsuyama **117** 36 3N 136 30 E
Kattegatt **97** 57 0N 11 20 E
Katwijk-aan-Zee **87** 52 12N 4 24 E
Katy **51** 29 47N 95 49W
Kauai **19** 22 3N 159 30W
Kauai Channel **19** 21 45N 158 50W
Kauai County ◇ **19** 22 0N 159 30W
Kaufman **51** 32 35N 96 19W
Kaufman County ◇ **51** 32 35N 96 20W
Kauhola Pt. **19** 20 15N 155 47W
Kaukauna **55** 44 17N 88 17W
Kaukonahua → **19** 21 35N 158 7W
Kaukonen **96** 67 31N 24 53 E
Kaula I. **19** 21 40N 160 33W
Kaulakahi Channel **19** 22 0N 159 55W
Kauliranta **96** 66 27N 23 41 E
Kaumalapau **19** 20 47N 156 59W
Kauna Pt. **19** 19 2N 155 53W
Kaunakakai **19** 21 6N 157 1W
Kaunas **98** 54 54N 23 54 E
Kaupo **19** 20 38N 156 8W
Kaura Namoda **120** 12 37N 6 33 E
Kautokeino **96** 69 0N 23 4 E
Kavacha **101** 60 16N 169 51 E
Kavalerovo **116** 44 15N 135 4 E
Kavali **108** 14 55N 80 1 E
Kaválla **95** 40 57N 24 28 E
Kavarna **95** 43 26N 28 22 E
Kavkaz, Bolshoi **99** 42 50N 44 0 E
Kaw **71** 4 30N 52 15W
Kaw City **43** 36 46N 96 50W
Kaw L. **43** 36 50N 96 55W
Kawagoe **117** 35 55N 139 29 E
Kawaguchi **117** 35 52N 139 45 E
Kawaihae **19** 20 3N 155 50W
Kawaihae B. **19** 20 0N 155 50W
Kawaihoa Pt. **19** 21 47N 160 12W
Kawaikimi **19** 22 5N 159 29W
Kawailoa Beach **19** 21 37N 158 5W
Kawambwa **122** 9 48 S 29 3 E
Kawanoe **117** 34 1N 133 34 E
Kawardha **109** 22 0N 81 17 E
Kawasaki **117** 35 35N 139 42 E
Kaweah, L. **15** 36 28N 118 52W
Kawela **19** 21 42N 158 1W
Kawene **60** 48 45N 91 15W
Kawerau **128** 38 7 S 176 42 E
Kawhia Harbour **128** 38 5 S 174 51 E
Kawio, Kepulauan **111** 4 30N 125 30 E
Kawkawlin **29** 43 39N 83 57W
Kawnro **109** 22 48N 99 8 E
Kawthaung **112** 10 5N 98 36 E
Kawthoolei □ =
Kawthule □ **109** 18 0N 97 30 E
Kawthule □ **109** 18 0N 97 30 E
Kay County ◇ **43** 36 50N 97 5W
Kaya **120** 13 4N 1 10W
Kayah □ **109** 19 15N 97 15 E
Kayak I. **11** 59 56N 144 23W
Kayan → **110** 2 55N 117 35 E
Kaycee **56** 43 43N 106 38W
Kayeli **111** 3 20 S 127 10 E
Kayenta **12** 36 44N 110 15W
Kayes **120** 14 25N 11 30W
Kaylor **47** 43 11N 97 50W
Kayoa **111** 0 1N 127 28 E
Kayseri **106** 38 45N 35 30 E
Kaysville **52** 41 2N 111 56W
Kayuagung **110** 3 24 S 104 50 E
Kazachinskoye **101** 56 16N 107 36 E
Kazachye **101** 70 52N 135 58 E
Kazakh S.S.R. □ **100** 50 0N 70 0 E
Kazan **98** 55 48N 49 3 E
Kazanlŭk **95** 42 38N 25 20 E
Kāzerūn **107** 29 38N 51 40 E
Kazumba **122** 6 25 S 22 5 E
Kazuno **116** 40 10N 140 45 E
Kazym → **100** 63 54N 65 50 E
Ké-Macina **120** 13 58N 5 22W
Kéa **95** 37 35N 24 22 E
Keaau **19** 19 37N 155 2W
Keahi Pt. **19** 21 19N 157 59W
Keahole Pt. **19** 19 44N 156 4W
Kealaikahiki Channel **19** 20 35N 156 50W
Kealaikahiki Pt. **19** 20 32N 156 42W
Kealakekua **19** 19 31N 155 55W
Kealia **19** 19 24N 155 53W
Keams Canyon **12** 35 49N 110 12W
Keansburg **37** 40 27N 74 8W
Kearney, Mo. **32** 39 22N 94 22W
Kearney, Nebr. **34** 40 42N 99 5W
Kearney County ◇ **34** 40 30N 99 0W
Kearneysville **54** 39 23N 77 53W
Kearns **52** 40 39N 112 0W
Kearny, Ariz. **12** 33 3N 110 55W
Kearny, N.J. **37** 40 46N 74 9W
Kearny County ◇ **24** 38 0N 101 15W
Kearsarge, Mt. **36** 43 22N 71 50W
Keatchie **25** 32 11N 93 54W
Keating **44** 44 53N 117 35W
Keats **24** 39 14N 96 43W
Keau **19** 19 38N 155 2W
Keawakapu **19** 20 43N 156 27W
Keban **99** 38 50N 38 50 E
Kebnekaise **96** 67 53N 18 33 E
Kebri Dehar **105** 6 45N 44 17 E
Kebumen **111** 7 42 S 109 40 E
Kechika → **62** 59 41N 127 12W
Kecskemét **89** 46 57N 19 42 E
Kedah □ **112** 5 50N 100 40 E
Keddie **14** 40 1N 120 58W
Kedgwick **61** 47 40N 67 20W
Kediri **111** 7 51 S 112 1 E
Kédougou **120** 12 35N 12 10W
Keedysville **27** 39 29N 77 40W
Keefers **62** 50 0N 121 40W
Keefeton **43** 35 36N 95 21W
Keehi Lagoon **19** 21 20N 157 54W
Keeley L. **63** 54 54N 108 8W
Keeling Is. = Cocos Is. **124** 12 10 S 96 55 E
Keene, N. Dak. **41** 47 56N 102 56W
Keene, N.H. **36** 42 56N 72 17W
Keene, Tex. **51** 32 24N 97 20W
Keenesburg **16** 40 7N 104 31W
Keensburg **21** 38 21N 87 52W
Keeper Hill **85** 52 46N 8 17W
Keer-Weer, C. **127** 14 0 S 141 32 E
Keetmanshoop **123** 26 35 S 18 8 E
Keewatin **30** 47 24N 93 5W
Keewatin □ **63** 63 20N 95 0W
Keewatin → **63** 56 29N 100 46W
Kefallinía **95** 38 20N 20 30 E
Kefamenanu **111** 9 28 S 124 29 E
Kefar 'Eqron **104** 31 52N 34 49 E
Kefar Ḥasīdim **104** 32 47N 35 5 E
Kefar Naḥum **104** 32 54N 35 34 E
Kefar Sava **104** 32 11N 34 54 E
Kefar Szold **104** 33 11N 35 39 E
Kefar Vitkin **104** 32 22N 34 53 E
Kefar Yehezqel **104** 32 34N 35 22 E
Kefar Yona **104** 32 20N 34 54 E
Kefar Zekharya **104** 31 43N 34 57 E
Kefar Zetim **104** 32 48N 35 27 E
Keffi **120** 8 55N 7 43 E
Keflavík **96** 64 2N 22 35W
Keg River **62** 57 54N 117 55W
Kegahka **61** 50 9N 61 18W
Keighley **82** 53 52N 1 54W
Keikiwaha Pt. **19** 19 31N 155 58W
Keith **84** 57 33N 2 58W
Keith Arm **58** 64 20N 122 15W
Keith County ◇ **34** 41 15N 101 40W
Keithsburg **21** 41 6N 90 56W
Keizer **44** 44 57N 123 1W
Kekaha **19** 21 58N 159 43W
Kekri **108** 26 0N 75 10 E
Kël **101** 69 30N 124 10 E
Kelan **114** 38 43N 111 31 E
Kelang **112** 3 2N 101 26 E
Kelantan □ **112** 5 10N 102 0 E
Kelantan → **112** 6 13N 102 14 E
Kelibia **121** 36 50N 11 3 E

Kildare Knox, C.

Kildare, Ga. **18** 32 32N 81 27W
Kildare, Okla. **43** 36 48N 97 3W
Kildare □ **85** 53 10N 6 50W
Kildeer **41** 47 22N 102 45W
Kilgore, Idaho **20** 44 24N 111 54W
Kilgore, Nebr. **34** 42 56N 100 57W
Kilgore, Tex. **51** 32 23N 94 53W
Kilimanjaro **122** 3 7S 37 20 E
Kilindini **122** 4 4S 39 40 E
Kilis **106** 36 50N 37 10 E
Kilju **114** 40 57N 129 25 E
Kilkee **85** 52 41N 9 40W
Kilkenny, Ireland **85** 52 40N 7 17W
Kilkenny, U.S.A. **30** 44 19N 93 34W
Kilkenny □ **85** 52 35N 7 15W
Kilkieran B. **85** 53 18N 9 45W
Kill Devil Hills **40** 36 1N 75 39W
Killala **85** 54 13N 9 12W
Killala B. **85** 54 20N 9 12W
Killaloe **85** 52 48N 8 28W
Killam **62** 52 47N 111 51W
Killarney, Canada **60** 45 55N 81 30W
Killarney, Ireland **85** 52 2N 9 30W
Killarney, Lakes of **85** 52 0N 9 30W
Killary Harbour **85** 53 38N 9 52W
Killbuck **42** 40 30N 81 59W
Killbuck → **42** 40 30N 81 59W
Killdeer **63** 49 6N 106 22W
Killeen **51** 31 7N 97 44W
Killen **10** 34 52N 87 32W
Killiecrankie, Pass of **84** 56 44N 3 46W
Killin **84** 56 28N 4 20W
Killingly **28** 41 0N 71 0W
Killingworth **28** 41 21N 72 30W
Killíni **95** 37 54N 22 25 E
Killybegs **85** 54 38N 8 26W
Kilmarnock, U.K. **84** 55 36N 4 30W
Kilmarnock, U.S.A. **54** 37 43N 76 23W
Kilmichael **31** 33 27N 89 34W
Kilosa **122** 6 48S 37 0 E
Kilrush **85** 52 39N 9 30W
Kilwa Kisiwani **122** 8 58S 39 32 E
Kilwa Kivinje **122** 8 45S 39 25 E
Kim **16** 37 15N 103 21W
Kimaam **111** 7 58S 138 53 E
Kimba **127** 33 8S 136 23 E
Kimball, Nebr. **34** 41 14N 103 40W
Kimball, S. Dak. **47** 43 45N 98 57W
Kimball, W. Va. **54** 37 26N 81 30W
Kimball County ◇ **34** 41 15N 103 40W
Kimballton **23** 41 38N 95 4W
Kimberley, Australia **126** 16 20S 127 0 E
Kimberley, Canada **62** 49 40N 115 59W
Kimberley, S. Africa **123** 28 43S 24 46 E
Kimberly, Idaho **20** 42 32N 114 22W
Kimberly, Oreg. **44** 44 46N 119 39W
Kimble County ◇ **51** 30 29N 99 46W
Kimbolton **42** 40 9N 81 34W
Kimbrough **10** 32 2N 87 34W
Kimchaek **114** 40 40N 129 10 E
Kimchŏn **114** 36 11N 128 4 E
Kimry **98** 56 55N 37 15 E
Kimsquit **62** 52 45N 126 57W
Kinabalu **110** 6 0N 116 0 E
Kinard **17** 30 16N 85 15W
Kinards **46** 34 23N 81 46W
Kinaskan L. **62** 57 38N 130 8W
Kincaid, Canada **63** 49 40N 107 0W
Kincaid, Ill. **21** 39 35N 89 25W
Kincaid, Kans. **24** 38 5N 95 9W
Kincaid, L. **21** 39 39N 89 29W
Kincardine **60** 44 10N 81 40W
Kinchafoonee Cr. → **18** 31 38N 84 10W
Kinde **29** 43 56N 83 0W
Kinder **25** 30 29N 92 51W
Kindersley **63** 51 30N 109 10W
Kindia **120** 10 0N 12 52W
Kindred **41** 46 39N 97 1W
Kindu **122** 2 55S 25 50 E
Kineshma **98** 57 30N 42 5 E
King **40** 36 17N 80 22W
King and Queen County ◇ **54** 37 40N 76 53W
King and Queen Court House **54** 37 40N 76 53W
King City, Calif. **15** 36 13N 121 8W
King City, Mo. **32** 40 3N 94 31W
King County ◇, Tex. **50** 33 37N 100 19W
King County ◇, Wash. **53** 47 25N 121 40W
King Cove **11** 55 3N 162 19W
King Frederick VI Land = Kong Frederik VI.s Kyst **4** 63 0N 43 0W
King George **54** 38 16N 77 11W
King George B. **78** 51 30S 60 30W
King George County ◇ **54** 38 16N 77 11W
King George I. **5** 60 0S 60 0W
King George Is. **59** 57 20N 80 30W
King George Sd. **126** 35 5S 118 0 E
King I. = Kadan Kyun **110** 12 30N 98 20 E
King I., Australia **127** 39 50S 144 0 E
King I., Canada **62** 52 10N 127 40W
King Leopold Ranges **126** 17 30S 125 45 E
King of Prussia **45** 40 5N 75 23W
King Salmon **11** 58 42N 156 40W
King Sd. **126** 16 50S 123 20 E
King William **54** 37 41N 77 1W
King William County ◇ **54** 37 41N 77 1W
King William I. **58** 69 10N 97 25W
King William's Town **123** 32 51S 27 22 E
Kingaroy **127** 26 32S 151 51 E
Kingfield **26** 44 58N 70 9W
Kingfisher **43** 35 52N 97 56W
Kingfisher County ◇ **43** 36 0N 98 0W
Kingman, Ariz. **12** 35 12N 114 4W
Kingman, Kans. **24** 37 39N 98 7W
Kingman County ◇ **24** 37 30N 98 0W
Kings →, Ark. **13** 36 30N 93 35W
Kings →, Calif. **15** 36 3N 119 50W
Kings →, Utah **52** 41 31N 118 8W
Kings Canyon National Park **15** 36 50N 118 40W
Kings County ◇, Calif. **15** 36 0N 119 50W
Kings County ◇, N.Y. **39** 40 37N 73 55W
King's Lynn **82** 52 45N 0 25 E
Kings Mountain **40** 35 15N 81 20W
Kings Peak **52** 40 46N 110 23W
Kings Valley **44** 44 42N 123 26W
Kingsbridge **83** 50 17N 3 46W
Kingsburg **15** 36 31N 119 33W
Kingsbury County ◇ **47** 44 23N 97 33W
Kingscourt **85** 53 55N 6 48W
Kingsdown **24** 37 32N 99 46W
Kingsford **29** 45 48N 88 4W
Kingsland, Ark. **13** 33 52N 92 18W
Kingsland, Ga. **18** 30 48N 81 41W
Kingsland, Tex. **51** 30 40N 98 26W
Kingsley, Iowa **23** 42 35N 95 58W
Kingsley, Mich. **29** 44 35N 85 32W
Kingsmill **50** 35 29N 101 4W
Kingsport **49** 36 33N 82 33W
Kingston, Canada **60** 44 14N 76 30W
Kingston, Jamaica **66** 18 0N 76 50W
Kingston, N.Z. **128** 45 20S 168 43 E
Kingston, Ark. **13** 36 3N 93 31W
Kingston, Ga. **18** 34 14N 84 57W
Kingston, Ky. **49** 37 39N 84 15W
Kingston, Mass. **28** 42 0N 70 43W
Kingston, Md. **27** 38 5N 75 46W
Kingston, Mich. **29** 43 25N 83 11W
Kingston, Minn. **30** 45 12N 94 19W
Kingston, Mo. **32** 39 39N 94 2W
Kingston, N.H. **36** 42 56N 71 3W
Kingston, N.Y. **39** 41 56N 73 59W
Kingston, Ohio **42** 39 28N 82 55W
Kingston, Okla. **43** 33 59N 96 45W
Kingston, Pa. **45** 41 16N 75 54W
Kingston, Tenn. **49** 35 52N 84 31W
Kingston, Utah **52** 38 13N 112 11W
Kingston, Wis. **55** 43 42N 89 8W
Kingston South East **127** 36 51S 139 55 E
Kingston Springs **48** 36 6N 87 7W
Kingston-upon-Thames **83** 51 23N 0 20W
Kingstown **67** 13 10N 61 10W
Kingstree **46** 33 40N 79 50W
Kingsville, Canada **60** 42 2N 82 45W
Kingsville, Md. **27** 39 27N 76 25W
Kingsville, Mo. **32** 38 45N 94 4W
Kingsville, Tex. **50** 27 31N 97 52W
Kingussie **84** 57 5N 4 2W
Kingwood **54** 39 28N 79 41W
Kinistino **63** 52 57N 105 2W
Kinkaid L. **21** 37 40N 89 25W
Kinkala **122** 4 18S 14 49 E
Kinki □ **117** 33 30N 136 0 E
Kinleith **128** 38 20S 175 56 E
Kinmundy **21** 38 46N 88 51W
Kinnaird **62** 49 17N 117 39W
Kinnairds Hd. **84** 57 40N 2 0W
Kinnelon **37** 41 0N 74 22W
Kinneret **104** 32 44N 35 34 E
Kinneret, Yam **104** 32 45N 35 35 E
Kinney **30** 47 31N 92 44W
Kinney County ◇ **50** 29 19N 100 25W
Kino **64** 28 45N 111 59W
Kinoje → **60** 52 8N 81 25W
Kinomoto **117** 35 30N 136 13 E
Kinross **84** 56 13N 3 25W
Kinsale, Ireland **85** 51 42N 8 31W
Kinsale, U.S.A. **54** 38 2N 76 35W
Kinsale, Old Hd. of **85** 51 37N 8 32W
Kinshasa **122** 4 20S 15 15 E
Kinsley **24** 37 55N 99 25W
Kinston, Ala. **10** 31 13N 86 10W
Kinston, N.C. **40** 35 16N 77 35W
Kinta **43** 35 8N 95 14W
Kintampo **120** 8 5N 1 41W
Kintap **110** 3 51S 115 13 E
Kintyre **84** 55 30N 5 35W
Kintyre, Mull of **84** 55 17N 5 55W
Kinushseo → **60** 55 15N 83 45W
Kinuso **62** 55 20N 115 25W
Kinwood **51** 29 55N 95 19W
Kinzua **44** 44 59N 120 3W
Kiosk **60** 46 6N 78 53W
Kiowa, Colo. **16** 39 21N 104 28W
Kiowa, Kans. **24** 37 1N 98 29W
Kiowa, Okla. **43** 34 43N 95 54W
Kiowa → **43** 36 46N 99 55W
Kiowa County ◇, Colo. **16** 38 25N 102 50W
Kiowa County ◇, Kans. **24** 37 30N 99 15W
Kiowa County ◇, Okla. **43** 35 0N 99 0W
Kiowa Cr. → **16** 40 20N 104 5W
Kipahigan L. **63** 55 20N 101 55W
Kipapa → **19** 21 24N 158 1W
Kiparissía **95** 37 15N 21 40 E
Kiparissiakós Kólpos **95** 37 25N 21 25 E
Kipembawe **122** 7 38S 33 27 E
Kipili **122** 7 28S 30 32 E
Kipling **63** 50 6N 102 38W
Kipnuk **11** 59 56N 164 3W
Kipp **24** 38 47N 97 27W
Kippure **85** 53 11N 6 23W
Kipushi **123** 11 48S 27 12 E
Kirby, Ark. **13** 34 15N 93 39W
Kirby, Tex. **51** 29 28N 98 23W
Kirby, Wyo. **56** 43 48N 108 11W
Kirbyville **51** 30 40N 93 54W
Kirensk **101** 57 50N 107 55 E
Kirgiz S.S.R. □ **100** 42 0N 75 0 E
Kirgiziya Steppe **99** 50 0N 55 0 E
Kiri **122** 1 29S 19 0 E
Kiribati ■ **124** 1 0N 176 0 E
Kırıkkale **106** 39 51N 33 32 E
Kirillov **98** 59 51N 38 14 E
Kirin = Jilin **114** 43 44N 126 30 E
Kirin □ = Jilin □ **114** 44 0N 124 0 E
Kiritimati **125** 1 58N 157 27W
Kirk, Colo. **16** 39 37N 102 36W
Kirk, Oreg. **44** 42 45N 121 50W
Kirkcaldy **84** 56 7N 3 10W
Kirkcudbright **84** 54 50N 4 3W
Kirkee **108** 18 34N 73 56 E
Kirkenes **96** 69 40N 30 5 E
Kirkintilloch **84** 55 57N 4 10W
Kirkjubœjarklaustur **96** 63 47N 18 4W
Kirkland, Ariz. **12** 34 25N 112 43W
Kirkland, Ill. **21** 42 6N 88 51W
Kirkland, Tex. **51** 34 23N 100 4W
Kirkland, Wash. **53** 47 41N 122 13W
Kirkland Junction **12** 34 22N 112 40W
Kirkland Lake **60** 48 9N 80 2W
Kırklareli **95** 41 44N 27 15 E
Kirklin **22** 40 12N 86 22W
Kirkman **23** 41 44N 95 16W
Kirkmansville **48** 37 1N 87 15W
Kirksey **48** 36 42N 88 24W
Kirksville **32** 40 12N 92 35W
Kirkūk **106** 35 30N 44 21 E
Kirkwall **84** 58 59N 2 59W
Kirkwood, Del. **27** 39 34N 75 42W
Kirkwood, Ill. **21** 40 52N 90 45W
Kirkwood, Mo. **32** 38 35N 90 24W
Kiron **23** 42 12N 95 20W
Kirov **100** 58 35N 49 40 E
Kirovabad **99** 40 45N 46 20 E
Kirovakan **99** 40 48N 44 30 E
Kirovograd **99** 48 35N 32 20 E
Kirovsk, R.S.F.S.R., U.S.S.R. **98** 67 48N 33 50 E
Kirovsk, Turkmen S.S.R., U.S.S.R. **100** 37 42N 60 23 E
Kirovskiy, R.S.F.S.R., U.S.S.R. **101** 54 27N 155 42 E
Kirovskiy, R.S.F.S.R., U.S.S.R. **116** 45 7N 133 30 E
Kirriemuir, Canada **63** 51 56N 110 20W
Kirriemuir, U.K. **84** 56 41N 3 0W
Kirsanov **98** 52 35N 42 40 E
Kırşehir **106** 39 14N 34 5 E
Kirteh **107** 32 15N 63 0 E
Kirthar Range **108** 27 0N 67 0 E
Kirtland **38** 36 44N 108 21W
Kiruna **96** 67 52N 20 15 E
Kirundu **122** 0 50S 25 35 E
Kirwin **24** 39 40N 99 7W
Kirwin Reservoir **24** 39 40N 99 8W
Kiryū **117** 36 24N 139 20 E
Kisalaya **66** 14 40N 84 3W
Kisangani **122** 0 35N 25 15 E
Kisar **111** 8 5S 127 10 E
Kisaran **110** 3 0N 99 37 E
Kisarazu **117** 35 23N 139 55 E
Kisatchie **25** 31 25N 93 10W
Kisatchie National Forest **25** 31 45N 92 30W
Kiselevsk **100** 54 5N 86 39 E
Kishanganj **109** 26 3N 88 14 E
Kishangarh **108** 27 50N 70 30 E
Kishinev **99** 47 0N 28 50 E
Kishiwada **117** 34 28N 135 22 E
Kishon **104** 32 49N 35 2 E
Kishtwar **108** 33 20N 75 48 E
Kisii **122** 0 40S 34 45 E
Kisiju **122** 7 23S 39 19 E
Kiska I. **11** 51 59N 177 30 E
Kiskatinaw → **62** 56 8N 120 10W
Kiskittogisu L. **63** 54 13N 98 20W
Kiskőrös **89** 46 37N 19 20 E
Kiskunfelégyháza **89** 46 42N 19 53 E
Kiskunhalas **89** 46 28N 19 37 E
Kislovodsk **99** 43 50N 42 45 E
Kismet **24** 37 12N 100 42W
Kiso-Gawa → **117** 35 20N 136 45 E
Kiso-Sammyaku **117** 35 45N 137 45 E
Kisofukushima **117** 35 52N 137 43 E
Kissidougou **120** 9 5N 10 0W
Kissimmee **17** 28 18N 81 24W
Kissimmee → **17** 27 9N 80 52W
Kissimmee, L. **17** 27 55N 81 17W
Kississing L. **63** 55 10N 101 20W
Kisumu **122** 0 3S 34 45 E
Kit Carson **16** 38 46N 102 48W
Kit Carson County ◇ **16** 39 15N 102 30W
Kita **120** 13 5N 9 25W
Kitab **100** 39 7N 66 52 E
Kitaibaraki **117** 36 50N 140 45 E
Kitakami **116** 39 20N 141 10 E
Kitakami-Gawa → **116** 38 25N 141 19 E
Kitakami-Sammyaku **116** 39 30N 141 30 E
Kitakata **116** 37 39N 139 52 E
Kitakyūshū **117** 33 50N 130 50 E
Kitale **122** 1 0N 35 0 E
Kitami **116** 43 48N 143 54 E
Kitami-Sammyaku **116** 44 22N 142 43 E
Kitchener **60** 43 27N 80 29W
Kitega = Gitega **122** 3 26S 29 56 E
Kitgum **122** 3 17N 32 52 E
Kíthira **95** 36 9N 23 0 E
Kíthnos **95** 37 26N 24 27 E
Kitikmeot □ **58** 70 0N 110 0W
Kitimat **62** 54 3N 128 38W
Kitinen → **96** 67 34N 26 40 E
Kitsap County ◇ **53** 47 30N 122 45W
Kitsuki **117** 33 25N 131 37 E
Kittanning **45** 40 49N 79 31W
Kittery, Maine **26** 43 5N 70 45W
Kittery, N.H. **36** 43 5N 70 45W
Kittitas **53** 46 59N 120 25W
Kittitas County ◇ **53** 47 10N 120 30W
Kitts Hummock **27** 39 8N 75 25W
Kittson County ◇ **30** 48 50N 96 50W
Kitui **122** 1 17S 38 0 E
Kitwe **123** 12 54S 28 13 E
Kitzmiller **27** 39 23N 79 10W
Kivalina **11** 67 44N 164 33W
Kivalo **96** 66 18N 26 0 E
Kivu, L. **122** 1 48S 29 0 E
Kiyev **99** 50 30N 30 28 E
Kiyevskoye Vdkhr. **99** 51 0N 30 0 E
Kizel **98** 59 3N 57 40 E
Kızıl Irmak → **99** 39 15N 36 0 E
Kizlyar **99** 43 51N 46 40 E
Kizyl-Arvat **100** 38 58N 56 15 E
Kladno **88** 50 10N 14 7 E
Klagenfurt **88** 46 38N 14 20 E
Klaipeda **98** 55 43N 21 10 E
Klamath **14** 41 32N 124 2W
Klamath → **14** 41 33N 124 5W
Klamath County ◇ **44** 42 40N 121 40W
Klamath Falls **44** 42 13N 121 46W
Klamath Marsh **44** 43 0N 121 40W
Klamath Mts. **14** 41 50N 123 20W
Klamath National Forest **14** 41 30N 123 20W
Klamath River **14** 41 52N 122 50W
Klappan → **62** 58 0N 129 43W
Klarälven → **97** 59 23N 13 32 E
Klaten **111** 7 43S 110 36 E
Klatovy **88** 49 23N 13 18 E
Klawer **123** 31 44S 18 36 E
Klawock **11** 55 33N 133 6W
Kleberg County ◇ **50** 27 31N 97 52W
Kleena Kleene **62** 52 0N 124 59W
Klein **33** 46 24N 108 33W
Klemme **23** 43 1N 93 36W
Klemtu **62** 52 35N 128 55W
Klerksdorp **123** 26 51S 26 38 E
Klickitat **53** 45 49N 121 9W
Klickitat County ◇ **53** 45 50N 120 30W
Klinaklini → **62** 51 21N 125 40W
Kline **46** 33 8N 81 21W
Klipplaat **123** 33 0S 24 22 E
Klisura **95** 42 40N 24 28 E
Kłodzko **88** 50 28N 16 38 E
Klondike **58** 64 0N 139 26W
Klouto **120** 6 57N 0 44 E
Kluane L. **58** 61 15N 138 40W
Klukwan **11** 59 24N 135 54W
Klyuchevskaya, Guba **101** 55 50N 160 30 E
Knapp **55** 44 57N 92 5W
Knaresborough **82** 54 1N 1 29W
Knee L., Man., Canada **63** 55 3N 94 45W
Knee L., Sask., Canada **63** 55 51N 107 0W
Kneeland **14** 40 45N 123 59W
Knezha **95** 43 30N 24 5 E
Knierim **23** 42 27N 94 27W
Knife → **41** 47 17N 101 20W
Knife River **30** 46 57N 91 47W
Knight I. **11** 60 21N 147 45W
Knight Inlet **62** 50 45N 125 40W
Knighton **83** 52 21N 3 2W
Knights Landing **14** 38 48N 121 43W
Knightstown **22** 39 48N 85 32W
Knob, C. **126** 34 32S 119 16 E
Knob Lick, Ky. **49** 37 5N 85 42W
Knob Lick, Mo. **32** 37 41N 90 22W
Knob Noster **32** 38 46N 93 33W
Knobel **13** 36 19N 90 36W
Knockmealdown Mts. **85** 52 16N 8 0W
Knokke **87** 51 20N 3 17 E
Knossos **95** 35 16N 25 10 E
Knott County ◇ **49** 37 20N 83 0W
Knotts Island **40** 36 31N 75 56W
Knowles **43** 36 53N 100 12W
Knox, Ind. **22** 41 18N 86 37W
Knox, N. Dak. **41** 48 20N 99 41W
Knox, Pa. **45** 41 14N 79 32W
Knox, C. **62** 54 11N 133 5W

Knox City Kūhpāyeh

Knox City, Mo. 32 40 9N 92 1W
Knox City, Tex. 51 33 25N 99 49W
Knox Coast 5 66 30S 108 0 E
Knox County ◇, Ill. 21 40 55N 90 10W
Knox County ◇, Ind. 22 38 40N 87 25W
Knox County ◇, Ky. 49 36 55N 83 50W
Knox County ◇, Maine 26 44 5N 69 5W
Knox County ◇, Mo. 32 40 10N 92 10W
Knox County ◇, Nebr. 34 42 40N 97 50W
Knox County ◇, Ohio 42 40 23N 82 29W
Knox County ◇, Tenn. 49 36 0N 83 0W
Knox County ◇, Tex. 51 33 35N 99 48W
Knoxville, Ga. 18 32 47N 83 59W
Knoxville, Ill. 21 40 55N 90 17W
Knoxville, Iowa 23 41 19N 93 6W
Knoxville, Pa. 45 41 57N 77 27W
Knoxville, Tenn. 49 35 58N 83 55W
Ko Chang 112 12 0N 102 20 E
Ko Kut 112 11 40N 102 32 E
Ko Phra Thong 112 9 6N 98 15 E
Ko Tao 112 10 6N 99 48 E
Koartac 59 60 55N 69 40W
Koba, Aru, Indonesia 111 6 37S 134 37 E
Koba, Bangka, Indonesia 110 2 26S 106 14 E
Kobarid 94 46 15N 13 30 E
Kobayashi 117 31 56N 130 59 E
Kōbe 117 34 45N 135 10 E
København 97 55 41N 12 34 E
Kōbi-Sho 117 25 56N 123 41 E
Koblenz 88 50 21N 7 36 E
Kobroor, Kepulauan 111 6 10S 134 30 E
Kobuk 11 66 55N 156 52W
Kobuk ◇ 11 66 0N 160 0W
Kobuk → 11 66 54N 160 38W
Kočani 95 41 55N 22 25 E
Kočevje 94 45 39N 14 50 E
Koch Bihar 109 26 22N 89 29 E
Kocheya 101 52 32N 120 42 E
Kōchi 117 33 30N 133 35 E
Kōchi □ 117 33 40N 133 30 E
Kochiu = Gejiu 113 23 20N 103 10 E
Kodiak 11 57 47N 152 24W
Kodiak I. 11 57 20N 154 0W
Kodiak Island ◇ 11 57 30N 154 0W
Kodiang 112 6 21N 100 18 E
Koehn Dry L. 15 35 20N 117 53W
Koes 123 26 0S 19 15 E
Kofa Mts. 12 33 15N 113 40W
Kofiau 111 1 11S 129 50 E
Koforidua 120 6 3N 0 17W
Kōfu 117 35 40N 138 30 E
Koga 117 36 11N 139 43 E
Kogaluk → 61 56 12N 61 44W
Koh-i-Bābā 107 34 30N 67 0 E
Kohala Mts. 19 20 5N 155 45W
Kohat 108 33 40N 71 29 E
Kohima 109 25 35N 94 10 E
Kohkīlūyeh va Būyer Aḥmadi □ 107 31 30N 50 30 E
Kohler Ra. 5 77 0S 110 0W
Kokand 100 40 30N 70 57 E
Kokanee Glacier Prov. Park 62 49 47N 117 10W
Kokas 111 2 42S 132 26 E
Kokchetav 100 53 20N 69 25 E
Kokemäenjoki 97 61 32N 21 44 E
Kokerite 71 7 12N 59 35W
Kokkola 96 63 50N 23 8 E
Koko Head 19 21 16N 157 43W
Koko Kyunzu 112 14 10N 93 25 E
Kokomo, Ind. 22 40 29N 86 8W
Kokomo, Miss. 31 31 12N 90 0W
Kokonau 111 4 43S 136 26 E
Koksoak → 59 58 30N 68 10W
Kokstad 123 30 32S 29 29 E
Kokubu 117 31 44N 130 46 E
Kokuora 101 71 35N 144 50 E
Kola, Indonesia 111 5 35S 134 30 E
Kola, U.S.S.R. 98 68 45N 33 8 E
Kola Pen. = Kolskiy Poluostrov 98 67 30N 38 0 E
Kolaka 111 4 3S 121 46 E
Kolar 108 13 12N 78 15 E
Kolar Gold Fields 108 12 58N 78 16 E
Kolari 96 67 20N 23 48 E
Kolarovgrad 95 43 18N 26 55 E
Kolayat 108 27 50N 72 50 E
Kolda 120 12 55N 14 57W
Kolding 97 55 30N 9 29 E
Kole 122 3 16S 22 42 E
Kolepom = Yos Sudarso, Pulau 111 8 0S 138 30 E
Kolguyev, Ostrov 98 69 20N 48 30 E
Kolhapur 108 16 43N 74 15 E
Koliganek 11 59 48N 157 25W
Kolín 88 50 2N 15 9 E
Köln 88 50 56N 6 58 E
Koło 89 52 14N 18 40 E
Koloa 19 21 55N 159 28W
Kołobrzeg 88 54 10N 15 35 E
Kolokani 120 13 35N 7 45W
Kolomna 98 55 8N 38 45 E
Kolomyya 99 48 31N 25 2 E
Kolonodale 111 2 3S 121 25 E
Kolosib 109 24 15N 92 45 E
Kolpashevo 100 58 20N 83 5 E
Kolskiy Poluostrov 98 67 30N 38 0 E
Kolskiy Zaliv 98 69 23N 34 0 E
Kolwezi 122 10 40S 25 25 E
Kolyma → 101 69 30N 161 0 E
Kolymskoye, Okhotsko 101 63 0N 157 0 E
Komárno 89 47 49N 18 5 E
Komatsu 117 36 25N 136 30 E
Komatsujima 117 34 0N 134 35 E
Komi A.S.S.R. □ 98 64 0N 55 0 E
Kommunizma, Pik 100 39 0N 72 2 E
Komodo 111 8 37S 119 20 E
Komono 122 3 10S 13 20 E
Komoran, Pulau 111 8 18S 138 45 E
Komoro 117 36 19N 138 26 E
Komotini 95 41 9N 25 26 E
Kompong Cham 112 12 0N 105 30 E
Kompong Chhnang 112 12 20N 104 35 E
Kompong Som 110 10 38N 103 30 E
Kompong Speu 112 11 26N 104 32 E
Kompong Thom 112 12 35N 104 51 E
Komsomolets, Ostrov 101 80 30N 95 0 E
Komsomolsk 101 50 30N 137 0 E
Konarhá □ 107 35 30N 71 3 E
Konawa 43 34 58N 96 45W
Konch 108 26 0N 79 10 E
Kondakovo 101 69 36N 152 0 E
Kondoa 122 4 55S 35 50 E
Kondopaga 98 62 12N 34 17 E
Kondratyevo 101 57 22N 98 15 E
Konduga 121 11 35N 13 26 E
Konevo 98 62 8N 39 20 E
Kong 120 8 54N 4 36W
Kong, Koh 112 11 20N 103 0 E
Kong Christian IX.s Land 4 68 0N 36 0W
Kong Christian X.s Land 4 74 0N 29 0W
Kong Franz Joseph Fd. 4 73 20N 24 30W
Kong Frederik IX.s Land 4 67 0N 52 0W
Kong Frederik VI.s Kyst 4 63 0N 43 0W
Kong Frederik VIII.s Land 4 78 30N 26 0W
Kong Oscar Fjord 4 72 20N 24 0W
Kongju 114 36 30N 127 0 E
Konglu 109 27 13N 97 57 E
Kongolo 122 5 22S 27 0 E
Kongor 121 7 1N 31 27 E
Kongsberg 97 59 39N 9 39 E
Kongsvinger 97 60 12N 12 2 E
Königsberg = Kaliningrad 98 54 42N 20 32 E
Konin 89 52 12N 18 15 E
Konjic 95 43 42N 17 58 E
Konosha 98 61 0N 40 5 E
Kōnosu 117 36 3N 139 31 E
Konotop 99 51 12N 33 7 E
Konqi He → 113 40 45N 90 10 E
Końskie 89 51 15N 20 23 E
Konstanz 88 47 39N 9 10 E
Kontagora 120 10 23N 5 27 E
Kontum 112 14 24N 108 0 E
Konya 106 37 52N 32 35 E
Konya Ovasi 106 38 30N 33 0 E
Konza 122 1 45S 37 7 E
Koochiching County ◇ 30 48 15N 93 50W
Koolan I. 126 16 0S 123 45 E
Koolau Range 19 21 35N 158 0W
Koosharem 52 38 31N 111 53W
Kooskia 20 46 9N 115 59W
Koostatak 63 51 26N 97 26W
Kootenai → 20 49 0N 116 30W
Kootenai County ◇ 20 47 45N 116 30W
Kootenai National Forest 33 48 30N 115 40W
Kootenay L. 62 49 45N 116 50W
Kootenay Nat. Park 62 51 0N 116 0W
Kopaonik Planina 95 43 10N 21 50 E
Kópavogur 96 64 6N 21 55W
Koper 94 45 31N 13 44 E
Kopervik 97 59 17N 5 17 E
Kopeysk 100 55 7N 61 37 E
Köping 97 59 31N 16 3 E
Kopparberg 97 59 52N 15 0 E
Kopparbergs län □ 97 61 20N 14 15 E
Koppeh Dāgh 107 38 0N 58 0 E
Kopperston 54 37 45N 81 35W
Koprivlen 95 41 36N 23 53 E
Koprivshtitsa 95 42 40N 24 19 E
Korab 95 41 44N 20 40 E
Korça 95 40 37N 20 50 E
Korčula 94 42 57N 17 8 E
Kordestan 106 35 30N 42 0 E
Kordestān □ 106 36 0N 47 0 E
Korea Bay 114 39 0N 124 0 E
Korea Strait 102 34 0N 129 30 E
Korhogo 120 9 29N 5 28W
Korim 111 0 58S 136 10 E
Korinthiakós Kólpos 95 38 16N 22 30 E
Kórinthos 95 37 56N 22 55 E
Kōriyama 116 37 24N 140 23 E
Koro, Fiji 128 17 19S 179 23 E
Koro, Ivory C. 120 8 32N 7 30W
Koro, Mali 120 14 1N 2 58W
Koro Sea 128 17 30S 179 45W
Korogwe 122 5 5S 38 25 E
Korona 17 29 25N 81 12W
Koror 112 7 20N 134 28 E
Körös → 89 46 43N 20 12 E
Korsakov 101 46 36N 142 42 E
Korshunovo 101 58 37N 110 10 E
Korsör 97 55 20N 11 9 E
Kortes Dam 56 42 12N 106 52W
Korti 121 18 6N 31 33 E
Kortrijk 87 50 50N 3 17 E
Koryakskiy Khrebet 101 61 0N 171 0 E
Kos 95 36 50N 27 15 E
Koschagyl 99 46 40N 54 0 E
Kościan 88 52 5N 16 40 E
Kosciusko 31 33 4N 89 35W
Kosciusko, Mt. 127 36 27S 148 16 E
Kosciusko County ◇ 22 41 15N 85 50W
Kosha 121 20 50N 30 30 E
K'oshih = Kashi 113 39 30N 76 2 E
Koshiki-Rettō 117 31 45N 129 49 E
Koshkonong 32 36 36N 91 39W
Koshkonong L. 55 42 52N 88 58W
Košice 89 48 42N 21 15 E
Koslan 98 63 28N 48 52 E
Kosŏng 114 38 40N 128 22 E
Kosovska-Mitrovica 95 42 54N 20 52 E
Kosse 51 31 18N 96 38W
Kossuth County ◇ 23 43 15N 94 10W
Kostamuksa 98 62 34N 32 44 E
Kostenets 95 42 15N 23 52 E
Kôstî 121 13 8N 32 43 E
Kostroma 98 57 50N 40 58 E
Kostrzyn 88 52 24N 17 14 E
Koszalin 88 53 50N 16 8 E
Kota 108 25 14N 75 49 E
Kota Baharu 112 6 7N 102 14 E
Kota Belud 110 6 21N 116 26 E
Kota Kinabalu 110 6 0N 116 4 E
Kota Tinggi 112 1 44N 103 53 E
Kotaagung 110 5 38S 104 29 E
Kotabaru 110 3 20S 116 20 E
Kotabumi 110 4 49S 104 54 E
Kotagede 111 7 54S 110 26 E
Kotamobagu 111 0 57N 124 31 E
Kotaneelee → 62 60 11N 123 42W
Kotawaringin 110 2 28S 111 27 E
Kotcho L. 62 59 7N 121 12W
Kotel 95 42 52N 26 26 E
Kotelnich 98 58 20N 48 10 E
Kotelnyy, Ostrov 101 75 10N 139 0 E
Kotka 97 60 28N 26 58 E
Kotlas 98 61 15N 47 0 E
Kotlenska Planina 95 42 56N 26 30 E
Kotli 108 33 30N 73 55 E
Kotlik 11 63 2N 163 33W
Kotor 95 42 25N 18 47 E
Kotri 108 25 22N 68 22 E
Kottayam 108 9 35N 76 33 E
Kotturu 108 14 45N 76 10 E
Kotuy → 101 71 54N 102 6 E
Kotzebue 11 66 53N 162 39W
Kotzebue Sound 11 66 20N 163 0W
Kouango 122 5 0N 20 10 E
Koudougou 120 12 10N 2 20W
Kouilou → 122 4 10S 12 5 E
Kouki 122 7 22N 17 3 E
Koula Moutou 122 1 15S 12 25 E
Koulen 112 13 50N 104 40 E
Koulikoro 120 12 40N 7 50W
Koumra 121 8 50N 17 35 E
Kounradskiy 100 46 59N 75 0 E
Kountze 51 30 22N 94 19W
Kourou 71 5 9N 52 39W
Kouroussa 120 10 45N 9 45W
Kousseri 121 12 0N 14 55 E
Koutiala 120 12 25N 5 23W
Kouts 22 41 19N 87 2W
Kovdor 98 67 34N 30 24 E
Kovel 98 51 10N 24 20 E
Kovrov 98 56 25N 41 25 E
Kowkash 60 50 20N 87 12W
Kowloon 115 22 20N 114 15 E
Koyabuti 111 2 36S 140 37 E
Koyuk 11 64 56N 161 9W
Koyukuk 11 64 53N 157 42W
Koyukuk → 11 64 55N 157 32W
Koza 117 26 19N 127 46 E
Kozan 106 37 35N 35 50 E
Kozáni 95 40 19N 21 47 E
Kozhikode = Calicut 108 11 15N 75 43 E
Kozhva 98 65 10N 57 0 E
Kozloduy 95 43 45N 23 42 E
Kozlovets 95 43 30N 25 20 E
Kpalimé 120 6 57N 0 44 E
Kra, Isthmus of = Kra, Kho Khot 112 10 15N 99 30 E
Kra, Kho Khot 112 10 15N 99 30 E
Kra Buri 112 10 22N 98 46 E
Kragan 111 6 43S 111 38 E
Kragerø 97 58 52N 9 25 E
Kragujevac 95 44 2N 20 56 E
Krakatau = Rakata, Pulau 110 6 10S 105 20 E
Kraków 89 50 4N 19 57 E
Kraksaan 111 7 43S 113 23 E
Kraljevo 95 43 44N 20 41 E
Kramatorsk 99 48 50N 37 30 E
Kramer 41 48 42N 100 40W
Kramfors 96 62 55N 17 48 E
Kranzburg 47 44 54N 96 55W
Krasavino 98 60 58N 46 29 E
Kraskino 101 42 44N 130 48 E
Kraśnik 89 50 55N 22 5 E
Krasnodar 99 45 5N 39 0 E
Krasnokamsk 98 58 4N 55 48 E
Krasnorechenskiy 116 44 41N 135 14 E
Krasnoselkupsk 100 65 20N 82 10 E
Krasnoturinsk 100 59 46N 60 12 E
Krasnoufimsk 98 56 57N 57 46 E
Krasnouralsk 98 58 21N 60 3 E
Krasnovishersk 98 60 23N 57 3 E
Krasnovodsk 99 40 0N 52 52 E
Krasnoyarsk 101 56 8N 93 0 E
Krasnyy Yar 99 46 43N 48 23 E
Kratie 112 12 32N 106 10 E
Krau 111 3 19S 140 5 E
Kravanh, Chuor Phnum 112 12 0N 103 32 E
Krawang 111 6 19N 107 18 E
Krebs 43 34 56N 95 43W
Krefeld 88 51 20N 6 32 E
Kremenchug 99 49 5N 33 25 E
Kremenchugskoye Vdkhr. 99 49 20N 32 30 E
Kremikovtsi 95 42 46N 23 28 E
Kremlin 43 36 33N 97 50W
Kremmling 16 40 4N 106 24W
Kremnica 89 48 45N 18 50 E
Kress 50 34 22N 101 45W
Kribi 122 2 57N 9 56 E
Krichem 95 42 8N 24 28 E
Krishna → 109 15 57N 80 59 E
Krishnanagar 109 23 24N 88 33 E
Kristiansand 97 58 9N 8 1 E
Kristianstad 97 56 2N 14 9 E
Kristianstads län □ 97 56 15N 14 0 E
Kristiansund 96 63 7N 7 45 E
Kristiinankaupunki 96 62 16N 21 21 E
Kristinehamn 97 59 18N 14 13 E
Kristinestad 96 62 16N 21 21 E
Kríti 95 35 15N 25 0 E
Krivoy Rog 99 47 51N 33 20 E
Krk 94 45 8N 14 40 E
Kronobergs län □ 97 56 45N 14 30 E
Kronprins Olav Kyst 5 69 0S 42 0 E
Kronprinsesse Märtha Kyst 5 73 30S 10 0 E
Kronshtadt 98 60 5N 29 45 E
Kroonstad 123 27 43S 27 19 E
Kropotkin, R.S.F.S.R., U.S.S.R. 101 59 0N 115 30 E
Kropotkin, R.S.F.S.R., U.S.S.R. 99 45 28N 40 28 E
Krosno 89 49 42N 21 46 E
Krotoszyn 89 51 42N 17 23 E
Krotz Springs 25 30 32N 91 45W
Krugersdorp 123 26 5S 27 46 E
Krum 51 33 16N 97 14W
Krumovgrad 95 41 29N 25 38 E
Krung Thep = Bangkok 112 13 45N 100 35 E
Krusenstern, C. 11 67 8N 163 45W
Kruševac 95 43 35N 21 28 E
Krymskiy P-ov. 99 45 0N 34 0 E
Ksar el Boukhari 120 35 51N 2 52 E
Ksar el Kebir 120 35 0N 6 0W
Ksar es Souk = Ar Rachidiya 120 31 58N 4 20W
Ku Tree Reservoir 19 21 30N 157 59W
Kuala 110 2 55N 105 47 E
Kuala Kangsar 112 4 46N 100 56 E
Kuala Kerai 112 5 30N 102 12 E
Kuala Kubu Baharu 112 3 34N 101 39 E
Kuala Lipis 112 4 10N 102 3 E
Kuala Lumpur 112 3 9N 101 41 E
Kuala Sedili Besar 112 1 55N 104 5 E
Kuala Terengganu 110 5 20N 103 8 E
Kualakapuas 110 2 55S 114 20 E
Kualakurun 110 1 10S 113 50 E
Kualapembuang 110 3 14S 112 38 E
Kualapuu 19 21 10N 157 2W
Kualasimpang 110 4 17N 98 3 E
Kualoa Pt. 19 21 31N 157 50W
Kuandang 111 0 56N 123 1 E
Kuandian 114 40 45N 124 45 E
Kuangchou = Guangzhou 115 23 5N 113 10 E
Kuantan 112 3 49N 103 20 E
Kuapa Pond 19 21 17N 157 43W
Kuba 99 41 21N 48 32 E
Kubak 107 27 10N 63 10 E
Kuban → 99 45 20N 37 30 E
Kubokawa 117 33 12N 133 8 E
Kubrat 95 43 49N 26 31 E
Kuchino-eruba-Jima 117 30 28N 130 12 E
Kuchino-Shima 117 29 57N 129 55 E
Kuchinotsu 117 32 36N 130 11 E
Kucing 110 1 33N 110 25 E
Kuda 108 23 10N 71 15 E
Kudat 110 6 55N 116 55 E
Kudus 111 6 48S 110 51 E
Kudymkar 100 59 1N 54 39 E
Kueiyang = Guiyang 115 26 32N 106 40 E
Kufrinjah 104 32 20N 35 41 E
Kufstein 88 47 35N 12 11 E
Kugong I. 60 56 18N 79 50W
Kūh-e 'Alijūq 107 31 30N 51 41 E
Kūh-e Dīnār 107 30 40N 51 0 E
Kūh-e-Hazārām 107 29 35N 57 20 E
Kūh-e-Jebāl Bārez 107 29 0N 58 0 E
Kūh-e Sorkh 107 35 30N 58 45 E
Kūh-e Taftān 107 28 40N 61 0 E
Kūhak 107 27 12N 63 10 E
Kūhhā-ye-Bashākerd 107 26 45N 59 0 E
Kūhhā-ye Sabalān 106 38 15N 47 45 E
Kūhpāyeh 107 32 44N 52 20 E

Kuile He Lake Alfred

Kuile He → 114 49 32N 124 42 E
Kuito 123 12 22 S 16 55 E
Kuiu I. 11 57 45N 134 10W
Kuji 116 40 11N 141 46 E
Kujū-San 117 33 5N 131 15 E
Kukawa 121 12 58N 13 27 E
Kukuihaele 19 20 5N 155 35W
Kulai 112 1 44N 103 35 E
Kulasekarappattinam 108 8 20N 78 0 E
Kuldja = Yining 113 43 58N 81 10 E
Kulm 41 46 18N 98 57W
Kulsary 100 46 59N 54 1 E
Kulunda 100 52 35N 78 57 E
Kulyab 100 37 55N 69 50 E
Kum Tekei 100 43 10N 79 30 E
Kuma → 99 44 55N 47 0 E
Kumagaya 117 36 9N 139 22 E
Kumai 110 2 44 S 111 43 E
Kumamba, Kepulauan 111 1 36 S 138 45 E
Kumamoto 117 32 45N 130 45 E
Kumamoto □ 117 32 55N 130 55 E
Kumanovo 95 42 9N 21 42 E
Kumara 128 42 37 S 171 12 E
Kumasi 120 6 41N 1 38W
Kumba 122 4 36N 9 24 E
Kume-Shima 117 26 20N 126 47 E
Kumertau 98 52 46N 55 47 E
Kumla 97 59 8N 15 10 E
Kumo 120 10 1N 11 12 E
Kumon Bum 109 26 30N 97 15 E
Kumukahi, C. 19 19 31N 154 49W
Kuna 20 43 30N 116 25W
Kunashir, Ostrov 101 44 0N 146 0 E
Kunghit I. 62 52 6N 131 3W
Kungrad 100 43 6N 58 54 E
Kungsbacka 97 57 30N 12 5 E
Kungur 98 57 25N 56 57 E
Kunia 19 21 28N 158 4W
Kuningan 111 6 59 S 108 29 E
Kunlong 109 23 20N 98 50 E
Kunlun Shan 109 36 0N 86 30 E
Kunming 113 25 1N 102 41 E
Kunsan 114 35 59N 126 45 E
Kunshan 115 31 22N 120 58 E
Kununurra 126 15 40 S 128 50 E
Kunya-Urgenoh 100 42 19N 59 10 E
Kuopio 96 62 53N 27 35 E
Kuopion lääni □ 96 63 25N 27 10 E
Kupa → 94 45 28N 16 24 E
Kupang 111 10 19 S 123 39 E
Kupreanof I. 11 56 50N 133 30W
Kuqa 113 41 35N 82 30 E
Kura → 99 39 50N 49 20 E
Kurashiki 117 34 40N 133 50 E
Kurayoshi 117 35 26N 133 50 E
Kŭrdzhali 95 41 38N 25 21 E
Kure 117 34 14N 132 32 E
Kure I. 19 28 25N 178 25W
Kurgaldzhino 100 50 35N 70 20 E
Kurgan 100 55 26N 65 18 E
Kuria Maria Is. = Khūrīyā Mūrīyā, Jazā 'ir 105 17 30N 55 58 E
Kurigram 109 25 49N 89 39 E
Kuril Is. = Kurilskiye Ostrova 101 45 0N 150 0 E
Kuril Trench 124 44 0N 153 0 E
Kurilsk 101 45 14N 147 53 E
Kurilskiye Ostrova 101 45 0N 150 0 E
Kurino 117 31 57N 130 43 E
Kurmuk 121 10 33N 34 21 E
Kurnool 108 15 45N 78 0 E
Kuro-Shima, Japan 117 30 50N 129 57 E
Kuro-Shima, Japan 117 24 14N 124 1 E
Kurow 128 44 44 S 170 29 E
Kursk 98 51 42N 36 11 E
Kuršumlija 95 43 9N 21 19 E
Kurthwood 25 31 20N 93 10W
Kurtistown 19 19 36N 155 4W
Kuruktag 113 41 0N 89 0 E
Kuruman 123 27 28 S 23 28 E
Kurume 117 33 15N 130 30 E
Kurunegala 108 7 30N 80 23 E
Kurupukari 71 4 43N 58 37W
Kurya 101 61 15N 108 10 E
Kusatsu 117 36 37N 138 36 E
Kusawa L. 62 60 20N 136 13W
Kushikino 117 31 44N 130 16 E
Kushima 117 31 29N 131 14 E
Kushimoto 117 33 28N 135 47 E
Kushiro 116 43 0N 144 25 E
Kushiro → 116 42 59N 144 23 E
Kushka 100 35 20N 62 18 E
Kushtia 109 23 55N 89 5 E
Kushva 98 58 18N 59 45 E
Kuskokwim → 11 60 5N 162 25W
Kuskokwim B. 11 59 45N 162 25W
Kuskokwim Mts. 11 62 30N 156 0W
Kussharo-Ko 116 43 38N 144 21 E
Kustanay 100 53 10N 63 35 E
Kütahya 106 39 30N 30 2 E
Kutaisi 99 42 19N 42 40 E
Kutaraja = Banda Aceh 110 5 35N 95 20 E
Kutch, Gulf of = Kachchh, Gulf of 108 22 50N 69 15 E
Kutch, Rann of = Kachchh, Rann of 108 24 0N 70 0 E
Kutno 89 52 15N 19 23 E
Kuttawa 48 37 4N 88 7W
Kutu 122 2 40 S 18 11 E
Kutum 121 14 10N 24 40 E
Kutztown 45 40 31N 75 47W
Kuwait = Al Kuwayt 106 29 30N 47 30 E
Kuwait ■ 106 29 30N 47 30 E
Kuwana 117 35 0N 136 43 E
Kuybyshev, R.S.F.S.R., U.S.S.R. 100 55 27N 78 19 E
Kuybyshev, R.S.F.S.R., U.S.S.R. 98 53 8N 50 6 E
Kuybyshevskoye Vdkhr. 98 55 2N 49 30 E
Küysanjaq 106 36 5N 44 38 E
Kuyto, Oz. 98 64 40N 31 0 E
Kuyumba 101 60 58N 96 59 E
Kuzey Anadolu Dağlari 106 41 30N 35 0 E
Kuzitrin → 11 65 10N 165 25W
Kuznetsk 98 53 12N 46 40 E
Kuzomen 98 66 22N 36 50 E
Kvœnangen 96 70 5N 21 15 E
Kvarner 94 44 50N 14 10 E
Kvarnerič 94 44 43N 14 37 E
Kvichak B. 11 58 48N 157 30W
Kwadacha → 62 57 28N 125 38W
Kwakoegron 71 5 12N 55 25W
Kwamouth 122 3 9 S 16 12 E
Kwando → 123 18 27 S 23 32 E
Kwangju 114 35 9N 126 54 E
Kwangsi-Chuang = Guangxi Zhuangzu Zizhiqu □ 115 24 0N 109 0 E
Kwangtung = Guangdong □ 115 23 0N 113 0 E
Kwataboahegan → 60 51 9N 80 50W
Kwatisore 111 3 18 S 134 50 E
Kweichow = Guizhou □ 115 27 0N 107 0 E
Kwekwe 123 18 58 S 29 48 E
Kwethluk 11 60 49N 161 26W
Kwigillingok 11 59 51N 163 8W
Kwiguk 11 62 46N 164 30W
Kwinana New Town 126 32 15 S 115 47 E
Kwoka 111 0 31 S 132 27 E
Kyabé 121 9 30N 19 0 E
Kyaikto 112 17 20N 97 3 E
Kyakhta 101 50 30N 106 25 E
Kyangin 109 18 20N 95 20 E
Kyaukpadaung 109 20 52N 95 8 E
Kyaukpyu 109 19 28N 93 30 E
Kyaukse 109 21 36N 96 10 E
Kyburz 14 38 47N 120 18W
Kyle, S. Dak. 47 43 26N 102 10W
Kyle, Tex. 51 29 59N 97 53W
Kyle Dam 123 20 15 S 31 0 E
Kyle of Lochalsh 84 57 17N 5 43W
Kyō-ga-Saki 117 35 45N 135 15 E
Kyoga, L. 122 1 35N 33 0 E
Kyongju 114 35 51N 129 14 E
Kyongpyaw 109 17 12N 95 10 E
Kyōto 117 35 0N 135 45 E
Kyōto □ 117 35 15N 135 45 E
Kyren 101 51 45N 101 45 E
Kyrenia 106 35 20N 33 20 E
Kystatyam 101 67 20N 123 10 E
Kytal Ktakh 101 65 30N 123 40 E
Kyulyunken 101 64 10N 137 5 E
Kyunhla 109 23 25N 95 15 E
Kyuquot 62 50 3N 127 25W
Kyūshū 117 33 0N 131 0 E
Kyūshū □ 117 33 0N 131 0 E
Kyūshū-Sanchi 117 32 35N 131 17 E
Kyustendil 95 42 16N 22 41 E
Kyusyur 101 70 39N 127 15 E
Kyzyl 101 51 50N 94 30 E
Kyzyl-Kiya 100 40 16N 72 8 E
Kyzylkum, Peski 100 42 30N 65 0 E
Kzyl-Orda 100 44 48N 65 28 E

L

La Barge 56 42 16N 110 12W
La Belle, Fla. 17 26 46N 81 26W
La Belle, Mo. 32 40 7N 91 55W
La Center 48 37 4N 88 58W
La Chorrera 57 8 53N 79 47W
La Conner 53 48 23N 122 30W
La Crescent 30 43 50N 91 18W
La Croix L. 30 48 20N 92 10W
La Crosse, Fla. 17 29 51N 82 24W
La Crosse, Kans. 24 38 32N 99 18W
La Crosse, Va. 54 36 42N 78 6W
La Crosse, Wash. 53 46 49N 117 53W
La Crosse, Wis. 55 43 48N 91 15W
La Crosse County ◇ 55 44 0N 91 0W
La Cygne 24 38 21N 94 46W
La Esperanza 57 18 23N 66 45W
La Farge 55 43 35N 90 38W
La Fayette, Ga. 18 34 42N 85 17W
La Fayette, Ky. 48 36 40N 87 40W
La Feria 50 26 9N 97 50W
La Follette 49 36 23N 84 7W
La Fontaine 22 40 40N 85 43W
La Garita 16 37 50N 106 15W
La Grande 44 45 20N 118 5W
La Grange, Ark. 13 34 39N 90 44W
La Grange, Ga. 18 33 2N 85 2W
La Grange, Ky. 49 38 25N 85 23W
La Grange, Mo. 32 40 3N 91 35W
La Grange, N.C. 40 35 19N 77 47W
La Grange, Tenn. 48 35 3N 89 15W
La Grange, Tex. 51 29 54N 96 52W
La Grange, Wyo. 56 41 38N 104 10W
La Harpe, Ill. 21 40 35N 90 58W
La Harpe, Kans. 24 37 55N 95 18W
La Jara, Colo. 16 37 16N 105 58W
La Jara, N. Mex. 38 36 5N 106 58W
La Joya 50 26 14N 98 27W
La Junta 16 37 59N 103 33W
La Luz 38 32 59N 105 57W
La Madera 38 36 23N 106 3W
La Marque 51 29 23N 94 58W
La Mesa, Calif. 15 32 46N 117 3W
La Mesa, N. Mex. 38 32 7N 106 42W
La Moille 21 41 32N 89 17W
La Moine → 21 39 59N 90 31W
La Monte 32 38 46N 93 26W
La Moure 41 46 21N 98 18W
La Moure County ◇ 41 46 23N 98 29W
La Palma 12 32 53N 111 31W
La Pine 44 43 40N 121 30W
La Place 25 30 4N 90 29W
La Plant 47 45 9N 100 39W
La Plata, Md. 27 38 32N 76 59W
La Plata, Mo. 32 40 2N 92 29W
La Plata, N. Mex. 38 36 56N 108 12W
La Plata County ◇ 16 37 15N 107 50W
La Porte 22 41 36N 86 43W
La Porte City 23 42 19N 92 12W
La Porte County ◇ 22 41 30N 86 45W
La Pryor 51 28 57N 99 51W
La Puente 38 36 42N 106 36W
La Push 53 47 55N 124 38W
La Sal 52 38 20N 109 15W
La Sal Mts. 52 38 30N 109 10W
La Salle, Colo. 16 40 21N 104 42W
La Salle, Ill. 21 41 20N 89 6W
La Salle, Minn. 30 44 4N 94 33W
La Salle County ◇, Ill. 21 41 20N 88 50W
La Salle County ◇, Tex. 51 28 26N 99 14W
La Salle Parish ◇ 25 31 41N 92 8W
La Santa, Cerro 57 18 7N 66 4W
La Union 38 31 57N 106 40W
La Vale 27 39 40N 78 48W
La Valle 55 43 35N 90 8W
La Vergne 48 36 1N 86 35W
La Verkin 52 37 12N 113 16W
La Vernia 51 29 21N 98 7W
La Veta 16 37 31N 105 0W
La Veta Pass 16 37 36N 105 13W
Laau Pt. 19 21 6N 157 19W
Labadieville 25 29 50N 90 57W
Labak 111 6 32N 124 5 E
Labé 120 11 24N 12 16W
Laberge, L. 62 61 11N 135 12W
Labette 24 37 14N 95 11W
Labette County ◇ 24 37 15N 95 15W
Labīs 112 2 22N 103 2 E
Laboulaye 76 34 10 S 63 30W
Labrador, Coast of □ 59 53 20N 61 0W
Labrador City 61 52 57N 66 55W
Lábrea 73 7 15 S 64 51W
Labuan, Pulau 110 5 21N 115 13 E
Labuha 111 0 30 S 127 30 E
Labuhan 111 6 22 S 105 50 E
Labuhanbaja 111 8 28 S 120 1 E
Labuk, Telok 110 6 10N 117 50 E
Labytnangi 100 66 39N 66 21 E
Lac Allard 61 50 33N 63 24W
Lac Bouchette 61 48 16N 72 11W
Lac Courte Oreilles Indian Reservation 55 45 50N 91 15W
Lac du Flambeau 55 45 58N 89 53W
Lac du Flambeau Indian Reservation 55 46 0N 89 50W
Lac Édouard 60 47 40N 72 16W
Lac la Biche 62 54 45N 111 58W
Lac la Martre 58 63 8N 117 16W
Lac-Mégantic 61 45 35N 70 53W
Lac qui Parle County ◇ 30 44 55N 96 0W
Lac Seul 63 50 28N 92 0W
Lacantúm → 65 16 36N 90 40W
Laccadive Is. = Lakshadweep Is. 102 10 0N 72 30 E
Lacepede Is. 126 16 55 S 122 0 E
Lacey 53 47 7N 122 49W
Lachay, Pta. 72 11 17 S 77 44W
Lachine 60 45 30N 73 40W
Lachlan → 127 34 22 S 143 55 E
Lachute 60 45 39N 74 21W
Lackawanna 39 42 50N 78 50W
Lackawanna County ◇ 45 41 30N 75 50W
Laclede County ◇ 32 37 40N 92 35W
Lacombe, Canada 62 52 30N 113 44W
Lacombe, U.S.A. 25 30 19N 89 56W
Lacon 21 41 2N 89 24W
Lacona, Iowa 23 41 12N 93 23W
Lacona, N.Y. 39 43 39N 76 10W
Laconia, Ind. 22 38 2N 86 5W
Laconia, N.H. 36 43 32N 71 28W
Lacoochee 17 28 28N 82 11W
Ladakh Ra. 108 34 0N 78 0 E
Ladário 73 19 1 S 57 35W
Ladd 21 41 23N 89 13W
Laddonia 32 39 15N 91 39W
Ladelle 13 33 28N 91 48W
Lādīz 107 28 55N 61 15 E
Ladoga 22 39 55N 86 48W
Ladoga, L. = Ladozhskoye Ozero 98 61 15N 30 30 E
Ladonia 51 33 25N 95 57W
Ladozhskoye Ozero 98 61 15N 30 30 E
Ladrillero, G. 78 49 20 S 75 35W
Ladson 46 32 59N 80 6W
Lady Grey 123 30 43 S 27 13 E
Lady Lake 17 28 55N 81 55W
Ladysmith, Canada 62 49 0N 123 49W
Ladysmith, S. Africa 123 28 32 S 29 46 E
Ladysmith, U.S.A. 55 45 28N 91 12W
Lae 124 6 40 S 147 2 E
Læsø 97 57 15N 10 53 E
Lafayette, Ala. 10 32 54N 85 24W
Lafayette, Calif. 14 37 53N 122 7W
Lafayette, Colo. 16 39 58N 105 12W
Lafayette, Ind. 22 40 25N 86 54W
Lafayette, La. 25 30 14N 92 1W
Lafayette, Minn. 30 44 27N 94 24W
Lafayette, Ohio 42 40 46N 83 57W
Lafayette, Oreg. 44 45 15N 123 7W
Lafayette, Tenn. 48 36 31N 86 2W
Lafayette, Mt. 36 44 10N 71 38W
Lafayette County ◇, Ark. 13 33 22N 93 43W
Lafayette County ◇, Fla. 17 30 0N 83 0W
Lafayette County ◇, Miss. 31 34 22N 89 31W
Lafayette County ◇, Mo. 32 39 5N 93 45W
Lafayette County ◇, Wis. 55 42 35N 90 10W
Lafayette Parish ◇ 25 30 14N 92 1W
Laferte → 62 61 53N 117 44W
Lafia 120 8 30N 8 34 E
Lafitte 25 29 40N 90 6W
Lafleche 63 49 45N 106 40W
Lafontaine 24 37 24N 95 51W
Lafourche Parish ◇ 25 29 34N 90 23W
Lagan → 85 54 35N 5 55W
Lagarfljót → 96 65 40N 14 18W
Lagarto 74 10 54 S 37 41W
Lågen → 97 61 8N 10 25 E
Laghmān □ 107 34 20N 70 0 E
Laghouat 120 33 50N 2 59 E
Lago Posadas 78 47 30 S 71 40W
Lago Ranco 78 40 19 S 72 30W
Lagonoy Gulf 111 13 50N 123 50 E
Lagos, Nigeria 120 6 25N 3 27 E
Lagos, Portugal 91 37 5N 8 41W
Lagos de Moreno 64 21 21N 101 55W
Lagrange, Australia 126 18 45 S 121 43 E
Lagrange, Ind. 22 41 39N 85 25W
Lagrange, Maine 26 45 11N 68 54W
Lagrange, Ohio 42 41 14N 82 7W
Lagrange County ◇ 22 41 35N 85 25W
Laguna, Brazil 77 28 30 S 48 50W
Laguna, U.S.A. 38 35 2N 107 25W
Laguna Beach 15 33 33N 117 47W
Laguna Indian Reservation 38 35 0N 107 20W
Laguna Limpia 76 26 32 S 59 45W
Laguna Mts. 15 33 0N 116 40W
Lagunas, Chile 76 21 0 S 69 45W
Lagunas, Peru 72 5 10 S 75 35W
Lagunillas 73 19 38 S 63 43W
Laha 114 48 12N 124 35 E
Lahad Datu 111 5 0N 118 20 E
Lahaina 19 20 53N 156 41W
Lahat 110 3 45 S 103 30 E
Lahewa 110 1 22N 97 12 E
Lahijan 106 37 10N 50 6 E
Lahilahi Pt. 19 21 28N 158 13W
Lahn → 88 50 52N 8 35 E
Laholm 97 56 30N 13 2 E
Lahoma 43 36 23N 98 5W
Lahontan Reservoir 35 39 28N 119 4W
Lahore 108 31 32N 74 22 E
Lahti 97 60 58N 25 40 E
Lahtis = Lahti 97 60 58N 25 40 E
Laï 121 9 25N 16 18 E
Lai Chau 112 22 5N 103 3 E
Laibin 115 23 42N 109 14 E
Laie 19 21 39N 157 56W
Laifeng 115 29 27N 109 20 E
Laingsburg 29 42 54N 84 21W
Lair 49 38 20N 84 18W
Lairg 84 58 1N 4 24W
Lais 110 3 35 S 102 0 E
Laiyang 114 36 59N 120 45 E
Laizhou Wan 114 37 30N 119 30 E
Laja → 64 20 55N 100 46W
Lajas 57 18 3N 67 4W
Lajere 120 11 58N 11 25 E
Lajes, Rio Grande d. N., Brazil 74 5 41 S 36 14W
Lajes, Sta. Catarina, Brazil 77 27 48 S 50 20W
Lajinha 75 20 9 S 41 37W
Lajitas 50 29 16N 103 46W
Lajoya 38 34 21N 106 51W
Lakar 111 8 15 S 128 17 E
Lake, Miss. 31 32 21N 89 20W
Lake, Wyo. 56 44 33N 110 24W
Lake Alfred 17 28 6N 81 44W

Lake Andes Las Termas

Lake Andes **47** 43 9N 98 32W
Lake Arthur, La. **25** 30 5N 92 41W
Lake Arthur, N. Mex. **38** 33 0N 104 22W
Lake Benton **30** 44 15N 96 17W
Lake Bird **17** 30 14N 83 37W
Lake Bronson **30** 48 44N 96 40W
Lake Butler **17** 30 1N 82 21W
Lake Cargelligo **127** 33 15 S 146 22 E
Lake Charles **25** 30 14N 93 13W
Lake Chelan National Recreation Area **53** 48 25N 120 52W
Lake City, Ark. **13** 35 49N 90 26W
Lake City, Calif. **14** 41 39N 120 13W
Lake City, Colo. **16** 38 2N 107 19W
Lake City, Fla. **17** 30 11N 82 38W
Lake City, Iowa **23** 42 16N 94 44W
Lake City, Kans. **24** 37 21N 98 49W
Lake City, Mich. **29** 44 20N 85 13W
Lake City, Minn. **30** 44 27N 92 16W
Lake City, Pa. **45** 42 1N 80 21W
Lake City, S.C. **46** 33 52N 79 45W
Lake City, S. Dak. **47** 45 44N 97 25W
Lake City, Tenn. **49** 36 13N 84 9W
Lake Clarke Shores **17** 26 39N 80 5W
Lake Clear Junction **39** 44 22N 74 14W
Lake County ◇, Calif. **14** 39 5N 122 45W
Lake County ◇, Colo. **16** 39 10N 106 20W
Lake County ◇, Fla. **17** 28 45N 81 45W
Lake County ◇, Ill. **21** 42 20N 88 0W
Lake County ◇, Ind. **22** 41 25N 87 25W
Lake County ◇, Mich. **29** 44 0N 85 50W
Lake County ◇, Minn. **30** 47 30N 91 20W
Lake County ◇, Mont. **33** 47 40N 114 10W
Lake County ◇, Ohio **42** 41 40N 81 21W
Lake County ◇, Oreg. **44** 44 45N 120 20W
Lake County ◇, S. Dak. **47** 44 0N 97 7W
Lake County ◇, Tenn. **48** 36 23N 89 29W
Lake Crystal **30** 44 6N 94 13W
Lake Delton **55** 43 35N 89 47W
Lake Forest **21** 42 15N 87 50W
Lake Fork **20** 44 50N 116 5W
Lake Fork Cr. → **52** 40 13N 110 7W
Lake Geneva **55** 42 36N 88 26W
Lake George, Colo. **16** 38 59N 105 22W
Lake George, Mich. **29** 43 58N 84 57W
Lake George, Minn. **30** 47 12N 94 59W
Lake George, N.Y. **39** 43 26N 73 43W
Lake Harbor **17** 26 42N 80 48W
Lake Harbour **59** 62 50N 69 50W
Lake Havasu City **12** 34 27N 114 22W
Lake Helen **17** 28 59N 81 14W
Lake Hughes **15** 34 41N 118 26W
Lake Isabella **15** 35 38N 118 28W
Lake Jackson **51** 29 3N 95 27W
Lake Lenore **63** 52 24N 104 59W
Lake Lillian **30** 44 57N 94 53W
Lake Linden **29** 47 11N 88 24W
Lake Louise **62** 51 30N 116 10W
Lake Lure **40** 35 25N 82 12W
Lake Mead National Recreation Area **12** 36 15N 114 30W
Lake Meredith National Recreation Area **50** 35 50N 101 50W
Lake Mills, Iowa **23** 43 25N 93 32W
Lake Mills, Wis. **55** 43 5N 88 55W
Lake Mohawk **37** 41 1N 74 39W
Lake Monroe **17** 28 50N 81 19W
Lake Nebagamon **55** 46 31N 91 42W
Lake Norden **47** 44 35N 97 13W
Lake Odessa **29** 42 47N 85 8W
Lake of the Woods County ◇ **30** 48 40N 94 50W
Lake Orion **29** 42 47N 83 14W
Lake Oswego **44** 45 25N 122 40W
Lake Ozark **32** 38 12N 92 38W
Lake Park, Fla. **17** 26 48N 80 3W
Lake Park, Ga. **18** 30 41N 83 11W
Lake Park, Iowa **23** 43 27N 95 19W
Lake Park, Minn. **30** 46 53N 96 6W
Lake Placid, Fla. **17** 27 18N 81 22W
Lake Placid, N.Y. **39** 44 17N 73 59W
Lake Pleasant **39** 43 28N 74 25W
Lake Preston **47** 44 22N 97 23W
Lake Providence **25** 32 48N 91 10W
Lake Range **35** 40 10N 119 20W
Lake River **60** 54 30N 82 31W
Lake Ronkonkoma **39** 40 50N 73 6W
Lake Shore **27** 39 7N 76 29W
Lake Stevens **53** 48 1N 122 4W
Lake Superior Prov. Park **60** 47 45N 84 45W
Lake Toxaway **40** 35 8N 82 56W
Lake View, Iowa **23** 42 18N 95 3W
Lake View, S.C. **46** 34 21N 79 10W
Lake Villa **21** 42 25N 88 5W
Lake Village **13** 33 20N 91 17W
Lake Wales **17** 27 54N 81 35W
Lake Wilson **30** 43 59N 95 57W
Lake Worth **17** 26 37N 80 3W
Lake Zurich **21** 42 12N 88 5W
Lakecreek **44** 42 26N 122 37W
Lakefield, Canada **60** 44 25N 78 16W
Lakefield, U.S.A. **30** 43 41N 95 10W
Lakehurst **37** 40 1N 74 19W
Lakeland, Fla. **17** 28 3N 81 57W
Lakeland, Ga. **18** 31 2N 83 4W
Lakemba **128** 18 13 S 178 47W
Lakemont **45** 40 28N 78 24W
Lakemount **18** 34 47N 83 25W
Lakeport, Calif. **14** 39 3N 122 55W
Lakeport, Mich. **29** 43 7N 82 30W
Lakeshore, Calif. **15** 37 15N 119 12W
Lakeshore, Miss. **31** 30 15N 89 26W
Lakeside, Ariz. **12** 34 9N 109 58W
Lakeside, Calif. **15** 32 52N 116 55W
Lakeside, Nebr. **34** 42 3N 102 26W
Lakeside, Oreg. **44** 43 35N 124 11W
Lakeside, Va. **54** 37 37N 77 28W
Laketon **50** 35 33N 100 38W
Laketown **52** 41 49N 111 19W
Lakeview, Mont. **33** 44 36N 111 49W
Lakeview, Ohio **42** 40 29N 83 56W
Lakeview, Oreg. **44** 42 11N 120 21W
Lakeview, Tex. **50** 34 40N 100 42W
Lakeview, Mich. **29** 42 17N 85 12W
Lakeview, Mich. **29** 43 27N 85 17W
Lakeville, Conn. **28** 41 58N 73 26W
Lakeville, Ind. **22** 41 31N 86 16W
Lakeville, Mass. **28** 41 50N 70 55W
Lakeville, Minn. **30** 44 39N 93 14W
Lakewood, Colo. **16** 39 44N 105 5W
Lakewood, N.J. **37** 40 6N 74 13W
Lakewood, N. Mex. **38** 32 38N 104 23W
Lakewood, N.Y. **39** 42 6N 79 19W
Lakewood, Ohio **42** 41 29N 81 48W
Lakewood, Wash. **53** 48 9N 122 13W
Lakewood, Wis. **55** 45 18N 88 31W
Lakewood Center **53** 47 11N 122 32W
Laki **96** 64 4N 18 14W
Lakin **24** 37 57N 101 15W
Lakitusaki → **60** 54 21N 82 25W
Lakonikós Kólpos **95** 36 40N 22 40 E
Lakota, Ivory C. **120** 5 50N 5 30W
Lakota, Iowa **23** 43 23N 94 6W
Lakota, N. Dak. **41** 48 2N 98 21W
Laksefjorden **96** 70 45N 26 50 E
Lakselv **96** 70 2N 24 56 E
Lakshadweep Is. **102** 10 0N 72 30 E
Lala Ghat **109** 24 30N 92 40 E
Lalibela **121** 12 2N 39 2 E
Lalin, China **114** 45 12N 127 0 E
Lalín, Spain **91** 42 40N 8 5W
Lalitapur = Patan **109** 27 40N 85 20 E
Lamaing **109** 15 25N 97 53 E
Lamar, Ark. **13** 35 27N 93 23W
Lamar, Colo. **16** 38 5N 102 37W
Lamar, Mo. **32** 37 30N 94 16W
Lamar, Nebr. **34** 40 34N 101 59W
Lamar, Okla. **43** 35 6N 96 8W
Lamar, S.C. **46** 34 10N 80 4W
Lamar County ◇, Ala. **10** 33 45N 88 7W
Lamar County ◇, Ga. **18** 33 5N 84 10W
Lamar County ◇, Miss. **31** 31 9N 89 25W
Lamar County ◇, Tex. **51** 33 40N 95 33W
Lamarque **78** 39 24 S 65 40W
Lamas **72** 6 28 S 76 31W
Lamb County ◇ **50** 34 0N 102 15W
Lambaréné **122** 0 41 S 10 12 E
Lambasa **128** 16 30 S 179 10 E
Lambay I. **85** 53 30N 6 0W
Lambayeque □ **72** 6 45 S 80 0W
Lambert, Miss. **31** 34 12N 90 17W
Lambert, Mont. **33** 47 41N 104 37W
Lambert Glacier **5** 71 0 S 70 0 E
Lamberton **30** 44 14N 95 16W
Lambertville, Mich. **29** 41 46N 83 35W
Lambertville, N.J. **37** 40 22N 74 57W
Lambi Kyun **112** 10 50N 98 20 E
Lame **120** 45 35N 106 40W
Lame Deer **33** 45 37N 106 40W
Lamego **91** 41 5N 7 52W
Lamèque **61** 47 45N 64 38W
Lamesa **50** 32 44N 101 58W
Lamía **95** 38 55N 22 26 E
Lamine → **32** 38 59N 92 51W
Lamison **10** 32 7N 87 34W
Lammermuir Hills **84** 55 50N 2 40W
Lamoille → **36** 44 38N 73 13W
Lamoille County ◇ **36** 44 40N 72 40W
Lamon Bay **111** 14 30N 122 20 E
Lamona **53** 47 22N 118 29W
Lamoni **23** 40 37N 93 56W
Lamont, Canada **62** 53 46N 112 50W
Lamont, Calif. **15** 35 15N 118 55W
Lamont, Fla. **17** 30 23N 83 49W
Lamont, Kans. **24** 38 7N 96 2W
Lamont, Miss. **31** 33 32N 91 5W
Lamont, Okla. **43** 36 42N 97 30W
Lamont, Wash. **53** 47 12N 117 54W
Lamont, Wyo. **56** 42 13N 107 29W
Lampa **72** 15 22 S 70 22W
Lampang **112** 18 16N 99 32 E
Lampasas **51** 31 4N 98 11W
Lampasas → **51** 30 59N 97 24W
Lampasas County ◇ **51** 31 5N 98 10W
Lampazos de Naranjo **64** 27 2N 100 32W
Lampedusa **94** 35 36N 12 40 E
Lampeter **83** 52 6N 4 6W
Lampman **63** 49 25N 102 50W
Lamprey **63** 58 33N 94 8W
Lampung □ **110** 5 30 S 104 30 E
Lamu **122** 2 16 S 40 55 E
Lamud **72** 6 10 S 77 57W
Lamut, Tg. **110** 3 50 S 105 58 E
Lamy **38** 35 29N 105 53W
Lan Xian **114** 38 15N 111 35 E
Lan Yu **115** 22 5N 121 35 E
Lanagan **32** 36 37N 94 27W
Lanai **19** 20 50N 156 55W
Lanai City **19** 20 50N 156 55W
Lanaihale **19** 20 49N 156 53W
Lanak La **108** 34 27N 79 32 E
Lanak'o Shank'ou = Lanak La **108** 34 27N 79 32 E
Lanao, L. **111** 7 52N 124 15 E
Lanark, U.K. **84** 55 40N 3 48W
Lanark, U.S.A. **21** 42 6N 89 50W
Lanark Village **17** 29 53N 84 36W
Lancashire □ **82** 53 40N 2 30W
Lancaster, U.K. **82** 54 3N 2 48W
Lancaster, Calif. **15** 34 42N 118 8W
Lancaster, Kans. **24** 39 34N 95 18W
Lancaster, Ky. **49** 37 37N 84 35W
Lancaster, Minn. **30** 48 52N 96 48W
Lancaster, Mo. **32** 40 31N 92 32W
Lancaster, N.H. **36** 44 29N 71 34W
Lancaster, N.Y. **39** 42 54N 78 40W
Lancaster, Ohio **42** 39 43N 82 36W
Lancaster, Pa. **45** 40 2N 76 19W
Lancaster, S.C. **46** 34 43N 80 46W
Lancaster, Tex. **51** 32 35N 96 45W
Lancaster, Va. **54** 37 46N 76 28W
Lancaster, Wis. **55** 42 51N 90 43W
Lancaster County ◇, Nebr. **34** 40 45N 96 45W
Lancaster County ◇, Pa. **45** 40 0N 76 19W
Lancaster County ◇, S.C. **46** 34 40N 80 40W
Lancaster County ◇, Va. **54** 37 45N 76 30W
Lancaster Sd. **4** 74 13N 84 0W
Lance Creek **56** 43 2N 104 39W
Lancer **63** 50 48N 108 53W
Lanchow = Lanzhou **114** 36 1N 103 52 E
Lanciano **94** 42 15N 14 22 E
Lanco **78** 39 24 S 72 46W
Lancones **72** 4 30 S 80 30W
Land Between The Lakes **48** 36 25N 88 0W
Land Between the Lakes Rec. Area **48** 36 55N 88 5W
Landa **41** 48 54N 100 55W
Lándana **122** 5 11 S 12 5 E
Landeck **88** 47 9N 10 34 E
Landen **87** 50 45N 5 5 E
Lander **56** 42 50N 108 44W
Lander County ◇ **35** 40 0N 117 0W
Landes □ **90** 43 57N 0 48W
Landes, Les **90** 44 20N 1 0W
Landi Kotal **108** 34 7N 71 6 E
Landis **40** 35 33N 80 37W
Landisburg **45** 40 21N 77 19W
Lando **46** 34 46N 81 1W
Landrum **46** 35 11N 82 11W
Land's End **83** 50 4N 5 43W
Landshut **88** 48 31N 12 10 E
Landskrona **97** 55 53N 12 50 E
Lane, Kans. **24** 38 26N 95 5W
Lane, S.C. **46** 33 32N 79 53W
Lane, S. Dak. **47** 44 4N 98 26W
Lane County ◇, Kans. **24** 38 30N 100 30W
Lane County ◇, Oreg. **44** 44 0N 123 0W
Lanesboro, Iowa **23** 42 11N 94 41W
Lanesboro, Mass. **28** 42 31N 73 14W
Lanesboro, Minn. **30** 43 43N 91 58W
Lanett **10** 32 52N 85 12W
Lang Bay **62** 49 45N 124 21W
Lang Shan **114** 41 0N 106 30 E
Lang Son **112** 21 52N 106 42 E
La'nga Co **109** 30 45N 81 15 E
Langara I. **62** 54 14N 133 1W
Langatabbetje **71** 4 59N 54 28W
Langdon, Kans. **24** 37 51N 98 19W
Langdon, N. Dak. **41** 48 45N 98 22W
Langenburg **63** 50 51N 101 43W
Langford **47** 45 36N 97 50W
Langholm **84** 55 9N 2 59W
Langjökull **96** 64 39N 20 12W
Langkawi, P. **112** 6 25N 99 45 E
Langkon **110** 6 30N 116 40 E
Langlade **61** 46 50N 56 20W
Langlade County ◇ **55** 45 15N 89 10W
Langley, Ark. **13** 34 19N 93 51W
Langley, Ky. **49** 37 32N 82 47W
Langley, Okla. **43** 36 28N 95 3W
Langlois **44** 42 56N 124 27W
Langøya **96** 68 45N 14 50 E
Langres **90** 47 52N 5 20 E
Langres, Plateau de **90** 47 45N 5 3 E
Langsa **110** 4 30N 97 57 E
Langston **43** 35 59N 97 18W
Langtry **50** 29 49N 101 34W
Languedoc **90** 43 58N 4 0 E
L'Anguille → **13** 34 44N 90 40W
Langxiangzhen **114** 39 43N 116 8 E
Langzhong **115** 31 38N 105 58 E
Lanier County ◇ **18** 31 0N 83 5W
Lanigan **63** 51 51N 105 2W
Lankao **115** 34 48N 114 50 E
Lankin **41** 48 19N 97 55W
Lansdale **45** 40 14N 75 17W
Lansdowne **27** 39 15N 76 40W
Lansdowne House **60** 52 14N 87 53W
L'Anse **29** 46 45N 88 27W
L'Anse Indian Reservation **29** 46 45N 88 20W
Lansford, N. Dak. **41** 48 38N 101 23W
Lansford, Pa. **45** 40 50N 75 53W
Lansing, Ill. **21** 41 34N 87 33W
Lansing, Iowa **23** 43 22N 91 13W
Lansing, Kans. **24** 39 15N 94 54W
Lansing, Mich. **29** 42 44N 84 33W
Lantana **17** 26 35N 80 3W
Lanus **76** 34 44 S 58 27W
Lanxi **115** 29 13N 119 28 E
Lanzarote **120** 29 0N 13 40W
Lanzhou **114** 36 1N 103 52 E
Lao Cai **112** 22 30N 103 57 E
Laoag **111** 18 7N 120 34 E
Laoang **111** 12 32N 125 8 E
Laoha He → **114** 43 25N 120 35 E
Laois □ **85** 53 0N 7 20W
Laon **90** 49 33N 3 35 E
Laona **55** 45 34N 88 40W
Laos ■ **112** 17 45N 105 0 E
Lapa **77** 25 46 S 49 44W
Laparan **111** 6 0N 120 0 E
Lapeer **29** 43 3N 83 19W
Lapeer County ◇ **29** 43 5N 83 15W
Lapel **22** 40 4N 85 51W
Lapi □ **96** 67 0N 27 0 E
Lapland = Lappland **96** 68 7N 24 0 E
Laporte, Colo. **16** 40 38N 105 8W
Laporte, Minn. **30** 47 13N 94 45W
Laporte, Pa. **45** 41 25N 76 30W
Lappans **27** 39 33N 77 43W
Lappland **96** 68 7N 24 0 E
Laprida **76** 37 34 S 60 45W
Laptev Sea **101** 76 0N 125 0 E
Lapwai **20** 46 24N 116 48W
Lār **107** 27 40N 54 14 E
Lara □ **70** 10 10N 69 50W
Larache **120** 35 10N 6 5W
Laramie **56** 41 19N 105 35W
Laramie → **56** 42 13N 104 33W
Laramie County ◇ **56** 41 15N 104 40W
Laramie Mts. **56** 42 0N 105 30W
Laramie Pk. **56** 42 17N 105 27W
Laranjeiras **74** 10 48 S 37 10W
Laranjeiras do Sul **77** 25 23 S 52 23W
Larantuka **111** 8 21 S 122 55 E
Larap **111** 14 18N 122 39 E
Larat **111** 7 0 S 132 0 E
Larchwood **23** 43 27N 96 26W
Larder Lake **60** 48 5N 79 40W
Laredo, Mo. **32** 40 2N 93 27W
Laredo, Tex. **50** 27 30N 99 30W
Laredo Sd. **62** 52 30N 128 53W
Lares **57** 18 18N 66 53W
Larga, L. **51** 27 30N 97 25W
Largo **17** 27 55N 82 47W
Largo Key **17** 25 15N 80 15W
Largs **84** 55 48N 4 51W
Lariang **111** 1 26 S 119 17 E
Larimer County ◇ **16** 40 40N 105 20W
Larimore **41** 47 54N 97 38W
Lárisa **95** 39 49N 22 28 E
Lark, N. Dak. **41** 46 27N 101 24W
Lark, Tex. **50** 35 12N 101 14W
Larkspur **16** 39 14N 104 53W
Larnaca **106** 35 0N 33 35 E
Larne **85** 54 52N 5 50W
Larned **24** 38 11N 99 6W
Larose **25** 29 34N 90 23W
Larrabee **23** 42 52N 95 33W
Larrimah **126** 15 35 S 133 12 E
Larsen Bay **11** 57 32N 153 59W
Larsen Ice Shelf **5** 67 0 S 62 0W
Larson **41** 48 53N 102 52W
Larue **42** 40 35N 83 23W
Larue County ◇ **49** 37 35N 85 40W
Larvik **97** 59 4N 10 0 E
Laryak **100** 61 15N 80 0 E
Las Animas **16** 38 4N 103 13W
Las Animas County ◇ **16** 37 15N 104 0W
Las Anod **105** 8 26N 47 19 E
Las Brenãs **76** 27 5 S 61 7W
Las Cascadas **57** 9 5N 79 41W
Las Coloradas **78** 39 34 S 70 36W
Las Cruces **38** 32 19N 106 47W
Las Flores **76** 36 10 S 59 7W
Las Heras **76** 32 51 S 68 49W
Las Horquetas **78** 48 14 S 71 11W
Las Khoreh **105** 11 10N 48 20 E
Las Lajas **78** 38 30 S 70 25W
Las Lomas **72** 4 40 S 80 10W
Las Lomitas **76** 24 43 S 60 35W
Las Marias **57** 18 15N 66 59W
Las Mercedes **70** 9 7N 66 24W
Las Nutrias **38** 34 28N 106 46W
Las Palmas, Argentina **76** 27 8 S 58 45W
Las Palmas, Canary Is. **120** 28 7N 15 26W
Las Palmas □ **120** 28 10N 15 28W
Las Piedras, Puerto Rico **57** 18 11N 65 52W
Las Piedras, Uruguay **77** 34 44 S 56 14W
Las Pipinas **76** 35 30 S 57 19W
Las Plumas **78** 43 40 S 67 15W
Las Rosas **76** 32 30 S 61 35W
Las Tablas **66** 7 49N 80 14W
Las Termas **76** 27 29 S 64 52W

Las Tunas, Pta. Leona

Las Tunas, Pta. 57 18 30N 66 38W
Las Varillas 76 31 50S 62 50W
Las Vegas, N. Mex. 38 35 36N 105 13W
Las Vegas, Nev. 35 36 10N 115 9W
Lascano 77 33 35S 54 12W
Lashburn 63 53 10N 109 40W
Lashio 109 22 56N 97 45E
Lassance 75 17 54S 44 34W
Lassen County ◇ 14 40 45N 120 30W
Lassen National Forest 14 40 30N 121 15W
Lassen Peak 14 40 29N 121 30W
Lassen Volcanic National Park 14 40 30N 121 20W
Last Chance 16 39 44N 103 36W
Last Mountain L. 63 51 5N 105 14W
Lastoursville 122 0 55S 12 38E
Lastovo 94 42 46N 16 55E
Lastrup 30 46 2N 94 4W
Latacunga 70 0 50S 78 35W
Latah County ◇ 20 46 45N 116 50W
Latakia = Al Lādhiqīyah 106 35 30N 35 45E
Latchford 60 47 20N 79 50W
Latham, Ill. 21 39 58N 89 10W
Latham, Kans. 24 37 32N 96 38W
Lathrop, Calif. 14 37 49N 121 16W
Lathrop, Mo. 32 39 33N 94 20W
Lathrop Wells 35 36 39N 116 24W
Latimer, Iowa 23 42 46N 93 22W
Latimer, Kans. 24 38 44N 96 51W
Latimer County ◇ 43 34 50N 95 10W
Latina 94 41 26N 12 53E
Latium = Lazio □ 94 42 10N 12 30E
Laton 15 36 26N 119 41W
Latouche Treville, C. 126 18 27S 121 49E
Latrobe 45 40 19N 79 23W
Latrun 104 31 50N 34 58E
Latta 46 34 21N 79 26W
Latvian S.S.R. □ 98 56 50N 24 0E
Lau 128 17 0S 178 30W
Lauca → 72 19 9S 68 10W
Lauchhammer 88 51 35N 13 48E
Lauderdale 31 32 31N 88 31W
Lauderdale County ◇, Ala. 10 34 56N 87 46W
Lauderdale County ◇, Miss. 31 32 22N 88 42W
Lauderdale County ◇, Tenn. 48 35 45N 89 23W
Lauenburg 88 53 23N 10 33E
Laugarbakki 96 65 20N 20 55W
Laughing Fish Pt. 29 46 32N 87 1W
Laughlin Pk. 38 36 40N 104 10W
Launceston, Australia 127 41 24S 147 8E
Launceston, U.K. 83 50 38N 4 21W
Laune → 85 52 5N 9 40W
Launglon Bok 112 13 50N 97 54E
Laura, Australia 127 15 32S 144 32E
Laura, U.S.A. 42 39 59N 84 22W
Laurel, Del. 27 38 33N 75 34W
Laurel, Fla. 17 27 8N 82 27W
Laurel, Iowa 23 41 53N 92 55W
Laurel, Md. 27 39 6N 76 51W
Laurel, Miss. 31 31 41N 89 8W
Laurel, Mont. 33 45 40N 108 46W
Laurel, Nebr. 34 42 26N 97 6W
Laurel, Wash. 53 45 57N 121 23W
Laurel Bay 46 32 27N 80 47W
Laurel County ◇ 49 37 5N 84 10W
Laurel Hill 40 34 49N 79 33W
Laurel River L. 49 36 57N 84 10W
Laureldale, N.J. 37 39 30N 74 41W
Laureldale, Pa. 45 40 23N 75 56W
Laurelville 42 39 28N 82 44W
Laurencekirk 84 56 50N 2 30W
Laurens, Iowa 23 42 51N 94 52W
Laurens, S.C. 46 34 30N 82 1W
Laurens County ◇, Ga. 18 32 30N 83 0W
Laurens County ◇, S.C. 46 34 30N 82 0W
Laurentian Plat. 61 52 0N 70 0W
Laurentides, Parc Prov. des 61 47 45N 71 15W
Laurie L. 63 56 35N 101 57W
Laurinburg 40 34 47N 79 28W
Laurium 29 47 14N 88 27W
Lausanne 88 46 32N 6 38E
Laut 110 4 45N 108 0E
Laut Ketil, Kepulauan 110 4 45S 115 40E
Lautaro 78 38 31S 72 27W
Lautoka 128 17 37S 177 27E
Lauzon 61 46 48N 71 10W
Lava Beds National Monument 14 41 40N 121 30W
Lava Hot Springs 20 42 37N 112 1W
Lavaca 13 35 20N 94 10W
Lavaca → 51 28 41N 96 35W
Lavaca County ◇ 51 29 27N 96 57W
Laval 90 48 4N 0 48W
Lavalle 76 28 15S 65 15W
Lavallette 37 39 58N 74 4W
Laverendrye Prov. Park 60 46 15N 17 15W
Laverne 43 36 43N 99 54W
Laverton 126 28 44S 122 29E
Lavi 104 32 47N 35 25E
Lavic L. 15 34 40N 116 21W
Lavina 33 46 18N 108 56W
Lavon L. 51 33 2N 96 28W
Lavonia 18 34 26N 83 6W
Lavras 75 21 20S 45 0W
Lavrentiya 101 65 35N 171 0W
Lávrion 95 37 40N 24 4E
Lawas 110 4 55N 115 25E
Lawele 111 5 16S 123 3E
Lawen 44 43 27N 118 48W
Lawler 23 43 4N 92 9W
Lawn 51 32 8N 99 45W
Lawndale 40 35 25N 81 34W
Lawng Pit 109 25 30N 97 25E
Lawrence, Ind. 22 39 50N 86 2W
Lawrence, Kans. 24 38 58N 95 14W
Lawrence, Mass. 28 42 43N 71 10W
Lawrence, Mich. 29 42 13N 86 3W
Lawrence, Nebr. 34 40 18N 98 16W
Lawrence County ◇, Ala. 10 34 29N 87 18W
Lawrence County ◇, Ark. 13 36 0N 91 0W
Lawrence County ◇, Ill. 21 38 45N 87 45W
Lawrence County ◇, Ind. 22 38 50N 86 30W
Lawrence County ◇, Ky. 49 38 5N 82 45W
Lawrence County ◇, Miss. 31 31 33N 90 7W
Lawrence County ◇, Mo. 32 37 10N 93 50W
Lawrence County ◇, Ohio 42 38 32N 82 41W
Lawrence County ◇, Pa. 45 41 0N 80 15W
Lawrence County ◇, S. Dak. 47 44 23N 103 44W
Lawrence County ◇, Tenn. 48 35 14N 87 20W
Lawrenceburg, Ind. 22 39 6N 84 52W
Lawrenceburg, Ky. 49 38 2N 84 54W
Lawrenceburg, Tenn. 48 35 14N 87 20W
Lawrenceville, Ga. 18 33 57N 83 59W
Lawrenceville, Ill. 21 38 44N 87 41W
Lawrenceville, N.J. 37 40 18N 74 44W
Lawrenceville, Pa. 45 41 59N 77 8W
Lawrenceville, Va. 54 36 46N 77 51W
Lawson 32 39 26N 94 12W
Lawtey 17 30 3N 82 5W
Lawton, Mich. 29 42 10N 85 50W
Lawton, N. Dak. 41 48 18N 98 22W
Lawton, Okla. 43 34 37N 98 25W
Lawu 111 7 40S 111 13E
Laxford, L. 84 58 25N 5 10W
Lay 16 40 32N 107 53W
Laylá 106 22 10N 46 40E
Laysan I., Pac. Oc. 125 25 30N 167 0W
Laysan I., U.S.A. 19 25 50N 171 50W
Layton, Fla. 17 24 50N 80 47W
Layton, N.J. 37 41 13N 74 50W
Layton, Utah 52 41 4N 111 58W
Laytonsville 27 39 13N 77 9W
Laytonville 14 39 41N 123 29W
Lazear 16 38 47N 107 47W
Lazio □ 94 42 10N 12 30E
Lazo 116 43 25N 133 55E
Le Center 30 44 23N 93 44W
Le Claire 23 41 36N 90 21W
Le Flore County ◇ 43 35 0N 94 45W
Le Grand, Calif. 14 37 14N 120 15W
Le Grand, Iowa 23 42 0N 92 47W
Le Loup 24 38 42N 95 10W
Le Mars 23 42 47N 96 10W
Le Moyen 25 30 48N 92 4W
Le Roy, Ill. 21 40 21N 88 46W
Le Roy, Kans. 24 38 5N 95 38W
Le Roy, Mich. 29 44 2N 85 27W
Le Roy, Minn. 30 43 31N 92 30W
Le Roy, N.Y. 39 42 58N 78 0W
Le Roy, Pa. 45 41 41N 76 43W
Le Sueur 30 44 28N 93 55W
Le Sueur County ◇ 30 44 20N 93 45W
Lea → 83 51 30N 0 10W
Lea County ◇ 38 32 50N 103 30W
Leachville 13 35 56N 90 16W
Lead 47 44 21N 103 46W
Lead Hill, Ark. 13 36 25N 92 55W
Lead Hill, Mo. 32 37 6N 92 38W
Leadbetter Pt. 53 46 39N 124 3W
Leader 63 50 50N 109 30W
Leadhills 84 55 25N 3 47W
Leadore 20 44 41N 113 21W
Leadpoint 53 48 55N 117 35W
Leadville 16 39 15N 106 18W
Leadwood 32 37 52N 90 36W
Leaf 31 31 2N 88 48W
Leaf → 31 30 59N 88 44W
League City 51 29 31N 95 6W
Leake County ◇ 31 32 42N 89 38W
Leakesville 31 31 9N 88 33W
Leakey 51 29 44N 99 46W
Leamington, Canada 60 42 3N 82 36W
Leamington, U.K. 83 52 18N 1 32W
Leamington, U.S.A. 52 39 32N 112 17W
Leandro Norte Alem 77 27 34S 55 15W
Learmonth 126 22 13S 114 10E
Leary 18 31 29N 84 31W
Leasburg, Mo. 32 38 5N 91 18W
Leasburg, N.C. 40 36 24N 79 10W
Leask 63 53 5N 106 45W
Leatherwood 49 37 2N 83 11W
Leavenworth, Ind. 22 38 12N 86 21W
Leavenworth, Kans. 24 39 19N 94 55W
Leavenworth, Wash. 53 47 36N 120 40W
Leavenworth County ◇ 24 39 15N 95 0W
Leavittsburg 42 41 14N 80 53W
Leawood 24 38 58N 94 37W
Lebam 53 46 34N 123 33W
Lebanon, Conn. 28 41 38N 72 13W
Lebanon, Ind. 22 40 3N 86 28W
Lebanon, Kans. 24 39 49N 98 33W
Lebanon, Ky. 49 37 34N 85 15W
Lebanon, Mo. 32 37 41N 92 40W
Lebanon, N.H. 36 43 39N 72 15W
Lebanon, Nebr. 34 40 3N 100 17W
Lebanon, Ohio 42 39 26N 84 13W
Lebanon, Okla. 43 33 59N 96 55W
Lebanon, Oreg. 44 44 32N 122 55W
Lebanon, Pa. 45 40 20N 76 26W
Lebanon, S. Dak. 47 45 4N 99 46W
Lebanon, Tenn. 48 36 12N 86 18W
Lebanon, Va. 54 36 54N 82 5W
Lebanon ■ 106 34 0N 36 0E
Lebanon County ◇ 45 40 20N 76 25W
Lebanon Junction 49 37 50N 85 44W
Lebanon State Forest 37 39 53N 74 30W
Lebec 15 34 50N 118 52W
Lebo 24 38 25N 95 51W
Lebrija 91 36 53N 6 5W
Lebu 76 37 40S 73 47W
Lecce 95 40 20N 18 10E
Lecco 94 45 50N 9 27E
Lechang 115 25 10N 113 20E
Lecompte 25 31 6N 92 24W
Łęczyca 89 52 5N 19 15E
Ledbury 83 52 3N 2 25W
Ledong 115 18 41N 109 5E
Leduc 62 53 15N 113 30W
Ledyard 23 43 25N 94 10W
Lee, Fla. 17 30 25N 83 18W
Lee, Ill. 21 41 48N 88 56W
Lee, Maine 26 45 22N 68 17W
Lee, Mass. 28 42 19N 73 15W
Lee → 85 51 50N 8 30W
Lee City 49 37 44N 83 20W
Lee County ◇, Ala. 10 32 39N 85 23W
Lee County ◇, Ark. 13 34 46N 90 46W
Lee County ◇, Fla. 17 26 30N 81 45W
Lee County ◇, Ga. 18 31 45N 84 5W
Lee County ◇, Ill. 21 41 45N 89 20W
Lee County ◇, Iowa 23 40 40N 91 30W
Lee County ◇, Ky. 49 37 35N 83 45W
Lee County ◇, Miss. 31 34 16N 88 43W
Lee County ◇, N.C. 40 35 30N 79 10W
Lee County ◇, S.C. 46 34 10N 80 15W
Lee County ◇, Tex. 51 30 17N 96 58W
Lee County ◇, Va. 54 36 45N 83 5W
Lee Vining 14 37 58N 119 7W
Leech L. 30 47 10N 94 24W
Leech Lake Indian Reservation 30 47 20N 94 10W
Leedey 43 35 52N 99 21W
Leeds, U.K. 82 53 48N 1 34W
Leeds, Ala. 10 33 33N 86 33W
Leeds, Maine 26 44 18N 70 7W
Leeds, N. Dak. 41 48 17N 99 27W
Leeds, Utah 52 37 14N 113 22W
Leek 82 53 7N 2 2W
Leektown 37 39 38N 74 26W
Leelanau County ◇ 29 44 55N 85 50W
Leelanau L. 29 44 55N 85 43W
Lees Summit 32 38 55N 94 23W
Leesburg, Fla. 17 28 49N 81 53W
Leesburg, Ga. 18 31 44N 84 10W
Leesburg, N.J. 37 39 15N 74 59W
Leesburg, Ohio 42 39 21N 83 33W
Leesburg, Va. 54 39 7N 77 34W
Leesport 45 40 27N 75 58W
Leesville, La. 25 31 9N 93 16W
Leesville, Ohio 42 40 27N 81 13W
Leesville L. 54 37 5N 79 25W
Leeton 127 34 33S 146 23E
Leeuwarden 87 53 15N 5 48E
Leeuwin, C. 126 34 20S 115 9E
Leeville 25 29 15N 90 12W
Leeward Is., Atl. Oc. 67 16 30N 63 30W
Leeward Is., Pac. Oc. 125 16 0S 147 0W
Leflore 43 34 54N 94 59W
Leflore County ◇ 31 33 30N 90 20W
Lefors 50 35 26N 100 48W
Lefroy, L. 126 31 21S 121 40E
Legal 62 53 55N 113 35W
Legazpi 111 13 10N 123 45E
Leggett, Calif. 14 39 52N 123 43W
Leggett, Tex. 51 30 49N 94 52W
Leghorn = Livorno 94 43 32N 10 18E
Legnica 88 51 12N 16 10E
Leh 108 34 9N 77 35E
Lehi 52 40 24N 111 51W
Lehigh, Iowa 23 42 22N 94 3W
Lehigh, Kans. 24 38 22N 97 18W
Lehigh, Okla. 43 34 28N 96 13W
Lehigh → 45 40 41N 75 12W
Lehigh Acres 17 26 36N 81 39W
Lehigh County ◇ 45 40 40N 75 50W
Lehighton 45 40 50N 75 43W
Lehliu 95 44 29N 26 20E
Lehr 41 46 17N 99 21W
Lehua I. 19 22 1N 160 6W
Leicester, U.K. 83 52 39N 1 9W
Leicester, Mass. 28 42 15N 71 55W
Leicester, Vt. 36 43 50N 73 8W
Leicester □ 83 52 40N 1 10W
Leichhardt → 127 17 35S 139 48E
Leiden 87 52 9N 4 30E
Leidy, Mt. 56 43 44N 110 24W
Leie → 87 51 2N 3 45E
Leigh 34 41 42N 97 14W
Leighton, Ala. 10 34 42N 87 32W
Leighton, Iowa 23 41 20N 92 47W
Leine → 88 52 20N 9 50E
Leinster □ 85 53 0N 7 10W
Leinster, Mt. 85 52 38N 6 47W
Leipsic, Del. 27 39 14N 75 31W
Leipsic, Ohio 42 41 6N 83 59W
Leipzig 88 51 20N 12 23E
Leiria 91 39 46N 8 53W
Leitchfield 48 37 29N 86 18W
Leitersburg 27 39 42N 77 37W
Leith, U.K. 84 55 59N 3 10W
Leith, U.S.A. 41 46 22N 101 38W
Leith Hill 83 51 10N 0 23W
Leitrim 85 54 0N 8 5W
Leitrim □ 85 54 8N 8 0W
Leiyang 115 26 27N 112 45E
Leizhou Bandao 115 21 0N 110 0E
Leizhou Wan 115 20 50N 110 20E
Lek → 87 52 0N 6 0E
Leksula 111 3 46S 126 31E
Lela 50 35 14N 100 21W
Leland, Ill. 21 41 37N 88 48W
Leland, Iowa 23 43 20N 93 38W
Leland, Mich. 29 45 1N 85 45W
Leland, Miss. 31 33 24N 90 54W
Leland, Oreg. 44 42 38N 123 27W
Leland, Wash. 53 47 53N 122 53W
Leland Lakes 63 60 0N 110 59W
Leleiwi Pt. 19 19 44N 155 0W
Leleque 78 42 28S 71 0W
Lelia Lake 50 34 54N 100 46W
Lelystad 87 52 30N 5 25E
Léman, Lac 88 46 26N 6 30E
Lemay 32 38 32N 90 16W
Lemery 111 13 51N 120 56E
Lemeta 11 64 52N 147 44W
Lemhi 20 44 52N 113 38W
Lemhi → 20 45 12N 113 53W
Lemhi County ◇ 20 45 0N 114 0W
Lemhi Range 20 44 0N 113 0W
Lemington 36 44 51N 71 36W
Lemitar 38 34 10N 106 55W
Lemmer 87 52 51N 5 43E
Lemmon 47 45 57N 102 10W
Lemon Grove 15 32 45N 117 2W
Lemoore 15 36 18N 119 46W
Lemoyne 34 41 17N 101 49W
Lempster 36 43 15N 72 12W
Lemvig 97 56 33N 8 20E
Lena, Ill. 21 42 23N 89 49W
Lena, Miss. 31 32 36N 89 36W
Lena → 101 72 52N 126 40E
Lena, Mt. 52 40 50N 109 20W
Lenapah 43 36 51N 95 38W
Lenawee County ◇ 29 41 50N 84 5W
Lençóis 75 12 35S 41 24W
Lengau de Vaca, Pta. 76 30 14S 71 38W
Lenggong 112 5 6N 100 58E
Leninabad 100 40 17N 69 37E
Leninakan 99 40 47N 43 50E
Leningrad 98 59 55N 30 20E
Leningradskaya 5 69 50S 160 0E
Leninogorsk 100 50 20N 83 30E
Leninsk 99 48 40N 45 15E
Leninsk-Kuznetskiy 100 54 44N 86 10E
Leninskoye 101 47 56N 132 38E
Lenkoran 99 39 45N 48 50E
Lenmalu 111 1 45S 130 15E
Lennep 33 46 25N 110 33W
Lennox 47 43 21N 96 53W
Lennox, I. 78 55 18S 66 50W
Lenoir 40 35 55N 81 32W
Lenoir City 49 35 48N 84 16W
Lenoir County ◇ 40 35 10N 77 40W
Lenora 24 39 37N 100 0W
Lenore 20 46 31N 116 33W
Lenore L. 63 52 30N 104 59W
Lenox, Ga. 18 31 16N 83 28W
Lenox, Iowa 23 40 53N 94 34W
Lenox, Mass. 28 42 22N 73 17W
Lenox, Mo. 32 37 39N 91 46W
Lens 90 50 26N 2 50E
Lensk 101 60 48N 114 55E
Lentini 94 37 18N 15 0E
Lenwood 15 34 53N 117 7W
Leoben 88 47 22N 15 5E
Leola, Ark. 13 34 10N 92 35W
Leola, S. Dak. 47 45 43N 98 56W
Leoma 48 35 10N 87 21W
Leominster, U.K. 83 52 15N 2 43W
Leominster, U.S.A. 28 42 32N 71 46W
León, Mexico 64 21 7N 101 30W
León, Nic. 66 12 20N 86 51W
León, Spain 91 42 38N 5 34W
Leon, Iowa 23 40 44N 93 45W
Leon, Kans. 24 37 42N 96 46W
Leon, Okla. 43 33 53N 97 26W
León □ 91 42 40N 5 55W
Leon → 51 31 14N 97 28W
León, Montañas de 91 42 30N 6 18W
Leon County ◇, Fla. 17 30 30N 84 15W
Leon County ◇, Tex. 51 31 16N 95 59W
Leon Valley 51 29 28N 98 38W
Leona, Kans. 24 39 47N 95 19W
Leona, Tex. 51 31 9N 95 58W

Leona Lineville

Leona → 51 28 45N 99 11W
Leonard, Minn. 30 47 39N 95 16W
Leonard, N. Dak. 41 46 39N 97 15W
Leonard, Tex. 51 33 23N 96 15W
Leonardtown 27 38 17N 76 38W
Leonardville 24 39 22N 96 51W
Leonia 17 30 55N 86 1W
Leonora 126 28 49 S 121 19 E
Léopold II, Lac = Mai-Ndombe, L. 122 2 0 S 18 20 E
Leopoldina 75 21 28 S 42 40W
Leopoldo Bulhões 75 16 37 S 48 46W
Leopoldsburg 87 51 7N 5 13 E
Léopoldville = Kinshasa 122 4 20 S 15 15 E
Leoti 24 38 29N 101 21W
Leoville 63 53 39N 107 33W
Lepanto 13 35 37N 90 20W
Lepel 98 54 50N 28 40 E
Lepikha 101 64 45N 125 55 E
Leping 115 28 47N 117 7 E
Leraysville 45 41 51N 76 11W
Lerdo 64 25 32N 103 32W
Léré 121 9 39N 14 13 E
Lérida 91 41 37N 0 39 E
Lerna 21 39 25N 88 17W
Lerwick 84 60 10N 1 10W
Lesbos, I. = Lésvos 95 39 10N 26 20 E
Leshukonskoye 98 64 54N 45 46 E
Leskov I. 5 56 0 S 28 0W
Leskovac 95 43 0N 21 58 E
Leslie, Ark. 13 35 50N 92 34W
Leslie, Ga. 18 31 57N 84 5W
Leslie, Mich. 29 42 27N 84 26W
Leslie County ◇ 49 37 5N 83 25W
Lesopilnoye 116 46 44N 134 20 E
Lesotho ■ 123 29 40 S 28 0 E
Lesozavodsk 101 45 30N 133 29 E
Lesse → 87 50 15N 4 54 E
Lesser Antilles 67 15 0N 61 0W
Lesser Slave L. 62 55 30N 115 25W
Lessines 87 50 42N 3 50 E
Lessley 31 31 10N 91 25W
Lester 54 37 44N 81 18W
Lesterville 47 43 2N 97 35W
Lestock 63 51 19N 103 59W
Lésvos 95 39 10N 26 20 E
Leszno 88 51 50N 16 30 E
Letart Falls 42 38 54N 81 56W
Letcher 47 43 54N 98 8W
Letcher County ◇ 49 37 5N 82 55W
Letchworth 83 51 58N 0 13W
Letea, Ostrov 95 45 18N 29 20 E
Letha 20 43 54N 116 39W
Lethbridge 62 49 45N 112 45W
Lethem 71 3 20N 59 50W
Leti, Kepulauan 111 8 10 S 128 0 E
Leticia 70 4 9 S 70 0W
Leting 114 39 23N 118 55 E
Letohatchee 10 32 8N 86 29W
Letpadan 109 17 45N 95 45 E
Letpan 109 19 28N 94 10 E
Letsôk-aw Kyun 112 11 30N 98 25 E
Letterkenny 85 54 57N 7 42W
Letts 23 41 20N 91 14W
Leu 95 44 10N 24 0 E
Leucadia 15 33 4N 117 18W
Leupp Corner 12 35 5N 110 52W
Leuser, G. 110 3 46N 97 12 E
Leuven 87 50 52N 4 42 E
Leuze, Hainaut, Belgium 87 50 36N 3 37 E
Leuze, Namur, Belgium 87 50 33N 4 54 E
Levan 52 39 33N 111 52W
Levanger 96 63 45N 11 19 E
Levelland 50 33 35N 102 23W
Levelock 11 59 7N 156 51W
Leven 84 56 12N 3 0W
Leven, L. 84 56 12N 3 22W
Leveque C. 126 16 20 S 123 0 E
Levering 29 45 38N 84 47W
Levin 128 40 37 S 175 18 E
Lévis 61 46 48N 71 9W
Levis, L. 62 62 37N 117 58W
Levisa Fork → 49 38 8N 82 37W
Levittown, N.Y. 39 40 44N 73 31W
Levittown, Pa. 45 40 9N 74 51W
Levka 95 41 52N 26 15 E
Levkás 95 38 40N 20 43 E
Levkôsia = Nicosia 106 35 10N 33 25 E
Levski 95 43 21N 25 10 E
Levskigrad 95 42 38N 24 47 E
Levy County ◇ 17 29 15N 82 45W
Lewellen 34 41 20N 102 9W
Lewes, U.K. 83 50 53N 0 2 E
Lewes, U.S.A. 27 38 46N 75 9W
Lewis, U.K. 84 58 10N 6 40W
Lewis, Colo. 16 37 30N 108 40W
Lewis, Iowa 23 41 18N 95 5W
Lewis, Kans. 24 37 56N 99 15W
Lewis → 53 45 51N 122 48W
Lewis, Butt of 84 58 30N 6 12W
Lewis and Clark County ◇ 33 47 25N 112 35W
Lewis And Clark L. 34 42 51N 97 29W
Lewis and Clark National Forest 33 47 0N 111 0W
Lewis County ◇, Idaho 20 46 15N 116 29W
Lewis County ◇, Ky. 49 38 30N 83 25W
Lewis County ◇, Mo. 32 40 5N 91 40W
Lewis County ◇, N.Y. 39 43 45N 75 30W
Lewis County ◇, Tenn. 48 35 33N 87 33W
Lewis County ◇, W. Va. 54 39 2N 80 28W
Lewis County ◇, Wash. 53 46 30N 122 0W
Lewis L. 56 44 18N 110 38W
Lewis Range 33 48 5N 113 5W
Lewis Run 45 41 52N 78 40W
Lewis Smith, L. 10 33 56N 87 6W
Lewisburg, Ky. 48 36 59N 86 57W
Lewisburg, Ohio 42 39 51N 84 33W
Lewisburg, Pa. 45 40 58N 76 54W
Lewisburg, Tenn. 48 35 27N 86 48W
Lewisburg, W. Va. 54 37 48N 80 27W
Lewisport 48 37 56N 86 54W
Lewisporte 61 49 15N 55 3W
Lewiston, Calif. 14 40 43N 122 48W
Lewiston, Idaho 20 46 25N 117 1W
Lewiston, Maine 26 44 6N 70 13W
Lewiston, Mich. 29 44 53N 84 18W
Lewiston, Minn. 30 43 59N 91 52W
Lewiston, N.C. 40 36 7N 77 10W
Lewiston, N.Y. 39 43 11N 79 3W
Lewiston, Nebr. 34 40 14N 96 25W
Lewiston, Utah 52 41 59N 111 51W
Lewistown, Ill. 21 40 24N 90 9W
Lewistown, Md. 27 39 32N 77 25W
Lewistown, Mo. 32 40 5N 91 49W
Lewistown, Mont. 33 47 4N 109 26W
Lewistown, Pa. 45 40 36N 77 34W
Lewisville, Ark. 13 33 22N 93 35W
Lewisville, Ohio 42 39 46N 81 13W
Lewisville, Tex. 51 33 5N 97 0W
Lexington, Ala. 10 34 58N 87 22W
Lexington, Ga. 18 33 52N 83 7W
Lexington, Ill. 21 40 39N 88 47W
Lexington, Ky. 49 38 3N 84 30W
Lexington, Mich. 29 43 16N 82 32W
Lexington, Miss. 31 33 7N 90 3W
Lexington, Mo. 32 39 11N 93 52W
Lexington, N.C. 40 35 49N 80 15W
Lexington, Nebr. 34 40 47N 99 45W
Lexington, Ohio 42 40 41N 82 35W
Lexington, Okla. 43 35 1N 97 20W
Lexington, Oreg. 44 45 27N 119 42W
Lexington, S.C. 46 33 59N 81 11W
Lexington, Tenn. 48 35 39N 88 24W
Lexington, Tex. 51 30 25N 97 1W
Lexington, Va. 54 37 47N 79 27W
Lexington, Wash. 53 46 11N 122 54W
Lexington County ◇ 46 33 50N 81 10W
Lexington Park 27 38 16N 76 27W
Leyte 111 11 0N 125 0 E
Lhasa 113 29 25N 90 58 E
Lhazê 113 29 5N 87 38 E
Lhokseumawe 110 5 10N 97 10 E
Lhuntsi Dzong 109 27 39N 91 10 E
Li Shui → 115 29 24N 112 1 E
Li Xian, Gansu, China 115 34 10N 105 5 E
Li Xian, Hunan, China 115 29 36N 111 42 E
Lianga 111 8 38N 126 6 E
Liangdang 115 33 56N 106 18 E
Lianhua 115 27 3N 113 54 E
Lianjiang 115 26 12N 119 27 E
Lianping 115 24 26N 114 30 E
Lianshanguan 114 40 53N 123 43 E
Lianyungang 115 34 40N 119 11 E
Liao He → 114 41 0N 121 50 E
Liaocheng 114 36 28N 115 58 E
Liaodong Bandao 114 40 0N 122 30 E
Liaodong Wan 114 40 20N 121 10 E
Liaoning □ 114 42 0N 122 0 E
Liaoyang 114 41 15N 122 58 E
Liaoyuan 114 42 58N 125 2 E
Liaozhong 114 41 23N 122 50 E
Liard → 62 61 51N 121 18W
Líbano 70 4 55N 75 4W
Libau = Liepaja 98 56 30N 21 0 E
Libby 33 48 23N 115 33W
Libenge 122 3 40N 18 55 E
Liberal, Kans. 24 37 3N 100 55W
Liberal, Mo. 32 37 34N 94 31W
Liberdade 72 10 5 S 70 20W
Liberdade → 73 9 40 S 52 17W
Liberec 88 50 47N 15 7 E
Liberia 66 10 40N 85 30W
Liberia ■ 120 6 30N 9 30W
Libertad 70 8 20N 69 37W
Libertad, La 66 16 47N 90 7W
Libertad, La □ 72 8 0 S 78 30W
Liberty, Ill. 21 39 53N 91 6W
Liberty, Ind. 22 39 38N 84 56W
Liberty, Kans. 24 37 9N 95 36W
Liberty, Ky. 49 37 19N 84 56W
Liberty, Maine 26 44 24N 69 18W
Liberty, Miss. 31 31 10N 90 49W
Liberty, Mo. 32 39 15N 94 25W
Liberty, N.C. 40 35 51N 79 34W
Liberty, N.Y. 39 41 48N 74 45W
Liberty, Nebr. 34 40 5N 96 29W
Liberty, Pa. 45 41 34N 77 6W
Liberty, S.C. 46 34 48N 82 42W
Liberty, Tex. 51 30 3N 94 48W
Liberty, Wash. 53 47 14N 120 42W
Liberty Center 42 41 27N 84 1W
Liberty County ◇, Fla. 17 30 15N 85 0W
Liberty County ◇, Ga. 18 31 50N 81 30W
Liberty County ◇, Mont. 33 48 40N 111 0W
Liberty County ◇, Tex. 51 30 7N 94 52W
Liberty Hill, S.C. 46 34 29N 80 48W
Liberty Hill, Tex. 51 30 40N 97 55W
Liberty Lake 27 39 23N 76 54W
Libertytown, Md. 27 39 30N 77 15W
Libertytown, Md. 27 38 18N 75 18W
Libertyville, Ill. 21 42 18N 87 57W
Libertyville, Iowa 23 40 57N 92 3W
Libo 115 25 22N 107 53 E
Libobo, Tanjung 111 0 54 S 128 28 E
Libonda 123 14 28 S 23 12 E
Libourne 90 44 55N 0 14W
Libramont 87 49 55N 5 23 E
Libreville 122 0 25N 9 26 E
Libya ■ 121 27 0N 17 0 E
Libyan Desert 118 25 0N 25 0 E
Licantén 76 35 55 S 72 0W
Licata 94 37 6N 13 55 E
Lichfield 82 52 40N 1 50W
Lichtenburg 123 26 8 S 26 8 E
Lichuan 115 30 18N 108 57 E
Licking 32 37 30N 91 54W
Licking → 49 39 6N 84 30W
Licking County ◇ 42 40 3N 82 24W
Lida 35 37 28N 117 30W
Lidderdale 23 42 8N 94 47W
Lidgerwood 41 46 5N 97 9W
Lidköping 97 58 31N 13 14 E
Liebenthal 24 38 39N 99 19W
Liechtenstein ■ 88 47 8N 9 35 E
Liège 87 50 38N 5 35 E
Liège □ 87 50 32N 5 35 E
Liegnitz = Legnica 88 51 12N 16 10 E
Lienyünchiangshih = Lianyungang 115 34 40N 119 11 E
Lienz 88 46 50N 12 46 E
Liepaja 98 56 30N 21 0 E
Lier 87 51 7N 4 34 E
Liești 95 45 38N 27 34 E
Lièvre → 60 45 31N 75 26W
Liffey → 85 53 21N 6 20W
Lifford 85 54 50N 7 30W
Lifudzin 116 44 21N 134 58 E
Lighthouse Point 17 26 15N 80 7W
Lighthouse Pt. 17 29 54N 84 21W
Lightning → 56 43 11N 104 44W
Lignite 41 48 53N 102 34W
Ligon 49 37 22N 82 41W
Ligonier, Ind. 22 41 28N 85 35W
Ligonier, Pa. 45 40 15N 79 14W
Ligua, La 76 32 30 S 71 16W
Liguria □ 94 44 30N 9 0 E
Ligurian Sea 94 43 20N 9 0 E
Lihou Reefs and Cays 127 17 25 S 151 40 E
Lihue 19 21 59N 159 23W
Lijiang 113 26 55N 100 20 E
Likasi 122 10 55 S 26 48 E
Likati 122 3 20N 24 0 E
Likely 14 41 14N 120 30W
Lilbourn 32 36 36N 89 37W
Liling 115 27 42N 113 29 E
Lille 90 50 38N 3 3 E
Lille Bælt 97 55 20N 9 45 E
Lillehammer 97 61 8N 10 30 E
Lillesand 97 58 15N 8 23 E
Lilleshall 83 52 45N 2 22W
Lillestrøm 97 59 58N 11 5 E
Lillie 25 32 56N 92 39W
Lillington 40 35 24N 78 49W
Lillooet → 62 49 15N 121 57W
Lilly 45 40 26N 78 37W
Lilongwe 123 14 0 S 33 48 E
Liloy 111 8 4N 122 39 E
Lily 47 45 11N 97 41W
Lima, Indonesia 111 3 37 S 128 4 E
Lima, Peru 72 12 0 S 77 0W
Lima, Ill. 21 40 11N 91 23W
Lima, Mont. 33 44 38N 112 36W
Lima, N.Y. 39 42 55N 77 37W
Lima, Ohio 42 40 44N 84 6W
Lima, Okla. 43 35 10N 96 36W
Lima □ 72 12 3 S 77 3W
Lima, Punta 57 18 11N 65 42W
Limassol 106 34 42N 33 1 E
Limavady 85 55 3N 6 58W
Limavady □ 85 55 0N 6 55W
Limay → 78 39 0 S 68 0W
Limay Mahuida 76 37 10 S 66 45W
Limbang 110 4 42N 115 6 E
Limbe 122 4 1N 9 10 E
Limburg □, Belgium 87 51 2N 5 25 E
Limburg □, Neth. 87 51 20N 5 55 E
Lime 44 44 24N 117 19W
Lime Ridge 55 43 28N 90 9W
Lime Springs 23 43 27N 92 17W
Lime Village 11 61 21N 155 28W
Limeira 77 22 35 S 47 28W
Limerick, Ireland 85 52 40N 8 38W
Limerick, U.S.A. 26 43 41N 70 48W
Limerick □ 85 52 30N 8 50W
Limestone, Maine 26 46 55N 67 50W
Limestone, N.Y. 39 42 2N 78 38W
Limestone, Tenn. 49 36 14N 82 38W
Limestone → 63 56 31N 94 7W
Limestone, L. 50 31 25N 96 22W
Limestone County ◇, Ala. 10 34 48N 86 58W
Limestone County ◇, Tex. 51 31 39N 96 31W
Limfjorden 97 56 55N 9 0 E
Limia → 91 41 41N 8 50W
Limmen Bight 126 14 40 S 135 35 E
Límnos 95 39 50N 25 5 E
Limoeiro 74 7 52 S 35 27W
Limoeiro do Norte 74 5 5 S 38 0W
Limoges 90 45 50N 1 15 E
Limón, C. Rica 66 10 0N 83 2W
Limon, U.S.A. 16 39 16N 103 41W
Limon B. 57 9 22N 79 56W
Limousin 90 46 0N 1 0 E
Limpopo → 123 25 15 S 33 30 E
Limuru 122 1 2 S 36 35 E
Linares, Chile 76 35 50 S 71 40W
Linares, Colombia 70 1 23N 77 31W
Linares, Mexico 65 24 50N 99 40W
Linares, Spain 91 38 10N 3 40W
Linares □ 76 36 0 S 71 0W
Linch 56 43 37N 106 12W
Lincheng 114 37 25N 114 30 E
Linchuan 115 27 57N 116 15 E
Lincoln, Argentina 76 34 55 S 61 30W
Lincoln, N.Z. 128 43 38 S 172 30 E
Lincoln, U.K. 82 53 14N 0 32W
Lincoln, Ark. 13 35 57N 94 25W
Lincoln, Calif. 14 38 54N 121 17W
Lincoln, Del. 27 38 52N 75 25W
Lincoln, Ill. 21 40 9N 89 22W
Lincoln, Iowa 23 42 16N 92 42W
Lincoln, Kans. 24 39 3N 98 9W
Lincoln, Maine 26 45 22N 68 30W
Lincoln, Mich. 29 44 41N 83 25W
Lincoln, Mo. 32 38 23N 93 20W
Lincoln, Mont. 33 46 58N 112 41W
Lincoln, N.H. 36 44 3N 71 40W
Lincoln, N. Mex. 38 33 30N 105 23W
Lincoln, Nebr. 34 40 49N 96 41W
Lincoln, Wash. 53 47 50N 118 25W
Lincoln □ 82 53 14N 0 32W
Lincoln City 44 44 57N 124 1W
Lincoln County ◇, Ark. 13 33 56N 91 51W
Lincoln County ◇, Colo. 16 39 0N 103 20W
Lincoln County ◇, Ga. 18 33 45N 82 20W
Lincoln County ◇, Idaho 20 43 0N 114 0W
Lincoln County ◇, Kans. 24 39 0N 98 10W
Lincoln County ◇, Ky. 49 37 25N 84 40W
Lincoln County ◇, Maine 26 44 0N 69 30W
Lincoln County ◇, Minn. 30 44 25N 96 10W
Lincoln County ◇, Miss. 31 31 35N 90 26W
Lincoln County ◇, Mo. 32 39 0N 91 0W
Lincoln County ◇, Mont. 33 48 45N 115 30W
Lincoln County ◇, N.C. 40 35 30N 81 10W
Lincoln County ◇, N. Mex. 38 33 40N 105 30W
Lincoln County ◇, Nebr. 34 41 0N 101 0W
Lincoln County ◇, Nev. 35 37 20N 115 0W
Lincoln County ◇, Okla. 43 35 40N 96 50W
Lincoln County ◇, Oreg. 44 44 40N 123 50W
Lincoln County ◇, S. Dak. 47 43 21N 96 53W
Lincoln County ◇, Tenn. 48 35 9N 86 34W
Lincoln County ◇, W. Va. 54 38 14N 81 59W
Lincoln County ◇, Wash. 53 47 45N 118 30W
Lincoln County ◇, Wis. 55 45 20N 89 45W
Lincoln County ◇, Wyo. 56 42 0N 110 30W
Lincoln National Forest 38 32 45N 105 40W
Lincoln Parish ◇ 25 32 32N 92 38W
Lincoln Park, Colo. 16 38 25N 105 10W
Lincoln Park, Ga. 18 32 52N 84 20W
Lincoln Park, Mich. 29 42 15N 83 11W
Lincoln Sea 4 84 0N 55 0W
Lincoln Wolds 82 53 20N 0 5W
Lincolnton, Ga. 18 33 48N 82 29W
Lincolnton, N.C. 40 35 29N 81 16W
Lincolnville, Kans. 24 38 30N 96 58W
Lincolnville, Maine 26 44 17N 69 1W
Lind 53 46 58N 118 37W
Linda 14 39 8N 121 34W
Lindale, Ga. 18 34 11N 85 11W
Lindale, Tex. 51 32 31N 95 25W
Linden, Guyana 72 6 0N 58 10W
Linden, Ala. 10 32 18N 87 48W
Linden, Calif. 14 38 1N 121 5W
Linden, Ind. 22 40 11N 86 54W
Linden, Mich. 29 42 49N 83 47W
Linden, N.J. 37 40 38N 74 15W
Linden, Tenn. 48 35 37N 87 50W
Linden, Tex. 51 33 1N 94 22W
Linden, Wis. 55 42 55N 90 16W
Lindenhurst 39 40 41N 73 23W
Lindenwold 37 39 49N 74 59W
Lindi 122 9 58 S 39 38 E
Lindian 114 47 11N 124 52 E
Lindley 39 42 1N 77 8W
Lindon 16 39 44N 103 24W
Lindsay, Canada 60 44 22N 78 43W
Lindsay, Calif. 15 36 12N 119 5W
Lindsay, Nebr. 34 41 42N 97 42W
Lindsay, Okla. 43 34 50N 97 38W
Lindsborg 24 38 35N 97 40W
Lindy 34 42 44N 97 44W
Línea de la Concepción, La 91 36 15N 5 23W
Linesville 45 41 39N 80 26W
Lineville, Ala. 10 33 19N 85 45W
Lineville, Iowa 23 40 35N 93 32W

Linfen Lomié

Linfen 114 36 3N 111 30 E
Ling Xian 114 37 22N 116 30 E
Lingao 115 19 56N 109 42 E
Lingayen 111 16 1N 120 14 E
Lingayen G. 111 16 10N 120 15 E
Lingchuan 115 25 26N 110 21 E
Lingen 88 52 32N 7 21 E
Lingga 110 0 12 S 104 37 E
Lingga, Kepulauan 110 0 10 S 104 30 E
Lingle 56 42 8N 104 21W
Lingling 115 26 17N 111 37 E
Lingshan 115 22 25N 109 18 E
Lingshi 114 36 48N 111 48 E
Lingshui 115 18 27N 110 0 E
Lingtai 115 35 0N 107 40 E
Linguéré 120 15 25N 15 5W
Lingyuan 114 41 10N 119 15 E
Lingyun 115 25 2N 106 35 E
Linh Cam 112 18 31N 105 31 E
Linhai 115 28 50N 121 8 E
Linhares 75 19 25 S 40 4W
Linhe 114 40 48N 107 20 E
Linjiang 114 41 50N 127 0 E
Linköping 97 58 28N 15 36 E
Linkou 114 45 15N 130 18 E
Linlithgow 84 55 58N 3 38W
Linn, Kans. 24 39 41N 97 5W
Linn, Mo. 32 38 29N 91 51W
Linn, Tex. 50 26 34N 98 7W
Linn County ◇, Iowa 23 42 5N 91 35W
Linn County ◇, Kans. 24 38 15N 94 45W
Linn County ◇, Mo. 32 39 50N 93 10W
Linn County ◇, Oreg. 44 44 30N 122 20W
Linn Creek 32 38 2N 92 43W
Linn Grove 23 42 53N 95 15W
Linneus, Maine 26 46 3N 67 52W
Linneus, Mo. 32 39 53N 93 11W
Linnhe, L. 84 56 36N 5 25W
Lino Lakes 30 45 12N 93 6W
Linqing 114 36 50N 115 42 E
Lins 77 21 40 S 49 44W
Lintao 114 35 18N 103 52 E
Lintlaw 63 52 4N 103 14W
Linton, Canada 61 47 15N 72 16W
Linton, Ind. 22 39 2N 87 10W
Linton, N. Dak. 41 46 16N 100 14W
Linville 40 36 4N 81 52W
Linwood, Ala. 10 31 56N 85 52W
Linwood, Kans. 24 39 0N 95 2W
Linwood, N.J. 37 39 21N 74 34W
Linwood, Nebr. 34 41 25N 96 56W
Linwu 115 25 19N 112 31 E
Linxi 114 43 36N 118 2 E
Linxia 113 35 36N 103 10 E
Linyi 115 35 5N 118 21 E
Linz, Austria 88 48 18N 14 18 E
Linz, Germany 88 50 33N 7 18 E
Lion, G. du 90 43 0N 4 0 E
Lion's Head 60 44 58N 81 15W
Lípari, Is. 94 38 30N 14 50 E
Lipetsk 98 52 37N 39 35 E
Liping 115 26 15N 109 7 E
Lipovcy Manzovka 116 44 12N 132 26 E
Lippe → 88 51 39N 6 38 E
Lipscomb 50 36 14N 100 16W
Lipscomb County ◇ 50 36 15N 100 15W
Lira 122 2 17N 32 57 E
Liria 91 39 37N 0 35W
Lisala 122 2 12N 21 38 E
Lisboa 91 38 42N 9 10W
Lisbon = Lisboa 91 38 42N 9 10W
Lisbon, Ill. 21 41 29N 88 29W
Lisbon, Maine 26 44 2N 70 6W
Lisbon, Md. 27 39 20N 77 4W
Lisbon, N. Dak. 41 46 27N 97 41W
Lisbon, N.H. 36 44 13N 71 55W
Lisbon, N.Y. 39 44 44N 75 19W
Lisbon, Ohio 42 40 46N 80 46W
Lisbon Falls 26 44 0N 70 4W
Lisburn 85 54 30N 6 9W
Lisburne, C. 11 68 53N 166 13W
Liscannor, B. 85 52 57N 9 24W
Lisco 34 41 30N 102 37W
Liscomb 23 42 11N 93 0W
Lishi 114 37 31N 111 8 E
Lishui 115 28 28N 119 54 E
Lisianski I., Pac. Oc. 124 26 2N 174 0W
Lisianski I., U.S.A. 19 26 2N 174 0W
Lisieux 90 49 10N 0 12 E
Lismore, Australia 127 28 44 S 153 21 E
Lismore, Ireland 85 52 8N 7 58W
Lismore, U.S.A. 30 43 45N 95 57W
Lisse 87 52 16N 4 33 E
Lista, Norway 97 58 7N 6 39 E
Lista, Sweden 97 59 19N 16 16 E
Lister, Mt. 5 78 0 S 162 0 E
Listowel, Canada 60 43 44N 80 58W
Listowel, Ireland 85 52 27N 9 30W
Litang, China 115 23 12N 109 8 E
Litang, Malaysia 111 5 27N 118 31 E
Litani →, Lebanon 104 33 20N 35 14 E
Litani →, Surinam 104 3 40N 54 0W
Litchfield, Conn. 28 41 45N 73 11W
Litchfield, Ill. 21 39 11N 89 39W
Litchfield, Mich. 29 42 3N 84 46W
Litchfield, Minn. 30 45 8N 94 32W
Litchfield, Nebr. 34 41 10N 99 9W
Litchfield County ◇ 28 41 40N 73 15W
Litchfield Park 12 33 30N 112 22W
Litchville 41 46 39N 98 12W
Lithgow 127 33 25 S 150 8 E
Líthinon, Ákra 95 34 55N 24 44 E
Lithuanian S.S.R. □ 98 55 30N 24 0 E
Lititz 45 40 9N 76 18W
Litoměřice 88 50 33N 14 10 E
Little →, Ark. 13 33 45N 94 3W
Little →, Ky. 48 36 51N 87 58W
Little →, N.C. 40 35 18N 78 42W
Little →, Tex. 51 30 51N 96 41W
Little Abaco I. 66 26 50N 77 30W
Little Andaman I. 112 10 40N 92 15 E
Little Barrier I. 128 36 12 S 175 8 E
Little Belt Mts. 33 46 40N 110 45W
Little Bighorn → 33 45 44N 107 34W
Little Blue → 24 39 42N 96 41W
Little Cadotte → 62 56 41N 117 6W
Little Cayman, I. 66 19 41N 80 3W
Little Churchill → 63 57 30N 95 22W
Little Chute 55 44 17N 88 16W
Little City 43 34 5N 96 36W
Little Colorado → 12 36 12N 111 48W
Little Creek 27 39 10N 75 27W
Little Current 60 45 55N 82 0W
Little Current → 60 50 57N 84 36W
Little Diomede I. 11 65 45N 168 56W
Little Eagle 47 45 40N 100 49W
Little Egg Harbor → 37 39 35N 74 18W
Little Falls, Minn. 30 45 59N 94 22W
Little Falls, N.J. 37 40 53N 74 14W
Little Falls, N.Y. 39 43 3N 74 51W
Little Fork → 30 48 31N 93 35W
Little Grand Rapids 63 52 0N 95 29W
Little Haw Cr. → 17 29 23N 81 24W
Little Humboldt → 35 41 1N 117 43W
Little Inagua I. 67 21 40N 73 50W
Little Kanawha → 54 39 16N 81 34W
Little Lake 15 35 56N 117 55W
Little Lost → 20 43 46N 112 58W
Little Minch 84 57 35N 6 45W
Little Missouri →, Ark. 13 33 49N 92 54W
Little Missouri →, N. Dak. 41 47 36N 102 25W
Little Missouri Badlands 41 47 5N 103 45W
Little Ouse → 83 52 25N 0 50 E
Little Pee Dee → 46 33 42N 79 11W
Little Powder → 33 45 28N 105 20W
Little Red → 13 35 11N 91 27W
Little River, N.Z. 128 43 45 S 172 49 E
Little River, U.S.A. 24 38 24N 98 1W
Little River County ◇ 13 33 40N 94 8W
Little Rock, Ark. 13 34 45N 92 17W
Little Rock, S.C. 46 34 29N 79 24W
Little Rocky Mts. 33 47 55N 108 30W
Little Sable Pt. 29 43 38N 86 33W
Little Salt L. 52 37 55N 112 53W
Little Sioux → 23 41 48N 96 4W
Little Sitkin 11 51 57N 178 31 E
Little Smoky → 62 54 44N 117 11W
Little Snake → 16 40 27N 108 26W
Little Tallapoosa → 18 33 18N 85 34W
Little Tennessee →, N.C. 40 35 47N 84 15W
Little Tennessee →, Tenn. 49 35 47N 84 16W
Little Traverse B. 29 45 25N 85 10W
Little Valley 39 42 15N 78 48W
Little White → 47 43 40N 100 40W
Little Wood → 20 42 57N 114 21W
Little York, Ill. 21 41 1N 90 45W
Little York, Ind. 22 38 42N 85 54W
Littlefield, Ariz. 12 36 53N 113 56W
Littlefield, Tex. 50 33 55N 102 20W
Littlefork 30 48 24N 93 34W
Littlehampton 83 50 48N 0 32W
Littlerock, Calif. 15 34 31N 117 59W
Littlerock, Wash. 53 46 54N 123 1W
Littlestown 45 39 45N 77 5W
Littleton, Colo. 16 39 37N 105 0W
Littleton, Ill. 21 40 14N 90 37W
Littleton, Maine 26 46 14N 67 51W
Littleton, N.C. 40 36 26N 77 54W
Littleton, N.H. 36 44 18N 71 46W
Littleton, W. Va. 54 39 42N 80 32W
Littleton Common 28 42 33N 71 28W
Littleville 10 34 36N 87 41W
Liuba 115 33 38N 106 55 E
Liucheng 115 24 38N 109 14 E
Liukang Tenggaja 111 6 45 S 118 50 E
Liuwa Plain 123 14 20 S 22 30 E
Liuyang 115 28 10N 113 37 E
Liuzhou 115 24 22N 109 22 E
Live Oak, Calif. 14 39 17N 121 40W
Live Oak, Fla. 17 30 18N 82 59W
Live Oak County ◇ 51 28 20N 98 7W
Livengood 11 65 32N 148 33W
Livermore, Calif. 14 37 41N 121 47W
Livermore, Colo. 16 40 47N 105 13W
Livermore, Iowa 23 42 52N 94 11W
Livermore, Ky. 48 37 29N 87 8W
Livermore, Mt. 50 30 38N 104 11W
Livermore Falls 26 44 29N 70 11W
Liverpool, Australia 127 33 54 S 150 58 E
Liverpool, Canada 61 44 5N 64 41W
Liverpool, U.K. 82 53 25N 3 0W
Liverpool, U.S.A. 39 43 6N 76 13W
Liverpool Plains 127 31 15 S 150 15 E
Liverpool Ra. 127 31 50 S 150 30 E
Livia 48 37 34N 87 6W
Livingston, Guat. 66 15 50N 88 50W
Livingston, Ala. 10 32 35N 88 11W
Livingston, Calif. 14 37 23N 120 43W
Livingston, Ill. 21 38 58N 89 46W
Livingston, Ky. 49 37 17N 84 13W
Livingston, La. 25 30 30N 90 45W
Livingston, Mont. 33 45 40N 110 34W
Livingston, N.J. 37 40 48N 74 19W
Livingston, Tenn. 49 36 23N 85 19W
Livingston, Tex. 51 30 43N 94 56W
Livingston, Wis. 55 42 54N 90 26W
Livingston, L. 51 30 50N 95 10W
Livingston County ◇, Ill. 21 40 55N 88 50W
Livingston County ◇, Ky. 48 37 10N 88 20W
Livingston County ◇, Mich. 29 42 35N 83 55W
Livingston County ◇, Mo. 32 39 50N 93 30W
Livingston County ◇, N.Y. 39 42 40N 77 45W
Livingston Manor 39 41 54N 74 50W
Livingston Parish ◇ 25 30 30N 90 45W
Livingstone 123 17 46 S 25 52 E
Livingstonia 122 10 38 S 34 5 E
Livny 98 52 30N 37 30 E
Livonia, Ind. 22 38 33N 86 17W
Livonia, La. 25 30 34N 91 33W
Livonia, Mich. 29 42 23N 83 23W
Livonia, Mo. 32 40 30N 92 42W
Livonia, N.Y. 39 42 49N 77 40W
Livorno 94 43 32N 10 18 E
Livramento 77 30 55 S 55 30W
Livramento do Brumado 75 13 39 S 41 50W
Liwale 122 9 48 S 37 58 E
Lizard Cr. → 23 42 30N 94 14W
Lizard Pt. 83 49 57N 5 11W
Lizarda 74 9 36 S 46 41W
Lizella 18 32 48N 83 49W
Lizemores 54 38 20N 81 11W
Ljubljana 94 46 4N 14 33 E
Ljungan → 96 62 18N 17 23 E
Ljungby 97 56 49N 13 55 E
Ljusdal 97 61 46N 16 3 E
Ljusnan → 97 61 12N 17 8 E
Ljusne 97 61 13N 17 7 E
Llamellín 72 9 0 S 76 54W
Llancanelo, Salina 76 35 40 S 69 8W
Llandeilo 83 51 53N 4 0W
Llandovery 83 51 59N 3 49W
Llandrindod Wells 83 52 15N 3 23W
Llandudno 82 53 19N 3 51W
Llanelli 83 51 41N 4 11W
Llanes 91 43 25N 4 50W
Llangollen 82 52 58N 3 10W
Llanidloes 83 52 28N 3 31W
Llano 51 30 45N 98 41W
Llano → 51 30 39N 98 26W
Llano County ◇ 51 30 45N 98 41W
Llano Estacado 38 33 30N 102 40W
Llanos 72 5 0N 71 35W
Llanquihue □ 78 41 30 S 73 0W
Llanquihue, L. 78 41 10 S 75 50W
Llera 65 23 19N 99 1W
Llica 72 19 52 S 68 16W
Llico 76 34 46 S 72 5W
Llobregat → 91 41 19N 2 9 E
Lloret de Mar 91 41 41N 2 53 E
Lloyd L. 63 57 22N 108 57W
Lloydminster 63 53 17N 110 0W
Lloyds 27 38 36N 76 12W
Llullaillaco, Volcán 76 24 43 S 68 30W
Loa 52 38 24N 111 39W
Loa → 76 21 26 S 70 41W
Loami 21 39 40N 89 51W
Lobatse 123 25 12 S 25 40 E
Lobelville 48 35 46N 87 47W
Lobería 76 38 10 S 58 40W
Lobito 123 12 18 S 13 35 E
Lobos 76 35 10 S 59 0W
Lobos, I. 64 27 15N 110 30W
Lobos, Is. 68 6 57 S 80 45W
Lobos de Tierra, I. 72 6 27 S 80 52W
Lobstick L. 61 54 0N 65 0W
Loc Binh 112 21 46N 106 54 E
Loc Ninh 112 11 50N 106 34 E
Locarno 88 46 10N 8 47 E
Loch Raven 27 39 26N 76 33W
Lochaber 84 56 55N 5 0W
Lochcarron 84 57 25N 5 30W
Loche, La 63 56 29N 109 26W
Lochearn 27 39 21N 76 43W
Lochem 87 52 9N 6 26 E
Loches 90 47 7N 1 0 E
Lochgelly 84 56 7N 3 18W
Lochgilphead 84 56 2N 5 37W
Lochinver 84 58 9N 5 15W
Lochloosa L. 17 29 30N 82 7W
Lochnagar 84 56 57N 3 14W
Lochsa → 20 46 9N 115 36W
Lochy → 84 56 52N 5 3W
Lock Haven 45 41 8N 77 28W
Lock Springs 32 39 51N 93 47W
Lockeford 14 38 10N 121 9W
Lockeport 61 43 47N 65 4W
Lockerbie 84 55 7N 3 21W
Lockesburg 13 33 58N 94 10W
Lockhart, S.C. 46 34 47N 81 28W
Lockhart, Tex. 51 29 53N 97 40W
Lockington 42 40 12N 84 14W
Lockney 50 34 7N 101 27W
Lockport, Ill. 21 41 35N 88 3W
Lockport, La. 25 29 39N 90 33W
Lockport, N.Y. 39 43 10N 78 42W
Lockridge 23 40 59N 91 45W
Lockwood 32 37 23N 93 57W
Loco 43 34 50N 97 38W
Locust 40 35 15N 80 25W
Locust Cr. → 32 39 40N 93 17W
Locust Fork → 10 33 33N 87 11W
Locust Grove, Ga. 18 33 21N 84 7W
Locust Grove, Okla. 43 36 12N 95 10W
Lod 104 31 57N 34 54 E
Loda 21 40 31N 88 4W
Lodeinoye Pole 98 60 44N 33 33 E
Lodge Grass 33 45 19N 107 22W
Lodgepole, Nebr. 34 41 9N 102 38W
Lodgepole, S. Dak. 47 45 48N 102 40W
Lodgepole → 34 41 2N 102 10W
Lodgepole Cr. → 16 40 57N 102 23W
Lodhran 108 29 32N 71 30 E
Lodi, Calif. 14 38 8N 121 16W
Lodi, Wis. 55 43 19N 89 32W
Lodja 122 3 30 S 23 23 E
Lodwar 122 3 10N 35 40 E
Łódź 89 51 45N 19 27 E
Lofoten 96 68 30N 15 0 E
Logan, Iowa 23 41 39N 95 47W
Logan, Kans. 24 39 40N 99 34W
Logan, N. Mex. 38 35 22N 103 25W
Logan, Ohio 42 39 32N 82 25W
Logan, Utah 52 41 44N 111 50W
Logan, W. Va. 54 37 51N 81 59W
Logan County ◇, Ark. 13 35 18N 93 44W
Logan County ◇, Colo. 16 40 45N 103 0W
Logan County ◇, Ill. 21 41 10N 89 20W
Logan County ◇, Kans. 24 39 0N 101 0W
Logan County ◇, Ky. 48 36 50N 86 50W
Logan County ◇, N. Dak. 41 46 28N 99 25W
Logan County ◇, Nebr. 34 41 30N 100 30W
Logan County ◇, Ohio 42 40 22N 83 46W
Logan County ◇, Okla. 43 36 0N 97 30W
Logan County ◇, W. Va. 54 37 58N 82 0W
Logan Martin Reservoir 10 33 26N 86 20W
Logandale 35 36 36N 114 29W
Logansport, Ind. 22 40 45N 86 22W
Logansport, La. 25 31 58N 94 0W
Loganton 45 41 2N 77 19W
Loganville, Ga. 18 33 50N 83 54W
Loganville, Wis. 55 43 27N 90 2W
Logroño 91 42 28N 2 27W
Lohardaga 109 23 27N 84 45 E
Lohrville 23 42 17N 94 33W
Loi-kaw 109 19 40N 97 17 E
Loimaa 97 60 50N 23 5 E
Loir → 90 47 33N 0 32W
Loir-et-Cher □ 90 47 40N 1 20 E
Loire □ 90 45 40N 4 5 E
Loire → 90 47 16N 2 10W
Loire-Atlantique □ 90 47 25N 1 40W
Loiret □ 90 47 58N 2 10 E
Loíza 57 18 26N 65 53W
Loíza, Lago 57 18 17N 66 0W
Loja, Ecuador 72 3 59 S 79 16W
Loja, Spain 91 37 10N 4 10W
Loja □ 70 4 0 S 79 13W
Loji 111 1 38 S 127 28 E
Lokandu 122 2 30 S 25 45 E
Lokeren 87 51 6N 3 59 E
Lokitaung 122 4 12N 35 48 E
Lokka 96 67 49N 27 45 E
Løkken Verk 96 63 7N 9 43 E
Lokoja 120 7 47N 6 45 E
Lokolama 122 2 35 S 19 50 E
Lokwei 115 19 5N 110 31 E
Lola 48 37 19N 88 18W
Lola, Mt. 14 39 26N 120 22W
Loliondo 122 2 2 S 35 39 E
Lolita 51 28 50N 96 33W
Lolland 97 54 45N 11 30 E
Lolo 33 46 45N 114 5W
Lolo Hot Springs 33 46 44N 114 32W
Lolo National Forest 33 47 8N 114 40W
Lolo Peak 33 46 41N 114 14W
Lom 95 43 48N 23 12 E
Loma, Colo. 16 39 12N 108 49W
Loma, Mont. 33 47 56N 110 30W
Loma, N. Dak. 41 48 38N 98 32W
Loma Prieta 14 37 6N 121 50W
Lomami → 122 0 46N 24 16 E
Loman 30 48 31N 93 49W
Lomas de Zamóra 76 34 45 S 58 25W
Lomax 21 40 41N 91 4W
Lombard 21 41 53N 88 1W
Lombardia □ 94 45 35N 9 45 E
Lombardy = Lombardia □ 94 45 35N 9 45 E
Lomblen 111 8 30 S 123 32 E
Lombok 110 8 45 S 116 30 E
Lomé 120 6 9N 1 20 E
Lomela 122 2 19 S 23 15 E
Lomela → 122 1 30 S 22 50 E
Lometa 51 31 13N 98 24W
Lomié 122 3 13N 13 38 E

Lomond **Lucerne**

Lomond **62** 50 24N 112 36W
Lomond, L. **84** 56 8N 4 38W
Lompobatang **111** 5 24S 119 56E
Lompoc **15** 34 38N 120 28W
Łomza **89** 53 10N 22 2E
Lonaconing **27** 39 34N 78 59W
Loncoche **78** 39 20S 72 50W
Loncopuè **78** 38 4S 70 37W
Londa **108** 15 30N 74 30E
London, Canada **60** 42 59N 81 15W
London, U.K. **83** 51 30N 0 5W
London, Ark. **13** 35 20N 93 15W
London, Ky. **49** 37 8N 84 5W
London, Ohio **42** 39 53N 83 27W
London, Greater □ **83** 51 30N 0 5W
London Mills **21** 40 43N 90 11W
Londonderry, U.K. **85** 55 0N 7 20W
Londonderry, Ohio **42** 39 16N 82 48W
Londonderry, Vt. **36** 43 14N 72 48W
Londonderry □ **85** 55 0N 7 20W
Londonderry, C. **126** 13 45S 126 55E
Londonderry, I. **78** 55 0S 71 0W
Londontowne **27** 38 55N 76 33W
Londrina **77** 23 18S 51 10W
Lone Grove **43** 34 11N 97 14W
Lone Mountain **49** 36 24N 83 35W
Lone Mt. **47** 45 23N 103 44W
Lone Oak, Ky. **48** 37 2N 88 40W
Lone Oak, Tex. **51** 33 0N 95 57W
Lone Pine **15** 36 36N 118 4W
Lone Star **51** 32 55N 94 43W
Lone Wolf **43** 34 59N 99 15W
Lonejack **32** 38 52N 94 10W
Lonepine **33** 47 42N 114 38W
Lonerock **44** 45 5N 119 53W
Long B. **46** 33 35N 78 45W
Long Beach, Calif. **15** 33 47N 118 11W
Long Beach, Miss. **31** 30 21N 89 9W
Long Beach, N.Y. **39** 40 35N 73 39W
Long Beach, Wash. **53** 46 21N 124 3W
Long Branch **37** 40 18N 74 0W
Long Branch L. **32** 39 50N 92 30W
Long County ◇ **18** 31 45N 81 45W
Long Creek **44** 44 43N 119 6W
Long Eaton **82** 52 54N 1 16W
Long I., Bahamas **67** 23 20N 75 10W
Long I., U.S.A. **39** 40 45N 73 30W
Long Island **24** 39 57N 99 32W
Long Island Sd. **28** 41 10N 73 0W
Long L., Canada **60** 49 30N 86 50W
Long L., Mich. **29** 45 13N 83 29W
Long L., N. Dak. **41** 46 44N 100 6W
Long L., N.Y. **39** 44 1N 74 24W
Long L., Wash. **53** 47 50N 117 51W
Long L., Maine **26** 47 13N 68 15W
Long L., Maine **26** 46 43N 69 23W
Long Lake **39** 43 58N 74 25W
Long Mt. **32** 36 43N 92 31W
Long Pine **34** 42 32N 99 42W
Long Pt. **61** 48 47N 58 46W
Long Point **21** 41 0N 88 54W
Long Pond **28** 41 48N 70 56W
Long Prairie **30** 45 59N 94 52W
Long Prairie → **30** 46 20N 94 36W
Long Pt **30** 48 59N 94 59W
Long Range Mts. **61** 49 30N 57 30W
Long Ridge **49** 38 35N 84 49W
Long Str. **4** 70 0N 175 0E
Long Xian **115** 34 55N 106 55E
Long Xuyen **112** 10 19N 105 28E
Long'an **115** 23 10N 107 40E
Longboat Key **17** 27 23N 82 39W
Longbranch **53** 47 13N 122 46W
Longchuan **115** 24 5N 115 17E
Longdale **43** 36 8N 98 33W
Longde **114** 35 30N 106 20E
Longford, Ireland **85** 53 43N 7 50W
Longford, U.S.A. **24** 39 10N 97 20W
Longford □ **85** 53 42N 7 45W
Longhua **114** 41 18N 117 45E
Longiram **110** 0 5S 115 45E
Longjiang **114** 47 20N 123 12E
Longkou **114** 37 40N 120 18E
Longlac **60** 49 45N 86 25W
Longlin **115** 24 47N 105 20E
Longmeadow **28** 42 3N 72 34W
Longmen **115** 23 40N 114 18E
Longmont **16** 40 10N 105 6W
Longnan **115** 24 55N 114 47E
Longnawan **110** 1 51N 114 55E
Longone → **121** 10 0N 15 40E
Longquan **115** 28 7N 119 10E
Longreach **127** 23 28S 144 14E
Longridge **27** 38 16N 75 37W
Longshan **115** 29 29N 109 25E
Longsheng **115** 25 48N 110 0E
Longstreet **25** 32 6N 93 57W
Longton **24** 37 23N 96 5W
Longtown, U.K. **83** 51 58N 2 59W
Longtown, U.S.A. **32** 37 40N 89 47W
Longview, Canada **62** 50 32N 114 10W
Longview, Ill. **21** 39 53N 88 4W
Longview, Miss. **31** 33 24N 88 55W
Longview, N.C. **40** 35 44N 81 23W
Longview, Tex. **51** 32 30N 94 44W
Longview, Wash. **53** 46 8N 122 57W
Longville, La. **25** 30 36N 93 14W
Longville, Minn. **30** 46 59N 94 13W
Longwood **17** 28 42N 81 21W
Longwoods **27** 38 52N 76 5W
Longxi **114** 34 53N 104 40E
Longzhou **115** 22 22N 106 50E
Lonoke **13** 34 47N 91 54W
Lonoke County ◇ **13** 34 47N 91 54W
Lonquimay **78** 38 26S 71 14W
Lons-le-Saunier **90** 46 40N 5 31E
Lonsdale **30** 44 29N 93 26W
Loogootee **22** 38 41N 86 55W
Lookeba **43** 35 22N 98 22W
Looking Glass → **29** 42 52N 84 54W
Lookout **14** 41 13N 121 9W
Lookout, C., N.C. **40** 34 35N 76 32W
Lookout, C., Oreg. **44** 45 20N 124 1W
Lookout, C., Canada **60** 55 18N 83 56W
Lookout, Pt. **29** 44 3N 83 35W
Lookout Mountain **49** 34 59N 85 21W
Lookout Mt., Ala. **10** 34 20N 85 45W
Lookout Mt., Oreg. **44** 45 21N 121 31W
Loomis, Nebr. **34** 40 29N 99 31W
Loomis, Wash. **53** 48 49N 119 38W
Loon →, Alta., Canada **62** 57 8N 115 3W
Loon →, Man., Canada **63** 55 53N 101 59W
Loon Lake, Canada **63** 54 2N 109 10W
Loon Lake, U.S.A. **53** 48 4N 117 38W
Loop Hd. **85** 52 34N 9 55W
Loose Creek **32** 38 31N 91 57W
Lop Nor = Lop Nur **113** 40 20N 90 10E
Lop Nur **113** 40 20N 90 10E
Lopatina, G. **101** 50 47N 143 10E
Lopez, C. **122** 0 47S 8 40E
Lopez Pt. **15** 36 1N 121 34W
Lopphavet **96** 70 27N 21 15E
Lora → **107** 32 0N 67 15E
Lora, Hamun-i- **107** 29 38N 64 58E
Lorain **42** 41 28N 82 11W
Lorain County ◇ **42** 41 14N 82 7W
Loraine, Ill. **21** 40 9N 91 13W
Loraine, Tex. **50** 32 25N 100 43W
Loralai **108** 30 20N 68 41E
Lorca **91** 37 41N 1 42W
Lord Howe I. **124** 31 33S 159 6E
Lord Howe Ridge **124** 30 0S 162 30E
Lordsburg **38** 32 21N 108 43W
Lore City **42** 39 59N 81 28W
Loreauville **25** 30 3N 91 44W
Lorenzo, Idaho **20** 43 44N 111 52W
Lorenzo, Tex. **50** 33 40N 101 32W
Loreto, Bolivia **73** 15 13S 64 40W
Loreto, Brazil **74** 7 5S 45 10W
Loreto, Italy **94** 43 26N 13 36E
Loreto, Mexico **64** 26 1N 111 21W
Loreto □ **70** 5 0S 75 0W
Loretta **24** 38 39N 99 12W
Loretto **48** 35 5N 87 26W
Lorica **70** 9 14N 75 49W
Lorient **90** 47 45N 3 23W
Lorimor **23** 41 8N 94 3W
Loris **46** 34 4N 78 53W
Loristān □ **106** 33 20N 47 0E
Lorman **31** 31 49N 91 3W
Lorn **84** 56 26N 5 10W
Lorn, Firth of **84** 56 20N 5 40W
Lorraine, France **90** 49 0N 6 0E
Lorraine, U.S.A. **24** 38 34N 98 19W
Lorrainville **60** 47 21N 79 23W
Lorton **34** 40 35N 96 1W
Los Alamos, Calif. **15** 34 44N 120 17W
Los Alamos, N. Mex. **38** 35 53N 106 19W
Los Alamos County ◇ **38** 35 55N 106 15W
Los Altos **14** 37 23N 122 7W
Los Andes **76** 32 50S 70 40W
Los Angeles, Chile **76** 37 28S 72 23W
Los Angeles, U.S.A. **15** 34 4N 118 15W
Los Angeles Aqueduct **15** 35 22N 118 5W
Los Angeles County ◇ **15** 34 20N 118 10W
Los Antiguos **78** 46 35S 71 40W
Los Banos **14** 37 4N 120 51W
Los Blancos **76** 23 40S 62 30W
Los Fresnos **50** 26 4N 97 29W
Los Gatos **14** 37 14N 121 59W
Los Hermanos **71** 11 45N 84 25W
Los Lagos **78** 39 51S 72 50W
Los Lamentos **64** 30 36N 105 50W
Los Lomas **72** 4 40S 80 10W
Los Lunas **38** 34 48N 106 44W
Los Menucos **78** 40 50S 68 10W
Los Mochis **64** 25 45N 109 5W
Los Molinos **14** 40 1N 122 6W
Los Monos **78** 46 1S 69 36W
Los Olivos **15** 34 40N 120 7W
Los Padillas **38** 34 57N 106 42W
Los Padres National Forest **15** 34 40N 119 40W
Los Palacios **66** 22 35N 83 15W
Los Pinas → **16** 36 56N 107 36W
Los Pinos **38** 36 59N 106 3W
Los Reyes **64** 19 34N 102 30W
Los Ríos □ **70** 1 30S 79 25W
Los Roques **70** 11 50N 66 45W
Los Teques **70** 10 21N 67 2W
Los Testigos **71** 11 23N 63 6W
Los Vilos **76** 32 10S 71 30W
Losada → **70** 2 12N 73 55W
Losantville **22** 40 2N 85 11W
Loshkalakh **101** 62 45N 147 20E
Lošinj **94** 44 30N 14 30E
Lossiemouth **84** 57 43N 3 17W
Lost →, Ind. **22** 38 33N 86 49W
Lost →, Oreg. **44** 41 56N 121 30W
Lost Chance Cr. → **40** 38 32N 110 55W
Lost Creek **54** 39 10N 80 21W
Lost Hills **15** 35 37N 119 41W
Lost Nation **23** 41 58N 90 49W
Lost Peak **52** 37 29N 113 55W
Lost River Range **20** 44 8N 113 47W
Lost Springs, Kans. **24** 38 34N 96 58W
Lost Springs, Wyo. **56** 42 46N 104 56W
Lostwood **41** 48 29N 102 25W
Lot □ **90** 44 39N 1 40E
Lot → **90** 44 18N 0 20E
Lot-et-Garonne □ **90** 44 22N 0 30E
Lota **76** 37 5S 73 10W
Lothair **33** 48 28N 111 14W
Lothian □ **84** 55 50N 3 0W
Lott **51** 31 12N 97 2W
Loubomo **122** 4 9S 12 47E
Loudon, N.H. **36** 43 16N 71 27W
Loudon, Tenn. **49** 35 45N 84 20W
Loudon County ◇ **49** 35 45N 84 20W
Loudonville **42** 40 38N 82 14W
Loudoun County ◇ **54** 39 5N 77 50W
Louga **120** 15 45N 16 5W
Loughborough **82** 52 46N 1 11W
Loughman **17** 28 14N 81 34W
Loughrea **85** 53 11N 8 33W
Loughros More B. **85** 54 48N 8 30W
Louin **31** 32 4N 89 16W
Louis Trichardt **123** 23 0S 29 43E
Louis XIV, Pte. **60** 54 37N 79 45W
Louisa, Ky. **49** 38 7N 82 36W
Louisa, Va. **54** 38 1N 78 0W
Louisa County ◇, Iowa **23** 41 15N 91 15W
Louisa County ◇, Va. **54** 38 1N 78 0W
Louisana □ **25** 31 0N 93 0W
Louisbourg **61** 45 55N 60 0W
Louisburg, Kans. **24** 38 37N 94 41W
Louisburg, Minn. **30** 45 10N 96 10W
Louisburg, Mo. **32** 37 46N 93 8W
Louisburg, N.C. **40** 36 6N 78 18W
Louise, Miss. **31** 32 59N 90 35W
Louise, Tex. **51** 29 6N 96 24W
Louise I. **62** 52 55N 131 50W
Louiseville **60** 46 20N 72 56W
Louisiade Arch. **124** 11 10S 153 0E
Louisiana **32** 39 27N 91 3W
Louisville, Ala. **10** 31 47N 85 33W
Louisville, Colo. **16** 39 59N 105 8W
Louisville, Ga. **18** 33 0N 82 25W
Louisville, Ill. **21** 38 46N 88 30W
Louisville, Kans. **24** 39 15N 96 18W
Louisville, Ky. **49** 38 15N 85 46W
Louisville, Miss. **31** 33 7N 89 3W
Louisville, Nebr. **34** 41 0N 96 10W
Louisville, Ohio **42** 40 50N 81 16W
Loulé **91** 37 9N 8 0W
Lount L. **63** 50 10N 94 20W
Loup → **34** 41 24N 97 19W
Loup City **34** 41 17N 98 58W
Loup County ◇ **34** 41 50N 99 30W
Lourdes **90** 43 6N 0 3W
Lourdes-du-Blanc-Sablon **61** 51 24N 57 12W
Lourenço **71** 2 30N 51 40W
Lourenço-Marques = Maputo **123** 25 58S 32 32E
Louth, Ireland **85** 53 47N 6 33W
Louth, U.K. **82** 53 23N 0 0E
Louth □ **85** 53 55N 6 30W
Louvain = Leuven **87** 50 52N 4 42E
Louvale **18** 32 10N 84 50W
Louvière, La **87** 50 27N 4 10E
Louviers **16** 39 28N 105 1W
Love **63** 53 29N 104 10W
Love County ◇ **43** 34 0N 97 15W
Love Point **27** 39 2N 76 19W
Lovech **95** 43 8N 24 42E
Lovelady **51** 31 8N 95 27W
Loveland, Colo. **16** 40 24N 105 5W
Loveland, Ohio **42** 39 16N 84 16W
Loveland, Okla. **43** 34 18N 98 46W
Loveland Pass **16** 39 40N 105 53W
Lovell, Maine **26** 44 7N 70 54W
Lovell, Wyo. **56** 44 50N 108 24W
Lovelock **35** 40 11N 118 28W
Loves Park **21** 42 19N 89 3W
Lovett **18** 32 38N 82 46W
Loviisa = Lovisa **97** 60 28N 26 12E
Lovilia **23** 41 8N 92 55W
Loving **38** 32 17N 104 6W
Loving County ◇ **50** 31 42N 103 36W
Lovingston **54** 37 46N 78 52W
Lovington, Ill. **21** 39 43N 88 38W
Lovington, N. Mex. **38** 32 57N 103 21W
Lovisa **97** 60 28N 26 12E
Low Rocky Pt. **127** 42 59S 145 29E
Lowa **122** 1 25S 25 47E
Lowden **23** 41 52N 90 56W
Lowell, Ark. **13** 36 15N 94 8W
Lowell, Fla. **17** 29 20N 82 12W
Lowell, Ind. **22** 41 18N 87 25W
Lowell, Mass. **28** 42 38N 71 19W
Lowell, N.C. **40** 35 16N 81 6W
Lowell, Oreg. **44** 43 55N 122 47W
Lowell, Vt. **36** 44 48N 72 27W
Lowell, L. **20** 43 35N 116 44W
Lower Arrow L. **62** 49 40N 118 5W
Lower Brule **47** 44 5N 99 34W
Lower Brule Indian Reservation **47** 44 5N 100 0W
Lower Gilmanton **36** 43 24N 71 24W
Lower Granite L. **53** 46 26N 117 14W
Lower Hutt **128** 41 10S 174 55E
Lower Kalskag **11** 61 31N 160 22W
Lower Klamath L. **14** 41 57N 121 42W
Lower L. **14** 41 16N 120 2W
Lower Lake **14** 38 55N 122 37W
Lower Marlboro **27** 38 39N 76 41W
Lower Monumental Dam **53** 46 32N 118 33W
Lower Neguac **61** 47 20N 65 10W
Lower New York B. **37** 40 33N 74 5W
Lower Paia **19** 20 55N 156 23W
Lower Post **62** 59 58N 128 30W
Lower Red L. **30** 47 58N 95 0W
Lowes **48** 36 53N 88 46W
Lowes Crossroads **27** 38 34N 75 24W
Lowestoft **83** 52 29N 1 44E
Lowgap **40** 36 32N 80 52W
Łowicz **89** 52 6N 19 55E
Lowland **40** 35 18N 76 35W
Lowman **20** 44 5N 115 37W
Lowmoor **54** 37 47N 79 53W
Lowndes County ◇, Ala. **10** 32 11N 86 35W
Lowndes County ◇, Ga. **18** 30 50N 83 15W
Lowndes County ◇, Miss. **31** 33 30N 88 25W
Lowndesboro **10** 32 17N 86 37W
Lowndesville **46** 34 13N 82 39W
Lowry, Minn. **30** 45 42N 95 31W
Lowry, S. Dak. **47** 45 20N 99 59W
Lowry City **32** 38 8N 93 44W
Lowrys **46** 34 47N 81 14W
Lowville **39** 43 47N 75 29W
Lowyar □ **107** 34 0N 69 0E
Loxley **10** 30 37N 87 45W
Loxton **127** 34 28S 140 31E
Loyal, Okla. **43** 35 59N 98 6W
Loyal, Wis. **55** 44 44N 90 30W
Loyal Valley **51** 30 35N 99 0W
Loyall **49** 36 51N 83 22W
Loyalton, Calif. **14** 39 41N 120 14W
Loyalton, S. Dak. **47** 45 17N 99 17W
Loyalty Is. = Loyauté, Is. **124** 21 0S 167 30E
Loyang = Luoyang **115** 34 40N 112 26E
Loyauté, Is. **124** 21 0S 167 30E
Lozère □ **90** 44 35N 3 30E
Lua Makiki **19** 20 33N 156 37W
Luachimo **122** 7 23S 20 48E
Luacono **122** 11 15S 21 37E
Lualaba → **122** 0 26N 25 20E
Lu'an **115** 31 45N 116 29E
Luan Chau **112** 21 38N 103 24E
Luan Xian **114** 39 40N 118 40E
Luanda **122** 8 50S 13 15E
Luang Prabang **112** 19 52N 102 10E
Luangwa **123** 15 35S 30 16E
Luangwa → **123** 14 25S 30 25E
Luanping **114** 40 53N 117 23E
Luanshya **123** 13 3S 28 28E
Luapula → **122** 9 26S 28 33E
Luarca **91** 43 32N 6 32W
Luashi **122** 10 50S 23 36E
Luau **122** 10 40S 22 10E
Lubalo **122** 9 10S 19 15E
Lubang Is. **111** 13 50N 120 12E
Lubbock **50** 33 35N 101 51W
Lubbock County ◇ **50** 33 35N 101 50W
Lubec **26** 44 52N 66 59W
Lübeck **88** 53 52N 10 41E
Lubefu **122** 4 47S 24 27E
Lubero = Luofu **122** 0 10S 29 15E
Lubicon L. **62** 56 23N 115 56W
Lublin, Poland **89** 51 12N 22 38E
Lublin, U.S.A. **55** 45 5N 90 43W
Lubran **106** 34 0N 36 0E
Lubuagan **111** 17 21N 121 10E
Lubuk Antu **110** 1 3N 111 50E
Lubuklinggau **110** 3 15S 102 55E
Lubuksikaping **110** 0 10N 100 15E
Lubumbashi **123** 11 40S 27 28E
Lubutu **122** 0 45S 26 30E
Lucama **40** 35 39N 78 0W
Lucapa **122** 8 20S 21 45E
Lucas, Kans. **24** 39 4N 98 32W
Lucas, Ky. **48** 36 53N 86 2W
Lucas, Ohio **42** 40 42N 82 25W
Lucas County ◇, Iowa **23** 41 0N 93 20W
Lucas County ◇, Ohio **42** 41 31N 83 48W
Lucasville **42** 38 53N 82 59W
Lucca **94** 43 50N 10 30E
Luce Bay **84** 54 45N 4 48W
Luce County ◇ **29** 46 30N 85 30W
Lucea **66** 18 25N 78 10W
Lucedale **31** 30 56N 88 35W
Lucena, Phil. **111** 13 56N 121 37E
Lucena, Spain **91** 37 27N 4 31W
Lučenec **89** 48 18N 19 42E
Lucerne = Luzern **88** 47 3N 8 18E

Lucerne McGehee

Lucerne 14 39 6N 122 48W
Lucerne L. 15 34 31N 116 58W
Lucerne Valley 15 34 27N 116 57W
Lucero 64 30 49N 106 30W
Lucero, L. 38 32 42N 106 27W
Lucie → 71 13 51 S 12 35 E
Lucile 20 45 32N 116 18W
Lucira 123 14 0 S 12 35 E
Luck 55 45 35N 92 29W
Luckenwalde 88 52 5N 13 11 E
Luckey 42 41 27N 83 29W
Lucknow 109 26 50N 81 0 E
Lüda = Dalian 114 38 50N 121 40 E
Luda Kamchiya → 95 43 3N 27 29 E
Ludden 41 46 1N 98 7W
Ludell 24 39 52N 100 58W
Lüderitz 123 26 41 S 15 8 E
Ludhiana 108 30 57N 75 56 E
Ludington 29 43 57N 86 27W
Ludlow, U.K. 83 52 23N 2 42W
Ludlow, Calif. 15 34 43N 116 10W
Ludlow, Colo. 16 37 20N 104 35W
Ludlow, Ill. 21 40 23N 88 8W
Ludlow, Mass. 28 42 10N 72 29W
Ludlow, Miss. 31 32 34N 89 43W
Ludlow, Mo. 32 39 39N 93 42W
Ludlow, Vt. 36 43 24N 72 42W
Ludowici 18 31 43N 81 45W
Ludus 95 46 29N 24 5 E
Ludvika 97 60 8N 15 14 E
Ludwigsburg 88 48 53N 9 11 E
Ludwigshafen 88 49 27N 8 27 E
Luebo 122 5 21 S 21 23 E
Lueders 51 32 48N 99 37W
Luepa 71 5 43N 61 31W
Lüeyang 115 33 22N 106 10 E
Lufeng 115 22 57N 115 38 E
Lufira → 122 9 30 S 27 0 E
Lufkin 51 31 21N 94 44W
Luga 98 58 40N 29 55 E
Lugang 115 24 4N 120 23 E
Lugano 88 46 0N 8 57 E
Lugansk = Voroshilovgrad 99 48 38N 39 15 E
Lugh Ganana 105 3 48N 42 34 E
Lugnaquilla 85 52 58N 6 28W
Lugo 91 43 2N 7 35W
Lugoff 46 34 13N 80 40W
Lugoj 89 45 42N 21 57 E
Lugovoye 100 42 55N 72 43 E
Luiana 123 17 25 S 22 59 E
Luis 64 26 36N 109 11W
Luís Correia 74 3 0 S 41 35W
Luís Gonçalves 74 5 37 S 50 25W
Luis Lopez 38 33 59N 106 53W
Luitpold Coast 5 78 30 S 32 0W
Luiza 122 7 40 S 22 30 E
Luján 76 34 45 S 59 5W
Lukachukai 12 36 25N 109 15W
Lukanga Swamps 123 14 30 S 27 40 E
Luke 27 39 30N 79 5W
Lukenie → 122 3 0 S 18 50 E
Lukeville 12 31 53N 112 49W
Lūki 95 41 50N 24 43 E
Lukolela 122 1 10 S 17 12 E
Lukovit 95 43 13N 24 11 E
Łukow 89 51 58N 22 22 E
Lula, Ga. 18 34 23N 83 40W
Lula, Miss. 31 34 27N 90 29W
Lule älv → 96 65 35N 22 10 E
Luleå 96 65 35N 22 10 E
Lüleburgaz 95 41 23N 27 22 E
Luling 51 29 41N 97 39W
Lulong 114 39 53N 118 51 E
Lulonga → 122 1 0N 19 0 E
Lulu 17 30 7N 82 29W
Lulua → 122 6 30 S 22 50 E
Luluabourg = Kananga 122 5 55 S 22 18 E
Lumai 123 13 13 S 21 25 E
Lumajang 111 8 8 S 113 13 E
Lumbala N'guimbo 123 14 18 S 21 18 E
Lumber → 40 34 12N 79 10W
Lumber City 18 31 56N 82 41W
Lumberton, Miss. 31 31 0N 89 27W
Lumberton, N.C. 40 34 37N 79 0W
Lumberton, N. Mex. 38 36 56N 106 56W
Lumby 62 50 10N 118 50W
Lummi Indian Reservation 53 48 52N 122 32W
Lumpkin 18 32 3N 84 48W
Lumpkin County ◇ 18 34 40N 84 0W
Lumsden 128 45 44 S 168 27 E
Lumut 112 4 13N 100 37 E
Luna County ◇ 38 32 15N 107 45W
Lund, Nev. 35 38 52N 115 0W
Lund, Utah 52 38 0N 113 26W
Lundazi 123 12 20 S 33 7 E
Lundu 110 1 40N 109 50 E
Lundy 83 51 10N 4 41W
Lune → 82 54 0N 2 51W
Lüneburg 88 53 15N 10 23 E
Lüneburg Heath =
Lüneburger Heide 88 53 0N 10 0 E
Lüneburger Heide 88 53 0N 10 0 E
Lunenburg, Canada 61 44 22N 64 18W
Lunenburg, Va. 54 36 58N 78 16W
Lunenburg, Vt. 36 44 26N 71 42W
Lunenburg County ◇ 54 36 58N 78 16W
Lunéville 90 48 36N 6 30 E
Lunglei 109 22 55N 92 45 E
Luni 108 26 0N 73 6 E
Lūni → 108 24 41N 71 14 E
Luning 35 38 30N 118 11W
Luo He → 115 34 35N 110 20 E
Luobei 114 47 35N 130 50 E
Luocheng 115 24 48N 108 53 E
Luochuan 114 35 45N 109 26 E
Luoding 115 22 45N 111 40 E
Luodong 115 24 41N 121 46 E
Luofu 122 0 10 S 29 15 E
Luoning 115 34 35N 111 40 E
Luoyang 115 34 40N 112 26 E
Luoyuan 115 26 28N 119 30 E
Luozi 122 4 54 S 14 0 E
Lupeni 95 45 21N 23 13 E
Łupków 90 49 15N 22 4 E
Lupton 12 35 21N 109 4W
Lupus 32 38 51N 92 27W
Luqa 94 35 48N 14 27 E
Luque 76 25 19 S 57 25W
Luquillo 57 18 23N 65 43W
Luquillo, Sierra de 57 18 20N 65 47W
Luray, Kans. 24 39 7N 98 41W
Luray, Mo. 32 40 27N 91 53W
Luray, S.C. 46 32 49N 81 14W
Luray, Va. 54 38 40N 78 28W
Luremo 122 8 30 S 17 50 E
Lurgan 85 54 28N 6 20W
Luribay 72 17 6 S 67 39W
Lurin 72 12 17 S 76 52W
Lusaka 123 15 28 S 28 16 E
Lusambo 122 4 58 S 23 28 E
Lusby 27 38 22N 76 26W
Luseland 63 52 5N 109 24W
Lushan 115 33 45N 112 55 E
Lushih 115 34 3N 111 3 E
Lushoto 122 4 47 S 38 20 E
Lushton 34 40 43N 97 44W
Lüshun 114 38 45N 121 15 E
Lusk 56 42 46N 104 27W
Lussanvira 75 20 42 S 51 7W
Luta = Lüda 114 38 50N 121 40 E
Lutcher 25 30 2N 90 42W
Lutesville 32 37 18N 89 59W
Luther, Iowa 23 41 58N 93 49W
Luther, Mich. 29 44 2N 85 41W
Luther, Okla. 43 35 40N 97 12W
Luthersville 18 33 13N 84 45W
Lutherville-Timonium 27 39 25N 76 38W
Lutie 50 35 1N 100 13W
Luton 83 51 53N 0 24W
Lutong 110 4 30N 114 0 E
Lutsen 30 47 39N 90 41W
Lutsk 98 50 50N 25 15 E
Luttrell 49 36 12N 83 45W
Lutts 48 35 9N 87 56W
Lutz 17 28 9N 82 28W
Lützow Holmbukta 5 69 10 S 37 30 E
Luverne, Ala. 10 31 43N 86 16W
Luverne, Iowa 23 42 55N 94 5W
Luverne, Minn. 30 43 39N 96 13W
Luverne, N. Dak. 41 47 16N 97 55W
Luwuk 111 0 56 S 122 47 E
Luxembourg 87 49 37N 6 9 E
Luxembourg □ 87 49 58N 5 30 E
Luxembourg ■ 87 50 0N 6 0 E
Luxemburg, Iowa 23 42 36N 91 5W
Luxemburg, Wis. 55 44 33N 87 42W
Luxi 115 28 20N 110 7 E
Luxor = El Uqsur 121 25 41N 32 38 E
Luxora 13 35 45N 89 56W
Luza 98 60 39N 47 10 E
Luzern 88 47 3N 8 18 E
Luzerne County ◇ 45 41 10N 76 0W
Luzhai 115 24 29N 109 42 E
Luzhou 115 28 52N 105 20 E
Luziânia 75 16 20 S 48 0W
Luzilândia 74 3 28 S 42 22W
Luzon 111 16 0N 121 0 E
Lvov 99 49 50N 24 0 E
Lyakhovskiye, Ostrova 101 73 40N 141 0 E
Lyallpur = Faisalabad 108 31 30N 73 5 E
Lyaskovets 95 43 6N 25 44 E
Lycan 16 37 37N 102 12W
Lycksele 96 64 38N 18 40 E
Lycoming County ◇ 45 41 20N 77 0W
Lydda = Lod 104 31 57N 34 54 E
Lydenburg 123 25 10 S 30 29 E
Lydia 46 34 17N 80 7W
Lyell 128 41 48 S 172 4 E
Lyell I. 62 52 40N 131 35W
Lyell Range 128 41 38 S 172 20 E
Lyerly 18 34 24N 85 24W
Lyford 50 26 25N 97 48W
Lykens 45 40 34N 76 42W
Lyle 30 43 30N 92 57W
Lyles 48 35 55N 87 21W
Lyman, Miss. 31 30 30N 89 7W
Lyman, Nebr. 34 41 55N 104 2W
Lyman, Wash. 53 48 32N 122 4W
Lyman, Wyo. 56 41 20N 110 18W
Lyman County ◇ 47 44 0N 100 0W
Lyman L. 12 34 22N 109 23W
Lyme 36 43 48N 72 12W
Lyme Regis 83 50 44N 2 57W
Lymington 83 50 46N 1 32W
Lyna → 89 54 17N 21 0 E
Lynch, Ky. 49 36 58N 82 54W
Lynch, Nebr. 34 42 50N 98 28W
Lynch Station 54 37 9N 79 18W
Lynchburg, Ohio 42 39 15N 83 48W
Lynchburg, S.C. 46 34 3N 80 4W
Lynchburg, Tenn. 48 35 17N 86 22W
Lynchburg, Va. 54 37 25N 79 9W
Lynches → 46 33 50N 79 22W
Lynd 30 44 23N 95 54W
Lynden 53 48 57N 122 27W
Lyndon, Ill. 21 41 43N 89 56W
Lyndon, Kans. 24 38 37N 95 41W
Lyndon B. Johnson, L. 51 30 33N 98 20W
Lyndon Station 55 43 43N 89 54W
Lyndonville, N.Y. 39 43 20N 78 23W
Lyndonville, Vt. 36 44 31N 72 1W
Lynn, Ala. 10 34 3N 87 33W
Lynn, Ind. 22 40 3N 84 56W
Lynn, Mass. 28 42 28N 70 57W
Lynn, Utah 52 41 53N 113 45W
Lynn Canal 11 58 50N 135 15W
Lynn County ◇ 50 33 10N 101 48W
Lynn Garden 49 36 35N 82 34W
Lynn Haven 17 30 15N 85 39W
Lynn Lake 63 56 51N 101 3W
Lynndyl 52 39 31N 112 22W
Lynne 17 29 12N 81 55W
Lynnville, Ky. 48 36 34N 88 34W
Lynnville, Tenn. 48 35 23N 87 0W
Lynnwood 53 47 49N 122 19W
Lynton 83 51 14N 3 50W
Lynx L. 63 62 25N 106 15W
Lynxville 55 43 15N 91 2W
Lyon, France 90 45 46N 4 50 E
Lyon, U.S.A. 31 34 13N 90 33W
Lyon County ◇, Iowa 23 43 20N 96 10W
Lyon County ◇, Kans. 24 38 30N 96 10W
Lyon County ◇, Ky. 48 37 0N 88 5W
Lyon County ◇, Minn. 30 44 25N 95 50W
Lyon County ◇, Nev. 35 38 45N 119 10W
Lyon Mountain 39 44 43N 73 55W
Lyonnais 90 45 45N 4 15 E
Lyons = Lyon 90 45 46N 4 50 E
Lyons, Colo. 16 40 14N 105 16W
Lyons, Ga. 18 32 12N 82 19W
Lyons, Ind. 22 38 59N 87 5W
Lyons, Kans. 24 38 21N 98 12W
Lyons, N.Y. 39 43 5N 77 0W
Lyons, Nebr. 34 41 56N 96 28W
Lyons, Ohio 42 41 42N 84 4W
Lyons, Oreg. 44 44 47N 122 37W
Lyons, Tex. 51 30 23N 96 34W
Lyons Falls 39 43 37N 75 22W
Lysva 98 58 7N 57 49 E
Lytle 51 29 14N 98 48W
Lyttelton 128 43 35 S 172 44 E
Lytton, Canada 62 50 13N 121 31W
Lytton, U.S.A. 23 42 25N 94 51W
Lyubimets 95 41 50N 26 5 E

M

Mā'ad 104 32 37N 35 36 E
Ma'alah 106 26 31N 47 20 E
Ma'ān 106 30 12N 35 44 E
Ma'anshan 115 31 44N 118 29 E
Maarianhamina 97 60 5N 19 55 E
Ma'arrat un Nu'man 106 35 38N 36 40 E
Maas → 87 51 45N 4 32 E
Maaseik 87 51 6N 5 45 E
Maassluis 87 51 56N 4 16 E
Maastricht 87 50 50N 5 40 E
Mabank 51 32 22N 96 6W
Mabaruma 71 8 10N 59 50W
Mabel 30 43 32N 91 46W
Mabel L. 62 50 35N 118 43W
Maben 54 37 38N 81 23W
Mablethorpe 82 53 21N 0 14 E
Mableton 18 33 49N 84 35W
Mabrouk 120 19 29N 1 15W
Mabton 53 46 13N 120 0W
Mac Nutt 63 51 5N 101 36W
Macachín 76 37 10 S 63 43W
McAdoo 45 40 55N 75 59W
Macaé 75 22 20 S 41 43W
Macaíba 74 5 51 S 35 21W
Macajuba 75 12 9 S 40 22W
McAlester 43 34 56N 95 46W
McAlister 38 34 42N 103 47W
McAllen 50 26 12N 98 14W
McAlpin 17 30 8N 82 57W
Macamic 60 48 45N 79 0W
Macao = Macau ■ 115 22 16N 113 35 E
Macapá 71 0 5N 51 4W
Macará 70 4 23 S 79 57W
Macarani 75 15 33 S 40 24W
Macarena, Serranía de la 70 2 45N 73 55W
McArthur, Calif. 14 41 3N 121 24W
McArthur, Ohio 42 39 15N 82 29W
McArthur → 127 15 54 S 136 40 E
McArthur River 127 16 27 S 136 7 E
Macas 70 2 19 S 78 7W
Macate 72 8 48 S 78 7W
Macau 74 5 0 S 36 40W
Macau ■ 115 22 16N 113 35 E
Macaúbas 75 13 2 S 42 42W
Macaya → 70 0 59N 72 20W
McBain 29 44 12N 85 13W
McBee 46 34 28N 80 15W
McBride, Canada 62 53 20N 120 19W
McBride, Mo. 32 37 50N 89 50W
McBride, Okla. 43 33 54N 96 36W
McBrides 29 43 21N 85 2W
McCall 20 44 55N 116 6W
McCallsburg 23 42 10N 93 23W
McCamey 50 31 8N 102 14W
McCammon 20 42 39N 112 12W
McCarthy 11 61 26N 142 56W
McCartys 38 35 4N 107 41W
McCauley I. 62 53 40N 130 15W
McCaysville 18 34 59N 84 23W
McClain County ◇ 43 35 0N 97 30W
McClave 16 38 8N 102 51W
McCleary 53 47 3N 123 16W
McClelland 23 41 20N 95 41W
McClellanville 46 33 5N 79 28W
Macclenny 17 30 17N 82 7W
Macclesfield, U.K. 82 53 16N 2 9W
Macclesfield, U.S.A. 40 35 45N 77 40W
McClintock 63 57 50N 94 10W
McCloud 14 41 15N 122 8W
McClure, Ohio 42 41 22N 83 57W
McClure, Pa. 45 40 42N 77 19W
McClure, L. 14 37 35N 120 16W
McClure Str. 4 75 0N 119 0W
McClusky 41 47 29N 100 27W
McColl 46 34 40N 79 33W
McComb, Miss. 31 31 15N 90 27W
McComb, Ohio 42 41 7N 83 48W
McConaughy, L. 34 41 14N 101 40W
McCone County ◇ 33 47 40N 105 50W
McConnells 46 34 52N 81 14W
McConnellsburg 45 39 56N 77 59W
McConnelsville 42 39 39N 81 51W
McCook 34 40 12N 100 38W
McCook County ◇ 47 43 44N 97 23W
McCool 31 33 12N 89 21W
McCool Junction 34 40 45N 97 36W
McCormick 46 33 55N 82 17W
McCormick County ◇ 46 33 50N 82 15W
McCoy 16 39 55N 106 44W
McCracken 24 38 36N 99 33W
McCracken County ◇ 48 37 5N 88 45W
McCreary County ◇ 49 37 45N 84 30W
McCrory 13 35 16N 91 12W
McCulloch County ◇ 51 31 9N 99 20W
McCune 24 37 21N 95 1W
McCurtain 43 35 9N 94 58W
McCurtain County ◇ 43 34 10N 94 45W
McCusker → 63 55 32N 108 39W
McDade 51 30 17N 97 14W
McDame 62 59 44N 128 59W
McDavid 17 30 52N 87 19W
McDermitt 35 41 59N 117 43W
Macdoel 14 41 50N 122 0W
McDonald, Kans. 24 39 47N 101 22W
McDonald, N. Mex. 38 33 9N 103 19W
McDonald, L. 33 48 35N 113 56W
McDonald County ◇ 32 36 40N 94 20W
McDonald Is. 3 54 0 S 73 0 E
Macdonald L. 126 23 30 S 129 0 E
Macdonnell Ranges 126 23 40 S 133 0 E
McDonough 18 33 27N 84 9W
McDonough County ◇ 21 40 30N 90 40W
McDougal 13 36 26N 90 23W
McDougall, Mt. 56 42 54N 110 36W
Macdougall L. 58 66 0N 98 27W
McDowell 54 38 20N 79 29W
McDowell County ◇, N.C. 40 35 40N 82 0W
McDowell County ◇,
W. Va. 54 37 22N 81 33W
MacDowell L. 60 52 15N 92 45W
Macduff 84 57 40N 2 30W
McDuffie County ◇ 18 33 20N 82 25W
Macedo de Cavaleiros 122 11 25 S 16 45 E
Macedonia = Makedhonía □ 95 40 39N 22 0 E
Macedonia = Makedonija □ 95 41 53N 21 40 E
Macedonia, Ill. 21 38 3N 88 42W
Macedonia, Iowa 23 41 12N 95 25W
Macedonia, Ohio 42 41 19N 81 31W
Maceió 74 9 40 S 35 41W
Macenta 120 8 35N 9 32W
Maceo 48 37 51N 87 0W
Macerata 94 43 19N 13 28 E
McEwen 48 36 7N 87 38W
McFadden 56 41 39N 106 8W
McFaddin 51 28 33N 97 1W
McFall 32 40 7N 94 13W
McFarland, Calif. 15 35 41N 119 14W
McFarland, Kans. 24 39 3N 96 14W
McFarland, Wis. 55 43 1N 89 17W
McFarlane → 63 59 12N 107 58W
Macfarlane, L. 127 32 0 S 136 40 E
McGee Creek Res. 43 34 22N 95 38W
McGehee 13 33 38N 91 24W

McGill Majari

McGill 35 39 23N 114 47W
Macgillycuddy's Reeks 85 52 2N 9 45W
McGrath 11 62 58N 155 36W
McGraw 39 42 36N 76 8W
MacGregor 63 49 57N 98 48W
McGregor, Iowa 23 43 1N 91 11W
McGregor, N. Dak. 41 48 36N 102 56W
McGregor, Tex. 51 31 27N 97 24W
McGregor → 62 55 10N 122 0W
McGrew 34 41 45N 103 25W
McGuffey 42 40 42N 83 47W
Mach 107 29 50N 67 20 E
Machacalis 75 17 5 S 40 45W
Machado = Jiparaná → 73 8 3 S 62 52W
Machagai 76 26 56 S 60 2W
Machakos 122 1 30 S 37 15 E
Machala 70 3 20 S 79 57W
Machattie, L. 127 24 50 S 139 48 E
Macheng 115 31 12N 115 2 E
McHenry, Ill. 21 42 21N 88 16W
McHenry, Md. 27 39 36N 79 22W
McHenry, Miss. 31 30 43N 89 8W
McHenry, N. Dak. 41 47 35N 98 35W
McHenry County ◇, Ill. 21 42 20N 88 25W
McHenry County ◇, N. Dak. 41 48 20N 100 45W
Machevna 101 61 20N 172 20 E
Machias 26 44 43N 67 28W
Machias → 26 44 43N 67 22W
Machichi → 63 57 3N 92 6W
Machilipatnam 109 16 12N 81 8 E
Machiques 70 10 4N 72 34W
Machupicchu 72 13 8 S 72 30W
Machynlleth 83 52 36N 3 51W
McIlwraith Ra. 127 13 50 S 143 20 E
Măcin 95 45 16N 28 8 E
McIntire 23 43 26N 92 36W
McIntosh, Ala. 10 31 16N 88 2W
McIntosh, Minn. 30 47 38N 95 53W
McIntosh, N. Mex. 38 34 52N 106 3W
McIntosh, S. Dak. 47 45 55N 101 21W
McIntosh County ◇, Ga. 18 31 30N 81 25W
McIntosh County ◇, N. Dak. 41 46 2N 99 20W
McIntosh County ◇, Okla. 43 35 20N 95 40W
McIntosh L. 63 55 45N 105 0W
Macintyre → 127 28 37 S 150 47 E
Mack 16 39 13N 108 52W
Mackay, Australia 127 21 8 S 149 11 E
Mackay, U.S.A. 20 43 55N 113 37W
Mackay → 62 57 10N 111 38W
Mackay, L. 126 22 30 S 129 0 E
McKean County ◇ 45 41 50N 78 45W
McKee 49 37 25N 84 0W
McKee City 37 39 26N 74 37W
McKee Cr. → 21 39 46N 90 36W
McKeesport 45 40 21N 79 52W
McKenney 54 36 59N 77 43W
Mackenzie, Canada 62 55 20N 123 5W
Mackenzie, Guyana 71 6 0N 58 17W
McKenzie, Ala. 10 31 33N 86 43W
McKenzie, N. Dak. 41 46 50N 100 25W
McKenzie, Tenn. 48 36 8N 88 31W
Mackenzie →, Australia 127 23 38 S 149 46 E
Mackenzie →, Canada 58 69 10N 134 20W
McKenzie → 44 44 7N 123 6W
McKenzie Bridge 44 44 11N 122 10W
Mackenzie City = Linden 72 6 0N 58 10W
McKenzie County ◇ 41 47 55N 103 30W
Mackenzie Highway 62 58 0N 117 15W
Mackenzie Mts. 58 64 0N 130 0W
Mackeys 40 35 56N 76 37W
McKibben 50 36 8N 101 20W
Mackinac, Straits of 29 45 50N 84 40W
Mackinac County ◇ 29 46 5N 85 0W
Mackinac Island 29 45 51N 84 37W
Mackinaw 21 40 32N 89 21W
Mackinaw → 21 40 33N 89 44W
Mackinaw City 29 45 47N 84 44W
McKinley, Mt. 11 63 4N 151 0W
McKinley County ◇ 38 35 30N 108 0W
McKinley Park 11 63 44N 148 55W
McKinley Sea 4 84 0N 10 0W
McKinleyville 14 40 57N 124 6W
McKinney 51 33 12N 96 37W
McKinney Mt. 50 29 50N 103 47W
McKinnon 18 31 25N 81 56W
McKittrick 32 38 44N 91 27W
Macksburg 23 41 13N 94 11W
Macksville 24 37 58N 98 58W
McLain 31 31 7N 88 50W
McLaughlin 47 45 49N 100 49W
McLaurin 31 31 10N 89 13W
Maclean 127 29 26 S 153 16 E
McLean, Ill. 21 40 19N 89 10W
McLean, Nebr. 34 42 23N 97 28W
McLean, Tex. 50 35 14N 100 36W
McLean County ◇, Ill. 21 40 30N 88 50W
McLean County ◇, Ky. 48 37 30N 87 15W
McLean County ◇, N. Dak. 41 47 30N 101 0W
McLeansboro 21 38 6N 88 32W
Maclear 123 31 2 S 28 23 E
Macleay → 127 30 56 S 153 0 E
McLennan 62 55 42N 116 50W
McLennan County ◇ 51 31 33N 97 9W
McLeod 41 46 24N 97 18W
MacLeod, B. 63 62 53N 110 0W
McLeod County ◇ 30 44 50N 94 15W
McLeod L. 128 24 9 S 113 47 E
MacLeod Lake 62 54 58N 123 0W
M'Clintock Chan. 58 72 0N 102 0W
McLoud 43 35 26N 97 6W
McLoughlin, Mt. 44 42 27N 122 19W
McLouth 24 39 12N 95 13W
McLure 62 51 2N 120 13W
McMillan, L. 38 32 36N 104 21W
McMinn County ◇ 49 35 27N 84 36W
McMinnville, Oreg. 44 45 13N 123 12W
McMinnville, Tenn. 49 35 41N 85 46W
McMorran 63 51 19N 108 42W
McMullen County ◇ 51 28 28N 98 33W
McMurdo Sd. 5 77 0 S 170 0 E
McMurray = Fort McMurray 62 56 44N 111 7W
McMurray 53 48 19N 122 14W
McNab 13 33 40N 93 50W
McNairy County ◇ 48 35 10N 88 36W
McNary, Ariz. 12 34 4N 109 51W
McNary, Tex. 50 31 15N 105 48W
*McNaughton L. 62 52 0N 118 10W
McNeal 12 31 36N 109 40W
McNeil 13 33 21N 93 13W
McNeill 31 30 40N 89 38W
Macomb, Ill. 21 40 27N 90 40W
Macomb, Okla. 43 35 10N 97 0W
Macomb County ◇ 29 42 40N 83 0W
Mâcon, France 90 46 19N 4 50 E
Macon, Ga. 18 32 51N 83 38W
Macon, Ill. 21 39 43N 89 0W
Macon, Miss. 31 33 7N 88 34W
Macon, Mo. 32 39 44N 92 28W
Macon, Nebr. 34 40 13N 98 55W
Macon County ◇, Ala. 10 32 25N 85 42W
Macon County ◇, Ga. 18 32 20N 84 0W
Macon County ◇, Ill. 21 39 50N 89 0W
Macon County ◇, Mo. 32 39 50N 92 30W
Macon County ◇, N.C. 40 35 15N 83 30W
Macon County ◇, Tenn. 48 36 31N 86 2W
Macondo 123 12 37 S 23 46 E
Macoun L. 63 56 32N 103 40W
Macoupin County ◇ 21 39 20N 89 55W
McPherson 24 38 22N 97 40W
McPherson County ◇, Kans. 24 38 20N 97 40W
McPherson County ◇, Nebr. 34 41 30N 101 0W
McPherson County ◇, S. Dak. 47 45 46N 99 0W
McQuady 48 37 42N 86 31W
Macquarie → 127 30 5 S 147 30 E
Macquarie Harbour 127 42 15 S 145 23 E
Macquarie Is. 124 54 36 S 158 55 E
McRae, Ark. 13 35 7N 91 49W
McRae, Ga. 18 32 4N 82 54W
McRoberts 49 37 12N 82 40W
MacRobertson Land 5 71 0 S 64 0 E
Macroom 85 51 54N 8 57W
Macujer 70 0 24N 73 10W
Macusani 72 14 4 S 70 29W
Macuspana 65 17 46N 92 36W
Mácuzari, Presa 64 27 10N 109 10W
McVeigh 49 37 32N 82 15W
McVeytown 45 40 30N 77 45W
McVille 41 47 46N 98 11W
Macwahoc 26 45 38N 68 16W
Macy 34 42 7N 96 21W
Mad →, Calif. 14 40 57N 124 7W
Mad →, Ohio 42 39 46N 84 12W
Mad →, Vt. 36 44 18N 72 41W
Madagali 121 10 56N 13 33 E
Madagascar ■ 123 20 0 S 47 0 E
Madā'in Sālih 106 26 46N 37 57 E
Madama 121 22 0N 13 40 E
Madame I. 61 45 30N 60 58W
Madan 95 41 30N 24 57 E
Madang 124 5 12 S 145 49 E
Madaoua 120 14 5N 6 27 E
Madaripur 109 23 19N 90 15 E
Madauk 109 17 56N 96 52 E
Madawaska 26 47 21N 68 20W
Madawaska → 60 45 27N 76 21W
Madaya 109 22 12N 96 10 E
Maddalena 94 41 15N 9 23 E
Madden Dam 57 9 13N 79 37W
Madden L. 57 9 15N 79 35W
Maddock 41 47 58N 99 32W
Maddox 27 38 20N 76 48W
Madeira 120 32 50N 17 0W
Madeira → 71 3 22 S 58 45W
Madeira Beach 17 27 48N 82 48W
Madeleine, Îs. de la 61 47 30N 61 40W
Madelia 30 44 3N 94 25W
Madeline 14 41 3N 120 28W
Madeline I. 55 46 49N 90 42W
Madera 15 36 57N 120 3W
Madera County ◇ 14 37 15N 119 35W
Madha 108 18 0N 75 30 E
Madhya Pradesh □ 108 21 50N 81 0 E
Madidi → 72 12 32 S 66 52W
Madikeri 108 12 30N 75 45 E
Madill 43 34 6N 96 46W
Madimba 122 5 0 S 15 0 E
Madīnat ash Sha'b 105 12 50N 45 0 E
Madingou 122 4 10 S 13 33 E
Madison, Ala. 10 34 42N 86 45W
Madison, Ark. 13 35 1N 90 43W
Madison, Fla. 17 30 28N 83 25W
Madison, Ga. 18 33 36N 83 28W
Madison, Ind. 22 38 44N 85 23W
Madison, Kans. 24 38 8N 96 8W
Madison, Maine 26 44 48N 69 53W
Madison, Md. 27 38 30N 76 13W
Madison, Minn. 30 45 1N 96 11W
Madison, Miss. 31 32 28N 90 7W
Madison, Mo. 32 39 28N 92 13W
Madison, N.C. 40 36 23N 79 58W
Madison, N.J. 37 40 46N 74 25W
Madison, Nebr. 34 41 50N 97 27W
Madison, Ohio 42 41 46N 81 3W
Madison, S. Dak. 47 44 0N 97 7W
Madison, Tenn. 48 36 16N 86 42W
Madison, Va. 54 38 23N 78 15W
Madison, W. Va. 54 38 4N 81 49W
Madison, Wis. 55 43 4N 89 24W
Madison → 33 45 56N 111 31W
Madison County ◇, Ala. 10 34 44N 86 35W
Madison County ◇, Ark. 13 36 5N 93 44W
Madison County ◇, Fla. 17 30 30N 83 30W
Madison County ◇, Ga. 18 34 10N 83 10W
Madison County ◇, Idaho 20 43 55N 111 50W
Madison County ◇, Ill. 21 38 50N 89 55W
Madison County ◇, Ind. 22 40 10N 85 45W
Madison County ◇, Iowa 23 41 20N 94 0W
Madison County ◇, Ky. 49 37 40N 84 20W
Madison County ◇, Miss. 31 32 37N 90 2W
Madison County ◇, Mo. 32 37 30N 90 20W
Madison County ◇, Mont. 33 45 12N 112 0W
Madison County ◇, N.C. 40 35 50N 82 50W
Madison County ◇, N.Y. 39 43 0N 75 45W
Madison County ◇, Nebr. 34 41 50N 97 30W
Madison County ◇, Ohio 42 39 53N 83 27W
Madison County ◇, Tenn. 48 35 37N 88 49W
Madison County ◇, Tex. 51 31 0N 96 0W
Madison County ◇, Va. 54 38 23N 78 15W
Madison Heights 54 37 25N 79 8W
Madison Lake 30 44 12N 93 49W
Madison Mills 42 39 39N 83 20W
Madison Parish ◇ 25 32 25N 91 11W
Madisonville, Ky. 48 37 20N 87 30W
Madisonville, La. 25 30 24N 90 10W
Madisonville, Tenn. 49 35 31N 84 22W
Madisonville, Tex. 51 30 57N 95 55W
Madiun 111 7 38 S 111 32 E
Madley 83 52 3N 2 51W
Madras = Tamil Nadu □ 108 11 0N 77 0 E
Madras, India 108 13 8N 80 19 E
Madras, U.S.A. 44 44 38N 121 8W
Madre, Laguna, Mexico 65 25 0N 97 30W
Madre, Laguna, U.S.A. 50 27 0N 97 30W
Madre, Sierra, Mexico 65 16 0N 93 0W
Madre, Sierra, Phil. 111 17 0N 122 0 E
Madre de Dios □ 72 12 0 S 70 15W
Madre de Dios → 72 10 59 S 66 8W
Madre de Dios, I. 78 50 20 S 75 10W
Madre del Sur, Sierra 65 17 30N 100 0W
Madre Occidental, Sierra 64 27 0N 107 0W
Madre Oriental, Sierra 64 25 0N 100 0W
Madrid, Spain 91 40 25N 3 45W
Madrid, Ala. 10 31 2N 85 24W
Madrid, Iowa 23 41 53N 93 49W
Madrid, N. Mex. 38 35 24N 106 9W
Madrid, N.Y. 39 44 45N 75 8W
Madrid, Nebr. 34 40 51N 101 33W
Madura, Selat 111 7 30 S 113 20 E
Madurai 108 9 55N 78 10 E
Madurantakam 108 12 30N 79 50 E
Mae Hong Son 112 19 16N 98 1 E
Mae Sot 112 16 43N 98 34 E
Maebashi 117 36 24N 139 4 E
Măeruş 95 45 53N 25 31 E
Maeser 52 40 28N 109 35W
Maesteg 83 51 36N 3 40W
Maestra, Sierra 66 20 15N 77 0W
Maestrazgo, Mts. del 91 40 30N 0 25W
Maevatanana 123 16 56N 46 49 E
Maeystown 21 38 13N 90 14W
Mafeking 63 52 40N 101 10W
Mafia 122 7 45 S 39 50 E
Mafikeng 123 25 50 S 25 38 E
Mafra, Brazil 77 26 10 S 50 0W
Mafra, Portugal 91 38 55N 9 20W
Magadan 101 59 38N 150 50 E
Magadi 122 1 54 S 36 19 E
Magallanes □ 78 52 0 S 72 0W
Magallanes, Estrecho de 78 52 30 S 75 0W
Magangué 70 9 14N 74 45W
Magazine 13 35 9N 93 48W
Magazine Mt. 13 35 10N 93 41W
Magburaka 120 8 47N 12 0W
Magdalena, Argentina 76 35 5 S 57 30W
Magdalena, Bolivia 73 13 13 S 63 57W
Magdalena, Malaysia 110 4 25N 117 55 E
Magdalena, Mexico 64 30 50N 112 0W
Magdalena, U.S.A. 38 34 7N 107 15W
Magdalena □ 70 10 0N 74 0W
Magdalena →, Colombia 70 11 6N 74 51W
Magdalena →, Mexico 64 30 40N 112 25W
Magdalena, B. 64 24 30N 112 10W
Magdalena, I., Chile 78 44 40 S 73 0W
Magdalena, I., Mexico 64 24 40N 112 15W
Magdalena, Llano de la 64 25 0N 111 30W
Magdalena Mts. 38 33 45N 107 15W
Magdeburg 88 52 8N 11 36 E
Magdi'el 104 32 10N 34 54 E
Magee 31 31 52N 89 44W
Magee, I. 85 54 48N 5 44W
Magelang 111 7 29 S 110 13 E
Magellan's Str. = Magallanes, Estrecho de 78 52 30 S 75 0W
Maggiore, L. 94 46 0N 8 35 E
Maghār 104 32 54N 35 24 E
Magherafelt 85 54 44N 6 37W
Magic Reservoir 20 43 15N 114 22W
Magna 52 40 42N 112 6W
Magnet 34 42 27N 97 28W
Magnetic Pole (North) 4 76 12N 100 12W
Magnetic Pole (South) 5 68 48 S 139 30 E
Magnitogorsk 98 53 27N 59 4 E
Magnolia, Ark. 13 33 16N 93 14W
Magnolia, Del. 27 39 4N 75 29W
Magnolia, Iowa 23 41 42N 95 52W
Magnolia, Ky. 49 37 27N 85 45W
Magnolia, Miss. 31 31 9N 90 28W
Magnolia, Ohio 42 40 39N 81 18W
Magnolia, Tex. 51 30 13N 95 45W
Magoffin County ◇ 49 37 45N 83 5W
Magog 61 45 18N 72 9W
Magosa = Famagusta 106 35 8N 33 55 E
Magpie L. 61 51 0N 64 41W
Magrath 62 49 25N 112 50W
Maguarinho, C. 74 0 15 S 48 30W
Maguse L. 63 61 40N 95 10W
Maguse Pt. 63 61 20N 93 50W
Magwe 109 20 10N 95 0 E
Mahābād 106 36 50N 45 45 E
Mahabo 123 20 23 S 44 40 E
Mahaffey 45 40 53N 78 44W
Mahagi 122 2 20N 31 0 E
Mahaicony 71 6 36N 57 48W
Mahajamba, Helodranon' i 123 15 24 S 47 5 E
Mahakam → 110 0 35 S 117 17 E
Mahalapye 123 23 1 S 26 51 E
Maḩallāt 107 33 55N 50 30 E
Mahanadi → 109 20 20N 86 25 E
Mahanoro 123 19 54 S 48 48 E
Mahanoy City 45 40 49N 76 9W
Maharashtra □ 108 20 30N 75 30 E
Mahaska 24 39 59N 97 20W
Mahaska County ◇ 23 41 20N 92 40W
Mahbubnagar 108 16 45N 77 59 E
Mahdia, Guyana 71 5 13N 59 8W
Mahdia, Tunisia 121 35 28N 11 0 E
Mahenge 122 8 45 S 36 41 E
Maheno 128 45 10 S 170 50 E
Mahesana 108 23 39N 72 26 E
Mahia Pen. 128 39 9 S 177 55 E
Mahmudia 95 45 5N 29 5 E
Mahnomen 30 47 19N 95 58W
Mahnomen County ◇ 30 47 20N 95 45W
Mahomet 21 40 12N 88 24W
Mahón 91 39 53N 4 16 E
Mahone Bay 61 44 30N 64 20W
Mahoning County ◇ 42 41 6N 80 48W
Mahtowa 30 46 34N 92 38W
Mai-Ndombe, L. 122 2 0 S 18 20 E
Maicao 70 11 23N 72 13W
Maici → 73 6 30 S 61 43W
Maicurú → 71 2 14 S 54 17W
Maiden 40 35 35N 81 13W
Maiden Rock 55 44 34N 92 18W
Maidenhead 83 51 31N 0 42W
Maidstone, Canada 63 53 5N 109 20W
Maidstone, U.K. 83 51 16N 0 31 E
Maiduguri 121 12 0N 13 20 E
Maigualida, Sierra 71 5 30N 65 10W
Maijdi 109 22 48N 91 10 E
Maikala Ra. 109 22 0N 81 0 E
Maili 19 21 25N 158 11W
Maili Pt 19 21 24N 158 11W
Main →, Germany 88 50 0N 8 18 E
Main →, U.K. 85 54 49N 6 20W
Main Centre 63 50 35N 107 21W
Maine 90 48 0N 0 0 E
Maine □ 26 45 15N 69 15W
Maine → 85 52 10N 9 40W
Maine-et-Loire □ 90 47 31N 0 30W
Maingkwan 109 26 15N 96 37 E
Mainit, L. 111 9 31N 125 30 E
Mainland, Orkney, U.K. 84 59 0N 3 10W
Mainland, Shetland, U.K. 84 60 15N 1 22W
Maintirano 123 18 3 S 44 1 E
Mainz 88 50 0N 8 17 E
Maipú 76 36 52 S 57 50W
Maiquetía 70 10 36N 66 57W
Mairabari 109 26 30N 92 22 E
Maire, Le, Est. de 78 54 50 S 65 0W
Mairipotaba 75 17 18 S 49 28W
Maisí 67 20 17N 74 9W
Maisi, Pta. de 67 20 10N 74 10W
Maitland, Australia 127 32 33 S 151 36 E
Maitland, Maine 26 40 12N 95 5W
Maitland, Mo. 32 40 12N 95 5W
Maiz, Islas del 66 12 15N 83 4W
Maizuru 117 35 25N 135 22 E
Majagual 70 8 33N 74 38W
Majalengka 111 6 55 S 108 14 E
Majari → 71 3 29N 60 58W

* Renamed Kinbasket L.

Majd el Kurūm

Mantalingajan, Mt.

Majd el Kurūm 104 32 56N 35 15 E
Majene 111 3 38 S 118 57 E
Majes → 72 16 40 S 72 44W
Maji 121 6 12N 35 30 E
Major 63 51 52N 109 37W
Major County ◇ 43 36 15N 98 30W
Majorca, I. = Mallorca 91 39 30N 3 0 E
Majunga 123 15 40 S 46 25 E
Majuriã 73 7 30 S 64 55W
Maka 120 13 40N 14 10W
Makah Indian Reservation 53 48 23N 124 29W
Makaha 19 21 29N 158 13W
Makahoa Pt. 19 21 41N 157 56W
Makahuena Pt. 19 21 52N 159 27W
Makakilo City 19 21 22N 158 5W
Makale 111 3 6 S 119 51 E
Makanda 21 37 37N 89 13W
Makapuu Pt. 19 21 19N 157 39W
Makari 122 12 35N 14 28 E
Makarikari = Makgadikgadi Salt Pans 123 20 40 S 25 45 E
Makarovo 101 57 40N 107 45 E
Makasar = Ujung Pandang 111 5 10 S 119 20 E
Makasar, Selat 111 1 0 S 118 20 E
Makat 100 47 39N 53 19 E
Makawao 19 20 52N 156 17W
Makedhonía □ 95 40 39N 22 0 E
Makedonija □ 95 41 53N 21 40 E
Makeni 120 8 55N 12 5W
Makeyevka 99 48 0N 38 0 E
Makgadikgadi Salt Pans 123 20 40 S 25 45 E
Makhachkala 99 43 0N 47 30 E
Makian 111 0 20N 127 20 E
Makindu 122 2 18 S 37 50 E
Makinsk 100 52 37N 70 26 E
Makkah 106 21 30N 39 54 E
Makkovik 61 55 10N 59 10W
Maklakovo 101 58 16N 92 29 E
Makó 89 46 14N 20 33 E
Makokou 122 0 40N 12 50 E
Makoti 41 47 58N 101 48W
Makoua 122 0 5 S 15 50 E
Makrai 108 22 2N 77 0 E
Makran 107 26 13N 61 30 E
Makran Coast Range 107 25 40N 64 0 E
Maksimkin Yar 100 58 42N 86 50 E
Mākū 106 39 15N 44 31 E
Makumbi 122 5 50 S 20 43 E
Makurazaki 117 31 15N 130 20 E
Makurdi 121 7 43N 8 35 E
Makushin Volcano 11 53 53N 166 55W
Mal B. 85 52 50N 9 30W
Mala 72 12 40 S 76 38W
Mala, Pta. 66 7 28N 80 2W
Malabang 111 7 36N 124 3 E
Malabar 17 28 0N 80 34W
Malabar Coast 108 11 0N 75 0 E
Malacca, Str. of 112 3 0N 101 0 E
Malad City 20 42 12N 112 15W
Malae Pt. 19 20 7N 155 53W
Málaga, Colombia 70 6 42N 72 44W
Málaga, Spain 91 36 43N 4 23W
Malaga, N. Mex. 38 32 14N 104 4W
Malaga, Ohio 42 39 51N 81 9W
Málaga □ 91 36 38N 4 58W
Malakâl 121 9 33N 31 40 E
Malakand 108 34 40N 71 55 E
Malakoff 51 32 10N 96 1W
Malamyzh 101 50 0N 136 50 E
Malang 111 7 59 S 112 45 E
Malanje 122 9 36 S 16 17 E
Mälaren 97 59 30N 17 10 E
Malargüe 76 35 32 S 69 30W
Malartic 60 48 9N 78 9W
Malaspina Glacier 11 59 50N 140 30W
Malatya 106 38 25N 38 20 E
Malawi ■ 123 13 0 S 34 0 E
Malawi, L. 123 12 30 S 34 30 E
Malay Pen. 112 7 25N 100 0 E
Malaybalay 111 8 5N 125 7 E
Malāyer 106 34 19N 48 51 E
Malaysia ■ 110 5 0N 110 0 E
Malazgirt 106 39 10N 42 33 E
Malbaie, La 61 47 40N 70 10W
Malbork 89 54 3N 19 1 E
Malcolm, Australia 126 28 51 S 121 25 E
Malcolm, U.S.A. 34 40 54N 96 52W
Malcom 23 41 43N 92 33W
Maldegem 87 51 14N 3 26 E
Malden, Ill. 21 41 25N 89 22W
Malden, Mass. 28 42 26N 71 4W
Malden, Mo. 32 36 34N 89 57W
Malden I. 125 4 3 S 155 1W
Maldives ■ 102 7 0N 73 0 E
Maldonado 77 35 0 S 55 0W
Maldonado, Punta 65 16 19N 98 35W
Malé Karpaty 88 48 30N 17 20 E
Maléa, Ákra 95 36 28N 23 7 E
Malebo, Pool 118 4 17 S 15 20 E
Malegaon 108 20 30N 74 38 E
Malema 123 14 57 S 37 20 E
Malesus 48 35 33N 88 50W
Malgomaj 96 64 40N 16 30 E
Malha 121 15 8N 25 10 E
Malhão, Sa. do 91 37 25N 8 0W
Malheur → 44 44 4N 116 59W
Malheur County ◇ 44 45 15N 117 45W
Malheur L. 44 43 20N 118 48W
Malheur National Forest 44 44 10N 119 15W
Mali ■ 120 15 0N 2 0W
Mali → 109 25 40N 97 40 E
Mali Kyun 112 13 0N 98 20 E
Malibu 15 34 2N 118 41W
Malih → 104 32 20N 35 34 E
Malik 111 0 39 S 123 16 E
Malili 111 2 42 S 121 6 E
Malin 44 42 1N 121 24W
Malinau 110 3 35N 116 40 E
Malindi 122 3 12 S 40 5 E
Malines = Mechelen 87 51 2N 4 29 E
Maling 111 1 0N 121 0 E
Malinta 42 41 19N 84 2W
Malita 111 6 19N 125 39 E
Maljamar 38 32 51N 103 46W
Malko Tŭrnovo 95 41 59N 27 31 E
Mallacoota Inlet 127 37 34 S 149 40 E
Mallaig 84 57 0N 5 50W
Mallard 23 42 56N 94 41W
Mallawi 121 27 44N 30 44 E
Malleco □ 78 38 10 S 72 20W
Mallorca 91 39 30N 3 0 E
Mallow 85 52 8N 8 40W
Malmberget 96 67 11N 20 40 E
Malmédy 87 50 25N 6 2 E
Malmö, Sweden 97 55 36N 12 59 E
Malmo, U.S.A. 34 41 16N 96 43W
Malmöhus län □ 97 55 45N 13 30 E
Malnaş 95 46 2N 25 49 E
Malo Konare 95 42 12N 24 24 E
Maloca 71 0 43N 55 57W
Malolos 111 14 50N 120 49 E
Malomir 95 42 16N 26 30 E
Malone, Fla. 17 30 57N 85 10W
Malone, N.Y. 39 44 51N 74 18W
Malone, L. 48 37 5N 87 2W
Maloney, L. 34 41 3N 100 48W
Malorad 95 43 28N 23 41 E
Malott 53 48 17N 119 42W
Maloy 23 40 40N 94 25W
Malozemelskaya Tundra 98 67 0N 50 0 E
Malpelo 72 4 3N 81 35W
Malta, Brazil 74 6 54 S 37 31W
Malta, Idaho 20 42 18N 113 22W
Malta, Ill. 21 41 56N 88 52W
Malta, Mont. 33 48 21N 107 52W
Malta ■ 94 35 50N 14 30 E
Malta Bend 32 39 12N 93 22W
Maltahöhe 123 24 55 S 17 0 E
Malton 82 54 9N 0 48W
Maluku 111 1 0 S 127 0 E
Maluku □ 111 3 0 S 128 0 E
Maluku, Kepulauan 111 3 0 S 128 0 E
Malvan 108 16 2N 73 30 E
Malvern, U.K. 83 52 7N 2 19W
Malvern, Ark. 13 34 22N 92 49W
Malvern, Iowa 23 41 0N 95 35W
Malvern, Ohio 42 40 42N 81 11W
Malvern Hills 83 52 0N 2 19W
Malvinas, Is. = Falkland Is. 78 51 30 S 59 0W
Malyy Lyakhovskiy, Ostrov 101 74 7N 140 36 E
Mama 101 58 18N 112 54 E
Mamahatun 106 39 50N 40 23 E
Mamaia 89 44 18N 28 37 E
Mamala B. 19 21 15N 157 55W
Mamanguape 74 6 50 S 35 4W
Mamaroneck 39 40 57N 73 44W
Mamasa 111 2 55 S 119 20 E
Mamayes 57 18 22N 65 46W
Mamberamo → 111 2 0 S 137 50 E
Mambilima Falls 122 10 31 S 28 45 E
Mamburao 111 13 13N 120 39 E
Mameigwess L. 60 52 35N 87 50W
Mamfe 120 5 50N 9 15 E
Mamiña 72 20 5 S 69 14W
Mammoth 12 32 43N 110 39W
Mammoth Cave National Park 48 37 8N 86 13W
Mammoth Hot Springs 56 44 59N 110 42W
Mammoth Lakes 14 37 39N 118 59W
Mammoth Pool Reservoir 14 37 20N 119 19W
Mammoth Spring 13 36 30N 91 33W
Mamoré → 73 10 23 S 65 53W
Mamou, Guinea 120 10 15N 12 0W
Mamou, U.S.A. 25 30 38N 92 25W
Mampawah 110 0 30N 109 5 E
Mamuil Malal, Paso 78 39 35 S 71 28W
Mamuju 111 2 41 S 118 50 E
Man, Ivory C. 120 7 30N 7 40W
Man, U.S.A. 54 37 45N 81 53W
Man, I. of 82 54 15N 4 30W
Man Na 109 23 27N 97 19 E
Mana, Fr. Gui. 71 5 45N 53 55W
Mana, U.S.A. 19 22 2N 159 47W
Mana → 71 5 45N 53 55W
Manaar, Gulf of = Mannar, G. of 108 8 30N 79 0 E
Manabí □ 70 0 40 S 80 5W
Manacacías → 70 4 23N 72 4W
Manacapuru 71 3 16 S 60 37W
Manacapuru → 71 3 18 S 60 37W
Manacor 91 39 34N 3 13 E
Manado 111 1 29N 124 51 E
Managua 66 12 6N 86 20W
Managua, L. 66 12 20N 86 30W
Manahawkin 37 39 42N 74 16W
Manakara 123 22 8 S 48 1 E
Manana I. 19 21 20N 157 40W
Mananara 123 16 10 S 49 46 E
Mananjary 123 21 13 S 48 20 E
Manantenina 123 24 17 S 47 19 E
Manaos = Manaus 71 3 0 S 60 0W
Manapire → 70 7 42N 66 7W
Manapouri 128 45 34 S 167 39 E
Manapouri, L. 128 45 32 S 167 32 E
Manas 113 44 17N 85 56 E
Manas → 109 26 12N 90 40 E
Manasir 107 24 30N 51 10 E
Manasquan 37 40 8N 74 3W
Manasquan → 37 40 6N 74 2W
Manassa 16 37 11N 105 56W
Manassas 54 38 45N 77 29W
Manatee County ◇ 17 27 30N 82 30W
Manati 57 18 26N 66 30W
Manaung 109 18 45N 93 40 E
Manaus 71 3 0 S 60 0W
Manawa 55 44 28N 88 55W
Manawan L. 63 55 24N 103 14W
Manay 111 7 17N 126 33 E
Mancelona 29 44 54N 85 4W
Mancha, La 91 39 10N 2 54W
Manche □ 90 49 10N 1 20W
Manchegorsk 98 67 40N 32 40 E
Manchester, U.K. 82 53 30N 2 15W
Manchester, Calif. 14 38 58N 123 41W
Manchester, Conn. 28 41 47N 72 31W
Manchester, Ga. 18 32 51N 84 37W
Manchester, Iowa 23 42 29N 91 27W
Manchester, Kans. 24 39 6N 97 19W
Manchester, Ky. 49 37 9N 83 46W
Manchester, Mass. 28 42 35N 70 46W
Manchester, Md. 27 39 40N 76 53W
Manchester, Mich. 29 42 9N 84 2W
Manchester, N.H. 36 42 59N 71 28W
Manchester, Ohio 42 38 41N 83 36W
Manchester, Tenn. 48 35 29N 86 5W
Manchester, Vt. 36 43 10N 73 4W
Manchester L. 63 61 28N 107 29W
Mancora, Pta. 72 4 9 S 81 1W
Mancos 16 37 21N 108 18W
Mand → 107 28 20N 52 30 E
Manda 122 10 30 S 34 40 E
Mandabé 123 21 0 S 44 55 E
Mandaguari 77 23 32 S 51 42W
Mandal 97 58 2N 7 25 E
Mandalay 109 22 0N 96 4 E
Mandale = Mandalay 109 22 0N 96 4 E
Mandalī 106 33 43N 45 28 E
Mandan 41 46 50N 100 54W
Mandar, Teluk 111 3 35 S 119 15 E
Mandaree 41 47 43N 102 41W
Mandasor = Mandsaur 108 24 3N 75 8 E
Manderson 56 44 16N 107 58W
Mandeville 25 30 22N 90 4W
Mandi 108 31 39N 76 58 E
Mandimba 123 14 20 S 35 40 E
Mandioli 111 0 40 S 127 20 E
Mandioré, L. 73 18 8 S 57 33W
Mandla 109 22 39N 80 30 E
Mandritsara 123 15 50 S 48 49 E
Mandsaur 108 24 3N 75 8 E
Mandvi 108 22 51N 69 22 E
Mandya 108 12 30N 77 0 E
Manfalût 121 27 20N 30 52 E
Manfredónia 94 41 40N 15 55 E
Manga 75 14 46 S 43 56W
Mangabeiras, Chapada das 74 10 0 S 46 30W
Mangaia 128 21 55 S 157 55W
Mangalia 89 43 50N 28 35 E
Mangalore 108 12 55N 74 47 E
Manggar 110 2 50 S 108 10 E
Manggawitu 111 4 8 S 133 32 E
Mangham 25 32 19N 91 47W
Mangkalihat, Tanjung 111 1 2N 118 59 E
Mangla Dam 108 33 9N 73 44 E
Manglares, C. 70 1 36N 79 2W
Mangnai 113 37 52N 91 43 E
Mango 120 10 20N 0 30 E
Mangoche 123 14 25 S 35 16 E
Mangole 111 1 50 S 125 55 E
Mangonia Park 17 26 45N 80 4W
Mangonui 128 35 1 S 173 32 E
Mangueigne 121 10 30N 21 15 E
Mangueira, Lagoa da 77 33 0 S 52 50W
Mangum 43 34 53N 99 30W
Manhasset 39 40 48N 73 42W
Manhattan, Kans. 24 39 11N 96 35W
Manhattan, Mont. 33 45 51N 111 20W
Manhattan, N.Y. 39 40 45N 73 59W
Manhuaçu 75 20 15 S 42 2W
Manhumirim 75 20 22 S 41 57W
Maní 70 4 49N 72 17W
Manicoré 73 5 48 S 61 16W
Manicoré → 73 5 51 S 61 19W
Manicouagan → 61 49 30N 68 30W
Manicouagan L. 61 51 25N 68 15W
Manīfah 106 27 44N 49 0 E
Manifest 25 31 43N 91 58W
Manigotagan 63 51 6N 96 18W
Manigotagan L. 63 50 52N 95 37W
Manihiki 125 10 24 S 161 1W
Manila, Phil. 111 14 40N 121 3 E
Manila, Ark. 13 35 53N 90 10W
Manila, Utah 52 40 59N 109 43W
Manila B. 111 14 0N 120 0 E
Manilla 23 41 53N 95 14W
Manipur □ 109 25 0N 94 0 E
Manipur → 109 23 45N 94 20 E
Manisa 106 38 38N 27 30 E
Manistee 29 44 15N 86 19W
Manistee → 29 44 15N 86 21W
Manistee County ◇ 29 44 20N 86 10W
Manistee National Forest 29 44 0N 86 0W
Manistique 29 45 57N 86 15W
Manistique → 29 45 57N 86 15W
Manistique L. 29 46 15N 85 46W
Manito 21 40 26N 89 47W
Manito L. 63 52 43N 109 43W
Manitoba □ 63 55 30N 97 0W
Manitoba, L. 63 51 0N 98 45W
Manitou, Canada 63 49 15N 98 32W
Manitou, U.S.A. 43 34 30N 98 59W
Manitou Beach 29 41 58N 84 19W
Manitou I. 29 47 25N 87 37W
Manitou L., Ont., Canada 63 49 15N 93 0W
Manitou L., Qué., Canada 61 50 55N 65 17W
Manitou Springs 16 38 52N 104 55W
Manitoulin I. 60 45 40N 82 30W
Manitowaning 60 45 46N 81 49W
Manitowish 55 46 8N 90 1W
Manitowish Waters 55 46 9N 89 53W
Manitowoc 55 44 5N 87 40W
Manitowoc County ◇ 55 44 10N 87 50W
Manitsauá-Missu → 73 10 58 S 53 20W
Manizales 70 5 5N 75 32W
Manja 123 21 26 S 44 20 E
Manjacaze 123 24 45 S 34 0 E
Manjhand 108 25 50N 68 10 E
Manjil 106 36 46N 49 30 E
Manjimup 126 34 15 S 116 6 E
Manjra → 108 18 49N 77 52 E
Mankato, Kans. 24 39 47N 98 13W
Mankato, Minn. 30 44 10N 94 0W
Mankono 120 8 1N 6 10W
Mankota 63 49 25N 107 5W
Manley 34 40 55N 96 10W
Manley Hot Springs 11 65 0N 150 38W
Manlius 21 41 27N 89 40W
Manly 23 43 17N 93 12W
Manmad 108 20 18N 74 28 E
Manna 110 4 25 S 102 55 E
Mannar 108 9 1N 79 54 E
Mannar, G. of 108 8 30N 79 0 E
Mannar I. 108 9 5N 79 45 E
Mannford 43 36 8N 96 24W
Mannheim 88 49 28N 8 29 E
Manning, Canada 62 56 53N 117 39W
Manning, Ark. 13 34 1N 92 48W
Manning, Iowa 23 41 55N 95 3W
Manning, N. Dak. 41 47 14N 102 46W
Manning, S.C. 46 33 42N 80 13W
Manning Prov. Park 62 49 5N 120 45W
Mannington, Ky. 48 37 8N 87 28W
Mannington, W. Va. 54 39 32N 80 21W
Manns Harbor 40 35 53N 75 46W
Mannsville, N.Y. 39 43 43N 76 4W
Mannsville, Okla. 43 34 11N 96 53W
Mano 120 8 3N 12 2W
Manoa 73 9 40 S 65 27W
Manokin 27 38 5N 75 55W
Manokotak 11 58 58N 159 3W
Manokwari 111 0 54 S 134 0 E
Manombo 123 22 57 S 43 28 E
Manono 122 7 15 S 27 25 E
Manouane L. 61 50 45N 70 45W
Manresa 91 41 48N 1 50 E
Mans, Le 90 48 0N 0 10 E
Mansa 122 11 13 S 28 55 E
Mansel I. 59 62 0N 80 0W
Mansfield, U.K. 82 53 8N 1 12W
Mansfield, Ark. 13 35 4N 94 15W
Mansfield, Ga. 18 33 31N 83 44W
Mansfield, Ill. 21 40 13N 88 31W
Mansfield, La. 25 32 2N 93 43W
Mansfield, Mass. 28 42 2N 71 13W
Mansfield, Mo. 32 37 6N 92 35W
Mansfield, Ohio 42 40 45N 82 31W
Mansfield, Pa. 45 41 48N 77 5W
Mansfield, S. Dak. 47 45 15N 98 34W
Mansfield, Tenn. 48 36 11N 88 17W
Mansfield, Tex. 51 32 34N 97 9W
Mansfield, Wash. 53 47 49N 119 38W
Mansfield, Mt. 36 44 33N 72 49W
Mansfield Hollow L. 28 41 45N 72 11W
Mansfield L. 22 39 43N 87 4W
Mansidão 74 10 43 S 44 2W
Manso → 75 13 50 S 47 0W
Manson, Iowa 23 42 32N 94 32W
Manson, Wash. 53 47 53N 120 9W
Manson Creek 62 55 37N 124 32W
Mansura 25 31 4N 92 3W
Manta 70 1 0 S 80 40W
Manta, B. de 70 0 54 S 80 44W
Mantador 41 46 10N 96 59W
Mantalingajan, Mt. 110 8 55N 117 45 E

Manteca Marshville

Manteca 14 37 48N 121 13W
Mantecal 70 7 34N 69 17W
Mantee 31 33 44N 89 3W
Mantena 75 18 47S 40 59W
Manteno 21 41 15N 87 50W
Manteo 40 35 55N 75 40W
Manter 24 37 31N 101 53W
Mantes-la-Jolie 90 49 0N 1 41 E
Manthani 108 18 40N 79 35 E
Manti 52 39 16N 111 38W
Manti-la Sal National Forest 52 37 50N 109 50W
Mantiqueira, Serra da 75 22 0S 44 0W
Mantoloking 37 40 4N 74 4W
Manton 29 44 25N 85 24W
Mantorville 30 44 5N 92 45W
Mántova 94 45 20N 10 42 E
Mänttä 96 62 0N 24 40 E
Mantua = Mántova 94 45 20N 10 42 E
Mantua, Ohio 42 41 17N 81 14W
Mantua, Utah 52 41 30N 111 57W
Manu 72 12 10S 70 51W
Manu → 72 12 16S 70 55W
Manua Is. 128 14 13S 169 35W
Manuae 125 19 30S 159 0W
Manuel Alves → 75 11 19S 48 28W
Manuel Alves Grande → 74 7 27S 47 35W
Manuel Urbano 72 8 53S 69 18W
Manuelito 38 35 24N 109 0W
Manui 111 3 35S 123 5 E
Manuripi → 72 11 6S 67 36W
Manvel 41 48 5N 97 11W
Manville, N.J. 37 40 33N 74 35W
Manville, Wyo. 56 42 47N 104 37W
Many 25 31 34N 93 29W
Manyara, L. 122 3 40S 35 50 E
Manych-Gudilo, Oz. 99 46 24N 42 38 E
Manyoni 122 5 45S 34 55 E
Manzai 108 32 12N 70 15 E
Manzanares 91 39 0N 3 22W
Manzanillo, Cuba 66 20 20N 77 31W
Manzanillo, Mexico 64 19 0N 104 20W
Manzanillo, Pta. 66 9 30N 79 40W
Manzanita 44 45 43N 123 56W
Manzano Mts. 38 34 40N 106 20W
Manzanola 16 38 6N 103 52W
Manzhouli 114 49 35N 117 25 E
Mao 121 14 4N 15 19 E
Maoke, Pegunungan 111 3 40S 137 30 E
Maoming 115 21 50N 110 54 E
Mapam Yumco 113 30 45N 81 28 E
Mapastepec 65 15 26N 92 54W
Mapia, Kepulauan 111 0 50N 134 20 E
Mapimí 64 25 50N 103 50W
Mapimí, Bolsón de 64 27 30N 104 15W
Mapire 71 7 45N 64 42W
Maple →, Iowa 23 42 0N 95 59W
Maple →, Mich. 29 42 59N 84 57W
Maple →, N. Dak. 41 46 56N 96 55W
Maple →, S. Dak. 47 45 48N 98 38W
Maple Creek 63 49 55N 109 29W
Maple Falls 53 48 56N 122 5W
Maple Hill, Kans. 24 39 5N 96 2W
Maple Hill, N.C. 40 34 40N 77 42W
Maple Rapids 29 43 6N 84 42W
Maple Shade 37 39 57N 74 58W
Maplesville 10 32 47N 86 52W
Mapleton, Iowa 23 42 10N 95 47W
Mapleton, Kans. 24 38 1N 94 53W
Mapleton, Minn. 30 43 56N 93 57W
Mapleton, Oreg. 44 44 2N 123 52W
Mapleton, Utah 52 40 8N 111 35W
Mapuera → 71 1 5S 57 2W
Maputo 123 25 58S 32 32 E
Maqnā 106 28 25N 34 50 E
Maquela do Zombo 122 6 0S 15 15 E
Maquinchao 78 41 15S 68 50W
Maquoketa 23 42 4N 90 40W
Maquoketa → 23 42 11N 90 19W
Maquon 21 40 48N 90 10W
Mar, Serra do 77 25 30S 49 0W
Mar Chiquita, L. 76 30 40S 62 50W
Mar del Plata 76 38 0S 57 30W
Mara 71 6 0N 57 36W
Maraā 70 1 52S 65 25W
Marabá 74 5 20S 49 5W
Maracá, I. de 74 2 10N 50 30W
Maracaibo 70 10 40N 71 37W
Maracaibo, Lago de 70 9 40N 71 30W
Maracaju 77 21 38S 55 9W
Maracajú, Serra de 73 23 57S 55 1W
Maracanã 74 0 46S 47 27W
Maracás 75 13 26S 40 18W
Maracay 70 10 15N 67 28W
Marādah 121 29 15N 19 15 E
Maradi 120 13 29N 8 10 E
Marāgheh 106 37 30N 46 12 E
Maragogipe 75 12 46S 38 55W
Marāh 106 25 0N 45 35 E
Marais des Cygnes → 24 38 2N 94 14W
Marajó, B. de 74 1 0S 48 30W
Marajó, Ilha de 74 1 0S 49 30W
Maralal 122 1 0N 36 38 E
Maralinga 126 30 13S 131 32 E
Maramec 43 36 15N 96 41W
Marampa 120 8 45N 12 28W
Marana 12 32 27N 111 13W
Marand 106 38 30N 45 45 E
Maranguape 74 3 55S 38 50W
Maranhão = São Luís 74 2 39S 44 15W
Maranhão □ 74 5 0S 46 0W
Maranoa → 127 27 50S 148 37 E
Marañón → 72 4 30S 73 35W
Marão 123 24 18S 34 2 E
Marapi → 71 0 37N 55 58W
Marari 72 5 43S 67 47W
Maraş 106 37 37N 36 53 E
Mărăşeşti 95 45 52N 27 14 E
Marathon, Canada 60 48 44N 86 23W
Marathón, Greece 95 38 11N 23 58 E
Marathon, Fla. 17 24 43N 81 5W
Marathon, Iowa 23 42 52N 94 59W
Marathon, N.Y. 39 42 27N 76 2W
Marathon, Tex. 50 30 12N 103 15W
Marathon, Wis. 55 44 56N 89 50W
Marathon County ◇ 55 44 50N 89 45W
Maratua 111 2 10N 118 35 E
Maraú 75 14 6S 39 0W
Maravatío 64 19 51N 100 25W
Maravillas Cr. → 50 29 34N 102 47W
Marbella 91 36 30N 4 57W
Marble, Ark. 13 36 8N 93 35W
Marble, Colo. 16 39 4N 107 12W
Marble, N.C. 40 35 10N 83 55W
Marble Bar 126 21 9S 119 44 E
Marble Canyon 12 36 49N 111 38W
Marble City 43 35 35N 94 49W
Marble Falls 51 30 35N 98 16W
Marble Hill 32 37 18N 89 58W
Marble Rock 23 42 58N 92 52W
Marblehead 28 42 30N 70 51W
Marblemount 53 48 32N 121 26W
Marbleton 56 42 34N 110 7W
Marburg 88 50 49N 8 36 E
Marbury 27 38 35N 77 10W
Marcapata 72 13 31S 70 52W
Marceline 32 39 43N 92 57W
Marcellus, Mich. 29 42 2N 85 49W
Marcellus, N.Y. 39 42 59N 76 20W
Marcellus, Wash. 53 47 14N 118 24W
March 83 52 33N 0 5 E
Marché 90 46 0N 1 20 E
Marche □ 94 43 22N 13 10 E
Marche-en-Famenne 87 50 14N 5 19 E
Marches = Marche □ 94 43 22N 13 10 E
Marco 17 25 58N 81 44W
Marcola 44 44 10N 122 52W
Marcona 72 15 10S 75 0W
Marcos Juárez 76 32 42S 62 5W
Marcus, Pac. Oc. 124 24 0N 153 45 E
Marcus, U.S.A. 23 42 50N 95 48W
Marcus Baker, Mt. 11 61 26N 147 45W
Marcus Necker Ridge 124 20 0N 175 0 E
Marcy, Mt. 39 44 7N 73 56W
Mardan 108 34 20N 72 0 E
Mardela Springs 27 38 28N 75 45W
Mardin 106 37 20N 40 43 E
Marechal Deodoro 74 9 43S 35 54W
Maree L. 84 57 40N 5 30W
Mareeba 127 16 59S 145 28 E
Marek = Stanke Dimitrov 95 42 17N 23 9 E
Marek 111 4 41S 120 24 E
Maremma 94 42 45N 11 15 E
Marengo, Ill. 21 42 15N 88 37W
Marengo, Ind. 22 38 22N 86 21W
Marengo, Iowa 23 41 48N 92 4W
Marengo, Ohio 42 40 24N 82 49W
Marengo, Wash. 53 47 1N 118 12W
Marengo County ◇ 10 32 18N 87 48W
Marenisco 29 46 23N 89 45W
Marfa 50 30 19N 104 1W
Margaret Bay 62 51 20N 126 35W
Margaret L. 62 58 56N 115 25W
Margaretville 39 42 9N 74 39W
Margarita 57 9 20N 79 55W
Margarita, Isla de 71 11 0N 64 0W
Margaritovo 116 43 25N 134 45 E
Margate, U.K. 83 51 23N 1 24 E
Margate, U.S.A. 17 26 15N 80 12W
Margate City 37 39 20N 74 30W
Marguerite 62 52 30N 122 25W
Mari A.S.S.R. □ 98 56 30N 48 0 E
María Elena 76 22 18S 69 40W
María Grande 76 31 45S 59 55W
Maria I. 126 14 52S 135 45 E
Maria van Diemen, C. 128 34 29S 172 40 E
Marian, L. 17 27 53N 81 6W
Marian L. 62 63 0N 116 15W
Mariana Trench 124 13 0N 145 0 E
Marianao 66 23 8N 82 24W
Marianna, Ark. 13 34 46N 90 46W
Marianna, Fla. 17 30 46N 85 14W
Marianna, Pa. 45 40 2N 80 6W
Marias → 33 47 56N 110 30W
Mariato, Punta 66 7 12N 80 52W
Ma'rib 105 15 25N 45 21 E
Maribor 94 46 36N 15 40 E
Maricao 57 18 11N 66 59W
Maricopa, Ariz. 12 33 4N 112 3W
Maricopa, Calif. 15 35 4N 119 24W
Maricopa County ◇ 12 33 15N 112 30W
Maricopa Indian Reservation 12 33 0N 112 10W
Maricopa Mts. 12 32 0N 112 30W
Marīdī 121 4 55N 29 25 E
Marié → 70 0 27S 66 26W
Marie-Galante 67 15 56N 61 16W
Mariecourt 59 61 30N 72 0W
Mariehamn 97 60 5N 19 55 E
Marienberg 87 52 30N 6 35 E
Marienbourg 87 50 6N 4 31 E
Mariental 123 24 36S 18 0 E
Marienthal 24 38 29N 101 13W
Marienville 45 41 28N 79 8W
Maries → 32 38 30N 92 1W
Maries County ◇ 32 38 10N 91 55W
Mariestad 97 58 43N 13 50 E
Marietta, Ga. 18 33 57N 84 33W
Marietta, Miss. 31 34 30N 88 28W
Marietta, Ohio 42 39 25N 81 27W
Marietta, Okla. 43 33 56N 97 7W
Marietta, S.C. 46 35 1N 82 30W
Mariinsk 100 56 10N 87 20 E
Marília 75 22 13S 50 0W
Marín 91 42 23N 8 42W
Marin County ◇ 14 38 0N 122 45W
Marina 14 36 41N 121 48W
Marinduque 111 13 25N 122 0 E
Marine 21 38 47N 89 47W
Marine City 29 42 43N 82 30W
Marine on St. Croix 30 45 12N 92 46W
Marinel, Le 122 10 25S 25 17 E
Marineland 17 29 40N 81 13W
Marinette 55 45 6N 87 38W
Marinette County ◇ 55 45 25N 88 10W
Maringá 77 23 26S 52 2W
Maringouin 25 30 29N 91 31W
Marion, Ala. 10 32 38N 87 19W
Marion, Ark. 13 35 13N 90 12W
Marion, Ill. 21 37 44N 88 56W
Marion, Ind. 22 40 32N 85 40W
Marion, Iowa 23 42 2N 91 36W
Marion, Kans. 24 38 21N 97 1W
Marion, Ky. 48 37 20N 88 5W
Marion, La. 25 32 54N 92 15W
Marion, Mass. 28 41 42N 70 46W
Marion, Mich. 29 44 6N 85 9W
Marion, Miss. 31 32 25N 88 39W
Marion, Mont. 33 48 6N 114 40W
Marion, N.C. 40 35 41N 82 1W
Marion, N. Dak. 41 46 37N 98 20W
Marion, Nebr. 34 40 1N 100 29W
Marion, Ohio 42 40 35N 83 8W
Marion, S.C. 46 34 11N 79 24W
Marion, S. Dak. 47 43 25N 97 16W
Marion, Va. 54 36 50N 81 31W
Marion, Wis. 55 44 39N 88 54W
Marion, L. 46 33 28N 80 10W
Marion County ◇, Ala. 10 34 9N 87 59W
Marion County ◇, Ark. 13 36 14N 92 41W
Marion County ◇, Fla. 17 29 15N 82 0W
Marion County ◇, Ga. 18 32 25N 84 35W
Marion County ◇, Ill. 21 38 40N 88 55W
Marion County ◇, Ind. 22 39 45N 86 10W
Marion County ◇, Iowa 23 41 20N 93 5W
Marion County ◇, Kans. 24 38 20N 97 0W
Marion County ◇, Ky. 49 37 30N 85 15W
Marion County ◇, Miss. 31 31 15N 89 50W
Marion County ◇, Mo. 32 39 50N 91 35W
Marion County ◇, Ohio 42 40 35N 83 8W
Marion County ◇, Oreg. 44 44 50N 122 50W
Marion County ◇, S.C. 46 34 10N 79 20W
Marion County ◇, Tenn. 49 35 5N 85 38W
Marion County ◇, Tex. 51 32 46N 94 21W
Marion County ◇, W. Va. 54 39 29N 80 9W
Marion Junction 10 32 26N 87 14W
Marion Lake 24 38 22N 97 5W
Marion Reef 127 19 10S 152 17 E
Marion Station 27 38 2N 75 46W
Marionville 32 37 0N 93 38W
Maripa 71 7 26N 65 9W
Maripasoula 71 3 40N 54 4W
Mariposa 14 37 29N 119 58W
Mariposa County ◇ 14 37 30N 120 0W
Mariscal Estigarribia 76 22 3S 60 40W
Marissa 21 38 15N 89 45W
Maritsa 95 42 1N 25 50 E
Maritsa → 95 42 15N 24 0 E
Marīvān 106 35 30N 46 25 E
Mark Twain National Forest 32 36 50N 92 0W
Markazī □ 107 35 0N 49 30 E
Marked Tree 13 35 32N 90 25W
Marken 87 52 26N 5 12 E
Markesan 55 43 42N 88 59W
Market Drayton 82 52 55N 2 30W
Market Harborough 83 52 29N 0 55W
Markham 51 28 58N 96 4W
Markham I. 4 84 0N 0 45W
Markham L. 63 62 30N 102 35W
Markham Mt. 5 83 0S 164 0 E
Markle 22 40 50N 85 20W
Markleeville 14 38 42N 119 47W
Markleville 22 39 59N 85 37W
Markleysburg 45 39 44N 79 27W
Markovo 101 64 40N 169 40 E
Marks, U.S.A. 31 34 16N 90 16W
Marks, U.S.S.R. 98 51 45N 46 50 E
Marks Butte 16 40 53N 102 23W
Marksville 25 31 8N 92 4W
Marland 43 36 34N 97 9W
Marlboro, N.J. 37 40 19N 74 15W
Marlboro, N.Y. 39 41 36N 73 59W
Marlboro County ◇ 46 34 40N 79 40W
Marlborough, Conn. 28 41 8N 72 27W
Marlborough, Mass. 28 42 21N 71 33W
Marlborough, N.H. 36 42 54N 72 13W
Marlborough □ 128 41 45S 173 33 E
Marlborough Downs 83 51 25N 1 55W
Marlette 29 43 20N 83 5W
Marlin, Tex. 51 31 18N 96 54W
Marlin, Wash. 53 47 25N 118 59W
Marlinton 54 38 13N 80 6W
Marlow, Ga. 18 32 16N 81 23W
Marlow, N.H. 36 43 9N 72 12W
Marlow, Okla. 43 34 39N 97 58W
Marlton 37 39 54N 74 55W
Marmaduke 13 36 11N 90 23W
Marmagao 108 15 25N 73 56 E
Marmara 95 40 35N 27 38 E
Marmara, Sea of = Marmara Denizi 106 40 45N 28 15 E
Marmara Denizi 106 40 45N 28 15 E
Marmaris 106 36 50N 28 14 E
Marmarth 41 46 18N 103 54W
Marmelos → 73 6 6S 61 46W
Marmion L. 60 48 55N 91 20W
Marmolada, Mte. 94 46 25N 11 55 E
Marmora, Canada 60 44 28N 77 41W
Marmora, U.S.A. 37 39 16N 74 39W
Marne 23 41 27N 95 6W
Marne □ 90 49 0N 4 10 E
Marne → 90 8 23N 18 36 E
Maro Reef 19 25 25N 170 35W
Maroa, U.S.A. 21 40 2N 88 57W
Maroa, Venezuela 70 2 43N 67 33W
Maroantsetra 123 15 26S 49 44 E
Marondera 123 18 5S 31 42 E
Maroni → 71 4 0N 52 0W
Maroua 121 10 40N 14 20 E
Marovoay 123 16 6S 46 39 E
Marowijne □ 71 4 0N 55 0W
Marowijne → 71 5 45N 53 58W
Marquand 32 37 26N 90 10W
Marquesas Is. 125 9 30S 140 0W
Marquesas Keys 17 24 35N 82 10W
Marquette, Iowa 23 43 3N 91 11W
Marquette, Kans. 24 38 33N 97 50W
Marquette, Mich. 29 46 33N 87 24W
Marquette County ◇, Mich. 29 46 20N 87 30W
Marquette County ◇, Wis. 55 43 50N 89 25W
Marquette I. 29 45 58N 84 24W
Marquez 51 31 14N 96 15W
Marra, Gebel 121 7 20N 27 35 E
Marrakech 120 31 9N 8 0W
Marrecas, Serra das 74 9 0S 41 0W
Marree 127 29 39S 138 1 E
Marrero 25 29 54N 90 6W
Marromeu 123 18 40S 36 25 E
Marrowbone 49 36 50N 85 30W
Marrupa 123 13 8S 37 30 E
Mars 45 40 42N 80 1W
Mars Hill, Maine 26 46 31N 67 52W
Mars Hill, N.C. 40 35 50N 82 33W
Marsá Susah 121 32 52N 21 59 E
Marsabit 122 2 18N 38 0 E
Marsala 94 37 48N 12 25 E
Marsaxlokk 94 35 47N 14 32 E
Marseille 90 43 18N 5 23 E
Marseilles = Marseille 90 43 18N 5 23 E
Marseilles 21 41 20N 88 43W
Marsh I. 25 29 34N 91 53W
Marsh Pass 12 36 36N 110 35W
Marsh Peak 52 40 43N 109 50W
Marshall = Fortuna Ledge 11 61 53N 162 5W
Marshall, Liberia 120 6 8N 10 22W
Marshall, Ark. 13 35 55N 92 38W
Marshall, Ill. 21 39 23N 87 42W
Marshall, Ind. 22 39 51N 87 11W
Marshall, Mich. 29 42 16N 84 58W
Marshall, Mo. 32 39 7N 93 12W
Marshall, N.C. 40 35 48N 82 41W
Marshall, Okla. 43 36 9N 97 38W
Marshall, Tex. 51 32 33N 94 23W
Marshall County ◇, Ala. 10 34 21N 86 18W
Marshall County ◇, Ill. 21 41 0N 89 20W
Marshall County ◇, Ind. 22 41 20N 86 15W
Marshall County ◇, Iowa 23 42 0N 93 0W
Marshall County ◇, Kans. 24 39 45N 96 30W
Marshall County ◇, Ky. 48 36 55N 88 20W
Marshall County ◇, Minn. 30 48 15N 96 15W
Marshall County ◇, Miss. 31 34 46N 89 27W
Marshall County ◇, Okla. 43 34 0N 96 50W
Marshall County ◇, S. Dak. 47 45 48N 97 45W
Marshall County ◇, Tenn. 48 35 27N 86 48W
Marshall County ◇, W. Va. 54 39 50N 80 34W
Marshall Is. 124 9 0N 171 0 E
Marshallberg 40 34 44N 76 31W
Marshallton 27 39 44N 75 39W
Marshalltown 23 42 3N 92 55W
Marshallville, Ga. 18 32 27N 89 56W
Marshallville, Ohio 42 40 54N 81 44W
Marshfield, Mo. 32 37 15N 92 54W
Marshfield, Vt. 36 44 20N 72 20W
Marshfield, Wis. 55 44 40N 90 10W
Marshfield Hills 28 42 9N 70 44W
Marshville 40 35 0N 80 25W

Marshyhope Mazīnān

Marshyhope → 27 38 32N 75 45W
Marsing 20 43 33N 116 48W
Marston 32 36 31N 89 37W
Marstrand 97 57 53N 11 35 E
Mart 51 31 33N 96 50W
Martaban 109 16 30N 97 35 E
Martaban, G. of 109 16 5N 96 30 E
Martapura, Kalimantan, Indonesia 110 3 22 S 114 47 E
Martapura, Sumatera, Indonesia 110 4 19 S 104 22 E
Marte 121 12 23N 13 46 E
Martelange 87 49 49N 5 43 E
Martelle 23 42 1N 91 22W
Martensdale 23 41 23N 93 45W
Martha's Vineyard 28 41 25N 70 38W
Marthasville 32 38 38N 91 4W
Marthaville 25 31 44N 93 24W
Martin, Mich. 29 42 32N 85 39W
Martin, N. Dak. 41 47 50N 100 7W
Martin, S. Dak. 47 43 11N 101 44W
Martin, Tenn. 48 36 21N 88 51W
Martin County ◇, Fla. 17 27 10N 80 20W
Martin County ◇, Ind. 22 38 40N 86 50W
Martin County ◇, Ky. 49 37 45N 82 30W
Martin County ◇, Minn. 30 43 40N 94 30W
Martin County ◇, N.C. 40 35 45N 77 0W
Martin County ◇, Tex. 50 32 18N 101 58W
Martin L. 10 32 41N 85 55W
Martin Pt. 11 70 8N 143 16W
Martinborough 128 41 14 S 175 29 E
Martinez 14 38 1N 122 8W
Martinez L. 12 32 59N 114 29W
Martinho Campos 75 19 20 S 45 13W
Martinique 67 14 40N 61 0W
Martinique Passage 67 15 15N 61 0W
Martinópolis 77 22 11 S 51 12W
Martins Ferry 42 40 6N 80 44W
Martinsburg, Md. 27 39 10N 77 28W
Martinsburg, Mo. 32 39 6N 91 39W
Martinsburg, Nebr. 34 42 30N 96 50W
Martinsburg, Ohio 42 40 16N 82 21W
Martinsburg, Pa. 45 40 19N 78 20W
Martinsburg, W. Va. 54 39 27N 77 58W
Martinsville, Ill. 21 39 20N 87 53W
Martinsville, Ind. 22 39 26N 86 25W
Martinsville, Va. 54 36 41N 79 52W
Martinton 21 40 55N 87 44W
Marton 128 40 4 S 175 23 E
Martos 91 37 44N 3 58W
Marudi 110 4 10N 114 19 E
Ma'ruf 107 31 30N 67 6 E
Marugame 117 34 15N 133 40 E
Maruim 74 10 45 S 37 5W
Marvel 16 37 7N 108 8W
Marvell 13 34 33N 90 55W
Marvin 47 45 16N 96 55W
Marvine, Mt. 52 38 40N 111 39W
Marwar 108 25 43N 73 45 E
Mary 100 37 40N 61 50 E
Mary Frances L. 63 63 19N 106 13W
Mary Kathleen 127 20 44 S 139 48 E
Maryborough = Port Laoise 85 53 2N 7 20W
Maryborough, Queens., Australia 127 25 31 S 152 37 E
Maryborough, Vic., Australia 127 37 0 S 143 44 E
Marydel 27 39 7N 75 45W
Maryfield 63 49 50N 101 35W
Maryhill 53 45 41N 120 49W
Maryland □ 27 39 0N 76 30W
Maryland City 27 39 6N 76 50W
Maryland Line 27 39 43N 76 40W
Maryland Point 27 38 22N 77 14W
Maryneal 50 32 14N 100 27W
Maryport 82 54 43N 3 30W
Marys → 35 41 4N 115 16W
Marys Corner 53 46 33N 122 49W
Mary's Harbour 61 52 18N 55 51W
Marys Pk. 44 44 30N 123 33W
Marystown 61 47 10N 55 10W
Marysvale 52 38 27N 112 14W
Marysville, Canada 62 49 35N 116 0W
Marysville, Calif. 14 39 9N 121 35W
Marysville, Kans. 24 39 51N 96 39W
Marysville, Mich. 29 42 54N 82 29W
Marysville, Ohio 42 40 14N 83 22W
Marysville, Pa. 45 40 21N 76 56W
Marysville, Wash. 53 48 3N 122 11W
Maryville, Mo. 32 40 21N 94 52W
Maryville, Tenn. 49 35 46N 83 58W
Marzo, Punta 70 6 50N 77 42W
Marzūq 121 25 53N 13 57 E
Masada = Mesada 104 31 20N 35 19 E
Masaka 122 0 21 S 31 45 E
Masalembo, Kepulauan 110 5 35 S 114 30 E
Masalima, Kepulauan 110 5 4 S 117 5 E
Masamba 111 2 30 S 120 15 E
Masan 114 35 11N 128 32 E
Masandam, Ras 107 26 30N 56 30 E
Masardis 26 46 30N 68 22W
Masaryktown 17 28 27N 82 27W
Masasi 122 10 45 S 38 52 E
Masaya 66 12 0N 86 7W
Masbate 111 12 21N 123 36 E
Mascara 120 35 26N 0 6 E
Mascot 49 36 4N 83 45W
Mascota 64 20 30N 104 50W
Mascoutah 21 38 29N 89 48W
Masela 111 8 9 S 129 51 E
Maseru 123 29 18 S 27 30 E
Mashābih 106 25 35N 36 30 E
Mashan 115 23 40N 108 11 E
Mashhad 107 36 20N 59 35 E
Mashkel, Hamun-i- 107 28 30N 63 0 E
Mashki Chāh 107 29 5N 62 30 E
Mashulaville 31 33 5N 88 45W
Masi 96 69 26N 23 40 E
Masi Manimba 122 4 40 S 17 54 E
Masindi 122 1 40N 31 43 E
Masisea 72 8 35 S 74 22W
Masjed Soleyman 106 31 55N 49 18 E
Mask, L. 85 53 36N 9 24W
Maskell 34 42 41N 96 59W
Maslen Nos 95 42 18N 27 48 E
Masoala, Tanjon' i 123 15 59 S 50 13 E
Masohi 111 3 2 S 128 15 E
Mason, Ill. 21 38 57N 88 38W
Mason, Mich. 29 42 35N 84 27W
Mason, N.H. 36 42 45N 71 47W
Mason, Ohio 42 39 22N 84 19W
Mason, Tenn. 48 35 25N 89 32W
Mason, Tex. 51 30 45N 99 14W
Mason, W. Va. 54 39 1N 82 2W
Mason, Wis. 55 46 26N 91 4W
Mason City, Ill. 21 40 12N 89 42W
Mason City, Iowa 23 43 9N 93 12W
Mason City, Nebr. 34 41 13N 99 18W
Mason County ◇, Ill. 21 40 15N 89 50W
Mason County ◇, Ky. 49 38 35N 83 50W
Mason County ◇, Mich. 29 44 0N 86 15W
Mason County ◇, Tex. 51 30 45N 99 15W
Mason County ◇, W. Va. 54 38 50N 82 8W
Mason County ◇, Wash. 53 47 20N 123 10W
Mason Springs 27 38 36N 77 10W
Masontown 54 39 33N 79 48W
Masonville, Colo. 16 40 29N 105 13W
Masonville, Iowa 23 42 29N 91 36W
Masqat 107 23 37N 58 36 E
Massa 94 44 2N 10 7 E
Massabesic L. 36 43 0N 71 23W
Massac County ◇ 21 37 15N 88 45W
Massachusetts □ 28 42 30N 72 0W
Massachusetts B. 28 42 20N 70 50W
Massacre L. 35 41 39N 119 36W
Massada 104 33 41N 35 36 E
Massaguet 121 12 28N 15 26 E
Massakory 121 13 0N 15 49 E
Massangena 123 21 34 S 33 0 E
Massapê 74 3 31 S 40 19W
Massapequa 39 40 41N 73 29W
Massawa = Mitsiwa 121 15 35N 39 25 E
Massena, Iowa 23 41 15N 94 46W
Massena, N.Y. 39 44 56N 74 54W
Massénya 121 11 21N 16 9 E
Masset 62 54 2N 132 10W
Massey 27 39 18N 75 49W
Massif Central 90 45 30N 2 21 E
Massillon 42 40 48N 81 32W
Massinga 123 23 15 S 35 22 E
Masson I. 5 66 10 S 93 20 E
Mastanli = Momchilgrad 95 41 33N 25 23 E
Masten's Corner 27 38 57N 75 37W
Masters 16 40 18N 104 15W
Masterton 128 40 56 S 175 39 E
Mastic 39 40 47N 72 54W
Mastuj 108 36 20N 72 36 E
Mastung 107 29 50N 66 56 E
Masuda 117 34 40N 131 51 E
Masvingo 123 20 8 S 30 49 E
Mata de São João 75 12 31 S 38 17W
Mataboor 111 1 41 S 138 3 E
Matachewan 60 47 56N 80 39W
Matacuni → 71 3 2N 65 16W
Matad 113 47 11N 115 27 E
Matadi 122 5 52 S 13 31 E
Matador 50 34 1N 100 49W
Matagalpa 66 13 0N 85 58W
Matagami 60 49 45N 77 34W
Matagami, L. 60 49 50N 77 40W
Matagorda 51 28 42N 95 58W
Matagorda B. 51 28 40N 96 0W
Matagorda County ◇ 51 29 0N 96 0W
Matagorda I. 51 28 15N 96 30W
Matagorda Peninsula 51 28 38N 96 0W
Matak, P. 110 3 18N 106 16 E
Matalaque 72 16 26 S 70 49W
Matam 120 15 34N 13 17W
Matamoros, Campeche, Mexico 65 18 50N 90 50W
Matamoros, Coahuila, Mexico 64 25 33N 103 15W
Matamoros, Puebla, Mexico 65 18 2N 98 17W
Matamoros, Tamaulipas, Mexico 65 25 50N 97 30W
Ma'ṭan as Sarra 121 21 45N 22 0 E
Matane 61 48 50N 67 33W
Matanuska-Susitna ◇ 11 62 30N 150 0W
Matanzas 66 23 0N 81 40W
Matapan, C. = Taínaron, Ákra 95 36 22N 22 27 E
Matapédia 61 48 0N 66 59W
Matara 108 5 58N 80 30 E
Mataram 110 8 41 S 116 10 E
Matarani 72 17 0 S 72 10W
Mataranka 126 14 55 S 133 4 E
Mataura 128 46 11 S 168 51 E
Matawan 37 40 25N 74 14W
Mategua 73 13 1 S 62 48W
Matehuala 64 23 40N 100 40W
Mateira 75 18 54 S 50 30W
Matera 94 40 40N 16 37 E
Matewan 54 37 37N 82 10W
Matfield Green 24 38 9N 96 31W
Matheson 16 39 10N 103 59W
Matheson Island 63 51 45N 96 56W
Mathews 54 37 26N 76 19W
Mathews, L. 15 33 51N 117 27W
Mathews County ◇ 54 37 26N 76 19W
Mathias 54 38 53N 78 52W
Mathis 51 28 6N 97 50W
Mathiston 31 33 32N 89 7W
Mathura 108 27 30N 77 40 E
Mati 111 6 55N 126 15 E
Matías Romero 65 16 53N 95 2W
Matinicus 26 43 52N 68 54W
Matlock, U.K. 82 53 8N 1 32W
Matlock, U.S.A. 23 43 15N 95 56W
Matmata 120 33 37N 9 59 E
Mato → 71 7 9N 65 7W
Mato, Serrania de 70 6 25N 65 25W
Mato Grosso □ 73 14 0 S 55 0W
Mato Grosso, Planalto do 73 15 0 S 59 57W
Matoaka 54 37 25N 81 15W
Matochkin Shar 100 73 10N 56 40 E
Matosinhos 91 41 11N 8 42W
Matrah 107 23 37N 58 30 E
Matrûh 121 31 19N 27 9 E
Matsue 117 35 25N 133 10 E
Matsumae 116 41 26N 140 7 E
Matsumoto 117 36 15N 138 0 E
Matsusaka 117 34 34N 136 32 E
Matsuura 117 33 20N 129 49 E
Matsuyama 117 33 45N 132 45 E
Mattagami → 60 50 43N 81 29W
Mattamuskeet, L. 40 35 30N 76 12W
Mattancheri 108 9 50N 76 15 E
Mattapoisett 28 41 40N 70 49W
Mattaponi → 54 37 31N 76 47W
Mattawa 60 46 20N 78 45W
Mattawamkeag 26 45 32N 68 21W
Matterhorn, Switz. 88 45 58N 7 39 E
Matterhorn, U.S.A. 35 41 49N 115 23W
Matthew Town 67 20 57N 73 40W
Matthews, Ind. 22 40 23N 85 30W
Matthews, Md. 27 38 49N 75 57W
Matthews, Mo. 32 36 46N 89 35W
Matthews, N.C. 40 35 7N 80 43W
Matthew's Ridge 71 7 37N 60 10W
Mattice 60 49 40N 83 20W
Mattituck 39 40 59N 72 32W
Mattole → 14 40 18N 124 21W
Mattoon, Ill. 21 39 29N 88 23W
Mattoon, Wis. 55 45 1N 89 2W
Mattson 31 34 6N 90 31W
Matua 110 2 58 S 110 46 E
Matucana 72 11 55 S 76 25W
Matun 108 33 22N 69 58 E
Matunuck 28 41 23N 71 32W
Maturín 71 9 45N 63 11W
Mau Ranipur 108 25 16N 79 8 E
Maud, Okla. 43 35 8N 96 46W
Maud, Tex. 51 33 20N 94 21W
Maudheim 5 71 5 S 11 0W
Maudin Sun 109 16 0N 94 30 E
Maués 71 3 20 S 57 45W
Mauganj 109 24 50N 81 55 E
Maui 19 20 48N 156 20W
Maui County ◇ 19 20 45N 156 20W
Mauke 128 20 9 S 157 20W
Maulamyaing 109 16 30N 97 40 E
Mauldin 46 34 47N 82 19W
Maule □ 76 36 5 S 72 30W
Maullín 78 41 38 S 73 37W
Maumee 42 41 34N 83 39W
Maumee → 42 41 42N 83 28W
Maumelle, L. 13 34 51N 92 29W
Maumere 111 8 38 S 122 13 E
Maun 123 20 0 S 23 26 E
Mauna Kea 19 19 50N 155 28W
Mauna Loa 19 19 30N 155 35W
Maunabo 57 18 1N 65 54W
Maunaloa 19 21 8N 157 13W
Maunalua B. 19 21 15N 157 45W
Maunawili 19 21 23N 157 46W
Maungmagan Kyunzu 112 14 0N 97 48 E
Maunie 21 38 2N 88 3W
Maupin 44 45 11N 121 5W
Maurepas, L. 25 30 15N 90 30W
Maures 90 43 15N 6 15 E
Maurice → 37 39 13N 75 2W
Maurice L. 126 29 30 S 131 0 E
Mauriceville 51 30 12N 93 52W
Mauritania ■ 120 20 50N 10 0W
Mauritius ■ 3 20 0 S 57 0 E
Maury 40 35 29N 77 35W
Maury → 54 37 50N 79 25W
Maury City 48 35 49N 89 14W
Maury County ◇ 48 35 37N 87 2W
Mauston 55 43 48N 90 5W
Mavaca → 71 2 31N 65 11W
Maverick County ◇ 50 28 55N 100 8W
Mavinga 123 15 50 S 20 21 E
Mavisdale 54 37 12N 81 59W
Mavqi'im 104 31 38N 34 32 E
Mawk Mai 109 20 14N 97 37 E
Mawlaik 109 23 40N 94 26 E
Mawson Base 5 67 30 S 62 53 E
Mawson Coast 5 68 30 S 63 0 E
Max 41 47 49N 101 18W
Maxbass 41 48 43N 101 9W
Maxcanú 65 20 40N 92 0W
Maxeys 18 33 45N 83 11W
Maxhamish L. 62 59 50N 123 17W
Maxinkuckee, L. 22 41 12N 86 24W
Maxixe 123 23 54 S 35 17 E
Maxton 40 34 44N 79 21W
Maxville 33 46 28N 113 14W
Maxwell, Calif. 14 39 17N 122 11W
Maxwell, Iowa 23 41 53N 93 24W
Maxwell, N. Mex. 38 36 32N 104 33W
Maxwell, Nebr. 34 41 5N 100 31W
May, Idaho 20 44 36N 113 55W
May, Okla. 43 36 37N 99 45W
May, C. 37 38 56N 74 58W
May Pen 66 17 58N 77 15W
Maya → 101 54 31N 134 41 E
Maya Mts. 65 16 30N 89 0W
Mayaguana 67 22 30N 72 44W
Mayaguez 57 18 13N 67 9W
Mayaguez ◇ 57 18 10N 67 0W
Mayaguez, Bahia de 57 18 15N 67 15W
Mayapán 65 20 28N 89 27W
Mayarí 67 20 40N 75 41W
Maybell 16 40 31N 108 5W
Maybeury 54 37 22N 81 22W
Mayenne 90 48 20N 0 38W
Mayenne □ 90 48 10N 0 40W
Mayer 12 34 24N 112 14W
Mayersville 31 32 54N 91 3W
Mayerthorpe 62 53 57N 115 8W
Mayes County ◇ 43 36 15N 95 10W
Mayesville 46 34 0N 80 12W
Mayetta, Kans. 24 39 20N 95 43W
Mayetta, N.J. 37 39 40N 74 18W
Mayfield, Ga. 18 33 21N 82 48W
Mayfield, Idaho 20 43 25N 115 54W
Mayfield, Kans. 24 37 16N 97 33W
Mayfield, Ky. 48 36 44N 88 38W
Mayfield, Utah 52 39 7N 111 43W
Mayflower 13 34 57N 92 26W
Mayhill 38 32 53N 105 29W
Maykop 99 44 35N 40 25 E
Maymyo 112 22 2N 96 28 E
Maynard, Ark. 13 36 25N 90 54W
Maynard, Iowa 23 42 47N 91 53W
Maynard, Mass. 28 42 26N 71 27W
Maynardville 49 36 15N 83 48W
Maynooth 85 53 22N 6 38W
Mayo, Canada 58 63 38N 135 57W
Mayo, Fla. 17 30 3N 83 10W
Mayo, S.C. 46 35 5N 81 52W
Mayo □ 85 53 47N 9 7W
Mayo →, Argentina 78 45 45 S 69 45W
Mayo →, Mexico 64 26 45N 109 47W
Mayo →, Peru 72 6 38 S 76 15W
Mayodan 40 36 25N 79 58W
Mayon Volcano 111 13 15N 123 41 E
Mayor I. 128 37 16 S 176 17 E
Mays Landing 37 39 27N 74 44W
Mays Lick 49 38 31N 83 50W
Mayson L. 63 57 55N 107 10W
Maysville, Ky. 49 38 39N 83 46W
Maysville, Mo. 32 39 53N 94 22W
Maysville, N.C. 40 34 54N 77 14W
Maysville, Okla. 43 34 49N 97 24W
Maythalūn 104 32 21N 35 16 E
Mayu 111 1 30N 126 30 E
Mayview 32 39 3N 93 50W
Mayville, Mich. 29 43 20N 83 21W
Mayville, N. Dak. 41 47 30N 97 20W
Mayville, N.Y. 39 42 15N 79 30W
Mayville, Wis. 55 43 30N 88 33W
Maywood 34 40 39N 100 37W
Mayya 101 61 44N 130 18 E
Maza 41 48 22N 99 12W
Mazabuka 123 15 52 S 27 44 E
Mazagān = El Jadida 120 33 11N 8 17W
Mazagão 71 0 7 S 51 16W
Mazama 53 48 36N 120 24W
Mazán 70 3 30 S 73 0W
Māzandarān □ 107 36 30N 52 0 E
Mazapil 64 24 38N 101 34W
Mazar-e Sharīf 107 36 41N 67 0 E
Mazarredo 78 47 10 S 66 50W
Mazarrón 91 37 38N 1 19W
Mazaruni → 71 6 25N 58 35W
Mazatán 64 29 0N 110 8W
Mazatenango 66 14 35N 91 30W
Mazatlán 64 23 10N 106 30W
Mazatzal Mts. 12 34 0N 111 30W
Māzhān 107 32 30N 59 0 E
Mazie, Ky. 49 38 2N 82 58W
Mazie, Okla. 43 36 6N 95 22W
Mazīnān 107 36 19N 56 56 E

Mazoe Merrick County

Mazoe → 123 16 45 S 32 30 E
Mazomanie 55 43 11N 89 48W
Mazon 21 41 14N 88 25W
Mazu Dao 115 26 10N 119 55 E
Mbabane 123 26 18 S 31 6 E
Mbaïki 122 3 53N 18 1 E
Mbala 122 8 46 S 31 24 E
Mbale 122 1 8N 34 12 E
Mbalmayo 122 3 33N 11 33 E
Mbamba Bay 122 11 13 S 34 49 E
Mbandaka 122 0 1N 18 18 E
Mbanza Congo 122 6 18 S 14 16 E
Mbanza Ngungu 122 5 12 S 14 53 E
Mbarara 122 0 35 S 30 40 E
Mbeya 122 8 54 S 33 29 E
Mbini □ 122 1 30N 10 0 E
Mbour 120 14 22N 16 54W
Mbout 120 16 1N 12 38W
Mbuji-Mayi 122 6 9 S 23 40 E
Mbulu 122 3 45 S 35 30 E
Mburucuyá 76 28 1 S 58 14W
Mchinji 123 13 47 S 32 58 E
Mdina 94 35 51N 14 25 E
Meacham 44 45 31N 118 25W
Mead, Nebr. 34 41 14N 96 29W
Mead, Okla. 43 34 0N 96 31W
Mead, Wash. 53 47 46N 117 21W
Mead, L. 12 36 1N 114 44W
Meade 24 37 17N 100 20W
Meade → 11 70 52N 155 55W
Meade County ◇, Kans. 24 37 15N 100 20W
Meade County ◇, Ky. 48 37 55N 86 10W
Meade County ◇, S. Dak. 47 44 30N 102 30W
Meade River 11 70 28N 157 24W
Meadow, S. Dak. 47 45 32N 102 13W
Meadow, Tex. 50 33 20N 102 12W
Meadow, Utah 52 38 53N 112 24W
Meadow → 54 38 12N 80 57W
Meadow Bridge 54 37 52N 80 51W
Meadow Grove 34 42 2N 97 44W
Meadow Lake 63 54 10N 108 26W
Meadow Lake Prov. Park 63 54 27N 109 0W
Meadow Valley Wash → 35 36 40N 114 34W
Meadow Vista 14 39 6N 121 1W
Meadowlands 30 47 4N 92 44W
Meadows 36 44 21N 71 28W
Meadowview 54 36 46N 81 52W
Meadville, Miss. 31 31 28N 90 54W
Meadville, Mo. 32 39 47N 93 18W
Meadville, Pa. 45 41 39N 80 9W
Meaford 60 44 36N 80 35W
Meagher County ◇ 33 46 40N 111 0W
Mealy Mts. 61 53 10N 58 0W
Meander River 62 59 2N 117 42W
Meansville 18 33 3N 84 18W
Mearim → 74 3 4 S 44 35W
Meath □ 85 53 32N 6 40W
Meath Park 63 53 27N 105 22W
Meaux 90 48 58N 2 50 E
Mebane 40 36 6N 79 16W
Mebechi-Gawa → 116 40 31N 141 31 E
Mecaya → 70 0 29N 75 11W
Mecca = Makkah 106 21 30N 39 54 E
Mecca 15 33 34N 116 5W
Mechanic Falls 26 44 7N 70 24W
Mechanicsburg, Ill. 21 39 49N 89 24W
Mechanicsburg, Ohio 42 40 4N 83 33W
Mechanicsburg, Pa. 45 40 13N 77 1W
Mechanicsville, Iowa 23 41 54N 91 16W
Mechanicsville, Md. 27 38 26N 76 44W
Mechanicsville, Va. 54 37 36N 77 22W
Mechanicville 39 42 54N 73 41W
Mechelen 87 51 2N 4 29 E
Mecheria 120 33 35N 0 18W
Mecklenburg County ◇, N.C. 40 35 10N 80 50W
Mecklenburg County ◇, Va. 54 36 55N 78 20W
Mecklenburger Bucht 88 54 20N 11 40 E
Meckling 47 42 51N 97 4W
Meconta 123 14 59 S 39 50 E
Mecosta 29 43 37N 85 14W
Mecosta County ◇ 29 43 35N 85 20W
Meda → 126 17 20 S 123 50 E
Medan 110 3 40N 98 38 E
Medanales 38 36 11N 106 11W
Médanos 78 38 50 S 62 42W
Medanosa, Pta. 78 48 8 S 66 0W
Medart 17 30 5N 84 23W
Medaryville 22 41 5N 86 55W
Medéa 120 36 12N 2 50 E
Medeiros Neto 75 17 20 S 40 14W
Medellín 70 6 15N 75 35W
Medemblik 87 52 46N 5 8 E
Mederdra 120 17 0N 15 38W
Medfield 28 42 11N 71 18W
Medford, Mass. 28 42 25N 71 7W
Medford, Minn. 30 44 11N 93 15W
Medford, N.J. 37 39 54N 74 50W
Medford, Okla. 43 36 48N 97 44W
Medford, Oreg. 44 42 19N 122 52W
Medford, Wis. 55 45 9N 90 20W
Medford Lakes 37 39 52N 74 48W
Medgidia 95 44 15N 28 19 E
Media 45 39 55N 75 23W
Media Agua 76 31 58 S 68 25W
Media Luna 76 34 45 S 66 44W
Mediapolis 23 41 0N 91 10W
Mediaş 89 46 9N 24 22 E
Medical Lake 53 47 34N 117 41W
Medicine Bow 56 41 54N 106 12W
Medicine Bow → 56 42 0N 106 40W
Medicine Bow Mts. 16 40 40N 106 0W
Medicine Bow National Forest 56 42 20N 105 38W
Medicine Cr. →, Mo. 32 39 43N 93 24W
Medicine Cr. →, Nebr. 34 40 17N 100 10W
Medicine Hat 63 50 0N 110 45W
Medicine L. 33 48 28N 104 24W
Medicine Lake 33 48 30N 104 30W
Medicine Lodge 24 37 17N 98 35W
Medicine Lodge → 24 36 49N 98 20W
Medina = Al Madīnah 106 24 35N 39 52 E
Medina, Brazil 75 16 15 S 41 29W
Medina, Colombia 70 4 30N 73 21W
Medina, N. Dak. 41 46 54N 99 18W
Medina, N.Y. 39 43 13N 78 23W
Medina, Ohio 42 41 8N 81 52W
Medina, Tenn. 48 35 48N 88 46W
Medina, Tex. 51 29 48N 99 15W
Medina → 51 29 16N 98 29W
Medina County ◇, Ohio 42 41 8N 81 52W
Medina County ◇, Tex. 51 29 21N 99 9W
Medina del Campo 91 41 18N 4 55W
Medina L. 51 29 32N 98 56W
Medina-Sidonia 91 36 28N 5 57W
Medinipur 109 22 25N 87 21 E
Medio Mundo, Punta 57 18 16N 65 37W
Mediterranean Sea 92 35 0N 15 0 E
Medley 63 54 25N 110 16W
Médoc 90 45 10N 0 56W
Medora, Ill. 21 39 11N 90 9W
Medora, Ind. 22 38 49N 86 10W
Medora, N. Dak. 41 46 55N 103 31W
Medport = Marsaxlokk 94 35 47N 14 32 E
Medstead 63 53 19N 108 5W
Medveditsa → 99 49 35N 42 41 E
Medvezhi, Ostrava 101 71 0N 161 0 E
Medvezhyegorsk 98 63 0N 34 25 E
Medway 28 42 8N 71 24W
Medway → 83 51 28N 0 45 E
Meekatharra 126 26 32 S 118 29 E
Meeker, Colo. 16 40 2N 107 55W
Meeker, Okla. 43 35 30N 96 54W
Meeker County ◇ 30 45 10N 94 30W
Meeks Bay 14 39 2N 120 8W
Meerut 108 29 1N 77 42 E
Meeteetse 56 44 9N 108 52W
Mega 121 3 57N 38 19 E
Mégara 95 37 58N 23 22 E
Megargel 51 33 27N 98 56W
Meghalaya □ 109 25 50N 91 0 E
Megiddo 104 32 36N 35 11 E
Mégiscane, L. 60 48 35N 75 55W
Megiste 93 36 8N 29 34 E
Mehadia 89 44 56N 22 23 E
Meharry, Mt. 126 22 59 S 118 35 E
Meherrin → 54 36 26N 76 57W
Mei Jiang → 115 24 25N 116 35 E
Mei Xian 115 24 16N 116 6 E
Meia Ponte → 75 18 32 S 49 36W
Meiganga 122 6 30N 14 25 E
Meigs 18 31 4N 84 6W
Meigs County ◇, Ohio 42 39 3N 82 8W
Meigs County ◇, Tenn. 49 35 31N 84 47W
Meiktila 109 20 53N 95 54 E
Meio → 75 13 36 S 44 7W
Me'ir Shefeya 104 32 35N 34 58 E
Meiss L. 14 41 52N 122 4W
Meissen 88 51 10N 13 29 E
Meitan 115 27 45N 107 29 E
Mejillones 76 23 10 S 70 30W
Mékambo 122 1 2N 13 50 E
Mekdela 121 11 24N 39 10 E
Mekhtar 108 30 30N 69 15 E
Mekinock 41 48 1N 97 22W
Meknès 120 33 57N 5 33W
Mekong → 112 9 30N 106 15 E
Mekongga 111 3 39 S 121 15 E
Mekoryuk 11 60 23N 166 11W
Melagiri Hills 108 12 20N 77 30 E
Melaka 112 2 15N 102 15 E
Melaka □ 112 2 20N 102 15 E
Melalap 110 5 10N 116 5 E
Melanesia 124 4 0 S 155 0 E
Melba 20 43 23N 116 32W
Melbourne, Australia 127 37 50 S 145 0 E
Melbourne, Ark. 13 36 4N 91 54W
Melbourne, Fla. 17 28 5N 80 37W
Melbourne, Iowa 23 41 57N 93 6W
Melcher 23 41 14N 93 15W
Melchor Múzquiz 64 27 50N 101 30W
Melchor Ocampo 64 24 52N 101 40W
Mélèzes → 59 57 30N 71 0W
Melfa 54 37 39N 75 45W
Melfi 121 11 0N 17 59 E
Melfort 63 52 50N 104 37W
Melilla 120 35 21N 2 57W
Melilot 104 31 22N 34 37 E
Melipilla 76 33 42 S 71 15W
Melissa 51 33 17N 96 34W
Melita 63 49 15N 101 0W
Melitopol 99 46 50N 35 22 E
Melitota 27 39 16N 76 9W
Melk 88 48 13N 15 20 E
Mellansel 96 63 25N 18 17 E
Mellen 55 46 20N 90 40W
Mellerud 97 58 41N 12 28 E
Mellette 47 45 9N 98 30W
Mellette County ◇ 47 43 35N 101 0W
Mellish Reef 127 17 25 S 155 50 E
Mellizo Sur, Cerro 78 48 33 S 73 10W
Mellott 22 40 10N 87 9W
Mellwood 13 34 12N 90 56W
Melnik 95 41 30N 23 25 E
Melo 77 32 20 S 54 10W
Melolo 111 9 53 S 120 40 E
Melrose, U.K. 84 53 35N 2 44W
Melrose, Iowa 23 40 59N 93 3W
Melrose, Mass. 28 42 27N 71 4W
Melrose, Minn. 30 45 40N 94 49W
Melrose, Mont. 33 45 38N 112 41W
Melrose, N. Mex. 38 34 26N 103 38W
Melrose, Wis. 55 44 8N 91 1W
Melstone 33 46 36N 107 52W
Melton Mowbray 82 52 46N 0 52W
Melun 90 48 32N 2 39 E
Melut 121 10 30N 32 13 E
Melvern 24 38 30N 95 38W
Melvern Lake 24 38 30N 95 50W
Melville, Canada 63 50 55N 102 50W
Melville, U.S.A. 25 30 42N 91 45W
Melville, C. 127 14 11 S 144 30 E
Melville, L. 61 53 30N 60 0W
Melville B. 127 12 0 S 136 45 E
Melville I., Australia 126 11 30 S 131 0 E
Melville I., Canada 4 75 30N 112 0W
Melville Pen. 59 68 0N 84 0W
Melvin, Ala. 10 31 56N 88 28W
Melvin, Ill. 21 40 34N 88 15W
Melvin, Tex. 51 31 12N 99 35W
Melvin → 62 59 11N 117 31W
Melvin Village 36 43 42N 71 28W
Melvina 55 43 48N 90 47W
Memba 123 14 11 S 40 30 E
Memboro 111 9 30 S 119 30 E
Memel = Klaipeda 98 55 43N 21 10 E
Memmingen 88 47 59N 10 12 E
Memphis, Fla. 17 27 32N 82 34W
Memphis, Mich. 29 42 54N 82 46W
Memphis, Mo. 32 40 28N 92 10W
Memphis, Nebr. 34 41 6N 96 26W
Memphis, Tenn. 48 35 8N 90 3W
Memphis, Tex. 50 34 44N 100 33W
Memphis Junction 48 36 57N 86 29W
Memphremagog, L. 36 45 0N 72 12W
Mena 13 34 35N 94 15W
Menahga 30 46 45N 95 6W
Menai Strait 82 53 14N 4 10W
Ménaka 120 15 59N 2 18 E
Menan = Chao Phraya → 112 13 32N 100 36 E
Menan 20 43 43N 111 59W
Menard, Mont. 33 45 59N 111 10W
Menard, Tex. 51 30 55N 99 47W
Menard County ◇, Ill. 21 40 0N 89 50W
Menard County ◇, Tex. 51 30 55N 99 45W
Menasha 55 44 13N 88 26W
Menate 110 0 12 S 113 3 E
Mendawai → 110 3 30 S 113 0 E
Mende 90 44 31N 3 30 E
Mendenhall 31 31 58N 89 52W
Mendenhall, C. 11 59 45N 166 10W
Menderes → 106 37 25N 28 45 E
Mendez 65 25 7N 98 34W
Mendham 37 40 47N 74 36W
Mendip Hills 83 51 17N 2 40W
Mendocino 14 39 19N 123 48W
Mendocino, C. 14 40 26N 124 25W
Mendocino, L. 14 39 12N 123 11W
Mendocino County ◇ 14 39 20N 123 20W
Mendocino National Forest 14 39 45N 122 50W
Mendocino Seascarp 125 41 0N 140 0W
Mendon, Mich. 29 42 0N 85 27W
Mendon, Mo. 32 39 36N 93 8W
Mendon, Ohio 42 40 40N 84 31W
Mendon, Vt. 36 43 40N 72 54W
Mendota, Calif. 15 36 45N 120 23W
Mendota, Ill. 21 41 33N 89 7W
Mendota, L. 55 43 7N 89 25W
Mendoza 76 32 50 S 68 52W
Mendoza □ 76 33 0 S 69 0W
Mene Grande 70 9 49N 70 56W
Menemen 106 38 34N 27 3 E
Menen 87 50 47N 3 7 E
Menéndez, L. 78 42 40 S 71 51W
Menfi 94 37 36N 12 57 E
Mengcheng 115 33 18N 116 31 E
Menggala 110 4 30 S 105 15 E
Mengshan 115 24 14N 110 55 E
Mengzi 113 23 20N 103 22 E
Menifee County ◇ 49 37 55N 83 35W
Menihek L. 61 54 0N 67 0W
Menin = Menen 87 50 47N 3 7 E
Menindee 127 32 20 S 142 25 E
Menlo, Ga. 18 34 29N 85 29W
Menlo, Iowa 23 41 31N 94 24W
Menlo, Kans. 24 39 21N 100 43W
Menlo, Wash. 53 46 38N 123 39W
Menlo Park 14 37 27N 122 12W
Menno 47 43 14N 97 34W
Meno 43 36 23N 98 11W
Menominee 29 45 6N 87 37W
Menominee → 55 45 6N 87 36W
Menominee County ◇, Mich. 29 45 30N 87 40W
Menominee County ◇, Wis. 55 45 0N 88 45W
Menominee Ind. Reservation 55 45 0N 88 45W
Menominee Ra. 29 46 0N 88 10W
Menomonee Falls 55 43 11N 88 7W
Menomonie 55 44 53N 91 55W
Menongue 123 14 48 S 17 52 E
Menorca 91 40 0N 4 0 E
Mentasta Lake 11 62 55N 143 45W
Mentawai, Kepulauan 110 2 0 S 99 0 E
Mentmore 38 35 31N 108 51W
Menton 90 43 50N 7 29 E
Mentone, Ind. 22 41 10N 86 2W
Mentone, Tex. 50 31 42N 103 36W
Mentor, Minn. 30 47 42N 96 9W
Mentor, Ohio 42 41 40N 81 21W
Mentor-on-the-Lake 42 41 43N 81 22W
Menzelinsk 98 55 53N 53 1 E
Menzies 126 29 40 S 120 58 E
Me'ona 104 33 1N 35 15 E
Meoqui 64 28 17N 105 29W
Meppel 87 52 42N 6 12 E
Mequon 55 43 14N 87 59W
Mer Rouge 25 32 47N 91 48W
Merabéllou, Kólpos 95 35 10N 25 50 E
Meramec → 32 38 24N 90 21W
Meran = Merano 94 46 40N 11 10 E
Merano 94 46 40N 11 10 E
Merauke 111 8 29 S 140 24 E
Merbabu 111 7 30 S 110 40 E
Merca 105 1 48N 44 50 E
Merced 14 37 18N 120 29W
Merced → 14 37 21N 120 59W
Merced County ◇ 14 37 15N 120 30W
Mercedes, Buenos Aires, Argentina 76 34 40 S 59 30W
Mercedes, Corrientes, Argentina 76 29 10 S 58 5W
Mercedes, San Luis, Argentina 76 33 40 S 65 21W
Mercedes, Uruguay 76 33 12 S 58 0W
Mercedes, U.S.A. 50 26 9N 97 55W
Merceditas 76 28 20 S 70 35W
Mercer, N.Z. 128 37 16 S 175 5 E
Mercer, Maine 26 44 41N 69 56W
Mercer, Mo. 32 40 31N 93 32W
Mercer, N. Dak. 41 47 29N 100 43W
Mercer, Pa. 45 41 14N 80 15W
Mercer, Tenn. 48 35 29N 89 2W
Mercer, Wis. 55 46 10N 90 4W
Mercer County ◇, Ill. 21 41 15N 90 40W
Mercer County ◇, Ky. 49 37 50N 84 50W
Mercer County ◇, Mo. 32 40 25N 93 30W
Mercer County ◇, N. Dak. 41 47 15N 102 0W
Mercer County ◇, N.J. 37 40 15N 74 40W
Mercer County ◇, Ohio 42 40 33N 84 35W
Mercer County ◇, Pa. 45 41 15N 80 10W
Mercer County ◇, W. Va. 54 37 22N 81 6W
Mercer Island 53 47 35N 122 15W
Mercersburg 45 39 50N 77 54W
Mercerville 37 40 14N 74 41W
Mercier 72 10 42 S 68 5W
Mercury 51 31 28N 99 10W
Mercy C. 59 65 0N 63 30W
Meredith, Colo. 16 39 22N 106 44W
Meredith, N.H. 36 43 39N 71 30W
Meredith, L. 50 35 43N 101 33W
Meredith C. 78 52 15 S 60 40W
Meredith L. 16 38 12N 103 43W
Meredosia 21 39 50N 90 34W
Merei 95 45 7N 26 43 E
Merga = Nukheila 121 19 1N 26 21 E
Mergui Arch. = Myeik Kyunzu 112 11 30N 97 30 E
Mérida, Mexico 65 20 9N 89 40W
Mérida, Spain 91 38 55N 6 25W
Mérida, Venezuela 70 8 24N 71 8W
Mérida □ 70 8 30N 71 10W
Mérida, Cord. de 68 9 0N 71 0W
Meriden, Conn. 28 41 32N 72 48W
Meriden, Iowa 23 42 48N 95 38W
Meriden, Kans. 24 39 11N 95 34W
Meriden, N.H. 36 43 36N 72 16W
Meridian, Ga. 18 31 27N 81 23W
Meridian, Idaho 20 43 37N 116 24W
Meridian, Miss. 31 32 22N 88 42W
Meridian, Okla. 43 35 48N 97 15W
Meridian, Tex. 51 31 56N 97 39W
Merigold 31 33 50N 90 43W
Meriruma 71 1 15N 54 50W
Meriwether County ◇ 18 33 0N 84 40W
Merkel 51 32 28N 100 1W
Merksem 87 51 16N 4 25 E
Merlin 44 42 31N 123 25W
Mermentau 25 30 11N 92 35W
Merna 34 41 29N 99 46W
Merowe 121 18 29N 31 46 E
Merredin 126 31 28 S 118 18 E
Merrick, U.K. 84 55 8N 4 30W
Merrick, U.S.A. 39 40 40N 73 33W
Merrick County ◇ 34 41 15N 98 0W

Merricourt **Millstone**

Merricourt **41** 46 12N 98 46W
Merrill, Iowa **23** 42 43N 96 15W
Merrill, Mich. **29** 43 25N 84 20W
Merrill, Miss. **31** 30 59N 88 43W
Merrill, Oreg. **44** 42 1N 121 36W
Merrill, Wis. **55** 45 11N 89 41W
Merrillan **55** 44 27N 90 50W
Merrillville, Ga. **18** 30 57N 83 53W
Merrillville, Ind. **22** 41 29N 87 20W
Merrimac, Ky. **49** 37 25N 85 8W
Merrimac, Mass. **28** 42 50N 71 0W
Merrimac, Wis. **55** 43 22N 89 37W
Merrimack **36** 42 49N 70 49W
Merrimack → **28** 42 49N 70 49W
Merrimack County ◇ **36** 43 15N 71 45W
Merriman **34** 42 55N 101 42W
Merrimon **40** 34 57N 76 38W
Merritt, Canada **62** 50 10N 120 45W
Merritt, U.S.A. **53** 47 47N 120 50W
Merritt Island **17** 28 21N 80 42W
Merritt Reservoir **34** 42 38N 100 53W
Merry I. **60** 55 29N 77 31W
Merryville **25** 30 45N 93 33W
Mersa Fatma **105** 14 57N 40 17 E
Mersch **87** 49 44N 6 7 E
Merseburg **88** 51 20N 12 0 E
Mersey → **82** 53 20N 2 56W
Merseyside □ **82** 53 25N 2 55W
Mershon **18** 31 28N 82 15W
Mersin **106** 36 51N 34 36 E
Mersing **112** 2 25N 103 50 E
Merthyr Tydfil **83** 51 45N 3 23W
Mértola **91** 37 40N 7 40 E
Mertzon **50** 31 16N 100 49W
Meru **122** 0 3N 37 40 E
Merwin, L. **53** 45 57N 122 33W
Mesa, Ariz. **12** 33 25N 111 50W
Mesa, Colo. **16** 39 10N 108 8W
Mesa, Wash. **53** 46 35N 119 0W
Mesa County ◇ **16** 39 0N 108 30W
Mesa Verde **16** 37 15N 108 45W
Mesa Verde National Park **16** 37 11N 108 29W
Mesabi Range **30** 47 40N 92 45W
Mesada **104** 31 20N 35 19 E
Mescalero **38** 33 9N 105 46W
Mescalero Indian Reservation **38** 33 12N 105 40W
Meservey **23** 42 55N 93 29W
Mesgouez, L. **60** 51 20N 75 0W
Meshed = Mashhad **107** 36 20N 59 35 E
Meshra er Req **121** 8 25N 29 18 E
Mesick **29** 44 24N 85 43W
Mesilinka → **62** 56 6N 124 30W
Mesilla **38** 32 16N 106 48W
Mesita **16** 37 6N 105 36W
Mesolóngion **95** 38 21N 21 28 E
Mesopotamia = Al Jazirah **106** 33 30N 44 0 E
Mesquite, N. Mex. **38** 32 10N 106 42W
Mesquite, Tex. **51** 32 46N 96 36W
Mesquite L. **15** 35 43N 115 35W
Mess Cr. → **62** 57 55N 131 14W
Messier, Canal **78** 48 20 S 74 33W
Messina, Italy **94** 38 10N 15 32 E
Messina, S. Africa **123** 22 20 S 30 0 E
Messina, Str. di **94** 38 5N 15 35 E
Messíni **95** 37 4N 22 1 E
Messiniakós, Kólpos **95** 36 45N 22 5 E
Mesta → **95** 41 30N 24 0 E
Mestre, Espigão **75** 12 30 S 46 10W
Meta **32** 38 19N 92 10W
Meta □ **70** 3 30N 73 0W
Meta → **70** 6 12N 67 28W
Metairie **25** 29 58N 90 10W
Metaline Falls **53** 48 52N 117 22W
Metamora, Ill. **21** 40 47N 89 22W
Metamora, Mich. **29** 42 57N 83 17W
Metán **76** 25 30 S 65 0W
Metangula **123** 12 40 S 34 50 E
Metcalf, Ga. **18** 30 43N 83 59W
Metcalf, Ill. **21** 39 48N 87 48W
Metcalfe County ◇ **49** 37 0N 85 40W
Metema **121** 12 56N 36 13 E
Methow **53** 48 8N 120 0W
Methow → **53** 48 5N 119 55W
Methuen **28** 42 44N 71 11W
Methven **128** 43 38 S 171 40 E
Methy L. **63** 56 28N 109 30W
Metil **123** 16 24 S 39 0 E
Metkovets **95** 43 37N 23 10 E
Metlakatla **11** 55 8N 131 35W
Metolius **44** 44 35N 121 11W
Metropolis **21** 37 9N 88 44W
Metter **18** 32 24N 82 3W
Mettur Dam **108** 11 45N 77 45 E
Metuchen **37** 40 32N 74 22W
Metulla **104** 33 17N 35 34 E
Metz, France **90** 49 8N 6 10 E
Metz, U.S.A. **32** 37 59N 94 27W
Meulaboh **110** 4 11N 96 3 E
Meureudu **110** 5 19N 96 10 E
Meurthe-et-Moselle □ **90** 48 52N 6 0 E
Meuse □ **90** 49 8N 5 25 E
Meuse → **87** 50 45N 5 41 E
Mexborough **82** 53 29N 1 18W
Mexia **51** 31 41N 96 29W
Mexiana, I. **74** 0 0 49 30W
Mexicali **64** 32 40N 115 30W
Mexican Hat **52** 37 9N 109 52W
Mexican Springs **38** 35 47N 108 50W
México, Mexico **65** 19 20N 99 10W
Mexico, Maine **26** 44 34N 70 33W
Mexico, Mo. **32** 39 10N 91 53W
México □ **64** 19 20N 99 10W
Mexico ■ **64** 20 0N 100 0W
Mexico, G. of **65** 25 0N 90 0W
Mexico B. **39** 43 35N 76 20W
Mexico Beach **17** 29 57N 85 25W
Meyers Chuck **11** 55 45N 132 15W
Meyersdale **45** 39 49N 79 2W
Meymaneh **107** 35 53N 64 38 E
Mezdra **95** 43 12N 23 42 E
Mezen **98** 65 50N 44 20 E
Mezen → **98** 66 11N 43 59 E
Mezőkövesd **89** 47 49N 20 35 E
Mezőtúr **89** 47 0N 20 41 E
Mezquital **64** 23 29N 104 23W
Mhow **108** 22 33N 75 50 E
Miahuatlán **65** 16 21N 96 36W
Miami, Ariz. **12** 33 24N 110 52W
Miami, Fla. **17** 25 47N 80 11W
Miami, Mo. **32** 39 19N 93 14W
Miami, N. Mex. **38** 36 21N 104 48W
Miami, Okla. **43** 36 53N 94 53W
Miami, Tex. **50** 35 42N 100 38W
Miami Beach **17** 25 47N 80 8W
Miami Canal **17** 26 30N 80 45W
Miami County ◇, Ind. **22** 40 45N 86 0W
Miami County ◇, Kans. **24** 38 30N 94 45W
Miami County ◇, Ohio **42** 40 9N 84 15W
Miami Shores **17** 25 52N 80 12W
Miami Springs **17** 25 49N 80 17W
Miamisburg **42** 39 38N 84 17W
Mian Xian **115** 33 10N 106 32 E
Mianchi **115** 34 48N 111 48 E
Mīāndow āb **106** 37 0N 46 5 E
Miandrivazo **123** 19 31 S 45 29 E
Mīāneh **106** 37 30N 47 40 E
Mianwali **108** 32 38N 71 28 E
Mianyang, Hubei, China **115** 30 25N 113 25 E
Mianyang, Sichuan, China **115** 31 22N 104 47 E
Miaoli **115** 24 37N 120 49 E
Miarinarivo **123** 18 57 S 46 55 E
Miass **98** 54 59N 60 6 E
Micanopy **17** 29 30N 82 17W
Micăsasa **95** 46 7N 24 7 E
Micaville **40** 35 55N 82 13W
Miccasukee, L. **17** 30 33N 83 53W
Micco **17** 27 53N 80 30W
Miccosukee **17** 30 36N 84 3W
Michie **48** 35 3N 88 26W
Michigamme, L. **29** 46 32N 88 5W
Michigamme Res. **29** 46 10N 88 10W
Michigan **41** 48 1N 98 7W
Michigan □ **29** 44 0N 85 0W
Michigan Center **29** 42 14N 84 20W
Michigan City **22** 41 43N 86 54W
Michigan I. **55** 46 53N 90 29W
Michigan L. **29** 44 0N 87 0W
Michigantown **22** 40 20N 86 24W
Michipicoten **60** 47 55N 84 55W
Michipicoten I. **60** 47 40N 85 40W
Michoacan □ **64** 19 0N 102 0W
Michurin **95** 42 9N 27 51 E
Michurinsk **98** 52 58N 40 27 E
Mico, Pta. **66** 12 0N 83 30W
Micronesia **124** 11 0N 160 0 E
Mid Glamorgan □ **83** 51 40N 3 25W
Mid-Indian Ridge **124** 40 0 S 75 0 E
Mid-Oceanic Ridge **124** 42 0 S 90 0 E
Midai, P. **110** 3 0N 107 47 E
Midale **63** 49 25N 103 20W
Middelburg, Neth. **87** 51 30N 3 36 E
Middelburg, S. Africa **123** 31 30 S 25 0 E
Middle Alkali L. **14** 41 27N 120 5W
Middle Andaman I. **112** 12 30N 92 30 E
Middle Concho → **50** 31 27N 100 25W
Middle Fork Feather → **14** 38 33N 121 30W
Middle Fork John Day → **44** 44 45N 119 38W
Middle Fork Salmon → **20** 45 18N 114 36W
Middle Fork Sappa Cr. → **24** 39 42N 100 51W
Middle Loup → **34** 41 17N 98 24W
Middle Pease → **50** 34 15N 100 7W
Middle Point **42** 40 51N 84 27W
Middle River, Md. **27** 39 20N 76 27W
Middle River, Minn. **30** 48 26N 96 10W
Middleberg **43** 35 6N 97 44W
Middleboro **28** 41 54N 70 55W
Middlebourne **54** 39 30N 80 54W
Middleburg, Fla. **17** 30 4N 81 52W
Middleburg, N.Y. **39** 42 36N 74 20W
Middleburg, Pa. **45** 40 47N 77 3W
Middleburg, Va. **54** 38 58N 77 44W
Middlebury, Conn. **28** 41 32N 73 7W
Middlebury, Ind. **22** 41 41N 85 42W
Middlebury, Vt. **36** 44 1N 73 10W
Middlefield, Mass. **28** 42 20N 73 2W
Middlefield, Ohio **42** 41 28N 81 5W
Middleport, N.Y. **39** 43 13N 78 29W
Middleport, Ohio **42** 39 0N 82 3W
Middlesboro **49** 36 36N 83 43W
Middlesbrough **82** 54 35N 1 14W
Middlesex, Belize **66** 17 2N 88 31W
Middlesex, U.S.A. **40** 35 47N 78 12W
Middlesex County ◇, Conn. **28** 41 25N 72 30W
Middlesex County ◇, Mass. **28** 42 20N 71 15W
Middlesex County ◇, N.J. **37** 40 30N 74 25W
Middlesex County ◇, Va. **54** 37 36N 76 36W
Middleton, Canada **61** 44 57N 65 4W
Middleton, Idaho **20** 43 42N 116 37W
Middleton, Mass. **28** 42 36N 71 1W
Middleton, Mich. **29** 43 11N 84 43W
Middleton, Tenn. **48** 35 4N 88 53W
Middleton, Wis. **55** 43 6N 89 30W
Middleton I. **11** 59 26N 146 20W
Middletown, Calif. **14** 38 45N 122 37W
Middletown, Conn. **28** 41 34N 72 39W
Middletown, Del. **27** 39 27N 75 43W
Middletown, Ill. **21** 40 11N 89 35W
Middletown, Ind. **22** 40 3N 85 32W
Middletown, Md. **27** 39 27N 77 33W
Middletown, Mo. **32** 39 8N 91 25W
Middletown, N.J. **37** 40 24N 74 8W
Middletown, N.Y. **39** 41 27N 74 25W
Middletown, Ohio **42** 39 31N 84 24W
Middletown, Pa. **45** 40 12N 76 44W
Middletown, R.I. **28** 41 32N 71 17W
Middletown, Va. **54** 39 2N 78 17W
Middletown Springs **36** 43 28N 73 8W
Middleville, Mich. **29** 42 43N 85 28W
Middleville, N.Y. **39** 43 8N 74 58W
Midi, Canal du **90** 43 45N 1 21 E
Midland, Canada **60** 44 45N 79 50W
Midland, Calif. **15** 33 52N 114 48W
Midland, Md. **27** 39 37N 78 55W
Midland, Mich. **29** 43 37N 84 14W
Midland, Oreg. **44** 42 8N 121 49W
Midland, S. Dak. **47** 44 4N 101 10W
Midland, Tex. **50** 32 0N 102 3W
Midland County ◇, Mich. **29** 43 35N 84 20W
Midland County ◇, Tex. **50** 32 0N 102 0W
Midleton **85** 51 52N 8 12W
Midlothian, Md. **27** 39 40N 78 58W
Midlothian, Tex. **51** 32 30N 97 0W
Midnight **31** 33 3N 90 35W
Midvale, Idaho **20** 44 28N 116 44W
Midvale, Ohio **42** 40 26N 81 23W
Midvale, Utah **52** 40 37N 111 54W
Midville **18** 32 49N 82 14W
Midway, Ala. **10** 32 5N 85 31W
Midway, Fla. **17** 30 30N 84 27W
Midway, Ky. **49** 38 9N 84 41W
Midway, Tex. **51** 31 2N 95 45W
Midway, Utah **52** 40 31N 111 28W
Midway Is., Pac. Oc. **124** 28 13N 177 22W
Midway Is., U.S.A. **19** 28 13N 177 22W
Midway Park **40** 34 44N 77 21W
Midwest **56** 43 25N 106 16W
Midwest City **43** 35 27N 97 24W
Midyat **106** 37 25N 41 23 E
Mie □ **117** 34 30N 136 10 E
Międzychód **88** 52 35N 15 53 E
Międzyrzec Podlaski **89** 51 58N 22 45 E
Miercurea Ciuc **89** 46 21N 25 48 E
Mieres **91** 43 18N 5 48W
Miesville **30** 44 36N 92 49W
Mifflintown **45** 40 34N 77 24W
Mifflin **42** 40 46N 82 22W
Mifflin County ◇ **45** 40 45N 77 45W
Mifflinburg **45** 40 55N 77 3W
Migdāl **104** 32 51N 35 30 E
Migdal Afeq **104** 32 5N 34 58 E
Miguel Alemán, Presa **65** 18 15N 96 40W
Miguel Alves **74** 4 11 S 42 55W
Miguel Calmon **74** 11 26 S 40 36W
Mihara **117** 34 24N 133 5 E
Mikhaylovgrad **95** 43 27N 23 16 E
Mikínai **95** 37 43N 22 46 E
Mikindani **122** 10 15 S 40 2 E
Mikkalo **44** 45 28N 120 14W
Mikkeli **97** 61 43N 27 15 E
Mikkeli □ **96** 62 0N 28 0 E
Mikkwa → **62** 58 25N 114 46W
Míkonos **95** 37 30N 25 25 E
Mikun **98** 62 20N 50 0 E
Milaca **30** 45 45N 93 39W
Milagro **70** 2 11 S 79 36W
Milam **51** 31 26N 93 51W
Milam County ◇ **51** 30 51N 96 59W
Milan = Milano **94** 45 28N 9 10 E
Milan, Ga. **18** 32 1N 83 4W
Milan, Ill. **21** 41 27N 90 34W
Milan, Ind. **22** 39 7N 85 8W
Milan, Mich. **29** 42 5N 83 41W
Milan, Minn. **30** 45 7N 95 55W
Milan, Mo. **32** 40 12N 93 7W
Milan, N.H. **36** 44 36N 71 12W
Milan, N. Mex. **38** 35 9N 107 54W
Milan, Ohio **42** 41 18N 82 37W
Milan, Tenn. **48** 35 55N 88 46W
Milan, Wash. **53** 47 58N 117 20W
Milano, Italy **94** 45 28N 9 10 E
Milano, U.S.A. **51** 30 43N 96 52W
Milâs **106** 37 20N 27 50 E
Milazzo **94** 38 13N 15 13 E
Milbank **47** 45 13N 96 38W
Milbridge **26** 44 32N 67 53W
Milburn, Nebr. **34** 41 43N 99 44W
Milburn, Okla. **43** 34 14N 96 33W
Milden **63** 51 29N 107 32W
Mildred **24** 38 1N 95 10W
Mildura **127** 34 13 S 142 9 E
Miles, Australia **127** 26 40 S 150 9 E
Miles, Tex. **50** 31 36N 100 11W
Miles, Wash. **53** 47 55N 118 18W
Miles City **33** 46 25N 105 51W
Milesburg **45** 40 57N 77 47W
Milestone **63** 49 59N 104 31W
Milford, Calif. **14** 40 10N 120 22W
Milford, Conn. **28** 41 14N 73 3W
Milford, Del. **27** 38 55N 75 26W
Milford, Ga. **18** 31 23N 84 33W
Milford, Ill. **21** 40 38N 87 42W
Milford, Ind. **22** 41 25N 85 51W
Milford, Iowa **23** 43 20N 95 9W
Milford, Kans. **24** 39 10N 96 55W
Milford, Ky. **49** 38 35N 84 9W
Milford, Maine **26** 44 57N 68 39W
Milford, Mass. **28** 42 8N 71 31W
Milford, Mich. **29** 42 35N 83 36W
Milford, Mo. **32** 37 35N 94 9W
Milford, N.H. **36** 42 50N 71 39W
Milford, N.J. **37** 40 34N 75 6W
Milford, N.Y. **39** 42 35N 74 57W
Milford, Nebr. **34** 40 47N 97 3W
Milford, Pa. **45** 41 19N 74 48W
Milford, Utah **52** 38 24N 113 1W
Milford Center **42** 40 11N 83 26W
Milford Haven **83** 51 43N 5 2W
Milford Haven, B. **83** 51 40N 5 10W
Milford Lake **24** 39 5N 96 54W
Milford Sd. **128** 44 41 S 167 47 E
Milḥ, Baḥr al **106** 32 40N 43 35 E
Milḥ, Ras al **121** 31 54N 25 6 E
Miliana **120** 27 20N 2 32 E
Mililani Town **19** 21 28N 158 1W
Milk → **33** 48 4N 106 19W
Milk River **62** 49 10N 112 5W
Mill → **29** 43 2N 82 35W
Mill City, Nev. **35** 40 41N 118 4W
Mill City, Oreg. **44** 44 45N 122 29W
Mill Creek **54** 38 44N 79 58W
Mill Hall **45** 41 6N 77 29W
Mill I. **5** 66 0 S 101 30 E
Mill Shoals **21** 38 15N 88 21W
Milladore **55** 44 36N 89 51W
Millard **32** 40 7N 92 33W
Millard County ◇ **52** 39 0N 113 0W
Millboro, S. Dak. **47** 43 4N 99 58W
Millboro, Va. **54** 37 59N 79 36W
Millbrook **39** 41 47N 73 42W
Millbury **28** 42 12N 71 46W
Millcreek **52** 40 42N 111 50W
Mille Lacs, L. des **60** 48 45N 90 35W
Mille Lacs County ◇ **30** 45 50N 93 45W
Mille Lacs L. **30** 46 15N 93 39W
Milledgeville, Ga. **18** 33 5N 83 14W
Milledgeville, Ill. **21** 41 58N 89 46W
Milledgeville, Ohio **42** 39 36N 83 35W
Milledgeville, Tenn. **48** 35 22N 88 22W
Millen **18** 32 48N 81 57W
Miller, Kans. **24** 38 38N 95 59W
Miller, Miss. **31** 34 55N 89 46W
Miller, Mo. **32** 37 13N 93 50W
Miller, Nebr. **34** 40 56N 99 23W
Miller, S. Dak. **47** 44 31N 98 59W
Miller County ◇, Ark. **13** 33 10N 93 58W
Miller County ◇, Ga. **18** 31 10N 84 45W
Miller County ◇, Mo. **32** 38 15N 92 25W
Millers → **28** 42 35N 72 30W
Millers Creek Res. **51** 33 30N 99 20W
Millers Falls **28** 42 35N 72 30W
Millers Ferry **10** 32 6N 87 22W
Millersburg, Ind. **22** 41 32N 85 42W
Millersburg, Iowa **23** 41 34N 92 10W
Millersburg, Mich. **29** 45 20N 84 4W
Millersburg, Ohio **42** 40 33N 81 55W
Millersburg, Pa. **45** 40 32N 76 58W
Millersport **42** 39 54N 82 32W
Millersville, Md. **27** 39 4N 76 39W
Millersville, Pa. **45** 40 0N 76 22W
Millerton, Iowa **23** 40 51N 93 18W
Millerton, N.Y. **39** 41 57N 73 31W
Millerton L. **15** 37 1N 119 41W
Millett **51** 28 35N 99 12W
Millheim **45** 40 54N 77 29W
Millicent **127** 37 34 S 140 21 E
Milligan, Fla. **17** 30 45N 86 38W
Milligan, Nebr. **34** 40 30N 97 23W
Millington, Md. **27** 39 16N 75 50W
Millington, Mich. **29** 43 17N 83 32W
Millinocket **26** 45 39N 68 43W
Millinocket L. **26** 45 46N 68 48W
Millis **28** 42 10N 71 22W
Millport **10** 33 34N 88 5W
Millry **10** 31 38N 88 19W
Mills, N. Mex. **38** 36 5N 104 15W
Mills, Nebr. **34** 42 57N 99 27W
Mills, Wyo. **56** 42 50N 106 22W
Mills County ◇, Iowa **23** 41 0N 95 35W
Mills County ◇, Tex. **51** 31 27N 98 34W
Mills L. **62** 61 30N 118 20W
Millsboro **27** 38 36N 75 18W
Millstadt **21** 38 28N 90 6W
Millstone **54** 38 48N 81 6W

Milltown Moju

Milltown, Ind. 22 38 21N 86 17W
Milltown, S. Dak. 47 43 25N 97 48W
Milltown, Wis. 55 45 32N 92 30W
Milltown Malbay 85 52 51N 9 25W
Millville, Del. 27 38 35N 75 8W
Millville, Iowa 23 42 42N 91 5W
Millville, Ky. 49 38 8N 84 49W
Millville, Mass. 28 42 2N 71 35W
Millville, N.J. 37 39 24N 75 2W
Millville, Ohio 42 39 23N 84 39W
Millville, Pa. 45 41 7N 76 32W
Millwood 18 31 16N 82 40W
Millwood L. 13 33 42N 93 58W
Milmay 37 39 26N 74 52W
Milne Inlet 59 72 30N 80 0W
Milner 16 40 29N 107 1W
Milnesand 38 33 39N 103 20W
Milnor 41 46 16N 97 27W
Milo, Canada 62 50 34N 112 53W
Milo, Iowa 23 41 17N 93 27W
Milo, Maine 26 45 15N 68 59W
Milo, Mo. 32 37 45N 94 18W
Milo, Oreg. 44 42 56N 123 3W
Milolii 19 19 11N 155 55W
Mílos 95 36 44N 24 25 E
Milpitas 14 37 26N 121 55W
Milroy, Ind. 22 39 30N 85 28W
Milroy, Minn. 30 44 25N 95 33W
Milroy, Pa. 45 40 43N 77 35W
Milton, N.Z. 128 46 7 S 169 59 E
Milton, U.K. 84 57 18N 4 32W
Milton, Del. 27 38 47N 75 19W
Milton, Fla. 17 30 38N 87 3W
Milton, Ill. 21 39 34N 90 39W
Milton, Iowa 23 40 41N 92 10W
Milton, Kans. 24 37 26N 97 46W
Milton, Ky. 49 38 43N 85 22W
Milton, Mass. 28 42 15N 71 5W
Milton, N. Dak. 41 48 38N 98 3W
Milton, N.H. 36 43 25N 70 59W
Milton, Pa. 45 41 1N 76 51W
Milton, Vt. 36 44 38N 73 7W
Milton, W. Va. 54 38 26N 82 8W
Milton, Wis. 55 42 47N 88 56W
Milton-Freewater 44 45 56N 118 23W
Milton Keynes 83 52 3N 0 42W
Milton Reservoir 16 40 14N 104 38W
Miltona 30 46 3N 95 18W
Miltonvale 24 39 21N 97 27W
Miltou 121 10 14N 17 26 E
Milwaukee 55 43 2N 87 55W
Milwaukee County ◇ 55 43 0N 88 0W
Milwaukie 44 45 27N 122 38W
Mimbres 38 32 51N 107 59W
Mimbres Mts. 38 32 50N 107 45W
Mimoso 75 15 10 S 48 5W
Mims 17 28 40N 80 51W
Min Jiang →, Fujian, China 115 26 0N 119 35 E
Min Jiang →, Sichuan, China 113 28 45N 104 40 E
Min Xian 115 34 25N 104 0 E
Mina 35 38 24N 118 7W
Mina Pirquitas 76 22 40 S 66 30W
Mīnā Su'ud 106 28 45N 48 28 E
Mīnā'al Aḥmadī 106 29 5N 48 10 E
Mīnāb 107 27 10N 57 1 E
Minago → 63 54 33N 98 59W
Minaki 63 49 59N 94 40W
Minam 44 45 38N 117 43W
Minamata 117 32 10N 130 30 E
Minas 77 34 20 S 55 10W
Minas, Sierra de las 66 15 9N 89 31W
Minas Basin 61 45 20N 64 12W
Minas de Rio Tinto 91 37 42N 6 35W
Minas Gerais □ 75 18 50 S 46 0W
Minas Novas 75 17 15 S 42 36W
Minatare 34 41 49N 103 30W
Minatitlán 65 17 58N 94 35W
Minbu 109 20 10N 94 52 E
Minburn 23 41 45N 94 2W
Minco 43 35 19N 97 57W
Mindanao 111 8 0N 125 0 E
Mindanao Trench 111 8 0N 128 0 E
Minden, Germany 88 52 18N 8 45 E
Minden, Iowa 23 41 28N 95 32W
Minden, La. 25 32 37N 93 17W
Minden, Nebr. 34 40 30N 98 57W
Minden, Nev. 35 38 57N 119 46W
Minden City 29 43 40N 82 47W
Mindenmines 32 37 28N 94 35W
Mindiptana 111 5 55 S 140 22 E
Mindoro 111 13 0N 121 0 E
Mindoro Strait 111 12 30N 120 30 E
Mindouli 122 4 12 S 14 28 E
Mine 117 34 12N 131 7 E
Minehead 83 51 12N 3 29W
Mineiros 73 17 34 S 52 34W
Mineola, N.Y. 39 40 45N 73 39W
Mineola, Tex. 51 32 40N 95 29W
Miner County ◇ 47 44 1N 97 36W
Mineral, Calif. 14 40 21N 121 36W
Mineral, Va. 54 38 1N 77 55W
Mineral, Wash. 53 46 43N 122 11W
Mineral Bluff 18 34 55N 84 17W
Mineral County ◇, Colo. 16 37 40N 106 50W
Mineral County ◇, Mont. 33 47 4N 115 0W
Mineral County ◇, Nev. 35 38 30N 118 25W
Mineral County ◇, W. Va. 54 39 21N 79 0W
Mineral Mts. 52 38 30N 112 45W
Mineral Point, Mo. 32 37 57N 90 44W
Mineral Point, Wis. 55 42 52N 90 11W
Mineral Springs 13 33 53N 93 55W
Mineral Wells 51 32 48N 98 7W
Minersville, Pa. 45 40 41N 76 16W
Minersville, Utah 52 38 13N 112 56W
Minerva, N.Y. 39 43 47N 73 59W
Minerva, Ohio 42 40 44N 81 6W
Mingan 61 50 20N 64 0W
Mingechaurskoye Vdkhr. 99 40 56N 47 20 E
Minggang 115 32 24N 114 3 E
Mingin 109 22 50N 94 30 E
Mingo County ◇ 54 37 43N 82 11W
Mingo Junction 42 40 19N 80 37W
Mingxi 115 26 18N 117 12 E
Minho □ 91 41 25N 8 20W
Minho → 91 41 58N 8 40W
Minidoka 20 42 45N 113 29W
Minidoka County ◇ 20 42 50N 113 38W
Minier 21 40 26N 89 19W
Minigwal L. 126 29 31 S 123 14 E
Minipi, L. 61 52 25N 60 45W
Mink L. 62 61 54N 117 40W
Minna 120 9 37N 6 30 E
Minneapolis, Kans. 24 39 8N 97 42W
Minneapolis, Minn. 30 44 59N 93 16W
Minnedosa 63 50 14N 99 50W
Minnehaha County ◇ 47 43 40N 96 49W
Minneiska 30 44 12N 91 52W
Minneola 24 37 26N 100 1W
Minneota 30 44 34N 95 59W
Minnesota □ 30 46 0N 94 15W
Minnesota → 30 44 54N 93 9W
Minnesota City 30 44 6N 91 46W
Minnesota Lake 30 43 51N 93 50W
Minnetonka 30 44 56N 93 27W
Minnewaukan 41 48 4N 99 15W
Minnitaki L. 60 49 57N 92 10W
Mino 117 35 32N 136 55 E
Miño → 91 41 52N 8 40W
Minong 55 46 6N 91 49W
Minonk 21 40 54N 89 2W
Minooka 21 41 27N 88 16W
Minor Hill 48 35 4N 87 9W
Minorca = Menorca 91 40 0N 4 0 E
Minot 41 48 14N 101 18W
Minqing 115 26 15N 118 50 E
Minsk 98 53 52N 27 30 E
Mińsk Mazowiecki 89 52 10N 21 33 E
Minster 42 40 24N 84 23W
Mint Hill 40 35 13N 80 41W
Mintaka Pass 108 37 0N 74 58 E
Minto, Alaska 11 64 53N 149 11W
Minto, N. Dak. 41 48 17N 97 22W
Minton 63 49 10N 104 35W
Minturn 16 39 35N 106 26W
Minusinsk 101 53 50N 91 20 E
Minutang 109 28 15N 96 30 E
Minvoul 122 2 9N 12 8 E
Mio 29 44 39N 84 8W
Mir 121 14 5N 11 59 E
Mira → 70 1 36N 79 1W
Mira por vos Cay 67 22 9N 74 30W
Miracema do Norte 74 9 33 S 48 24W
Mirador 74 6 22 S 44 22W
Miraflores, Colombia 70 1 25N 72 13W
Miraflores, Mexico 64 23 21N 109 45W
Miraflores Locks 57 9 0N 79 36W
Miraj 108 16 50N 74 45 E
Miram Shah 108 33 0N 70 2 E
Miramar, Argentina 76 38 15 S 57 50W
Miramar, U.S.A. 17 25 59N 80 15W
Miramichi B. 61 47 15N 65 0W
Miranda 73 20 10 S 56 15W
Miranda □ 70 10 15N 66 25W
Miranda → 73 19 25 S 57 20W
Miranda de Ebro 91 42 41N 2 57W
Mirando City 50 27 26N 99 0W
Mirandópolis 77 21 9 S 51 6W
Mirassol 77 20 46 S 49 28W
Mirbāţ 105 17 0N 54 45 E
Miri 110 4 18N 114 0 E
Mirim, Lagoa 77 32 45 S 52 50W
Mirimire 70 11 10N 68 43W
Miriti 73 6 15 S 59 0W
Mirnyy, Antarct. 5 66 33 S 93 1 E
Mirnyy, U.S.S.R. 101 62 33N 113 53 E
Mirond L. 63 55 6N 102 47W
Mirpur Khas 108 25 30N 69 0 E
Mirror 62 52 30N 113 7W
Mîrşani 95 44 1N 23 59 E
Miryang 114 35 31N 128 44 E
Mirzapur 109 25 10N 82 34 E
Mirzapur-cum-Vindhyachal = Mirzapur 109 25 10N 82 34 E
Misantla 65 19 56N 96 50W
Misawa 116 40 41N 141 24 E
Miscou I. 61 47 57N 64 31W
Misenheimer 40 35 29N 80 17W
Mish'āb, Ra'as al 106 28 15N 48 43 E
Mishagua → 72 11 12 S 72 58W
Mishan 114 45 37N 131 48 E
Mishawaka 22 41 40N 86 11W
Mishima 117 35 10N 138 52 E
Mishmar Ayyalon 104 31 52N 34 57 E
Mishmar Ha' Emeq 104 32 37N 35 7 E
Mishmar Ha Negev 104 31 22N 34 48 E
Mishmar Ha Yarden 104 33 0N 35 36 E
Misión, La 64 32 5N 116 50W
Misión Fagnano 78 54 32 S 67 17W
Misiones □, Argentina 77 27 0 S 55 0W
Misiones □, Paraguay 76 27 0 S 56 0W
Miskīn 107 23 44N 56 52 E
Miskitos, Cayos 66 14 26N 82 50W
Miskolc 89 48 7N 20 50 E
Misool 111 1 52 S 130 10 E
Misquah Hills 30 47 50N 90 30W
Misquamicut 28 41 20N 71 49W
Misrātah 121 32 24N 15 3 E
Misriç 106 37 55N 41 40 E
Missanabie 60 48 20N 84 6W
Missão Velha 74 7 15 S 39 10W
Missaukee County ◇ 29 44 20N 85 10W
Missinaibi → 60 50 43N 81 29W
Missinaibi L. 60 48 23N 83 40W
Mission, S. Dak. 47 43 18N 100 39W
Mission, Tex. 50 26 13N 98 20W
Mission City 62 49 10N 122 15W
Mission Hill 47 42 55N 97 17W
Mission Indian Reservations 15 33 20N 116 50W
Mission Viejo 15 33 36N 117 40W
Missiquoi B. 36 45 5N 73 10W
Missisa L. 60 52 20N 85 7W
Missisquoi → 36 45 0N 73 8W
Mississagi → 60 46 15N 83 9W
Mississinewa L. 22 40 42N 85 52W
Mississippi □ 31 32 0N 90 0W
Mississippi → 25 29 9N 89 15W
Mississippi County ◇, Ark. 13 35 45N 90 5W
Mississippi County ◇, Mo. 32 36 50N 89 15W
Mississippi River Delta 25 29 10N 89 15W
Mississippi Sd. 31 30 20N 89 0W
Missoula 33 46 52N 114 1W
Missoula County ◇ 33 47 4N 114 0W
Missouri □ 32 38 0N 92 0W
Missouri → 32 38 49N 90 7W
Missouri Buttes 56 44 37N 104 47W
Missouri City 32 39 14N 94 18W
Missouri Valley 23 41 34N 95 53W
Mistake B. 63 62 8N 93 0W
Mistassini → 61 48 42N 72 20W
Mistassini L. 60 51 0N 73 30W
Mistastin L. 61 55 57N 63 20W
Mistatim 63 52 52N 103 22W
Mistretta 94 37 56N 14 20 E
Misty L. 63 58 53N 101 40W
Mitchell, Australia 127 26 29 S 147 58 E
Mitchell, Ga. 18 33 13N 82 42W
Mitchell, Ind. 22 38 44N 86 28W
Mitchell, Iowa 23 43 19N 92 53W
Mitchell, Nebr. 34 41 57N 103 49W
Mitchell, Oreg. 44 44 34N 120 9W
Mitchell, S. Dak. 47 43 43N 98 2W
Mitchell → 127 15 12 S 141 35 E
Mitchell, Mt. 40 35 46N 82 16W
Mitchell County ◇, Ga. 18 31 15N 84 10W
Mitchell County ◇, Iowa 23 43 20N 92 45W
Mitchell County ◇, Kans. 24 39 30N 98 10W
Mitchell County ◇, N.C. 40 36 5N 82 10W
Mitchell County ◇, Tex. 50 32 24N 100 52W
Mitchell L. 10 32 48N 86 27W
Mitchellsburg 49 37 36N 84 57W
Mitchellville 23 41 40N 93 22W
Mitchelstown 85 52 16N 8 18W
Mitiaro, I. 128 19 49 S 157 43W
Mitla 65 16 55N 96 24W
Mito 117 36 20N 140 30 E
Mitsinjo 123 16 1 S 45 52 E
Mitsiwa 121 15 35N 39 25 E
Mitsukaidō 117 36 1N 139 59 E
Mitú 70 1 8N 70 3W
Mituas 70 3 52N 68 49W
Mitumba, Chaîne des 122 6 0 S 29 0 E
Mitwaba 122 8 2 S 27 17 E
Mitzic 122 0 45N 11 40 E
Mixteco → 65 18 11N 98 30W
Miyagi □ 116 38 15N 140 45 E
Miyake-Jima 117 34 0N 139 30 E
Miyako 116 39 40N 141 59 E
Miyako-Jima 117 24 45N 125 20 E
Miyako-Rettō 117 24 24N 125 0 E
Miyakonojō 117 31 40N 131 5 E
Miyanoura-Dake 117 30 20N 130 31 E
Miyazaki 117 31 56N 131 30 E
Miyazaki □ 117 32 30N 131 30 E
Miyazu 117 35 35N 135 10 E
Miyoshi 117 34 48N 132 51 E
Miyun 114 40 28N 116 50 E
Mizal 106 23 59N 45 11 E
Mizamis = Ozamis 111 8 15N 123 50 E
Mizdah 121 31 30N 13 0 E
Mize 31 31 52N 89 33W
Mizen Hd., Cork, Ireland 85 51 27N 9 50W
Mizen Hd., Wicklow, Ireland 85 52 52N 6 4W
Mizhi 114 37 47N 110 12 E
Mizil 95 44 59N 26 29 E
Mizoram □ 109 23 30N 92 40 E
Mizpah, Minn. 30 47 55N 94 12W
Mizpah, Mont. 33 46 14N 105 16W
Miẓpe Ramon 104 30 34N 34 49 E
Mizuho 5 70 30 S 41 0 E
Mizusawa 116 39 8N 141 8 E
Mjölby 97 58 20N 15 10 E
Mjøsa 97 60 48N 11 0 E
Mkushi 123 14 25 S 29 15 E
Mladá Boleslav 88 50 27N 14 53 E
Mława 89 53 9N 20 25 E
Mo i Rana 96 66 15N 14 7 E
Moa 111 8 0 S 128 0 E
Moab 52 38 35N 109 33W
Moabi 122 2 24 S 10 59 E
Moaco → 72 7 41 S 68 18W
Moala 128 18 36 S 179 53 E
Moapa 35 36 40N 114 37W
Moba 122 7 0 S 29 48 E
Mobaye 122 4 25N 21 5 E
Mobayi 122 4 15N 21 8 E
Mobeetie 50 35 31N 100 26W
Moberly 32 39 25N 92 26W
Moberly → 62 56 12N 120 55W
Mobile, Ala. 10 30 41N 88 3W
Mobile, Ariz. 12 33 3N 112 16W
Mobile B. 10 30 30N 88 0W
Mobile County ◇ 10 30 41N 88 3W
Mobridge 47 45 32N 100 26W
Mobutu Sese Seko, L. 122 1 30N 31 0 E
Moca 57 18 24N 67 10W
Mocajuba 74 2 35 S 49 30W
Moçambique 123 15 3 S 40 42 E
Moçâmedes = Namibe 123 15 7 S 12 11 E
Mocapra → 70 7 56N 66 46W
Moccasin 12 36 55N 112 46W
Moccasin Gap 54 36 38N 82 33W
Mocha, I. 78 38 22 S 73 56W
Mochudi 123 24 27 S 26 7 E
Mocimboa da Praia 122 11 25 S 40 20 E
Mocksville 40 35 54N 80 34W
Moclips 53 47 14N 124 13W
Mocoa 70 1 7N 76 35W
Mococa 77 21 28 S 47 0W
Mocorito 64 25 30N 107 53W
Moctezuma 64 29 50N 109 0W
Moctezuma → 65 21 59N 98 34W
Mocuba 123 16 54 S 36 57 E
Modane 90 45 12N 6 40 E
Model 16 37 22N 104 15W
Módena, Italy 94 44 39N 10 55 E
Modena, U.S.A. 52 37 48N 113 56W
Modesto 14 37 39N 121 0W
Módica 94 36 52N 14 45 E
Modoc, Ga. 18 32 37N 82 19W
Modoc, S.C. 46 33 44N 82 13W
Modoc County ◇ 14 41 40N 120 50W
Modoc Point 44 42 27N 121 52W
Moe 127 38 12 S 146 19 E
Moei → 112 17 25N 98 10 E
Moengo 71 5 45N 54 20W
Moenkopi 12 36 7N 111 13W
Moffat, U.K. 84 55 20N 3 27W
Moffat, U.S.A. 16 37 58N 105 56W
Moffat County ◇ 16 40 45N 108 10W
Mogadishu = Muqdisho 105 2 2N 45 25 E
Mogador = Essaouira 120 31 32N 9 42W
Mogami → 116 38 45N 140 0 E
Mogaung 109 25 20N 97 0 E
Mogi das Cruzes 77 23 31 S 46 11W
Mogi-Guaçu → 77 20 53 S 48 10W
Mogi-Mirim 77 22 29 S 47 0W
Mogilev 98 53 55N 30 18 E
Mogilev-Podolskiy 99 48 20N 27 40 E
Mogincual 123 15 35 S 40 25 E
Mogocha 101 53 40N 119 50 E
Mogoi 111 1 55 S 133 10 E
Mogok 109 23 0N 96 40 E
Mogollon Mts. 38 33 25N 108 40W
Mogollon Rim 12 34 10N 110 50W
Mohács 89 45 58N 18 41 E
Mohall 41 48 46N 101 31W
Moḩammadābād 107 37 52N 59 5 E
Mohave, L. 12 35 12N 114 34W
Mohave County ◇ 12 35 0N 114 0W
Mohave Mts. 12 34 35N 114 10W
Mohawk, Mich. 29 47 18N 88 21W
Mohawk, N.Y. 39 43 0N 75 0W
Mohawk → 39 42 47N 73 41W
Mohawk Mts. 12 32 30N 113 35W
Mohe 114 53 28N 122 17 E
Mohican → 42 40 22N 82 9W
Mohican, C. 11 60 12N 167 25W
Mohicanville Reservoir 42 40 45N 82 0W
Mohon Pk. 12 34 57N 113 9W
Mohoro 122 8 6 S 39 8 E
Moidart, L. 84 56 47N 5 40W
Moineşti 95 46 28N 26 31 E
Mointy 100 47 10N 73 18 E
Moisie 61 50 12N 66 1W
Moisie → 61 50 14N 66 5W
Moïssala 121 8 21N 17 46 E
Mojave 15 35 3N 118 10W
Mojave → 15 35 6N 116 4W
Mojave Desert 15 35 0N 117 20W
Mojo 76 21 48 S 65 33W
Mojokerto 111 7 29 S 112 25 E
Mojos, Llanos de 73 15 0 S 65 0W
Moju → 74 1 40 S 48 25W

Mokai Moose Jaw Cr.

Mokai 128 38 32 S 175 56 E
Mokane 32 38 41N 91 53W
Mokapu Peninsula 19 21 25N 157 45W
Mokelumne → 14 38 13N 121 28W
Mokelumne Hill 14 38 18N 120 43W
Mokokchung 109 26 15N 94 30 E
Mokolea Rock 19 21 27N 157 44W
Moku Manu 19 21 29N 157 43W
Mokuaeae I. 19 22 14N 159 25W
Mokuauia I. 19 21 40N 157 56W
Mokulua Is. 19 21 24N 157 42W
Mol 87 51 11N 5 5 E
Molalla 44 45 9N 122 35W
Molchanovo 100 57 40N 83 50 E
Mold 82 53 10N 3 10W
Moldavia = Moldova 95 46 30N 27 0 E
Moldavian S.S.R. □ 99 47 0N 28 0 E
Molde 96 62 45N 7 9 E
Moldova 95 46 30N 27 0 E
Moldoveanu 95 45 36N 24 45 E
Molena 18 33 1N 84 30W
Molepolole 123 24 28 S 25 28 E
Molfetta 94 41 12N 16 35 E
Molii Pond 19 21 31N 157 51W
Molina 16 39 11N 108 4W
Moline, Ill. 21 41 30N 90 31W
Moline, Kans. 24 37 22N 96 18W
Molino 17 30 43N 87 20W
Molinos 76 25 28 S 66 15W
Moliro 122 8 12 S 30 30 E
Molise □ 94 41 45N 14 30 E
Mollendo 72 17 0 S 72 0W
Mölndal 97 57 40N 12 3 E
Molokai 19 21 8N 157 0W
Molokini I. 19 20 38N 156 30W
Molopo → 123 28 30 S 20 13 E
Molotov = Perm 98 58 0N 57 10 E
Moloundou 122 2 8N 15 15 E
Molson L. 63 54 22N 96 40W
Molu 111 6 45 S 131 40 E
Molucca Sea 111 4 0 S 124 0 E
Moluccas = Maluku 111 1 0 S 127 0 E
Moma 123 16 47 S 39 4 E
Mombaça 74 5 43 S 39 45W
Mombasa 122 4 2 S 39 43 E
Mombetsu 116 44 21N 143 22 E
Momchilgrad 95 41 33N 25 23 E
Momence 21 41 10N 87 40W
Mompós 70 9 14N 74 26W
Møn 97 54 57N 12 15 E
Mon → 109 20 25N 94 30 E
Mona 52 39 49N 111 51W
Mona, Canal de la 67 18 30N 67 45W
Mona, I. 67 18 5N 67 54W
Mona, Isla 57 18 5N 67 54W
Mona, Pta. 66 9 37N 82 36W
Monach Is. 84 57 32N 7 40W
Monaco ■ 90 43 46N 7 23 E
Monadhliath Mts. 84 57 10N 4 4W
Monadnock, Mt. 36 42 52N 72 7W
Monagas □ 71 9 20N 63 0W
Monaghan 85 54 15N 6 58W
Monaghan □ 85 54 10N 7 0W
Monahans 50 31 36N 102 54W
Monango 41 46 10N 98 36W
Monarch 46 34 42N 81 34W
Monarch Mt. 62 51 55N 125 57W
Monarch Pass 16 38 30N 106 20W
Monastir = Bitola 95 41 5N 21 10 E
Monastir 121 35 50N 10 49 E
Moncayo, Sierra del 91 41 48N 1 50W
Mönchengladbach 88 51 12N 6 23 E
Monchique 91 37 19N 8 38W
Monchique, Sa. de 91 37 18N 8 39W
Moncks Corner 46 33 12N 80 1W
Monclova 64 26 50N 101 30W
Moncton 61 46 7N 64 51W
Mondamin 23 41 42N 96 1W
Mondego → 91 40 9N 8 52W
Mondeodo 111 3 34 S 122 9 E
Mondovì, Italy 94 44 23N 7 49 E
Mondovi, U.S.A. 55 44 34N 91 40W
Monee 21 41 25N 87 44W
Monero 38 36 55N 106 52W
Monessen 45 40 9N 79 54W
Moneta 23 43 13N 95 24W
Monett 32 36 55N 93 55W
Monette 13 35 53N 90 21W
Monforte 91 39 6N 7 25W
Mong Cai 112 21 27N 107 54 E
Mong Hsu 109 21 54N 98 30 E
Mong Kung 109 21 35N 97 35 E
Mong Lang 112 21 29N 97 52 E
Mong Nai 109 20 32N 97 46 E
Mong Pawk 109 22 4N 99 16 E
Mong Ton 109 20 17N 98 45 E
Mong Wa 109 21 26N 100 27 E
Mong Yai 109 22 21N 98 3 E
Mongalla 121 5 8N 31 42 E
Mongers, L. 126 29 25 S 117 5 E
Monghyr = Munger 109 25 23N 86 30 E
Mongo 121 12 14N 18 43 E
Mongolia ■ 113 47 0N 103 0 E
Mongororo 121 12 3N 22 26 E
Mongu 123 15 16 S 23 12 E
Monhegan I. 26 43 46N 69 19W
Moniac 18 30 31N 82 14W
Monico 55 45 35N 89 9W
Monida 33 44 34N 112 19W
Moniteau County ◇ 32 38 35N 92 35W
Monitor 53 47 29N 120 25W
Monitor Range 35 38 40N 118 45W
Monkey River 65 16 22N 88 29W
Monkoto 122 1 38 S 20 35 E
Monkstown 51 33 48N 95 56W
Monkton 27 39 35N 76 37W
Monmouth, U.K. 83 51 48N 2 43W
Monmouth, Ill. 21 40 55N 90 39W
Monmouth, Oreg. 44 44 51N 123 14W
Monmouth County ◇ 37 40 15N 74 15W
Monmouth Junction 37 40 23N 74 33W
Mono County ◇ 14 38 0N 119 0W
Mono L. 14 38 1N 119 1W
Monocary → 27 39 13N 77 27W
Monolith 15 35 7N 118 22W
Monomoy I. 28 41 36N 69 59W
Monomoy Point 28 41 33N 70 2W
Monon 22 40 52N 86 53W
Monona, Iowa 23 43 3N 91 23W
Monona, Wis. 55 43 4N 89 20W
Monona County ◇ 23 42 0N 96 0W
Monongah 54 39 28N 80 13W
Monongahela 45 40 12N 79 56W
Monongahela → 45 40 27N 80 1W
Monongahela National Forest 54 38 30N 79 57W
Monongalia County ◇ 54 39 39N 80 1W
Monópoli 94 40 57N 17 18 E
Monowi 34 42 50N 98 20W
Monqoumba 122 3 33N 18 40 E
Monroe, Ark. 13 34 44N 91 6W
Monroe, Ga. 18 33 47N 83 43W
Monroe, Ind. 22 40 45N 84 56W
Monroe, Iowa 23 41 31N 93 6W
Monroe, La. 25 32 30N 92 7W
Monroe, Mich. 29 41 55N 83 24W
Monroe, N.C. 40 34 59N 80 33W
Monroe, N.Y. 39 41 20N 74 11W
Monroe, Nebr. 34 41 28N 97 36W
Monroe, Ohio 42 39 27N 84 22W
Monroe, Okla. 43 34 59N 94 30W
Monroe, Oreg. 44 44 19N 123 18W
Monroe, S. Dak. 47 43 29N 97 13W
Monroe, Utah 52 38 38N 112 7W
Monroe, Va. 54 37 30N 79 8W
Monroe, Wash. 53 47 51N 121 58W
Monroe, Wis. 55 42 36N 89 38W
Monroe, L. 17 28 50N 81 19W
Monroe City 32 39 39N 91 44W
Monroe County ◇, Ala. 10 31 31N 87 20W
Monroe County ◇, Ark. 13 34 42N 91 19W
Monroe County ◇, Fla. 17 25 30N 81 0W
Monroe County ◇, Ga. 18 33 0N 83 55W
Monroe County ◇, Ill. 21 38 15N 90 10W
Monroe County ◇, Ind. 22 39 10N 86 30W
Monroe County ◇, Iowa 23 41 0N 92 50W
Monroe County ◇, Ky. 49 36 45N 85 45W
Monroe County ◇, Mich. 29 41 50N 83 35W
Monroe County ◇, Miss. 31 33 49N 88 33W
Monroe County ◇, Mo. 32 39 30N 92 0W
Monroe County ◇, N.Y. 39 43 10N 77 40W
Monroe County ◇, Ohio 42 39 46N 81 7W
Monroe County ◇, Pa. 45 41 0N 75 15W
Monroe County ◇, Tenn. 49 35 31N 84 22W
Monroe County ◇, W. Va. 54 37 36N 80 33W
Monroe County ◇, Wis. 55 43 50N 90 40W
Monroe L. 22 39 1N 86 31W
Monroeton 45 41 43N 76 29W
Monroeville, Ala. 10 31 31N 87 20W
Monroeville, Ind. 22 40 59N 84 52W
Monroeville, Ohio 42 41 15N 82 42W
Monroeville, Pa. 45 40 26N 79 45W
Monrovia 120 6 18N 10 47W
Mons 87 50 27N 3 58 E
Monse 111 4 0 S 123 10 E
Monsefú 72 6 52 S 79 52W
Monson 26 45 17N 69 30W
Mont Alto 45 39 51N 77 34W
Mont Belvieu 51 29 51N 94 53W
Mont-de-Marsan 90 43 54N 0 31W
Mont Ida 24 38 13N 95 22W
Mont-Joli 61 48 37N 68 10W
Mont Laurier 60 46 35N 75 30W
Mont-St-Michel, Le 90 48 40N 1 30W
Mont Tremblant Prov. Park 60 46 30N 74 30W
Mont Vernon 36 42 50N 71 42W
Montagu I. 5 58 25 S 26 20W
Montague, Canada 61 46 10N 62 39W
Montague, Calif. 14 41 44N 122 32W
Montague, Mass. 28 42 32N 72 32W
Montague, Mich. 29 43 25N 86 22W
Montague, Tex. 51 33 42N 97 48W
Montague, I. 64 31 40N 114 56W
Montague County ◇ 51 33 47N 97 44W
Montague I. 11 60 0N 147 30W
Montague Sd. 126 14 28 S 125 20 E
Montalba 51 31 53N 95 44W
Montalbán 91 40 50N 0 45W
Montaña 72 6 0 S 73 0W
Montana □ 33 47 0N 110 0W
Montañita 70 1 22N 75 28W
Montargis 90 48 0N 2 43 E
Montauban 90 44 0N 1 21 E
Montauk 39 41 3N 71 57W
Montbéliard 90 47 31N 6 48 E
Montcalm County ◇ 29 43 15N 85 10W
Montclair 37 40 49N 74 13W
Monte Albán 65 17 2N 96 45W
Monte Alegre 71 2 0 S 54 0W
Monte Alegre de Goiás 75 13 14 S 47 10W
Monte Alegre de Minas 75 18 52 S 48 52W
Monte Azul 75 15 9 S 42 53W
Monte Bello Is. 126 20 30 S 115 45 E
Monte-Carlo 90 43 46N 7 23 E
Monte Carmelo 75 18 43 S 47 29W
Monte Caseros 76 30 10 S 57 50W
Monte Comán 76 34 40 S 67 53W
Monte Cristi 67 19 52N 71 39W
Monte Dinero 78 52 18 S 68 33W
Monte Lindo → 76 23 56 S 57 12W
Monte Quemado 76 25 53 S 62 41W
Monte Sant' Ángelo 94 41 42N 15 59 E
Monte Santu, C. di 94 40 5N 9 42 E
Monte Vista 16 37 35N 106 9W
Monteagle 49 35 15N 85 50W
Monteagudo, Argentina 77 27 14 S 54 8W
Monteagudo, Bolivia 73 19 49 S 63 59W
Montebello 60 45 40N 74 55W
Montecito 15 34 26N 119 40W
Montecristi 70 1 0 S 80 40W
Montego Bay 66 18 30N 78 0W
Montegut 25 29 28N 90 33W
Monteiro 74 7 48 S 37 2W
Montelíbano 70 8 5N 75 29W
Montélimar 90 44 33N 4 45 E
Montello, Nev. 35 41 16N 114 12W
Montello, Wis. 55 43 48N 89 20W
Montemorelos 65 25 11N 99 42W
Montenegro = Crna Gora □ 95 42 40N 19 20 E
Montenegro 77 29 39 S 51 29W
Montepuez 123 13 8 S 38 59 E
Monterey, Calif. 14 36 37N 121 55W
Monterey, Ky. 49 38 25N 84 52W
Monterey, Mass. 28 42 11N 73 13W
Monterey, Tenn. 49 36 9N 85 16W
Monterey, Va. 54 38 25N 79 35W
Monterey B. 14 36 45N 122 0W
Monterey County ◇ 15 36 15N 121 20W
Montería 70 8 46N 75 53W
Montero 73 17 20 S 63 15W
Monteros 76 27 11 S 65 30W
Monterrey 64 25 40N 100 30W
Montes Altos 74 5 50 S 47 4W
Montes Claros 75 16 30 S 43 50W
Montesano 53 46 59N 123 36W
Montevallo 10 33 6N 86 52W
Montevideo, Uruguay 77 34 50 S 56 11W
Montevideo, U.S.A. 30 44 57N 95 43W
Monteview 20 43 56N 112 32W
Montezuma, Ga. 18 32 18N 84 2W
Montezuma, Ind. 22 39 48N 87 22W
Montezuma, Iowa 23 41 35N 92 32W
Montezuma, Kans. 24 37 36N 100 27W
Montezuma County ◇ 16 37 20N 108 30W
Montezuma Cr. → 52 37 17N 109 20W
Montfort 55 42 58N 90 26W
Montgomery = Sahiwal 108 30 45N 73 8 E
Montgomery, U.K. 83 52 34N 3 9W
Montgomery, Ala. 10 32 23N 86 19W
Montgomery, Ga. 18 31 57N 81 7W
Montgomery, La. 25 31 40N 92 53W
Montgomery, Minn. 30 44 26N 93 35W
Montgomery, Pa. 45 41 10N 76 53W
Montgomery, Tex. 51 30 23N 95 42W
Montgomery, W. Va. 54 38 11N 81 19W
Montgomery Center 36 44 53N 73 40W
Montgomery City 32 38 59N 91 30W
Montgomery County ◇, Ala. 10 32 15N 86 18W
Montgomery County ◇, Ark. 13 34 34N 93 38W
Montgomery County ◇, Ga. 18 32 15N 82 35W
Montgomery County ◇, Ill. 21 39 10N 89 30W
Montgomery County ◇, Ind. 22 40 5N 86 55W
Montgomery County ◇, Iowa 23 41 0N 95 10W
Montgomery County ◇, Kans. 24 37 15N 95 45W
Montgomery County ◇, Ky. 49 38 0N 83 55W
Montgomery County ◇, Md. 27 39 15N 77 15W
Montgomery County ◇, Miss. 31 33 29N 89 44W
Montgomery County ◇, Mo. 32 38 55N 91 30W
Montgomery County ◇, N.C. 40 35 20N 79 50W
Montgomery County ◇, N.Y. 39 42 50N 74 30W
Montgomery County ◇, Ohio 42 39 45N 84 12W
Montgomery County ◇, Pa. 45 40 10N 75 10W
Montgomery County ◇, Tenn. 48 36 32N 87 21W
Montgomery County ◇, Tex. 51 30 19N 95 27W
Montgomery County ◇, Va. 54 37 8N 80 25W
Montgomery Village 27 39 12N 77 13W
Monticello, Ark. 13 33 38N 91 47W
Monticello, Fla. 17 30 33N 83 52W
Monticello, Ga. 18 33 18N 83 40W
Monticello, Ill. 21 40 1N 88 34W
Monticello, Ind. 22 40 45N 86 46W
Monticello, Iowa 23 42 15N 91 12W
Monticello, Ky. 49 36 50N 84 51W
Monticello, Maine 26 46 19N 67 51W
Monticello, Minn. 30 45 18N 93 48W
Monticello, Miss. 31 31 33N 90 7W
Monticello, Mo. 32 40 7N 91 43W
Monticello, N. Mex. 38 33 24N 107 27W
Monticello, N.Y. 39 41 39N 74 42W
Monticello, Utah 52 37 52N 109 21W
Monticello, Wis. 55 42 45N 89 36W
Montijo 91 38 52N 6 39W
Montilla 91 37 36N 4 40W
Montluçon 90 46 22N 2 36 E
Montmagny 61 46 58N 70 34W
Montmartre 63 50 14N 103 27W
Montmorency 61 46 53N 71 11W
Montmorency County ◇ 29 45 0N 84 10W
Monto 127 24 52 S 151 6 E
Montoro 91 38 1N 4 27W
Montour, Idaho 20 43 55N 116 20W
Montour, Iowa 23 41 59N 92 43W
Montour County ◇ 45 41 0N 76 40W
Montour Falls 39 42 21N 76 51W
Montoursville 45 41 15N 76 55W
Montoya 38 35 6N 104 4W
Montpelier, Idaho 20 42 19N 111 18W
Montpelier, Ind. 22 40 33N 85 17W
Montpelier, La. 25 30 41N 90 39W
Montpelier, Miss. 31 33 43N 88 57W
Montpelier, N. Dak. 41 46 42N 98 35W
Montpelier, Ohio 42 41 35N 84 37W
Montpelier, Vt. 36 44 16N 72 35W
Montpellier 90 43 37N 3 52 E
Montréal 60 45 31N 73 34W
Montreal L. 63 54 20N 105 45W
Montreal Lake 63 54 3N 105 46W
Montreuil 90 50 27N 1 45 E
Montreux 88 46 26N 6 55 E
Montrose, U.K. 84 56 43N 2 28W
Montrose, Ark. 13 33 18N 91 30W
Montrose, Colo. 16 38 29N 107 53W
Montrose, Ill. 21 39 10N 88 23W
Montrose, Iowa 23 40 31N 91 25W
Montrose, Mich. 29 43 11N 83 54W
Montrose, Miss. 31 32 8N 89 14W
Montrose, Mo. 32 38 16N 93 59W
Montrose, Pa. 45 41 50N 75 53W
Montrose, S. Dak. 47 43 42N 97 11W
Montrose, W. Va. 54 39 4N 79 49W
Montrose County ◇ 16 38 30N 108 15W
Montross 54 38 6N 76 50W
Monts, Pte. des 61 49 20N 67 12W
Montserrat 67 16 40N 62 10W
Montvale 54 37 23N 79 44W
Montville 28 41 27N 72 8W
Monument, Kans. 24 39 6N 101 1W
Monument, Oreg. 44 44 49N 119 25W
Monument Draw → 50 32 29N 102 20W
Monument Pass 12 36 58N 110 5W
Monument Pk. 20 42 7N 114 14W
Monument Valley 12 37 0N 110 0W
Monveda 122 2 52N 21 30 E
Monywa 109 22 7N 95 11 E
Monze 123 16 17 S 27 29 E
Monze, C. 108 24 47N 66 37 E
Monzón 91 41 52N 0 10 E
Moody, Mo. 32 36 32N 91 59W
Moody, Tex. 51 31 18N 97 21W
Moody County ◇ 47 44 3N 96 36W
Mooleyville 48 38 1N 86 28W
Moon L. 14 41 10N 121 10W
Moonbeam 60 49 20N 82 10W
Moonie → 127 29 19 S 148 43 E
Moorcroft 56 44 16N 104 57W
Moore, Idaho 20 43 44N 113 22W
Moore, Mont. 33 46 59N 109 42W
Moore, Okla. 43 35 20N 97 29W
Moore, Tex. 51 29 3N 99 1W
Moore, Utah 52 38 58N 111 10W
Moore, L. 126 29 50 S 117 35 E
Moore County ◇, N.C. 40 35 20N 79 20W
Moore County ◇, Tenn. 48 35 17N 86 22W
Moore County ◇, Tex. 50 35 55N 101 59W
Moore Haven 17 26 50N 81 6W
Moore Reservoir 36 44 20N 71 53W
Moorefield, Nebr. 34 40 41N 100 24W
Moorefield, W. Va. 54 39 4N 78 58W
Moorefield → 54 39 5N 78 59W
Mooreland 43 36 26N 99 12W
Moorestown 37 39 58N 74 57W
Mooresville, Ind. 22 39 37N 86 22W
Mooresville, N.C. 40 35 35N 80 48W
Mooreton 41 46 16N 96 53W
Moorfoot Hills 84 55 44N 3 8W
Moorhead, Iowa 23 41 56N 95 51W
Moorhead, Minn. 30 46 53N 96 45W
Moorhead, Miss. 31 33 27N 90 30W
Mooringsport 25 32 41N 93 58W
Moorland 23 42 26N 94 18W
Moose →, Canada 60 51 20N 80 25W
Moose →, N.Y. 39 43 38N 75 24W
Moose →, Vt. 36 44 24N 72 1W
Moose Factory 60 51 16N 80 32W
Moose I. 63 51 42N 97 10W
Moose Jaw 63 50 24N 105 30W
Moose Jaw Cr. → 63 50 34N 105 18W

Moose Lake Mountain

Moose Lake, Canada 63 53 43N 100 20W
Moose Lake, U.S.A. 30 46 27N 92 46W
Moose Mountain Cr. → 63 49 13N 102 12W
Moose Mountain Prov. Park 63 49 48N 102 25W
Moose Pass 11 60 29N 149 22W
Moose River, Canada 60 50 48N 81 17W
Moose River, U.S.A. 26 45 39N 70 16W
Moosehead L. 26 45 38N 69 40W
Mooselookmeguntic L. 26 44 55N 70 49W
Moosilauke, Mt. 36 44 3N 71 40W
Moosomin 63 50 9N 101 40W
Moosonee 60 51 17N 80 39W
Moosup 28 41 43N 71 53W
Mopeia 123 17 30 S 35 40 E
Mopti 120 14 30N 4 0W
Moquegua 72 17 15 S 70 46W
Moquegua □ 72 16 50 S 70 55W
Mora, Puerto Rico 57 18 28N 67 2W
Mora, Sweden 97 61 2N 14 38 E
Mora, Ga. 18 31 25N 82 57W
Mora, Minn. 30 45 53N 93 18W
Mora, N. Mex. 38 35 58N 105 20W
Mora County ◊ 38 36 0N 104 0W
Morada Nova 74 5 7 S 38 23W
Morada Nova de Minas 75 18 37 S 45 22W
Moradabad 108 28 50N 78 50 E
Morafenobe 123 17 50 S 44 53 E
Morales, Colombia 70 2 45N 76 38W
Morales, U.S.A. 51 29 8N 96 46W
Moramanga 123 18 56 S 48 12 E
Moran, Kans. 24 37 55N 95 10W
Moran, Mich. 29 46 0N 84 50W
Moran, Tex. 51 32 33N 99 10W
Morant Cays 66 17 22N 76 0W
Morant Pt. 66 17 55N 76 12W
Morar L. 84 56 57N 5 40W
Moratuwa 108 6 45N 79 55 E
Morava → 88 48 10N 16 59 E
Moravia, Iowa 23 40 53N 92 49W
Moravia, N.Y. 39 42 43N 76 25W
Moravian Hts. = Ceskomoravská Vrchovina 88 49 30N 15 40 E
Morawhanna 71 8 30N 59 40W
Moray Firth 84 57 50N 3 30W
Morbihan □ 90 47 55N 2 50W
Morden 63 49 15N 98 10W
Mordovian A.S.S.R.□ 98 54 20N 44 30 E
Møre og Romsdal fylke □ 96 62 30N 8 0 E
Moreau → 47 45 18N 100 43W
Morecambe 82 54 5N 2 52W
Morecambe B. 82 54 7N 3 0W
Moree 127 29 28 S 149 54 E
Morehead 49 38 11N 83 26W
Morehead City 40 34 43N 76 43W
Morehouse 32 36 51N 89 41W
Morehouse Parish ◊ 25 32 47N 91 48W
Moreland, Ga. 18 33 17N 84 46W
Moreland, Ky. 49 37 30N 84 49W
Morelia 64 19 40N 101 11W
Morella 91 40 35N 0 5W
Morelos 64 26 42N 107 40W
Morelos □ 65 18 40N 99 10W
Morena, Sierra 91 38 20N 4 0W
Morenci, Ariz. 12 33 5N 109 22W
Morenci, Mich. 29 41 43N 84 13W
Moreni 95 44 59N 25 36 E
Morero 73 11 9 S 66 15W
Moreru → 73 10 10 S 59 15W
Moresby I. 62 52 30N 131 40W
Moreton B. 127 27 10 S 153 10 E
Moreton I. 127 27 10 S 153 25 E
Morgan, Ga. 18 31 32N 84 36W
Morgan, Ky. 49 38 36N 84 24W
Morgan, Minn. 30 44 25N 94 56W
Morgan, Utah 52 41 2N 111 41W
Morgan, Vt. 36 44 53N 73 2W
Morgan, Mt. 15 37 31N 118 47W
Morgan City, Ala. 10 34 28N 86 34W
Morgan City, La. 25 29 42N 91 12W
Morgan County ◊, Ala. 10 34 27N 86 56W
Morgan County ◊, Colo. 16 40 15N 103 50W
Morgan County ◊, Ga. 18 33 40N 83 25W
Morgan County ◊, Ill. 21 39 45N 90 10W
Morgan County ◊, Ind. 22 39 30N 86 25W
Morgan County ◊, Ky. 49 37 55N 83 15W
Morgan County ◊, Mo. 32 38 25N 92 50W
Morgan County ◊, Ohio 42 39 39N 81 51W
Morgan County ◊, Tenn. 49 36 6N 84 36W
Morgan County ◊, Utah 52 41 10N 111 45W
Morgan County ◊, W. Va. 54 39 35N 78 16W
Morgan Hill 14 37 8N 121 39W
Morgan L. 38 36 52N 108 41W
Morgan Mill 51 32 23N 98 10W
Morganfield 48 37 41N 87 55W
Morganton 40 35 45N 81 41W
Morgantown, Ind. 22 39 22N 86 16W
Morgantown, Ky. 48 37 14N 86 41W
Morgantown, Md. 27 38 21N 76 58W
Morgantown, Ohio 42 39 8N 83 12W
Morgantown, W. Va. 54 39 38N 79 57W
Morganville, Ga. 18 34 56N 85 27W
Morganville, Kans. 24 39 28N 97 12W
Morganza 25 30 44N 91 36W
Moriah Mt. 35 39 17N 114 12W
Moriarty 38 34 59N 106 3W
Morice L. 62 53 50N 127 40W
Morichal 70 2 10N 70 34W
Morichal Largo → 71 9 27N 62 25W
Morinville 62 53 49N 113 41W
Morioka 116 39 45N 141 8 E
Moris 64 28 8N 108 32W
Morlaix 90 48 36N 3 52W
Morland 24 39 21N 100 5W
Morley, Mich. 29 43 29N 85 27W
Morley, Mo. 32 37 3N 89 37W
Mormon L. 12 34 57N 111 29W
Mormon Lake 12 34 55N 111 28W
Mormon Mts. 35 37 0N 114 0W
Morning Sun 23 41 5N 91 15W
Morningside 27 38 50N 76 54W
Mornington, I. 78 49 50 S 75 30W
Mornington I. 127 16 30 S 139 30 E
Moro, Ark. 13 34 48N 90 59W
Moro, Oreg. 44 45 29N 120 44W
Moro → 13 33 17N 92 21W
Moro G. 111 6 30N 123 0 E
Morocco 22 40 57N 87 27W
Morocco ■ 120 32 0N 5 50W
Morococha 72 11 40 S 76 5W
Morogoro 122 6 50 S 37 40 E
Morokweng 123 26 12 S 23 45 E
Moroleón 64 20 8N 101 32W
Morombe 123 21 45 S 43 22 E
Moron, Argentina 76 34 39 S 58 37W
Morón, Cuba 66 22 8N 78 39W
Mörön → 113 47 14N 110 37 E
Morón de la Frontera 91 37 6N 5 28W
Morona → 70 4 40 S 77 10W
Morona-Santiago □ 70 2 30 S 78 0W
Morondava 123 20 17 S 44 17 E
Moroni 52 39 32N 111 35W
Morotai 111 2 10N 128 30 E
Moroto 122 2 28N 34 42 E
Morovis 57 18 20N 66 25W
Morozov 95 42 30N 25 10 E
Morpeth 82 55 11N 1 41W
Morphou 106 35 12N 32 59 E
Morral 42 40 41N 83 13W
Morrill, Kans. 24 39 56N 95 42W
Morrill, Nebr. 34 41 58N 103 56W
Morrill County ◊ 34 41 45N 103 0W
Morrilton 13 35 9N 92 44W
Morrinhos, Ceara, Brazil 74 3 14 S 40 7W
Morrinhos, Minas Gerais, Brazil 75 17 45 S 49 10W
Morrinsville 128 37 40 S 175 32 E
Morris, Canada 63 49 25N 97 22W
Morris, Conn. 28 41 43N 73 15W
Morris, Ga. 18 31 48N 84 57W
Morris, Ill. 21 41 22N 88 26W
Morris, Minn. 30 45 35N 95 55W
Morris, N.Y. 39 42 33N 75 15W
Morris, Okla. 43 35 36N 95 51W
Morris County ◊, Kans. 24 38 30N 96 40W
Morris County ◊, N.J. 37 40 45N 74 30W
Morris County ◊, Tex. 51 33 2N 94 44W
Morrisburg 60 44 55N 75 7W
Morrison, Ill. 21 41 49N 89 58W
Morrison, Okla. 43 36 18N 97 1W
Morrison, Tenn. 49 35 36N 85 55W
Morrison County ◊ 30 46 0N 94 10W
Morrisonville 21 39 25N 89 27W
Morristown, Ariz. 12 33 51N 112 37W
Morristown, Ind. 22 39 40N 85 42W
Morristown, Minn. 30 44 14N 93 27W
Morristown, N.J. 37 40 48N 74 29W
Morristown, N.Y. 39 44 35N 75 39W
Morristown, S. Dak. 47 45 56N 101 43W
Morristown, Tenn. 49 36 13N 83 18W
Morrisville, Mo. 32 37 29N 93 25W
Morrisville, N.C. 40 35 49N 78 50W
Morrisville, N.Y. 39 42 53N 75 35W
Morrisville, Vt. 36 44 34N 72 36W
Morro, Pta. 76 27 6 S 71 0W
Morro Bay 15 35 22N 120 51W
Morro do Chapéu 75 11 33 S 41 9W
Morros 74 2 52 S 44 3W
Morrosquillo, Golfo de 66 9 35N 75 40W
Morrow, La. 25 30 50N 92 5W
Morrow, Ohio 42 39 21N 84 8W
Morrow County ◊, Ohio 42 40 33N 82 50W
Morrow County ◊, Oreg. 44 45 25N 119 40W
Morrowville 24 39 51N 97 10W
Morrumbene 123 23 31 S 35 16 E
Morse 50 36 4N 101 29W
Morse Bluff 34 41 26N 96 46W
Morse Res. 22 40 7N 86 3W
Morshansk 98 53 28N 41 50 E
Morteros 76 30 50 S 62 0W
Mortes, L. Aux 41 48 20N 99 7W
Mortes, R. das → 75 11 45 S 50 44W
Morton, Ill. 21 40 37N 89 28W
Morton, Minn. 30 44 33N 94 59W
Morton, Miss. 31 32 21N 89 39W
Morton, Tex. 50 33 44N 102 46W
Morton, Wash. 53 46 34N 122 17W
Morton County ◊, Kans. 24 37 15N 101 45W
Morton County ◊, N. Dak. 41 46 45N 101 30W
Mortons Gap 48 37 14N 87 28W
Morvan, Mts. du 90 47 5N 4 0 E
Morven, Ga. 18 30 57N 83 30W
Morven, N.C. 40 34 52N 80 0W
Morvern 84 56 38N 5 44W
Morwell 127 38 10 S 146 22 E
Morzhovets, Ostrov 98 66 44N 42 35 E
Mosby 33 47 0N 107 52W
Mosca 16 37 39N 105 52W
Moscos Is. 112 14 0N 97 30 E
Moscow = Moskva 98 55 45N 37 35 E
Moscow, Idaho 20 46 44N 117 0W
Moscow, Kans. 24 37 20N 101 12W
Moscow, Ky. 48 36 37N 89 2W
Moscow, Ohio 42 38 52N 84 14W
Moscow, Pa. 45 41 20N 75 31W
Moscow, Tenn. 48 35 4N 89 24W
Moscow Mills 32 38 57N 90 55W
Mosel → 90 50 22N 7 36 E
Moselle = Mosel → 90 50 22N 7 36 E
Moselle 31 31 30N 89 17W
Moselle □ 90 48 59N 6 33 E
Moses Lake 53 47 8N 119 17W
Mosgiel 128 45 53 S 170 21 E
Mosheim 49 36 11N 82 57W
Mosher 47 43 28N 100 18W
Moshi 122 3 22 S 37 18 E
Mosier 44 45 41N 121 24W
Mosinee 55 44 47N 89 43W
Mosjøen 96 65 51N 13 12 E
Moskenesøya 96 67 58N 13 0 E
Moskenstraumen 96 67 47N 12 45 E
Moskva 98 55 45N 37 35 E
Moskva → 98 55 5N 38 51 E
Mosquera 70 2 35N 78 24W
Mosquero 38 35 47N 103 58W
Mosquitia 66 15 20N 84 10W
Mosquito Creek L. 42 41 18N 80 46W
Mosquitos, Golfo de los 66 9 15N 81 10W
Moss, Norway 97 59 27N 10 40 E
Moss, U.S.A. 49 36 36N 85 37W
Moss Bluff 25 30 18N 93 11W
Moss Point 31 30 25N 88 30W
Mossaka 122 1 15 S 16 45 E
Mossâmedes 75 16 7 S 50 11W
Mossbank 63 49 56N 105 56W
Mossburn 128 45 41 S 168 15 E
Mosselbaai 123 34 11 S 22 8 E
Mossendjo 122 2 55 S 12 42 E
Mossman 127 16 21 S 145 15 E
Mossoró 74 5 10 S 37 15W
Mossuril 123 14 58 S 40 42 E
Mossy → 63 54 5N 102 58W
Mossy Head 17 30 45N 86 19W
Mossyrock 53 46 32N 122 29W
Most 88 50 31N 13 38 E
Mosta 94 35 54N 14 24 E
Mostaganem 120 35 54N 0 5 E
Mostar 95 43 22N 17 50 E
Mostardas 77 31 2 S 50 51W
Mosul = Al Mawşil 106 36 15N 43 5 E
Motagua → 66 15 44N 88 14W
Motala 97 58 32N 15 1 E
Motherwell 84 55 48N 4 0W
Motihari 109 26 30N 84 55 E
Motley 30 46 20N 94 40W
Motley County ◊ 50 34 1N 100 50W
Motocurunya 71 4 24N 64 5W
Motozintla de Mendoza 65 15 21N 92 14W
Motru → 95 44 44N 22 59 E
Mott 41 46 23N 102 20W
Motters 27 39 40N 77 20W
Motueka 128 41 7 S 173 1 E
Motul 65 21 0N 89 20W
Mouanda 122 1 28 S 13 7 E
Mouchalagane → 61 50 56N 68 41W
Moúdhros 95 39 50N 25 18 E
Moudjeria 120 17 50N 12 28W
Mouila 122 1 50 S 11 0 E
Moule 67 16 20N 61 22W
Moulins 90 46 35N 3 19 E
Moulmein 109 16 30N 97 40 E
Moulton, Ala. 10 34 29N 87 18W
Moulton, Iowa 23 40 41N 92 41W
Moulton, Tex. 51 29 35N 97 9W
Moultonboro 36 43 45N 71 10W
Moultrie 18 31 11N 83 47W
Moultrie, L. 46 33 20N 80 5W
Moultrie County ◊ 21 39 40N 88 35W
Mound 25 32 21N 91 1W
Mound Bayou 31 33 53N 90 44W
Mound City, Ill. 21 37 5N 89 10W
Mound City, Kans. 24 38 8N 94 49W
Mound City, Mo. 32 40 7N 95 14W
Mound City, S. Dak. 47 45 44N 100 4W
Mound Valley 24 37 12N 95 24W
Moundou 121 8 40N 16 10 E
Moundridge 24 38 12N 97 31W
Mounds, Ill. 21 37 7N 89 12W
Mounds, Okla. 43 35 53N 96 4W
Moundsville 54 39 55N 80 44W
Moundville, Ala. 10 33 1N 87 37W
Moundville, Mo. 32 37 46N 94 27W
Mount Airy, Md. 27 39 22N 77 10W
Mount Airy, N.C. 40 36 31N 80 37W
Mount Angel 44 45 4N 122 48W
Mount Auburn 23 42 15N 92 6W
Mount Ayr, Ind. 22 40 57N 87 18W
Mount Ayr, Iowa 23 40 43N 94 14W
Mount Baker National Forest 53 48 10N 121 15W
Mount Barker 126 34 38 S 117 40 E
Mount Blanchard 42 40 54N 83 34W
Mount Calm 51 31 46N 96 53W
Mount Carmel, Ill. 21 38 25N 87 46W
Mount Carmel, Utah 52 37 15N 112 40W
Mount Carroll 21 42 6N 89 59W
Mount Clemens 29 42 35N 82 53W
Mount Darwin 123 16 47 S 31 38 E
Mount Desert I. 26 44 21N 68 20W
Mount Dora, Fla. 17 28 48N 81 38W
Mount Dora, N. Mex. 38 36 31N 103 29W
Mount Eaton 42 40 42N 81 42W
Mount Eden 49 38 3N 85 9W
Mount Edgecumbe 11 57 3N 135 21W
Mount Enid 126 21 42 S 116 26 E
Mount Enterprise 51 31 55N 94 41W
Mount Erie 21 38 31N 88 14W
Mount Etna 22 40 45N 85 34W
Mount Forest 60 43 59N 80 43W
Mount Gambier 127 37 50 S 140 46 E
Mount Gay 54 37 51N 82 0W
Mount Gilead, N.C. 40 35 13N 80 0W
Mount Gilead, Ohio 42 40 33N 82 50W
Mount Holly, N.C. 40 35 18N 81 1W
Mount Holly, N.J. 37 39 59N 74 47W
Mount Holly Springs 45 40 7N 77 12W
Mount Hood National Forest 44 45 15N 122 0W
Mount Hope, Kans. 24 37 52N 97 40W
Mount Hope, W. Va. 54 37 54N 81 10W
Mount Horeb 55 43 1N 89 44W
Mount Ida 13 34 34N 93 38W
Mount Isa 127 20 42 S 139 26 E
Mount Jackson 54 38 45N 78 39W
Mount Jewett 45 41 44N 78 39W
Mount Joy 45 40 7N 76 30W
Mount Juliet 48 36 12N 86 31W
Mount Kisco 39 41 12N 73 44W
Mount Laguna 15 32 52N 116 25W
Mount Lebanon 45 40 23N 80 3W
Mount Liberty 42 40 21N 82 38W
Mount Lofty Ra. 127 34 35 S 139 5 E
Mount McKinley National Park 11 63 30N 150 0W
Mount Magnet 126 28 2 S 117 47 E
Mount Maunganui 128 37 40 S 176 14 E
Mount Montgomery 35 37 58N 118 20W
Mount Morgan 127 23 40 S 150 25 E
Mount Moriah 32 40 20N 93 48W
Mount Morris, Ill. 21 42 3N 89 26W
Mount Morris, Mich. 29 43 7N 83 42W
Mount Morris, N.Y. 39 42 44N 77 52W
Mount Nicholas 126 22 54 S 120 27 E
Mount Olive, Ill. 21 39 4N 89 44W
Mount Olive, Miss. 31 31 46N 89 39W
Mount Olive, N.C. 40 35 12N 78 4W
Mount Olivet 49 38 32N 84 2W
Mount Orab 42 39 2N 83 55W
Mount Pearl 61 47 31N 52 47W
Mount Pleasant, Del. 27 39 32N 75 43W
Mount Pleasant, Iowa 23 40 58N 91 33W
Mount Pleasant, Mich. 29 43 36N 84 46W
Mount Pleasant, Pa. 45 40 9N 79 33W
Mount Pleasant, S.C. 46 32 47N 79 52W
Mount Pleasant, Tenn. 48 35 32N 87 12W
Mount Pleasant, Tex. 51 33 9N 94 58W
Mount Pleasant, Utah 52 39 33N 111 27W
Mount Pocono 45 41 7N 75 22W
Mount Prospect 21 42 4N 87 56W
Mount Pulaski 21 40 1N 89 17W
Mount Rainier National Park 53 46 55N 121 50W
Mount Revelstoke Nat. Park 62 51 5N 118 30W
Mount Robson 62 52 56N 119 15W
Mount Robson Prov. Park 62 53 0N 119 0W
Mount Savage 27 39 42N 78 53W
Mount Shasta 14 41 19N 122 19W
Mount Solon 54 38 21N 79 5W
Mount Sterling, Ill. 21 39 59N 90 45W
Mount Sterling, Ky. 49 38 4N 83 56W
Mount Sterling, Ohio 42 39 43N 83 16W
Mount Storm 54 39 17N 79 15W
Mount Storm L. 54 39 13N 79 16W
Mount Summit 22 40 0N 85 23W
Mount Sunapee 36 43 19N 72 6W
Mount Trumbull 12 36 25N 113 19W
Mount Union, Iowa 23 41 3N 91 23W
Mount Union, Pa. 45 40 23N 77 53W
Mount Vernon, Ala. 10 31 5N 88 1W
Mount Vernon, Ark. 13 35 14N 92 8W
Mount Vernon, Ga. 18 32 11N 82 36W
Mount Vernon, Ill. 21 38 19N 88 55W
Mount Vernon, Ind. 22 37 56N 87 54W
Mount Vernon, Iowa 23 41 55N 91 23W
Mount Vernon, Ky. 49 37 21N 84 21W
Mount Vernon, Md. 27 38 47N 77 6W
Mount Vernon, Mo. 32 37 6N 93 49W
Mount Vernon, N.Y. 39 40 55N 73 50W
Mount Vernon, Ohio 42 40 23N 82 29W
Mount Vernon, Oreg. 44 44 25N 119 7W
Mount Vernon, S. Dak. 47 43 43N 98 16W
Mount Vernon, Tenn. 49 35 25N 84 22W
Mount Vernon, Tex. 51 33 11N 95 13W
Mount Vernon, Wash. 53 48 25N 122 20W
Mount Whaleback 126 23 18 S 119 44 E
Mount Wolf 45 40 4N 76 43W
Mount Zion 21 39 46N 88 53W
Mountain, N. Dak. 41 48 41N 97 52W

Mountain Nacaome

Mountain, Wis. 55 45 11N 88 28W
Mountain Brook 10 33 30N 86 45W
Mountain City, Ga. 18 34 55N 83 23W
Mountain City, Nev. 35 41 50N 115 58W
Mountain City, Tenn. 49 36 29N 81 48W
Mountain Creek 10 32 43N 86 29W
Mountain Grove 32 37 8N 92 16W
Mountain Home, Ark. 13 36 20N 92 23W
Mountain Home, Idaho 20 43 8N 115 41W
Mountain Home, N.C. 40 35 23N 82 30W
Mountain Home, Tex. 51 30 10N 99 22W
Mountain Iron 30 47 32N 92 37W
Mountain Lake 30 43 57N 94 56W
Mountain Lake Park 27 39 24N 79 23W
Mountain Meadows Reservoir 14 40 17N 120 49W
Mountain Park 43 34 42N 98 57W
Mountain Park 62 52 50N 117 15W
Mountain Pine 13 34 34N 93 10W
Mountain View, Ark. 13 35 52N 92 7W
Mountain View, Calif. 14 37 23N 122 5W
Mountain View, Hawaii 19 19 33N 155 7W
Mountain View, Mo. 32 37 0N 91 42W
Mountain View, Okla. 43 35 6N 98 45W
Mountain Village 11 62 5N 163 43W
Mountainair 38 34 31N 106 15W
Mountainaire 12 35 9N 111 40W
Mountainburg 13 35 38N 94 10W
Mountainview 56 41 16N 110 20W
Mountlake Terrace 53 47 47N 122 19W
Mountmellick 85 53 7N 7 20W
Mountrail County ◊ 41 48 10N 102 30W
Moura 71 1 32S 61 38W
Mourdi Depression 121 18 10N 23 0E
Mourdiah 120 14 35N 7 25W
Mourne → 85 54 45N 7 39W
Mourne Mts. 85 54 10N 6 0W
Mouscron 87 50 45N 3 12E
Mousie 49 37 25N 82 53W
Moussoro 121 13 41N 16 35E
Moutong 111 0 28N 121 13E
Movas 64 28 10N 109 25W
Moville, Ireland 85 55 11N 7 3W
Moville, U.S.A. 23 42 29N 96 4W
Moweaqua 21 39 38N 89 1W
Mower County ◊ 30 43 40N 92 45W
Mowrystown 42 39 2N 83 45W
Moxee City 53 46 33N 120 23W
Moxotó → 74 9 19S 38 14W
Moy → 85 54 5N 8 50W
Moyahua 64 21 16N 103 10W
Moyale, Ethiopia 105 3 34N 39 4E
Moyale, Kenya 122 3 30N 39 0E
Moyamba 120 8 4N 12 30W
Moyen Atlas 120 32 0N 5 0W
Moyers 43 34 19N 95 39W
Moyie Springs 20 48 44N 116 11W
Moyle □ 85 55 10N 6 15W
Moylie → 20 48 43N 116 11W
Moyo 110 8 10S 117 40E
Moyobamba 72 6 0S 77 0W
Moyyero → 101 68 44N 103 42E
Mozambique = Moçambique 123 15 3S 40 42E
Mozambique ■ 123 19 0S 35 0E
Mozambique Chan. 123 20 0S 39 0E
Mozdok 99 43 45N 44 48E
Mozyr 98 52 0N 29 15E
Mpanda 122 6 23S 31 1E
Mpika 123 11 51S 31 25E
Mpwapwa 122 6 23S 36 30E
Msaken 121 35 49N 10 33E
Msoro 123 13 35S 31 50E
Mt. Everest = Qomolangma Feng 113 28 0N 86 45E
Mtwara 122 10 20S 40 20E
Mu Us Shamo 114 39 0N 109 0E
Muaná 74 1 25S 49 15W
Muang Chiang Rai 112 19 52N 99 50E
Muang Lamphun 112 18 40N 99 2E
Muang Phichit 112 16 29N 100 21E
Muar = Bandar Maharani 112 2 3N 102 34E
Muar → 112 2 15N 102 48E
Muarabungo 110 1 28S 102 52E
Muaraenim 110 3 40S 103 50E
Muarajuloi 110 0 12S 114 3E
Muarakaman 110 0 2S 116 45E
Muaratebo 110 1 30S 102 26E
Muaratembesi 110 1 42S 103 8E
Muaratewe 110 0 58S 114 52E
Mubende 122 0 33N 31 22E
Mubi 121 10 18N 13 16E
Mucajaí → 71 2 25N 60 52W
Mucajaí, Serra do 71 2 23N 61 10W
Muck 84 56 50N 6 15W
Muckalee Cr. → 18 31 38N 84 9W
Muco → 70 4 15N 70 21W
Muconda 122 10 31S 21 15E
Mucuim → 73 6 33S 64 18W
Mucura 71 2 31S 62 43W
Mucuri 75 18 0S 39 36W
Mucurici 75 18 6S 40 31W
Mud → 48 37 13N 86 54W
Mud Butte 47 45 0N 102 54W
Mud Cr. →, Okla. 43 33 55N 97 28W
Mud Cr. →, S. Dak. 47 45 11N 98 24W
Mud L. 35 37 52N 117 4W
Mud Lake Reservoir 47 45 47N 98 15W
Mudanjiang 114 44 38N 129 30E
Muddy →, Ill. 21 37 33N 89 32W
Muddy →, Nev. 35 36 31N 114 24W
Muddy Boggy Cr. → 43 34 3N 95 47W
Muddy Cr. →, Utah 52 38 24N 110 42W
Muddy Cr. →, Wyo. 56 41 35N 109 58W
Muddy Creek Reservoir 16 37 45N 103 15W
Muddy Gap 56 42 21N 107 28W
Mudgee 127 32 32S 149 31E
Mudjatik → 63 56 1N 107 36W
Muenster 51 33 39N 97 23W
Muerto, Mar 65 16 10N 94 10W
Mufulira 123 12 32S 28 15E
Mugi 117 33 40N 134 25E
Muğla 106 37 15N 28 22E
Mŭglizh 95 42 37N 25 32E
Mugu 109 29 45N 82 30E
Muhammad Qol 121 20 53N 37 9E
Muharraqa = Sa'ad 104 31 28N 34 33E
Muhlenberg County ◊ 48 37 10N 87 10W
Mühlig Hofmann fjella 5 72 30S 5 0E
Mui Bai Bung 112 8 35N 104 42E
Mui Ron 112 18 7N 106 27E
Muikamachi 117 37 15N 138 50E
Muine Bheag 85 52 42N 6 57W
Muir 29 43 0N 84 56W
Muir Woods National Monument 14 37 55N 122 35W
Mukah 110 2 55N 112 5E
Mukden = Shenyang 114 41 48N 123 27E
Mukhtuya = Lensk 101 60 48N 114 55E
Mukilteo 53 47 57N 122 18W
Mukomuko 110 2 30S 101 10E
Muktsar 108 30 30N 74 30E
Mukur 108 32 50N 67 42E
Mukutawa → 63 53 10N 97 24W
Mukwonago 55 42 52N 88 20W
Mulberry, Ark. 13 35 30N 94 3W
Mulberry, Fla. 17 27 54N 81 59W
Mulberry Fork → 10 33 33N 87 11W
Mulberry Grove 21 38 56N 89 16W
Mulchatna → 11 59 40N 157 7W
Mulchén 76 37 45S 72 20W
Mulde → 88 51 10N 12 48E
Muldoon 51 29 49N 97 4W
Muldraugh 49 37 56N 85 59W
Muldrow 43 35 24N 94 36W
Mule Creek, N. Mex. 38 33 7N 108 57W
Mule Creek, Wyo. 56 43 19N 104 8W
Mulegé 64 26 53N 112 1W
Muleshoe 50 34 13N 102 43W
Mulgrave 61 45 38N 61 31W
Mulhacén 91 37 4N 3 20W
Mulhall 43 36 4N 97 25W
Mülheim 88 51 26N 6 53E
Mulhouse 90 47 40N 7 20E
Muling He → 114 45 53N 133 30E
Mull 84 56 27N 6 0W
Mullaittvu 108 9 15N 80 49E
Mullan 20 47 28N 115 48W
Mullen 34 42 3N 101 1W
Mullens 54 37 35N 81 23W
Muller, Pegunungan 110 0 30N 113 30E
Mullet Pen. 85 54 10N 10 2W
Mullett L. 29 45 31N 84 31W
Mullett Lake 29 45 34N 84 32W
Mullewa 126 28 29S 115 30E
Mullica → 37 39 33N 74 25W
Mullin 51 31 33N 98 40W
Mullingar 85 53 31N 7 20W
Mullins 46 34 12N 79 15W
Mullinville 24 37 35N 99 29W
Multan 108 30 15N 71 36E
Multnomah County ◊ 44 45 30N 122 10W
Mulvane 24 37 29N 97 15W
Mumbwa 123 15 0S 27 0E
Mun → 112 15 17N 103 0E
Muna 111 5 0S 122 30E
München 88 48 8N 11 33E
Munchen-Gladbach = Mönchengladbach 88 51 12N 6 23E
Muncho Lake 62 59 0N 125 50W
Muncie 22 40 12N 85 23W
Muncy 45 41 12N 76 47W
Mundala 111 4 30S 141 0E
Mundare 62 53 35N 112 20W
Munday 51 33 27N 99 38W
Mundelein 21 42 16N 88 0W
Münden, Germany 88 51 25N 9 42E
Munden, U.S.A. 24 39 55N 97 32W
Mundo Novo 75 11 50S 40 29W
Munducurus 71 4 47S 58 16W
Munford 48 35 27N 89 49W
Munfordville 49 37 16N 85 54W
Mungbere 122 2 36N 28 28E
Munger 109 25 23N 86 30E
Mungindi 127 28 58S 149 1E
Munhango 123 12 10S 18 38E
Munhango → 123 11 30S 19 30E
Munich = München 88 48 8N 11 33E
Munich 41 48 40N 98 50W
Munising 29 46 25N 86 40W
Munjor 24 38 49N 99 16W
Munku-Sardyk 101 51 45N 100 20E
Munnsville 39 42 59N 75 35W
Muñoz Gamero, Pen. 78 52 30S 73 5E
Munroe L. 63 59 13N 98 35W
Munson 17 30 52N 86 52W
Münster 88 51 58N 7 37E
Munster □ 85 52 20N 8 40W
Munsungan L. 26 46 22N 69 0W
Muntele Mare 95 46 30N 23 12E
Muntok 110 2 5S 105 10E
Munyak 100 43 30N 59 15E
Muon Pak Beng 112 19 51N 101 4E
Muonio 96 67 57N 23 40E
Mupa 123 16 5S 15 50E
Muping 114 37 22N 121 36E
Muqdisho 105 2 2N 45 25E
Mûr → 88 47 7N 13 55E
Murakami 116 38 14N 139 29E
Murallón, Cuerro 78 49 48S 73 30W
Murang'a 122 0 45S 37 9E
Murashi 98 59 30N 49 0E
Murayama 116 38 30N 140 25E
Murchison → 126 27 45S 114 0E
Murchison, Mt. 5 73 0S 168 0E
Murchison Falls = Kabarega Falls 122 2 15N 31 30E
Murchison Ra. 126 20 0S 134 10E
Murcia 91 38 20N 1 10W
Murcia □ 91 37 50N 1 30W
Murdo 47 43 53N 100 43W
Murdock, Kans. 24 37 37N 97 56W
Murdock, Minn. 30 45 13N 95 24W
Murdock, Nebr. 34 40 55N 96 17W
Mureş □ 95 46 45N 24 40E
Mureş → 89 46 15N 20 13E
Mureşul = Mureş → 89 46 15N 20 13E
Murfatlar 95 44 10N 28 26E
Murfreesboro, Ark. 13 34 4N 93 41W
Murfreesboro, N.C. 40 36 27N 77 6W
Murfreesboro, Tenn. 48 35 51N 86 24W
Murgab 100 38 10N 74 2E
Murgeni 95 46 12N 28 1E
Murgon 127 26 15S 151 54E
Muriaé 75 21 8S 42 23W
Murici 74 9 19S 35 56W
Müritz See 88 53 25N 12 40E
Murmansk 98 68 57N 33 10E
Murom 98 55 35N 42 3E
Muroran 116 42 25N 141 0E
Muroto 117 33 18N 134 9E
Muroto-Misaki 117 33 15N 134 10E
Murphy, Idaho 20 43 13N 116 33W
Murphy, N.C. 40 35 5N 84 2W
Murphy, Oreg. 44 42 21N 123 20W
Murphys Corner 53 47 53N 122 12W
Murphysboro 21 37 46N 89 20W
Murray, Iowa 23 41 3N 93 57W
Murray, Ky. 48 36 37N 88 19W
Murray, Utah 52 40 40N 111 53W
Murray →, Australia 127 35 20S 139 22E
Murray →, Canada 62 56 11N 120 45W
Murray, L., Okla. 43 34 2N 97 3W
Murray, L., S.C. 46 34 3N 81 13W
Murray Bridge 127 35 6S 139 14E
Murray City 42 39 31N 82 10W
Murray County ◊, Ga. 18 34 50N 84 45W
Murray County ◊, Minn. 30 44 0N 95 45W
Murray County ◊, Okla. 43 34 30N 97 0W
Murray Harbour 61 46 0N 62 28W
Murray Seascarp 125 30 0N 135 0W
Murraysburg 123 31 58S 23 47E
Murrayville 21 39 35N 90 15W
Murree 108 33 56N 73 28E
Murrells Inlet 46 33 33N 79 2W
Murrumbidgee → 127 34 43S 143 12E
Mursala 110 1 41N 98 28E
Murtaugh 20 42 30N 114 10W
Murtle L. 62 52 8N 119 38W
Muru → 72 8 9S 70 45W
Murvaul L. 51 32 2N 94 25W
Murwara 109 23 46N 80 28E
Murwillumbah 127 28 18S 153 27E
Muryo 111 6 36S 110 53E
Mürzzuschlag 88 47 36N 15 41E
Muş 106 38 45N 41 30E
Mûsa, G. 106 28 33N 33 59E
Musa Khel 108 30 59N 69 52E
Mūsá Qal'eh 107 32 20N 64 50E
Musaffargarh 108 30 10N 71 10E
Musala 95 42 13N 23 37E
Musan 114 42 12N 129 12E
Musay'īd 107 25 0N 51 33E
Muscat = Masqat 107 23 37N 58 36E
Muscat & Oman = Oman ■ 105 23 0N 58 0E
Muscatine 23 41 25N 91 3W
Muscatine County ◊ 23 41 30N 91 0W
Muscle Shoals 10 34 45N 87 40W
Muscoda 55 43 11N 90 27W
Muscogee County ◊ 18 32 30N 84 58W
Musconetcong → 37 40 36N 75 11W
Muscotah 24 39 33N 95 31W
Musella 18 32 48N 84 2W
Musgrave Ras. 126 26 0S 132 0E
Mushie 122 2 56S 16 55E
Musi → 110 2 20S 104 56E
Muskeg → 62 60 20N 123 20W
Muskeg B. 30 48 55N 95 10W
Muskeget Channel 28 41 25N 70 25W
Muskego 55 42 55N 88 8W
Muskegon 29 43 14N 86 16W
Muskegon → 29 43 14N 86 21W
Muskegon County ◊ 29 43 15N 86 15W
Muskegon Heights 29 43 12N 86 16W
Muskingum → 42 40 3N 81 59W
Muskingum County ◊ 42 39 56N 82 1W
Muskogee 43 35 45N 95 22W
Muskogee County ◊ 43 35 40N 95 25W
Muskwa → 62 58 47N 122 48W
Musmar 121 18 13N 35 40E
Musoma 122 1 30S 33 48E
Musquaro, L. 61 50 38N 61 5W
Musquodoboit Harbour 61 44 50N 63 9W
Musselburgh 84 55 57N 3 3W
Mussell Cr. → 32 39 26N 92 57W
Musselshell → 33 47 21N 107 57W
Musselshell County ◊ 33 46 35N 108 30W
Mussoorie 108 30 27N 78 6E
Mustang, Nepal 109 29 10N 83 55E
Mustang, U.S.A. 43 35 24N 97 42W
Mustang Draw → 50 31 58N 102 40W
Mustang I. 51 27 52N 97 3W
Musters, L. 78 45 20S 69 25W
Mustinka → 30 45 45N 96 38W
Muswellbrook 127 32 16S 150 56E
Mût, Egypt 121 25 28N 28 58E
Mut, Turkey 106 36 40N 33 28E
Mutaray 101 60 56N 101 0E
Mutare 123 18 58S 32 38E
Muting 111 7 23S 140 20E
Mutsu 116 41 5N 140 55E
Mutsu-Wan 116 41 5N 140 55E
Muttaburra 127 22 38S 144 29E
Mutual, Ohio 42 40 5N 83 38W
Mutual, Okla. 43 36 14N 99 9W
Mutunópolis 75 13 40S 49 15W
Muxima 122 9 33S 13 58E
Muy Muy 66 12 39N 85 36W
Muya 101 56 27N 115 50E
Muzaffarabad 108 34 25N 73 30E
Muzaffarnagar 108 29 26N 77 40E
Muzaffarpur 109 26 7N 85 23E
Muzhi 100 65 25N 64 40E
Muzon, C. 11 54 40N 132 42W
Muztag 113 36 20N 87 28E
Mvuma 123 19 16S 30 30E
Mwanza, Tanzania 122 2 30S 32 58E
Mwanza, Zaïre 122 7 55S 26 43E
Mwaya 122 9 32S 33 55E
Mweelrea 85 53 37N 9 48W
Mweka 122 4 50S 21 34E
Mwenezi 123 21 15S 30 48E
Mwenga 122 3 1S 28 28E
Mweru, L. 122 9 0S 28 40E
Mwinilunga 123 11 43S 24 25E
My Tho 112 10 29N 106 23E
Myakka → 17 26 56N 82 11W
Myanaung 109 18 18N 95 22E
Myaungmya 109 16 30N 94 40E
Mycenae = Mikínai 95 37 43N 22 46E
Myeik Kyunzu 112 11 30N 97 30E
Myerstown 45 40 22N 76 19W
Myingyan 109 21 30N 95 20E
Myitkyina 109 25 24N 97 26E
Mylo 41 48 38N 99 37W
Mymensingh 109 24 45N 90 24E
Mynydd Du 83 51 45N 3 45W
Mýrdalsjökull 96 63 40N 19 6W
Myrtle, Miss. 31 34 34N 89 7W
Myrtle, Mo. 32 36 31N 91 16W
Myrtle, W. Va. 54 37 46N 82 12W
Myrtle Beach 46 33 42N 78 53W
Myrtle Creek 44 43 1N 123 17W
Myrtle Point 44 43 4N 124 8W
Myrtlewood 10 32 16N 87 57W
Mysore 108 12 17N 76 41E
Mysore □ = Karnataka □ 108 13 15N 77 0E
Mystic, Conn. 28 41 21N 71 58W
Mystic, Iowa 23 40 47N 92 57W
Mystic Island 37 39 34N 74 22W
Myton 52 40 12N 110 4W
Mývatn 96 65 36N 17 0W
Mzimvubu → 123 31 38S 29 33E

N

Naab → 88 49 1N 12 2E
Naalehu 19 19 4N 155 35W
Na'an 104 31 53N 34 52E
Naantali 97 60 29N 22 2E
Naas 85 53 12N 6 40W
Nabadwip = Navadwip 109 23 34N 88 20E
Nabari 117 34 37N 136 5E
Nabesna 11 62 22N 143 0W
Nabeul 121 36 30N 10 44E
Nabire 111 3 15S 135 26E
Nabisipi → 61 50 14N 62 13W
Nablus = Nābulus 104 32 14N 35 15E
Nābulus 104 32 14N 35 15E
Nacala-Velha 123 14 32S 40 34E
Nacaome 66 13 31N 87 30W

Nebraska **Newark-on-Trent**

Nebraska □ **34** 41 30N 99 30W
Nebraska City **34** 40 41N 95 52W
Nebraska National Forest **34** 42 45N 103 10W
Nébrodi, Monti **94** 37 55N 14 50 E
Necedah **55** 44 2N 90 4W
Nechako → **62** 53 30N 122 44W
Neche **41** 48 59N 97 33W
Neches → **51** 29 58N 93 51W
Neckar → **88** 49 31N 8 26 E
Necker I. **19** 23 35N 164 42W
Necochea **76** 38 30 S 58 50W
Nederland, Colo. **16** 39 58N 105 31W
Nederland, Tex. **51** 29 59N 94 0W
Neebish I. **29** 46 16N 84 9W
Needham **28** 42 17N 71 14W
Needle Range **52** 38 25N 113 55W
Needles **15** 34 51N 114 37W
Needles, The **83** 50 39N 1 35W
Needmore, Ga. **18** 30 41N 82 43W
Needmore, Tex. **50** 34 2N 102 45W
Needville **51** 29 24N 95 50W
Neely **31** 31 10N 88 45W
Neely Henry L. **10** 33 55N 86 2W
Neelyville **32** 36 34N 90 30W
Ñeembucú □ **76** 27 0 S 58 0W
Neemuch = Nimach **108** 24 30N 74 56 E
Neenah **55** 44 11N 88 28W
Neepawa **63** 50 15N 99 30W
Neeses **46** 33 33N 81 7W
Neft-chala = imeni 26 Bakinskikh Komissarov **99** 39 19N 49 12 E
Nefta **120** 33 53N 7 50 E
Neftyannyye Kamni **99** 40 20N 50 55 E
Negapatam = Nagappattinam **108** 10 46N 79 51 E
Negaunee **29** 46 30N 87 36W
Negba **104** 31 40N 34 41 E
Negele **105** 5 20N 39 36 E
Negeri Sembilan □ **112** 2 50N 102 10 E
Negev = Hanegev **104** 30 50N 35 0 E
Negoiu **95** 45 35N 24 32 E
Negoiu, Vf. **89** 43 35N 24 31 E
Negombo **108** 7 12N 79 50 E
Negotin **95** 44 16N 22 37 E
Negra, La **76** 23 46 S 70 18W
Negra, Pta. **72** 6 6 S 81 10W
Negra Pt. **111** 18 40N 120 50 E
Negreet **25** 31 28N 93 35W
Negro →, Argentina **78** 41 2 S 62 47W
Negro →, Bolivia **73** 14 11 S 63 7W
Negro →, Brazil **71** 3 0 S 60 0W
Negro →, Uruguay **77** 33 24 S 58 22W
Negros **111** 10 0N 123 0 E
Negru Vodă **95** 43 47N 28 21 E
Nehalem → **44** 45 40N 123 56W
Nehawka **34** 40 50N 95 59W
Nehbandān **107** 31 35N 60 5 E
Nehoiaşu **95** 45 24N 26 20 E
Nei Monggol Zizhiqu □ **114** 42 0N 112 0 E
Neidpath **63** 50 12N 107 20W
Neijiang **115** 29 35N 104 55 E
Neillsville **55** 44 34N 90 36W
Neilton **53** 47 25N 123 53W
Neisse → **88** 52 4N 14 46 E
Neiva **70** 2 56N 75 18W
Neixiang **115** 33 10N 111 52 E
Nejanilini L. **63** 59 33N 97 48W
Nekemte **121** 9 4N 36 30 E
Nekoma, Kans. **24** 38 28N 99 27W
Nekoma, N. Dak. **41** 48 35N 98 22W
Nekoosa **55** 44 19N 89 54W
Neksø **97** 55 4N 15 8 E
Nelhart **33** 46 56N 110 44W
Neligh **34** 42 8N 98 2W
Nelkan **101** 57 40N 136 4 E
Nellore **108** 14 27N 79 59 E
Nelma **101** 47 39N 139 0 E
Nelson, Canada **62** 49 30N 117 20W
Nelson, N.Z. **128** 41 18 S 173 16 E
Nelson, U.K. **82** 53 50N 2 14W
Nelson, Ariz. **12** 35 31N 113 19W
Nelson, Mo. **32** 38 59N 93 3W
Nelson, N.H. **36** 42 58N 72 8W
Nelson, Nebr. **34** 40 12N 98 4W
Nelson, Wis. **55** 44 25N 92 0W
Nelson □ **128** 42 11 S 172 15 E
Nelson → **63** 54 33N 98 2W
Nelson, Estrecho **78** 51 30 S 75 0W
Nelson County ◇, Ky. **49** 37 50N 85 30W
Nelson County ◇, N. Dak. **41** 48 0N 98 5W
Nelson County ◇, Va. **54** 37 50N 78 52W
Nelson Forks **62** 59 30N 124 0W
Nelson House **63** 55 47N 98 51W
Nelson L. **63** 55 48N 100 7W
Nelson Reservoir **33** 48 32N 107 31W
Nelspruit **123** 25 29 S 30 59 E
Néma **120** 16 40N 7 15W
Nemah **53** 46 31N 123 53W
Nemaha, Iowa **23** 42 31N 95 6W
Nemaha, Nebr. **34** 40 20N 95 41W
Nemaha County ◇, Kans. **24** 39 45N 96 0W
Nemaha County ◇, Nebr. **34** 40 20N 95 45W
Neman → **98** 55 25N 21 10 E
Nemeiben L. **63** 55 20N 105 20W
Nemira **95** 46 17N 26 19 E
Nemunas = Neman → **98** 55 25N 21 10 E
Nemuro **116** 43 20N 145 35 E
Nemuro-Kaikyō **116** 43 30N 145 30 E
Nemuy **101** 55 40N 136 9 E
Nen Jiang → **114** 45 28N 124 30 E
Nenagh **85** 52 52N 8 11W
Nenana **11** 64 34N 149 5W
Nene → **82** 52 38N 0 13 E
Nenjiang **114** 49 10N 125 10 E
Nenusa, Kepulauan **111** 4 45N 127 1 E
Nenzel **34** 42 56N 101 6W
Neodesha **24** 37 25N 95 41W
Neoga **21** 39 19N 88 27W
Neola, Iowa **23** 41 27N 95 37W
Neola, Utah **52** 40 26N 110 2W
Neopit **55** 44 59N 88 50W
Neópolis **74** 10 18 S 36 35W
Neosho **32** 36 52N 94 22W
Neosho → **43** 36 48N 95 18W
Neosho County ◇ **24** 37 30N 95 15W
Neosho Falls **24** 37 59N 95 33W
Neosho Rapids **24** 38 22N 95 59W
Nepal ■ **109** 28 0N 84 30 E
Nepalganj **109** 28 5N 81 40 E
Nephi **52** 39 43N 111 50W
Nephin **85** 54 1N 9 21W
Neptune **37** 40 13N 74 2W
Nerchinsk **101** 52 0N 116 39 E
Nerchinskiy Zavod **101** 51 20N 119 40 E
Nereju **95** 45 43N 26 43 E
Néret L. **61** 54 45N 70 44W
Neretva → **95** 43 1N 17 27 E
Nerstrand **30** 44 20N 93 4W
Nerva **91** 37 42N 6 30W
Nes **96** 65 53N 17 24W
Nes Ziyyona **104** 31 56N 34 48W
Nesbit **31** 34 53N 90 1W
Nesebůr **95** 42 41N 27 46 E
Neshkoro **55** 43 58N 89 13W
Neshoba **31** 32 37N 89 8W
Neshoba County ◇ **31** 32 46N 89 7W
Neskaupstaður **96** 65 9N 13 42W
Nesmith **46** 33 39N 79 31W
Nespelem **53** 48 10N 118 59W
Ness, Loch **84** 57 15N 4 30W
Ness City **24** 38 27N 99 54W
Ness County ◇ **24** 38 30N 100 0W
Nesttun **97** 60 19N 5 21 E
Netanya **104** 32 20N 34 51 E
Netarts **44** 45 26N 123 57W
Netawaka **24** 39 36N 95 43W
Netcong **37** 40 54N 74 42W
Nète → **87** 51 7N 4 14 E
Nether Stowey **83** 51 0N 3 10W
Netherbury **83** 50 46N 2 45W
Netherdale **127** 21 10 S 148 33 E
Netherlands ■ **87** 52 0N 5 30 E
Netherlands Antilles ■ **70** 12 15N 69 0W
Netherlands Guiana = Surinam ■ **71** 4 0N 56 0W
Nett L. **30** 48 7N 93 7W
Nett Lake Indian Reservation **30** 48 5N 93 5W
Nettilling L. **59** 66 30N 71 0W
Nettleton **31** 34 5N 88 37W
Netzahualcoyotl, Presa **65** 17 10N 93 30W
Neubrandenburg **88** 53 33N 13 17 E
Neuchâtel **88** 47 0N 6 55 E
Neuchâtel, Lac de **88** 46 53N 6 50 E
Neufchâteau **87** 49 50N 5 25 E
Neumünster **88** 54 4N 9 58 E
Neunkirchen **88** 49 23N 7 12 E
Neuquén **78** 38 55 S 68 0 E
Neuquén □ **76** 38 0 S 69 50W
Neuquén → **78** 38 59 S 68 0W
Neuruppin **88** 52 56N 12 48 E
Neuse → **40** 35 6N 76 29W
Neusiedler See **88** 47 50N 16 47 E
Neustrelitz **88** 53 22N 13 4 E
Neuville **51** 31 41N 94 9W
Neva → **98** 59 50N 30 30 E
Nevada, Iowa **23** 42 1N 93 27W
Nevada, Mo. **32** 37 51N 94 22W
Nevada □ **35** 39 0N 117 0W
Nevada, Sierra **91** 37 3N 3 15W
Nevada City **14** 39 16N 121 1W
Nevada County ◇, Ark. **13** 33 36N 93 17W
Nevada County ◇, Calif. **14** 39 15N 121 0W
Nevada de Sta. Marta, Sa. **72** 10 55N 73 50W
Nevado, Cerro **76** 35 30 S 68 32W
Nevanka **101** 56 31N 98 55 E
Nevers **90** 47 0N 3 9 E
Neversink → **39** 41 21N 74 42W
Neversink Res. **39** 41 48N 74 42W
Neville **63** 49 58N 107 39W
Nevis, U.S.A. **30** 46 58N 94 51W
Nevis, W. Indies **67** 17 0N 62 30W
Nevrokop = Gotse Delchev **95** 41 43N 23 46 E
Nevşehir **106** 38 33N 34 40 E
Nevyansk **98** 57 30N 60 13 E
New →, Guyana **71** 3 20N 57 37W
New →, Fla. **17** 29 50N 84 40W
New →, W. Va. **54** 38 10N 81 12W
New Albany, Ind. **22** 38 18N 85 49W
New Albany, Kans. **24** 37 34N 95 56W
New Albany, Miss. **31** 34 29N 89 0W
New Albany, Pa. **45** 41 36N 76 27W
New Alluwe **43** 36 37N 95 29W
New Almelo **24** 39 36N 100 7W
New Amsterdam **71** 6 15N 57 36W
New Athens, Ill. **21** 38 19N 89 53W
New Athens, Ohio **42** 40 11N 81 0W
New Auburn, Minn. **30** 44 40N 94 14W
New Auburn, Wis. **55** 45 12N 91 33W
New Augusta **31** 31 12N 89 2W
New Baden **21** 38 32N 89 42W
New Baltimore, Mich. **29** 42 41N 82 44W
New Baltimore, Pa. **45** 39 59N 78 46W
New Bavaria **42** 41 12N 84 10W
New Bedford **28** 41 38N 70 56W
New Berlin, Ill. **21** 39 44N 89 55W
New Berlin, N.Y. **39** 42 37N 75 20W
New Berlin, Wis. **55** 42 59N 88 6W
New Bern **40** 35 7N 77 3W
New Bethlehem **45** 41 0N 79 20W
New Bloomfield, Mo. **32** 38 43N 92 5W
New Bloomfield, Pa. **45** 40 25N 77 11W
New Boston, Ill. **21** 41 10N 91 0W
New Boston, Mass. **28** 42 6N 73 5W
New Boston, N.H. **36** 42 59N 71 41W
New Boston, Ohio **42** 38 45N 82 56W
New Boston, Tex. **51** 33 28N 94 25W
New Braunfels **51** 29 42N 98 8W
New Bremen **42** 40 26N 84 23W
New Brighton **128** 43 29 S 172 43 E
New Britain, Papua N. G. **124** 5 50 S 150 20 E
New Britain, U.S.A. **28** 41 40N 72 47W
New Brockton **10** 31 23N 85 56W
New Brunswick **37** 40 30N 74 27W
New Brunswick □ **61** 46 50N 66 30W
New Buffalo **29** 41 47N 86 45W
New Caledonia = Nouvelle Calédonie **124** 21 0 S 165 0 E
New Cambria **24** 38 53N 97 30W
New Canaan **28** 41 9N 73 30W
New Canton **54** 37 42N 78 18W
New Carlisle **42** 39 56N 84 2W
New Carrollton **27** 38 58N 76 53W
New Castile = Castilla La Nueva **91** 39 45N 3 20W
New Castle, Colo. **16** 39 34N 107 32W
New Castle, Del. **27** 39 40N 75 34W
New Castle, Ind. **22** 39 55N 85 22W
New Castle, Ky. **49** 38 26N 85 10W
New Castle, Pa. **45** 41 0N 80 21W
New Castle, Va. **54** 37 30N 80 7W
New Castle County ◇ **27** 39 30N 75 40W
New City **39** 41 9N 73 59W
New Concord, Ky. **48** 36 33N 88 9W
New Concord, Ohio **42** 39 59N 81 54W
New Cumberland **54** 40 30N 80 36W
New Deal **50** 33 44N 101 50W
New Delhi **108** 28 37N 77 13 E
New Denver **62** 50 0N 117 25W
New Don Pedro Reservoir **14** 37 43N 120 24W
New Edinburg **13** 33 46N 92 14W
New Effington **47** 45 51N 96 55W
New Egypt **37** 40 4N 74 32W
New Ellenton **46** 33 28N 81 41W
New England **41** 46 32N 102 52W
New England Ra. **127** 30 20 S 151 45 E
New Era **29** 43 34N 86 21W
New Fairfield **28** 41 27N 73 14W
New Florence, Mo. **32** 38 55N 91 27W
New Florence, Pa. **45** 40 23N 79 5W
New Forest **83** 50 53N 1 40W
New Fork Lakes **56** 43 6N 109 57W
New Franklin **32** 39 1N 92 44W
New Freedom **45** 39 44N 76 42W
New Glarus **55** 42 49N 89 38W
New Glasgow **61** 45 35N 62 36W
New Guinea **124** 4 0 S 136 0 E
New Hampshire □ **36** 44 0N 71 30W
New Hampton, Iowa **23** 43 3N 92 19W
New Hampton, Mo. **32** 40 16N 94 12W
New Hampton, N.H. **36** 43 36N 71 39W
New Hanover County ◇ **40** 34 15N 77 50W
New Harmony, Ind. **22** 38 8N 87 56W
New Harmony, Utah **52** 37 29N 113 19W
New Hartford, Conn. **28** 41 53N 72 59W
New Hartford, Iowa **23** 42 34N 92 37W
New Hartford, N.Y. **39** 43 4N 75 18W
New Haven, Conn. **28** 41 18N 72 55W
New Haven, Ill. **21** 37 55N 88 8W
New Haven, Ind. **22** 41 4N 85 1W
New Haven, Ky. **49** 37 40N 85 36W
New Haven, Mich. **29** 42 44N 82 48W
New Haven, Mo. **32** 38 37N 91 13W
New Haven, N.Y. **39** 43 29N 76 19W
New Haven, W. Va. **54** 38 59N 81 58W
New Haven County ◇ **28** 41 25N 72 50W
New Hazelton **62** 55 20N 127 30W
New Hebrides = Vanuatu ■, Pac. Oc. **124** 15 0 S 168 0 E
New Hebrides = Vanuatu ■, Pac. Oc. **124** 15 0 S 168 0 E
New Hebron **31** 31 44N 89 59W
New Hogan L. **14** 38 9N 120 49W
New Holstein **55** 43 57N 88 5W
New Hope, Ala. **10** 34 32N 86 24W
New Hope, Pa. **45** 40 22N 74 57W
New Iberia **25** 30 1N 91 49W
New Ipswich **36** 42 46N 71 51W
New Ireland **124** 3 20 S 151 50 E
New Jersey □ **37** 40 0N 74 30W
New Johnsonville **48** 36 1N 87 58W
New Kensington **45** 40 34N 79 46W
New Kent **54** 37 31N 76 59W
New Kent County ◇ **54** 37 31N 76 59W
New L. **40** 35 39N 76 20W
New Leipzig **41** 46 22N 101 57W
New Lexington **42** 39 43N 82 13W
New Lisbon **55** 43 53N 90 10W
New Liskeard **60** 47 31N 79 41W
New London, Conn. **28** 41 22N 72 6W
New London, Iowa **23** 40 55N 91 24W
New London, Md. **27** 39 25N 77 16W
New London, Minn. **30** 45 18N 94 56W
New London, Mo. **32** 39 35N 91 24W
New London, N.H. **36** 43 25N 71 59W
New London, Ohio **42** 41 5N 82 24W
New London, Wis. **55** 44 23N 88 45W
New London County ◇ **28** 41 30N 72 15W
New Madison **42** 39 58N 84 43W
New Madrid **32** 36 36N 89 32W
New Madrid County ◇ **32** 36 40N 89 35W
New Market, Ala. **10** 34 55N 86 26W
New Market, Ind. **22** 39 57N 86 55W
New Market, Iowa **23** 40 44N 94 54W
New Market, Md. **27** 39 23N 77 16W
New Market, Tenn. **49** 36 6N 83 33W
New Market, Va. **54** 38 39N 78 40W
New Martinsville **54** 39 39N 80 52W
New Matamoras **42** 39 31N 81 4W
New Meadows **20** 44 58N 116 18W
New Melle **32** 38 43N 90 53W
New Melones L. **14** 37 57N 120 31W
New Mexico □ **38** 34 30N 106 0W
New Miami **42** 39 26N 84 32W
New Milford, Conn. **28** 41 35N 73 25W
New Milford, Pa. **45** 41 52N 75 44W
New Munich **30** 45 38N 94 45W
New Norfolk **127** 42 46 S 147 2 E
New Orleans **25** 29 58N 90 4W
New Oxford **45** 39 52N 77 4W
New Paltz **39** 41 45N 74 5W
New Paris **42** 39 51N 84 48W
New Philadelphia, Ohio **42** 40 30N 81 27W
New Philadelphia, Pa. **45** 40 43N 76 7W
New Pine Creek **44** 42 0N 120 18W
New Plymouth, N.Z. **128** 39 4 S 174 5 E
New Plymouth, U.S.A. **20** 43 58N 116 49W
New Port Richey **17** 28 16N 82 43W
New Prague **30** 44 32N 93 35W
New Preston **28** 41 40N 73 21W
New Princeton **44** 43 15N 118 35W
New Providence, Bahamas **66** 25 25N 78 35W
New Providence, U.S.A. **22** 38 28N 85 57W
New Radnor **83** 52 15N 3 10W
New Raymer **16** 40 36N 103 51W
New Richland **30** 43 54N 93 30W
New Richmond, Ohio **42** 38 57N 84 17W
New Richmond, Wis. **55** 45 7N 92 32W
New Riegel **42** 41 3N 83 19W
New Roads **25** 30 42N 91 26W
New Rochelle **39** 40 55N 73 47W
New Rockford **41** 47 41N 99 8W
New Ross **85** 52 24N 6 58W
New Salem, Mass. **28** 42 30N 72 20W
New Salem, N. Dak. **41** 46 51N 101 25W
New Sharon **23** 41 28N 92 39W
New Siberian Is. = Novosibirskiye Ostrava **101** 75 0N 142 0 E
New Smyrna Beach **17** 29 1N 80 56W
New South Wales □ **127** 33 0 S 146 0 E
New Straitsville **42** 39 35N 82 14W
New Stuyahok **11** 59 29N 157 20W
New Tazewell **49** 36 27N 83 36W
New Town **41** 47 59N 102 30W
New Tulsa **43** 36 9N 95 48W
New Ulm **30** 44 19N 94 28W
New Underwood **47** 44 6N 102 50W
New Vienna, Iowa **23** 42 33N 91 7W
New Vienna, Ohio **42** 39 19N 83 42W
New Vineyard **26** 44 48N 70 7W
New Virginia **23** 41 11N 93 44W
New Washington **42** 40 58N 82 51W
New Waterford **61** 46 13N 60 4W
New Waverly **51** 30 32N 95 29W
New Westminster **62** 49 13N 122 55W
New Whiteland **22** 39 33N 86 5W
New Windsor **27** 39 34N 77 9W
New Woodville **43** 33 56N 96 36W
New York **39** 40 43N 74 0W
New York □ **39** 43 0N 75 0W
New York County ◇ **39** 40 45N 73 59W
New York Mills **30** 46 31N 95 22W
New Zealand ■ **128** 40 0 S 176 0 E
New Zion **46** 33 51N 80 2W
Newala **122** 10 58 S 39 18 E
Newark, Ark. **13** 35 42N 91 27W
Newark, Calif. **14** 37 32N 122 2W
Newark, Del. **27** 39 41N 75 46W
Newark, Md. **27** 38 15N 75 17W
Newark, N.J. **37** 40 44N 74 10W
Newark, N.Y. **39** 43 3N 77 6W
Newark, Ohio **42** 40 3N 82 24W
Newark, Tex. **51** 33 0N 97 29W
Newark L. **35** 39 42N 115 44W
Newark-on-Trent **82** 53 6N 0 48W

Newark Valley Nong Khai

Newark Valley 39 42 14N 76 11W
Newaygo 29 43 25N 85 48W
Newaygo County ◇ 29 43 30N 85 50W
Newberg 44 45 18N 122 58W
Newbern, Ala. 10 32 36N 87 32W
Newbern, Tenn. 48 36 7N 89 16W
Newberry, Fla. 17 29 39N 82 37W
Newberry, Ind. 22 38 55N 87 1W
Newberry, Mich. 29 46 21N 85 30W
Newberry, S.C. 46 34 17N 81 37W
Newberry County ◇ 46 34 20N 81 40W
Newberry Springs 15 34 50N 116 41W
Newbrook 62 54 24N 112 57W
Newburg, Md. 27 38 22N 76 37W
Newburg, Mo. 32 37 55N 91 54W
Newburg, N. Dak. 41 48 43N 100 55W
Newburg, Pa. 45 40 8N 77 33W
Newburg, W. Va. 54 39 23N 79 51W
Newburgh, Ind. 22 37 57N 87 24W
Newburgh, N.Y. 39 41 30N 74 1W
Newbury, U.K. 83 51 24N 1 19W
Newbury, U.S.A. 36 43 19N 72 3W
Newburyport 28 42 49N 70 53W
Newcastle, Australia 127 33 0 S 151 46 E
Newcastle, Canada 61 47 1N 65 38W
Newcastle, S. Africa 123 27 45 S 29 58 E
Newcastle, U.K. 85 54 13N 5 54W
Newcastle, Calif. 14 38 53N 121 8W
Newcastle, Maine 26 44 2N 69 32W
Newcastle, Nebr. 34 42 39N 96 53W
Newcastle, Okla. 43 35 15N 97 36W
Newcastle, Tex. 51 33 12N 98 44W
Newcastle, Utah 52 37 40N 113 33W
Newcastle, Wyo. 56 43 50N 104 11W
Newcastle Emlyn 83 52 2N 4 29W
Newcastle Ra. 127 15 45 S 130 15 E
Newcastle-under-Lyme 82 53 2N 2 15W
Newcastle-upon-Tyne 82 54 59N 1 37W
Newcastle Waters 126 17 30 S 133 28 E
Newcomb, Md. 27 38 45N 76 12W
Newcomb, N. Mex. 38 36 17N 108 42W
Newcomb, N.Y. 39 43 58N 74 10W
Newcomerstown 42 40 16N 81 36W
Newdegate 126 33 6 S 119 0 E
Newe Etan 104 32 30N 35 32 E
Newe Sha'anan 104 32 47N 34 59 E
Newe Zohar 104 31 9N 35 21 E
Newell, Ark. 13 33 10N 92 45W
Newell, Iowa 23 42 36N 95 0W
Newell, S. Dak. 47 44 43N 103 25W
Newellton 25 32 4N 91 14W
Newenham, C. 11 58 39N 162 11W
Newfane 39 43 17N 78 43W
Newfield 37 39 33N 75 1W
Newfolden 30 48 21N 96 20W
Newfound L. 36 43 40N 71 47W
Newfoundland, Canada 61 48 30N 56 0W
Newfoundland, U.S.A. 49 38 8N 83 6W
Newfoundland □ 61 53 0N 58 0W
Newfoundland Mts. 52 41 10N 113 20W
Newhalem 53 48 40N 121 15W
Newhalen 11 59 43N 154 54W
Newhall, Calif. 15 34 23N 118 32W
Newhall, Iowa 23 41 59N 91 59W
Newham 83 51 31N 0 2 E
Newhaven 83 50 47N 0 4 E
Newington, Conn. 28 41 43N 72 45W
Newington, Ga. 18 32 35N 81 30W
Newkirk, N. Mex. 38 35 4N 104 16W
Newkirk, Okla. 43 36 53N 97 3W
Newland 40 36 5N 81 56W
Newllano 25 31 7N 93 16W
Newman, Calif. 14 37 19N 121 1W
Newman, Ill. 21 39 48N 87 59W
Newman Grove 34 41 45N 97 47W
Newmans L. 17 29 40N 82 12W
Newmarket, Ireland 85 52 13N 9 0W
Newmarket, U.K. 83 52 15N 0 23 E
Newmarket, U.S.A. 36 43 5N 70 56W
Newnan 18 33 23N 84 48W
Newport, Gwent, U.K. 83 51 35N 3 0W
Newport, I. of W., U.K. 83 50 42N 1 18W
Newport, Salop, U.K. 83 52 47N 2 22W
Newport, Ark. 13 35 37N 91 16W
Newport, Del. 27 39 43N 75 37W
Newport, Ind. 22 39 53N 87 25W
Newport, Ky. 49 39 5N 84 30W
Newport, Maine 26 44 50N 69 17W
Newport, N.C. 40 34 48N 76 52W
Newport, N.H. 36 43 22N 72 10W
Newport, N.J. 37 39 18N 75 11W
Newport, N.Y. 39 43 11N 75 1W
Newport, Nebr. 34 42 36N 99 20W
Newport, Oreg. 44 44 39N 124 3W
Newport, Pa. 45 40 29N 77 8W
Newport, R.I. 28 41 29N 71 19W
Newport, Tenn. 49 35 58N 83 11W
Newport, Vt. 36 44 56N 72 13W
Newport, Wash. 53 48 11N 117 3W
Newport Beach 15 33 37N 117 56W
Newport County ◇ 28 41 30N 71 20W
Newport News 54 36 59N 76 25W
Newquay 83 50 24N 5 6W
Newry 85 54 10N 6 20W
Newry & Mourne □ 85 54 10N 6 15W
Newsoms 54 36 38N 77 8W
Newtok 11 60 56N 164 38W
Newton, Ga. 18 31 19N 84 20W
Newton, Ill. 21 38 59N 88 10W
Newton, Iowa 23 41 42N 93 3W
Newton, Kans. 24 38 3N 97 21W
Newton, Mass. 28 42 21N 71 12W
Newton, Miss. 31 32 19N 89 10W
Newton, N.C. 40 35 40N 81 13W
Newton, N.J. 37 41 3N 74 45W
Newton, Tex. 51 30 51N 93 46W
Newton, Utah 52 41 52N 112 0W
Newton Abbot 83 50 32N 3 37W
Newton County ◇, Ark. 13 35 50N 93 13W
Newton County ◇, Ga. 18 33 30N 83 50W
Newton County ◇, Ind. 22 41 0N 87 25W
Newton County ◇, Miss. 31 32 26N 89 7W
Newton County ◇, Mo. 32 36 55N 94 20W
Newton County ◇, Tex. 51 30 32N 93 49W
Newton Falls, N.Y. 39 44 13N 74 59W
Newton Falls, Ohio 42 41 11N 80 59W
Newton Grove 40 35 14N 78 21W
Newton L. 21 38 55N 88 15W
Newton Stewart 84 54 57N 4 30W
Newtonia 32 36 53N 94 11W
Newtonmore 84 57 4N 4 7W
Newtonsville 42 39 11N 84 5W
Newtonville 10 33 33N 87 48W
Newtown, U.K. 83 52 31N 3 19W
Newtown, Conn. 28 41 25N 73 19W
Newtown, Md. 27 39 18N 76 9W
Newtown, Mo. 32 40 22N 93 20W
Newtown, Pa. 45 40 14N 74 57W
Newtownabbey 85 54 40N 5 55W
Newtownabbey □ 85 54 45N 6 0W
Newtownards 85 54 37N 5 40W
Newville 45 40 10N 77 24W
Ney 42 41 23N 84 32W
Neya 98 58 21N 43 49 E
Neyrīz 107 29 15N 54 19 E
Neyshābūr 107 36 10N 58 50 E
Nez Perce County ◇ 20 46 10N 116 55W
Nez Perce Indian Reservation 20 46 15N 116 30W
Nezhin 99 51 5N 31 55 E
Nezperce 20 46 14N 116 14W
Nezperce National Forest 20 45 50N 115 20W
Ngabang 110 0 23N 109 55 E
Ngabordamlu, Tanjung 111 6 56 S 134 11 E
Ngami Depression 123 20 30 S 22 46 E
Nganglong Kangri 109 33 0N 81 0 E
Nganjuk 111 7 32 S 111 55 E
Ngaoundéré 122 7 15N 13 35 E
Ngapara 128 44 57 S 170 46 E
Ngawi 111 7 24 S 111 26 E
Ngha Lo 112 21 33N 104 28 E
Ngoring Hu 113 34 55N 97 5 E
Ngudu 122 2 58 S 33 25 E
Nguigmi 121 14 20N 13 20 E
Nguru 120 12 56N 10 29 E
Nha Trang 112 12 16N 109 10 E
Nhambiquara 73 12 50 S 59 49W
Nhamundá 71 2 14 S 56 43W
Nhamundá → 71 2 12 S 56 41W
Nhecolândia 73 19 17 S 56 58W
Niafounké 120 16 0N 4 5W
Niagara 41 48 0N 97 54W
Niagara → 39 43 16N 79 4W
Niagara County ◇ 39 43 15N 78 45W
Niagara Falls, Canada 60 43 7N 79 5W
Niagara Falls, U.S.A. 39 43 5N 79 4W
Niah 110 3 58N 113 46 E
Niamey 120 13 27N 2 6 E
Niangara 122 3 42N 27 50 E
Niangua 32 37 23N 92 50W
Niangua → 32 38 58N 92 48W
Niantic 28 41 20N 72 11W
Nianzishan 114 47 31N 122 53 E
Niarada 33 47 49N 114 36W
Nias 110 1 0N 97 30 E
Nibong Tebal 112 5 10N 100 29 E
Nicaragua ■ 66 11 40N 85 30W
Nicaragua, Lago de 66 12 0N 85 30W
Nicastro 94 39 0N 16 18 E
Nicatous L. 26 45 5N 68 9W
Nice, France 90 43 42N 7 14 E
Nice, U.S.A. 14 39 7N 122 51W
Niceville 17 30 31N 86 30W
Nichinan 117 31 38N 131 23 E
Nicholás, Canal 66 23 30N 80 5W
Nicholas County ◇, Ky. 49 38 20N 84 0W
Nicholas County ◇, W. Va. 54 38 17N 80 51W
Nicholasville 49 37 53N 84 34W
Nicholls 18 31 31N 82 38W
Nichols, Iowa 23 41 29N 91 19W
Nichols, N.Y. 39 42 1N 76 22W
Nichols, S.C. 46 34 14N 79 9W
Nichols, Wis. 55 44 40N 88 28W
Nicholson, Ga. 18 34 7N 83 26W
Nicholson, Miss. 31 30 29N 89 43W
Nickel Creek 50 31 55N 104 45W
Nickerie □ 71 4 0N 57 0W
Nickerie → 71 5 58N 57 0W
Nickerson, Kans. 24 38 8N 98 5W
Nickerson, Nebr. 34 41 32N 96 28W
Nicobar Is. 102 9 0N 93 0 E
Nicoclí 70 8 26N 76 48W
Nicodemus 24 39 24N 99 37W
Nicola 62 50 12N 120 40W
Nicolet 60 46 17N 72 35W
Nicolet National Forest 55 45 35N 88 45W
Nicollet 30 44 17N 94 11W
Nicollet County ◇ 30 44 20N 94 15W
Nicolls Town 66 25 8N 78 0W
Nicoma Park 43 35 30N 97 19W
Nicosia 106 35 10N 33 25 E
Nicoya 66 10 9N 85 27W
Nicoya, G. de 66 10 0N 85 0W
Nicoya, Pen. de 66 9 45N 85 40W
Nidd → 82 54 1N 1 32W
Nielsville 30 47 32N 96 49W
Nienburg 88 52 38N 9 15 E
Nieuw Amsterdam 71 5 53N 55 5W
Nieuw Nickerie 71 6 0N 56 59W
Nieuwpoort 87 51 8N 2 45 E
Nièvre □ 90 47 10N 3 40 E
Niğde 106 38 0N 34 40 E
Niger ■ 120 13 30N 10 0 E
Niger → 120 5 33N 6 33 E
Nigeria ■ 120 8 30N 8 0 E
Nightcaps 128 45 57 S 168 2 E
Nighthawk 53 48 58N 119 38W
Nightmute 11 60 29N 164 44W
Nihoa 19 23 6N 161 58W
Nii-Jima 117 34 20N 139 15 E
Niigata 116 37 58N 139 0 E
Niigata □ 117 37 15N 138 45 E
Niihama 117 33 55N 133 16 E
Niihau 19 21 54N 160 9W
Niimi 117 34 59N 133 28 E
Niitsu 116 37 48N 139 7 E
Nijkerk 87 52 13N 5 30 E
Nijmegen 87 51 50N 5 52 E
Nijverdal 87 52 22N 6 28 E
Nikel 96 69 24N 30 12 E
Nikep 37 29 32N 79 1W
Nikiniki 111 9 49 S 124 30 E
Nikki 120 9 58N 3 12 E
Nikkō 117 36 45N 139 35 E
Nikolai 11 62 58N 154 10W
Nikolayev 99 46 58N 32 0 E
Nikolayevsk 99 50 0N 45 35 E
Nikolayevsk-na-Amur 101 53 8N 140 44 E
Nikolski 11 52 56N 168 52W
Nikolskoye 101 55 12N 166 0 E
Nikopol, Bulgaria 95 43 43N 24 54 E
Nikopol, U.S.S.R. 99 47 35N 34 25 E
Nīkshahr 107 26 15N 60 10 E
Nîl, Nahr en → 121 30 10N 31 6 E
Nîl el Abyad → 121 15 38N 32 31 E
Nîl el Azraq → 121 15 38N 32 31 E
Niland 15 33 14N 115 31W
Nile = Nîl, Nahr en → 121 30 10N 31 6 E
Niles, Kans. 24 38 58N 97 28W
Niles, Mich. 29 41 50N 86 15W
Niles, Ohio 42 41 11N 80 46W
Nill 19 21 19N 157 44W
Nilo Peçanha 75 13 37 S 39 6W
Nimach 108 24 30N 74 56 E
Nîmes 90 43 50N 4 23 E
Nimneryskiy 101 57 50N 125 10 E
Nimrod 30 46 38N 94 53W
Nimrod L. 13 34 57N 93 10W
Nīmrūz □ 107 30 0N 62 0 E
Nimule 122 3 32N 32 3 E
Ninaview 16 37 39N 103 15W
Nīnawá 106 36 25N 43 10 E
Ninety Mile Beach, The 127 38 15 S 147 24 E
Ninety Six 46 34 11N 82 1W
Nineveh = Nīnawá 106 36 25N 43 10 E
Ning'an 114 44 22N 129 20 E
Ningbo 115 29 51N 121 28 E
Ningde 115 26 38N 119 23 E
Ningdu 115 26 25N 115 59 E
Ningjin 114 37 35N 114 57 E
Ningming 115 22 8N 107 4 E
Ningpo = Ningbo 115 29 51N 121 28 E
Ningqiang 115 32 47N 106 15 E
Ningshan 115 33 21N 108 21 E
Ningsia Hui A.R. = Ningxia Huizu Zizhiqu □ 114 38 0N 106 0 E
Ningwu 114 39 0N 112 18 E
Ningxia Huizu Zizhiqu □ 114 38 0N 106 0 E
Ningxiang 115 28 15N 112 30 E
Ningyuan 115 25 37N 111 57 E
Ninh Binh 112 20 15N 105 55 E
Ninini Pt. 19 21 58N 159 20W
Ninnekah 43 34 57N 97 56W
Ninnescah → 24 37 20N 97 10W
Ninove 87 50 51N 4 2 E
Nioaque 77 21 5 S 55 50W
Niobrara 34 42 45N 98 2W
Niobrara → 34 42 46N 98 3W
Niobrara County ◇ 56 43 0N 104 25W
Nioro du Sahel 120 15 15N 9 30W
Niort 90 46 19N 0 29W
Ni ta 49 35 31N 84 33W
Nipawin 63 53 20N 104 0W
Nipawin Prov. Park 63 54 0N 104 37W
Nipigon 60 49 0N 88 17W
Nipigon, L. 60 49 50N 88 30W
Nipin → 63 55 46N 108 35W
Nipishish L. 61 54 12N 60 45W
Nipissing L. 60 46 20N 80 0W
Nipomo 15 35 3N 120 29W
Nipton 15 35 28N 115 16W
Niquelândia 75 14 33 S 48 23W
Nirasaki 117 35 42N 138 27 E
Nirmal 108 19 3N 78 20 E
Nirmali 109 26 20N 86 35 E
Niš 95 43 19N 21 58 E
Nişāb 105 14 25N 46 29 E
Nishinomiya 117 34 45N 135 20 E
Nishin'omote 117 30 43N 130 59 E
Nishiwaki 117 34 59N 134 58 E
Niskibi → 60 56 29N 88 9W
Nisland 47 44 40N 103 33W
Nisswa 30 46 31N 94 17W
Nisutlin → 62 60 14N 132 34W
Niţā' 106 27 15N 48 35 E
Nitchequon 61 53 10N 70 58W
Niterói 75 22 52 S 43 0W
Nith → 84 55 20N 3 5W
Nitra 89 48 19N 18 4 E
Nitra → 89 47 46N 18 10 E
Nitro 54 38 25N 81 51W
Nitta Yuma 31 33 2N 90 51W
Niuafo'ou 128 15 30 S 175 58W
Niue I. 125 19 2 S 169 54W
Niut 110 0 55N 110 6 E
Nivelles 87 50 35N 4 20 E
Nivernais 90 47 0N 3 40 E
Niwot 16 40 6N 105 10W
Nixa 32 37 3N 93 18W
Nixon, Tenn. 48 35 7N 88 16W
Nixon, Tex. 51 29 16N 97 46W
Nizamabad 108 18 45N 78 7 E
Nizamghat 109 28 20N 95 45 E
Nizhne Kolymsk 101 68 34N 160 55 E
Nizhne-Vartovskoye 100 60 56N 76 38 E
Nizhneangarsk 101 55 47N 109 30 E
Nizhneudinsk 101 54 54N 99 3 E
Nizhneyansk 101 71 26N 136 4 E
Nizhniy Novgorod = Gorkiy 98 56 20N 44 0 E
Nizhniy Tagil 98 57 55N 59 57 E
Nizhnyaya Tunguska → 101 64 20N 93 0 E
Nizip 106 37 5N 37 50 E
Nizké Tatry 89 48 55N 20 0 E
Njombe 122 9 20 S 34 50 E
Nkambe 120 6 35N 10 40 E
Nkawkaw 120 6 36N 0 49W
Nkhata Bay 122 11 33 S 34 16 E
Nkhota Kota 123 12 56 S 34 15 E
Nkongsamba 122 4 55N 9 55 E
Nmai → 109 25 30N 97 25 E
Noakhali = Maijdi 109 22 48N 91 10 E
Noank 28 41 19N 72 1W
Noatak 11 67 34N 162 58W
Nobeoka 117 32 36N 131 41 E
Noble, Ill. 21 38 42N 88 14W
Noble, La. 25 31 41N 93 41W
Noble, Okla. 43 35 8N 97 24W
Noble County ◇, Ind. 22 41 25N 85 25W
Noble County ◇, Ohio 42 39 45N 81 31W
Noble County ◇, Okla. 43 36 20N 97 10W
Nobles County ◇ 30 43 45N 95 45W
Noblesville 22 40 3N 86 1W
Nocatee 17 27 10N 81 53W
Nocera Inferiore 94 40 45N 14 37 E
Nochixtlán 65 17 28N 97 14W
Nocona 51 33 47N 97 44W
Nocrich 95 45 55N 24 26 E
Noda 117 35 56N 139 52 E
Nodaway 23 40 56N 94 54W
Nodaway → 32 39 54N 94 58W
Nodaway County ◇ 32 40 20N 94 50W
Noel 32 36 33N 94 29W
Nogales, Mexico 64 31 20N 110 56W
Nogales, U.S.A. 12 31 20N 110 56W
Nōgata 117 33 48N 130 44 E
Noginsk 101 64 30N 90 50 E
Nogoa → 127 23 40 S 147 55 E
Nogoyá 76 32 24 S 59 48W
Nohili Pt. 19 22 4N 159 47W
Noi → 112 14 50N 100 15 E
Noirmoutier, Î. de 90 46 58N 2 10W
Nojima-Zaki 117 34 54N 139 53 E
Nok Kundi 107 28 50N 62 45 E
Nokhtuysk 101 60 0N 117 45 E
Nokomis, Canada 63 51 35N 105 0W
Nokomis, Fla. 17 27 7N 82 27W
Nokomis, Ill. 21 39 18N 89 18W
Nokomis L. 63 57 0N 103 0W
Nola 122 3 35N 16 4 E
Nolan County ◇ 50 32 28N 100 25W
Nolensville 48 35 57N 86 40W
Nolin River L. 48 37 17N 86 15W
Noma 17 30 59N 85 37W
Noman L. 63 62 15N 108 55W
Nomans Land 28 41 15N 70 49W
Nombre de Dios 66 9 34N 79 28W
Nome, Alaska 11 64 30N 165 25W
Nome, Tex. 51 30 2N 94 25W
Nome ◇ 11 64 30N 165 0W
Nomo-Zaki 117 32 35N 129 44 E
Nonacho L. 63 61 42N 109 40W
Nondalton 11 59 58N 154 51W
Nong Khae 112 14 29N 100 53 E
Nong Khai 112 17 50N 102 46 E

Nong'an Nouâdhibou

Nong'an 114 44 25N 125 5 E
Nonoava 64 27 28N 106 44W
Noonan 41 48 54N 103 1W
Noord Brabant □ 87 51 40N 5 0 E
Noord Holland □ 87 52 30N 4 45 E
Noordbeveland 87 51 35N 3 50 E
Noordoostpolder 87 52 45N 5 45 E
Noordwijk aan Zee 87 52 14N 4 26 E
Noorvik 11 66 50N 161 3W
Noorvik Indian Reservation 11 66 50N 161 5W
Nootka 62 49 38N 126 38W
Nootka I. 62 49 32N 126 42W
Nopah Range 15 36 10N 116 10W
Nóqui 122 5 55 S 13 30 E
Nora 34 40 10N 97 58W
Nora Springs 23 43 9N 93 1W
Noranda 60 48 20N 79 0W
Norborne 32 39 18N 93 40W
Norcatur 24 39 50N 100 11W
Norco 15 33 56N 117 33W
Norcross, Ga. 18 33 56N 84 13W
Norcross, Minn. 30 45 52N 96 12W
Nord □ 90 50 15N 3 30 E
Nord-Ostsee Kanal 88 54 15N 9 40 E
Nord-Trøndelag fylke □ 96 64 20N 12 0 E
Nordaustlandet 4 79 14N 23 0 E
Nordegg 62 52 29N 116 5W
Norden 34 42 52N 100 5W
Nordhausen 88 51 29N 10 47 E
Nordheim 51 28 55N 97 37W
Nordkapp, Norway 96 71 10N 25 44 E
Nordkapp, Svalbard 4 80 31N 20 0 E
Nordland fylke □ 96 65 40N 13 0 E
Nordman 20 48 38N 116 57W
Nordrhein-Westfalen □ 88 51 45N 7 30 E
Nordvik 101 74 2N 111 32 E
Nore → 85 52 40N 7 20W
Norembega 60 48 59N 80 43W
Norfolk, Conn. 28 41 59N 73 12W
Norfolk, N.Y. 39 44 50N 71 1W
Norfolk, Nebr. 34 42 2N 97 25W
Norfolk, Va. 54 36 51N 76 17W
Norfolk □ 82 52 39N 1 0 E
Norfolk Broads 82 52 30N 1 15 E
Norfolk County ◇ 28 42 10N 71 20W
Norfolk I. 124 28 58 S 168 3 E
Norfork 13 36 13N 92 17W
Norfork L. 13 36 15N 92 14W
Norge 43 34 59N 98 0W
Norias 50 26 47N 97 47W
Norilsk 101 69 20N 88 6 E
Norlina 40 36 27N 78 12W
Normal, Ala. 10 34 47N 86 34W
Normal, Ill. 21 40 31N 88 59W
Norman, Ark. 13 34 27N 93 41W
Norman, N.C. 40 35 10N 79 43W
Norman, Nebr. 34 40 29N 98 48W
Norman, Okla. 43 35 13N 97 26W
Norman → 127 17 28 S 140 49 E
Norman, L. 40 35 26N 80 57W
Norman County ◇ 30 47 20N 96 30W
Norman Park 18 31 16N 83 41W
Norman Wells 58 65 17N 126 51W
Normanby → 127 14 23 S 144 10 E
Normandie 90 48 45N 0 10 E
Normandin 60 48 49N 72 31W
Normandy = Normandie 90 48 45N 0 10 E
Normandy 50 28 55N 100 36W
Normangee 51 31 2N 96 7W
Normanton 127 17 40 S 141 10 E
Norphlet 13 33 19N 92 40W
Norquay 63 51 53N 102 5W
Norquinco 78 41 51 S 70 55W
Norrbotten □ 96 66 30N 22 30 E
Norrby 96 64 55N 18 15 E
Nørresundby 97 57 5N 9 52 E
Norris, Mont. 33 45 34N 111 41W
Norris, S. Dak. 47 43 28N 101 12W
Norris, Tenn. 49 36 12N 84 4W
Norris City 21 37 59N 88 20W
Norris L. 49 36 14N 84 6W
Norristown, Ga. 18 32 30N 82 30W
Norristown, Pa. 45 40 7N 75 21W
Norrköping 97 58 37N 16 11 E
Norrland □ 96 66 50N 18 0 E
Norrtälje 97 59 46N 18 42 E
Norsk 101 52 30N 130 0 E
Norte, Pta. 78 42 5 S 63 46W
Norte de Santander □ 70 8 0N 73 0W
Nortelândia 73 14 25 S 56 48W
North 46 33 37N 81 6W
North → 28 42 37N 72 44W
North Adams, Mass. 28 42 42N 73 7W
North Adams, Mich. 29 41 58N 84 32W
North America 6 40 0N 100 0W
North Amherst 28 42 25N 72 32W
North Andaman I. 112 13 15N 92 40 E
North Andover 28 42 42N 71 8W
North Anna → 54 37 48N 77 25W
North Atlanta 18 33 52N 84 21W
North Attleboro 28 41 59N 71 20W
North Augusta 46 33 30N 81 59W
North Battleford 63 52 50N 108 17W
North Bay 60 46 20N 79 30W
North Beach 27 38 43N 76 32W
North Belcher Is. 60 56 50N 79 50W
North Bend, Canada 62 49 50N 121 27W
North Bend, Nebr. 34 41 28N 96 47W
North Bend, Oreg. 44 43 24N 124 14W
North Bennington 36 42 56N 73 15W
North Bergen 37 40 48N 74 1W
North Berwick, U.K. 84 56 4N 2 44W
North Berwick, U.S.A. 26 43 18N 70 44W
North Bonneville 53 45 39N 121 57W
North Branch, Mich. 29 43 14N 83 12W
North Branch, Minn. 30 45 31N 92 59W
North Branch Elkhorn → 34 41 59N 97 27W
North Branch Potomac → 27 39 32N 78 35W
North Branch Shenandoah → 54 38 59N 78 22W
North Branford 28 41 20N 72 46W
North Brookfield 28 42 16N 72 5W
North Brunswick 37 40 28N 74 28W
North Buena Vista 23 42 41N 90 58W
North Butte 56 43 54N 105 57W
North Canadian → 43 35 16N 95 31W
North Canton 42 40 53N 81 24W
North C., Canada 61 47 2N 60 20W
North C., N.Z. 128 34 23 S 173 4 E
North Cape May 37 38 59N 74 57W
North Caribou L. 60 52 50N 90 40W
North Carolina □ 40 35 30N 80 0W
North Cascades National Park 53 48 45N 121 10W
North Channel, Br. Is. 84 55 0N 5 30W
North Channel, Canada 60 46 0N 83 0W
North Channel, U.S.A. 29 46 5N 83 30W
North Charleston, N.H. 36 43 18N 72 24W
North Charleston, S.C. 46 32 53N 79 58W
North Chelmsford 28 42 38N 71 23W
North Chicago 21 42 19N 87 51W
North Chichester 36 43 15N 71 22W
North College Hill 42 39 13N 84 33W
North Collins 39 42 36N 78 56W
North Concho → 50 31 27N 100 25W
North Conway 36 44 3N 71 8W
North Dakota □ 41 47 30N 100 15W
North Dartmouth 28 41 36N 70 59W
North Down □ 85 54 40N 5 45W
North Downs 83 51 17N 0 30 E
North Druid Hills 18 33 49N 84 19W
North East, Md. 27 39 36N 75 57W
North East, Pa. 45 42 13N 79 50W
North East Cape Fear → 40 34 11N 77 57W
North East Frontier Agency = Arunachal Pradesh □ 109 28 0N 95 0 E
North East Providence Chan. 66 26 0N 76 0W
North Eastham 28 41 52N 69 59W
North Easton 28 42 4N 71 6W
North English 23 41 31N 92 5W
North Enid 43 36 26N 97 52W
North Esk → 84 56 44N 2 25W
North European Plain 80 55 0N 20 0 E
North Fabius → 32 39 54N 91 30W
North Fairfield 42 41 6N 82 37W
North Fond du Lac 55 43 48N 88 29W
North Foreland 83 51 22N 1 28 E
North Fork 20 45 25N 113 59W
North Fork American → 14 38 57N 120 59W
North Fork Cuivre → 32 39 2N 90 59W
North Fork Edisto → 46 33 16N 80 54W
North Fork Feather → 14 38 33N 121 30W
North Fork Grand → 47 45 47N 102 16W
North Fork Humboldt → 35 40 56N 115 32W
North Fork John Day → 44 44 45N 119 38W
North Fork Moreau → 47 45 9N 102 50W
North Fork Red → 43 34 24N 99 14W
North Fork Shoshone → 56 44 29N 109 18W
North Fork Smoky Hill → 24 38 54N 101 18W
North Fork Solomon → 24 39 28N 98 26W
North Fork South Platte → 16 39 25N 105 10W
North Fort Myers 17 26 41N 81 53W
North Fox I. 29 45 29N 85 47W
North Freedom 55 43 28N 89 52W
North Grafton 28 42 14N 71 42W
North Grosvenor Dale 28 41 59N 71 54W
North Hampton 36 42 57N 70 48W
North Haven, Conn. 28 41 23N 72 52W
North Haven, Maine 26 44 8N 68 53W
North Henik L. 63 61 45N 97 40W
North Hero 36 44 49N 73 18W
North Highlands 14 38 40N 121 23W
North I., N.Z. 128 38 0 S 175 0 E
North I., U.S.A. 46 33 17N 79 11W
North Judson 22 41 13N 86 46W
North Kingsville 42 41 54N 80 42W
North Knife → 63 58 53N 94 45W
North Korea ■ 114 40 0N 127 0 E
North Lakhimpur 109 27 14N 94 7 E
North Las Vegas 35 36 12N 115 7W
North Lewisburg 42 40 13N 83 33W
North Liberty, Ind. 22 41 32N 86 26W
North Liberty, Iowa 23 41 46N 91 35W
North Little Rock 13 34 45N 92 16W
North Loon Mt. 20 45 7N 115 52W
North Loup 34 41 30N 98 46W
North Loup → 34 41 17N 98 24W
North Manchester 22 41 0N 85 46W
North Manitou I. 29 45 7N 86 1W
North Mankato 30 44 10N 94 0W
North Miami 17 25 54N 80 11W
North Miami Beach 17 25 56N 80 10W
North Middletown 49 38 9N 84 7W
North Minch 84 58 5N 5 55W
North Muskegon 29 43 15N 86 17W
North Myrtle Beach 46 33 48N 78 42W
North Nahanni → 62 62 15N 123 20W
North Naples 17 26 12N 81 48W
North New River Canal 17 26 30N 80 30W
North Oaks 15 34 25N 118 31W
North Ogden 52 41 19N 111 58W
North Olmsted 42 41 25N 81 56W
North Ossetian A.S.S.R. □ 99 43 30N 44 30 E
North Palisade 15 37 6N 118 31W
North Pease → 50 34 15N 100 7W
North Perry 42 41 47N 81 9W
North Plains, N. Mex. 38 34 45N 108 10W
North Plains, Oreg. 44 45 37N 123 0W
North Platte 34 41 8N 100 46W
North Platte → 34 41 7N 100 42W
North Pt. 61 47 5N 64 0W
North Pole, Arctic 4 90 0N 0 0 E
North Pole, U.S.A. 11 64 45N 147 21W
North Portal 63 49 0N 102 33W
North Powder 44 45 2N 117 55W
North Prairie 55 42 56N 88 24W
North Providence 28 41 50N 71 25W
North Pt., Mich. 29 45 2N 83 16W
North Pt., Mich. 29 45 22N 83 30W
North Richland Hills 51 32 50N 97 14W
North Rim 12 36 12N 112 3W
North Ronaldsay 84 59 20N 2 30W
North Salem 22 39 52N 86 39W
North Salt Lake 52 40 50N 111 55W
North Santiam → 44 44 41N 123 0W
North Saskatchewan → 63 53 15N 105 5W
North Schell Peak 35 39 25N 114 36W
North Sea 86 56 0N 4 0 E
North Sentinel I. 112 11 35N 92 15 E
North Sioux City 47 42 32N 96 29W
North Slope ◇ 11 69 0N 154 0W
North Sporades = Voríai Sporádhes 95 39 15N 23 30 E
North Springfield, Pa. 45 41 59N 80 26W
North Springfield, Vt. 36 43 20N 72 32W
North Stonington 28 41 20N 72 0W
North Stradbroke I. 127 27 35 S 153 28 E
North Stratford 36 44 45N 71 38W
North Sulphur → 51 33 23N 95 18W
North Sutton 36 43 22N 71 56W
North Sydney 61 46 12N 60 15W
North Syracuse 39 43 8N 76 7W
North Terre Haute 22 39 31N 87 22W
North Thompson → 62 50 40N 120 20W
North Toe → 40 36 0N 82 16W
North Tonawanda 39 43 2N 78 53W
North Troy 36 45 0N 72 24W
North Truro 28 42 2N 70 5W
North Twin I. 60 53 20N 80 0W
North Tyne → 82 54 59N 2 7W
North Uist 84 57 40N 7 15W
North Umpqua → 44 43 16N 123 27W
North Vancouver 62 49 25N 123 3W
North Vernon 22 39 0N 85 38W
North Wabiskaw L. 62 56 0N 113 55W
North Wales 45 40 13N 75 17W
North Walsham 82 52 49N 1 22 E
North Washington 23 43 7N 92 25W
North West Basin 126 25 45 S 115 0 E
North West C. 126 21 45 S 114 9 E
North West Christmas I. Ridge 125 6 30N 165 0W
North West Frontier □ 108 34 0N 71 0 E
North West Highlands 84 57 35N 5 2W
North West Providence Channel 66 26 0N 78 0W
North West River 61 53 30N 60 10W
North West Territories □ 58 67 0N 110 0W
North Wichita → 51 33 43N 99 29W
North Wildwood 37 39 0N 74 48W
North Wilkesboro 40 36 10N 81 9W
North Windham 26 43 50N 70 26W
North York Moors 82 54 25N 0 50W
North Yorkshire □ 82 54 15N 1 25W
Northallerton 82 54 20N 1 26W
Northam 126 31 35 S 116 42 E
Northampton, Australia 126 28 27 S 114 33 E
Northampton, U.K. 83 52 14N 0 54W
Northampton, Mass. 28 42 19N 72 38W
Northampton, Pa. 45 40 41N 75 30W
Northampton □ 83 52 16N 0 55W
Northampton County ◇, N.C. 40 36 20N 77 30W
Northampton County ◇, Pa. 45 40 50N 75 20W
Northampton County ◇, Va. 54 37 15N 75 55W
Northborough 28 42 19N 71 39W
Northbridge 28 42 9N 71 39W
Northeast C. 11 63 18N 168 42W
Northern Cheyenne Indian Reservation 33 45 30N 106 40W
Northern Circars 109 17 30N 82 30 E
Northern Group 128 10 0 S 160 0W
Northern Indian L. 63 57 20N 97 20W
Northern Ireland □ 85 54 45N 7 0W
Northern Light, L. 60 48 15N 90 39W
Northern Marianas 124 17 0N 145 0 E
Northern Territory □ 126 16 0 S 133 0 E
Northfield, Maine 26 44 52N 67 34W
Northfield, Mass. 28 42 42N 72 27W
Northfield, Minn. 30 44 27N 93 9W
Northfield, N.H. 36 43 26N 71 36W
Northfield, N.J. 37 39 22N 74 33W
Northfield, Vt. 36 44 9N 72 40W
Northford 28 41 24N 72 48W
Northglenn 16 39 53N 104 58W
Northland □ 128 35 30 S 173 30 E
Northome 30 47 52N 94 17W
Northport, Ala. 10 33 14N 87 35W
Northport, Mich. 29 45 8N 85 37W
Northport, N.Y. 39 40 54N 73 21W
Northport, Nebr. 34 41 41N 103 5W
Northport, Wash. 53 48 55N 117 48W
Northrop 30 43 44N 94 26W
Northumberland 45 40 54N 76 48W
Northumberland □ 82 55 12N 2 0W
Northumberland, C. 127 38 5 S 140 40 E
Northumberland County ◇, Pa. 45 40 55N 76 50W
Northumberland County ◇, Va. 54 37 55N 76 29W
Northumberland Str. 61 46 20N 64 0W
Northview 32 37 17N 93 0W
Northville, N.Y. 39 43 13N 74 11W
Northville, S. Dak. 47 45 9N 98 35W
Northway 11 62 58N 141 56W
Northwest Territories □ 58 65 0N 100 0W
Northwich 82 53 16N 2 30W
Northwood, Iowa 23 43 27N 93 13W
Northwood, N. Dak. 41 47 44N 97 34W
Northwood, N.H. 36 43 12N 71 9W
Northwye 32 37 59N 91 46W
Norton, Kans. 24 39 50N 99 53W
Norton, Mass. 28 41 58N 71 11W
Norton, Va. 54 36 56N 82 38W
Norton, Vt. 36 45 0N 71 48W
Norton B. 11 64 45N 161 15W
Norton County ◇ 24 39 45N 99 50W
Norton Reservoir 24 39 48N 99 56W
Norton Sd. 11 63 50N 164 0W
Nortonville, Kans. 24 39 25N 95 20W
Nortonville, Ky. 48 37 12N 87 27W
Norwalk, Calif. 15 33 54N 118 5W
Norwalk, Conn. 28 41 7N 73 22W
Norwalk, Iowa 23 41 29N 93 41W
Norwalk, Ohio 42 41 15N 82 37W
Norway, Iowa 23 41 54N 91 55W
Norway, Kans. 24 39 42N 97 47W
Norway, Maine 26 44 13N 70 32W
Norway, Mich. 29 45 47N 87 55W
Norway, S.C. 46 33 27N 81 7W
Norway ■ 97 63 0N 11 0 E
Norway House 63 53 59N 97 50W
Norwegian Dependency □ 5 66 0 S 15 0 E
Norwegian Sea 97 66 0N 1 0 E
Norwich, U.K. 82 52 38N 1 17 E
Norwich, Conn. 28 41 31N 72 5W
Norwich, Kans. 24 37 27N 97 51W
Norwich, N.Y. 39 42 32N 75 32W
Norwich, Vt. 36 43 42N 72 18W
Norwood, Colo. 16 38 8N 108 20W
Norwood, La. 25 30 58N 91 6W
Norwood, Mass. 28 42 12N 71 12W
Norwood, Minn. 30 44 46N 93 55W
Norwood, Mo. 32 37 7N 92 24W
Norwood, N.C. 40 35 14N 80 7W
Norwood, N.Y. 39 44 45N 75 0W
Norwood, Ohio 42 39 10N 84 27W
Norwoodville 23 41 39N 93 33W
Nos Kaliakra 95 43 21N 28 30 E
Noshiro 116 40 12N 140 0 E
Nosok 100 70 10N 82 20 E
Noşratābād 107 29 55N 60 0 E
Noss Hd. 84 58 29N 3 4W
Nossa Senhora da Glória 74 10 14 S 37 25W
Nossa Senhora das Dores 74 10 29 S 37 13W
Nossa Senhora do Livramento 73 15 48 S 56 22W
Nossob → 123 26 55 S 20 37 E
Nosy Bé 123 13 25 S 48 15 E
Nosy Boraha 123 16 50 S 49 55 E
Nosy Mitsio 123 12 54 S 48 36 E
Nosy Varika 123 20 35 S 48 32 E
Notasulga 10 32 34N 85 41W
Notch Peak 52 39 9N 113 25W
Notigi Dam 63 56 40N 99 10W
Notikewin → 62 57 2N 117 38W
Noto 94 36 52N 15 4 E
Notre-Dame 61 46 18N 64 46W
Notre Dame B. 61 49 45N 55 30W
Notre Dame de Koartac = Koartac 59 60 55N 69 40W
Notre Dame d'Ivugivic = Ivugivik 59 62 24N 77 55W
Notrees 50 31 55N 102 45W
Nottaway → 60 51 22N 78 55W
Nottely L. 18 34 58N 84 5W
Nottingham, U.K. 82 52 57N 1 10W
Nottingham, U.S.A. 36 43 7N 71 6W
Nottingham □ 82 53 10N 1 0W
Nottoway → 54 36 33N 76 55W
Nottoway County ◇ 54 37 8N 78 5W
Nottoway Court House 54 37 8N 78 5W
Notus 20 43 43N 116 48W
Nouâdhibou 120 20 54N 17 0W

Ogdensburg Oracle

Ogdensburg, N.J. 37 41 5N 74 36W
Ogdensburg, N.Y. 39 44 42N 75 30W
Ogeechee → 18 31 50N 81 3W
Ogema 30 47 6N 95 56W
Ogemaw 13 33 28N 93 2W
Ogemaw County ◇ 29 44 15N 84 10W
Ogilvie 30 45 50N 93 26W
Oglala 47 43 17N 102 44W
Oglala National Grassland 34 42 55N 103 45W
Ogle County ◇ 21 42 0N 89 20W
Oglesby, Ill. 21 41 18N 89 4W
Oglesby, Tex. 51 31 25N 97 30W
Oglethorpe 18 32 18N 84 4W
Oglethorpe County ◇ 18 33 50N 83 0W
Oglio → 94 45 2N 10 39 E
Ogoki → 60 51 38N 85 57W
Ogoki L. 60 50 50N 87 10W
Ogoki Res. 60 50 45N 88 15W
Ogooué → 122 1 0S 10 0 E
Ogosta → 95 43 48N 23 55 E
Ogowe = Ogooué → 122 1 0S 10 0 E
Ohai 128 44 55 S 168 0 E
Ohakune 128 39 24 S 175 24 E
Ohanet, Oued → 120 28 44N 8 46 E
Ohata 116 41 24N 141 10 E
Ohatchee 10 33 47N 86 0W
Ohau, L. 128 44 15 S 169 53 E
Ohey 87 50 26N 5 8 E
Ohio, Colo. 16 38 34N 106 37W
Ohio, Ill. 21 41 34N 89 28W
Ohio □ 42 40 15N 82 45W
Ohio → 48 36 59N 89 8W
Ohio City 42 40 46N 84 37W
Ohio County ◇, Ind. 22 38 55N 85 0W
Ohio County ◇, Ky. 48 37 30N 86 50W
Ohio County ◇, W. Va. 54 40 6N 80 34W
Ohioville 45 40 41N 80 30W
Ohre → 88 50 30N 14 10 E
Ohridsko, Jezero 95 41 8N 20 52 E
Oiapoque → 71 4 8N 51 40W
Oil Center 38 32 30N 103 16W
Oil City, La. 25 32 45N 93 58W
Oil City, Pa. 45 41 26N 79 42W
Oil Trough 13 35 38N 91 28W
Oildale 15 35 25N 119 1W
Oilmont 33 48 44N 111 51W
Oilton 43 36 5N 96 35W
Oise □ 90 49 28N 2 30 E
Ōita 117 33 14N 131 36 E
Ōita □ 117 33 15N 131 30 E
Oiticica 74 5 3 S 41 5W
Ojai 15 34 27N 119 15W
Ojinaga 64 29 34N 104 25W
Ojiya 117 37 18N 138 48 E
Ojo Feliz 38 36 4N 105 7W
Ojo Sarco 38 36 7N 105 47W
Ojos del Salado, Cerro 76 27 0S 68 40W
Okaba 111 8 6 S 139 42 E
Okabena 30 43 44N 95 19W
Okahandja 123 22 0S 16 59 E
Okahukura 124 38 48 S 175 14 E
Okaloosa County ◇ 17 30 30N 86 40W
Okanagan L. 62 50 0N 119 30W
Okanagan Ra. 53 48 40N 119 45W
Okandja 122 0 35 S 13 45 E
Okanogan 53 48 22N 119 35W
Okanogan → 53 48 6N 119 44W
Okanogan County ◇ 53 48 30N 120 0W
Okanogan National Forest 53 48 30N 120 10W
Okarche 43 35 44N 97 58W
Okarito 128 43 15 S 170 9 E
Okaton 47 43 53N 100 53W
Okaukuejo 123 19 10 S 16 0 E
Okavango Swamps 123 18 45 S 22 45 E
Okay 43 35 51N 95 19W
Okaya 117 36 0N 138 10 E
Okayama 117 34 40N 133 54 E
Okayama □ 117 35 0N 133 50 E
Okazaki 117 34 57N 137 10 E
O'Kean 13 36 10N 90 49W
Okeechobee 17 27 15N 80 50W
Okeechobee, L. 17 27 0N 80 50W
Okeechobee County ◇ 17 27 30N 81 0W
Okeene 43 36 7N 98 19W
Okefenokee Swamp 18 30 40N 82 20W
Okehampton 83 50 44N 4 1W
Okemah 43 35 26N 96 19W
Okemos 29 42 43N 84 26W
Okene 120 7 32N 6 11 E
Oketo 24 39 58N 96 36W
Okfuskee County ◇ 43 35 25N 96 15W
Okha 101 53 40N 143 0 E
Okhotsk 101 59 20N 143 10 E
Okhotsk, Sea of 101 55 0N 145 0 E
Okhotskiy Perevoz 101 61 52N 135 35 E
Okhotsko Kolymskoye 101 63 0N 157 0 E
Oki-Shotō 117 36 5N 133 15 E
Okiep 123 29 39 S 17 53 E
Okinawa □ 117 26 40N 128 0 E
Okinawa-Guntō 117 26 40N 128 0 E
Okinawa-Jima 117 26 32N 128 0 E
Okino-erabu-Shima 117 27 21N 128 33 E
Oklahoma □ 43 36 0N 97 0W
Oklahoma City 43 35 30N 97 30W
Oklahoma County ◇ 43 35 35N 97 20W
Oklaunion 51 34 8N 99 9W
Oklawaha → 17 29 28N 81 41W
Oklawaha, L. 17 29 30N 81 45W
Oklee 30 47 50N 95 51W
Okmulgee 43 35 37N 95 58W
Okmulgee County ◇ 43 35 40N 96 0W
Okoboji 23 43 23N 95 8W
Okolona, Ark. 13 34 0N 93 20W
Okolona, Ky. 49 38 8N 85 41W
Okolona, Miss. 31 34 0N 88 45W
Okrika 120 4 40N 7 10 E
Oktabrsk 100 49 28N 57 25 E
Oktaha 43 35 35N 95 29W
Oktibbeha County ◇ 31 33 28N 88 49W
Oktyabrskiy 98 54 28N 53 28 E
Oktyabrskoy Revolyutsii, Os. 101 79 30N 97 0 E
Oktyabrskoye 100 62 28N 66 3 E
Okuru 128 43 55 S 168 55 E
Okushiri-Tō 116 42 15N 139 30 E
Ola, Ark. 13 35 2N 93 13W
Ola, Idaho 20 44 11N 116 18W
Ólafsfjörður 96 66 4N 18 39W
Ólafsvík 96 64 53N 23 43W
Olamon 26 45 7N 68 37W
Olancha 15 36 17N 118 1W
Olanchito 66 15 30N 86 30W
Öland 97 56 45N 16 38 E
Olanta 46 33 56N 79 56W
Olar 46 33 11N 81 11W
Olascoaga 76 35 15 S 60 39W
Olathe, Colo. 16 38 36N 107 59W
Olathe, Kans. 24 38 53N 94 49W
Olavarría 76 36 55 S 60 20W
Olberg 12 33 6N 111 41W
Ólbia 94 40 55N 9 30 E
Old Bahama Chan. = Bahama, Canal Viejo de 66 22 10N 77 30W
Old Bridge 37 40 25N 74 22W
Old Castile = Castilla La Vieja 91 41 55N 4 0W
Old Castle 85 53 46N 7 10W
Old Crow 58 67 30N 140 5 E
Old Faithful 56 44 28N 110 50W
Old Forge, N.Y. 39 43 43N 74 58W
Old Forge, Pa. 45 41 22N 75 45W
Old Fort 40 35 38N 82 11W
Old Fort → 63 58 36N 110 24W
Old Harbor 11 57 12N 153 18W
Old Hickory L. 48 36 18N 86 40W
Old Logan Cr. → 34 41 37N 96 30W
Old Lyme 28 41 19N 72 20W
Old Mines 32 38 1N 90 45W
Old Monroe 32 38 56N 90 45W
Old Ocean 51 29 5N 95 45W
Old Orchard Beach 26 43 31N 70 23W
Old Saybrook 28 41 18N 72 23W
Old Speck Mt. 26 44 34N 70 57W
Old Town, Fla. 17 29 36N 82 59W
Old Town, Maine 26 44 56N 68 39W
Old Washington 42 40 2N 81 27W
Old Wives L. 63 50 5N 106 0W
Old Woman Mts. 15 34 20N 115 0W
Oldbury 83 51 38N 2 30W
Oldenburg, Germany 88 53 10N 8 10 E
Oldenburg, U.S.A. 22 39 21N 85 12W
Oldenzaal 87 52 19N 6 53 E
Oldham, U.K. 82 53 33N 2 8W
Oldham, U.S.A. 47 44 14N 97 19W
Oldham County ◇, Ky. 49 38 25N 85 30W
Oldham County ◇, Tex. 50 35 30N 102 30W
Oldman → 62 49 57N 111 42W
Olds 62 51 50N 114 10W
Oldsmar 17 28 2N 82 40W
Oldtown 27 39 33N 78 37W
Olean, Mo. 32 38 25N 92 32W
Olean, N.Y. 39 42 5N 78 26W
Olekma → 101 60 22N 120 42 E
Olekminsk 101 60 25N 120 30 E
Olenegorsk 98 68 9N 33 18 E
Olenek 101 68 28N 112 18 E
Olenek → 101 73 0N 120 10 E
Olentangy → 42 39 58N 83 2W
Oléron, Île d' 90 45 55N 1 15W
Oleśnica 89 51 13N 17 22 E
Olex 44 45 30N 120 11W
Olga 101 43 50N 135 14 E
Olga, L. 60 49 47N 77 15W
Olga, Mt. 126 25 20 S 130 50 E
Olgastretet 4 78 35N 25 0 E
Olifants → 123 24 5 S 31 20 E
Ólimbos, Óros 95 40 6N 22 23 E
Olímpia 77 20 44 S 48 54W
Olimpo □ 76 20 30 S 58 45W
Olinda 74 8 1 S 34 51W
Olindiná 74 11 22 S 38 21W
Oliva 76 32 0 S 63 38W
Olive Branch 31 34 58N 89 50W
Olive Hill 49 38 18N 83 13W
Olivehurst 14 39 6N 121 34W
Oliveira 75 20 39 S 44 50W
Oliveira dos Brejinhos 75 12 19 S 42 54W
Olivenza 91 38 41N 7 9W
Oliver, Canada 62 49 13N 119 37W
Oliver, Ga. 18 32 31N 81 32W
Oliver, Wis. 55 46 40N 92 12W
Oliver County ◇ 41 47 2N 101 25W
Oliver L. 63 56 56N 103 22W
Oliver Springs 49 36 3N 84 20W
Olivet, Kans. 24 38 29N 95 45W
Olivet, Md. 27 38 20N 76 26W
Olivet, Mich. 29 42 27N 84 56W
Olivet, S. Dak. 47 43 14N 97 40W
Olivia, Minn. 30 44 47N 94 59W
Olivia, N.C. 40 35 22N 79 7W
Olla 25 31 54N 92 14W
Ollagüe 76 21 15 S 68 10W
Ollie 23 41 12N 92 6W
Olmos 72 5 59 S 79 46W
Olmstead, Ill. 21 37 11N 89 5W
Olmstead, Ky. 48 36 45N 87 1W
Olmsted County ◇ 30 44 0N 92 30W
Olney, Ill. 21 38 44N 88 5W
Olney, Md. 27 39 9N 77 4W
Olney, Mont. 33 48 33N 114 35W
Olney, Tex. 51 33 22N 98 45W
Olney Springs 16 38 10N 103 57W
Olomane → 61 50 14N 60 37W
Olomouc 88 49 38N 17 12 E
Olonets 98 61 10N 33 0 E
Olongapo 111 14 50N 120 18 E
Olovyannaya 101 50 58N 115 35 E
Olowalu 19 20 49N 156 38W
Oloy → 101 66 29N 159 29 E
Olpe 24 38 16N 96 10W
Olsburg 24 39 26N 96 37W
Olsztyn 89 53 48N 20 29 E
Olt □ 95 44 20N 24 30 E
Olt → 89 43 50N 24 40 E
Olteniţa 89 44 7N 26 42 E
Olton 50 34 11N 102 8W
Oltu 106 40 35N 41 58 E
Olustee, Fla. 17 30 12N 82 26W
Olustee, Okla. 43 34 33N 99 25W
Olympia, Greece 95 37 39N 21 39 E
Olympia, U.S.A. 53 47 3N 122 53W
Olympic Mts. 53 47 55N 123 45W
Olympic National Forest 53 47 25N 123 35W
Olympus, Mt. = Ólimbos, Óros 95 40 6N 22 23 E
Olympus, Mt. 53 47 48N 123 43W
Om → 100 54 59N 73 22 E
Ōma, Japan 116 41 45N 141 5 E
Oma, U.S.A. 31 31 44N 90 9W
Ōmachi 117 36 30N 137 50 E
Omae-Zaki 117 34 36N 138 14 E
Ōmagari 116 39 27N 140 29 E
Omagh 85 54 36N 7 20W
Omagh □ 85 54 35N 7 15W
Omaha, Ark. 13 36 27N 93 11W
Omaha, Nebr. 34 41 17N 96 1W
Omaha, Tex. 51 33 11N 94 45W
Omaha Indian Reservation 34 42 10N 96 30W
Omak 53 48 25N 119 31W
Omak L. 53 48 17N 119 24W
Oman ■ 105 23 0N 58 0 E
Oman, G. of 107 24 30N 58 30 E
Omaruru 123 21 26 S 16 0 E
Omate 72 16 45 S 71 0W
Ombai, Selat 111 8 30 S 124 50 E
Omboué 122 1 35 S 9 15 E
Ombrone → 94 42 39N 11 0 E
Omdurmân 121 15 40N 32 28 E
Omega 18 31 21N 83 36W
Omemee 41 48 42N 100 22W
Omer 29 44 3N 83 51W
Ometepe, Isla de 66 11 32N 85 35W
Ometepec 65 16 39N 98 23W
Omez 104 32 22N 35 0 E
Ominato 116 41 17N 141 10 E
Omineca → 62 56 3N 124 16W
Ōmiya 117 35 54N 139 38 E
Ommaney, C. 11 56 10N 134 40W
Ommen 87 52 31N 6 26 E
Omo → 121 6 25N 36 10 E
Omolon → 101 68 42N 158 36 E
Omono-Gawa → 116 39 46N 140 3 E
Ompompanoosuc → 36 43 45N 72 14W
Omro 55 44 2N 88 45W
Omsk 100 55 0N 73 12 E
Omsukchan 101 62 32N 155 48 E
Ōmu 116 44 34N 142 58 E
Omul, Vf. 89 45 27N 25 29 E
Ōmura 117 32 56N 130 0 E
Omuramba → 123 19 10 S 19 20 E
Omurtag 95 43 8N 26 26 E
Ōmuta 117 33 0N 130 26 E
Ona 17 27 29N 81 55W
Onaga 24 39 29N 96 10W
Onaka 47 45 12N 99 28W
Onalaska 55 43 53N 91 14W
Onamia 30 46 4N 93 40W
Onancock 54 37 43N 75 45W
Onang 111 3 2 S 118 49 E
Onaping L. 60 47 3N 81 30W
Onarga 21 40 43N 88 1W
Onarhā 107 35 30N 71 0 E
Onavas 64 28 28N 109 30W
Onawa 23 42 2N 96 6W
Onaway, Idaho 20 46 56N 116 53W
Onaway, Mich. 29 45 21N 84 14W
Oncesti 95 43 56N 25 52 E
Oncócua 123 16 30 S 13 25 E
Onda 91 39 55N 0 17W
Ondangua 123 17 57 S 16 4 E
Ondas → 75 12 8 S 45 0W
Ondo 120 7 4N 4 47 E
Öndörhaan 113 47 19N 110 39 E
Öndverðarnes 96 64 52N 24 0W
Onega 98 64 0N 38 10 E
Onega → 98 63 58N 37 55 E
Onega, G. of = Onezhskaya Guba 98 64 30N 37 0 E
Onega, L. = Onezhskoye Ozero 98 62 0N 35 30 E
Onehunga 128 36 55 S 174 48 E
Oneida, Ill. 21 41 4N 90 13W
Oneida, Iowa 23 42 33N 91 21W
Oneida, Kans. 24 39 52N 95 56W
Oneida, N.Y. 39 43 6N 75 39W
Oneida, Tenn. 49 36 30N 84 31W
Oneida County ◇, Idaho 20 42 10N 112 30W
Oneida County ◇, N.Y. 39 43 20N 75 30W
Oneida County ◇, Wis. 55 45 40N 89 35W
Oneida Indian Reservation 55 44 25N 88 10W
Oneida L. 39 43 12N 75 54W
O'Neill 34 42 27N 98 39W
Onekama 29 44 22N 86 12W
Onekotan, Ostrov 101 49 25N 154 45 E
Oneonta, Ala. 10 33 57N 86 28W
Oneonta, N.Y. 39 42 27N 75 4W
Onezhskaya Guba 98 64 30N 37 0 E
Onezhskoye Ozero 98 62 0N 35 30 E
Ongarue 128 38 42 S 175 19 E
Ongniud Qi 114 43 0N 118 38 E
Ongole 108 15 33N 80 2 E
Onguren 101 53 38N 107 36 E
Onida 47 44 42N 100 4W
Onilahy → 123 23 34 S 43 45 E
Onitsha 120 6 6N 6 42 E
Onley 54 37 41N 75 43W
Ono 14 40 29N 122 37W
Onoda 117 34 2N 131 25 E
Onondaga County ◇ 39 43 0N 76 15W
Onondaga Indian Reservation 39 42 55N 76 10W
Onset 28 41 45N 70 39W
Onslow, Australia 126 21 40 S 115 12 E
Onslow, U.S.A. 23 42 6N 91 1W
Onslow B. 40 34 20N 77 15W
Onslow County ◇ 40 34 50N 77 30W
Onstwedde 87 53 2N 7 4 E
Ontake-San 117 35 53N 137 29 E
Ontario, Calif. 15 34 4N 117 39W
Ontario, Oreg. 44 44 2N 116 58W
Ontario, Wis. 55 43 45N 90 35W
Ontario □ 60 52 0N 88 10W
Ontario, L., U.S.A. 39 43 20N 78 0W
Ontario County ◇ 39 42 50N 77 20W
Ontonagon 29 46 52N 89 19W
Ontonagon County ◇ 29 46 40N 89 25W
Oodnadatta 126 27 33 S 135 30 E
Ookala 19 20 1N 155 17W
Ooldea 126 30 27 S 131 50 E
Oolitic 22 38 54N 86 31W
Oologah 43 36 27N 95 43W
Oologah L. 43 36 26N 95 41W
Ooltewah 49 35 4N 85 4W
Oona River 62 53 57N 130 16W
Oost-Vlaanderen □ 87 51 5N 3 50 E
Oostburg 55 43 37N 87 48W
Oostende 87 51 15N 2 50 E
Oosterhout 87 51 39N 4 47 E
Oosterschelde 87 51 33N 4 0 E
Ootacamund 108 11 30N 76 44 E
Ootsa L. 62 53 50N 126 2W
Opaka 95 43 28N 26 10 E
Opala, U.S.S.R. 101 51 58N 156 30 E
Opala, Zaïre 122 0 40 S 24 20 E
Opan 95 42 13N 25 41 E
Opanake 108 6 35N 80 40 E
Opasatika 60 49 30N 82 50W
Opasquia 63 53 16N 93 34W
Opava 89 49 57N 17 58 E
Opelika 10 32 39N 85 23W
Opelousas 25 30 32N 92 5W
Opémisca, L. 60 49 56N 74 52W
Opheim 33 48 51N 106 24W
Ophir, Alaska 11 63 10N 156 31W
Ophir, Oreg. 44 42 34N 124 23W
Ophthalmia Ra. 126 23 15 S 119 30 E
Opihikao 19 19 26N 154 53W
Opinaca → 60 52 15N 78 2W
Opinaca L. 60 52 39N 76 20W
Opiskotish, L. 61 53 10N 67 50W
Opole 89 50 42N 17 58 E
Oporto = Porto 91 41 8N 8 40W
Opotiki 128 38 1 S 177 19 E
Opp 10 31 17N 86 16W
Oppland fylke □ 97 61 15N 9 40 E
Opportunity, Mont. 33 46 6N 112 50W
Opportunity, Wash. 53 47 39N 117 15W
Optima 43 36 46N 101 21W
Opua 128 35 19 S 174 9 E
Opunake 128 39 26 S 173 52 E
Oquawka 21 40 56N 90 57W
Or Yehuda 104 32 2N 34 50 E
Ora 104 30 55N 35 1 E
Oracle 12 32 37N 110 46W

Oradea Oulu

Oradea 89 47 2N 21 58 E
Öræfajökull 96 64 2N 16 39W
Orai 108 25 58N 79 30 E
Oraibi 12 35 53N 110 37W
Oran, Algeria 120 35 45N 0 39W
Oran, Argentina 76 23 10 S 64 20W
Oran, U.S.A. 32 37 5N 89 39W
Orange, Australia 127 33 15 S 149 7 E
Orange, France 90 44 8N 4 47 E
Orange, Calif. 15 33 47N 117 51W
Orange, Conn. 28 41 17N 73 2W
Orange, Mass. 28 42 35N 72 19W
Orange, Tex. 51 30 6N 93 44W
Orange, Va. 54 38 15N 78 7W
Orange, C. 71 4 20N 51 30W
Orange City, Fla. 17 28 57N 81 18W
Orange City, Iowa 23 43 0N 96 4W
Orange County ◇, Calif. 15 33 30N 117 45W
Orange County ◇, Fla. 17 28 30N 81 15W
Orange County ◇, Ind. 22 38 30N 86 30W
Orange County ◇, N.C. 40 36 0N 79 10W
Orange County ◇, N.Y. 39 41 20N 74 15W
Orange County ◇, Tex. 51 30 12N 93 52W
Orange County ◇, Va. 54 38 15N 78 7W
Orange County ◇, Vt. 36 44 0N 72 20W
Orange Cove 15 36 38N 119 19W
Orange Free State = Oranje Vrystaat □ 123 28 30 S 27 0 E
Orange Grove 51 27 58N 97 56W
Orange Lake 17 29 25N 82 13W
Orange Park 17 30 10N 81 42W
Orange Walk 65 18 6N 88 33W
Orangeburg 46 33 30N 80 52W
Orangeburg County ◇ 46 33 20N 80 30W
Orangevale 14 38 41N 121 13W
Orangeville, Canada 60 43 55N 80 5W
Orangeville, Ill. 21 42 28N 89 39W
Orangeville, Pa. 45 41 5N 76 25W
Orangeville, Utah 52 39 14N 111 3W
Oranienburg 88 52 45N 13 15 E
Oranje → 123 28 41 S 16 28 E
Oranje Vrystaat □ 123 28 30 S 27 0 E
Oranjemund 123 28 38 S 16 29 E
Or'Aquiva 104 32 30N 34 54 E
Oras 111 12 9N 125 28 E
Orăştie 95 45 50N 23 10 E
Oraşul Stalin = Braşov 89 45 38N 25 35 E
Oraya, La 72 11 32 S 75 54W
Orbetello 94 42 26N 11 11 E
Orbisonia 45 40 15N 77 54W
Orbost 127 37 40 S 148 29 E
Orcadas 5 60 44 S 44 37W
Orcas 53 48 36N 122 57W
Orcas I. 53 48 42N 122 56W
Orchard, Colo. 16 40 20N 104 7W
Orchard, Idaho 20 43 19N 116 2W
Orchard, Iowa 23 43 14N 92 47W
Orchard, Nebr. 34 42 20N 98 15W
Orchard City 16 38 50N 107 58W
Orchard Homes 33 46 55N 114 4W
Orchard Park 39 42 46N 78 45W
Orchard Valley 56 41 6N 104 49W
Orchards 53 45 40N 122 34W
Orchila, Isla 70 11 48N 66 10W
Orcopampa 72 15 20 S 72 23W
Ord 34 41 36N 98 56W
Ord → 126 15 33 S 138 15 E
Ord, Mt., Australia 126 17 20 S 125 34 E
Ord, Mt., U.S.A. 50 30 18N 103 30W
Orderville 52 37 17N 112 38W
Ordos = Mu Us Shamo 114 39 0N 109 0 E
Ordu 106 40 55N 37 53 E
Ordway 16 38 13N 103 46W
Ordzhonikidze 99 43 0N 44 35 E
Ore City 51 32 48N 94 43W
Ore Mts. = Erzgebirge 88 50 25N 13 0 E
Orealla 71 5 15N 57 23W
Oreana, Idaho 20 43 3N 116 24W
Oreana, Ill. 21 39 56N 88 52W
Oreana, Nev. 35 40 20N 118 19W
Örebro 97 59 20N 15 18 E
Örebro län □ 97 59 27N 15 0 E
Oregon, Ill. 21 42 1N 89 20W
Oregon, Mo. 32 39 59N 95 9W
Oregon, Ohio 42 41 38N 83 25W
Oregon, Wis. 55 42 56N 89 23W
Oregon □ 44 44 0N 121 0W
Oregon Butte 53 46 7N 117 41W
Oregon Caves National Monument 44 42 6N 123 24W
Oregon City 44 45 21N 122 36W
Oregon County ◇ 32 36 40N 91 25W
Oregon Dunes Nat. Rec. Area 44 42 3N 123 26W
Orekhovo-Zuyevo 98 55 50N 38 55 E
Orel 98 52 57N 36 3 E
Orem 52 40 19N 111 42W
Orenburg 98 51 45N 55 6 E
Orense 91 42 19N 7 55W
Orepuki 128 46 19 S 167 46 E
Orford Ness 83 52 6N 1 31 E
Organ 38 32 26N 106 36W
Organ Pipe Cactus National Monument 12 32 0N 113 10W
Orgün 107 32 55N 69 12 E
Orhon Gol → 113 49 30N 106 0 E
Orick 14 41 17N 124 4W
Orient, Iowa 23 41 12N 94 25W
Orient, Maine 26 45 49N 67 50W
Orient, S. Dak. 47 44 54N 99 5W
Orient, Wash. 53 48 52N 118 12W
Oriental 40 35 2N 76 42W
Oriental, Cordillera, Bolivia 73 17 0 S 66 0W
Oriental, Cordillera, Colombia 70 6 0N 73 0W
Oriente 76 38 44 S 60 37W
Orihuela 91 38 7N 0 55W
Orin 56 42 39N 105 12W
Orinda 14 37 53N 122 11W
Orinduik 71 4 40N 60 3W
Orinoco → 71 9 15N 61 30W
Orion, Ala. 10 31 58N 86 0W
Orion, Ill. 21 41 21N 90 23W
Orion, Okla. 43 36 13N 98 47W
Oriska 41 46 56N 97 47W
Oriskany 39 43 10N 75 20W
Orissa □ 109 20 0N 84 0 E
Oristano 94 39 54N 8 35 E
Oristano, Golfo di 94 39 50N 8 22 E
Orituco → 70 8 45N 67 27W
Orizaba 65 18 50N 97 10W
Orizare 95 42 44N 27 39 E
Orizona 75 17 3 S 48 18W
Orkanger 96 63 18N 9 52 E
Orkla → 96 63 18N 9 51 E
Orkney □ 84 59 0N 3 0W
Orkney Is. 84 59 0N 3 0W
Orla 50 31 50N 103 55W
Orland 14 39 45N 122 12W
Orlando, Fla. 17 28 33N 81 23W
Orlando, Okla. 43 36 9N 97 23W
Orléanais 90 48 0N 2 0 E
Orléans, France 90 47 54N 1 52 E
Orleans, Calif. 14 41 18N 123 32W
Orleans, Ind. 22 38 40N 86 27W
Orleans, Mass. 28 41 47N 69 59W
Orleans, Nebr. 34 40 8N 99 27W
Orleans, Vt. 36 44 49N 72 12W
Orléans, Î. d' 61 46 54N 70 58W
Orleans County ◇, N.Y. 39 43 15N 78 10W
Orleans County ◇, Vt. 36 44 45N 72 15W
Orleans Parish ◇ 25 29 58N 90 4W
Orlik 101 52 30N 99 55 E
Orlinda 48 36 36N 86 43W
Ormara 107 25 16N 64 33 E
Ormoc 111 11 0N 124 37 E
Ormond 128 38 33 S 177 56 E
Ormond Beach 17 29 17N 81 3W
Ormond-by-the-Sea 17 29 21N 81 4W
Ormsby 30 43 51N 94 42W
Orne □ 90 48 40N 0 5 E
Örnsköldsvik 96 63 17N 18 40 E
Oro → 64 25 35N 105 2W
Oro Grande 15 34 36N 117 20W
Orocovis 57 18 14N 66 23W
Orocué 70 4 48N 71 20W
Orofino 20 46 29N 116 15W
Orogrande 38 32 24N 106 5W
Oromocto 61 45 54N 66 29W
Orono 26 44 53N 68 40W
Oronoco 30 44 10N 92 32W
Oroqen Zizhiqi 114 50 34N 123 43 E
Oroquieta 111 8 32N 123 44 E
Orós 74 6 15 S 38 55W
Orosei 94 40 20N 9 40 E
Orotukan 101 62 16N 151 42 E
Orovada 35 41 34N 117 47W
Oroville, Calif. 14 39 31N 121 33W
Oroville, Wash. 53 48 56N 119 26W
Oroville, L. 14 39 33N 121 29W
Oroville Dam 14 39 33N 121 29W
Orpha 56 42 51N 105 30W
Orr, Minn. 30 48 3N 92 50W
Orr, Okla. 43 34 2N 97 32W
Orrick 32 39 13N 94 7W
Orrin 41 48 6N 100 10W
Orrville 42 40 50N 81 46W
Orsha 98 54 30N 30 25 E
Orsk 98 51 12N 58 34 E
Orşova 89 44 41N 22 25 E
Ortegal, C. 91 43 43N 7 52W
Orteguaza → 70 0 43N 75 16W
Orthez 90 43 29N 0 48W
Ortigueira 91 43 40N 7 50W
Orting 53 47 6N 122 12W
Ortles 94 46 31N 10 33 E
Ortley 47 45 20N 97 12W
Ortón → 72 10 50 S 67 0W
Ortona 94 42 21N 14 24 E
Ortonville 30 45 19N 96 27W
Orūmīyeh 106 37 40N 45 0 E
Orūmīyeh, Daryācheh-ye 106 37 50N 45 30 E
Oruro 72 18 0 S 67 9W
Oruro □ 72 18 40 S 67 30W
Oruzgān □ 107 33 30N 66 0 E
Orvieto 94 42 43N 12 8 E
Orwell 42 41 32N 80 52W
Orwell → 83 52 2N 1 12 E
Oryakhovo 95 43 40N 23 57 E
Osa 98 57 17N 55 26 E
Osa, Pen. de 66 8 0N 84 0W
Osage, Ark. 13 36 11N 93 24W
Osage, Iowa 23 43 17N 92 49W
Osage, Okla. 43 36 19N 96 24W
Osage, W. Va. 54 39 39N 80 1W
Osage, Wyo. 56 43 59N 104 25W
Osage → 32 38 36N 92 57W
Osage Beach 32 38 9N 92 37W
Osage City, Kans. 24 38 38N 95 50W
Osage City, Mo. 32 38 33N 92 2W
Osage County ◇, Kans. 24 38 40N 95 40W
Osage County ◇, Mo. 32 38 30N 91 45W
Osage County ◇, Okla. 43 36 40N 96 30W
Ōsaka 117 34 40N 135 30 E
Osakis 30 45 52N 95 9W
Osakis, L. 30 45 54N 95 7W
Osawatomie 24 38 31N 94 57W
Osborne 24 39 26N 98 42W
Osborne County ◇ 24 39 30N 98 45W
Osburn 20 47 30N 116 0W
Osceola, Ark. 13 35 42N 89 58W
Osceola, Iowa 23 41 2N 93 46W
Osceola, Mo. 32 38 3N 93 42W
Osceola, Nebr. 34 41 11N 97 33W
Osceola, Wis. 55 45 19N 92 42W
Osceola County ◇, Fla. 17 28 0N 81 0W
Osceola County ◇, Iowa 23 43 20N 95 35W
Osceola County ◇, Mich. 29 44 0N 85 20W
Osceola Mills 45 40 51N 78 16W
Osceola National Forest 17 30 20N 82 30W
Oscoda 29 44 26N 83 20W
Oscoda County ◇ 29 44 40N 84 10W
Oscura 38 33 29N 106 3W
Ösel = Saaremaa 98 58 30N 22 30 E
Osgood, Ind. 22 39 8N 85 18W
Osgood, Ohio 42 40 20N 84 30W
Osgood Mts. 35 41 10N 117 20W
Osh 100 40 37N 72 49 E
Oshawa 60 43 50N 78 50W
Oshkosh, Nebr. 34 41 24N 102 21W
Oshkosh, Wis. 55 44 1N 88 33W
Oshogbo 120 7 48N 4 37 E
Oshwe 122 3 25 S 19 28 E
Osica de Jos 95 44 14N 24 20 E
Osierfield 18 31 40N 83 7W
Osijek 95 45 34N 18 41 E
Osipenko = Berdyansk 99 46 45N 36 50 E
Oskaloosa, Iowa 23 41 18N 92 39W
Oskaloosa, Kans. 24 39 13N 95 19W
Oskarshamn 97 57 15N 16 27 E
Oskélanéo 60 48 5N 75 15W
Oslo, Norway 97 59 55N 10 45 E
Oslo, U.S.A. 30 48 12N 97 8W
Oslob 111 9 31N 123 26 E
Oslofjorden 97 59 20N 10 35 E
Osmanabad 108 18 5N 76 10 E
Osmaniye 106 37 5N 36 10 E
Osmond 34 42 22N 97 36W
Osnabrock 41 48 40N 98 9W
Osnabrück 88 52 16N 8 2 E
Osorio 77 29 53 S 50 17W
Osorno 78 40 25 S 73 0W
Osorno □ 78 40 34 S 73 9W
Osorno, Vol. 78 41 0 S 72 30W
Osoyoos 62 49 0N 119 30W
Ospika → 62 56 20N 124 0W
Osprey 17 27 12N 82 29W
Osprey Reef 127 13 52 S 146 36 E
Oss 87 51 46N 5 32 E
Ossa, Mt. 127 41 52 S 146 3 E
Óssa, Oros 95 39 47N 22 42 E
Ossabaw I. 18 31 50N 81 5W
Ossabaw Sd. 18 31 50N 81 6W
Osseo, Mich. 29 41 53N 84 33W
Osseo, Wis. 55 44 35N 91 13W
Ossian, Ind. 22 40 53N 85 10W
Ossian, Iowa 23 43 9N 91 46W
Ossineke 29 44 55N 83 26W
Ossining 39 41 10N 73 55W
Ossipee 36 43 41N 71 7W
Ossipee L. 36 43 42N 71 10W
Ossokmanuan L. 61 53 25N 65 0W
Ossora 101 59 20N 163 13 E
Ostend = Oostende 87 51 15N 2 50 E
Österdalälven → 97 61 30N 13 45 E
Östergötlands län □ 97 58 35N 15 45 E
Östersund 96 63 10N 14 38 E
Osterville 28 41 38N 70 22W
Østfold fylke □ 97 59 25N 11 25 E
Ostfriesische Inseln 88 53 45N 7 15 E
Ostia 94 41 40N 12 20 E
Ostrander 30 43 37N 92 26W
Ostrava 89 49 51N 18 18 E
Ostróda 89 53 42N 19 58 E
Ostrołeka 89 53 4N 21 32 E
Ostrov, Bulgaria 95 43 40N 24 9 E
Ostrov, Romania 95 44 6N 27 24 E
Ostrów Mazowiecka 89 52 50N 21 51 E
Ostrów Wielkopolski 89 51 36N 17 44 E
Ostrowiec-Świętokrzyski 89 50 55N 21 22 E
O'Sullivan Dam 53 46 59N 119 16W
Osum → 95 43 40N 24 50 E
Ōsumi-Kaikyō 117 30 55N 131 0 E
Ōsumi-Shotō 117 30 30N 130 0 E
Osuna 91 37 14N 5 8W
Oswegatchie → 39 44 42N 75 30W
Oswego, Ill. 21 41 41N 88 21W
Oswego, Kans. 24 37 10N 95 6W
Oswego, N.Y. 39 43 27N 76 31W
Oswego → 39 43 27N 76 30W
Oswego County ◇ 39 43 25N 76 10W
Oswestry 82 52 52N 3 3W
Osyka 31 31 0N 90 28W
Otago □ 128 44 44 S 169 10 E
Otago Harb. 128 45 47 S 170 42 E
Ōtake 117 34 12N 132 13 E
Otaki 128 40 45 S 175 10 E
Otaru 116 43 10N 141 0 E
Otaru-Wan = Ishikari-Wan 116 43 25N 141 1 E
Otavalo 70 0 13N 78 20W
Otavi 123 19 40 S 17 24 E
Otero County ◇, Colo. 16 38 0N 103 45W
Otero County ◇, N. Mex. 38 32 30N 105 45W
Othello 53 46 50N 119 10W
Otho 23 42 25N 94 9W
Otira Gorge 128 42 53 S 171 33 E
Otis, Colo. 16 40 9N 102 58W
Otis, Kans. 24 38 32N 99 3W
Otis, Mass. 28 42 12N 73 6W
Otisville 29 43 10N 83 31W
Otjiwarongo 123 20 30 S 16 33 E
Oto 23 42 17N 95 54W
Otoe 34 40 43N 96 7W
Otoe County ◇ 34 40 40N 96 0W
Otoineppu 116 44 44N 142 16 E
Otorohanga 128 38 12 S 175 14 E
Otoskwin → 60 52 13N 88 6W
Otosquen 63 53 17N 102 1W
Otranto 95 40 9N 18 28 E
Otranto, C. d' 95 40 7N 18 30 E
Otranto, Str. of 95 40 15N 18 40 E
Otsego 29 42 27N 85 42W
Otsego County ◇, Mich. 29 45 0N 84 40W
Otsego County ◇, N.Y. 39 42 40N 75 0W
Otsego L. 39 42 45N 74 52W
Ōtsu 117 35 0N 135 50 E
Ōtsuki 117 35 36N 138 57 E
Ottawa = Outaouais → 60 45 27N 74 8W
Ottawa, Canada 60 45 27N 75 42W
Ottawa, Ill. 21 41 21N 88 51W
Ottawa, Kans. 24 38 37N 95 16W
Ottawa, Ohio 42 41 1N 84 3W
Ottawa County ◇, Kans. 24 39 15N 97 45W
Ottawa County ◇, Mich. 29 42 50N 86 0W
Ottawa County ◇, Ohio 42 41 30N 83 9W
Ottawa County ◇, Okla. 43 36 50N 94 50W
Ottawa Is. 59 59 35N 80 10W
Ottawa National Forest 29 46 25N 89 15W
Otter 33 45 12N 106 12W
Otter Cr. →, Utah 52 38 10N 112 2W
Otter Cr. →, Vt. 36 44 13N 73 17W
Otter Creek 17 29 19N 82 46W
Otter Creek Reservoir 52 38 10N 112 1W
Otter L. 63 55 35N 104 39W
Otter Lake, Ill. 21 39 28N 89 56W
Otter Lake, Mich. 29 43 13N 83 28W
Otter Rapids, Ont., Canada 60 50 11N 81 39W
Otter Rapids, Sask., Canada 63 55 38N 104 44W
Otter Tail → 30 46 16N 96 36W
Otter Tail County ◇ 30 46 20N 95 45W
Otter Tail L. 30 46 24N 95 40W
Otterbein 22 40 29N 87 6W
Ottertail 30 46 26N 95 33W
Otterville 32 38 42N 93 0W
Ottosen 23 42 54N 94 23W
Ottumwa 23 41 1N 92 25W
Oturkpo 120 7 16N 8 8 E
Otway 42 38 52N 83 11W
Otway, Bahía 78 53 30 S 74 0W
Otway, C. 127 38 52 S 143 30 E
Otwock 89 52 5N 21 20 E
Ötztaler Alpen 88 46 45N 11 0 E
Ou → 112 20 4N 102 13 E
Ou-Sammyaku 116 39 20N 140 35 E
Ouachita 13 33 51N 92 50W
Ouachita → 25 31 38N 91 49W
Ouachita, L. 13 34 34N 93 12W
Ouachita County ◇ 13 33 35N 92 50W
Ouachita Mts. 43 34 40N 94 25W
Ouachita National Forest 43 34 50N 94 50W
Ouachita Parish ◇ 25 32 30N 92 7W
Ouadâne 120 20 50N 11 40W
Ouadda 121 8 15N 22 20 E
Ouagadougou 120 12 25N 1 30W
Ouahran = Oran 120 35 45N 0 39W
Ouallene 120 24 41N 1 11 E
Ouanda Djallé 121 8 55N 22 53 E
Ouango 122 4 19N 22 30 E
Ouargla 120 31 59N 5 16 E
Ouarzazate 120 30 55N 6 50W
Oubangi → 122 1 0N 17 50 E
Ouddorp 87 51 50N 3 57 E
Oude Rijn → 87 52 12N 4 24 E
Oudenaarde 87 50 50N 3 37 E
Oudtshoorn 123 33 35 S 22 14 E
Ouessant, Île d' 90 48 28N 5 6W
Ouesso 122 1 37N 16 5 E
Ouest, Pte. 61 49 52N 64 40W
Ouezzane 120 34 51N 5 35W
Ouidah 120 6 25N 2 0 E
Oujda 120 34 41N 1 55W
Oujeft 120 20 2N 13 0W
Ouled Djellal 120 34 28N 5 2 E
Oulu 96 65 1N 25 29 E

Oulu Pampas

Oulu □ 96 65 10N 27 20 E
Oulujärvi 96 64 25N 27 15 E
Oulujoki → 96 65 1N 25 30 E
Oum Chalouba 121 15 48N 20 46 E
Ounianga-Kébir 121 19 4N 20 29 E
Ounianga Sérir 121 18 54N 19 51 E
Our → 87 49 55N 6 5 E
Ouray, Colo. 16 38 1N 107 40W
Ouray, Utah 52 40 6N 109 41W
Ouray County ◇ 16 38 10N 107 45W
Ourém 74 1 33 S 47 6W
Ouricuri 74 7 53 S 40 5W
Ourinhos 77 23 0 S 49 54W
Ouro Fino 77 22 16 S 46 25W
Ouro Prêto 75 20 20 S 43 30W
Ourthe → 87 50 29N 5 35 E
Ouse →, E. Sussex, U.K. 83 50 43N 0 3 E
Ouse →, N. Yorks., U.K. 82 54 3N 0 7 E
Outagamie County ◇ 55 44 20N 88 30W
Outaouais → 60 45 27N 74 8W
Outardes → 61 49 24N 69 30W
Outer Hebrides 84 57 30N 7 40W
Outer I., Canada 61 51 10N 58 35W
Outer I., U.S.A. 55 47 2N 90 26W
Outer Santa Barbara Passage 15 33 15N 118 40W
Outjo 123 20 5 S 16 7 E
Outlook, Canada 63 51 30N 107 0W
Outlook, U.S.A. 33 48 53N 104 47W
Ouyen 127 35 1 S 142 22 E
Ouzinkie 11 57 56N 152 30W
Ovalau 128 17 40 S 178 48 E
Ovalle 76 30 33 S 71 18W
Ovando 33 47 1N 113 8W
Ovar 91 40 51N 8 40W
Ovejas 70 9 32N 75 14W
Over Flakkee 87 51 45N 4 5 E
Overbrook 24 38 47N 95 33W
Overijssel □ 87 52 25N 6 35 E
Overland 32 38 41N 90 22W
Overland Park 24 38 58N 94 40W
Overlea 27 39 22N 76 32W
Overly 41 48 41N 100 9W
Overpelt 87 51 12N 5 20 E
Overton, Nebr. 34 40 44N 99 32W
Overton, Nev. 35 36 33N 114 27W
Overton, Tex. 51 32 16N 94 59W
Overton County ◇ 49 36 23N 85 19W
Övertorneå 96 66 23N 23 38 E
Ovett 31 31 29N 89 2W
Ovid, Colo. 16 40 58N 102 23W
Ovid, Mich. 29 43 1N 84 22W
Ovid, N.Y. 39 42 41N 76 49W
Oviedo, Spain 91 43 25N 5 50W
Oviedo, U.S.A. 17 28 40N 81 13W
Owaka 128 46 27 S 169 40 E
Owambo 123 17 20 S 16 30 E
Owanka 47 44 1N 102 35W
Owasa 23 42 26N 93 12W
Owasco L. 39 42 50N 76 31W
Owase 117 34 7N 136 12 E
Owasso 43 36 16N 95 51W
Owatonna 30 44 5N 93 14W
Owbeh 107 34 28N 63 10 E
Owego 39 42 6N 76 16W
Owen 55 44 57N 90 33W
Owen County ◇, Ind. 22 39 20N 86 50W
Owen County ◇, Ky. 49 38 30N 84 50W
Owen Sound 60 44 35N 80 55W
Owendo 122 0 17N 9 30 E
Owens → 15 36 32N 117 59W
Owens L. 15 36 26N 117 57W
Owensboro 48 37 46N 87 7W
Owensville, Ark. 13 34 37N 92 49W
Owensville, Ind. 22 38 16N 87 41W
Owensville, Mo. 32 38 21N 91 30W
Owensville, Ohio 42 39 7N 84 8W
Owenton 49 38 32N 84 50W
Owings Mills 27 39 25N 76 47W
Owingsville 49 38 9N 83 46W
Owl → 63 57 51N 92 44W
Owl Creek Mts. 56 43 40N 108 55W
Owls Head 26 44 5N 69 4W
Owo 120 7 10N 5 39 E
Owosso 29 43 0N 84 10W
Owsley County ◇ 49 37 25N 83 40W
Owyhee 35 41 57N 116 6W
Owyhee → 44 43 49N 117 2W
Owyhee, L. 44 43 38N 117 14W
Owyhee County ◇ 20 42 45N 116 0W
Owyhee Mts. 20 42 45N 116 20W
Ox Mts. 85 54 6N 9 0W
Oxapampa 72 10 33 S 75 26W
Oxbow 26 46 25N 68 28W
Oxelösund 97 58 43N 17 15 E
Oxford, N.Z. 128 43 18 S 172 11 E
Oxford, U.K. 83 51 45N 1 15W
Oxford, Ala. 10 33 36N 85 51W
Oxford, Ark. 13 36 13N 91 56W
Oxford, Colo. 16 37 10N 107 43W
Oxford, Ind. 22 40 31N 87 15W
Oxford, Iowa 23 41 43N 91 47W
Oxford, Kans. 24 37 17N 97 10W
Oxford, La. 25 31 56N 93 38W
Oxford, Maine 26 44 8N 70 30W
Oxford, Mass. 28 42 7N 71 52W
Oxford, Md. 27 38 41N 76 11W
Oxford, Mich. 29 42 49N 83 16W
Oxford, Miss. 31 34 22N 89 31W
Oxford, N.C. 40 36 19N 78 35W
Oxford, N.Y. 39 42 27N 75 36W
Oxford, Nebr. 34 40 15N 99 38W
Oxford, Ohio 42 39 31N 84 45W
Oxford, Pa. 45 39 47N 75 59W
Oxford □ 83 51 45N 1 15W
Oxford County ◇ 26 44 30N 70 30W
Oxford Junction 23 41 59N 90 57W
Oxford L. 63 54 51N 95 37W
Oxford Pk. 20 42 16N 112 6W
Oxnard 15 34 12N 119 11W
Oxon Hill 27 38 48N 76 59W
Oya 110 2 55N 111 55 E
Oyama 117 36 18N 139 48 E
Oyapock → 71 4 8N 51 40W
Oyem 122 1 34N 11 31 E
Oyen 63 51 22N 110 28W
Oykel → 84 57 55N 4 26W
Oymyakon 101 63 25N 142 44 E
Oyo 120 7 46N 3 56 E
Oyón 72 10 37 S 76 47W
Oyster Bay 39 40 52N 73 32W
Ōyūbari 116 43 1N 142 5 E
Ozamis 111 8 15N 123 50 E
Ozan 13 33 51N 93 43W
Ozark, Ala. 10 31 28N 85 39W
Ozark, Ark. 13 35 29N 93 50W
Ozark, Mo. 32 37 1N 93 12W
Ozark County ◇ 32 36 40N 92 25W
Ozark National Forest 13 35 40N 93 20W
Ozark Plateau 32 37 0N 93 0W
Ozark Reservoir 13 35 30N 94 10W
Ozarks, L. of the 32 38 12N 92 38W
Ozarks Nat. Scenic Riverways 32 37 25N 91 12W
Ozaukee County ◇ 55 43 20N 88 0W
Ozette L. 53 48 6N 124 38W
Ozona 50 30 43N 101 12W
Ozone 49 35 53N 84 49W
Ozuluama 65 21 40N 97 50W
Ozun 95 45 47N 25 50 E

P

Pa-an 109 16 51N 97 40 E
Pa Sak → 112 15 30N 101 0 E
Paarl 123 33 45 S 18 56 E
Paatsi → 96 68 55N 29 0 E
Paauilo 19 20 2N 155 22W
Pab Hills 108 26 30N 66 45 E
Pablo 33 47 36N 114 7W
Pabna 109 24 1N 89 18 E
Pacaás Novos, Serra dos 73 10 45 S 64 15W
Pacaipampa 72 5 35 S 79 39W
Pacaja → 74 1 56 S 50 50W
Pacajus 74 4 10 S 38 31W
Pacaraima, Sierra 71 4 0N 62 30W
Pacarán 72 12 50 S 76 3W
Pacaraos 72 11 12 S 76 42W
Pacasmayo 72 7 20 S 79 35W
Pace 17 30 36N 87 10W
Pachacamac 72 12 14 S 77 53W
Pachitea → 72 8 46 S 74 33W
Pachiza 72 7 16 S 76 46W
Pacho 70 5 8N 74 10W
Pachpadra 108 25 58N 72 10 E
Pachuca 65 20 10N 98 40W
Pachuta 31 32 2N 88 53W
Pacific, Canada 62 54 48N 128 28W
Pacific, U.S.A. 32 38 29N 90 45W
Pacific-Antarctic Basin 125 46 0 S 95 0W
Pacific-Antarctic Ridge 125 43 0 S 115 0W
Pacific Beach 53 47 13N 124 12W
Pacific City 44 45 12N 123 57W
Pacific County ◇ 53 46 30N 123 55W
Pacific Grove 14 36 38N 121 56W
Pacific Ocean 124 10 0N 140 0W
Pacific Palisades 19 21 25N 157 58W
Pacifica 14 37 36N 122 30W
Pacitan 111 8 12 S 111 7 E
Packwood, Iowa 23 41 8N 92 5W
Packwood, Wash. 53 46 36N 121 40W
Pacofi 62 53 0N 132 30W
Pacolet 46 34 54N 81 46W
Pacolet Mills 46 34 55N 81 45W
Pacuí → 75 16 46 S 45 1W
Padaido, Kepulauan 111 1 5 S 138 0 E
Padang 110 1 0 S 100 20 E
Padangpanjang 110 0 40 S 100 20 E
Padangsidempuan 110 1 30N 99 15 E
Padauari → 71 0 15 S 64 5W
Padcaya 73 21 52 S 64 48W
Paddockwood 63 53 30N 105 30W
Paden 43 35 30N 96 34W
Paderborn 88 51 42N 8 44 E
Padilla 73 19 19 S 64 20W
Padina 95 44 50N 27 8 E
Padloping Island 59 67 0N 62 50W
Pádova 94 45 24N 11 52 E
Padre I. 50 27 10N 97 25W
Padre Island National Seashore 50 27 0N 97 25W
Padroni 16 40 47N 103 10W
Padstow 82 50 33N 4 57W
Padua = Pádova 94 45 24N 11 52 E
Paducah, Ky. 48 37 5N 88 37W
Paducah, Tex. 50 34 1N 100 18W
Paeroa 128 37 23 S 175 41 E
Pag 94 44 30N 14 50 E
Pagadian 111 7 55N 123 30 E
Pagai Selatan 110 3 0 S 100 15W
Pagai Utara 110 2 35 S 100 0 E
Pagalu 119 1 25 S 5 36 E
Pagastikós Kólpos 95 39 15N 23 0 E
Pagatan 110 3 33 S 115 59 E
Page, Ariz. 12 36 57N 111 27W
Page, N. Dak. 41 47 10N 97 34W
Page, Nebr. 34 42 26N 98 25W
Page City 24 39 5N 101 9W
Page County ◇, Iowa 23 40 45N 95 10W
Page County ◇, Va. 54 38 40N 78 28W
Pageland 46 34 46N 80 24W
Pago Pago 128 14 16 S 170 43W
Pagosa Springs 16 37 16N 107 1W
Paguate 38 35 8N 107 23W
Pagwa River 60 50 2N 85 14W
Pahala 19 19 12N 155 29W
Pahang □ 112 3 40N 102 20 E
Pahang → 112 3 30N 103 9 E
Pahaska 56 44 30N 109 58W
Pahiatua 128 40 27 S 175 50 E
Pahoa 19 19 30N 154 57W
Pahokee 17 26 50N 80 40W
Pahrump 35 36 12N 115 59W
Pahute Mesa 35 37 20N 116 45W
Paia 19 20 54N 156 22W
Paige 51 30 13N 97 7W
Paignton 83 50 26N 3 33W
Paiján 72 7 42 S 79 20W
Päijänne, L. 97 61 30N 25 30 E
Pailin 112 12 46N 102 36 E
Pailolo Channel 19 21 0N 156 40W
Painan 110 1 21 S 100 34 E
Paincourtville 25 29 59N 91 3W
Painesdale 29 47 3N 88 40W
Painesville 42 41 43N 81 15W
Paint → 42 45 58N 88 15W
Paint Hills = Nouveau Comptoir 60 53 0N 78 49W
Paint I. 63 55 28N 97 57W
Paint Rock, Ala. 10 34 40N 86 20W
Paint Rock, Tex. 51 31 31N 99 55W
Paint Rock → 10 34 28N 86 28W
Painted Desert 12 36 0N 111 0W
Painted Post 39 42 10N 77 6W
Paintsville 49 37 49N 82 48W
Pais Vasco 91 43 0N 2 30W
Paisley, U.K. 84 55 51N 4 27W
Paisley, U.S.A. 44 42 42N 120 32W
Paita 72 5 11 S 81 9W
Pajarito 38 34 59N 106 42W
Pak Lay 112 18 15N 101 27 E
Pakanbaru 110 0 30N 101 15 E
Pakaraima Mts. 71 6 0N 60 0W
Pakistan ■ 107 30 0N 70 0 E
Pakokku 109 21 20N 95 0 E
Pakse 112 15 5N 105 52 E
Paktīā □ 107 33 0N 69 15 E
Pala, Chad 121 9 25N 15 5 E
Pala, U.S.A. 15 33 22N 117 5W
Palacios 51 28 42N 96 13W
Palagruža 94 42 24N 16 15 E
Palam 108 19 0N 77 0 E
Palamós 91 41 50N 3 10 E
Palampur 108 32 10N 76 30 E
Palana 101 59 10N 159 59 E
Palanan 111 17 8N 122 29 E
Palanan Pt. 111 17 17N 122 30 E
Palangkaraya 110 2 16 S 113 56 E
Palani Hills 108 10 14N 77 33 E
Palanpur 108 24 10N 72 25 E
Palaoa Pt. 19 20 44N 156 58W
Palapye 123 22 30 S 27 7 E
Palatine 21 42 7N 88 3W
Palatka, U.S.A. 17 29 39N 81 38W
Palatka, U.S.S.R. 101 60 6N 150 54 E
Palauk 112 13 10N 98 40 E
Palawan 110 9 30N 118 30 E
Palayankottai 108 8 45N 77 45 E
Palca 72 19 7 S 69 9W
Palco 24 39 15N 99 34W
Paleleh 111 1 10N 121 50 E
Palembang 110 3 0 S 104 50 E
Palen Dry L. 15 33 46N 115 13W
Palena → 78 43 50 S 73 50W
Palena, L. 78 43 55 S 71 40W
Palencia 91 42 1N 4 34W
Palermo, Colombia 70 2 54N 75 26W
Palermo, Italy 94 38 8N 13 20 E
Palermo, Calif. 14 39 26N 121 33W
Palermo, N. Dak. 41 48 21N 102 14W
Palestine, Asia 104 32 0N 35 0 E
Palestine, Ark. 13 34 58N 90 54W
Palestine, Ill. 21 39 0N 87 37W
Palestine, Ohio 42 40 3N 84 45W
Palestine, Tex. 51 31 46N 95 38W
Palestine, L. 51 32 6N 95 27W
Paletwa 109 21 10N 92 50 E
Palghat 108 10 46N 76 42 E
Pali 108 25 50N 73 20 E
Palikea Pk. 19 21 25N 158 6W
Palisade, Colo. 16 39 7N 108 21W
Palisade, Nebr. 34 40 21N 101 7W
Palisades, Idaho 20 43 21N 111 13W
Palisades, Wash. 53 47 25N 119 54W
Palisades Reservoir 20 43 20N 111 12W
Palitana 108 21 32N 71 49 E
Palito Blanco 50 27 35N 98 11W
Palizada 65 18 18N 92 8W
Palk Bay 108 9 30N 79 15 E
Palk Strait 108 10 0N 79 45 E
Palm Bay 17 28 2N 80 35W
Palm Beach 17 26 43N 80 2W
Palm Beach County ◇ 17 26 45N 80 20W
Palm Desert 15 33 43N 116 22W
Palm Is. 127 18 40 S 146 35 E
Palm Springs 15 33 50N 116 33W
Palma, Canary Is. 120 28 40N 17 50W
Palma, Mozam. 122 10 46 S 40 29 E
Palma → 75 12 33 S 47 52W
Palma, B. de 91 39 30N 2 39 E
Palma, La, Canary Is. 120 28 40N 17 50W
Palma, La, Panama 66 8 15N 78 0W
Palma, La, Spain 91 37 21N 6 38W
Palma de Mallorca 91 39 35N 2 39 E
Palma Soriano 66 20 15N 76 0W
Palmaḥim 104 31 56N 34 44 E
Palmares 74 8 41 S 35 28W
Palmarito 70 7 37N 70 10W
Palmas 77 26 29 S 52 0W
Palmas, C. 120 4 27N 7 46W
Pálmas, G. di 94 39 0N 8 30 E
Palmas de Monte Alto 75 14 16 S 43 10W
Palmdale, Calif. 15 34 35N 118 7W
Palmdale, Fla. 17 26 57N 81 19W
Palmeira 75 25 25 S 50 0W
Palmeira dos Índios 74 9 25 S 36 37W
Palmeirais 74 6 0 S 43 0W
Palmeiras → 75 12 22 S 47 8W
Palmeirinhas, Pta. das 122 9 2 S 12 57 E
Palmelo 75 17 20 S 48 27W
Palmer, Alaska 11 61 36N 149 7W
Palmer, Iowa 23 42 38N 94 36W
Palmer, Kans. 24 39 38N 97 8W
Palmer, Mass. 28 42 9N 72 20W
Palmer, Nebr. 34 41 13N 98 15W
Palmer, Tenn. 49 35 21N 85 34W
Palmer → 126 24 46 S 133 25 E
Palmer Arch. 5 64 15 S 65 0W
Palmer Lake 16 39 7N 104 55W
Palmer Land 5 73 0 S 60 0W
Palmers Crossing 31 31 16N 89 15W
Palmerston, C. 127 21 32 S 149 29 E
Palmerston North 128 40 21 S 175 39 E
Palmerton 45 40 48N 75 37W
Palmetto, Fla. 17 27 31N 82 34W
Palmetto, Ga. 18 33 31N 84 40W
Palmetto, La. 25 30 43N 91 55W
Palmi 94 38 21N 15 51 E
Palmira, Argentina 76 32 59 S 68 34W
Palmira, Colombia 70 3 32N 76 16W
Palmyra = Tudmur 106 34 36N 38 15 E
Palmyra, Ill. 21 39 26N 90 0W
Palmyra, Ind. 22 38 24N 86 7W
Palmyra, Mo. 32 39 48N 91 32W
Palmyra, N.J. 37 40 1N 75 1W
Palmyra, Nebr. 34 40 42N 96 23W
Palmyra, Pa. 45 40 18N 76 36W
Palmyra, Va. 54 37 52N 78 16W
Palmyra Is. 125 5 52N 162 5W
Palo 23 42 4N 91 48W
Palo Alto 14 37 27N 122 10W
Palo Alto County ◇ 23 43 5N 94 40W
Palo Duro Cr. → 50 35 0N 101 55W
Palo Pinto 51 32 46N 98 18W
Palo Pinto County ◇ 51 32 45N 98 20W
Palo Verde, Ariz. 12 33 21N 112 41W
Palo Verde, Calif. 15 33 26N 114 44W
Paloma, La 76 30 35 S 71 0W
Palopo 111 3 0 S 120 16 E
Palos, Cabo de 91 37 38N 0 40W
Palouse 53 46 55N 117 4W
Palouse → 53 46 35N 118 13W
Palpa 72 14 30 S 75 15W
Palu, Indonesia 111 1 0 S 119 52 E
Palu, Turkey 106 38 45N 40 0 E
Paluan 111 13 26N 120 29 E
Pama 120 11 19N 0 44 E
Pamanukan 111 6 16 S 107 49 E
Pamekasan 111 7 10 S 113 28 E
Pamirs 100 37 40N 73 0 E
Pamlico → 40 35 20N 76 28W
Pamlico County ◇ 40 35 10N 76 45W
Pamlico Sd. 40 35 20N 76 0W
Pampa 50 35 32N 100 58W
Pampa, La □ 76 36 50 S 66 0W
Pampa de Agma 78 43 45 S 69 40W
Pampa de las Salinas 76 32 1 S 66 58W
Pampa Grande 73 18 5 S 64 6W
Pampa Hermosa 72 7 7 S 75 4W
Pampanua 111 4 16 S 120 8 E
Pampas, Argentina 76 35 0 S 63 0W

Pampas

Patrocínio

Pampas, Peru 72 12 20 S 74 50W
Pampas → 72 13 24 S 73 12W
Pamplico 46 34 0N 79 34W
Pamplin City 54 37 16N 78 41W
Pamplona, Colombia 70 7 23N 72 39W
Pamplona, Spain 91 42 48N 1 38W
Pamunkey → 54 37 32N 76 48W
Pana 21 39 23N 89 5W
Panaca 35 37 47N 114 23W
Panacea 17 30 2N 84 23W
Panagyurishte 95 42 30N 24 15 E
Panaitan 111 6 35 S 105 10 E
Panaji 108 15 25N 73 50 E
Panama, Panama 57 8 48N 79 55W
Panamá, Panama 66 9 0N 79 25W
Panama, Nebr. 34 40 36N 96 31W
Panama, Okla. 43 35 10N 94 40W
Panama ■ 66 8 48N 79 55W
Panama, Bay of 57 8 50N 79 20W
Panama Canal, Panama 57 9 20N 79 55W
Panama City 17 30 10N 85 40W
Panama City Beach 17 30 11N 85 48W
Panamint Range 15 36 20N 117 20W
Panamint Valley 15 36 15N 117 20W
Panão 72 9 55 S 75 55W
Panarukan 111 7 40 S 113 52 E
Panay 111 11 10N 122 30 E
Panay, G. 111 11 0N 122 30 E
Pancake Range 35 38 30N 115 50W
Pančevo 95 44 52N 20 41 E
Panciu 95 45 54N 27 8 E
Pancorbo, Paso 91 42 32N 3 5W
Pandan 111 11 45N 122 10 E
Pandegelang 111 6 25 S 106 0 E
Pandharpur 108 17 41N 75 20 E
Pando 77 34 44 S 56 0W
Pando □ 72 11 20 S 67 40W
Pandora 42 40 57N 83 58W
Panfilov 100 44 10N 80 0 E
Pang-Long 109 23 11N 98 45 E
Pang-Yang 109 22 7N 98 48 E
Pangani 122 5 25 S 38 58 E
Pangburn 13 35 26N 91 50W
Pangfou = Bengbu 115 32 58N 117 20 E
Pangil 122 3 10 S 26 35 E
Pangkah, Tanjung 111 6 51 S 112 33 E
Pangkajene 111 4 46 S 119 34 E
Pangkalanberandan 110 4 1N 98 20 E
Pangkalanbuun 110 2 41 S 111 37 E
Pangkalansusu 110 4 2N 98 13 E
Pangkalpinang 110 2 0 S 106 0 E
Pangkoh 110 3 5 S 114 8 E
Pangnirtung 59 66 8N 65 54W
Pangong Tso 108 34 0N 78 20 E
Pangrango 111 6 46 S 107 1 E
Panguipulli 78 39 38 S 72 20W
Panguitch 52 37 50N 112 26W
Pangutaran Group 111 6 18N 120 34 E
Panhandle 50 35 21N 101 23W
Paniau 19 21 56N 160 5W
Panjgur 107 27 0N 64 5 E
Panjim = Panaji 108 15 25N 73 50 E
Panjinad Barrage 107 29 22N 71 15 E
Panna 108 24 40N 80 15 E
Panola 10 32 57N 88 16W
Panola County ◇, Miss. 31 34 19N 89 57W
Panola County ◇, Tex. 51 32 9N 94 20W
Panora 23 41 42N 94 22W
Panorama 77 21 21 S 51 51W
Panshan 114 41 3N 122 2 E
Panshi 114 42 58N 126 5 E
Pantar 111 8 28 S 124 10 E
Pantelleria 94 36 52N 12 0 E
Pánuco 65 22 0N 98 15W
Panyam 120 9 27N 9 8 E
Panyu 115 22 51N 113 20 E
Pao →, Anzoátegui, Venezuela 71 8 6N 64 17W
Pao →, Apure, Venezuela 70 8 33N 68 1W
Paola 24 38 35N 94 53W
Paoli, Colo. 16 40 37N 102 28W
Paoli, Ind. 22 38 33N 86 28W
Paoli, Okla. 43 34 50N 97 15W
Paonia 16 38 52N 107 36W
Paoshan 109 25 7N 99 9 E
Paoting = Baoding 114 38 50N 115 28 E
Paot'ou = Baotou 114 40 32N 110 2 E
Paoua 122 7 9N 16 20 E
Papá, Hungary 89 47 22N 17 30 E
Papa, U.S.A. 19 19 13N 155 52W
Papaaloa 19 19 59N 155 13W
Papagayo → 65 16 36N 99 43W
Papagayo, Golfo de 66 10 30N 85 50W
Papago Indian Reservation 12 32 15N 112 0W
Papaikou 19 19 47N 155 6W
Papakura 128 37 4 S 174 59 E
Papantla 65 20 30N 97 30W
Papar 110 5 45N 116 0 E
Paparoa 128 36 6 S 174 16 E
Papawai Pt. 19 20 47N 156 32W
Papien Chiang = Da → 112 21 15N 105 20 E
Papigochic → 64 29 9N 109 40W
Papillion 34 41 9N 96 3W
Papineau 21 40 58N 87 43W
Paposo 76 25 0 S 70 30W
Papua New Guinea ■ 124 8 0 S 145 0 E
Papudo 76 32 29 S 71 27W
Papun 109 18 0N 97 30 E
Pará = Belém 74 1 20 S 48 30W
Pará □, Brazil 73 3 20 S 52 0W
Pará □, Surinam 71 40 0 S 53 0W
Paraburdoo 126 23 14 S 117 32 E
Paracas, Pen. 72 13 53 S 76 20W
Paracatu 75 17 10 S 46 50W
Paracatu → 75 16 30 S 45 4W
Parachinar 108 33 55N 70 5 E
Paracuru 74 3 24 S 39 4W
Parada, Punta 72 15 22 S 75 11W
Paradip 109 20 15N 86 35 E
Paradise, Calif. 14 39 46N 121 37W
Paradise, Kans. 24 39 7N 98 55W
Paradise, Mich. 29 46 38N 85 2W
Paradise, Mont. 33 47 23N 114 48W
Paradise, Nev. 35 36 9N 115 10W
Paradise, Utah 52 41 34N 111 50W
Paradise → 61 53 27N 57 19W
Paradise Hill 43 35 40N 95 5W
Paradise Valley, Ariz. 12 33 32N 111 57W
Paradise Valley, Nev. 35 41 30N 117 32W
Paradise Valley, Wyo. 56 42 49N 106 23W
Parado 111 8 42 S 118 30 E
Paragon 22 39 24N 86 34W
Paragonah 52 37 53N 112 46W
Paragould 13 36 3N 90 29W
Paraguá →, Bolivia 73 13 34 S 61 53W
Paragua →, Venezuela 71 6 55N 62 55W
Paragua, La 71 6 50N 63 20W
Paraguaçu → 75 12 45 S 38 54W
Paraguaçu Paulista 77 22 22 S 50 35W
Paraguaipoa 70 11 21N 71 57W
Paraguaná, Pen. de 70 12 0N 70 0W
Paraguarí 76 25 36 S 57 0W
Paraguarí □ 76 26 0 S 57 10W
Paraguay ■ 76 23 0 S 57 0W
Paraguay → 76 27 18 S 58 38W
Paraíba = João Pessoa 74 7 10 S 34 52W
Paraíba □ 74 7 0 S 36 0W
Paraíba do Sul → 75 21 37 S 41 3W
Parainen 97 60 18N 22 18 E
Paraiso, Mexico 65 18 24N 93 14W
Paraiso, Panama 57 9 3N 79 38W
Parakou 120 9 25N 2 40 E
Paramaribo 71 5 50N 55 10W
Parambu 74 6 13 S 40 43W
Paramillo, Nudo del 70 7 4N 75 55W
Paramirim 75 13 26 S 42 15W
Paramirim → 75 11 34 S 43 18W
Paramus 37 40 55N 74 4W
Paramushir, Ostrov 101 50 24N 156 0 E
Paran → 104 30 20N 35 10 E
Paraná, Argentina 76 31 45 S 60 30W
Paranã, Brazil 75 12 30 S 47 48W
Paraná □ 77 24 30 S 51 0W
Paraná → 76 33 43 S 59 15W
Paranaguá 77 25 30 S 48 30W
Paranaíba → 75 20 6 S 51 4W
Paranapanema → 77 22 40 S 53 9W
Paranapiacaba, Serra do 77 24 31 S 48 35W
Paranavaí 77 23 4 S 52 56W
Parang, Jolo, Phil. 111 5 55N 120 54 E
Parang, Mindanao, Phil. 111 7 23N 124 16 E
Parangaba 74 3 45 S 38 33W
Paratinga 75 12 40 S 43 10W
Paraúna 75 16 55 S 50 26W
Parbhani 108 19 8N 76 52 E
Parchim 88 53 25N 11 50 E
Parchment 29 42 20N 85 34W
Pardee Reservoir 14 38 16N 120 51W
Pardeeville 55 43 32N 89 18W
Pardes Hanna 104 32 28N 34 57 E
Pardo →, Bahia, Brazil 75 15 40 S 39 0W
Pardo →, Mato Grosso, Brazil 75 21 46 S 52 9W
Pardo →, Minas Gerais, Brazil 75 15 48 S 44 48W
Pardo →, São Paulo, Brazil 75 20 10 S 48 38W
Pardubice 88 50 3N 15 45 E
Pare 111 7 43 S 112 12 E
Parecis, Serra dos 73 13 0 S 60 0W
Parelhas 74 6 41 S 36 39W
Paren 101 62 30N 163 15 E
Parent 60 47 55N 74 35W
Parent, Lac 60 48 31N 77 1W
Parepare 111 4 0 S 119 40 E
Parfuri 123 22 28 S 31 17 E
Parguba 98 62 20N 34 27 E
Parguera 57 17 59N 67 3W
Paria → 12 36 52N 111 36W
Paria, Golfo de 70 10 20N 62 0W
Paria, Pen. de 71 10 50N 62 30W
Paria Plateau 12 36 50N 111 50W
Pariaguán 71 8 51N 64 34W
Pariaman 110 0 47 S 100 11 E
Paricatuba 71 4 26 S 61 53W
Paricutín, Cerro 64 19 28N 102 15W
Parigi, Java, Indonesia 111 7 42 S 108 29 E
Parigi, Sulawesi, Indonesia 111 0 50 S 120 5 E
Parika 71 6 50N 58 20W
Parima, Serra 71 2 30N 64 0W
Parinari 72 4 35 S 74 25W
Parincea 95 46 27N 27 9 E
Paring 95 45 20N 23 37 E
Paringul-Mare 89 45 20N 23 37 E
Parintins 71 2 40 S 56 50W
Pariparit Kyun 109 14 55 S 93 45 E
Paris, Canada 60 43 12N 80 25W
Paris, France 90 48 50N 2 20 E
Paris, Ark. 13 35 18N 93 44W
Paris, Idaho 20 42 14N 111 24W
Paris, Ill. 21 39 36N 87 42W
Paris, Ky. 49 38 13N 84 15W
Paris, Maine 26 44 16N 70 30W
Paris, Mo. 32 39 29N 92 0W
Paris, Tenn. 48 36 18N 88 19W
Paris, Tex. 51 33 40N 95 33W
Paris, Ville de □ 90 48 50N 2 20 E
Parish 39 43 25N 76 8W
Parishville 39 44 38N 74 49W
Pariti 111 10 15 S 123 45 E
Park 24 39 7N 100 22W
Park → 41 48 28N 97 9W
Park City, Kans. 24 37 48N 97 20W
Park City, Ky. 48 37 6N 86 3W
Park City, Mont. 33 45 38N 108 55W
Park City, Utah 52 40 39N 111 30W
Park County ◇, Colo. 16 39 0N 105 45W
Park County ◇, Mont. 33 45 30N 110 30W
Park County ◇, Wyo. 56 44 30N 109 30W
Park Falls 55 45 56N 90 27W
Park Forest 21 41 29N 87 40W
Park Range 16 40 0N 106 30W
Park Rapids 30 46 55N 95 4W
Park Ridge, Ill. 21 42 2N 87 51W
Park Ridge, N.J. 37 41 2N 74 2W
Park River 41 48 24N 97 45W
Park Valley 52 41 49N 113 20W
Parkdale, Ark. 13 33 7N 91 33W
Parkdale, Colo. 16 38 29N 105 23W
Parkdale, Oreg. 44 45 31N 121 36W
Parke County ◇ 22 39 45N 87 10W
Parker, Ariz. 12 34 9N 114 17W
Parker, Colo. 16 39 31N 104 46W
Parker, Kans. 24 38 18N 95 0W
Parker, S. Dak. 47 43 24N 97 8W
Parker, Wash. 53 46 30N 120 28W
Parker City 22 40 11N 85 12W
Parker County ◇ 51 32 46N 97 48W
Parker Dam 12 34 18N 114 8W
Parkers Prairie 30 46 9N 95 20W
Parkersburg, Ill. 21 38 36N 88 3W
Parkersburg, Iowa 23 42 35N 92 47W
Parkersburg, W. Va. 54 39 16N 81 34W
Parkerview 63 51 21N 103 18W
Parkerville 24 38 46N 96 40W
Parkes, A.C.T., Australia 127 35 18 S 149 8 E
Parkes, N.S.W., Australia 127 33 9 S 148 11 E
Parkesburg 45 39 58N 75 55W
Parkin 13 35 16N 90 34W
Parkland 53 47 9N 122 26W
Parkrose 44 45 34N 122 33W
Parks, Ark. 13 34 48N 93 58W
Parks, Nebr. 34 40 3N 101 44W
Parkside 63 53 10N 106 33W
Parksley 54 37 47N 75 39W
Parkston 47 43 24N 97 59W
Parksville, Canada 62 49 20N 124 21W
Parksville, U.S.A. 46 33 47N 82 13W
Parkton 27 39 40N 76 40W
Parkville 27 39 23N 76 33W
Parle, L. qui 30 45 1N 95 52W
Parlier 15 36 37N 119 32W
Parma, Italy 94 44 50N 10 20 E
Parma, Idaho 20 43 47N 116 57W
Parma, Mich. 29 42 16N 84 36W
Parma, Mo. 32 36 37N 89 48W
Parma, Ohio 42 41 23N 81 43W
Parmelee 47 43 19N 101 2W
Parmer County ◇ 50 34 38N 102 45W
Parnaguá 74 10 10 S 44 38W
Parnaíba, Piauí, Brazil 74 2 54 S 41 47W
Parnaíba, São Paulo, Brazil 73 19 34 S 51 14W
Parnaíba → 74 3 0 S 41 50W
Parnamirim 74 8 5 S 39 34W
Parnarama 74 5 31 S 43 6W
Parnassós 95 38 35N 22 30 E
Parnell, Iowa 23 41 35N 92 0W
Parnell, Mo. 32 40 26N 94 37W
Pärnu 98 58 28N 24 33 E
Paroo → 127 31 28 S 143 32 E
Paroo Chan. 127 30 50 S 143 35 E
Páros 95 37 5N 25 12 E
Parowan 52 37 51N 112 50W
Parral 76 36 10 S 71 52W
Parramore I. 54 37 32N 75 39W
Parras 64 25 30N 102 20W
Parrett → 83 51 7N 2 58W
Parris I. 46 32 20N 80 41W
Parrish, Ala. 10 33 44N 87 17W
Parrish, Fla. 17 27 35N 82 26W
Parrott 18 31 54N 84 31W
Parrsboro 61 45 30N 64 25W
Parry Is. 4 77 0N 110 0W
Parry Sound 60 45 20N 80 0W
Parshall, Colo. 16 40 3N 106 11W
Parshall, N. Dak. 41 47 57N 102 8W
Parsippany 37 40 52N 74 26W
Parsnip → 62 55 10N 123 2W
Parsons, Kans. 24 37 20N 95 16W
Parsons, Tenn. 48 35 39N 88 8W
Parsons, W. Va. 54 39 6N 79 41W
Parsonsburg 27 38 22N 75 28W
Partridge 24 37 58N 98 5W
Paru →, Brazil 71 1 33 S 52 38W
Parú →, Venezuela 70 4 20N 66 27W
Paru de Oeste → 71 1 30N 56 0W
Parucito → 71 5 18N 65 59W
Paruro 72 13 45 S 71 50W
Parvān □ 107 35 0N 69 0 E
Parvatipuram 109 18 50N 83 25 E
Pas-de-Calais □ 90 50 30N 2 30 E
Pasadena, Calif. 15 34 9N 118 9W
Pasadena, Tex. 51 29 43N 95 13W
Pasaje 70 3 23 S 79 50W
Pasaje → 76 25 39 S 63 56W
Pascagoula 31 30 21N 88 33W
Pascagoula → 31 30 23N 88 37W
Pasco 53 46 14N 119 6W
Pasco □ 72 10 40 S 75 0W
Pasco, Cerro de 72 10 45 S 76 10W
Pasco County ◇ 17 28 20N 82 30W
Pascoag 28 41 57N 71 42W
Pasfield L. 63 58 24N 105 20W
Pashmakli = Smolyan 95 41 36N 24 38 E
Pasir Mas 112 6 2N 102 8 E
Pasir Putih 112 5 50N 102 24 E
Pasirian 111 8 13 S 113 8 E
Paskenta 14 39 53N 122 33W
Pasley, C. 126 33 52 S 123 35 E
Pasni 107 25 15N 63 27 E
Paso de Indios 78 43 55 S 69 0W
Paso de los Libres 76 29 44 S 57 10W
Paso de los Toros 76 32 45 S 56 30W
Paso Flores 78 40 35 S 70 38W
Paso Robles 15 35 38N 120 41W
Pasorapa 73 18 16 S 64 37W
Paspébiac 61 48 3N 65 17W
Pasquotank County ◇ 40 36 15N 76 10W
Pass Christian 31 30 19N 89 15W
Passaconaway 36 43 59N 71 22W
Passadumkeag 26 45 11N 68 37W
Passage West 85 51 52N 8 20W
Passaic, Mo. 32 38 19N 94 21W
Passaic, N.J. 37 40 51N 74 7W
Passaic County ◇ 37 41 0N 74 20W
Passau 88 48 34N 13 27 E
Passero, C. 94 36 42N 15 8 E
Passo Fundo 77 28 10 S 52 20W
Passos 75 20 45 S 46 37W
Passumpsic → 36 44 18N 72 3W
Pastaza □ 70 2 0 S 77 0W
Pastaza → 70 4 50 S 76 52W
Pasto 70 1 13N 77 17W
Pastol B. 11 63 7N 163 15W
Pastora Peak 12 36 47N 109 10W
Pastos Bons 74 6 36 S 44 5W
Pastura 38 34 47N 104 57W
Pasuruan 111 7 40 S 112 44 E
Pat Mayse L. 51 33 51N 95 33W
Patagonia, Argentina 78 45 0 S 69 0W
Patagonia, U.S.A. 12 31 33N 110 45W
Patan, India 108 23 54N 72 14 E
Patan, Nepal 109 27 40N 85 20 E
Patani 111 0 20N 128 50 E
Patapsco 27 39 32N 76 54W
Patapsco → 27 39 11N 76 28W
Patch Grove 55 42 56N 90 58W
Patchogue 39 40 46N 73 1W
Patea 128 39 45 S 174 30 E
Pategi 120 8 50N 5 45 E
Paternò 94 37 34N 14 53 E
Pateros 53 48 3N 119 54W
Paterson, N.J. 37 40 55N 74 11W
Paterson, Wash. 53 45 56N 119 36W
Patesville 48 37 47N 86 43W
Pathankot 108 32 18N 75 45 E
Pathfinder Reservoir 56 42 28N 106 51W
Pathfork 49 36 45N 83 28W
Pati 111 6 45 S 111 3 E
Patía 70 2 4N 77 4W
Patía → 70 2 13N 78 40W
Patiala 108 30 23N 76 26 E
Patillas 57 18 1N 66 1W
Patillas, Puerto 57 17 57N 66 0W
Pativilca 72 10 42 S 77 48W
Patkai Bum 109 27 0N 95 30 E
Patman, L. 51 33 19N 94 10W
Pátmos 95 37 21N 26 36 E
Patna 109 25 35N 85 12 E
Patoka 21 38 45N 89 6W
Patoka L. 22 38 20N 86 40W
Paton 23 42 10N 94 16W
Patos 74 6 55 S 37 16W
Patos, Lag. dos 77 31 20 S 51 0 E
Patos de Minas 75 18 35 S 46 32W
Patquía 76 25 30N 102 11W
Pátrai 95 38 14N 21 47 E
Pátraikós, Kólpos 95 38 17N 21 30 E
Patricia 50 32 33N 102 1W
Patricio Lynch, I. 78 48 35 S 75 30W
Patrick 46 34 34N 80 3W
Patrick County ◇ 54 36 55N 80 10W
Patrocínio 75 18 57 S 47 0W

Patsaliga **Perley**

Patsaliga → **10** 31 22N 86 31W
Pattani **112** 6 48N 101 15 E
Patten **26** 46 0N 68 38W
Patterson, Calif. **14** 37 28N 121 8W
Patterson, Ga. **18** 31 23N 82 8W
Patterson, Idaho **20** 44 32N 113 43W
Patterson, La. **25** 29 42N 91 18W
Patterson, Mo. **32** 37 11N 90 33W
Patterson, Pt. **29** 45 58N 85 39W
Patti **94** 38 8N 14 57 E
Pattison **31** 31 53N 90 53W
Patton **45** 40 38N 78 39W
Pattonsburg **32** 40 3N 94 8W
Patu **74** 6 6 S 37 38W
Patuakhali **109** 22 20N 90 25 E
Patuca → **66** 15 50N 84 18W
Patuca, Punta **66** 15 49N 84 14W
Patuxent → **27** 38 18N 76 25W
Pátzcuaro **64** 19 30N 101 40W
Pau **90** 43 19N 0 25W
Pau d' Arco **74** 7 30 S 49 22W
Pau dos Ferros **74** 6 7 S 38 10W
Paucartambo **72** 13 19 S 71 35W
Pauillac **90** 45 11N 0 46W
Pauini **72** 7 40 S 66 58W
Pauini → **71** 1 42 S 62 50W
Pauk **109** 21 27N 94 30 E
Paul **20** 42 36N 113 47W
Paul I. **61** 56 30N 61 20W
Paul Isnard **71** 4 47N 54 1W
Paul Spur **12** 31 22N 109 44W
Paulden **12** 34 53N 112 28W
Paulding, Miss. **31** 32 2N 89 2W
Paulding, Ohio **42** 41 8N 84 35W
Paulding County ◇, Ga. **18** 34 0N 84 50W
Paulding County ◇, Ohio **42** 41 8N 84 35W
Paulina **44** 44 8N 119 58W
Paulina Marsh **44** 43 15N 121 0W
Paulina Pk. **44** 43 41N 121 15W
Paulins Kill → **37** 40 55N 75 5W
Paulis = Isiro **122** 2 53N 27 40 E
Paulista **74** 7 57 S 34 53W
Paulistana **74** 8 9 S 41 9W
Paullina **23** 42 59N 95 41W
Paulo Afonso **74** 9 21 S 38 15W
Paulo de Faria **75** 20 2 S 49 24W
Pauls Valley **43** 34 44N 97 13W
Paulsboro **37** 39 50N 75 15W
Pausa **72** 15 16 S 73 22W
Pauto → **70** 5 9N 70 55W
Pauwela **19** 20 56N 156 19W
Pavant Range **52** 39 10N 112 5W
Pavia **94** 45 10N 9 10 E
Pavillion **56** 43 15N 108 42W
Pavlikeni **95** 43 14N 25 20 E
Pavlodar **100** 52 33N 77 0 E
Pavlograd **99** 48 30N 35 52 E
Pavlovo, Gorkiy, U.S.S.R. **98** 55 58N 43 5 E
Pavlovo, Yakut A.S.S.R., U.S.S.R. **101** 63 5N 115 25 E
Pavlovsk **99** 50 26N 40 5 E
Pavo **18** 30 58N 83 45W
Paw Creek **40** 35 17N 80 56W
Paw Paw, Mich. **29** 42 13N 85 53W
Paw Paw, W. Va. **54** 39 32N 78 28W
Paw Paw Lake **29** 42 13N 86 16W
Pawcatuck **28** 41 22N 71 52W
Pawhuska **43** 36 40N 96 20W
Pawlet **36** 43 20N 73 12W
Pawling **39** 41 34N 73 36W
Pawnee, Ill. **21** 39 36N 89 35W
Pawnee, Okla. **43** 36 20N 96 48W
Pawnee → **24** 38 10N 99 6W
Pawnee City **34** 40 7N 96 9W
Pawnee County ◇, Kans. **24** 38 10N 99 15W
Pawnee County ◇, Nebr. **34** 40 10N 96 20W
Pawnee County ◇, Okla. **43** 36 20N 96 50W
Pawnee Cr. → **16** 40 34N 103 14W
Pawnee National Grassland **16** 40 40N 104 20W
Pawnee Rock **24** 38 16N 99 1W
Pawpaw **21** 41 41N 88 59W
Pawtucket **28** 41 53N 71 23W
Paxico **24** 39 4N 96 10W
Paxson **11** 63 2N 145 30W
Paxton, Ill. **21** 40 27N 88 6W
Paxton, Mass. **28** 42 19N 71 56W
Paxton, Nebr. **34** 41 7N 101 21W
Paya Bakri **112** 2 3N 102 44 E
Payakumbuh **110** 0 20 S 100 35 E
Payette **20** 44 5N 116 56W
Payette → **20** 44 5N 116 57W
Payette County ◇ **20** 44 0N 116 55W
Payette L. **20** 44 55N 116 7W
Payette National Forest **20** 45 10N 115 30W
Payne **42** 41 5N 84 44W
Payne Bay = Bellin **59** 60 0N 70 0W
Payne County ◇ **43** 36 5N 97 0W
Payne L. **59** 59 30N 74 30W
Paynesville **30** 45 23N 94 43W
Paysandú **76** 32 19 S 58 8W
Payson, Ariz. **12** 34 14N 111 20W
Payson, Ill. **21** 39 49N 91 15W
Payson, Utah **52** 40 3N 111 44W
Paytes **54** 38 13N 77 49W
Paz → **66** 13 44N 90 10W
Paz, Bahía de la **64** 24 15N 110 25W
Paz, La, Entre Ríos, Argentina **76** 30 50 S 59 45W
Paz, La, San Luis, Argentina **76** 33 30 S 67 20W
Paz, La, Bolivia **72** 16 20 S 68 10W
Paz, La, Hond. **66** 14 20N 87 47W
Paz, La, Mexico **64** 24 10N 110 20W
Paz, La □ **72** 15 30 S 68 0W
Paz Centro, La **66** 12 20N 86 41W
Pazar **106** 41 10N 40 50 E
Pazardzhik **95** 42 12N 24 20 E
Pazña **72** 18 36 S 66 55W
Pe Ell **53** 46 34N 123 18W
Pea → **17** 31 1N 85 51W
Pea Ridge **13** 36 27N 94 7W
Peabody, Kans. **24** 38 10N 97 7W
Peabody, Mass. **28** 42 31N 70 56W
Peace →, Canada **62** 59 0N 111 25W
Peace →, U.S.A. **17** 26 56N 82 6W
Peace Dale **28** 41 27N 71 30W
Peace Point **62** 59 7N 112 27W
Peace River **62** 56 15N 117 18W
Peach County ◇ **18** 32 30N 83 50W
Peach Creek **54** 37 53N 81 59W
Peach Orchard **13** 36 17N 90 40W
Peach Springs **12** 35 32N 113 25W
Peachtree City **18** 33 25N 84 35W
Peak, The **82** 53 24N 1 53W
Peak Range **127** 22 50 S 148 20 E
Peale, Mt. **52** 38 26N 109 14W
Pearblossom **15** 34 30N 117 55W
Pearce **12** 31 54N 109 49W
Pearisburg **54** 37 20N 80 44W
Pearl, Ill. **21** 39 28N 90 38W
Pearl, Miss. **31** 32 18N 90 12W
Pearl → **31** 30 11N 89 32W
Pearl and Hermes Reef **19** 27 55N 175 45W
Pearl City, Hawaii **19** 21 24N 157 59W
Pearl City, Ill. **21** 42 16N 89 50W
Pearl Harbor **19** 21 21N 157 57W
Pearl River, La. **25** 30 23N 89 45W
Pearl River, N.Y. **39** 41 4N 74 2W
Pearl River County ◇ **31** 30 40N 89 38W
Pearland **51** 29 34N 95 17W
Pearsall **51** 28 54N 99 6W
Pearse I. **62** 54 52N 130 14W
Pearson **18** 31 18N 82 51W
Peary Land **4** 82 40N 33 0W
Pease **30** 45 42N 93 39W
Pease → **51** 34 12N 99 2W
Pebane **123** 17 10 S 38 8 E
Pebas **70** 3 10 S 71 46W
Pebble, I. **78** 51 20 S 59 40W
Pebble Beach **14** 36 34N 121 57W
Peč **95** 42 40N 20 17 E
Peçanha **75** 18 33 S 42 34W
Pecatonica **21** 42 19N 89 22W
Pecatonica → **21** 42 26N 89 12W
Pechea **95** 45 36N 27 49 E
Pechenga **98** 69 30N 31 25 E
Pechora → **98** 68 13N 54 15 E
Pechorskaya Guba **98** 68 40N 54 0 E
Peck **29** 43 16N 82 49W
Peckerwood L. **13** 34 40N 91 30W
Pecos, N. Mex. **38** 35 35N 105 41W
Pecos, Tex. **50** 31 26N 103 30W
Pecos → **50** 29 42N 101 22W
Pecos County ◇ **50** 30 53N 102 53W
Pecos Plains **38** 33 15N 104 10W
Pécs **89** 46 5N 18 15 E
Peculiar **32** 38 43N 94 28W
Pédernales **67** 18 2N 71 44W
Pedernales → **51** 30 26N 98 4W
Pedra Azul **75** 16 2 S 41 17W
Pedra Grande, Recifes de **75** 17 45 S 38 58W
Pedras Negras **72** 12 51 S 62 54W
Pedreiras **74** 4 32 S 44 40W
Pedrera, La **70** 1 18 S 69 43W
Pedro Afonso **74** 9 0 S 48 10W
Pedro Antonio Santos **65** 18 54N 88 15W
Pedro Bay **11** 59 47N 154 7W
Pedro Cays **66** 17 5N 77 48W
Pedro Chico **70** 1 4N 70 25W
Pedro de Valdivia **76** 22 55 S 69 38W
Pedro Juan Caballero **77** 22 30 S 55 40W
Pedro Miguel **57** 9 2N 79 37W
Pedro Miguel Locks **57** 9 1N 79 36W
Peduyim **104** 31 20N 34 37 E
Pee Dee → **46** 33 22N 79 16W
Peebles, U.K. **84** 55 40N 3 12W
Peebles, U.S.A. **42** 38 57N 83 24W
Peekskill **39** 41 17N 73 55W
Peel **82** 54 14N 4 40W
Peel → **58** 67 0N 135 0W
Peerless **33** 48 47N 105 50W
Peers **62** 53 40N 116 0W
Peetz **16** 40 58N 103 7W
Peever **47** 45 33N 96 57W
Pegasus Bay **128** 43 20 S 173 10 E
Pegram **48** 36 6N 87 3W
Pegu **109** 17 20N 96 29 E
Pegu Yoma **109** 19 0N 96 0 E
Pehuajó **76** 35 45 S 62 0W
Peine **76** 23 45 S 68 8W
Peixe **75** 12 0 S 48 40W
Peixe → **75** 21 31 S 51 58W
Peixoto de Azeredo → **73** 10 6 S 55 31W
Pekalongan **111** 6 53 S 109 40 E
Pekan **112** 3 30N 103 25 E
Pekin, Ill. **21** 40 35N 89 40W
Pekin, Ind. **22** 38 30N 86 0W
Pekin, N. Dak. **41** 47 48N 98 20W
Peking = Beijing **114** 39 55N 116 20 E
Pelabuhan Kelang **110** 3 0N 101 23 E
Pelabuhan Ratu, Teluk **111** 7 5 S 106 30 E
Pelabuhanratu **111** 7 0 S 106 32 E
Pelahatchie **31** 32 19N 89 48W
Pelaihari **110** 3 55 S 114 45 E
Peleaga **89** 45 22N 22 55 E
Pelechuco **72** 14 48 S 69 4W
Pelée, Mt. **67** 14 48N 61 0W
Pelee, Pt. **60** 41 54N 82 31W
Pelee I. **60** 41 47N 82 40W
Pelejo **72** 6 10 S 75 49W
Peleng **111** 1 20 S 123 30 E
Pelham, Ga. **18** 31 8N 84 9W
Pelham, Mass. **28** 42 24N 72 24W
Pelham, N.C. **40** 36 31N 79 28W
Pelican, Alaska **11** 57 58N 136 14W
Pelican, La. **25** 31 53N 93 35W
Pelican L., Canada **63** 52 28N 100 20W
Pelican L., U.S.A. **30** 48 4N 92 55W
Pelican Narrows **63** 55 10N 102 56W
Pelican Portage **62** 55 51N 112 35W
Pelican Rapids, Canada **63** 52 45N 100 42W
Pelican Rapids, U.S.A. **30** 46 34N 96 5W
Pelion **46** 33 46N 81 15W
Pelkosenniemi **96** 67 6N 27 28 E
Pell City **10** 33 35N 86 17W
Pella **23** 41 25N 92 55W
Pellston **29** 45 33N 84 47W
Pellville **48** 37 45N 86 49W
Pelly → **58** 62 47N 137 19W
Pelly Bay **59** 68 38N 89 50W
Pelly L. **58** 66 0N 102 0W
Peloncillo Mts. **12** 32 20N 109 0W
Peloponnes = Pelopónnisos □ **95** 37 10N 22 0 E
Pelopónnisos □ **95** 37 10N 22 0 E
Peloro, C. **94** 38 15N 15 40 E
Pelorus Sound **128** 40 59 S 173 59 E
Pelotas **77** 31 42 S 52 23W
Pelòvo **95** 43 26N 24 17 E
Pelvoux, Massif de **90** 44 52N 6 20 E
Pemadumcook L. **26** 45 42N 68 57W
Pemalang **111** 6 53 S 109 23 E
Pematang **110** 0 12 S 102 4 E
Pematangsiantar **110** 2 57N 99 5 E
Pemba **123** 5 0 S 39 45 E
Pemberton, Australia **126** 34 30 S 116 0 E
Pemberton, Canada **62** 50 25N 122 50W
Pemberton, Minn. **30** 44 1N 93 47W
Pemberton, N.J. **37** 39 58N 74 41W
Pemberville **42** 41 25N 83 28W
Pembina **41** 48 58N 97 15W
Pembina →, Canada **63** 49 0N 98 12W
Pembina →, U.S.A. **41** 48 58N 97 14W
Pembina County ◇ **41** 48 48N 97 37W
Pembine **55** 45 38N 87 59W
Pembroke, Canada **60** 45 50N 77 7W
Pembroke, U.K. **83** 51 41N 4 57W
Pembroke, Ga. **18** 32 8N 81 37W
Pembroke, Ky. **48** 36 47N 87 21W
Pembroke, Mass. **28** 42 5N 70 48W
Pembroke, N.C. **40** 34 41N 79 12W
Pembroke Pines **17** 26 0N 80 14W
Pemigewasset → **36** 43 26N 71 40W
Pemiscot County ◇ **32** 36 10N 89 50W
Pen Argyl **45** 40 52N 75 16W
Pen-y-Ghent **82** 54 10N 2 15W
Peña de Francia, Sierra de **91** 40 32N 6 10W
Peñalara, Pico **91** 40 51N 3 57W
Penalosa **24** 37 43N 98 19W
Penalva **74** 3 18 S 45 10W
Penang = Pinang **112** 5 25N 100 15 E
Penápolis **77** 21 30 S 50 0W
Peñarroya-Pueblonuevo **91** 38 19N 5 16W
Peñas, C. de **91** 43 42N 5 52W
Penas, G. de **78** 47 0 S 75 0W
Peñas, Pta. **71** 11 17N 62 0W
Penasco **38** 36 10N 105 41W
Pench'i = Benxi **114** 41 20N 123 48 E
Pend Oreille → **53** 49 4N 117 37W
Pend Oreille County ◇ **53** 48 30N 117 10W
Pend Oreille L. **20** 48 10N 116 21W
Pendembu **120** 9 7N 12 14W
Pendências **74** 5 15 S 36 43W
Pender **34** 42 7N 96 43W
Pender County ◇ **40** 34 30N 78 0W
Pendergrass **18** 34 10N 83 41W
Pendleton, Ind. **22** 40 0N 85 45W
Pendleton, Oreg. **44** 45 40N 118 47W
Pendleton, S.C. **46** 34 39N 82 47W
Pendleton County ◇, Ky. **49** 38 40N 84 20W
Pendleton County ◇, W. Va. **54** 38 47N 79 17W
Pendroy **33** 48 4N 112 18W
Penedo **74** 10 15 S 36 36W
Penelope **51** 31 52N 96 56W
Penetanguishene **60** 44 50N 79 55W
Penfield **45** 41 13N 78 35W
Pengalengan **111** 7 9 S 107 30 E
Penglai **114** 37 48N 120 42 E
Pengshui **115** 29 17N 108 12 E
Peniche **91** 39 19N 9 22W
Penicuik **84** 55 50N 3 14W
Penida **110** 8 45 S 115 30 E
Peninsular Malaysia □ **112** 4 0N 102 0 E
Penitente, Serra dos **74** 8 45 S 46 20W
Penmarch, Pte. de **90** 47 48N 4 22W
Penn Hills **45** 40 28N 79 52W
Penn Yan **39** 42 40N 77 3W
Pennant **63** 50 32N 108 14W
Pennell, Mt. **52** 37 58N 110 47W
Penner → **108** 14 35N 80 10 E
Pennines **82** 54 50N 2 20W
Pennington, Ala. **10** 32 13N 88 3W
Pennington, N.J. **37** 40 19N 74 48W
Pennington County ◇, Minn. **30** 48 5N 96 0W
Pennington County ◇, S. Dak. **47** 44 0N 103 0W
Pennington Gap **54** 36 46N 83 2W
Pennock **30** 45 9N 95 10W
Penns Grove **37** 39 44N 75 28W
Pennsauken **37** 39 58N 75 3W
Pennsboro **54** 39 17N 80 58W
Pennsburg **45** 40 23N 75 29W
Pennsville **37** 39 39N 75 31W
Pennsylvania □ **45** 40 45N 77 30W
Pennville **22** 40 30N 85 9W
Penny **62** 53 51N 121 20W
Penobscot → **26** 44 30N 68 48W
Penobscot B. **26** 44 35N 68 50W
Penobscot County ◇ **26** 45 0N 69 0W
Penola **127** 37 25 S 140 21 E
Penong **126** 31 59 S 133 5 E
Penonomé **66** 8 31N 80 21W
Penrhyn Is. **125** 9 0 S 158 30W
Penrith, Australia **127** 33 43 S 150 38 E
Penrith, U.K. **82** 54 40N 2 45W
Pensacola, Fla. **17** 30 25N 87 13W
Pensacola, Okla. **43** 36 28N 95 7W
Pensacola Mts. **5** 84 0 S 40 0W
Pense **63** 50 25N 104 59W
Pentecoste **74** 3 48 S 39 17W
Penticton **62** 49 30N 119 38W
Pentland **127** 20 32 S 145 25 E
Pentland Firth **84** 58 43N 3 10W
Pentland Hills **84** 55 48N 3 25W
Pentwater **29** 43 47N 86 26W
Penuelas **57** 18 4N 66 43W
Penwell **50** 31 45N 102 36W
Penylan L. **63** 61 50N 106 20W
Penza **98** 53 15N 45 5 E
Penzance **83** 50 7N 5 32W
Penzhino **101** 63 30N 167 55 E
Penzhinskaya Guba **101** 61 30N 163 0 E
Peoria, Ariz. **12** 33 35N 112 14W
Peoria, Ill. **21** 40 42N 89 36W
Peoria, Okla. **43** 36 54N 94 41W
Peoria County ◇ **21** 40 45N 89 45W
Peoria Heights **21** 40 45N 89 35W
Peotone **21** 41 20N 87 48W
Pep **38** 33 50N 103 20W
Pepacton Reservoir **39** 42 5N 74 58W
Pepeekeo **19** 19 51N 155 6W
Pepin **55** 44 27N 92 9W
Pepin County ◇ **55** 44 30N 92 10W
Pepperell **28** 42 40N 71 35W
Pequest → **37** 40 50N 75 5W
Pequop Mts. **35** 40 45N 114 40W
Pequot Lakes **30** 46 36N 94 19W
Perabumilih **110** 3 27 S 104 15 E
Perak → **112** 5 10N 101 4 E
Peralta **38** 34 50N 106 41W
Percé **61** 48 31N 64 13W
Perche **90** 48 31N 1 1 E
Perche Cr. → **32** 38 49N 92 24W
Percy **31** 33 7N 90 53W
Perdido **10** 31 0N 87 38W
Perdido →, Argentina **78** 42 55 S 67 0W
Perdido →, U.S.A. **10** 30 27N 87 23W
Perdido, Mte. **90** 42 40N 0 5 E
Perdido B. **10** 30 20N 87 30W
Pereira **70** 4 49N 75 43W
Pereira Barreto **75** 20 38 S 51 7W
Perekop **99** 46 10N 33 42 E
Perené → **72** 11 9 S 74 14W
Pereyaslav Khmelnitskiy **99** 50 3N 31 28 E
Pérez, I. **65** 22 24N 89 42W
Pergamino **76** 33 52 S 60 30W
Perham **30** 46 36N 95 34W
Perhentian, Kepulauan **112** 5 54N 102 42 E
Péribonca → **61** 48 45N 72 5W
Péribonca, L. **61** 50 1N 71 10W
Perico **76** 24 20 S 65 5W
Pericos **64** 25 3N 107 42W
Peridot **12** 33 18N 110 28W
Périgord **90** 45 0N 0 40 E
Périgueux **90** 45 10N 0 42 E
Perijá, Sierra de **70** 9 30N 73 3W
Perito Moreno **78** 46 36 S 70 56W
Peritoró **74** 4 20 S 44 18W
Perkasie **45** 40 22N 75 18W
Perkins **43** 35 58N 97 2W
Perkins County ◇, Nebr. **34** 40 45N 101 45W
Perkins County ◇, S. Dak. **47** 45 30N 102 30W
Perkinston **31** 30 47N 89 8W
Perlas, Arch. de las **66** 8 41N 79 7W
Perlas, Punta de **66** 12 30N 83 30W
Perley **30** 47 11N 96 48W

Perlis Pine Apple

Perlis □ 112 6 30N 100 15 E
Perm 98 58 0N 57 10 E
Perma 33 47 22N 114 35W
Pernambuco = Recife 74 8 0S 35 0W
Pernambuco □ 74 8 0S 37 0W
Pernell 43 34 34N 97 31W
Perouse Str., La 116 45 40N 142 0 E
Perow 62 54 35N 126 10W
Perpignan 90 42 42N 2 53 E
Perquimans County ◇ 40 36 10N 76 30W
Perrin 51 33 2N 98 4W
Perrine 17 25 36N 80 21W
Perris 15 33 47N 117 14W
Perro, L. del 38 34 41N 105 58W
Perry, Ark. 13 35 3N 92 48W
Perry, Fla. 17 30 7N 83 35W
Perry, Ga. 18 32 28N 83 44W
Perry, Ill. 21 39 47N 90 45W
Perry, Iowa 23 41 51N 94 6W
Perry, Kans. 24 39 5N 95 24W
Perry, Maine 26 44 58N 67 5W
Perry, Mich. 29 42 50N 84 13W
Perry, Mo. 32 39 26N 91 40W
Perry, N.Y. 39 42 43N 78 0W
Perry, Okla. 43 36 17N 97 14W
Perry, S.C. 46 33 38N 81 19W
Perry, Utah 52 41 28N 112 2W
Perry County ◇, Ala. 10 32 38N 87 19W
Perry County ◇, Ark. 13 35 0N 92 48W
Perry County ◇, Ill. 21 38 5N 89 20W
Perry County ◇, Ind. 22 38 5N 86 40W
Perry County ◇, Ky. 49 37 15N 83 15W
Perry County ◇, Miss. 31 31 12N 89 2W
Perry County ◇, Mo. 32 37 45N 89 50W
Perry County ◇, Ohio 42 39 43N 82 13W
Perry County ◇, Pa. 45 40 35N 77 5W
Perry County ◇, Tenn. 48 35 39N 87 50W
Perry Hall 27 39 25N 76 28W
Perry Lake 24 39 7N 95 26W
Perrydale 44 45 3N 123 16W
Perrysburg 42 41 34N 83 38W
Perrysville 42 40 40N 82 19W
Perryton 50 36 24N 100 48W
Perryville, Alaska 11 55 55N 159 9W
Perryville, Ark. 13 35 0N 92 48W
Perryville, Ky. 49 37 39N 84 57W
Perryville, Md. 27 39 34N 76 4W
Perryville, Mo. 32 37 43N 89 52W
Persepolis 107 29 55N 52 50 E
Perseverancia 73 14 44S 62 48W
Pershing County ◇ 35 40 20N 118 10W
Persia = Iran ■ 107 33 0N 53 0 E
Persia 23 41 35N 95 33W
Persian Gulf = The Gulf 107 27 0N 50 0 E
Person County ◇ 40 36 15N 79 0W
Perth, Australia 126 31 57S 115 52 E
Perth, Canada 60 44 55N 76 15W
Perth, U.K. 84 56 24N 3 27W
Perth, Kans. 24 37 11N 97 31W
Perth, N. Dak. 41 48 43N 99 28W
Perth Amboy 37 40 31N 74 16W
Peru, Ill. 21 41 20N 89 8W
Peru, Ind. 22 40 45N 86 4W
Peru, Kans. 24 37 5N 96 6W
Peru, N.Y. 39 44 35N 73 32W
Peru, Nebr. 34 40 29N 95 44W
Peru, Vt. 36 43 14N 72 54W
Peru ■ 70 8 0S 75 0W
Peru-Chile Trench 125 20 0S 72 0W
Perúgia 94 43 6N 12 24 E
Pervomaysk 99 48 10N 30 46 E
Pervouralsk 98 56 55N 60 0 E
Pésaro 94 43 55N 12 53 E
Pesca, La 65 23 46N 97 47W
Pescara 94 42 28N 14 13 E
Peshawar 108 34 2N 71 37 E
Peshtera 95 42 2N 24 18 E
Peshtigo → 55 44 58N 87 40W
Pesotum 21 39 55N 88 16W
Pesqueira 74 8 20S 36 42W
Pesqueria → 64 25 54N 99 11W
Petah Tiqwa 104 32 6N 34 53 E
Petal 31 31 21N 89 16W
Petaling Jaya 112 3 4N 101 42 E
Petaluma 14 38 14N 122 39W
Petange 87 49 33N 5 55 E
Petatlán 64 17 31N 101 16W
Petauke 123 14 14S 31 20 E
Petawawa 60 45 54N 77 17W
Petén Itzá, Lago 66 16 58N 89 50W
Petenwell L. 55 44 4N 90 1W
Peter 1st, I. 5 69 0S 91 0W
Peter Pond L. 63 55 55N 108 44W
Peterbell 60 48 36N 83 21W
Peterborough, Australia 127 32 58S 138 51 E
Peterborough, U.K. 83 52 35N 0 14W
Peterborough, U.S.A. 36 42 53N 71 57W
Peterhead 84 57 30N 1 49W
Peter's Mine 71 6 14N 59 20W
Petersburg, Alaska 11 56 48N 132 58W
Petersburg, Ill. 21 40 1N 89 51W
Petersburg, Ind. 22 38 30N 87 17W
Petersburg, Mich. 29 41 54N 83 43W
Petersburg, N. Dak. 41 48 0N 98 0W
Petersburg, N.J. 37 39 15N 74 43W
Petersburg, Nebr. 34 41 51N 98 5W
Petersburg, Ohio 42 40 55N 80 32W
Petersburg, Pa. 45 40 34N 78 3W
Petersburg, Tenn. 48 35 19N 86 38W
Petersburg, Tex. 50 33 52N 101 36W
Petersburg, Va. 54 37 14N 77 24W
Petersburg, W. Va. 54 39 1N 79 5W
Petersham 28 42 29N 72 11W
Peterson, Iowa 23 42 55N 95 21W
Peterson, Minn. 30 43 47N 91 50W
Peterstown 54 37 24N 80 48W
Petersville 49 38 27N 83 30W
Petit Bois I. 31 30 12N 88 26W
Petit-Cap 61 48 3N 64 30W
Petit Goâve 67 18 27N 72 51W
Petit Manan Pt. 26 44 24N 67 54W
Petitcodiac 61 45 57N 65 11W
Petite Baleine → 60 56 0N 76 45W
Petite Saguenay 61 48 15N 70 4W
Petitsikapau, L. 61 54 37N 66 25W
Petlad 108 22 30N 72 45 E
Peto 65 20 10N 88 53W
Petone 128 41 13S 174 53 E
Petoskey 29 45 22N 84 57W
Petra 104 30 20N 35 22 E
Petra, Ostrova 4 76 15N 118 30 E
Petra Velikogo, Zaliv 116 42 40N 132 0 E
Petrey 10 31 51N 86 13W
Petrich 95 41 24N 23 13 E
Petrified Forest National Park 12 35 0N 109 30W
Petrila 95 45 29N 23 29 E
Petrolândia 74 9 5S 38 20W
Petroleum 54 39 11N 81 16W
Petroleum County ◇ 33 47 7N 108 25W
Petrolia, Canada 60 42 54N 82 9W
Petrolia, Kans. 24 37 45N 95 29W
Petrolia, Tex. 51 34 1N 98 14W
Petrolina 74 9 24S 40 30W
Petropavlovsk 100 54 53N 69 13 E
Petropavlovsk-Kamchatskiy 101 53 3N 158 43 E
Petrópolis 75 22 33S 43 9W
Petros 49 36 6N 84 27W
Petroşeni 89 45 28N 23 20 E
Petrovaradin 95 45 16N 19 55 E
Petrovsk 98 52 22N 45 19 E
Petrovsk-Zabaykalskiy 101 51 20N 108 55 E
Petrozavodsk 98 61 41N 34 20 E
Pettibone 41 47 7N 99 31W
Pettis County ◇ 32 38 40N 93 15W
Pettus 51 28 37N 97 48W
Peumo 76 34 21S 71 12W
Peureulak 110 4 48N 97 45 E
Pevek 101 69 41N 171 19 E
Pfeifer 24 38 43N 99 10W
Pforzheim 88 48 53N 8 43 E
Phagwara 108 31 10N 75 40 E
Phala 123 23 45S 26 50 E
Phalodi 108 27 12N 72 24 E
Phan Rang 112 11 34N 109 0 E
Phan Thiet 112 11 1N 108 9 E
Phangan, Ko 112 9 45N 100 0 E
Phangnga 112 8 28N 98 30 E
Phanh Bho Ho Chi Minh 112 10 58N 106 40 E
Pharr 50 26 12N 98 11W
Phatthalung 112 7 39N 100 6 E
Pheba 31 33 35N 88 57W
Phelps, Ky. 49 37 32N 82 9W
Phelps, N.Y. 39 42 58N 77 3W
Phelps, Wis. 55 46 4N 89 5W
Phelps County ◇, Mo. 32 37 55N 91 45W
Phelps County ◇, Nebr. 34 40 30N 99 30W
Phelps L., Canada 63 59 15N 103 15W
Phelps L., U.S.A. 40 35 46N 76 27W
Phenix 54 37 5N 78 45W
Phenix City 10 32 28N 85 0W
Phetchabun 112 16 25N 101 8 E
Phetchabun, Thiu Khao 112 16 0N 101 20 E
Phetchaburi 112 13 1N 99 55 E
Phichai 112 17 22N 100 10 E
Phil Campbell 10 34 21N 87 42W
Philadelphia, Miss. 31 32 46N 89 7W
Philadelphia, N.Y. 39 44 9N 75 43W
Philadelphia, Pa. 45 39 57N 75 10W
Philadelphia, Tenn. 49 35 41N 84 24W
Philadelphia County ◇ 45 39 57N 75 10W
Philip 47 44 2N 101 40W
Philip Smith Mts. 11 68 0N 148 0W
Philippeville 87 50 12N 4 33 E
Philippi 54 39 9N 80 3W
Philippines ■ 111 12 0N 123 0 E
Philippopolis = Plovdiv 95 42 8N 24 44 E
Philipsburg, Mont. 33 46 20N 113 18W
Philipsburg, Pa. 45 40 54N 78 13W
Phillip, I. 127 38 30S 145 12 E
Phillips, Maine 26 44 49N 70 21W
Phillips, Nebr. 34 40 54N 98 13W
Phillips, Okla. 43 34 30N 96 12W
Phillips, Tex. 50 35 42N 101 22W
Phillips, Wis. 55 45 42N 90 24W
Phillips County ◇, Ark. 13 34 19N 90 51W
Phillips County ◇, Colo. 16 40 40N 102 20W
Phillips County ◇, Kans. 24 39 45N 99 15W
Phillips County ◇, Mont. 33 48 12N 108 0W
Phillipsburg, Ga. 18 31 25N 83 30W
Phillipsburg, Kans. 24 39 45N 99 19W
Phillipsburg, Mo. 32 37 33N 92 47W
Phillipsburg, N.J. 37 40 42N 75 12W
Phillipsburg, Ohio 42 39 54N 84 24W
Philmont 39 42 15N 73 39W
Philo, Calif. 14 39 4N 123 26W
Philo, Ill. 21 40 1N 88 9W
Philomath, Ga. 18 33 44N 82 59W
Philomath, Oreg. 44 44 32N 123 22W
Philpott L. 54 36 47N 80 2W
Phippsburg 16 40 14N 106 57W
Phitsanulok 112 16 50N 100 12 E
Phnom Dangrek 112 14 20N 104 0 E
Phnom Penh 112 11 33N 104 55 E
Phnom Thbeng 112 13 50N 104 56 E
Phoenix, Ariz. 12 33 27N 112 4W
Phoenix, La. 25 29 39N 89 56W
Phoenix, N.Y. 39 43 14N 76 18W
Phoenix, Oreg. 44 42 16N 122 49W
Phoenix Is. 124 3 30S 172 0W
Phoenixville 45 40 8N 75 31W
Phong Saly 112 21 42N 102 9 E
Phra Chedi Sam Ong 112 15 16N 98 23 E
Phra Nakhon Si Ayutthaya 112 14 25N 100 30 E
Phrae 112 18 7N 100 9 E
Phrao 112 19 23N 99 15 E
Phu Doan 112 21 40N 105 10 E
Phu Loi 112 20 14N 103 14 E
Phu Ly 112 20 35N 105 50 E
Phuket 112 7 52N 98 22 E
Piacá 74 7 42S 47 18W
Piacenza 94 45 2N 9 42 E
Piaçubaçu 74 10 24S 36 25W
Pialba 127 25 20S 152 45 E
Piapot 63 49 59N 109 8W
Piatã 75 13 9S 41 48W
Piatra 95 43 51N 25 9 E
Piatra Neamţ 89 46 56N 26 21 E
Piatra Olt 95 44 22N 24 16 E
Piatt County ◇ 21 40 0N 88 35W
Piauí □ 74 7 0S 43 0W
Piaui → 74 6 38S 42 42W
Piave → 94 45 32N 12 44 E
Piazza Ármerina 94 37 21N 14 20 E
Pibor Post 121 6 47N 33 3 E
Pica 72 20 35S 69 25W
Picacho, Ariz. 12 32 43N 111 30W
Picacho, N. Mex. 38 33 21N 105 9W
Picardie 90 50 0N 2 15 E
Picardy = Picardie 90 50 0N 2 15 E
Picayune 31 30 32N 89 41W
Piceance Cr. → 16 40 5N 108 14W
Picher 43 36 59N 94 50W
Pichilemu 76 34 22S 72 0W
Pichincha, □ 70 0 10S 78 40W
Pickaway County ◇ 42 39 43N 82 59W
Pickens, Ark. 13 33 51N 91 29W
Pickens, Miss. 31 32 53N 89 58W
Pickens, Okla. 43 34 23N 95 2W
Pickens, S.C. 46 34 53N 82 42W
Pickens, W. Va. 54 38 39N 80 13W
Pickens County ◇, Ala. 10 33 16N 88 6W
Pickens County ◇, Ga. 18 34 30N 84 25W
Pickens County ◇, S.C. 46 34 50N 82 45W
Pickerel L. 60 48 40N 91 25W
Pickering 32 40 27N 94 49W
Pickett County ◇ 49 36 34N 85 8W
Pickford 29 46 10N 84 22W
Pickle Lake 60 51 30N 90 12W
Pickrell 34 40 23N 96 44W
Pickstown 47 43 4N 98 32W
Pickwick L. 10 35 4N 88 15W
Pico Truncado 78 46 40S 68 0W
Picos 74 7 5S 41 28W
Picota 72 6 54S 76 24W
Picton, Canada 60 44 1N 77 9W
Picton, N.Z. 128 41 18S 174 3 E
Picton, I. 78 55 2S 66 57W
Pictou 61 45 41N 62 42W
Picture Butte 62 49 55N 112 45W
Pictured Rocks Nat. Lakeshore 29 46 30N 86 30W
Picuí 74 6 31S 36 21W
Picún Leufú 78 39 30S 69 5W
Pidurutalagala 108 7 10N 80 50 E
Pie Town 38 34 18N 108 9W
Piedad, La 64 20 20N 102 1W
Piedecuesta 70 6 59N 73 3W
Piedmont = Piemonte □ 94 45 0N 7 30 E
Piedmont, Ala. 10 33 55N 85 37W
Piedmont, Kans. 24 37 37N 96 22W
Piedmont, Mo. 32 37 9N 90 42W
Piedmont, Okla. 43 35 39N 97 44W
Piedmont, S.C. 46 34 42N 82 28W
Piedmont, S. Dak. 47 44 14N 103 24W
Piedmont L. 42 40 11N 81 13W
Piedra del Anguila 78 40 2S 70 4W
Piedra Lais 70 3 10N 65 50W
Piedras, R. de las → 72 12 30S 69 15W
Piedras Negras 64 28 35N 100 35W
Piemonte □ 94 45 0N 7 30 E
Pierce, Colo. 16 40 38N 104 45W
Pierce, Idaho 20 46 30N 115 48W
Pierce, Nebr. 34 42 12N 97 32W
Pierce City 32 36 57N 94 0W
Pierce County ◇, Ga. 18 31 20N 82 10W
Pierce County ◇, N. Dak. 41 48 0N 100 0W
Pierce County ◇, Nebr. 34 42 20N 97 40W
Pierce County ◇, Wash. 53 47 0N 122 0W
Pierce County ◇, Wis. 55 44 45N 92 25W
Pierceton 22 41 12N 85 42W
Pierceville 24 37 53N 100 40W
Piercy 14 39 59N 123 48W
Pierpont 47 45 30N 97 50W
Pierre 47 44 22N 100 21W
Pierron 21 38 47N 89 36W
Pierson, Fla. 17 29 14N 81 28W
Pierson, Iowa 23 42 33N 95 52W
Pierz 30 45 59N 94 6W
Piet Retief 123 27 1S 30 50 E
Pietarsaari = Jakobstad 96 63 40N 22 43 E
Pietermaritzburg 123 29 35S 30 25 E
Pietersburg 123 23 54S 29 25 E
Pietrosul 89 47 35N 24 43 E
Pigeon, La. 25 30 4N 91 17W
Pigeon, Mich. 29 43 50N 83 16W
Pigeon →, Ind. 22 41 47N 85 49W
Pigeon →, Tenn. 49 36 2N 83 17W
Pigeon Cove 28 42 41N 70 38W
Pigeon Cr. → 10 31 20N 86 42W
Pigeon Falls 55 44 26N 91 13W
Pigeon Forge 49 35 48N 83 33W
Pigg → 54 37 0N 79 29W
Piggott 13 36 23N 90 11W
Pigüe 76 37 36S 62 25W
Pike 54 39 17N 81 5W
Pike County ◇, Ala. 10 31 48N 85 58W
Pike County ◇, Ark. 13 34 14N 93 45W
Pike County ◇, Ga. 18 33 5N 84 20W
Pike County ◇, Ill. 21 39 35N 90 50W
Pike County ◇, Ind. 22 38 25N 87 10W
Pike County ◇, Ky. 49 37 30N 82 25W
Pike County ◇, Miss. 31 31 15N 90 27W
Pike County ◇, Mo. 32 39 20N 91 10W
Pike County ◇, Ohio 42 39 4N 83 1W
Pike County ◇, Pa. 45 41 20N 75 0W
Pike National Forest 16 39 15N 105 20W
Pike Road 10 32 17N 86 6W
Pikes Peak 16 38 50N 105 3W
Pikesville 27 39 23N 76 43W
Piketberg 123 32 55S 18 40 E
Piketon 42 39 4N 83 1W
Pikeville, Ky. 49 37 29N 82 31W
Pikeville, N.C. 40 35 30N 77 59W
Pikeville, Tenn. 49 35 36N 85 11W
Pikwitonei 63 55 35N 97 9W
Pilão Arcado 74 10 9S 42 26W
Pilar, Brazil 74 9 36S 35 56W
Pilar, Paraguay 76 26 50S 58 20W
Pilas 111 6 39N 121 37 E
Pilaya → 73 20 55S 64 4W
Pilbara 126 21 15S 118 16 E
Pilcomayo → 76 25 21S 57 42W
Pilger 34 42 0N 97 3W
Pilibhit 108 28 40N 79 50 E
Pilica → 89 51 25N 20 45 E
Pillager 30 46 20N 94 28W
Pillaro 70 1 10S 78 32W
Pillsbury 41 47 13N 97 48W
Pillsbury, L. 14 39 25N 122 57W
Pillsbury Sd. 57 18 20N 64 50W
Pílos 95 36 55N 21 42 E
Pilot Grove 32 38 53N 92 55W
Pilot Knob, Ark. 13 35 42N 93 57W
Pilot Knob, Ky. 48 36 50N 86 41W
Pilot Knob, Mo. 32 37 40N 90 40W
Pilot Mound 63 49 15N 98 54W
Pilot Mountain 40 36 23N 80 28W
Pilot Pk. 56 44 58N 109 53W
Pilot Point, Alaska 11 57 34N 157 35W
Pilot Point, Tex. 51 33 24N 96 58W
Pilot Rock 44 45 29N 118 50W
Pilot Station 11 61 56N 162 53W
Pilsen = Plzen 88 49 45N 13 22 E
Pima 12 32 54N 109 50W
Pima County ◇ 12 32 0N 112 0W
Pimba 127 31 18S 136 46 E
Pimenta Bueno 73 11 35S 61 10W
Pimentel 72 6 45S 79 55W
Pinal County ◇ 12 33 0N 111 15W
Pinang 112 5 25N 100 15 E
Pinar del Río 66 22 26N 83 40W
Pinaroo 127 35 17S 140 53 E
Pinas, Mt. 15 34 50N 119 9W
Pincher Creek 62 49 30N 113 57W
Pinchi L. 62 54 38N 124 30W
Pinckard 10 31 19N 85 33W
Pinckneyville, Ill. 21 38 5N 89 23W
Pinckneyville, Miss. 31 31 1N 91 29W
Pinconning 29 43 51N 83 58W
Pinczów 89 50 30N 20 35 E
Pindall 13 36 4N 92 53W
Pindaré → 74 3 17S 44 47W
Pindaré Mirim 74 3 37S 45 21W
Pindiga 120 9 58N 10 53 E
Pindobal 74 3 16S 48 25W
Pindos Óros 95 40 0N 21 0 E
Pindus Mts. = Pindos Óros 95 40 0N 21 0 E
Pine, Ariz. 12 34 23N 111 27W
Pine, Oreg. 44 44 52N 117 5W
Pine →, Canada 63 58 50N 105 38W
Pine →, U.S.A. 29 43 35N 84 8W
Pine, C. 61 46 37N 53 32W
Pine Apple 10 31 52N 87 0W

Pine Barrens Pocatalico

Pine Barrens 37 39 30N 74 30W
Pine Bluff 13 34 13N 92 1W
Pine Bluffs 56 41 11N 104 4W
Pine Castle 17 28 28N 81 22W
Pine City, Minn. 30 45 50N 92 59W
Pine City, Wash. 53 47 12N 117 31W
Pine County ◇ 30 46 5N 92 50W
Pine Cr. →, Nev. 35 40 36N 116 12W
Pine Cr. →, Pa. 45 41 10N 77 16W
Pine Creek 126 13 50 S 132 10 E
Pine Creek L. 43 34 7N 95 5W
Pine Falls 63 50 34N 96 11W
Pine Flat L. 15 36 50N 119 20W
Pine Forest Range 35 41 45N 118 50W
Pine Grove, La. 25 30 43N 90 45W
Pine Grove, Pa. 45 40 33N 76 23W
Pine Grove, W. Va. 54 39 34N 80 41W
Pine Hill 37 39 47N 74 59W
Pine Is. 17 26 36N 82 7W
Pine Island 30 44 12N 92 39W
Pine Knot 49 36 39N 84 26W
Pine Level 10 32 4N 86 4W
Pine Log 18 34 21N 84 44W
Pine Mountain 18 32 52N 84 51W
Pine Mt., Ga. 18 34 56N 83 12W
Pine Mt., Ky. 49 37 0N 83 45W
Pine Mt., Wyo. 56 41 2N 109 1W
Pine Pass 62 55 25N 122 42W
Pine Point 62 60 50N 114 28W
Pine Prairie 25 30 47N 92 25W
Pine Ridge, S. Dak. 47 42 30N 102 40W
Pine Ridge, S. Dak. 47 43 2N 102 33W
Pine Ridge Indian Reservation 47 43 30N 102 0W
Pine River, Canada 63 51 45N 100 30W
Pine River, U.S.A. 30 46 43N 94 24W
Pine Springs 50 31 54N 104 49W
Pine Valley 52 38 20N 113 45W
Pinebluff 40 35 6N 79 28W
Pinedale, Calif. 15 36 50N 119 48W
Pinedale, Wyo. 56 42 52N 109 52W
Pinega → 98 64 8N 46 54 E
Pinehurst, Ga. 18 32 12N 83 46W
Pinehurst, N.C. 40 35 12N 79 28W
Pineland 51 31 15N 93 58W
Pinellas County ◇ 17 28 0N 82 45W
Pinellas Park 17 27 50N 82 43W
Pinerolo 94 44 47N 7 21 E
Pines, Lake O The 51 32 45N 94 30W
Pinetop 12 34 8N 109 56W
Pinetops 40 35 46N 77 38W
Pinetown, S. Africa 123 29 48 S 30 54 E
Pinetown, U.S.A. 40 35 37N 76 52W
Pinetta 17 30 36N 83 21W
Pineview 18 32 7N 83 30W
Pineville, Iowa 23 36 36N 94 23W
Pineville, Ky. 49 36 46N 83 42W
Pineville, La. 25 31 19N 92 26W
Pineville, N.C. 40 35 5N 80 53W
Pineville, S.C. 46 33 26N 80 1W
Pineville, W. Va. 54 37 35N 81 32W
Pinewood 46 33 44N 80 27W
Piney → 32 37 54N 92 4W
Piney Buttes 33 47 35N 106 45W
Piney Grove 27 39 42N 78 24W
Piney Point 27 38 9N 76 31W
Piney Woods 31 32 2N 90 0W
Ping → 112 15 42N 100 9 E
Pingding 114 37 47N 113 38 E
Pingdingshan 115 33 43N 113 27 E
Pingdong 115 22 39N 120 30 E
Pingdu 114 36 42N 119 59 E
Pingguo 115 23 19N 107 36 E
Pinghe 115 24 17N 117 21 E
Pingjiang 115 28 45N 113 36 E
Pingle 115 24 40N 110 40 E
Pingliang 114 35 35N 106 31 E
Pingluo 114 38 52N 106 30 E
Pingnan 115 23 33N 110 22 E
Pingree 41 47 10N 98 55W
Pingtan Dao 115 25 29N 119 47 E
Pingwu 115 32 25N 104 30 E
Pingxiang, Guangxi Zhuangzu, China 115 22 6N 106 46 E
Pingxiang, Jiangxi, China 115 27 43N 113 48 E
Pingyao 114 37 12N 112 10 E
Pinhal 77 22 10 S 46 46W
Pinheiro 74 2 31 S 45 5W
Pinhel 91 40 50N 7 1W
Pinhuá → 73 6 21 S 65 0W
Pini 110 0 10N 98 40 E
Piniós → 95 39 55N 22 10 E
Pinjarra 126 32 37 S 115 52 E
Pink 43 35 18N 97 6W
Pink → 63 56 50N 103 50W
Pink Cliffs 52 37 25N 112 20W
Pink Hill 40 35 3N 77 45W
Pinnacle 40 36 20N 80 26W
Pinnacle Buttes 56 43 44N 109 57W
Pinnacle Peak 56 43 23N 110 32W
Pinnacles National Monument 15 36 25N 121 12W
Pino Hachado, Paso 78 38 39 S 70 54W
Pinola 31 31 53N 89 58W
Pinole 14 38 0N 122 17W
Pinon 12 36 6N 110 14W
Pinos 64 22 20N 101 40W
Pinotepa Nacional 65 16 19N 98 3W
Pinrang 111 3 46 S 119 41 E
Pinsk 98 52 10N 26 1 E
Pinson, Ala. 10 33 41N 86 41W
Pinson, Tenn. 48 35 29N 88 43W
Pinta, Sierra 12 32 15N 113 30W
Pintados 72 20 35 S 69 40W
Pintlalla Cr. → 10 32 21N 86 30W
Pinyang 115 27 42N 120 31 E
Pinyug 98 60 5N 48 0 E
Pio XII 74 3 53 S 45 17W
Pioche 35 37 56N 114 27W
Piombino 94 42 54N 10 30 E
Pioneer, Iowa 23 42 39N 94 23W
Pioneer, La. 25 32 44N 91 26W
Pioneer, Ohio 42 41 41N 84 33W
Pioneer, Tenn. 49 36 25N 84 19W
Pioner, Os. 101 79 50N 92 0 E
Piorini → 71 3 23 S 63 30W
Piorini, L. 71 3 15 S 62 35W
Piotrków Trybunalski 89 51 23N 19 43 E
Pīp 107 26 45N 60 10 E
Pipe Creek 51 29 43N 98 56W
Pipe Spring National Monument 12 36 50N 112 55W
Pipestone 30 44 0N 96 19W
Pipestone → 60 52 53N 89 23W
Pipestone County ◇ 30 44 0N 96 15W
Pipestone Cr. → 63 49 42N 100 45W
Pipmuacan, Rés. 61 49 45N 70 30W
Piqua, Kans. 24 37 56N 95 32W
Piqua, Ohio 42 40 9N 84 15W
Piquet Carneiro 74 5 48 S 39 25W
Piquiri → 77 24 3 S 54 14W
Piracanjuba 75 17 18 S 49 1W
Piracicaba 77 22 45 S 47 40W
Piracuruca 74 3 50 S 41 50W
Piræus = Piraiévs 95 37 57N 23 42 E
Piraiévs 95 37 57N 23 42 E
Pirajuí 77 21 59 S 49 29W
Pirané 76 25 42 S 59 6W
Piranhas 74 9 27 S 37 46W
Pirapemas 74 3 43 S 44 14W
Pirapora 75 17 20 S 44 56W
Pirata, Monte 57 18 6N 65 33W
Piray → 73 16 32 S 63 45W
Pirdop 95 42 40N 24 10 E
Pires do Rio 75 17 18 S 48 17W
Pírgos 95 37 40N 21 27 E
Pirgovo 95 43 44N 25 43 E
Piribebuy 76 25 26 S 57 2W
Pirin Planina 95 41 40N 23 30 E
Pirineos 91 42 40N 1 0 E
Piripiri 74 4 15 S 41 46W
Piritu 70 9 23N 69 12W
Pirot 95 43 9N 22 39 E
Piru 111 3 4 S 128 12 E
Pisa 94 43 43N 10 23 E
Pisac 72 13 25 S 71 50W
Pisagua 72 19 40 S 70 15W
Piscataquis → 26 45 15N 68 58W
Piscataquis County ◇ 26 46 0N 69 0W
Piscataway, Md. 27 38 42N 76 58W
Piscataway, N.J. 37 40 34N 74 27W
Pisco 72 13 50 S 76 12W
Piscu 95 45 30N 27 43 E
Písek, Czech. 88 49 19N 14 10 E
Pisek, U.S.A. 41 48 19N 97 43W
Pisgah, Iowa 23 41 50N 95 55W
Pisgah, Md. 27 38 32N 77 8W
Pisgah Forest 40 35 15N 82 44W
Pisgah National Forest 40 35 50N 82 0W
Pishan 113 37 30N 78 33 E
Pising 111 5 8 S 121 53 E
Pisinimo 12 32 2N 112 19W
Pismo Beach 15 35 9N 120 38W
Pistóia 94 43 57N 10 53 E
Pistol B. 63 62 25N 92 37W
Pistol River 44 42 17N 124 24W
Pisuerga → 91 41 33N 4 52W
Pit → 14 40 47N 122 6W
Pitalito 70 1 51N 76 2W
Pitanga 75 24 46 S 51 44W
Pitangui 75 19 40 S 44 54 E
Pitcairn I. 125 25 5 S 130 5W
Pite älv → 96 65 20N 21 25 E
Piteå 96 65 20N 21 25 E
Piteşti 89 44 52N 24 54 E
Pithapuram 109 17 10N 82 15 E
Pitiquito 64 30 42N 112 2W
Pitkin, Colo. 16 38 37N 106 31W
Pitkin, La. 25 30 56N 92 56W
Pitkin County ◇ 16 39 10N 106 50W
Pitlochry 84 56 43N 3 43W
Pitman 37 39 44N 75 8W
Pitrufquén 78 38 59 S 72 39W
Pitt County ◇ 40 35 30N 77 20W
Pitt I. 62 53 30N 129 50W
Pittsboro, Ind. 22 39 52N 86 28W
Pittsboro, Miss. 31 33 56N 89 20W
Pittsboro, N.C. 40 35 43N 79 11W
Pittsburg, Calif. 14 38 2N 121 53W
Pittsburg, Ill. 21 37 47N 88 51W
Pittsburg, Kans. 24 37 25N 94 42W
Pittsburg, N.H. 36 45 3N 71 24W
Pittsburg, Okla. 43 34 43N 95 52W
Pittsburg, Tex. 51 33 0N 94 59W
Pittsburg County ◇ 43 34 50N 95 50W
Pittsburgh 45 40 26N 80 1W
Pittsfield, Ill. 21 39 36N 90 49W
Pittsfield, Maine 26 44 47N 69 23W
Pittsfield, Mass. 28 42 27N 73 15W
Pittsfield, N.H. 36 43 18N 71 20W
Pittsfield, Vt. 36 43 46N 72 48W
Pittsford 36 43 42N 73 3W
Pittsgrove 37 39 37N 75 14W
Pittston 45 41 19N 75 47W
Pittstown 37 40 36N 74 56W
Pittsview 10 32 11N 85 10W
Pittsville, Md. 27 38 24N 75 52W
Pittsville, Mo. 32 38 50N 93 0W
Pittsville, Wis. 55 44 27N 90 8W
Pittsylvania County ◇ 54 36 55N 79 15W
Piuí 75 20 28 S 45 58W
Pium 74 10 27 S 49 11W
Piura 72 5 15 S 80 38W
Piura □ 72 5 10 S 80 0W
Piute County ◇ 52 38 20N 112 10W
Pivijay 70 10 28N 74 37W
Pixley 15 35 58N 119 18W
Pizarro 70 4 58N 77 22W
Pizzo 94 38 44N 16 10 E
Placedo 51 28 41N 96 50W
Placentia 61 47 20N 54 0W
Placentia B. 61 47 0N 54 40W
Placer County ◇ 14 39 10N 120 30W
Placerville, Calif. 14 38 44N 120 48W
Placerville, Colo. 16 38 1N 108 3W
Placerville, Idaho 20 43 57N 115 57W
Placetas 66 22 15N 79 44W
Placid, L. 17 27 15N 81 22W
Placitas 38 35 18N 106 25W
Plain City 52 41 18N 112 6W
Plain Dealing 25 32 54N 93 42W
Plainfield, Conn. 28 41 41N 71 56W
Plainfield, Ind. 22 39 42N 86 24W
Plainfield, Iowa 23 42 51N 92 32W
Plainfield, Mass. 28 42 0N 72 0W
Plainfield, N.H. 36 43 32N 72 21W
Plainfield, N.J. 37 40 37N 74 25W
Plainfield, Vt. 36 44 17N 72 26W
Plainfield, Wis. 55 44 13N 89 30W
Plainfield Heights 29 43 1N 85 37W
Plains, Ga. 18 32 2N 84 24W
Plains, Kans. 24 37 16N 100 35W
Plains, Mont. 33 47 28N 114 53W
Plains, Pa. 45 41 15N 75 37W
Plains, Tex. 50 33 11N 102 50W
Plainview, Ark. 13 35 2N 93 18W
Plainview, Minn. 30 44 10N 92 10W
Plainview, N.Y. 39 40 46N 73 29W
Plainview, Nebr. 34 42 21N 97 47W
Plainview, Tex. 50 34 11N 101 43W
Plainville, Conn. 28 41 41N 72 51W
Plainville, Ga. 18 34 24N 85 2W
Plainville, Ind. 22 38 48N 87 9W
Plainville, Kans. 24 39 14N 99 18W
Plainwell 29 42 27N 85 38W
Plaistow 36 42 50N 71 6W
Pláka 95 40 0N 25 24 E
Plakhino 100 67 45N 86 5 E
Plana Cays 67 22 38N 73 30W
Planada 14 37 16N 120 19W
Planeta Rica 70 8 25N 75 36W
Plankinton 47 43 43N 98 29W
Plano, Ill. 21 41 40N 88 32W
Plano, Tex. 51 33 1N 96 42W
Plant City 17 28 1N 82 7W
Plantation 17 26 8N 80 15W
Plantersville, Ala. 10 32 40N 86 56W
Plantersville, Miss. 31 34 12N 88 40W
Plantersville, S.C. 46 33 33N 79 13W
Plantsite 12 33 2N 109 21W
Plaquemine 25 30 17N 91 14W
Plaquemines Parish ◇ 25 29 29N 89 42W
Plasencia 91 40 3N 6 8W
Plaster Rock 61 46 53N 67 22W
Plastun 116 44 45N 136 19 E
Plata, La, Argentina 76 35 0 S 57 55W
Plata, La, Colombia 70 2 23N 75 53W
Plata, La, L. 78 44 55 S 71 50W
Plata, Rio de la 57 18 29N 66 15W
Plata, Río de la → 76 34 45 S 57 30W
Platani → 94 37 23N 13 16 E
Platí, Ákra- 95 40 27N 24 0 E
Platina 14 40 22N 122 53W
Platinum 11 59 1N 161 49W
Plato 70 9 47N 74 47W
Platte 47 43 23N 98 51W
Platte →, Mo. 32 39 16N 94 50W
Platte →, Nebr. 34 41 4N 95 53W
Platte Center 34 41 32N 97 29W
Platte City 32 39 22N 94 47W
Platte County ◇, Mo. 32 39 20N 94 45W
Platte County ◇, Nebr. 34 41 30N 97 30W
Platte County ◇, Wyo. 56 42 0N 105 0W
Platteville, Colo. 16 40 13N 104 49W
Platteville, Wis. 55 42 44N 90 29W
Plattsburg 32 39 34N 94 27W
Plattsburgh 39 44 42N 73 28W
Plattsmouth 34 41 1N 95 53W
Plauen 88 50 29N 12 9 E
Playa Azul 64 17 59N 102 24W
Playa de Guayanés 57 18 4N 65 49W
Playa de Humacao 57 18 10N 65 45W
Playas L. 38 31 51N 108 35W
Playgreen L. 63 54 0N 98 15W
Plaza, N. Dak. 41 48 1N 101 58W
Plaza, Wash. 53 47 19N 117 23W
Pleasant, L. 12 33 51N 112 16W
Pleasant B. 28 41 40N 69 57W
Pleasant Bay 61 46 51N 60 48W
Pleasant Dale 34 40 48N 96 56W
Pleasant Garden 40 35 58N 79 46W
Pleasant Grove 52 40 22N 111 44W
Pleasant Hill, Calif. 14 37 57N 122 4W
Pleasant Hill, Ill. 21 39 27N 90 52W
Pleasant Hill, La. 25 31 49N 93 31W
Pleasant Hill, Mo. 32 38 47N 94 16W
Pleasant Hill, N. Mex. 38 34 31N 103 4W
Pleasant Hill, Ohio 42 40 3N 84 21W
Pleasant Hill, Tenn. 49 35 59N 85 12W
Pleasant Lake 30 45 40N 94 17W
Pleasant Plains, Ark. 13 35 33N 91 38W
Pleasant Plains, Ill. 21 39 52N 89 55W
Pleasant Site 10 34 33N 88 4W
Pleasant View, Colo. 16 37 35N 108 46W
Pleasant View, Wash. 53 46 29N 118 20W
Pleasanton, Iowa 23 40 35N 93 45W
Pleasanton, Kans. 24 38 11N 94 43W
Pleasanton, N. Mex. 38 33 17N 108 53W
Pleasanton, Nebr. 34 40 58N 99 5W
Pleasanton, Tex. 51 28 58N 98 29W
Pleasants County ◇ 54 39 22N 81 12W
Pleasantville, Iowa 23 41 23N 93 18W
Pleasantville, N.J. 37 39 24N 74 32W
Pleasantville, Ohio 42 39 49N 82 32W
Pleasure Ridge Park 49 38 9N 85 50W
Pleasureville 49 38 21N 85 7W
Pleiku 112 13 57N 108 0 E
Pleniţa 95 44 14N 23 10 E
Plenty, Bay of 128 37 45 S 177 0 E
Plentywood 33 48 47N 104 34W
Plesetsk 98 62 40N 40 10 E
Plessisville 61 46 14N 71 47W
Pletipi L. 61 51 44N 70 6W
Pleven 95 43 26N 24 37 E
Plevlja 95 43 21N 19 21 E
Plevna, Kans. 24 37 59N 98 19W
Plevna, Mont. 33 46 25N 104 31W
Ploieşti 89 44 57N 26 5 E
Plonge, Lac La 63 55 8N 107 20W
Plovdiv 95 42 8N 24 44 E
Plover, Iowa 23 42 53N 94 38W
Plover, Wis. 55 44 27N 89 32W
Plover → 55 44 29N 89 35W
Plum 45 40 29N 79 47W
Plum City 55 44 38N 92 11W
Plum I., Mass. 28 42 45N 70 48W
Plum I., N.Y. 39 41 11N 72 12W
Plum Point 27 38 0N 76 0W
Plum Springs 48 37 0N 86 20W
Plumas County ◇ 14 40 0N 121 0W
Plumas National Forest 14 39 50N 120 40W
Plumerville 13 35 10N 92 38W
Plummer, Idaho 20 47 20N 116 53W
Plummer, Minn. 30 47 55N 96 3W
Plumtree 123 20 27 S 27 55 E
Plush 44 42 25N 119 54W
Plymouth, U.K. 83 50 23N 4 9W
Plymouth, Calif. 14 38 29N 120 51W
Plymouth, Ill. 21 40 18N 90 58W
Plymouth, Ind. 22 41 21N 86 19W
Plymouth, Iowa 23 43 15N 93 7W
Plymouth, Kans. 24 38 25N 96 20W
Plymouth, Mass. 28 41 57N 70 40W
Plymouth, Minn. 30 45 2N 93 27W
Plymouth, N.C. 40 35 52N 76 43W
Plymouth, N.H. 36 43 46N 71 41W
Plymouth, Nebr. 34 40 18N 97 0W
Plymouth, Pa. 45 41 14N 75 57W
Plymouth, Utah 52 41 53N 112 9W
Plymouth, Vt. 36 43 34N 72 45W
Plymouth, W. Va. 54 38 31N 81 51W
Plymouth, Wis. 55 43 45N 87 59W
Plymouth Bay 28 41 57N 70 37W
Plymouth County ◇, Iowa 23 42 45N 96 10W
Plymouth County ◇, Mass. 28 41 45N 70 45W
Plymouth Sd. 83 50 20N 4 10W
Plynlimon = Pumlumon Fawr 83 52 29N 3 47W
Plzen 88 49 45N 13 22 E
Po → 94 44 57N 12 4 E
Po Hai = Bo Hai 114 39 0N 120 0 E
Pobeda 101 65 12N 146 12 E
Pobedino 101 49 51N 142 49 E
Pobedy Pik 100 40 45N 79 58 E
Poca 54 38 28N 81 49W
Pocahontas, Ark. 13 36 16N 90 58W
Pocahontas, Ill. 21 38 50N 89 33W
Pocahontas, Iowa 23 42 44N 94 40W
Pocahontas County ◇, Iowa 23 42 45N 94 40W
Pocahontas County ◇, W. Va. 54 38 10N 80 2W
Pocasset, Mass. 28 41 41N 70 37W
Pocasset, Okla. 43 35 12N 97 58W
Pocatalico 54 38 29N 81 40W

Pocatalico Porter L.

Pocatalico → 54 38 29N 81 49W
Pocatello 20 42 52N 112 27W
Pochontas 62 53 10N 117 51W
Pochutla 65 15 50N 96 31W
Poci 71 5 57N 61 29W
Pocinhos 74 7 4S 36 3W
Pocito Casas 64 28 32N 111 6W
Poções 75 14 31S 40 21W
Pocomoke → 27 37 58N 75 39W
Pocomoke City 27 38 5N 75 34W
Pocomoke Sd. 54 37 50N 75 50W
Pocomoke Sound 27 37 56N 75 45W
Poconé 73 16 15S 56 37W
Pocono Mts. 45 41 7N 75 22W
Poços de Caldas 75 21 50S 46 33W
Podgorica = Titograd 95 42 30N 19 19E
Podkamennaya Tunguska → 101 61 50N 90 13E
Podolsk 98 55 25N 37 30E
Podor 120 16 40N 15 2W
Podporozhy 98 60 55N 34 2E
Podu Turcului 95 46 11N 27 25E
Pofadder 123 29 10S 19 22E
Pogamasing 60 46 55N 81 50W
Pogoanele 95 44 55N 27 0E
Pogranitšnyi 116 44 25N 131 24E
Poh 111 0 46S 122 51E
Pohang 114 36 1N 129 23E
Pohue B. 19 19 0N 155 48W
Poiana Mare 95 43 57N 23 5E
Poinsett, C. 5 65 42S 113 18E
Poinsett, L. 47 44 34N 97 5W
Poinsett County ◇ 13 35 34N 90 43W
Point Arena 14 38 55N 123 41W
Point au Fer I. 25 29 18N 91 15W
Point Baker 11 56 21N 133 37W
Point Comfort 51 28 41N 96 33W
Point Edward 60 43 0N 82 30W
Point Hope 11 68 21N 166 47W
Point Lay 11 69 46N 163 3W
Point Lookout 27 38 5N 76 18W
Point of Rocks 56 41 41N 108 47W
Point Pedro 108 9 50N 80 15E
Point Pleasant, N.J. 37 40 5N 74 3W
Point Pleasant, W. Va. 54 38 51N 82 8W
Point Reyes National Seashore 14 38 10N 122 55W
Point Stephens 127 32 38S 152 12E
Pointblank 51 30 45N 95 13W
Pointe a la Hache 25 29 35N 89 48W
Pointe-à-Pitre 67 16 10N 61 30W
Pointe Coupee Parish ◇ 25 30 36N 91 37W
Pointe Noire 122 4 48S 11 53E
Poitiers 90 46 35N 0 20E
Pojoaque Valley 38 35 54N 106 1W
Pokai B. 19 21 27N 158 12W
Pokaran 108 27 0N 71 50E
Pokegama L. 30 47 12N 93 35W
Poko 122 5 41N 31 55E
Pokrovsk 101 61 29N 126 12E
Polacca 12 35 50N 110 23W
Polacca Wash → 12 35 22N 110 50W
Polan 107 25 30N 61 10E
Poland, N.Y. 39 43 14N 75 4W
Poland, Ohio 42 41 1N 80 37W
Poland ■ 89 52 0N 20 0E
Polar Sub-Glacial Basin 5 85 0S 110 0E
Polcura 76 37 17S 71 43W
Polden Hills 83 51 7N 2 50W
Pole Mt. 56 41 14N 105 23W
Polesye 98 52 0N 28 10E
Polevskoy 98 56 26N 60 11E
Polewali, Sulawesi, Indonesia 111 4 8S 119 43E
Polewali, Sulawesi, Indonesia 111 3 21S 119 23E
Poli 122 8 34N 13 15E
Polillo Is. 111 14 56N 122 0E
Políyiros 95 40 23N 23 25E
Polk, Nebr. 34 41 5N 97 46W
Polk, Ohio 42 40 57N 82 13W
Polk, Pa. 45 41 22N 79 56W
Polk City 23 41 46N 93 43W
Polk County ◇, Ark. 13 34 35N 94 15W
Polk County ◇, Fla. 17 28 0N 81 45W
Polk County ◇, Ga. 18 34 0N 85 10W
Polk County ◇, Iowa 23 41 40N 93 35W
Polk County ◇, Minn. 30 47 40N 96 30W
Polk County ◇, Mo. 32 37 35N 93 25W
Polk County ◇, N.C. 40 35 15N 82 10W
Polk County ◇, Nebr. 34 41 15N 97 40W
Polk County ◇, Oreg. 44 44 55N 123 20W
Polk County ◇, Tenn. 49 35 10N 84 39W
Polk County ◇, Tex. 51 30 43N 94 56W
Polk County ◇, Wis. 55 45 30N 92 30W
Polkton 40 35 1N 80 12W
Polkville, Miss. 31 32 11N 89 42W
Polkville, N.C. 40 35 25N 81 39W
Pollachi 108 10 35N 77 0E
Pollock, Idaho 20 45 19N 116 21W
Pollock, La. 25 31 32N 92 25W
Pollock, Mo. 32 40 21N 93 5W
Pollock, S. Dak. 47 45 55N 100 17W
Pollock Pines 14 38 46N 120 34W
Pollocksville 40 35 0N 77 14W
Polnovat 100 63 50N 65 54E
Polo, Ill. 21 41 59N 89 35W
Polo, Mo. 32 39 33N 94 3W
Polotsk 98 55 30N 28 50E
Polski Trŭmbesh 95 43 20N 25 38E
Polsko Kosovo 95 43 23N 25 38E
Polson 33 47 41N 114 9W
Poltava 99 49 35N 34 35E
Polunochnoye 98 60 52N 60 25E
Polvadera 38 34 12N 106 55W
Polyanovgrad 95 42 39N 26 59E
Polyarny 98 69 8N 33 20E
Polynesia 125 10 0S 162 0W
Pomaria 46 34 16N 81 25W
Pomaro 64 18 20N 103 18W
Pombal, Brazil 74 6 45S 37 50W
Pombal, Portugal 91 39 55N 8 40W
Pomeroy, Iowa 23 42 33N 94 41W
Pomeroy, Ohio 42 39 2N 82 2W
Pomeroy, Wash. 53 46 28N 117 36W
Pomfret, Conn. 28 41 54N 71 58W
Pomfret, Md. 27 38 0N 77 0W
Pomme de Terre →, Minn. 30 45 10N 96 5W
Pomme de Terre →, Mo. 32 38 11N 93 25W
Pomme de Terre L. 32 37 54N 93 19W
Pomona, Calif. 15 34 4N 117 45W
Pomona, Kans. 24 38 36N 95 27W
Pomona, Md. 27 39 10N 76 7W
Pomona, Mo. 32 36 52N 91 55W
Pomona, N.J. 37 39 29N 74 35W
Pomona Lake 24 38 39N 95 34W
Pomona Park 17 29 30N 81 36W
Pomorie 95 42 32N 27 41E
Pompano Beach 17 26 14N 80 8W
Pompeys Pillar 33 45 59N 107 57W
Pompton Lakes 37 41 0N 74 17W
Ponape 124 6 55N 158 10E
Ponask, L. 60 54 0N 92 41W
Ponass L. 63 52 16N 103 58W
Ponca 34 42 34N 96 43W
Ponca City 43 36 42N 97 5W
Ponca Cr. → 34 42 48N 98 5W
Ponce 57 18 1N 66 37W
Ponce ◇ 57 18 10N 66 30W
Ponce de Leon 17 30 44N 85 56W
Ponce de Leon B. 17 25 15N 81 10W
Poncha Springs 16 38 31N 106 5W
Ponchatoula 25 30 26N 90 26W
Poncheville, L. 60 50 10N 76 55W
Pond Creek 43 36 40N 97 48W
Pond Inlet 59 72 40N 77 0W
Pondera County ◇ 33 48 12N 112 30W
Ponderosa 38 35 40N 106 40W
Pondicherry 108 11 59N 79 50E
Pondosa 14 41 12N 121 41W
Ponds, I. of 61 53 27N 55 52W
Poneto 22 40 39N 85 13W
Ponferrada 91 42 32N 6 35W
Ponnani 108 10 45N 75 59E
Ponnyadaung 109 22 0N 94 10E
Ponoi 98 67 0N 41 0E
Ponoi → 98 66 59N 41 17E
Ponoka 62 52 42N 113 40W
Ponorogo 111 7 52S 111 29E
Ponta de Pedras 74 1 23S 48 52W
Ponta Grossa 77 25 7S 50 10W
Ponta Pora 77 22 20S 55 35W
Pontal → 74 9 8S 40 12W
Pontalina 75 17 31S 49 27W
Pontarlier 90 46 54N 6 20E
Pontchartrain L. 25 30 5N 90 5W
Ponte Alta, Serra do 75 19 42S 47 40W
Ponte Alta do Norte 74 10 45S 47 34W
Ponte Branca 73 16 27S 52 40W
Ponte Macassar 111 9 30S 123 58E
Ponte Nova 75 20 25S 42 54W
Ponte Vedra Beach 17 30 15N 81 23W
Pontedera 94 43 40N 10 37E
Pontefract 82 53 42N 1 19W
Ponteix 63 49 46N 107 29W
Pontevedra 91 42 26N 8 40W
Pontiac, Ill. 21 40 53N 88 38W
Pontiac, Mich. 29 42 38N 83 18W
Pontian Kecil 112 1 29N 103 23E
Pontianak 110 0 3S 109 15E
Pontine Is. = Ponziane, Isole 94 40 55N 13 0E
Ponton → 62 58 27N 116 11W
Pontotoc 31 34 15N 89 0W
Pontotoc County ◇, Miss. 31 34 15N 89 0W
Pontotoc County ◇, Okla. 43 34 45N 96 45W
Pontypool 83 51 42N 3 1W
Pontypridd 83 51 36N 3 21W
Ponziane, Isole 94 40 55N 13 0E
Poole, U.K. 83 50 42N 1 58W
Poole, Ky. 48 37 38N 87 39W
Poole, Nebr. 34 40 58N 98 58W
Pooler 18 32 7N 81 15W
Pooles I. 27 39 17N 76 16W
Poolesville 27 39 9N 77 25W
Pooley I. 62 52 45N 128 15W
Poona = Pune 108 18 29N 73 57E
Poopó 72 18 23S 66 59W
Poopó, Lago de 72 18 30S 67 35W
Popayán 70 2 27N 76 36W
Pope 31 34 13N 89 57W
Pope County ◇, Ark. 13 35 28N 92 59W
Pope County ◇, Ill. 21 37 25N 88 35W
Pope County ◇, Minn. 30 45 40N 95 25W
Pope Cr. → 21 41 8N 90 58W
Popejoy 23 42 36N 93 26W
Poperinge 87 50 51N 2 42E
Popes Creek 27 38 24N 76 58W
Popigay 101 72 1N 110 39E
Popina 95 44 7N 26 57E
Poplar, Mont. 33 48 7N 105 12W
Poplar, N.C. 40 36 4N 82 21W
Poplar, Wis. 55 46 35N 91 48W
Poplar →, Man., Canada 63 53 0N 97 19W
Poplar →, N.W.T., Canada 62 61 22N 121 52W
Poplar →, U.S.A. 33 48 5N 105 11W
Poplar Bluff 32 36 46N 90 24W
Poplar Branch 40 36 17N 75 53W
Poplar Grove 21 42 22N 88 49W
Poplar I. 27 38 46N 76 23W
Poplar Mt. 49 36 43N 85 3W
Poplar Plains 49 38 21N 83 41W
Poplarville 31 30 51N 89 32W
Popo Aggie → 56 43 1N 108 21W
Popocatepetl 65 19 10N 98 40W
Popokabaka 122 5 41S 16 40E
Popovo 95 43 21N 26 18E
Poquetanuck 28 41 29N 72 3W
Poquonock Bridge 28 41 19N 72 11W
Poquoson 54 37 8N 76 24W
Porangaba 72 8 48S 70 36W
Porangatu 75 13 26S 49 10W
Porbandar 108 21 44N 69 43E
Porce → 70 7 28N 74 53W
Porcher I. 62 53 50N 130 30W
Porco 73 19 50S 65 59W
Porcos → 75 12 42S 45 7W
Porcupine →, Canada 63 59 11N 104 46W
Porcupine →, U.S.A. 11 66 34N 145 19W
Porcupine Mts. 29 46 40N 89 40W
Pordim 95 43 23N 24 51E
Porecatu 75 22 43S 51 24W
Pori 97 61 29N 21 48E
Porjus 96 66 57N 19 50E
Porkkala 97 59 59N 24 26E
Porlamar 71 10 57N 63 51W
Poronaysk 101 49 13N 143 0E
Poroshiri-Dake 116 42 41N 142 52E
Porpoise B. 5 66 0S 127 0E
Porreta Pass 94 44 0N 11 10E
Porsangen 96 70 40N 25 40E
Port Alberni 62 49 40N 124 50W
Port Alexander 11 56 15N 134 38W
Port Alfred, Canada 61 48 18N 70 53W
Port Alfred, S. Africa 123 33 36S 26 55E
Port Alice 62 50 20N 127 25W
Port Allegany 45 41 48N 78 17W
Port Allen 25 30 27N 91 12W
Port Angeles 53 48 7N 123 27W
Port Antonio 66 18 10N 76 30W
Port Aransas 51 27 50N 97 4W
Port Arthur = Lüshun 114 38 45N 121 15E
Port Arthur, Australia 127 43 7S 147 50E
Port Arthur, U.S.A. 51 29 54N 93 56W
Port au Port B. 61 48 40N 58 50W
Port-au-Prince 67 18 40N 72 20W
Port Augusta 127 32 30S 137 50E
Port Augusta West 127 32 29S 137 29E
Port Austin 29 44 3N 83 1W
Port Barre 25 30 34N 91 57W
Port Bergé Vaovao 123 15 33S 47 40E
Port Blair 112 11 40N 92 30E
Port Blandford 61 48 20N 54 10W
Port Bradshaw 127 12 30S 137 20E
Port Burwell 60 42 40N 80 48W
Port-Cartier 61 50 2N 66 50W
Port Chalmers 128 45 49S 170 30E
Port Charlotte 17 26 59N 82 6W
Port Chester 39 41 0N 73 40W
Port Clements 62 53 40N 132 10W
Port Clinton 42 41 31N 82 56W
Port Clyde 26 43 56N 69 16W
Port Colborne 60 42 50N 79 10W
Port Coquitlam 62 49 15N 122 45W
Port Darwin, Australia 126 12 24S 130 45E
Port Darwin, Falk. Is. 78 51 50S 59 0W
Port Davey 127 43 16S 145 55E
Port-de-Paix 67 19 50N 72 50W
Port Dickson 112 2 30N 101 49E
Port Edward 62 54 12N 130 10W
Port Edwards 55 44 21N 89 52W
Port Elgin 60 44 25N 81 25W
Port Elizabeth, S. Africa 123 33 58S 25 40E
Port Elizabeth, U.S.A. 37 39 19N 74 59W
Port Ellen 84 55 38N 6 10W
Port-en-Bessin 90 49 21N 0 45W
Port Erin 82 54 5N 4 45W
Port Etienne = Nouâdhibou 120 20 54N 17 0W
Port Ewen 39 41 54N 73 59W
Port Fairy 127 38 22S 142 12E
Port Gamble 53 47 51N 122 35W
Port-Gentil 122 0 40S 8 50E
Port Gibson 31 31 58N 90 59W
Port Glasgow 84 55 57N 4 40W
Port Harcourt 120 4 40N 7 10E
Port Hardy 62 50 41N 127 30W
Port Harrison = Inoucdjouac 59 58 25N 78 15W
Port Hawkesbury 61 45 36N 61 22W
Port Hedland 126 20 25S 118 35E
Port Heiden 11 56 55N 158 41W
Port Henry 39 44 3N 73 28W
Port Hood 61 46 0N 61 32W
Port Hope, Canada 60 43 56N 78 20W
Port Hope, U.S.A. 29 43 57N 82 43W
Port Hueneme 15 34 7N 119 12W
Port Huron 29 42 58N 82 26W
Port Isabel 50 26 5N 97 12W
Port Jackson 127 33 50S 151 18E
Port Jefferson, N.Y. 39 40 57N 73 3W
Port Jefferson, Ohio 42 40 20N 84 6W
Port Jervis 39 41 22N 74 41W
Port-la-Nouvelle 90 43 1N 3 3E
Port Laoise 85 53 2N 7 20W
Port Lavaca 51 28 37N 96 38W
Port Lincoln 126 34 42S 135 52E
Port Lions 11 57 52N 152 53W
Port Loko 120 8 48N 12 46W
Port Ludlow 53 47 56N 122 41W
Port Lyautey = Kenitra 120 34 15N 6 40W
Port Macquarie 127 31 25S 152 25E
Port Mansfield 50 26 34N 97 26W
Port Maria 66 18 25N 77 5W
Port Matilda 45 40 48N 78 3W
Port Mayaca 17 26 59N 80 36W
Port Mellon 62 49 32N 123 31W
Port-Menier 61 49 51N 64 15W
Port Moller 11 55 59N 160 34W
Port Morant 66 17 54N 76 19W
Port Moresby 124 9 24S 147 8E
Port Mourant 71 6 15N 57 20W
Port Mouton 61 43 58N 64 50W
Port Musgrave 127 11 55S 141 50E
Port Neches 51 30 0N 93 59W
Port Nelson 63 57 3N 92 36W
Port Nolloth 123 29 17S 16 52E
Port Norris 37 39 15N 75 2W
Port Nouveau-Québec 59 58 30N 65 59W
Port of Spain 67 10 40N 61 31W
Port Orange 17 29 9N 80 59W
Port Orchard 53 47 32N 122 38W
Port Orford 44 42 45N 124 30W
Port Pegasus 128 47 12S 167 41E
Port Penn 27 39 31N 75 35W
Port Perry 60 44 6N 78 56W
Port Phillip B. 127 38 10S 144 50E
Port Pirie 127 33 10S 138 1E
Port Radium = Echo Bay 58 66 5N 117 55W
Port Renfrew 62 48 30N 124 20W
Port Republic, Md. 27 38 30N 76 33W
Port Republic, N.J. 37 39 31N 74 29W
Port Rowan 60 42 40N 80 30W
Port Royal, Ky. 49 38 33N 85 5W
Port Royal, Va. 54 38 10N 77 12W
Port Royal Sd. 46 32 15N 80 40W
Port Safaga = Bûr Safâga 121 26 43N 33 57E
Port Said = Bûr Sa'îd 121 31 16N 32 18E
Port St. Joe 17 29 49N 85 18W
Port-St-Louis-du-Rhône 90 43 23N 4 49E
Port Salerno 17 27 9N 80 12W
Port Sanilac 29 43 26N 82 33W
Port Saunders 61 50 40N 57 18W
Port Shepstone 123 30 44S 30 28E
Port Simpson 62 54 30N 130 20W
Port Stanley 60 42 40N 81 10W
Port Sudan = Bûr Sûdân 121 19 32N 37 9E
Port Sulphur 25 29 29N 89 42W
Port Susan 53 48 5N 122 15W
Port Talbot 83 51 35N 3 48W
Port Tobacco 27 38 27N 77 2W
Port Townsend 53 48 7N 122 45W
Port-Vendres 90 42 32N 3 8E
Port Vincent 25 30 20N 90 51W
Port Vladimir 98 69 25N 33 6E
Port Washington, N.Y. 39 40 50N 73 41W
Port Washington, Ohio 42 40 20N 81 31W
Port Washington, Wis. 55 43 23N 87 53W
Port Weld 112 4 50N 100 38E
Port Wentworth 18 32 9N 81 10W
Port Wing 55 46 47N 91 23W
Portachuelo 73 17 10S 63 20W
Portadale 18 30 34N 83 54W
Portadown 85 54 27N 6 26W
Portage, Ind. 22 41 34N 87 11W
Portage, Maine 26 46 46N 68 29W
Portage, Mich. 29 42 12N 85 35W
Portage, Pa. 45 40 23N 78 41W
Portage, Utah 52 41 59N 112 14W
Portage, Wis. 55 43 33N 89 28W
Portage → 42 41 31N 83 5W
Portage County ◇, Ohio 42 41 9N 81 15W
Portage County ◇, Wis. 55 44 25N 89 30W
Portage La Prairie 63 49 58N 98 18W
Portageville 32 36 26N 89 42W
Portal, Ariz. 12 31 55N 109 9W
Portal, Ga. 18 32 33N 81 56W
Portal, N. Dak. 41 48 59N 102 33W
Portalegre 91 39 19N 7 25W
Portalegre □ 91 39 20N 7 40W
Portales 38 34 11N 103 20W
Portarlington 85 53 10N 7 10W
Porteirinha 75 15 44S 43 2W
Portel 74 1 57S 50 49W
Porter, Minn. 30 44 38N 96 10W
Porter, Okla. 43 35 52N 95 31W
Porter, Wash. 53 46 56N 123 18W
Porter County ◇ 22 41 25N 87 5W
Porter L., N.W.T., Canada 63 61 41N 108 5W

Porter L. **Priština**

Porter L., Sask., Canada **63** 56 20N 107 20W
Porterville, Calif. **15** 36 4N 119 1W
Porterville, Miss. **31** 32 41N 88 28W
Porthcawl **83** 51 28N 3 42W
Porthill **20** 48 59N 116 30W
Portile de Fier **89** 44 42N 22 30 E
Portimão **91** 37 8N 8 32W
Portis **24** 39 34N 98 41W
Portland, Australia **127** 38 20 S 141 35 E
Portland, Ark. **13** 33 14N 91 31W
Portland, Conn. **28** 41 34N 72 38W
Portland, Fla. **17** 30 31N 86 12W
Portland, Ind. **22** 40 26N 84 59W
Portland, Maine **26** 43 39N 70 16W
Portland, Mich. **29** 42 52N 84 54W
Portland, Mo. **32** 38 43N 91 43W
Portland, N. Dak. **41** 47 30N 97 22W
Portland, Oreg. **44** 45 32N 122 37W
Portland, Tenn. **48** 36 35N 86 31W
Portland, Tex. **51** 27 53N 97 20W
Portland, Bill of **83** 50 31N 2 27W
Portland, C. **127** 40 46 S 148 0 E
Portland, I. of **83** 50 32N 2 25W
Portland Prom. **59** 58 40N 78 33W
Portneuf **61** 46 43N 71 55W
Portneuf → **20** 42 58N 112 35W
Portneuf Range **20** 42 50N 112 0W
Pôrto, Brazil **74** 3 54 S 42 42W
Porto, Portugal **91** 41 8N 8 40W
Pôrto Acre **72** 9 34 S 67 31W
Pôrto Alegre, Pará, Brazil **71** 4 22 S 52 44W
Pôrto Alegre, Rio Grande do Sul, Brazil **77** 30 5 S 51 10W
Porto Amboim = Gunza **122** 10 50 S 13 50 E
Pôrto Cajueiro **73** 11 3 S 55 53W
Pôrto da Fôlha **74** 9 55 S 37 17W
Pôrto de Móz **74** 1 41 S 52 13W
Pôrto de Pedras **74** 9 10 S 35 17W
Pôrto des Meinacos **73** 12 33 S 53 7W
Porto Empédocle **94** 37 18N 13 30 E
Pôrto Esperança **73** 19 37 S 57 29W
Pôrto Esperidião **73** 15 51 S 58 28W
Pôrto Franco **74** 6 20 S 47 24W
Pôrto Grande **71** 0 42N 51 24W
Pôrto Jofre **73** 17 20 S 56 48W
Porto Mendes **77** 24 30 S 54 15W
Pôrto Murtinho **73** 21 45 S 57 55W
Pôrto Nacional **74** 10 40 S 48 30W
Porto Novo **120** 6 23N 2 42 E
Pôrto Santana **71** 0 3 S 51 11W
Porto Santo **120** 33 45N 16 25W
Pôrto São José **77** 22 43 S 53 10W
Pôrto Seguro **75** 16 26 S 39 5W
Pôrto Tórres **94** 40 50N 8 23 E
Pôrto União **77** 26 10 S 51 10W
Pôrto Válter **72** 8 15 S 72 40W
Porto-Vecchio **90** 41 35N 9 16 E
Pôrto Velho **73** 8 46 S 63 54W
Portobelo **66** 9 35N 79 42W
Portoferráio **94** 42 50N 10 20 E
Portola **14** 39 49N 120 28W
Portoscuso **94** 39 12N 8 22 E
Portoviejo **70** 1 7 S 80 28W
Portpatrick **84** 54 50N 5 7W
Portree **84** 57 25N 6 11W
Portrush **85** 55 13N 6 40W
Portsmouth, Domin. **67** 15 34N 61 27W
Portsmouth, U.K. **83** 50 48N 1 6W
Portsmouth, N.H. **36** 43 5N 70 45W
Portsmouth, Ohio **42** 38 44N 82 57W
Portsmouth, R.I. **28** 41 36N 71 15W
Portsmouth, Va. **54** 36 50N 76 18W
Portsoy **84** 57 41N 2 41W
Porttipahta **96** 68 5N 26 40 E
Portugal ■ **91** 40 0N 7 0W
Portuguesa □ **70** 9 10N 69 15W
Portuguese-Guinea = Guinea-Bissau ■ **120** 12 0N 15 0W
Portuguese Timor □ = Timor **111** 9 0 S 125 0 E
Portumna **85** 53 5N 8 12W
Portville **39** 42 3N 78 20W
Porum **43** 35 22N 95 16W
Porvenir, Bolivia **72** 11 10 S 68 50W
Porvenir, Chile **78** 53 10 S 70 16W
Porvoo **97** 60 24N 25 40 E
Posadas **77** 27 30 S 55 50W
Posen **29** 45 16N 83 42W
Posey County ◇ **22** 38 0N 87 50W
Poseyville **22** 38 10N 87 47W
Poshan = Boshan **114** 36 28N 117 49 E
Poso **111** 1 20 S 120 55 E
Posoegroenoe **71** 4 23N 55 43W
Posse **75** 14 4 S 46 18W
Possel **122** 5 5N 19 10 E
Possession I. **5** 72 4 S 172 0 E
Possum Kingdom L. **51** 32 52N 98 26W
Post, Oreg. **44** 44 10N 120 29W
Post, Tex. **50** 33 12N 101 23W
Post Falls **20** 47 43N 116 57W
Poste Maurice Cortier **120** 22 14N 1 2 E
Postojna **89** 45 46N 14 12 E
Poston **46** 33 53N 79 26W
Postville **23** 43 5N 91 34W
Potagannissing B. **29** 46 5N 83 50W
Potatch → **20** 46 26N 116 47W
Potawatomi Indian Reservation **24** 39 20N 95 52W
Potchefstroom **123** 26 41 S 27 7 E
Potcoava **95** 44 30N 24 39 E
Poté **75** 17 49 S 41 49W
Poteau **43** 35 3N 94 37W
Poteau → **43** 35 23N 94 26W
Poteet **51** 29 2N 98 35W
Potelu, Lacul **95** 43 44N 24 20 E
Potenza **94** 40 40N 15 50 E
Poteriteri, L. **128** 46 5 S 167 10 E
Potgietersrus **123** 24 10 S 28 55 E
Poth **51** 29 4N 98 5W
Potholes Reservoir **53** 46 59N 119 16W
Poti **99** 42 10N 41 38 E
Potiraguá **75** 15 36 S 39 53W
Potiskum **120** 11 39N 11 2 E
Potlatch **20** 46 55N 116 54W
Potlogi **95** 44 34N 25 34 E
Potomac, Ill. **21** 40 18N 87 48W
Potomac, Md. **27** 39 1N 77 13W
Potomac → **27** 38 0N 76 23W
Potomac Heights **27** 38 36N 77 8W
Potosí, Bolivia **73** 19 38 S 65 50W
Potosi, U.S.A. **32** 37 56N 90 47W
Potosí □ **72** 20 31 S 67 0W
Pototan **111** 10 54N 122 38 E
Potrerillos **76** 26 30 S 69 30W
Potsdam, Germany **88** 52 23N 13 4 E
Potsdam, U.S.A. **39** 44 40N 74 59W
Pottawatomie County ◇, Kans. **24** 39 20N 96 15W
Pottawatomie County ◇, Okla. **43** 35 10N 97 0W
Pottawattamie County ◇ **23** 41 20N 95 30W
Potter, Kans. **24** 39 26N 95 9W
Potter, Nebr. **34** 41 13N 103 19W
Potter County ◇, Pa. **45** 41 50N 78 0W
Potter County ◇, S. Dak. **47** 45 0N 100 0W
Potter County ◇, Tex. **50** 35 22N 101 50W
Potterville, Ga. **18** 32 31N 84 7W
Potterville, Mich. **29** 42 38N 84 45W
Potts Camp **31** 34 39N 89 18W
Pottsboro **51** 33 46N 96 40W
Pottstown **45** 40 15N 75 39W
Pottsville **45** 40 41N 76 12W
Pottuvil **108** 6 55N 81 50 E
Potwin **24** 37 56N 97 1W
Pouce Coupé **62** 55 40N 120 10W
Poughkeepsie **39** 41 42N 73 56W
Poulan **18** 31 31N 83 47W
Poulaphouca Res. **85** 53 8N 6 30W
Poulsbo **53** 47 44N 122 39W
Poultney **36** 43 31N 73 14W
Pound **54** 37 8N 82 36W
Pouso Alegre, Mato Grosso, Brazil **73** 11 46 S 57 16W
Pouso Alegre, Minas Gerais, Brazil **77** 22 14 S 45 57W
Povenets **98** 62 50N 34 50 E
Poverty Bay **128** 38 43 S 178 2 E
Póvoa de Varzim **91** 41 25N 8 46W
Powassan **60** 46 5N 79 25W
Poway **15** 32 58N 117 2W
Powder →, Mont. **33** 46 45N 105 26W
Powder →, Oreg. **44** 44 45N 117 3W
Powder River **56** 43 2N 106 59W
Powder River County ◇ **33** 45 20N 105 40W
Powder Springs **18** 33 52N 84 41W
Powderhorn **16** 38 17N 107 7W
Powell **56** 44 45N 108 46W
Powell → **49** 36 29N 83 52W
Powell Butte **44** 44 15N 121 1W
Powell County ◇, Ky. **49** 37 50N 83 50W
Powell County ◇, Mont. **33** 47 0N 113 0W
Powell Creek **126** 18 6 S 133 46 E
Powell L. **52** 36 57N 111 29W
Powell River **62** 49 50N 124 35W
Powellville **27** 38 20N 75 22W
Powelton **18** 33 26N 82 52W
Power County ◇ **20** 42 50N 112 50W
Powers, Mich. **29** 45 41N 87 32W
Powers, Oreg. **44** 42 53N 124 4W
Powers Lake **41** 48 34N 102 39W
Powersville **32** 40 33N 93 15W
Poweshiek County ◇ **23** 41 40N 92 30W
Powhatan, Ark. **13** 36 5N 91 7W
Powhatan, Va. **54** 37 32N 77 55W
Powhatan County ◇ **54** 37 32N 77 55W
Powhatan Point **42** 39 52N 80 49W
Powhattan **24** 39 46N 95 38W
Pownal **36** 42 46N 73 14W
Powys □ **83** 52 20N 3 20W
Poxoreu **73** 15 50 S 54 23W
Poyang Hu **115** 29 5N 116 20 E
Poyarkovo **101** 49 36N 128 41 E
Poygan L. **55** 44 19N 88 50W
Poynette **55** 43 24N 89 24W
Poza Rica **65** 20 33N 97 27W
Požarevac **95** 44 35N 21 18 E
Poznań **88** 52 25N 16 55 E
Pozo Almonte **72** 20 10 S 69 50W
Pozo Colorado **76** 23 30 S 58 45W
Pozo del Dátil **64** 30 0N 112 15W
Pozoblanco **91** 38 23N 4 51W
Pozuzo **72** 10 5 S 75 35W
Prachin Buri **112** 14 0N 101 25 E
Prachuap Khiri Khan **112** 11 49N 99 48 E
Pradera **70** 3 25N 76 15W
Prado **75** 17 20 S 39 13W
Prague = Praha **88** 50 5N 14 22 E
Prague, Nebr. **34** 41 19N 96 49W
Prague, Okla. **43** 35 29N 96 41W
Praha **88** 50 5N 14 22 E
Prahova □ **95** 45 10N 26 0 E
Prahova → **95** 44 50N 25 50 E
Praid **89** 46 32N 25 10 E
Prainha, Amazonas, Brazil **73** 7 10 S 60 30W
Prainha, Pará, Brazil **71** 1 45 S 53 30W
Prairie **31** 33 48N 88 40W
Prairie City, Iowa **23** 41 36N 93 14W
Prairie City, Oreg. **44** 44 28N 118 43W
Prairie City, S. Dak. **47** 45 32N 102 48W
Prairie County ◇, Ark. **13** 34 47N 91 35W
Prairie County ◇, Mont. **33** 46 57N 105 30W
Prairie Dog Cr. → **24** 40 0N 99 18W
Prairie Dog Town Ford Red → **50** 34 27N 99 21W
Prairie du Chien **55** 43 3N 91 9W
Prairie du Rocher **21** 38 5N 90 6W
Prairie du Sac **55** 43 17N 89 43W
Prairie Farm **55** 45 14N 91 59W
Prairie Grove **13** 35 59N 94 19W
Prairie Hill **32** 39 31N 92 44W
Prairie Home **32** 38 49N 92 35W
Prairie View, Kans. **24** 39 50N 99 34W
Prairie View, Tex. **51** 30 6N 95 59W
Prairie Village **24** 38 58N 94 38W
Prapat **110** 2 41N 98 58 E
Prata **75** 19 25 S 48 54W
Prato **94** 43 53N 11 5 E
Pratt **24** 37 39N 98 44W
Pratt County ◇ **24** 37 35N 98 45W
Prattville **10** 32 28N 86 29W
Pravia **91** 43 30N 6 12W
Praya **110** 8 39 S 116 17 E
Preble **39** 42 44N 76 9W
Preble County ◇ **42** 39 45N 84 38W
Precordillera **76** 30 0 S 69 1W
Preeceville **63** 51 57N 102 40W
Pregonero **70** 8 1N 71 46W
Prelate **63** 50 51N 109 24W
Premier **62** 56 4N 129 56W
Premier Downs **126** 30 30 S 126 30 E
Premont **50** 27 22N 98 7W
Prentice **55** 45 33N 90 17W
Prentiss **31** 31 36N 89 52W
Prentiss County ◇ **31** 34 39N 88 34W
Prenzlau **88** 53 19N 13 51 E
Preobrazheniye **116** 42 54N 133 54 E
Prepansko Jezero **95** 40 55N 21 0 E
Preparis North Channel **112** 15 12N 93 40 E
Preparis South Channel **112** 14 36N 93 40 E
Přerov **89** 49 28N 17 27 E
Prescott, Canada **60** 44 45N 75 30W
Prescott, Ariz. **12** 34 33N 112 28W
Prescott, Ark. **13** 33 48N 93 23W
Prescott, Iowa **23** 41 1N 94 37W
Prescott, Kans. **24** 38 4N 94 42W
Prescott, Mich. **29** 44 11N 83 56W
Prescott, Wash. **53** 46 18N 118 19W
Prescott National Forest **12** 34 30N 112 30W
Preservation Inlet **128** 46 8 S 166 35 E
Presho **47** 43 54N 100 3W
Presidencia de la Plaza **76** 27 0 S 29 50W
Presidencia Roque Saenz Peña **76** 26 45 S 60 30W
Presidente Epitácio **75** 21 56 S 52 6W
Presidente Hayes □ **76** 24 0 S 59 0W
Presidente Hermes **73** 11 17 S 61 55W
Presidente Prudente **75** 22 5 S 51 25W
Presidential Lakes **37** 39 54N 74 35W
Presidio, Mexico **64** 29 29N 104 23W
Presidio, U.S.A. **50** 29 34N 104 22W
Presidio County ◇ **50** 30 0N 104 0W
Preslav **95** 43 10N 26 52 E
Preslavska Planina **95** 43 10N 26 45 E
Prespa **95** 41 44N 24 55 E
Prespa, L. = Prepansko Jezero **95** 40 55N 21 0 E
Presque Isle, Maine **26** 46 41N 68 1W
Presque Isle, Mich. **29** 45 18N 83 29W
Presque Isle County ◇ **29** 45 15N 84 0W
Prestbury **83** 51 54N 2 2W
Presteigne **83** 52 17N 3 0W
Presto **73** 18 55 S 64 56W
Preston, U.K. **82** 53 46N 2 42W
Preston, Ga. **18** 32 4N 84 32W
Preston, Idaho **20** 42 6N 111 53W
Preston, Iowa **23** 42 3N 90 24W
Preston, Kans. **24** 37 46N 98 33W
Preston, Md. **27** 38 43N 75 55W
Preston, Minn. **30** 43 40N 92 5W
Preston, Nev. **35** 38 55N 115 4W
Preston, Okla. **43** 35 43N 95 59W
Preston, C. **126** 20 51 S 116 12 E
Preston City **28** 41 33N 72 57W
Preston County ◇ **54** 39 31N 79 48W
Prestonpans **84** 55 58N 3 0W
Prestonsburg **49** 37 40N 82 47W
Prestwick **84** 55 30N 4 38W
Prêto →, Amazonas, Brazil **71** 0 8 S 64 6W
Prêto →, Bahia, Brazil **74** 11 21 S 43 52W
Prêto do Igapó-Açu → **71** 4 26 S 59 48W
Pretoria **123** 25 44 S 28 12 E
Pretty Prairie **24** 37 47N 98 1W
Prettyboy Reservoir **27** 39 37N 76 43W
Préveza **95** 38 57N 20 47 E
Prewitt **38** 35 22N 108 3W
Prewitt Reservoir **16** 40 26N 103 22W
Prey-Veng **112** 11 35N 105 29 E
Pribilof Is., Bering S. **4** 56 0N 170 0W
Pribilof Is., U.S.A. **11** 57 0N 170 0W
Příbram **88** 49 41N 14 2 E
Price, Md. **27** 39 6N 75 58W
Price, Tex. **51** 32 8N 94 57W
Price, Utah **52** 39 36N 110 49W
Price → **52** 39 10N 110 6W
Price County ◇ **55** 45 45N 90 20W
Price I. **62** 52 23N 128 41W
Prichard, Ala. **10** 30 44N 88 5W
Prichard, W. Va. **54** 38 15N 82 36W
Prichett **16** 37 22N 102 52W
Priddy **51** 31 41N 98 31W
Pride **48** 37 34N 87 53W
Prieska **123** 29 40 S 22 42 E
Priest → **20** 48 12N 116 54W
Priest L. **20** 48 35N 116 52W
Priest Rapids Dam **53** 46 39N 119 54W
Priestly **62** 54 8N 125 20W
Prieta Loma **14** 37 7N 121 50W
Prikaspiyskaya Nizmennost **99** 47 0N 48 0 E
Prikumsk **99** 44 50N 44 10 E
Prilep **95** 41 21N 21 37 E
Priluki **99** 50 30N 32 24 E
Primeira Cruz **74** 2 30 S 43 26W
Primghar **23** 43 5N 95 38W
Primorsko **95** 42 15N 27 44 E
Primrose **34** 41 38N 98 14W
Primrose L. **63** 54 55N 109 45W
Prince Albert **63** 53 15N 105 50W
Prince Albert Mts. **5** 76 0 S 161 30 E
Prince Albert Nat. Park **63** 54 0N 106 25W
Prince Albert Pen. **58** 72 30N 116 0W
Prince Albert Sd. **58** 70 25N 115 0W
Prince Alfred C. **4** 74 20N 124 40W
Prince Charles I. **59** 67 47N 76 12W
Prince Charles Mts. **5** 72 0 S 67 0 E
Prince Edward County ◇ **54** 37 15N 78 25W
Prince Edward I. □ **61** 46 20N 63 20W
Prince Edward Is. **3** 45 15 S 39 0 E
Prince Frederick **27** 38 33N 76 35W
Prince George, Canada **62** 53 55N 122 50W
Prince George, U.S.A. **54** 37 13N 77 17W
Prince George County ◇ **54** 37 13N 77 17W
Prince Georges County ◇ **27** 38 45N 76 50W
Prince of Wales, C. **11** 65 36N 168 5W
Prince of Wales I., Canada **58** 73 0N 99 0W
Prince of Wales I., U.S.A. **11** 55 47N 132 50W
Prince of Wales Is. **127** 10 40 S 142 10 E
Prince of Wales-Outer Ketchikan ◇ **11** 55 0N 131 30W
Prince Patrick I. **4** 77 0N 120 0W
Prince Regent Inlet **4** 73 0N 90 0W
Prince Rupert **62** 54 20N 130 20W
Prince William County ◇ **54** 38 45N 77 29W
Prince William Sd. **11** 60 40N 147 0W
Princesa Isabel **74** 7 44 S 38 0W
Princess Anne **27** 38 12N 75 42W
Princess Charlotte B. **127** 14 25 S 144 0 E
Princess Royal I. **62** 53 0N 128 40W
Princeton, Canada **62** 49 27N 120 30W
Princeton, Ark. **13** 33 59N 92 38W
Princeton, Calif. **14** 39 24N 122 1W
Princeton, Ill. **21** 41 23N 89 28W
Princeton, Ind. **22** 38 21N 87 34W
Princeton, Iowa **23** 41 40N 90 20W
Princeton, Kans. **24** 38 29N 95 16W
Princeton, Ky. **48** 37 7N 87 53W
Princeton, Maine **26** 45 13N 67 34W
Princeton, Mass. **28** 42 0N 71 0W
Princeton, Mich. **29** 46 17N 87 29W
Princeton, Minn. **30** 45 34N 93 35W
Princeton, Mo. **32** 40 24N 93 35W
Princeton, N.C. **40** 35 28N 78 10W
Princeton, N.J. **37** 40 21N 74 39W
Princeton, S.C. **46** 34 30N 82 17W
Princeton, W. Va. **54** 37 22N 81 6W
Princeton, Wis. **55** 43 51N 89 8W
Princeville **21** 40 56N 89 46W
Principe, I. de **119** 1 37N 7 27 E
Principe Chan. **62** 53 28N 130 0W
Principe da Beira **73** 12 20 S 64 30W
Prineville **44** 44 18N 120 51W
Prineville Reservoir **44** 44 7N 120 47W
Pringle, S. Dak. **47** 43 37N 103 36W
Pringle, Tex. **50** 35 57N 101 27W
Prins Harald Kyst **5** 70 0 S 35 1 E
Prinsburg **30** 44 56N 95 11W
Prinsesse Astrid Kyst **5** 70 45 S 12 30 E
Prinsesse Ragnhild Kyst **5** 70 15 S 27 30 E
Prinzapolca **66** 13 20N 83 35W
Prior Lake **30** 44 43N 93 25W
Priozersk **98** 61 2N 30 7 E
Pripet = Pripyat → **98** 51 20N 30 9 E
Pripet Marshes = Polesye **98** 52 0N 28 10 E
Pripyat → **98** 51 20N 30 9 E
Priština **95** 42 40N 21 13 E

Privas

Qo

Privas **90** 44 45N 4 37 E
Privolzhskaya Vozvyshennost **99** 51 0N 46 0 E
Prizren **95** 42 13N 20 45 E
Probolinggo **111** 7 46 S 113 13 E
Proctor, Colo. **16** 40 48N 102 57W
Proctor, Minn. **30** 46 45N 92 14W
Proctor, Vt. **36** 43 40N 73 2W
Proctor, W. Va. **54** 39 43N 80 49W
Proctor L. **51** 31 58N 98 29W
Proctorsville **36** 43 23N 72 40W
Proctorville **42** 38 26N 82 23W
Proddatur **108** 14 45N 78 30 E
Prof. Van Blommestein Meer **71** 4 45N 55 5W
Progreso **65** 21 20N 89 40W
Prokopyevsk **100** 54 0N 86 45 E
Prome = Pyè **109** 18 49N 95 13 E
Promise City **23** 40 45N 93 9W
Promontory Mts. **52** 41 30N 112 30W
Prophet → **62** 58 48N 122 40W
Prophetstown **21** 41 40N 89 56W
Propriá **74** 10 13 S 36 51W
Proserpine **127** 20 21 S 148 36 E
Prospect, Conn. **28** 41 30N 72 59W
Prospect, Ohio **42** 40 27N 83 11W
Prospect, Oreg. **44** 42 45N 122 29W
Prospect, Pa. **45** 40 54N 80 3W
Prosperity **46** 34 12N 81 32W
Prosser, Nebr. **34** 40 41N 98 34W
Prosser, Wash. **53** 46 12N 119 46W
Prostějov **88** 49 30N 17 9 E
Protection **24** 37 12N 99 29W
Protem **32** 36 32N 92 51W
Protivin **23** 43 13N 92 6W
Provadiya **95** 43 12N 27 30 E
Provence **90** 43 40N 5 46 E
Providence, Ky. **48** 37 24N 87 46W
Providence, R.I. **28** 41 49N 71 24W
Providence, Utah **52** 41 43N 111 49W
Providence Bay **60** 45 41N 82 15W
Providence County ◇ **28** 41 50N 71 40W
Providence Mts. **15** 35 10N 115 15W
Providencia **70** 0 28 S 76 28W
Providencia, I. de **66** 13 25N 81 26W
Provideniya **101** 64 23N 173 18W
Provincetown **28** 42 3N 70 11W
Provins **90** 48 33N 3 15 E
Provo, S. Dak. **47** 43 12N 103 50W
Provo, Utah **52** 40 14N 111 39W
Provost **63** 52 25N 110 20W
Prowers County ◇ **16** 38 0N 102 30W
Prudence I. **28** 41 37N 71 19W
Prudentópolis **75** 25 12 S 50 57W
Prudhoe Bay **11** 70 18N 148 22W
Prud'homme **63** 52 20N 105 54W
Prue **43** 36 15N 96 15W
Pruszków **89** 52 9N 20 49 E
Prut → **89** 46 3N 28 10 E
Prydz B. **5** 69 0 S 74 0 E
Pryor **43** 36 19N 95 19W
Przemyśl **89** 49 50N 22 45 E
Przeworsk **89** 50 6N 22 32 E
Przhevalsk **100** 42 30N 78 20 E
Pskov **98** 57 50N 28 25 E
Puaena Pt. **19** 21 36N 158 6W
Puán **76** 37 30 S 62 45W
Pucacuro → **70** 3 20 S 74 58W
Pucallpa **72** 8 25 S 74 30W
Pucará, Bolivia **73** 18 43 S 64 11W
Pucará, Peru **72** 15 5 S 70 24W
Pucarani **72** 16 23 S 68 30W
Pucheng **115** 27 59N 118 31 E
Pucheni **95** 45 12N 25 17 E
Puckaway L. **55** 43 45N 89 10W
Puckett **31** 32 5N 89 47W
Pudozh **98** 61 48N 36 32 E
Pudukkottai **108** 10 28N 78 47 E
Puebla **65** 19 0N 98 10W
Puebla □ **65** 18 30N 98 0W
Pueblo **16** 38 16N 104 37W
Pueblo Colorado Wash → **12** 35 5N 110 22W
Pueblo County ◇ **16** 38 15N 104 30W
Pueblo Hundido **76** 26 20 S 70 5W
Pueblo Mt. **44** 42 6N 118 39W
Pueblo Nuevo, Puerto Rico **57** 18 28N 66 51W
Pueblo Nuevo, Venezuela **70** 8 26N 71 26W
Puelches **76** 38 5 S 65 51W
Puelén **76** 37 32 S 67 38W
Puente Alto **76** 33 32 S 70 35W
Puente-Genil **91** 37 22N 4 47W
Pueo Pt. **19** 21 54N 160 4W
Puerca, Pta. **57** 18 13N 65 36W
Puerco →, Ariz. **12** 34 54N 110 2W
Puerco →, N. Mex. **38** 34 22N 107 50W
Puerto Acosta **72** 15 32 S 69 15W
Puerto Aisén **78** 45 27 S 73 0W
Puerto Ángel **65** 15 40N 96 29W
Puerto Arista **65** 15 56N 93 48W
Puerto Armuelles **66** 8 20N 82 51W
Puerto Ayacucho **70** 5 40N 67 35W
Puerto Barrios **66** 15 40N 88 32W
Puerto Bermejo **76** 26 55 S 58 34W
Puerto Bermúdez **72** 10 20 S 75 0W
Puerto Bolívar **70** 3 19 S 79 55W
Puerto Cabello **70** 10 28N 68 1W
Puerto Cabezas **66** 14 0N 83 30W
Puerto Cabo Gracias á Dios **66** 15 0N 83 10W
Puerto Carreño **70** 6 12N 67 22W
Puerto Castilla **66** 16 0N 86 0W
Puerto Chicama **72** 7 45 S 79 20W
Puerto Coig **78** 50 54 S 69 15W
Puerto Cortes, C. Rica **66** 8 55N 84 0W
Puerto Cortés, Hond. **66** 15 51N 88 0W
Puerto Cumarebo **70** 11 29N 69 30W
Puerto de Santa María **91** 36 36N 6 13W
Puerto del Rosario **120** 28 30N 13 52W
Puerto Deseado **78** 47 55 S 66 0W
Puerto Guaraní **73** 21 18 S 57 55W
Puerto Heath **72** 12 34 S 68 39W
Puerto Huitoto **70** 0 18N 74 3W
Puerto Inca **72** 9 22 S 74 54W
Puerto Juárez **65** 21 11N 86 49W
Puerto La Cruz **71** 10 13N 64 38W
Puerto Leguízamo **70** 0 12 S 74 46W
Puerto Libertad **64** 29 55N 112 41W
Puerto Limón **70** 3 23N 73 30W
Puerto Lobos **78** 42 0 S 65 3W
Puerto López **70** 4 5N 72 58W
Puerto Madryn **78** 42 48 S 65 4W
Puerto Maldonado **72** 12 30 S 69 10W
Puerto Manotí **66** 21 22N 76 50W
Puerto Mercedes **70** 1 11N 72 53W
Puerto Miraña **70** 1 20 S 70 19W
Puerto Montt **78** 41 28 S 73 0W
Puerto Morelos **65** 20 49N 86 52W
Puerto Nariño **70** 4 56N 67 48W
Puerto Natales **78** 51 45 S 72 15W
Puerto Nuevo **70** 5 53N 69 56W
Puerto Nuevo, Pta. **57** 18 30N 66 24W
Puerto Nutrias **70** 8 5N 69 18W
Puerto Ordaz **71** 8 16N 62 44W
Puerto Padre **66** 21 13N 76 35W
Puerto Páez **70** 6 13N 67 28W
Puerto Peñasco **64** 31 20N 113 33W
Puerto Pinasco **76** 22 36 S 57 50W
Puerto Pirámides **78** 42 35 S 64 20W
Puerto Plata **67** 19 48N 70 45W
Puerto Portillo **72** 9 45 S 72 42W
Puerto Princesa **111** 9 46N 118 45 E
Puerto Quellón **78** 43 7 S 73 37W
Puerto Quepos **66** 9 29N 84 6W
Puerto Rico **72** 11 5 S 67 38W
Puerto Rico ■ **57** 18 15N 66 30W
Puerto Saavedra **78** 38 47 S 73 24W
Puerto Sastre **76** 22 2 S 57 55W
Puerto Siles **73** 12 48 S 65 5W
Puerto Suárez **73** 18 58 S 57 52W
Puerto Tejada **70** 3 14N 76 24W
Puerto Umbría **70** 0 52N 76 33W
Puerto Vallarta **64** 20 36N 105 15W
Puerto Varas **78** 41 19 S 72 59W
Puerto Villazón **73** 13 32 S 61 57W
Puerto Wilches **70** 7 21N 73 54W
Puertollano **91** 38 43N 4 7W
Puesto Cunambo **70** 2 10 S 76 0W
Pueyrredón, L. **78** 47 20 S 72 0W
Pugachev **98** 52 0N 48 49 E
Puget Sound **53** 47 50N 122 30W
Púglia □ **94** 41 0N 16 30 E
Puica **72** 15 0 S 72 33W
Puieşti **95** 46 25N 27 33 E
Puigcerdá **91** 42 24N 1 50 E
Pujilí **70** 0 57 S 78 41W
Pukaki L. **128** 44 4 S 170 1 E
Pukalani **19** 20 51N 156 20W
Pukapuka **125** 10 53 S 165 49W
Pukatawagan **63** 55 45N 101 20W
Pukekohe **128** 37 12 S 174 55 E
Pukoo **19** 21 4N 156 48W
Pukou **115** 32 7N 118 38 E
Pula **94** 39 0N 9 0 E
Pulacayo **72** 20 25 S 66 41W
Pulaski, Ill. **21** 37 12N 89 10W
Pulaski, Iowa **23** 40 45N 92 12W
Pulaski, N.Y. **39** 43 34N 76 8W
Pulaski, Tenn. **48** 35 12N 87 2W
Pulaski, Va. **54** 37 3N 80 47W
Pulaski, Wis. **55** 44 41N 88 14W
Pulaski County ◇, Ark. **13** 34 45N 92 20W
Pulaski County ◇, Ga. **18** 32 15N 83 30W
Pulaski County ◇, Ill. **21** 37 15N 89 5W
Pulaski County ◇, Ind. **22** 41 0N 86 40W
Pulaski County ◇, Ky. **49** 37 5N 84 35W
Pulaski County ◇, Mo. **32** 37 50N 92 10W
Pulaski County ◇, Va. **54** 37 0N 80 45W
Pulicat, L. **108** 13 40N 80 15 E
Pullman **53** 46 44N 117 10W
Pulog, Mt. **111** 16 40N 120 50 E
Puloraja **110** 4 55N 95 24 E
Pumlumon Fawr **83** 52 29N 3 47W
Pumpville **50** 29 53N 101 45W
Puna **73** 19 45 S 65 28W
Puná, I. **70** 2 55 S 80 5W
Punakha **109** 27 42N 89 52 E
Punaluu **19** 21 35N 157 53W
Punata **73** 17 32 S 65 50W
Punch **108** 33 48N 74 4 E
Pune **108** 18 29N 73 57 E
Pungo L. **40** 35 42N 76 33W
Puning **115** 23 20N 116 12 E
Punjab □, India **108** 31 0N 76 0 E
Punjab □, Pakistan **108** 30 0N 72 0 E
Puno **72** 15 55 S 70 3W
Punta, Cerro de **57** 18 10N 66 37W
Punta Alta **78** 38 53 S 62 4W
Punta Arenas **78** 53 10 S 71 0W
Punta Cardón **70** 11 38N 70 14W
Punta Coles **72** 17 43 S 71 23W
Punta de Agua → **50** 35 32N 102 27W
Punta de Bombón **72** 17 10 S 71 48W
Punta de Díaz **76** 28 0 S 70 45W
Punta de Piedras **70** 10 54N 64 6W
Punta Delgado **78** 42 43 S 63 38W
Punta Gorda, Belize **65** 16 10N 88 45W
Punta Gorda, U.S.A. **17** 26 56N 82 3W
Punta Prieta **64** 28 58N 114 17W
Punta Rassa **17** 26 26N 81 59W
Puntarenas **66** 10 0N 84 50W
Punto Fijo **70** 11 50N 70 13W
Punxsatawney **45** 40 57N 78 59W
Puolo Pt. **19** 21 54N 159 36W
Puqi **115** 29 40N 113 50 E
Puquio **72** 14 45 S 74 10W
Pur → **100** 67 31N 77 55 E
Purace, Vol. **70** 2 21N 76 23W
Purbeck, Isle of **83** 50 40N 2 5W
Purcell **43** 35 1N 97 22W
Purcell Mts. **33** 48 30N 115 0W
Purcellville **54** 39 8N 77 43W
Purdin **32** 39 57N 93 10W
Purdon **51** 31 57N 96 37W
Purdy, Mo. **32** 36 49N 93 55W
Purdy, Okla. **43** 34 43N 97 35W
Purdy, Va. **54** 36 49N 77 36W
Purgatoire → **16** 38 4N 103 11W
Puri **109** 19 50N 85 58 E
Purificación **70** 3 51N 74 55W
Purísima, La **64** 26 10N 112 4W
Purmerend **87** 52 30N 4 58 E
Purnia **109** 25 45N 87 31 E
Pursat **112** 12 34N 103 50 E
Purukcau **110** 0 35 S 114 35 E
Puruliya **109** 23 17N 86 24 E
Purus → **71** 3 42 S 61 28W
Purvis **31** 31 9N 89 25W
Půrvomay **95** 42 8N 25 17 E
Purwakarta **111** 6 35 S 107 29 E
Purwodadi, Jawa, Indonesia **111** 7 7 S 110 55 E
Purwodadi, Jawa, Indonesia **111** 7 51 S 110 0 E
Purwokerto **111** 7 25 S 109 14 E
Purworejo **111** 7 43 S 110 2 E
Puryear **48** 36 27N 88 20W
Pusan **114** 35 5N 129 0 E
Pushaw L. **26** 44 56N 68 48W
Pushchino **101** 54 10N 158 0 E
Pushkino **99** 51 16N 47 0 E
Pushmataha County ◇ **43** 34 25N 95 20W
Put-in Bay **42** 41 39N 82 49W
Putahow L. **63** 59 54N 100 40W
Putao **109** 27 28N 97 30 E
Putaruru **128** 38 2 S 175 50 E
Puţeni **95** 45 49N 27 42 E
Puthein Myit → **109** 15 56N 94 18 E
Putian **115** 25 23N 119 0 E
Putignano **94** 40 50N 17 5 E
Putina **72** 14 55 S 69 55W
Puting, Tanjung **110** 3 31 S 111 46 E
Putna → **95** 45 42N 27 26 E
Putnam, Conn. **28** 41 55N 71 55W
Putnam, Okla. **43** 35 51N 98 58W
Putnam, Tex. **51** 32 22N 99 12W
Putnam County ◇, Fla. **17** 29 35N 81 45W
Putnam County ◇, Ga. **18** 33 20N 83 15W
Putnam County ◇, Ill. **21** 41 10N 89 15W
Putnam County ◇, Ind. **22** 39 40N 86 50W
Putnam County ◇, Mo. **32** 40 30N 93 0W
Putnam County ◇, N.Y. **39** 41 25N 73 45W
Putnam County ◇, Ohio **42** 40 59N 84 12W
Putnam County ◇, Tenn. **49** 36 10N 85 30W
Putnam County ◇, W. Va. **54** 38 32N 81 54W
Putney, Ga. **18** 31 29N 84 8W
Putney, S. Dak. **47** 45 34N 98 11W
Putney, Vt. **36** 42 58N 72 31W
Putorana, Gory **101** 69 0N 95 0 E
Putre **72** 18 12 S 69 35W
Puttalam **108** 8 1N 79 55 E
Putten **87** 52 16N 5 36 E
Puttgarden **88** 54 28N 11 15 E
Putumayo → **70** 3 7 S 67 58W
Putussibau **110** 0 50N 112 56 E
Puu Kaaumakua **19** 21 30N 157 54W
Puu Keahiakahoe **19** 21 23N 157 49W
Puu o Keokeo **19** 19 13N 155 44W
Puuanahulu **19** 19 49N 155 51W
Puukolii **19** 20 56N 156 41W
Puunene **19** 20 53N 156 23W
Puuwai **19** 21 54N 160 12W
Puxico **32** 36 57N 90 10W
Puy, Le **90** 45 3N 3 52 E
Puy-de-Dôme **90** 45 46N 2 57 E
Puy-de-Dôme □ **90** 45 47N 3 0 E
Puyallup **53** 47 12N 122 18W
Puyang **114** 35 40N 115 1 E
Puyehue **78** 40 40 S 72 37W
Puyo **70** 1 28 S 77 59W
Pweto **122** 8 25 S 28 51 E
Pwllheli **82** 52 54N 4 26W
Pya-ozero **98** 66 5N 30 58 E
Pyapon **109** 16 20N 95 40 E
Pyasina → **101** 73 30N
Pyatigorsk **99** 44 2N
Pyè **109** 18 49N
Pyinmana **109** 19 45N
Pymatuning Reservoir **42** 41 30N
Pyŏngyang **114** 39 0N
Pyote **50** 31 32N
Pyramid L. **35** 40 1N
Pyramid Lake Indian Reservation **35** 40 20N
Pyramid Pk. **56** 43 27N
Pyrenees = Pyrénées **90** 42 45N
Pyrénées **90** 42 45N
Pyrénées-Atlantiques □ **90** 43 15N
Pyrénées-Orientales □ **90** 42 35N
Pyu **109** 18 30N

Q

Qabalān **104** 32 8N
Qabātiyah **104** 32 25N
Qādib **105** 12 35N
Qā'emshahr **107** 36 30N
Qahremānshahr **106** 34 23N
Qaidam Pendi **113** 37 0N
Qa'iya **106** 24 33N
Qalāt **107** 32 15N
Qal'at al Akhḑar **106** 28 0N
Qal'at al Mu'azzam **106** 27 45N
Qal'eh Shaharak **108** 34 10N
Qal'eh-ye Now **107** 35 0N
Qalqīlya **104** 32 12N
Qam **104** 32 36N
Qamar, Ghubbat al **105** 16 20N
Qamruddin Karez **108** 31 45N
Qāna **104** 33 12N
Qandahār **108** 31 32N
Qandahār □ **108** 31 0N
Qâra **121** 29 38N
Qarachuk **106** 37 0N
Qārah **106** 29 55N
Qarqan **113** 38 5N
Qarqan He → **113** 39 30N
Qasim, Si. Arabia **106** 26 0N
Qāsim, Syria **104** 32 59N
Qaşr-e Qand **107** 26 15N
Qasr Farâfra **121** 27 0N
Qatar ■ **107** 25 30N
Qattâra, Munkhafed el **121** 29 30N
Qattâra Depression = Qattâra, Munkhafed el **121** 29 30N
Qāyen **107** 33 40N
Qazvin **106** 36 15N
Qena **121** 26 10N
Qeshm **107** 26 55N
Qezi'ot **104** 30 52N
Qian Xian **115** 34 31N
Qianshan **115** 30 37N
Qianxi **115** 27 3N
Qianyang **115** 27 18N
Qijiang **115** 28 57N
Qila Safed **107** 29 0N
Qila Saifullāh **108** 30 45N
Qilian Shan **113** 38 30N
Qin Ling = Qinling Shandi **115** 33 50N
Qin'an **115** 34 48N
Qingdao **114** 36 5N
Qinghai □ **113** 36 0N
Qinghai Hu **113** 36 40N
Qingjiang, Jiangsu, China **115** 33 30N
Qingjiang, Jiangxi, China **115** 28 4N
Qingliu **115** 26 11N
Qingshuihe **114** 39 55N
Qingyang **114** 36 2N
Qingyuan **115** 23 40N
Qinhuangdao **114** 39 56N
Qinling Shandi **115** 33 50N
Qinyang **115** 35 7N
Qinyuan **114** 36 29N
Qinzhou **115** 21 58N
Qiongshan **115** 19 51N
Qiongzhou Haixia **115** 20 10N
Qiqihar **114** 47 26N
Qiryat 'Anavim **104** 31 49N
Qiryat Ata **104** 32 47N
Qiryat Bialik **104** 32 50N
Qiryat Gat **104** 31 32N
Qiryat Ḩayyim **104** 32 49N
Qiryat Mal'akhi **104** 31 44N
Qiryat Shemona **104** 33 13N
Qiryat Yam **104** 32 51N
Qishan **115** 22 52N
Qishon → **104** 32 49N
Qitai **113** 44 2N
Qiyahe **114** 53 0N
Qiyang **115** 26 35N
Qizān **105** 17 0N
Qom **107** 34 40N
Qomolangma Feng **113** 28 0N
Qomsheh **107** 32 0N
Qondūz **107** 36 50N
Qondūz □ **107** 36 50N

Qu Jiang → **115** 30 1N 106 24 E
Qu Xian, Sichuan, China **115** 30 48N 106 58 E
Qu Xian, Zhejiang, China **115** 28 57N 118 54 E
Quabbin Reservoir **28** 42 20N 72 20W
Quail **50** 34 55N 100 30W
Quakertown **45** 40 26N 75 21W
Quan Long **112** 9 7N 105 8 E
Quanah **51** 34 18N 99 44W
Quang Ngai **112** 15 13N 108 58 E
Quang Yen **112** 20 56N 106 52 E
Quantico **27** 38 23N 75 44W
Quantock Hills **83** 51 8N 3 10W
Quanzhou, Fujian, China **115** 24 55N 118 34 E
Quanzhou, Guangxi Zhuangzu, China **115** 25 57N 111 5 E
Quapaw **43** 36 58N 94 50W
Quaraí **76** 30 15 S 56 20W
Quarryville **45** 39 54N 76 10W
Quartz Hill **15** 34 39N 118 13W
Quartzsite **12** 33 40N 114 13W
Quatsino **62** 50 30N 127 40W
Quatsino Sd. **62** 50 25N 127 58W
Quay **38** 34 56N 103 45W
Quay County ◇ **38** 35 0N 103 30W
Qubab = Mishmar Ayyalon **104** 31 52N 34 57 E
Qūchān **107** 37 10N 58 27 E
Queanbeyan **127** 35 17 S 149 14 E
Québec **61** 46 52N 71 13W
Québec □ **61** 50 0N 70 0W
Quebradillas **57** 18 29N 66 56W
Quechee **36** 43 40N 72 25W
Queen Alexandra Ra. **5** 85 0 S 170 0 E
Queen Anne **27** 38 55N 75 57W
Queen Annes County ◇ **27** 39 10N 76 0W
Queen Charlotte **62** 53 15N 132 2W
Queen Charlotte Bay **78** 51 50 S 60 40W
Queen Charlotte Is. **62** 53 20N 132 10W
Queen Charlotte Sd. **128** 41 10 S 174 15 E
Queen Charlotte Str. **62** 51 0N 128 0W
Queen City, Mo. **32** 40 25N 92 34W
Queen City, Tex. **51** 33 9N 94 9W
Queen Creek **12** 33 15N 111 35W
Queen Elizabeth Is. **6** 76 0N 95 0W
Queen Mary Coast **5** 70 0 S 95 0 E
Queen Maud G. **58** 68 15N 102 30W
Queen Maud Ra. **5** 86 0 S 160 0W
Queens Chan. **126** 15 0 S 129 30 E
Queens County ◇ **39** 40 40N 73 50W
Queenscliff **127** 38 16 S 144 39 E
Queensland **18** 31 46N 83 14W
Queensland □ **127** 22 0 S 142 0 E
Queenstown, Australia **127** 42 4 S 145 35 E
Queenstown, N.Z. **128** 45 1 S 168 40 E
Queenstown, S. Africa **123** 31 52 S 26 52 E
Queenstown, U.S.A. **27** 38 59N 76 9W
Queets → **53** 47 33N 124 21W
Queguay Grande → **76** 32 9 S 58 9W
Queimadas **74** 11 0 S 39 38W
Quela **122** 9 10 S 16 56 E
Quelimane **123** 17 53 S 36 58 E
Quelpart = Cheju Do **115** 33 29N 126 34 E
Quemado **38** 34 20N 108 30W
Quemú-Quemú **76** 36 3 S 63 36W
Quenemo **24** 38 35N 95 30W
Quequén **76** 38 30 S 58 30W
Querco **72** 13 50 S 74 52W
Querétaro **64** 20 40N 100 23W
Querétaro □ **64** 20 30N 100 0W
Queshan **115** 32 55N 114 2 E
Quesnel **62** 53 0N 122 30W
Quesnel → **62** 52 58N 122 29W
Quesnel L. **62** 52 30N 121 20W
Questa **38** 36 42N 105 36W
Quetena **72** 22 10 S 67 25W
Quetico Prov. Park **60** 48 30N 91 45W
Quetrequile **78** 41 33 S 69 22W
Quetta **107** 30 15N 66 55 E
Quevedo **70** 1 2 S 79 29W
Quezaltenango **66** 14 50N 91 30W
Quezon City **111** 14 38N 121 0 E
Qui Nhon **112** 13 40N 109 13 E
Quiaca, La **76** 22 5 S 65 35W
Quibaxe **122** 8 24 S 14 27 E
Quibdo **70** 5 42N 76 40W
Quiberon **90** 47 29N 3 9W
Quíbor **70** 9 56N 69 37W
Quick **62** 54 36N 126 54W
Quidnet **28** 41 18N 69 58W
Quiet L. **62** 61 5N 133 5W
Quiindy **76** 25 58 S 57 14W
Quila **64** 24 23N 107 13W
Quilán, C. **78** 43 15 S 74 30W
Quilcene **53** 47 49N 122 53W
Quilengues **123** 14 12 S 14 12 E
Quilimarí **76** 32 5 S 71 30W
Quilino **76** 30 14 S 64 29W
Quillabamba **72** 12 50 S 72 50W
Quillacollo **72** 17 26 S 66 17W
Quillagua **76** 21 40 S 69 40W
Quillaicillo **76** 31 17 S 71 40W
Quillota **76** 32 54 S 71 16W
Quilmes **76** 34 43 S 58 15W
Quilon **108** 8 50N 76 38 E
Quilpie **127** 26 35 S 144 11 E
Quilpué **76** 33 5 S 71 33W
Quimby **23** 42 38N 95 38W
Quime **72** 17 2 S 67 15W
Quimilí **76** 27 40 S 62 30W
Quimper **90** 48 0N 4 9W
Quimperlé **90** 47 53N 3 33W
Quinault **53** 47 28N 123 51W
Quinault → **53** 47 21N 124 18W
Quinault Indian Reservation **53** 47 30N 124 5W
Quincemil **72** 13 15 S 70 40W
Quincy, Calif. **14** 39 56N 120 57W
Quincy, Fla. **17** 30 35N 84 34W
Quincy, Ill. **21** 39 56N 91 23W
Quincy, Mass. **28** 42 15N 71 0W
Quincy, Mich. **29** 41 57N 84 53W
Quincy, Ohio **42** 10 18N 83 58W
Quinebaug **28** 42 1N 71 57W
Quinebaug → **28** 41 33N 72 3W
Quines **76** 32 13 S 65 48W
Quinga **123** 15 49 S 40 15 E
Quinhagak **11** 59 45N 161 54W
Quinlan, Okla. **43** 36 27N 99 3W
Quinlan, Tex. **51** 32 55N 96 8W
Quinn → **35** 40 53N 119 3W
Quintana Roo □ **65** 19 0N 88 0W
Quintanar de la Orden **91** 39 36N 3 5W
Quintanar de la Sierra **91** 41 57N 2 55W
Quinter **24** 39 4N 100 14W
Quintero **76** 32 45 S 71 30W
Quinton **43** 35 7N 95 22W
Quinwood **54** 38 4N 80 42W
Quipungo **123** 14 37 S 14 40 E
Quirihue **76** 36 15 S 72 35W
Quiriquire **70** 9 59N 63 13W
Quiruvilca **72** 8 1 S 78 19W
Quissanga **123** 12 24 S 40 28 E
Quitaque **50** 34 22N 101 4W
Quitilipi **76** 26 50 S 60 13W
Quitman, Ark. **13** 35 23N 92 13W
Quitman, Ga. **18** 30 47N 83 34W
Quitman, La. **25** 32 21N 92 43W
Quitman, Miss. **31** 32 2N 88 44W
Quitman, Tex. **51** 32 48N 95 27W
Quitman County ◇, Ga. **18** 31 50N 85 0W
Quitman County ◇, Miss. **31** 34 12N 90 17W
Quitman Mts. **50** 31 0N 105 10W
Quito **70** 0 15 S 78 35W
Quixadá **74** 4 55 S 39 0W
Quixeramobim **74** 5 12 S 39 17W
Qulin **32** 36 36N 90 15W
Qumrān **104** 31 43N 35 27 E
Quneitra **104** 33 7N 35 48 E
Quonochontaug **28** 41 21N 71 43W
Quorn **127** 32 25 S 138 0 E
Qûs **121** 25 55N 32 50 E
Quseir **121** 26 7N 34 16 E
Qusrah **104** 32 5N 35 20 E

R

Raahe **96** 64 40N 24 28 E
Ra'ananna **104** 32 12N 34 52 E
Raasay **84** 57 25N 6 4W
Raasay, Sd. of **84** 57 30N 6 8W
Raba **111** 8 36 S 118 55 E
Rabat, Malta **94** 35 53N 14 25 E
Rabat, Morocco **120** 34 2N 6 48W
Rabaul **124** 4 24 S 152 18 E
Rabbit → **62** 59 41N 127 12W
Rabbit Cr. → **47** 45 13N 102 10W
Rabbit Lake **63** 53 8N 107 46W
Rabbitskin → **62** 61 47N 120 42W
Rābigh **106** 22 50N 39 5 E
Rabun County ◇ **18** 34 50N 83 30W
Raccoon →, Iowa **23** 41 35N 93 37W
Raccoon →, Ohio **42** 40 2N 82 24W
Race, C. **61** 46 40N 53 5W
Race Point **28** 42 4N 70 14W
Raceland, Ky. **49** 38 32N 82 44W
Raceland, La. **25** 29 44N 90 36W
Rach Gia **112** 10 5N 105 5 E
Racine **30** 43 48N 92 31W
Rădăuţi **89** 47 50N 25 59 E
Radcliff **49** 37 51N 85 57W
Radcliffe **23** 42 20N 93 25W
Radford **54** 37 8N 80 34W
Radhwa, Jabal **106** 24 34N 38 18 E
Radisson, Canada **63** 52 30N 107 20W
Radisson, U.S.A. **55** 45 45N 91 14W
Radium **24** 38 12N 98 56W
Radium Hill **127** 32 30 S 140 42 E
Radium Hot Springs **62** 50 35N 116 2W
Radium Springs **38** 32 30N 106 55W
Radnevo **95** 42 17N 25 58 E
Radnor **42** 40 23N 83 9W
Radnor Forest **83** 52 17N 3 10W
Radom **89** 51 23N 21 12 E
Radomir **95** 42 37N 23 4 E
Radomsko **89** 51 5N 19 28 E
Radstock **83** 51 17N 2 25W
Radstock, C. **126** 33 12 S 134 20 E
Radville **63** 49 30N 104 15W
Rae **62** 62 50N 116 3W
Rae Bareli **109** 26 18N 81 20 E
Rae Isthmus **59** 66 40N 87 30W
Raeren **87** 50 41N 6 7 E
Raeside, L. **126** 29 20 S 122 0 E
Raetihi **128** 39 25 S 175 17 E
Rafaela **76** 31 10 S 61 30W
Rafai **122** 4 59N 23 58 E
Rafḥā **106** 29 35N 43 35 E
Rafsanjān **107** 30 30N 56 5 E
Raft → **20** 42 37N 113 15W
Raft River Mts. **52** 41 55N 113 25W
Ragama **108** 7 0N 79 50 E
Ragan **34** 40 19N 99 15W
Raglan **128** 37 55 S 174 55 E
Ragland **10** 33 45N 86 9W
Ragley **25** 30 30N 93 15W
Rago **24** 37 26N 98 4W
Ragusa **94** 36 56N 14 42 E
Raha **111** 4 55 S 123 0 E
Rahad al Bardī **121** 11 20N 23 40 E
Rahaeng = Tak **112** 16 52N 99 8 E
Rahway **37** 40 37N 74 17W
Raichur **108** 16 10N 77 20 E
Raiford **17** 30 4N 82 14W
Raigarh **109** 21 56N 83 25 E
Raiis **106** 23 33N 38 43 E
Raijua **111** 10 37 S 121 36 E
Railroad Valley **35** 38 25N 115 40W
Rainbow City **10** 33 57N 86 0W
Rainbow Lake **62** 58 30N 119 23W
Rainbow Plateau **12** 36 55N 111 0W
Rainelle **54** 37 58N 80 47W
Rainier **53** 46 53N 122 41W
Rainier, Mt. **53** 46 52N 121 46W
Rains County ◇ **51** 32 52N 95 46W
Rainsburg **45** 39 54N 78 30W
Rainsville **10** 34 30N 85 50W
Rainy → **30** 48 50N 94 42W
Rainy L. **63** 48 42N 93 10W
Rainy River **63** 48 43N 94 29W
Raipur **109** 21 17N 81 45 E
Raj Nandgaon **109** 21 0N 81 0 E
Raja, Ujung **110** 3 40N 96 25 E
Raja Ampat, Kepulauan **111** 0 30 S 130 0 E
Rajahmundry **109** 17 1N 81 48 E
Rajang → **110** 2 30N 112 0 E
Rajapalaiyam **108** 9 25N 77 35 E
Rajasthan □ **108** 26 45N 73 30 E
Rajasthan Canal **108** 28 0N 72 0 E
Rajgarh **108** 24 2N 76 45 E
Rajkot **108** 22 15N 70 56 E
Rajojooseppi **96** 68 25N 28 30 E
Rajpipla **108** 21 50N 73 30 E
Rajshahi **109** 24 22N 88 39 E
Rajshahi □ **109** 25 0N 89 0 E
Rakaia **128** 43 45 S 172 1 E
Rakaia → **128** 43 36 S 172 15 E
Rakan, Ra's **107** 26 10N 51 20 E
Rakaposhi **108** 36 10N 74 25 E
Rakata, Pulau **110** 6 10 S 105 20 E
Rake **23** 43 35N 93 50W
Rakitnoye **116** 45 36N 134 17 E
Rakitovo **95** 41 59N 24 5 E
Rakovski **95** 42 21N 24 57 E
Raleigh, Fla. **17** 29 25N 82 32W
Raleigh, N.C. **40** 35 47N 78 39W
Raleigh, N. Dak. **41** 46 20N 101 20W
Raleigh B. **40** 34 50N 76 15W
Raleigh County ◇ **54** 37 45N 81 10W
Ralls **50** 33 41N 101 24W
Ralls County ◇ **32** 39 30N 91 30W
Ralston, Nebr. **34** 41 12N 96 3W
Ralston, Okla. **43** 36 30N 96 44W
Ralston, Pa. **45** 41 30N 76 57W
Ralston, Wyo. **56** 44 43N 108 52W
Ram → **62** 62 1N 123 41W
Rām Allāh **104** 31 55N 35 10 E
Rama, Israel **104** 32 56N 35 21 E
Rama, Nic. **66** 12 9N 84 15W
Ramah **16** 39 7N 104 10W
Ramalho, Serra do **75** 13 45 S 44 0W
Ramanathapuram **108** 9 25N 78 55 E
Ramat Gan **104** 32 4N 34 48 E
Ramat HaSharon **104** 32 7N 34 50 E
Rambipuji **111** 8 12 S 113 37 E
Ramea **61** 47 31N 57 23W
Ramechhap **109** 27 25N 86 10 E
Ramelau **111** 8 55 S 126 22 E
Ramer, Ala. **10** 32 3N 86 13W
Ramer, Tenn. **48** 35 4N 88 37W
Ramey **45** 40 48N 78 24W
Ramgarh, Bihar, India **109** 23 40N 85 35 E
Ramgarh, Raj., India **108** 27 30N 70 36 E
Rāmhormoz **106** 31 15N 49 35 E
Ramla **104** 31 55N 34 52 E
Rammūn **104** 31 55N 35 17 E
Ramnad = Ramanathapuram **108** 9 25N 78 55 E
Ramon, Har **104** 30 30N 34 38 E
Ramona, Calif. **15** 33 2N 116 52W
Ramona, Kans. **24** 38 36N 97 4W
Ramona, Okla. **43** 36 32N 95 55W
Ramona, S. Dak. **47** 44 7N 97 13W
Ramore **60** 48 30N 80 25W
Ramos → **64** 25 35N 105 3W
Rampart **11** 65 30N 150 10W
Rampur **108** 28 50N 79 5 E
Rampur Hat **109** 24 10N 87 50 E
Ramree Kyun **109** 19 0N 94 0 E
Ramsay, Mich. **29** 46 28N 90 0W
Ramsay, Mont. **33** 46 1N 112 42W
Ramseur **40** 35 44N 79 39W
Ramsey, Canada **60** 47 25N 82 20W
Ramsey, U.K. **82** 54 20N 4 21W
Ramsey, Ill. **21** 39 8N 89 7W
Ramsey, N.J. **37** 41 4N 74 9W
Ramsey County ◇, Minn. **30** 45 0N 93 5W
Ramsey County ◇, N. Dak. **41** 48 15N 98 50W
Ramsgate **83** 51 20N 1 25 E
Ramtek **108** 21 20N 79 15 E
Ranaghat **109** 23 15N 88 35 E
Ranau **110** 6 2N 116 40 E
Rancagua **76** 34 10 S 70 50W
Rancharia **75** 22 15 S 50 55W
Rancheria → **62** 60 13N 129 7W
Ranches of Taos **38** 36 22N 105 37W
Ranchester **56** 44 54N 107 10W
Ranchi **109** 23 19N 85 27 E
Rancho Cordova **14** 38 36N 121 18W
Ranco, L. **78** 40 15 S 72 25W
Rancu **95** 44 32N 24 15 E
Rand, Colo. **16** 40 27N 106 11W
Rand, W. Va. **54** 38 17N 81 34W
Randalia **23** 42 52N 91 53W
Randall, Iowa **23** 42 14N 93 35W
Randall, Kans. **24** 39 38N 98 3W
Randall, Minn. **30** 46 5N 94 30W
Randall County ◇ **50** 34 59N 101 55W
Randallstown **27** 39 22N 76 48W
Randers **97** 56 29N 10 1 E
Randle **53** 46 32N 121 57W
Randleman **40** 35 49N 79 48W
Randlett **43** 34 11N 98 28W
Randolph, Iowa **23** 40 52N 95 34W
Randolph, Kans. **24** 39 26N 96 46W
Randolph, Maine **26** 44 14N 69 46W
Randolph, Mass. **28** 42 10N 71 2W
Randolph, Miss. **31** 34 11N 89 10W
Randolph, N.Y. **39** 42 10N 78 59W
Randolph, Nebr. **34** 42 23N 97 22W
Randolph, Utah **52** 41 40N 111 11W
Randolph, Vt. **36** 43 55N 72 40W
Randolph Center **36** 43 55N 72 37W
Randolph County ◇, Ala. **10** 33 20N 85 25W
Randolph County ◇, Ark. **13** 36 20N 91 0W
Randolph County ◇, Ga. **18** 31 45N 84 45W
Randolph County ◇, Ill. **21** 38 0N 89 50W
Randolph County ◇, Ind. **22** 40 10N 85 0W
Randolph County ◇, Mo. **32** 39 25N 92 30W
Randolph County ◇, N.C. **40** 35 40N 79 50W
Randolph County ◇, W. Va. **54** 38 45N 80 0W
Råne älv → **96** 65 50N 22 20 E
Rangaunu B. **128** 34 51 S 173 15 E
Rangeley **26** 44 58N 70 39W
Rangeley L. **26** 44 55N 70 43W
Rangely **16** 40 5N 108 48W
Ranger **51** 32 28N 98 41W
Rangia **109** 26 28N 91 38 E
Rangiora **128** 43 19 S 172 36 E
Rangitaiki → **128** 37 54 S 176 49 E
Rangitata → **128** 43 45 S 171 15 E
Rangkasbitung **111** 6 22 S 106 16 E
Rangon → **109** 16 28N 96 40 E
Rangoon **109** 16 45N 96 20 E
Rangpur **109** 25 42N 89 22 E
Ranibennur **108** 14 35N 75 30 E
Ranier **30** 48 36N 93 20W
Raniganj **109** 23 40N 87 5 E
Raniwara **108** 24 50N 72 10 E
Rankin, Ill. **21** 40 28N 87 54W
Rankin, Tex. **50** 31 13N 101 56W
Rankin County ◇ **31** 32 15N 90 0W
Rankin Inlet **58** 62 30N 93 0W
Rannoch, L. **84** 56 41N 4 20W
Rannoch Moor **84** 56 38N 4 48W
Ranohira **123** 22 29 S 45 24 E
Ranong **112** 9 56N 98 40 E
Ransiki **111** 1 30 S 134 10 E
Ransom, Ill. **21** 41 9N 88 39W
Ransom, Kans. **24** 38 38N 99 58W
Ransom County ◇ **41** 46 30N 97 40W
Rantau **110** 2 56 S 115 9 E
Rantauprapat **110** 2 15N 99 50 E
Rantekombola **111** 3 15 S 119 57 E
Rantīs **104** 32 4N 35 3 E
Rantoul, Ill. **21** 40 19N 88 9W
Rantoul, Kans. **24** 38 33N 95 7W
Raohe **114** 46 47N 134 0 E
Rapa Iti **125** 27 35 S 144 20W
Rapang **111** 3 45 S 119 55 E
Rāpch **107** 25 40N 59 15 E
Rapelje **33** 45 58N 109 14W
Rapid →, Canada **62** 59 15N 129 5W
Rapid →, U.S.A. **30** 48 42N 94 26W
Rapid City **47** 44 5N 103 14W
Rapid Cr. → **47** 43 54N 102 37W
Rapid River **29** 45 55N 86 58W
Rapidan → **54** 38 22N 77 37W
Rapides des Joachims **60** 46 13N 77 43W
Rapides Parish ◇ **25** 31 15N 92 30W
Rappahannock → **54** 37 34N 76 18W
Rappahannock County ◇ **54** 38 40N 78 10W
Raquette → **39** 45 0N 74 42W
Rarden **42** 38 55N 83 12W

Raritan Reynolds

Raritan 37 40 34N 74 38W
Raritan → 37 40 29N 74 17W
Raritan Bay 37 40 27N 74 15W
Rarotonga 125 21 30 S 160 0W
Ra's al Khaymah 107 25 50N 56 5 E
Ra's al-Unuf 121 30 25N 18 15 E
Ras Bânâs 121 23 57N 35 59 E
Ras Dashen 122 13 8N 38 26 E
Ra's Tannūrah 106 26 40N 50 10 E
Râs Timirist 120 19 21N 16 30W
Rasa, Punta 78 40 50 S 62 15W
Rashad 121 11 55N 31 0 E
Rashîd 121 31 21N 30 22 E
Rasht 106 37 20N 49 40 E
Rason, L. 126 28 45 S 124 25 E
Raşova 95 44 15N 27 55 E
Rasovo 95 43 42N 23 17 E
Rastu 95 43 53N 23 16 E
Rat Buri 112 13 30N 99 54 E
Rat Islands 11 52 0N 178 0W
Rat River 62 61 7N 112 36W
Ratangarh 108 28 5N 74 35 E
Ratcliff 51 31 24N 95 8W
Rath Luirc 85 52 21N 8 40W
Rathbun 23 40 50N 92 50W
Rathbun L. 23 40 54N 93 5W
Rathdrum 85 52 57N 6 13W
Rathenow 88 52 38N 12 23 E
Rathkeale 85 52 32N 8 57W
Rathlin I. 85 55 18N 6 14W
Rathlin O'Birne I. 85 54 40N 8 50W
Ratlam 108 23 20N 75 0 E
Ratliff City 43 34 25N 97 30W
Ratnagiri 108 16 57N 73 18 E
Raton 38 36 54N 104 24W
Rattan 43 34 12N 95 25W
Rattlesnake Cr. → 44 42 44N 117 47W
Rattlesnake Hills 56 42 45N 107 10W
Rattray Hd. 84 57 38N 1 50W
Ratz, Mt. 62 57 23N 132 12W
Raub 112 3 47N 101 52 E
Rauch 76 36 45 S 59 5W
Raufarhöfn 96 66 27N 15 57W
Raukumara Ra. 128 38 5 S 177 55 E
Raul Soares 75 20 5 S 42 22W
Rauma 97 61 10N 21 30 E
Rausu-Dake 116 44 4N 145 7 E
Ravalli 33 47 17N 114 11W
Ravalli County ◇ 33 46 0N 114 0W
Rāvar 107 31 20N 56 51 E
Ravena 39 42 28N 73 49W
Ravendale 14 40 48N 120 22W
Ravenel 46 32 46N 80 15W
Ravenna, Italy 94 44 28N 12 15 E
Ravenna, Nebr. 34 41 1N 98 55W
Ravenna, Ohio 42 41 9N 81 15W
Ravenna, Tex. 51 33 40N 96 15W
Ravensburg 88 47 48N 9 38 E
Ravenshoe 127 17 37 S 145 29 E
Ravensthorpe 126 33 35 S 120 2 E
Ravenswood 54 38 57N 81 46W
Ravenwood 32 40 22N 94 41W
Ravi → 108 30 35N 71 49 E
Ravinia 47 43 8N 98 26W
Rawalpindi 108 33 38N 73 8 E
Rawāndūz 106 36 40N 44 30 E
Rawang 112 3 20N 101 35 E
Rawdon 60 46 3N 73 40W
Rawene 128 35 25 S 173 32 E
Rawlinna 126 30 58 S 125 28 E
Rawlins 56 41 47N 107 14W
Rawlins County ◇ 24 39 45N 101 0W
Rawlinson Range 126 24 40 S 128 30 E
Rawson 78 43 15 S 65 0W
Rawsonville 36 43 10N 72 50W
Ray, Minn. 30 48 25N 93 13W
Ray, N. Dak. 41 48 21N 103 10W
Ray, C. 61 47 33N 59 15W
Ray City 18 31 5N 83 11W
Ray County ◇ 32 39 20N 94 0W
Ray Mts. 11 66 0N 152 0W
Rayadurg 108 14 40N 76 50 E
Rayagada 109 19 15N 83 20 E
Raychikhinsk 101 49 46N 129 25 E
Rayle 18 33 48N 82 54W
Raymond, Canada 62 49 30N 112 35W
Raymond, Calif. 14 37 13N 119 54W
Raymond, Ga. 18 33 20N 84 43W
Raymond, Ill. 21 39 19N 89 34W
Raymond, Kans. 24 38 17N 98 25W
Raymond, Minn. 30 45 2N 95 14W
Raymond, Miss. 31 32 16N 90 25W
Raymond, N.H. 36 43 2N 71 11W
Raymond, Nebr. 34 40 57N 96 47W
Raymond, S. Dak. 47 44 55N 97 56W
Raymond, Wash. 53 46 41N 123 44W
Raymondville, Mo. 32 37 20N 91 50W
Raymondville, Tex. 50 26 29N 97 47W
Raymore 63 51 25N 104 31W
Rayne 25 30 14N 92 16W
Rayón 64 29 43N 110 35W
Rayong 112 12 40N 101 20 E
Raystown Branch → 45 40 27N 77 59W
Raystown L. 45 40 25N 78 5W
Raytown 32 39 1N 94 28W
Rayville, La. 25 32 29N 91 46W
Rayville, Mo. 32 39 21N 94 4W
Raz, Pte. du 90 48 2N 4 47W
Razdelna 95 43 13N 27 41 E
Razdolnoye 116 43 30N 131 52 E
Razelm, Lacul 95 44 50N 29 0 E
Razgrad 95 43 33N 26 34 E
Razlog 95 41 53N 23 28 E
Ré, Île de 90 46 12N 1 30W
Reader 13 33 46N 93 6W
Reading, U.K. 83 51 27N 0 57W
Reading, Kans. 24 38 31N 95 58W
Reading, Mass. 28 42 32N 71 6W
Reading, Mich. 29 41 50N 84 45W
Reading, Ohio 42 39 13N 84 26W
Reading, Pa. 45 40 20N 75 56W
Readland 13 33 4N 91 13W
Readlyn 23 42 42N 92 14W
Readsboro 36 42 46N 72 57W
Readstown 55 43 27N 90 45W
Reagan 48 35 31N 88 20W
Reagan County ◇ 50 31 25N 101 34W
Real, Cordillera 72 17 0 S 67 10W
Real County ◇ 51 29 55N 99 55W
Realicó 76 35 0 S 64 15W
Realitos 50 27 27N 98 32W
Ream 112 10 34N 103 39 E
Reardan 53 47 40N 117 53W
Reasnor 23 41 35N 93 1W
Reata 64 26 8N 101 5W
Rebi 111 6 23 S 134 7 E
Rebiana 121 24 12N 22 10 E
Rebun-Tō 116 45 23N 141 2 E
Recherche, Arch. of the 126 34 15 S 122 50 E
Recife 74 8 0 S 35 0W
Reconquista 76 29 10 S 59 45W
Recreio 73 8 0 S 58 25W
Recreo 76 29 25 S 65 10W
Rector 13 36 16N 90 17W
Recuay 72 9 43 S 77 28W
Red →, Canada 63 50 24N 96 48W
Red →, Ky. 49 37 51N 84 5W
Red →, La. 25 31 1N 91 45W
Red →, N. Dak. 41 49 0N 97 15W
Red →, Tenn. 48 36 32N 87 22W
Red Bank, N.J. 37 40 21N 74 5W
Red Bank, Tenn. 49 35 7N 85 17W
Red Bay 61 51 44N 56 25W
Red Bluff 14 40 11N 122 15W
Red Bluff L. 38 31 54N 103 55W
Red Boiling Springs 49 36 32N 85 51W
Red Bud 21 38 13N 89 59W
Red Cedar → 55 44 42N 91 53W
Red Cliff Ind. Reservation 55 46 50N 90 47W
Red Cloud 34 40 5N 98 32W
Red Cr. → 31 30 41N 88 40W
Red Deer 62 52 20N 113 50W
Red Deer →, Alta., Canada 63 50 58N 110 0W
Red Deer →, Man., Canada 63 52 53N 101 1W
Red Deer L. 63 52 55N 101 20W
Red Devil 11 61 46N 157 19W
Red Feather Lakes 16 40 48N 105 35W
Red Head 17 30 29N 85 51W
Red Hills 24 37 40N 98 50W
Red Hook 39 41 55N 73 53W
Red Indian L. 61 48 35N 57 0W
Red L., Ariz. 12 35 40N 114 4W
Red L., S. Dak. 47 43 44N 99 13W
Red Lake 63 51 3N 93 49W
Red Lake → 30 47 55N 97 1W
Red Lake County ◇ 30 47 50N 96 0W
Red Lake Falls 30 47 53N 96 16W
Red Lake Indian Reservation 30 48 0N 95 20W
Red Level 10 31 24N 86 36W
Red Lion, N.J. 37 39 53N 74 45W
Red Lion, Pa. 45 39 54N 76 36W
Red Lodge 33 45 11N 109 15W
Red Mountain 15 35 37N 117 38W
Red Oak, Iowa 23 41 1N 95 14W
Red Oak, N.C. 40 36 2N 77 54W
Red Oak, Okla. 43 34 57N 95 5W
Red River County ◇ 51 33 37N 95 3W
Red River Parish ◇ 25 32 1N 93 21W
Red River Valley 41 48 0N 96 50W
Red Rock, Canada 60 48 55N 88 15W
Red Rock, Ariz. 12 36 36N 109 3W
Red Rock, Mont. 33 44 55N 112 50W
Red Rock, Okla. 43 36 28N 97 11W
Red Rock, L. 23 41 22N 92 59W
Red Rock Cr. → 43 36 30N 96 59W
Red Sea 105 25 0N 36 0 E
Red Springs, N.C. 40 34 49N 79 11W
Red Springs, Tex. 51 33 37N 99 25W
Red Sucker L. 63 54 9N 93 40W
Red Tower Pass = Turnu Rosu Pasul 89 45 33N 24 17 E
Red Willow County ◇ 34 40 15N 100 30W
Red Willow Cr. → 34 40 13N 100 29W
Red Wing 30 44 34N 92 31W
Redbay 17 30 35N 85 57W
Redbird 43 35 54N 95 36W
Redbridge 83 51 35N 0 7 E
Redcar 82 54 37N 1 4W
Redcliff, Canada 63 50 10N 110 50W
Redcliff, U.S.A. 16 39 31N 106 22W
Reddell 25 30 40N 92 25W
Reddick, Fla. 17 29 22N 82 12W
Reddick, Ill. 21 41 6N 88 15W
Redding, Calif. 14 40 35N 122 24W
Redding, Iowa 23 40 36N 94 23W
Redding Ridge 28 41 19N 73 21W
Redditch 83 52 18N 1 57W
Redenção 74 4 13 S 38 43W
Redfield, Ark. 13 34 27N 92 11W
Redfield, Iowa 23 41 35N 94 12W
Redfield, Kans. 24 37 50N 94 53W
Redfield, S. Dak. 47 44 53N 98 31W
Redford 50 29 27N 104 11W
Redkey 22 40 21N 85 9W
Redknife → 62 61 14N 119 22W
Redlake 30 47 53N 95 1W
Redlands 15 34 4N 117 11W
Redmesa 16 37 6N 108 11W
Redmon 21 39 39N 87 52W
Redmond, Oreg. 44 44 17N 121 11W
Redmond, Utah 52 39 0N 111 52W
Redmond, Wash. 53 47 41N 122 7W
Redonda 67 16 58N 62 19W
Redondela 91 42 15N 8 38W
Redondo 91 38 39N 7 37W
Redondo Beach 15 33 50N 118 23W
Redoubt Volcano 11 60 29N 152 45W
Redrock 38 32 41N 108 44W
Redrock Pt. 62 62 11N 115 2W
Redruth 83 50 14N 5 14W
Redstone 16 39 11N 107 14W
Redstone Cr. → 47 44 4N 98 5W
Redvale 16 38 10N 108 25W
Redvers 63 49 35N 101 40W
Redwater 62 53 55N 113 6W
Redwater → 33 48 3N 105 13W
Redwood 31 32 29N 90 48W
Redwood → 30 44 34N 95 5W
Redwood City 14 37 30N 122 15W
Redwood County ◇ 30 44 20N 95 15W
Redwood Cr. → 14 41 18N 124 5W
Redwood Falls 30 44 32N 95 7W
Redwood National Park 14 41 40N 124 5W
Ree, L. 85 53 35N 8 0W
Ree Heights 47 44 31N 99 12W
Reece 24 37 48N 96 27W
Reed, Ky. 48 37 51N 87 21W
Reed, Okla. 43 34 54N 99 42W
Reed, L. 63 54 38N 100 30W
Reed City 29 43 53N 85 31W
Reeder 41 46 7N 102 57W
Reedley 15 36 36N 119 27W
Reeds 32 37 7N 94 10W
Reeds Pk. 38 33 9N 107 51W
Reeds Spring 32 36 45N 93 23W
Reedsburg 55 43 32N 90 0W
Reedsport 44 43 42N 124 6W
Reedsville, Va. 54 37 51N 76 17W
Reedsville, W. Va. 54 39 31N 79 48W
Reedy 54 38 54N 81 26W
Reedy → 46 28 4N 81 21W
Reefton 128 42 6 S 171 51 E
Reelfoot L. 48 36 25N 89 22W
Reese 29 43 27N 83 42W
Reese → 35 40 48N 117 4W
Reeves 25 30 31N 93 3W
Reeves County ◇ 50 31 13N 103 45W
Reform 10 33 23N 88 1W
Refugio 51 28 18N 97 17W
Refugio County ◇ 51 28 14N 97 20W
Regan 41 47 10N 100 32W
Regavim 104 32 32N 35 2 E
Regeneração 74 6 15 S 42 41W
Regensburg 88 49 1N 12 7 E
Regent 41 46 25N 102 33W
Réggio di Calábria 94 38 7N 15 38 E
Réggio nell' Emilia 94 44 42N 10 38 E
Regina, Canada 63 50 27N 104 35W
Régina, Fr. Gui. 71 4 19N 52 8W
Register 18 32 22N 81 53W
Registro 77 24 29 S 47 49W
Rehoboth, Namibia 123 23 15 S 17 4 E
Rehoboth, U.S.A. 38 35 32N 108 39W
Rehoboth Bay 27 38 40N 75 6W
Rehoboth Beach 27 38 43N 131 15W
Rehovot 104 31 54N 34 48 E
Rei-Bouba 121 8 40N 14 15 E
Reichenbach 88 50 36N 12 19 E
Reidsville, Ga. 18 32 6N 82 7W
Reidsville, N.C. 40 36 21N 79 40W
Reigate 83 51 14N 0 11W
Reims 90 49 15N 4 0 E
Reina 104 32 43N 35 18 E
Reina Adelaida, Arch. 78 52 20 S 74 0W
Reinbeck 23 42 19N 92 36W
Reindeer → 63 55 36N 103 11W
Reindeer I. 63 52 30N 98 0W
Reindeer L. 63 57 15N 102 15W
Reinga, C. 128 34 25 S 172 43 E
Reisterstown 27 39 28N 76 50W
Rekinniki 101 60 51N 163 40 E
Reliance, Canada 63 63 0N 109 20W
Reliance, Del. 27 38 38N 75 43W
Reliance, S. Dak. 47 43 53N 99 36W
Reliance, Wyo. 56 41 40N 109 12W
Remanso 74 9 41 S 42 4W
Rembang 111 6 42 S 111 21 E
Rembert 46 34 6N 80 32W
Rembrandt 23 42 50N 95 10W
Remedios, Colombia 70 7 2N 74 41W
Remedios, Panama 66 8 15N 81 50W
Remer 30 47 4N 93 55W
Remeshk 107 26 55N 58 50 E
Remetea 95 46 45N 25 29 E
Remich 87 49 32N 6 22 E
Remington, Ind. 22 40 46N 87 9W
Remington, Va. 54 38 32N 77 49W
Rémire 71 4 53N 52 17W
Remscheid 88 51 11N 7 12 E
Remsen, Iowa 23 42 49N 95 58W
Remsen, N.Y. 39 43 20N 75 11W
Renascença 70 3 50 S 66 21W
Rend Lake 21 38 2N 88 58W
Rendsburg 88 54 18N 9 41 E
Rene 101 66 2N 179 25W
Renfrew, Canada 60 45 30N 76 40W
Renfrew, U.K. 84 55 52N 4 24W
Renfroe 18 32 14N 84 43W
Rengat 110 0 30 S 102 45 E
Rengo 76 34 24 S 70 50W
Renhuai 115 27 48N 106 24 E
Renick 54 38 1N 80 22W
Renk 121 11 50N 32 50 E
Renkum 87 51 58N 5 43 E
Renmark 127 34 11 S 140 43 E
Rennell Sd. 62 53 23N 132 35W
Renner Springs T.O. 126 18 20 S 133 47 E
Rennes 90 48 7N 1 41W
Reno, Minn. 30 43 36N 91 17W
Reno, Nev. 35 39 31N 119 48W
Reno → 94 44 37N 12 17 E
Reno County ◇ 24 38 0N 98 0W
Renovo 45 41 20N 77 45W
Rensselaer, Ind. 22 40 57N 87 9W
Rensselaer, N.Y. 39 42 38N 73 45W
Rensselaer County ◇ 39 42 40N 73 30W
Rentiesville 43 35 35N 95 30W
Renton 53 47 29N 122 12W
Rentz 18 32 25N 82 59W
Renville 30 44 48N 95 13W
Renville County ◇, Minn. 30 44 45N 95 0W
Renville County ◇, N. Dak. 41 48 37N 101 35W
Renwick 23 42 50N 93 59W
Repton 10 31 25N 87 14W
Republic, Kans. 24 39 55N 97 49W
Republic, Mich. 29 46 25N 87 59W
Republic, Mo. 32 37 7N 93 29W
Republic, Ohio 42 41 8N 83 1W
Republic, Wash. 53 48 39N 118 44W
Republic County ◇ 24 39 45N 97 40W
Republican → 24 39 4N 96 48W
Republican City 34 40 6N 99 13W
Republiek 71 5 30N 55 13W
Repulse B., Antarct. 5 64 30 S 99 30 E
Repulse B., Australia 127 20 31 S 148 45 E
Repulse Bay 59 66 30N 86 30W
Requena, Peru 72 5 5 S 73 52W
Requena, Spain 91 39 30N 1 4W
Reserve, Canada 63 52 28N 102 39W
Reserve, Kans. 24 39 59N 95 34W
Reserve, La. 25 30 3N 90 33W
Reserve, N. Mex. 38 33 43N 108 45W
Resht = Rasht 106 37 20N 49 40 E
Resistencia 76 27 30 S 59 0W
Reşiţa 89 45 18N 21 53 E
Resolution I., Canada 59 61 30N 65 0W
Resolution I., N.Z. 128 45 40 S 166 40 E
Resplandes 74 6 17 S 45 13W
Resplendor 75 19 20 S 41 15W
Reston 63 49 33N 101 6W
Retalhuleu 66 14 33N 91 46W
Réthímnon 95 35 18N 24 30 E
Réunion 3 22 0 S 56 0 E
Reutlingen 88 48 28N 9 13 E
Reval = Tallinn 98 59 22N 24 48 E
Revda 98 56 48N 59 57 E
Revelstoke 62 51 0N 118 10W
Reventazón 72 6 10 S 80 58W
Revere, Mass. 28 42 25N 71 1W
Revere, Mo. 32 40 35N 91 41W
Revilla Gigedo, Is. 125 18 40N 112 0W
Revillo 47 45 1N 96 34W
Rewa 109 24 33N 81 25 E
Rewa → 71 3 19N 58 42W
Rewari 108 28 15N 76 40 E
Rewey 55 42 51N 90 24W
Rexburg 20 43 49N 111 47W
Rexford, Kans. 24 39 28N 100 45W
Rexford, Mont. 33 48 53N 115 13W
Rey Malabo 122 3 45N 8 50 E
Reydon 43 35 39N 99 55W
Reyes 72 14 19 S 67 23W
Reyes, Pt. 14 38 0N 123 0W
Reykjahlið 96 65 40N 16 55W
Reykjanes 96 63 48N 22 40W
Reykjavík 96 64 10N 21 57 E
Reynolds, Canada 63 49 40N 95 55W
Reynolds, Ga. 18 32 33N 84 6W
Reynolds, Ill. 21 41 20N 90 40W
Reynolds, Ind. 22 40 45N 86 52W
Reynolds, N. Dak. 41 47 40N 97 7W
Reynolds, Nebr. 34 40 4N 97 20W

Reynolds County Robbinsville

Reynolds County 32 37 20N 91 0W
Reynolds Ra. 126 22 30 S 133 0 E
Reynoldsville 18 30 51N 84 47W
Reynosa 65 26 5N 98 18W
Reynosa Draz 50 26 15N 98 30W
Rezovo 95 42 0N 28 0 E
Rhame 41 46 14N 103 39W
Rhayader 83 52 19N 3 30W
Rhea County ◇ 49 35 30N 85 0W
Rheden 87 52 0N 6 3 E
Rhein 63 51 25N 102 15W
Rhein → 87 51 52N 6 20 E
Rheine 88 52 17N 7 25 E
Rheinland-Pfalz □ 88 50 0N 7 0 E
Rhin = Rhein → 87 51 52N 6 20 E
Rhine = Rhein → 87 51 52N 6 20 E
Rhine 18 31 59N 83 12W
Rhinelander 55 45 38N 89 25W
Rhode Island 28 41 30N 71 15W
Rhode Island □ 28 41 40N 71 30W
Rhode Island Sd. 28 41 20N 71 10W
Rhodes = Ródhos 95 36 15N 28 10 E
Rhodesia = Zimbabwe ■ 123 20 0 S 30 0 E
Rhodhiss L. 40 35 47N 81 26W
Rhodope Mts. = Rhodopi Planina 95 41 40N 24 20 E
Rhodopi Planina 95 41 40N 24 20 E
Rhome 51 33 3N 97 28W
Rhön 88 50 24N 9 58 E
Rhondda 83 51 39N 3 30W
Rhône □ 90 45 54N 4 35 E
Rhône → 90 43 28N 4 42 E
Rhum 84 57 0N 6 20W
Rhumney 83 51 32N 3 7W
Rhyl 82 53 19N 3 29W
Riachão 74 7 20 S 46 37W
Riacho de Santana 75 13 37 S 42 57W
Rialma 75 15 18 S 49 34W
Riasi 108 33 10N 74 50 E
Riau □ 110 0 0 102 35 E
Riau, Kepulauan 110 0 30N 104 20 E
Rib Lake 55 45 19N 90 12W
Ribadeo 91 43 35N 7 5W
Ribamar 74 2 33 S 44 3W
Ribas do Rio Pardo 73 20 27 S 53 46W
Ribat 123 29 50N 60 55 E
Ribatejo □ 91 39 15N 8 30W
Ribble → 82 54 13N 2 20W
Ribe 97 55 19N 8 44 E
Ribeira do Pombal 74 10 50 S 38 32W
Ribeirão Prêto 75 21 10 S 47 50W
Ribeiro Gonçalves 74 7 32 S 45 14W
Ribera 38 35 23N 105 27W
Riberalta 73 11 0 S 66 0W
Ricardo 50 27 25N 97 51W
Riccarton 128 43 32 S 172 37 E
Rice, Calif. 15 34 5N 114 51W
Rice, Minn. 30 45 45N 94 13W
Rice, Tex. 51 32 14N 96 30W
Rice County ◇, Kans. 24 38 25N 98 10W
Rice County ◇, Minn. 30 44 20N 93 15W
Rice Lake 55 45 30N 91 44W
Riceboro 18 31 44N 81 26W
Riceville, Iowa 23 43 22N 92 33W
Riceville, Ky. 49 37 44N 82 55W
Riceville, Tenn. 49 35 23N 84 42W
Rich County ◇ 52 41 30N 111 10W
Rich Fountain 32 38 24N 91 53W
Rich Hill 32 38 6N 94 22W
Rich Square 40 36 16N 77 17W
Richards, Mo. 32 37 54N 94 33W
Richards, Tex. 51 30 32N 95 51W
Richards L. 63 59 10N 107 10W
Richardson 51 32 57N 96 44W
Richardson → 63 58 25N 111 14W
Richardson County ◇ 34 40 15N 95 45W
Richardson Lakes 26 44 46N 70 58W
Richardton 41 46 53N 102 19W
Richey 33 47 39N 105 4W
Richfield, Idaho 20 43 3N 114 9W
Richfield, Kans. 24 37 16N 101 47W
Richfield, Minn. 30 44 53N 93 17W
Richfield, Pa. 45 40 41N 77 7W
Richfield, Utah 52 38 46N 112 5W
Richfield Springs 39 42 51N 74 59W
Richford 36 45 0N 72 40W
Richgrove 15 35 48N 119 7W
Richibucto 61 46 42N 64 54W
Richland, Ga. 18 32 5N 84 40W
Richland, Mich. 29 42 22N 85 27W
Richland, Mo. 32 37 51N 92 26W
Richland, Nebr. 34 41 26N 97 13W
Richland, Oreg. 44 44 46N 117 10W
Richland, S. Dak. 47 42 46N 96 39W
Richland, Tex. 51 31 57N 96 26W
Richland, Wash. 53 46 17N 119 18W
Richland Center 55 43 21N 90 23W
Richland County ◇, Ill. 21 38 45N 88 5W
Richland County ◇, Mont. 33 47 48N 104 40W
Richland County ◇, N. Dak. 41 46 15N 97 0W
Richland County ◇, Ohio 42 40 45N 82 31W
Richland County ◇, S.C. 46 34 10N 81 0W
Richland County ◇, Wis. 55 43 20N 90 30W
Richland Parish ◇ 25 32 22N 91 52W
Richland Springs 51 31 16N 98 57W
Richlands, N.C. 40 34 54N 77 34W
Richlands, Va. 54 37 6N 81 48W
Richmond, Australia 127 20 43 S 143 8 E
Richmond, N.Z. 128 41 20 S 173 12 E
Richmond, S. Africa 123 29 51 S 30 18 E
Richmond, N. Yorks., U.K. 82 54 24N 1 43W
Richmond, Surrey, U.K. 83 51 28N 0 18W
Richmond, Calif. 14 37 56N 122 21W
Richmond, Ill. 21 42 29N 88 18W
Richmond, Ind. 22 39 50N 84 53W
Richmond, Kans. 24 38 24N 95 15W
Richmond, Ky. 49 37 45N 84 18W
Richmond, Maine 26 44 5N 69 48W
Richmond, Mich. 29 42 49N 82 45W
Richmond, Mo. 32 39 17N 93 58W
Richmond, N.H. 36 42 45N 72 18W
Richmond, Tex. 51 29 35N 95 46W
Richmond, Utah 52 41 56N 111 48W
Richmond, Va. 54 37 33N 77 27W
Richmond, Vt. 36 44 24N 72 59W
Richmond County ◇, Ga. 18 33 15N 82 5W
Richmond County ◇, N.C. 40 35 0N 79 45W
Richmond County ◇, N.Y. 39 40 40N 74 15W
Richmond County ◇, Va. 54 37 58N 76 46W
Richmond Heights 17 25 38N 80 23W
Richmond Highlands 53 47 46N 122 21W
Richmond Hill 18 31 56N 81 18W
Richmond Ra. 128 41 32 S 173 22 E
Richmondville 39 42 38N 74 34W
Richton 31 31 16N 88 56W
Richville, Minn. 30 46 31N 95 38W
Richville, N.Y. 39 44 25N 75 22W
Richwood, Ohio 42 40 26N 83 18W
Richwood, W. Va. 54 38 14N 80 32W
Richwoods 32 38 10N 90 50W
Ricketts 23 42 8N 95 35W
Rico 16 37 42N 108 2W
Riddle, Idaho 20 42 11N 116 7W
Riddle, Oreg. 44 42 57N 123 22W
Ridge 27 38 8N 76 24W
Ridge Farm 21 39 54N 87 39W
Ridge Spring 46 33 51N 81 40W
Ridgecrest 15 35 38N 117 40W
Ridgedale 63 53 0N 104 10W
Ridgefield, Conn. 28 41 17N 73 30W
Ridgefield, Wash. 53 45 49N 122 45W
Ridgeland, Miss. 31 32 26N 90 8W
Ridgeland, S.C. 46 32 29N 80 59W
Ridgeland, Wis. 55 45 12N 91 54W
Ridgely 48 36 16N 89 29W
Ridgetop 48 36 24N 86 46W
Ridgetown 60 42 26N 81 52W
Ridgeville, Ind. 22 40 18N 85 2W
Ridgeville, S.C. 46 33 6N 80 19W
Ridgeway, Iowa 23 43 18N 91 59W
Ridgeway, Mo. 32 40 23N 93 57W
Ridgeway, Ohio 42 40 31N 83 35W
Ridgeway, S.C. 46 34 18N 80 58W
Ridgeway, Va. 54 36 35N 79 52W
Ridgeway, Wis. 55 43 1N 90 1W
Ridgewood 37 40 59N 74 7W
Ridgway, Colo. 16 38 9N 107 46W
Ridgway, Ill. 21 37 48N 88 16W
Ridgway, Pa. 45 41 25N 78 44W
Riding Mt. Nat. Park 63 50 50N 100 0W
Ried 88 48 14N 13 30 E
Rienzi 31 34 46N 88 32W
Riesco, I. 78 52 55 S 72 40W
Riesel 51 31 29N 96 55W
Rieth 44 45 40N 118 54W
Rieti 94 42 23N 12 50 E
Riffe L. 53 46 32N 122 26W
Rifle 16 39 32N 107 47W
Rifstangi 96 66 32N 16 12W
Rig Rig 121 14 13N 14 25 E
Riga 98 56 53N 24 8 E
Riga, G. of = Rīgas Jūras Līcis 98 57 40N 23 45 E
Rīgas Jūras Līcis 98 57 40N 23 45 E
Rigby 20 43 40N 111 55W
Rīgestān □ 107 30 15N 65 0 E
Riggins 20 45 25N 116 19W
Rigolet 61 54 10N 58 23W
Riihimäki 97 60 45N 24 48 E
Riiser-Larsen-halvøya 5 68 0 S 35 0 E
Rijeka 94 45 20N 14 21 E
Rijn → 87 52 12N 4 21 E
Rijssen 87 52 19N 6 30 E
Rijswijk 87 52 4N 4 22 E
Rikuzentakada 116 39 0N 141 40 E
Rila 95 42 7N 23 7 E
Riley, Ind. 22 39 23N 87 18W
Riley, Kans. 24 39 18N 96 50W
Riley, Oreg. 44 43 32N 119 28W
Riley County ◇ 24 39 20N 96 40W
Rillito 12 32 25N 111 9W
Rimah, Wadi ar → 106 26 5N 41 30 E
Rimbey 62 52 35N 114 15W
Rimersburg 45 41 3N 79 30W
Rîmini, Italy 94 44 3N 12 33 E
Rimini, U.S.A. 46 33 40N 80 30W
Rîmna → 95 45 36N 27 3 E
Rîmnicu Sărat 89 45 26N 27 3 E
Rîmnicu Vîlcea 89 45 9N 24 21 E
Rimouski 61 48 27N 68 30W
Rinard 23 42 20N 94 29W
Rinca 111 8 45 S 119 35 E
Rincon, Puerto Rico 57 18 20N 67 15W
Rincon, U.S.A. 18 32 18N 81 14W
Rincon, Bahia de 57 17 55N 66 20W
Rincón de Romos 64 22 14N 102 18W
Rinconada 76 22 26 S 66 10W
Rineanna 85 52 42N 85 7W
Rineyville 49 37 45N 85 58W
Ringgold, Ga. 18 34 55N 85 7W
Ringgold, La. 25 32 20N 93 17W
Ringgold, Nebr. 34 41 31N 100 47W
Ringgold County ◇ 23 40 45N 94 15W
Ringkøbing 97 56 5N 8 15 E
Ringling, Mont. 33 46 16N 110 49W
Ringling, Okla. 43 34 11N 97 36W
Ringoes 37 40 26N 74 52W
Ringsted 23 43 18N 94 31W
Ringvassøy 96 69 56N 19 15 E
Ringwood, N.J. 37 41 7N 74 15W
Ringwood, Okla. 43 36 23N 98 15W
Rinía 95 37 23N 25 13 E
Rinjani 110 8 24 S 116 28 E
Rio, Ill. 21 41 7N 90 24W
Rio, Wis. 55 43 27N 89 14W
Rio Arriba County ◇ 38 36 30N 106 45W
Rio Blanco 16 39 44N 107 57W
Rio Blanco County ◇ 16 40 0N 108 15W
Rio Branco, Brazil 72 9 58 S 67 49W
Río Branco, Uruguay 77 32 40 S 53 40W
Rio Brilhante 77 21 48 S 54 33W
Río Bueno 78 40 19 S 72 58W
Río Chico 70 10 19N 65 59W
Rio Claro, Brazil 77 22 19 S 47 35W
Rio Claro, Trin. & Tob. 67 10 20N 61 25W
Río Colorado 78 39 0 S 64 0W
Río Cuarto 76 33 10 S 64 25W
Rio de Contas 75 13 36 S 41 48W
Rio de Janeiro 75 23 0 S 43 12W
Rio de Janeiro □ 75 22 50 S 43 0W
Rio Dell 14 40 30N 124 6W
Rio do Prado 75 16 35 S 40 34W
Rio do Sul 77 27 13 S 49 37W
Río Gallegos 78 51 35 S 69 15W
Río Grande, Argentina 78 53 50 S 67 45W
Río Grande, Bolivia 72 20 51 S 67 17W
Rio Grande, Brazil 77 32 0 S 52 20W
Río Grande, Mexico 64 23 50N 103 2W
Río Grande, Nic. 66 12 54N 83 33W
Río Grande, Puerto Rico 57 18 23N 65 50W
Rio Grande, N.J. 37 39 1N 74 53W
Rio Grande, Ohio 42 38 56N 82 21W
Rio Grande City 50 26 23N 98 49W
Rio Grande County ◇ 16 37 40N 106 20W
Rio Grande do Norte □ 74 5 40 S 36 0W
Rio Grande do Sul □ 77 30 0 S 53 0W
Rio Grande National Forest 16 37 30N 106 30W
Río Hato 66 8 22N 80 10W
Rio Hondo 50 26 14N 97 35W
Río Lagartos 65 21 36N 88 10W
Rio Largo 74 9 28 S 35 50W
Río Mayo 78 45 40 S 70 15W
Río Mulatos 72 19 40 S 66 50W
Río Muni = Mbini □ 122 1 30N 10 0 E
Rio Negro, Brazil 77 26 0 S 50 0W
Río Negro, Chile 78 40 47 S 73 14W
Rio Negro, Pantanal do 73 19 0 S 56 0W
Rio Pardo 77 30 0 S 52 30W
Río Pico 78 44 0 S 70 22W
Rio Piedras 57 18 24N 66 3W
Rio Real 75 11 28 S 37 56W
Río Segundo 76 31 40 S 63 59W
Río Tercero 76 32 15 S 64 8W
Rio Tinto 74 6 48 S 35 5W
Rio Verde, Brazil 75 17 50 S 51 0W
Río Verde, Mexico 65 21 56N 99 59W
Rio Verde de Mato Grosso 73 18 56 S 54 52W
Rio Vista 14 38 10N 121 42W
Ríobamba 70 1 50 S 78 45W
Ríohacha 70 11 33N 72 55W
Rioja 72 6 11 S 77 5W
Rioja, La 76 29 20 S 67 0W
Rioja, La □, Argentina 76 29 30 S 67 0W
Rioja, La □, Spain 91 42 20N 2 20W
Rion 46 34 18N 81 8W
Rionegro 70 6 9N 75 22W
Riosucio, Caldas, Colombia 70 5 30N 75 40W
Ríosucio, Choco, Colombia 70 7 27N 77 7W
Riou L. 63 59 7N 106 25W
Riozinho → 70 2 55 S 67 7W
Ripley, Ill. 21 40 1N 90 38W
Ripley, Miss. 31 34 44N 88 57W
Ripley, N.Y. 39 42 16N 79 43W
Ripley, Ohio 42 38 45N 83 51W
Ripley, Okla. 43 36 1N 96 54W
Ripley, Tenn. 48 35 45N 89 32W
Ripley, W. Va. 54 38 49N 81 43W
Ripley County ◇, Ind. 22 39 5N 85 15W
Ripley County ◇, Mo. 32 36 40N 90 50W
Ripon, U.K. 82 54 8N 1 31W
Ripon, Calif. 14 37 44N 121 7W
Ripon, Wis. 55 43 51N 88 50W
Rippey 23 41 56N 94 12W
Ririe 20 43 38N 111 47W
Ririe L. 20 43 30N 111 43W
Risaralda □ 70 5 0N 76 10W
Risco 32 36 33N 89 49W
Rishiri-Tō 116 45 11N 141 15 E
Rishon le Ẕiyyon 104 31 58N 34 48 E
Rishpon 104 32 12N 34 49 E
Rising City 34 41 12N 97 18W
Rising Fawn 18 34 46N 85 32W
Rising Star 51 32 6N 98 58W
Rising Sun, Ind. 22 38 57N 84 51W
Rising Sun, Md. 27 39 42N 76 4W
Rîsnov 95 45 35N 25 27 E
Rison 13 33 58N 92 11W
Risør 97 58 43N 9 13 E
Rita Blanca Cr. → 50 35 40N 102 29W
Rita Blanca National Grassland 50 36 20N 102 30W
Ritchie County ◇ 54 39 13N 81 3W
Ritchies Archipelago 112 12 5N 94 0 E
Ritter, Mt. 14 37 41N 119 12W
Rittman 42 40 58N 81 47W
Ritzville 53 47 8N 118 23W
Riva 27 38 57N 76 35W
Rivadavia, Buenos Aires, Argentina 76 35 29 S 62 59W
Rivadavia, Mendoza, Argentina 76 33 13 S 68 30W
Rivadavia, Salta, Argentina 76 24 5 S 62 54W
Rivadavia, Chile 76 29 57 S 70 35W
Rivas 66 11 30N 85 50W
River Falls 55 44 52N 92 38W
Rivera 77 31 0 S 55 50W
Riverbank 14 37 44N 120 56W
Riverdale, Calif. 15 36 26N 119 52W
Riverdale, Ga. 18 33 34N 84 25W
Riverdale, N. Dak. 41 47 30N 101 22W
Riverdale, Nebr. 34 40 47N 99 10W
Riverdsale 123 34 7 S 21 15 E
Riverhead 39 40 55N 72 40W
Riverhurst 63 50 55N 106 50W
Riverina 127 35 30 S 145 20 E
Rivers 63 50 2N 100 14W
Rivers, L. of the 63 49 49N 105 44W
Rivers Inlet 62 51 40N 127 20W
Riverside, Calif. 15 33 59N 117 22W
Riverside, Iowa 23 41 29N 91 35W
Riverside, Md. 27 38 22N 77 11W
Riverside, N.J. 37 40 2N 74 58W
Riverside, Oreg. 44 43 32N 118 10W
Riverside, Tex. 51 30 51N 95 24W
Riverside, Wash. 53 48 30N 119 30W
Riverside, Wyo. 56 41 13N 106 47W
Riverside County ◇ 15 33 45N 116 0W
Riverside Reservoir 16 40 20N 104 15W
Riverton, Canada 63 51 1N 97 0W
Riverton, N.Z. 128 46 21 S 168 0 E
Riverton, Ill. 21 39 51N 89 33W
Riverton, Iowa 23 40 41N 95 34W
Riverton, Kans. 24 37 5N 94 42W
Riverton, La. 25 32 10N 92 6W
Riverton, Nebr. 34 40 5N 98 46W
Riverton, Oreg. 44 43 10N 124 16W
Riverton, Utah 52 40 31N 111 56W
Riverton, W. Va. 54 38 45N 79 26W
Riverton, Wyo. 56 43 2N 108 23W
Riverton Heights 53 47 28N 122 17W
Riverview 17 27 52N 82 20W
Rivesville 54 39 32N 80 7W
Riviera, Ariz. 12 35 8N 114 32W
Riviera, Tex. 50 27 18N 97 49W
Riviera Beach, Fla. 17 26 47N 80 3W
Riviera Beach, Md. 27 39 10N 76 31W
Rivière-à-Pierre 61 46 59N 72 11W
Rivière-au-Renard 61 48 59N 64 23W
Rivière-du-Loup 61 47 50N 69 30W
Rivière-Pentecôte 61 49 57N 67 1W
Rivière-Pilot 67 14 26N 60 53W
Riyadh = Ar Riyāḑ 106 24 41N 46 42 E
Rize 106 41 0N 40 30 E
Rizhao 115 35 25N 119 30 E
Rizzuto, C. 94 38 54N 17 5 E
Rjukan 97 59 54N 8 33 E
Roach L. 35 35 41N 115 22W
Roachdale 22 39 51N 86 48W
Roag, L. 84 58 10N 6 55W
Roan Cliffs 52 39 20N 109 40W
Roan Cr. → 16 39 20N 108 13W
Roan Mountain 49 36 12N 82 4W
Roan Plateau 52 39 20N 109 20W
Roanaoke I. 40 35 53N 75 39W
Roane County ◇, Tenn. 49 35 52N 84 31W
Roane County ◇, W. Va. 54 38 48N 81 21W
Roanne 90 46 3N 4 4 E
Roanoke, Ala. 10 33 9N 85 22W
Roanoke, Ill. 21 40 48N 89 12W
Roanoke, Ind. 22 40 58N 85 22W
Roanoke, Tex. 51 33 0N 97 10W
Roanoke, Va. 54 37 16N 79 56W
Roanoke → 40 35 57N 76 42W
Roanoke County ◇ 54 37 16N 79 56W
Roanoke Rapids 40 36 28N 77 40W
Roanoke Rapids L. 40 36 29N 77 40W
Roaring Spring 45 40 20N 78 24W
Roaring Springs 50 33 54N 100 52W
Roatán 66 16 18N 86 35W
Robards 48 37 41N 87 33W
Robbins, N.C. 40 35 26N 79 35W
Robbins, Tenn. 49 36 21N 84 35W
Robbinsville 40 35 19N 83 48W

Robe Ross Ice Shelf

Robe → 85 53 38N 9 10W
Robersonville 40 35 50N 77 15W
Robert Lee 50 31 54N 100 29W
Robert S. Kerr Reservoir 43 35 21N 94 47W
Roberta 18 32 43N 84 1W
Roberts, Idaho 20 43 43N 112 8W
Roberts, Ill. 21 40 37N 88 11W
Roberts, Mont. 33 45 22N 109 10W
Roberts County ◇, S. Dak. 47 45 33N 96 57W
Roberts County ◇, Tex. 50 35 55N 100 55W
Robertsdale 10 30 33N 87 43W
Robertson 123 33 46 S 19 50 E
Robertson County ◇, Ky. 49 38 30N 84 5W
Robertson County ◇, Tenn. 48 36 31N 86 53W
Robertson County ◇, Tex. 51 31 2N 96 29W
Robertson I. 5 65 15 S 59 30W
Robertsport 120 6 45N 11 26W
Robertsville 37 40 21N 74 17W
Roberval 61 48 32N 72 15W
Robeson Ch. 4 82 0N 61 30W
Robeson County ◇ 40 34 30N 79 10W
Robesonia 45 40 21N 76 8W
Robinson, Ill. 21 39 0N 87 44W
Robinson, Kans. 24 39 49N 95 25W
Robinson, N. Dak. 41 47 9N 99 47W
Robinson, Tex. 51 31 28N 97 7W
Robinson, L. 46 34 30N 80 12W
Robinson Crusoe I. 125 33 38 S 78 52W
Robinson Mt. 33 48 58N 115 25W
Robinson Ranges 126 25 40 S 119 0 E
Robla, La 91 42 50N 5 41W
Roblin 63 51 14N 101 21W
Roboré 73 18 10 S 59 45W
Robson, Mt. 62 53 10N 119 10W
Robstown 51 27 47N 97 40W
Roby, Mo. 32 37 31N 92 8W
Roby, Tex. 50 32 45N 100 23W
Roca 34 40 39N 96 40W
Roca, C. da 91 38 40N 9 31W
Roca Partida, I. 64 19 1N 112 2W
Rocas, I. 74 4 0 S 34 1W
Rocha 77 34 30 S 54 25W
Rochdale, U.K. 82 53 36N 2 10W
Rochdale, U.S.A. 28 42 12N 71 54W
Roche, La 90 46 4N 6 19 E
Rochedo 73 19 57 S 54 52W
Rochefort, Belgium 87 50 9N 5 12 E
Rochefort, France 90 45 56N 0 57W
Rochelle, Ga. 18 31 57N 83 27W
Rochelle, Ill. 21 41 56N 89 4W
Rochelle, Tex. 51 31 14N 99 13W
Rochelle, La 90 46 10N 1 9W
Rocheport 32 38 59N 92 34W
Rocher River 62 61 23N 112 44W
Rochester, Canada 62 54 22N 113 27W
Rochester, U.K. 83 51 22N 0 30 E
Rochester, Ill. 21 39 45N 89 32W
Rochester, Ind. 22 41 4N 86 13W
Rochester, Ky. 48 37 13N 86 53W
Rochester, Mass. 28 41 44N 70 49W
Rochester, Mich. 29 42 41N 83 8W
Rochester, Minn. 30 44 1N 92 28W
Rochester, N.H. 36 43 18N 70 59W
Rochester, N.Y. 39 43 10N 77 37W
Rochester, Ohio 42 41 8N 82 18W
Rochester, Tex. 51 33 19N 99 51W
Rochester, Vt. 36 43 51N 72 48W
Rochester, Wash. 53 46 49N 123 6W
Rociu 95 44 43N 25 2 E
Rock 29 46 4N 87 10W
Rock →, Canada 62 60 7N 127 7W
Rock →, U.S.A. 21 41 29N 90 37W
Rock Cave 54 38 50N 80 21W
Rock County ◇, Minn. 30 43 45N 96 15W
Rock County ◇, Nebr. 34 42 30N 99 30W
Rock County ◇, Wis. 55 42 45N 89 10W
Rock Cr. →, Ill. 21 41 42N 90 3W
Rock Cr. →, Nev. 35 40 39N 116 55W
Rock Cr. →, Oreg. 44 45 34N 120 25W
Rock Cr. →, S. Dak. 47 43 44N 97 58W
Rock Cr. →, Utah 52 40 17N 110 30W
Rock Cr. →, Mont. 33 46 43N 113 40W
Rock Cr. →, Mont. 33 48 27N 107 6W
Rock Creek 42 41 40N 80 52W
Rock Creek Butte 44 44 49N 118 7W
Rock Falls, Ill. 21 41 47N 89 41W
Rock Falls, Iowa 23 43 13N 93 5W
Rock Hall 27 39 8N 76 14W
Rock Hill 46 34 56N 81 1W
Rock Island, Ill. 21 41 30N 90 34W
Rock Island, Wash. 53 47 22N 120 8W
Rock Island County ◇ 21 41 25N 90 30W
Rock Island Dam 53 47 23N 120 4W
Rock Point 27 38 16N 76 50W
Rock Rapids 23 43 26N 96 10W
Rock River 56 41 44N 105 58W
Rock Sound 66 24 54N 76 12W
Rock Spring 18 34 50N 85 14W
Rock Springs, Mont. 33 46 49N 106 15W
Rock Springs, Wyo. 56 41 35N 109 14W
Rock Valley 23 43 12N 96 18W
Rockall 80 57 37N 13 42W
Rockaway 44 45 37N 123 57W
Rockbridge 21 39 16N 90 12W
Rockbridge County ◇ 54 37 55N 79 20W
Rockcastle → 49 36 58N 84 21W
Rockcastle County ◇ 49 37 20N 84 20W
Rockdale 51 30 39N 97 0W
Rockdale County ◇ 18 33 40N 84 0W
Rockefeller Plat. 5 80 0 S 140 0W
Rockford, Ala. 10 32 53N 86 13W
Rockford, Ill. 21 42 16N 89 6W
Rockford, Iowa 23 43 3N 92 57W
Rockford, Mich. 29 43 7N 85 34W
Rockford, Minn. 30 45 5N 93 44W
Rockford, Ohio 42 40 41N 84 39W
Rockford, Wash. 53 47 27N 117 8W
Rockglen 63 49 11N 105 57W
Rockham 47 44 55N 98 49W
Rockhampton 127 23 22 S 150 32 E
Rockingham 40 34 57N 79 46W
Rockingham County ◇, N.C. 40 36 20N 79 50W
Rockingham County ◇, N.H. 36 43 0N 71 10W
Rockingham County ◇, Va. 54 38 27N 78 52W
Rockingham Forest 83 52 28N 0 42W
Rocklake 41 48 47N 99 15W
Rockland, Idaho 20 42 34N 112 53W
Rockland, Maine 26 44 6N 69 7W
Rockland, Mass. 28 42 8N 70 55W
Rockland, Mich. 29 46 44N 89 11W
Rockland, Wis. 55 43 54N 90 55W
Rockland County ◇ 39 41 10N 74 5W
Rockledge 17 28 20N 80 43W
Rocklin 14 38 48N 121 14W
Rockmart 18 34 0N 85 3W
Rockport, Calif. 14 39 44N 123 49W
Rockport, Ind. 22 37 53N 87 3W
Rockport, Mass. 28 42 39N 70 37W
Rockport, Mo. 32 40 25N 95 31W
Rockport, Tex. 51 28 2N 97 3W
Rockport, Wash. 53 48 29N 121 36W
Rocksprings 50 30 1N 100 13W
Rockton 21 42 27N 89 4W
Rockville, Conn. 28 41 52N 72 28W
Rockville, Ind. 22 39 46N 87 14W
Rockville, Md. 27 39 5N 77 9W
Rockville, Mo. 32 38 4N 94 5W
Rockville, Nebr. 34 41 7N 98 50W
Rockwall 51 32 56N 96 28W
Rockwall County ◇ 51 32 56N 96 28W
Rockwell, Iowa 23 42 59N 93 11W
Rockwell, N.C. 40 35 33N 80 25W
Rockwell City 23 42 24N 94 38W
Rockwood, Maine 26 45 41N 69 45W
Rockwood, Pa. 45 39 55N 79 9W
Rockwood, Tenn. 49 35 52N 84 41W
Rocky 43 35 9N 99 3W
Rocky → 40 35 9N 80 4W
Rocky Boy 33 48 16N 109 47W
Rocky Boys Indian Reservation 33 48 25N 109 30W
Rocky Comfort Cr. → 18 32 59N 82 25W
Rocky Ford, Colo. 16 38 3N 103 43W
Rocky Ford, Ga. 18 32 40N 81 50W
Rocky Fork 49 36 2N 82 33W
Rocky Hill 28 41 40N 72 39W
Rocky Lane 62 58 31N 116 22W
Rocky Mount, N.C. 40 35 57N 77 48W
Rocky Mount, Va. 54 37 12N 79 57W
Rocky Mountain House 62 52 22N 114 55W
Rocky Mountain National Park 16 40 25N 105 45W
Rocky Mts., N. Amer. 62 55 0N 121 0W
Rocky Mts., U.S.A. 16 39 0N 106 0W
Rocky Pt. 126 33 30 S 123 57 E
Rocky Point 40 34 26N 77 53W
Rocky Ridge 27 39 38N 77 20W
Rocky Top 44 44 47N 122 17W
Rockyford 62 51 14N 113 10W
Rod 107 28 10N 63 5 E
Roda, La 91 39 13N 2 15W
Rødbyhavn 97 54 39N 11 22 E
Roddickton 61 50 51N 56 8W
Rodeo 38 31 50N 109 2W
Roderick I. 62 52 38N 128 22W
Rodez 90 44 21N 2 33 E
Ródhos 95 36 15N 28 10 E
Rodman 23 43 2N 94 32W
Rodney 23 42 12N 95 57W
Rodney, C. 128 36 17 S 174 50 E
Rodoni, C. 95 41 32N 19 30 E
Rodriguez 3 19 45 S 63 20 E
Roe → 85 55 10N 6 59W
Roebling 37 40 7N 74 47W
Roebourne 126 20 44 S 117 9 E
Roebuck B. 126 18 5 S 122 20 E
Roeland Park 24 39 2N 94 39W
Roermond 87 51 12N 6 0 E
Roes Welcome Sd. 59 65 0N 87 0W
Roeselare 87 50 57N 3 7 E
Roff 43 34 38N 96 50W
Rogagua, L. 72 13 43 S 66 50W
Rogaland fylke □ 97 59 12N 6 20 E
Roger Mills County ◇ 43 35 45N 99 45W
Rogers, Ark. 13 36 20N 94 7W
Rogers, La. 25 31 32N 92 14W
Rogers, N. Dak. 41 47 4N 98 12W
Rogers, Nebr. 34 41 28N 96 55W
Rogers, Tex. 51 30 56N 97 14W
Rogers, Mt. 54 36 40N 81 33W
Rogers City 29 45 25N 83 49W
Rogers County ◇ 43 36 20N 95 40W
Rogers L. 15 34 55N 117 50W
Rogerson 20 42 13N 114 36W
Rogersville, Ala. 10 34 50N 87 18W
Rogersville, Mo. 32 37 7N 93 3W
Rogersville, Tenn. 49 36 24N 83 1W
Roggan 60 54 25N 79 32W
Roggen 16 40 10N 104 22W
Rogoaguado, L. 73 13 0 S 65 30W
Rogue → 44 42 26N 124 26W
Rogue River 44 42 26N 123 10W
Rogue River Nat. Forest 44 42 54N 122 22W
Rohnerville 14 40 34N 124 8W
Rohri 108 27 45N 68 51 E
Rohtak 108 28 55N 76 43 E
Roi Et 112 16 4N 103 40 E
Rojas 76 34 10 S 60 45W
Rojo, Cabo 57 17 56N 67 12W
Rojo, C. 65 21 33N 97 20W
Rokan → 110 2 0N 100 50 E
Roland, Iowa 23 42 10N 93 30W
Roland, Okla. 43 35 25N 94 31W
Rolândia 77 23 18 S 51 23W
Rolette 41 48 40N 99 51W
Rolette County ◇ 41 48 55N 99 55W
Rolfe 23 42 49N 94 31W
Roll 12 32 45N 113 59W
Rolla, Kans. 24 37 7N 101 38W
Rolla, Mo. 32 37 57N 91 46W
Rolla, N. Dak. 41 48 52N 99 37W
Rolling Fork 31 32 55N 90 53W
Rolling Fork → 49 37 55N 85 50W
Roma, Australia 127 26 32 S 148 49 E
Roma, Italy 94 41 54N 12 30 E
Roma, Sweden 97 57 32N 18 26 E
Roma-Los Saenz 50 26 24N 99 5W
Romain C. 46 33 0N 79 22W
Roman, Bulgaria 95 43 8N 23 54 E
Roman, Romania 89 46 57N 26 55 E
Roman, U.S.S.R. 101 66 4N 112 14 E
Romana, La 67 18 27N 68 57W
Romang 111 7 30 S 127 20 E
Romania ■ 89 46 0N 25 0 E
Romano, Cayo 66 22 0N 77 30W
Romano C. 17 25 51N 81 41W
Romanzof C. 11 61 49N 166 6W
Romblon 111 12 33N 122 17 E
Rome = Roma 94 41 54N 12 30 E
Rome, Ga. 18 34 15N 85 10W
Rome, Ill. 21 40 53N 89 30W
Rome, N.Y. 39 43 13N 75 27W
Rome, Pa. 45 41 51N 76 21W
Rome City 22 41 30N 85 23W
Romeo, Colo. 16 37 10N 105 59W
Romeo, Mich. 29 42 48N 83 1W
Romeoville 21 41 39N 88 3W
Romero 50 35 44N 102 56W
Romîni 95 44 59N 24 11 E
Romney 54 39 21N 78 45W
Romney Marsh 83 51 0N 1 0 E
Romorantin-Lanthenay 90 47 21N 1 45 E
Romsdalen 96 62 25N 8 0 E
Rona 84 57 33N 6 0W
Ronan 33 47 32N 114 6W
Roncador, Cayos 66 13 32N 80 4W
Roncador, Serra do 75 12 30 S 52 30W
Ronceverte 54 37 45N 80 28W
Ronda 91 36 46N 5 12W
Rondane 97 61 57N 9 50 E
Rondón 70 6 17N 71 6W
Rondônia 73 10 52 S 61 57W
Rondônia □ 73 11 0 S 63 0W
Rondonópolis 73 16 28 S 54 38W
Rondout Res. 39 41 50N 74 29W
Rong, Koh 112 10 45N 103 15 E
Rong Xian 115 29 23N 104 22 E
Rong'an 115 25 14N 109 22 E
Ronge, L. la 63 55 6N 105 17W
Ronge, La 63 55 5N 105 20W
Rongshui 115 25 5N 109 12 E
Ronkonkoma 39 40 48N 73 7W
Ronne Ice Shelf 5 78 0 S 60 0W
Ronse 87 50 45N 3 35 E
Ronuro → 73 11 56 S 53 33W
Roodepoort-Maraisburg 123 26 8 S 27 52 E
Roodhouse 21 39 29N 90 24W
Roof Butte 12 36 28N 109 5W
Rooks County ◇ 24 39 20N 99 15W
Roopville 18 33 27N 85 8W
Roorkee 108 29 52N 77 59 E
Roosendaal 87 51 32N 4 29 E
Roosevelt, Ariz. 12 33 41N 111 9W
Roosevelt, Minn. 30 48 48N 95 6W
Roosevelt, Okla. 43 34 51N 99 1W
Roosevelt, Utah 52 40 18N 109 59W
Roosevelt → 73 7 35 S 60 20W
Roosevelt, Mt. 62 58 26N 125 20W
Roosevelt County ◇, Mont. 33 48 20N 105 20W
Roosevelt County ◇, N. Mex. 38 34 0N 103 30W
Roosevelt I. 5 79 30 S 162 0W
Roosevelt National Forest 16 40 45N 105 40W
Roper 40 35 53N 76 37W
Roper → 126 14 43 S 135 27 E
Ropesville 50 33 26N 102 9W
Roque Pérez 76 35 25 S 59 24W
Roraima □ 71 2 0N 61 30W
Roraima, Mt. 71 5 10N 60 40W
Rorketon 63 51 24N 99 35W
Røros 96 62 35N 11 23 E
Rosa 122 9 33 S 31 15 E
Rosa, Monte 88 45 57N 7 53 E
Rosalia 53 47 14N 117 22W
Rosamond L. 15 34 50N 118 4W
Rosario, Argentina 76 33 0 S 60 40W
Rosário, Brazil 74 3 0 S 44 15W
Rosario, Baja Calif. N., Mexico 64 30 0N 115 50W
Rosario, Durango, Mexico 64 26 30N 105 35W
Rosario, Sinaloa, Mexico 64 23 0N 105 52W
Rosario, Paraguay 76 24 30 S 57 35W
Rosario, Villa del 70 10 19N 72 19W
Rosario de la Frontera 76 25 50 S 65 0W
Rosario de Lerma 76 24 59 S 65 35W
Rosario del Tala 76 32 20 S 59 10W
Rosário do Sul 77 30 15 S 54 55W
Rosário Oeste 73 14 50 S 56 25W
Rosarito 64 28 38N 114 4W
Rosas 91 42 19N 3 10 E
Rosas, G. de 91 42 10N 3 15 E
Rosburg 53 46 20N 123 38W
Roscoe, Ill. 21 42 25N 89 1W
Roscoe, S. Dak. 47 45 27N 99 20W
Roscoe, Tex. 50 32 27N 100 32W
Roscommon, Ireland 85 53 38N 8 11W
Roscommon, U.S.A. 29 44 30N 84 35W
Roscommon □ 85 53 40N 8 15W
Roscommon County ◇ 29 44 15N 84 40W
Roscrea 85 52 58N 7 50W
Rose 34 42 9N 99 28W
Rose, Mt. 35 39 21N 119 55W
Rose Blanche 61 47 38N 58 45W
Rose Bud 13 35 20N 92 5W
Rose City 29 44 25N 84 7W
Rose Creek 30 43 36N 92 50W
Rose Harbour 62 52 15N 131 10W
Rose Hill, Ill. 21 39 6N 88 9W
Rose Hill, Iowa 23 41 19N 92 28W
Rose Hill, Kans. 24 37 34N 97 7W
Rose Hill, N.C. 40 34 50N 78 2W
Rose Pk. 12 33 25N 109 21W
Rose Pt. 62 54 11N 131 39W
Rose Valley 63 52 19N 103 49W
Roseau, Domin. 67 15 20N 61 24W
Roseau, U.S.A. 30 48 51N 95 46W
Roseau → 30 49 0N 96 30W
Roseau County ◇ 30 48 45N 95 50W
Roseboro 40 34 58N 78 31W
Rosebud, Mo. 32 38 23N 91 25W
Rosebud, Mont. 33 46 16N 106 27W
Rosebud, S. Dak. 47 43 14N 100 51W
Rosebud, Tex. 51 31 4N 96 59W
Rosebud County ◇ 33 46 30N 106 45W
Rosebud Indian Reservation 47 43 10N 101 0W
Roseburg 44 43 13N 123 20W
Rosebush 29 43 42N 84 46W
Rosedale, Md. 27 39 19N 76 31W
Rosedale, Miss. 31 33 51N 91 2W
Rosedale, Okla. 43 34 55N 97 11W
Rosedale, W. Va. 54 38 44N 80 57W
Roseglen 41 47 45N 101 50W
Roseland, La. 25 30 46N 90 31W
Roseland, Nebr. 34 40 28N 98 34W
Rosemary 62 50 46N 112 5W
Rosemont 27 39 20N 77 37W
Rosemount 30 44 45N 93 8W
Rosenberg 51 29 34N 95 49W
Rosendale 30 45 2N 94 43W
Rosenhayn 37 39 29N 75 8W
Rosenheim 88 47 51N 12 9 E
Rosepine 25 30 55N 93 17W
Rosetown 63 51 35N 107 59W
Rosetta = Rashîd 121 31 21N 30 22 E
Rosette 52 41 49N 113 25W
Roseville, Calif. 14 38 45N 121 17W
Roseville, Ill. 21 40 44N 90 40W
Roseville, Mich. 29 42 30N 82 56W
Roseville, Minn. 30 45 1N 93 10W
Roseville, Ohio 42 39 49N 82 5W
Roseville, Pa. 45 41 52N 76 58W
Rosh Haniqra, Kefar 104 33 5N 35 5 E
Rosh Pinna 104 32 58N 35 32 E
Rosharon 51 29 21N 95 28W
Rosholt, S. Dak. 47 45 52N 96 44W
Rosholt, Wis. 55 44 38N 89 18W
Rosiclare 21 37 26N 88 21W
Rosier 18 32 59N 82 15W
Rosignol 71 6 15N 57 30W
Roşiori de Vede 95 44 9N 25 0 E
Rositsa 95 43 57N 27 57 E
Rositsa → 95 43 10N 25 30 E
Roskilde 97 55 38N 12 3 E
Roslavl 98 53 57N 32 55 E
Roslyn, S. Dak. 47 45 30N 97 29W
Roslyn, Wash. 53 47 13N 120 59W
Rosman 40 35 9N 82 49W
Ross, N.Z. 128 42 53 S 170 49 E
Ross, U.S.A. 41 48 19N 102 33W
Ross County ◇ 42 39 20N 82 59W
Ross Dependency □ 5 70 0 S 170 5W
Ross I. 5 77 30 S 168 0 E
Ross Ice Shelf 5 80 0 S 180 0 E

Ross L. Sage Cr.

Ross L. 53 48 44N 121 4W
Ross Lake National
Recreation Area 53 48 43N 121 4W
Ross on Wye 83 51 55N 2 34W
Ross R. Barnett Reservoir 31 32 24N 90 4W
Ross Sea 5 74 0S 178 0E
Rossan Pt. 85 54 42N 8 47W
Rossburg 42 40 17N 84 38W
Rossburn 63 50 40N 100 49W
Rossford 42 41 36N 83 34W
Rossie 23 43 1N 95 11W
Rossignol, L., N.S., Canada 61 44 12N 65 10W
Rossignol, L., Qué., Canada 60 52 43N 73 40W
Rossiter 45 40 54N 78 56W
Rossland 62 49 6N 117 50W
Rosslare 85 52 17N 6 23W
Rosso 120 16 40N 15 45W
Rossosh 99 50 15N 39 28 E
Rossport 60 48 50N 87 30W
Rosston, Ark. 13 33 36N 93 17W
Rosston, Okla. 43 36 49N 99 56W
Røssvatnet 96 65 45N 14 5 E
Rossville, Ill. 21 40 23N 87 40W
Rossville, Ind. 22 40 25N 86 36W
Rossville, Kans. 24 39 8N 95 57W
Rosthern 63 52 40N 106 20W
Rostock 88 54 4N 12 9 E
Rostov, Don, U.S.S.R. 99 47 15N 39 45 E
Rostov, Moskva, U.S.S.R. 98 57 14N 39 25 E
Roswell, Ga. 18 34 2N 84 22W
Roswell, N. Mex. 38 33 24N 104 32W
Rosyth 84 56 2N 3 26W
Rotan 50 32 51N 100 28W
Rothaargebirge 88 51 0N 8 20 E
Rother ⟶ 83 50 59N 0 40 E
Rotherham 82 53 26N 1 21W
Rothes 84 57 31N 3 12W
Rothesay, Canada 61 45 23N 66 0W
Rothesay, U.K. 84 55 50N 5 3W
Rothsay 30 46 28N 96 17W
Rothschild 55 44 53N 89 37W
Roti 111 10 50 S 123 0 E
Roto 127 33 0 S 145 30 E
Rotoroa, L. 128 41 55 S 172 39 E
Rotorua 128 38 9 S 176 16 E
Rotorua, L. 128 38 5 S 176 18 E
Rotterdam, Neth. 87 51 55N 4 30 E
Rotterdam, U.S.A. 39 42 48N 74 1W
Rottumeroog 87 53 33N 6 34 E
Rottweil 88 48 9N 8 38 E
Rotuma 124 12 25 S 177 5 E
Roubaix 90 50 40N 3 10 E
Rouen 90 49 27N 1 4 E
Rougemont 40 36 13N 78 56W
Rough River L. 48 37 37N 86 30W
Rouleau 63 50 10N 104 56W
Roulette 45 41 47N 78 9W
Round Hill 54 39 8N 77 46W
Round Lake 30 43 32N 95 28W
Round Mt. 127 30 26 S 152 16 E
Round Mountain, Nev. 35 38 43N 117 4W
Round Mountain, Tex. 51 30 26N 98 21W
Round Oak 18 33 7N 83 37W
Round Rock, Ariz. 12 36 31N 109 28W
Round Rock, Tex. 51 30 31N 97 41W
Round Top 51 30 4N 96 42W
Round Valley Indian
Reservation 14 39 50N 123 20W
Roundup 33 46 27N 108 33W
Roura 71 4 44N 52 20W
Rousay 84 59 10N 3 2W
Rouses Point 39 44 59N 73 22W
Rouseville 45 41 28N 79 42W
Roussillon 90 42 30N 2 35 E
Routt County ◇ 16 40 30N 107 0W
Routt National Forest 16 40 45N 107 0W
Rouyn 60 48 20N 79 0W
Rovaniemi 96 66 29N 25 41 E
Rover 48 35 40N 86 36W
Rovereto 94 45 53N 11 3 E
Rovigo 94 45 4N 11 48 E
Rovinj 94 45 5N 13 40 E
Rovira 70 4 15N 75 20W
Rovno 99 50 40N 26 10 E
Rovuma ⟶ 122 10 29 S 40 28 E
Rowan 23 42 45N 93 33W
Rowan County ◇, Ky. 49 38 10N 83 25W
Rowan County ◇, N.C. 40 35 40N 80 30W
Rowe 38 35 30N 105 41W
Rowena 51 31 39N 100 3W
Rowesville 46 33 22N 80 50W
Rowland 40 34 32N 79 18W
Rowlesburg 54 39 21N 79 40W
Rowlett 51 32 54N 96 34W
Rowley 23 42 22N 91 51W
Rowley Shoals 126 17 30 S 119 0 E
Roxana 27 38 30N 75 10W
Roxas 111 11 36N 122 49 E
Roxboro 40 36 24N 78 59W
Roxburgh 128 45 33 S 169 19 E
Roxbury, Conn. 28 41 45N 73 11W
Roxbury, Kans. 24 38 33N 97 26W
Roxbury, N.Y. 39 42 17N 74 34W
Roxbury, Vt. 36 44 8N 72 44W
Roxie 31 31 30N 91 4W
Roxton 51 33 33N 95 44W
Roy, Fla. 17 29 37N 81 29W
Roy, Mont. 33 47 20N 108 58W
Roy, N. Mex. 38 35 57N 104 12W
Roy, Utah 52 41 10N 112 2W
Roy, Wash. 53 47 0N 122 33W
Royal 23 43 4N 95 17W
Royal Center 22 40 52N 86 30W
Royal City 53 46 54N 119 38W
Royal Oak, Md. 27 38 44N 76 11W
Royal Oak, Mich. 29 42 30N 83 9W
Royalston 28 42 40N 72 12W
Royalton 30 45 50N 94 18W
Royalty 50 31 22N 102 52W
Royan 90 45 37N 1 2W
Royersford 45 40 11N 75 33W
Royse City 51 32 59N 96 20W
Royston 18 34 17N 83 7W
Rozel 24 38 12N 99 24W
Rtishchevo 98 55 16N 43 50 E
Ruahine Ra. 128 39 55 S 176 2 E
Ruapehu 128 39 17 S 175 35 E
Ruapuke I. 128 46 46 S 168 31 E
Rub' al Khali 105 18 0N 48 0 E
Rubh a' Mhail 84 55 55N 6 10W
Rubha Hunish 84 57 42N 6 20W
Rubiataba 75 15 8 S 49 48W
Rubicone ⟶ 94 44 8N 12 28 E
Rubinéia 75 20 13 S 51 2W
Rubio 70 7 43N 72 22W
Rubtsovsk 100 51 30N 81 10 E
Ruby, Alaska 11 64 45N 155 30W
Ruby, S.C. 46 34 44N 80 11W
Ruby Dome 35 40 37N 115 28W
Ruby L. 35 40 10N 115 28W
Ruby Mts. 35 40 30N 115 20W
Ruby Valley 35 40 30N 115 21W
Rudnichnyy 98 59 38N 52 26 E
Rudnik 95 42 36N 27 30 E
Rudnogorsk 101 57 15N 103 42 E
Rudnyy 100 52 57N 63 7 E
Rudolf, Ostrov 100 81 45N 58 30 E
Rudolph 55 44 30N 89 48W
Rudozem 95 41 29N 24 51 E
Rudy 13 35 31N 94 16W
Rudyard, Mich. 29 46 14N 84 36W
Rudyard, Mont. 33 48 34N 110 33W
Rufa'a 121 14 44N 33 22 E
Rufflin 46 33 0N 80 49W
Rufiji ⟶ 122 7 50 S 39 15 E
Rufino 76 34 20 S 62 50W
Rufisque 120 14 40N 17 15W
Rufus 44 45 42N 120 44W
Rugao 115 32 23N 120 31 E
Rugby, U.K. 83 52 23N 1 16W
Rugby, U.S.A. 41 48 22N 100 0W
Rügen 88 54 22N 13 25 E
Ruḩama 104 31 31N 34 43 E
Ruhr ⟶ 88 51 25N 6 44 E
Rui Barbosa 75 12 18 S 40 27W
Rui'an 115 27 47N 120 40 E
Ruidosa 50 29 59N 104 41W
Ruidoso 38 33 20N 105 41W
Ruidoso Downs 38 33 20N 105 32W
Rukwa L. 122 8 0 S 32 20 E
Rule 51 33 11N 99 54W
Ruleville 31 33 44N 90 33W
Rulo 34 40 3N 95 26W
Rum ⟶ 30 45 11N 93 23W
Rum Cay 66 23 40N 74 58W
Rum Jungle 126 13 0 S 130 59 E
Rumāḩ 106 25 29N 47 10 E
Rumania = Romania ■ 89 46 0N 25 0 E
Rumbêk 121 6 54N 29 37 E
Rumbley 27 38 6N 75 51W
Rumford 26 44 33N 70 33W
Rumney 36 43 47N 71 48W
Rumoi 116 43 56N 141 39W
Rump Mt. 26 45 12N 71 4W
Rumsey 62 51 51N 112 48W
Rumson 37 40 23N 74 0W
Runan 115 33 0N 114 30 E
Runanga 128 42 25 S 171 15 E
Runcorn 82 53 20N 2 44W
Runge 51 28 53N 97 43W
Rungwa 122 6 55 S 33 32 E
Runnells 23 41 31N 93 21W
Runnels County ◇ 51 31 51N 99 57W
Running Water ⟶ 50 34 0N 101 30W
Ruoqiang 113 38 55N 88 10 E
Rupa 109 27 15N 92 21 E
Rupat 110 1 45N 101 40 E
Rupea 95 46 2N 25 13 E
Rupert, Idaho 20 42 37N 113 41W
Rupert, Vt. 36 43 16N 73 13W
Rupert, W. Va. 54 37 58N 80 41W
Rupert ⟶ 60 51 29N 78 45W
Rupert House = Fort Rupert 60 51 30N 78 40W
Rupununi ⟶ 71 4 3N 58 35W
Rural Hall 40 36 15N 80 18W
Rural Retreat 54 36 54N 81 17W
Rurrenabaque 72 14 30 S 67 32W
Rusape 123 18 35 S 32 8 E
Ruschuk = Ruse 95 43 48N 25 59 E
Ruse 95 43 48N 25 59 E
Ruşeţu 95 44 57N 27 14 E
Rush 49 38 20N 82 46W
Rush Center 24 38 28N 99 19W
Rush City 30 45 41N 92 58W
Rush County ◇, Ind. 22 39 35N 85 30W
Rush County ◇, Kans. 24 38 30N 99 15W
Rush Cr. ⟶ 16 38 22N 102 32W
Rush Springs 43 34 47N 97 58W
Rushden 83 52 17N 0 37W
Rushford 30 43 49N 91 46W
Rushmore, Mt. 47 43 53N 103 28W
Rushville, Ill. 21 40 7N 90 34W
Rushville, Ind. 22 39 37N 85 27W
Rushville, Mo. 32 39 35N 95 1W
Rushville, Nebr. 34 42 43N 102 28W
Rusk 51 31 48N 95 9W
Rusk County ◇, Tex. 51 32 9N 94 48W
Rusk County ◇, Wis. 55 45 25N 91 10W
Ruskin, Fla. 17 27 43N 82 26W
Ruskin, Nebr. 34 40 9N 97 52W
Ruso 41 47 50N 100 56W
Russas 74 4 55 S 37 50W
Russell, Canada 63 50 50N 101 20W
Russell, N.Z. 128 35 16 S 174 10 E
Russell, Fla. 17 30 3N 81 45W
Russell, Kans. 24 38 54N 98 52W
Russell County ◇, Ala. 10 32 18N 85 10W
Russell County ◇, Kans. 24 39 0N 98 45W
Russell County ◇, Ky. 49 37 0N 85 0W
Russell County ◇, Va. 54 36 0N 82 0W
Russell Cr. ⟶ 49 37 14N 85 30W
Russell L., Man., Canada 63 56 15N 101 30W
Russell L., N.W.T., Canada 62 63 5N 115 44W
Russell Springs, Kans. 24 38 55N 101 11W
Russell Springs, Ky. 49 37 3N 85 5W
Russellkonda 109 19 57N 84 42 E
Russellville, Ala. 10 34 30N 87 44W
Russellville, Ark. 13 35 17N 93 8W
Russellville, Ky. 48 36 51N 86 53W
Russellville, Mo. 32 38 31N 92 26W
Russellville, Ohio 42 38 52N 83 47W
Russellville, Tenn. 49 36 15N 83 12W
Russian ⟶ 14 38 27N 123 8W
Russian Mission 11 61 47N 161 19W
Russian S.F.S.R. □ 101 62 0N 105 0 E
Russiaville 22 40 25N 86 16W
Russkaya Polyana 100 53 47N 73 53 E
Russkoye Ustie 4 71 0N 149 0 E
Rustburg 54 37 17N 79 6W
Rustenburg 123 25 41 S 27 14 E
Ruston 25 32 32N 92 38W
Ruteng 111 8 35 S 120 30 E
Ruth, Miss. 31 31 23N 90 19W
Ruth, Nev. 35 39 17N 114 59W
Rutherford 48 36 8N 88 59W
Rutherford County ◇, N.C. 40 35 20N 81 50W
Rutherford County ◇, Tenn. 48 35 51N 86 24W
Rutherfordton 40 35 22N 81 58W
Rutherglen 84 55 50N 4 11W
Ruthsburg 27 39 0N 75 58W
Ruthton 30 44 11N 96 6W
Ruthven 23 43 8N 94 54W
Rutland, Ill. 21 40 59N 89 3W
Rutland, Iowa 23 42 46N 94 18W
Rutland, Mass. 28 42 23N 71 57W
Rutland, N. Dak. 41 46 3N 97 30W
Rutland, Ohio 42 39 3N 82 8W
Rutland, S. Dak. 47 44 5N 96 58W
Rutland, Vt. 36 43 37N 72 58W
Rutland County ◇ 36 43 35N 73 0W
Rutland I. 112 11 25N 92 40 E
Rutledge, Ga. 18 33 38N 83 37W
Rutledge, Minn. 30 46 16N 92 52W
Rutledge, Tenn. 49 36 17N 83 31W
Rutledge ⟶ 63 61 4N 112 0W
Rutledge L. 63 61 33N 110 47W
Rutshuru 122 1 13 S 29 25 E
Ruurlo 87 52 5N 6 24 E
Ruwenzori 122 0 30N 29 55 E
Růzhevo Konare 95 42 23N 24 46 E
Ružomberok 89 49 3N 19 17 E
Rwanda ■ 122 2 0 S 30 0 E
Ryakhovo 95 44 0N 26 18 E
Ryan, Iowa 23 42 21N 91 29W
Ryan, Okla. 43 34 1N 97 57W
Ryan, L. 84 55 0N 5 2W
Ryazan 98 54 40N 39 40 E
Ryazhsk 98 53 45N 40 3 E
Rybache 100 46 40N 81 20 E
Rybachiy Poluostrov 98 69 43N 32 0 E
Rybinsk = Andropov 98 58 5N 38 50 E
Rybinskoye Vdkhr. 98 58 30N 38 25 E
Ryde 83 50 44N 1 9W
Ryder 41 47 55N 101 40W
Ryderwood 53 46 23N 123 3W
Rye, U.K. 83 50 57N 0 46 E
Rye, Ark. 13 33 45N 91 59W
Rye, Colo. 16 37 55N 104 56W
Rye, N.H. 36 43 2N 70 50W
Rye ⟶ 82 54 12N 0 53W
Rye Beach 36 42 59N 70 46W
Rye Patch Reservoir 35 40 28N 118 19W
Ryegate 33 46 18N 109 15W
Ryōthu 116 38 5N 138 26 E
Rypin 89 53 3N 19 25 E
Ryūgasaki 117 35 54N 140 11 E
Ryūkyū Is. = Nansei-Shotō 117 26 0N 128 0 E
Rzeszów 89 50 5N 21 58 E
Rzhev 98 56 20N 34 20 E

S

Sa Dec 112 10 20N 105 46 E
Sa'ad 104 31 28N 34 33 E
Sa'ādatābād 107 30 10N 53 5 E
Saale ⟶ 88 51 57N 11 56 E
Saar ⟶ 88 49 41N 6 32 E
Saarbrücken 88 49 15N 6 58 E
Saaremaa 98 58 30N 22 30 E
Saariselkä 96 68 16N 28 15 E
Saba 67 17 42N 63 26W
Sabadell 91 41 28N 2 7 E
Sabagalet 110 1 36 S 98 40 E
Sabah □ 110 6 0N 117 0 E
Sábana de la Mar 67 19 7N 69 24W
Sabana Grande 57 18 5N 66 58W
Sábanalarga 70 10 38N 74 55W
Sabang 110 5 50N 95 15 E
Sabará 75 19 55 S 43 46W
Sabarania 111 2 5 S 138 18 E
Sabasţiyah 104 32 17N 35 12 E
Sabáudia 94 41 17N 13 2 E
Sabaya 72 19 1 S 68 23W
Sabetha 24 39 54N 95 48W
Sabhah 121 27 9N 14 29 E
Sabin 30 46 47N 96 39W
Sabina 42 39 29N 83 38W
Sabinal, Mexico 64 30 58N 107 25W
Sabinal, U.S.A. 51 29 19N 99 28W
Sabinas 64 27 50N 101 10W
Sabinas ⟶ 64 27 37N 100 42W
Sabinas Hidalgo 64 26 33N 100 10W
Sabine ⟶ 25 29 59N 93 47W
Sabine County ◇ 51 31 20N 93 51W
Sabine L. 25 29 53N 93 51W
Sabine National Forest 51 31 38N 94 0W
Sabine Parish ◇ 25 31 38N 93 39W
Sabine Pass 51 29 44N 93 54W
Sabinópolis 75 18 40 S 43 6W
Sabinoso 38 35 42N 104 24W
Sablayan 111 12 50N 120 50 E
Sable, C., U.S.A. 17 25 9N 81 8W
Sable, C., Canada 61 43 29N 65 38W
Sable I. 61 44 0N 60 0W
Sables-d'Olonne, Les 90 46 30N 1 45W
Saboeiro 74 6 32 S 39 54W
Sabolev 101 54 20N 155 30 E
Sabrina Coast 5 68 0 S 120 0 E
Sabula, Iowa 23 42 4N 90 10W
Sabula, Mo. 32 37 27N 90 42W
Sabzevār 107 36 15N 57 40 E
Sabzvārān 107 28 45N 57 50 E
Sac ⟶ 32 38 1N 93 43W
Sac City 23 42 25N 95 0W
Sac County ◇ 23 42 25N 95 5W
Sacajawea, L. 53 46 20N 118 45W
Sacajawea Peak 44 45 15N 117 17W
Sacandaga Reservoir 39 43 6N 74 16W
Sacaton 12 33 5N 111 44W
Sachigo ⟶ 60 55 6N 88 58W
Sachigo, L. 60 53 50N 92 12W
Sackets Harbor 39 43 57N 76 7W
Saco, Maine 26 43 30N 70 27W
Saco, Mont. 33 48 28N 107 21W
Saco ⟶ 26 43 28N 70 23W
Sacramento, Brazil 75 19 53 S 47 27W
Sacramento, Calif. 14 38 35N 121 29W
Sacramento, Ky. 48 37 25N 87 16W
Sacramento, N. Mex. 38 32 48N 105 34W
Sacramento ⟶ 14 38 3N 121 56W
Sacramento County ◇ 14 38 20N 121 20W
Sacramento Mts. 38 32 30N 105 30W
Sacramento South 14 38 32N 121 26W
Sacramento Valley 14 39 30N 122 0W
Sacramento Wash ⟶ 12 34 43N 114 28W
Sádaba 91 42 19N 1 12W
Sadani 122 5 58 S 38 35 E
Sadao 112 6 38N 100 26 E
Sadd el Aali 121 23 54N 32 54 E
Saddle Mt., Oreg. 44 45 58N 123 41W
Saddle Mt., Wyo. 56 44 43N 109 59W
Saddle Mts. 53 46 55N 120 0W
Saddle Peak 53 48 58N 120 9W
Sadieville 49 38 23N 84 32W
Sado 116 38 0N 138 25 E
Sadon 109 25 28N 98 0 E
Sadorus 21 39 58N 88 21W
Saegerstown 45 41 43N 80 9W
Säffle 97 59 8N 12 55 E
Safford 12 32 50N 109 43W
Saffron Walden 83 52 2N 0 15 E
Safi 120 32 18N 9 20W
Safīd Kūh 107 34 45N 63 0 E
Sag Harbor 39 41 0N 72 18W
Saga, Indonesia 111 2 40 S 132 55 E
Saga, Japan 117 33 15N 130 16 E
Saga □ 117 33 15N 130 20 E
Sagadahoc County ◇ 26 44 0N 70 0W
Sagae 116 38 22N 140 17 E
Sagaing □ 109 23 55N 95 56 E
Sagala 120 14 9N 6 38W
Sagamore 28 41 45N 70 33W
Sagavanirktok ⟶ 11 70 19N 147 53W
Sage 56 41 49N 110 58W
Sage Cr. ⟶ 33 47 16N 109 43W

Sagerton **Salālah**

Sagerton **51** 33 5N 99 58W
Sageville **23** 42 36N 90 43W
Sagil **113** 50 15N 91 15 E
Saginaw **29** 43 26N 83 56W
Saginaw → **29** 43 39N 83 51W
Saginaw B. **29** 43 50N 83 40W
Saginaw County ◇ **29** 43 20N 84 0W
Sagīr, Zab al **106** 35 10N 43 20 E
Saglouc **59** 62 14N 75 38W
Sagra, La **91** 37 57N 2 35W
Sagres **91** 37 0N 8 58W
Sagua la Grande **66** 22 50N 80 10W
Saguache **16** 38 5N 106 8W
Saguache County ◇ **16** 38 10N 106 15W
Saguaro Nat. Monument **12** 32 12N 110 38W
Saguenay → **61** 48 22N 71 0W
Sagunto **91** 39 42N 0 18W
Sahagún, Colombia **70** 8 57N 75 27W
Sahagún, Spain **91** 42 18N 5 2W
Saham **104** 32 42N 35 46 E
Saḥam al Jawlān **104** 32 45N 35 55 E
Sahand, Kūh-e **106** 37 44N 46 27 E
Sahara **120** 23 0N 5 0 E
Saharan Atlas **118** 34 9N 3 29 E
Saharanpur **108** 29 58N 77 33 E
Saharien, Atlas **120** 33 30N 1 0 E
Sahiwal **108** 30 45N 73 8 E
Sahtaneh → **62** 59 2N 122 28W
Sahuaripa **64** 29 0N 109 13W
Sahuarita **12** 31 57N 110 58W
Sahuayo **64** 20 4N 102 43W
Sai-Cinza **73** 6 17 S 57 42W
Sa'id Bundas **121** 8 24N 24 48 E
Saïda **120** 34 50N 0 11 E
Saīdābād **107** 29 30N 55 45 E
Sa'idiyeh **106** 36 20N 48 55 E
Saidu **108** 34 43N 72 24 E
Saigon = Phanh Bho Ho Chi Minh, Vietnam **112** 10 58N 106 40 E
Saigon = Phanh Bho Ho Chi Minh, Vietnam **112** 10 58N 106 40 E
Saigon = Phanh Bho Ho Chi Minh, Vietnam **112** 10 58N 106 40 E
Saih-al-Malih **107** 23 37N 58 31 E
Saijō **117** 33 55N 133 11 E
Saikhoa Ghat **109** 27 50N 95 40 E
Saiki **117** 32 58N 131 51 E
Sailolof **111** 1 7 S 130 46 E
Sailor Springs **21** 38 46N 88 22W
St. Abb's Head **84** 55 55N 2 10W
St. Alban's, Canada **61** 47 51N 55 50W
St. Albans, U.K. **83** 51 44N 0 19W
St. Albans, Vt. **36** 44 49N 73 5W
St. Albans, W. Va. **54** 38 23N 81 50W
St. Alban's Head **83** 50 34N 2 3W
St. Albert **62** 53 37N 113 32W
St. Andrew Sd. **18** 31 0N 81 25W
St. Andrew's, Canada **61** 47 45N 59 15W
St. Andrews, U.K. **84** 56 20N 2 48W
St. Ann B. **61** 46 22N 60 25W
St. Anne **21** 41 1N 87 43W
St. Ann's Bay **66** 18 26N 77 15W
St. Ansgar **23** 43 23N 92 55W
St. Anthony, Canada **61** 51 22N 55 35W
St. Anthony, U.S.A. **20** 43 58N 111 41W
St. Arnaud Ra. **128** 42 1 S 172 53 E
St. Arthur **61** 47 33N 67 46W
St. Asaph **82** 53 15N 3 27W
St-Augustin-Saguenay **61** 51 13N 58 38W
St. Augustine **17** 29 54N 81 19W
St. Augustine Beach **17** 29 51N 81 16W
St. Austell **83** 50 20N 4 48W
St.-Barthélemy, I. **67** 17 50N 62 50W
St. Bee's Hd. **82** 54 30N 3 38 E
St. Benedict **24** 39 53N 96 6W
St. Bernard Parish ◇ **25** 29 55N 89 10W
St. Boniface **63** 49 53N 97 5W
St. Bride's **61** 46 56N 54 10W
St. Bride's B. **83** 51 48N 5 15W
St-Brieuc **90** 48 30N 2 46W
St. Catharines **60** 43 10N 79 15W
St. Catherines I. **18** 31 40N 81 10W
St. Catherine's Pt. **83** 50 34N 1 18W
St. Charles, Ark. **13** 34 23N 91 8W
St. Charles, Idaho **20** 42 7N 111 23W
St. Charles, Ill. **21** 41 54N 88 19W
St. Charles, Iowa **23** 41 17N 93 49W
St. Charles, Mich. **29** 43 18N 84 9W
St. Charles, Minn. **30** 43 58N 92 4W
St. Charles, Mo. **32** 38 47N 90 29W
St. Charles, S. Dak. **47** 43 5N 99 6W
St. Charles, Va. **54** 36 48N 83 4W
St. Charles County ◇ **32** 38 45N 90 40W
St. Charles Parish ◇ **25** 29 59N 90 25W
St. Christopher-Nevis ■ **67** 17 20N 62 40W
St. Clair, Ga. **18** 33 9N 82 13W
St. Clair, Mich. **29** 42 50N 82 30W
St. Clair, Minn. **30** 44 5N 93 51W
St. Clair, Mo. **32** 38 21N 90 59W
St. Clair, Pa. **45** 40 43N 76 12W
St. Clair → **29** 42 38N 82 31W
St. Clair, L., Canada **60** 42 30N 82 45W
St. Clair, L., U.S.A. **29** 42 27N 82 39W
St. Clair County ◇, Ala. **10** 33 35N 86 17W
St. Clair County ◇, Ill. **21** 38 30N 89 55W
St. Clair County ◇, Mich. **29** 43 0N 82 30W
St. Clair County ◇, Mo. **32** 38 0N 93 45W
St. Clair Shores **29** 42 30N 82 53W
St. Clairsville **42** 40 5N 80 54W
St. Claude **63** 49 40N 98 20W
St. Cloud, Fla. **17** 28 15N 81 17W
St. Cloud, Minn. **30** 45 34N 94 10W
St-Coeur de Marie **61** 48 39N 71 43W
St. Croix →, Maine **26** 45 4N 67 5W
St. Croix →, Wis. **55** 44 45N 92 48W
St. Croix County ◇ **55** 45 0N 92 20W
St. Croix Falls **55** 45 24N 92 38W
St. Croix Flowage **55** 46 15N 91 56W
St. Croix L. **30** 44 57N 92 45W
St. David, Ariz. **12** 31 54N 110 13W
St. David, Ill. **21** 40 30N 90 3W
St. David's, Canada **61** 48 12N 58 52W
St. David's, U.K. **83** 51 54N 5 16W
St. David's Head **83** 51 55N 5 16W
St-Denis **90** 48 56N 2 22 E
St. Donatus **23** 42 22N 90 33W
St. Edward **34** 41 34N 97 52W
St. Elias, Mt. **11** 60 18N 140 56W
St. Elias Mts., Canada **62** 60 33N 139 28W
St. Elias Mts., U.S.A. **11** 60 0N 138 0W
St.-Elie **71** 4 49N 53 17W
St. Elizabeth **32** 38 15N 92 16W
St. Elmo **21** 39 2N 88 51W
St-Étienne **90** 45 27N 4 22 E
St. Eustatius **67** 17 20N 63 0W
St-Félicien **60** 48 40N 72 25W
St-Flour **90** 45 2N 3 6 E
St. Frances **47** 43 9N 100 54W
St. Francis, Kans. **24** 39 47N 101 48W
St. Francis, Maine **26** 47 10N 68 54W
St. Francis, Minn. **30** 45 23N 93 22W
St. Francis, Wis. **55** 42 58N 87 52W
St. Francis → **13** 34 38N 90 36W
St. Francis, C. **123** 34 14 S 24 49 E
St. Francis County ◇ **13** 35 1N 90 47W
St. Francisville, Ill. **21** 38 36N 87 39W
St. Francisville, La. **25** 30 47N 91 23W
St. Francois County ◇ **32** 37 50N 90 30W
St. Francois Mts. **32** 37 30N 90 35W
St. Froid, L. **26** 46 57N 68 37W
St. Gabriel **25** 30 16N 91 6W
St-Gabriel-de-Brandon **60** 46 17N 73 24W
St. Gallen **88** 47 25N 9 20 E
St. Genevieve County ◇ **32** 37 50N 90 10W
St. George, Australia **127** 28 1 S 148 30 E
St. George, Canada **61** 45 11N 66 50W
St. George, Ga. **18** 30 31N 82 2W
St. George, Kans. **24** 39 12N 96 25W
St. George, S.C. **46** 33 11N 80 35W
St. George, Utah **52** 37 6N 113 35W
St. George, C. **61** 48 30N 59 16W
St. George, Pt. **14** 41 47N 124 15W
St. George I., Alaska **11** 56 35N 169 35W
St. George I., Fla. **17** 29 35N 84 55W
St. George Island **27** 38 7N 76 29W
St-Georges **87** 50 37N 5 20 E
St. George's, Newf., Canada **61** 48 26N 58 31W
St. Georges, Qué., Canada **60** 46 42N 72 35W
St-Georges **61** 46 8N 70 40W
St. Georges, Fr. Gui. **71** 4 0N 52 0W
St. George's, Grenada **67** 12 5N 61 43W
St. George's B. **61** 48 24N 58 53W
St. George's Channel **86** 52 0N 6 0W
St. Helena, Atl. Oc. **2** 15 55 S 5 44W
St. Helena, Calif. **14** 38 30N 122 28W
St. Helena, Nebr. **34** 42 49N 97 15W
St. Helena Parish ◇ **25** 30 50N 90 40W
St. Helena Sd. **46** 32 15N 80 25W
St. Helenabaai **123** 32 40 S 18 10 E
St. Helens, U.K. **82** 53 28N 2 44W
St. Helens, U.S.A. **44** 45 52N 122 48W
St. Helens, Mt. **53** 46 12N 122 12W
St. Helier **83** 49 11N 2 6W
St. Henry **42** 40 25N 84 38W
St. Hilaire **30** 48 1N 96 14W
St-Hubert **87** 50 2N 5 23 E
St-Hyacinthe **60** 45 40N 72 58W
St. Ignace **29** 45 52N 84 44W
St. Ignace I. **60** 48 45N 88 0W
St. Ignatius **33** 47 19N 114 6W
St. Ives, Cambs., U.K. **83** 52 20N 0 5W
St. Ives, Cornwall, U.K. **83** 50 13N 5 29W
St. James, Mich. **29** 45 45N 85 31W
St. James, Minn. **30** 43 59N 94 38W
St. James, Mo. **32** 38 0N 91 37W
St. James, N.Y. **39** 40 53N 73 9W
St. James City **17** 26 29N 82 5W
St. James Parish ◇ **25** 30 1N 90 50W
St. Jean **60** 45 20N 73 20W
St-Jean → **61** 50 17N 64 20W
St-Jean, L. **61** 48 40N 72 0W
St. Jean Baptiste **63** 49 15N 97 20W
St-Jean-Port-Joli **61** 47 15N 70 13W
St-Jérôme, Qué., Canada **60** 45 47N 74 0W
St-Jérôme, Qué., Canada **61** 48 26N 71 53W
St. Jo **51** 33 42N 97 31W
St. Joe, Ark. **13** 36 2N 92 48W
St. Joe, Idaho **20** 47 19N 116 21W
St. Joe National Forest **20** 47 5N 115 30W
St. John, Canada **61** 45 20N 66 8W
St. John, Kans. **24** 38 0N 98 46W
St. John, N. Dak. **41** 48 57N 99 43W
St. John, Wash. **53** 47 6N 117 35W
St. John →, Canada **61** 45 15N 66 4W
St. John →, U.S.A. **26** 45 12N 66 5W
St. John, C. **61** 50 0N 55 32W
St. John I. **57** 18 20N 64 42W
St. John The Baptist Parish ◇ **25** 30 3N 90 33W
St. John's, Antigua **67** 17 6N 61 51W
St. John's, Canada **61** 47 35N 52 40W
St. Johns, Ariz. **12** 34 30N 109 22W
St. Johns, Mich. **29** 43 0N 84 33W
St. Johns → **17** 30 24N 81 24W
St. Johns County ◇ **17** 29 45N 81 25W
St. Johnsbury **36** 44 25N 72 1W
St. Joseph, Ill. **21** 40 7N 88 2W
St. Joseph, La. **25** 31 55N 91 14W
St. Joseph, Mich. **29** 42 6N 86 29W
St. Joseph, Mo. **32** 39 46N 94 50W
St. Joseph, Tenn. **48** 35 2N 87 30W
St. Joseph →, Ind. **22** 41 5N 85 8W
St. Joseph →, Mich. **29** 42 7N 86 29W
St. Joseph, I. **60** 46 12N 83 58W
St. Joseph, L. **60** 51 10N 90 35W
St. Joseph County ◇ **22** 41 35N 86 15W
St. Joseph Pt. **17** 29 52N 85 24W
St-Jovite **60** 46 8N 74 38W
St. Kilda **128** 45 53 S 170 31 E
St. Kitts = St. Christopher **67** 17 20N 62 40W
St. Kitts-Nevis ■ **67** 17 20N 62 40W
St. Landry Parish ◇ **25** 30 40N 92 0W
St. Laurent **63** 50 25N 97 58W
St-Laurent **71** 5 29N 54 3W
St. Lawrence, Canada **61** 46 54N 55 23W
St. Lawrence, U.S.A. **47** 44 31N 98 56W
St. Lawrence → **61** 49 30N 66 0W
St. Lawrence, Gulf of **61** 48 25N 62 0W
St. Lawrence County ◇ **39** 44 30N 75 0W
St. Lawrence I. **11** 63 30N 170 30W
St. Leo **30** 44 43N 96 3W
St. Leonard, Canada **61** 47 12N 67 58W
St. Leonard, U.S.A. **27** 38 28N 76 30W
St. Lewis → **61** 52 26N 56 11W
St. Libory **34** 41 5N 98 21W
St-Lô **90** 49 7N 1 5W
St-Louis **120** 16 8N 16 27W
St. Louis, Mich. **29** 43 25N 84 36W
St. Louis, Mo. **32** 38 37N 90 12W
St. Louis, Okla. **43** 35 5N 96 53W
St. Louis → **30** 46 44N 92 9W
St. Louis County ◇, Minn. **30** 47 40N 92 20W
St. Louis County ◇, Mo. **32** 38 40N 90 25W
St. Louis Park **30** 44 57N 93 21W
St. Louisville **42** 40 10N 82 25W
St. Lucia ■ **67** 14 0N 60 50W
St. Lucia, Lake **123** 28 5 S 32 30 E
St. Lucia Channel **67** 14 15N 61 0W
St. Lucie **17** 27 29N 80 20W
St. Lucie Canal **17** 27 10N 80 18W
St. Lucie County ◇ **17** 27 25N 80 30W
St. Lunaire-Griquet **61** 51 31N 55 28W
St. Maarten **67** 18 0N 63 5W
St-Malo **90** 48 39N 2 1W
St-Marc **67** 19 10N 72'41W
St. Marie **21** 38 56N 88 1W
St. Maries **20** 47 19N 116 35W
St. Maries → **20** 47 19N 116 33W
St. Marks **17** 30 9N 84 12W
St. Marks → **17** 30 8N 84 12W
St-Martin, I. **67** 18 0N 63 0W
St. Martin I. **29** 45 30N 86 46W
St. Martin L. **63** 51 40N 98 30W
St. Martin Parish ◇ **25** 30 7N 91 50W
St. Martins **61** 45 22N 65 34W
St. Martinville **25** 30 7N 91 50W
St. Mary B. **61** 46 50N 53 50W
St. Mary Parish ◇ **25** 29 48N 91 30W
St. Mary Pk. **127** 31 32 S 138 34 E
St. Marys, Australia **127** 41 35 S 148 11 E
St. Mary's, U.K. **83** 49 55N 6 17W
St. Mary's, Alaska **11** 62 4N 163 10W
St. Marys, Ga. **18** 30 44N 81 33W
St. Marys, Iowa **23** 41 19N 93 44W
St. Marys, Kans. **24** 39 12N 96 4W
St. Marys, Mo. **32** 37 53N 89 57W
St. Marys, Ohio **42** 40 33N 84 24W
St. Marys, Pa. **45** 41 26N 78 34W
St. Marys, W. Va. **54** 39 23N 81 12W
St. Marys →, Ga. **18** 30 43N 81 27W
St. Marys →, Ind. **22** 41 5N 85 8W
St. Marys →, Mich. **29** 46 0N 83 55W
St. Mary's, C. **61** 46 50N 54 12W
St. Marys Bay **61** 44 25N 66 10W
St. Marys City **27** 38 11N 76 26W
St. Marys County ◇ **27** 38 15N 76 40W
St-Mathieu, Pte. de **90** 48 20N 4 45W
St. Matthew I. **11** 60 24N 172 42W
St. Matthews, Ky. **49** 38 15N 85 39W
St. Matthews, S.C. **46** 33 40N 80 46W
St. Matthews, I. = Zadetkyi Kyun **110** 10 0N 98 25 E
St-Maurice → **60** 46 21N 72 31W
St. Meinrad **22** 38 10N 86 49W
St. Michael **11** 63 29N 162 2W
St. Michaels **27** 38 47N 76 14W
St. Michael's Mt. **83** 50 7N 5 30W
St-Nazaire **90** 47 17N 2 12W
St. Nazianz **55** 44 0N 87 55W
St. Neots **83** 52 14N 0 16W
St. Olaf **23** 42 56N 91 23W
St-Omer **90** 50 45N 2 15 E
St. Onge **47** 44 33N 103 43W
St-Pacome **61** 47 24N 69 58W
St-Pamphile **61** 46 58N 69 48W
St. Paris **42** 40 8N 83 58W
St. Pascal **61** 47 32N 69 48W
St. Patrick Peak **33** 46 59N 114 51W
St. Paul, Canada **62** 54 0N 111 17W
St. Paul, Ind. Oc. **3** 30 40 S 77 34 E
St. Paul, Alaska **11** 57 7N 170 17W
St. Paul, Ark. **13** 35 50N 93 46W
St. Paul, Ind. **22** 39 26N 85 38W
St. Paul, Iowa **23** 40 46N 91 31W
St. Paul, Kans. **24** 37 31N 95 10W
St. Paul, Minn. **30** 44 57N 93 6W
St. Paul, Nebr. **34** 41 13N 98 27W
St. Paul, Va. **54** 36 54N 82 19W
St. Paul, I. **61** 47 12N 60 9W
St. Paul I. **11** 57 10N 170 15W
St. Pauls **40** 34 48N 78 58W
St. Peter, Ill. **21** 38 52N 88 51W
St. Peter, Minn. **30** 44 20N 93 57W
St. Peter Port **83** 49 27N 2 31W
St. Peters, N.S., Canada **61** 45 40N 60 53W
St. Peters, P.E.I., Canada **61** 46 25N 62 35W
St. Petersburg **17** 27 46N 82 39W
St. Petersburg Beach **17** 27 45N 82 45W
St. Phillip **33** 46 50N 104 9W
St Pierre **61** 46 46N 56 12W
St-Pierre, L. **60** 46 12N 72 52W
St-Pierre et Miquelon □ **61** 46 55N 56 10W
St-Quentin **90** 49 50N 3 16 E
St. Regis **33** 47 18N 115 6W
St. Regis Falls **39** 44 41N 74 33W
St. Sebastien, Tanjon' i **123** 12 26 S 48 44 E
St-Siméon **61** 47 51N 69 54W
St. Simons I. **18** 31 12N 81 15W
St. Stephen, Canada **61** 45 16N 67 17W
St. Stephen, U.S.A. **46** 33 24N 79 55W
St. Tammany Parish ◇ **25** 30 29N 90 2W
St. Thomas, Canada **60** 42 45N 81 10W
St. Thomas, Mo. **32** 38 23N 92 13W
St. Thomas, N. Dak. **41** 48 37N 97 27W
St. Thomas I. **57** 18 20N 64 55W
St-Tite **60** 46 45N 72 34W
St-Tropez **90** 43 17N 6 38 E
St. Troud = Sint Truiden **87** 50 48N 5 10 E
St-Valéry **90** 50 10N 1 38 E
St. Vincent, U.S.A. **30** 48 58N 97 14W
St. Vincent, W. Indies **67** 13 10N 61 10W
St. Vincent, G. **127** 35 0 S 138 0 E
St. Vincent and the Grenadines ■ **67** 13 0N 61 10W
St. Vincent I. **17** 29 42N 85 3W
St. Vincent Passage **67** 13 30N 61 0W
St-Vith **87** 50 17N 6 9 E
St. Vrain **38** 34 25N 103 29W
Ste-Agathe-des-Monts **60** 46 3N 74 17W
Ste Anne de Beaupré **61** 47 2N 70 58W
Ste-Anne-des-Monts **61** 49 8N 66 30W
Ste-Marguerite → **61** 50 9N 66 36W
Ste Marie **67** 14 48N 61 1W
Ste-Marie de la Madeleine **61** 46 26N 71 0W
Ste-Rose **67** 16 20N 61 45W
Ste.-Rose du Lac **63** 51 4N 99 30W
Saintes **90** 45 45N 0 37W
Saintes, Île des **67** 15 50N 61 35W
Saintonge **90** 45 40N 0 50W
Sairang **109** 23 50N 92 45 E
Sairecábur, Cerro **76** 22 43 S 67 54W
Saitama □ **117** 36 25N 139 30 E
Sajama **72** 18 7 S 69 0W
Sakai **117** 34 30N 135 30 E
Sakaide **117** 34 15N 133 50 E
Sakaiminato **117** 35 38N 133 11 E
Sakākah **106** 30 0N 40 8 E
Sakakawea, L. **41** 47 30N 101 25W
Sakami, L. **60** 53 15N 77 0W
Sakania **123** 12 43 S 28 30 E
Sakarya → **99** 41 7N 30 39 E
Sakashima-Guntō **117** 24 46N 124 0 E
Sakata **116** 38 55N 139 50 E
Sakhalin, Ostrov **101** 51 0N 143 0 E
Sakhalinskiy Zaliv **101** 54 0N 141 0 E
Sakhnīn **104** 32 52N 35 12 E
Sakon Nakhon **112** 17 10N 104 9 E
Sakuma **117** 35 3N 137 49 E
Sakurai **117** 34 30N 135 51 E
Sala **97** 59 58N 16 35 E
Sala-y-Gómez **125** 26 28 S 105 28W
Salaberry-de-Valleyfield **60** 45 15N 74 8W
Salada, La **64** 24 30N 111 30W
Saladas **76** 28 15 S 58 40W
Saladillo **76** 35 40 S 59 55W
Salado **13** 35 42N 91 36W
Salado →, Buenos Aires, Argentina **76** 35 44 S 57 22W
Salado →, La Pampa, Argentina **78** 37 30 S 67 0W
Salado →, Río Negro, Argentina **78** 41 34 S 65 3W
Salado →, Santa Fe, Argentina **76** 31 40 S 60 41W
Salado →, Mexico **64** 26 52N 99 19W
Salado, Rio → **38** 34 16N 106 52W
Salaga **120** 8 31N 0 31W
Salālah **105** 16 56N 53 59 E

San Jose I.
Santa Isabel

San Jose I. 51 27 59N 96 59W
San Juan, Argentina 76 31 30 S 68 30W
San Juan, Colombia 70 8 46N 76 32W
San Juan, Mexico 64 21 20N 102 50W
San Juan, Ica, Peru 72 15 22 S 75 7W
San Juan, Puno, Peru 72 14 2 S 69 19W
San Juan, Phil. 111 8 25N 126 20 E
San Juan, Puerto Rico 57 18 28N 66 7W
San Juan ◇ 57 18 20N 66 10W
San Juan □, Argentina 76 31 9 S 69 0W
San Juan □, Dom. Rep. 67 18 45N 71 25W
San Juan →, Argentina 76 32 20 S 67 25W
San Juan →, Bolivia 73 21 2 S 65 19W
San Juan →, Colombia 70 4 3N 77 27W
San Juan →, Nic. 66 10 56N 83 42W
San Juan →, U.S.A. 52 37 16N 110 26W
San Juan →, Venezuela 71 10 14N 62 38W
San Juan, C. 122 1 5N 9 20 E
San Juan Basin 38 36 20N 108 10W
San Juan Bautista, Paraguay 76 26 37 S 57 6W
San Juan Bautista, U.S.A. 14 36 51N 121 32W
San Juan Capistrano 15 33 30N 117 40W
San Juan County ◇, Colo. 16 37 50N 107 40W
San Juan County ◇, N. Mex. 38 36 30N 108 30W
San Juan County ◇, Utah 52 38 0N 109 30W
San Juan County ◇, Wash. 53 48 32N 123 5W
San Juan Cr. → 15 35 40N 120 22W
San Juan de Guadalupe 64 24 38N 102 44W
San Juan de los Morros 70 9 55N 67 21W
San Juan del César 70 10 46N 73 1W
San Juan del Norte 66 10 58N 83 40W
San Juan del Norte, B. de 66 11 0N 83 40W
San Juan del Río 65 20 25N 100 0W
San Juan del Sur 66 11 20N 85 51W
San Juan I. 53 48 32N 123 5W
San Juan Indian Reservation 38 36 0N 106 10W
San Juan Mts. 16 37 30N 107 0W
San Juan National Forest 16 37 30N 108 0W
San Juan Pueblo 38 36 3N 106 4W
San Julián 78 49 15 S 67 45W
San Justo 76 30 47 S 60 30W
San Lázaro, C. 64 24 50N 112 18W
San Lázaro, Sa. de 64 23 25N 110 0W
San Leandro 14 37 44N 122 9W
San Lorenzo, Argentina 76 32 45 S 60 45W
San Lorenzo, Beni, Bolivia 73 15 22 S 65 48W
San Lorenzo, Tarija, Bolivia 73 21 26 S 64 47W
San Lorenzo, Ecuador 70 1 15N 78 50W
San Lorenzo, Paraguay 76 25 20 S 57 32W
San Lorenzo, Puerto Rico 57 18 11N 65 58W
San Lorenzo, Venezuela 70 9 47N 71 4W
San Lorenzo → 64 24 15N 107 24W
San Lorenzo, I., Mexico 64 28 35N 112 50W
San Lorenzo, I., Peru 72 12 7 S 77 15W
San Lorenzo, Mt. 78 47 40 S 72 20W
San Lucas, Bolivia 73 20 5 S 65 7W
San Lucas, Baja Calif. S., Mexico 64 22 53N 109 54W
San Lucas, Baja Calif. S., Mexico 64 27 10N 112 14W
San Lucas, U.S.A. 15 36 8N 121 1W
San Lucas, C. de 64 22 50N 110 0W
San Luis, Argentina 76 33 20 S 66 20W
San Luis, Cuba 66 22 17N 83 46W
San Luis, Guat. 66 16 14N 89 27W
San Luis, Ariz. 12 32 29N 114 47W
San Luis, Colo. 16 37 12N 105 25W
San Luis □ 76 34 0 S 66 0W
San Luis, I. 64 29 58N 114 26W
San Luis, L. de 73 13 45 S 64 0W
San Luis, Sierra de 76 32 30 S 66 10W
San Luis Cr. → 16 37 42N 105 44W
San Luís de la Loma 64 17 18N 100 55W
San Luis de la Paz 64 21 19N 100 32W
San Luis Obispo 15 35 17N 120 40W
San Luis Obispo County ◇ 15 35 30N 120 30W
San Luis Peak 16 37 59N 106 56W
San Luis Potosí 64 22 9N 100 59W
San Luis Potosí □ 64 22 10N 101 0W
San Luis Reservoir 14 37 4N 121 5W
San Luis Rey → 15 33 12N 117 24W
San Luis Río Colorado 64 32 29N 114 58W
San Luis Valley 16 37 45N 105 50W
San Manuel 12 32 36N 110 38W
San Marcos, Colombia 70 8 39N 75 8W
San Marcos, Guat. 66 14 59N 91 52W
San Marcos, Mexico 64 27 13N 112 6W
San Marcos, Calif. 15 33 9N 117 10W
San Marcos, Tex. 51 29 53N 97 56W
San Marino 94 43 56N 12 25 E
San Marino ■ 94 43 56N 12 25 E
San Martin, Antarct. 5 68 11 S 67 0W
San Martín, Argentina 76 33 5 S 68 28W
San Martín, Colombia 70 3 42N 73 42W
San Martin, U.S.A. 14 37 5N 121 37W
San Martín → 73 13 8 S 63 43W
San Martin, C. 15 35 53N 121 28W
San Martín, L. 78 48 50 S 72 50W
San Martín de los Andes 78 40 10 S 71 20W
San Mateo, Calif. 14 37 34N 122 19W
San Mateo, N. Mex. 38 35 20N 107 39W
San Mateo County ◇ 14 37 30N 122 25W
San Mateo Mts. 38 33 45N 107 25W
San Matías 73 16 25 S 58 20W
San Matías, Golfo 78 41 30 S 64 0W
San Miguel, El Salv. 66 13 30N 88 12W
San Miguel, Panama 66 8 27N 78 55W
San Miguel, Calif. 15 35 45N 120 42W
San Miguel, N. Mex. 38 32 9N 106 44W
San Miguel, Venezuela 70 9 40N 65 11W
San Miguel →, Bolivia 73 13 52 S 63 56W
San Miguel →, S. Amer. 70 0 25N 76 30W
San Miguel →, U.S.A. 16 38 23N 108 48W
San Miguel County ◇, Colo. 16 38 0N 108 30W
San Miguel County ◇, N. Mex. 38 35 30N 105 0W
San Miguel de Huachi 72 15 40 S 67 15W
San Miguel de Tucumán 76 26 50 S 65 20W
San Miguel del Monte 76 35 23 S 58 50W
San Miguel I. 15 34 2N 120 23W
San Narciso 111 15 2N 120 3 E
San Nicolás de los Arroyas 76 33 25 S 60 10W
San Nicolas I. 15 33 15N 119 30W
San Onofre 70 9 44N 75 32W
San Pablo, Bolivia 76 21 43 S 66 38W
San Pablo, Calif. 14 37 58N 122 21W
San Pablo, Colo. 16 37 9N 105 24W
San Pablo B. 14 38 5N 122 20W
San Patricio 38 33 25N 105 20W
San Patricio County ◇ 51 28 2N 97 31W
San Pedro, Buenos Aires, Argentina 77 26 30 S 54 10W
San Pedro, Jujuy, Argentina 76 24 12 S 64 55W
San Pedro, Colombia 70 4 56N 71 53W
San-Pédro, Ivory C. 120 4 50N 6 33W
San Pedro, Mexico 64 23 55N 110 17W
San Pedro, Peru 72 14 49 S 74 5W
San Pedro, U.S.A. 51 27 48N 97 41W
San Pedro □ 76 24 0 S 57 0W
San Pedro →, Chihuahua, Mexico 64 28 20N 106 10W
San Pedro →, Michoacan, Mexico 64 19 23N 103 51W
San Pedro →, Nayarit, Mexico 64 21 45N 105 30W
San Pedro →, U.S.A. 12 32 59N 110 47W
San Pedro, Pta. 76 25 30 S 70 38W
San Pedro Channel 15 33 30N 118 25W
San Pedro de Arimena 70 4 37N 71 42W
San Pedro de Atacama 76 22 55 S 68 15W
San Pedro de Jujuy 76 24 12 S 64 55W
San Pedro de las Colonias 64 25 50N 102 59W
San Pedro de Lloc 72 7 15 S 79 28W
San Pedro de Macorís 67 18 30N 69 18W
San Pedro del Norte 66 13 4N 84 33W
San Pedro del Paraná 76 26 43 S 56 13W
San Pedro Mártir, Sierra 64 31 0N 115 30W
San Pedro Mixtepec 65 16 2N 97 7W
San Pedro Ocampo = Melchor Ocampo 64 24 52N 101 40W
San Pedro Sula 66 15 30N 88 0W
San Perlita 50 26 30N 97 39W
San Pitch → 52 39 3N 111 51W
San Quintín 64 30 29N 115 57W
San Rafael, Argentina 76 34 40 S 68 21W
San Rafael, Calif. 14 37 58N 122 32W
San Rafael, N. Mex. 38 35 7N 107 53W
San Rafael, Venezuela 70 10 58N 71 46W
San Rafael → 52 38 47N 110 7W
San Rafael Mts. 15 34 40N 119 50W
San Rafael Swell 52 38 45N 110 45W
San Ramón, Bolivia 73 13 17 S 64 43W
San Ramón, Peru 72 11 8 S 75 20W
San Ramón de la Nueva Orán 76 23 10 S 64 20W
San Remo 94 43 48N 7 47 E
San Román, C. 70 12 12N 70 0W
San Roque 76 28 25 S 58 45W
San Rosendo 76 37 16 S 72 43W
San Saba 51 31 12N 98 43W
San Saba → 51 31 15N 98 36W
San Saba County ◇ 51 31 13N 98 47W
San Salvador, Bahamas 67 24 0N 74 40W
San Salvador, El Salv. 66 13 40N 89 10W
San Salvador de Jujuy 76 24 10 S 64 48W
San Salvador I. 67 24 0N 74 32W
San Sebastián, Argentina 78 53 10 S 68 30W
San Sebastian, Puerto Rico 57 18 20N 66 59W
San Sebastián, Spain 91 43 17N 1 58W
San Sebastián, Venezuela 70 9 57N 67 11W
San Simeon 15 35 39N 121 11W
San Simon 12 32 16N 109 14W
San Simon → 12 32 50N 109 39W
San Telmo 64 30 58N 116 6W
San Tiburcio 64 24 8N 101 32W
San Valentin, Mte. 78 46 30 S 73 30W
San Vicente de la Barquera 91 43 23N 4 29W
San Vicente del Caguán 70 2 7N 74 46W
San Xavier Indian Reservation 12 32 10N 111 0W
San Yanaro 70 2 47N 69 42W
San Ygnacio 50 27 3N 99 26W
San Ysidro 38 35 34N 106 46W
Saña, Peru 72 6 54 S 79 36W
Sana', Yemen 105 15 27N 44 12 E
Sana → 94 45 3N 16 23 E
Sanaga → 122 3 35N 9 38 E
Sanak I. 11 54 25N 162 40W
Sanaloa, Presa 64 24 50N 107 20W
Sanana 111 2 5 S 125 59 E
Sanandaj 106 35 18N 47 1 E
Sanandita 76 21 40 S 63 45W
Sanborn, Minn. 30 44 13N 95 8W
Sanborn, N. Dak. 41 46 57N 98 14W
Sanborn County ◇ 47 44 0N 98 0W
Sanbornville 36 43 33N 71 2W
Sancha He → 115 26 48N 106 7 E
Sánchez 67 19 15N 69 36W
Sanco, Pt. 111 8 15N 126 24 E
Sancti-Spíritus 66 21 52N 79 33W
Sand Cr. →, Ind. 22 39 3N 85 51W
Sand Cr. →, Wyo. 56 43 20N 105 2W
Sand Fork 54 38 55N 80 45W
Sand Hill → 30 47 36N 96 52W
Sand Hills 34 42 10N 101 30W
Sand I., Hawaii 19 21 19N 157 53W
Sand I., Wis. 55 46 59N 90 58W
Sand Lake 29 43 18N 85 31W
Sand Point 11 55 20N 160 30W
Sand Pt. 29 43 55N 83 24W
Sand Res. 43 36 45N 96 10W
Sand Springs 43 36 9N 96 7W
Sand Tank Mts. 12 32 45N 112 30W
Sanda 117 34 53N 135 14 E
Sandakan 110 5 53N 118 4 E
Sandan 112 12 46N 106 0 E
Sandanski 95 41 35N 23 16 E
Sanday 84 59 15N 2 30W
Sandborn 22 38 54N 87 11W
Sanders 12 35 13N 109 20W
Sanders County ◇ 33 47 40N 115 30W
Sanderson, Fla. 17 30 15N 82 16W
Sanderson, Tex. 50 30 9N 102 24W
Sandersville, Ga. 18 32 59N 82 48W
Sandersville, Miss. 31 31 47N 89 2W
Sandfly L. 63 55 43N 106 6W
Sandía, Peru 72 14 10 S 69 30W
Sandia, U.S.A. 51 28 1N 97 53W
Sandıklı 106 38 30N 30 20 E
Sandnes 97 58 50N 5 45 E
Sandness 84 60 18N 1 38W
Sandoa 122 9 41 S 23 0 E
Sandomierz 89 50 40N 21 43 E
Sandona 70 1 17N 77 28W
Sandoval 21 38 37N 89 7W
Sandoval County ◇ 38 35 45N 106 45W
Sandover → 127 21 43 S 136 32 E
Sandoway 109 18 20N 94 30 E
Sandpoint 20 48 17N 116 33W
Sandringham 82 52 50N 0 30 E
Sandspit 62 53 14N 131 49W
Sandston 54 37 31N 77 19W
Sandstone, Australia 126 27 59 S 119 16 E
Sandstone, U.S.A. 30 46 8N 92 52W
Sandtown 27 39 4N 75 44W
Sandusky, Mich. 29 43 25N 82 50W
Sandusky, Ohio 42 41 27N 82 42W
Sandusky → 42 41 27N 83 0W
Sandusky County ◇ 42 41 21N 83 7W
Sandviken 97 60 38N 16 46 E
Sandwich, Ill. 21 41 39N 88 37W
Sandwich, Mass. 28 41 46N 70 30W
Sandwich B. 61 53 40N 57 15W
Sandwip Chan. 109 22 35N 91 35 E
Sandy, Oreg. 44 45 24N 122 16W
Sandy, Pa. 45 41 6N 78 46W
Sandy, Utah 52 40 35N 111 50W
Sandy C., Queens., Australia 127 24 42 S 153 15 E
Sandy C., Tas., Australia 127 41 25 S 144 45 E
Sandy Cay 67 23 13N 75 18W
Sandy Cr. → 56 41 51N 109 47W
Sandy Hook, Ky. 49 38 5N 83 8W
Sandy Hook, Miss. 31 31 2N 89 49W
Sandy Hook, N.J. 37 40 26N 74 0W
Sandy L. 60 53 2N 93 0W
Sandy Lake 60 53 0N 93 15W
Sandy Narrows 63 55 5N 103 4W
Sandy Ridge 40 36 30N 80 6W
Sandy Springs 18 33 56N 84 23W
Sandyville 54 38 54N 81 40W
Sanford, Colo. 16 37 16N 105 54W
Sanford, Fla. 17 28 48N 81 16W
Sanford, Maine 26 43 27N 70 47W
Sanford, Miss. 31 31 29N 89 26W
Sanford, N.C. 40 35 29N 79 10W
Sanford, Tex. 50 35 42N 101 32W
Sanford → 126 27 22 S 115 53 E
Sanford, Mt. 11 62 13N 144 8W
Sanga → 122 1 5 S 17 0 E
Sanga-Tolon 101 61 50N 149 40 E
Sangamner 108 19 37N 74 15 E
Sangamon → 21 40 7N 90 20W
Sangamon County ◇ 21 39 45N 89 40W
Sangar 101 64 2N 127 31 E
Sangasangadalam 110 0 36 S 117 13 E
Sangay 70 2 0 S 78 20W
Sangeang 111 8 12 S 119 6 E
Sanger, Calif. 15 36 42N 119 33W
Sanger, Tex. 51 33 22N 97 10W
Sanggan He → 114 38 12N 117 15 E
Sanggau 110 0 5N 110 30 E
Sangihe, Kepulauan 111 3 0N 126 0 E
Sangihe, P. 111 3 45N 125 30 E
Sangkapura 110 5 52 S 112 40 E
Sangli 108 16 55N 74 33 E
Sangmélina 122 2 57N 12 1 E
Sangonera → 91 37 59N 1 4W
Sangre de Cristo 38 36 40N 105 15W
Sangre de Cristo Mts. 16 37 30N 105 20W
Sangudo 62 53 50N 114 54W
Sangue → 73 11 1 S 58 39W
Sangzhi 115 29 25N 110 12 E
Sanibel I. 17 26 26N 82 6W
Sanilac County ◇ 29 43 25N 82 50W
Sanjiang 115 25 48N 109 37 E
Sanjo 116 37 37N 138 57 E
Sankt Gotthard P. = San Gottardo, Passo del 88 46 33N 8 33 E
Sankt Moritz 88 46 30N 9 50 E
Sankuru → 122 4 17 S 20 25 E
Sanlúcar de Barrameda 91 36 46N 6 21W
Sanmenxia 115 34 47N 111 12 E
Sannicandro Gargánico 94 41 50N 15 34 E
Sanok 89 49 35N 22 10 E
Sanpete County ◇ 52 39 30N 111 40W
Sanpoil → 53 47 57N 118 41W
Sanquhar 84 55 21N 3 56W
Sanshui 115 23 10N 112 56 E
Sant Joseph County ◇ 29 41 50N 85 30W
Santa, Peru 72 8 59 S 78 40W
Santa, U.S.A. 20 47 9N 116 27W
Santa Ana, Beni, Bolivia 73 13 50 S 65 40W
Santa Ana, Santa Cruz, Bolivia 73 18 43 S 58 44W
Santa Ana, Santa Cruz, Bolivia 73 16 37 S 60 43W
Santa Ana, Ecuador 70 1 16 S 80 20W
Santa Ana, El Salv. 66 14 0N 89 31W
Santa Ana, Mexico 64 30 31N 111 8W
Santa Ana, U.S.A. 15 33 46N 117 52W
Santa Ana → 70 9 30N 71 57W
Santa Ana Indian Reservation 38 35 26N 106 37W
Santa Ana Mts. 15 33 40N 117 30W
Santa Ana Pueblo 38 35 26N 106 37W
Santa Anna 51 31 45N 99 20W
Santa Bárbara, Colombia 70 5 53N 75 35W
Santa Barbara, Hond. 66 14 53N 88 14W
Santa Bárbara, Mexico 64 26 48N 105 50W
Santa Barbara, U.S.A. 15 34 25N 119 42W
Santa Bárbara, Venezuela 70 7 47N 71 10W
Santa Barbara Channel 15 34 15N 120 0W
Santa Barbara County ◇ 15 34 40N 120 0W
Santa Barbara I. 15 33 29N 119 2W
Santa Catalina, Colombia 70 10 36N 75 17W
Santa Catalina, Mexico 64 25 40N 110 50W
Santa Catalina, Gulf of 15 33 10N 117 50W
Santa Catalina I. 15 33 23N 118 25W
Santa Catarina □ 77 27 25 S 48 30W
Santa Catarina, I. de 77 27 30 S 48 40W
Santa Cecília 77 26 56 S 50 18W
Santa Clara, Cuba 66 22 20N 80 0W
Santa Clara, Calif. 14 37 21N 121 57W
Santa Clara, N.Y. 39 44 38N 74 27W
Santa Clara, Oreg. 44 44 6N 123 8W
Santa Clara, Utah 52 37 8N 113 39W
Santa Clara → 15 34 14N 119 16W
Santa Clara County ◇ 14 37 15N 121 40W
Santa Clara de Olimar 77 32 50 S 54 54W
Santa Clara Valley 15 36 50N 121 30W
Santa Clotilde 70 2 33 S 73 45W
Santa Cruz, Argentina 78 50 0 S 68 32W
Santa Cruz, Bolivia 73 17 43 S 63 10W
Santa Cruz, Brazil 74 6 13 S 36 1W
Santa Cruz, Chile 76 34 38 S 71 27W
Santa Cruz, C. Rica 66 10 15N 85 35W
Santa Cruz, Peru 72 5 40 S 75 56W
Santa Cruz, Phil. 111 14 20N 121 24 E
Santa Cruz, U.S.A. 15 36 58N 122 1W
Santa Cruz, Venezuela 71 8 3N 64 27W
Santa Cruz □, Argentina 78 49 0 S 70 0W
Santa Cruz □, Bolivia 73 17 43 S 63 10W
Santa Cruz →, Argentina 78 50 10 S 68 20W
Santa Cruz →, U.S.A. 12 33 20N 112 16W
Santa Cruz, Is. 124 10 30 S 166 0 E
Santa Cruz Cabrália 75 16 17 S 39 2W
Santa Cruz County ◇, Ariz. 12 31 30N 110 45W
Santa Cruz County ◇, Calif. 14 37 0N 122 0W
Sta. Cruz de Tenerife 120 28 28N 16 15W
Santa Cruz del Norte 66 23 9N 81 55W
Santa Cruz del Sur 66 20 44N 78 0W
Santa Cruz do Rio Pardo 77 22 54 S 49 37W
Santa Cruz do Sul 77 29 42 S 52 25W
Santa Cruz I. 15 34 1N 119 43W
Santa Cruz Mts. 14 37 15N 122 0W
Santa Cruz Wash → 12 33 23N 112 12W
Santa Domingo, Cay 66 21 25N 75 15W
Santa Elena, Argentina 76 30 58 S 59 47W
Santa Elena, Ecuador 70 2 16 S 80 52W
Santa Elena, U.S.A. 50 26 46N 98 29W
Santa Elena, C. 66 10 54N 85 56W
Santa Fe, Argentina 76 31 35 S 60 41W
Santa Fe, U.S.A. 38 35 41N 105 57W
Santa Fé □ 76 31 50 S 60 55W
Santa Fe → 17 29 53N 82 53W
Santa Fe, L. 17 29 45N 82 5W
Santa Fe Baldy 38 35 50N 105 46W
Santa Fe County ◇ 38 35 30N 106 0W
Santa Fe Nat. Forest 38 36 31N 106 42W
Santa Filomena 74 9 6 S 45 50W
Santa Genoveva 64 23 18N 109 52W
Santa Helena 74 2 14 S 42 45W
Santa Helena de Goiás 75 17 53 S 50 35W
Santa Inês 75 13 17 S 39 48W
Santa Inés, I. 78 54 0 S 73 0W
Santa Isabel = Rey Malabo 122 3 45N 8 50 E
Santa Isabel, Argentina 76 36 10 S 66 54W
Santa Isabel, Brazil 75 11 45 S 51 30W

Santa Isabel Savona

Santa Isabel, Puerto Rico ... 57 17 58N 66 24W
Santa Isabel do Araguaia.... 74 6 7 S 48 19W
Santa Isabel do Morro ...... 75 11 34 S 50 40W
Santa Lucía, Corrientes, Argentina .... 76 28 58 S 59 5W
Santa Lucía, San Juan, Argentina .... 76 31 30 S 68 30W
Santa Lucia, Uruguay....... 76 34 27 S 56 24W
Santa Lucia Range 15 36 0N 121 20W
Santa Margarita, Argentina.. 76 38 28 S 61 35W
Santa Margarita, Mexico 64 24 30N 111 50W
Santa Margarita L. 15 35 20N 120 30W
Santa María, Argentina ..... 76 26 40 S 66 0W
Santa Maria, Brazil......... 77 29 40 S 53 48W
Santa Maria, U.S.A. 15 34 57N 120 26W
Santa María →, Mexico.... 64 31 0N 107 14W
Santa Maria →, U.S.A...... 12 34 19N 114 31W
Santa María, Bahía de 64 25 10N 108 40W
Santa Maria da Vitória...... 75 13 24 S 44 12W
Santa María de Ipire......... 71 8 49N 65 19W
Santa María del Oro........ 64 25 58N 105 20W
Santa Maria di Leuca, C. ... 95 39 48N 18 20 E
Santa Maria do Suaçuí ...... 75 18 12 S 42 25W
Santa Maria dos Marmelos .. 73 6 7 S 61 51W
Santa Marta 70 11 15N 74 13W
Santa Marta, Sierra Nevada de 70 10 55N 73 50W
Santa Marta Grande, C. ..... 77 28 43 S 48 50W
Santa Maura = Levkás ..... 95 38 40N 20 43 E
Santa Monica 15 34 1N 118 29W
Santa Paula................ 15 34 21N 119 4W
Santa Quitéria .... 74 4 20 S 40 10W
Santa Rita, Mont. 33 48 42N 112 19W
Santa Rita, N. Mex. 38 32 48N 108 4W
Santa Rita, Guarico, Venezuela 70 8 8N 66 16W
Santa Rita, Zulia, Venezuela 70 10 32N 71 32W
Santa Rita do Araquaia ..... 73 17 20 S 53 12W
Santa Rosa, La Pampa, Argentina .... 76 36 40 S 64 17W
Santa Rosa, San Luis, Argentina .... 76 32 21 S 65 10W
Santa Rosa, Bolivia .... 72 10 36 S 67 20W
Santa Rosa, Brazil .... 77 27 52 S 54 29W
Santa Rosa, Colombia 70 3 32N 69 48W
Santa Rosa, Ecuador .... 70 3 27 S 79 58W
Santa Rosa, Peru........... 72 14 30 S 70 50W
Santa Rosa, Calif........... 14 38 26N 122 43W
Santa Rosa, N. Mex. 38 34 57N 104 41W
Santa Rosa, Tex............ 50 26 16N 97 50W
Santa Rosa, Venezuela 70 1 29N 66 55W
Santa Rosa Beach 17 30 22N 86 14W
Santa Rosa County ◇ 17 30 45N 87 0W
Santa Rosa de Cabal 70 4 52N 75 38W
Santa Rosa de Copán....... 66 14 47N 88 46W
Santa Rosa de Osos 70 6 39N 75 28W
Santa Rosa de Río Primero.. 76 31 8 S 63 20W
Santa Rosa de Viterbo 70 5 53N 72 59W
Santa Rosa del Palmar...... 73 16 54 S 62 24W
Santa Rosa I., Calif......... 15 33 58N 120 6W
Santa Rosa I., Fla. 17 30 20N 86 50W
Santa Rosa Mts. 15 33 20N 116 15W
Santa Rosa Range........... 35 41 45N 117 40W
Santa Rosa Wash →....... 12 33 0N 112 0W
Santa Rosalía 64 27 20N 112 20W
Santa Sylvina .... 76 27 50 S 61 10W
Santa Tecla = Nueva San Salvador 66 13 40N 89 18W
Santa Teresa, Argentina .... 76 33 25 S 60 47W
Santa Teresa, Brazil .... 75 19 55 S 40 36W
Santa Teresa, Mexico 65 25 17N 97 51W
Santa Teresa, Venezuela 71 4 43N 61 4W
Santa Vitória .... 75 18 50 S 50 8W
Santa Vitória do Palmar .... 77 33 32 S 53 25W
Santa Ynez → 15 35 41N 120 36W
Santa Ynez Mts. 15 34 30N 120 0W
Santai...................... 115 31 5N 104 58 E
Santaluz.................... 74 11 15 S 39 22W
Santana .... 75 13 2 S 44 5W
Santana, Coxilha de .... 77 30 50 S 55 35W
Santana do Ipanema .... 74 9 22 S 37 14W
Santana do Livramento ..... 77 30 55 S 55 30W
Santander, Colombia 70 3 1N 76 28W
Santander, Spain 91 43 27N 3 51W
Santander Jiménez 65 24 11N 98 29W
Santaquin 52 39 59N 111 47W
Santarém, Brazil .... 73 2 25 S 54 42W
Santarém, Portugal 91 39 12N 8 42W
Santaren Channel 66 24 0N 79 30W
Sante Genevieve 32 37 59N 90 3W
Santee, Calif. 15 32 50N 116 58W
Santee, Nebr. 34 42 51N 97 50W
Santee → 46 33 7N 79 17W
Santee Indian Reservation... 34 42 50N 97 50W
Santiago, Bolivia .... 73 18 19 S 59 34W
Santiago, Brazil .... 77 29 11 S 54 52W
Santiago, Chile .... 76 33 24 S 70 40W
Santiago, Panama 66 8 0N 81 0W
Santiago, Peru .... 72 14 11 S 75 43W
Santiago □ .... 76 33 30 S 70 50W
Santiago →................ 70 4 27 S 77 38W
Santiago, C. .... 78 50 46 S 75 27W
Santiago, Serranía de .... 73 18 25 S 59 25W
Santiago de Chuco .... 72 8 9 S 78 11W
Santiago de Compostela..... 91 42 52N 8 37W
Santiago de Cuba 66 20 0N 75 49W
Santiago de los Cabelleros... 67 19 30N 70 40W
Santiago del Estero......... 76 27 50 S 64 15W
Santiago del Estero □ ...... 76 27 40 S 63 15W
Santiago Ixcuintla 64 21 50N 105 11W
Santiago Mts. 50 29 55N 103 22W
Santiago Papasquiaro 64 25 0N 105 20W
Santiago Peak 50 29 47N 103 25W
Santiaguillo, L. de.......... 64 24 50N 104 50W
Santiam Pass 44 44 25N 121 55W
Santo → .... 72 8 56 S 78 37W
Santo Amaro .... 75 12 30 S 38 43W
Santo Anastácio............ 77 21 58 S 51 39W
Santo André................ 77 23 39 S 46 29W
Santo Ângelo .... 77 28 15 S 54 15W
Santo Antonio .... 73 15 50 S 56 0W
Santo Antônio de Jesus ..... 75 12 58 S 39 16W
Santo Antônio do Içá....... 70 3 5 S 67 57W
Santo Antônio do Leverger.. 73 15 52 S 56 5W
Santo Corazón .... 73 18 0 S 58 45W
Santo Domingo, Dom. Rep.. 67 18 30N 64 54W
Santo Domingo, Baja Calif. N., Mexico.... 64 30 43N 116 2W
Santo Domingo, Baja Calif. S., Mexico 64 25 32N 112 2W
Santo Domingo, Nic. 66 12 14N 84 59W
Santo Domingo de los Colorados .... 70 0 15 S 79 9W
Santo Domingo Indian Reservation 38 35 30N 106 30W
Santo Domingo Pueblo 38 35 31N 106 22W
Santo Tomás, Mexico....... 64 31 33N 116 24W
Santo Tomás, Peru .... 72 14 26 S 72 8W
Santo Tomé .... 77 28 40 S 56 5W
Santo Tomé de Guayana 71 8 22N 62 40W
Santoña 91 43 29N 3 27W
Santos .... 77 24 0 S 46 20W
Santos Dumont .... 77 22 55 S 43 10W
Sānūr .... 104 32 22N 35 15 E
Sanyuan.................... 115 34 35N 108 58 E
Sanza Pombo .... 122 7 18 S 15 56 E
São Anastácio .... 77 22 0 S 51 40W
São Benedito .... 74 4 3 S 40 53W
São Bento .... 74 2 42 S 44 50W
São Bento do Norte .... 74 5 4 S 36 2W
São Borja .... 77 28 39 S 56 0W
São Caitano .... 74 8 21 S 36 6W
São Carlos .... 77 22 0 S 47 50W
São Cristóvão .... 74 11 1 S 37 15W
São Domingos .... 75 13 25 S 46 19W
São Domingos do Maranhão. 74 5 42 S 44 22W
São Félix .... 75 11 36 S 50 39W
São Francisco .... 75 16 0 S 44 50W
São Francisco → .... 74 10 30 S 36 24W
São Francisco do Maranhão . 74 6 15 S 42 52W
São Francisco do Sul ...... 77 26 15 S 48 36W
São Gabriel .... 77 30 20 S 54 20W
São Gabriel da Palha ...... 75 18 47 S 40 39W
São Gonçalo .... 75 22 48 S 43 5W
São Gotardo .... 75 19 19 S 46 3W
São João da Boa Vista ..... 77 22 0 S 46 52W
São João da Ponte .... 75 15 56 S 44 1W
São João del Rei .... 75 21 8 S 44 15W
São João do Araguaia ...... 74 5 23 S 48 46W
São João do Paraíso .... 75 15 19 S 42 1W
São João do Piauí .... 74 8 21 S 42 15W
São João dos Patos .... 74 6 30 S 43 42W
São Joaquim da Barra ...... 75 20 35 S 47 53W
São José, B. de .... 74 2 38 S 44 4W
São José da Laje .... 74 9 1 S 36 3W
São José de Mipibu......... 74 6 5 S 35 15W
São José do Peixe .... 74 7 24 S 42 34W
São José do Rio Prêto ..... 77 20 50 S 49 20W
São José dos Campos ...... 77 23 7 S 45 52W
São Leopoldo .... 77 29 50 S 51 10W
São Lourenço .... 75 22 7 S 45 3W
São Lourenço →........... 73 17 53 S 57 27W
São Lourenço, Pantanal do .. 73 17 30 S 56 20W
São Luís .... 74 2 39 S 44 15W
São Luís do Curu .... 74 3 40 S 39 14W
São Luís Gonzaga .... 77 28 25 S 55 0W
São Marcos →............. 75 18 15 S 47 37W
São Marcos, B. de .... 74 2 0 S 44 0W
São Mateus................ 75 18 44 S 39 50W
São Mateus →............. 75 18 35 S 39 44W
São Miguel do Araguaia .... 75 13 19 S 50 13W
São Miguel dos Campos..... 74 9 47 S 36 5W
São Nicolau → .... 74 5 45 S 42 2W
São Paulo .... 77 23 32 S 46 37W
São Paulo □............... 77 22 0 S 49 0W
São Paulo, I. 2 0 50N 31 40W
São Paulo de Olivença ...... 70 3 27 S 68 48W
São Rafael .... 74 5 47 S 36 55W
São Raimundo das Mangabeiras .... 74 7 1 S 45 29W
São Raimundo Nonato ...... 74 9 1 S 42 42W
São Romão................. 75 16 22 S 45 4W
São Roque, C. de .... 74 5 30 S 35 16W
São Sebastião, I. de .... 77 23 50 S 45 18W
São Sebastião do Paraíso ... 77 20 54 S 46 59W
São Simão................. 75 18 56 S 50 30W
São Tomé, Atl. Oc. .... 119 0 10N 6 39 E
São Tomé, Brazil .... 74 5 58 S 36 4W
São Tomé, C. de .... 75 22 0 S 40 59W
São Tomé & Principe ■ ..... 119 0 12N 6 39 E
São Vicente .... 77 23 57 S 46 23W
São Vicente, Cabo de....... 91 37 0N 9 0W
Saona, I. 67 18 10N 68 40W
Saône → .... 90 45 44N 4 50 E
Saône-et-Loire □ .... 90 46 25N 4 50 E
Saonek..................... 111 0 22 S 130 55 E
Sapão → .... 74 11 1 S 45 32W
Saparua .... 111 3 33 S 128 40 E
Sapé....................... 74 7 6 S 35 13W
Sapele .... 120 5 50N 5 40 E
Sapelo I. 18 31 25N 81 12W
Sapelo Island 18 31 23N 81 17W
Sapelo Sound 18 31 30N 81 10W
Saposoa .... 72 6 55 S 76 45W
Sappa Cr. → 34 40 7N 99 39W
Sappho 53 48 4N 124 16W
Sappington 33 45 48N 111 46W
Sapporo................... 116 43 0N 141 21 E
Sapudi .... 111 7 2 S 114 17 E
Sapulpa 43 35 59N 96 5W
Saqqez..................... 106 36 15N 46 20 E
Sar-e Pol .... 107 36 10N 66 0 E
Sar Planina .... 95 42 10N 21 0 E
Sara, L. 21 39 8N 88 36W
Sarāb .... 106 38 0N 47 30 E
Sarada → .... 109 27 21N 81 23 E
Saragosa 50 31 2N 103 39W
Saragossa = Zaragoza 91 41 39N 0 53W
Saraguro .... 70 3 35 S 79 16W
Sarah 31 34 34N 90 13W
Sarajevo .... 95 43 52N 18 26 E
Saraland 10 30 50N 88 4W
Saralu .... 95 44 43N 28 10 E
Saramacca □ 71 5 0N 56 0W
Saramacca → 71 5 50N 55 55W
Saran, G. .... 110 0 30 S 111 25 E
Saranac, Mich. 29 42 56N 85 13W
Saranac, N.Y. 39 44 39N 73 45W
Saranac → 39 44 42N 73 27W
Saranac L. 39 44 20N 74 10W
Saranac Lake 39 44 20N 74 8W
Sarandí del Yi .... 77 33 18 S 55 38W
Sarandí Grande .... 76 33 44 S 56 20W
Sarangani B................ 111 6 0N 125 13 E
Sarangani Is. .... 111 5 25N 125 25 E
Sarangarh .... 109 21 30N 83 5 E
Saransk .... 98 54 10N 45 10 E
Sarapul .... 98 56 28N 53 48 E
Sarasota................... 17 27 20N 82 32W
Sarasota County ◇ 17 27 15N 82 20W
Saratoga, Calif. 14 37 16N 122 2W
Saratoga, Ind. 22 40 14N 84 55W
Saratoga, N.C. 40 35 39N 77 47W
Saratoga, Tex. 51 30 17N 94 31W
Saratoga, Wyo. 56 41 27N 106 49W
Saratoga County ◇ 39 43 10N 73 50W
Saratoga L. 39 43 1N 73 45W
Saratoga Springs 39 43 5N 73 47W
Saratov .... 98 51 30N 46 2 E
Saravane .... 112 15 43N 106 25 E
Sarawak □ .... 110 2 0N 113 0 E
Sarbāz .... 107 26 38N 61 19 E
Sarbīsheh .... 107 32 30N 59 40 E
Sarcoxie................... 32 37 3N 94 7W
Sardalas................... 120 25 50N 10 34 E
Sardarshahr .... 108 28 30N 74 29 E
Sardegna .... 94 39 57N 9 0 E
Sardinata.................. 70 8 5N 72 48W
Sardinia = Sardegna .... 94 39 57N 9 0 E
Sardinia 42 39 0N 83 49W
Sardis, Ala. 10 32 17N 86 59W
Sardis, Ga. 18 32 58N 81 46W
Sardis, Miss. 31 34 26N 89 55W
Sardis L. 31 34 25N 89 48W
Sardis Res. 43 34 40N 95 25W
Sarepta 25 32 54N 93 27W
Sargeant 30 43 48N 92 48W
Sargent, Ga. 18 33 26N 84 52W
Sargent, Nebr. 34 41 39N 99 22W
Sargent County ◇.......... 41 46 3N 97 45W
Sargents................... 16 38 25N 106 24W
Sargodha .... 108 32 10N 72 40 E
Sarh .... 121 9 5N 18 23 E
Sārī....................... 107 36 30N 53 4 E
Sarida →................. 104 32 4N 34 45 E
Sarikamiş .... 106 40 22N 42 35 E
Sarikei .... 110 2 8N 111 30 E
Sarina .... 127 21 22 S 149 13 E
Sarita 50 27 13N 97 47W
Sariyer .... 95 41 10N 29 3 E
Sark 83 49 25N 2 20W
Sarlat-la-Canéda .... 90 44 54N 1 13 E
Sarmi .... 111 1 49 S 138 44 E
Sarmiento .... 78 45 35 S 69 5W
Sarnia 60 42 58N 82 23W
Sarny .... 98 51 17N 26 40 E
Sarolangun .... 110 2 19 S 102 42 E
Saronikós Kólpos .... 95 37 45N 23 45 E
Saros Körfezi .... 95 40 30N 26 15 E
Sarpsborg .... 97 59 16N 11 12 E
Sarpy County ◇ 34 41 10N 96 10W
Sarre = Saar →............ 88 49 41N 6 32 E
Sarre, La 60 48 45N 79 15W
Sarro 120 13 40N 5 15W
Sartell 30 45 37N 94 12W
Sartène .... 94 41 38N 8 58 E
Sarthe □.................. 90 47 58N 0 10 E
Sarthe → 90 47 33N 0 31W
Sartynya .... 100 63 22N 63 11 E
Sarvestān................. 107 29 20N 53 10 E
Sary-Tash .... 100 39 44N 73 15 E
Saryshagan .... 100 46 12N 73 38 E
Sasa .... 104 33 2N 35 23 E
Sasabe 12 31 29N 111 33W
Sasabeneh .... 105 7 59N 44 43 E
Sasakwa................... 43 34 57N 96 31W
Sasaram................... 109 24 57N 84 5 E
Sasebo .... 117 33 10N 129 43 E
Saser Mt. .... 108 34 50N 77 50 E
Saskatchewan □ 63 54 40N 106 0W
Saskatchewan → 63 53 37N 100 40W
Saskatoon 63 52 10N 106 38W
Saskylakh .... 101 71 55N 114 1 E
Sasovo .... 98 54 25N 41 55 E
Sassafras 27 39 22N 75 20W
Sassandra 120 5 0N 6 8W
Sassandra → 120 4 58N 6 5W
Sássari .... 94 40 44N 8 33 E
Sasser 18 31 43N 84 21W
Sassnitz .... 88 54 29N 13 39 E
Sasyk, Ozero .... 95 45 45N 30 0 E
Sata-Misaki .... 117 30 59N 130 40 E
Satadougou 120 12 25N 11 25W
Satanta 24 37 26N 100 59W
Satara .... 82 17 44N 73 58 E
Satartia 31 32 40N 90 33W
Satellite Beach 17 28 10N 80 36W
Satilla →.................. 18 30 59N 81 29W
Satipo .... 72 11 15 S 74 25W
Satka .... 98 55 3N 59 1 E
Satmala Hills .... 108 20 15N 74 40 E
Satna .... 109 24 35N 80 50 E
Satolah 18 34 59N 83 11W
Sátoraljaújhely............. 89 48 25N 21 41 E
Satpura Ra. .... 108 21 25N 76 10 E
Satsuma 10 30 51N 88 4W
Satsuna-Shotō .... 117 30 0N 130 0 E
Satu Mare .... 89 47 46N 22 55 E
Satui...................... 110 3 50 S 115 27 E
Satun .... 112 6 43N 100 2 E
Saturnina →............... 73 12 15 S 58 10W
Sauce .... 76 30 5 S 58 46W
Sauceda 64 25 55N 101 18W
Sauceda Mts. 12 32 35N 112 35W
Saucier.................... 31 30 39N 89 8W
Saucillo 64 28 1N 105 17W
Sauda .... 97 59 40N 6 20 E
Saúde...................... 74 10 56 S 40 24W
Sauðarkrókur 96 65 45N 19 40W
Saudi Arabia ■ .... 105 26 0N 44 0 E
Saugatuck 29 42 40N 86 12W
Saugatuck → 28 41 7N 73 22W
Saugerties 39 42 5N 73 57W
Saugus, Calif. 15 34 25N 118 32W
Saugus, Mass. 28 42 28N 71 1W
Sauk Centre 30 45 44N 94 57W
Sauk City 55 43 17N 89 43W
Sauk County ◇ 55 43 25N 89 50W
Sauk Rapids 30 45 35N 94 10W
Saukville 55 43 23N 87 56W
Saül 71 3 37N 53 12W
Saulsbury 48 35 3N 89 5W
Sault Ste. Marie, Canada.... 60 46 30N 84 20W
Sault Ste. Marie, U.S.A. 29 46 30N 84 21W
Saumlaki .... 111 7 55 S 131 20 E
Saumur 90 47 15N 0 5W
Saunders C. .... 128 45 53 S 170 45 E
Saunders County ◇ 34 41 15N 96 40W
Saunders I. .... 5 57 48 S 26 28W
Saunemin 21 40 54N 88 24W
Sauquoit 39 43 0N 75 16W
Saurbœr, Borgarfjarðarsýsla, Iceland 96 64 24N 21 35W
Saurbœr, Eyjafjarðarsýsla, Iceland 96 65 27N 18 13W
Sauri .... 120 11 42N 6 44 E
Saurimo .... 122 9 40 S 20 12 E
Sautatá 70 7 50N 77 4W
Savá 66 15 32N 86 15W
Sava → .... 95 44 50N 20 26 E
Savage, Md. 27 39 8N 76 50W
Savage, Mont. 33 47 27N 104 21W
Savage I. = Niue I. .... 125 19 2 S 169 54W
Savai'i .... 128 13 28 S 172 24W
Savalou .... 120 7 57N 1 58 E
Savana I. 57 18 21N 65 5W
Savanna, Ill. 21 42 5N 90 8W
Savanna, Okla. 43 34 50N 95 51W
Savanna la Mar 66 18 10N 78 10W
Savannah, Ga. 18 32 5N 81 6W
Savannah, Mo. 32 39 56N 94 50W
Savannah, Ohio 42 40 58N 82 22W
Savannah, Tenn. 48 35 14N 88 15W
Savannah →............... 46 32 2N 80 53W
Savannah Beach 18 32 1N 80 51W
Savannakhet .... 112 16 30N 104 49 E
Savant L. 60 50 16N 90 44W
Savant Lake 60 50 14N 90 40W
Savanur .... 108 14 59N 75 21 E
Savé .... 120 8 2N 2 29 E
Save → .... 123 21 16 S 34 0 E
Sāveh .... 106 35 2N 50 20 E
Savelugu 120 9 38N 0 54W
Savoie □.................. 90 45 26N 6 35 E
Savona .... 94 44 19N 8 29 E

Savonburg
Senador Pompeu

Savonburg 24 37 45N 95 9W
Savonlinna 98 61 52N 28 53 E
Savoonga 11 63 42N 170 29W
Savoy 21 40 3N 88 15W
Saw Pit 16 37 56N 108 6W
Sawahlunto 110 0 40 S 100 52 E
Sawai 111 3 0 S 129 5 E
Sawai Madhopur 108 26 0N 76 25 E
Sawara 117 35 55N 140 30 E
Sawatch Range 16 39 0N 106 30W
Sawel, Mt. 85 54 48N 7 5W
Sawknah 121 29 4N 15 47 E
Sawmills 123 19 30 S 28 2 E
Sawtooth Mts. 30 47 30N 91 0W
Sawtooth Nat. Rec. Area 20 44 0N 114 50W
Sawtooth National Forest 52 41 50N 113 20W
Sawtooth Range 20 44 3N 114 58W
Sawu 111 10 35 S 121 50 E
Sawu Sea 111 9 30 S 121 50 E
Sawyer, Kans. 24 37 30N 98 41W
Sawyer, Mich. 29 41 53N 86 35W
Sawyer, N. Dak. 41 48 5N 101 3W
Sawyer, Okla. 43 34 1N 95 23W
Sawyer County ◇ 55 45 50N 91 0W
Sawyers Bar 14 41 18N 123 7W
Saxapahaw 40 35 57N 79 19W
Saxonburg 45 40 45N 79 49W
Saxton, Ky. 49 36 38N 84 7W
Saxton, Pa. 45 40 13N 78 15W
Say 120 13 8N 2 22 E
Sayabec 61 48 35N 67 41W
Sayán 72 11 8 S 77 12W
Sayan, Vostochnyy 101 54 0N 96 0 E
Sayan, Zapadnyy 101 52 30N 94 0 E
Saybrook 21 40 26N 88 32W
Saydā 106 33 35N 35 25 E
Sayghān 107 35 10N 67 55 E
Sayḩut 105 15 12N 51 10 E
Saylorville L. 23 41 48N 93 46W
Saynshand 113 44 55N 110 11 E
Sayre, Okla. 43 35 18N 99 38W
Sayre, Pa. 45 41 59N 76 32W
Sayreville 37 40 28N 74 22W
Sayula 64 19 50N 103 40W
Sayville 39 40 44N 73 5W
Sazan 95 40 30N 19 20 E
Sázava → 88 49 53N 14 24 E
Sazin 108 35 35N 73 30 E
Sazlika → 95 41 59N 25 50 E
Sca Fell 86 54 27N 3 14W
Scafell Pikes 82 54 26N 3 14W
Scaggsville 27 39 9N 76 54W
Scales Mound 21 42 29N 90 15W
Scalpay 84 57 51N 6 40W
Scammon 24 37 17N 94 49W
Scammon Bay 11 61 51N 165 35W
Scandia, Canada 62 50 20N 112 0W
Scandia, U.S.A. 24 39 48N 97 47W
Scandinavia, Europe 80 64 0N 12 0 E
Scandinavia, U.S.A. 55 44 27N 89 9W
Scanlon 30 46 42N 92 26W
Scapa Flow 84 58 52N 3 6W
Scappoose 44 45 45N 122 53W
Scarborough, Trin. & Tob. 67 11 11N 60 42W
Scarborough, U.K. 82 54 17N 0 24W
Scarsdale 39 40 59N 73 49W
Scarville 23 43 28N 93 37W
Scenic 47 43 47N 102 33W
Schaffhausen 88 47 42N 8 39 E
Schagen 87 52 49N 4 48 E
Schaller 23 42 30N 95 18W
Schefferville 61 54 48N 66 50W
Schelde → 87 51 15N 4 16 E
Schell City 32 38 1N 94 7W
Schell Creek Range 35 39 25N 114 40W
Schellsburg 45 40 3N 78 39W
Schenectady 39 42 49N 73 57W
Schenectady County ◇ 39 42 50N 74 0W
Scheveningen 87 52 6N 4 16 E
Schiedam 87 51 55N 4 25 E
Schiermonnikoog 87 53 30N 6 15 E
Schio 94 45 42N 11 21 E
Schlater 31 33 39N 90 21W
Schleicher County ◇ 50 30 52N 100 36W
Schleswig, Germany 88 54 32N 9 34 E
Schleswig, U.S.A. 23 42 10N 95 26W
Schleswig-Holstein □ 88 54 10N 9 40 E
Schley County ◇ 18 32 15N 84 15W
Schoenchen 24 38 43N 99 20W
Schofield 55 44 54N 89 36W
Schoharie 39 42 40N 74 19W
Schoharie → 39 42 57N 74 18W
Schoharie County ◇ 39 42 35N 74 30W
Schoharie Res. 39 42 22N 74 26W
Schoodic L. 26 45 23N 68 56W
Schoolcraft 29 42 7N 85 38W
Schoolcraft County ◇ 29 46 10N 86 15W
Schouwen 87 51 43N 3 45 E
Schreiber 60 48 45N 87 20W
Schroon L. 39 43 47N 73 47W
Schroon Lake 39 43 50N 73 46W
Schulenburg 51 29 41N 96 54W
Schuler 63 50 20N 110 6W
Schumacher 60 48 30N 81 16W
Schurz 35 38 57N 118 49W
Schuylkill Haven 45 40 38N 76 10W
Schuyler, Nebr. 34 41 27N 97 4W
Schuyler, Va. 54 37 47N 78 42W
Schuyler County ◇, Ill. 21 40 10N 90 40W
Schuyler County ◇, Mo. 32 40 25N 92 30W
Schuyler County ◇, N.Y. 39 42 20N 76 50W
Schuylkill → 45 39 53N 75 12W
Schuylkill County ◇ 45 40 48N 76 50W
Schwäbische Alb 88 48 30N 9 30 E
Schwarzwald 88 48 0N 8 0 E
Schwatka Mts. 11 67 20N 156 30W
Schweinfurt 88 50 3N 10 12 E
Schwerin 88 53 37N 11 22 E
Schwyz 88 47 2N 8 39 E
Sciacca 94 37 30N 13 3 E
Scie, La 61 49 57N 55 36W
Science Hill 49 37 11N 84 38W
Scilla 94 38 18N 15 44 E
Scilly, Isles of 83 49 55N 6 15W
Scio, Ohio 42 40 24N 81 5W
Scio, Oreg. 44 44 42N 122 51W
Scioto → 42 38 44N 83 1W
Scioto County ◇ 42 38 53N 82 59W
Scipio, Okla. 43 35 3N 95 58W
Scipio, Utah 52 39 15N 112 6W
Scituate 28 42 12N 70 44W
Scituate Reservoir 28 41 45N 71 35W
Scobey 33 48 47N 105 25W
Scofield 52 39 44N 111 10W
Scofield Reservoir 52 39 49N 111 8W
Scone 84 56 25N 3 26W
Scooba 31 32 50N 88 29W
Scoresbysund 4 70 20N 23 0W
Scotch Plains 37 40 39N 74 24W
Scotia, Calif. 14 40 29N 124 6W
Scotia, N.Y. 39 42 50N 73 58W
Scotia, Nebr. 34 41 28N 98 42W
Scotia, S.C. 46 32 41N 81 15W
Scotia Sea 5 56 5 S 56 0W
Scotland, Ark. 13 35 32N 92 37W
Scotland, Conn. 28 41 42N 72 7W
Scotland, Md. 27 38 5N 76 22W
Scotland, S. Dak. 47 43 9N 97 43W
Scotland □ 83 57 0N 4 0W
Scotland County ◇, Mo. 32 40 25N 92 10W
Scotland County ◇, N.C. 40 34 50N 79 30W
Scotland Neck 40 36 8N 77 25W
Scotlandville 25 30 31N 91 11W
Scott, Antarct. 5 77 0 S 165 0 E
Scott, Ark. 13 34 42N 92 6W
Scott, Miss. 31 33 36N 91 5W
Scott, Ohio 42 40 59N 84 35W
Scott → 14 41 48N 123 2W
Scott, Mt. 44 42 56N 122 1W
Scott Bar Mts. 14 41 50N 123 0W
Scott City, Kans. 24 38 29N 100 54W
Scott City, Mo. 32 37 12N 89 30W
Scott County ◇, Ark. 13 34 54N 94 5W
Scott County ◇, Ill. 21 39 40N 90 30W
Scott County ◇, Ind. 22 38 40N 85 45W
Scott County ◇, Iowa 23 41 35N 90 35W
Scott County ◇, Kans. 24 38 30N 101 0W
Scott County ◇, Ky. 49 38 15N 84 35W
Scott County ◇, Minn. 30 44 40N 93 30W
Scott County ◇, Miss. 31 32 22N 89 29W
Scott County ◇, Mo. 32 37 0N 89 35W
Scott County ◇, Tenn. 49 36 25N 84 29W
Scott County ◇, Va. 54 36 55N 82 45W
Scott Glacier 5 66 15 S 100 5 E
Scott I. 5 67 0 S 179 0 E
Scott Inlet 59 71 0N 71 0W
Scott Is. 62 50 48N 128 40W
Scott L. 63 59 55N 106 18W
Scott Mts. 14 41 15N 122 45W
Scott Peak 20 44 21N 112 49W
Scott Reef 126 14 0 S 121 50 E
Scottdale 45 40 6N 79 35W
Scotts Bluff County ◇ 34 41 50N 103 45W
Scotts Bluff National
Monument 34 41 50N 103 40W
Scotts Hill 48 35 31N 88 15W
Scottsbluff 34 41 52N 103 40W
Scottsboro 10 34 40N 86 2W
Scottsburg, Ind. 22 38 41N 85 47W
Scottsburg, Oreg. 44 43 39N 123 49W
Scottsburg, Va. 54 36 45N 78 48W
Scottsdale, Australia 127 41 9 S 147 31 E
Scottsdale, U.S.A. 12 33 29N 111 56W
Scottsville, Kans. 24 39 32N 97 57W
Scottsville, Ky. 48 36 45N 86 11W
Scottville 29 43 58N 86 17W
Scranton, Iowa 23 42 1N 94 33W
Scranton, Kans. 24 38 47N 95 44W
Scranton, N. Dak. 41 46 9N 103 9W
Scranton, Pa. 45 41 25N 75 40W
Screven 18 31 29N 82 1W
Screven County ◇ 18 32 45N 81 40W
Scribner 34 41 40N 96 40W
Scunthorpe 82 53 35N 0 38W
Scurry 51 32 31N 96 23W
Scurry County ◇ 50 32 44N 100 55W
Scusciuban 105 10 18N 50 12 E
Scutari = Üsküdar 106 41 0N 29 5 E
Sea Breeze 37 39 18N 75 20W
Sea Bright 37 40 22N 73 59W
Sea Isle City 37 39 9N 74 42W
Seaboard 40 36 29N 77 26W
Seabra 75 12 25 S 41 46W
Seabrook, N.H. 36 42 53N 70 52W
Seabrook, Tex. 51 29 34N 95 2W
Seadrift 51 28 25N 96 43W
Seaford, Del. 27 38 39N 75 37W
Seaford, Va. 54 37 12N 76 26W
Seaforth, Canada 60 43 35N 81 25W
Seaforth, U.S.A. 30 44 29N 95 20W
Seagoville 51 32 38N 96 32W
Seagraves 50 32 57N 102 34W
Seagrove 40 35 33N 79 46W
Seal → 63 58 50N 97 30W
Seal Cove 61 49 57N 56 22W
Seal I. 26 43 53N 68 45W
Seal L. 61 54 20N 61 30W
Seale 10 32 18N 85 10W
Sealevel 40 34 52N 76 23W
Sealy 51 29 47N 96 9W
Seaman 42 38 57N 83 34W
Searchlight 35 35 28N 114 55W
Searcy 13 35 15N 91 44W
Searcy County ◇ 13 35 55N 92 38W
Searles L. 15 35 44N 117 21W
Searsboro 23 41 35N 92 42W
Searsburg 36 42 52N 72 58W
Searsport 26 44 28N 68 56W
Seaside, Calif. 14 36 37N 121 50W
Seaside, Oreg. 44 46 0N 123 56W
Seaside Heights 37 39 55N 74 6W
Seaside Park 37 39 55N 74 5W
Seat Pleasant 27 38 54N 76 55W
Seattle 53 47 36N 122 20W
Seaview Ra. 127 18 40 S 145 45 E
Seaville 37 39 12N 74 42W
Sebago L. 26 43 52N 70 34W
Sebastian 17 27 49N 80 28W
Sebastian, C. 44 42 20N 124 26W
Sebastian County ◇ 13 35 10N 94 10W
Sebastián Vizcaíno, Bahía 64 28 0N 114 30W
Sebastopol = Sevastopol 99 44 35N 33 30 E
Sebastopol, Calif. 14 38 24N 122 49W
Sebastopol, Miss. 31 32 34N 89 20W
Sebec L. 26 45 16N 69 15W
Sebeka 30 46 38N 95 5W
Sebeş 95 45 58N 23 34 E
Sebeşului, Munţii 95 45 36N 23 40 E
Sebewaing 29 43 44N 83 27W
Şebinkarahisar 106 40 22N 38 28 E
Seboeis 26 45 22N 68 43W
Seboeis L. 26 45 28N 68 53W
Seboomook L. 26 45 56N 69 51W
Seboyeta 38 35 12N 107 23W
Sebree 48 37 36N 87 32W
Sebrell 54 36 47N 77 8W
Sebring 17 27 30N 81 27W
Sebta = Ceuta 120 35 52N 5 18W
Sebuku 110 3 30 S 116 25 E
Sebuku, Teluk 110 4 0N 118 10 E
Secession L. 46 34 18N 82 39W
Sechelt 62 49 25N 123 42W
Sechura 72 5 39 S 80 50W
Sechura, Desierto de 72 6 0 S 80 30W
Second L. 36 45 9N 71 10W
Secor 21 40 45N 89 8W
Secretary 27 38 37N 75 57W
Secretary I. 128 45 15 S 166 56 E
Section 10 34 35N 85 59W
Secunderabad 108 17 28N 78 30 E
Sécure → 73 15 10 S 64 52W
Security 16 38 45N 104 45W
Sedalia, Colo. 16 39 26N 104 58W
Sedalia, Mo. 32 38 42N 93 14W
Sedan, France 90 49 43N 4 57 E
Sedan, Kans. 24 37 8N 96 11W
Sedan, Minn. 30 45 35N 95 15W
Sedan, N. Mex. 38 36 9N 103 8W
Seddon 128 41 40 S 174 7 E
Seddonville 128 41 33 S 172 1 E
Sede Ya'aqov 104 32 43N 35 7 E
Sedgefield 40 36 1N 79 54W
Sedgewick 62 52 48N 111 41W
Sedgewick, Mt. 38 35 11N 108 6W
Sedgwick, Colo. 16 40 56N 102 32W
Sedgwick, Kans. 24 37 55N 97 26W
Sedgwick, Maine 26 44 18N 68 37W
Sedgwick County ◇, Colo. 16 40 50N 102 15W
Sedgwick County ◇, Kans. 24 37 30N 97 20W
Sedhiou 120 12 44N 15 30W
Sedienie 95 42 16N 24 33 E
Sedley 63 50 10N 104 0W
Sedom 104 31 5N 35 20 E
Sedona 12 34 52N 111 46W
Sedova, Pik 100 73 29N 54 58 E
Sedro-Woolley 53 48 30N 122 14W
Seeheim 123 26 50 S 17 45 E
Seekonk 28 41 49N 71 20W
Seeley Lake 33 47 11N 113 29W
Se'elim, Nahal 104 31 21N 35 24 E
Seelyville 22 39 30N 87 16W
Seg-ozero 98 63 0N 33 10 E
Segamat 112 2 30N 102 50 E
Segarcea 95 44 6N 23 43 E
Seget 111 1 24 S 130 58 E
Segezha 98 63 44N 34 19 E
Ségou 120 13 30N 6 16W
Segovia = Coco → 66 15 0N 83 8W
Segovia, Colombia 70 7 7N 74 42W
Segovia, Spain 91 40 57N 4 10W
Segre → 91 41 40N 0 43 E
Seguam I. 11 52 19N 172 30W
Seguam Pass 11 52 0N 172 30W
Séguéla 120 7 55N 6 40W
Seguin 51 29 34N 97 58W
Segundo → 76 30 53 S 62 44W
Segura → 91 38 6N 0 54W
Sehithwa 123 20 30 S 22 30 E
Sehore 108 23 10N 77 5 E
Seibert 16 39 18N 102 53W
Şeica Mare 95 46 1N 24 7 E
Seiland 96 70 25N 23 15 E
Seiling 43 36 9N 98 56W
Seinäjoki → 96 62 40N 22 45 E
Seine → 90 49 26N 0 26 E
Seine-et-Marne □ 90 48 45N 3 0 E
Seine-Maritime □ 90 49 40N 1 0 E
Seine-Saint-Denis □ 90 48 58N 2 24 E
Seistan 107 30 50N 61 0 E
Seistan, Daryācheh-ye 107 31 0N 61 0 E
Sekayu 110 2 51 S 103 51 E
Sekondi-Takoradi 120 4 58N 1 45W
Selah 53 46 39N 120 32W
Selama 112 5 12N 100 42 E
Selangor □ 112 3 20N 101 30 E
Selaru 111 8 9 S 131 0 E
Selawik 11 66 36N 160 0W
Selawik L. 11 66 30N 160 45W
Selby, U.K. 82 53 47N 1 5W
Selby, U.S.A. 47 45 31N 100 2W
Selbyville 27 38 28N 75 14W
Selden, Kans. 24 39 33N 100 34W
Selden, N.Y. 39 40 52N 73 2W
Seldovia 11 59 26N 151 43W
Sele → 94 40 27N 14 58 E
Selemdzha → 101 51 42N 128 53 E
Selenge → 113 49 25N 103 59 E
Seletan, Tg. 110 4 10 S 114 40 E
Selfridge 41 46 2N 100 56W
Sélibabi 120 15 10N 12 15W
Seligman, Ariz. 12 35 20N 112 53W
Seligman, Mo. 32 36 31N 93 56W
Selîma, El Wâhât el 121 21 22N 29 19 E
Selinsgrove 45 40 48N 76 52W
Selkirk, Canada 63 50 10N 96 55W
Selkirk, U.K. 84 55 33N 2 50W
Selkirk, U.S.A. 24 38 29N 101 32W
Selkirk I. 63 53 20N 99 6W
Selkirk Mts., Canada 62 51 15N 117 40W
Selkirk Mts., U.S.A. 20 48 30N 116 40W
Selleck 53 47 23N 121 52W
Sellers 46 34 17N 79 28W
Sellersburg 22 38 24N 85 45W
Sells 12 31 55N 111 53W
Selma, Ala. 10 32 25N 87 1W
Selma, Ark. 13 33 42N 91 34W
Selma, Calif. 15 36 34N 119 37W
Selma, N.C. 40 35 32N 78 17W
Selma, Oreg. 44 42 17N 123 37W
Selman 43 36 48N 99 30W
Selmer 48 35 10N 88 36W
Selpele 111 0 1 S 130 5 E
Selsey Bill 83 50 44N 0 47W
Selu 111 7 32 S 130 55 E
Selva 76 29 50 S 62 0W
Selvas 72 6 30 S 67 0W
Selway → 20 46 9N 115 36W
Selwyn 127 21 32 S 140 30 E
Selwyn L. 63 60 0N 104 30W
Selwyn Ra. 127 21 10 S 140 0 E
Selz 41 47 52N 99 54W
Seman → 95 40 45N 19 50 E
Semarang 111 7 0 S 110 26 E
Semau 111 10 13 S 123 22 E
Semeru 111 8 4 S 112 55 E
Semichi Is. 11 52 42N 174 0 E
Seminary 31 31 34N 89 30W
Seminoe Reservoir 56 42 9N 106 55W
Seminole, Fla. 17 27 50N 82 47W
Seminole, Okla. 43 35 14N 96 41W
Seminole, Tex. 50 32 43N 102 39W
Seminole, L. 18 30 43N 84 52W
Seminole County ◇, Fla. 17 28 40N 81 15W
Seminole County ◇, Ga. 18 31 0N 84 55W
Seminole County ◇, Okla. 43 35 10N 96 40W
Semiozernoye 100 52 22N 64 8 E
Semipalatinsk 100 50 30N 80 10 E
Semirara Is. 111 12 0N 121 20 E
Semisopochnoi I. 11 51 55N 179 36 E
Semitau 110 0 29N 111 57 E
Semiyarskoye 100 50 55N 78 23 E
Semmering Pass 88 47 41N 15 45 E
Semmes 10 30 47N 88 16W
Semnān 107 35 55N 53 25 E
Semnān □ 107 36 0N 54 0 E
Semois → 87 49 53N 4 44 E
Semporna 111 4 30N 118 33 E
Semuda 110 2 51 S 112 58 E
Sen → 112 13 45N 105 12 E
Sena 72 11 32 S 67 11W
Sena → 72 11 31 S 67 11W
Sena Madureira 72 9 5 S 68 45W
Senachwine L. 21 41 10N 89 20W
Senador Pompeu 74 5 40 S 39 20W

Senai Shenandoah

Senai 112 1 38N 103 38 E
Senaja 110 6 45N 117 3 E
Senanga 123 16 2 S 23 14 E
Senath 32 36 8N 90 10W
Senatobia 31 34 37N 89 58W
Sendai, Kagoshima, Japan 117 31 50N 130 20 E
Sendai, Miyagi, Japan 116 38 15N 140 53 E
Sendai-Wan 116 38 15N 141 0 E
Seneca, Ill. 21 41 19N 88 37W
Seneca, Kans. 24 39 50N 96 4W
Seneca, Md. 27 39 5N 77 20W
Seneca, Mo. 32 36 51N 94 37W
Seneca, Nebr. 34 42 3N 100 50W
Seneca, Oreg. 44 44 8N 118 58W
Seneca, S.C. 46 34 41N 82 57W
Seneca, S. Dak. 47 45 4N 99 31W
Seneca County ◇, N.Y. 39 42 45N 76 45W
Seneca County ◇, Ohio 42 41 7N 83 11W
Seneca Falls 39 42 55N 76 48W
Seneca L. 39 42 40N 76 54W
Senecaville L. 42 39 55N 81 25W
Senegal ■ 120 14 30N 14 30W
Senegal → 120 15 48N 16 32W
Senegambia 118 12 45N 12 0W
Senge Khambab = Indus → 108 24 20N 67 47 E
Sengkang 111 4 8 S 120 1 E
Senguerr → 78 45 35 S 68 50W
Senhor-do-Bonfim 74 10 30 S 40 10W
Senigállia 94 43 42N 13 12 E
Senj 94 45 0N 14 58 E
Senja 96 69 25N 17 30 E
Senlis 90 49 13N 2 35 E
Senmonorom 112 12 27N 107 12 E
Sennâr 121 13 30N 33 35 E
Senneterre 60 48 25N 77 15W
Senoia 18 33 18N 84 33W
Sens 90 48 11N 3 15 E
Senta 95 45 55N 20 3 E
Sentinel, Ariz. 12 32 52N 113 13W
Sentinel, Okla. 43 35 9N 99 11W
Sentinel Butte 41 46 55N 103 51W
Sento Sé 74 9 40 S 41 18W
Sentola 111 7 55 S 110 13 E
Seo de Urgel 91 42 22N 1 23 E
Seoul = Sŏul 114 37 31N 126 58 E
Separation Point 61 53 37N 57 25W
Sepīdān 107 30 20N 52 5 E
Sepone 112 16 45N 106 13 E
Sept-Îles 61 50 13N 66 22W
Septemvri 95 42 13N 24 6 E
Sepulga → 10 31 11N 86 46W
Sequatchie County ◇ 49 35 23N 85 23W
Sequim 53 48 5N 123 6W
Sequoia National Forest 15 36 0N 118 20W
Sequoia National Park 15 36 30N 118 30W
Sequoyah County ◇ 43 35 30N 94 45W
Serafina 38 35 24N 105 19W
Seraing 87 50 35N 5 32 E
Seram 111 3 10 S 129 0 E
Seram Laut, Kepulauan 111 4 5 S 131 25 E
Seram Sea 111 2 30 S 128 30 E
Serang 111 6 8 S 106 10 E
Serasan 110 2 29N 109 4 E
Serbia = Srbija □ 95 43 30N 21 0 E
Sercaia 95 45 49N 25 9 E
Serdobsk 98 52 28N 44 10 E
Seremban 112 2 43N 101 53 E
Serena, La 76 29 55 S 71 10W
Serenje 123 13 14 S 30 15 E
Sereth = Siret → 89 47 58N 26 5 E
Sergeant Bluff 23 42 24N 96 22W
Sergino 100 62 30N 65 38 E
Sergipe □ 74 10 30 S 37 30W
Seria 110 4 37N 114 23 E
Serian 110 1 10N 110 31 E
Seribu, Kepulauan 110 5 36 S 106 33 E
Sermata 111 8 15 S 128 50 E
Serny Zavod 100 39 59N 58 50 E
Serov 100 59 29N 60 35 E
Serowe 123 22 25 S 26 43 E
Serpukhov 98 54 55N 37 28 E
Serra do Navio 71 0 59N 52 3W
Serra Talhada 74 7 59 S 38 18W
Sérrai 95 41 5N 23 31 E
Serrezuela 76 30 40 S 65 20W
Serrinha 75 11 39 S 39 0W
Serrita 74 7 56 S 39 19W
Sertânia 74 8 5 S 37 20W
Sertanópolis 77 23 4 S 51 2W
Serua 111 6 18 S 130 1 E
Serui 111 1 53 S 136 10 E
Serule 123 21 57 S 27 20 E
Sesepe 111 1 30 S 127 59 E
Sesfontein 123 19 7 S 13 39 E
Sesheke 123 17 29 S 24 13 E
Sesser 21 38 5N 89 1W
Sestao 91 43 18N 3 0W
Setana 116 42 26N 139 51 E
Sète 90 43 25N 3 42 E
Sete Lagôas 75 19 27 S 44 16W
Seth Ward 50 34 13N 101 42W
Sétif 120 36 9N 5 26 E
Seto 117 35 14N 137 6 E
Setonaikai 117 34 20N 133 30 E
Settat 120 33 0N 7 40W
Setté-Cama 122 2 32 S 9 45 E
Setting L. 63 55 0N 98 38W
Settle 82 54 5N 2 18W
Setúbal 91 38 30N 8 58W
Setúbal, B. de 91 38 40N 8 56W
Seul, Lac-Rés. 60 50 25N 92 30W
Seul Choix Pt. 29 45 55N 85 55W
Seulimeum 110 5 27N 95 15 E
Sevan, Ozero 99 40 30N 45 20 E
Sevastopol 99 44 35N 33 30 E
Seven Devils Mts. 20 44 45N 116 40W
Seven Sisters 62 54 56N 128 10W
Seven Springs 40 35 14N 77 51W
Seven Troughs Range 35 40 30N 118 40W
Seven Valleys 45 39 51N 76 46W
Severn 40 36 31N 77 11W
Severn →, Canada 60 56 2N 87 36W
Severn →, U.K. 83 51 35N 2 38W
Severn L. 60 53 54N 90 48W
Severna Park 27 39 4N 76 33W
Severnaya Zemlya 101 79 0N 100 0 E
Severnyye Uvaly 98 58 0N 48 0 E
Severo-Kurilsk 101 50 40N 156 8 E
Severo-Yeniseyskiy 101 60 22N 93 1 E
Severodinsk 98 64 27N 39 58 E
Severomorsk 98 69 5N 33 27 E
Severouralsk 98 60 9N 59 57 E
Severy 24 37 37N 96 14W
Sevier → 52 39 4N 113 6W
Sevier Bridge Reservoir 52 39 22N 112 2W
Sevier County ◇, Ark. 13 33 58N 94 10W
Sevier County ◇, Tenn. 49 35 48N 83 33W
Sevier County ◇, Utah 52 38 45N 111 50W
Sevier Desert 52 39 40N 112 45W
Sevier L. 52 38 54N 113 9W
Sevier Plateau 52 38 20N 112 10W
Sevierville 49 35 52N 83 34W
Sevilla, Colombia 70 4 16N 75 57W
Sevilla, Spain 91 37 23N 6 0W
Seville = Sevilla 91 37 23N 6 0W
Seville, Fla. 17 29 19N 81 30W
Seville, Ga. 18 31 58N 83 36W
Sevlievo 95 43 2N 25 3 E
Sewanee 49 35 12N 85 55W
Seward, Alaska 11 60 7N 149 27W
Seward, Ill. 21 42 14N 89 22W
Seward, Kans. 24 38 11N 98 48W
Seward, Nebr. 34 40 55N 97 6W
Seward, Pa. 45 40 25N 79 1W
Seward County ◇, Kans. 24 37 15N 100 45W
Seward County ◇, Nebr. 34 40 50N 97 10W
Seward Peninsula 11 65 30N 166 0W
Sewell 76 34 10 S 70 23W
Sewer 111 5 53 S 134 40 E
Sewickley 45 40 32N 80 12W
Sexsmith 62 55 21N 118 47W
Seychelles ■ 3 5 0 S 56 0 E
Seyðisfjörður 96 65 16N 14 0W
Seyhan → 99 36 38N 35 8 E
Seymchan 101 62 54N 152 30 E
Seymour, Conn. 28 41 24N 73 4W
Seymour, Ind. 22 38 58N 85 53W
Seymour, Iowa 23 40 45N 93 7W
Seymour, Mo. 32 37 9N 92 46W
Seymour, Tex. 51 33 35N 99 16W
Seymour, Wis. 55 44 31N 88 20W
Seymourville 25 30 16N 91 14W
Sfax 121 34 49N 10 48 E
Sfîntu Gheorghe 89 45 52N 25 48 E
Sha Xian 115 26 23N 117 45 E
Shaanxi □ 115 35 0N 109 0 E
Shaba □ 122 8 0 S 25 0 E
Shabla 95 43 31N 28 32 E
Shabunda 122 2 40 S 27 16 E
Shache 113 38 20N 77 10 E
Shackelford County ◇ 51 32 45N 99 18W
Shackleton Ice Shelf 5 66 0 S 100 0 E
Shackleton Inlet 5 83 0 S 160 0 E
Shadehill Reservoir 47 45 45N 102 12W
Shadow Mt. Nat. Rec. Area 16 40 7N 105 48W
Shadrinsk 100 56 5N 63 32 E
Shady Cove 44 42 37N 122 49W
Shady Dale 18 33 24N 83 36W
Shady Grove, Fla. 17 30 17N 83 38W
Shady Grove, Ky. 48 37 20N 87 53W
Shady Point 43 35 8N 94 40W
Shady Side 27 38 50N 76 31W
Shady Spring 54 37 42N 81 6W
Shafer, L. 22 40 46N 86 46W
Shafter, Calif. 15 35 30N 119 16W
Shafter, Tex. 50 29 49N 104 18W
Shaftesbury 83 51 0N 2 12W
Shaftsbury 36 43 1N 73 11W
Shageluk 11 62 41N 159 34W
Shāhābād 107 37 40N 56 50 E
Shahdād 107 30 30N 57 40 E
Shahdadkot 108 27 50N 67 55 E
Shahgarh 108 27 15N 69 50 E
Shaḥḥāt 121 32 48N 21 54 E
Shahr Kord 107 32 15N 50 55 E
Shahrig 108 30 15N 67 40 E
Shahsād, Namakzār-e 107 30 20N 58 20 E
Shaikhabad 108 34 2N 68 45 E
Shajapur 108 23 27N 76 21 E
Shaker Heights 42 41 29N 81 32W
Shakhty 99 47 40N 40 16 E
Shakhunya 98 57 40N 46 46 E
Shaki 120 8 41N 3 21 E
Shakopee 30 44 48N 93 32W
Shaktoolik 11 64 20N 161 9W
Shala, L. 121 7 30N 38 30 E
Shalimar 17 30 27N 86 36W
Shallotte 40 33 58N 78 23W
Shallow Water 24 38 23N 100 55W
Shallowater 50 33 36N 102 0W
Sham, J. ash 107 23 10N 57 5 E
Shamâl Dârfûr □ 121 15 0N 25 0 E
Shamâl Kordofân □ 121 15 0N 30 0 E
Shamattawa 63 55 51N 92 5W
Shamattawa → 60 55 1N 85 23W
Shambaugh 23 40 42N 95 3W
Shamīl 107 27 30N 56 55 E
Shammar, Jabal 106 27 40N 41 0 E
Shamo = Gobi 114 44 0N 111 0 E
Shamo, L. 121 5 45N 37 30 E
Shamokin 45 40 47N 76 34W
Shamrock, Okla. 43 35 56N 96 35W
Shamrock, Tex. 50 35 13N 100 15W
Shamva 123 17 20 S 31 32 E
Shan □ 109 21 30N 98 30 E
Shanchengzhen 114 42 20N 125 20 E
Shandon 15 35 39N 120 23W
Shandong □ 114 36 0N 118 0 E
Shang Xian 115 33 50N 109 58 E
Shangani → 123 18 41 S 27 10 E
Shangbancheng 114 40 50N 118 1 E
Shangcheng 115 31 47N 115 26 E
Shangchuan Dao 115 21 40N 112 50 E
Shangdu 114 41 30N 113 30 E
Shanggao 115 28 17N 114 55 E
Shanghai 115 31 15N 121 26 E
Shangqiu 115 34 26N 115 36 E
Shangrao 115 28 25N 117 59 E
Shangshui 115 33 42N 114 35 E
Shangsi 115 22 8N 107 58 E
Shangyou 115 25 48N 114 32 E
Shangzhi 114 45 22N 127 56 E
Shaniko 44 45 0N 120 45W
Shannon, Greenland 4 75 10N 18 30W
Shannon, N.Z. 128 40 33 S 175 25 E
Shannon, Ga. 18 34 20N 85 4W
Shannon, Ill. 21 42 9N 89 44W
Shannon, Miss. 31 34 7N 88 43W
Shannon → 85 52 35N 9 30W
Shannon, L. 53 48 33N 121 45W
Shannon County ◇, Mo. 32 37 10N 91 20W
Shannon County ◇, S. Dak. 47 43 15N 102 35W
Shannontown 46 33 53N 80 21W
Shansi = Shanxi □ 114 37 0N 112 0 E
Shantar, Ostrov Bolshoy 101 55 9N 137 40 E
Shantou 115 23 18N 116 40 E
Shantung = Shandong □ 114 36 0N 118 0 E
Shanxi □ 114 37 0N 112 0 E
Shanyang 115 33 31N 109 55 E
Shaoguan 115 24 48N 113 35 E
Shaowu 115 27 22N 117 28 E
Shaoxing 115 30 0N 120 35 E
Shaoyang 115 27 14N 111 25 E
Shapinsay 84 59 2N 2 50W
Shaqrā', S. Yemen 105 13 22N 45 44 E
Shaqra', Si. Arabia 106 25 15N 45 16 E
Shari 116 43 55N 144 40 E
Sharjah = Ash Shāriqah 107 25 23N 55 26 E
Shark B. 126 25 55 S 113 32 E
Sharkey County ◇ 31 32 55N 90 53W
Sharon, Conn. 28 41 53N 73 29W
Sharon, Kans. 24 37 15N 98 25W
Sharon, Mass. 28 42 7N 71 11W
Sharon, N. Dak. 41 47 36N 97 54W
Sharon, Okla. 43 36 17N 99 20W
Sharon, Pa. 45 41 14N 80 31W
Sharon, Tenn. 48 36 14N 88 50W
Sharon, Vt. 36 43 47N 72 25W
Sharon, Wis. 55 42 30N 88 44W
Sharon, Plain of = Hasharon 104 32 12N 34 49 E
Sharon Springs 24 38 54N 101 45W
Sharonville 42 39 16N 84 25W
Sharp County ◇ 13 36 4N 91 37W
Sharpe, L. 47 44 1N 99 23W
Sharpe L. 63 54 5N 93 40W
Sharpes 17 28 26N 80 46W
Sharpsburg, Iowa 23 40 48N 94 38W
Sharpsburg, Md. 27 39 28N 77 45W
Sharpsburg, N.C. 40 35 53N 77 50W
Sharpsville, Ind. 22 40 23N 86 5W
Sharpsville, Pa. 45 41 15N 80 29W
Sharptown, Md. 27 38 0N 75 0W
Sharptown, N.J. 37 39 40N 75 22W
Sharq el Istiwa'iya □ 121 5 0N 33 0 E
Sharya 98 58 22N 45 20 E
Shashi, Botswana 123 21 15 S 27 27 E
Shashi, China 115 30 25N 112 14 E
Shasta 14 40 36N 122 29W
Shasta, Mt. 14 41 25N 122 12W
Shasta County ◇ 14 40 40N 122 0W
Shasta Dam 14 40 43N 122 25W
Shasta L. 14 40 43N 122 25W
Shasta National Forest 14 41 10N 122 20W
Shattuck 43 36 16N 99 53W
Shaunavon 63 49 35N 108 25W
Shaver L. 15 37 9N 119 18W
Shaw 31 33 36N 90 47W
Shaw → 126 20 21 S 119 17 E
Shawan 113 44 34N 85 50 E
Shawangunk Mts. 39 41 35N 74 30W
Shawano 55 44 47N 88 36W
Shawano County ◇ 55 44 45N 88 40W
Shawboro 40 36 24N 76 6W
Shawhan 49 38 18N 84 16W
Shawinigan 60 46 35N 72 50W
Shawnee, Ga. 18 32 29N 81 25W
Shawnee, Kans. 24 39 1N 94 43W
Shawnee, Ohio 42 39 36N 82 13W
Shawnee, Okla. 43 35 20N 96 55W
Shawnee County ◇ 24 39 0N 95 45W
Shawnee National Forest 21 37 40N 88 20W
Shawneetown 21 37 42N 88 8W
Shcherbakov = Rybinsk 98 58 5N 38 50 E
Shchuchiosk 100 52 56N 70 12 E
She Xian 115 29 50N 118 25 E
Shea 71 2 48N 59 4W
Shebele, Wabi → 105 2 0N 44 0 E
Sheboygan 55 43 46N 87 45W
Sheboygan County ◇ 55 43 45N 87 50W
Sheboygan Falls 55 43 44N 87 49W
Shechem 104 32 13N 35 21 E
Shedd 44 44 28N 123 7W
Shediac 61 46 14N 64 32W
Sheelin, Lough 85 53 48N 7 20W
Sheenjek → 11 66 45N 144 33W
Sheep Haven 85 55 12N 7 55W
Sheep Hole Mts. 15 34 10N 117 40W
Sheep Mt. 56 43 31N 110 28W
Sheep Range 35 36 35N 115 15W
Sheerness 83 51 26N 0 47 E
Sheet Harbour 61 44 56N 62 31W
Shefar'am 104 32 48N 35 10 E
Sheffield, U.K. 82 53 23N 1 28W
Sheffield, Ala. 10 34 46N 87 41W
Sheffield, Ill. 21 41 21N 89 44W
Sheffield, Iowa 23 42 54N 93 13W
Sheffield, Mass. 28 42 5N 73 21W
Sheffield, Tex. 50 30 41N 101 49W
Sheho 63 51 35N 103 13W
Shehuen → 78 49 35 S 69 34W
Shekhupura 108 31 42N 73 58 E
Shelbiana 49 37 26N 82 30W
Shelbina 32 39 47N 92 2W
Shelburn 22 39 11N 87 24W
Shelburne, N.S., Canada 61 43 47N 65 20W
Shelburne, Ont., Canada 60 44 4N 80 15W
Shelburne, U.S.A. 36 44 23N 73 14W
Shelburne B. 127 11 50 S 142 50 E
Shelburne Falls 28 42 36N 72 45W
Shelby, Iowa 23 41 31N 95 27W
Shelby, Mich. 29 43 37N 86 22W
Shelby, Miss. 31 33 57N 90 46W
Shelby, Mont. 33 48 30N 111 51W
Shelby, N.C. 40 35 17N 81 32W
Shelby, Nebr. 34 41 12N 97 26W
Shelby, Ohio 42 40 53N 82 40W
Shelby County ◇, Ala. 10 33 15N 86 49W
Shelby County ◇, Ill. 21 39 25N 88 45W
Shelby County ◇, Ind. 22 39 30N 85 50W
Shelby County ◇, Iowa 23 41 40N 95 20W
Shelby County ◇, Ky. 49 38 10N 85 10W
Shelby County ◇, Mo. 32 39 50N 92 0W
Shelby County ◇, Ohio 42 40 17N 84 9W
Shelby County ◇, Tenn. 48 35 5N 89 55W
Shelby County ◇, Tex. 51 31 48N 94 11W
Shelbyville, Ill. 21 39 24N 88 48W
Shelbyville, Ind. 22 39 31N 85 47W
Shelbyville, Ky. 49 38 13N 85 14W
Shelbyville, Mo. 32 39 48N 92 2W
Shelbyville, Tenn. 48 35 29N 86 28W
Shelbyville, Tex. 51 31 46N 94 5W
Shelbyville, L. 21 39 26N 88 46W
Sheldahl 23 41 52N 93 42W
Sheldon, Iowa 23 43 11N 95 51W
Sheldon, Mo. 32 37 40N 94 18W
Sheldon, N. Dak. 41 46 35N 97 30W
Sheldon, S.C. 46 32 36N 80 48W
Sheldon, Wis. 55 45 19N 90 58W
Sheldon Point 11 62 32N 164 52W
Sheldrake 61 50 20N 64 51W
Shelikhova, Zaliv 101 59 30N 157 0 E
Shelikof Strait 11 57 30N 155 0W
Shell Lake, Canada 63 53 19N 107 2W
Shell Lake, U.S.A. 55 45 45N 91 55W
Shell Rock 23 42 43N 92 35W
Shellbrook 63 53 13N 106 24W
Shelley 20 43 23N 112 7W
Shellharbour 127 34 31 S 150 51 E
Shelling Rocks 85 51 45N 10 35W
Shellman 18 31 46N 84 37W
Shellman Bluff 18 31 35N 81 19W
Shellrock → 23 42 35N 92 25W
Shellsburg 23 42 6N 91 52W
Shelltown 27 37 58N 75 40W
Shelly 30 47 28N 96 49W
Shelton, Conn. 28 41 19N 73 5W
Shelton, Nebr. 34 40 47N 98 44W
Shelton, S.C. 46 34 30N 81 25W
Shelton, Wash. 53 47 13N 123 6W
Shemakha 99 40 38N 48 37 E
Shenandoah, Iowa 23 40 46N 95 22W
Shenandoah, Pa. 45 40 49N 76 12W
Shenandoah, Va. 54 38 29N 78 37W
Shenandoah → 54 39 19N 77 44W

Silver L. Sneads Ferry

Silver L., Calif. 15 35 21N 116 7W
Silver L., Wash. 53 46 17N 122 47W
Silver L., Oreg. 44 43 22N 119 25W
Silver L., Oreg. 44 43 6N 120 53W
Silver Lake, Kans. 24 39 6N 95 52W
Silver Lake, Minn. 30 44 54N 94 12W
Silver Lake, Oreg. 44 43 8N 121 3W
Silver Lake, Wis. 55 44 4N 89 14W
Silver Run 27 39 42N 77 3W
Silver Spring 27 38 59N 77 2W
Silver Springs, Fla. 17 29 13N 82 3W
Silver Springs, Nev. 35 39 25N 119 14W
Silverdale 24 37 3N 96 54W
Silverstreet 46 34 13N 81 43W
Silverton, Colo. 16 37 49N 107 40W
Silverton, N.J. 37 40 1N 74 10W
Silverton, Oreg. 44 45 1N 122 47W
Silverton, Tex. 50 34 28N 101 19W
Silverton, Wash. 53 48 5N 121 35W
Silvia 70 2 37N 76 21W
Silvies → 44 43 34N 119 2W
Silwād 104 31 59N 35 15 E
Simanggang 110 1 15N 111 32 E
Simão Dias 74 10 44 S 37 49W
Simard, L. 60 47 40N 78 40W
Simărtin 95 46 19N 25 58 E
Simcoe 60 42 50N 80 20W
Simcoe, L. 60 44 25N 79 20W
Simenga 101 62 42N 108 25 E
Simeulue 110 2 45N 95 45 E
Simferopol 99 44 55N 34 3 E
Simi Valley 15 34 16N 118 47W
Simikot 109 30 0N 81 50 E
Simití 70 7 58N 73 57W
Simla, India 108 31 2N 77 9 E
Simla, U.S.A. 16 39 9N 104 5W
Simmesport 25 30 59N 91 49W
Simmie 63 49 56N 108 6W
Simms 33 47 30N 111 56W
Simnasho 44 44 58N 121 21W
Simões 74 7 36 S 40 49W
Simojärvi 96 66 5N 27 3 E
Simojoki → 96 65 35N 25 1 E
Simojovel 65 17 12N 92 38W
Simonette → 62 55 9N 118 15W
Simonton Lake 22 41 44N 85 59W
Simpang, Indonesia 110 1 16 S 104 5 E
Simpang, Malaysia 112 4 50N 100 40 E
Simplício Mendes 74 7 51 S 41 54W
Simplon Pass 88 46 15N 8 0 E
Simpson, Kans. 24 39 23N 97 56W
Simpson, La. 25 31 16N 93 1W
Simpson County ◇, Ky. 48 36 45N 86 35W
Simpson County ◇, Miss. 31 31 53N 89 58W
Simpson Des. 127 25 0 S 137 0 E
Simpson Park Range 35 39 50N 116 35W
Simpsonville, Ky. 49 38 13N 85 22W
Simpsonville, S.C. 46 34 44N 82 15W
Sims 21 38 22N 88 32W
Simsbury 28 41 53N 72 48W
Simunjan 110 1 25N 110 45 E
Simushir, Ostrov 101 46 50N 152 30 E
Sinabang 110 2 30N 96 24 E
Sinadogo 105 5 50N 47 0 E
Sinai = Es Sînâ' 121 29 0N 34 0 E
Sinai 47 44 15N 97 3W
Sinai, Mt. = Mûsa, G. 106 28 33N 33 59 E
Sinaia 95 45 21N 25 38 E
Sinaloa 64 25 50N 108 20W
Sinaloa □ 64 25 0N 107 30W
Sinan 115 27 56N 108 13 E
Sīnāwan 120 31 0N 10 37 E
Sincé 70 9 15N 75 9W
Sincelejo 70 9 18N 75 24W
Sinclair 56 41 47N 107 7W
Sinclair, L. 18 33 8N 83 12W
Sinclair Mills 62 54 5N 121 40W
Sinclairville 39 42 16N 79 16W
Sincorá, Serra do 75 13 30 S 41 0W
Sind □ 108 26 0N 69 0 E
Sind Sagar Doab 108 32 0N 71 30 E
Sindangan 111 8 10N 123 5 E
Sindangbarang 111 7 27 S 107 1 E
Sines 91 37 56N 8 51W
Singa 121 13 10N 33 57 E
Singapore ■ 112 1 17N 103 51 E
Singapore, Straits of 112 1 15N 104 0 E
Singaraja 110 8 6 S 115 10 E
Singer 25 30 39N 93 25W
Singida 122 4 49 S 34 48 E
Singitikós Kólpos 95 40 6N 24 0 E
Singkaling Hkamti 109 26 0N 95 39 E
Singkawang 110 1 0N 108 57 E
Singkep 110 0 30 S 104 20 E
Singleton 127 32 33 S 151 0 E
Singleton, Mt. 126 29 27 S 117 15 E
Singora = Songkhla 112 7 13N 100 37 E
Sinjai 111 5 7 S 120 20 E
Sinjār 106 36 19N 41 52 E
Sinjil 104 32 3N 35 15 E
Sinkat 121 18 55N 36 49 E
Sinkiang Uighur = Xinjiang Uygur Zizhiqu □ 113 42 0N 86 0 E
Sinking Spring 42 39 4N 83 23W
Sinnemahoning 45 41 19N 78 6W
Sinni → 94 40 9N 16 42 E
Sinnuris 121 29 26N 30 31 E
Sinoe, L. 95 44 35N 28 50 E
Sinop 106 42 1N 35 11 E
Sinskoye 101 61 8N 126 48 E
Sint Eustatius, I. 67 17 30N 62 59W
Sint Maarten, I. 67 18 4N 63 4W
Sint Niklaas 87 51 10N 4 9 E
Sint Truiden 87 50 48N 5 10 E
Sintang 110 0 5N 111 35 E
Sinton 51 28 2N 97 31W
Sintra 91 38 47N 9 25W
Sinŭiju 114 40 5N 124 24 E
Siocon 111 7 40N 122 10 E
Sioma 123 16 25 S 23 28 E
Sion 88 46 14N 7 20 E
Sioux Center 23 43 5N 96 11W
Sioux City 23 42 30N 96 24W
Sioux County ◇, Iowa 23 43 5N 96 10W
Sioux County ◇, N. Dak. 41 46 0N 101 0W
Sioux County ◇, Nebr. 34 42 30N 103 45W
Sioux Falls 47 43 33N 96 44W
Sioux Lookout 60 50 10N 91 50W
Sioux Rapids 23 42 53N 95 9W
Siping 114 43 8N 124 21 E
Sipiwesk L. 63 55 5N 97 35W
Siple 5 75 0 S 74 0 E
Sipora 110 2 18 S 99 40 E
Sipsey → 10 33 0N 88 10W
Siquia → 66 12 10N 84 20W
Siquijor 111 9 12N 123 35 E
Siquirres 66 10 6N 83 30W
Siquisique 70 10 34N 69 42W
Sir Edward Pellew Group 127 15 40 S 137 10 E
Siracusa 94 37 4N 15 17 E
Sirajganj 109 24 25N 89 47 E
Siren 55 45 47N 92 24W
Siret → 89 47 58N 26 5 E
Sirmans 17 30 21N 83 39W
Sirohi 108 24 52N 72 53 E
Sironj 108 24 5N 77 39 E
Síros 95 37 28N 24 57 E
Sirsa 108 29 33N 75 4 E
Sisak 94 45 30N 16 21 E
Sisaket 112 15 8N 104 23 E
Sishui 115 34 48N 113 15 E
Sisipuk L. 63 55 45N 101 50W
Siskiyou County ◇ 14 41 40N 122 40W
Siskiyou Mts. 14 42 0N 122 40W
Siskiyou National Forest 44 42 20N 124 0W
Sisophon 112 13 38N 102 59 E
Sisquoc → 15 34 54N 120 18W
Sisseton 47 45 40N 97 3W
Sisseton Indian Reservation 41 46 0N 126 30W
Sissonville 54 38 32N 81 38W
Sīstān va Balūchestān □ 107 27 0N 62 0 E
Sister Bay 55 45 11N 87 7W
Sisters 44 44 18N 121 33W
Sisterville 54 39 34N 80 59W
Sitapur 109 27 38N 80 45 E
Sitges 91 41 17N 1 47 E
Sítio da Abadia 75 14 48 S 46 16W
Sitka, Alaska 11 57 3N 135 20W
Sitka, Kans. 24 37 11N 99 39W
Sitka ◇ 11 57 0N 135 0W
Sitkinak I. 11 56 33N 154 10W
Sittang → 109 17 10N 96 58 E
Sittang Myit → 109 17 20N 96 45 E
Sittard 87 51 0N 5 52 E
Sittwe 109 20 18N 92 45 E
Situbondo 111 7 45 S 114 0 E
Siuna 66 13 37N 84 45W
Siuri 109 23 50N 87 34 E
Siuslaw → 44 44 1N 124 8W
Siuslaw National Forest 44 44 15N 123 50W
Sīvand 107 30 5N 52 55 E
Sivas 106 39 43N 36 58 E
Siverek 106 37 50N 39 19 E
Sivomaskinskiy 98 66 40N 62 35 E
Sivrihisar 106 39 30N 31 35 E
Sîwa 121 29 11N 25 31 E
Siwalik Range 109 28 0N 83 0 E
Siwan 109 26 13N 84 21 E
Sizewell 83 52 13N 1 38 E
Sjælland 97 55 30N 11 30 E
Sjíptjenski P. 95 42 46N 25 33 E
Sjumen = Kolarovgrad 95 43 18N 26 55 E
Skagafjörður 96 65 54N 19 35W
Skagastølstindane 97 61 28N 7 52 E
Skagen 97 68 37N 14 27 E
Skagerrak 97 57 30N 9 0 E
Skagit → 53 48 23N 122 22W
Skagit County ◇ 53 48 30N 121 30W
Skagway 11 59 28N 135 19W
Skagway-Yakutat-Angoon ◇ 11 59 0N 139 0W
Skaidi 96 70 26N 24 30 E
Skalni Dol = Kamenyak 95 43 24N 26 57 E
Skamania County ◇ 53 46 0N 122 0W
Skaneateles 39 42 57N 76 26W
Skara 97 58 25N 13 30 E
Skaraborgs län □ 97 58 20N 13 30 E
Skardu 108 35 20N 75 44 E
Skedee 43 36 23N 96 42W
Skeena → 62 54 9N 130 5W
Skeena Mts. 62 56 40N 128 30W
Skegness 82 53 9N 0 20 E
Skeldon 71 5 55N 57 20W
Skellefte älv → 96 64 45N 21 10 E
Skellefteå 96 64 45N 20 58 E
Skelleftehamn 96 64 47N 20 59 E
Skellytown 50 35 34N 101 11W
Skerries, The 82 53 27N 4 40W
Skhwaner, Pegunungan 110 1 0 S 112 30 E
Skiatook 43 36 20N 96 0W
Skiatook Res. 43 36 20N 96 10W
Skibbereen 85 51 33N 9 16W
Skiddaw 82 54 39N 3 9W
Skidmore, Mo. 32 40 17N 95 5W
Skidmore, Tex. 51 28 15N 97 41W
Skien 97 59 12N 9 35 E
Skierniewice 89 51 58N 20 10 E
Skikda 120 36 50N 6 58 E
Skillet → 21 38 5N 88 5W
Skipton 82 53 57N 2 1W
Skíros 95 38 55N 24 34 E
Skive 97 56 33N 9 2 E
Skjálfandafljót → 96 65 59N 17 25W
Skjálfandi 96 66 5N 17 30W
Skoghall 97 59 20N 13 30 E
Skokie 21 42 3N 87 45W
Skopje 95 42 1N 21 32 E
Skövde 97 58 15N 13 59 E
Skovorodino 101 54 0N 125 0 E
Skowhegan 26 44 46N 69 43W
Skownan 63 51 58N 99 35W
Skudeneshavn 97 59 10N 5 10 E
Skull 85 51 32N 9 40W
Skull Valley 12 34 30N 112 41W
Skull Valley Indian Reservation 52 40 24N 112 45W
Skuna → 31 33 54N 89 41W
Skunk → 23 40 42N 91 7W
Skwierzyna 88 52 33N 15 30 E
Skye 84 57 15N 6 10W
Skykomish 53 47 42N 121 22W
Skyland 40 35 29N 82 32W
Skyros = Skíros 95 38 55N 24 34 E
Slagle 25 31 12N 93 8W
Slamet 110 7 16 S 109 8 E
Slaney → 85 52 52N 6 45W
Slănic 95 45 14N 25 58 E
Slask 88 51 0N 16 30 E
Slate Is. 60 48 40N 87 0W
Slate Spring 31 33 44N 89 22W
Slater, Iowa 23 41 53N 93 41W
Slater, Mo. 32 39 13N 93 4W
Slatina 89 44 28N 24 22 E
Slaton 50 33 26N 101 39W
Slaughter 25 30 43N 91 9W
Slaughter Beach 27 38 52N 75 18W
Slaughters 48 37 29N 87 30W
Slaughterville 43 35 5N 97 20W
Slave → 62 61 18N 113 39W
Slave Coast 118 6 0N 2 30 E
Slave Lake 62 55 17N 114 43W
Slave Pt. 62 61 11N 115 56W
Slavgorod 100 53 1N 78 37 E
Slavkov 88 49 10N 16 52 E
Slavyanka 116 42 53N 131 21 E
Slavyansk 99 48 55N 37 36 E
Slayden 31 34 57N 89 27W
Slayton 30 43 59N 95 45W
Sleaford 82 53 0N 0 22W
Sleat, Sd. of 84 57 5N 5 47W
Sledge 31 34 26N 90 13W
Sleeper 32 37 46N 92 36W
Sleeper Is. 59 58 30N 81 0W
Sleeping Bear Dunes Nat. Lakeshore 29 44 50N 86 5W
Sleeping Bear Pt. 29 44 55N 86 3W
Sleepy Eye 30 44 18N 94 43W
Sleetmute 11 61 42N 157 10W
Sleman 111 7 40 S 110 20 E
Slemon L. 62 63 13N 116 4W
Slemp 49 37 5N 83 6W
Slick 43 35 47N 96 16W
Slick Rock 16 38 3N 108 54W
Slide Mt. 39 42 0N 74 25W
Slidell 25 30 17N 89 47W
Sliedrecht 87 51 50N 4 45 E
Slieve Aughty 85 53 4N 8 30W
Slieve Bloom 85 53 4N 7 40W
Slieve Donard 85 54 10N 5 57W
Slieve Gullion 85 54 8N 6 26W
Slieve Mish 85 52 12N 9 50W
Slievenamon 85 52 25N 7 37W
Sligo, Ireland 85 54 17N 8 28W
Sligo, U.S.A. 45 41 6N 79 29W
Sligo □ 85 54 10N 8 35W
Sligo B. 85 54 20N 8 40W
Slim Buttes 47 45 20N 103 15W
Slite 97 57 42N 18 48 E
Sliven 95 42 42N 26 19 E
Sloan 23 42 14N 96 14W
Sloat 14 39 52N 120 44W
Slobodskoy 98 58 40N 50 6 E
Slobozia, Argeş, Romania 95 44 30N 25 14 E
Slobozia, Ialomiţa, Romania 95 44 34N 27 23 E
Slocan 62 49 48N 117 28W
Slochteren 87 53 12N 6 48 E
Slocomb 10 31 7N 85 36W
Slocum 28 41 32N 71 31W
Slope County ◇ 41 46 20N 103 30W
Slough 83 51 30N 0 35W
Slovakia = Slovensko □ 89 48 30N 19 0 E
Slovakian Ore Mts. = Slovenské Rudohorie 89 48 45N 20 0 E
Slovenia = Slovenija □ 94 45 58N 14 30 E
Slovenija □ 94 45 58N 14 30 E
Slovenské Rudohorie 89 48 45N 20 0 E
Slovensko □ 89 48 30N 19 0 E
Sluis 87 51 18N 3 23 E
Slunchev Bryag 95 42 40N 27 41 E
Slyne Hd. 85 53 25N 10 10W
Slyudyanka 101 51 40N 103 40 E
Smakover 13 33 22N 92 44W
Small, C. 26 43 42N 69 51W
Smalltree L. 63 61 0N 105 0W
Smallwood Reservoir 61 54 20N 63 10W
Smara 120 32 9N 8 16W
Smarr 18 32 59N 83 53W
Smarts Mt. 36 43 48N 72 3W
Smartville 14 39 13N 121 18W
Smeaton 63 53 30N 104 49W
Smederevo 95 44 40N 20 57 E
Smethport 45 41 49N 78 27W
Smidovich 101 48 36N 133 49 E
Smiley, Canada 63 51 38N 109 29W
Smiley, U.S.A. 51 29 16N 97 38W
Smilyan 95 41 29N 24 46 E
Smith, Canada 62 55 10N 114 0W
Smith, U.S.A. 35 38 48N 119 20W
Smith →, Canada 62 59 34N 126 30W
Smith →, Mont. 33 47 25N 111 29W
Smith →, N.C. 40 36 27N 79 43W
Smith Arm 58 66 15N 123 0W
Smith B. 11 70 30N 154 20W
Smith Center 24 39 47N 98 47W
Smith County ◇, Kans. 24 39 45N 98 45W
Smith County ◇, Miss. 31 32 1N 89 23W
Smith County ◇, Tenn. 48 36 5N 86 0W
Smith County ◇, Tex. 51 32 21N 95 18W
Smith I., Md. 27 38 0N 76 0W
Smith I., N.C. 40 33 53N 77 59W
Smith I., Va. 54 37 9N 75 53W
Smith Mountain L. 54 37 2N 79 30W
Smith Pk. 20 48 51N 116 40W
Smith River 14 41 56N 124 9W
Smith Sund 4 78 30N 74 0W
Smithburg, N.J. 37 40 13N 74 21W
Smithburg, W. Va. 54 39 17N 80 44W
Smithers 62 54 45N 127 10W
Smithfield, N.C. 40 35 31N 78 21W
Smithfield, Nebr. 34 40 34N 99 45W
Smithfield, Utah 52 41 50N 111 50W
Smithfield, Va. 54 36 59N 76 38W
Smithland, Iowa 23 42 14N 95 56W
Smithland, Ky. 48 37 9N 88 24W
Smiths 10 32 32N 85 6W
Smiths Falls 60 44 55N 76 0W
Smiths Ferry 20 44 18N 116 5W
Smiths Grove 48 37 3N 86 12W
Smithsburg 27 39 39N 77 35W
Smithton 32 38 41N 93 5W
Smithtown 39 40 51N 73 12W
Smithville, Ga. 18 31 54N 84 15W
Smithville, Md. 27 38 26N 75 45W
Smithville, Miss. 31 34 4N 88 23W
Smithville, Mo. 32 39 23N 94 35W
Smithville, Okla. 43 34 28N 94 39W
Smithville, Tenn. 49 35 58N 85 49W
Smithville, Tex. 51 30 1N 97 10W
Smithville, W. Va. 54 39 4N 81 6W
Smoaks 46 33 5N 80 49W
Smoke Bend 25 30 7N 91 1W
Smoke Creek Desert 35 40 30N 119 40W
Smoky → 62 56 10N 117 21W
Smoky Dome 20 43 30N 114 56W
Smoky Falls 60 50 4N 82 10W
Smoky Hill → 24 39 4N 96 48W
Smoky Hills 24 39 15N 99 30W
Smoky Lake 62 54 10N 112 30W
Smøla 96 63 23N 8 3 E
Smolan 24 38 44N 97 41W
Smolensk 98 54 45N 32 0 E
Smolikas, Óros 95 40 9N 20 58 E
Smolyan 95 41 36N 24 38 E
Smoot 56 42 37N 110 55W
Smooth Rock Falls 60 49 17N 81 37W
Smoothstone L. 63 54 40N 106 50W
Smulţi 95 45 57N 27 44 E
Smyadovo 95 43 2N 27 1 E
Smyrna = İzmir 99 38 25N 27 8 E
Smyrna, Del. 27 39 18N 75 36W
Smyrna, Ga. 18 33 53N 84 31W
Smyrna, Tenn. 48 35 59N 86 31W
Smyrna Mills 26 46 8N 68 10W
Smyth County ◇ 54 36 55N 81 25W
Snaefell 82 54 18N 4 26W
Snaefellsjökull 96 64 45N 23 46W
Snake →, Nebr. 34 42 47N 100 47W
Snake →, Wash. 53 46 12N 119 2W
Snake →, Minn. 30 48 26N 97 7W
Snake →, Minn. 30 45 49N 92 46W
Snake L. 63 55 32N 106 35W
Snake Range 35 39 0N 114 20W
Snake River Plain 20 42 50N 114 0W
Snake Valley 52 39 30N 113 55W
Sneads Ferry 40 34 33N 77 24W

Sneedville South Webster

Sneedville 49 36 32N 83 13W
Sneek 87 53 2N 5 40 E
Snelling, Calif. 14 37 31N 120 26W
Snelling, S.C. 46 33 15N 81 27W
Snizort, L. 84 57 33N 6 28W
Snøhetta 96 62 19N 9 16 E
Snohomish 53 47 55N 122 6W
Snohomish County ◇ 53 48 0N 121 30W
Snoqualmie 53 47 31N 121 49W
Snoqualmie National Forest 53 47 35N 121 20W
Snoqualmie Pass 53 47 25N 121 25W
Snover 29 43 28N 82 58W
Snow Hill, Ala. 10 32 0N 87 0W
Snow Hill, Md. 27 38 11N 75 24W
Snow Hill, N.C. 40 35 27N 77 40W
Snow Lake 63 54 52N 100 3W
Snow Mt., Calif. 14 39 23N 122 45W
Snow Mt., Maine 26 45 18N 70 48W
Snow Shoe 45 41 2N 77 57W
Snow Water L. 35 40 48N 114 59W
Snowball 13 35 55N 92 49W
Snowbird L. 63 60 45N 103 0W
Snowdon 82 53 4N 4 8W
Snowdoun 10 32 15N 86 18W
Snowdrift 63 62 24N 110 44W
Snowdrift → 63 62 24N 110 44W
Snowflake 12 34 30N 110 5W
Snowmass 16 39 20N 106 59W
Snowmass Mt. 16 39 8N 107 5W
Snowshoe Pk. 33 48 13N 115 41W
Snowville 52 41 58N 112 43W
Snowy → 127 37 46 S 148 30 E
Snowy Mt. 39 43 42N 74 23W
Snowyside Pk. 20 43 57N 114 58W
Snug Corner 67 22 33N 73 52W
Snyder, Colo. 16 40 20N 103 36W
Snyder, Nebr. 34 41 43N 96 47W
Snyder, Okla. 43 34 40N 98 57W
Snyder, Tex. 50 32 44N 100 55W
Snyder County ◇ 45 40 50N 77 0W
Soacha 70 4 35N 74 13W
Soalala 123 16 6 S 45 20 E
Soap Lake 53 47 23N 119 29W
Sobat, Nahr → 121 9 22N 31 33 E
Sobral 74 3 50 S 40 20W
Soc Trang 112 9 37N 105 50 E
Sochi 99 43 35N 39 40 E
Social Circle 18 33 39N 83 43W
Société, Is. de la 125 17 0 S 151 0W
Society Hill, Ala. 10 32 26N 85 27W
Society Hill, S.C. 46 34 31N 79 51W
Society Is. = Société, Is. de la 125 17 0 S 151 0W
Socompa, Portezuelo de 76 24 27 S 68 18W
Socorro, Colombia 70 6 29N 73 16W
Socorro, U.S.A. 38 34 4N 106 54W
Socorro, I. 64 18 45N 110 58W
Socorro County ◇ 38 34 0N 107 0W
Socotra 105 12 30N 54 0 E
Soda L. 15 35 10N 116 4W
Soda Plains 108 35 30N 79 0 E
Soda Springs, Calif. 14 39 20N 120 23W
Soda Springs, Idaho 20 42 39N 111 36W
Soddy-Daisy 49 35 17N 85 10W
Söderhamn 97 61 18N 17 10 E
Söderköping 97 58 31N 16 20 E
Södermanlands län □ 97 59 10N 16 30 E
Södertälje 97 59 12N 17 39 E
Sodiri 121 14 27N 29 0 E
Sodo 121 7 0N 37 41 E
Sodus 39 43 14N 77 4W
Sodus Point 39 43 16N 76 59W
Soest 87 52 9N 5 19 E
Sofia = Sofiya 95 42 45N 23 20 E
Sofia → 123 15 27 S 47 23 E
Sofiiski 101 52 15N 133 59 E
Sofiya 95 42 45N 23 20 E
Sōfu-Gan 117 29 49N 140 21 E
Sogamoso 70 5 43N 72 56W
Sogn og Fjordane fylke □ 97 61 40N 6 0 E
Sogndalsfjøra 97 61 14N 7 5 E
Sognefjorden 97 61 10N 5 50 E
Sohâg 121 26 33N 31 43 E
Soignies 87 50 35N 4 5 E
Soissons 90 49 25N 3 19 E
Sōja 117 34 40N 133 45 E
Söke 106 37 48N 27 28 E
Sokodé 120 9 0N 1 11 E
Sokol 98 59 30N 40 5 E
Sokółka 89 53 25N 23 30 E
Sokolo 120 14 53N 6 8W
Sokoto 120 13 2N 5 16 E
Sol Iletsk 98 51 10N 55 0 E
Solano 111 16 31N 121 15 E
Solano County ◇ 14 38 20N 121 50W
Solapur 108 17 43N 75 56 E
Soldier, Iowa 23 41 59N 95 46W
Soldier, Kans. 24 39 32N 95 58W
Soldier Summit 52 39 56N 111 5W
Soldiers Grove 55 43 24N 90 47W
Soldotna 11 60 29N 151 3W
Soledad, Colombia 70 10 55N 74 46W
Soledad, U.S.A. 14 36 26N 121 20W
Soledad, Venezuela 71 8 10N 63 34W
Solen 41 46 23N 100 48W
Solent, The 83 50 45N 1 25W
Solfonn 97 60 2N 6 57 E
Soligalich 98 59 5N 42 10 E
Solikamsk 100 59 38N 56 50 E
Solimões → = Amazonas → 71 0 5 S 50 0W
Sollefteå 96 63 12N 17 20 E
Sóller 91 39 46N 2 43 E
Sologne 90 47 40N 2 0 E
Solok 110 0 45 S 100 40 E
Sololá 66 14 49N 91 10 E
Solomon, Ariz. 12 32 49N 109 38W
Solomon, Kans. 24 38 55N 97 22W
Solomon → 24 38 55N 97 22W
Solomon Is. ■ 124 6 0 S 155 0 E
Solomons 27 38 19N 76 27W
Solomon's Pools = Birak Sulaymān 104 31 42N 35 7 E
Solon, China 114 46 32N 121 10 E
Solon, Iowa 23 41 48N 91 30W
Solon, Maine 26 44 57N 69 52W
Solon Springs 55 46 22N 91 49W
Solonópole 74 5 44 S 39 1W
Solor 111 8 27 S 123 0 E
Solothurn 88 47 13N 7 32 E
Solṭānābād 107 36 29N 58 5 E
Solunska Glava 95 41 44N 21 31 E
Solvang 15 34 36N 120 8W
Solvay 39 43 3N 76 13W
Solvychegodsk 98 61 21N 46 56 E
Solway 49 35 59N 84 11W
Solway Firth 82 54 45N 3 38W
Solwezi 123 12 11 S 26 21 E
Sōma 116 37 40N 140 50 E
Somali Rep. ■ 105 7 0N 47 0 E
Sombor 95 45 46N 19 9 E
Sombrerete 64 23 40N 103 40W
Sombrero 67 18 37N 63 30W
Somers, Conn. 28 41 59N 72 27W
Somers, Iowa 23 42 23N 94 26W
Somers, Mont. 33 48 5N 114 13W
Somers Point 37 39 20N 74 36W
Somerset, Canada 63 49 25N 98 39W
Somerset, Colo. 16 38 56N 107 28W
Somerset, Ky. 49 37 5N 84 36W
Somerset, Mass. 28 41 47N 71 8W
Somerset, Ohio 42 39 48N 82 18W
Somerset, Pa. 45 40 1N 79 5W
Somerset, Tex. 51 29 14N 98 40W
Somerset □ 83 51 9N 3 0W
Somerset County ◇, Maine 26 45 30N 70 0W
Somerset County ◇, Md. 27 38 10N 75 50W
Somerset County ◇, N.J. 37 40 35N 74 35W
Somerset County ◇, Pa. 45 40 0N 79 0W
Somerset East 123 32 42 S 25 35 E
Somerset I. 58 73 30N 93 0W
Somerset Res. 36 43 0N 72 57W
Somersworth 36 43 16N 70 52W
Somerton 12 32 36N 114 43W
Somervell County ◇ 51 32 14N 97 45W
Somerville, Mass. 28 42 23N 71 6W
Somerville, N.J. 37 40 35N 74 38W
Somerville, Ohio 42 39 34N 84 38W
Somerville, Tenn. 48 35 15N 89 21W
Somerville, Tex. 51 30 21N 96 32W
Somerville L. 51 30 19N 96 31W
Someş → 89 47 15N 23 45 E
Somes Bar 14 41 23N 123 29W
Somme □ 90 50 0N 2 20 E
Somoto 66 13 28N 86 37W
Somovit 95 43 40N 24 45 E
Somport, Puerto de 91 42 48N 0 31W
Somuncurá, Meseta de 78 41 30 S 67 0W
Son La 112 21 20N 103 50 E
Soná 66 8 0N 81 20W
Sønderborg 97 54 55N 9 49 E
Sondheimer 25 32 33N 91 11W
Sonepur 109 20 55N 83 50 E
Song Cau 112 13 27N 109 18 E
Song Xian 115 34 12N 112 8 E
Songea 122 10 40 S 35 40 E
Songhua Hu 114 43 35N 126 50 E
Songhua Jiang → 114 47 45N 132 30 E
Songjiang 115 31 1N 121 12 E
Songkhla 112 7 13N 100 37 E
Songling 114 48 2N 121 9 E
Songpan 113 32 40N 103 30 E
Songtao 115 28 11N 109 10 E
Songzi 115 30 12N 111 45 E
Sonipat 108 29 0N 77 5 E
Sonmiani 108 25 25N 66 40 E
Sono →, Goiás, Brazil 74 9 58 S 48 11W
Sono →, Minas Gerais, Brazil 75 17 2 S 45 32W
Sonoma 14 38 18N 122 28W
Sonoma County ◇ 14 38 30N 123 0W
Sonoma Peak 35 40 52N 117 36W
Sonora, Calif. 14 37 59N 120 23W
Sonora, Ky. 49 37 32N 85 54W
Sonora, Tex. 50 30 34N 100 39W
Sonora □ 64 29 0N 111 0W
Sonora → 64 28 50N 111 33W
Sonora Desert 12 33 40N 114 15W
Sonoyta 64 31 51N 112 50W
Sonsomate 66 13 43N 89 44W
Sontag 31 31 39N 90 12W
Sopachuy 73 19 29 S 64 31W
Sopchoppy 17 30 4N 84 29W
Soper 43 34 2N 95 42W
Soperton 18 32 23N 82 35W
Sophia 40 35 50N 79 52W
Sopi 111 2 34N 128 28 E
Sopot 89 54 27N 18 31 E
Sop's Arm 61 49 46N 56 56W
Sør-Rondane 5 72 0 S 25 0 E
Sør-Trøndelag fylke □ 96 63 0N 10 0 E
Sorata 72 15 50 S 68 40W
Sorel 60 46 0N 73 10W
Sorento 21 39 1N 89 35W
Soreq, N. → 104 31 57N 34 43 E
Sorgono 94 40 0N 9 0 E
Soria 91 41 43N 2 32W
Soriano 76 33 24 S 58 19W
Sorkh, Kuh-e 107 35 40N 58 30 E
Sorocaba 77 23 31 S 47 27W
Sorochinsk 98 52 26N 53 10 E
Sorong 111 0 55 S 131 15 E
Soroti 122 1 43N 33 35 E
Sørøya 96 70 40N 22 30 E
Sørøysundet 96 70 25N 23 0 E
Sorrento, Italy 94 40 38N 14 23 E
Sorrento, U.S.A. 25 30 11N 90 51W
Sorsele 96 65 31N 17 30 E
Sorsogon 111 13 0N 124 0 E
Sortavala 98 61 42N 30 41 E
Soscumica, L. 60 50 15N 77 27W
Sosnogorsk 98 63 37N 53 51 E
Sosnovka 101 54 9N 109 35 E
Sosnowiec 89 50 20N 19 10 E
Soso 31 31 45N 89 17W
Sosva 98 59 10N 61 50 E
Soto la Marina → 65 23 40N 97 40W
Sotuta 65 20 29N 89 43W
Souanké 122 2 10N 14 3 E
Souderton 45 40 19N 75 19W
Soúdhas, Kólpos 95 35 25N 24 10 E
Souhegan → 36 42 51N 71 29W
Sŏul 114 37 31N 126 58 E
Sound, The 97 56 7N 12 30 E
Sour Lake 51 30 9N 94 25W
Sources, Mt. aux 123 28 45 S 28 50 E
Soure 74 0 35 S 48 30W
Souris, Man., Canada 63 49 40N 100 20W
Souris, P.E.I., Canada 61 46 21N 62 15W
Souris, U.S.A. 41 48 55N 100 40W
Souris →, Canada 63 49 40N 99 34W
Souris →, U.S.A. 41 49 0N 100 57W
Sousa 74 6 45 S 38 10W
Sousel 74 2 38 S 52 29W
Sousse 121 35 50N 10 38 E
South → 40 34 20N 78 3W
South Africa, Rep. of, ■ 123 32 0 S 17 0 E
South Amboy 37 40 29N 74 18W
South America 68 10 0 S 60 0W
South Anna → 54 37 48N 77 25W
South Ashburnam 28 42 37N 71 57W
South Aulatsivik I. 61 56 45N 61 30W
South Australia □ 126 32 0 S 139 0 E
South Baldy 38 33 59N 107 11W
South Bay 17 26 40N 80 43W
South Beloit 21 42 29N 89 2W
South Bend, Ind. 22 41 41N 86 15W
South Bend, Wash. 53 46 40N 123 48W
South Bloomfield 42 39 43N 82 59W
South Boardman 29 44 38N 85 17W
South Boston 54 36 42N 78 54W
South Branch 61 47 55N 59 2W
South Branch Potomac → 54 39 32N 78 35W
South Brook 61 49 26N 56 5W
South Burlington 36 44 28N 73 13W
South Carolina □ 46 34 0N 81 0W
South Carver 28 41 51N 70 54W
South Chaplin 28 41 46N 72 9W
South Charleston, Ohio 42 39 50N 83 38W
South Charleston, W. Va. 54 38 22N 81 44W
South Charlestown 36 43 12N 72 26W
South China 26 44 24N 69 34W
South China Sea 112 10 0N 113 0 E
South Coffeyville 43 36 59N 95 37W
South Congaree 46 33 53N 81 9W
South Dakota □ 47 44 15N 100 0W
South Dartmouth 28 41 36N 70 57W
South Daytona 17 29 10N 81 0W
South Deerfield, Mass. 28 42 29N 72 37W
South Deerfield, N.H. 36 43 6N 71 18W
South Downs 83 50 53N 0 10W
South East C. 127 43 40 S 146 50 E
South-East Fairbanks ◇ 11 64 0N 144 0W
South-East Indian Rise 124 43 0 S 80 0 E
South Easton 28 42 3N 71 5W
South Egremont 28 42 10N 73 25W
South Elgin 21 42 0N 88 18W
South English 23 41 27N 92 5W
South Esk → 84 56 44N 3 3W
South Fabius → 32 39 54N 91 30W
South Foreland 83 51 7N 1 23 E
South Fork, Colo. 16 37 40N 106 37W
South Fork, Pa. 45 40 22N 78 48W
South Fork American → 14 38 57N 120 59W
South Fork Edisto → 46 33 16N 80 54W
South Fork Grand → 47 45 43N 102 17W
South Fork Indian Reservation 35 40 45N 115 40W
South Fork John Day → 44 44 28N 119 31W
South Fork Moreau 47 45 9N 102 50W
South Fork Owyhee → 20 42 16N 116 53W
South Fork Powder → 56 43 40N 106 30W
South Fork Republican → 34 40 3N 101 31W
South Fork Salmon → 20 45 23N 115 31W
South Fork Sappa Cr. → 24 39 47N 100 35W
South Fork Selway → 20 46 10N 115 58W
South Fork Shenandoah → 54 38 57N 78 12W
South Fork Shoshone → 56 44 27N 109 14W
South Fork Solomon → 24 39 28N 98 26W
South Fork Spring → 13 36 19N 91 30W
South Fox I. 29 45 25N 85 51W
South Fulton 48 36 30N 88 52W
South Georgia 5 54 30 S 37 0W
South Glamorgan □ 83 51 30N 3 20W
South Grand → 32 38 17N 93 25W
South Greensburg 45 40 17N 79 33W
South Hadley 28 42 16N 72 35W
South Hadley Falls 28 42 14N 72 36W
South Hamilton 28 42 37N 70 53W
South Haven, Kans. 24 37 3N 97 24W
South Haven, Mich. 29 42 24N 86 16W
South Henik, L. 63 61 30N 97 30W
South Hero 36 44 39N 73 19W
South Hill 54 36 44N 78 8W
South Holston L. 49 36 31N 82 5W
South Honshu Ridge 124 23 0N 143 0 E
South Horr 122 2 12N 36 56 E
South Houston 51 29 40N 95 14W
South Hutchinson 24 38 2N 97 56W
South I., N.Z. 128 44 0 S 170 0 E
South I., U.S.A. 46 33 10N 79 14W
South Invercargill 128 46 26 S 168 23 E
South Jacksonville 21 39 44N 90 12W
South Jordan 52 40 34N 111 55W
South Junction 44 44 51N 121 5W
South Knife → 63 58 55N 94 37W
South Korea ■ 114 36 0N 128 0 E
South Lake Tahoe 14 38 57N 119 59W
South Lancaster 28 42 27N 71 41W
South Lebanon 42 39 22N 84 13W
South Loup → 34 41 4N 98 39W
South Lyon 29 42 28N 83 39W
South Magnetic Pole 5 65 36 S 139 24 E
South Manitou I. 29 45 2N 86 8W
South Marsh I. 27 38 6N 76 2W
South Merrimac 36 42 49N 71 34W
South Miami 17 25 42N 80 18W
South Middleboro 28 41 45N 70 50W
South Mills 40 36 27N 76 20W
South Milwaukee 55 42 55N 87 52W
South Molton 83 51 1N 3 50W
South Mountain 27 39 30N 77 40W
South Mt. 20 42 44N 116 54W
South Nahanni → 62 61 3N 123 21W
South Negril Pt. 66 18 14N 78 30W
South Newport 18 31 38N 81 24W
South Newtane 36 42 55N 72 42W
South Ogden 52 41 12N 112 0W
South Orkney Is. 5 63 0 S 45 0W
South Otselic 39 42 39N 75 47W
South Paris 26 44 14N 70 31W
South Passage 126 26 7 S 113 9 E
South Pekin 21 40 30N 89 39W
South Pittsburg 49 35 1N 85 42W
South Platte → 34 41 7N 100 42W
South Pole 5 90 0 S 0 0 E
South Pomfret 36 43 40N 72 33W
South Ponte Vedra Beach 17 30 3N 81 20W
South Porcupine 60 48 30N 81 12W
South Portland 26 43 38N 70 15W
South Range 29 47 4N 88 38W
South River, Canada 60 45 52N 79 23W
South River, U.S.A. 37 40 27N 74 23W
South Ronaldsay 84 58 46N 2 58W
South Royalton 36 43 49N 72 32W
South St. Paul 30 44 53N 93 2W
South San Francisco 14 37 39N 122 24W
South Sandwich Is. 2 57 0 S 27 0W
South Saskatchewan → 63 53 15N 105 5W
South Seal → 63 58 48N 98 8W
South Seaville 37 39 11N 74 46W
South Sentinel I. 112 11 1N 92 16 E
South Shetland Is. 5 62 0 S 59 0W
South Shields 82 54 59N 1 26W
South Shore, Ky. 49 38 43N 82 59W
South Shore, S. Dak. 47 45 7N 96 56W
South Sioux City 34 42 28N 96 24W
South Skunk → 23 41 15N 92 2W
South Stoddard 36 43 4N 72 7W
South Strafford 36 43 49N 72 23W
South Sulphur → 51 33 23N 95 18W
South Superior 56 41 46N 108 58W
South Taranaki Bight 128 39 40 S 174 5 E
South Thompson → 62 50 40N 120 20W
South Torrington 56 42 3N 104 11W
South Tucson 12 32 12N 110 58W
South Twin I. 60 53 7N 79 52W
South Tyne → 82 54 46N 2 25W
South Uist 84 57 20N 7 15W
South Umpqua → 44 43 16N 123 27W
South Venice 17 27 3N 82 25W
South Wayne 55 42 34N 89 53W
South Weare 36 43 5N 71 45W
South Webster 42 38 49N 82 44W

Staunton
Sublette County

Staunton, Ill. 21 39 1N 89 47W
Staunton, Va. 54 38 9N 79 4W
Stavanger 97 58 57N 5 40 E
Staveley 128 43 40 S 171 32 E
Stavelot 87 50 23N 5 55 E
Staveren 87 52 53N 5 22 E
Stavern 97 59 0N 10 1 E
Stavropol 99 45 5N 42 0 E
Stawell 127 37 5 S 142 47 E
Stayton 44 44 48N 122 48W
Staytonville 27 38 50N 75 32W
Stead 38 36 6N 103 12W
Steamboat Canyon 12 35 45N 109 51W
Steamboat Rock 23 42 25N 93 4W
Steamboat Springs 16 40 29N 106 50W
Stearns County ◇ 30 45 35N 94 30W
Stebbins 11 63 31N 162 17W
Stedman 40 35 0N 78 41W
Steel, Mt. 56 41 50N 107 0W
Steele, Ala. 10 33 56N 86 12W
Steele, Mo. 32 36 5N 89 50W
Steele, N. Dak. 41 46 51N 99 55W
Steele City 34 40 2N 97 2W
Steele County ◇, Minn. 30 44 0N 93 10W
Steele County ◇, N. Dak. 41 47 31N 97 50W
Steeleville 21 38 0N 89 40W
Steelton 45 40 14N 76 50W
Steelville 32 37 58N 91 22W
Steen 30 43 31N 96 16W
Steen River 62 59 40N 117 12W
Steenkool = Bintuni 111 2 7 S 133 32 E
Steens Mt. 44 42 35N 118 40W
Steenwijk 87 52 47N 6 7 E
Steep Pt. 126 26 8 S 113 8 E
Steep Rock 63 51 30N 98 48W
Stefanie L. = Chew Bahir 121 4 40N 36 50 E
Stefansson Bay 5 67 20 S 59 8 E
Stehekin 53 48 19N 120 39W
Steiermark □ 88 47 26N 15 0 E
Steinauer 34 40 12N 96 14W
Steinbach 63 49 32N 96 40W
Steinfort 87 49 39N 5 55 E
Steinhatchee 17 29 40N 83 23W
Steinkjer 96 63 59N 11 31 E
Steinkopf 123 29 15 S 17 48 E
Stella, Ky. 48 36 38N 88 24W
Stella, Mo. 32 36 46N 94 12W
Stella, Nebr. 34 40 14N 95 46W
Stella, Tenn. 48 35 2N 87 5W
Stellarton 61 45 32N 62 30W
Stellenbosch 123 33 58S 18 50 E
Stelvio, Paso dello 94 46 32N 10 27 E
Stem 40 36 12N 78 43W
Stendal 88 52 36N 11 50 E
Stensele 96 65 3N 17 8 E
Stepanakert 99 39 40N 46 25 E
Stephen 30 48 27N 96 53W
Stephens 13 33 25N 93 4W
Stephens City 54 39 5N 78 13W
Stephens County ◇, Ga. 18 34 35N 83 15W
Stephens County ◇, Okla. 43 34 30N 97 50W
Stephens County ◇, Tex. 51 32 45N 98 54W
Stephens I. 62 54 10N 130 45W
Stephens Knob 49 36 37N 84 20W
Stephenson 29 45 25N 87 36W
Stephenson County ◇ 21 42 20N 89 40W
Stephenville, Canada 61 48 31N 58 35W
Stephenville, U.S.A. 51 32 13N 98 12W
Stepnoi = Elista 99 46 16N 44 14 E
Stepnyak 100 52 50N 70 50 E
Steppe 102 50 0N 50 0 E
Steptoe 53 47 0N 117 21W
Steptoe Valley 35 39 50N 114 45W
Sterling, Alaska 11 60 32N 150 46W
Sterling, Colo. 16 40 37N 103 13W
Sterling, Ga. 18 31 16N 81 34W
Sterling, Idaho 20 43 2N 112 44W
Sterling, Ill. 21 41 48N 89 42W
Sterling, Kans. 24 38 13N 98 12W
Sterling, Mass. 28 42 26N 71 46W
Sterling, Mich. 29 44 2N 84 2W
Sterling, N. Dak. 41 46 49N 100 17W
Sterling, Nebr. 34 40 28N 96 23W
Sterling, Okla. 43 34 45N 98 10W
Sterling, Utah 52 39 12N 111 42W
Sterling, Va. 54 39 1N 77 26W
Sterling City 50 31 51N 101 0W
Sterling County ◇ 50 32 0N 101 0W
Sterling Reservoir 16 40 47N 103 16W
Sterlington 25 32 42N 92 5W
Sterlitamak 98 53 40N 56 0 E
Stetsonville 55 45 4N 90 19W
Stettin = Szczecin 88 53 27N 14 27 E
Stettler 62 52 19N 112 40W
Steuben County ◇, Ind. 22 41 40N 85 0W
Steuben County ◇, N.Y. 39 42 15N 77 20W
Steubens 55 43 11N 90 52W
Steubenville, Ky. 49 36 53N 84 48W
Steubenville, Ohio 42 40 22N 80 37W
Stevens County ◇, Kans. 24 37 15N 101 20W
Stevens County ◇, Minn. 30 45 40N 96 0W
Stevens County ◇, Wash. 53 48 30N 118 0W
Stevens Point 55 44 31N 89 34W
Stevens Pottery 18 32 57N 83 17W
Stevens Village 11 66 1N 149 6W
Stevenson, Ala. 10 34 52N 85 50W
Stevenson, Wash. 53 45 42N 121 53W
Stevenson L. 63 53 55N 96 0W
Stevensville, Md. 27 38 59N 76 19W
Stevensville, Mont. 33 46 30N 114 5W
Steward 21 41 51N 89 1W
Stewardson 21 39 16N 88 38W
Stewart, B.C., Canada 62 55 56N 129 57W
Stewart, N.W.T., Canada 58 63 19N 139 26W
Stewart, Ga. 18 33 25N 83 52W
Stewart, Minn. 30 44 43N 94 29W
Stewart, Miss. 31 33 27N 89 26W
Stewart, I. 78 54 50 S 71 15W
Stewart County ◇, Ga. 18 32 5N 84 50W
Stewart County ◇, Tenn. 48 36 20N 87 55W
Stewart I. 128 46 58 S 167 54 E
Stewarts Point 14 38 39N 123 24W
Stewartstown, N.H. 36 45 0N 71 31W
Stewartstown, Pa. 45 39 45N 76 36W
Stewartsville 32 39 45N 94 30W
Stewartville 30 43 51N 92 29W
Stewiacke 61 45 9N 63 22W
Steyr 88 48 3N 14 25 E
Stickney 47 43 35N 98 26W
Stidham 43 35 22N 95 42W
Stigler 43 35 15N 95 8W
Stikine → 62 56 40N 132 30W
Stiles 50 31 25N 101 34W
Stilesville 22 39 38N 86 38W
Still Pond 27 39 20N 76 3W
Stillhouse Hollow L. 51 31 2N 97 32W
Stillmore 18 32 27N 82 13W
Stillwater, N.Z. 128 42 27 S 171 20 E
Stillwater, Minn. 30 45 3N 92 49W
Stillwater, Nev. 35 39 31N 118 33W
Stillwater, Okla. 43 36 7N 97 4W
Stillwater County ◇ 33 45 48N 109 15W
Stillwater Range 35 39 50N 118 5W
Stillwater Reservoir 39 43 54N 75 3W
Stillwell 18 32 23N 81 15W
Stilwell, Kans. 24 38 46N 94 39W
Stilwell, Okla. 43 35 49N 94 38W
Stinnett 50 35 50N 101 27W
Stinson Lake 36 43 51N 71 48W
Stip 95 41 42N 22 10 E
Stirling, Canada 62 49 30N 112 30W
Stirling, U.K. 84 56 7N 3 57W
Stirling City 14 39 54N 121 32W
Stirling Ra. 126 34 23 S 118 0 E
Stirrat 54 37 44N 82 0W
Stites 20 46 6N 115 59W
Stock Island 17 24 32N 81 34W
Stockbridge, Ga. 18 33 33N 84 14W
Stockbridge, Mass. 28 42 17N 73 19W
Stockbridge, Mich. 29 42 27N 84 11W
Stockbridge Indian Reservation 55 44 50N 88 50W
Stockdale 51 29 14N 97 58W
Stockerau 88 48 24N 16 12 E
Stockett 33 47 21N 111 10W
Stockham 34 40 43N 97 56W
Stockholm, Sweden 97 59 20N 18 3 E
Stockholm, Maine 26 47 3N 68 8W
Stockholm, S. Dak. 47 45 6N 96 48W
Stockholm, Wis. 55 44 29N 92 16W
Stockland 21 40 37N 87 36W
Stockly 27 38 40N 75 20W
Stockport, U.K. 82 53 25N 2 11W
Stockport, Iowa 23 40 51N 91 50W
Stockport, Ohio 42 39 33N 81 48W
Stockton, Ala. 10 31 0N 87 52W
Stockton, Calif. 14 37 58N 121 17W
Stockton, Ill. 21 42 21N 90 1W
Stockton, Kans. 24 39 26N 99 16W
Stockton, Md. 27 38 3N 75 25W
Stockton, Minn. 30 44 2N 91 46W
Stockton, Mo. 32 37 42N 93 48W
Stockton, N.J. 37 40 24N 74 58W
Stockton, Utah 52 40 27N 112 22W
Stockton I. 55 46 57N 90 35W
Stockton L. 32 37 42N 93 46W
Stockton-on-Tees 82 54 34N 1 20W
Stockton Plateau 50 30 30N 102 30W
Stockville 34 40 32N 100 23W
Stoddard 55 43 40N 91 13W
Stoddard County ◇ 32 36 50N 90 0W
Stoke-on-Trent 82 53 1N 2 11W
Stokes Bay 60 45 0N 81 28W
Stokes County ◇ 40 36 20N 80 10W
Stokkseyri 96 63 50N 21 2W
Stokksnes 96 64 14N 14 58W
Stolac 95 43 8N 17 59 E
Stolbovaya 101 64 50N 153 50 E
Stolbovoy, Ostrov 101 56 44N 163 14 E
Stolnici 95 44 31N 24 48 E
Stone 20 42 1N 112 42W
Stone County ◇, Ark. 13 35 52N 92 7W
Stone County ◇, Miss. 31 30 47N 89 8W
Stone County ◇, Mo. 32 36 45N 93 25W
Stone Harbor 37 39 3N 74 45W
Stone Mountain 18 33 49N 84 10W
Stone Mt. 36 44 34N 71 40W
Stoneboro 45 41 20N 80 7W
Stonega 54 36 57N 82 48W
Stoneham 16 40 36N 103 40W
Stonehaven 84 56 58N 2 11W
Stoner 16 37 35N 108 19W
Stoneville 40 36 28N 79 54W
Stonewall, Canada 63 50 10N 97 19W
Stonewall, Ark. 13 36 14N 90 32W
Stonewall, Colo. 16 37 9N 105 1W
Stonewall, La. 25 32 17N 93 50W
Stonewall, Miss. 31 32 8N 88 47W
Stonewall, Okla. 43 34 39N 96 32W
Stonewall County ◇ 50 33 8N 100 14W
Stonington, Colo. 16 37 18N 102 11W
Stonington, Ill. 21 39 44N 89 12W
Stonington, Maine 26 44 9N 68 40W
Stony Creek 54 36 57N 77 24W
Stony Gorge Reservoir 14 39 35N 122 32W
Stony I. 39 43 54N 76 20W
Stony L. 63 58 51N 98 40W
Stony Point, Mich. 29 41 57N 83 16W
Stony Point, N.C. 40 35 52N 81 3W
Stony Pt. 39 43 50N 76 18W
Stony Rapids 63 59 16N 105 50W
Stony Ridge 42 41 31N 83 30W
Stony River 11 61 47N 156 35W
Stony Tunguska = Tunguska, Nizhnyaya → 101 65 48N 88 4 E
Stonyford 14 39 23N 122 33W
Stora Lulevatten 96 67 10N 19 30 E
Stora Sjöfallet 96 67 29N 18 40 E
Storavan 96 65 45N 18 10 E
Store Bælt 97 55 20N 11 0 E
Støren 96 63 3N 10 18 E
Storey County ◇ 35 39 30N 119 35W
Storm B. 127 43 10 S 147 30 E
Storm L. 23 42 38N 95 13W
Storm Lake 23 42 39N 95 13W
Stormberg 123 31 16 S 26 17 E
Stormy Mt. 53 47 54N 120 21W
Stornoway 84 58 12N 6 23W
Storrs 28 41 49N 72 15W
Storsjön 96 62 50N 13 8 E
Storuman 96 65 5N 17 10 E
Storuman,sjö 96 65 13N 16 50 E
Story 56 44 35N 106 53W
Story City 23 42 11N 93 36W
Story County ◇ 23 42 0N 93 25W
Stotesbury 32 37 59N 94 34W
Stoughton, Canada 63 49 40N 103 0W
Stoughton, Mass. 28 42 8N 71 6W
Stoughton, Wis. 55 42 55N 89 13W
Stour →, Dorset, U.K. 83 50 48N 2 7W
Stour →, Hereford & Worcs., U.K. 83 52 25N 2 13W
Stour →, Kent, U.K. 83 51 15N 1 20 E
Stour →, Suffolk, U.K. 83 51 55N 1 5 E
Stourbridge 83 52 28N 2 8W
Stout 23 42 32N 92 43W
Stout, L. 63 52 0N 94 40W
Stoutland 32 37 49N 92 31W
Stoutsville, Mo. 32 39 33N 91 51W
Stoutsville, Ohio 42 39 36N 82 50W
Stovall, Ga. 18 32 58N 84 51W
Stovall, N.C. 40 36 27N 78 35W
Stover 32 38 27N 92 59W
Stowe 36 44 28N 72 41W
Stowell 51 29 47N 94 23W
Stowmarket 83 52 11N 1 0 E
Strabane 85 54 50N 7 28W
Strabane □ 85 54 45N 7 25W
Strafford, Mo. 32 37 16N 93 7W
Strafford, N.H. 36 43 19N 71 12W
Strafford County ◇ 36 43 15N 71 0W
Strahan 127 42 9 S 145 20 E
Straldzha 95 42 35N 26 40 E
Stralsund 88 54 17N 13 5 E
Strand 123 34 9 S 18 48 E
Strandburg 47 45 3N 96 46W
Strandquist 30 48 29N 96 27W
Strang 34 40 25N 97 35W
Strangford, L. 85 54 30N 5 37W
Stranraer 84 54 54N 5 0W
Strasbourg, Canada 63 51 4N 104 55W
Strasbourg, France 90 48 35N 7 42 E
Strasburg, Colo. 16 39 44N 104 20W
Strasburg, Mo. 32 38 46N 94 10W
Strasburg, N. Dak. 41 46 8N 100 10W
Strasburg, Ohio 42 40 36N 81 32W
Strasburg, Pa. 45 39 59N 76 11W
Strasburg, Va. 54 38 59N 78 22W
Stratford, Canada 60 43 23N 81 0W
Stratford, N.Z. 128 39 20 S 174 19 E
Stratford, Calif. 15 36 11N 119 49W
Stratford, Conn. 28 41 12N 73 8W
Stratford, Iowa 23 42 16N 93 56W
Stratford, N.H. 36 44 42N 71 36W
Stratford, Okla. 43 34 48N 96 58W
Stratford, S. Dak. 47 45 19N 98 18W
Stratford, Tex. 50 36 20N 102 4W
Stratford, Wis. 55 44 48N 90 4W
Stratford-on-Avon 83 52 12N 1 42W
Strath Spey 84 57 15N 3 40W
Stratham 36 43 3N 70 55W
Strathclyde □ 84 56 0N 4 50W
Strathcona 30 48 33N 96 10W
Strathcona Prov. Park 62 49 38N 125 40W
Strathmere 37 39 12N 74 40W
Strathmore, Canada 62 51 5N 113 18W
Strathmore, U.K. 84 56 40N 3 4W
Strathmore, U.S.A. 15 36 9N 119 4W
Strathnaver 62 53 20N 122 33W
Strathpeffer 84 57 35N 4 32W
Strathroy 60 42 58N 81 38W
Strathy Pt. 84 58 35N 4 0W
Stratton, U.K. 82 51 41N 1 45W
Stratton, Colo. 16 39 19N 102 36W
Stratton, Maine 26 45 8N 70 26W
Stratton, Nebr. 34 40 9N 101 14W
Stratton, Vt. 36 43 4N 72 55W
Stratton Meadows 16 38 45N 104 48W
Straumnes 96 66 26N 23 8W
Strawberry 13 35 58N 91 19W
Strawberry →, Ark. 13 35 53N 91 13W
Strawberry →, Utah 52 40 10N 110 24W
Strawberry Mt. 44 44 19N 118 43W
Strawberry Point 23 42 41N 91 32W
Strawberry Reservoir 52 40 8N 111 9W
Strawn, Ill. 21 40 39N 88 24W
Strawn, Tex. 51 32 33N 98 30W
Streaky Bay 126 32 48 S 134 13 E
Streator 21 41 8N 88 50W
Streeter 41 46 39N 99 21W
Streetman 51 31 53N 96 19W
Streetsboro 42 41 14N 81 21W
Strehaia 95 44 37N 23 10 E
Strelcha 95 42 25N 24 19 E
Strelka 101 58 5N 93 3 E
Strezhevoy 100 60 42N 77 34 E
Stringer 31 31 52N 89 16W
Stroeder 78 40 12 S 62 37W
Strómboli 94 38 48N 15 12 E
Stromeferry 84 57 20N 5 33W
Stromness 84 58 58N 3 18W
Ströms vattudal 96 64 15N 14 55 E
Stromsburg 34 41 7N 97 36W
Strömstad 97 58 55N 11 15 E
Strömsund 96 63 51N 15 33 E
Strong 13 33 7N 92 21W
Strong → 31 31 51N 90 8W
Strong City, Kans. 24 38 24N 96 32W
Strong City, Okla. 43 35 40N 99 36W
Stronghurst 21 40 45N 90 55W
Strongville 42 41 19N 81 50W
Stronsay 84 59 8N 2 38W
Stroud, U.K. 83 51 44N 2 12W
Stroud, U.S.A. 43 35 45N 96 40W
Stroudsburg 45 40 59N 75 12W
Struer 97 56 30N 8 35 E
Strum 55 44 33N 91 24W
Strumica 95 41 28N 22 41 E
Struthers, Canada 60 48 41N 85 51W
Struthers, U.S.A. 42 41 4N 80 39W
Stryama 95 42 16N 24 54 E
Stryker, Mont. 33 48 41N 114 46W
Stryker, Ohio 42 41 30N 84 25W
Strzelecki Cr. → 127 29 37 S 139 59 E
Stuart, Fla. 17 27 12N 80 15W
Stuart, Iowa 23 41 30N 94 19W
Stuart, Nebr. 34 42 36N 99 8W
Stuart, Okla. 43 34 54N 96 6W
Stuart, Va. 54 36 38N 80 16W
Stuart → 62 54 0N 123 35W
Stuart, Mt. 53 47 29N 120 54W
Stuart I. 11 63 35N 162 30W
Stuart L. 62 54 30N 124 30W
Stuart Range 126 29 10 S 134 56 E
Studen Kladenets, Yazovir 95 41 37N 25 30 E
Studley 24 39 21N 100 10W
Stull, L. 63 54 24N 92 34W
Stump L. 41 47 54N 98 24W
Stumpy Point 40 35 42N 75 44W
Stung Treng 112 13 31N 105 58 E
Stupart → 63 56 0N 93 25W
Sturgeon 32 39 14N 92 17W
Sturgeon →, Mich. 29 45 24N 84 38W
Sturgeon →, Mich. 29 47 2N 88 30W
Sturgeon B., Canada 63 52 0N 97 50W
Sturgeon B., U.S.A. 29 45 45N 85 0W
Sturgeon Bay 55 44 50N 87 23W
Sturgeon Falls 60 46 25N 79 57W
Sturgeon L., Alta., Canada 62 55 6N 117 32W
Sturgeon L., Ont., Canada 60 50 0N 90 45W
Sturgeon Lake 30 46 23N 92 49W
Sturgis, Ky. 48 37 33N 87 59W
Sturgis, Mich. 29 41 48N 85 25W
Sturgis, S. Dak. 47 44 25N 103 31W
Sturt Cr. → 126 20 8 S 127 24 E
Sturtevant 55 42 42N 87 54W
Stutsman County ◇ 41 47 0N 99 0W
Stutterheim 123 32 33 S 27 28 E
Stuttgart, Germany 88 48 46N 9 10 E
Stuttgart, U.S.A. 13 34 30N 91 33W
Stykkishólmur 96 65 2N 22 40W
Styria = Steiermark □ 88 47 26N 15 0 E
Styx → 10 30 31N 87 27W
Su Xian 115 33 41N 116 59 E
Suakin 121 19 8N 37 20 E
Suapure → 70 6 48N 67 1W
Suaqui 64 29 12N 109 41W
Suatá → 71 7 52N 65 22W
Subang 111 6 34 S 107 45 E
Subansiri → 109 26 48N 93 50 E
Subi 110 2 58N 108 50 E
Sublette, Ill. 21 41 39N 89 14W
Sublette, Kans. 24 37 29N 100 51W
Sublette County ◇ 56 43 0N 110 0W

Subotica Svishtov

Subotica **95** 46 6N 19 49 E
Sucarnoochee → **10** 32 25N 88 2W
Success, Canada **63** 50 28N 108 6W
Success, U.S.A. **13** 36 27N 90 43W
Success, L. **15** 36 4N 118 55W
Success, Mt. **36** 44 27N 71 5W
Succor Cr. → **20** 43 37N 116 57W
Suceava **89** 47 38N 26 16 E
Suchan **116** 43 8N 133 9 E
Suchil **64** 23 38N 103 55W
Suchitoto **66** 13 56N 89 0W
Suchou = Suzhou **115** 31 19N 120 38 E
Süchow = Xuzhou **115** 34 18N 117 10 E
Sucio → **70** 7 27N 77 7W
Suck → **85** 53 17N 8 18W
Sucre, Bolivia **73** 19 0 S 65 15W
Sucre, Colombia **70** 8 49N 74 44W
Sucre □, Colombia **70** 8 50N 75 40W
Sucre □, Venezuela **71** 10 25N 63 30W
Sucuaro **70** 4 34N 68 50W
Sucuriju **74** 1 39N 49 57W
Sucuriú → **73** 20 47 S 51 38W
Sud, Pte. **61** 49 3N 62 14W
Sud-Ouest, Pte. du **61** 49 23N 63 36W
Sudair **106** 26 0N 45 0 E
Sudan ■ **121** 15 0N 30 0 E
Sudbury, Canada **60** 46 30N 81 0W
Sudbury, U.K. **83** 52 2N 0 44 E
Sudbury, U.S.A. **28** 42 23N 71 25W
Sûdd **121** 8 20N 30 0 E
Suddie **71** 7 8N 58 29W
Sudetan Mts. = Sudety **88** 50 20N 16 45 E
Sudety **88** 50 20N 16 45 E
Sudirman, Pegunungan **111** 4 30 S 137 0 E
Sudiţi **95** 44 35N 27 38 E
Sudlersville **27** 39 11N 75 52W
Sueca **91** 39 12N 0 21W
Suez = El Suweis **121** 29 58N 32 31 E
Sûf **104** 32 19N 35 49 E
Suffield, Canada **63** 50 12N 111 10W
Suffield, U.S.A. **28** 41 59N 72 39W
Suffolk **54** 36 44N 76 35W
Suffolk □ **83** 52 16N 1 0 E
Suffolk County ◇, Mass. **28** 42 21N 71 5W
Suffolk County ◇, N.Y. **39** 40 50N 73 0W
Sufuk **107** 23 50N 51 50 E
Sugag **95** 45 47N 23 37 E
Sugar →, Ill. **21** 42 26N 89 12W
Sugar →, N.H. **36** 43 24N 72 24W
Sugar City, Colo. **16** 38 14N 103 40W
Sugar City, Idaho **20** 43 52N 111 45W
Sugar Cr. →, Ill. **21** 40 50N 87 45W
Sugar Cr. →, Iroquois, Ind. **22** 39 51N 87 21W
Sugar Cr. →, Mason, Ill. **21** 40 9N 89 38W
Sugar Creek **45** 41 47N 76 27W
Sugar Grove, N.C. **40** 36 15N 81 47W
Sugar Grove, Ohio **42** 39 38N 82 33W
Sugar Hill **18** 34 6N 84 2W
Sugar I. **29** 46 25N 84 12W
Sugar Land **51** 29 37N 95 38W
Sugar Notch **45** 41 12N 75 56W
Sugarloaf Mt. **43** 35 2N 94 28W
Sugartown **25** 30 50N 93 1W
Sugarville **52** 39 28N 112 39W
Sugden **43** 34 5N 97 59W
Sugluk = Saglouc **59** 62 14N 75 38W
Suhaia, L. **95** 43 45N 25 15 E
Suhār **107** 24 20N 56 40 E
Suhbaatar **113** 50 17N 106 10 E
Sui Xian, Henan, China **115** 34 25N 115 2 E
Sui Xian, Henan, China **115** 31 42N 113 24 E
Suiá Missu → **73** 11 13 S 53 15W
Suichang **115** 28 29N 119 15 E
Suichuan **115** 26 20N 114 32 E
Suide **114** 37 30N 110 12 E
Suifenhe **114** 44 25N 131 10 E
Suihua **114** 46 32N 126 55 E
Suining, Hunan, China **115** 26 35N 110 10 E
Suining, Sichuan, China **115** 30 26N 105 35 E
Suiping **115** 33 10N 113 59 E
Suir → **85** 52 15N 7 10W
Suisun B. **14** 38 5N 122 0W
Suisun City **14** 38 15N 122 2W
Suitland **27** 38 51N 76 56W
Suixi **115** 21 19N 110 18 E
Suizhong **114** 40 21N 120 20 E
Sukabumi **111** 6 56 S 106 50 E
Sukadana, Kalimantan, Indonesia **110** 1 10 S 110 0 E
Sukadana, Sumatera, Indonesia **110** 5 5 S 105 33 E
Sukagawa **117** 37 17N 140 23 E
Sukaraja **110** 2 28 S 110 25 E
Sukarnapura = Jayapura **111** 2 28 S 140 38 E
Sukhindol **95** 43 11N 25 10 E
Sukhona → **98** 60 30N 45 0 E
Sukhumi **99** 43 0N 41 0 E
Sukkur **108** 27 42N 68 54 E
Sukkur Barrage **108** 27 50N 68 45 E
Sukumo **117** 32 56N 132 44 E
Sukunka → **62** 55 45N 121 15W
Sul, Canal do **74** 0 10 S 48 30W
Sula, Kepulauan **111** 1 45 S 125 0 E
Sulaco → **66** 15 2N 87 44W
Sulaiman Range **108** 30 30N 69 50 E
Sulam Tsor **104** 33 4N 35 6 E
Sulawesi □ **111** 2 0 S 120 0 E
Sulima **120** 6 58N 11 32W
Sulina **89** 45 10N 29 40 E
Sulitälma **96** 67 17N 17 28 E
Sulitjelma **96** 67 9N 16 3 E
Sullana **72** 4 52 S 80 39W
Sulligent **10** 33 54N 88 8W
Sullivan, Ill. **21** 39 36N 88 37W
Sullivan, Ind. **22** 39 6N 87 24W
Sullivan, Ky. **48** 37 30N 87 57W
Sullivan, Mo. **32** 38 13N 91 10W
Sullivan Bay **62** 50 55N 126 50W
Sullivan County ◇, Ind. **22** 39 5N 87 25W
Sullivan County ◇, Mo. **32** 40 10N 93 5W
Sullivan County ◇, N.H. **36** 43 20N 72 15W
Sullivan County ◇, N.Y. **39** 41 45N 74 45W
Sullivan County ◇, Pa. **45** 41 30N 76 35W
Sullivan County ◇, Tenn. **49** 36 32N 82 19W
Sullivan I. = Lambi Kyun **112** 10 50N 98 20 E
Sully County ◇ **47** 44 45N 100 0W
Sulphur, La. **25** 30 14N 93 23W
Sulphur, Okla. **43** 34 31N 96 58W
Sulphur →, Ark. **13** 33 7N 93 52W
Sulphur →, S. Dak. **47** 44 45N 102 0W
Sulphur →, Tex. **51** 33 7N 93 52W
Sulphur Draw → **50** 33 12N 102 17W
Sulphur Pt. **62** 60 56N 114 48W
Sulphur Rock **13** 35 45N 91 30W
Sulphur Springs, Ark. **13** 36 29N 94 28W
Sulphur Springs, Ind. **22** 40 0N 85 27W
Sulphur Springs, Tex. **51** 33 8N 95 36W
Sulphur Springs Draw → **50** 32 12N 101 36W
Sultan, Canada **60** 47 36N 82 47W
Sultan, U.S.A. **53** 47 52N 121 49W
Sultanpur **109** 26 18N 82 4 E
Sultsa **98** 63 27N 46 2 E
Sulu Arch. **111** 6 0N 121 0 E
Sulu Sea **111** 8 0N 120 0 E
Suluq **121** 31 44N 20 14 E
Sulzberger Ice Shelf **5** 78 0 S 150 0 E
Sumac **18** 34 53N 84 48W
Sumalata **111** 1 0N 122 31 E
Sumampa **76** 29 25 S 63 29W
Sumas **53** 48 59N 122 15W
Sumatera □ **110** 0 40N 100 20 E
Sumatra = Sumatera □ **110** 0 40N 100 20 E
Sumatra, Fla. **17** 30 1N 84 59W
Sumatra, Mont. **33** 46 37N 107 33W
Sumba **111** 9 45 S 119 35 E
Sumba, Selat **111** 9 0 S 118 40 E
Sumbawa **110** 8 26 S 117 30 E
Sumbawa Besar **110** 8 30 S 117 26 E
Sumbe **122** 11 10 S 13 48 E
Sumburgh Hd. **84** 59 52N 1 17W
Sumé **74** 7 39 S 36 55W
Sumedang **111** 6 52 S 107 55 E
Sumenep **111** 7 1 S 113 52 E
Summer I. **29** 45 34N 86 39W
Summer L. **44** 42 50N 120 45W
Summer Lake **44** 42 58N 120 47W
Summerdale **10** 30 28N 87 55W
Summerfield, Kans. **24** 39 59N 96 21W
Summerfield, Ohio **42** 39 48N 81 20W
Summerfield, Tex. **50** 34 44N 102 31W
Summerland **62** 49 32N 119 41W
Summerland Key **17** 24 40N 81 27W
Summers County ◇ **54** 37 40N 80 54W
Summerside **61** 46 24N 63 47W
Summersville, Mo. **32** 37 11N 91 40W
Summersville, W. Va. **54** 38 17N 80 51W
Summersville L. **54** 38 13N 80 53W
Summerton **46** 33 36N 80 20W
Summertown, Ga. **18** 32 45N 82 16W
Summertown, Tenn. **48** 35 26N 87 18W
Summerville, Ga. **18** 34 29N 85 21W
Summerville, S.C. **46** 33 1N 80 11W
Summit, Alaska **11** 63 20N 149 7W
Summit, Ill. **21** 41 48N 87 48W
Summit, Ky. **48** 37 34N 86 5W
Summit, Miss. **31** 31 17N 90 28W
Summit, N.J. **37** 40 43N 74 22W
Summit, Okla. **43** 35 40N 95 26W
Summit, Oreg. **44** 44 38N 123 35W
Summit, S. Dak. **47** 45 18N 97 2W
Summit, Utah **52** 37 48N 112 56W
Summit County ◇, Colo. **16** 39 30N 106 0W
Summit County ◇, Ohio **42** 41 8N 81 29W
Summit County ◇, Utah **52** 40 55N 111 0W
Summit L. **35** 41 31N 119 4W
Summit Lake **62** 54 20N 122 40W
Summit Lake Indian Reservation **35** 41 33N 119 2W
Summit Peak **16** 37 21N 106 42W
Sumner, Iowa **23** 42 51N 92 6W
Sumner, Miss. **31** 33 58N 90 22W
Sumner, Mo. **32** 39 39N 93 15W
Sumner, Nebr. **34** 40 57N 99 31W
Sumner, L. **38** 34 40N 104 25W
Sumner County ◇, Kans. **24** 37 15N 97 20W
Sumner County ◇, Tenn. **48** 36 24N 86 27W
Sumoto **117** 34 21N 134 54 E
Sumperk **88** 49 59N 17 0 E
Sumpter **44** 44 45N 118 12W
Sumrall **31** 31 25N 89 33W
Sumter **46** 33 55N 80 21W
Sumter County ◇, Ala. **10** 32 35N 88 11W
Sumter County ◇, Fla. **17** 28 45N 82 10W
Sumter County ◇, Ga. **18** 32 0N 84 10W
Sumter County ◇, S.C. **46** 33 50N 80 30W
Sumter National Forest **46** 34 50N 83 0W
Sumy **99** 50 57N 34 50 E
Sun **25** 30 39N 89 54W
Sun → **33** 47 29N 111 19W
Sun City, Ariz. **12** 33 36N 112 17W
Sun City, Calif. **15** 33 42N 117 11W
Sun City, Kans. **24** 37 23N 98 55W
Sun Prairie **55** 43 11N 89 13W
Sun River **33** 47 32N 111 43W
Sun Valley **20** 43 42N 114 21W
Sunagawa **116** 43 29N 141 55 E
Sunapee **36** 43 23N 72 7W
Sunapee L. **36** 43 23N 72 5W
Sunart, L. **84** 56 42N 5 43W
Sunbright **49** 36 15N 84 40W
Sunburg **30** 45 21N 95 14W
Sunburst **33** 48 53N 111 55W
Sunbury, N.C. **40** 36 27N 76 37W
Sunbury, Pa. **45** 40 52N 76 48W
Sunchales **76** 30 58 S 61 35W
Suncho Corral **76** 27 55 S 63 27W
Sunchon **115** 34 52N 127 31 E
Suncook **36** 43 8N 71 27W
Suncook → **36** 43 8N 71 28W
Sunda, Selat **110** 6 20 S 105 30 E
Sunda Is. **124** 5 0 S 105 0 E
Sundance **56** 44 24N 104 23W
Sundarbans, The **109** 22 0N 89 0 E
Sundargarh **109** 22 4N 84 5 E
Sunderland, U.K. **82** 54 54N 1 22W
Sunderland, U.S.A. **27** 38 40N 76 36W
Sundre **62** 51 49N 114 38W
Sundridge **60** 45 45N 79 25W
Sundsvall **96** 62 23N 17 17 E
Sunflower **31** 33 33N 90 32W
Sunflower → **31** 32 40N 90 40W
Sunflower, Mt. **24** 39 6N 102 2W
Sunflower County ◇ **31** 33 44N 90 33W
Sungaigerung **110** 2 59 S 104 52 E
Sungailiat **110** 1 51 S 106 8 E
Sungaipakning **110** 1 19N 102 0 E
Sungaipenuh **110** 2 1 S 101 20 E
Sungaitiram **110** 0 45 S 117 8 E
Sungei Patani **112** 5 38N 100 29 E
Sungei Siput **112** 4 51N 101 6 E
Sungguminasa **111** 5 17 S 119 30 E
Sunghua Chiang = Songhua Jiang → **114** 47 45N 132 30 E
Sungtao Hu **115** 19 20N 109 35 E
Sungurlu **106** 40 12N 34 21 E
Sunland Park **38** 31 50N 106 40W
Sunman **22** 39 14N 85 6W
Sunnyside, Utah **52** 39 34N 110 23W
Sunnyside, Wash. **53** 46 20N 120 0W
Sunnyvale **14** 37 23N 122 2W
Sunol **34** 41 9N 102 46W
Sunray, Okla. **43** 34 25N 97 58W
Sunray, Tex. **50** 36 1N 101 49W
Sunrise **56** 42 20N 104 42W
Sunrise Manor **35** 36 12N 115 3W
Sunset, La. **25** 30 25N 92 4W
Sunset, Utah **52** 41 10N 112 0W
Sunset Beach **19** 21 40N 158 3W
Sunset Crater National Monument **12** 35 20N 111 20W
Suntar **101** 62 15N 117 30 E
Suntrana **11** 63 52N 148 51W
Suoyarvi **98** 62 12N 32 23 E
Supai **12** 36 15N 112 41W
Supamo → **71** 6 48N 61 50W
Supaul **109** 26 10N 86 40 E
Supe **72** 11 0 S 77 30W
Superior, Ariz. **12** 33 18N 111 6W
Superior, Iowa **23** 43 26N 94 57W
Superior, Mont. **33** 47 12N 114 53W
Superior, Nebr. **34** 40 1N 98 4W
Superior, Wis. **55** 46 44N 92 6W
Superior, L. **55** 47 0N 90 0W
Superior National Forest **30** 47 40N 92 45W
Suphan Buri **112** 14 14N 100 10 E
Suphan Daği **106** 38 54N 42 48 E
Suphur Springs Range **35** 40 15N 116 0W
Supriori, Kepulauan **111** 1 0 S 136 0 E
Suqian **115** 33 54N 118 8 E
Suqualena **31** 32 27N 88 50W
Sūr, Lebanon **104** 33 19N 35 16 E
Sūr, Oman **107** 22 34N 59 32 E
Sur, Pt. **14** 36 18N 121 54W
Sura → **98** 56 6N 46 0 E
Surabaja = Surabaya **111** 7 17 S 112 45 E
Surabaya **111** 7 17 S 112 45 E
Suraia **95** 45 40N 27 25 E
Surakarta **111** 7 35 S 110 48 E
Surat **108** 21 12N 72 55 E
Surat Thani **112** 9 6N 99 20 E
Suratgarh **108** 29 18N 73 55 E
Surduc Pasul **95** 45 21N 23 23 E
Sûre → **87** 49 44N 6 31 E
Surf City, N.C. **40** 34 26N 77 33W
Surf City, N.J. **37** 39 40N 74 10W
Surfside **17** 25 53N 80 8W
Surfside Beach **46** 33 37N 78 57W
Surgut **100** 61 14N 73 20 E
Surianu **95** 45 33N 23 31 E
Suriapet **108** 17 10N 79 40 E
Şūrīf **104** 31 40N 35 4 E
Surigao **111** 9 47N 125 29 E
Surin **112** 14 50N 103 34 E
Surinam ■ **71** 4 0N 56 0W
Suriname □ **71** 5 30N 55 0W
Suriname → **71** 5 50N 55 15W
Suring **55** 44 59N 88 22W
Surprise, Ariz. **12** 33 38N 112 19W
Surprise, Nebr. **34** 41 6N 97 19W
Surprise L. **62** 59 40N 133 15W
Surrency **18** 31 44N 82 12W
Surrey **41** 48 14N 101 6W
Surrey □ **83** 51 16N 0 30W
Surry, N.H. **36** 43 3N 72 18W
Surry, Va. **54** 37 8N 76 50W
Surry County ◇, N.C. **40** 36 20N 80 45W
Surry County ◇, Va. **54** 37 8N 76 50W
Surt **121** 31 11N 16 39 E
Surt, Khalīj **121** 31 40N 18 30 E
Surtsey **96** 63 20N 20 30W
Surubim **74** 7 50 S 35 45W
Suruga-Wan **117** 34 45N 138 30 E
Surumu → **71** 3 22N 60 19W
Susa **94** 45 8N 7 3 E
Susaki **117** 33 22N 133 17 E
Sūsangerd **106** 31 35N 48 6 E
Susanino **101** 52 50N 140 14 E
Susank **24** 38 38N 98 46W
Susanville **14** 40 25N 120 39W
Susquehanna → **45** 39 33N 76 5W
Susquehanna County ◇ **45** 41 55N 75 50W
Susquehanna Depot **45** 41 57N 75 36W
Susques **76** 23 35 S 66 25W
Sussex, Canada **61** 45 45N 65 37W
Sussex, N.J. **37** 41 13N 74 37W
Sussex, Va. **54** 36 55N 77 17W
Sussex, Wis. **55** 43 8N 88 13W
Sussex, Wyo. **56** 43 42N 106 18W
Sussex, E. □ **83** 51 0N 0 20 E
Sussex, W. □ **83** 51 0N 0 30W
Sussex County ◇, Del. **27** 38 45N 75 20W
Sussex County ◇, N.J. **37** 41 15N 74 45W
Sussex County ◇, Va. **54** 36 55N 77 17W
Sustut → **62** 56 20N 127 30W
Susuman **101** 62 47N 148 10 E
Susunu **111** 3 20 S 133 25 E
Sutcliffe **35** 39 57N 119 36W
Şuţeşti **95** 45 13N 27 27 E
Sutherland, S. Africa **123** 32 33 S 20 40 E
Sutherland, Iowa **23** 42 58N 95 29W
Sutherland, Nebr. **34** 41 10N 101 8W
Sutherland Falls **128** 44 48 S 167 46 E
Sutherland Pt. **127** 28 15 S 153 35 E
Sutherland Reservoir **34** 41 6N 101 10W
Sutherlin **44** 43 23N 123 19W
Sutlej → **108** 29 23N 71 3 E
Sutter **14** 39 10N 121 45W
Sutter County ◇ **14** 39 0N 121 45W
Sutter Creek **14** 38 24N 120 48W
Suttle **10** 32 32N 87 11W
Sutton, N. Dak. **41** 47 24N 98 27W
Sutton, Nebr. **34** 40 36N 97 52W
Sutton, Vt. **36** 44 39N 72 3W
Sutton, W. Va. **54** 38 40N 80 43W
Sutton → **60** 55 15N 83 45W
Sutton County ◇ **50** 30 34N 100 39W
Sutton-in-Ashfield **82** 53 7N 1 20W
Sutton L. **54** 38 40N 80 41W
Suttsu **116** 42 48N 140 14 E
Sutwik I. **11** 56 34N 157 12W
Suva **124** 18 6 S 178 30 E
Suva Planina **95** 43 10N 22 5 E
Suvorov Is. = Suwarrow Is. **125** 15 0 S 163 0W
Suvorovo **95** 43 20N 27 35 E
Suwałki **89** 54 8N 22 59 E
Suwanee **18** 34 3N 84 4W
Suwannee **17** 29 20N 83 9W
Suwannee → **17** 29 17N 83 10W
Suwannee County ◇ **17** 30 15N 83 0W
Suwannee Sd. **17** 29 20N 83 15W
Suwanose-Jima **117** 29 38N 129 43 E
Suwarrow Is. **125** 15 0 S 163 0W
Suweis, Khalîg el **121** 28 40N 33 0 E
Suwŏn **114** 37 17N 127 1 E
Suzdal **98** 56 29N 40 26 E
Suzhou **115** 31 19N 120 38 E
Suzu **117** 37 25N 137 17 E
Suzu-Misaki **117** 37 31N 137 21 E
Suzuka **117** 34 55N 136 36 E
Svalbard **4** 78 0N 17 0 E
Svalbarð **96** 66 12N 15 43W
Svanvik **96** 69 25N 30 3 E
Svappavaara **96** 67 40N 21 3 E
Svartisen **96** 66 40N 13 50 E
Svay Rieng **112** 11 9N 105 45 E
Svealand □ **97** 59 55N 15 0 E
Sveg **97** 62 2N 14 21 E
Svendborg **97** 55 4N 10 35 E
Sverdlovsk **98** 56 50N 60 30 E
Sverdrup Is. **4** 79 0N 97 0W
Svetlaya **116** 46 33N 138 18 E
Svilengrad **95** 41 49N 26 12 E
Svir → **98** 60 30N 32 48 E
Svishtov **95** 43 36N 25 23 E

Svobodnyy Tamburâ

Svobodnyy 101 51 20N 128 0 E
Svoge 95 42 59N 23 23 E
Svolvœr 96 68 15N 14 34 E
Swabian Alps = Schwäbische Alb 88 48 30N 9 30 E
Swain 13 35 51N 93 20W
Swain County ◇ 40 35 30N 83 20W
Swain Reefs 127 21 45 S 152 20 E
Swainsboro 18 32 36N 82 20W
Swakopmund 123 22 37 S 14 30 E
Swale → 82 54 5N 1 20W
Swaledale 23 42 59N 93 19W
Swan → 126 32 3 S 115 45 E
Swan Hill 127 35 20 S 143 33 E
Swan Hills 62 54 42N 115 24W
Swan Islands 66 17 22N 83 57W
Swan L., Canada 63 52 30N 100 40W
Swan L., U.S.A. 47 45 17N 99 51W
Swan Lake 33 47 56N 113 51W
Swan Ra. 33 48 0N 113 45W
Swan River 63 52 10N 101 16W
Swan Valley 20 43 27N 111 20W
Swanage 83 50 36N 1 59W
Swandale 54 38 30N 80 57W
Swannanoa 40 35 36N 82 24W
Swanquarter 40 35 25N 76 20W
Swans I. 26 44 10N 68 26W
Swansboro 40 34 39N 77 7W
Swansea, U.K. 83 51 37N 3 57W
Swansea, U.S.A. 46 33 44N 81 6W
Swanson L. 34 40 10N 101 4W
Swanton, Md. 27 39 27N 79 14W
Swanton, Vt. 36 44 55N 73 8W
Swanville 30 45 55N 94 38W
Swartberge 118 33 20 S 22 0 E
Swartswood 37 41 8N 74 50W
Swartz Creek 29 42 58N 83 50W
Swasey Peak 52 39 23N 113 19W
Swastika 60 48 7N 80 6W
Swatow = Shantou 115 23 18N 116 40 E
Swayzee 22 40 30N 85 50W
Swaziland ■ 123 26 30 S 31 30 E
Swea City 23 43 23N 94 19W
Sweatman 31 33 38N 89 35W
Swedeborg 32 37 55N 92 20W
Sweden 26 46 57N 68 8W
Sweden ■ 97 57 0N 15 0 E
Swedesboro 37 39 45N 75 19W
Swedish Knoll 52 39 0N 111 0W
Sweeny 51 29 3N 95 42W
Sweet Air 27 39 31N 76 32W
Sweet Briar 54 37 33N 79 4W
Sweet Grass County ◇ 33 46 0N 110 0W
Sweet Home, Ark. 13 34 41N 92 15W
Sweet Home, Oreg. 44 44 24N 122 44W
Sweet Springs 32 38 58N 93 25W
Sweetgrass 33 48 59N 111 58W
Sweetwater, Okla. 43 35 25N 99 55W
Sweetwater, Tenn. 49 35 36N 84 28W
Sweetwater, Tex. 50 32 28N 100 25W
Sweetwater → 56 42 31N 107 2W
Sweetwater County ◇ 56 42 0N 109 0W
Sweetwater L. 41 48 13N 98 50W
Swellendam 123 34 1 S 20 26 E
Swenson 50 33 13N 100 19W
Świdnica 88 50 50N 16 30 E
Świebodzin 88 52 15N 15 31 E
Swift County ◇ 30 45 15N 95 45W
Swift Current 63 50 20N 107 45W
Swift Reservoir 53 46 4N 122 3W
Swiftcurrent → 63 50 38N 107 44W
Swifton 13 35 49N 91 8W
Swilly, L. 85 55 12N 7 35W
Swindle, I. 62 52 30N 128 35W
Swindon 83 51 33N 1 47W
Swinemünde = Świnoujście 88 53 54N 14 16 E
Swink, Colo. 16 38 1N 103 38W
Swink, Okla. 43 34 1N 95 12W
Swinomish Indian Reservation 53 48 23N 122 32W
Świnoujście 88 53 54N 14 16 E
Swisher 23 41 50N 91 42W
Swisher County ◇ 50 34 32N 101 46W
Swisshome 44 44 4N 123 48W
Switzerland ■ 88 46 30N 8 0 E
Switzerland County ◇ 22 38 50N 85 0W
Swords, Ireland 85 53 27N 6 15W
Swords, U.S.A. 18 33 33N 83 18W
Swoyerville 45 41 18N 75 53W
Sycamore, Ga. 18 31 40N 83 38W
Sycamore, Ill. 21 41 59N 88 41W
Sycamore, Kans. 24 37 20N 95 43W
Sycamore, Ohio 42 40 57N 83 10W
Sycamore, S.C. 46 33 2N 81 13W
Sycan Marsh 44 42 45N 121 5W
Sydney, Australia 127 33 53 S 151 10 E
Sydney, Canada 61 46 7N 60 7W
Sydney, U.S.A. 41 46 44N 98 46W
Sydney Mines 61 46 18N 60 15W
Sydprøven 4 60 30N 45 35W
Sykeston 41 47 28N 99 24W
Sykesville, Md. 27 39 22N 76 58W
Sykesville, Pa. 45 41 3N 78 50W
Syktyvkar 98 61 45N 50 40 E
Sylacauga 10 33 10N 86 15W
Sylarna 96 63 2N 12 13 E
Sylhet 109 24 54N 91 52 E
Sylva 40 35 23N 83 13W
Sylvan Grove 24 39 1N 98 24W
Sylvan Lake 62 52 20N 114 3W
Sylvania, Ga. 18 32 45N 81 38W
Sylvania, Ohio 42 41 43N 83 42W
Sylvarena 31 32 1N 89 23W
Sylvester, Ga. 18 31 32N 83 50W
Sylvester, Tex. 50 32 43N 100 15W
Sylvia 24 37 57N 98 25W
Sym 100 60 20N 88 18 E
Symerton 21 41 20N 88 3W
Symmes → 42 38 26N 82 27W
Symón 64 24 42N 102 35W
Symsonia 48 36 55N 88 31W
Syracuse, Ind. 22 41 26N 85 45W
Syracuse, Kans. 24 37 59N 101 45W
Syracuse, Mo. 32 38 40N 92 53W
Syracuse, N.Y. 39 43 3N 76 9W
Syracuse, Nebr. 34 40 39N 96 11W
Syrdarya → 100 46 3N 61 0 E
Syria ■ 106 35 0N 38 0 E
Syrian Desert 102 31 0N 40 0 E
Syul'dzhyukyor 101 63 14N 113 32 E
Syutkya 95 41 50N 24 16 E
Syzran 98 53 12N 48 30 E
Szczecin 88 53 27N 14 27 E
Szczecinek 88 53 43N 16 41 E
Szechwan = Sichuan □ 115 31 0N 104 0 E
Szeged 89 46 16N 20 10 E
Székesfehérvár 89 47 15N 18 25 E
Szekszárd 89 46 22N 18 42 E
Szentes 89 46 39N 20 21 E
Szolnok 89 47 10N 20 15 E
Szombathely 88 47 14N 16 38 E

T

Tabacal 76 23 15 S 64 15W
Tabaco 111 13 22N 123 44 E
Ţābah 106 26 55N 42 38 E
Tabajara 73 8 56 S 62 8W
Tabalos 72 6 26 S 76 37W
Tabarka 120 36 56N 8 46 E
Ţabas, Khorāsān, Iran 107 32 48N 60 12 E
Ţabas, Khorāsān, Iran 107 33 35N 56 55 E
Tabasará, Serranía de 66 8 35N 81 40W
Tabasco □ 65 17 45N 93 30W
Tabatinga, Serra da 74 10 30 S 44 0W
Tabelkaza 120 29 50N 0 55 E
Taber 62 49 47N 112 8W
Tabernash 16 39 57N 105 52W
Tabiona 52 40 21N 110 43W
Tabira 74 7 35 S 37 33W
Tablas 111 12 25N 122 2 E
Table B. = Tafelbaai, S. Africa 123 33 35 S 18 25 E
Table B. = Tafelbaai, S. Africa 123 33 35 S 18 25 E
Table B. 61 53 40N 56 25W
Table Mt., S. Africa 123 34 0 S 18 22 E
Table Mt., Ariz. 12 32 49N 110 31W
Table Mt., N. Dak. 41 45 57N 103 48W
Table Rock 34 40 11N 96 6W
Table Rock L. 32 36 36N 93 19W
Table Top 12 32 45N 112 8W
Tábor, Czech. 88 49 25N 14 39 E
Tabor, Israel 104 32 42N 35 24 E
Tabor, Iowa 23 40 54N 95 40W
Tabor, Minn. 30 48 5N 96 52W
Tabor, S. Dak. 47 42 57N 97 40W
Tabor City 40 34 10N 78 52W
Tabora 122 5 2 S 32 50 E
Tabou 120 4 30N 7 20W
Tabrīz 106 38 7N 46 20 E
Tabūk 106 28 23N 36 36 E
Tacámbaro de Codallos 64 19 14N 101 28W
Tacheng 113 46 40N 82 58 E
Tach'ing Shan = Daqing Shan 114 40 40N 111 0 E
Tachira 70 8 7N 72 15 E
Táchira □ 70 8 7N 72 15W
Tacloban 111 11 15N 124 58 E
Tacna, Peru 72 18 0 S 70 20W
Tacna, U.S.A. 12 32 41N 114 1W
Tacna □ 72 17 40 S 70 20W
Tacoma 53 47 14N 122 26W
Taconite Harbor 30 47 32N 90 55W
Tacuarembó 77 31 45 S 56 0W
Tacutu → 71 3 1N 60 29W
Tademaït, Plateau du 120 28 30N 2 30 E
Tadjoura 105 11 50N 42 55 E
Tadmor 128 41 27 S 172 45 E
Tadoule, L. 63 58 36N 98 20W
Tadoussac 61 48 11N 69 42W
Tadzhik S.S.R. □ 100 35 30N 70 0 E
Taegu 114 35 50N 128 37 E
Taejŏn 114 36 20N 127 28 E
Tafalla 91 42 30N 1 41W
Ţafas 104 32 44N 36 5 E
Tafelbaai 123 33 35 S 18 25 E
Tafermaar 111 6 47 S 134 10 E
Tafí Viejo 76 26 43 S 65 17W
Taft, Phil. 111 11 57N 125 30 E
Taft, Calif. 15 35 8N 119 28W
Taft, Fla. 17 28 26N 81 22W
Taft, Okla. 43 35 46N 95 32W
Taft, Tenn. 48 35 1N 86 43W
Taft, Tex. 51 27 59N 97 24W
Taga Dzong 109 27 5N 89 55 E
Taganrog 99 47 12N 38 50 E
Tagbilaran 111 9 39N 123 51 E
Tagish 62 60 19N 134 16W
Tagish L. 62 60 10N 134 20W
Tagliamento → 94 45 38N 13 5 E
Tagna 70 2 24 S 70 37W
Tagua, La 70 0 3N 74 40W
Taguatinga 75 12 16 S 42 26W
Tagum 111 7 33N 125 53 E
Tagus = Tajo → 91 38 40N 9 24W
Tahakopa 128 46 30 S 169 23 E
Tahan, Gunong 112 4 34N 102 17 E
Tahat 120 23 18N 5 33 E
Tāherī 107 27 43N 52 20 E
Tahiti 125 17 37 S 149 27W
Tahlequah 43 35 55N 94 58W
Tahoe, L. 35 39 6N 120 2W
Tahoe City 14 39 10N 120 9W
Tahoe National Forest 14 39 20N 120 30W
Tahoka 50 33 10N 101 48W
Taholah 53 47 21N 124 17W
Tahoua 120 14 57N 5 16 E
Tahquamenon → 29 46 34N 85 2W
Tahta 121 26 44N 31 32 E
Tahuamanu → 72 11 6 S 67 36W
Tahulandang 111 2 27N 125 23 E
Tahuna 111 3 38N 125 30 E
Taï 120 5 55N 7 30W
Tai Hu 115 31 5N 120 10 E
Tai Shan 114 36 25N 117 20 E
Tai'an 114 36 12N 117 8 E
Taiban 38 34 26N 104 1W
Taibei 115 25 4N 121 29 E
Taibus Qi 114 41 54N 115 22 E
T'aichung = Taizhong 115 24 12N 120 35 E
Taidong 115 22 43N 121 9 E
Taieri → 128 46 3 S 170 12 E
Taigu 114 37 28N 112 30 E
Taihang Shan 114 36 0N 113 30 E
Taihape 128 39 41 S 175 48 E
Taihe 115 26 47N 114 52 E
Taihu 115 30 22N 116 20 E
Taijiang 115 26 39N 108 21 E
Taikang, Heilongjiang, China 114 46 50N 124 25 E
Taikang, Henan, China 115 34 5N 114 50 E
Tailai 114 46 23N 123 24 E
Taimyr = Taymyr, Poluostrov 101 75 0N 100 0 E
Taimyr, Oz. 101 74 20N 102 0 E
Tain 84 57 49N 4 4W
Tainan 115 23 17N 120 18 E
Taínaron, Ákra 95 36 22N 22 27 E
Taining 115 26 54N 117 9 E
Taiobeiras 75 15 49 S 42 14W
T'aipei = Taibei 115 25 4N 121 29 E
Taiping 112 4 51N 100 44 E
Taipu 74 5 37 S 35 36W
Taishan 115 22 14N 112 41 E
Taishun 115 27 30N 119 42 E
Taitao, C. 78 45 53 S 75 5W
Taitao, Pen. de 78 46 30 S 75 0W
Taivalkoski 96 65 33N 28 12 E
Taiwan ■ 115 23 30N 121 0 E
Taïyetos Óros 95 37 0N 22 23 E
Taiyib → 104 31 55N 35 17 E
Taiyiba 104 32 36N 35 27 E
Taiyuan 114 37 52N 112 33 E
Taizhong 115 24 12N 120 35 E
Taizhou 115 32 28N 119 55 E
Ta'izz 105 13 35N 44 2 E
Tajapuru, Furo do 74 1 50 S 50 25W
Tajima 117 37 12N 139 46 E
Tajique 38 34 45N 106 17W
Tajitos 64 30 58N 112 18W
Tajo → 91 38 40N 9 24W
Tajumulco, Volcán de 65 15 2N 91 50W
Tājūrā 121 32 51N 13 21 E
Tak 112 16 52N 99 8 E
Takachiho 117 32 42N 131 18 E
Takada 117 37 7N 138 15 E
Takahagi 117 36 43N 140 45 E
Takaka 128 40 51 S 172 50 E
Takamatsu 117 34 20N 134 5 E
Takaoka 117 36 47N 137 0 E
Takapuna 128 36 47 S 174 47 E
Takasaki 117 36 20N 139 0 E
Takatsuki 117 34 51N 135 37 E
Takaungu 122 3 38 S 39 52 E
Takayama 117 36 18N 137 11 E
Take-Shima 117 30 49N 130 26 E
Takefu 117 35 50N 136 10 E
Takeo, Cambodia 112 10 59N 104 47 E
Takeo, Japan 117 33 12N 130 1 E
Tākestān 106 36 0N 49 40 E
Taketa 117 32 58N 131 24 E
Takhār □ 107 36 40N 70 0 E
Takikawa 116 43 33N 141 54 E
Takingeun 110 4 45N 96 50 E
Takla L. 62 55 15N 125 45W
Takla Landing 62 55 30N 125 50W
Takla Makan 102 39 0N 83 0 E
Takoma Park 27 38 59N 77 0W
Takotna 11 62 59N 156 4W
Taku → 62 58 30N 133 50W
Takua Pa 112 7 18N 9 59 E
Takum 120 7 18N 9 36 E
Takutu → 71 3 1N 60 29W
Tala 77 34 21 S 55 46W
Talagante 76 33 40 S 70 50W
Talala 43 36 32N 95 42W
Talamanca, Cordillera de 66 9 20N 83 20W
Talara 72 4 38 S 81 18 E
Talas 100 42 30N 72 13 E
Talaud, Kepulauan 111 4 30N 127 10 E
Talavera de la Reina 91 39 55N 4 46W
Talayan 111 6 52N 124 24 E
Talbert 49 37 25N 83 28W
Talbot, C. 126 13 48 S 126 43 E
Talbot County ◇, Ga. 18 32 45N 84 40W
Talbot County ◇, Md. 27 38 45N 76 0W
Talbotton 18 32 41N 84 32W
Talca 76 35 28 S 71 40W
Talca □ 76 35 20 S 71 46W
Talcahuano 76 36 40 S 73 10W
Talcher 109 21 0N 85 18 E
Talco 51 33 22N 95 6W
Taldy Kurgan 100 45 10N 78 45 E
Talent 44 42 15N 122 47W
Ţalesh, Kūhhā-ye 106 39 0N 48 30 E
Talfīt 104 32 5N 35 17 E
Talguppa 108 14 10N 74 45 E
Tali Post 121 5 55N 30 44 E
Taliabu 111 1 45 S 125 0 E
Taliaferro County ◇ 18 33 35N 82 50W
Talibon 111 10 9N 124 20 E
Talihina 43 34 45N 95 3W
Taling Sung 112 15 5N 99 11 E
Taliwang 110 8 50 S 116 55 E
Talkeetna 11 62 20N 150 6W
Talking Rock 18 34 31N 84 30W
Tall 104 33 0N 35 6 E
Tall 'Afar 106 36 22N 42 27 E
Tall 'Asūr 104 31 59N 35 17 E
Talladega 10 33 26N 86 6W
Talladega County ◇ 10 33 26N 86 6W
Talladega National Forest 10 32 55N 87 15W
Tallahala → 31 31 12N 89 5W
Tallahassee 17 30 27N 84 17W
Tallahatchie County ◇ 31 33 58N 90 22W
Tallahtchie → 31 33 33N 90 10W
Tallapoosa 18 33 45N 85 17W
Tallapoosa → 10 32 30N 86 16W
Tallapoosa County ◇ 10 32 50N 85 46W
Tallassee 10 32 32N 85 54W
Tallering Pk. 126 28 6 S 115 37 E
Talleyville 27 39 48N 75 33W
Tallinn 98 59 22N 24 48 E
Tallmadge 42 41 6N 81 27W
Tallula 21 39 56N 89 56W
Tallulah 25 32 25N 91 11W
Tallulah Falls 18 34 44N 83 24W
Ţallūzā 104 32 17N 35 18 E
Tălmaciu 95 45 38N 24 19 E
Talmage, Kans. 24 39 2N 97 16W
Talmage, Nebr. 34 40 32N 96 1W
Talodi 121 10 35N 30 22 E
Taloga 43 36 2N 98 58W
Talowah 31 31 4N 89 26W
Talpa 51 31 47N 99 43W
Talpa de Allende 64 20 23N 104 51W
Talquin, L. 17 30 23N 84 39W
Taltal 76 25 23 S 70 33W
Taltson → 62 61 24N 112 46W
Taltson L. 63 61 30N 110 15W
Tama 23 41 58N 92 35W
Tama County ◇ 23 42 5N 92 30W
Tamaha 43 35 20N 94 59W
Tamalameque 70 8 52N 73 49W
Tamale 120 9 22N 0 50W
Tamano 117 34 29N 133 59 E
Tamanrasset 120 22 50N 5 30 E
Tamaqua 45 40 48N 75 58W
Tamar → 83 50 33N 4 15W
Támara 70 5 50N 72 10W
Tamarac 17 26 12N 80 10W
Tamarack 30 46 39N 93 8W
Tamaroa 21 38 8N 89 14W
Tamashima 117 34 32N 133 40 E
Tamaské 120 14 49N 5 43 E
Tamaulipas □ 65 24 0N 99 0W
Tamaulipas, Sierra de 65 23 30N 98 20W
Tamazula 64 24 55N 106 58W
Tamazunchale 65 21 16N 98 47W
Tambacounda 120 13 45N 13 40W
Tambelan, Kepulauan 110 1 0N 107 30 E
Tambo 72 12 57 S 74 1W
Tambo → 72 10 42 S 73 47W
Tambo de Mora 72 13 30 S 76 8W
Tambobamba 72 13 54 S 72 8W
Tambopata → 72 13 21 S 69 36W
Tambora 110 8 12 S 118 5 E
Tambov 98 52 45N 41 28 E
Tambuku 111 7 8 S 113 40 E
Tamburâ 121 5 40N 27 25 E

Tâmchekket Tekonsha

Tâmchekket **120** 17 25N 10 40W
Tame **70** 6 28N 71 44W
Tamega → **91** 41 5N 8 21W
Tamenglong **109** 25 0N 93 35 E
Tamgak, Mts. **120** 19 12N 8 35 E
Tamiahua, Laguna de **65** 21 30N 97 30W
Tamiami Canal **17** 25 50N 81 0W
Tamil Nadu □ **108** 11 0N 77 0 E
Tammerfors = Tampere **97** 61 30N 23 50 E
Tammisaari **97** 60 0N 23 26 E
Tamms **21** 37 14N 89 16W
Ţammūn **104** 32 18N 35 23 E
Tamo Abu, Pegunungan **110** 3 10N 115 0 E
Tamora **34** 40 54N 97 14W
Tampa, Fla. **17** 27 57N 82 27W
Tampa, Kans. **24** 38 33N 97 9W
Tampa B. **17** 27 50N 82 30W
Tampere **97** 61 30N 23 50 E
Tampico, Mexico **65** 22 20N 97 50W
Tampico, U.S.A. **21** 41 38N 89 47W
Tampin **112** 2 28N 102 13 E
Tamrida = Qādib **105** 12 35N 54 2 E
Tamsagbulag **113** 47 14N 117 21 E
Tamu **109** 24 13N 94 12 E
Tamworth, Australia **127** 31 7 S 150 58 E
Tamworth, U.K. **83** 52 38N 1 41W
Tamworth, U.S.A. **36** 43 50N 71 18W
Tana **96** 70 26N 28 14 E
Tana →, Kenya **122** 2 32 S 40 31 E
Tana →, Norway **96** 70 30N 28 23 E
Tana, L. **121** 13 5N 37 30 E
Tanabe **117** 33 44N 135 22 E
Tanabi **75** 20 37 S 49 37W
Tanacross **11** 63 23N 143 21W
Tanafjorden **96** 70 45N 28 25 E
Tanaga I. **11** 51 48N 177 53W
Tanaga Volcano **11** 51 53N 178 8W
Tanahbala **110** 0 30 S 98 30 E
Tanahgrogot **110** 1 55 S 116 15 E
Tanahjampea **111** 7 10 S 120 35 E
Tanahmasa **110** 0 12 S 98 39 E
Tanahmerah **111** 6 5 S 140 16 E
Tanakura **117** 37 10N 140 20 E
Tanama → **57** 18 25N 66 42W
Tanami Des. **126** 18 50 S 132 0 E
Tanana **11** 65 10N 152 4W
Tanana → **11** 65 10N 151 58W
Tananarive = Antananarivo **123** 18 55 S 47 31 E
Tánaro → **94** 45 1N 8 47 E
Tanchŏn **114** 40 27N 128 54 E
Tandag **111** 9 4N 126 9 E
Tăndărei **95** 44 39N 27 40 E
Tandil **76** 37 15 S 59 6W
Tandil, Sa. del **76** 37 30 S 59 0W
Tando Adam **108** 25 45N 68 40 E
Tane-ga-Shima **117** 30 30N 131 0 E
Taneatua **128** 38 4 S 177 1 E
Tanen Tong Dan **109** 16 30N 98 30 E
Taney County ◇ **32** 36 40N 93 0W
Taneytown **27** 39 40N 77 11W
Taneyville **32** 36 44N 93 2W
Tanezrouft **120** 23 9N 0 11 E
Tanga **122** 5 5 S 39 2 E
Tanganyika, L. **122** 6 40 S 30 0 E
Tangent **44** 44 33N 123 7W
Tanger **120** 35 50N 5 49W
Tangerang **111** 6 12 S 106 39 E
Tanggu **114** 39 2N 117 40 E
Tanggula Shan **113** 32 40N 92 10 E
Tanghe **115** 32 47N 112 50 E
Tangier = Tanger **120** 35 50N 5 49W
Tangier I. **54** 37 55N 75 59W
Tangier Sd. **27** 38 0N 75 57W
Tangipahoa, La. **25** 30 52N 90 30W
Tangipahoa, La. **25** 30 53N 90 31W
Tangipahoa Parish ◇ **25** 30 30N 90 28W
Tangkak **112** 2 18N 102 34 E
Tangshan **114** 39 38N 118 10 E
Tanimbar, Kepulauan **111** 7 30 S 131 30 E
Tanjay **111** 9 30N 123 5 E
Tanjore = Thanjavur **108** 10 48N 79 12 E
Tanjung **110** 2 10 S 115 25 E
Tanjungbalai **110** 2 55N 99 44 E
Tanjungbatu **110** 2 23N 118 3 E
Tanjungkarang **110** 5 20 S 105 10 E
Tanjungpandan **110** 2 43 S 107 38 E
Tanjungpinang **110** 1 5N 104 30 E
Tanjungpriok **111** 6 8 S 106 55 E
Tanjungredeb **110** 2 9N 117 29 E
Tanjungselor **110** 2 55N 117 25 E
Tankersley **50** 31 21N 100 39W
Tanner **54** 38 59N 80 57W
Tannu-Ola **101** 51 0N 94 0 E
Tanout **120** 14 50N 8 55 E
Tanquinho **75** 11 58 S 39 6W
Tanta **121** 30 45N 30 57 E
Tantoyuca **65** 21 21N 98 10W
Tantung = Dandong **114** 40 10N 124 20 E
Tantūra = Dor **104** 32 37N 34 55 E
Tanzania ■ **122** 6 40 S 34 0 E
Tanzilla → **62** 58 8N 130 43W
Tao'an **114** 45 22N 122 40 E
Taopi **30** 43 34N 92 38W
Taos **38** 36 24N 105 35W
Taos County ◇ **38** 36 30N 105 40W
Taos Indian Reservation **38** 36 35N 105 25W
Taos Pueblo **38** 36 24N 105 33W
Taoudenni **120** 22 40N 3 55W
Taourirt **120** 34 25N 2 53W
Taoyuan, China **115** 28 55N 111 16 E
Taoyuan, Taiwan **115** 25 0N 121 13 E
Tapa Shan = Daba Shan **115** 32 0N 109 0 E
Tapachula **65** 14 54N 92 17W
Tapah **112** 4 12N 101 15 E
Tapajós → **71** 2 24 S 54 41W
Tapaktuan **110** 3 15N 97 10 E
Tapanahoni → **71** 4 20N 54 25W
Tapanui **128** 45 56 S 169 18 E
Tapauá **73** 5 40 S 64 20W
Tapauá → **73** 5 40 S 64 21W
Tapeta **120** 6 29N 8 52W
Tapi → **108** 21 8N 72 41 E
Tapiraí **75** 19 52 S 46 1W
Tapirapé → **74** 10 41 S 50 38W
Tapirapecó, Serra **71** 1 10N 65 0W
Tapirapuã **73** 14 51 S 57 45W
Tapoeripa **71** 5 22N 56 34W
Tappahannock **54** 37 56N 76 52W
Tappan L. **42** 40 22N 81 14W
Tappen **41** 46 52N 99 38W
Tapuaenuku, Mt. **128** 42 0 S 173 39 E
Tapul Group **111** 5 35N 120 50 E
Tapurucuará **71** 0 24 S 65 2W
Taquara **77** 29 36 S 50 46W
Taquari → **73** 19 15 S 57 17W
Taquaritinga **75** 21 24 S 48 30W
Tar → **40** 35 33N 77 6W
Tar Island **62** 57 3N 111 40W
Tara **100** 56 55N 74 24 E
Tara →, U.S.S.R. **100** 56 42N 74 36 E
Tara →, Yugoslavia **95** 43 21N 18 51 E
Tarabagatay, Khrebet **100** 48 0N 83 0 E
Tarabuco **73** 19 10 S 64 57W
Tarābulus, Lebanon **106** 34 31N 35 50 E
Tarābulus, Libya **121** 32 49N 13 7 E
Tarakan **110** 3 20N 117 35 E
Tarama-Jima **117** 24 39N 124 42 E
Taranaki □ **128** 39 5 S 174 51 E
Taranga Hill **108** 24 0N 72 40 E
Táranto **94** 40 30N 17 11 E
Táranto, G. di **94** 40 0N 17 15 E
Tarapacá **70** 2 56 S 69 46W
Tarapacá □ **76** 20 45 S 69 30W
Tarapoto **72** 6 30 S 76 20W
Taraquá **70** 0 6N 68 28W
Tararua Range **128** 40 45 S 175 25 E
Tarat **120** 25 55N 9 3 E
Tarata **72** 17 27 S 70 2W
Tarauacá **72** 8 6 S 70 48W
Tarauacá → **72** 6 42 S 69 48W
Tarawera **128** 39 2 S 176 36 E
Tarawera L. **128** 38 13 S 176 27 E
Tarbat Ness **84** 57 52N 3 48W
Tarbela Dam **108** 34 8N 72 52 E
Tarbert, Strathclyde, U.K. **84** 55 55N 5 25W
Tarbert, W. Isles, U.K. **84** 57 54N 6 49W
Tarbes **90** 43 15N 0 3 E
Tarboro, Ga. **18** 31 1N 81 48W
Tarboro, N.C. **40** 35 54N 77 32W
Tarcoola **126** 30 44 S 134 36 E
Taree **127** 31 50 S 152 30 E
Tarentaise **90** 45 30N 6 35 E
Tarfaya **120** 27 55N 12 55W
Targhee National Forest **20** 44 15N 111 20W
Táriba **70** 7 49N 72 13W
Tarifa **91** 36 1N 5 36W
Tarija **76** 21 30 S 64 40W
Tarija □ **76** 21 30 S 63 30W
Tariku → **111** 2 55 S 138 26 E
Tarim He → **113** 39 30N 88 30 E
Tarim Pendi **113** 40 0N 84 0 E
Taritatu → **111** 2 54 S 138 27 E
Tarkhankut, Mys **99** 45 25N 32 30 E
Tarkio, Mo. **32** 40 27N 95 23W
Tarkio, Mont. **33** 47 1N 114 44W
Tarkio → **32** 40 27N 95 23W
Tarko Sale **100** 64 55N 77 50 E
Tarkwa **120** 5 20N 2 0W
Tarlac **111** 15 29N 120 35 E
Tarlton **42** 39 33N 82 47W
Tarma **72** 11 25 S 75 45W
Tarn □ **90** 43 49N 2 8 E
Tarn → **90** 44 5N 1 6 E
Tarn-et-Garonne □ **90** 44 8N 1 20 E
Tarnov **34** 41 37N 97 30W
Tarnów **89** 50 3N 21 0 E
Tarnowskie Góry **89** 50 27N 18 54 E
Taroom **127** 25 36 S 149 48 E
Taroudannt **120** 30 30N 8 52W
Tarpon Springs **17** 28 9N 82 45W
Tarqūmiyah **104** 31 35N 35 1 E
Tarragona **91** 41 5N 1 17 E
Tarrant City **10** 33 34N 86 47W
Tarrant County ◇ **51** 32 44N 97 7W
Tarrasa **91** 41 34N 2 1 E
Tarryall **16** 39 7N 105 29W
Tarryall Cr. → **16** 39 5N 105 19W
Tarrytown, Ga. **18** 32 19N 82 34W
Tarrytown, N.Y. **39** 41 4N 73 52W
Tarshiha = Me'ona **104** 33 1N 35 15 E
Tarso Emissi **121** 21 27N 18 36 E
Tarsus **106** 36 58N 34 55 E
Tartagal **76** 22 30 S 63 50W
Tartu **98** 58 20N 26 44 E
Tarţūs **106** 34 55N 35 55 E
Tarumirim **75** 19 16 S 41 59W
Tarumizu **117** 31 29N 130 42 E
Tarutao, Ko **112** 6 33N 99 40 E
Tarutung **110** 2 0N 98 54 E
Tarzan **50** 32 18N 101 58W
Tasāwah **121** 26 0N 13 30 E
Taschereau **60** 48 40N 78 40W
Taseko → **62** 52 4N 123 9W
Tash-Kumyr **100** 41 40N 72 10 E
Tashauz **100** 41 49N 59 58 E
Tashi Chho Dzong = Thimphu **109** 27 31N 89 45 E
Tashkent **100** 41 20N 69 10 E
Tashtagol **100** 52 47N 87 53 E
Tasikmalaya **111** 7 18 S 108 12 E
Tåsjön **96** 64 15N 16 0 E
Taskan **101** 62 59N 150 20 E
Tasman B. **128** 40 59 S 173 25 E
Tasman Mts. **128** 41 3 S 172 25 E
Tasman Pen. **127** 43 10 S 148 0 E
Tasman Sea **124** 36 0 S 160 0 E
Tasmania □ **127** 42 0 S 146 30 E
Tasu Sd. **62** 52 47N 132 2W
Tatar A.S.S.R. □ **98** 55 30N 51 30 E
Tatarsk **100** 55 14N 76 0 E
Tate **18** 34 25N 84 23W
Tate County ◇ **31** 34 37N 89 58W
Tateyama **117** 35 0N 139 50 E
Tathlina L. **62** 60 33N 117 39W
Tatinnai L. **63** 60 55N 97 40W
Tatitlek **11** 60 52N 146 41W
Tatnam, C. **63** 57 16N 91 0W
Tatra = Tatry **89** 49 20N 20 0 E
Tatry **89** 49 20N 20 0 E
Tatsuno **117** 34 52N 134 33 E
Tatta **108** 24 42N 67 55 E
Tattnall County ◇ **18** 32 0N 82 0W
Tatuī **77** 23 25 S 47 53W
Tatum, N. Mex. **38** 33 16N 103 19W
Tatum, Tex. **51** 32 19N 94 31W
Tatum Cr. → **18** 30 43N 82 32W
Tat'ung = Datong **114** 40 6N 113 18 E
Tatvan **106** 38 31N 42 15 E
Tauá **74** 6 1 S 40 26W
Taubaté **77** 23 0 S 45 36W
Tauern **88** 47 15N 12 40 E
Taum Sauk Mt. **32** 37 34N 90 44W
Taumarunui **128** 38 53 S 175 15 E
Taumaturgo **72** 8 54 S 72 51W
Taungdwingyi **109** 20 1N 95 40 E
Taunggyi **109** 20 50N 97 0 E
Taungup **109** 18 51N 94 14 E
Taungup Pass **109** 18 40N 94 45 E
Taungup Taunggya **109** 18 20N 93 40 E
Taunton, U.K. **83** 51 1N 3 7W
Taunton, Mass. **28** 41 54N 71 6W
Taunton, Minn. **30** 44 36N 96 4W
Taunton Lakes **37** 39 51N 74 52W
Taunus **88** 50 15N 8 20 E
Taupo **128** 38 41 S 176 7 E
Taupo, L. **128** 38 46 S 175 55 E
Tauranga **128** 37 42 S 176 11 E
Tauranga Harb. **128** 37 30 S 176 5 E
Taurianova **94** 38 22N 16 1 E
Taurus Mts. = Toros Daglari **106** 37 0N 35 0 E
Tavares **17** 28 48N 81 44W
Tavda **100** 58 7N 65 8 E
Tavda → **100** 59 20N 63 28 E
Tavernier **17** 25 1N 80 31W
Taveta **122** 3 23 S 37 37 E
Taveuni **128** 16 51 S 179 58W
Taviche **65** 16 38N 96 32W
Tavira **91** 37 8N 7 40W
Tavistock **83** 50 33N 4 9W
Tavoy **112** 14 2N 98 12 E
Taw → **83** 17 37 S 177 55 E
Tawakoni, L. **51** 32 49N 95 55W
Tawas City **29** 44 16N 83 31W
Tawau **110** 4 20N 117 55 E
Tawitawi **111** 5 10N 120 0 E
Tay → **84** 56 37N 3 38W
Tay, Firth of **84** 56 25N 3 8W
Tay, L. **84** 56 30N 4 10W
Tay Ninh **112** 11 20N 106 5 E
Tayabamba **72** 8 15 S 77 16W
Taylakovy **100** 59 13N 74 0 E
Taylor, Canada **62** 56 13N 120 40W
Taylor, Ariz. **12** 34 28N 110 5W
Taylor, Ark. **13** 33 6N 93 28W
Taylor, Fla. **17** 30 26N 82 18W
Taylor, Mich. **29** 42 14N 83 16W
Taylor, Miss. **31** 34 16N 89 35W
Taylor, N. Dak. **41** 46 54N 102 26W
Taylor, Nebr. **34** 41 46N 99 23W
Taylor, Tex. **51** 30 34N 97 25W
Taylor, Wis. **55** 44 19N 91 7W
Taylor → **16** 38 32N 106 55W
Taylor, Mt. **38** 35 14N 107 37W
Taylor County ◇, Fla. **17** 30 0N 83 30W
Taylor County ◇, Ga. **18** 32 35N 84 15W
Taylor County ◇, Iowa **23** 40 45N 94 40W
Taylor County ◇, Ky. **49** 37 20N 85 20W
Taylor County ◇, Tex. **51** 32 21N 99 53W
Taylor County ◇, W. Va. **54** 39 21N 80 2W
Taylor County ◇, Wis. **55** 45 10N 90 30W
Taylor Mill **49** 38 55N 84 32W
Taylor Park Reservoir **16** 38 49N 106 36W
Taylor Ridge **18** 34 35N 85 12W
Taylors Bridge **27** 39 23N 75 36W
Taylors Island **27** 38 28N 76 18W
Taylorsville, Ind. **22** 39 18N 85 57W
Taylorsville, Ky. **49** 38 2N 85 21W
Taylorsville, Md. **27** 39 27N 77 8W
Taylorsville, Miss. **31** 31 50N 89 26W
Taylorsville, N.C. **40** 35 55N 81 11W
Taylorville **21** 39 33N 89 18W
Taymā **106** 27 35N 38 45 E
Taymyr, Poluostrov **101** 75 0N 100 0 E
Tayport **84** 56 27N 2 52W
Ţayr Zibnā **104** 33 14N 35 23 E
Tayshet **101** 55 58N 98 1 E
Tayside □ **84** 56 25N 3 30W
Taytay **111** 10 45N 119 30 E
Taz → **100** 67 32N 78 40 E
Taza **120** 34 16N 4 6W
Tazawa-Ko **116** 39 43N 140 40 E
Tazewell, Tenn. **49** 36 27N 83 34W
Tazewell, Va. **54** 37 7N 81 31W
Tazewell County ◇, Ill. **21** 40 30N 89 30W
Tazewell County ◇, Va. **54** 37 7N 81 31W
Tazin → **63** 60 26N 110 45W
Tazin L. **63** 59 44N 108 42W
Tazlina **11** 62 4N 146 27W
Tazovskiy **100** 67 30N 78 44 E
Tbilisi **99** 41 43N 44 50 E
Tchad = Chad ■ **121** 12 30N 17 15 E
Tchad, L. **121** 13 30N 14 30 E
Tch'eng-tou = Chengdu **113** 30 38N 104 2 E
Tchentlo L. **62** 55 15N 125 0W
Tchibanga **122** 2 45 S 11 0 E
Tch'ong-k'ing = Chongqing **115** 29 35N 106 25 E
Tchula **31** 33 11N 90 13W
Te Anau, L. **128** 45 15 S 167 45 E
Te Aroha **128** 37 32 S 175 44 E
Te Awamutu **128** 38 1 S 175 20 E
Te Kuiti **128** 38 20 S 175 11 E
Te Puke **128** 37 46 S 176 22 E
Te Waewae B. **128** 46 13 S 167 33 E
Tea **47** 43 27N 96 50W
Tea → **70** 0 30 S 65 9W
Teague **51** 31 38N 96 17W
Teaneck **37** 40 53N 74 1W
Teapa **65** 18 35N 92 56W
Teasdale **52** 38 17N 111 29W
Tebakang **110** 1 6N 110 30 E
Tébessa **120** 35 22N 8 8 E
Tebicuary → **76** 26 36 S 58 16W
Tebingtinggi, Bengkulu, Indonesia **110** 3 38 S 103 9 E
Tebingtinggi, Sumatera Utara, Indonesia **110** 3 20N 99 9 E
Tecate **64** 32 34N 116 38W
Techirghiol **95** 44 4N 28 32 E
Tecka **78** 7 35N 1 43W
Tecomán **64** 18 55N 103 53W
Tecopa **15** 35 51N 116 13W
Tecoripa **64** 28 37N 109 57W
Tecuala **64** 22 23N 105 27W
Tecuci **89** 45 51N 27 27 E
Tecumseh, Mich. **29** 42 0N 83 57W
Tecumseh, Nebr. **34** 40 22N 96 11W
Tecumseh, Okla. **43** 35 15N 96 56W
Tecumseh, Mt. **36** 43 57N 71 34W
Tedzhen **100** 37 23N 60 31 E
Teec Nos Pas **12** 36 55N 109 6W
Tees → **82** 54 36N 1 25W
Teesside **82** 54 37N 1 13W
Tefé **71** 3 25 S 64 50W
Tefé → **71** 3 35 S 64 47W
Tegal **111** 6 52 S 109 8 E
Tegelen **87** 51 20N 6 9 E
Tegid, L. **82** 52 53N 3 38W
Tegina **120** 10 5N 6 11 E
Tegucigalpa **66** 14 5N 87 14W
Tehachapi **15** 35 8N 118 27W
Tehachapi Mts. **15** 35 0N 118 30W
Tehachapi Pass **15** 35 6N 118 18W
Tehama **14** 40 2N 122 7W
Tehama County ◇ **14** 40 5N 122 15W
Tehrān **107** 35 44N 51 30 E
Tehuacán **65** 18 30N 97 30W
Tehuantepec **65** 16 21N 95 13W
Tehuantepec, Golfo de **65** 15 50N 95 0W
Tehuantepec, Istmo de **65** 17 0N 94 30W
Teifi → **83** 52 4N 4 14W
Teign → **83** 50 41N 3 42W
Teignmouth **83** 50 33N 3 30W
Teiuş **95** 46 12N 23 40 E
Teixeira **74** 7 13 S 37 15W
Tejo → **91** 38 40N 9 24W
Tejon Pass **15** 34 49N 118 53W
Tekamah **34** 41 47N 96 13W
Tekapo, L. **128** 43 53 S 170 33 E
Tekax **65** 20 11N 89 18W
Tekeli **100** 44 50N 79 0 E
Tekirdağ **106** 40 58N 27 30 E
Tekkali **109** 18 37N 84 15 E
Tekoa **53** 47 14N 117 4W
Tekonsha **29** 42 5N 84 59W

Tel Adashim Throckmorton

Tel Adashim **104** 32 30N 35 17 E
Tel Aviv-Yafo **104** 32 4N 34 48 E
Tel Lakhish **104** 31 34N 34 51 E
Tel Megiddo **104** 32 35N 35 11 E
Tel Mond **104** 32 15N 34 56 E
Tela **66** 15 40N 87 28W
Telanaipura = Jambi **110** 1 38 S 103 30 E
Telavi **99** 42 0N 45 30 E
Telegraph Cr. **62** 58 0N 131 10W
Telemark fylke □ **97** 59 25N 8 30 E
Telén **76** 36 15 S 65 31W
Teleorman □ **95** 44 0N 25 0 E
Teleorman → **95** 44 15N 25 20 E
Teles Pires → **73** 7 21 S 58 3W
Telescope Pk. **15** 36 10N 117 5W
Telfair County ◇ **18** 31 55N 83 0W
Telford **82** 52 42N 2 31W
Telida **11** 63 23N 153 16W
Télimélé **120** 10 54N 13 2W
Telkwa **62** 54 41N 127 5W
Tell City **22** 37 57N 86 46W
Teller **11** 65 16N 166 22W
Teller County ◇ **16** 38 50N 105 10W
Tellicherry **108** 11 45N 75 30 E
Tellico Plains **49** 35 22N 84 18W
Telluride **16** 37 56N 107 49W
Telocaset **44** 45 6N 117 49W
Telogia **17** 30 21N 84 49W
Teloloapán **65** 18 21N 99 51W
Telom → **112** 4 20N 101 46 E
Telpos Iz **98** 63 35N 57 30 E
Telsen **78** 42 30 S 66 50W
Teluk Intan **110** 4 3N 101 0 E
Telukbetung **110** 5 29 S 105 17 E
Telukbutun **110** 4 13N 108 12 E
Telukdalem **110** 0 33N 97 50 E
Tema **120** 5 41N 0 0 E
Temanggung **111** 7 18 S 110 10 E
Temapache **65** 21 4N 97 38W
Temax **65** 21 10N 88 50W
Tembeling → **112** 4 20N 102 23 E
Temblador **71** 8 59N 62 44W
Temblor Range **15** 35 20N 119 50W
Teme → **83** 52 23N 2 15W
Temecula **15** 33 30N 117 9W
Temerloh **112** 3 27N 102 25 E
Temir **100** 49 21N 57 3 E
Temirtau, Kazakh S.S.R., U.S.S.R. **100** 50 5N 72 56 E
Temirtau, R.S.F.S.R., U.S.S.R. **100** 53 10N 87 30 E
Témiscaming **60** 46 44N 79 5W
Temosachic **64** 28 58N 107 50W
Tempe **12** 33 25N 111 56W
Temperance **29** 41 47N 83 34W
Tempino **110** 1 42 S 103 30 E
Tempiute **35** 37 39N 115 38W
Temple, N.H. **36** 42 48N 71 50W
Temple, Okla. **43** 34 16N 98 14W
Temple, Tex. **51** 31 6N 97 21W
Temple B. **127** 12 15 S 143 3 E
Temple Hill **49** 36 53N 85 51W
Temple Terrace **17** 28 2N 82 23W
Templemore **85** 52 48N 7 50W
Templeton, Calif. **15** 35 33N 120 42W
Templeton, Mass. **28** 42 33N 72 4W
Tempoal **65** 21 31N 98 23W
Temuco **78** 38 45 S 72 40W
Temuka **128** 44 14 S 171 17 E
Ten Thousand Is. **17** 25 55N 81 45W
Tena **70** 0 59 S 77 49W
Tenabo **65** 20 2N 90 12W
Tenaha **51** 31 57N 94 15W
Tenakee Springs **11** 57 47N 135 13W
Tenali **108** 16 15N 80 35 E
Tenancingo **65** 19 0N 99 33W
Tenango **65** 19 7N 99 33W
Tenasserim **112** 12 6N 99 3 E
Tenasserim □ **112** 14 0N 98 30 E
Tenby **83** 51 40N 4 42W
Tendaho **105** 11 48N 40 54 E
Tendoy **20** 44 57N 113 38W
Tenente Marques → **73** 11 10 S 59 56W
Tenerife **120** 28 15N 16 35W
Teng → **112** 20 30N 98 10 E
Teng Xian, Guangxi Zhuangzu, China **115** 23 21N 110 56 E
Teng Xian, Shandong, China **115** 35 5N 117 10 E
Tengah □ **111** 2 0 S 122 0 E
Tengah Kepulauan **110** 7 5 S 118 15 E
Tengchong **113** 25 0N 98 28 E
Tengchowfu = Penglai **114** 37 48N 120 42 E
Tenggara □ **111** 3 0 S 122 0 E
Tenggarong **110** 0 24 S 116 58 E
Tengiz, Ozero **100** 50 30N 69 0 E
Tenino **53** 46 51N 122 51W
Tenkasi **108** 8 55N 77 20 E
Tenke **122** 10 32 S 26 7 E
Tenkiller Ferry L. **43** 35 35N 95 2W
Tenkodogo **120** 11 54N 0 19W
Tennant **23** 41 35N 95 26W
Tennant Creek **126** 19 30 S 134 15 E
Tennessee **21** 40 18N 90 52W
Tennessee □ **48** 35 50N 85 30W
Tennessee → **48** 37 4N 88 34W
Tennessee Pass **16** 39 22N 106 19W
Tennessee Ridge **48** 36 19N 87 47W
Tennille **18** 32 56N 82 48W
Tennyson, Ind. **22** 38 5N 87 7W
Tennyson, Wis. **55** 42 41N 90 41W
Tenom **110** 5 4N 115 57 E
Tenosique **65** 17 30N 91 24W
Tenryū-Gawa → **117** 35 39N 137 48 E
Tensas → **25** 31 38N 91 49W
Tensas Parish ◇ **25** 32 0N 91 10W
Tensed **20** 47 10N 116 55W
Tensleep **56** 44 2N 107 27W
Tenstrike **30** 47 39N 94 41W
Tent L. **63** 62 25N 107 54W
Tenterfield **127** 29 0 S 152 0 E
Teófilo Otoni **75** 17 50 S 41 30W
Teotihuacán **65** 19 44N 98 50W
Tepa **111** 7 52 S 129 31 E
Tepalcatepec → **64** 18 35N 101 59W
Tepehuanes **64** 25 21N 105 44W
Tepequem, Serra **71** 3 45N 61 45W
Tepetongo **64** 22 28N 103 9W
Tepic **64** 21 30N 104 54W
Teplice **88** 50 40N 13 48 E
Tepoca, C. **64** 30 20N 112 25W
Tequila **64** 20 54N 103 47W
Ter → **91** 42 0N 3 12 E
Ter Apel **87** 52 53N 7 5 E
Téra **120** 14 0N 0 45 E
Teraina, I. **125** 4 43N 160 25W
Téramo **94** 42 40N 13 40 E
Tercero → **76** 32 58 S 61 47W
Terek → **99** 44 0N 47 30 E
Terengganu □ **112** 4 55N 103 0 E
Terenos **73** 20 26 S 54 50W
Teresina **74** 5 9 S 42 45W
Teresinha **71** 0 58N 52 2W
Terhazza **120** 23 38N 5 22W
Terlingua **50** 29 19N 103 36W
Terlingua Cr. → **50** 29 10N 103 36W
Terlton **43** 36 8N 96 29W
Termez **100** 37 15N 67 15 E
Términos, Laguna de **65** 18 35N 91 30W
Térmoli **94** 42 0N 15 0 E
Ternate **111** 0 45N 127 25 E
Terneuzen **87** 51 20N 3 50 E
Terney **101** 45 3N 136 37 E
Terni **94** 42 34N 12 38 E
Terra Alta **54** 39 27N 79 33W
Terra Bella **15** 35 58N 119 3W
Terra Nova B. **5** 74 50 S 164 40 E
Terrace **62** 54 30N 128 35W
Terrace Bay **60** 48 47N 87 5W
Terracina **94** 41 17N 13 12 E
Terral **43** 33 54N 97 57W
Terralba **94** 39 42N 8 38 E
Terranova = Ólbia **94** 40 55N 9 30 E
Terre Haute **22** 39 28N 87 25W
Terrebonne **44** 44 21N 121 11W
Terrebonne B. **25** 29 5N 90 35W
Terrebonne Parish ◇ **25** 29 20N 91 0W
Terrell **51** 32 44N 96 17W
Terrell County ◇, Ga. **18** 31 50N 84 25W
Terrell County ◇, Tex. **50** 30 0N 102 0W
Terrenceville **61** 47 40N 54 44W
Terreton **20** 43 51N 112 26W
Terril **23** 43 18N 94 58W
Terry, La. **25** 32 56N 91 21W
Terry, Miss. **31** 32 6N 90 18W
Terry, Mont. **33** 46 47N 105 19W
Terry County ◇ **50** 33 11N 102 17W
Terry Pk. **47** 44 19N 103 50W
Terryville **28** 41 41N 73 3W
Terschelling **87** 53 25N 5 20 E
Teruel **91** 40 22N 1 8W
Tervel **95** 43 45N 27 28 E
Tervola **96** 66 6N 24 49 E
Tešanj **95** 44 38N 17 59 E
Tescott **24** 39 1N 97 53W
Teshekpuk L. **11** 70 35N 153 26W
Teshio **116** 44 53N 141 44 E
Teshio-Gawa → **116** 44 53N 141 45 E
Tesiyn Gol → **113** 50 40N 93 20 E
Teslin **62** 60 10N 132 43W
Teslin → **62** 61 34N 134 35W
Teslin L. **62** 60 15N 132 57W
Tesouro **73** 16 4 S 53 34W
Tessalit **120** 20 12N 1 0 E
Tessaoua **120** 13 47N 7 56 E
Test → **83** 51 7N 1 30W
Tetachuck L. **62** 53 18N 125 55W
Tetas, Pta. **76** 23 31 S 70 38W
Tete **123** 16 13 S 33 33 E
Teteven **95** 42 58N 24 17 E
Tethul → **62** 60 35N 112 12W
Tetlin **11** 63 8N 142 31W
Tetlin Indian Reservation **11** 63 0N 142 30W
Teton **20** 43 53N 111 40W
Teton →, Idaho **20** 43 54N 111 51W
Teton →, Mont. **33** 47 56N 110 31W
Teton County ◇, Idaho **20** 43 55N 111 5W
Teton County ◇, Mont. **33** 47 52N 112 20W
Teton County ◇, Wyo. **56** 44 0N 110 30W
Teton Pass **56** 43 30N 110 57W
Teton Range **56** 43 45N 111 0W
Tetonia **20** 43 49N 111 10W
Tétouan **120** 35 35N 5 21W
Tetovo **95** 42 1N 21 2 E
Tetuán = Tétouan **120** 35 35N 5 21W
Tetyukhe Pristan **116** 44 22N 135 48 E
Teuco → **76** 25 35 S 60 11W
Teulon **63** 50 23N 97 16W
Teun **111** 6 59 S 129 8 E
Teutoburger Wald **88** 52 5N 8 20 E
Teutopolis **21** 39 8N 88 29W
Tevere → **94** 41 44N 12 14 E
Teverya **104** 32 47N 35 32 E
Teviot → **84** 55 21N 2 51W
Tewkesbury **83** 51 59N 2 8W
Tewksbury **28** 42 37N 71 14W
Texada I. **62** 49 40N 124 25W
Texana, L. **51** 29 0N 96 35W
Texarkana, Ark. **13** 33 26N 94 2W
Texarkana, Tex. **51** 33 26N 94 3W
Texas □ **50** 31 0N 101 0W
Texas City **51** 29 24N 94 54W
Texas County ◇, Mo. **32** 37 20N 92 0W
Texas County ◇, Okla. **43** 36 45N 101 30W
Texel **87** 53 5N 4 50 E
Texhoma **43** 36 30N 101 47W
Texico **38** 34 24N 103 3W
Texline **50** 36 23N 103 2W
Texola **43** 35 12N 99 59W
Texoma, L. **51** 33 50N 96 34W
Texon **50** 31 13N 101 42W
Teyvareh **107** 33 30N 64 24 E
Teziutlán **65** 19 50N 97 22W
Tezpur **109** 26 40N 92 45 E
Tezzeron L. **62** 54 43N 124 30W
Tha-anne → **63** 60 31N 94 37W
Tha Nun **112** 8 12N 98 17 E
Thabana Ntlenyana **123** 29 30 S 29 16 E
Thabazimbi **123** 24 40 S 27 21 E
Thackerville **43** 33 48N 97 9W
Thai Hoa **112** 19 20N 105 20 E
Thai Nguyen **112** 21 35N 105 55 E
Thailand ■ **110** 16 0N 102 0 E
Thailand, G. of **112** 11 30N 101 0 E
Thakhek **112** 17 25N 104 45 E
Thal **108** 33 28N 70 33 E
Thala La **109** 28 25N 97 23 E
Thalia **51** 33 59N 99 32W
Thalmann **18** 31 18N 81 41W
Thame → **83** 51 35N 1 8W
Thames **128** 37 7 S 175 34 E
Thames →, Canada **60** 42 20N 82 25W
Thames →, U.K. **83** 51 30N 0 35 E
Thames →, U.S.A. **28** 41 18N 72 5W
Thane **108** 19 12N 72 59 E
Thanet, I. of **83** 51 21N 1 20 E
Thang Binh **112** 15 50N 108 20 E
Thanh Hoa **112** 19 48N 105 46 E
Thanjavur **108** 10 48N 79 12 E
Thanlwin Myit → **109** 20 0N 98 0 E
Thar Desert **108** 28 0N 72 0 E
Tharad **108** 24 30N 71 44 E
Thargomindah **127** 27 58 S 143 46 E
Tharrawaddy **109** 17 38N 95 48 E
Thásos **95** 40 40N 24 40 E
Thatcher, Ariz. **12** 32 51N 109 46W
Thatcher, Colo. **16** 37 33N 104 7W
Thaton **109** 16 55N 97 22 E
Thaungdut **109** 24 30N 94 40 E
Thawville **21** 40 41N 88 7W
Thaxton **31** 34 18N 89 11W
Thayer, Kans. **24** 37 29N 95 28W
Thayer, Mo. **32** 36 31N 91 33W
Thayer, Nebr. **34** 40 58N 97 30W
Thayer County ◇ **34** 40 15N 97 40W
Thayetmyo **109** 19 20N 95 10 E
Thayne **56** 42 55N 111 0W
Thazi **109** 21 0N 96 5 E
The Bight **67** 24 19N 75 24W
The Dalles **44** 45 36N 121 10W
The English Company's Is. **127** 11 50 S 136 32 E
The Granites **126** 20 35 S 130 21 E
The Grenadines, Is. **67** 12 40N 61 20W
The Grove **51** 31 16N 97 32W
The Hamilton → **126** 26 40 S 135 19 E
The Macumba → **127** 27 52 S 137 12 E
The Pas **63** 53 45N 101 15W
The Plains **54** 38 52N 77 47W
The Village **43** 35 35N 97 33W
Theba **12** 32 55N 112 53W
Thebes = Thívai **95** 38 19N 23 19 E
Thebes **21** 37 13N 89 28W
Thedford **34** 41 59N 100 35W
Thekulthili L. **63** 61 3N 110 0W
Thelon → **63** 62 35N 104 3W
Theodore, Australia **127** 24 55 S 150 3 E
Theodore, U.S.A. **10** 30 33N 88 10W
Theodore Roosevelt L. **12** 33 40N 111 10W
Theodore Roosevelt National Memorial Park **41** 47 0N 103 25W
Theodosia **32** 36 35N 92 39W
Theresa **39** 44 13N 75 48W
Theressa **17** 29 50N 82 4W
Theriot **25** 29 28N 90 45W
Thermaïkos Kólpos **95** 40 15N 22 45 E
Thermal **15** 33 39N 116 9W
Thermalito **14** 39 31N 121 36W
Thermopolis **56** 43 39N 108 13W
Thermopylae P. **95** 38 48N 22 35 E
Thessalía □ **95** 39 30N 22 0 E
Thessalon **60** 46 20N 83 30W
Thessaloníki **95** 40 38N 22 58 E
Thessaly = Thessalía □ **95** 39 30N 22 0 E
Theta **48** 35 47N 87 3W
Thetford **83** 52 25N 0 44 E
Thetford Mines **61** 46 8N 71 18W
Thibodaux **25** 29 48N 90 49W
Thicket Portage **63** 55 19N 97 42W
Thief L. **30** 48 30N 95 54W
Thief River Falls **30** 48 7N 96 10W
Thiel Mts. **5** 85 15 S 91 0W
Thielsen, Mt. **44** 43 9N 122 4W
Thiérache **90** 49 51N 3 45 E
Thies **120** 14 50N 16 51W
Thika **122** 1 1 S 37 5 E
Thikombia **128** 15 44 S 179 55W
Thimphu **109** 27 31N 89 45 E
þingvallavatn **96** 64 11N 21 9W
Thionville **90** 49 20N 6 10 E
Thíra **95** 36 23N 25 27 E
Thirsk **82** 54 15N 1 20W
Thisted **97** 56 58N 8 40 E
Thistle I. **126** 35 0 S 136 8 E
Thívai **95** 38 19N 23 19 E
þjórsá → **96** 63 47N 20 48W
Thlewiaza →, Man., Canada **63** 59 43N 100 5W
Thlewiaza →, N.W.T., Canada **63** 60 29N 94 40W
Thoa → **63** 60 31N 109 47W
Thomas, Md. **27** 38 36N 76 18W
Thomas, Okla. **43** 35 45N 98 45W
Thomas, W. Va. **54** 39 9N 79 30W
Thomas A. Edison, L. **15** 37 25N 119 0W
Thomas County ◇, Ga. **18** 30 50N 83 55W
Thomas County ◇, Kans. **24** 39 20N 101 0W
Thomas County ◇, Nebr. **34** 41 50N 100 30W
Thomas Hill Reservoir **32** 39 34N 92 39W
Thomasboro **21** 40 15N 88 11W
Thomaston, Ala. **10** 32 16N 87 38W
Thomaston, Conn. **28** 41 41N 73 4W
Thomaston, Ga. **18** 32 53N 84 20W
Thomaston, Maine **26** 44 5N 69 11W
Thomaston Res. **28** 41 42N 73 5W
Thomastown **31** 32 52N 89 40W
Thomasville, Ala. **10** 31 55N 87 44W
Thomasville, Ga. **18** 30 50N 83 59W
Thomasville, N.C. **40** 35 53N 80 5W
Thompson, Canada **63** 55 45N 97 52W
Thompson, Iowa **23** 43 22N 93 46W
Thompson, N. Dak. **41** 47 47N 97 6W
Thompson, Pa. **45** 41 52N 75 31W
Thompson, Utah **52** 38 58N 109 43W
Thompson →, Canada **62** 50 15N 121 24W
Thompson →, U.S.A. **32** 39 46N 93 37W
Thompson Falls **33** 47 36N 115 21W
Thompson Landing **63** 62 56N 110 40W
Thompson Pk. **14** 41 0N 123 0W
Thompsons Cr. → **31** 31 10N 88 55W
Thompsonville, Ill. **21** 37 55N 88 46W
Thompsonville, Mich. **29** 44 31N 85 56W
Thomson, Ga. **18** 33 28N 82 30W
Thomson, Ill. **21** 41 58N 90 6W
Thomson → **127** 25 11 S 142 53 E
Thomson's Falls = Nyahururu **122** 0 2N 36 27 E
Thon Buri **112** 13 43N 100 29 E
Thoreau **38** 35 24N 108 13W
þórisvatn **96** 64 20N 18 55W
þorlákshöfn **96** 63 51N 21 22W
Thornaby on Tees **82** 54 36N 1 19W
Thornapple →, Mich. **29** 42 56N 85 28W
Thornapple →, Wis. **55** 45 28N 91 16W
Thornburg **23** 41 27N 92 20W
Thorndale **51** 30 37N 97 12W
Thornton, Colo. **16** 39 52N 104 58W
Thornton, Idaho **20** 43 45N 111 51W
Thornton, Iowa **23** 42 57N 93 23W
Thornton, Miss. **31** 33 5N 90 19W
Thornton, Tex. **51** 31 25N 96 34W
Thornton, Wash. **53** 47 7N 117 23W
Thorntown **22** 40 8N 86 36W
Thornville **42** 39 54N 82 25W
Thorny Mt. **32** 37 6N 91 10W
Thorp, Wash. **53** 47 4N 120 40W
Thorp, Wis. **55** 44 58N 90 48W
Thorsby **10** 32 55N 86 43W
þórshöfn **96** 66 12N 15 20W
Thousand Oaks **15** 34 10N 118 50W
Thousand Springs Cr. → **35** 41 17N 113 51W
Thrace = Thráki □ **95** 41 9N 25 30 E
Thráki □ **95** 41 9N 25 30 E
Thrall **51** 30 35N 97 18W
Thrashers **31** 34 43N 88 32W
Three Forks **33** 45 54N 111 33W
Three Hills **62** 51 43N 113 15W
Three Lakes **55** 45 48N 89 10W
Three Oaks **29** 41 48N 86 36W
Three Points, C. **120** 4 42N 2 6W
Three Rivers, Calif. **15** 36 26N 118 54W
Three Rivers, Mich. **29** 41 57N 85 38W
Three Rivers, N. Mex. **38** 33 19N 106 5W
Three Rivers, Tex. **51** 28 28N 98 11W
Three Sisters **44** 44 4N 121 51W
Throckmorton **51** 33 11N 99 11W

Throckmorton County
Tombigee National Forest

Throckmorton County ◇ 51 33 10N 99 10W
Throssell Ra. 126 22 3S 121 43E
Thubun Lakes 63 61 30N 112 0W
Thuin 87 50 20N 4 17E
Thule, Antarct. 5 59 27S 27 19W
Thule, Greenland 4 77 40N 69 0W
Thun 88 46 45N 7 38E
Thunder B. 29 45 0N 83 20W
Thunder Basin National Grassland 56 43 45N 105 5W
Thunder Bay 60 48 20N 89 15W
Thunder Butte 47 45 19N 101 53W
Thunder Hawk 47 45 56N 101 58W
Thunderbird, L. 43 35 14N 97 18W
Thunderbolt 18 32 3N 81 4W
Thung Song 112 8 10N 99 40E
Thunkar 109 27 55N 91 0E
Thüringer Wald 88 50 35N 11 0E
Thurles 85 52 40N 7 53W
Thurman 23 40 49N 95 45W
Thurmont 27 39 37N 77 25W
Thursday I. 127 10 30S 142 3E
Thurso, Canada 60 45 36N 75 15W
Thurso, U.K. 84 58 34N 3 31W
Thurston, Nebr. 34 42 11N 96 42W
Thurston, Ohio 42 39 50N 82 33W
Thurston County ◇, Nebr. 34 42 15N 96 40W
Thurston County ◇, Wash. 53 46 58N 122 59W
Thurston I. 5 72 0S 100 0W
Thutade L. 62 57 0N 126 55W
Thysville = Mbanza Ngungu 122 5 12S 14 53E
Tiahuanacu 72 16 33S 68 42W
Tian Shan 113 43 0N 84 0E
Tiandu 115 18 18N 109 36E
Tian'e 115 25 1N 107 9E
Tianguá 74 3 44S 40 59W
Tianhe 115 24 48N 108 40E
Tianjin 114 39 8N 117 10E
Tianshui 115 34 32N 105 40E
Tianyang 115 23 42N 106 53E
Tianzhen 114 40 24N 114 5E
Tiaret 120 35 20N 1 21E
Tiassalé 120 5 58N 4 57W
Tibagi 77 24 30S 50 24W
Tibagi → 77 22 47S 51 1W
Tibati 121 6 22N 12 30E
Tibble 10 31 22N 88 15W
Tiber = Tevere → 94 41 44N 12 14E
Tiber Reservoir 33 48 19N 111 6W
Tiberias, L. = Kinneret, Yam 104 32 45N 35 35E
Tiberias, L. = Yam Kinneret 104 32 45N 35 35E
Tibesti 121 21 0N 17 30E
Tibet = Xizang □ 113 32 0N 88 0E
Tibnīn 104 33 12N 35 24E
Tibooburra 127 29 26S 142 1E
Tibugá, Golfo de 70 5 45N 77 20W
Tiburón 64 29 0N 112 30W
Tice 17 26 40N 81 49W
Tichît 120 18 21N 9 29W
Tichnor 13 34 8N 91 16W
Ticino □ 88 46 20N 8 45E
Ticino → 94 45 9N 9 14E
Ticonderoga 39 43 51N 73 26W
Ticul 65 20 20N 89 31W
Tiddim 109 23 28N 93 45E
Tidewater 54 37 51N 76 42W
Tidioute 45 41 41N 79 24W
Tidjikja 120 18 29N 11 35W
Tidore 111 0 40N 127 25E
Tie Plant 31 33 44N 89 47W
Tiel, Neth. 87 51 53N 5 26E
Tiel, Senegal 120 14 55N 15 5W
Tieling 114 42 20N 123 55E
Tielt 87 51 0N 3 20E
Tien Shan 107 42 0N 80 0E
Tienen 87 50 48N 4 57E
Tientsin = Tianjin 114 39 8N 117 10E
Tierra Amarilla, Chile 76 27 28S 70 18W
Tierra Amarilla, U.S.A. 38 36 42N 106 33W
Tierra Blanca Cr. → 50 34 58N 101 55W
Tierra Colorada 65 17 10N 99 35W
Tierra de Campos 91 42 10N 4 50W
Tierra del Fuego □ 78 54 0S 67 45W
Tierra del Fuego, I. Gr. de 78 54 0S 69 0W
Tierralta 70 8 11N 76 4W
Tiétar → 91 39 50N 6 1W
Tieté → 77 20 40S 51 35W
Tieton 53 46 42N 120 46W
Tiffany 16 37 2N 107 32W
Tiffany Mt. 53 48 40N 119 56W
Tiffin, Iowa 23 41 42N 91 40W
Tiffin, Ohio 42 41 7N 83 11W
Tiflis = Tbilisi 99 41 43N 44 50E
Tifrah 104 31 19N 34 42E
Tift County ◇ 18 31 30N 83 30W
Tifton 18 31 27N 83 31W
Tifu 111 3 39S 126 24E
Tigalda I. 11 54 6N 165 5W
Tigard 44 45 26N 122 46W
Tiger 53 48 42N 117 24W
Tigil 101 57 49N 158 40E
Tignall 18 33 52N 82 44W
Tignish 61 46 58N 64 2W
Tigre →, Peru 72 4 30S 74 10W
Tigre →, Venezuela 71 9 20N 62 30W
Tigris = Dijlah, Nahr → 106 31 0N 47 25E
Tigveni 95 45 10N 24 31E
Tigyaing 109 23 45N 96 10E
Tîh, Gebel el 121 29 32N 33 26E
Tihāmah 106 22 0N 39 0E
Tijeras 38 35 5N 106 23W
Tijuana 64 32 30N 117 10W
Tikal 66 17 13N 89 24W
Tikamgarh 108 24 44N 78 50E
Tikhoretsk 99 45 56N 40 5E
Tikrīt 106 34 35N 43 37E
Tiksi 101 71 40N 128 45E
Tilamuta 111 0 32N 122 23E
Tilburg 87 51 31N 5 6E
Tilbury, Canada 60 42 17N 82 23W
Tilbury, U.K. 83 51 27N 0 24E
Tilcara 76 23 36S 65 23W
Tilden, Ill. 21 38 13N 89 41W
Tilden, Nebr. 34 42 3N 97 50W
Tilden, Tex. 51 28 28N 98 33W
Tilghman 27 38 43N 76 20W
Tilichiki 101 60 27N 166 5E
Tiline 48 37 11N 88 15W
Till → 82 55 35N 2 3W
Tillabéri 120 14 28N 1 28E
Tillamook 44 45 27N 123 51W
Tillamook B. 44 45 30N 123 53W
Tillamook County ◇ 44 45 20N 123 45W
Tillamook Head 44 45 57N 124 0W
Tillar 13 33 43N 91 27W
Tiller 44 42 56N 122 57W
Tillery, L. 40 35 12N 80 4W
Tillman 46 32 28N 81 6W
Tillman County ◇ 43 34 25N 99 0W
Tillmans Corner 10 30 46N 88 8W
Tillsonburg 60 42 53N 80 44W
Tílos 95 36 27N 27 27E
Tilsit = Sovetsk 98 55 6N 21 50E
Tilt → 84 56 50N 3 50W
Tilton, Ga. 18 34 40N 84 56W
Tilton, Ill. 21 40 6N 87 38W
Tilton, N.H. 36 43 27N 71 36W
Timagami L. 60 47 0N 80 10W
Timanskiy Kryazh 98 65 58N 50 5E
Timaru 128 44 23S 171 14E
Timbalier B. 25 29 3N 90 20W
Timbalier I. 25 29 3N 90 28W
Timbaúba 74 7 31S 35 19W
Timbedgha 120 16 17N 8 16W
Timber 44 45 43N 123 18W
Timber Lake 47 45 26N 101 5W
Timberlake 40 36 17N 78 57W
Timbío 70 2 20N 76 40W
Timbiqui 70 2 46N 77 42W
Timbo 13 35 52N 92 19W
Timbuktu = Tombouctou 120 16 50N 3 0W
Timimoun 120 29 14N 0 16E
Timişoara 89 45 43N 21 15E
Timken 24 38 29N 99 11W
Timmins 60 48 28N 81 25W
Timmonsville 46 34 8N 79 57W
Timnath 16 40 32N 104 59W
Timok → 95 44 10N 22 40E
Timon 74 5 8S 42 52W
Timor 111 9 0S 125 0E
Timor □ 111 9 0S 125 0E
Timor Sea 127 10 0S 127 0E
Timpas 16 37 49N 103 46W
Timpson 51 31 54N 94 24W
Tims Ford L. 48 35 15N 86 10W
Tin Mt. 15 36 50N 117 10W
Tina 32 39 32N 93 27W
Tinaca Pt. 111 5 30N 125 25E
Tinaco 70 9 42N 68 26W
Tinaquillo 70 9 55N 68 18W
Tindall 32 40 10N 93 36W
Tindouf 120 27 42N 8 10W
Tinemaha Reservoir 15 37 3N 118 13W
Tingley 23 40 51N 94 12W
Tingo Maria 72 9 10S 75 54W
Tinharé, I. de 75 13 30S 38 58W
Tinjoub 120 29 45N 5 40W
Tinmouth 36 43 26N 73 4W
Tinnevelly = Tirunelveli 108 8 45N 77 45E
Tinnoset 97 59 55N 9 3E
Tinogasta 76 28 5S 67 32W
Tínos 95 37 33N 25 8E
Tinsley 31 32 44N 90 28W
Tinsman 13 33 38N 92 21W
Tinta 72 14 3S 71 20W
Tintah 30 46 1N 96 19W
Tintina 76 27 2S 62 45W
Tioga, N. Dak. 41 48 24N 102 56W
Tioga, Pa. 45 41 55N 77 8W
Tioga, Tex. 51 33 28N 96 55W
Tioga, W. Va. 54 38 25N 80 40W
Tioga County ◇, N.Y. 39 42 10N 76 20W
Tioga County ◇, Pa. 45 41 50N 77 10W
Tioga Pass 14 37 54N 119 15W
Tioman, Pulau 112 2 50N 104 10E
Tionesta 45 41 30N 79 28W
Tipongpani 109 27 20N 95 55E
Tipp City 42 39 58N 84 11W
Tippah County ◇ 31 34 44N 88 57W
Tippecanoe County ◇ 22 40 25N 86 55W
Tipperary 85 52 28N 8 10W
Tipperary □ 85 52 37N 7 55W
Tipton, U.K. 83 52 32N 2 4W
Tipton, Calif. 15 36 4N 119 19W
Tipton, Ind. 22 40 17N 86 2W
Tipton, Iowa 23 41 46N 91 8W
Tipton, Kans. 24 39 21N 98 28W
Tipton, Mo. 32 38 39N 92 47W
Tipton, Okla. 43 34 30N 99 8W
Tipton County ◇, Ind. 22 40 20N 86 5W
Tipton County ◇, Tenn. 48 35 29N 89 43W
Tipton Mt. 12 35 32N 114 12W
Tiptonville 48 36 23N 89 29W
Tiquié → 70 0 5N 68 25W
Tiracambu, Serra do 74 3 15S 46 30W
Tīrān 107 32 45N 51 8E
Tirana 95 41 18N 19 49E
Tiraspol 99 46 55N 29 35E
Tirat Karmel 104 32 46N 34 58E
Tirat Yehuda 104 32 1N 34 56E
Tirat Ẕevi 104 32 26N 35 31E
Tire 106 38 5N 27 50E
Tirebolu 106 40 58N 38 45E
Tiree 84 56 31N 6 55W
Tîrgovişte 89 44 55N 25 27E
Tîrgu-Jiu 89 45 5N 23 19E
Tîrgu Mureş 89 46 31N 24 38E
Tîrgu Ocna 95 46 16N 26 39E
Tîrgu Secuiesc 95 46 0N 26 10E
Tirich Mir 107 36 15N 71 55E
Tiririca, Serra da 75 17 6S 47 6W
Tîrnava Mare → 95 46 15N 24 30E
Tîrnava Mică → 95 46 17N 24 30E
Tîrnăveni 95 46 19N 24 13E
Tirodi 108 21 40N 79 44E
Tirol □ 88 47 3N 10 43E
Tiros 75 19 0S 45 58W
Tirso → 94 39 52N 8 33E
Tiruchchirappalli 108 10 45N 78 45E
Tirunelveli 108 8 45N 77 45E
Tirupati 108 13 39N 79 25E
Tiruvannamalai 108 12 15N 79 5E
Tisa → 89 45 15N 20 17E
Tisdale 63 52 50N 104 0W
Tishomingo, Miss. 31 34 38N 88 14W
Tishomingo, Okla. 43 34 14N 96 41W
Tishomingo County ◇ 31 34 49N 88 12W
Tiskilwa 21 41 18N 89 30W
Tit-Ary 101 71 55N 127 2E
Titicaca, L. 72 15 30S 69 30W
Titograd 95 42 30N 19 19E
Titonka 23 43 14N 94 3W
Titov Veles 95 41 46N 21 47E
Titovo Užice 95 43 55N 19 50E
Tittabawassee → 29 43 23N 83 59W
Titule 122 3 15N 25 31E
Titumate 70 8 19N 77 5W
Titus County ◇ 51 33 9N 94 58W
Titusville, Fla. 17 28 37N 80 49W
Titusville, Pa. 45 41 38N 79 41W
Tivaouane 120 14 56N 16 45W
Tiverton, U.K. 83 50 54N 3 30W
Tiverton, U.S.A. 28 41 38N 71 12W
Tívoli, Italy 94 41 58N 12 45E
Tivoli, U.S.A. 51 28 27N 96 53W
Tīwī 107 22 45N 59 12E
Tizi-Ouzou 120 36 42N 4 3E
Tizimín 65 21 0N 88 1W
Tiznados → 70 8 16N 67 47W
Tiznit 120 29 48N 9 45W
Tjeggelvas 96 66 37N 17 45E
Tjirebon = Cirebon 111 6 45S 108 32E
Tlacolula 65 16 57N 96 23W
Tlacotalpan 65 18 37N 95 40W
Tlahualilo 64 26 20N 103 30W
Tlaquepaque 64 20 39N 103 19W
Tlaxcala 65 19 20N 98 14W
Tlaxcala □ 65 19 30N 98 20W
Tlaxiaco 65 17 18N 97 40W
Tlell 62 53 34N 131 56W
Tlemcen 120 34 52N 1 21W
Tmassah 121 26 19N 15 51E
Toa Alta 57 18 23N 66 15W
Toa Baja 57 18 27N 66 15W
Toad → 62 59 25N 124 57W
Toamasina 123 18 10S 49 25E
Toana Range 35 40 50N 114 20W
Toano 54 37 23N 76 48W
Toast 40 36 30N 80 38W
Toay 76 36 43S 64 38W
Toba 117 34 30N 136 51E
Toba Kakar 108 31 30N 69 0E
Tobago 67 11 10N 60 30W
Tobelo 111 1 45N 127 56E
Tobermory, Canada 60 45 12N 81 40W
Tobermory, U.K. 84 56 37N 6 4W
Tobias 34 40 25N 97 20W
Tobin L. 63 53 35N 103 30W
Tobin Range 35 40 20N 117 30W
Toboali 110 3 0S 106 25E
Tobol 100 52 40N 62 39E
Toboli 111 0 38S 120 5E
Tobolsk 100 58 15N 68 10E
Tobruk = Tubruq 121 32 7N 23 55E
Tobyhanna 45 41 11N 75 25W
Tocache Nuevo 72 8 9S 76 26W
Tocantínia 74 9 33S 48 22W
Tocantinópolis 74 6 20S 47 25W
Tocantins → 74 1 45S 49 10W
Toccoa 18 34 35N 83 19W
Toccopola 31 34 15N 89 14W
Tochigi 117 36 25N 139 45E
Tochigi □ 117 36 45N 139 45E
Tocopilla 76 22 5S 70 10W
Tocuyo → 70 11 3N 68 23W
Tocuyo de la Costa 70 11 2N 68 23W
Todd County ◇, Ky. 48 36 50N 87 10W
Todd County ◇, Minn. 30 46 10N 94 50W
Todd County ◇, S. Dak. 47 43 5N 101 0W
Toddville 27 38 18N 76 4W
Todeli 111 1 38S 124 34E
Todenyang 122 4 35N 35 56E
Todos os Santos, Baía de 75 12 48S 38 38W
Todos Santos 64 23 27N 110 13W
Tofield 62 53 25N 112 40W
Tofino 62 49 11N 125 55W
Tofte 30 47 35N 90 50W
Tofua 128 19 45S 175 5W
Tōgane 117 35 33N 140 22E
Togba 120 17 26N 10 12W
Togiak 11 59 4N 160 24W
Togian, Kepulauan 111 0 20S 121 50E
Togliatti 98 53 32N 49 24E
Togo ■ 120 6 15N 1 35E
Togowatee Pass 56 43 45N 110 4W
Togtoh 114 40 15N 111 10E
Tohatchi 38 35 52N 108 47W
Tōhoku □ 116 39 50N 141 45E
Tohopekaliga L. 17 28 12N 81 24W
Toinya 121 6 17N 29 46E
Toiyabe National Forest 35 38 40N 117 0W
Toiyabe Range 35 39 30N 117 0W
Tojo, Indonesia 111 1 20S 121 15E
Tōjō, Japan 117 34 53N 133 16E
Tok 11 63 20N 142 59W
Toka 71 3 58N 59 17W
Tokachi-Dake 116 43 17N 142 5E
Tokachi-Gawa → 116 42 44N 143 42E
Tokaj 89 48 8N 21 27E
Tokala 111 1 30S 121 40E
Tōkamachi 117 37 8N 138 43E
Tokanui 128 46 34S 168 56E
Tokar 121 18 27N 37 56E
Tokara-Rettō 117 29 37N 129 43E
Tokarahi 128 44 56S 170 39E
Tokashiki-Shima 117 26 11N 127 21E
Tokat 106 40 22N 36 35E
Tokeland 53 46 42N 123 59W
Tokelau Is. 124 9 0S 171 45W
Tokmak 100 42 49N 75 15E
Tokong 112 5 27N 100 23E
Tokoro-Gawa → 116 44 7N 144 5E
Toksook Bay 11 60 32N 165 0W
Tokuno-Shima 117 27 56N 128 55E
Tokushima 117 34 4N 134 34E
Tokushima □ 117 34 15N 134 0E
Tokuyama 117 34 3N 131 50E
Tōkyō 117 35 45N 139 45E
Tolbert 51 34 13N 99 24W
Tolbukhin 95 43 37N 27 49E
Tolchester Beach 27 39 13N 76 14W
Toledo, Spain 91 39 50N 4 2W
Toledo, Ill. 21 39 16N 88 15W
Toledo, Iowa 23 42 0N 92 35W
Toledo, Ohio 42 41 39N 83 33W
Toledo, Oreg. 44 44 37N 123 56W
Toledo, Wash. 53 46 26N 122 51W
Toledo, Montes de 91 39 33N 4 20W
Toledo Bend Reservoir 25 31 11N 93 34W
Tolga 120 34 40N 5 22E
Toliara 123 23 21S 43 40E
Tolima □ 70 3 45N 75 15W
Tolima, Vol. 70 4 40N 75 19W
Tolitoli 111 1 5N 120 50E
Tolland 28 41 52N 72 22W
Tolland County ◇ 28 41 45N 72 20W
Tolleson 12 33 27N 112 16W
Tolley 41 48 44N 101 50W
Tolna 41 47 50N 98 26W
Tolo 122 2 55S 18 34E
Tolo, Teluk 111 2 20S 122 10E
Tolono 21 39 59N 88 16W
Tolosa 91 43 8N 2 5W
Toltén 78 39 13S 74 14W
Tolu 48 37 26N 88 15W
Toluca 65 19 20N 99 40W
Tom 43 33 44N 94 35W
Tom Green County ◇ 50 31 28N 100 26W
Tom Price 126 22 40S 117 48E
Tom Steed Res. 43 34 46N 98 50W
Tomah 55 43 59N 90 30W
Tomahawk 55 45 28N 89 44W
Tomakomai 116 42 38N 141 36E
Tomales Pt. 14 38 14N 122 59W
Tomar 91 39 36N 8 25W
Tomás Barrón 72 17 35S 67 31W
Tomaszów Mazowiecki 89 51 30N 19 57E
Tomatlán 64 19 56N 105 15W
Tombador, Serra do 73 12 0S 58 0W
Tomball 51 30 6N 95 37W
Tombé 121 5 53N 31 40E
Tombigbee → 10 31 8N 87 57W
Tombigee National Forest 31 33 10N 89 0W

Tombouctou
Trinity

Tombouctou 120 16 50N 3 0W
Tombstone 12 31 43N 110 4W
Tombua 123 15 55S 11 55E
Tomé, Chile 76 36 36S 72 57W
Tome, U.S.A. 38 34 44N 106 44W
Tomé-Açu 74 2 25S 48 9W
Tomelloso 91 39 10N 3 2W
Tomichi → 16 38 31N 106 58W
Tomini 111 0 30N 120 30E
Tomini, Teluk 111 0 10S 122 0E
Tommot 101 59 4N 126 20E
Tomnavoulin 84 57 19N 3 18W
Tomo 70 2 38N 67 32W
Tomo → 70 5 20N 67 48W
Tomorrit 95 40 40N 20 30E
Tompkins County ◇ 39 42 30N 76 30W
Tompkinsville, Ky. 49 36 42N 85 41W
Tompkinsville, Md. 27 38 18N 76 54W
Toms → 37 39 57N 74 7W
Toms Brook 54 38 57N 78 26W
Toms River 37 39 58N 74 12W
Tomsk 100 56 30N 85 5E
Tonalá 65 16 8N 93 41W
Tonalea 12 36 19N 110 56W
Tonantins 70 2 45S 67 45W
Tonasket 53 48 42N 119 26W
Tonate 71 5 0N 52 28W
Tonawanda 39 43 1N 78 53W
Tonawanda Indian Reservation 39 43 5N 78 25W
Tonbridge 83 51 12N 0 18E
Tondano 111 1 35N 124 54E
Tonekābon 107 36 45N 51 12E
Tong Xian 114 39 55N 116 35E
Tonga ■ 128 19 50S 174 30W
Tonga Trench 124 18 0S 175 0W
Tonganoxie 24 39 7N 95 5W
Tongareva 125 9 0S 158 0W
Tongass National Forest 11 56 30N 134 0W
Tongatapu 128 21 10S 174 0W
Tongcheng 115 31 4N 116 56E
Tongchuan 115 35 6N 109 3E
Tongdao 115 26 10N 109 42E
Tongeren 87 50 47N 5 28E
Tongguan 115 34 40N 110 25E
Tonghua 114 41 42N 125 58E
Tongjiang, Heilongjiang, China 114 47 40N 132 27E
Tongjiang, Sichuan, China 115 31 58N 107 11E
Tongking, G. of 112 20 0N 108 0E
Tongliao 114 43 38N 122 18E
Tongling 115 30 55N 117 48E
Tonglu 115 29 45N 119 37E
Tongnan 115 30 9N 105 50E
Tongoy 76 30 16S 71 31W
Tongren 115 27 43N 109 11E
Tongres = Tongeren 87 50 47N 5 28E
Tongsa Dzong 109 27 31N 90 31E
Tongue 84 58 29N 4 25W
Tongue → 33 46 25N 105 52W
Tongue River Reservoir 33 45 8N 106 46W
Tongyu 114 44 45N 123 4E
Tongzi 115 28 9N 106 49E
Tonica 21 41 13N 89 4W
Tonk 108 26 6N 75 54E
Tonkawa 43 36 41N 97 18W
Tonkin = Bac Phan 112 22 0N 105 0E
Tonlé Sap 112 13 0N 104 0E
Tono 116 39 19N 141 32E
Tonopah, Ariz. 12 33 30N 112 56W
Tonopah, Nev. 35 38 4N 117 14W
Tonosí 66 7 20N 80 20W
Tønsberg 97 59 19N 10 25E
Tonsina 11 61 39N 145 11W
Tontitown 13 36 11N 94 14W
Tonto National Forest 12 34 0N 111 20W
Tooele 52 40 32N 112 18W
Tooele County ◇ 52 40 25N 113 0W
Toole County ◇ 33 48 48N 111 50W
Toombs County ◇ 18 32 10N 82 15W
Toomsboro 18 32 50N 83 5W
Toone 48 35 21N 88 57W
Toora-Khem 101 52 28N 96 17E
Toowoomba 127 27 32S 151 56E
Top 108 34 15N 68 35E
Top-ozero 98 65 35N 32 0E
Topalu 95 44 31N 28 3E
Topawa 12 31 48N 111 51W
Topaz L. 35 38 41N 119 33W
Topeka, Ind. 22 41 32N 85 32W
Topeka, Kans. 24 39 3N 95 40W
Topki 100 55 20N 85 35E
Topley 62 54 49N 126 18W
Topocalma, Pta. 76 34 10S 72 2W
Topolnitsa → 95 42 11N 24 18E
Topolobampo 64 25 40N 109 4W
Topolovgrad 95 42 5N 26 20E
Toponas 16 40 4N 106 48W
Toppenish 53 46 23N 120 19W
Topsail Beach 40 34 23N 77 37W
Topsfield, Maine 26 45 25N 67 44W
Topsfield, Mass. 28 42 38N 70 57W
Topton, N.C. 40 35 15N 83 42W
Topton, Pa. 45 40 30N 75 42W
Toquepala 72 17 24S 70 25W
Toquerville 52 37 15N 113 17W
Toquima Range 35 38 55N 116 50W
Tor Bay 126 35 5S 117 50E
Toraka Vestale 123 16 20S 43 58E
Torata 72 17 23S 70 1W
Torbat-e Heydārīyeh 107 35 15N 59 12E
Torbat-e Jām 107 35 16N 60 35E
Torbay, Canada 61 47 40N 52 42W
Torbay, U.K. 83 50 26N 3 31W
Torch L. 29 44 58N 85 18W
Tordesillas 91 41 30N 5 0W
Torey 101 50 33N 104 50E
Torfajökull 96 63 54N 19 0W
Torgau 88 51 32N 13 0E
Torhout 87 51 5N 3 7E
Tori-Shima 117 30 29N 140 19E
Torin 64 27 33N 110 15W
Torino 94 45 4N 7 40E
Torit 121 4 27N 32 31E
Tormentine 61 46 6N 63 46W
Tormes → 91 41 18N 6 29W
Tornado Mt. 62 49 55N 114 40W
Torne älv → 96 65 50N 24 12E
Torneå = Tornio 96 65 50N 24 12E
Torneträsk 96 68 24N 19 15E
Tornillo 50 31 27N 106 5W
Tornio 96 65 50N 24 12E
Tornionjoki → 96 65 50N 24 12E
Tornquist 76 38 8S 62 15W
Toro 25 31 17N 93 33W
Toro, Cerro del 76 29 10S 69 50W
Toronìos Kólpos 95 40 5N 23 30E
Toronto, Canada 60 43 39N 79 20W
Toronto, Iowa 23 41 54N 90 52W
Toronto, Kans. 24 37 48N 95 57W
Toronto, Ohio 42 40 28N 80 36W
Toronto, S. Dak. 47 44 34N 96 39W
Toronto, L. 64 27 40N 105 30W
Toronto Lake 24 37 46N 95 57W
Toropets 98 56 30N 31 40E
Tororo 122 0 45N 34 12E
Toros Daglari 106 37 0N 35 0E
Torotoro 73 18 7S 65 46W
Torquay, Canada 63 49 9N 103 30W
Torquay, U.K. 83 50 27N 3 31W
Torrance 15 33 50N 118 19W
Torrance County ◇ 38 34 40N 106 0W
Torre Annunziata 94 40 45N 14 26E
Tôrre de Moncorvo 91 41 12N 7 8W
Torrelavega 91 43 20N 4 5W
Torremolinos 91 36 38N 4 30W
Torrens, L. 127 31 0S 137 50E
Torréon 64 25 33N 103 25W
Torres 64 28 46N 110 47W
Torres Strait 127 9 50S 142 20E
Torres Vedras 91 39 5N 9 15W
Torrevieja 91 37 59N 0 42W
Torrey 52 38 18N 111 25W
Torridge → 83 50 51N 4 10W
Torridon, L. 84 57 35N 5 50W
Torrington, Conn. 28 41 48N 73 7W
Torrington, Wyo. 56 42 4N 104 11W
Tortilla Flat 12 33 32N 111 23W
Tortosa 91 40 49N 0 31E
Tortosa, C. 91 40 41N 0 52E
Tortue, Î. de la 67 20 5N 72 57W
Tortuga, La 71 11 0N 65 22W
Tortuguero, L. 57 18 28N 66 26W
Ţorūd 107 35 25N 55 5E
Toruń 89 53 0N 18 39E
Tory I. 85 55 17N 8 12W
Tosa 117 33 24N 133 23E
Tosa-Shimizu 117 32 52N 132 58E
Tosa-Wan 117 33 15N 133 30E
Toscana 94 43 30N 11 5E
Tostado 76 29 15S 61 50W
Toston 33 46 11N 111 26W
Tosu 117 33 22N 130 31E
Tosya 106 41 1N 34 2E
Toteng 123 20 22S 22 58E
Totma 98 60 0N 42 40E
Totnes 83 50 26N 3 41W
Totness 71 5 53N 56 19W
Totonicapán 66 14 58N 91 12W
Totora 73 17 42S 65 9W
Totten Glacier 5 66 45S 116 10E
Tottori 117 35 30N 134 15E
Tottori □ 117 35 30N 134 12E
Touba 120 8 22N 7 40W
Toubkal, Djebel 120 31 0N 8 0W
Tougan 120 13 11N 2 58W
Touggourt 120 33 6N 6 4E
Toughy 34 41 8N 96 50W
Tougué 120 11 25N 11 50W
Toul 90 48 40N 5 53E
Toulepleu 120 6 32N 8 24W
Toulon, France 90 43 10N 5 55E
Toulon, U.S.A. 21 41 6N 89 52W
Toulouse 90 43 37N 1 27E
Toummo 121 22 45N 14 8E
Toungoo 109 19 0N 96 30E
Touraine 90 47 20N 0 30E
Tourane = Da Nang 112 16 4N 108 13E
Tourcoing 90 50 42N 3 10E
Tournai 87 50 35N 3 25E
Tournon 90 45 4N 4 50E
Touros 74 5 12S 35 28W
Tours 90 47 22N 0 40E
Tovar 70 8 20N 71 46W
Towada 116 40 37N 141 13E
Towada-Ko 116 40 28N 140 55E
Towanda, Kans. 24 37 44N 97 0W
Towanda, Pa. 45 41 46N 76 27W
Towang 109 27 37N 91 50E
Towaoc 16 37 12N 108 44W
Tower 30 47 48N 92 17W
Tower City, N. Dak. 41 46 56N 97 40W
Tower City, Pa. 45 40 35N 76 33W
Tower Hill 21 39 23N 88 58W
Towner, Colo. 16 38 28N 102 5W
Towner, N. Dak. 41 48 21N 100 25W
Towner County ◇ 41 48 45N 99 10W
Towns 18 32 0N 82 45W
Towns County ◇ 18 34 55N 83 45W
Townsend, Del. 27 39 24N 75 41W
Townsend, Ga. 18 31 33N 81 31W
Townsend, Mass. 28 42 40N 71 42W
Townsend, Mont. 33 46 19N 111 31W
Townshend 36 43 3N 72 41W
Townshend, C. 127 22 18S 150 30E
Townshend I. 127 22 10S 150 31E
Townsville, Australia 127 19 15S 146 45E
Townsville, U.S.A. 40 36 30N 78 25W
Townville 45 41 41N 79 53W
Towson 27 39 24N 76 36W
Towyn 83 52 36N 4 5W
Toxey 10 31 55N 88 19W
Toya-Ko 116 42 35N 140 51E
Toyah 50 31 19N 103 48W
Toyah Cr. → 50 31 18N 103 27W
Toyah L. 50 31 15N 103 20W
Toyahvale 50 30 57N 103 47W
Toyama 117 36 40N 137 15E
Toyama □ 117 36 45N 137 30E
Toyama-Wan 117 37 0N 137 30E
Toyohashi 117 34 45N 137 25E
Toyokawa 117 34 48N 137 27E
Toyonaka 117 34 50N 135 28E
Toyooka 117 35 35N 134 48E
Toyota 117 35 3N 137 7E
Tozeur 120 33 56N 8 8E
Trabzon 106 41 0N 39 45E
Tracadie 61 47 30N 64 55W
Tracy, Calif. 14 37 44N 121 26W
Tracy, Minn. 30 44 14N 95 37W
Tracy City 49 35 16N 85 44W
Tradewater → 48 37 31N 88 3W
Tradovoye 116 43 17N 132 5E
Traer 23 42 12N 92 28W
Trafalgar 22 39 25N 86 9W
Trafalgar, C. 91 36 10N 6 2W
Traian 95 45 2N 28 15E
Traiguén 78 38 15S 72 41W
Trail, Canada 62 49 5N 117 40W
Trail, U.S.A. 30 47 47N 95 42W
Traill County ◇ 41 47 30N 97 20W
Trainor L. 62 60 24N 120 17W
Traíra → 70 1 4S 69 26W
Tralee 85 52 16N 9 42W
Tralee B. 85 52 17N 9 55W
Trammel 54 37 1N 82 18W
Tramore 85 52 10N 7 10W
Tramway 40 35 27N 79 13W
Tran Ninh, Cao Nguyen 112 19 30N 103 10E
Tranås 97 58 3N 14 59E
Trancas 76 26 11S 65 20W
Trang 112 7 33N 99 38E
Trangan 111 6 40S 134 20E
Trani 94 41 17N 16 24E
Tranqueras 77 31 13S 55 45W
Tranquillity 15 36 39N 120 15W
Transantarctic Mts. 5 85 0S 170 0W
Transcona 63 49 55N 97 0W
Transilvania 89 46 19N 25 0E
Transkei 123 32 15S 28 15E
Transvaal □ 123 25 0S 29 0E
Transylvania = Transilvania 89 46 19N 25 0E
Transylvania 25 32 41N 91 11W
Transylvania County ◇ 40 35 10N 82 50W
Transylvanian Alps 95 45 30N 25 0E
Trápani 94 38 1N 12 30E
Trappe 27 38 40N 76 4W
Trapper Pk. 33 45 54N 114 18W
Traralgon 127 38 12S 146 34E
Tras os Montes e Alto Douro □ 91 41 25N 7 20W
Trăscău, Munţii 95 46 14N 23 14E
Trasimeno, L. 94 43 10N 12 5E
Trask Mt. 44 45 22N 123 27W
Traskwood 13 34 27N 92 39W
Trat 112 12 14N 102 33E
Travelers Rest 46 34 58N 82 27W
Travers, Mt. 128 42 1S 172 45E
Traversay Is. 5 57 0S 28 0W
Traverse, L. 47 45 46N 96 38W
Traverse City 29 44 46N 85 38W
Traverse County ◇ 30 45 45N 96 25W
Traverse Pt. 29 47 9N 88 14W
Travis, L. 51 30 24N 97 55W
Travis County ◇ 51 30 17N 97 45W
Travnik 95 44 17N 17 39E
Treasure County ◇ 33 46 15N 107 20W
Treasure Island 17 27 46N 82 46W
Trébbia → 94 45 4N 9 41E
Trebinje 95 42 44N 18 22E
Třeboň 88 48 59N 14 48E
Tredegar 83 51 47N 3 16W
Treece 24 37 0N 94 51W
Tregaron 83 52 14N 3 56W
Trego 33 48 42N 114 52W
Trego County ◇ 24 38 55N 99 50W
Tréguier 90 48 47N 3 16W
Treherne 63 49 38N 98 42W
Treinta y Tres 77 33 16S 54 17W
Trelew 78 43 10S 65 20W
Trelleborg 97 55 20N 13 10E
Tremont, Ill. 21 40 28N 89 29W
Tremont, Miss. 31 34 14N 88 16W
Tremonton 52 41 43N 112 10W
Tremp 91 42 10N 0 52E
Trempealeau 55 44 0N 91 26W
Trempealeau County ◇ 55 44 15N 91 20W
Trenche → 60 47 46N 72 53W
Trenggalek 111 8 5S 111 38E
Trenque Lauquen 76 36 5S 62 45W
Trent 47 43 54N 96 39W
Trent →, U.K. 82 53 33N 0 44W
Trent →, U.S.A. 40 35 5N 77 2W
Trentino-Alto Adige □ 94 46 30N 11 0E
Trento 94 46 5N 11 8E
Trenton, Canada 60 44 10N 77 34W
Trenton, Fla. 17 29 37N 82 49W
Trenton, Ga. 18 34 52N 85 31W
Trenton, Ill. 21 38 36N 89 41W
Trenton, Ky. 48 36 43N 87 16W
Trenton, Maine 26 44 27N 68 22W
Trenton, Mich. 29 42 8N 83 11W
Trenton, Mo. 32 40 5N 93 37W
Trenton, N.C. 40 35 4N 77 21W
Trenton, N. Dak. 41 48 4N 103 51W
Trenton, N.J. 37 40 14N 74 46W
Trenton, Nebr. 34 40 11N 101 1W
Trenton, Ohio 42 39 29N 84 28W
Trenton, S.C. 46 33 45N 81 51W
Trenton, Tenn. 48 35 59N 88 56W
Trepassey 61 46 43N 53 25W
Tréport, Le 90 50 3N 1 20E
Tres Arroyos 76 38 26S 60 20W
Três Corações 75 21 44S 45 15W
Três Lagoas 75 20 50S 51 43W
Tres Lagos → 78 49 35S 71 25W
Tres Marías 64 21 25N 106 28W
Três Marias, Reprêsa 75 18 12S 45 15W
Tres Montes, C. 78 46 50S 75 30W
Tres Palacios B. 51 28 30N 96 25W
Tres Piedras 38 36 39N 105 58W
Tres Pinos 14 36 48N 121 19W
Três Pontas 75 21 23S 45 29W
Tres Puentes 76 27 50S 70 15W
Tres Puntas, C. 78 47 0S 66 0W
Três Rios 75 22 6S 43 15W
Tres Valles 65 18 15N 96 8W
Treungen 97 59 1N 8 31E
Treutlen County ◇ 18 32 25N 82 30W
Treviso 94 45 40N 12 15E
Trevorton 45 40 47N 76 41W
Treynor 23 41 14N 95 36W
Trezevant 48 36 1N 88 37W
Triangle 54 38 33N 77 20W
Tribbey 43 35 7N 97 4W
Tribly 17 28 28N 82 12W
Tribulation, C. 127 16 5S 145 29E
Tribune 24 38 28N 101 45W
Trichinopoly = Tiruchchirappalli 108 10 45N 78 45E
Trichur 108 10 30N 76 18E
Trident 33 45 57N 111 28W
Trident Peak 35 41 54N 118 25W
Trier 88 49 45N 6 37E
Trieste 94 45 39N 13 45E
Trigg County ◇ 48 36 50N 87 55W
Triglav 94 46 21N 13 50E
Trigo Mountains 12 33 15N 114 40W
Tríkkala 95 39 34N 21 47E
Trikora, Puncak 111 4 15S 138 45E
Trim 85 53 34N 6 48W
Trimble, Mo. 32 39 28N 94 34W
Trimble, Tenn. 48 36 12N 89 11W
Trimble County 49 38 35N 85 20W
Trimont 30 43 46N 94 43W
Trinchera 16 37 2N 104 3W
Trincomalee 108 8 38N 81 15E
Trindade 75 16 40S 49 30W
Trindade, I. 2 20 20S 29 50W
Trinidad, Bolivia 73 14 46S 64 50W
Trinidad, Colombia 70 5 25N 71 40W
Trinidad, Cuba 66 21 48N 80 0W
Trinidad, Uruguay 76 33 30S 56 50W
Trinidad, Calif. 14 41 4N 124 9W
Trinidad, Colo. 16 37 10N 104 31W
Trinidad, Tex. 51 32 9N 96 6W
Trinidad, W. Indies 67 10 30N 61 15W
Trinidad → 65 17 49N 95 9W
Trinidad, G. 78 49 55S 75 25W
Trinidad, I. 78 39 10S 62 0W
Trinidad & Tobago ■ 67 10 30N 61 20W
Trinidad Head 14 41 3N 124 9W
Trinity, Canada 61 48 59N 53 55W
Trinity, U.S.A. 51 30 57N 95 22W

Trinity Tuscumbia

Trinity →, Calif. 14 41 11N 123 42W
Trinity →, Tex. 51 29 45N 94 43W
Trinity B., Australia 127 16 30S 146 0 E
Trinity B., Canada 61 48 20N 53 10W
Trinity B., U.S.A. 51 29 42N 94 55W
Trinity Center 14 41 0N 122 41W
Trinity County ◇, Calif. 14 40 40N 123 0W
Trinity County ◇, Tex. 51 31 4N 95 8W
Trinity Is. 11 56 33N 154 25W
Trinity Mt. 20 43 36N 115 26W
Trinity Mts. 14 40 50N 122 40W
Trinity National Forest 14 40 40N 123 15W
Trinity Range 35 40 15N 118 45W
Trinkitat 121 18 45N 37 51 E
Trinway 42 40 9N 82 1W
Trion 18 34 33N 85 19W
Triplett 32 39 30N 93 12W
Tripoli = Tarābulus, Lebanon 106 34 31N 35 50 E
Tripoli = Tarābulus, Libya 121 32 49N 13 7 E
Tripoli 23 42 49N 92 16W
Trípolis 95 37 31N 22 25 E
Tripp 47 43 13N 97 58W
Tripp County ◇ 47 43 20N 100 0W
Tripura □ 109 24 0N 92 0 E
Tristan da Cunha 2 37 6S 12 20W
Triumph 25 29 20N 89 30W
Trivandrum 108 8 41N 77 0 E
Trnava 89 48 23N 17 35 E
Trochu 62 51 50N 113 13W
Trodely I. 60 52 15N 79 26W
Troglav 94 43 56N 16 36 E
Troilus, L. 60 50 50N 74 35W
Trois-Pistoles 61 48 5N 69 10W
Trois-Riviéres 60 46 25N 72 34W
Troitsk 100 54 10N 61 35 E
Troitsko Pechorsk 98 62 40N 56 10 E
Trölladyngja 96 64 54N 17 16W
Trollhättan 97 58 17N 12 20 E
Trombetas → 71 1 55S 55 35W
Troms fylke □ 96 68 56N 19 0 E
Tromsø 96 69 40N 18 56 E
Trona 15 35 46N 117 23W
Tronador 78 41 10S 71 50W
Trondheim 96 63 36N 10 25 E
Trondheimsfjorden 96 63 35N 10 30 E
Troon 84 55 33N 4 40W
Tropic 52 37 37N 112 5W
Trossachs, The 84 56 14N 4 24W
Trostan 85 55 4N 6 10W
Trotternish 84 57 32N 6 15W
Troup 51 32 9N 95 7W
Troup County ◇ 18 33 0N 85 0W
Trousdale 24 37 49N 99 5W
Trousdale County ◇ 48 36 24N 86 10W
Trout → 62 61 19N 119 51W
Trout Cr. →, Oreg. 44 42 23N 118 3W
Trout Cr. →, Oreg. 44 44 48N 121 3W
Trout Creek, Mich. 29 46 29N 89 1W
Trout Creek, Mont. 33 47 50N 115 36W
Trout Creek, Utah 52 39 42N 113 50W
Trout Dale 54 36 42N 81 26W
Trout L., N.W.T., Canada 62 60 40N 121 40W
Trout L., Ont., Canada 63 51 20N 93 15W
Trout Lake, Mich. 29 46 12N 85 1W
Trout Lake, Wash. 53 46 0N 121 32W
Trout Pk. 56 44 36N 109 32W
Trout River 61 49 29N 58 8W
Troutmans 40 35 42N 80 53W
Troutville 54 37 25N 79 53W
Trouville 90 49 21N 0 5 E
Trowbridge 83 51 18N 2 12W
Troy, Turkey 106 39 57N 26 12 E
Troy, Ala. 10 31 48N 85 58W
Troy, Idaho 20 46 44N 116 46W
Troy, Ind. 22 37 59N 86 55W
Troy, Kans. 24 39 47N 95 5W
Troy, Mich. 29 42 37N 83 9W
Troy, Miss. 31 34 7N 88 53W
Troy, Mo. 32 38 59N 90 59W
Troy, Mont. 33 48 28N 115 53W
Troy, N.C. 40 35 22N 79 53W
Troy, N.H. 36 42 49N 72 11W
Troy, N.Y. 39 42 44N 73 41W
Troy, Ohio 42 40 2N 84 12W
Troy, Oreg. 44 45 57N 117 27W
Troy, Pa. 45 41 47N 76 47W
Troy, S.C. 46 33 59N 82 17W
Troy, S. Dak. 47 45 2N 96 52W
Troy, Tenn. 48 36 20N 89 10W
Troy, Tex. 51 31 12N 97 18W
Troy, Vt. 36 44 52N 72 25W
Troy Peak 35 38 19N 115 30W
Troyan 95 42 57N 24 43 E
Troyes 90 48 19N 4 3 E
Truchas 38 36 3N 105 49W
Truchas Peak 38 35 58N 105 39W
Trucial States = United Arab Emirates ■ 107 23 50N 54 0 E
Truckee 14 39 20N 120 11W
Truckee → 35 39 51N 119 24W
Truesdale 23 42 44N 95 11W
Trufant 29 43 19N 85 21W
Trujillo, Colombia 70 4 10N 76 19W
Trujillo, Hond. 66 16 0N 86 0W
Trujillo, Peru 72 8 6S 79 0W
Trujillo, Spain 91 39 28N 5 55W
Trujillo, U.S.A. 38 35 32N 104 42W
Trujillo, Venezuela 70 9 22N 70 38W
Trujillo □ 70 9 25N 70 30W
Trujillo Alto 57 18 21N 66 1W
Truk 124 7 25N 151 46 E
Truman 30 43 50N 94 26W
Trumann 13 35 41N 90 31W
Trumansburg 39 42 33N 76 40W
Trumbull, Conn. 28 41 15N 73 12W
Trumbull, Nebr. 34 40 41N 98 16W
Trumbull County ◇ 42 41 14N 80 49W
Trung-Phan 110 16 0N 108 0 E
Truro, Canada 61 45 21N 63 14W
Truro, U.K. 83 50 17N 5 2W
Truro, U.S.A. 28 42 0N 70 3W
Truscott 51 33 45N 99 49W
Trussville 10 33 37N 86 35W
Truth or Consequences 38 33 8N 107 15W
Trutnov 88 50 37N 15 54 E
Truxton 12 35 29N 113 34W
Tryavna 95 42 54N 25 25 E
Tryon, N.C. 40 35 13N 82 14W
Tryon, Nebr. 34 41 33N 100 57W
Tryon, Okla. 43 35 52N 96 58W
Tsala Apopka L. 17 28 53N 82 19W
Tsaratanana 123 16 47S 47 39 E
Tsarevo = Michurin 95 42 9N 27 51 E
Tsau 123 20 8S 22 22 E
Tschida L. 41 46 36N 101 49W
Tselinograd 100 51 10N 71 30 E
Tsetserleg 113 47 36N 101 32 E
Tshabong 123 26 2S 22 29 E
Tshane 123 24 5S 21 54 E
Tshela 122 4 57S 13 4 E
Tshikapa 122 6 28S 20 48 E
Tshofa 122 5 13S 25 16 E
Tshwane 123 22 24S 22 1 E
Tsihombe 123 25 10S 45 41 E
Tsimlyanskoye Vdkhr. 99 48 0N 43 0 E
Tsinan = Jinan 114 36 38N 117 1 E
Tsinghai = Qinghai □ 113 36 0N 98 0 E
Tsingtao = Qingdao 114 36 5N 120 20 E
Tsivory 123 24 4S 46 5 E
Tskhinvali 99 42 14N 44 1 E
Tsna → 98 54 55N 41 58 E
Tsu 117 34 45N 136 25 E
Tsu L. 62 60 40N 111 52W
Tsuchiura 117 36 5N 140 15 E
Tsugaru-Kaikyō 116 41 35N 141 0 E
Tsumeb 123 19 9S 17 44 E
Tsumis 123 23 39S 17 29 E
Tsuruga 117 35 45N 136 2 E
Tsurugi-San 117 33 51N 134 6 E
Tsuruoka 116 38 44N 139 50 E
Tsushima, Gifu, Japan 117 35 10N 136 43 E
Tsushima, Nagasaki, Japan 117 34 20N 129 20 E
Tual 111 5 38S 132 44 E
Tuam 85 53 30N 8 50W
Tuamotu Arch. 125 17 0S 144 0W
Tuamotu Ridge 125 20 0S 138 0W
Tuao 111 17 55N 122 22 E
Tuapse 99 44 5N 39 10 E
Tuatapere 128 46 8S 167 41 E
Tuba City 12 36 8N 111 14W
Tubac 12 31 37N 111 3W
Tuban 111 6 54S 112 3 E
Tubarão 77 28 30S 49 0W
Tūbās 104 32 20N 35 22 E
Tubau 110 3 10N 113 40 E
Tübingen 88 48 31N 9 4 E
Tubruq 121 32 7N 23 55 E
Tubuaeran I. 125 3 51N 159 22W
Tubuai Is. 125 25 0S 150 0W
Tucacas 70 10 48N 68 19W
Tucano 74 10 58S 38 48W
Tuchodi → 62 58 17N 123 42W
Tuckahoe 37 39 17N 74 45W
Tuckahoe → 27 38 0N 75 0W
Tucker, Ark. 13 34 26N 91 57W
Tucker, Ga. 18 33 51N 84 13W
Tucker County ◇ 54 39 9N 79 30W
Tuckerman 13 35 44N 91 12W
Tuckernuck Island 28 41 18N 70 15W
Tuckerton 37 39 36N 74 20W
Tucson 12 32 13N 110 58W
Tucumán □ 76 26 48S 66 2W
Tucumcari 38 35 10N 103 44W
Tucunaré 73 5 18S 55 51W
Tucupido 70 9 17N 65 47W
Tucupita 71 9 2N 62 3W
Tucuruí 74 3 42S 49 44W
Tudela 91 42 4N 1 39W
Tudmur 106 34 36N 38 15 E
Tudor, Lac 61 55 50N 65 25W
Tueré → 74 2 48S 50 59W
Tuftonboro 36 43 42N 71 13W
Tug Fork → 54 38 7N 82 36W
Tugidak I. 11 56 30N 154 40W
Tuguegarao 111 17 35N 121 42 E
Tugur 101 53 44N 136 45 E
Tukangbesi, Kepulauan 111 6 0S 124 0 E
Tukarak I. 60 56 15N 78 45W
Tūkrah 121 32 30N 20 37 E
Tuktoyaktuk 58 69 27N 133 2W
Tukuyu 122 9 17S 33 35 E
Tukzar 108 35 55N 66 25 E
Tula, Hidalgo, Mexico 65 20 0N 99 20W
Tula, Tamaulipas, Mexico 65 23 0N 99 40W
Tula, U.S.A. 31 34 14N 89 22W
Tula, U.S.S.R. 98 54 13N 37 38 E
Tulak 107 33 55N 63 40 E
Tulalip Indian Reservation 53 48 4N 122 13W
Tulancingo 65 20 5N 99 22W
Tulare, Calif. 15 36 13N 119 21W
Tulare, S. Dak. 47 44 44N 98 31W
Tulare County ◇ 15 36 10N 118 50W
Tulare Lake Bed 15 36 0N 119 48W
Tularosa 38 33 5N 106 1W
Tularosa Mts. 38 33 45N 108 40W
Tularosa Valley 38 32 45N 106 0W
Tulbagh 123 33 16S 19 6 E
Tulcán 70 0 48N 77 43W
Tulcea 89 45 13N 28 46 E
Tulcea □ 95 45 0N 29 0 E
Tule → 15 36 3N 119 50W
Tule Cr. → 50 34 40N 101 14W
Tule L. 14 41 53N 121 30W
Tule River Indian Reservation 15 36 0N 118 50W
Tule Valley 52 39 25N 113 30W
Tulelake 14 41 57N 121 29W
Tulemalu L. 63 62 58N 99 25W
Tuli, Indonesia 111 1 24S 122 26 E
Tuli, Zimbabwe 123 21 58S 29 13 E
Tulia 50 34 32N 101 46W
Ţūlkarm 104 32 19N 35 2 E
Tullahassee 43 35 50N 95 26W
Tullahoma 48 35 22N 86 13W
Tullamore 85 53 17N 7 30W
Tulle 90 45 16N 1 46 E
Tulloch Reservoir 14 37 53N 120 36W
Tullos 25 31 49N 92 19W
Tullow 85 52 48N 6 45W
Tully 39 42 48N 76 7W
Ţulmaythah 121 32 40N 20 55 E
Tulnici 95 45 51N 26 38 E
Tulovo 95 42 33N 25 32 E
Tulsa 43 36 10N 95 55W
Tulsa County ◇ 43 36 0N 95 55W
Tulsequah 62 58 39N 133 35W
Tulua 70 4 6N 76 11W
Tuluksak 11 61 6N 160 58W
Tulun 101 54 32N 100 35 E
Tulungagung 110 8 5S 111 54 E
Tum 111 3 36S 130 21 E
Tuma → 66 13 6N 84 35W
Tumaco 70 1 50N 78 45W
Tumaco, Ensenada 70 1 55N 78 45W
Tumatumari 71 5 20N 58 55W
Tumba, L. 122 0 50S 18 0 E
Tumbaya 76 23 50S 65 26W
Túmbes 72 3 37S 80 27W
Tumbes □ 72 3 50S 80 30W
Tumen 114 43 0N 129 50 E
Tumen Jiang → 114 42 20N 130 35 E
Tumeremo 71 7 18N 61 30W
Tumiritinga 75 18 58S 41 38W
Tumkur 108 13 18N 77 6 E
Tummel, L. 84 56 43N 3 55W
Tump 107 26 7N 62 16 E
Tumpat 112 6 11N 102 10 E
Tumu 120 10 56N 1 56W
Tumucumaque, Serra 71 2 0N 55 0W
Tumupasa 72 14 9S 67 55W
Tumut 127 35 16S 148 13 E
Tumwater 53 47 1N 122 54W
Tunas de Zaza 66 21 39N 79 34W
Tunbridge Wells 83 51 7N 0 16 E
Tunduru 122 11 8S 37 25 E
Tundzha → 95 41 40N 26 35 E
Tunga Pass 109 29 0N 94 14 E
Tungabhadra → 108 15 57N 78 15 E
Tungaru 121 10 9N 30 52 E
Tungla 66 13 24N 84 21W
Tungnafellsjökull 96 64 45N 17 55W
Tungsten 62 61 57N 128 16W
Tungurahua □ 70 1 15S 78 35W
Tunguska, Nizhnyaya → 101 65 48N 88 4 E
Tunguska, Podkamennaya → 101 61 36N 90 18 E
Tunia 70 2 41N 76 31W
Tunica, La. 25 30 56N 91 33W
Tunica, Miss. 31 34 41N 90 23W
Tunica County ◇ 31 34 41N 90 23W
Tunis 120 36 50N 10 11 E
Tunis Mills 27 38 49N 76 10W
Tunisia ■ 120 33 30N 9 10 E
Tunja 70 5 33N 73 25W
Tunkhannock 45 41 32N 75 57W
Tunliu 114 36 13N 112 52 E
Tunnell Hill 21 37 32N 88 50W
Tunnelton 54 39 24N 79 45W
Tunnsjøen 96 64 45N 13 25 E
Tuntutuliak 11 60 22N 162 38W
Tununak 11 60 37N 165 15W
Tunungayualok I. 61 56 0N 61 0W
Tunuyán 76 33 35S 69 0W
Tunuyán → 76 33 33S 67 30W
Tunxi 115 29 42N 118 25 E
Tuolumne 14 37 58N 120 15W
Tuolumne County ◇ 14 38 0N 120 0W
Tuoy-Khaya 101 62 32N 111 25 E
Tupã 77 21 57S 50 28W
Tupaciguara 75 18 35S 48 42W
Tupelo, Miss. 31 34 16N 88 43W
Tupelo, Okla. 43 34 36N 96 26W
Tupik 101 54 26N 119 57 E
Tupinambaranas 71 3 0S 58 0W
Tupirama 74 8 58S 48 12W
Tupiratins 74 8 23S 48 8W
Tupiza 76 21 30S 65 40W
Tupper 62 55 32N 120 1W
Tupper L. 39 44 12N 74 35W
Tupper Lake 39 44 14N 74 28W
Tupungato, Cerro 76 33 15S 69 50W
Tuquan 114 45 18N 121 38 E
Tuque, La 60 47 30N 72 50W
Túquerres 70 1 5N 77 37W
Tura 101 64 20N 100 17 E
Turabah 106 28 20N 43 15 E
Turagua, Serranía 71 7 20N 64 35W
Tūrān, Iran 107 35 39N 56 42 E
Turan, U.S.S.R. 101 51 55N 95 0 E
Turayf 106 31 41N 38 39 E
Turbeville 46 33 54N 80 1W
Turda 95 46 34N 23 47 E
Turek 89 52 3N 18 30 E
Turen 70 9 17N 69 6W
Turfan = Turpan 113 43 58N 89 10 E
Turfan Depression = Turpan Hami 113 42 40N 89 25 E
Turfan Depression 113 42 45N 89 0 E
Tŭrgovishte 95 43 17N 26 38 E
Turgutlu 106 38 30N 27 48 E
Turhal 106 40 24N 36 5 E
Turia → 91 39 27N 0 19W
Turiaçu 74 1 40S 45 19W
Turiaçu → 74 1 36S 45 19W
Turin = Torino 94 45 4N 7 40 E
Turin, Canada 62 49 47N 112 24W
Turin, U.S.A. 23 42 1N 95 58W
Turkana, L. 122 3 30N 36 5 E
Turkestan 100 43 17N 68 16 E
Turkey, Ky. 49 37 29N 83 31W
Turkey, Tex. 50 34 24N 100 54W
Turkey ■ 106 39 0N 36 0 E
Turkey → 23 42 43N 91 2W
Turkey Cr. → 43 35 58N 97 56W
Turkey Creek 25 30 53N 92 25W
Turkey Mt. 50 29 22N 100 12W
Turkey Ridge 47 43 25N 97 25W
Turkmen S.S.R. □ 100 39 0N 59 0 E
Turks Is. 67 21 20N 71 20W
Turks Island Passage 67 21 30N 71 30W
Turku 97 60 30N 22 19 E
Turlock 14 37 30N 120 51W
Turlock L. 14 37 37N 120 35W
Turnagain → 62 59 12N 127 35W
Turnagain, C. 128 40 28S 176 38 E
Turneffe Is. 65 17 20N 87 50W
Turner, Mich. 29 44 9N 83 47W
Turner, Mont. 33 48 51N 108 24W
Turner, Oreg. 44 44 51N 122 57W
Turner, Wash. 53 46 25N 117 51W
Turner County ◇, Ga. 18 31 45N 83 45W
Turner County ◇, S. Dak. 47 43 17N 97 5W
Turner Valley 62 50 40N 114 17W
Turners Falls 28 42 36N 72 33W
Turnhout 87 51 19N 4 57 E
Turnor L. 63 56 35N 108 35W
Tŭrnovo 95 43 5N 25 41 E
Turnu Măgurele 89 43 46N 24 56 E
Turnu Rosu Pasul 89 45 33N 24 17 E
Turnu-Severin 89 44 39N 22 41 E
Turon 24 37 48N 98 26W
Turpan 113 43 58N 89 10 E
Turpan Hami 113 42 40N 89 25 E
Turpin 43 36 52N 100 52W
Turrell 13 35 23N 90 15W
Turriff 84 57 32N 2 28W
Turtle → 47 44 55N 98 29W
Turtle-Flambeau Flowage 55 46 4N 90 14W
Turtle L. 63 53 36N 108 38W
Turtle Lake, N. Dak. 41 47 31N 100 53W
Turtle Lake, Wis. 55 45 24N 92 8W
Turtle Mountain Indian Reservation 41 48 58N 99 58W
Turtle Mountains 41 48 58N 100 0W
Turtle River 30 47 35N 94 46W
Turtleford 63 53 23N 108 57W
Turukhansk 101 65 21N 88 5 E
Turun ja Porin lääni □ 97 60 27N 22 15 E
Tuscaloosa 10 33 12N 87 34W
Tuscaloosa County ◇ 10 33 11N 87 27W
Tuscany = Toscana 94 43 30N 11 5 E
Tuscarawas 42 40 24N 81 25W
Tuscarawas County ◇ 42 40 22N 81 26W
Tuscarora 35 41 19N 116 14W
Tuscarora Indian Reservation 39 43 10N 78 55W
Tuscarora Mt. 45 40 55N 77 55W
Tuscarora Mts. 35 41 0N 116 20W
Tuscola, Ill. 21 39 48N 88 17W
Tuscola, Tex. 51 32 12N 99 48W
Tuscola County ◇ 29 43 25N 83 20W
Tusculum 49 36 10N 82 46W
Tuscumbia, Ala. 10 34 44N 87 42W
Tuscumbia, Mo. 32 38 14N 92 28W

Tushar Mts. Uralsk

Tushar Mts. 52 38 20N 112 30W
Tushka 43 34 19N 96 10W
Tuskahoma 43 34 37N 95 17W
Tuskar Rock 85 52 12N 6 10W
Tuskegee 10 32 25N 85 42W
Tustin 29 44 6N 85 28W
Tutóia 74 2 45 S 42 20W
Tutong 110 4 47N 114 40 E
Tutova → 95 46 20N 27 30 E
Tutrakan 95 44 2N 26 40 E
Tutshi L. 62 59 56N 134 30W
Tuttle, N. Dak. 41 47 9N 100 0W
Tuttle, Okla. 43 35 17N 97 49W
Tuttle Creek Lake 24 39 15N 96 36W
Tuttlingen 88 47 59N 8 50 E
Tutuala 111 8 25 S 127 15 E
Tutuila 128 14 19 S 170 50W
Tututepec 65 16 9N 97 38W
Tutwiler 31 34 1N 90 26W
Tuva A.S.S.R. □ 101 51 30N 95 0 E
Tuvalu ■ 124 8 0 S 178 0 E
Tuweep 12 36 25N 113 4W
Tuxpan 65 20 58N 97 23W
Tuxtla Gutiérrez 65 16 50N 93 10W
Tuy 91 42 3N 8 39W
Tuy Hoa 112 13 5N 109 10 E
Tuya L. 62 59 7N 130 35W
Tuyen Hoa 112 17 50N 106 10 E
Tuz Gölü 106 38 45N 33 30 E
Ţūz Khurmātū 106 34 56N 44 38 E
Tuzla 95 44 34N 18 41 E
Tvŭrditsa 95 42 42N 25 53 E
Twain Harte 14 38 2N 120 14W
Tweed → 84 55 42N 2 10W
Tweedsmuir Prov. Park 62 53 0N 126 20W
Twentynine Palms 15 34 8N 116 3W
Twiggs County ◇ 18 32 40N 83 30W
Twillingate 61 49 42N 54 45W
Twin Bridges 33 45 33N 112 20W
Twin Brooks 47 45 12N 96 47W
Twin Buttes Reservoir 50 31 22N 100 32W
Twin City 18 32 35N 82 10W
Twin Falls 20 42 34N 114 28W
Twin Falls County ◇ 20 42 30N 114 45W
Twin Hills 11 59 23N 159 58W
Twin Lakes, Colo. 16 39 5N 106 23W
Twin Lakes, Ga. 18 30 43N 83 13W
Twin Lakes, Minn. 30 43 34N 93 25W
Twin Mountain 36 44 16N 71 32W
Twin Mts. 50 30 25N 103 50W
Twin Oaks 43 36 10N 94 51W
Twin Peaks 20 44 35N 114 29W
Twin Rivers 37 40 15N 74 32W
Twin Valley 30 47 16N 96 16W
Twisp 53 48 22N 120 7W
Twitchell Reservoir 15 34 59N 120 19W
Twitty 50 35 19N 100 14W
Two Butte → 16 38 2N 102 9W
Two Buttes 16 37 34N 102 24W
Two Buttes Reservoir 16 37 38N 102 32W
Two Harbors 30 47 2N 91 40W
Two Hills 62 53 43N 111 52W
Two Medicine → 33 48 29N 112 14W
Two Rivers 55 44 9N 87 34W
Twofold B. 127 37 8 S 149 59 E
Ty Ty 18 31 28N 83 39W
Tyaskin 27 38 18N 75 52W
Tye 51 32 27N 99 52W
Tygart L. 54 39 19N 80 2W
Tyger → 46 34 28N 81 26W
Tygh Valley 44 45 15N 121 10W
Tyhee 20 42 57N 112 28W
Tyler, Tex. 51 32 21N 95 18W
Tyler, Wash. 53 47 26N 117 47W
Tyler County ◇, Tex. 51 30 47N 94 25W
Tyler County ◇, W. Va. 54 39 30N 80 54W
Tylertown 31 31 7N 90 9W
Tymochtee → 42 40 57N 83 16W
Tynan 51 28 10N 97 45W
Tynda 101 55 10N 124 43 E
Tyndall 47 43 0N 97 50W
Tyne → 82 54 58N 1 28W
Tyne & Wear □ 82 54 55N 1 35W
Tynemouth 82 55 1N 1 27W
Tyner 40 36 13N 76 37W
Tyonek 11 61 4N 151 8W
Tyonek Indian Reservation 11 61 5N 151 10W
Tyre = Sūr 104 33 19N 35 16 E
Tyrifjorden 97 60 2N 10 8 E
Tyro, Ark. 13 33 50N 91 43W
Tyro, Kans. 24 37 2N 95 49W
Tyro, Miss. 31 34 35N 89 42W
Tyrol = Tirol □ 88 47 3N 10 43 E
Tyrone, N. Mex. 38 32 40N 108 22W
Tyrone, Okla. 43 36 57N 101 4W
Tyrone, Pa. 45 40 40N 78 14W
Tyrrell Arm 63 62 27N 97 30W
Tyrrell County ◇ 40 35 50N 76 10W
Tyrrell L. 63 63 7N 105 27W
Tyrrhenian Sea 94 40 0N 12 30 E
Tysfjorden 96 68 7N 16 25 E
Tyson 36 43 27N 72 44W
Tyulgan 98 52 22N 56 12 E
Tyumen 100 57 11N 65 29 E
Tywi → 83 51 48N 4 20W
Tzaneen 123 23 47 S 30 9 E
Tzukong = Zigong 115 29 15N 104 48 E

U

Uachadi, Sierra 71 4 54N 65 18W
Uainambi 70 1 43N 69 51W
Uarsciek 105 2 28N 45 55 E
Uato-Udo 111 9 7 S 125 36 E
Uatumã → 71 2 26 S 57 37W
Uauá 74 9 50 S 39 28W
Uaupés 70 0 8 S 67 5W
Uaxactún 66 17 25N 89 29W
Ubá 77 21 8 S 43 0W
Ubaitaba 75 14 18 S 39 20W
Ubangi = Oubangi → 122 1 0N 17 50 E
Ubaté 70 5 19N 73 49W
Ubauro 108 28 15N 69 45 E
Ube 117 33 56N 131 15 E
Ubeda 91 38 3N 3 23W
Uberaba 75 19 50 S 47 55W
Uberaba, L. 73 17 30 S 57 50W
Uberlândia 75 19 0 S 48 20W
Ubly 29 43 43N 82 56W
Ubon Ratchathani 112 15 15N 104 50 E
Ubundu 122 0 22 S 25 30 E
Ucayali → 72 4 30 S 73 30W
Uchi Lake 63 51 5N 92 35W
Uchiura-Wan 116 42 25N 140 40 E
Uchiza 72 8 25 S 76 20W
Uchur → 101 58 48N 130 35 E
Ucluelet 62 48 57N 125 32W
Ucon 20 43 36N 111 58W
Uda → 101 54 42N 135 14 E
Udaipur 108 24 36N 73 44 E
Udaipur Garhi 109 27 0N 86 35 E
Udall 24 37 23N 97 7W
Uddevalla 97 58 21N 11 55 E
Uddjaur 96 65 25N 21 15 E
Udell 23 40 47N 92 45W
Udgir 108 18 25N 77 5 E
Udhampur 108 33 0N 75 5 E
Udi 120 6 23N 7 21 E
Údine 94 46 5N 13 10 E
Udmurt A.S.S.R. □ 98 57 30N 52 30 E
Udon Thani 112 17 29N 102 46 E
Udupi 108 13 25N 74 42 E
Udvoy Balkan 95 42 50N 26 50 E
Ueda 117 36 24N 138 16 E
Uedineniya, Os. 4 78 0N 85 0 E
Uehling 34 41 44N 96 30W
Uelen 101 66 10N 170 0W
Uelzen 88 53 0N 10 33 E
Uere → 122 3 45N 24 45 E
Ufa 98 54 45N 55 55 E
Ufa → 98 54 40N 56 0 E
Ugad → 123 20 55 S 14 30 E
Ugalla → 122 5 8 S 30 42 E
Uganda ■ 122 2 0N 32 0 E
Uglegorsk 101 49 5N 142 2 E
Ugolyak 101 64 33N 120 30 E
Ugŭrchin 95 43 6N 24 26 E
Uhrichsville 42 40 24N 81 21W
Uíge 122 7 30 S 14 40 E
Uiju 114 40 15N 124 35 E
Uinta → 52 40 14N 109 51W
Uinta County ◇ 56 41 15N 110 30W
Uinta Mts. 52 40 45N 110 30W
Uinta National Forest 52 40 10N 111 20W
Uintah and Ouray Indian Reservation 52 40 15N 110 20W
Uintah County ◇ 52 40 20N 109 30W
Uitenhage 123 33 40 S 25 28 E
Uithuizen 87 53 24N 6 41 E
Uji-guntō 117 31 15N 129 25 E
Ujjain 108 23 9N 75 43 E
Újpest 89 47 32N 19 6 E
Ujung Pandang 111 5 10 S 119 20 E
Uka 101 57 50N 162 0 E
Uke-Shima 117 28 2N 129 14 E
Ukerewe I. 122 2 0 S 33 0 E
Ukhrul 109 25 10N 94 25 E
Ukhta 98 63 55N 54 0 E
Ukiah, Calif. 14 39 9N 123 13W
Ukiah, Oreg. 44 45 8N 118 56W
Ukrainian S.S.R. □ 99 49 0N 32 0 E
Ulaanbaatar 113 47 55N 106 53 E
Ulaangom 113 50 0N 92 10 E
Ulak I. 11 51 22N 178 57W
Ulan Bator = Ulaanbaatar 113 47 55N 106 53 E
Ulan Ude 101 51 45N 107 40 E
Ulcinj 95 41 58N 19 10 E
Ulen 30 47 5N 96 16W
Ulhasnagar 108 19 15N 73 10 E
Ullapool 84 57 54N 5 10W
Ullin 21 37 17N 89 11W
Ullswater 82 54 35N 2 52W
Ullung-do 114 37 30N 130 30 E
Ulm 88 48 23N 10 0 E
Ulmeni 95 45 4N 26 40 E
Ulonguè 123 14 37 S 34 19 E
Ulricehamn 97 57 46N 13 26 E
Ulster □ 85 54 35N 6 30W
Ulster County ◇ 39 41 50N 74 15W
Ulstrem 95 42 1N 26 27 E
Ulungur He → 113 47 1N 87 24 E
Ulupalakua 19 20 39N 156 24W
Ulutau 100 48 39N 67 1 E
Ulverston 82 54 13N 3 7W
Ulverstone 127 41 11 S 146 11 E
Ulya 101 59 10N 142 0 E
Ulyanovsk 98 54 20N 48 25 E
Ulyasutay 113 47 56N 97 28 E
Ulysses, Kans. 24 37 35N 101 22W
Ulysses, Nebr. 34 41 4N 97 12W
Ulysses, Pa. 45 41 54N 77 46W
Umala 72 17 25 S 68 5W
Uman 99 48 40N 30 12 E
Umaria 109 23 35N 80 50 E
Umarkot 108 25 15N 69 40 E
Umatilla 44 45 55N 119 21W
Umatilla → 44 45 55N 119 20W
Umatilla, L. 53 45 53N 119 40W
Umatilla County ◇ 44 45 40N 118 45W
Umatilla Indian Reservation 44 45 41N 118 31W
Umatilla National Forest 44 45 0N 118 50W
Umba 98 66 50N 34 20 E
Umbagog L. 36 44 46N 71 3W
Umbarger 50 34 57N 102 7W
Umbrella Mts. 128 45 35 S 169 5 E
Umbria □ 94 42 53N 12 30 E
Ume älv → 96 63 45N 20 20 E
Umeå 96 63 45N 20 20 E
Umera 111 0 12 S 129 37 E
Umiat 11 69 22N 152 8W
Umm al Qaywayn 107 25 30N 55 35 E
Umm az Zamul 107 22 42N 55 18 E
Umm Bel 121 13 35N 28 0 E
Umm el Fahm 104 32 31N 35 9 E
Umm Lajj 106 25 0N 37 23 E
Umm Qays 104 32 40N 35 41 E
Umm Ruwaba 121 12 50N 31 20 E
Umnak I. 11 53 15N 168 20W
Umniati → 123 16 49 S 28 45 E
Umpang 112 16 3N 98 54 E
Umpire 13 34 17N 94 3W
Umpqua 44 43 22N 123 28W
Umpqua → 44 43 40N 124 12W
Umpqua National Forest 44 43 10N 122 40W
Umtata 123 31 36 S 28 49 E
Unac → 94 44 30N 16 9 E
Unadilla, Ga. 18 32 16N 83 44W
Unadilla, N.Y. 39 42 20N 75 19W
Unadilla, Nebr. 34 40 41N 96 16W
Unadilla → 39 42 20N 75 25W
Unalakleet 11 63 52N 160 47W
Unalaska 11 53 53N 166 32W
Unalaska I. 11 53 35N 166 50W
Uncía 72 18 25 S 66 40W
Uncompahgre → 16 38 45N 108 6W
Uncompahgre National Forest 16 38 30N 108 30W
Uncompahgre Peak 16 38 4N 107 28W
Uncompahgre Plateau 16 38 20N 108 15W
Underhill Flats 36 44 33N 72 56W
Underwood 41 47 27N 101 9W
Uneiuxi → 70 0 37 S 65 34W
Unga I. 11 55 15N 160 40W
Ungava B. 59 59 30N 67 30W
Ungava Pen. 59 60 0N 74 0W
Unggi 114 42 16N 130 28 E
União da Vitória 77 26 13 S 51 5W
União dos Palmares 74 9 10 S 36 2W
Unicoi 49 36 12N 82 21W
Unicoi County ◇ 49 36 9N 82 25W
Unimak I. 11 54 45N 164 0W
Unimak Pass 11 54 15N 164 30W
Unini → 71 1 41 S 61 31W
Union, Iowa 23 42 15N 93 4W
Union, La. 25 30 5N 90 54W
Union, Maine 26 44 13N 69 17W
Union, Miss. 31 32 34N 89 7W
Union, Mo. 32 38 27N 91 0W
Union, N.J. 37 40 42N 74 17W
Union, Nebr. 34 40 49N 95 55W
Union, Oreg. 44 45 13N 117 52W
Union, S.C. 46 34 43N 81 37W
Union, W. Va. 54 37 36N 80 33W
Union, Wash. 53 47 22N 123 6W
Unión, La, Chile 78 40 10 S 73 0W
Unión, La, Colombia 70 1 35N 77 5W
Unión, La, El Salv. 66 13 20N 87 50W
Unión, La, Mexico 64 17 58N 101 49W
Unión, La, Peru 72 9 43 S 76 45W
Union Bridge 27 39 34N 77 11W
Union Center, S. Dak. 47 44 34N 102 40W
Union Center, Wis. 55 43 41N 90 16W
Union City, Calif. 14 37 36N 122 1W
Union City, Ga. 18 33 35N 84 33W
Union City, Ind. 22 40 12N 84 49W
Union City, Mich. 29 42 4N 85 8W
Union City, N.J. 37 40 45N 74 2W
Union City, Ohio 42 40 12N 84 48W
Union City, Okla. 43 35 23N 97 57W
Union City, Pa. 45 41 54N 79 51W
Union City, Tenn. 48 36 26N 89 3W
Union County ◇, Ark. 13 33 12N 92 40W
Union County ◇, Fla. 17 30 0N 82 25W
Union County ◇, Ga. 18 34 50N 84 0W
Union County ◇, Ill. 21 37 30N 89 15W
Union County ◇, Ind. 22 39 35N 84 55W
Union County ◇, Iowa 23 41 0N 94 15W
Union County ◇, Ky. 48 37 40N 87 55W
Union County ◇, Miss. 31 34 29N 89 0W
Union County ◇, N.C. 40 35 0N 80 40W
Union County ◇, N.J. 37 40 40N 74 20W
Union County ◇, N. Mex. 38 36 30N 103 30W
Union County ◇, Ohio 42 40 14N 83 22W
Union County ◇, Oreg. 44 45 15N 118 0W
Union County ◇, Pa. 45 41 0N 77 0W
Union County ◇, S.C. 46 34 45N 81 45W
Union County ◇, S. Dak. 47 42 51N 96 45W
Union County ◇, Tenn. 49 36 15N 83 48W
Union Creek 44 42 55N 122 27W
Union Gap 53 46 33N 120 28W
Union Grove 55 42 41N 88 3W
Union of Soviet Socialist Republics ■ 101 60 0N 100 0 E
Union Parish ◇ 25 32 47N 92 24W
Union Park 17 28 34N 81 17W
Union Point 18 33 37N 83 4W
Union Springs, Ala. 10 32 9N 85 43W
Union Springs, N.Y. 39 42 51N 76 42W
Union Star 32 39 59N 94 36W
Union Valley Reservoir 14 38 52N 120 26W
Uniondale, Ind. 22 40 50N 85 15W
Uniondale, N.Y. 39 40 43N 73 36W
Uniondale, Pa. 45 41 43N 75 30W
Uniontown, Ala. 10 32 27N 87 31W
Uniontown, Kans. 24 37 51N 94 59W
Uniontown, Ky. 48 37 47N 87 56W
Uniontown, Md. 27 39 36N 77 7W
Uniontown, Pa. 45 39 54N 79 44W
Uniontown, Wash. 53 46 32N 117 5W
Unionville, Ga. 18 31 26N 83 30W
Unionville, Iowa 23 40 49N 92 42W
Unionville, Md. 27 39 28N 77 12W
Unionville, Mich. 29 43 39N 83 28W
Unionville, Mo. 32 40 29N 93 1W
Unionville, N.Y. 39 41 18N 74 34W
Unionville, Nev. 35 40 27N 118 8W
Unionville, Pa. 45 40 55N 77 53W
Unionville, Va. 54 38 16N 77 58W
Uniopolis 42 40 36N 84 5W
Unirea 95 44 15N 27 35 E
United 45 40 13N 79 30W
United Arab Emirates ■ 107 23 50N 54 0 E
United Kingdom ■ 86 55 0N 3 0W
United States Trust Terr. of the Pacific Is. 124 10 0N 160 0 E
Unity, Canada 63 52 30N 109 5W
Unity, Maine 26 44 37N 69 20W
Unity, Md. 27 39 13N 77 5W
Unity, Oreg. 44 44 26N 118 12W
Unity, Wis. 55 44 51N 90 19W
Universal City 51 29 33N 98 17W
University City 32 38 40N 90 20W
University Park 38 32 17N 106 45W
Unnao 109 26 35N 80 30 E
Unst 84 60 50N 0 55W
Unuk → 62 56 5N 131 3W
Ünye 106 41 5N 37 15 E
Uozu 117 36 48N 137 24 E
Upata 71 8 1N 62 24W
Upatoie → 18 32 22N 84 58W
Upemba, L. 122 8 30 S 26 20 E
Upernavik 4 72 49N 56 20W
Upham 41 48 35N 100 44W
Upington 123 28 25 S 21 15 E
Upland, Calif. 15 34 6N 117 39W
Upland, Ind. 22 40 28N 85 30W
Upland, Nebr. 34 40 19N 98 54W
Upolu 128 13 58 S 172 0W
Upolu Pt. 19 20 16N 155 52W
Upper Arlington 42 40 0N 83 4W
Upper Arrow L. 62 50 30N 117 50W
Upper Crossroads 27 39 33N 76 29W
Upper Darby 45 39 58N 75 16W
Upper Foster L. 63 56 47N 105 20W
Upper Hutt 128 41 8 S 175 5 E
Upper Iowa → 23 43 29N 91 14W
Upper Klamath L. 44 42 25N 121 55W
Upper L. 14 41 45N 120 9W
Upper L. Erne 85 54 14N 7 22W
Upper Lake 14 39 10N 122 54W
Upper Marlboro 27 38 49N 76 45W
Upper Musquodoboit 61 45 10N 62 58W
Upper Preoria L. 21 40 52N 89 24W
Upper Red L. 30 48 8N 94 45W
Upper Sandusky 42 40 50N 83 17W
Upper Taimyr → 101 74 15N 99 48 E
Upper Tract 54 38 47N 79 17W
*Upper Volta ■ 120 12 0N 1 0W
Uppsala 97 59 53N 17 38 E
Uppsala län □ 97 60 0N 17 30 E
Upshur County ◇, Tex. 51 32 44N 94 57W
Upshur County ◇, W. Va. 54 39 0N 80 8W
Upson 55 46 22N 90 24W
Upson County ◇ 18 32 50N 84 20W
Upton, Ky. 49 37 28N 85 54W
Upton, Maine 26 44 42N 71 1W
Upton, Mass. 28 42 11N 71 37W
Upton, Wyo. 56 44 6N 104 38W
Upton County ◇ 50 31 15N 102 0W
Ur 106 30 55N 46 25 E
Urabá, Golfo de 70 8 25N 76 53W
Uracara 72 2 20 S 57 50W
Urad Qianqi 114 40 40N 108 30 E
Urakawa 116 42 9N 142 47 E
Ural → 100 47 0N 51 48 E
Ural Mts. = Uralskie Gory 98 60 0N 59 0 E
Uralsk 98 51 20N 51 20 E

*Renamed Burkina Faso

Vasht Vilyuy

Vasht = Khāsh 108 28 15N 61 15 E
Vaslui 89 46 38N 27 42 E
Vaslui □ 95 46 30N 27 45 E
Vass 40 35 15N 79 17W
Vassar, Canada 63 49 10N 95 55W
Vassar, Kans. 24 38 42N 95 37W
Vassar, Mich. 29 43 22N 83 35W
Västerås 97 59 37N 16 38 E
Västerbottens län □ 96 64 58N 18 0 E
Västernorrlands län □ 96 63 30N 17 30 E
Västervik 97 57 43N 16 43 E
Västmanlands län □ 97 59 45N 16 20 E
Vasto 94 42 8N 14 40 E
Vatnajökull 96 64 30N 16 48W
Vatneyri 96 65 35N 24 0W
Vatoa 128 19 50 S 178 13W
Vatomandry 123 19 20 S 48 59 E
Vatra-Dornei 89 47 22N 25 22 E
Vättern 97 58 25N 14 30 E
Vaucluse 46 33 37N 81 49W
Vaucluse □ 90 44 3N 5 10 E
Vaughan 31 32 48N 90 3W
Vaughn, Mont. 33 47 33N 111 33W
Vaughn, N. Mex. 38 34 36N 105 13W
Vaupe □ 70 1 0N 71 0W
Vaupés → 70 0 2N 67 16W
Vauxhall 62 50 5N 112 9W
Vava'u 128 18 36 S 174 0W
Växjö 97 56 52N 14 50 E
Vaygach, Ostrov 100 70 0N 60 0 E
Vazovgrad 95 42 39N 24 45 E
Veadeiros 75 14 7 S 47 31W
Veblen 47 45 52N 97 17W
Vechte → 87 52 34N 6 6 E
Vedea → 89 44 0N 25 20 E
Vedia 76 34 30 S 61 31W
Veedersburg 22 40 7N 87 16W
Veendam 87 53 5N 6 52 E
Veenendaal 87 52 2N 5 34 E
Vefsna → 96 65 48N 13 10 E
Vega, Norway 96 65 40N 11 55 E
Vega, U.S.A. 50 35 15N 102 26W
Vega, La, Dom. Rep. 67 19 20N 70 30W
Vega, La, Peru 72 10 41 S 77 44W
Vega Alta 57 18 25N 66 20W
Vega Baja 57 18 27N 66 23W
Vegafjorden 96 65 37N 12 0 E
Veghel 87 51 37N 5 32 E
Vegreville 62 53 30N 112 5W
Veguita 38 34 31N 106 46W
Vejer de la Frontera 91 36 15N 5 59W
Vejle 97 55 43N 9 30 E
Vela, La 70 11 27N 69 34W
Velas, C. 66 10 21N 85 52W
Velasco, Sierra de 76 29 20 S 67 10W
Velay, Mts. du 90 45 0N 3 40 E
Velebit Planina 94 44 50N 15 20 E
Veleka → 95 42 4N 27 58 E
Vélez 70 6 1N 73 41W
Vélez Málaga 91 36 48N 4 5W
Vélez Rubio 91 37 41N 2 5W
Velhas → 75 17 13 S 44 49W
Velikaya → 98 57 48N 28 20 E
Velikaya Kema 116 45 30N 137 12 E
Veliki Ustyug 98 60 47N 46 20 E
Velikiye Luki 98 56 25N 30 32 E
Velikonda Range 108 14 45N 79 10 E
Velingrad 95 42 4N 23 58 E
Velletri 94 41 43N 12 43 E
Vellore 108 12 57N 79 10 E
Velma 43 34 28N 97 40W
Velsen-Noord 87 52 27N 4 40 E
Velsk 98 61 10N 42 5 E
Velva 41 48 4N 100 56W
Venado 64 22 56N 101 10W
Venado Tuerto 76 33 50 S 62 0W
Venango County ◇ 45 41 20N 79 50W
Vendée □ 90 46 50N 1 35W
Vendée, Collines de 90 46 35N 0 45W
Venedocia 42 40 47N 84 28W
Veneta 44 44 3N 123 21W
Venetie 11 67 1N 146 25W
Venetie Indian Reservation 11 67 20N 146 0W
Véneto □ 94 45 40N 12 0 E
Venézia 94 45 27N 12 20 E
Venézia, Golfo di 94 45 20N 13 0 E
Venezuela ■ 70 8 0N 65 0W
Venezuela, Golfo de 70 11 30N 71 0W
Vengurla 108 15 53N 73 45 E
Venice = Venézia 94 45 27N 12 20 E
Venice, Fla. 17 27 6N 82 27W
Venice, La. 25 29 17N 89 22W
Venkatapuram 109 18 20N 80 30 E
Venleer 48 36 14N 87 27W
Venlo 87 51 22N 6 11 E
Venraij 87 51 31N 6 0 E
Venta, La 65 18 8N 94 3W
Ventana, Punta de la 64 24 4N 109 48W
Ventana, Sa. de la 76 38 0 S 62 30W
Ventnor 83 50 35N 1 12W
Ventnor City 37 39 20N 74 29W
Venton 27 38 12N 75 18W
Ventspils 98 57 25N 21 32 E
Ventuarí → 70 3 58N 67 2W
Ventura 15 34 17N 119 18W
Ventura, La 64 24 38N 100 54W
Ventura County ◇ 15 34 30N 119 0W
Venturosa, La 70 6 8N 68 48W
Venus 17 27 4N 81 22W
Vera, Argentina 76 29 30 S 60 20W
Vera, Spain 91 37 15N 1 51W
Vera, U.S.A. 43 36 27N 95 53W
Veracruz 65 19 10N 96 10W
Veracruz □ 65 19 0N 96 15W
Veraval 108 20 53N 70 27 E
Verbena 10 32 45N 86 31W
Vercelli 94 45 19N 8 25 E
Verda 25 31 42N 92 46W
Verdalsøra 96 63 48N 11 30 E
Verde →, Argentina 78 41 56 S 65 5W
Verde →, Goiás, Brazil 75 19 11 S 50 44W
Verde →, Goiás, Brazil 75 18 1 S 50 14W
Verde →, Mato Grosso, Brazil 73 11 54 S 55 48W
Verde →, Mato Grosso, Brazil 73 21 25 S 56 20W
Verde →, Chihuahua, Mexico 64 26 29N 107 58W
Verde →, Oaxaca, Mexico 65 15 59N 97 50W
Verde →, Veracruz, Mexico 64 21 10N 102 50W
Verde →, Paraguay 76 23 9 S 57 37W
Verde →, U.S.A. 12 33 33N 111 40W
Verde, Cay 66 23 0N 75 5W
Verde Grande → 75 16 13 S 43 49W
Verde Pequeno → 75 14 48 S 43 31W
Verdel 34 42 49N 98 12W
Verden, Germany 89 52 58N 9 18 E
Verden, U.S.A. 43 35 5N 98 5W
Verdery 46 34 7N 82 15W
Verdi 35 39 31N 119 59W
Verdigre 34 42 36N 98 2W
Verdigre Cr. → 34 42 42N 98 3W
Verdigris → 43 35 48N 95 19W
Verdon 34 40 9N 95 43W
Verdon-sur-Mer, Le 90 45 33N 1 4W
Verdun 90 49 12N 5 24 E
Vereeniging 123 26 38 S 27 57 E
Vérendrye, Parc Prov. de la 60 47 20N 76 40W
Verga, C. 120 10 30N 14 10W
Vergas 30 46 40N 95 48W
Vergennes 36 44 10N 73 15W
Verkhnevilyuysk 101 63 27N 120 18 E
Verkhneye Kalinino 101 59 54N 108 8 E
Verkhniy Baskunchak 99 48 14N 46 44 E
Verkhoyansk 101 67 35N 133 25 E
Verkhoyansk Ra. 102 66 0N 129 0 E
Verkhoyanskiy Khrebet 101 66 0N 129 0 E
Verlo 63 50 19N 108 35W
Vermilion, Canada 63 53 20N 110 50W
Vermilion, Ill. 21 39 35N 87 35W
Vermilion, Ohio 42 41 25N 82 22W
Vermilion →, Alta., Canada 63 53 22N 110 51W
Vermilion →, Qué., Canada 60 47 38N 72 56W
Vermilion →, U.S.A. 21 41 19N 89 4W
Vermilion B. 25 29 42N 92 0W
Vermilion Bay 63 49 51N 93 34W
Vermilion Chutes 62 58 22N 114 51W
Vermilion Cliffs 52 37 10N 112 30W
Vermilion County ◇ 21 40 10N 87 45W
Vermilion L. 30 47 53N 92 26W
Vermilion Parish ◇ 25 29 55N 92 15W
Vermilion Ra. 30 47 50N 92 0W
Vermillion 47 42 47N 96 56W
Vermillion → 47 42 44N 96 53W
Vermillion Bluffs 16 40 50N 108 20W
Vermillion County ◇ 22 39 50N 87 30W
Vermont □ 36 44 0N 73 0W
Verna 17 27 23N 82 16W
Vernal 52 40 27N 109 32W
Verndale 30 46 24N 95 1W
Verner 60 46 25N 80 8W
Vernon, Canada 62 50 20N 119 15W
Vernon, Ala. 10 33 45N 88 7W
Vernon, Colo. 16 39 57N 102 19W
Vernon, Conn. 28 41 50N 72 28W
Vernon, Ill. 21 38 48N 89 5W
Vernon, Ind. 22 38 59N 85 36W
Vernon, Tex. 51 34 9N 99 17W
Vernon, Utah 52 40 6N 112 26W
Vernon Center 30 43 58N 94 10W
Vernon County ◇, Mo. 32 37 50N 94 20W
Vernon County ◇, Wis. 55 43 30N 90 50W
Vernon Parish ◇ 25 31 9N 93 16W
Vernonia 44 45 52N 123 11W
Vero Beach 17 27 38N 80 24W
Véroia 95 40 34N 22 12 E
Verona, Italy 94 45 27N 11 0 E
Verona, Miss. 31 34 12N 88 43W
Verona, N.C. 40 34 40N 77 28W
Verona, N. Dak. 41 46 22N 98 4W
Verona, Wis. 55 42 59N 89 32W
Veropol 101 65 15N 168 40 E
Verret, L. 25 29 53N 91 10W
Versailles, France 90 48 48N 2 8 E
Versailles, Ill. 21 39 53N 90 39W
Versailles, Ind. 22 39 4N 85 15W
Versailles, Ky. 49 38 3N 84 44W
Versailles, Mo. 32 38 26N 92 51W
Versailles, Ohio 42 40 13N 84 29W
Versalles 73 12 44 S 63 18W
Vert, C. 120 14 45N 17 30W
Verviers 87 50 37N 5 52 E
Verwood 63 49 30N 105 40W
Veseliye 95 42 18N 27 38 E
Veselovskoye Vdkhr. 99 47 0N 41 0 E
Vesoul 90 47 40N 6 11 E
Vesper, Kans. 24 39 2N 98 17W
Vesper, Wis. 55 44 29N 89 58W
Vest-Agder fylke □ 97 58 30N 7 15 E
Vesta, C. Rica 66 9 43N 83 3W
Vesta, Ga. 18 33 58N 82 56W
Vesta, Nebr. 34 40 21N 96 20W
Vesterålen 96 68 45N 15 0 E
Vestfjorden 96 67 55N 14 0 E
Vestfold fylke □ 97 59 15N 10 0 E
Vestmannaeyjar 96 63 27N 20 15W
Vestspitsbergen 4 78 40N 17 0 E
Vestvågøy 96 68 18N 13 50 E
Vesuvio 94 40 50N 14 22 E
Vesuvius, Mt. = Vesuvio 94 40 50N 14 22 E
Veszprém 89 47 8N 17 57 E
Vetal 47 43 13N 101 23W
Vetlanda 97 57 24N 15 3 E
Vetovo 95 43 42N 26 16 E
Vetren 95 42 15N 24 3 E
Veurne 87 51 5N 2 40 E
Vevay 22 38 45N 85 4W
Veys 106 31 30N 49 0 E
Vezhen 95 42 50N 24 20 E
Viacha 72 16 39 S 68 18W
Vian 43 35 30N 94 58W
Viana, Brazil 74 3 13 S 45 0W
Viana, Portugal 91 38 20N 8 0W
Viana do Castelo 91 41 42N 8 50W
Vianópolis 75 16 40 S 48 35W
Vibank 63 50 20N 103 56W
Viborg, Denmark 97 56 27N 9 23 E
Viborg, U.S.A. 47 43 10N 97 5W
Viburnum 32 37 43N 91 8W
Vicco 49 37 13N 83 4W
Vicenza 94 45 32N 11 31 E
Vich 91 41 58N 2 19 E
Vichada □ 70 5 0N 69 30W
Vichada → 70 4 55N 67 50W
Vichy 90 46 9N 3 26 E
Vici 43 36 9N 99 18W
Vick 13 33 20N 92 6W
Vicksburg, Mich. 29 42 7N 85 32W
Vicksburg, Miss. 31 32 21N 90 53W
Viçosa 74 9 28 S 36 14W
Viçosa do Ceará 74 3 34 S 41 5W
Victor, India 108 21 0N 71 30 E
Victor, Colo. 16 38 43N 105 9W
Victor, Idaho 20 43 36N 111 7W
Victor, Iowa 23 41 44N 92 18W
Victor, Mont. 33 46 25N 114 9W
Victor Harbor 127 35 30 S 138 37 E
Victoria, Argentina 76 32 40 S 60 10W
Victoria, Canada 62 48 30N 123 25W
Victoria, Chile 78 38 13 S 72 20W
Victoria, Guinea 120 10 50N 14 32W
Victoria, H.K. 115 22 16N 114 15 E
Victoria, Malaysia 110 5 20N 115 14 E
Victoria, Ill. 21 41 2N 90 6W
Victoria, Kans. 24 38 52N 99 9W
Victoria, Tex. 51 28 48N 97 0W
Victoria, Va. 54 36 59N 78 8W
Victoria □ 127 37 0 S 144 0 E
Victoria → 126 15 10 S 129 40 E
Victoria, Grand L. 60 47 31N 77 30W
Victoria, L. 122 1 0 S 33 0 E
Victoria, La 70 10 14N 67 20W
Victoria Beach 63 50 40N 96 35W
Victoria County ◇ 51 28 45N 96 55W
Victoria de las Tunas 66 20 58N 76 59W
Victoria Falls 123 17 58 S 25 52 E
Victoria Harbour 60 44 45N 79 45W
Victoria I. 58 71 0N 111 0W
Victoria Ld. 5 75 0 S 160 0 E
Victoria Ra. 128 42 12 S 172 7 E
Victoria Res. 61 48 20N 57 27W
Victoria River Downs 126 16 25 S 131 0 E
Victoria Taungdeik 109 21 15N 93 55 E
Victoria West 123 31 25 S 23 4 E
Victoriaville 61 46 4N 71 56W
Victorica 76 36 20 S 65 30W
Victorville 15 34 32N 117 18W
Vicuña 76 30 0 S 70 50W
Vicuña Mackenna 76 33 53 S 64 25W
Vidal 15 34 7N 114 31W
Vidalia, Ga. 18 32 13N 82 25W
Vidalia, La. 25 31 34N 91 26W
Vidauri 51 28 26N 97 8W
Vidette 18 33 2N 82 15W
Vidin 95 43 59N 22 50 E
Vidisha 108 23 28N 77 53 E
Vidor 51 30 7N 94 1W
Vidra 95 45 56N 26 55 E
Viedma 78 40 50 S 63 0W
Viedma, L. 78 49 30 S 72 30W
Vieja, Sierra 50 30 35N 104 40W
Vien Pou Kha 112 20 45N 101 5 E
Vienna = Wien 88 48 12N 16 22 E
Vienna, Ga. 18 32 6N 83 47W
Vienna, Ill. 21 37 25N 88 54W
Vienna, Md. 27 38 29N 75 50W
Vienna, Mo. 32 38 11N 91 57W
Vienna, S. Dak. 47 44 42N 97 30W
Vienna, W. Va. 54 39 20N 81 33W
Vienne 90 45 31N 4 53 E
Vienne □ 90 46 30N 0 42 E
Vienne → 90 47 13N 0 5 E
Vientiane 112 17 58N 102 36 E
Vientos, Paso de los 67 20 0N 74 0W
Vieques, Isla de 57 18 8N 65 25W
Vieques, Pasaje de 57 18 10N 65 35W
Vieques, Sonda de 57 18 15N 65 15W
Vierzon 90 47 13N 2 5 E
Vietnam ■ 112 19 0N 106 0 E
Vieux Desert, L. 29 46 8N 89 7W
Vigan 111 17 35N 120 28 E
Vigia 74 0 50 S 48 5W
Vigía Chico 65 19 46N 87 35W
Vigo 91 42 12N 8 41W
Vigo County ◇ 22 39 25N 87 25W
Vigo Park 50 34 39N 101 30W
Vijayawada 109 16 31N 80 39 E
Viking, Canada 62 53 7N 111 50W
Viking, U.S.A. 30 48 13N 96 24W
Vikna 96 64 55N 10 58 E
Vikulovo 100 56 50N 70 40 E
Vila da Maganja 123 17 18 S 37 30 E
Vila de João Belo = Xai-Xai 123 25 6 S 33 31 E
Vila de Manica 123 18 58 S 32 59 E
Vila Franca de Xira 91 38 57N 8 59W
Vila Machado 123 19 15 S 34 14 E
Vila Real 91 41 17N 7 48W
Vila Real de Santo António 91 37 10N 7 28W
Vila Velha, Amapá, Brazil 71 3 13N 51 13W
Vila Velha, Espírito Santo, Brazil 75 20 20 S 40 17W
Vilaine → 90 47 30N 2 27W
Vilanculos 123 22 1 S 35 17 E
Vilas, Colo. 16 37 22N 102 27W
Vilas, S. Dak. 47 44 1N 97 36W
Vilas County ◇ 55 46 0N 89 30W
Vilcabamba, Cordillera 72 13 0 S 73 0W
Vilcanchos 72 13 40 S 74 25W
Vîlcea □ 95 45 0N 24 10 E
Vilhelmina 96 64 35N 16 39 E
Vilhena 73 12 40 S 60 5W
Viliga 101 61 36N 156 56 E
Villa Abecia 76 21 0 S 68 18W
Villa Ahumada 64 30 38N 106 30W
Villa Ana 76 28 28 S 59 40W
Villa Ángela 76 27 34 S 60 45W
Villa Bella 73 10 25 S 65 22W
Villa Bens = Tarfaya 120 27 55N 12 55W
Villa Cañás 76 34 0 S 61 35W
Villa Cisneros = Dakhla 120 23 50N 15 53W
Villa Colón 76 31 38 S 68 20W
Villa Constitución 76 33 15 S 60 20W
Villa de Cura 70 10 2N 67 29W
Villa de María 76 29 55 S 63 43W
Villa del Rosario 70 10 19N 72 19W
Villa Dolores 76 31 58 S 65 15W
Villa Frontera 64 26 56N 101 27W
Villa Grove, Colo. 16 38 15N 105 59W
Villa Grove, Ill. 21 39 52N 88 10W
Villa Guillermina 76 28 15 S 59 29W
Villa Hayes 76 25 0 S 57 20W
Villa Iris 76 38 12 S 63 12W
Villa María 76 32 20 S 63 10W
Villa Mazán 76 28 40 S 66 30W
Villa Montes 76 21 10 S 63 30W
Villa Ocampo, Argentina 76 28 30 S 59 20W
Villa Ocampo, Mexico 64 26 29N 105 30W
Villa Ojo de Agua 76 29 30 S 63 44W
Villa Pérez 57 18 12N 66 47W
Villa Rica 18 33 44N 84 55W
Villa San José 76 32 12 S 58 15W
Villa San Martín 76 28 15 S 64 9W
Villa Unión 64 23 12N 106 14W
Villach 88 46 37N 13 51 E
Villagarcía de Arosa 91 42 34N 8 46W
Village of Superior 55 46 40N 92 6W
Villagrán 65 24 29N 99 29W
Villaguay 76 32 0 S 59 0W
Villahermosa 65 18 0N 92 50W
Villalba, Puerto Rico 57 18 8N 66 30W
Villalba, Spain 91 43 26N 7 40W
Villanueva, Colombia 70 10 37N 72 59W
Villanueva, U.S.A. 38 35 16N 105 22W
Villanueva de la Serena 91 38 59N 5 50W
Villard 30 45 43N 95 16W
Villarreal 91 39 55N 0 3W
Villarrica, Chile 78 39 15 S 72 15W
Villarrica, Paraguay 76 25 40 S 56 30W
Villarrobledo 91 39 18N 2 36W
Villas 37 39 2N 74 56W
Villavicencio, Argentina 76 32 28 S 69 0W
Villavicencio, Colombia 70 4 9N 73 37W
Villaviciosa 91 43 32N 5 27W
Villazón 76 22 0 S 65 35W
Ville-Marie 60 47 20N 79 30W
Ville Platte 25 30 41N 92 17W
Villegrande 73 18 30 S 64 10W
Villegreen 16 37 18N 103 31W
Villena 91 38 39N 0 52W
Villisca 23 40 56N 94 59W
Vilna 62 54 7N 111 55W
Vilnius 98 54 38N 25 19 E
Vilonia 13 35 5N 92 13W
Vilskutskogo, Proliv 101 78 0N 103 0 E
Vilvoorde 87 50 56N 4 26 E
Vilyuy → 101 64 24N 126 26 E

Vilyuysk **Walker**

Vilyuysk 101 63 40N 121 35 E
Vina 10 34 23N 88 4W
Viña del Mar 76 33 0 S 71 30W
Vinalhaven 26 44 3N 68 50W
Vinalhaven I. 26 44 5N 68 51W
Vinaroz 91 40 30N 0 27 E
Vincennes 22 38 41N 87 32W
Vincent, Ala. 10 33 23N 86 25W
Vincent, Iowa 23 42 36N 94 1W
Vincentown 37 39 56N 74 45W
Vinces 70 1 32 S 79 45W
Vinchina 76 28 45 S 68 15W
Vindel älven → 96 63 55N 19 50 E
Vindeln 96 64 12N 19 43 E
Vindhya Ra. 108 22 50N 77 0 E
Vine Grove 49 37 49N 85 59W
Vineland 37 39 29N 75 2W
Vinemont 10 34 15N 86 52W
Vineyard Haven 28 41 27N 70 36W
Vineyard Sd. 28 41 25N 70 45W
Vinh 112 18 45N 105 38 E
Vining 30 46 16N 95 32W
Vinita 43 36 39N 95 9W
Vinkovci 95 45 19N 18 48 E
Vinnitsa 99 49 15N 28 30 E
Vinson 43 34 54N 99 52W
Vinson Massif 5 78 35 S 85 25W
Vinton, Calif. 14 39 48N 120 10W
Vinton, Iowa 23 42 10N 92 1W
Vinton, La. 25 30 11N 93 35W
Vinton, Ohio 42 38 59N 82 21W
Vinton County ◇ 42 39 15N 82 29W
Vințu de Jos 95 46 0N 23 30 E
Viola, Ark. 13 36 24N 91 59W
Viola, Del. 27 39 5N 75 34W
Viola, Ill. 21 41 12N 90 35W
Viola, Kans. 24 37 29N 97 39W
Viola, Tenn. 49 35 32N 85 52W
Viola, Wis. 55 43 31N 90 40W
Violet 25 29 54N 89 54W
Viqueque 111 8 52 S 126 23 E
Virac 111 13 30N 124 20 E
Virago Sd. 62 54 0N 132 30W
Viramgam 108 23 5N 72 0 E
Viranşehir 106 37 13N 39 45 E
Virden, Canada 63 49 50N 100 56W
Virden, Ill. 21 39 30N 89 46W
Virden, N. Mex. 38 32 41N 109 0W
Vire 90 48 50N 0 53W
Virgem da Lapa 75 16 49 S 42 21W
Vírgenes, C. 78 52 19 S 68 21W
Virgil, Kans. 24 37 59N 96 1W
Virgil, S. Dak. 47 44 17N 98 25W
Virgilina 54 36 33N 78 47W
Virgin 52 37 12N 113 11W
Virgin →, Canada 63 57 2N 108 17W
Virgin →, U.S.A. 35 36 28N 114 21W
Virgin Islands □ 57 18 30N 64 25W
Virginia, Idaho 20 42 30N 112 10W
Virginia, Ill. 21 39 57N 90 13W
Virginia, Minn. 30 47 31N 92 32W
Virginia □ 54 37 30N 78 45W
Virginia Beach 54 36 51N 75 59W
Virginia City, Mont. 33 45 18N 111 56W
Virginia City, Nev. 35 39 19N 119 39W
Virginia Falls 62 61 38N 125 42W
Virginia Mts. 35 39 50N 119 30W
Virginiatown 60 48 9N 79 36W
Viroqua 55 43 34N 90 53W
Virton 87 49 35N 5 32 E
Virú 72 8 25 S 78 45W
Virudunagar 108 9 30N 78 0 E
Vis 94 43 0N 16 10 E
Visalia 15 36 20N 119 18W
Visayan Sea 111 11 30N 123 30 E
Visby 97 57 37N 18 18 E
Viscount Melville Sd. 4 74 10N 108 0W
Visé 87 50 44N 5 41 E
Višegrad 95 43 47N 19 17 E
Viseu, Brazil 74 1 10 S 46 5W
Viseu, Portugal 91 40 40N 7 55W
Vishakhapatnam 109 17 45N 83 20 E
Visikoi I. 5 56 43 S 27 15W
Viso, Mte. 94 44 38N 7 5 E
Vista, Calif. 15 33 12N 117 14W
Vista, Mo. 32 37 58N 93 40W
Vistula = Wisła → 89 54 22N 18 55 E
Vit → 95 43 30N 24 30 E
Vitebsk 98 55 10N 30 15 E
Viterbo 94 42 25N 12 8 E
Viti Levu 128 17 30 S 177 30 E
Vitim 101 59 28N 112 35 E
Vitim → 101 59 26N 112 34 E
Vitória, Brazil 75 20 20 S 40 22W
Vitoria, Spain 91 42 50N 2 41W
Vitória da Conquista 75 14 51 S 40 51W
Vitória de São Antão 74 8 10 S 35 20W
Vitorino Friere 74 4 4 S 45 10W
Vittória 94 36 58N 14 30 E
Vittório Véneto 94 45 59N 12 18 E
Vivero 91 43 39N 7 38W
Vivian, La. 25 32 53N 93 59W
Vivian, S. Dak. 47 43 56N 100 18W
Vizcaíno, Desierto de 64 27 40N 113 50W
Vizcaíno, Sierra 64 27 30N 114 0W
Vizianagaram 109 18 6N 83 30 E
Viziru 95 45 0N 27 43 E
Vlaardingen 87 51 55N 4 21 E
Vladimir 98 56 15N 40 30 E
Vladimirovo 95 43 32N 23 22 E
Vladivostok 101 43 10N 131 53 E
Vlieland 87 53 16N 4 55 E
Vlissingen 87 51 26N 3 34 E
Vlonë = Vlórë 95 40 32N 19 28 E
Vlórë 95 40 32N 19 28 E
Vltava → 88 50 21N 14 30 E
Vogelkop = Doberai, Jazirah 111 1 25 S 133 0 E
Vogelsberg 88 50 37N 9 15 E
Vohibinany 123 18 49 S 49 4 E
Vohimarina 123 13 25 S 50 0 E
Vohimena, Tanjon' i 123 25 36 S 45 8 E
Vohipeno 123 22 22 S 47 51 E
Voi 122 3 25 S 38 32 E
Voineşti 95 45 5N 25 14 E
Voisey B. 61 56 15N 61 50W
Vojmsjön 96 64 55N 16 40 E
Volborg 33 45 51N 105 41W
Volcano 19 19 26N 155 14W
Volcano Is. 124 25 0N 141 0 E
Volchayevka 101 48 40N 134 30 E
Volda 96 62 9N 6 5 E
Volga, Iowa 23 42 48N 91 33W
Volga, S. Dak. 47 44 19N 96 56W
Volga → 99 48 30N 46 0 E
Volga Hts. = Privolzhskaya Vozvyshennost 99 51 0N 46 0 E
Volgograd 99 48 40N 44 25 E
Volgogradskoye Vdkhr. 99 50 0N 45 20 E
Volin 47 42 58N 97 11W
Volkhov → 98 60 8N 32 20 E
Vollenhove 87 52 40N 5 58 E
Volochanka 101 71 0N 94 28 E
Vologda 98 59 10N 40 0 E
Vólos 95 39 24N 22 59 E
Volsk 98 52 5N 47 22 E
Volta → 118 5 46N 0 41 E
Volta, L. 120 7 30N 0 15 E
Volta Redonda 75 22 31 S 44 5W
Volterra 94 43 24N 10 50 E
Volturno → 94 41 1N 13 55 E
Voluntown 28 41 34N 71 52W
Volusia County ◇ 17 29 0N 81 15W
Volzhskiy 99 48 56N 44 46 E
Vona 16 39 18N 102 45W
Vonore 49 35 36N 84 14W
Voorburg 87 52 5N 4 24 E
Voorheesville 39 42 39N 73 56W
Vopnafjörður 96 65 45N 14 40W
Vorarlberg □ 88 47 20N 10 0 E
Voríai Sporádhes 95 39 15N 23 30 E
Vorkuta 98 67 48N 64 20 E
Voronezh 98 51 40N 39 10 E
Voroshilovgrad 99 48 38N 39 15 E
Vorovskoye 101 54 30N 155 50 E
Vosges 90 48 20N 7 10 E
Vosges □ 90 48 12N 6 20 E
Voss 97 60 38N 6 26 E
Vostochnyy Sayan 101 54 0N 96 0 E
Vostok I. 125 10 5 S 152 23W
Votkinsk 98 57 0N 53 55 E
Votkinskoye Vdkhr. 98 57 30N 55 0 E
Vouga → 91 40 41N 8 40W
Voyageurs Nat. Park 30 48 32N 93 0W
Vozhe Oz. 98 60 45N 39 0 E
Voznesenka 101 56 40N 95 3 E
Voznesensk 99 47 35N 31 21 E
Voznesenye 98 61 0N 35 45 E
Vrancea □ 95 45 50N 26 45 E
Vrancei, Munţii 95 46 0N 26 30 E
Vrangelya, Ostrov 101 71 0N 180 0 E
Vranje 95 42 34N 21 54 E
Vratsa 95 43 13N 23 30 E
Vrbas → 95 45 8N 17 29 E
Vrede 123 27 24 S 29 6 E
Vredenburg 123 32 51 S 18 0 E
Vršac 95 45 8N 21 18 E
Vryburg 123 26 55 S 24 45 E
Vryheid 123 27 45 S 30 47 E
Vucha → 95 42 10N 24 26 E
Vught 87 51 38N 5 20 E
Vulcan, Canada 62 50 25N 113 15W
Vulcan, Romania 95 45 23N 23 17 E
Vulcan, U.S.A. 29 45 47N 87 53W
Vulcano 94 38 25N 14 58 E
Vŭlchedruma 95 43 42N 23 27 E
Vulture Mts. 12 33 45N 113 0W
Vung Tau 112 10 21N 107 4 E
Vŭrbitsa 95 42 59N 26 40 E
Vurshets 95 43 15N 23 23 E
Vutcani 95 46 26N 27 59 E
Vya 35 41 35N 119 52W
Vyatka → 98 56 30N 51 0 E
Vyatskiye Polyany 98 56 5N 51 0 E
Vyazemskiy 101 47 32N 134 45 E
Vyazma 98 55 10N 34 15 E
Vyborg 98 60 43N 28 47 E
Vychegda → 98 61 18N 46 36 E
Vychodné Beskydy 89 49 30N 22 0 E
Vyg-ozero 98 63 30N 34 0 E
Vyrnwy, L. 82 52 48N 3 30W
Vyshniy Volochek 98 57 30N 34 30 E
Vyshzha = imeni 26 Bakinskikh Komissarov 99 39 22N 54 10 E
Vytegra 98 61 0N 36 27 E

W

W.A.C. Bennett Dam 62 56 2N 122 6W
Wa 120 10 7N 2 25W
Waal → 87 51 59N 4 30 E
Wabakimi L. 60 50 38N 89 45W
Wabana 61 47 40N 53 0W
Wabasca 62 55 57N 113 56W
Wabash 22 40 48N 85 49W
Wabash → 22 37 48N 88 2W
Wabash County ◇, Ill. 21 38 30N 87 50W
Wabash County ◇, Ind. 22 40 50N 85 45W
Wabasha 30 44 23N 92 2W
Wabasha County ◇ 30 44 15N 92 15W
Wabasso, Fla. 17 27 45N 80 26W
Wabasso, Minn. 30 44 24N 95 15W
Wabaunsee 24 39 9N 96 21W
Wabaunsee County ◇ 24 39 0N 96 15W
Wabeno 55 45 26N 88 39W
Wabigoon L. 63 49 44N 92 44W
Wabowden 63 54 55N 98 38W
Wąbrzeźno 89 53 16N 18 57 E
Wabuk Pt. 60 55 20N 85 5W
Wabush 61 52 55N 66 52W
Wabuska 35 39 9N 119 11W
Waccamaw, L. 40 34 18N 78 31W
Waccasassa B. 17 29 10N 82 50W
Wachapreague 54 37 36N 75 42W
Wachusett Reservoir 28 42 24N 71 41W
Wacissa 17 30 22N 83 59W
Waco, Nebr. 34 40 54N 97 28W
Waco, Tex. 51 31 33N 97 9W
Waco L. 51 31 35N 97 12W
Waconda Lake 24 39 29N 98 19W
Waconichi, L. 60 50 8N 74 0W
Wad Banda 121 13 10N 27 56 E
Wad Hamid 121 16 30N 32 45 E
Wâd Medanî 121 14 28N 33 30 E
Wadayama 117 35 19N 134 52 E
Waddeneilanden 87 53 25N 5 10 E
Waddenzee 87 53 6N 5 10 E
Waddington 39 44 52N 75 12W
Waddington, Mt. 62 51 23N 125 15W
Wade 40 35 10N 78 44W
Wade Hampton ◇ 11 62 0N 164 0W
Wadena, Canada 63 51 57N 103 47W
Wadena, U.S.A. 30 46 26N 95 8W
Wadena County ◇ 30 46 30N 95 0W
Wadesboro 40 34 58N 80 5W
Wadhams 62 51 30N 127 30W
Wadi Halfa 121 21 53N 31 19 E
Wadi Şabāḩ 106 23 50N 48 30 E
Wading River 37 39 38N 74 31W
Wadley, Ala. 10 33 7N 85 34W
Wadley, Ga. 18 32 52N 82 24W
Wadsworth, Nev. 35 39 38N 119 17W
Wadsworth, Ohio 42 41 2N 81 44W
Wadsworth, Tex. 51 28 50N 95 56W
Waelder 51 29 42N 97 18W
Wafrah 106 28 33N 47 56 E
Wagener 46 33 39N 81 22W
Wageningen, Neth. 87 51 58N 5 40 E
Wageningen, Surinam 71 5 50N 56 50W
Wager B. 59 65 26N 88 40W
Wager Bay 59 65 56N 90 49W
Wagga Wagga 127 35 7 S 147 24 E
Waghete 111 4 10 S 135 50 E
Wagin 126 33 17 S 117 25 E
Wagner 47 43 5N 98 18W
Wagon Mound 38 36 1N 104 42W
Wagon Wheel Gap 16 37 46N 106 49W
Wagoner 43 35 58N 95 22W
Wagoner County ◇ 43 36 0N 95 30W
Wagontire 44 43 15N 119 52W
Wagontire Mt. 44 43 21N 119 53W
Wagram 40 34 54N 79 22W
Wah Wah Mts. 52 38 25N 113 40W
Wahai 111 2 48 S 129 35 E
Wahiawa 19 21 30N 158 2W
Wahiawa Reservoir 19 21 30N 158 3W
Wahkiakum County ◇ 53 46 10N 123 30W
Wahkon 30 46 7N 93 31W
Wahoo 34 41 13N 96 37W
Wahpeton 41 46 16N 96 36W
Waialee 19 21 41N 158 1W
Waialua 19 21 34N 158 8W
Waialua B. 19 21 35N 158 5W
Waianae 19 21 27N 158 11W
Waianae Mts. 19 21 30N 158 10W
Waiau → 128 42 47 S 173 22 E
Waiawa → 19 21 23N 157 59W
Waibeem 111 0 30 S 132 59 E
Waigeo 111 0 20 S 130 40 E
Waihi 128 37 23 S 175 52 E
Waihou → 128 37 15 S 175 40 E
Waikabubak 111 9 45 S 119 25 E
Waikaremoana 128 38 42 S 177 12 E
Waikari 128 42 58 S 172 41 E
Waikato → 128 37 23 S 174 43 E
Waikiki 19 21 17N 157 50W
Waikokopu 128 39 3 S 177 52 E
Waikouaiti 128 45 36 S 170 41 E
Wailua, Hawaii 19 22 3N 159 20W
Wailua, Hawaii 19 20 51N 156 8W
Wailuku 19 20 53N 156 30W
Waimanalo 19 21 21N 157 43W
Waimanalo B. 19 21 20N 157 40W
Waimanalo Beach 19 21 21N 157 42W
Waimano → 19 21 25N 157 58W
Waimate 128 44 45 S 171 3 E
Waimea, Hawaii 19 21 39N 158 3W
Waimea, Hawaii 19 21 58N 159 40W
Waimea B. 19 21 40N 158 5W
Wainganga → 108 18 50N 79 55 E
Waingapu 111 9 35 S 120 11 E
Waini → 71 8 20N 59 50W
Wainwright, Canada 63 52 50N 110 50W
Wainwright, Alaska 11 70 38N 160 2W
Wainwright, Okla. 43 35 37N 95 34W
Waiouru 128 39 28 S 175 41 E
Waipahu 19 21 23N 158 1W
Waipara 128 43 3 S 172 46 E
Waipawa 128 39 56 S 176 38 E
Waipio Acres 19 21 28N 158 1W
Waipio Peninsula 19 21 20N 158 0W
Waipiro 128 38 2 S 178 22 E
Waipu 128 35 59 S 174 29 E
Waipukurau 128 40 1 S 176 33 E
Wairakei 128 38 37 S 176 6 E
Wairarapa, L. 128 41 14 S 175 15 E
Wairoa 128 39 3 S 177 25 E
Waita Reservoir 19 21 55N 159 28W
Waitaki → 128 44 56 S 171 7 E
Waitara 128 38 59 S 174 15 E
Waite 26 45 20N 67 42W
Waite Park 30 45 33N 94 14W
Waits → 36 43 59N 72 8W
Waitsburg 53 46 16N 118 9W
Waitsfield 36 44 42N 72 50W
Waiuku 128 37 15 S 174 45 E
Wajima 117 37 30N 137 0 E
Wajir 122 1 42N 40 5 E
Waka 50 36 17N 101 3W
Wakarusa 22 41 32N 86 1W
Wakasa 117 35 20N 134 24 E
Wakasa-Wan 117 35 40N 135 30 E
Wakatipu, L. 128 45 5 S 168 33 E
Wakaw 63 52 39N 105 44W
Wakayama 117 34 15N 135 15 E
Wakayama-ken □ 117 33 50N 135 30 E
Wake County ◇ 40 35 40N 78 45W
Wake Forest 40 35 59N 78 30W
Wake I. 124 19 18N 166 36 E
WaKeeney 24 39 1N 99 53W
Wakefield, N.Z. 128 41 24 S 173 5 E
Wakefield, U.K. 82 53 41N 1 31W
Wakefield, Kans. 24 39 13N 97 1W
Wakefield, Mass. 28 42 30N 71 4W
Wakefield, Mich. 29 46 29N 89 56W
Wakefield, N.H. 36 43 35N 71 4W
Wakefield, Nebr. 34 42 16N 96 52W
Wakefield, R.I. 28 41 26N 71 30W
Wakefield, Va. 54 36 58N 76 59W
Wakema 109 16 30N 95 11 E
Wakita 43 36 53N 97 55W
Wakkanai 116 45 28N 141 35 E
Wakonda 47 43 0N 97 6W
Wakpala 47 45 40N 100 32W
Wakre 111 0 19 S 131 5 E
Wakuach L. 61 55 34N 67 32W
Wakulla 17 30 14N 84 14W
Wakulla Beach 17 30 6N 84 16W
Wakulla County ◇ 17 30 15N 84 20W
Wałbrzych 88 50 45N 16 18 E
Walbury Hill 83 51 22N 1 28W
Walcheren 87 51 30N 3 35 E
Walcott, Iowa 23 41 35N 90 47W
Walcott, N. Dak. 41 46 33N 96 56W
Walcott, Wyo. 56 41 46N 106 51W
Walcott L. 20 42 40N 113 29W
Walden, Colo. 16 40 44N 106 17W
Walden, N.Y. 39 41 34N 74 11W
Walden Reservoir 16 40 43N 106 17W
Walden Ridge 49 35 30N 85 15W
Waldo, Ark. 13 33 21N 93 18W
Waldo, Fla. 17 29 48N 82 10W
Waldo, Maine 26 44 31N 69 5W
Waldo, Ohio 42 40 28N 83 5W
Waldo County ◇ 26 44 25N 69 0W
Waldoboro 26 44 6N 69 23W
Waldorf, Md. 27 38 38N 76 55W
Waldorf, Minn. 30 43 56N 93 42W
Waldport 44 44 26N 124 4W
Waldron, Canada 63 50 53N 102 35W
Waldron, Ark. 13 34 54N 94 5W
Waldron, Ind. 22 39 27N 85 40W
Waldron, Mich. 29 41 44N 84 25W
Waldwick 37 41 1N 74 7W
Wales, Alaska 11 65 37N 168 5W
Wales, N. Dak. 41 48 54N 98 36W
Wales, Utah 52 39 29N 111 38W
Wales □ 86 52 30N 3 30W
Walford 23 41 53N 91 50W
Walgett 127 30 0 S 148 5 E
Walgreen Coast 5 75 15 S 105 0W
Walhalla, N. Dak. 41 48 55N 97 55W
Walhalla, S.C. 46 34 46N 83 4W
Walk, L. 50 29 31N 100 59W
Walker, Iowa 23 42 17N 91 47W
Walker, Mich. 29 42 58N 85 46W
Walker, Minn. 30 47 6N 94 35W
Walker, Mo. 32 37 54N 94 14W

Walker Watertown

Walker, S. Dak. **47** 45 55N 101 5W
Walker → **35** 38 54N 118 47W
Walker County ◇, Ala. **10** 33 50N 87 17W
Walker County ◇, Ga. **18** 34 45N 85 15W
Walker County ◇, Tex. **51** 30 43N 95 33W
Walker L., Man., Canada **63** 54 42N 95 57W
Walker L., Qué., Canada **61** 50 20N 67 11W
Walker L., U.S.A. **35** 38 42N 118 43W
Walker River Indian Reservation **35** 39 0N 118 50W
Walkers Pt. **26** 43 21N 70 28W
Walkersville **27** 39 29N 77 21W
Walkerton **22** 41 28N 86 29W
Walkertown **40** 36 10N 80 10W
Walkerville **29** 43 43N 86 8W
Wall, S. Dak. **47** 44 0N 102 8W
Wall, Tex. **50** 31 22N 100 18W
Wall Lake **23** 42 16N 95 5W
Walla Walla **53** 46 4N 118 20W
Walla Walla County ◇ **53** 46 18N 118 37W
Wallace, Idaho **20** 47 28N 115 56W
Wallace, Kans. **24** 38 58N 101 36W
Wallace, N.C. **40** 34 44N 77 59W
Wallace, Nebr. **34** 40 50N 101 10W
Wallace, S. Dak. **47** 45 5N 97 29W
Wallace County ◇ **24** 38 50N 101 45W
Wallaceburg **60** 42 34N 82 23W
Wallachia = Valahia **89** 44 35N 25 0 E
Walland **49** 35 44N 83 49W
Wallaroo **127** 33 56 S 137 39 E
Wallasey **82** 53 26N 3 2W
Wallenpaupack, L. **45** 41 25N 75 15W
Waller **51** 30 4N 95 56W
Waller County ◇ **51** 30 0N 96 0W
Wallingford, U.K. **82** 51 40N 1 15W
Wallingford, Conn. **28** 41 27N 72 50W
Wallingford, Iowa **23** 43 19N 94 48W
Wallingford, Vt. **36** 43 28N 72 59W
Wallis **51** 29 38N 96 4W
Wallis & Futuna **124** 13 18 S 176 10W
Wallisville L. **51** 29 57N 94 54W
Walloon L. **29** 45 17N 85 0W
Wallowa **44** 45 34N 117 32W
Wallowa → **44** 45 43N 117 47W
Wallowa County ◇ **44** 45 30N 117 10W
Wallowa Mts. **44** 45 20N 117 30W
Wallowa-Whitman National Forest **44** 45 15N 117 20W
Walls **31** 34 58N 90 9W
Wallsburg **52** 40 23N 111 25W
Wallsend **82** 54 59N 1 30W
Wallula **53** 46 5N 118 54W
Wallula, L. **53** 46 2N 118 59W
Walmsley, L. **63** 63 25N 108 36W
Walney, Isle of **82** 54 5N 3 15W
Walnut, Ill. **21** 41 33N 89 36W
Walnut, Iowa **23** 41 29N 95 13W
Walnut, Kans. **24** 37 36N 95 5W
Walnut, Miss. **31** 34 57N 88 54W
Walnut, N.C. **40** 35 51N 82 44W
Walnut → **24** 37 3N 97 0W
Walnut Canyon National Monument **12** 35 15N 111 20W
Walnut Cove **40** 36 18N 80 9W
Walnut Creek **14** 37 54N 122 4W
Walnut Grove, Ala. **10** 34 4N 86 18W
Walnut Grove, Miss. **31** 32 36N 89 28W
Walnut Grove, Mo. **32** 37 25N 93 33W
Walnut Hill **17** 30 53N 87 30W
Walnut Ridge **13** 36 4N 90 57W
Walnut Springs **51** 32 3N 97 45W
Walpole, Mass. **28** 42 9N 71 15W
Walpole, N.H. **36** 43 5N 72 26W
Walsall **83** 52 36N 1 59W
Walsenburg **16** 37 38N 104 47W
Walsh **16** 37 23N 102 17W
Walsh County ◇ **41** 48 24N 97 45W
Walter F. George Reservoir **10** 31 38N 85 4W
Walterboro **46** 32 55N 80 40W
Walters **43** 34 22N 98 19W
Walterville **44** 44 4N 122 48W
Walthall **31** 33 37N 89 17W
Walthall County ◇ **31** 31 7N 90 9W
Waltham, Maine **26** 44 43N 68 20W
Waltham, Mass. **28** 42 23N 71 14W
Waltham Sta. **60** 45 57N 76 57W
Walthill **34** 42 9N 96 30W
Waltman **56** 43 4N 107 12W
Walton, Ind. **22** 40 40N 86 15W
Walton, Kans. **24** 38 7N 97 15W
Walton, Ky. **49** 38 52N 84 37W
Walton, N.Y. **39** 42 10N 75 8W
Walton County ◇, Fla. **17** 30 30N 86 10W
Walton County ◇, Ga. **18** 33 45N 83 45W
Waltonville **21** 38 13N 89 2W
Walvisbaai **123** 23 0 S 14 28 E
Walworth County ◇, S. Dak. **47** 45 30N 100 0W
Walworth County ◇, Wis. **55** 42 40N 88 30W
Wamac **21** 38 31N 89 8W
Wamba **122** 2 10N 27 57 E
Wamego **24** 39 12N 96 18W
Wamena **111** 4 4 S 138 57 E
Wampsville **39** 43 5N 75 42W
Wampum **45** 40 54N 80 21W
Wamsasi **111** 3 27 S 126 7 E
Wamsutter **56** 41 40N 107 58W
Wana **108** 32 20N 69 32 E
Wanaka L. **128** 44 33 S 169 7 E
Wanamingo **30** 44 18N 92 47W
Wan'an **115** 26 26N 114 49 E
Wanapiri **111** 4 30 S 135 59 E
Wanapitei L. **60** 46 45N 80 40W
Wanaque **37** 41 2N 74 18W
Wanaque Reservoir **37** 41 2N 74 18W
Wanatah **22** 41 26N 86 54W
Wanblee **47** 43 34N 101 40W
Wanchese **40** 35 51N 75 38W
Wanda **30** 44 19N 95 13W
Wanda Shan **114** 46 0N 132 0 E
Wandaik **71** 4 27N 59 35W
Wandoan **127** 26 5 S 149 55 E
Wanette **43** 34 58N 97 2W
Wang Saphung **112** 17 18N 101 46 E
Wangal **111** 6 8 S 134 9 E
Wanganui **128** 39 56 S 175 3 E
Wangaratta **127** 36 21 S 146 19 E
Wangdu **114** 38 40N 115 7 E
Wangerooge **88** 53 47N 7 52 E
Wangiwangi **111** 5 22 S 123 37 E
Wangjiang **115** 30 10N 116 42 E
Wango **27** 38 20N 75 25W
Wangqing **114** 43 12N 129 42 E
Wanless **63** 54 11N 101 21W
Wann **43** 36 55N 95 48W
Wanning **115** 18 48N 110 22 E
Wanquan **114** 40 50N 114 40 E
Wanxian **115** 30 42N 108 20 E
Wanyuan **115** 32 4N 108 3 E
Wanzai **115** 28 7N 114 30 E
Wapakoneta **42** 40 34N 84 12W
Wapanucka **43** 34 23N 96 26W
Wapato **53** 46 27N 120 25W
Wapawekka L. **63** 54 55N 104 40W
Wapello **23** 41 11N 91 11W
Wapello County ◇ **23** 41 0N 92 25W
Wapikopa L. **60** 52 56N 87 53W
Wapinitia Pass **44** 45 14N 121 42W
Wapiti **56** 44 28N 109 26W
Wappapello, L. **32** 36 56N 90 17W
Wappingers Falls **39** 41 36N 73 55W
Wapsipinicon → **23** 41 44N 90 19W
War **54** 37 18N 81 41W
Warangal **108** 17 58N 79 35 E
Warburton → **127** 28 4 S 137 28 E
Ward, N.Z. **128** 41 49 S 174 11 E
Ward, U.S.A. **47** 44 9N 96 28W
Ward County ◇, N. Dak. **41** 48 5N 101 30W
Ward County ◇, Tex. **50** 31 32N 103 8W
Wardell **32** 36 21N 89 49W
Warden **53** 46 58N 119 2W
Wardensville **54** 39 5N 78 36W
Wardha **108** 20 45N 78 39 E
Wardha → **108** 19 57N 79 11 E
Wardlow **62** 50 56N 111 31W
Wardsville **32** 38 29N 92 11W
Ware, Canada **62** 57 26N 125 41W
Ware, U.S.A. **28** 42 16N 72 14W
Ware → **28** 42 11N 72 22W
Ware County ◇ **18** 31 10N 82 20W
Ware Shoals **46** 34 24N 82 15W
Wareham **28** 41 46N 70 43W
Warehouse Point **28** 41 56N 72 37W
Waresboro **18** 31 15N 82 28W
Warialda **127** 29 29 S 150 33 E
Wariap **111** 1 30 S 134 5 E
Warkopi **111** 1 12 S 134 9 E
Warley **83** 52 30N 2 0W
Warm Springs, Ga. **18** 32 53N 84 41W
Warm Springs, Oreg. **44** 44 46N 121 16W
Warm Springs, Va. **54** 38 3N 79 47W
Warm Springs Indian Reservation **44** 45 0N 121 25W
Warm Springs Reservoir **44** 43 35N 118 13W
Warman **63** 52 19N 106 30W
Warmbad, Namibia **123** 28 25 S 18 42 E
Warmbad, S. Africa **123** 24 51 S 28 19 E
Warnemünde **88** 54 9N 12 5 E
Warner, Canada **62** 49 17N 112 12W
Warner, N.H. **36** 43 17N 71 49W
Warner, Okla. **43** 35 30N 95 18W
Warner, S. Dak. **47** 45 20N 98 30W
Warner Mts. **14** 41 40N 120 15W
Warner Range **44** 42 25N 120 5W
Warner Robins **18** 32 37N 83 36W
Warner Valley **44** 42 25N 119 50W
Warnes **73** 17 30 S 63 10W
Warr Acres **43** 35 31N 97 37W
Warrego → **127** 30 24 S 145 21 E
Warrego Ra. **127** 24 58 S 146 0 E
Warren, Ark. **13** 33 37N 92 4W
Warren, Conn. **28** 41 0N 73 0W
Warren, Idaho **20** 45 16N 115 41W
Warren, Ill. **21** 42 29N 90 0W
Warren, Ind. **22** 40 41N 85 26W
Warren, Minn. **30** 48 12N 96 46W
Warren, N.H. **36** 43 56N 71 54W
Warren, Ohio **42** 41 14N 80 49W
Warren, Pa. **45** 41 51N 79 9W
Warren, R.I. **28** 41 43N 71 17W
Warren, Tex. **51** 30 37N 94 24W
Warren, Vt. **36** 44 7N 72 50W
Warren County ◇, Ga. **18** 33 20N 82 40W
Warren County ◇, Ill. **21** 40 50N 90 35W
Warren County ◇, Ind. **22** 40 20N 87 25W
Warren County ◇, Iowa **23** 41 20N 93 35W
Warren County ◇, Ky. **48** 37 0N 86 25W
Warren County ◇, Miss. **31** 32 21N 90 53W
Warren County ◇, Mo. **32** 38 45N 91 10W
Warren County ◇, N.C. **40** 36 15N 78 0W
Warren County ◇, N.J. **37** 40 50N 75 0W
Warren County ◇, N.Y. **39** 43 35N 73 45W
Warren County ◇, Ohio **42** 39 26N 84 13W
Warren County ◇, Pa. **45** 41 50N 79 15W
Warren County ◇, Tenn. **49** 35 41N 85 46W
Warren County ◇, Va. **54** 38 55N 78 12W
Warren Grove **37** 39 44N 74 22W
Warren Pks. **56** 44 29N 104 28W
Warrenpoint **85** 54 7N 6 15W
Warrens **55** 44 8N 90 30W
Warrensburg, Ill. **21** 39 56N 89 4W
Warrensburg, Mo. **32** 38 46N 93 44W
Warrensburg, N.Y. **39** 43 29N 73 46W
Warrenton, S. Africa **123** 28 9 S 24 47 E
Warrenton, Ga. **18** 33 24N 82 40W
Warrenton, Mo. **32** 38 49N 91 9W
Warrenton, N.C. **40** 36 24N 78 9W
Warrenton, Oreg. **44** 46 10N 123 56W
Warrenton, Va. **54** 38 43N 77 48W
Warrenville **46** 33 32N 81 48W
Warri **120** 5 30N 5 41 E
Warrick County ◇ **22** 38 5N 87 15W
Warrina **126** 28 12 S 135 50 E
Warrington, U.K. **82** 53 25N 2 38W
Warrington, U.S.A. **17** 30 23N 87 17W
Warrior **10** 33 49N 86 49W
Warrnambool **127** 38 25 S 142 30 E
Warroad **30** 48 54N 95 19W
Warsa **111** 0 47 S 135 55 E
Warsaw = Warszawa **89** 52 13N 21 0 E
Warsaw, Ill. **21** 40 22N 91 26W
Warsaw, Ind. **22** 41 14N 85 51W
Warsaw, Ky. **49** 38 47N 84 54W
Warsaw, Mo. **32** 38 15N 93 23W
Warsaw, N.C. **40** 35 0N 78 5W
Warsaw, N.Y. **39** 42 45N 78 8W
Warsaw, Va. **54** 37 58N 76 46W
Warszawa **89** 52 13N 21 0 E
Warta → **88** 52 35N 14 39 E
Wartburg **49** 36 6N 84 36W
Warthe = Warta → **88** 52 35N 14 39 E
Warthen **18** 33 6N 82 48W
Wartrace **48** 35 32N 86 20W
Waru **111** 3 30 S 130 36 E
Warwick, Australia **127** 28 10 S 152 1 E
Warwick, U.K. **83** 52 17N 1 36W
Warwick, Ga. **18** 31 50N 83 57W
Warwick, Mass. **28** 42 0N 72 0W
Warwick, Md. **27** 39 25N 75 47W
Warwick, N. Dak. **41** 47 51N 98 43W
Warwick, N.Y. **39** 41 16N 74 22W
Warwick, R.I. **28** 41 42N 71 28W
Warwick □ **83** 52 20N 1 30W
Wasa **62** 49 45N 115 50W
Wasatch County ◇ **52** 40 20N 111 15W
Wasatch National Forest **52** 40 50N 110 40W
Wasatch Plateau **52** 39 20N 111 30W
Wasatch Range **52** 40 0N 111 30W
Wasco, Calif. **15** 35 36N 119 20W
Wasco, Oreg. **44** 45 36N 120 42W
Wasco County ◇ **44** 45 15N 121 15W
Waseca **30** 44 5N 93 30W
Waseca County ◇ **30** 44 0N 93 40W
Wasekamio L. **63** 56 45N 108 45W
Wash, The **82** 52 58N 0 20 E
Washakie County ◇ **56** 44 0N 107 40W
Washburn, Ill. **21** 40 55N 89 17W
Washburn, Maine **26** 46 47N 68 9W
Washburn, Mo. **32** 36 35N 93 58W
Washburn, N. Dak. **41** 47 17N 101 2W
Washburn, Tex. **50** 35 11N 101 34W
Washburn, Wis. **55** 46 40N 90 54W
Washburn County ◇ **55** 45 50N 91 50W
Washim **108** 20 3N 77 0 E
Washington, Ark. **13** 33 47N 93 41W
Washington, Conn. **28** 41 39N 73 19W
Washington, D.C. **27** 38 54N 77 2W
Washington, Ga. **18** 33 44N 82 44W
Washington, Ill. **21** 40 42N 89 24W
Washington, Ind. **22** 38 40N 87 10W
Washington, Iowa **23** 41 18N 91 42W
Washington, Kans. **24** 39 49N 97 3W
Washington, Ky. **49** 38 37N 83 49W
Washington, La. **25** 30 37N 92 4W
Washington, Maine **26** 44 16N 69 22W
Washington, Mo. **32** 38 33N 91 1W
Washington, N.C. **40** 35 33N 77 3W
Washington, N.H. **36** 43 11N 72 8W
Washington, N.J. **37** 40 46N 74 59W
Washington, Nebr. **34** 41 24N 96 13W
Washington, Okla. **43** 35 4N 97 29W
Washington, Pa. **45** 40 10N 80 15W
Washington, Utah **52** 37 8N 113 31W
Washington, Va. **54** 38 43N 78 10W
Washington □ **53** 47 30N 120 30W
Washington, Mt. **36** 44 16N 71 18W
Washington County ◇, Ala. **10** 31 22N 88 15W
Washington County ◇, Ark. **13** 36 4N 94 10W
Washington County ◇, Colo. **16** 40 0N 103 10W
Washington County ◇, Fla. **17** 30 30N 85 45W
Washington County ◇, Ga. **18** 33 0N 82 50W
Washington County ◇, Idaho **20** 44 30N 116 50W
Washington County ◇, Ill. **21** 38 20N 89 25W
Washington County ◇, Ind. **22** 38 35N 86 5W
Washington County ◇, Iowa **23** 41 20N 91 40W
Washington County ◇, Kans. **24** 39 45N 97 0W
Washington County ◇, Ky. **49** 37 45N 85 10W
Washington County ◇, Maine **26** 45 0N 67 30W
Washington County ◇, Md. **27** 39 40N 78 0W
Washington County ◇, Minn. **30** 45 10N 92 55W
Washington County ◇, Miss. **31** 33 16N 90 53W
Washington County ◇, Mo. **32** 38 0N 90 50W
Washington County ◇, N.C. **40** 35 50N 76 30W
Washington County ◇, N.Y. **39** 43 20N 73 25W
Washington County ◇, Nebr. **34** 41 30N 96 15W
Washington County ◇, Ohio **42** 39 25N 81 27W
Washington County ◇, Okla. **43** 36 40N 95 55W
Washington County ◇, Oreg. **44** 45 30N 123 0W
Washington County ◇, Pa. **45** 40 8N 80 8W
Washington County ◇, R.I. **28** 41 30N 71 40W
Washington County ◇, Tenn. **49** 36 18N 82 29W
Washington County ◇, Tex. **51** 30 10N 96 24W
Washington County ◇, Utah **52** 37 20N 113 30W
Washington County ◇, Va. **54** 36 55N 82 0W
Washington County ◇, Vt. **36** 44 15N 72 40W
Washington County ◇, Wis. **55** 43 20N 88 15W
Washington Court House **42** 39 32N 83 26W
Washington Grove **27** 39 8N 77 11W
Washington I. **55** 45 23N 86 54W
Washington Island **55** 45 24N 86 56W
Washington Parish ◇ **25** 30 51N 90 9W
Washington Terrace **52** 41 11N 111 59W
Washir **108** 32 15N 63 50 E
Washita → **43** 34 8N 96 36W
Washita County ◇ **43** 35 15N 99 0W
Washoe City **35** 39 19N 119 49W
Washoe County ◇ **35** 41 0N 119 40W
Washoe L. **35** 39 16N 119 48W
Washta **23** 42 35N 95 43W
Washtenaw County ◇ **29** 42 15N 83 50W
Washtucna **53** 46 45N 118 19W
Wasian **111** 1 47 S 133 19 E
Wasilla **11** 61 35N 149 26W
Wasior **111** 2 43 S 134 30 E
Waskaiowaka, L. **63** 56 33N 96 23W
Waskesiu Lake **63** 53 55N 106 5W
Waskish **30** 48 10N 94 31W
Waskom **51** 32 29N 94 4W
Wassaw I. **18** 31 53N 80 58W
Wassaw Sd. **18** 31 55N 80 55W
Wassenaar **87** 52 8N 4 24 E
Wassuk Range **35** 38 40N 118 50W
Wasta **47** 44 4N 102 27W
Waswanipi **60** 49 40N 76 29W
Waswanipi, L. **60** 49 35N 76 40W
Watangpone **111** 4 29 S 120 25 E
Watauga County ◇ **40** 36 15N 81 45W
Watauga L. **49** 36 19N 82 7W
Water Valley, Ky. **48** 36 34N 88 49W
Water Valley, Miss. **31** 34 10N 89 38W
Waterberg **123** 20 30 S 17 18 E
Waterbury, Conn. **28** 41 33N 73 3W
Waterbury, Nebr. **34** 42 27N 96 44W
Waterbury, Vt. **36** 44 20N 72 46W
Waterbury Center **36** 44 22N 72 43W
Waterbury L. **63** 58 10N 104 22W
Wateree → **46** 33 45N 80 37W
Wateree L. **46** 34 20N 80 42W
Waterflow **38** 36 45N 108 27W
Waterford, Ireland **85** 52 16N 7 8W
Waterford, Calif. **14** 37 38N 120 46W
Waterford, Conn. **28** 41 20N 72 9W
Waterford, Maine **26** 44 14N 70 46W
Waterford, Miss. **31** 34 39N 89 28W
Waterford, Pa. **45** 41 57N 79 59W
Waterford, Wis. **55** 42 46N 88 13W
Waterford □ **85** 52 10N 7 40W
Waterford Harb. **85** 52 10N 6 58W
Watergap **49** 37 38N 82 45W
Waterhen L., Man., Canada **63** 52 10N 99 40W
Waterhen L., Sask., Canada **63** 54 28N 108 25W
Waterloo, Belgium **87** 50 43N 4 25 E
Waterloo, Canada **60** 43 30N 80 32W
Waterloo, S. Leone **120** 8 26N 13 8W
Waterloo, Ala. **10** 34 55N 88 4W
Waterloo, Ark. **13** 33 33N 93 15W
Waterloo, Ill. **21** 38 20N 90 9W
Waterloo, Ind. **22** 41 26N 85 1W
Waterloo, Iowa **23** 42 30N 92 21W
Waterloo, Mont. **33** 45 43N 112 12W
Waterloo, N.Y. **39** 42 54N 76 52W
Waterloo, Wis. **55** 43 11N 88 59W
Waterman **21** 41 46N 88 47W
Waterproof **25** 31 48N 91 23W
Watersmeet **29** 46 16N 89 11W
Waterton-Glacier International Peace Park **33** 48 45N 115 0W
Waterton Lakes Nat. Park **62** 49 5N 114 15W
Watertown, Conn. **28** 41 36N 73 7W
Watertown, Fla. **17** 30 11N 82 36W
Watertown, Mass. **28** 42 22N 71 11W

Watertown West Frankfort

Watertown, N.Y. 39 43 59N 75 55W
Watertown, S. Dak. 47 44 54N 97 7W
Watertown, Tenn. 48 36 6N 86 8W
Watertown, Wis. 55 43 12N 88 43W
Waterville, Kans. 24 39 42N 96 45W
Waterville, Maine 26 44 33N 69 38W
Waterville, Minn. 30 44 13N 93 34W
Waterville, N.Y. 39 42 56N 75 23W
Waterville, Ohio 42 41 30N 83 43W
Waterville, Vt. 36 44 42N 72 47W
Waterville, Wash. 53 47 39N 120 4W
Waterville Valley 36 43 57N 71 31W
Watervliet 39 42 44N 73 42W
Wates 111 7 53 S 110 6 E
Watford 83 51 38N 0 23W
Watford City 41 47 48N 103 17W
Wathaman → 63 57 16N 102 59W
Wathena 24 39 46N 94 57W
Watkins 30 45 19N 94 24W
Watkins Glen 39 42 23N 76 52W
Watkinsville 18 33 52N 83 25W
Watonga 43 35 51N 98 25W
Watonwan County ◇ 30 44 0N 94 40W
Watova 43 36 37N 95 39W
Watrous, Canada 63 51 40N 105 25W
Watrous, U.S.A. 38 35 48N 104 59W
Watsa 122 3 4N 29 30 E
Watseka 21 40 47N 87 44W
Watson, Canada 63 52 10N 104 30W
Watson, Ark. 13 33 54N 91 15W
Watson, Ill. 21 39 2N 88 34W
Watson, Minn. 30 45 1N 95 48W
Watson, Mo. 32 40 29N 95 40W
Watson Lake 62 60 6N 128 49W
Watsontown 45 41 5N 76 52W
Watsonville 14 36 55N 121 45W
Watts 43 36 7N 94 34W
Watts Bar L. 49 35 37N 84 47W
Wattsburg 45 42 0N 79 49W
Wattsville 46 34 31N 82 2W
Watuata = Batuata 111 6 12 S 122 42 E
Watubela, Kepulauan 111 4 28 S 131 35 E
Watuppa Pond 28 41 42N 71 6W
Waubay 47 45 20N 97 18W
Waubay L. 47 45 25N 97 24W
Waubun 30 47 11N 95 57W
Wauchula 17 27 33N 81 49W
Waucoba Mt. 15 37 1N 118 0W
Waucoma 23 43 2N 92 1W
Waugh 63 49 40N 95 11W
Waugoshance Pt. 29 45 46N 85 1W
Waukee 23 41 37N 93 53W
Waukeenah 17 30 25N 83 57W
Waukegan 21 42 22N 87 50W
Waukesha 55 43 1N 88 14W
Waukesha County ◇ 55 43 0N 88 15W
Waukomis 43 36 17N 97 54W
Waukon 23 43 16N 91 29W
Waunakee 55 43 11N 89 27W
Wauneta 34 40 25N 101 23W
Waupaca 55 44 21N 89 5W
Waupaca County ◇ 55 44 25N 89 0W
Waupun 55 43 38N 88 44W
Waurika 43 34 10N 98 0W
Waurika Res. 43 34 10N 98 0W
Wausa 34 42 30N 97 32W
Wausau, Fla. 17 30 38N 85 35W
Wausau, Wis. 55 44 58N 89 38W
Wausaukee 55 45 23N 87 57W
Wauseon 42 41 33N 84 8W
Waushara County ◇ 55 44 10N 89 15W
Wautoma 55 44 4N 89 18W
Wauwatosa 55 43 3N 88 0W
Wauzeka 55 43 5N 90 53W
Wave Hill 126 17 32 S 131 0 E
Waveland, Ind. 22 39 53N 87 3W
Waveland, Miss. 31 30 17N 89 23W
Waveney → 83 52 24N 1 20 E
Waverley 128 39 46 S 174 37 E
Waverley Hall 18 32 41N 84 44W
Waverly, Ala. 10 32 44N 85 35W
Waverly, Fla. 17 27 59N 81 37W
Waverly, Ga. 18 31 6N 81 43W
Waverly, Ill. 21 39 36N 89 57W
Waverly, Iowa 23 42 44N 92 29W
Waverly, Kans. 24 38 23N 95 36W
Waverly, Ky. 48 37 43N 87 48W
Waverly, Mo. 32 39 13N 93 31W
Waverly, N.Y. 39 42 1N 76 32W
Waverly, Nebr. 34 40 55N 96 32W
Waverly, Tenn. 48 36 5N 87 48W
Waverly, Va. 54 37 2N 77 6W
Waverly, Wash. 53 47 21N 117 14W
Wavre 87 50 43N 4 38 E
Wâw 121 7 45N 28 1 E
Waw al Kabir 121 25 20N 17 20 E
Wawa 60 47 59N 84 47W
Wawanesa 63 49 36N 99 40W
Wawasee, L. 22 41 24N 85 42W
Wawona 14 37 32N 119 39W
Waxahachie 51 32 24N 96 51W
Waxhaw 40 34 56N 80 45W
Way 31 32 45N 90 2W
Wayabula Rau 111 2 29N 128 17 E
Wayan 20 42 58N 111 23W
Waycross 18 31 13N 82 21W
Wayland, Iowa 23 41 8N 91 40W
Wayland, Ky. 49 37 27N 82 48W
Wayland, Mass. 28 42 22N 71 22W
Wayland, Mich. 29 42 40N 85 39W
Wayland, N.Y. 39 42 34N 77 35W
Wayne, Kans. 24 39 43N 97 33W
Wayne, Mich. 29 42 17N 83 23W
Wayne, N.J. 37 40 55N 74 17W
Wayne, Nebr. 34 42 14N 97 1W
Wayne, Ohio 42 41 18N 83 29W
Wayne, Okla. 43 34 55N 97 19W
Wayne, W. Va. 54 38 13N 82 27W
Wayne County ◇, Ga. 18 31 30N 82 0W
Wayne County ◇, Ill. 21 38 25N 88 25W
Wayne County ◇, Ind. 22 39 50N 85 0W
Wayne County ◇, Iowa 23 40 45N 93 20W
Wayne County ◇, Ky. 49 36 45N 84 50W
Wayne County ◇, Mich. 29 42 15N 83 15W
Wayne County ◇, Miss. 31 31 40N 88 39W
Wayne County ◇, Mo. 32 37 5N 90 30W
Wayne County ◇, N.C. 40 35 20N 78 0W
Wayne County ◇, N.Y. 39 43 10N 77 0W
Wayne County ◇, Nebr. 34 42 15N 97 5W
Wayne County ◇, Ohio 42 40 48N 81 56W
Wayne County ◇, Pa. 45 41 35N 75 15W
Wayne County ◇, Tenn. 48 35 10N 87 44W
Wayne County ◇, Utah 52 38 15N 111 0W
Wayne County ◇, W. Va. 54 38 13N 82 27W
Wayne National Forest 42 39 33N 81 4W
Waynesboro, Ga. 18 33 6N 82 1W
Waynesboro, Miss. 31 31 40N 88 39W
Waynesboro, Pa. 45 39 45N 77 35W
Waynesboro, Tenn. 48 35 19N 87 46W
Waynesboro, Va. 54 38 4N 78 53W
Waynesburg 45 39 54N 80 11W
Waynesville, Ill. 21 40 15N 89 8W
Waynesville, Mo. 32 37 50N 92 12W
Waynesville, N.C. 40 35 28N 82 58W
Waynesville, Ohio 42 39 32N 84 5W
Waynetown 22 40 5N 87 4W
Waynoka 43 36 35N 98 53W
Wayside, Ga. 18 33 4N 83 37W
Wayside, Miss. 31 33 16N 91 2W
Wayside, Wis. 55 44 15N 87 57W
Waza 108 33 22N 69 22 E
Wazirabad 108 32 30N 74 8 E
We 110 5 51N 95 18 E
Weakley County ◇ 48 36 14N 88 50W
Weald, The 83 51 7N 0 9 E
Wear → 82 54 55N 1 22W
Weare 36 43 6N 71 44W
Weatherby 32 39 55N 94 14W
Weatherford, Okla. 43 35 32N 98 43W
Weatherford, Tex. 51 32 46N 97 48W
Weatherly 45 40 57N 75 50W
Weathersby 31 31 56N 89 50W
Weaubleau 32 37 54N 93 32W
Weaverville, Calif. 14 40 44N 122 56W
Weaverville, N.C. 40 35 42N 82 34W
Webb, Iowa 23 42 57N 95 1W
Webb, Miss. 31 33 57N 90 21W
Webb City, Mo. 32 37 9N 94 28W
Webb City, Okla. 43 36 48N 96 42W
Webb County ◇ 51 27 30N 99 10W
Webber 24 39 56N 98 2W
Webbville 49 38 11N 82 52W
Weber → 52 41 10N 112 10W
Weber County ◇ 52 41 20N 111 40W
Webster, Fla. 17 28 37N 82 3W
Webster, Iowa 23 41 26N 92 10W
Webster, Mass. 28 42 3N 71 53W
Webster, N. Dak. 41 48 17N 98 53W
Webster, N.Y. 39 43 13N 77 26W
Webster, S. Dak. 47 45 20N 97 31W
Webster, Wis. 55 45 53N 92 22W
Webster City 23 42 28N 93 49W
Webster County ◇, Ga. 18 32 0N 84 35W
Webster County ◇, Iowa 23 42 25N 94 10W
Webster County ◇, Ky. 48 37 30N 87 40W
Webster County ◇, Miss. 31 33 37N 89 17W
Webster County ◇, Mo. 32 37 15N 92 50W
Webster County ◇, Nebr. 34 40 15N 98 30W
Webster County ◇, W. Va. 54 38 29N 80 25W
Webster Parish ◇ 25 32 40N 93 20W
Webster Reservoir 24 39 25N 99 26W
Webster Springs 54 38 29N 80 25W
Weda 111 0 21N 127 50 E
Weda, Teluk 111 0 30N 127 50 E
Weddell I. 78 51 50 S 61 0W
Weddell Sea 5 72 30 S 40 0W
Wedgefield 46 33 53N 80 31W
Wedgeport 61 43 44N 65 59W
Wedowee 10 33 19N 85 29W
Weed, Calif. 14 41 25N 122 23W
Weed, N. Mex. 38 32 48N 105 31W
Weed Heights 35 38 59N 119 13W
Weedville 45 41 17N 78 30W
Weekapaug 28 41 20N 71 45W
Weeks 25 29 48N 91 49W
Weekstown 37 39 37N 74 37W
Weeksville 40 36 13N 76 10W
Weeping Water 34 40 52N 96 8W
Weert 87 51 15N 5 43 E
Wei He →, Hebei, China 114 36 10N 115 45 E
Wei He →, Shaanxi, China 115 34 38N 110 15 E
Weifang 114 36 44N 119 7 E
Weihai 114 37 30N 122 6 E
Weimar, Germany 88 51 0N 11 20 E
Weimar, Calif. 14 39 2N 120 59W
Weimar, Tex. 51 29 42N 96 47W
Weinan 115 34 31N 109 29 E
Weiner 13 35 37N 90 54W
Weipa 127 12 40 S 141 50 E
Weippe 20 46 23N 115 56W
Weir, Kans. 24 37 19N 94 46W
Weir, Ky. 48 37 7N 87 13W
Weir, Miss. 31 33 16N 89 18W
Weir → 63 56 54N 93 21W
Weir, L. 17 29 0N 81 57W
Weir River 63 56 49N 94 6W
Weirsdale 17 28 59N 81 55W
Weirton 54 40 24N 80 35W
Weiser 20 44 45N 116 58W
Weiser → 20 44 14N 116 58W
Weishan 115 34 47N 117 5 E
Weiss L. 10 34 8N 85 48W
Weissert 34 41 28N 99 27W
Weiyuan 114 35 7N 104 10 E
Weizhou Dao 115 21 0N 109 5 E
Wejherowo 89 54 35N 18 12 E
Wekusko 63 54 30N 99 45W
Wekusko L. 63 54 40N 99 50W
Welby 63 50 33N 101 29W
Welch, Okla. 43 36 52N 95 6W
Welch, Tex. 50 32 56N 102 8W
Welch, W. Va. 54 37 26N 81 35W
Welcome, Md. 27 38 28N 77 8W
Welcome, Minn. 30 43 40N 94 37W
Welcome, N.C. 40 35 55N 80 15W
Weld 26 44 42N 70 25W
Weld County ◇ 16 40 45N 104 15W
Welda 24 38 10N 95 18W
Weldon, Ill. 21 40 7N 88 45W
Weldon, Iowa 23 40 54N 93 44W
Weldon, N.C. 40 36 25N 77 36W
Weldon Spring 32 38 43N 90 41W
Weldona 16 40 21N 103 58W
Weleetka 43 35 20N 96 8W
Welkom 123 28 0 S 26 50 E
Welland 60 43 0N 79 15W
Welland → 82 52 43N 0 10W
Wellborn 51 30 32N 96 18W
Wellesley 28 42 18N 71 18W
Wellesley Is. 127 16 42 S 139 30 E
Wellfleet, Mass. 28 41 56N 70 2W
Wellfleet, Nebr. 34 40 45N 100 44W
Wellin 87 50 5N 5 6 E
Wellingborough 83 52 18N 0 41W
Wellington, Australia 127 32 35 S 148 59 E
Wellington, Canada 60 43 57N 77 20W
Wellington, N.Z. 128 41 19 S 174 46 E
Wellington, Salop, U.K. 82 52 42N 2 31W
Wellington, Somerset, U.K. 83 50 58N 3 13W
Wellington, Colo. 16 40 42N 105 0W
Wellington, Ill. 21 40 32N 87 41W
Wellington, Kans. 24 37 16N 97 24W
Wellington, Maine 26 45 2N 69 36W
Wellington, Mo. 32 39 8N 93 59W
Wellington, Nev. 35 38 45N 119 23W
Wellington, Ohio 42 41 10N 82 13W
Wellington, Tex. 50 34 51N 100 13W
Wellington, Utah 52 39 32N 110 44W
Wellington □ 128 40 8 S 175 36 E
Wellington, I. 78 49 30 S 75 0W
Wellman, Iowa 23 41 28N 91 50W
Wellman, Tex. 50 33 3N 102 26W
Wellpinit 53 47 53N 117 59W
Wells, Norfolk, U.K. 82 52 57N 0 51 E
Wells, Somerset, U.K. 83 51 12N 2 39W
Wells, Kans. 24 39 5N 97 33W
Wells, Maine 26 43 20N 70 35W
Wells, Minn. 30 43 45N 93 44W
Wells, N.Y. 39 43 24N 74 17W
Wells, Nev. 35 41 7N 114 58W
Wells, Tex. 51 31 29N 94 56W
Wells, Vt. 36 43 25N 73 10W
Wells → 36 44 10N 72 3W
Wells County ◇, Ind. 22 40 45N 85 15W
Wells County ◇, N. Dak. 41 47 35N 99 45W
Wells Gray Prov. Park 62 52 30N 120 15W
Wells L. 126 26 44 S 123 15 E
Wellsboro 45 41 45N 77 18W
Wellsburg, Iowa 23 42 26N 92 56W
Wellsburg, N.Y. 39 42 1N 76 44W
Wellsburg, W. Va. 54 40 16N 80 37W
Wellsford 24 37 37N 99 2W
Wellston, Mich. 29 44 13N 85 58W
Wellston, Ohio 42 39 7N 82 32W
Wellston, Okla. 43 35 42N 97 4W
Wellsville, Kans. 24 38 43N 95 5W
Wellsville, Mo. 32 39 4N 91 34W
Wellsville, N.Y. 39 42 7N 77 57W
Wellsville, Ohio 42 40 36N 80 39W
Wellsville, Pa. 45 40 3N 76 56W
Wellsville, Utah 52 41 38N 111 56W
Wellton 12 32 40N 114 8W
Wels 88 48 9N 14 1 E
Welsh 25 30 14N 92 49W
Welshpool 83 52 40N 3 9W
Welton 23 41 55N 90 36W
Welwyn 63 50 20N 101 30W
Wem 82 52 52N 2 45W
Wen Xian 115 32 43N 104 36 E
Wenatchee 53 47 25N 120 19W
Wenatchee → 53 47 27N 120 19W
Wenatchee Mts. 53 47 15N 120 30W
Wenatchee National Forest 53 47 55N 120 55W
Wenchang 115 19 38N 110 42 E
Wenchi 120 7 46N 2 8W
Wenchow = Wenzhou 115 28 0N 120 38 E
Wendell, Idaho 20 42 47N 114 42W
Wendell, Minn. 30 46 2N 96 6W
Wendell, N.C. 40 35 47N 78 22W
Wendell, N.H. 36 43 22N 72 9W
Wenden 12 33 49N 113 33W
Wendeng 114 37 15N 122 5 E
Wendesi 111 2 30 S 134 17 E
Wendover 52 40 44N 114 2W
Wengcheng 115 24 22N 113 50 E
Wenlock → 127 12 2 S 141 55 E
Wenona, Ill. 21 41 3N 89 3W
Wenona, Md. 27 38 8N 75 57W
Wensu 113 41 15N 80 10 E
Wentworth, Australia 127 34 2 S 141 54 E
Wentworth, Mo. 32 36 59N 94 4W
Wentworth, N.C. 40 36 24N 79 46W
Wentworth, N.H. 36 43 52N 71 55W
Wentzville 32 38 49N 90 51W
Wenut 111 3 11 S 133 19 E
Wenxi 115 35 20N 111 10 E
Wenzhou 115 28 0N 120 38 E
Weott 14 40 20N 123 55W
Wepener 123 29 42 S 27 3 E
Werda 123 25 24 S 23 15 E
Werder 105 6 58N 45 1 E
Weri 111 3 10 S 132 38 E
Werley 55 43 1N 90 46W
Wersar 111 1 30 S 131 55 E
Weser → 88 53 33N 8 30 E
Wesiri 111 7 30 S 126 30 E
Weskan 24 38 52N 101 57W
Weslaco 50 26 10N 97 58W
Wesley, Ga. 18 32 29N 82 20W
Wesley, Iowa 23 43 5N 93 59W
Wesley, Maine 26 44 57N 67 40W
Wesleyville, Canada 61 49 8N 53 36W
Wesleyville, U.S.A. 45 42 9N 80 0W
Wessel Is. 127 11 10 S 136 45 E
Wessington 47 44 27N 98 42W
Wessington Springs 47 44 5N 98 34W
Wesson, Ark. 13 33 7N 92 46W
Wesson, Miss. 31 31 42N 90 24W
West 51 31 48N 97 6W
West → 36 42 52N 72 33W
West Acton 28 42 29N 71 29W
West Alexandria 42 39 45N 84 32W
West Allis 55 43 1N 88 0W
West Arlington 36 43 8N 73 12W
West Arm Grand Traverse B. 29 44 50N 85 40W
West B., Fla. 17 30 10N 85 45W
West B., La. 25 29 3N 89 22W
West B., Tex. 51 29 14N 95 0W
West Babylon 39 40 42N 73 21W
West Baton Rouge Parish ◇ 25 30 27N 91 12W
West Bend, Iowa 23 42 57N 94 27W
West Bend, Wis. 55 43 25N 88 11W
West Bengal □ 109 23 0N 88 0 E
West Blocton 10 33 7N 87 7W
West Boylston 28 42 22N 71 47W
West Branch, Iowa 23 41 42N 91 20W
West Branch, Mich. 29 44 17N 84 14W
West Branch Susquehanna → 45 40 53N 76 48W
West Bridgewater 28 42 1N 71 0W
West Bromwich 83 52 32N 2 1W
West Brookfield 28 42 14N 72 9W
West Burke 36 44 39N 71 59W
West Burlington 23 40 49N 91 9W
West Campton 36 43 40N 71 41W
West Canaan 36 43 40N 72 2W
West Cape May 37 38 56N 74 56W
West Carroll Parish ◇ 25 32 30N 92 52W
West Carthage 39 43 59N 75 37W
West Chester, Iowa 23 41 20N 91 49W
West Chester, Pa. 45 39 58N 75 36W
West Columbia, S.C. 46 34 0N 81 4W
West Columbia, Tex. 51 29 9N 95 39W
West Concord 30 44 9N 92 54W
West Cote Blanche B. 25 29 45N 91 55W
West Covina 15 34 4N 117 54W
West Creek 37 39 38N 74 18W
West Cummington 28 42 29N 72 57W
West Des Moines 23 41 35N 93 43W
West Dover 36 42 56N 72 51W
West Dummerston 36 42 55N 72 38W
West Elk Mts. 16 38 35N 107 15W
West Elkton 42 39 35N 84 33W
West End, Bahamas 66 26 41N 78 58W
West End, U.S.A. 40 35 15N 79 34W
West Fairlee 36 43 54N 72 16W
West Falkland 78 51 40 S 60 0W
West Fargo 41 46 52N 96 54W
West Feliciana Parish ◇ 25 30 50N 91 23W
West Fork Cuivre → 32 39 2N 90 59W
West Fork Poplar → 33 48 31N 105 22W
West Fork Trinity → 51 32 48N 96 54W
West Forks 26 45 20N 69 58W
West Frankfort 21 37 54N 88 55W

West Germany

Whitesboro

West Germany ■ 88 52 0N 9 0 E
West Glacier 33 48 30N 113 59W
West Glamorgan □ 83 51 40N 3 55W
West Grand L. 26 45 14N 67 51W
West Green 18 31 37N 82 44W
West Hamlin 54 38 17N 82 12W
West Hartford 28 41 45N 72 44W
West Haven 28 41 17N 72 57W
West Helena 13 34 33N 90 38W
West Ice Shelf 5 67 0S 85 0E
West Indies 67 15 0N 70 0W
West Jefferson, N.C. 40 36 24N 81 30W
West Jefferson, Ohio 42 39 57N 83 17W
West Kingston 28 41 29N 71 34W
West Lafayette 22 40 27N 86 55W
West Lebanon 22 40 16N 87 23W
West Leipsic 42 41 7N 84 0W
West Liberty, Iowa 23 41 34N 91 16W
West Liberty, Ky. 49 37 55N 83 16W
West Liberty, Ohio 42 40 15N 83 45W
West Looe 83 50 21N 4 29W
West Louisville 48 37 42N 87 17W
West Mansfield 42 40 24N 83 33W
West Mayfield 45 40 47N 80 20W
West Memphis 13 35 9N 90 11W
West Midlands □ 83 52 30N 1 55W
West Mifflin 45 40 22N 79 52W
West Milan 36 44 37N 71 18W
West Milford 54 39 12N 80 24W
West Millgrove 42 41 15N 83 30W
West Milton 42 39 58N 84 20W
West Mineral 24 37 17N 94 55W
West Monroe 25 32 31N 92 9W
West Moors 82 50 49N 1 50W
West Newbury 28 42 48N 70 0W
West Nicholson 123 21 2S 29 20 E
West Nishnabotna → 23 40 39N 95 38W
West Nueces → 51 29 16N 99 56W
West Okoboji L. 23 43 23N 95 9W
West Orange 51 30 5N 93 46W
West Ossipee 36 43 48N 71 12W
West Palm Beach 17 26 43N 80 3W
West Palm Beach Canal 17 26 40N 80 15W
West Panama City Beach 17 30 13N 85 53W
West Pawlet 36 43 21N 73 15W
West Pensacola 17 30 25N 87 16W
West Plains 32 36 44N 91 51W
West Plymouth 36 43 45N 71 45W
West Point, Calif. 14 38 24N 120 32W
West Point, Ga. 18 32 53N 85 11W
West Point, Ill. 21 40 15N 91 11W
West Point, Iowa 23 40 43N 91 27W
West Point, Ky. 49 37 59N 85 57W
West Point, Miss. 31 33 36N 88 39W
West Point, N.Y. 39 41 24N 73 58W
West Point, Nebr. 34 41 51N 96 43W
West Point, Va. 54 37 32N 76 48W
West Point L. 10 33 0N 85 5W
West Richland 53 46 18N 119 20W
West Rindge 36 42 47N 72 3W
West River 27 38 52N 76 31W
West Road → 62 53 18N 122 53W
West Rutland 36 43 36N 73 3W
West Sacramento 14 38 35N 121 32W
West Salem, Ill. 21 38 31N 88 1W
West Salem, Ohio 42 40 58N 82 7W
West Salem, Wis. 55 43 54N 91 5W
West Schelde → = Westerschelde → 87 51 25N 3 25 E
West Seneca 39 42 51N 78 48W
West Siberian Plain 102 62 0N 75 0 E
West Siloam Springs 43 36 12N 94 39W
West Springfield 28 42 6N 72 38W
West Stewartstown 36 44 59N 71 32W
West Sussex □ 83 50 55N 0 30W
West Tavaputs Plateau 52 39 50N 110 20W
West Terre Haute 22 39 28N 87 27W
West-Terschelling 87 53 22N 5 13 E
West Thompson Res. 28 41 57N 71 54W
West Thorton 36 43 55N 71 42W
West Thumb 56 44 25N 110 34W
West Tisbury 28 41 23N 70 41W
West Topsham 36 44 7N 72 19W
West Union, Iowa 23 42 57N 91 49W
West Union, Minn. 30 45 48N 95 5W
West Union, Ohio 42 38 48N 83 33W
West Union, W. Va. 54 39 18N 80 47W
West Unity 42 41 35N 84 26W
West University Place 51 29 42N 95 26W
West Valley 52 40 42N 111 58W
West Virginia □ 54 38 45N 80 30W
West-Vlaanderen □ 87 51 0N 3 0 E
West Warwick 28 41 43N 71 32W
West Winfield 39 42 53N 75 12W
West Yarmouth 28 41 39N 70 15W
West Yellowstone 33 44 40N 111 6W
West York 45 39 57N 76 46W
West Yorkshire □ 82 53 45N 1 40W
Westbay 17 30 18N 85 52W
Westboro 32 40 32N 95 19W
Westborough 28 42 16N 71 37W
Westbrook, Conn. 28 41 17N 72 27W
Westbrook, Maine 26 43 41N 70 22W
Westbrook, Minn. 30 44 3N 95 26W
Westbrook, Tex. 50 32 21N 101 1W
Westby, Mont. 33 48 52N 104 3W
Westby, Wis. 55 43 39N 90 51W
Westchester County ◇ 39 41 40N 73 45W
Westcliffe 16 38 9N 105 28W
Westend 15 35 42N 117 24W
Westerly 28 41 22N 71 50W
Western 34 40 24N 97 12W
Western □ 123 15 15 S 24 30 E
Western Australia □ 128 25 0 S 118 0 E
Western Ghats 108 14 0N 75 0 E
Western Grove 13 36 6N 92 57W
Western Isles □ 84 57 30N 7 10W
Western Sahara ■ 120 25 0N 13 0W
Western Samoa ■ 128 14 0 S 172 0W
Westernport 27 39 29N 79 3W
Westerschelde → 87 51 25N 3 25 E
Westerville, Nebr. 34 41 24N 99 23W
Westerville, Ohio 42 40 8N 82 56W
Westerwald 88 50 39N 8 0 E
Westfall 44 43 59N 117 48W
Westfield, Ill. 21 39 27N 88 0W
Westfield, Ind. 22 40 2N 86 8W
Westfield, Iowa 23 42 45N 96 36W
Westfield, Maine 26 46 34N 67 55W
Westfield, Mass. 28 42 7N 72 45W
Westfield, N.J. 37 40 39N 74 21W
Westfield, N.Y. 39 42 20N 79 35W
Westfield, Pa. 45 41 55N 77 32W
Westfield, Wis. 55 43 53N 89 30W
Westfield → 28 42 5N 72 35W
Westfir 44 43 46N 122 31W
Westford 28 42 35N 71 26W
Westgate 23 42 46N 92 0W
Westhoff 51 29 12N 97 28W
Westhope 41 48 55N 101 1W
Westland □ 128 43 33 S 169 59 E
Westland Bight 128 42 55 S 170 5 E
Westlock 62 54 9N 113 55W
Westmeath □ 85 53 30N 7 30W
Westminster, Calif. 15 33 46N 118 1W
Westminster, Colo. 16 39 50N 105 2W
Westminster, Mass. 28 42 33N 71 55W
Westminster, Md. 27 39 34N 76 59W
Westminster, S.C. 46 34 40N 83 6W
Westminster, Vt. 36 43 5N 72 27W
Westmont 45 40 19N 78 58W
Westmore 36 44 0N 72 0W
Westmoreland, Kans. 24 39 24N 96 25W
Westmoreland, N.H. 36 42 57N 72 25W
Westmoreland, Tenn. 48 36 34N 86 15W
Westmoreland County ◇, Pa. 45 40 20N 79 25W
Westmoreland County ◇, Va. 54 38 6N 76 50W
Westmorland 15 33 2N 115 37W
Weston, Malaysia 110 5 10N 115 35 E
Weston, Colo. 16 37 8N 104 48W
Weston, Mo. 32 39 25N 94 54W
Weston, Nebr. 34 41 12N 96 45W
Weston, Oreg. 44 45 49N 118 26W
Weston, Vt. 36 43 18N 72 38W
Weston, W. Va. 54 39 2N 80 28W
Weston, Wis. 55 44 49N 92 4W
Weston County ◇ 56 43 55N 104 35W
Weston I. 60 52 33N 79 36W
Weston-super-Mare 83 51 20N 2 59W
Westover, Md. 27 38 7N 75 42W
Westover, Pa. 45 40 45N 78 40W
Westover, S. Dak. 47 43 45N 100 40W
Westover, Tenn. 48 35 37N 88 53W
Westphalia, Mich. 29 42 56N 84 48W
Westphalia, Mo. 32 38 26N 92 0W
Westpoint 48 35 8N 87 32W
Westport, Ireland 85 53 44N 9 31W
Westport, N.Z. 128 41 46 S 171 37 E
Westport, Calif. 14 39 38N 123 47W
Westport, Conn. 28 41 9N 73 22W
Westport, Ind. 22 39 11N 85 34W
Westport, Minn. 30 45 43N 95 10W
Westport, N.H. 36 42 49N 72 20W
Westport, N.Y. 39 44 11N 73 26W
Westport, Okla. 43 36 8N 96 20W
Westport, Oreg. 44 46 8N 123 23W
Westport, Wash. 53 46 53N 124 6W
Westray, Canada 63 53 36N 101 24W
Westray, U.K. 84 59 18N 3 0W
Westree 60 47 26N 81 34W
Westview 62 49 50N 124 31W
Westville, Fla. 17 30 46N 85 51W
Westville, Ill. 21 40 2N 87 38W
Westville, Okla. 43 35 58N 94 40W
Westville, S.C. 46 34 27N 80 36W
Westwego 25 29 54N 90 8W
Westwood, Calif. 14 40 18N 121 0W
Westwood, Ky. 49 38 30N 82 50W
Westwood, Mass. 28 42 13N 71 14W
Westwood, Md. 27 38 40N 76 45W
Westwood, N.J. 37 40 58N 74 2W
Westwood Lakes 17 25 44N 80 23W
Wet Mts. 16 38 0N 105 10W
Wetar 111 7 30 S 126 30 E
Wetaskiwin 62 52 55N 113 24W
Wethersfield 28 41 42N 72 40W
Wetmore, Colo. 16 38 14N 105 5W
Wetmore, Kans. 24 39 38N 95 49W
Wetteren 87 51 0N 3 53 E
Wetumka 43 35 14N 96 15W
Wetumpka 10 32 32N 86 13W
Wetzel County ◇ 54 39 34N 80 41W
Wetzlar 88 50 33N 8 30 E
Wewahitchka 17 30 7N 85 12W
Wewoka 43 35 9N 96 30W
Wexford 85 52 20N 6 28W
Wexford □ 85 52 20N 6 25W
Wexford County ◇ 29 44 20N 85 40W
Wexford Harb. 85 52 20N 6 25W
Weyauwega 55 44 19N 88 56W
Weyburn 63 49 40N 103 50W
Weyburn L. 62 63 0N 117 59W
Weyerhaeuser 55 45 26N 91 25W
Weymouth, Canada 61 44 30N 66 1W
Weymouth, U.K. 83 50 36N 2 28W
Weymouth, U.S.A. 28 42 13N 70 58W
Weymouth, C. 127 12 37 S 143 27 E
Whakatane 128 37 57 S 177 1 E
Whalan 30 43 44N 91 55W
Whale → 61 58 15N 67 40W
Whale Cove 58 62 11N 92 36W
Whales, B. of 5 78 0 S 165 0W
Whaleysville 27 38 24N 75 18W
Whalsay 84 60 22N 1 0W
Whangamomona 128 39 8 S 174 44 E
Whangarei 128 35 43 S 174 21 E
Whangarei Harbour 128 35 45 S 174 28 E
Wharfe → 82 53 55N 1 30W
Wharfedale 82 54 7N 2 4W
Wharton, N.J. 37 40 54N 74 35W
Wharton, Ohio 42 40 52N 83 28W
Wharton, Tex. 51 29 19N 96 6W
Wharton County ◇ 51 29 12N 96 16W
Wharton State Forest 37 39 45N 74 40W
What Cheer 23 41 24N 92 21W
Whatcom, L. 53 48 44N 122 20W
Whatcom County ◇ 53 48 56N 122 0W
Whatley 10 31 39N 87 42W
Wheat Ridge 16 39 46N 105 5W
Wheatcroft 48 37 30N 87 52W
Wheatland, Calif. 14 39 1N 121 25W
Wheatland, Ind. 22 38 40N 87 19W
Wheatland, Iowa 23 41 50N 90 51W
Wheatland, Mo. 32 37 57N 93 24W
Wheatland, Wyo. 56 42 3N 104 58W
Wheatland County ◇ 33 46 30N 109 50W
Wheatland Reservoir No.2 56 41 50N 105 38W
Wheatley 13 34 55N 91 7W
Wheaton, Ill. 21 41 52N 88 6W
Wheaton, Kans. 24 39 30N 96 19W
Wheaton, Md. 27 39 3N 77 3W
Wheaton, Minn. 30 45 48N 96 30W
Wheeler, Ill. 21 39 3N 88 19W
Wheeler, Kans. 24 39 46N 101 43W
Wheeler, Miss. 31 34 35N 88 37W
Wheeler, Oreg. 44 45 41N 123 53W
Wheeler, Tex. 50 35 27N 100 16W
Wheeler, Wis. 55 45 3N 91 55W
Wheeler → 63 57 25N 105 30W
Wheeler County ◇, Ga. 18 32 5N 82 45W
Wheeler County ◇, Nebr. 34 41 50N 98 30W
Wheeler County ◇, Oreg. 44 44 45N 120 0W
Wheeler County ◇, Tex. 50 35 30N 100 15W
Wheeler L. 10 34 48N 87 23W
Wheeler Peak, N. Mex. 38 36 33N 105 25W
Wheeler Peak, Nev. 35 38 59N 114 19W
Wheeler Ridge 15 35 0N 118 57W
Wheelersburg 42 38 44N 82 51W
Wheeling, Ill. 21 42 8N 87 55W
Wheeling, W. Va. 54 40 4N 80 43W
Wheelock 41 48 18N 103 15W
Wheelwright 49 37 20N 82 43W
Whelen Springs 13 33 50N 93 7W
Whernside 82 54 14N 2 24W
Whidbey I. 53 48 12N 122 17W
Whidbey Is. 126 34 30 S 135 3 E
Whiskey Gap 62 49 0N 113 3W
Whiskey Jack L. 63 58 23N 101 55W
Whiskey Pk. 56 42 18N 107 35W
Whiskeytown-Shasta-Trinity Nat. Rec. Area 14 40 45N 122 15W
Whispering Pines 40 35 17N 79 26W
Whitakers 40 36 6N 77 43W
Whitby 82 54 29N 0 37W
White, Ga. 18 34 17N 84 45W
White, S. Dak. 47 44 26N 96 39W
White →, Ariz. 12 33 44N 110 13W
White →, Ark. 13 33 57N 91 5W
White →, Ind. 22 38 25N 87 45W
White →, Nev. 35 37 19N 115 8W
White →, S. Dak. 47 43 42N 99 27W
White →, Tex. 50 33 14N 100 56W
White →, Utah 52 40 4N 109 41W
White →, Vt. 36 43 37N 72 20W
White Apple 31 31 27N 91 4W
White B. 61 50 0N 56 35W
White Bear Lake 30 45 5N 93 1W
White Bear Res. 61 48 10N 57 5W
White Bird 20 45 46N 116 18W
White Bluff 48 36 6N 87 13W
White Butte, N. Dak. 41 46 23N 103 18W
White Butte, S. Dak. 47 45 56N 102 22W
White Canyon 52 37 49N 110 26W
White Castle 25 30 10N 91 9W
White City, Fla. 17 29 53N 85 13W
White City, Kans. 24 38 48N 96 44W
White City, Ky. 49 37 35N 85 40W
White City, Oreg. 44 42 26N 122 51W
White Cloud, Kans. 24 39 59N 95 18W
White Cloud, Mich. 29 43 33N 85 46W
White County ◇, Ark. 13 35 15N 91 44W
White County ◇, Ga. 18 34 40N 83 45W
White County ◇, Ill. 21 38 5N 88 10W
White County ◇, Ind. 22 40 45N 86 50W
White County ◇, Tenn. 49 35 56N 85 28W
White Deer 50 35 26N 101 10W
White Earth 41 48 23N 102 46W
White Earth → 41 48 9N 102 42W
White Earth Indian Reservation 30 47 20N 95 45W
White Hall, Ala. 10 32 20N 86 43W
White Hall, Ill. 21 39 26N 90 24W
White Haven 45 41 4N 75 47W
White Horse 37 40 11N 74 42W
White I. 128 37 30 S 177 13 E
White L. 25 29 44N 92 30W
White Lake, N.C. 40 34 39N 78 30W
White Lake, S. Dak. 47 43 43N 98 43W
White Lake, Wis. 55 45 10N 88 46W
White Mountain 11 64 41N 163 24W
White Mountain National Forest 36 44 10N 71 25W
White Mountain Peak 15 37 38N 118 15W
White Mts., Alaska 11 65 30N 146 30W
White Mts., Calif. 15 37 30N 118 15W
White Mts., N.H. 36 44 10N 71 20W
White Nile = Nîl el Abyad → 121 15 38N 32 31 E
White Oak, Ga. 18 31 2N 81 43W
White Oak, S.C. 46 34 28N 81 7W
White Oak, Tex. 51 32 32N 94 52W
White Oak Cr. → 51 33 14N 94 42W
White Otter L. 60 49 5N 91 55W
White Owl 47 44 36N 102 26W
White Pass, Canada 62 59 40N 135 3W
White Pass, U.S.A. 53 46 38N 121 24W
White Pigeon 29 41 48N 85 39W
White Pine, Mich. 29 46 45N 89 35W
White Pine, Mont. 33 47 45N 115 29W
White Pine, Tenn. 49 36 7N 83 17W
White Pine County ◇ 35 39 30N 115 0W
White Pine Range 35 39 10N 115 20W
White Plains, Ga. 18 33 28N 83 1W
White Plains, Md. 27 38 36N 76 55W
White Plains, N.Y. 39 41 2N 73 46W
White River, Canada 60 48 35N 85 20W
White River, U.S.A. 47 43 34N 100 45W
White River Junction 36 43 39N 72 19W
White River National Forest 16 39 20N 106 45W
White River Reservoir 50 33 27N 101 5W
White Rock 49 36 48N 83 26W
White Rock Cr. → 24 39 55N 97 50W
White Russia = Byelorussian S.S.R. □ 98 53 30N 27 0 E
White Salmon 53 45 44N 121 29W
White Sands National Monument 38 32 46N 106 20W
White Sea = Beloye More 98 66 30N 38 0 E
White Springs 17 30 20N 82 45W
White Stone 54 37 39N 76 23W
White Sulphur Springs, Mont. 33 46 33N 110 54W
White Sulphur Springs, W. Va. 54 37 48N 80 18W
White Swan 53 46 23N 120 44W
Whiteburg 27 38 12N 75 32W
Whiteclay 34 42 57N 102 33W
Whitecliffs 128 43 26 S 171 55 E
Whitecourt 62 54 10N 115 45W
Whiteface 50 33 36N 102 37W
Whiteface → 30 46 32N 92 48W
Whiteface Reservoir 30 47 17N 92 11W
Whitefield, Maine 26 44 10N 69 38W
Whitefield, N.H. 36 44 23N 71 37W
Whitefish 33 48 25N 114 20W
Whitefish → 29 45 55N 86 57W
Whitefish B. 29 46 40N 84 55W
Whitefish Bay 55 43 23N 87 54W
Whitefish L. 63 62 41N 106 48W
Whitefish Point 29 46 45N 84 59W
Whitefish Pt. 29 46 46N 84 57W
Whiteford 27 39 42N 76 21W
Whitegull, L. 61 55 27N 64 17W
Whitehall, Ark. 13 35 29N 90 44W
Whitehall, Mich. 29 43 24N 86 21W
Whitehall, Mont. 33 45 52N 112 6W
Whitehall, N.Y. 39 43 33N 73 24W
Whitehall, Wis. 55 44 22N 91 19W
Whitehaven 82 54 33N 3 35W
Whitehorse 62 60 43N 135 3W
Whitehorse, Vale of 83 51 37N 1 30W
Whitehouse 42 41 31N 83 48W
Whiteland 22 39 33N 86 5W
Whitelaw 55 44 9N 87 49W
Whiteleysburg 27 38 57N 75 45W
Whitemouth 63 49 57N 95 58W
Whiteriver 12 33 50N 109 58W
Whites City 38 32 11N 104 22W
Whitesail, L. 62 53 35N 127 45W
Whitesboro, N.Y. 39 43 7N 75 18W
Whitesboro, Okla. 43 34 41N 94 53W
Whitesboro, Tex. 51 33 39N 96 54W

Winona **Xi Xian**

Winona, Wash. **53** 46 57N 117 48W
Winona County ◇ **30** 44 0N 91 50W
Winona Lake **22** 41 14N 85 49W
Winooski **36** 44 29N 73 11W
Winooski → **36** 44 32N 73 17W
Winschoten **87** 53 9N 7 3 E
Winside **34** 42 11N 97 10W
Winslow, Ariz. **12** 35 2N 110 42W
Winslow, Ark. **13** 35 48N 94 8W
Winslow, Ind. **22** 38 23N 87 13W
Winslow, Maine **26** 44 33N 69 37W
Winslow, Nebr. **34** 41 37N 96 30W
Winslow, Wash. **53** 47 38N 122 31W
Winsted, Conn. **28** 41 55N 73 4W
Winsted, Minn. **30** 44 58N 94 3W
Winston, N. Mex. **38** 33 20N 107 39W
Winston, Oreg. **44** 45 7N 123 25W
Winston County ◇, Ala. **10** 34 9N 87 24W
Winston County ◇, Miss. **31** 33 7N 89 3W
Winston-Salem **40** 36 6N 80 15W
Winter **55** 45 49N 91 1W
Winter Beach **17** 27 43N 80 25W
Winter Garden **17** 28 34N 81 35W
Winter Harbor **26** 44 24N 68 5W
Winter Haven **17** 28 1N 81 44W
Winter Park, Colo. **16** 39 53N 105 46W
Winter Park, Fla. **17** 28 36N 81 20W
Winters **51** 31 58N 99 58W
Winterset **23** 41 20N 94 1W
Wintersville **42** 40 23N 80 42W
Winterswijk **87** 51 58N 6 43 E
Winterthur **88** 47 30N 8 44 E
Winterville, Maine **26** 46 58N 68 34W
Winterville, N.C. **40** 35 32N 77 24W
Winthrop, Ark. **13** 33 50N 94 21W
Winthrop, Iowa **23** 42 28N 91 44W
Winthrop, Maine **26** 44 18N 69 58W
Winthrop, Minn. **30** 44 32N 94 22W
Winthrop, Wash. **53** 48 28N 120 10W
Winthrop Harbor **21** 42 29N 87 50W
Winton, Australia **127** 22 24 S 143 3 E
Winton, N.Z. **128** 46 8 S 168 20 E
Winton, Calif. **14** 37 23N 120 37W
Winton, Minn. **30** 47 56N 91 48W
Winton, N.C. **40** 36 24N 76 56W
Winton, Wyo. **56** 41 45N 109 10W
Wiota, Iowa **23** 41 24N 94 54W
Wiota, Wis. **55** 42 39N 89 57W
Wirral **82** 53 25N 3 0W
Wirt County ◇ **54** 39 4N 81 24W
Wisacky **46** 34 9N 80 12W
Wisbech **82** 52 39N 0 10 E
Wiscasset **26** 44 0N 69 40W
Wisconsin □ **55** 44 45N 89 30W
Wisconsin → **55** 43 0N 91 15W
Wisconsin Dells **55** 43 38N 89 46W
Wisconsin L. **55** 43 19N 89 44W
Wisconsin Rapids **55** 44 23N 89 49W
Wisdom **33** 45 37N 113 27W
Wise, N.C. **40** 36 29N 78 10W
Wise, Va. **54** 36 59N 82 35W
Wise County ◇, Tex. **51** 33 14N 97 35W
Wise County ◇, Va. **54** 37 0N 82 45W
Wise River **33** 45 48N 112 57W
Wiseman **11** 67 25N 150 6W
Wishaw **84** 55 46N 3 55W
Wishek **41** 46 16N 99 33W
Wishon Res. **15** 36 50N 118 50W
Wishram **53** 45 40N 120 58W
Wisła → **89** 54 22N 18 55 E
Wismar, Germany **88** 53 53N 11 23 E
Wismar, Guyana **71** 5 59N 58 18W
Wisner, La. **25** 31 59N 91 39W
Wisner, Nebr. **34** 41 59N 96 55W
Wissota L. **55** 44 56N 91 20W
Wister **43** 34 58N 94 43W
Witbank **123** 25 51 S 29 14 E
Witham → **82** 53 3N 0 8W
Withee **55** 44 57N 90 36W
Withernsea **82** 53 43N 0 2 E
Withington Mt. **38** 33 53N 107 29W
Withlacoochee →, Fla. **17** 29 0N 82 45W
Withlacoochee →, Fla. **17** 30 24N 83 10W
Withrow **53** 47 42N 119 48W
Witney **83** 51 47N 1 29W
Witt **21** 39 15N 89 21W
Witten **47** 43 26N 100 5W
Wittenberg, Germany **88** 51 51N 12 39 E
Wittenberg, Mo. **32** 37 39N 89 31W
Wittenberg, Wis. **55** 44 49N 89 10W
Wittenberge **88** 53 0N 11 44 E
Wittenoom **126** 22 15 S 118 20 E
Wittman **27** 38 48N 76 18W
Wittmann **12** 33 47N 112 32W
Wixom **29** 42 32N 83 32W
Wkra → **89** 52 45N 20 30 E
Wlingi **111** 8 5 S 112 25 E
Woburn **28** 42 29N 71 9W
Woëvre, Plaine de la **90** 49 15N 5 45 E
Wokam **111** 5 45 S 134 28 E
Woking **62** 55 35N 118 50W
Wolbach **34** 41 24N 98 24W
Wolcott, Colo. **16** 39 42N 106 40W
Wolcott, Conn. **28** 41 36N 72 59W
Wolcott, Ind. **22** 40 46N 87 3W
Wolcott, N.Y. **39** 43 13N 76 49W
Wolcottville **22** 41 32N 85 22W
Wolf **24** 38 2N 101 6W
Wolf →, Canada **62** 60 17N 132 33W
Wolf →, Miss. **31** 30 22N 89 18W
Wolf →, Okla. **43** 36 34N 99 34W
Wolf →, Tenn. **48** 35 10N 89 5W
Wolf →, Wis. **55** 44 11N 88 48W
Wolf Cr. → **33** 47 37N 109 38W
Wolf Creek, Mont. **33** 47 0N 112 4W
Wolf Creek, Oreg. **44** 42 42N 123 24W
Wolf Creek Pass **16** 37 29N 106 48W
Wolf L. **62** 60 24N 131 40W
Wolf Lake, Mich. **29** 43 15N 86 7W
Wolf Lake, Minn. **30** 46 48N 95 21W
Wolf Point **33** 48 5N 105 39W
Wolfe City **51** 33 22N 96 4W
Wolfe County ◇ **49** 37 45N 83 30W
Wolfe I. **60** 44 7N 76 20W
Wolfeboro **36** 43 35N 71 13W
Wolfenden **62** 52 0N 119 25W
Wolfforth **50** 33 30N 102 1W
Wolford **41** 48 30N 99 42W
Wolfsville **27** 39 37N 77 35W
Wolin **88** 53 50N 14 37 E
Wollaston, Islas **78** 55 40 S 67 30W
Wollaston L. **63** 58 7N 103 10W
Wollaston Pen. **58** 69 30N 115 0W
Wollongong **127** 34 25 S 150 54 E
Wolseley **63** 50 25N 103 15W
Wolsey **47** 44 25N 98 28W
Wolstenholme Fjord **4** 76 0N 70 0W
Wolvega **87** 52 52N 6 0 E
Wolverhampton **86** 52 35N 2 6W
Wolverine **29** 45 17N 84 36W
Wolverine Peak **56** 42 59N 109 22W
Wolverton **30** 46 34N 96 44W
Wonalancet **36** 43 44N 71 21W
Wondai **127** 26 20 S 151 49 E
Wŏnju **114** 37 22N 127 58 E
Wonosari **111** 7 58 S 110 36 E
Wŏnsan **114** 39 11N 127 27 E
Wonthaggi **127** 38 37 S 145 37 E
Wood **47** 43 30N 100 29W
Wood → **34** 41 2N 98 5W
Wood Buffalo Nat. Park **62** 59 0N 113 41W
Wood County ◇, Ohio **42** 41 23N 83 39W
Wood County ◇, Tex. **51** 32 48N 95 27W
Wood County ◇, W. Va. **54** 39 14N 81 34W
Wood County ◇, Wis. **55** 44 20N 90 0W
Wood L. **63** 55 17N 103 17W
Wood Lake, Minn. **30** 44 39N 95 32W
Wood Lake, Nebr. **34** 42 38N 100 14W
Wood River, Ill. **21** 38 52N 90 5W
Wood River, Nebr. **34** 40 49N 98 36W
Woodall Mt. **31** 34 47N 88 15W
Woodberry **13** 33 35N 92 31W
Woodbine, Ga. **18** 30 58N 81 44W
Woodbine, Iowa **23** 41 44N 95 43W
Woodbine, Kans. **24** 38 48N 96 57W
Woodbine, Ky. **49** 36 54N 84 5W
Woodbine, Md. **27** 39 22N 77 4W
Woodbine, N.J. **37** 39 15N 74 49W
Woodbourne **39** 41 46N 74 36W
Woodbridge, Conn. **28** 41 21N 73 2W
Woodbridge, Va. **54** 38 40N 77 15W
Woodburn, Ind. **22** 41 8N 84 51W
Woodburn, Iowa **23** 41 1N 93 36W
Woodburn, Ky. **48** 36 50N 86 32W
Woodburn, Oreg. **44** 45 9N 122 51W
Woodbury, Conn. **28** 41 33N 73 13W
Woodbury, Ga. **18** 32 59N 84 35W
Woodbury, Ky. **48** 37 11N 86 38W
Woodbury, N.J. **37** 39 50N 75 9W
Woodbury, Tenn. **48** 35 50N 86 4W
Woodbury County ◇ **23** 42 25N 96 0W
Woodfin **40** 35 38N 82 36W
Woodford, S.C. **46** 33 40N 81 7W
Woodford, Vt. **36** 42 52N 73 6W
Woodford County ◇, Ill. **21** 40 50N 89 10W
Woodford County ◇, Ky. **49** 38 0N 84 45W
Woodfords **14** 38 47N 119 50W
Woodhull **21** 41 11N 90 20W
Woodlake **15** 36 25N 119 6W
Woodland, Calif. **14** 38 41N 121 46W
Woodland, Ill. **21** 40 43N 87 44W
Woodland, Maine **26** 45 9N 67 25W
Woodland, Miss. **31** 33 47N 89 3W
Woodland, N.C. **40** 36 19N 77 12W
Woodland, Tex. **51** 33 48N 95 17W
Woodland, Wash. **53** 45 54N 122 45W
Woodland Beach **27** 39 20N 75 28W
Woodland Park **16** 38 57N 105 12W
Woodlawn **27** 39 19N 76 44W
Woodman **55** 43 7N 90 48W
Woodpecker **62** 53 30N 122 40W
Woodridge, Canada **63** 49 20N 96 9W
Woodridge, U.S.A. **39** 41 43N 74 34W
Woodroffe, Mt. **126** 26 20 S 131 45 E
Woodrow **50** 33 27N 101 50W
Woodruff, Kans. **24** 39 59N 99 19W
Woodruff, S.C. **46** 34 45N 82 2W
Woodruff, Utah **52** 41 31N 111 10W
Woodruff, Wis. **55** 45 54N 89 42W
Woodruff, L. **17** 29 6N 81 24W
Woodruff County ◇ **13** 35 9N 91 21W
Woodruff Narrows Reservoir **56** 41 31N 111 1W
Woods, L., Australia **126** 17 50 S 133 30 E
Woods, L., Canada **61** 54 30N 65 13W
Woods, L. of the, Canada **63** 49 15N 94 45W
Woods, L. of the, U.S.A. **30** 49 0N 94 0W
Woods County ◇ **43** 36 45N 98 50W
Woods Cross **52** 40 52N 111 58W
Woods Hole **28** 41 31N 70 40W
Woodsboro, Md. **27** 39 32N 77 19W
Woodsboro, Tex. **51** 28 14N 97 20W
Woodsfield **42** 39 46N 81 7W
Woodson, Ark. **13** 34 32N 92 13W
Woodson, Tex. **51** 33 1N 99 3W
Woodson County ◇ **24** 37 50N 95 45W
Woodstock, N.B., Canada **61** 46 11N 67 37W
Woodstock, Ont., Canada **60** 43 10N 80 45W
Woodstock, U.K. **83** 51 51N 1 20W
Woodstock, Conn. **28** 41 0N 72 0W
Woodstock, Ga. **18** 34 6N 84 31W
Woodstock, Ill. **21** 42 19N 88 27W
Woodstock, N.H. **36** 43 57N 71 42W
Woodstock, Ohio **42** 40 10N 83 32W
Woodstock, Va. **54** 38 53N 78 30W
Woodstock, Vt. **36** 43 37N 72 31W
Woodston **24** 39 27N 99 6W
Woodstown **37** 39 39N 75 20W
Woodsville **36** 44 9N 72 2W
Woodville, N.Z. **128** 40 20 S 175 53 E
Woodville, Ala. **10** 34 38N 86 17W
Woodville, Fla. **17** 30 19N 84 15W
Woodville, Ga. **18** 33 40N 83 7W
Woodville, Miss. **31** 31 6N 91 18W
Woodville, Tex. **51** 30 47N 94 25W
Woodward, Iowa **23** 41 51N 93 55W
Woodward, Okla. **43** 36 26N 99 24W
Woodward County ◇ **43** 36 25N 99 15W
Woodway **51** 31 30N 97 13W
Woodworth, La. **25** 31 9N 92 30W
Woodworth, N. Dak. **41** 47 9N 99 23W
Woody Creek **16** 39 17N 106 54W
Woolridge **32** 38 55N 92 32W
Woolstock **23** 42 34N 93 51W
Woomera **127** 31 30 S 137 10 E
Woonsocket, R.I. **28** 42 0N 71 31W
Woonsocket, S. Dak. **47** 44 3N 98 17W
Wooramel → **126** 25 47 S 114 10 E
Wooster, Ark. **13** 35 12N 92 27W
Wooster, Ohio **42** 40 48N 81 56W
Worcester, S. Africa **123** 33 39 S 19 27 E
Worcester, U.K. **83** 52 12N 2 12W
Worcester, Mass. **28** 42 16N 71 48W
Worcester, N.Y. **39** 42 36N 74 45W
Worcester, Vt. **36** 44 20N 72 40W
Worcester County ◇, Mass. **28** 42 25N 72 0W
Worcester County ◇, Md. **27** 38 15N 75 20W
Worden, Ill. **21** 38 56N 89 50W
Worden, Mont. **33** 45 58N 108 10W
Worden, Oreg. **44** 42 2N 121 52W
Workington **82** 54 39N 3 34W
Worksop **82** 53 19N 1 9W
Workum **87** 52 59N 5 26 E
Worland **56** 44 1N 107 57W
Worley **20** 47 24N 116 55W
Worms **88** 49 37N 8 21 E
Woronoco **28** 42 10N 72 50W
Worth **32** 40 24N 94 27W
Worth County ◇, Ga. **18** 31 30N 83 50W
Worth County ◇, Iowa **23** 43 20N 93 15W
Worth County ◇, Mo. **32** 40 30N 94 25W
Wortham **51** 31 47N 96 28W
Worthing, U.K. **83** 50 49N 0 21W
Worthing, U.S.A. **47** 43 20N 96 46W
Worthington, Ind. **22** 39 7N 86 59W
Worthington, Iowa **23** 42 24N 91 7W
Worthington, Minn. **30** 43 37N 95 36W
Worthington, Ohio **42** 40 5N 83 1W
Worthington, Pa. **45** 40 50N 79 38W
Worton **27** 39 17N 76 6W
Wosi **111** 0 15 S 128 0 E
Wou-han = Wuhan **115** 30 31N 114 18 E
Wounded Knee **47** 43 8N 102 22W
Wour **121** 21 14N 16 0 E
Wowoni **111** 4 5 S 123 5 E
Wrangel I. **102** 71 0N 180 0 E
Wrangell **11** 56 28N 132 23W
Wrangell I. **11** 56 16N 132 12W
Wrangell Mts. **11** 61 30N 142 0W
Wrangell-Petersburg ◇ **11** 57 0N 134 0W
Wrath, C. **84** 58 38N 5 0W
Wray **16** 40 5N 102 13W
Wrekin, The **82** 52 41N 2 35W
Wren, Ala. **10** 34 26N 87 18W
Wren, Ohio **42** 40 48N 84 47W
Wrens **18** 33 12N 82 23W
Wrenshall **30** 46 37N 92 23W
Wrentham **28** 42 4N 71 20W
Wrexham **82** 53 5N 3 0W
Wright, Canada **62** 51 52N 121 40W
Wright, Phil. **111** 11 42N 125 2 E
Wright, U.S.A. **24** 37 47N 99 54W
Wright City, Mo. **32** 38 50N 91 1W
Wright City, Okla. **43** 34 5N 95 0W
Wright County ◇, Iowa **23** 42 45N 93 40W
Wright County ◇, Minn. **30** 45 10N 94 0W
Wright County ◇, Mo. **32** 37 15N 92 30W
Wrightson Mt. **12** 31 42N 110 51W
Wrightstown, N.J. **37** 40 2N 74 37W
Wrightstown, Wis. **55** 44 20N 88 10W
Wrightsville, Ark. **13** 34 36N 92 13W
Wrightsville, Ga. **18** 32 44N 82 43W
Wrightsville Beach **40** 34 12N 77 48W
Wrigley, Canada **58** 63 16N 123 37W
Wrigley, U.S.A. **48** 35 54N 87 21W
Wrocław **88** 51 5N 17 5 E
Września **89** 52 21N 17 36 E
Wu Jiang → **115** 29 40N 107 20 E
Wuchang **114** 44 55N 127 5 E
Wuchuan **115** 28 25N 108 3 E
Wuding He → **114** 37 2N 110 23 E
Wugang **115** 26 44N 110 35 E
Wugong Shan **115** 27 30N 114 0 E
Wuhan **115** 30 31N 114 18 E
Wuhsi = Wuxi **115** 31 33N 120 18 E
Wuhu **115** 31 22N 118 21 E
Wukari **120** 7 51N 9 42 E
Wuliaru **111** 7 27 S 131 0 E
Wulumuchi = Ürümqi **113** 43 45N 87 45 E
Wum **120** 6 24N 10 2 E
Wuning **115** 29 17N 115 5 E
Wunnummin L. **60** 52 55N 89 10W
Wuntho **109** 23 55N 95 45 E
Wupatki National Monument **12** 35 35N 111 20W
Wuping **115** 25 5N 116 5 E
Wuppertal **88** 51 15N 7 8 E
Wuqing **114** 39 23N 117 4 E
Würzburg **88** 49 46N 9 55 E
Wushan **115** 31 7N 109 54 E
Wusuli Jiang = Ussuri → **116** 48 27N 135 0 E
Wuting = Huimin **114** 37 27N 117 28 E
Wutongqiao **113** 29 22N 103 50 E
Wuwei, Anhui, China **115** 31 18N 117 54 E
Wuwei, Gansu, China **113** 37 57N 102 34 E
Wuxi, Jiangsu, China **115** 31 33N 120 18 E
Wuxi, Sichuan, China **115** 31 23N 109 35 E
Wuxing **115** 30 51N 120 8 E
Wuyi, Hebei, China **114** 37 46N 115 56 E
Wuyi, Zhejiang, China **115** 28 52N 119 50 E
Wuyi Shan **113** 27 0N 117 0 E
Wuying **114** 47 53N 129 56 E
Wuyuan **114** 41 2N 108 20 E
Wuzhai **114** 38 54N 111 48 E
Wuzhi Shan **115** 18 45N 109 45 E
Wuzhong **114** 38 2N 106 12 E
Wuzhou **115** 23 30N 111 18 E
Wyaconda **32** 40 24N 91 55W
Wyalusing **45** 41 40N 76 16W
Wyandot County ◇ **42** 40 50N 83 17W
Wyandotte, Mich. **29** 42 12N 83 9W
Wyandotte, Okla. **43** 36 48N 94 44W
Wyandotte County ◇ **24** 39 10N 94 45W
Wyandra **127** 27 12 S 145 56 E
Wyarno **56** 44 49N 106 46W
Wyatt, La. **25** 32 9N 92 42W
Wyatt, Mo. **32** 36 55N 89 13W
Wye → **83** 51 36N 2 40W
Wyeville **55** 44 2N 90 23W
Wykoff **30** 43 42N 92 16W
Wylie **51** 33 1N 96 33W
Wylie, L. **46** 35 1N 81 1W
Wymondham **83** 52 45N 0 42W
Wymore **34** 40 7N 96 40W
Wyndham, Australia **126** 15 33 S 128 3 E
Wyndham, N.Z. **128** 46 20 S 168 51 E
Wyndmere **41** 46 16N 97 8W
Wynne **13** 35 14N 90 47W
Wynnewood **43** 34 39N 97 10W
Wynona **43** 36 33N 96 20W
Wynot **34** 42 45N 97 10W
Wynyard **63** 51 45N 104 10W
Wyocena **55** 43 30N 89 17W
Wyoconda → **32** 40 2N 91 34W
Wyodak **56** 44 17N 105 22W
Wyoming, Del. **27** 39 7N 75 34W
Wyoming, Ill. **21** 41 4N 89 47W
Wyoming, Iowa **23** 42 4N 91 0W
Wyoming, Mich. **29** 42 54N 85 42W
Wyoming □ **56** 43 0N 107 30W
Wyoming County ◇, N.Y. **39** 42 40N 78 15W
Wyoming County ◇, Pa. **45** 41 30N 76 5W
Wyoming County ◇, W. Va. **54** 37 35N 81 32W
Wyoming Pk. **56** 42 36N 110 37W
Wyoming Range **56** 42 55N 110 52W
Wyomissing **45** 40 20N 75 59W
Wythe County ◇ **54** 37 0N 81 5W
Wytheville **54** 36 57N 81 5W

X

Xai-Xai **123** 25 6 S 33 31 E
Xainza **113** 30 58N 88 35 E
Xambioá **74** 6 25 S 48 40W
Xangongo **123** 16 45 S 15 0 E
Xánthi **95** 41 10N 24 58 E
Xapuri **72** 10 35 S 68 35W
Xavantina **77** 21 15 S 52 48W
Xenia, Ill. **21** 38 38N 88 38W
Xenia, Ohio **42** 39 41N 83 56W
Xi Jiang → **115** 22 5N 113 20 E
Xi Xian **114** 36 41N 110 58 E

Xiachengzi **York, Kap**

Xiachengzi **114** 44 40N 130 18 E
Xiachuan Dao **115** 21 40N 112 40 E
Xiaguan **113** 25 32N 100 16 E
Xiajiang **115** 27 30N 115 10 E
Xiamen **114** 24 25N 118 4 E
Xi'an **115** 34 15N 109 0 E
Xianfeng **115** 29 40N 109 8 E
Xiang Jiang → **115** 28 55N 112 50 E
Xiangfan **115** 32 2N 112 8 E
Xiangning **114** 35 58N 110 50 E
Xiangtan **115** 27 51N 112 54 E
Xiangxiang **115** 27 43N 112 28 E
Xiangyang **115** 32 1N 112 8 E
Xiangyin **115** 28 38N 112 54 E
Xiangzhou **115** 23 58N 109 40 E
Xianju **115** 28 51N 120 44 E
Xianyang **115** 34 20N 108 40 E
Xiao Hinggan Ling **114** 49 0N 127 0 E
Xiaogan **115** 30 52N 113 55 E
Xiapu **115** 26 54N 119 59 E
Xichang **113** 27 51N 102 19 E
Xichuan **115** 33 0N 111 30 E
Xieng Khouang **112** 19 17N 103 25 E
Xifeng **115** 27 7N 106 42 E
Xigazê **113** 29 5N 88 45 E
Xihe **115** 34 2N 105 20 E
Xiliao He → **114** 43 32N 123 35 E
Xilin **115** 24 30N 105 6 E
Xin Xian **114** 38 22N 112 46 E
Xinavane **123** 25 2 S 32 47 E
Xinbin **114** 41 40N 125 2 E
Xincheng **115** 24 5N 108 39 E
Xinfeng **115** 25 27N 114 58 E
Xing'an, Guangxi Zhuangzu, China **115** 25 38N 110 40 E
Xingan, Jiangxi, China **115** 27 46N 115 20 E
Xingcheng **114** 40 40N 120 45 E
Xingguo **115** 26 21N 115 21 E
Xinghua **115** 32 58N 119 48 E
Xinghua Wan **115** 25 15N 119 20 E
Xingning **115** 24 3N 115 42 E
Xingren **113** 25 24N 105 11 E
Xingshan **115** 31 15N 110 45 E
Xingtai **114** 37 3N 114 32 E
Xingu → **71** 1 30 S 51 53W
Xingyang **115** 34 45N 112 52 E
Xinhua **115** 27 42N 111 13 E
Xining **113** 36 34N 101 40 E
Xinjiang **114** 35 34N 111 11 E
Xinjiang Uygur Zizhiqu □ **113** 42 0N 86 0 E
Xinjin **114** 39 25N 121 58 E
Xinle **114** 38 25N 114 40 E
Xinmin **114** 41 59N 122 50 E
Xinning **115** 26 28N 110 50 E
Xinxiang **115** 35 18N 113 50 E
Xinyang **115** 32 6N 114 3 E
Xinzheng **115** 34 20N 113 45 E
Xinzhou **115** 19 43N 109 17 E
Xinzhu **115** 24 49N 120 57 E
Xiongyuecheng **114** 40 12N 122 5 E
Xiping **115** 33 22N 114 0 E
Xique-Xique **74** 10 50 S 42 40W
Xiruá → **72** 6 3 S 67 50W
Xiuyan **114** 40 18N 123 11 E
Xixabangma Feng **109** 28 20N 85 40 E
Xixiang **115** 33 0N 107 44 E
Xizang □ **113** 32 0N 88 0 E
Xuancheng **115** 30 56N 118 43 E
Xuan'en **115** 30 0N 109 30 E
Xuanhan **115** 31 18N 107 38 E
Xuanhua **114** 40 40N 115 2 E
Xuchang **115** 34 2N 113 48 E
Xuguit Qi **114** 49 17N 120 44 E
Xunke **114** 49 35N 128 27 E
Xupu **115** 27 53N 110 32 E
Xuwen **115** 20 20N 110 10 E
Xuyong **115** 28 10N 105 22 E
Xuzhou **115** 34 18N 117 10 E

Y

Ya 'Bad **104** 32 27N 35 10 E
Yaak **33** 48 50N 115 43W
Ya'an **113** 29 58N 103 5 E
Yabelo **121** 4 50N 38 8 E
Yablanitsa **95** 43 2N 24 5 E
Yablonovy Khrebet **101** 53 0N 114 0 E
Yablonovyy Ra. **102** 53 0N 114 0 E
Yabucoa **57** 18 3N 65 53W
Yabucoa, Puerto **57** 18 8N 65 48W
Yachats **44** 44 19N 124 6W
Yacheng **115** 18 22N 109 6 E
Yacolt **53** 45 51N 122 24W
Yacuiba **76** 22 0 S 63 43W
Yacuma → **73** 13 38 S 65 23W
Yadgir **108** 16 45N 77 5 E
Yadkin → **40** 35 29N 80 9W
Yadkin County ◇ **40** 36 10N 80 40W
Yadkinville **40** 36 8N 80 39W
Yagodnoye **101** 62 33N 149 40 E
Yagoua **122** 10 20N 15 13 E
Yaguas → **70** 2 45 S 70 10W
Yagur **104** 32 45N 35 4 E
Yahk **62** 49 6N 116 10W
Yahuma **122** 1 0N 23 10 E
Yaita **117** 36 48N 139 56 E
Yakima **53** 46 36N 120 31W
Yakima → **53** 46 15N 119 14W
Yakima County ◇ **53** 46 30N 120 30W
Yakima Indian Reservation **53** 46 10N 120 30W
Yakoruda **95** 42 1N 23 39 E
Yakovlevka **116** 44 26N 133 28 E
Yaku-Shima **117** 30 20N 130 30 E
Yakut A.S.S.R. □ **101** 62 0N 130 0 E
Yakutat **11** 59 33N 139 44W
Yakutat B. **11** 59 45N 140 45W
Yakutsk **101** 62 5N 129 50 E
Yala **112** 6 33N 101 18 E
Yale, Ill. **21** 39 7N 88 2W
Yale, Iowa **23** 41 47N 94 21W
Yale, Mich. **29** 43 8N 82 48W
Yale, Okla. **43** 36 7N 96 42W
Yale, S. Dak. **47** 44 26N 97 59W
Yale, Va. **54** 36 51N 77 17W
Yale L. **53** 45 58N 122 20W
Yalgoo **126** 28 16 S 116 39 E
Yalinga **122** 6 33N 23 10 E
Yalkubul, Punta **65** 21 32N 88 37W
Yalobusha → **31** 33 33N 90 10W
Yalobusha County ◇ **31** 33 59N 89 41W
Yalong Jiang → **113** 26 40N 101 55 E
Yalpukh, Oz. **95** 45 30N 28 41 E
Yalta **99** 44 30N 34 10 E
Yalu Chiang → **114** 41 30N 126 30 E
Yalu He → **114** 46 56N 123 30 E
Yalu Jiang → **114** 40 0N 124 22 E
Yalutorovsk **100** 56 41N 66 12 E
Yam Ha Melaḥ = Dead Sea **106** 31 30N 35 30 E
Yam Kinneret **104** 32 45N 35 35 E
Yamada **117** 33 33N 130 49 E
Yamagata **116** 38 15N 140 15 E
Yamagata □ **116** 38 30N 140 0 E
Yamaguchi **117** 34 10N 131 32 E
Yamaguchi □ **117** 34 20N 131 40 E
Yamal, Poluostrov **100** 71 0N 70 0 E
Yamanashi □ **117** 35 40N 138 40 E
Yamantau **98** 54 20N 57 40 E
Yamantau, Gora **98** 54 15N 58 6 E
Yâmbiô **121** 4 35N 28 16 E
Yambol **95** 42 30N 26 36 E
Yamdena **111** 7 45 S 131 20 E
Yame **117** 33 13N 130 35 E
Yamethin **109** 20 29N 96 18 E
Yamhill County ◇ **44** 45 15N 123 10W
Yamma-Yamma, L. **127** 26 16 S 141 20 E
Yampa **16** 40 9N 106 55W
Yampa → **16** 40 32N 108 59W
Yampi Sd. **126** 16 8 S 123 38 E
Yamrukchal **95** 42 44N 24 52 E
Yamsay Mt. **44** 42 56N 121 22W
Yamuna → **109** 25 30N 81 53 E
Yamzho Yumco **113** 28 48N 90 35 E
Yana → **101** 71 30N 136 0 E
Yanagawa **117** 33 10N 130 24 E
Yanai **117** 33 58N 132 7 E
Yan'an **114** 36 35N 109 26 E
Yanaul **98** 56 25N 55 0 E
Yanbu 'al Baḥr **106** 24 0N 38 5 E
Yancey **51** 29 8N 99 9W
Yancey County ◇ **40** 35 50N 82 20W
Yanceyville **40** 36 24N 79 20W
Yanchang **114** 36 43N 110 1 E
Yancheng, Henan, China **115** 33 35N 114 0 E
Yancheng, Jiangsu, China **115** 33 23N 120 8 E
Yanchi **114** 37 48N 107 20 E
Yanchuan **114** 36 51N 110 10 E
Yandoon **109** 17 0N 95 40 E
Yangambi **122** 0 47N 24 20 E
Yangch'ü = Taiyuan **114** 37 52N 112 33 E
Yangchun **115** 22 11N 111 48 E
Yanggao **114** 40 21N 113 55 E
Yangi-Yer **100** 40 17N 68 48 E
Yangjiang **115** 21 50N 110 59 E
Yangquan **114** 37 58N 113 31 E
Yangshan **115** 24 30N 112 40 E
Yangshuo **115** 24 48N 110 29 E
Yangtze Kiang = Chang Jiang → **115** 31 48N 121 10 E
Yangxin **115** 29 50N 115 12 E
Yangzhou **115** 32 21N 119 26 E
Yanhee Res. **112** 17 30N 98 45 E
Yanji **114** 42 59N 129 30 E
Yankton **47** 42 53N 97 23W
Yankton County ◇ **47** 43 0N 97 30W
Yanqi **113** 42 5N 86 35 E
Yanqing **114** 40 30N 115 58 E
Yanshan **115** 28 15N 117 41 E
Yantai **114** 37 34N 121 22 E
Yanting **115** 31 11N 105 24 E
Yantra → **95** 43 40N 25 37 E
Yanush **43** 34 43N 95 19W
Yanzhou **114** 35 35N 116 49 E
Yao **121** 12 56N 17 33 E
Yaoundé **122** 3 50N 11 35 E
Yap **124** 9 31N 138 6 E
Yapen **111** 1 50 S 136 0 E
Yapen, Selat **111** 1 20 S 136 10 E
Yaqui → **64** 27 37N 110 39W
Yaquina Head **44** 44 41N 124 5W
Yar-Sale **100** 66 50N 70 50 E
Yaracuy □ **70** 10 20N 68 45W
Yaracuy → **70** 10 33N 68 15W
Yaraka **127** 24 53 S 144 3 E
Yarangüme **106** 37 35N 29 8 E
Yaransk **98** 57 22N 47 49 E
Yarbo **10** 31 32N 88 17W
Yardville **37** 40 11N 74 40W
Yare → **83** 52 36N 1 28 E
Yarensk **98** 61 10N 49 8 E
Yarí → **70** 0 20 S 72 20W
Yaritagua **70** 10 5N 69 8W
Yarkand = Shache **113** 38 20N 77 10 E
Yarkhun → **108** 36 17N 72 30 E
Yarmouth, Canada **61** 43 50N 66 7W
Yarmouth, U.S.A. **26** 43 48N 70 11W
Yarmūk → **104** 32 42N 35 40 E
Yarnell **12** 34 13N 112 45W
Yaroslavl **98** 57 35N 39 55 E
Yartsevo **101** 60 20N 90 0 E
Yarumal **70** 6 58N 75 24W
Yasawa Group **128** 17 0 S 177 23 E
Yasinski, L. **60** 53 16N 77 35W
Yasothon **112** 15 50N 104 10 E
Yass **127** 34 49 S 148 54 E
Yas'ur **104** 32 54N 35 10 E
Yata → **73** 10 29 S 65 26W
Yates Center **24** 37 53N 95 44W
Yates City **21** 40 47N 90 1W
Yates County ◇ **39** 42 40N 77 10W
Yatesboro **45** 40 48N 79 20W
Yatesville **18** 32 55N 84 9W
Yathkyed L. **63** 62 40N 98 0W
Yatsushiro **117** 32 30N 130 40 E
Yaṭṭah **104** 31 27N 35 6 E
Yauca **72** 15 39 S 74 35W
Yauco **57** 18 2N 66 51W
Yauco, Rio → **57** 17 59N 66 49W
Yauya **72** 8 59 S 77 17W
Yauyos **72** 12 19 S 75 50W
Yavapai County ◇ **12** 34 30N 112 30W
Yavari → **72** 4 21 S 70 2W
Yavatmal **108** 20 20N 78 15 E
Yavne **104** 31 52N 34 45 E
Yawatahama **117** 33 27N 132 24 E
Yayama-Rettō **117** 24 30N 123 40 E
Yazd **107** 31 55N 54 27 E
Yazd □ **107** 32 0N 55 0 E
Yazdān **107** 33 30N 60 50 E
Yazoo → **31** 32 22N 90 54W
Yazoo City **31** 32 51N 90 25W
Yazoo County ◇ **31** 32 50N 90 25W
Yding Skovhøj **97** 55 59N 9 46 E
Ye Xian **114** 37 8N 119 57 E
Yeager **43** 35 9N 96 21W
Yebyu **109** 14 15N 98 13 E
Yecla **91** 38 35N 1 5W
Yécora **64** 28 20N 108 58W
Yegros **76** 26 20 S 56 25W
Yeguas, Punta **57** 18 1N 65 50W
Yehuda, Midbar **104** 31 35N 35 15 E
Yei **121** 4 9N 30 40 E
Yelabuga **98** 55 45N 52 4 E
Yelanskoye **101** 61 25N 128 0 E
Yelcho, L. **78** 43 18 S 72 18W
Yelets **98** 52 40N 38 30 E
Yell **84** 60 35N 1 5W
Yell County ◇ **13** 35 3N 93 24W
Yell Sd. **84** 60 33N 1 15W
Yellow →, Fla. **17** 30 30N 87 0W
Yellow →, Ind. **22** 41 16N 86 50W
Yellow →, Wis. **55** 46 1N 92 22W
Yellow →, Wis. **55** 44 58N 91 18W
Yellow Jacket **16** 37 32N 108 43W
Yellow Medicine County ◇ **30** 44 40N 95 45W
Yellow Pine **20** 44 58N 115 30W
Yellow Sea **114** 35 0N 123 0 E
Yellow Springs **42** 39 48N 83 53W
Yellowhead P. **62** 52 53N 118 25W
Yellowknife **62** 62 27N 114 29W
Yellowknife → **58** 62 31N 114 19W
Yellowstone → **33** 47 59N 103 59W
Yellowstone County ◇ **33** 46 10N 108 0W
Yellowstone L. **56** 44 27N 110 22W
Yellowstone National Park **56** 44 40N 110 30W
Yellville **13** 36 14N 92 41W
Yelm **53** 46 57N 122 36W
Yemassee **46** 32 41N 80 51W
Yemen ■ **105** 15 0N 44 0 E
Yenangyaung **109** 20 30N 95 0 E
Yenisey → **100** 71 50N 82 40 E
Yeniseysk **101** 58 27N 92 13 E
Yeniseyskiy Zaliv **100** 72 20N 81 0 E
Yenyuka **101** 57 57N 121 15 E
Yeo, L. **126** 28 0 S 124 30 E
Yeola **108** 20 0N 74 30 E
Yeoman **22** 40 40N 86 44W
Yeovil **83** 50 57N 2 38W
Yeppoon **127** 23 5 S 150 47 E
Yerbent **100** 39 30N 58 50 E
Yerbogachen **101** 61 16N 108 0 E
Yerevan **99** 40 10N 44 31 E
Yerington **35** 38 59N 119 10W
Yermak **100** 52 2N 76 55 E
Yermakovo **101** 52 25N 126 20 E
Yermo **15** 34 54N 116 50W
Yerofey Pavlovich **101** 54 0N 122 0 E
Yershov **99** 51 22N 48 16 E
Yerunaja, Cerro **72** 10 16 S 76 55W
Yerushalayim **104** 31 47N 35 10 E
Yes Tor **83** 50 41N 3 59W
Yeso **38** 34 26N 104 37W
Yessey **101** 68 29N 102 10 E
Yetter **23** 42 19N 94 51W
Yeu, I. d' **90** 46 42N 2 20W
Yevpatoriya **99** 45 15N 33 20 E
Yeysk **99** 46 40N 38 12 E
Yezd = Yazd **107** 31 55N 54 27 E
Yhati **76** 25 45 S 56 35W
Yhú **77** 25 0 S 56 0W
Yi → **76** 33 7 S 57 8W
Yi Xian **114** 41 30N 121 22 E
Yiannitsa **95** 40 46N 22 24 E
Yibin **113** 28 45N 104 32 E
Yichang **115** 30 40N 111 20 E
Yicheng **114** 35 42N 111 40 E
Yichuan **114** 36 2N 110 10 E
Yichun, Heilongjiang, China **114** 47 44N 128 52 E
Yichun, Jiangxi, China **115** 27 48N 114 22 E
Yidu **114** 36 43N 118 28 E
Yihuang **115** 27 30N 116 12 E
Yijun **114** 35 28N 109 8 E
Yilan, China **114** 46 19N 129 34 E
Yilan, Taiwan **115** 24 51N 121 44 E
Yilehuli Shan **114** 51 20N 124 20 E
Yimianpo **114** 45 7N 128 2 E
Yinchuan **114** 38 30N 106 15 E
Ying He → **115** 32 30N 116 30 E
Ying Xian **114** 39 32N 113 10 E
Yingcheng **115** 30 56N 113 35 E
Yingde **115** 24 10N 113 25 E
Yingkou **114** 40 37N 122 18 E
Yingshan **115** 30 41N 115 32 E
Yingshang **115** 32 38N 116 12 E
Yingtan **113** 28 12N 117 0 E
Yining **113** 43 58N 81 10 E
Yinjiang **115** 28 1N 108 21 E
Yinmabin **109** 22 10N 94 55 E
Yinnietharra **126** 24 39 S 116 12 E
Yipinglang **113** 25 10N 101 52 E
Yirshi **114** 47 18N 119 49 E
Yishan **115** 24 28N 108 38 E
Yíthion **95** 36 46N 22 34 E
Yitong **114** 43 13N 125 20 E
Yitulihe **114** 50 38N 121 34 E
Yixing **115** 31 21N 119 48 E
Yiyang, Henan, China **115** 34 27N 112 10 E
Yiyang, Hunan, China **115** 28 35N 112 18 E
Yizhang **115** 25 27N 112 57 E
Yizre'el **104** 32 34N 35 19 E
Ylitornio **96** 66 19N 23 39 E
Ylivieska **96** 64 4N 24 28 E
Ynykchanskiy **101** 60 15N 137 35 E
Yoakum **51** 29 17N 97 9W
Yoakum County ◇ **50** 33 11N 102 50W
Yocona → **31** 34 11N 90 10W
Yoder **56** 41 55N 104 18W
Yog Pt. **111** 14 6N 124 12 E
Yogyakarta **111** 7 49 S 110 22 E
Yoho Nat. Park **62** 51 25N 116 30W
Yojoa, L. de **66** 14 53N 88 0W
Yokadouma **122** 3 26N 15 6 E
Yokkaichi **117** 35 0N 136 38 E
Yoko **121** 5 32N 12 20 E
Yokohama **117** 35 27N 139 28 E
Yokosuka **117** 35 20N 139 40 E
Yokote **116** 39 20N 140 30 E
Yola **121** 9 10N 12 29 E
Yolaina, Cordillera de **66** 11 30N 84 0W
Yolo County ◇ **14** 38 45N 121 50W
Yonago **117** 35 25N 133 19 E
Yonaguni-Jima **117** 24 27N 123 0 E
Yoncalla **44** 43 36N 123 17W
Yonezawa **116** 37 57N 140 4 E
Yong Peng **112** 2 0N 103 3 E
Yong'an **115** 25 59N 117 25 E
Yongchun **115** 25 16N 118 20 E
Yongding **115** 24 43N 116 45 E
Yongfeng **115** 27 20N 115 22 E
Yongfu **115** 24 59N 109 59 E
Yonghe **114** 36 46N 110 38 E
Yongji **115** 34 52N 110 28 E
Yongshun **115** 29 2N 109 51 E
Yongxin **115** 26 58N 114 15 E
Yongxing **115** 26 9N 113 8 E
Yongxiu **115** 29 2N 115 42 E
Yonibana **120** 8 30N 12 19W
Yonkers **39** 40 56N 73 54W
Yonne □ **90** 47 50N 3 40 E
Yonne → **90** 48 23N 2 58 E
Yoqne'am **104** 32 40N 35 6 E
York, Australia **126** 31 52 S 116 47 E
York, U.K. **82** 53 58N 1 7W
York, Ala. **10** 32 29N 88 18W
York, N. Dak. **41** 48 19N 99 34W
York, Nebr. **34** 40 52N 97 36W
York, Pa. **45** 39 58N 76 44W
York, S.C. **46** 35 0N 81 12W
York → **54** 37 15N 76 23W
York, C. **127** 10 42 S 142 31 E
York, Kap **4** 75 55N 66 25W

York County Zyryanovsk

York County ◇, Maine 26 43 25N 70 50W
York County ◇, Nebr. 34 40 45N 97 40W
York County ◇, Pa. 45 39 58N 76 44W
York County ◇, S.C. 46 34 55N 81 10W
York County ◇, Va. 54 37 14N 76 30W
York Sd. 126 14 50 S 125 5 E
York Springs 45 40 0N 77 7W
Yorke Pen. 127 34 50 S 137 40 E
Yorkshire Wolds 82 54 0N 0 30W
Yorkton 63 51 11N 102 28W
Yorktown, Ark. 13 34 1N 91 49W
Yorktown, Ind. 22 40 10N 85 30W
Yorktown, Tex. 51 28 59N 97 30W
Yorktown, Va. 54 37 14N 76 30W
Yorkville, Ga. 18 33 55N 84 58W
Yorkville, Ill. 21 41 38N 88 27W
Yoro 66 15 9N 87 7W
Yoron-Jima 117 27 2N 128 26 E
Yos Sudarso, Pulau 111 8 0 S 138 30 E
Yosemite 49 37 21N 84 50W
Yosemite National Park 14 37 45N 119 40W
Yosemite Village 14 37 45N 119 35W
Yoshkar Ola 98 56 38N 47 55 E
Yost 52 41 58N 113 33W
Yŏsu 115 34 47N 127 45 E
Yotala 73 19 10 S 65 17W
Yotvata 104 29 55N 35 2 E
You Jiang → 115 23 22N 110 3 E
Youbou 62 48 53N 124 13W
Youghal 85 51 58N 7 51W
Youghal B. 85 51 55N 7 50W
Youghiogheny → 45 40 22N 79 52W
Youghiogheny Reservoir 27 39 48N 79 22W
Young, Australia 127 34 19 S 148 18 E
Young, Canada 63 51 47N 105 45W
Young, Uruguay 76 32 44 S 57 36W
Young County ◇ 51 33 12N 98 44W
Young Harris 18 34 56N 83 51W
Youngstown, Canada 63 51 35N 111 10W
Youngstown, Fla. 17 30 22N 85 26W
Youngstown, N.Y. 39 43 15N 79 3W
Youngstown, Ohio 42 41 6N 80 39W
Youngsville, La. 25 30 3N 92 0W
Youngsville, N.C. 40 36 1N 78 29W
Youngsville, N. Mex. 38 36 11N 106 34W
Youngsville, Pa. 45 41 51N 79 19W
Yountville 14 38 24N 122 22W
Youyang 115 28 47N 108 42 E
Youyu 114 40 10N 112 20 E
Yozgat 106 39 51N 34 47 E
Ypané → 76 23 29 S 57 19W
Ypres = Ieper 87 50 51N 2 53 E
Ypsilanti, Mich. 29 42 14N 83 37W
Ypsilanti, N. Dak. 41 46 47N 98 34W
Yreka 14 41 44N 122 38W
Ystad 97 55 26N 13 50 E
Ythan → 84 57 26N 2 12W
Ytyk-Kel 101 62 30N 133 45 E
Yu Shan 115 23 30N 120 58 E
Yu Xian, Hebei, China 114 39 50N 114 35 E
Yu Xian, Henan, China 115 34 10N 113 28 E
Yuan Jiang → 115 28 55N 111 50 E
Yuanling 115 28 29N 110 22 E
Yuanyang 113 23 10N 102 43 E
Yuba 55 43 33N 90 26W
Yuba City 14 39 8N 121 37W
Yuba County ◇ 14 39 15N 121 30W
Yūbari 116 43 4N 141 59 E
Yūbetsu 116 43 13N 144 5 E
Yucatán □ 65 21 30N 86 30W
Yucatán, Canal de 66 22 0N 86 30W
Yucca 12 34 52N 114 9W
Yucca House National Monument 16 37 16N 108 38W
Yucca L. 35 36 57N 116 2W
Yucca Valley 15 34 8N 116 27W
Yucheng 114 36 55N 116 32 E
Yuci 114 37 42N 112 46 E
Yudino 100 55 10N 67 55 E
Yudu 115 25 59N 115 30 E
Yueqing 115 28 9N 120 59 E
Yueyang 115 29 21N 113 5 E
Yugan 115 28 43N 116 37 E
Yugoslavia ■ 95 44 0N 20 0 E
Yuhuan 115 28 9N 121 12 E
Yujiang 115 28 10N 116 43 E
Yukon 43 35 31N 97 45W
Yukon → 11 62 32N 163 54W
Yukon-Koyukuk ◇ 11 65 0N 154 0W
Yukon Territory □ 58 63 0N 135 0W
Yukti 101 63 26N 105 42 E
Yukuhashi 117 33 44N 130 59 E
Yule → 126 20 41 S 118 17 E
Yulee 17 30 38N 81 36W
Yülin, China 115 18 10N 109 31 E
Yulin, Guangxi Zhuangzu, China 115 22 40N 110 8 E
Yulin, Shaanxi, China 114 38 20N 109 30 E
Yuma, Ariz. 12 32 43N 114 37W
Yuma, Colo. 16 40 8N 102 43W
Yuma, B. de 67 18 20N 68 35W
Yuma County ◇, Ariz. 12 33 30N 114 0W
Yuma County ◇, Colo. 16 40 0N 102 20W
Yuma Desert 12 32 25N 114 30W
Yumbo 70 1 20 S 26 15 E
Yumen 113 39 50N 97 30 E
Yun Xian 115 32 50N 110 46 E
Yunaska I. 11 52 38N 170 40W
Yungas 73 17 0 S 66 0W
Yungay, Chile 76 37 10 S 72 5W
Yungay, Peru 72 9 2 S 77 45W
Yunhe 115 28 8N 119 33 E
Yunlin 115 23 42N 120 30 E
Yunnan □ 113 25 0N 102 0 E
Yunxiao 115 23 59N 117 18 E
Yupukarri 71 3 45N 59 20W
Yur 101 59 52N 137 41 E
Yurgao 100 55 42N 84 51 E
Yuribei 100 71 8N 76 58 E
Yurimaguas 72 5 55 S 76 7W
Yuscarán 66 13 58N 86 45W
Yushu, Jilin, China 114 44 43N 126 38 E
Yushu, Qinghai, China 113 33 5N 96 55 E
Yutan 34 41 15N 96 24W
Yuyao 115 30 3N 121 10 E
Yuzawa 116 39 10N 140 30 E
Yuzhno-Sakhalinsk 101 46 58N 142 45 E
Yvelines □ 90 48 40N 1 45 E
Yvetot 90 49 37N 0 44 E

Z

Zaandam 87 52 26N 4 49 E
Zabaykalskiy 101 49 40N 117 25 E
Zabid 105 14 0N 43 10 E
Zābol 107 31 0N 61 32 E
Zābol □ 107 32 0N 67 0 E
Zābolī 107 27 10N 61 35 E
Zabrze 89 50 18N 18 50 E
Zacapa 66 14 59N 89 31W
Zacapu 64 19 50N 101 43W
Zacatecas 64 22 49N 102 34W
Zacatecas □ 64 23 30N 103 0W
Zacatecoluca 66 13 29N 88 51W
Zachary 25 30 39N 91 9W
Zacoalco 64 20 14N 103 33W
Zacualtipán 65 20 39N 98 36W
Zadar 94 44 8N 15 14 E
Zadetkyi Kyun 110 10 0N 98 25 E
Zafra 91 38 26N 6 30W
Zafriya 104 31 59N 34 51 E
Żagań 88 51 39N 15 22 E
Zagazig 121 30 40N 31 30 E
Zagreb 94 45 50N 16 0 E
Zāgros, Kuhhā-ye 107 33 45N 47 0 E
Zāhedān 107 29 30N 60 50 E
Zahl 41 48 34N 103 42W
Zahlah 106 33 52N 35 50 E
Zaïre ■ 122 3 0 S 23 0 E
Zaïre → 122 6 4 S 12 24 E
Zaječar 95 43 53N 22 18 E
Zakamensk 101 50 23N 103 17 E
Zakavkazye 99 42 0N 44 0 E
Zākhū 106 37 10N 42 50 E
Zákinthos 95 37 47N 20 57 E
Zaleski 42 39 17N 82 24W
Zalingei 121 12 51N 23 29 E
Zalma 32 37 9N 90 5W
Zama 31 32 59N 89 23W
Zambeze → 123 18 55 S 36 4 E
Zambezi = Zambeze → 123 18 55 S 36 4 E
Zambezi 123 13 30 S 23 15 E
Zambia ■ 123 15 0 S 28 0 E
Zamboanga 111 6 59N 122 3 E
Zambrano 70 9 45N 74 49W
Zamora, Ecuador 70 4 4 S 78 58W
Zamora, Mexico 64 20 0N 102 21W
Zamora, Spain 91 41 30N 5 45W
Zamora-Chinchipe □ 70 4 15 S 78 50W
Zamość 89 50 43N 23 15 E
Zamuro, Sierra del 71 4 0N 62 30W
Zanaga 122 2 48 S 13 48 E
Zandvoort 87 52 22N 4 32 E
Zanesville 42 39 56N 82 1W
Zanjan 106 36 40N 48 35 E
Zanjān □ 106 37 20N 49 30 E
Zante = Zákinthos 95 37 47N 20 57 E
Zanthus 126 31 2 S 123 34 E
Zanzibar 122 6 12 S 39 12 E
Zaouiet El-Kala = Bordj Omar Driss 120 28 10N 6 40 E
Zaouiet Reggane 120 26 32N 0 3 E
Zap 41 47 17N 101 55W
Zapadnaya Dvina → 98 57 4N 24 3 E
Západné Beskydy 89 49 30N 19 0 E
Zapadni Rodopi 95 41 50N 24 0 E
Zapadnyy Sayan 101 52 30N 94 0 E
Zapala 78 39 0 S 70 5W
Zapaleri, Cerro 76 22 49 S 67 11W
Zapata 50 26 55N 99 16W
Zapata County ◇ 50 27 0N 99 0W
Zapiga 72 19 40 S 79 0W
Zapolyarnyy 98 69 26N 30 51 E
Zaporozhye 99 47 50N 35 10 E
Zara 106 39 58N 37 43 E
Zaragoza, Colombia 70 7 30N 74 52W
Zaragoza, Coahuila, Mexico 64 28 30N 101 0W
Zaragoza, Nuevo León, Mexico 65 24 0N 99 46W
Zaragoza, Spain 91 41 39N 0 53W
Zaragoza □ 91 41 35N 1 0W
Zarand 107 30 46N 56 34 E
Zaranj 107 30 55N 61 55 E
Zarate 76 34 7 S 59 0W
Zaraza 71 9 21N 65 19W
Zaria 120 11 0N 7 40 E
Zarqā' → 104 32 10N 35 37 E
Zaruma 70 3 40 S 79 38W
Zary 88 51 37N 15 10 E
Zarzal 70 4 24N 76 4W
Zarzis 121 33 31N 11 2 E
Zashiversk 101 67 25N 142 40 E
Zaskar Mountains 108 33 15N 77 30 E
Zavala County ◇ 51 28 57N 99 51W
Zavalla 51 31 10N 94 26W
Zavāreh 107 33 29N 52 28 E
Zavitinsk 101 50 10N 129 20 E
Zavodoski 5 56 0 S 27 45W
Zawiercie 89 50 30N 19 24 E
Zāwiyat al Bayḍā 121 32 30N 21 40 E
Zāyandeh → 107 32 35N 52 0 E
Zayarsk 101 56 12N 102 55 E
Zaysan 100 47 28N 84 52 E
Zaysan, Oz. 100 48 0N 83 0 E
Zaytā 104 32 23N 35 2 E
Zduńska Wola 89 51 37N 18 59 E
Zearing 23 42 10N 93 18W
Zeballos 62 49 59N 126 50W
Zebulon, Ga. 18 33 6N 84 21W
Zebulon, Ky. 49 37 32N 82 28W
Zebulon, N.C. 40 35 49N 78 19W
Zeebrugge 87 51 19N 3 12 E
Zeehan 127 41 52 S 145 25 E
Zeeland, Mich. 29 42 49N 86 1W
Zeeland, N. Dak. 41 45 58N 99 50W
Zeeland □ 87 51 30N 3 50 E
Ze'elim 104 31 13N 34 32 E
Zeerust 123 25 31 S 26 4 E
Zefat 104 32 58N 35 29 E
Zeigler 21 37 54N 89 3W
Zeila 105 11 21N 43 30 E
Zeist 87 52 5N 5 15 E
Zeitz 88 51 3N 12 9 E
Zelienople 45 40 48N 80 8W
Zell 47 44 54N 98 44W
Zelzate 87 51 13N 3 47 E
Zémio 122 5 2N 25 5 E
Zemlya Frantsa Iosifa 4 81 0N 55 0 E
Zemun 95 44 51N 20 25 E
Zenda 24 37 27N 98 17W
Zephyr Cove 35 39 0N 119 57W
Zephyrhills 17 28 14N 82 11W
Zerbst 88 51 59N 12 8 E
Zeya 101 53 48N 127 14 E
Zeya → 101 53 13N 127 35 E
Zhailma 100 51 37N 61 33 E
Zhangguangcai Ling 114 45 0N 129 0 E
Zhanghua 115 24 6N 120 29 E
Zhangjiakou 114 40 48N 114 55 E
Zhangping 115 25 17N 117 23 E
Zhangpu 115 24 8N 117 35 E
Zhangwu 114 42 43N 123 52 E
Zhangye 113 38 50N 100 23 E
Zhangzhou 115 24 30N 117 35 E
Zhanhua 114 37 40N 118 8 E
Zhanjiang 115 21 15N 110 20 E
Zhanyi 113 25 38N 103 48 E
Zhanyu 114 44 30N 122 30 E
Zhao Xian 114 37 43N 114 45 E
Zhao'an 115 23 41N 117 10 E
Zhaoping 115 24 11N 110 48 E
Zhaoqing 115 23 0N 112 20 E
Zhaotong 113 27 20N 103 44 E
Zhaoyuan 114 37 20N 120 23 E
Zhdanov 99 47 5N 37 31 E
Zhecheng 115 34 7N 115 20 E
Zhejiang □ 115 29 0N 120 0 E
Zheleznodorozhny 98 62 35N 50 55 E
Zheleznogorsk-Ilimskiy 101 56 34N 104 8 E
Zhen'an 115 33 27N 109 9 E
Zhenfeng 115 25 22N 105 40 E
Zheng'an 115 28 32N 107 27 E
Zhengding 114 38 8N 114 32 E
Zhenghe 115 27 20N 118 50 E
Zhengyang 115 32 37N 114 22 E
Zhengyangguan 115 32 30N 116 29 E
Zhengzhou 115 34 45N 113 34 E
Zhenjiang 115 32 11N 119 26 E
Zhenlai 114 45 50N 123 5 E
Zhenning 115 26 4N 105 45 E
Zhenyuan, Gansu, China 114 35 35N 107 30 E
Zhenyuan, Guizhou, China 115 27 4N 108 21 E
Zhigansk 101 66 48N 123 27 E
Zhijiang 115 27 27N 109 42 E
Zhitomir 99 50 20N 28 40 E
Zhlobin 98 52 55N 30 0 E
Zhokhova, Ostrov 101 76 4N 152 40 E
Zhong Xian 115 30 21N 108 1 E
Zhongdian 113 27 48N 99 42 E
Zhongshan 115 22 26N 113 20 E
Zhongwei 114 37 30N 105 12 E
Zhongxiang 115 31 12N 112 34 E
Zhoushan Dao 115 28 5N 122 10 E
Zhouzhi 115 34 10N 108 12 E
Zhuanghe 114 39 40N 123 0 E
Zhucheng 114 36 0N 119 27 E
Zhugqu 115 33 40N 104 30 E
Zhuji 115 29 40N 120 10 E
Zhumadian 115 32 59N 114 2 E
Zhuo Xian 114 39 28N 115 58 E
Zhupanovo 101 53 40N 159 52 E
Zhushan 115 32 15N 110 13 E
Zhuxi 115 32 25N 109 40 E
Zhuzhou 115 27 49N 113 12 E
Zia Indian Reservation 38 35 30N 106 50W
Zibo 114 36 47N 118 3 E
Zidarovo 95 42 20N 27 24 E
Ziebach County ◇ 47 45 0N 101 50W
Zielona Góra 88 51 57N 15 31 E
Zierikzee 87 51 40N 3 55 E
Zigey 121 14 43N 15 50 E
Zigong 115 29 15N 104 48 E
Zigui 115 31 0N 110 40 E
Ziguinchor 120 12 35N 16 20W
Zihuatanejo 64 17 38N 101 33W
Zikhron Ya'Aqov 104 32 34N 34 56 E
Ẑile 106 40 15N 35 52 E
Žilina 89 49 12N 18 42 E
Zillah, Libya 121 28 30N 17 33 E
Zillah, U.S.A. 53 46 24N 120 16W
Zima 101 54 0N 102 5 E
Zimapán 65 20 54N 99 20W
Zimbabwe ■ 123 20 0 S 30 0 E
Zimmerman 30 45 37N 93 34W
Zimnicea 95 43 40N 25 22 E
Zinder 120 13 48N 9 0 E
Zion 21 42 27N 87 50W
Zion National Park 52 37 15N 113 5W
Zion Reservoir 12 34 37N 109 29W
Zionsville 22 39 57N 86 16W
Zipaquirá 70 5 0N 74 0W
Ẓippori 104 32 45N 35 16 E
Zirkel, Mt. 16 40 50N 106 40W
Zirko 107 25 0N 53 40 E
Zitácuaro 64 19 28N 100 21W
Ziway, L. 121 8 0N 38 50 E
Zixi 115 27 45N 117 4 E
Ziyang 115 32 32N 108 31 E
Zizhong 115 29 48N 104 47 E
Zlataritsa 95 43 2N 25 55 E
Zlatitsa 95 42 41N 24 7 E
Zlatna 95 46 8N 23 11 E
Zlatograd 95 41 22N 25 7 E
Zlatoust 98 55 10N 59 40 E
Zlin = Gottwaldov 89 49 14N 17 40 E
Ẓlītan 121 32 32N 14 35 E
Zmeinogorsk 100 51 10N 82 13 E
Znojmo 88 48 50N 16 2 E
Zolfo Springs 17 27 30N 81 48W
Zomba 123 15 22 S 35 19 E
Zongo 122 4 20N 18 35 E
Zonguldak 106 41 28N 31 50 E
Zorleni 95 46 14N 27 44 E
Zornitsa 95 42 23N 26 58 E
Zorra I. 57 9 18N 79 52W
Zorritos 72 3 43 S 80 40W
Zou Xiang 115 35 30N 116 58 E
Zouar 121 20 30N 16 32 E
Zouérate 120 22 44N 12 21W
Zoutkamp 87 53 20N 6 18 E
Zrenjanin 95 45 22N 20 23 E
Zudáñez 73 19 6 S 64 44W
Zuetina 121 30 58N 20 7 E
Zufar 105 17 40N 54 0 E
Zug 88 47 10N 8 31 E
Zuid-Holland □ 87 52 0N 4 35 E
Zuidhorn 87 53 15N 6 23 E
Zula 121 15 17N 39 40 E
Zulia □ 70 10 0N 72 10W
Zumbo 123 15 35 S 30 26 E
Zumbro Falls 30 44 17N 92 26W
Zumbrota 30 44 17N 92 40W
Zumpango 65 19 48N 99 6W
Zungeru 120 9 48N 6 8 E
Zunhua 114 40 18N 117 58 E
Zuni 38 35 4N 108 51W
Zuni → 12 34 39N 109 40W
Zuni Indian Reservation 38 35 0N 108 50W
Zuni Mts. 38 35 10N 108 30W
Zunyi 115 27 42N 106 53 E
Zürich, Switz. 88 47 22N 8 32 E
Zurich, U.S.A. 24 39 14N 99 26W
Zutphen 87 52 9N 6 12 E
Zuwārah 121 32 58N 12 1 E
Zverinogolovskoye 100 54 23N 64 40 E
Zvezdets 95 42 6N 27 26 E
Zvishavane 123 20 17 S 30 2 E
Zvolen 89 48 33N 19 10 E
Zwettl 88 48 35N 15 9 E
Zwickau 88 50 43N 12 30 E
Zwingle 23 42 18N 90 41W
Zwolle, Neth. 87 52 31N 6 6 E
Zwolle, U.S.A. 25 31 38N 93 39W
Zymoetz → 62 54 33N 128 31W
Żyrardów 89 52 3N 20 28 E
Zyryanka 101 65 45N 150 51 E
Zyryanovsk 100 49 43N 84 20 E